Prepare, Apply, and Confirm

- **Enhanced eText**—The Pearson eText gives students access to their textbook anytime, anywhere. In addition to notetaking, highlighting, and bookmarking, the Pearson eText offers interactive and sharing features. Students actively read and learn, through embedded and auto-graded practice, animations, author videos, and more. Instructors can share comments or highlights, and students can add their own, for a tight community of learners in any class.

- **Dynamic Study Modules**—Work by continuously assessing student performance and activity, then using data and analytics to provide personalized content in real time to reinforce concepts that target each student's particular strengths and weaknesses.

- **Hallmark Features**—Personalized Learning Aids, like Help Me Solve This, View an Example, and instant feedback are available for further practice and mastery when students need the help most!

- **Learning Catalytics**—Generates classroom discussion, guides lecture, and promotes peer-to-peer learning with real-time analytics. Now, students can use any device to interact in the classroom.

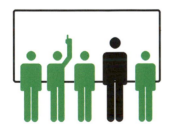

- **Adaptive Study Plan**—Assists students in monitoring their own progress by offering them a customized study plan powered by Knewton, based on Homework, Quiz, and Test results. Includes regenerated exercises with unlimited practice and the opportunity to prove mastery through quizzes on recommended learning objectives.

with MyFinanceLab™

- **Worked Solutions**—Provide step-by-step explanations on how to solve select problems using the exact numbers and data that were presented in the problem. Instructors will have access to the Worked Solutions in preview and review mode.

- **Algorithmic Test Bank**—Instructors have the ability to create multiple versions of a test or extra practice for students.

- **Financial Calculator**—The Financial Calculator is available as a smartphone application, as well as on a computer, and includes important functions such as cash flow, net present value, and internal rate of return. Fifteen helpful tutorial videos show the many ways to use the Financial Calculator in MyFinanceLab.

- **Reporting Dashboard**—View, analyze, and report learning outcomes clearly and easily. Available via the Gradebook and fully mobile-ready, the Reporting Dashboard presents student performance data at the class, section, and program levels in an accessible, visual manner.

- **LMS Integration**—Link from any LMS platform to access assignments, rosters, and resources, and synchronize MyLab grades with your LMS gradebook. For students, new direct, single sign-on provides access to all the personalized learning MyLab resources that make studying more efficient and effective.

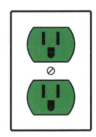

- **Mobile Ready**—Students and instructors can access multimedia resources and complete assessments right at their fingertips, on any mobile device.

Fundamentals
of Investing

The Pearson Series in Finance

Berk/DeMarzo
Corporate Finance*
Corporate Finance: The Core*

Berk/DeMarzo/Harford
Fundamentals of Corporate Finance*

Brooks
Financial Management: Core Concepts*

Copeland/Weston/Shastri
Financial Theory and Corporate Policy

Dorfman/Cather
Introduction to Risk Management and Insurance

Eakins/McNally
Corporate Finance Online*

Eiteman/Stonehill/Moffett
Multinational Business Finance*

Fabozzi
Bond Markets: Analysis and Strategies

Foerster
Financial Management: Concepts and Applications*

Frasca
Personal Finance

Gitman/Zutter
Principles of Managerial Finance*
Principles of Managerial Finance—Brief Edition*

Haugen
The Inefficient Stock Market: What Pays Off and Why
Modern Investment Theory

Holden
Excel Modeling in Corporate Finance
Excel Modeling in Investments

Hughes/MacDonald
International Banking: Text and Cases

Hull
Fundamentals of Futures and Options Markets Options, Futures, and Other Derivatives

Keown
Personal Finance: Turning Money into Wealth*

Keown/Martin/Petty
Foundations of Finance: The Logic and Practice of Financial Management*

Madura
Personal Finance*

Marthinsen
Risk Takers: Uses and Abuses of Financial Derivatives

McDonald
Derivatives Markets
Fundamentals of Derivatives Markets

Mishkin/Eakins
Financial Markets and Institutions

Moffett/Stonehill/Eiteman
Fundamentals of Multinational Finance

Nofsinger
Psychology of Investing

Pennacchi
Theory of Asset Pricing

Rejda/McNamara
Principles of Risk Management and Insurance

Smart/Gitman/Joehnk
Fundamentals of Investing*

Solnik/McLeavey
Global Investments

Titman/Keown/Martin
Financial Management: Principles and Applications*

Titman/Martin
Valuation: The Art and Science of Corporate Investment Decisions

Weston/Mitchell/Mulherin
Takeovers, Restructuring, and Corporate Governance

*denotes titles with MyFinanceLab.   Log onto http://www.myfinancelab.com to learn more.

Fundamentals of Investing

Thirteenth Edition

SCOTT B. SMART
Indiana University

LAWRENCE J. GITMAN, CFP®
San Diego State University

MICHAEL D. JOEHNK, CFA
Arizona State University

PEARSON

Boston Columbus Indianapolis New York San Francisco
Amsterdam Cape Town Dubai London Madrid Milan Munich Paris Montréal Toronto
Delhi Mexico City São Paulo Sydney Hong Kong Seoul Singapore Taipei Tokyo

Vice President, Business Publishing: Donna Battista
Editor-in-Chief: Adrienne D'Ambrosio
Acquisitions Editor: Kate Fernandes
Editorial Assistant: Kathryn Brightney
Vice President, Product Marketing: Maggie Moylan
Director of Marketing, Digital Services and Products: Jeanette Koskinas
Senior Product Marketing Manager: Alison Haskins
Executive Field Marketing Manager: Adam Goldstein
Product Marketing Assistant: Jessica Quazza
Team Lead, Program Management: Ashley Santora
Program Manager: Kathryn Dinovo
Team Lead, Project Management: Jeff Holcomb
Project Manager: Alison Kalil
Operations Specialist: Carol Melville
Creative Director: Blair Brown
Art Director: Jonathan
Vice President, Director of Digital Strategy and Assessment: Paul Gentile

Manager of Learning Applications: Paul DeLuca
Digital Editor: Brian Hyland
Director, Digital Studio: Sacha Laustsen
Digital Studio Manager: Diane Lombardo
Digital Studio Project Managers: Melissa Honig and Andra Skaalrud
Digital Studio Project Manager: Alana Coles
Digital Studio Project Manager: Robin Lazrus
Digital Content Team Lead: Noel Lotz
Digital Content Project Lead: Miguel Leonarte
Full-Service Project Management, Interior Designer, and Composition: Cenveo® Publisher Services
Cover Designer: Jonathan Boylan
Cover Art: Can Yesil/Fotolia; Oez/Fotolia; ukix21/ Shutterstock
Printer/Binder: LSC Communications/Harrisonburg
Cover Printer: LSC Communications/Harrisonburg

Cataloging-in-Publication Data is on File at the Library of Congress

10

ISBN 10: 0-13-408330-X
ISBN 13: 978-0-13-408330-8

Dedicated To
Susan R. Smart,
Robin F. Gitman, and
Charlene W. Joehnk

Brief Contents

Detailed Contents viii
Preface xvii

Part One **Preparing to Invest**
1   **The Investment Environment**   1
2   **Securities Markets and Transactions**   37
3   **Investment Information and Securities Transactions**   74

Part Two **Important Conceptual Tools**
4   **Return and Risk**   121
4A **The Time Value of Money**   157
5   **Modern Portfolio Concepts**   170

Part Three **Investing in Common Stocks**
6   **Common Stocks**   215
7   **Analyzing Common Stocks**   254
8   **Stock Valuation**   297
9   **Market Efficiency and Behavioral Finance**   335

Part Four **Investing in Fixed-Income Securities**
10 **Fixed-Income Securities**   378
11 **Bond Valuation**   425

Part Five **Portfolio Management**
12 **Mutual Funds and Exchange-Traded Funds**   468
13 **Managing Your Own Portfolio**   511

Part Six **Derivative Securities**
14 **Options: Puts and Calls**   549
15 **Futures Markets and Securities**   592

Glossary G-1
Index I-1

Web Chapters (at http://www.pearsonhighered.com/smart)
16 **Investing in Preferred Stocks**
17 **Tax-Advantaged Investments**
18 **Real Estate and Other Tangible Investments**

Contents

Part One　Preparing to Invest

Chapter 1
The Investment Environment 1

■ FAMOUS FAILURES IN FINANCE
Ethical Failure—Massaging the
Numbers 21

■ FAMOUS FAILURES IN FINANCE
A Run for the Money 22

Opening Vignette 1

Investments and the Investment Process 2
Attributes of Investments 2 / The Structure of the Investment
Process 5

Types of Investments 7
Short-Term Investments 7 / Common Stock 8 / Fixed-Income
Securities 9 / Mutual Funds 10 / Exchange-Traded
Funds 11 / Hedge Funds 12 / Derivative Securities 12 / Other
Popular Investments 13

Making Your Investment Plan 14
Writing an Investment Policy Statement 14 / Considering Personal
Taxes 16 / Investing over the Life Cycle 19 / Investing over the
Business Cycle 20

Meeting Liquidity Needs with Short-Term Investments 22
The Role of Short-Term Investments 22 / Common Short-Term
Investments 23 / Investment Suitability 23

Careers in Finance 27

**Summary 30 / Discussion Questions 32 / Problems 33 / Case
Problem 1.1 34 / Case Problem 1.2 35 / Excel@Investing 36**

Chapter 2
Securities Markets and Transactions 37

■ FAMOUS FAILURES IN FINANCE
Short Sellers Tip 60 Minutes 63

Opening Vignette 37

Securities Markets 38

Types of Securities Markets 38 / Broker Markets and Dealer Markets 44 / Alternative Trading Systems 48 / General Market Conditions: Bull or Bear 48

Globalization of Securities Markets 49

Growing Importance of International Markets 50 / International Investment Performance 50 / Ways to Invest in Foreign Securities 51 / Risks of Investing Internationally 51

Trading Hours and Regulation of Securities Markets 53

Trading Hours of Securities Markets 53 / Regulation of Securities Markets 53

Basic Types of Securities Transactions 55

Long Purchase 55 / Margin Trading 56 / Short Selling 62

Summary 65 / Discussion Questions 68 / Problems 68 / Case Problem 2.1 71 / Case Problem 2.2 72 / Excel@Investing 72

Chapter 3
Investment Information and Securities Transactions 74

FAMOUS FAILURES IN FINANCE
PIIGS Feast on Wall Street 97

FAMOUS FAILURES IN FINANCE
Bond Yields Hit Historic Lows 99

FAMOUS FAILURES IN FINANCE
Hello, I Am Tim, an Insider Trader 103

Opening Vignette 74

Investment Research and Planning 75

Getting Started in Investment Research 75 / Pros and Cons of the Internet as an Investment Tool 79

Types and Sources of Investment Information 80

Types of Information 82 / Sources of Information 82

Understanding Market Averages and Indexes 94

Stock Market Averages and Indexes 94 / Bond Market Indicators 98

Making Securities Transactions 100

The Role of Stockbrokers 100 / Basic Types of Orders 104 / Online Transactions 106 / Transaction Costs 108 / Investor Protection: SIPC and Arbitration 108

Investment Advisors and Investment Clubs 110

Using an Investment Advisor 110 / Investment Clubs 111

Summary 112 / Discussion Questions 115 / Problems 116 / Case Problem 3.1 118 / Case Problem 3.2 119 / Excel@Investing 120

Part Two   Important Conceptual Tools

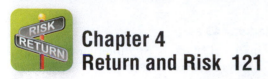

Chapter 4
Return and Risk 121

■ **FAMOUS FAILURES IN FINANCE**
Fears of Deflation Worry Investors 125

Opening Vignette 121

The Concept of Return 122

Components of Return 122 / Why Return Is Important 123 / Level of Return 124 / Historical Returns 126 / The Time Value of Money and Returns 126

Measuring Return 128

Real, Risk-Free, and Required Returns 129 / Holding Period Return 131 / The Internal Rate of Return 133 / Finding Growth Rates 137

Risk: The Other Side of the Coin 138

Sources of Risk 138 / Risk of a Single Asset 141 / Assessing Risk 144 / Steps in the Decision Process: Combining Return and Risk 146

Summary 147 / **Discussion Questions** 149 / **Problems 149 / Case Problem 4.1** 153 / **Case Problem 4.2** 154 / **Excel@Investing** 155 / **Chapter-Opening Problem** 156

Appendix 4A
The Time Value of Money 157

Opening Vignette 157

Interest: The Basic Return to Savers 157

Simple Interest 157 / Compound Interest 157

Computational Aids for Use in Time Value Calculations 159

Financial Calculators 159 / Computers and Spreadsheets 160

Future Value: An Extension of Compounding 160

Future Value of an Annuity 162

Present Value: An Extension of Future Value 162

Present Value of a Stream of Returns 163

Present Value of a Mixed Stream 164 / Present Value of an Annuity 165

Summary 166 / **Problems** 166

Chapter 5
Modern Portfolio Concepts 170

■ **FAMOUS FAILURES IN FINANCE**
Bulging Betas 187

Opening Vignette 170

Principles of Portfolio Planning 171

Portfolio Objectives 171 / Portfolio Return and Standard
Deviation 171 / Correlation and Diversification 174 / International
Diversification 180

The Capital Asset Pricing Model 182

Components of Risk 182 / Beta: A Measure of Undiversifiable
Risk 183 / The CAPM: Using Beta to Estimate Return 187

Traditional Versus Modern Portfolio Management 190

The Traditional Approach 190 / Modern Portfolio
Theory 191 / Reconciling the Traditional Approach and MPT 196

**Summary 197 / Discussion Questions 199 / Problems 200 / Case
Problem 5.1 207 / Case Problem 5.2 209 / Excel@Investing 210 /
Chapter-Opening Problem 211**

CFA Exam Questions 213

Part Three   Investing in Common Stocks

Chapter 6
Common Stocks 215

■ **FAMOUS FAILURES IN FINANCE**
Beware of the Lumbering Bear 217

Opening Vignette 215

What Stocks Have to Offer 216

The Appeal of Common Stocks 216 / Putting Stock Price Behavior
in Perspective 216 / From Stock Prices to Stock Returns 216 / A
Real Estate Bubble Goes Bust and So Does the Market 218 / The
Pros and Cons of Stock Ownership 219

Basic Characteristics of Common Stock 221

Common Stock as a Corporate Security 221 / Buying and Selling
Stocks 225 / Common Stock Values 226

Common Stock Dividends 228

The Dividend Decision 229 / Types of Dividends 230 / Dividend
Reinvestment Plans 232

Types and Uses of Common Stock 234

Types of Stocks 234 / Investing in Foreign Stocks 238 / Alternative Investment Strategies 242

Summary 245 / Discussion Questions 247 / Problems 248 / Case Problem 6.1 251 / Case Problem 6.2 252 / Excel@Investing 253

Chapter 7
Analyzing Common Stocks 254

■ FAMOUS FAILURES IN FINANCE
Staying on Top a Challenge for Fund Managers 257

■ FAMOUS FAILURES IN FINANCE
Cooking the Books: What Were They Thinking? 271

Opening Vignette 254

Security Analysis 255

Principles of Security Analysis 255 / Who Needs Security Analysis in an Efficient Market? 256

Economic Analysis 258

Economic Analysis and the Business Cycle 259 / Key Economic Factors 259 / Developing an Economic Outlook 260

Industry Analysis 263

Key Issues 263 / Developing an Industry Outlook 265

Fundamental Analysis 266

The Concept 266 / Financial Statements 267 / Financial Ratios 270 / Interpreting the Numbers 283

Summary 287 / Discussion Questions 288 / Problems 288 / Case Problem 7.1 292 / Case Problem 7.2 294 / Excel@Investing 295 / Chapter-Opening Problem 296

Chapter 8
Stock Valuation 297

■ FAMOUS FAILURES IN FINANCE
P/E Ratios Can Be Misleading 302

■ FAMOUS FAILURES IN FINANCE
Ethical Conflicts Faced by Stock Analysts: Don't Always Believe the Hype 310

Opening Vignette 297

Valuation: Obtaining a Standard of Performance 298

Valuing a Company and Its Future Performance 298 / Developing a Forecast of Universal's Financial Performance 304 / The Valuation Process 307

Stock Valuation Models 308

The Dividend Valuation Model 309 / Other Approaches to Stock Valuation 317 / Other Price-Relative Procedures 322

Summary 324 / Discussion Questions 326 / Problems 327 / Case Problem 8.1 332 / Case Problem 8.2 333 / Excel@Investing 333 / Chapter-Opening Problem 334

Chapter 9
Market Efficiency and Behavioral Finance 335

■ FAMOUS FAILURES IN FINANCE
Loss Aversion and Trading Volume 350

■ FAMOUS FAILURES IN FINANCE
Buying High and Selling Low 353

Opening Vignette 335

Efficient Markets 336
The Efficient Markets Hypothesis 338 / Market
Anomalies 344 / Possible Explanations 346

**Behavioral Finance: A Challenge to the Efficient Markets
Hypothesis 348**
Investor Behavior and Security Prices 348 / Implications of
Behavioral Finance for Security Analysis 355

Technical Analysis 356
Measuring the Market 357 / Trading Rules and
Measures 360 / Charting 363

**Summary 367 / Discussion Questions 368 / Problems 369 / Case
Problem 9.1 372 / Case Problem 9.2 374 / Excel@Investing 375**

CFA Exam Questions 376

Part Four
Investing in Fixed-Income Securities

Chapter 10
Fixed-Income Securities 378

■ FAMOUS FAILURES IN FINANCE
Rating Agencies Miss a Big One 393

■ FAMOUS FAILURES IN FINANCE
Yield Spreads Approach Records 396

■ FAMOUS FAILURES IN FINANCE
Implicit Guarantee Becomes
Explicit 397

Opening Vignette 378

Why Invest in Bonds? 379
A Brief History of Bond Prices, Returns, and Interest
Rates 380 / Exposure to Risk 384

Essential Features of a Bond 386
Bond Interest and Principal 386 / Maturity Date 386 / Principles of
Bond Price Behavior 387 / Quoting Bond Prices 389 / Call Features—
Let the Buyer Beware! 389 / Sinking Funds 390 / Secured or
Unsecured Debt 390 / Bond Ratings 391

The Market for Debt Securities 394
Major Market Segments 394 / Specialty Issues 402 / A Global View
of the Bond Market 406

Convertible Securities 408
Convertibles as Investment Outlets 408 / Sources of
Value 411 / Measuring the Value of a Convertible 411

Summary 415 / Discussion Questions 417 / Problems 418 / Case Problem 10.1 421 / Case Problem 10.2 422 / Excel@Investing 423 / Chapter-Opening Problem 424

Chapter 11
Bond Valuation 425

■ **FAMOUS FAILURES IN FINANCE**
Signs of a Recession 427

Opening Vignette 425

The Behavior of Market Interest Rates 426

Keeping Tabs on Market Interest Rates 426 / What Causes Rates to Move? 427 / The Term Structure of Interest Rates and Yield Curves 429

The Pricing of Bonds 434

The Basic Bond Valuation Model 435 / Annual Compounding 435 / Semiannual Compounding 437 / Accrued Interest 438

Measures of Yield and Return 439

Current Yield 439 / Yield to Maturity 440 / Yield to Call 444 / Expected Return 445 / Valuing a Bond 447

Duration and Immunization 447

The Concept of Duration 448 / Measuring Duration 449 / Bond Duration and Price Volatility 451 / Effective Duration 452 / Uses of Bond Duration Measures 453

Bond Investment Strategies 455

Passive Strategies 455 / Trading on Forecasted Interest Rate Behavior 456 / Bond Swaps 456

Summary 458 / Discussion Questions 459 / Problems 460 / Case Problem 11.1 463 / Case Problem 11.2 463 / Excel@Investing 464

CFA Exam Questions 466

Part Five   Portfolio Management

Chapter 12
Mutual Funds and Exchange-Traded Funds 468

■ **FAMOUS FAILURES IN FINANCE**
When Mutual Funds Behaved Badly 474

■ **FAMOUS FAILURES IN FINANCE**
Breaking the Buck 487

Opening Vignette 468

The Mutual Fund Concept 469

An Overview of Mutual Funds 469 / Exchange-Traded Funds 477 / Some Important Considerations 479 / Other Types of Investment Companies 481

Types of Funds and Services 484

Types of Mutual Funds 484 / Investor Services 489

Investing in Mutual Funds 492

Investor Uses of Mutual Funds 492 / The Selection Process 493 / Investing in Closed-End Funds 495 / Measuring Performance 498

Summary 503 / Discussion Questions 505 / Problems 505 / Case Problem 12.1 508 / Case Problem 12.2 509 / Excel@Investing 509 / Chapter-Opening Problem 510

Chapter 13
Managing Your Own Portfolio 511

Opening Vignette 511

Constructing a Portfolio Using an Asset Allocation Scheme 512

Investor Characteristics and Objectives 512 / Portfolio Objectives and Policies 512 / Developing an Asset Allocation Scheme 513

Evaluating the Performance of Individual Investments 516

Obtaining Data 516 / Indexes of Investment Performance 517 / Measuring the Performance of Investments 517 / Comparing Performance to Investment Goals 520

Assessing Portfolio Performance 521

Measuring Portfolio Return 522 / Comparison of Return with Overall Market Measures 525 / Portfolio Revision 528

Timing Transactions 529

Formula Plans 529 / Using Limit and Stop-Loss Orders 533 / Warehousing Liquidity 533 / Timing Investment Sales 534

Summary 535 / Discussion Questions 537 / Problems 539 / Case Problem 13.1 543 / Case Problem 13.2 544 / Excel@Investing 545

CFA Exam Questions 547

Part Six

Derivative Securities

Chapter 14
Options: Puts and Calls 549

■ FAMOUS FAILURES IN FINANCE
Ethical Lapse or Extraordinarily Good Timing? 561

■ FAMOUS FAILURES IN FINANCE
The Volatility Index 566

Opening Vignette 549

Call and Put Options 550

Basic Features of Calls and Puts 550 / Options Markets 553 / Stock Options 554

Options Pricing and Trading 557

The Profit Potential from Puts and Calls *558* / Intrinsic Value *559* / What Drives Option Prices *564* / Trading Strategies *568*

Stock-Index and Other Types of Options 576

Contract Provisions of Stock-Index Options *576* / Investment Uses *579* / Other Types of Options *580*

Summary 583 / Discussion Questions 584 / Problems 585 / Case Problem 14.1 588 / Case Problem 14.2 588 / Excel@Investing 589 / Chapter-Opening Problem 590

Chapter 15
Futures Markets and Securities 591

■ **FAMOUS FAILURES IN FINANCE**
Shady Trading at Enron 603

■ **FAMOUS FAILURES IN FINANCE**
Diving Oil Prices Send Cal Dive into Bankruptcy 605

Opening Vignette 591

The Futures Market 592

Market Structure *592* / Trading in the Futures Market *595*

Commodities 598

Basic Characteristics *598* / Trading Commodities *603*

Financial Futures 606

The Financial Futures Market *606* / Trading Techniques *610* / Financial Futures and the Individual Investor *613* / Options on Futures *614*

Summary 616 / Discussion Questions 618 / Problems 619 / Case Problem 15.1 621 / Case Problem 15.2 622 / Excel@Investing 623

CFA Exam Questions 624

Glossary G-1
Index I-1

Web Chapters   (at http://www.pearsonhighered.com/smart)

Chapter 16   Investing in Preferred Stocks

Chapter 17   Tax-Advantaged Investments

Chapter 18   Real Estate and Other Tangible Investments

Preface

"Great firms aren't great investments unless the price is right." Those words of wisdom come from none other than Warren Buffett, who is, without question, one of the greatest investors ever. The words of Mr. Buffett sum up very nicely the essence of this book—namely, to help students learn to make informed investment decisions, not only when buying stocks but also when investing in bonds, mutual funds, or any other type of investment.

The fact is, investing may sound simple, but it's not. Investors in today's turbulent financial markets confront many challenges when deciding how to invest their money. Nearly a decade after the 2008 meltdown in financial markets, investors are still more wary of risk than they were before the crisis. This book is designed to help students understand the risks inherent in investing and to give them the tools they need to answer the fundamental questions that help shape a sound investment strategy. For example, students want to know, what are the best investments for me? Should I buy individual securities, mutual funds, or exchange-traded funds? How do I make judgments about risk? Do I need professional help with my investments, and can I afford it? Clearly, investors need answers to questions like these to make informed decisions.

The language, concepts, and strategies of investing are foreign to many. In order to become informed investors, students must first become conversant with the many aspects of investing. Building on that foundation, they can learn how to make informed decisions in the highly dynamic investment environment. This thirteenth edition of *Fundamentals of Investing* provides the information and guidance needed by individual investors to make such informed decisions and to achieve their investment goals.

This book meets the needs of professors and students in the first investments course offered at colleges and universities, junior and community colleges, professional certification programs, and continuing education courses. Focusing on both individual securities and portfolios, *Fundamentals of Investing* explains how to develop, implement, and monitor investment goals after considering the risk and return of different types of investments. A conversational tone and liberal use of examples guide students through the material and demonstrate important points.

New for the Thirteenth Edition

Our many adopters are interested in how we have changed the content from the twelfth to the thirteenth edition. We hope that this information will also interest potential adopters because it indicates our mandate to stay current in the field of investments and to continue to craft a book that will truly meet the needs of students and professors.

Some of the major changes made in the thirteenth edition are the following:

- Updated all real-world data through 2015 (or 2014 if 2015 numbers were not yet available), including text, tables, and figures.

- Created new videos of worked-out solutions to in-text examples that students can see on MyFinanceLab and use as a guide for the end-of-chapter problems as well as related assignments made by their professors.

- Revised many end-of-chapter problems.

- Expanded coverage of mutual funds, ETFs, and hedge funds in Chapter 1, and introduced new coverage on formulating a personal investment policy statement.

- Replaced the previous Markets in Crisis feature, which focused on various causes and consequences of the 2007 to 2008 financial crisis and recession, with a new Famous Failures in Finance boxed item. Famous Failures shares some lessons from the financial crisis, but it also highlights other "problem areas" in the investments world such as market crashes, ethical scandals, and failures of financial service providers to act in their clients' best interests.

- Updated QR codes in the margins of each chapter. Students can scan these codes with their smart phones to gain access to videos and other web content that enhance the topical coverage of each chapter.

- Added a new feature called Watch Your Behavior. These boxes appear in the margins of most chapters and highlight investment lessons gleaned from the behavioral finance literature.

- Updated numerous Investor Facts boxes from the twelfth edition and incorporated entirely new ones in most chapters.

- Expanded the use of real-world data in examples.

- Added new coverage of the free-cash-flow-to-equity stock valuation model in Chapter 8.

- Expanded and updated coverage of behavioral finance, particularly but not exclusively in Chapter 9. Also added new content on the role of arbitrage in moving financial markets toward efficiency.

- Included new historical data on interest rates and bond returns in Chapter 10, highlighting the link between changes in interest rates and total returns earned on bonds.

- Revised or replaced every chapter opener, and in many chapters, included an end-of-chapter problem that ties back to the chapter opener.

- Created a new feature called Excel@Investing, which provides students with online access to electronic copies of most tables in the text that involve calculations. Students can explore these Excel files to better understand the calculations embedded in the printed tables, and students make the textbook's tables dynamic by using these spreadsheets to change key assumptions to see how doing so affects the key results.

Hallmarks of *Fundamentals of Investing*

Using information gathered from academicians and practicing investment professionals, plus feedback from adopters, the thirteenth edition reflects the realities of today's investment environment. At the same time, the following characteristics provide a structured framework for successful teaching and learning.

Clear Focus on the Individual Investor

According to a Gallup poll, today about 55% of all U.S. households own stock either directly or indirectly through mutual funds or participation in 401(k)s. That percentage peaked at 65% in 2008 but if fell for six consecutive years in the aftermath of the financial crisis and has only recently started rising again. The focus of *Fundamentals of*

Investing has always been on the individual investor. This focus gives students the information they need to develop, implement, and monitor a successful investment program. It also provides students with a solid foundation of basic concepts, tools, and techniques. Subsequent courses can build on that foundation by presenting the advanced concepts, tools, and techniques used by institutional investors and money managers.

Comprehensive Yet Flexible Organization

The text provides a firm foundation for learning by first describing the overall investment environment, including the various investment markets, information, and transactions. Next, it presents conceptual tools needed by investors—the concepts of return and risk and the basic approaches to portfolio management. It then examines the most popular types of investments—common stocks, bonds, and mutual funds. Following this series of chapters on investment vehicles is a chapter on how to construct and administer one's own portfolio. The final section of the book focuses on derivative securities—options and futures—which require more expertise. Although the first two parts of the textbook are best covered at the start of the course, instructors can cover particular investment types in just about any sequence. The comprehensive yet flexible nature of the book enables instructors to customize it to their own course structure and teaching objectives.

We have organized each chapter according to a decision-making perspective, and we have been careful always to point out the pros and cons of the various investments and strategies we present. With this information, individual investors can select the investment actions that are most consistent with their objectives. In addition, we have presented the various investments and strategies in such a way that students learn the decision-making implications and consequences of each investment action they contemplate.

Timely Topics

Various issues and developments constantly reshape financial markets and investment vehicles. Virtually all topics in this book take into account changes in the investment environment. For example, in every chapter we've added a new feature called Famous Failures in Finance. This feature highlights various aspects of the recent and historic financial crisis, as well as other "failures" in financial markets such as bank runs and ethical lapses by corporate managers and rogue traders. Fundamentally, investing is about the tradeoff between risk and return, and the Famous Failures in Finance feature serves as a reminder to students that they should not focus exclusively on an investment's returns.

In addition, the thirteenth edition provides students access to short video clips from professional investment advisors. In these clips, which are carefully integrated into the content of each chapter, students will hear professionals sharing the lessons that they have learned through years of experience working as advisors to individual investors.

Globalization

One issue that is reshaping the world of investing is the growing globalization of securities markets. As a result, *Fundamentals of Investing* continues to stress the global aspects of investing. We initially look at the growing importance of international markets, investing in foreign securities (directly or indirectly), international investment performance, and the risks of international investing. In later chapters, we describe popular international investment opportunities and strategies as part of the coverage of each specific type of investment vehicle. This integration of international topics helps students understand the importance of maintaining a global focus when planning, building, and managing an investment portfolio. Global topics are highlighted by a globe icon in the margin.

Comprehensive, Integrated Learning System

Another feature of the thirteenth edition is its comprehensive and integrated learning system, which makes clear to students what they need to learn in the chapter and helps them focus their study efforts as they progress through the chapter. For more detailed discussion of the learning system, see the feature walkthrough later in the preface (beginning on page xxi).

CFA Exam Questions

We are pleased to include CFA exam questions in the thirteenth edition, both in the written text and in MyFinanceLab. CFA exam questions appear in the text at the end of five of the book's six parts. Due to the nature of the material in some of the early chapters, the CFA questions for Parts One and Two are combined and appear at the end of Part Two. These questions offer students an opportunity to test their investment knowledge against that required for the CFA Level-I exam.

In MyFinanceLab on the Course Home page, there are three Sample CFA Exams. Each of these exams is patterned after the CFA Level-I exam and comes with detailed guideline answers. The exams deal only with topics that are actually covered in the thirteenth edition of *Fundamentals of Investing* and are meant to replicate as closely as possible the types of questions that appear on the standard Level-I Exam. The Sample CFA Exams on MyFinanceLab come in three lengths: 30 questions, 40 questions, and 50 questions. Each exam is unique and consists of a different set of questions, so students can take any one or all of the exams without running into any duplicate questions. For the most part, these questions are adapted from past editions of the CFA Candidate Study Notes. Answers are included for immediate reinforcement.

MyFinanceLab

MyFinanceLab is a fully integrated online homework and tutorial system that offers flexible instructor tools like the easy-to-use homework manager for test, quiz, and homework assignments, automatic grading, and a powerful online Gradebook. Students can take preloaded Sample Tests for each chapter and their results generate an individualized Study Plan that helps focus and maximize their study time. Please visit http://www.myfinancelab.com for more information or to register.

The Smart, Gitman & Joehnk

PROVEN
TEACHING/LEARNING/MOTIVATIONAL SYSTEM

Users of *Fundamentals of Investing* have praised the effectiveness of the Smart/Gitman/Joehnk teaching and learning system, which has been hailed as one of its hallmarks. In the thirteenth edition we have retained and polished the system, which is driven by a set of carefully developed learning goals. Users have also praised the rich motivational framework that underpins each chapter. Key elements of the pedagogical and motivational features are illustrated and described below.

THE LEARNING GOAL SYSTEM

The Learning Goal system begins each chapter with **six Learning Goals**, labeled with numbered icons. These goals anchor the most important concepts and techniques to be learned. The Learning Goal icons are then tied to key points in the chapter's structure, including:

- First-level headings
- Summary
- Discussion Questions
- Problems
- Cases

This tightly knit structure provides a clear road map for students—they know what they need to learn, where they can find it, and whether they've mastered it by the end of the chapter.

An **opening story** sets the stage for the content that follows by focusing on an investment situation involving a real company or real event, which is in turn linked to the chapter topics. Students see the relevance of the vignette to the world of investments.

In many cases, an end-of-chapter problem draws students back to the chapter opener and asks them to use the data in the opener to make a calculation or draw a conclusion to demonstrate what they learned in the chapter.

What Is Inflation?

In the margins of each chapter students will find **QR codes**. By scanning these codes with their smart phones, students will be taken to websites with useful information to enhance their understanding of the topics covered in the textbook. For example, many of these QR codes link students with free online video tutorials covering a range of topics.

Also new to this edition, **Watch Your Behavior** boxes appear in the margins of most chapters and highlight investment lessons gleaned from the behavioral finance literature.

Each chapter contains a handful of **Investor Facts**—brief sidebar items that give an interesting statistic or cite an unusual investment experience. These facts add a bit of seasoning to the concepts under review and capture a real-world flavor. The Investor Facts sidebars include material focused on topics such as art as an investment, the downgrade of the U.S. government's credit rating, the use of financial statements to detect accounting fraud, and recent issues of unusual securities such as bonds with 100-year maturities.

An Advisor's Perspective consists of short video clips of professional investment advisers discussing the investments topics covered in each chapter. Students can access the video clips on MyFinanceLab.

WATCH YOUR BEHAVIOR

Short-Lived Growth So-called value stocks are stocks that have low price-to-book ratios, and growth stocks are stocks that have relatively high price-to-book ratios. Many studies demonstrate that value stocks outperform growth stocks, perhaps because investors overestimate the odds that a firm that has grown rapidly in the past will continue to do so.

AN ADVISOR'S PERSPECTIVE

Ed Slott
CEO, Ed Slott and Company

"The greatest money making asset any individual can possess is time."

MyFinanceLab

INVESTOR FACTS

A Steady Stream York Water Company raised its dividend for the 17th consecutive year in February 2015. That's an impressive run, but it's not the most notable fact about York's dividend stream. The company paid dividends without missing a single year since 1816, the year that Indiana was admitted as the 19th U.S. state! No other U.S. company can match York's record of nearly two centuries of uninterrupted dividend payments.

FAMOUS FAILURES IN FINANCE

Fears of Deflation Worry Investors

For most of your lifetime, prices of most goods and services have been rising. There are important exceptions, such as the prices of consumer electronics and computers, but from one year to the next, the overall price level rose continuously in the United States from 1955 through 2007. However, as the recession deepened in 2008, consumer prices in the United States began to decline, falling in each of the last five months that year. Countries in the European Union experienced a brief deflationary period around the same time. The news raised fears among some investors that the recession might turn into a depression like the one that had brought about a price decline of −27% from November 1929 to March 1933. Although prices began to rise again, fears of deflation resurfaced again in late 2014 and early 2015. Prices in the United States were flat or down in the first three months of 2015, while countries in the European Union experienced falling prices for four consecutive months starting in December 2015.

Critical Thinking Question Suppose you own an investment that pays a fixed return in dollars year after year. How do you think inflation (rising prices) or deflation (falling prices) would influence the value of this type of investment?

Famous Failures in Finance boxes—short, boxed discussions of real-life scenarios in the investments world, many of which focus on ethics—appear in selected chapters and on the book's website. Many of these boxes contain a Critical Thinking Question for class discussion, with guideline answers given in the Instructor's Manual.

WITHIN THE CHAPTER

Key Equations are screened in yellow throughout the text to help readers identify the most important mathematical relationships. Select key equations also appear in the text's rear endpapers.

Equation 8.4	$$\frac{\text{Estimated dividends}}{\text{per share in year } t} = \frac{\text{Estimated EPS}}{\text{for year } t} \times \frac{\text{Estimated}}{\text{payout ratio}}$$

Calculator Keystrokes At appropriate spots in the text the student will find sections on the use of financial calculators, with marginal calculator graphics that show the inputs and functions to be used.

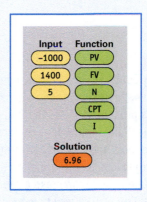

CONCEPTS IN REVIEW

Answers available at
http://www.pearsonhighered.com/smart

3.1 Discuss the impact of the Internet on the individual investor and summarize the types of resources it provides.

3.2 Identify the four main types of online investment tools. How can they help you become a better investor?

3.3 What are the pros and cons of using the Internet to choose and manage your investments?

Concepts in Review questions appear at the end of each section of the chapter. These review questions allow students to test their understanding of each section before moving on to the next section of the chapter. Answers for these questions are available in the Multimedia Library of MyFinanceLab, at the book's website, and by review of the preceding text.

The **end-of-chapter summary** makes *Fundamentals of Investing* an efficient study tool by integrating chapter contents with online learning resources available in **MyFinanceLab**. A thorough summary of the key concepts—What You Should Know—is directly linked with the text and online resources—Where to Practice. **Learning Goal** icons precede each summary item, which begins with a boldfaced restatement of the learning goal.

Discussion Questions, keyed to Learning Goals, guide students to integrate, investigate, and analyze the key concepts presented in the chapter. Many questions require that students apply the tools and techniques of the chapter to investment information they have obtained and then make a recommendation with regard to a specific investment strategy or vehicle. These project-type questions are far broader than the Concepts in Review questions within the chapter. Answers to odd-numbered questions are available to students in MyFinanceLab and on the book's website.

Expanded and Revised Problem Sets offer additional review and homework opportunities and are keyed to Learning Goals. Answers to odd-numbered Problems are available to students in MyFinanceLab and on the book's website, while all answers/solutions are available for instructors in the Instructor's Manual.

MyFinanceLab | Here is what you should know after reading this chapter. MyFinanceLab will help you identify what you know and where to go when you need to practice.

What You Should Know	Key Terms	Where to Practice
LG1 **Explain the behavior of market interest rates and identify the forces that cause interest rates to change.** The behavior of interest rates is the most important force in the bond market. It determines not only the amount of current income an investor will receive but also the investor's capital gains (or losses). Changes in market interest rates can have a dramatic impact on the total returns obtained from bonds over time.	yield spreads, p. 426	MyFinanceLab Study Plan 11.1
LG2 **Describe the term structure of interest rates and note how investors can use yield curves.** Many forces drive the behavior of interest rates over time, including inflation, the cost and availability of funds, and the level of interest rates in major foreign markets. One particularly important force is the term structure of interest rates, which relates yield to maturity to term to maturity. Yield curves essentially plot the term structure and are often used by investors as a way to get a handle on the future behavior of interest rates.	expectations hypothesis, p. 432 liquidity preference theory, p. 433 market segmentation theory, p. 433 term structure of interest rates, p. 429 yield curve, p. 429	MyFinanceLab Study Plan 11.2
LG3 **Understand how investors value bonds in the marketplace.** Bonds are valued (priced) in the	accrued interest, p. 438 clean price, p. 439	MyFinanceLab Study Plan 11.3

Discussion Questions

LG1 **Q11.1** Briefly describe each of the following theories of the term structure of interest rates.
a. Expectations hypothesis
b. Liquidity preference theory
c. Market segmentation theory

According to these theories, what conditions would result in a downward-sloping yield curve? What conditions would result in an upward-sloping yield curve? Which theory do you think is most valid, and why?

LG2 **Q11.2** Using the *Wall Street Journal*, *Barron's*, or an online source, find the bond yields for Treasury securities with the following maturities: 3 months, 6 months, 1 year, 3 years, 5 years, 10 years, 15 years, and 20 years. Construct a yield curve based on these reported yields, putting term to maturity on the horizontal (x) axis and yield to maturity on the vertical (y) axis. Briefly discuss the general shape of your yield curve. What conclusions might you draw about future interest rate movements from this yield curve?

LG5 **Q11.3** Briefly explain what will happen to a bond's duration measure if each of the following events occur.
a. The yield to maturity on the bond falls from 8.5% to 8%.
b. The bond rate 1 year closer to its maturity.

Problems

All problems are available on http://www.myfinancelab.com

LG3 **P11.1** You are considering the purchase of a $1,000 par value bond with an 6.5% coupon rate (with interest paid semiannually) that matures in 12 years. If the bond is priced to provide a required return of 8%, what is the bond's current price?

LG3 **P11.2** Two bonds have par values of $1,000. One is a 5%, 15-year bond priced to yield 8%. The other is a 7.5%, 20-year bond priced to yield 6%. Which of these has the lower price? (Assume annual compounding in both cases.)

LG3 **P11.3** Using semiannual compounding, find the prices of the following bonds.
a. A 10.5%, 15-year bond priced to yield 8%
b. A 7%, 10-year bond priced to yield 8%
c. A 12%, 20-year bond priced at 10%

Repeat the problem using annual compounding. Then comment on the differences you found in the prices of the bonds.

LG3 **P11.4** You have the opportunity to purchase a 25-year, $1,000 par value bond that has an annual coupon rate of 9%. If you require a YTM of 7.6%, how much is the bond worth to you?

LG3 **P11.5** A $1,000 par value bond has a current price of $800 and a maturity value of $1,000 and matures in five years. If interest is paid semiannually and the bond is priced to yield 8%, what is the bond's annual coupon rate?

LG3 **P11.6** A 20-year bond has a coupon of 10% and is priced to yield 8%. Calculate the price per $1,000 par value using semiannual compounding. If an investor purchases this bond two months before a scheduled coupon payment, how much accrued interest must be paid to the seller?

AT CHAPTER END

Case Problem 4.2   The Risk-Return Tradeoff: Molly O'Rourke's Stock Purchase Decision

LG3 LG6   Over the past 10 years, Molly O'Rourke has slowly built a diversified portfolio of common stock. Currently her portfolio includes 20 different common stock issues and has a total market value of $82,500.

Molly is at present considering the addition of 50 shares of either of two common stock issues—X or Y. To assess the return and risk of each of these issues, she has gathered dividend income and share price data for both over the last 10 years (2007–2016). Molly's investigation of the outlook for these issues suggests that each will, on average, tend to behave in the future just as it has in the past. She therefore believes that the expected return can be estimated by finding the average HPR over the past 10 years for each of the stocks. The historical dividend income and stock price data collected by Molly are given in the accompanying table.

Two **Case Problems**, keyed to the Learning Goals, encourage students to use higher-level critical thinking skills: to apply techniques presented in the chapter, to evaluate alternatives, and to recommend how an investor might solve a specific problem. Again, Learning Goals show the student the chapter topics on which the case problems focus.

Excel@Investing problems, appearing at the end of all chapters, challenge students to solve financial problems and make decisions through the creation of spreadsheets. In addition, in this edition we provide electronic versions of many in-text tables so students can see how the calculations in the tables work, and they can alter the baseline assumption in the printed tables to see how changing assumptions affects the main results of each table. In Chapter 1 students are directed to the website http://www.myfinancelab.com, where they can complete a spreadsheet tutorial, if needed. In addition, this tutorial and selected tables within the text carrying a spreadsheet icon are available in spreadsheet form on the text's website.

Excel@Investing

Excel@Investing   The cash flow component of bond investments is made up of the annual interest payments and the future redemption value or its par value. Just like other time-value-of-money considerations, the bond cash flows are discounted back in order to determine their present value.

In comparing bonds to stocks, many investors look at the respective returns. The total returns in the bond market are made up of both current income and capital gains. Bond investment analysis should include the determination of the current yield as well as a specific holding period return.

On January 13, 2016, you gather the following information on three corporate bonds issued by the General Pineapple Corporation (GPC). Remember that corporate bonds are quoted as a percentage of their par value. Assume the par value of each bond to be $1,000. These debentures are quoted in eighths of a point. Create a spreadsheet that will model and answer the following bond investment problems.

Bonds	Current Yield	Volume	Close
GPC 5.3 13	?	25	$105^7/_8$
GPC 6.65s 20	?	45	103
GPC 7.4 22	?	37	$104^6/_8$

CFA Exam Questions

Investing in Common Stocks

Following is a sample of 11 Level-I CFA exam questions that deal with many topics covered in Chapters 6, 7, 8, and 9 of this text, including the use of financial ratios, various stock valuation models, and efficient market concepts. (*Note:* When answering some of the questions, remember: "Forward P/E" is the same as a P/E based on estimated earnings one year out.) When answering the questions, give yourself 1½ minutes for each question; the objective is to correctly answer 8 of the 11 questions in a period of 16½ minutes.

1. Holding constant all other variables and excluding any interactions among the determinants of value, which of the following would most likely increase a firm's price-to-earnings multiple?
   a. The risk premium increases.
   b. The retention rate increases.
   c. The beta of the stock increases.

2. A rationale for the use of the price-to-sales (P/S) approach is:
   a. Sales are more volatile than earnings.
   b. P/S ratios assess cost structures accurately.
   c. Revenues are less subject to accounting manipulation than earnings.

3. A cyclical company tends to
   a. have earnings that track the overall economy.
   b. have a high price-to-earnings ratio.
   c. have less volatile earnings than the overall market.

4. Consider a company that earned $4.00 per share last year and paid a dividend of $1.00. The firm has maintained a consistent payout ratio over the years and analysts expect this to continue. The firm is expected to earn $4.40 per share next year, and the stock is expected to sell for $30.00. The required rate of return is 12%. What is the best estimate of the stock's current value?
   a. $44.00
   b. $22.67
   c. $27.77

5. A stock's current dividend is $1 and its expected dividend is $1.10 next year. If the investor's required rate of return is 15% and the stock is currently trading at $20.00, what is the implied expected price in one year?
   a. $21.90
   b. $22.00
   c. $23.00

6. A firm has total revenues of $187,500, net income of $15,000, total current liabilities of $50,000, total common equity of $75,000, and total assets of $150,000. What is the firm's ROE?
   a. 15%
   b. 20%
   c. 24%

CFA Exam Questions from the 2010 Level One Curriculum and the *CFA Candidate Study Notes, Level 1, Volume 4* are now at the end of each part of the book, starting at Part Two. These questions are also assignable in MyFinanceLab.

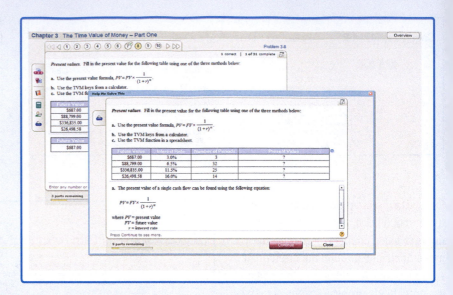

MyFinanceLab is a fully integrated homework and tutorial system which solves one of the biggest teaching problems in finance courses—students learn better with lots of practice, but grading complex multipart problems is time-consuming for the instructor. In MyFinanceLab, students can work the end-of-chapter problems with algorithmically generated values for unlimited practice and instructors can create assignments that are automatically graded and recorded in an online Gradebook.

MyFinanceLab also contains brief videos of author Scott Smart walking students through step-by-step solutions of select problems.

MyFinanceLab: hands-on practice, hands-off grading.

Supplemental Materials

We recognize the key role of a complete and creative package of materials to supplement a basic textbook. We believe that the following materials, offered with the thirteenth edition, will enrich the investments course for both students and instructors.

Fundamentals of Investing Companion Website

The book's Companion Website offers students and professors an up-to-date source of supplemental materials. This resource is located at http://www.pearsonhighered.com/smart. Visitors will find answers to Concepts in Review questions and answers to odd-numbered Discussion Questions and Problems and spreadsheets of selected tables within the text carrying the Excel@Investing icon.

Instructor's Manual

Revised by Robert J. Hartwig of Worcester State College, the *Instructor's Manual* contains chapter outlines; lists of key concepts discussed in each chapter; detailed chapter overviews; answers/suggested answers to all Concepts in Review and Discussion Questions, Problems, and Critical Thinking Questions to Famous Failures in Finance boxes; solutions to the Case Problems; and ideas for outside projects.

Test Bank

Revised for the thirteenth edition, also by Robert J. Hartwig of Worcester State College, the *Test Bank* includes a substantial number of questions. Each chapter features true-false and multiple-choice questions, as well as several problems and short-essay questions. The *Test Bank* is also available in Test Generator Software (TestGen with QuizMaster). Fully networkable, this software is available for Windows and Macintosh. TestGen's graphical interface enables instructors to easily view, edit, and add questions; export questions to create tests; and print tests in a variety of fonts and forms. Search and sort features let the instructor quickly locate questions and arrange them in a preferred order. QuizMaster, working with your school's computer network, automatically grades the exams, saves results, and allows the instructor to view or print a variety of reports.

PowerPoint Lecture Slides

To facilitate classroom presentations, PowerPoint slides of all text images and classroom lecture notes are available for Windows and Macintosh. The slides were revised by textbook author Scott Smart.

Acknowledgments

Many people gave their generous assistance during the initial development and revisions of *Fundamentals of Investing*. The expertise, classroom experience, and general advice of both colleagues and practitioners have been invaluable. Reactions and suggestions from students throughout the country—comments we especially enjoy receiving—sustained our belief in the need for a fresh, informative, and teachable investments text.

A few individuals provided significant subject matter expertise in the initial development of the book. They are Terry S. Maness of Baylor University, Arthur L. Schwartz, Jr., of the University of South Florida at St. Petersburg, and Gary W. Eldred. Their contributions are greatly appreciated. In addition, Pearson obtained the advice of a large group of experienced reviewers. We appreciate their many suggestions and criticisms, which have had a strong influence on various aspects of this volume. Our special thanks go to the following people, who reviewed all or part of the manuscript for the previous twelve editions of the book.

Kevin Ahlgrim	Albert J. Fredman	Wendy Ku	Rathin Rathinasamy
M. Fall Ainina	John Gerlach	George Kutner	William A. Richard
Joan Anderssen	Tom Geurts	Blake LeBaron	Linda R. Richardson
Felix O. Ayadi	Chaim Ginsberg	Robert T. LeClair	William A. Rini
Gary Baker	Joel Gold	Chun I. Lee	Roy A. Roberson
Harisha Batra	Terry Grieb	William Lepley	Tammy Rogers
Anand K. Bhattacharya	Frank Griggs	Steven Lifland	Edward Rozalewicz
Richard B. Bellinfante	Brian Grinder	Ralph Lim	William J. Ruckstuhl
Cecil C. Bigelow	Arthur S. Guarino	James Lock	David Russo
Robert J. Boldin	Harry P. Guenther	Larry A. Lynch	Arthur L. Schwartz, Jr.
Paul Bolster	Tom Guerts	Barry Marchman	William Scroggins
Denis O. Boudreaux	John Guess	Weston A. McCormac	Daniel Singer
A. David Brummett	Robert Hartwig	David J. McLaughlin	Keith V. Smith
Gary P. Cain	Mahboubul Hassan	Anne Macy	Pat R. Stout
Gary Carman	Gay Hatfield	James Mallett	Nancy E. Strickler
Daniel J. Cartell	Dan Hess	Keith Manko	Glenn T. Sweeney
P. R. Chandy	Robert D. Hollinger	Timothy Manuel	Amir Tavakkol
Steven P. Clark	Sue Beck Howard	Kathy Milligan	Phillip D. Taylor
William Compton	Ping Hsiao	Warren E. Moeller	Wenyuh Tsay
David M. Cordell	Roland Hudson, Jr.	Homer Mohr	Robert C. Tueting
Timothy Cowling	Raad Jassim	Majed R. Muhtaseb	Howard E. Van Auken
Robert M. Crowe	Donald W. Johnson	Joseph Newhouse	P. V. Viswanath
Richard F. DeMong	Samuel Kyle Jones	Michael Nugent	Doug Waggle
Clifford A. Diebold	Rajiv Kalra	Joseph F. Ollivier	Hsinrong Wei
Steven Dolvin	Ravindra R. Kamath	Michael Palermo	John R. Weigel
James Dunn	Bill Kane	John Palffy	Sally Wells
Betty Marie Dyatt	Daniel J. Kaufmann, Jr.	John Park	Peter M. Wichert
Scott Ehrhorn	Burhan Kawosa	Thomas Patrick	John C. Woods
Steven J. Elbert	Nancy Kegelman	Michael Polakoff	Michael D. Woodworth
Robert Eldridge	Phillip T. Kolbe	Barbara Poole	Robert J. Wright
Imad Elhaj	Sheri Kole	Ronald S. Pretekin	Richard H. Yanow
Thomas Eyssell	Christopher M. Korth	Stephen W. Pruitt	Ali E. Zadeh
Frank J. Fabozzi	Marie A. Kratochvil	Mark Pyles	Edward Zajicek
Robert A. Ford	Thomas M. Krueger	S. P. Umamaheswar Rao	

The following people provided extremely useful reviews and input to the thirteenth edition:

James DeMello, Western Michigan University

Matthew Haertzen, Northern Arizona University

Jeffrey Jones, College of Southern Nevada

Lynn Kugele, University of Mississippi

Michael G. Nugent, Stony Brook University

James Pandjiris, University of Missouri-St. Louis

Daniel Wolman, Nassau Community College

Dazhi Zheng, West Chester University

Because of the wide variety of topics covered in the book, we called upon many experts for advice. We thank them and their firms for allowing us to draw on their insights and awareness of recent developments to ensure that the text is as current as possible. In particular, we want to mention Bill Bachrach, Bachrach & Associates, San Diego, CA; John Markese, President, American Association of Individual Investors, Chicago, IL; Frank Hatheway, CFA, Chief Economist, Nasdaq, New York, NY; George Ebenhack, Oppenheimer & Co., Los Angeles, CA; Mark D. Erwin, ChFC, Commonwealth Financial Network, San Diego, CA; David M. Love, C. P. Eaton and Associates, La Jolla, CA; Michael R. Murphy, Sceptre Investment Counsel, Toronto, Ontario, Canada; Richard Russell, Dow Theory Letters, La Jolla, CA; and Michael J. Steelman, Merrill Lynch, Bonsall, CA.

To create the video feature An Advisor's Perspective, we relied on the generosity of many investment professionals from around the country. We are especially thankful to David Hays of CFCI and Ed Slott of Ed Slott and Company for helping us to do a great deal of the videotaping for this feature at the Ed Slott conference in Phoenix, Arizona. We are thankful to all of the investment professionals who participated in this project on video:

Catherine Censullo, Founder, CMC Wealth Management

Joseph A. Clark, Managing Partner, Financial Enhancement Group

Ron Courser, CFO, Ron Courser and Associates

Bob Grace, President, Grace Tax Advisory Group

James Grant, Founder, Grant's Interest Rate Observer

Bill Harris, Founder, WH Cornerstone Investments

James Johnson, President, All Mark Insurance Services

Mary Kusske, President, Kusske Financial Management

Rick Loek, CEO, Calrima Financial and Insurance Agency

Ryan McKeown, Senior VP, Wealth Enhancement Group

Thomas O'Connell, President, International Financial Advisory Group

Phil Putney, Owner, AFS Wealth Management

Tom Riquier, Owner, The Retirement Center

Rob Russell, CEO, Russell and Company

Carol Schmidlin, President, Franklin Planning

Ed Slott, CEO, Ed Slott and Company

Bryan Sweet, Owner, Sweet Financial Services

Steve Wright, Managing Member, The Wright Legacy Group

Special thanks to Robert Hartwig of Worcester State College for revising and updating the *Test Bank* and *Instructor's Manual*.

The staff at Pearson, particularly Donna Battista, contributed their creativity, enthusiasm, and commitment to this textbook. Pearson Program Manager Kathryn Dinovo and Project Manager Alison Kalil managed and pulled together the various strands of the project. Other dedicated Pearson staff, including Acquisitions Editor Kate Fernandes, Digital Studios Project Managers Melissa Honig and Andra Skaalrud, Digital Content Team Lead for MyFinanceLab Miguel Leonarte, Senior Product Marketing Manager Alison Haskins, warrant special thanks for shepherding the project through the development, production, marketing, and website construction stages. Without their care and concern, this text would not have evolved into the teachable and interesting text and package we believe it to be.

Finally, our wives, Susan, Robin, and Charlene, played important roles by providing support and understanding during the book's development, revision, and production. We are forever grateful to them, and we hope that this edition will justify the sacrifices required during the many hours we were away from them working on this book.

SCOTT B. SMART
LAWRENCE J. GITMAN
MICHAEL D. JOEHNK

1

The Investment Environment

LEARNING GOALS

After studying this chapter, you should be able to:

LG1 Understand the meaning of the term *investment* and list the attributes that distinguish one investment from another.

LG2 Describe the investment process and types of investors.

LG3 Discuss the principal types of investments.

LG4 Describe the purpose and content of an investment policy statement, review fundamental tax considerations, and discuss investing over the life cycle.

LG5 Describe the most common types of short-term investments.

LG6 Describe some of the main careers available to people with financial expertise and the role that investments play in each.

You have worked hard for your money. Now it is time to make your money work for you. Welcome to the world of investments. There are literally thousands of investments, from all around the world, from which to choose. How much should you invest, when should you invest, and which investments are right for you? The answers depend upon the knowledge and financial circumstances of each investor.

Financial news is plentiful, and finding financial information has become easier than ever. Today investors are bombarded with financial news. Cable TV networks such as CNBC, Bloomberg Television, and Fox Business Network specialize in business and financial news, and the print-based financial media has expanded beyond traditional powerhouses such as *The Wall Street Journal* and *The Financial Times* to include periodicals like *Money Magazine* and *Smart Money*, which focus on financial advice for individual investors. Clearly the Internet has played a major role in opening up the world of investing to millions of experienced and novice investors. The Internet makes enormous amounts of information readily available and enables investors to trade securities with the click of a mouse. Free and low-cost access to tools that were once restricted to professional investors helps create a more level playing field—yet at the same time, such easy access can increase the risks for inexperienced investors.

Regardless of whether you are an experienced investor or a newcomer to the field, the same investment fundamentals apply. Perhaps the most fundamental principle in investing, and one that you would be wise to keep in mind whenever you invest, is this—there is a tradeoff between an investment's risk and its return. Most people would like their investments to be as profitable as possible, but there is an almost unavoidable tendency for investments with the greatest profit potential to be associated with the highest degree of risk. You will see examples of the link between risk and return throughout this text.

This chapter provides a broad overview of the investments field. It introduces the various types of investments, the investment process, the role of investment plans, the importance of meeting liquidity needs, and careers in finance. Becoming familiar with investment alternatives and developing realistic investment plans should greatly increase your chance of achieving financial success.

Investments and the Investment Process

LG1 LG2

NOTE The Learning Goals shown at the beginning of the chapter are keyed to text discussions using these icons.

You are probably already an investor. If you have money in a savings account, you already have at least one investment to your name. An **investment** is simply any asset into which funds can be placed with the expectation that it will generate positive income and/or increase its value, and a collection of different investments is called a **portfolio**.

The rewards, or **returns**, from investing come in two basic forms: income and increased value. Money invested in a savings account provides *income* in the form of periodic interest payments. A share of common stock may also provide income (in the form of dividends), but investors often buy stock because they expect its price to rise. That is, common stock offers both income and the chance of an *increased value*. In the United States since 1900, the average annual return on a savings account has been a little more than 3%. The average annual return on common stock has been about 9.6%. Of course, during major market downturns (such as the one that occurred in 2008), the returns on nearly all investments fall well below these long-term historical averages.

Is cash placed in a simple (no-interest) checking account an investment? No, because it fails both tests of the definition: It does not provide added income and its value does not increase. In fact, over time inflation erodes the purchasing power of money left in a non-interest-bearing checking account.

We begin our study of investments by looking at types of investments and at the structure of the investment process.

Attributes of Investments

When you invest, the organization in which you invest—whether it is a company or a government entity—offers you the prospect of a future benefit in exchange for the use of your funds. You are giving up the use of your money, or the opportunity to use that money to consume goods and services today, in exchange for the prospect of having more money, and thus the ability to consume goods and services, in the future. Organizations compete for the use of your funds, and just as retailers compete for customers' dollars by offering a wide variety of products with different characteristics, organizations attempting to raise funds from investors offer a wide variety of investments with different attributes. As a result, investments of every type are available, from virtually zero-risk savings accounts at banks, which in recent years offered returns hovering barely above 0%, to shares of common stock in high-risk companies that might triple in value in a short time. The investments you choose will depend on your resources, your goals, and your willingness to take risk. We can describe a number of attributes that distinguish one type of investment from another.

NOTE Investor Facts offer interesting or entertaining tidbits of information.

INVESTOR FACTS

Art as an Asset Securities don't necessarily perform better than property. Over the decade ending in 2011, fine art produced an average annual return of 4.6%, compared to about 3.0% for stocks in the S&P 500.

Sources: (1) http://www.artasanasset.com; (2) "Paint by Numbers," Time, January 30, 2012.

Securities or Property Securities are investments issued by firms, governments, or other organizations that represent a financial claim on the resources of the issuer. The most common types of securities are stocks and bonds, but more exotic types such as stock options are available as well. One benefit of investing in securities is that they often have a high degree of **liquidity**, meaning that you can sell securities and convert them into cash quickly without incurring substantial transaction costs and without having an adverse impact on the security's price. Stocks issued by large companies, for example, tend to be highly liquid, and investors trade billions of shares of stock each day in the markets all over the world. The focus of this text is primarily on the most basic types of securities.

Property, on the other hand, consists of investments in real property or tangible personal property. *Real property* refers to land, buildings, and that which is permanently affixed to the land. *Tangible personal property* includes items such as gold, artwork, antiques, and other collectibles. In most cases, property is not as easy to buy or sell as are securities, so we would say that property tends to be a relatively *illiquid* type of investment. Investors who want to sell a building or a painting may have to hire (and compensate) a real estate agent or an art dealer to locate a buyer, and it may take weeks or months to sell the property.

Direct or Indirect A **direct investment** is one in which an investor directly acquires a claim on a security or property. If you buy shares of common stock in a company such as Apple Inc., then you have made a direct investment, and you are a part owner of that firm. An **indirect investment** is an investment in a collection of securities or properties managed by a professional investor. For example, when you send your money to a mutual fund company such as Vanguard or Fidelity, you are making an indirect investment in the assets held by these mutual funds.

Direct ownership of common stock has been on the decline in the United States for many years. For example, in 1945 households owned (directly) more than 90% of the common stocks listed in the United States. Over time that percentage dropped to its 2013 level of about 14% (by comparison, 36% of U.S. households own a dog). The same trend has occurred in most of the world's larger economies. In the United Kingdom, for example, households' direct ownership of shares fell from roughly 66% to 14% in the last half century. Today, households directly hold less than one-quarter of outstanding shares in most of the world's major stock markets, as Figure 1.1 shows.

Just as direct stock ownership by households has been falling, indirect ownership has been rising. One way to examine this trend is to look at the

INVESTOR FACTS

Smart people own stocks The stock market participation rate refers to the percentage of households who invest in stocks directly or indirectly. A study of investors from Finland found a remarkable connection between IQ and stock market participation— people with higher IQ scores were much more likely to invest in stocks than were people with lower IQ scores. More remarkable still, the IQ measure used in this study was the score on a test given to Finnish males when they were 19 or 20 years old as part of their induction to military service. IQ scores measured at that early age were a very strong predictor of whether these men would invest in stocks much later in life.

(Source: "IQ and Stock Market Participation," *Journal of Finance,* 2011, Vol. 66, Issue 6, pp. 2121–2164.)

FIGURE 1.1

Direct Stock Ownership by Households

The figure shows the percentage of common stocks in each country that is owned directly by households. In most countries, households' direct ownership accounts for less than one-quarter of listed common stocks in the country.

(Source: Data from "Government Policy and Ownership of Equity Securities, *Journal of Financial Economics,* 2014, Vol. 111, Issue 1, pp. 70–85.)

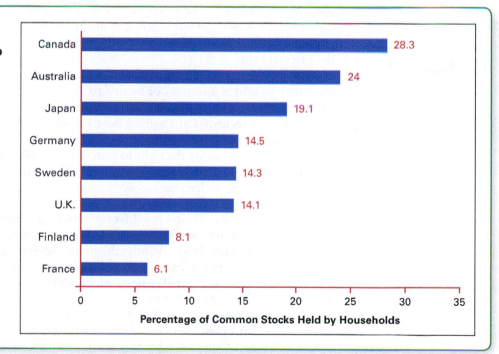

Country	Percentage
Canada	28.3
Australia	24
Japan	19.1
Germany	14.5
Sweden	14.3
U.K.	14.1
Finland	8.1
France	6.1

Percentage of Common Stocks Held by Households

WATCH YOUR BEHAVIOR

Surprisingly Low Stock Ownership
An important determinant in investment success is being willing to take some risk. One measure of risk-taking is stock ownership. Numerous studies have documented that only about 50% of U.S. households have direct or indirect investments in stocks. Given that stocks have historically earned a higher return than safer invest-ments, such as bonds, households that avoid stocks altogether may not accumulate as much wealth over time as they could if they were willing to take more risk.

Bonds vs. Stocks

direct ownership held by institutions that manage money on behalf of households. In 1945 institutional investors such as pension funds, hedge funds, and mutual funds combined held just less than 2% of the outstanding stock in the United States, but today their direct ownership is approaching 70%.

Tax policy helps to explain the decline in direct stock ownership by individuals and the related rise in direct ownership by institutions such as mutual funds and pension funds. Starting in 1978, section 401(k) of the Internal Revenue Code allowed employees to avoid paying tax on earnings that they elect to receive as deferred compensation, such as in a retirement savings plan. Since then, most large companies have adopted so-called 401(k) plans, which allow employees to avoid paying current taxes on the income that they contribute to a 401(k) plan. Employees are taxed on this income when they withdraw it during their retirement years. Typically, mutual fund companies such as T. Rowe Price and Franklin Templeton manage these 401(k) plans, so stocks held in these plans represent indirect ownership for the workers and direct ownership for the mutual fund companies.

An important element of this trend is that individuals who trade stocks often deal with professional investors who sell the shares those individuals want to buy or buy what individuals want to sell. For instance, in 2015 Fidelity had almost $2 trillion in assets in its various mutual funds, trusts, and other accounts, and the company employed approximately 41,000 people, many of whom had advanced investments training and access to a tremendous amount of information about the companies in which they invest. Given the prepon-derance of institutional investors in the market today, individuals are wise to consider the advantages possessed by the people with whom they are trading.

Debt, Equity, or Derivative Securities Most investments fall into one of two broad categories—debt or equity. **Debt** is simply a loan that obligates the borrower to make periodic interest payments and to repay the full amount of the loan by some future date. When companies or governments need to borrow money, they issue securities called *bonds*. When you buy a bond, in effect you lend money to the issuer. The issuer agrees to pay you interest for a specified time, at the end of which the issuer will repay the original loan.

Equity represents ongoing ownership in a business or property. An equity invest-ment may be held as a security or by title to a specific property. The most common type of equity security is *common stock*.

Derivative securities are neither debt nor equity. Instead, they derive their value from an underlying security or asset. Stock *options* are an example. A stock option is an investment that grants the right to purchase (or sell) a share of stock in a company at a fixed price for a limited period of time. The value of this option depends on the market price of the underlying stock.

Low- or High-Risk Investments Investments also differ on the basis of risk. **Risk** reflects the uncertainty surrounding the return that a particular investment will gen-erate. To oversimplify things slightly, the more uncertain the return associated with an investment, the greater is its risk. One of the most important strategies that investors use to manage risk is **diversification**, which simply means holding different types of assets in an investment portfolio.

As you invest over your lifetime, you will be confronted with a continuum of investments that range from low risk to high risk. For example, stocks are generally considered riskier than bonds because stock returns vary over a much wider range and are harder to predict than are bond returns. However, it is not difficult to find high-risk bonds that are riskier than the stock of a financially sound firm.

In general, investors face a tradeoff between risk and return—to obtain higher returns, investors usually have to accept greater risks. *Low-risk investments* provide a relatively predictable, but also relatively low, return. *High-risk investments* provide much higher returns on average, but they also have the potential for much larger losses.

Short- or Long-Term Investments   The life of an investment may be either short or long. **Short-term investments** typically mature within one year. **Long-term investments** are those with longer maturities or, like common stock, with no maturity at all.

Domestic or Foreign   As recently as 25 years ago, U.S. citizens invested almost exclusively in purely **domestic investments**: the debt, equity, and derivative securities of U.S.–based companies and governments. The same could be said of investors in many other countries. In the past, most people invested the vast majority of their money in securities issued by entities located in their home countries. Today investors routinely also look for **foreign investments** (both direct and indirect) that might offer more attractive returns than purely domestic investments. Even when the returns offered by foreign investments are not higher than those found in domestic securities, investors may still choose to make foreign investments because they help them build more diversified portfolios, which in turn helps limit exposure to risk. Information on foreign companies is now readily available, and it is now relatively easy to make foreign investments.

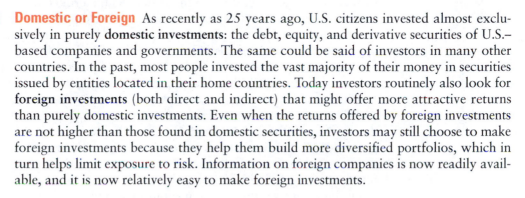

How Much Debt Has the U.S. Government Issued?

The Structure of the Investment Process

The investment process brings together *suppliers* who have extra funds and *demanders* who need funds. Households, governments, and businesses are the key participants in the investment process, and each of these participants may act as a supplier or a demander of funds at a particular time. However, there are some general tendencies. Households who spend less than their income have savings, and they want to invest those surplus funds to earn a return. Households, then, are generally *net suppliers* of funds in the investment process. Governments, on the other hand, often spend more than they take in through tax revenue, so they issue bonds and other debt securities to raise additional funds. Governments are typically *net demanders* of funds. Businesses are also *net demanders* of funds most of the time. They issue debt or equity securities to finance new investments and other activities.

Suppliers and demanders of funds usually come together by means of a financial institution or a financial market. **Financial institutions** are organizations, such as banks and insurance companies, that pool the resources of households and other savers and use those funds to make loans and to invest in securities such as short-term bonds issued by the U.S. government. **Financial markets** are markets in which suppliers and demanders of funds trade financial assets, typically with the assistance of intermediaries such as securities brokers and dealers. All types of investments, including stocks, bonds, commodities, and foreign currencies, trade in financial markets.

The dominant financial market in the United States is the *securities market*. It includes stock markets, bond markets, and options markets. Similar markets exist in most major economies throughout the world. The prices of securities traded in these markets are determined by the interactions of buyers and sellers, just as other prices are established in other kinds of markets. For example, if the number of Facebook shares that investors want to buy is greater than the number that investors want to sell, the price of Facebook stock will rise. As new information about the company becomes available, changes in supply (investors who want to sell) and demand (investors who want to buy) may result in a new market price. Financial markets streamline the process of bringing together buyers and sellers so that investors can transact with each other quickly and without incurring exorbitant transaction costs. Financial markets provide another valuable function by establishing market prices for securities that are easy for market participants to monitor. For example, a firm that launches a new product may get an early indication of how that product will be received in the market by seeing whether investors drive the firm's stock price up or down when they learn about the new product.

Figure 1.2 is a diagram of the investment process. Note that the suppliers of funds may transfer their resources to the demanders through financial institutions, through financial markets, or in direct transactions. As the broken lines show, financial institutions can participate in financial markets as either suppliers or demanders of funds. For the economy to grow and prosper, funds must flow to those with attractive investment opportunities. If individuals began suddenly hoarding their excess funds rather than putting them to work in financial institutions and markets, then organizations in need of funds would have difficulty obtaining them. As a result, government spending, business expansion, and consumer purchases would decline, and economic activity would slow.

When households have surplus funds to invest, they must decide whether to make the investment decisions themselves or to delegate some or all of that responsibility to professionals. This leads to an important distinction between two types of investors in the financial markets. **Individual investors** manage their own funds to achieve their financial goals. Individual investors usually concentrate on earning a return on idle funds, building a source of retirement income, and providing security for their families.

Individuals who lack the time or expertise to make investment decisions often employ **institutional investors**—investment professionals who earn their living by managing other people's money. These professionals trade large volumes of securities for individuals, as well as for businesses and governments. Institutional investors include banks, life insurance companies, mutual funds, pension funds, and hedge funds. For example, a life insurance company invests the premiums it receives from policyholders to earn returns that will cover death benefits paid to beneficiaries.

FIGURE 1.2

The Investment Process

Financial institutions participate in the financial markets as well as transfer funds between suppliers and demanders. Although the arrows go only from suppliers to demanders, for some transactions (e.g., the sale of a bond or a college loan), the principal amount borrowed by the demander from the supplier (the lender) is eventually returned.

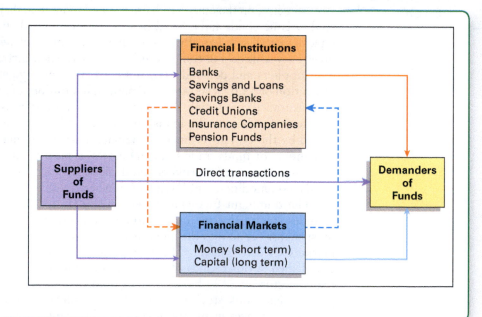

Both individual and institutional investors apply similar fundamental principles when deciding how to invest money. However, institutional investors generally control larger sums of money and have more sophisticated analytical skills than do most individual investors. *The information presented in this text is aimed primarily at you—the individual investor.* Mastering this material represents only the first step that you need to take to develop the expertise to become an institutional investor.

CONCEPTS IN REVIEW
Answers available at
http://www.pearsonhighered.com/smart

NOTE The Concepts in Review questions at the end of each text section encourage you, before you move on, to test your understanding of the material you've just read.

1.1 Define the term *investment*, and explain why individuals invest.

1.2 Differentiate among the following types of investments, and cite an example of each: (a) securities and property investments; (b) direct and indirect investments; (c) debt, equity, and derivative securities; and (d) short-term and long-term investments.

1.3 What is the relation between an investment's risk and its return?

1.4 Define the term *risk*, and explain how risk is used to differentiate among investments.

1.5 What are *foreign investments*, and what role do they play for the individual investor?

1.6 Describe the structure of the overall investment process. Explain the role played by *financial institutions* and *financial markets*.

1.7 Classify the roles of (a) government, (b) business, and (c) individuals as net suppliers or net demanders of funds.

1.8 Differentiate between *individual investors* and *institutional investors*.

Types of Investments

LG3 A wide variety of investments is available to individual investors. As you have seen, investments differ in terms of risk, maturity, and many other characteristics. We devote the bulk of this text to describing the characteristics of different investments and the strategies that you may use when you buy and sell these investments. Table 1.1 summarizes some basic information about the major types of investments that we will study.

Short-Term Investments

Short-term investments have a life of one year or less and usually (but not always) carry little or no risk. People buy these investments as a temporary "warehouse" for idle funds before transferring the money into a long-term investment. Short-term investments are also popular among conservative investors who may be reluctant to lock up their funds in riskier, long-term assets such as stocks or bonds.

Short-term investments also provide liquidity because they can be converted into cash quickly and with little or no loss in value. Liquidity is important to investors because it is impossible to know when an emergency or other unplanned event will make it necessary to obtain cash by selling an investment. At such a time, the speed at which the investment can be sold is particularly important. Of course, almost any investment can be sold quickly if the owner is willing to lower the price enough, but having to sell an investment at a bargain price only compounds the problem that led to the need to sell in the first place. Liquid investments give investors peace of mind that

TABLE 1.1   MAJOR TYPES OF INVESTMENTS

Type	Description	Examples	Where Covered in This Book
Short-term investments	Savings instruments with lives of 1 year or less. Used to warehouse idle funds and to provide liquidity.	Deposit accounts, U.S. Treasury bills (T-bills), Certificates of deposit (CDs), Commercial paper, Money market mutual funds	Ch. 1
Common stock	Equity investments that represent ownership in a corporation.		Chs. 6–9
Fixed-income securities	Investments that make fixed cash payments at regular intervals.	Bonds, Convertible securities Preferred stock	Chs. 10, 11 Web Ch. 16
Mutual funds	Companies that pool money from many investors and invest funds in a diversified portfolio of securities.	Large-cap funds, Growth funds	Ch. 1
Exchange-traded funds	Investment funds, typically index funds, that are exchange listed and, therefore, exchange traded.	Stock index funds, Bond index funds	Ch. 12
Hedge funds	Alternative investments, usually in pools of underlying securities, available only to sophisticated investors, such as institutions and individuals with significant assets.	Long and short equities, Funds of funds	Ch. 12
Derivative securities	Securities that are neither debt nor equity but are structured to exhibit the characteristics of the underlying assets from which they derive their value.	Options Futures	Ch. 14 Ch. 15
Other popular investments	Various other investments that are widely used by investors.	Tax-advantaged investments Real estate Tangibles	Web Ch. 17 Web Ch. 18 Web Ch. 18

they will be able to get their hands on cash quickly if they need it, without having to sell their investments at fire-sale prices.

Common Stock

Common stock is an equity investment that represents ownership in a corporation. Each share of common stock represents a fractional ownership interest in the firm. For example, if you buy 1 share of common stock in a corporation that has 10,000 shares outstanding, you would be a 1/10,000th owner in the firm. Today, roughly half of all U.S. households own some common stock, either directly or indirectly.

The return on investment in common stock comes from two sources: dividends and capital gains. **Dividends** are payments the corporation makes to its shareholders. Companies are not required to pay dividends to their shareholders, and most firms that are small or are growing very rapidly do not pay dividends. As firms grow and accumulate cash, they often start paying dividends, just as Dollar General did in 2015. Companies that pay dividends usually pay them quarterly. **Capital gains** occur when the stock price rises above an investor's initial purchase price. Capital gains may be *realized* or *unrealized*. If you sell a stock for more than you paid for it, you have realized a capital gain. If you continue to hold the stock rather than sell it, you have an unrealized capital gain.

Example

> Suppose you purchased a single share of Whirlpool Corporation common stock for $155 on January 2, 2014, the first day that the stock market was open for trading that year. During 2014 you received $2.87 in cash dividends. At the end of the year, you sold the stock for $195. You earned $2.87 in dividends and you realized a $40 capital gain ($195 sale price − $155 purchase price) for a total dollar return of $42.87. On a percentage basis, the return on Whirlpool shares in 2014 is calculated as $42.87 ÷ $155 = 0.277 or 27.7%. If you continued to hold the stock rather than sell it, at the end of the year you would have earned the same return but your capital gain would have been unrealized.

As mentioned earlier, since 1900 the average annual rate of return on common stocks has been about 9.6%, so 2014 was a good year for Whirlpool. As a producer of durable consumer products such as refrigerators, washing machines, and the iconic KitchenAid stand mixer, Whirlpool's stock generally performs best when the economy is growing (as it was in 2014) and consumers are making major purchases of new appliances.

Fixed-Income Securities

Fixed-income securities are investments that offer a periodic cash payment that may be fixed in dollar terms or may vary according to a predetermined formula (for example, the formula might dictate that cash payments rise if a general rise in market interest rates occurs). Some offer contractually guaranteed returns, meaning that the issuer of the security (i.e., the borrower) must fulfill a promise to make payments to investors or risk being sued. Other fixed-income securities come with the expectation of regular payments even if a contractual obligation is absent. Because of their relatively predictable cash payments, fixed-income securities tend to be popular during periods of economic uncertainty when investors are reluctant to invest in riskier securities such as common stocks. Fixed-income securities are also attractive during periods of high interest rates when investors seek to "lock in" high returns. The most common fixed-income securities are bonds, convertible securities, and preferred stock.

Bonds Bonds are long-term debt instruments (in other words, an IOU, or promise to pay) issued by corporations and governments. A bondholder has a contractual right to receive periodic interest payments plus return of the bond's *face*, or *par*, *value* (the stated value given on the certificate) at maturity (typically 10 to 30 years from the date issued).

If you purchased a $1,000 bond paying 9% interest in semiannual installments, you would receive an interest payment equal to $1,000 × 9% × ½ year = $45 every six months. At maturity you would also receive the bond's $1,000 face value. Bonds vary a great deal in terms of liquidity, so they may or may not be easy to sell prior to maturity.

Since 1900 the average annual rate of return on long-term government bonds has been about 5%. Corporate bonds are riskier because they are not backed by the full faith and credit of the U.S. government and, therefore, tend to offer slightly higher returns than government bonds provide.

Convertible Securities A **convertible security** is a special type of fixed-income investment. It has a feature permitting the investor to convert it into a specified number of shares of common stock. Convertibles provide the fixed-income benefit of a bond (interest) while offering the price-appreciation (capital gain) potential of common stock.

Preferred Stock Like common stock, **preferred stock** represents an ownership interest in a corporation and has no maturity date. Unlike common stock, preferred stock has a fixed dividend rate. Firms are generally required to pay dividends on preferred shares before they are allowed to pay dividends on their common shares. Furthermore, if a firm is having financial difficulties and decides to stop paying preferred dividends, it must usually make up all of the dividend payments that it skipped before paying dividends on common shares. Investors typically purchase preferred stocks for the dividends they pay, but preferred shares may also provide capital gains.

Mutual Funds

A **mutual fund** is a portfolio of stocks, bonds, or other assets that were purchased with a pool of funds contributed by many different investors and that are managed by an investment company on behalf of its clients. Investors in a mutual fund own an interest in the fund's collection of securities. Most individual investors who invest in stocks do so indirectly by purchasing mutual funds that hold stocks. When they send money to a mutual fund, investors buy shares in the fund (as opposed to shares in the companies in which the fund invests), and the prices of the mutual fund shares reflect the value of the assets that the fund holds. Mutual funds allow investors to construct well-diversified portfolios without having to invest a large sum of money. After all, it's cheaper to buy shares in a fund that holds 500 stocks than it is to buy shares in 500 companies on your own. In the last three decades, the mutual fund industry has experienced tremendous growth. The number of equity mutual funds (i.e., funds that invest mainly or exclusively in common stock) has more than quadrupled since 1980.

Most mutual managers follow one of two broad approaches when selecting specific securities for their funds. In an *actively managed fund*, managers try to identify and purchase securities that are undervalued and are therefore likely to perform particularly well in the future. Or managers try to identify overvalued securities that may perform poorly and simply avoid those investments. The goal of an actively managed fund is typically to earn a higher return than some sort of benchmark. For a mutual fund that invests in stocks, a common goal is to earn a return that is higher than the return on a market index like the Standard and Poor's 500 Stock Index (S&P 500). In a *passively managed fund*, managers make no attempt to identify under or overvalued securities. Instead, they buy a diversified portfolio of stocks and try to mimic or match the return on a market index. Because these funds try to provide returns that are as close as possible to the returns on a market index, they usually referred to as *index funds*.

In return for the services that they provide, mutual funds (or rather the investment companies that run the mutual funds) charge investors fees, and some of those fees are rolled together in a figure known as the *expense ratio*. The expense ratio is a fee charged to investors based on a percentage of the assets invested in a fund. It accrues daily and represents one of the primary costs that investors pay when they purchase mutual fund shares. For example, if an individual has $10,000 invested in a mutual fund with an expense ratio of 1%, then the fund will charge $100 per year to manage the individual's money.

Expense ratios are generally higher for funds that invest in riskier securities. For example, in 2014 the average expense ratio among mutual funds investing in stocks was 0.70%, meaning that investors would pay expenses equal to $70 per $10,000 invested. For funds that invest in bonds, the average expense ratio was 0.57%. **Money**

market mutual funds (also called **money funds**) are mutual funds that invest solely in short-term investments. The average expense ratio for money market mutual funds in 2014 was just 0.13%.

Expense ratios also tend to be higher for actively managed funds than for index funds. That shouldn't be surprising because actively managed funds are more expensive to operate. For many years, expense ratios have been on the decline. The average expense ratio for equity mutual funds fell 25 basis points (or one quarter of one percent) in the last decade, from 9.95% in 2004 to 0.70% in 2014. Falling expense ratios is good news for mutual fund investors. Even so, there is considerable variation in expense ratios from one fund to another, so investors need to pay close attention to expenses before they choose a fund.

In addition to the expense ratio, some funds charge a fee called a *load*. A load may be charged up front when the investor initially buys shares in the fund, in which case it is called a *sales load*. Alternatively, when investors sell their shares the fund may charge a fee known as a *redemption fee* or *back-end load*. Typically, redemption fees are reduced or waived entirely if investors keep their money in the fund for a long period of time.

Exchange-Traded Funds

Like mutual funds, **exchange-traded funds** (ETFs) hold portfolios of securities, and investors buy shares in the ETF. ETFs are very similar to mutual funds. They allow investors to form well-diversified portfolios with low initial investments, and the fees charged by ETFs are generally quite low. However, there are some important distinctions between these two popular investments. The main distinction is that ETFs trade on exchanges, so investors can buy and sell shares in an ETF at its current market price at any time during regular trading hours. Mutual fund shares are not traded on exchanges, and when an investor buys (or sells) shares in a fund from an investment company, the transaction occurs at the end of the trading day using the fund's closing price. The mutual fund's closing price is determined by adding up the values of all of the securities that the fund holds at the end of the day and dividing by the number of shares in the fund. If stock prices are rising or falling rapidly during the day, ETF investors may be able to take advantage of this by purchasing or selling their shares before prices hit their peak (or bottom). Investors in mutual funds have to wait until the end of the day to learn the price at which they can buy or sell shares in the fund.

Another important difference has to do with what happens to the money when investors buy or sell shares. When you buy shares in a mutual fund, the fund has more resources than it had before, so the fund's managers will likely use those funds to invest in more securities. Similarly, if you sell shares in the fund, then the fund's managers may have to sell some of the securities that the fund holds to raise the cash to pay you when you redeem your shares. If many investors want to sell their shares simultaneously, that may trigger a *fire sale*—the fund manager has to accept lower prices to quickly convert the fund's assets into cash. In contrast, ETF shares represent a fixed number of claims on a fixed portfolio of securities. When you buy ETF shares, you are simply acquiring them from other investors who want to sell their shares. There is no net inflow or outflow of money into the company that manages the ETF, and therefore there is no need to buy or sell additional securities in response to investors' transactions.

Launched in 1993, the very first ETF was a broad-based equity fund designed to track the Standard and Poor's 500 Stock Index. Since then, both the number of ETFs and the amount of money invested in them has grown explosively. From 2003 to 2014, the number of ETFs grew by a factor of 12, and assets invested in those funds grew at a rate that exceeded 26% per year. Even so, for every $1 invested in ETFs today, about $9 are invested in mutual funds.

Hedge Funds

Like mutual funds, **hedge funds** are investment funds that pool resources from many different investors and invest those funds in securities. Hedge funds are generally open to a narrower group of investors than are mutual funds. For example, the minimum investment required by a mutual fund might be a few hundred dollars whereas the minimum investment required to participate in a hedge fund runs into the hundreds of thousands of dollars. Some hedge funds have a minimum investment of $1 million. Despite the high minimum investment, hedge funds have grown in importance in recent years, with assets under management approaching $3 trillion in 2015.

Hedge funds generally charge investors much higher fees than do mutual funds. Traditionally, hedge fund fees follow the "two and twenty" rule, which means that investors pay the hedge fund annual fees equal to 2% of the assets they manage plus 20% of any investment gains that the fund can achieve. The first component of the fee is known as the management fee and is independent of the fund's performance. The second component is known as the incentive fee. Investors in hedge funds do not pay incentive fees if a fund earns a negative return in a particular year, and it is common for the incentive fee to have a feature known as the "high-water mark." The high-water mark specifies that the incentive fee is not payable until a hedge fund passes its previous peak value. For example, if the hedge fund loses 6% in one year and earns 10% the following year, the incentive fee will not be paid on the second year's entire 10% return. Instead, the fee will only apply to the increase in fund value above and beyond its previous peak. In other words, the fund has to earn back the 6% that it previously lost before new incentive fees kick in.

Hedge funds are not as closely regulated as are mutual funds, and they tend to invest in riskier and less liquid securities. The very name "hedge fund" suggests that these funds try to limit or hedge the risks that they take, and, indeed, some hedge funds do operate with that goal in mind. However, some hedge funds adopt very high-risk investment strategies. Nonetheless, the hedge fund industry experienced dramatic growth in the last decade.

Derivatives Securities

As the name suggests, *derivative securities* derive their value from an underlying security or asset. Many derivatives are among the most risky financial assets because they are designed to magnify price changes of the underlying asset. For example, when the price of oil moves up or down by $1 per barrel, the value of an oil futures contract (an agreement between two parties to trade oil on a future date at a specified price) moves $1,000 in the same direction. Investors may buy or sell derivatives to speculate on the future movements of another asset, but corporations also buy and sell derivatives to hedge against some of the risks they face. For example, a cereal company may purchase wheat futures contracts as a kind of insurance against the possibility that wheat prices will rise.

Options Options are securities that give the investor an opportunity to sell or buy another security at a specified price over a given period of time. Investors purchase options to take advantage of an anticipated change in the price of common stock. However, the purchaser of an option is not guaranteed a return and could even lose the entire amount invested if the option does not become attractive enough to use. Two common types of options are *calls* and *puts*. Call options grant the right to buy another security at a fixed price, and put options grant the right to sell another security at a fixed price.

Futures **Futures** are legally binding obligations stipulating that the seller of the futures contract will make delivery and the buyer of the contract will take delivery of an asset at some specific date and at a price agreed on at the time the contract is sold. Examples of *commodities futures* include soybeans, pork bellies, platinum, and cocoa contracts. Examples of *financial futures* are contracts for Japanese yen, U.S. Treasury securities, interest rates, and stock indexes. Trading in commodity and financial futures is generally a highly specialized, high-risk proposition.

Other Popular Investments

Because the U.S. federal income tax rate for an individual can be as high as 39.6%, many investors look for **tax-advantaged investments**. These are investments that provide higher after-tax returns by reducing the amount of taxes that investors must pay. For instance, municipal bonds, which are bonds issued by state and local governments, make interest payments that are not subject to federal income taxation. Because investors do not have to pay taxes on the interest they receive on municipal bonds, they will accept lower interest rates on these investments than they will on similar bonds that make taxable interest payments.

Real estate consists of assets such as residential homes, raw land, and a variety of forms of income property, including warehouses, office and apartment buildings, and condominiums. The appeal of real estate investment is the potential returns in the forms of rental income, tax write-offs, and capital gains.

Tangibles are investment assets, other than real estate, that can be seen or touched. They include gold and other precious metals, gemstones, and collectibles such as coins, stamps, artwork, and antiques. People purchase these assets as investments in anticipation of price increases.

CONCEPTS IN REVIEW

Answers available at
http://www.pearsonhighered.com/smart

1.9 What are *short-term investments*? How do they provide *liquidity*?

1.10 What is *common stock*, and what are its two sources of potential return?

1.11 Briefly define and differentiate among the following investments. Which offer fixed returns? Which are derivative securities? Which offer professional investment management?

   a. Bonds
   b. Convertible securities
   c. Preferred stock
   d. Mutual funds
   e. Hedge funds
   f. Options
   g. Futures

Making Your Investment Plan

 Investing can be conducted on a strictly intuitive basis or on the basis of plans carefully developed to achieve specific goals. Evidence favors the planned approach. Developing a well thought-out investment plan encourages you to follow a disciplined approach to managing money. That discipline will help you avoid many common investment mistakes by keeping you focused on your investment goals during market swings. A good investment plan is a reminder of the goals that you are trying to achieve with your money, and it provides a kind of strategic roadmap to guide investment decisions over a lifetime. We suggest that your investment plan should begin with an Investment Policy Statement.

Writing an Investment Policy Statement

Large corporations typically have an investment policy statement (IPS) that spells out how the corporation will invest funds in the company retirement plan. Financial advisors write them for their clients. Our view is that an IPS is equally important for individual investors like you. Writing such a statement forces you to think carefully about all aspects of your investment plan, a particularly useful exercise for a novice investor. If you have a spouse or partner, an IPS can help you work out (in advance) disagreements about how much money the two of you should save and how that money should be invested. In middle age, an IPS helps you assess the progress toward your long-term financial goals. Below we outline the major elements of a well-crafted IPS. Most of the tools and concepts covered in this text can be applied in a thorough IPS.

Summarize your current situation. In the opening section of the IPS, list the assets that you currently own. Set a target for how much money you think you can save and invest each month. Describe where the money that you plan to invest will come from. Given your income and your current spending habits, is it reasonable to expect that you will have surplus funds to invest? What tax rate do you face today, and how do you expect that to change in the future? Establish some broad guidelines for the initial asset allocation in your portfolio. What percentage of your funds do you want to invest in stocks, bonds, and other types of investments? Ask yourself how much money you think you can afford to lose, both in the short term (over a few months) and the long term (over a few years), and articulate your action plan when losses occur. Will you sell some of your investments, simply hold onto them, or continue making new investments each month according to the plan? Try to define your investment horizon. Will you need to access the funds you are investing in a year, in a decade, or at the end of your working life? If you plan to enlist the help of a professional investment advisor, describe the process that you will use to select that person. If you have already selected an advisor, list that person's contact information in your IPS and discuss the statement with him or her, perhaps even getting his or her signature on the document.

Specify your investment goals. Once you have outlined your current situation, write out your investment goals. **Investment goals** are the financial objectives you wish to achieve by investing. Are you trying to reach a specific target savings goal, such as accumulating enough money to make a down payment on a house? Or do you have a goal that is further out in the future, such as saving enough money to send your children to college or even to provide enough income for your own retirement? Is your investment goal to generate more cash flow in the form of interest or dividends, or are you trying to shelter income from taxation? Achieving each of these goals may call for a different type of investment strategy. For each goal that you specify, try to determine how many years you will need to save and invest to achieve that goal, and how much money you need to invest each year to reach your goal.

Articulate your investment philosophy. In this part of the IPS, you'll want to spell out your investment philosophy, your views about the types of investments you're willing to make, how often you are willing to adjust your portfolio through trading, and other matters that will shape your investment portfolio. Perhaps the most important aspect of your investment philosophy is your tolerance for risk. Your investment philosophy should indicate how much volatility in the value of your portfolio that you are willing to tolerate. For example, you might say that your portfolio should be designed in such a way that a loss in a single year of more than 20% is highly unlikely. Your policy should indicate how important diversification is to you and how many types of investments you plan to own. Your philosophy will specify certain types of investments that you are not willing to purchase. Perhaps you will choose not to invest in certain industries for ethical reasons, or you will declare that only "plain vanilla" investments like stocks and bonds should be part of your portfolio (no derivatives or exotic investments, please). If you are working with a financial advisor, you may want to specify how frequently you want to make changes in the portfolio by trading, or you may want to provide guidelines about the trading costs or (in the case of mutual funds and ETFs) the management fees you're willing to pay. In this section of the IPS you may choose to articulate your assumptions about the returns that you expect different types of investments to earn over time.

Set investment selection guidelines. For each type of investment, or asset class, that you expect to hold in your portfolio (e.g., stocks, bonds, mutual funds), establish guidelines for how specific investments in that asset class will be selected. For example, if you plan to hold mutual funds, will you invest in actively or passively managed funds? In your selection process, how much importance will you place on a fund's track record (i.e., its past performance or the experience and education of the fund manager) and how much on its expense ratio and other costs of investing in the fund? If you plan to invest directly in stocks, will you focus on large, well-known companies, or are you more interested in emerging high-tech companies? Does it matter to you whether the stocks you invest in pay dividends? When you are deciding which bonds to invest in, will you focus more heavily on the creditworthiness of the bond issuer or on other features of the bond such as its maturity or the interest rate that it promises to pay?

Assign responsibility for selecting and monitoring investments. In this part of the IPS, you indicate whether you will make your own investment selections or whether you will enlist the help of an advisor to do that. Likewise, you establish a plan for monitoring your investments. Do you plan to evaluate your investment performance quarterly, semiannually, or just once a year?

What criteria will you use to determine whether your investments are meeting your expectations or not? Any risky investment is bound to have periods when it performs poorly, so your IPS should provide some guidance about how long you are willing to tolerate subpar performance before making a change in the portfolio. Similarly, an investment that performs particularly well for a year or two will inevitably account for a rising fraction of the portfolio's overall value. Your IPS may describe the conditions under which you might sell some of your better performing investments simply to rebalance the portfolio.

WATCH YOUR BEHAVIOR

Watch your investments, but not too closely. Researchers have uncovered an interesting aspect of investor behavior. Individuals who monitor their portfolios most frequently tend to invest less in risky assets. Almost by definition, risky investments will frequently experience periods of low or even negative returns, even though over long periods of time risky assets tend to earn higher returns than safe assets do. When investors check their portfolios frequently, they apparently find it uncomfortable to observe the periods when risky investments perform badly, so they simply take less risk. In the long run, taking very little risk leads to very low returns, so it is not clear that watching investments too closely is a good thing.

(Source: "Myopic Loss Aversion and the Equity Premium Puzzle," *Quarterly Journal of Economics*, 1995, Vol. 110, pp. 75–92.)

Considering Personal Taxes

Knowledge of the tax laws can help you reduce taxes and increase the amount of after-tax dollars you have for investing. Because tax laws are complicated and subject to frequent revision, we present only the key concepts and how they apply to popular investment transactions.

Basic Sources of Taxation The two major types of taxes to consider when forming your investment plans are those levied by the federal government and those levied by state and local governments. The federal *income tax* is the major form of personal taxation. Federal rates currently range from 10% to 39.6% of taxable income, although with rising federal budget deficits, many experts believe that those tax rates will rise in the future.

State and local taxes vary from area to area. Top earners in California face a tax rate of 13.3%, and six other states have tax rates on high-income households that range from 8% to 11%. Some cities, especially large East Coast cities, also have local income taxes that typically range between 1% and 5%. In addition to income taxes, state and local governments rely heavily on sales and property taxes as a source of revenue.

Income taxes at the federal, state, and local levels have a great impact on the returns that investors earn from security investments. Property taxes can have a sizable impact on real estate and other forms of property investment.

Types of Income The income of individuals is classified into *three basic categories*:

- *Active income* consists of everything from wages and salaries to bonuses, tips, pension income, and alimony. Active income is made up of income earned on the job as well as most other forms of *noninvestment* income.

- *Portfolio income* includes earnings generated from various types of investments. This category covers most (but not all) types of investments from savings accounts, stocks, bonds, and mutual funds to options and futures. For the most part, portfolio income consists of interest, dividends, and capital gains (the profit on the sale of an investment).

- *Passive income* is a special category of income composed chiefly of income derived from real estate, limited partnerships, and other forms of tax-advantaged investments.

Tax laws limit the amount of deductions (write-offs) that can be taken for each category, particularly for portfolio and passive income. The amount of allowable deductions for portfolio and passive income is *limited to the amount of income derived from these two sources*. For example, if you had a total of $380 in portfolio income for the year, you could deduct no more than $380 in investment-related interest expense. For deduction purposes, the portfolio and passive income categories cannot be mixed or combined with each other or with active income. *Investment-related expenses can be used only to offset portfolio income*, and (with a few exceptions) *passive investment expenses can be used only to offset the income from passive investments*.

Ordinary Income Whether it's classified as active, portfolio, or passive, ordinary income is taxed at the federal level at one of seven rates: 10%, 15%, 25%, 28%, 33%, 35%, or 39.6%. There is one structure of tax rates for taxpayers who file *individual* returns and another for those who file *joint* returns with a spouse. Table 1.2 shows the 2015 tax rates and income brackets for these two categories. Note that the rates are *progressive*; that is, income is taxed in a tiered progression—the first portion of a taxpayer's income is taxed at one rate, the next portion at a higher rate, and so on. An example will demonstrate how ordinary income is taxed.

TABLE 1.2   FEDERAL INCOME TAX RATES AND BRACKETS FOR INDIVIDUAL AND JOINT RETURNS (DUE BY APRIL 15, 2015)

	Taxable Income	
Tax Rates	Individual Returns	Joint Returns
10.0%	$0 to $9,075	$0 to $18,150
15.0%	$9,076 to $36,900	$18,151 to $73,800
25.0%	$36,901 to $89,350	$73,801 to $148,850
28.0%	$89,351 to $186,350	$148,851 to $226,850
33.0%	$186,351 to $405,100	$226,851 to $405,100
35.0%	$405,101 to $406,750	$405,101 to $457,600
39.6%	Over $406,750	Over $457,600

NOTE Excel Spreadsheet exercises at the end of each chapter will assist you in learning some useful applications of this tool in the personal investing process.

Consider the Ellis sisters, Joni and Cara. Both are single. Joni's taxable income is $25,000. Cara's is $50,000. Using the tax rates and income brackets in Table 1.2, we can calculate their taxes as follows:

Joni:

$(0.10 \times \$9,075) + [0.15 \times (\$25,000 - \$9,075)] = \$907.50 + \$2,388.75 = \underline{\$3,296.25}$

Cara:

$(0.10 \times \$9,075) + [0.15 \times (\$36,900 - \$9,075)] + [0.25 \times (\$50,000 - \$36,900)]$

$= \$907.50 + \$4,173.75 + \$3,275 = \underline{\$8,356.25}$

Notice that Joni pays about 13.2% of her income in taxes ($3,296.25 ÷ $25,000) while Cara's taxes amount to 16.7% of her income ($8,356.25 ÷ $50,000). The progressive nature of the federal income tax structure means that Cara pays a higher fraction of her income in taxes—although her taxable income is twice Joni's, Cara's income tax is about 2.5 times Joni's. You can build a spreadsheet model like the one below to automate these calculations, so you can calculate the tax bill for an individual taxpayer with any income level.

Example

Excel@Investing

NOTE This icon indicates that there is a downloadable Excel file available on MyFinanceLab that matches the text's content at the point where the icon appears.

	A	B	C	D	E	F	G
1	TAX RATES, INCOME BRACKETS, AND INCOME TAX FOR INDIVIDUAL RETURNS (2014)						
2							
3					Individual Returns		
4	Tax Rates (% of income)	Taxable Income			Base Tax + (Marginal rate x amount over base bracket)		
5	10.0%	$0 to $9,075			$0.00 + (10% x amount over $0)		
6	15.0%	$9,076 to $36,900			$907.50 + (15% x amount over $9,075)		
7	25.0%	$36,901 to $89,350			$5,081.25 + (25% x amount over $36,900)		
8	28.0%	$89,351 to $186,350			$18,193.75 + (28% x amount over $89,350)		
9	33.0%	$186,351 to $405,100			$45,353.75 + (33% x amount over $186,350)		
10	35.0%	$405,101 to $406,750			$117,541.25 + (35% x amount over $405,100)		
11	39.6%	Over $406,750			$118,118.75 + (39.6% x amount over $406,750)		
12							
13				Joni's Income	$25,000		
14				Joni's Income Tax	$3,296.25		
15							
16				Cara's Income	$50,000		
17				Joni's Income Tax	$8,356.25		

Capital Gains and Losses   A *capital asset* is property owned and used by the taxpayer for personal reasons, pleasure, or investment. The most common types are securities and real estate, including one's home. A *capital gain* represents the amount by which the proceeds from the sale of a capital asset *exceed* its original purchase price. How heavily capital gains should be taxed is a contentious political issue, so tax rates on gains change frequently, especially when political power shifts between parties, as it did in 2008. At the time this text was going to press in late 2015, several tax rates applied to capital gains income depending on the length of the investment holding period and the tax-payer's income.

For assets held more than 12 months, capital gains are classified as long-term, and the capital gains tax rate is 0% for taxpayers in the 10% and 15% tax brackets. For taxpayers in the 25%, 28%, 33%, and 35% tax brackets, the tax rate on long-term capital gains income is 15%. For taxpayers in the 39.6% tax bracket, the tax rate on long-term capital gains is 20%. Dividends on stock in domestic corporations is essen-tially tax using the same rates that apply to long-term capital gains. If the asset is held for fewer than 12 months, then the amount of any capital gain realized is added to other sources of income, and the total is taxed at the rates given in Table 1.2.

Example

> For example, imagine that James McFail, a single person who has other tax-able income totaling $75,000, sold 500 shares of stock at $12 per share. He pur-chased this stock at $10 per share. The total capital gain on this transaction was $1,000 [500 shares × ($12/share − $10/share)]. James's taxable income totals $76,000, and he is in the 25% tax bracket (see Table 1.2).
>
> If the $1,000 capital gain resulted from an asset that was held for more than 12 months, the capital gain would be taxed at the maximum rate of 15%. His total tax would be calculated as follows:
>
> Ordinary income ($75,000)
>
> $$(0.10 \times \$9,075) + [0.15 \times (\$36,900 - \$9,075)] + [0.25 \times (\$75,000 - \$36,900)]$$
> $$= \$907.50 + \$4,173.75 + \$9,525 = \$14,606.25$$
>
> Capital gain ($1,000)
>
> $$(0.15 \times \$1,000) = \$150$$
>
> Total tax
>
> $$\$14,606.25 + \$150 = \underline{\$14,756.25}$$
>
> James's total tax would be $14,756.25. Had his other taxable income been below $36,900 (i.e., in the 15% bracket), the $1,000 capital gain would have been taxed at 0% rather than 15%. Had James held the asset for fewer than 12 months, his $1,000 capital gain would have been taxed as ordinary income, which in James's case would result in a 25% rate.

Capital gains are appealing because they are not taxed until you actually realize them. For example, if you own a stock originally purchased for $50 per share that at the end of the tax year has a market price of $60 per share, you have a "paper gain" of $10 per share. This *paper (unrealized) gain* is not taxable because you still own the stock. *Only realized gains are taxed.* If you sold the stock for $60 per share during the tax year, you would have a realized—and therefore taxable—gain of $10 per share.

A **capital loss** results when a capital asset is sold for *less than* its original purchase price. Before taxes are calculated, all gains and losses must be netted out. Taxpayers can apply up to $3,000 of **net losses** against ordinary income in any year. Losses that cannot be applied in the current year may be carried forward and used to offset future income, subject to certain conditions.

A final tax issue arises from the Affordable Care Act's Net Investment Income Tax. This tax applies to married taxpayers with incomes exceeding $250,000 and single taxpayers with incomes over $200,000. For these taxpayers, investment income that they receive is subject to an addition 3.8% tax rate.

Investments and Taxes The opportunities created by the tax laws make tax planning important in the investment process. **Tax planning** involves looking at your earnings, both current and projected, and developing strategies that will defer and minimize the level of taxes. The tax plan should guide your investment activities so that over the long run you will achieve maximum after-tax returns for an acceptable level of risk.

For example, the fact that capital gains are not taxed until actually realized allows you to defer tax payments on them as well as control the timing of these payments. However, investments that are likely to produce the largest capital gains generally have higher risk than those that provide significant current income. Therefore, you should not choose investments solely on tax considerations. Instead you must strike a balance of tax benefits, investment returns, and risk. *It is the after-tax return and associated risk that matter.*

Tax-Advantaged Retirement Savings Plans The federal government has established a number of plans that offer special tax incentives designed to encourage people to save for retirement. Those that are employer sponsored include profit-sharing plans, thrift and savings plans, and 401(k) plans. These plans allow employees to defer paying taxes on funds that they save and invest during their working years until they withdraw those funds during retirement. Individuals who are self-employed can set up their own tax-sheltered retirement programs such as Keogh plans and SEP-IRAs. Other savings plans with tax advantages are not tied directly to the employer. Almost anyone can set up an individual retirement arrangement (IRA), although the law limits the tax benefits of these plans for high-income taxpayers. In a traditional IRA, contributions to the plan as well as investment earnings generated on those contributions are not taxed until the participant withdraws funds during retirement. In a Roth IRA, contributions are taxed up front, but subsequent investment earnings and withdrawals are tax-free. For most investors, these plans offer an attractive way to both accumulate funds for retirement and reduce taxes.

Investing over the Life Cycle

Investors tend to follow different investment philosophies as they move through different stages of life. Generally speaking, most investors tend to be more aggressive when they're young and more conservative as they grow older. Typically, investors move through these investment stages:

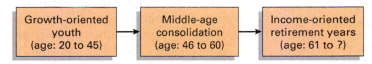

Most young investors in their twenties and thirties prefer growth-oriented investments that stress capital gains rather than current income. Often young investors don't have much in the way of investable funds, so they view capital gains as the quickest (if not necessarily the surest) way to build capital. Young investors tend to favor growth-oriented and speculative investments, particularly high-risk common stocks.

As investors approach middle age, family demands and responsibilities such as educational expenses and retirement contributions become more important. The whole portfolio often shifts to a less aggressive posture. Stocks that offer a balance between growth and income—high-grade bonds, preferred stocks, convertibles, and mutual funds—are all widely used at this stage.

Finally, when investors approach their retirement years, preservation of capital and current income become the principal concerns. A secure, high level of income is paramount. Investors place less emphasis on growing their portfolio. Instead, they structure their portfolios to generate regular cash flow with relatively low exposure to risk. The investment portfolio now becomes *highly conservative*. It consists of low-risk income stocks and mutual funds, government bonds, quality corporate bonds, bank certificates of deposit (CDs), and other short-term investments. At this stage, investors reap the rewards of a lifetime of saving and investing.

Investing over the Business Cycle

Common stocks and other equity-related securities (convertible securities, stock mutual funds, stock options, and stock index futures) are highly responsive to conditions in the economy. The *business cycle* refers to the recurring sequence of growth and decline, boom and recession that characterizes economies around the world. The business cycle reflects the current status of a variety of economic variables, including gross domestic product (GDP), industrial production, personal disposable income, the unemployment rate, and more.

A strong economy is reflected in an expanding business cycle. Stocks tend to be a leading indicator of the business cycle, meaning that stock prices tend to rise prior to periods when business is good and profits are up. Growth-oriented and speculative stocks tend to do especially well in strong markets. To a lesser extent, so do low-risk and income-oriented stocks. In contrast, stock values often fall several months before periods when economic activity is declining. The reason that stocks tend to move ahead of changes in the business cycle is that stock prices reflect investors' beliefs about the future prospects of companies. When investors believe that business conditions will deteriorate, stock prices will fall even before those poor business conditions materialize. Of course, the same thing happens in reverse when investors believe the economy will perform better. Stock prices rise in anticipation of strong future economic performance.

Bonds and other forms of fixed-income securities (bond funds and preferred stocks) are also sensitive to the business cycle because they are highly sensitive to movements in interest rates. In fact, interest rates represent the most important variable in determining bond price behavior and returns to investors. Interest rates and bond prices move in opposite directions (Chapters 10 and 11). Therefore, rising interest rates are unfavorable for bonds already held in an investor's portfolio. Of course, high interest rates enhance the attractiveness of new bonds because these bonds must offer high returns to attract investors.

If you had a crystal ball and could foresee the future, our advice to you would be to load up on high-risk investments each time the economy was nearing the end of a recession and to discard those investments in favor of safer assets near the end of each economic boom. Of course, no one has such a crystal

FAMOUS FAILURES IN FINANCE

Ethical Failure—Massaging the Numbers

In recent years, business headlines were full of allegations of massive financial fraud committed by prominent business leaders. These allegations shocked the investment community and resulted in spectacular bankruptcies of large corporations. Civil and criminal charges against the key executives involved in the fraud soon followed. Among the list of business leaders charged or convicted of financial fraud were Bernie Madoff, Ramalinga Raju of Satyam Computer Services, Hank Greenberg of American International Group (AIG), and David Glenn of Freddie Mac.

In many cases, the primary weapon of fraudulent CEOs was the use of corporate accounting to report huge, fictitious profits or hide financial problems. To cite just one example, prior to its 2008 bankruptcy, the investment banking firm Lehman Brothers had repeatedly engaged in a transaction known as Repo 105. In this transaction, just before it issued a quarterly financial report, Lehman Brothers essentially borrowed money on a short-term basis (usually for 7 to 10 days) from another entity. However, on Lehman's balance sheet that loan was recorded as an asset sale. On Lehman's publicly released financial statements, this transaction made it appear that Lehman Brothers had more cash and less debt than it actually did. More than 13 years after the passage of the Sarbanes-Oxley Act, legislation designed to prevent this kind of corporate fraud, investors have learned the hard way that corporate fraud is a significant risk that remains difficult to anticipate or detect until it is too late.

Critical Thinking Question Why do you think Lehman engaged in Repo 105 transactions?

NOTE Famous Failures in Finance boxes highlight important problems that sometimes occur in the investments field. These problems may deal with ethical lapses, as in the box above, or they may involve various kinds of failures that take place in the marketplace.

ball, and unfortunately professional economic forecasters and investment professionals do not have a particularly strong record at predicting turns in the economy and financial markets. Perhaps the best advice that we can offer regarding investments and the business cycle is this: Do not overreact to the ups and downs that appear to be an unavoidable (and unpredictable) part of economic life. Investors who load up on risky assets after the market has already risen from its bottom and who dump their stocks after the market has begun a slide will probably perform worse than investors who apply a consistent investment strategy over many years through many business cycles.

CONCEPTS IN REVIEW

Answers available at
http://www.pearsonhighered.com/smart

1.12 What should an investor establish before developing and executing an investment program? Briefly describe the elements of an investment policy statement.

1.13 Define and differentiate among the following. Explain how each is related to federal income taxes.

a. Active income
b. Portfolio and passive income
c. Capital gain
d. Capital loss
e. Tax planning
f. Tax-advantaged retirement investments

1.14 Describe the differing investment philosophies typically applied during each of the following stages of an investor's life cycle.

a. Youth (ages 20 to 45)
b. Middle age (ages 46 to 60)
c. Retirement years (age 61 and older)

1.15 Discuss the relation between stock prices and the business cycle.

Meeting Liquidity Needs with Short-Term Investments

LG5 *Liquidity* is the ability to convert an investment into cash quickly with little or no loss in value. A checking account is highly liquid. Stocks and bonds are a little less liquid because there is no assurance that you will be able to quickly sell them without having to cut the price to attract a buyer and because selling these securities usually triggers various transactions costs. Real estate is even less liquid and may take weeks or months to sell even if you are willing to accept a very low price. Unexpected life events such as illness and unemployment sometimes require individuals to draw on their savings to meet daily expenses, so planning for and providing for adequate liquidity is an important part of an investment plan.

The Role of Short-Term Investments

Short-term investments represent an important part of most savings and investment programs. They generate income, although with the prevailing near-zero interest rates in recent years, the income provided by these investments has been quite low. However, their primary function is to provide a pool of reserves for emergencies or simply to accumulate funds for some specific purpose. As a rule of thumb, financial planners often suggest that you hold cash reserves equivalent to three to six months of your after-tax salary, and typically this type of emergency fund would be invested in safe, liquid, short-term investments.

Some individuals choose to hold short-term investments because they simply do not want to take the risk inherent in many types of long-term investments. Certainly there are periods when these low-risk investments perform better than stocks and bonds. Regardless of your motives for holding short-term investments, you should evaluate them in terms of their risk and return, just as you would longer-term investments.

FAMOUS FAILURES IN FINANCE

A Run for the Money

During the Great Depression, individuals became fearful about the ability of banks to survive, and this prompted a great number of bank runs. One of these featured prominently in Frank Capra's classic film, *It's A Wonderful Life.* In a bank run many of a bank's depositors attempt to withdraw money from their accounts at the same time. Because the bank holds only a small fraction of its deposits as cash in a vault, a run can cause a bank to run out of cash quickly and fail as a result. In fact, thousands of banks failed in the 1930s for this reason. To protect banks against runs, the U.S. government created a deposit insurance program via the Banking Act of 1933, which guaranteed that each depositor's money (up to $2,500) would be returned to him or her in the event of a bank failure. This led to fewer bank runs and fewer bank failures. In 1934 only 9 banks failed, compared to more than 9,000 from 1929 to 1933.

In the recent financial crisis, depositors began to question the safety of banks and other financial institutions not only in the United States but also in many other countries. In an attempt to reassure depositors and to prevent a classic bank run, several countries increased the limit on their deposit insurance programs. In 2008 the Federal Deposit Insurance Corporation (FDIC) increased the amount of insured deposits from $100,000 to $250,000. Greece, Poland, Sweden, Denmark, and the United Kingdom all increased their limits on insured deposits. In Greece and Ireland the limit was entirely eliminated, committing those governments to cover 100% of customers' deposits at insured financial institutions. As part of the Dodd-Frank Wall Street Reform and Consumer Protection Act, the FDIC announced in 2010 that it would temporarily provide unlimited insurance for non-interest-bearing accounts at all FDIC-insured institutions. Today the deposit insurance limit is $250,000 per depositor at each bank.

Interest on Short-Term Investments Short-term investments earn interest in one of two ways. Some investments, such as savings accounts, pay a *stated rate of interest*. In this case, you can easily find the interest rate—it's the stated rate on the account.

Alternatively, some short-term investments earn interest on a **discount basis**. This means that you buy the security at a price below its redemption value (or face value), and the difference between what you pay to acquire the asset and what you receive when it matures is the interest the investment will earn. U.S. Treasury bills (T-bills), for example, are issued on a discount basis.

Risk Characteristics Short-term investments are generally not very risky. Their primary risk results from *inflation risk*—the potential loss of purchasing power that may occur if the rate of return on these investments is less than the inflation rate. Investors holding money in bank savings accounts have experienced this outcome in each of the last several years. The average interest rate on bank money market savings accounts has been below 0.5% since 2010, but over that same period, the average annual inflation rate has been about 2%. Usually, short-term investments provide rates of return that are slightly higher than the inflation rate, but actions by the U.S. Federal Reserve have kept short-term interest rates at historically low levels in recent years.

The *risk of default*—nonpayment—is almost nonexistent with short-term investments. The reason is that issuers of most short-term investments are highly reputable institutions, such as the U.S. Treasury, large banks, and major corporations. In addition, government agencies insure deposits in commercial banks, savings and loans, savings banks, and credit unions for up to $250,000 per account. Finally, because the value of short-term investments does not change much in response to changing interest rates, exposure to capital loss is correspondingly low.

Advantages and Disadvantages of Short-Term Investments As noted, the major advantages of short-term investments are their high liquidity and low risk. Most are available from local financial institutions and can be readily converted to cash with minimal inconvenience. Finally, because the returns on most short-term investments usually vary with inflation and market interest rates, investors can readily capture higher returns as rates move up. On the negative side, when interest rates go down, returns drop as well.

Although a decline in market rates has undesirable effects on most short-term investments, perhaps their biggest disadvantage is their relatively low return. Because these securities are generally so low in risk, you can expect the returns on short-term investments to average less than the returns on long-term investments.

Common Short-Term Investments

A variety of short-term investments are available to the individual investor. Some are deposit-type accounts where investors can place money, earn a relatively low rate of interest, and conveniently withdraw funds at their discretion. Part A of Table 1.3 summarizes the popular deposit-type accounts. Another group of short-term investments are those issued by the federal government. Basic features of many of those instruments are summarized in Part B of Table 1.3. The final group of short-term investments includes nongovernment instruments, typically issued by a financial institution or a corporation. Part C of Table 1.3 summarizes these investments.

Investment Suitability

Individual investors use short-term investments for both savings and investment. When the savings motive is paramount, investors use these assets to maintain a

TABLE 1.3   COMMON SHORT-TERM INVESTMENTS

Part A. Deposit-Type Accounts

Type of Account	Description	Minimum Balance	Interest Rate	Federal Insurance
Passbook savings account	Savings accounts offered by banks.* Used primarily for convenience or if investors lack sufficient funds to purchase other short-term investments.	Typically none	0.25%–4% depending on economy	Up to $250,000 per deposit.
NOW (negotiated order of withdrawal) account	Bank checking account that pays interest on balances.	No legal minimum but often set at $500 to $1,000	At or near passbook rates	Up to $250,000 per deposit.
Money market deposit account (MMDA)	Bank deposit account with limited check-writing privileges.	No legal minimum, but often set at about $2,500	Typically slightly above passbook rate	Up to $250,000 per deposit.
Asset management account	Deposit account at bank, brokerage house, mutual fund, or insurance company that combines checking, investing, and borrowing. Automatically "sweeps" excess balances into short-term investments and borrows to meet shortages.	Typically $5,000 to $20,000	Similar to MMDAs	Up to $250,000 per deposit in banks. Varies in other institutions.

Part B. Federal Government Issues

Security	Issuer	Description	Initial Maturity	Risk and Return
I bonds	U.S. Treasury	Savings bonds issued by the U.S. Treasury in denominations as low as $25; earn an interest rate that varies with the inflation rate; interest is exempt from state and local taxes.	30 years, but redeemable after 1 year	Lowest, virtually risk free
Treasury bills	U.S. Treasury	Issued weekly at auction; sold at a discount; strong secondary market; exempt from local and state income taxes.	1 year or less	Lowest, virtually risk free

Part C. Nongovernment Issues

Security	Issuer	Description	Initial Maturity	Risk and Return
Certificates of deposit (CDs)	Commercial banks	Cash deposits in commercial banks; amounts and maturities tailored to investor's needs.	1 month and longer	Higher than U.S. Treasury issues and comparable to commercial paper
Commercial paper	Corporation with a high credit standing	Unsecured note of issuer; large denominations.	3 to 270 days	Higher than U.S. Treasury issues and comparable to CDs

Banker's acceptances	Banks	Analogous to a post-dated check on an account with over-draft protection; a time draft drawn on a customer's account, guaranteed by a bank; bank's "acceptance" makes the trade a tradable instrument.	30 to 180 days	About the same as CDs and commercial paper but higher than U.S. Treasury issues
Money market mutual funds (money funds)	Professional portfolio manage-ment companies	Professionally man-aged portfolios of marketable securi-ties; provide instant liquidity.	None—depends on wishes of investor	Vary, but gener-ally higher than U.S. Treasury issues and comparable to CDs and com-mercial paper

*The term *bank* refers to commercial banks, savings and loans (S&Ls), savings banks, and credit unions.

desired level of savings that will be readily available if the need arises—in essence, to provide *safety and security*. For this purpose, an investment's return is less important than its safety, liquidity, and convenience. Passbook savings accounts and NOW accounts are examples of short-term investments that fulfill investors' short-term savings needs.

When investors use short-term securities for *investment purposes*, the return that these instruments provide is often just as important as their liquidity. Most investors will hold at least a part of their portfolio in short-term, highly liquid securities, if for no other reason than to be able to act on unanticipated investment opportunities. Some investors, in fact, devote all or most of their portfolios to such securities.

Investors also use short-term securities as a temporary place to "park" funds before deciding where to invest the money on a long-term basis. For example, if you have just sold some stock but do not have a suitable long-term investment alternative, you might place the proceeds in a money fund until you find a longer-term use for them. Or if you feel that interest rates are about to rise sharply, you might sell some long-term bonds that you have and use the proceeds to buy T-bills. The securities offering the highest returns—like money market deposit accounts (MMDAs), CDs, commercial paper, banker's acceptances, and money funds—are generally preferred for this warehousing function, as are asset management accounts at major brokerage firms.

To decide which securities are most appropriate for a particular situation, you need to consider such characteristics as availability, safety, liquidity, and rate of return. Although all investments we have discussed satisfy the basic liquidity demand, they do so to varying degrees. A NOW account is unquestionably the most liquid of all. You can write as many checks on the account as you wish and for any amount. A certificate of deposit, on the other hand, is not so liquid because early redemption involves an interest penalty. Table 1.4 summarizes the key characteristics of the short-term investments described in Table 1.3. The letter grade assigned for each characteristic reflects

TABLE 1.4   A SCORECARD FOR SHORT-TERM INVESTMENT

Type of Investment	Availability	Safety	Liquidity	Typical Rate in 2015
NOW account	A–	A+	A+	0.03%
Passbook savings account	A+	A+	A	0.06%
Money market mutual fund (money fund)	B	A/A+	B+	0.07%
Money market deposit account (MMDA)	B	A+	A	0.08%
Asset management account	B–	A	A+	0.20%
U.S. Treasury bill (1 year)	B–	A++	A–	0.20%
Banker's acceptance (90 day)	B–	A	B	0.23%
Commercial paper (90 day)	B–	A–	B–	0.50%
Certificate of deposit (1 year, large denomination)	B	A±	B	0.70%
I bonds	A+	A++	C–	1.50%

an estimate of the investment's quality in that area. For example, money market mutual funds (money funds) rate only a B+ on liquidity because withdrawals must usually be made in a minimum amount of $250 to $500. NOW accounts are somewhat better in this respect because a withdrawal can be for any amount. Rates on short-term investments tend to be low. Among the investments listed in Table 1.4, the rates on NOW and passbook savings accounts are typically lowest, and the rates on I bonds are the highest. However, in 2015 as the economy continued its slow recovery from a recession, rates on all of these instruments were barely above zero. For example, a large, 1-year CD offered investors a return of 0.7%. You should note, though, that if an investment scores lower on availability, safety, or liquidity, it will generally offer a higher rate.

CONCEPTS IN REVIEW

Answers available at
http://www.pearsonhighered.com/smart

1.16 What makes an asset liquid? Why hold liquid assets? Would 100 shares of IBM stock be considered a liquid investment? Explain.

1.17 Explain the characteristics of short-term investments with respect to purchasing power and default risk.

1.18 Briefly describe the key features and differences among the following deposit accounts.

a. Passbook savings account
b. NOW account
c. Money market deposit account
d. Asset management account

1.19 Define, compare, and contrast the following short-term investments.

a. I bonds
b. U.S. Treasury bills
c. Certificates of deposit
d. Commercial paper
e. Banker's acceptances
f. Money market mutual funds (money funds)

Careers in Finance

LG6

Choosing an Index Fund

AN ADVISOR'S PERSPECTIVE

Bryan Sweet *Founder and CEO*, **Sweet Financial Services**

"The CFP gives you confidence when speaking to clients."

MyFinanceLab

Regardless of the job title, a career in finance requires you to understand the investment environment. The principles presented throughout this text will provide an initial foundation in investments essential to pursuing one of the many rewarding career paths within the field of finance. If you are well prepared and enthusiastic about a career in finance, you will find a wide variety of job opportunities. Many people who pursue a career in the investments field obtain one of two professional certifications: Certified Financial Planner (CFP®) or Chartered Financial Analyst (CFA). Each of these certifications can help advance your career, although the requirements and the focus of each certification are somewhat different.

The CFP® program is primarily designed for people who want to work directly with clients, helping them develop investment plans and executing those plans. To obtain the CFP® credential, you must have a bachelor's degree in finance or a related field. You must pass the six-hour CFP® Certification Exam, which in 2014 had a pass rate of 66%. The exam focuses heavily on aspects of the advisor-client relationship including establishing and defining client relationships, analyzing a client's current financial position, and developing, communicating, implementing, and monitoring investment recommendations. In addition to passing the exam, to earn the CFP® you must have three years of professional work experience in financial planning, and you must agree to abide by a code of ethics established by the CFP® Board. People with the CFP® credential typically work as financial advisors, either in their own practice or as part of a larger team.

The CFA program's focus is more appropriate for people who want to work as institutional investors, for example as a financial analyst on Wall Street. To earn the CFA credential, you must pass a series of three, grueling, six-hour exams (Level 1, Level 2, and Level 3), each of which usually requires hundreds of hours of study. Typically the pass rate on these exams is 50% or less. Examples of CFA exam questions appear scattered throughout this text and on MyFinanceLab. You also need a bachelor's degree (in any field) simply to register for the exam. In addition, you must have four years of qualified investment work experience, and you must adhere to the CFA Institute's Code of Ethics and Professional Conduct. The most common job held by CFAs is portfolio manager, but people with this certification also work as consultants, financial analysts inside corporations, traders, risk managers, and more.

Whether you hold any of these professional credentials, there are many career opportunities open to you if you are well trained in investments. Some of the industries with investments-oriented career opportunities are commercial banking, corporate finance, financial planning, insurance, investment banking, and investment management.

Commercial Banking Commercial banks provide banking services to individuals and businesses alike. In spite of considerable consolidation within the banking sector, more people work in commercial banking than in any other area of the financial services industry.

Due to the vast range of services provided by commercial banks, banks offer a tremendous variety of finance career opportunities, many of which require training in investments. In a commercial bank you might find yourself working in mortgage lending, mortgage underwriting, corporate lending, asset management, leasing, consumer credit, trade credit, and international finance. Some of the job titles that you might hold in the commercial banking sector include personal banker, portfolio manager, short-term securities manager, financial analyst, credit analyst, home loan officer, corporate loan officer, and mortgage underwriter.

Corporate Finance Within the corporate finance setting, you will find several rewarding job opportunities. Among other things, corporations require financial professionals to manage cash and short-term investments, raise and manage long-term financing, evaluate and undertake investments, and interface with investors and the financial community. These critical finance functions exist within virtually every firm regardless of size

The top finance job in a corporation is that of the chief financial officer (CFO). The CFO's primary responsibilities are to manage the firm's capital resources and capital investments. Investment principles are important to CFOs because so much of a CFO's job revolves around communication with investors. A CFO must understand how investors view the firm and value the securities the firm has issued. A CFO's job (and most other corporate finance jobs) is typically focused on increasing a firm's value through successful business decisions. More so than other finance-related jobs, corporate finance jobs require a broad understanding of the various functional areas within the corporate setting (e.g., operations, marketing, and accounting) and how these areas contribute to the corporate finance goals.

Financial Planning A financial planner counsels clients on how to deal with their specific situations and meet their particular goals, both short-term and long-term. As a personal financial planner, you provide financial advice relating to education, retirement, investment, insurance, tax, and estate planning. You may be consulted by business owners for advice on issues such as cash flow management, investment planning, risk management and insurance planning, tax planning, and business succession planning.

An ability to clarify objectives, assess risks, and develop strategic plans is essential for financial planners. For example, if a client desires to send a child to college someday, what savings or investment strategies are best suited to meet that client's goals? Financial planners can work within a large financial services company such as ING, within a small practice, or for themselves.

Insurance The insurance business is a trillion-dollar industry that serves both individual and business clients. There are two prominent finance jobs in insurance. The first involves providing individuals or businesses with products that provide cash payments when unfavorable events (e.g., sickness, death, property damage due to fire or natural disaster) occur, and the second involves investing the premiums that customers pay when they buy insurance. Individuals and businesses purchase insurance products in order to protect themselves from catastrophic losses or to guarantee certain outcomes. Insurers collect premiums and fees for the services they provide and they invest those funds in assets so that when customers submit claims, the insurance company will have the cash to fulfill the financial promises they made to their customers. The insurance industry has vast sums under management and therefore requires highly trained investment specialists.

Investment Banking Investment banks assist firms and governments when issuing financial securities, such as stocks and bonds, and they facilitate the purchase of securities by both institutional and retail investors. Their in-house security analysts provide research on both equity and fixed-income securities. Investment banks also make markets for financial securities (e.g., stocks and bonds) and provide financial advice to and manage financial assets for high net worth individuals, firms, institutions, and governments. Investment banks even provide their clients with quantitative analysis or program trading and consultation on mergers and acquisitions.

The investment banking industry changed dramatically during the 2008 financial crisis. Many investment banks invested heavily in securities tied to U.S. real estate values, and when home prices began to drop, the losses on banks' investments began to mount. Several prominent investment banks either went bankrupt or were acquired by other banks. Since then, the industry has recovered to a degree, but there are fewer professionals working in investment banks today than there were a decade ago.

Investment Management As the name implies, investment management is all about managing money for clients. The role of an investment manager includes elements of financial analysis, asset selection, security (e.g., stock or bond) selection, and investment implementation and monitoring. Most investment management is done on behalf of a pool of investors whose investments comprise a fund. Some common examples of managed funds are bank trust funds, pension funds, mutual funds, exchange-traded funds, and hedge funds.

Money managers often specialize in managing a portfolio of a particular type of security. Some money managers buy and hold fixed-income securities, including mortgage-backed securities, corporate bonds, municipal bonds, agency securities, and asset-backed securities. Others focus on equities, including small stocks, large caps, and emerging market stocks. Some managers invest only in domestic securities while others buy securities in markets all over the world.

Table 1.5 lists average salaries and required years of experience for a variety of jobs in the commercial banking, corporate finance, investment banking, and

TABLE 1.5	AVERAGE SALARIES FOR VARIOUS FINANCE JOBS (2015)	
Job Title	Salary	Years of Experience
Commercial Banking		
Commercial credit analyst, Jr.	$ 43,254	0
Commercial credit analyst, Sr.	$ 85,532	7
Lending office, Jr.	$ 81,713	8
Lending officer, Sr.	$151,722	12
Corporate Finance		
Financial analyst, Jr.	$ 51,848	0
Financial analyst, Sr.	$ 93,724	7
Assistant controller	$112,876	7
Investor relations director	$145,796	10
Treasurer	$179,029	7
Chief financial officer	$300,571	15
Investment Banking		
Analyst	$ 85,300	0
Associate	$120,000	3
Managing director	$273,400	10
Investment Management		
Securities analyst	$ 62,780	2
Investment specialist	$ 78,757	2
Portfolio manager	$101,031	5
Investment operations manager	$125,366	7

(Sources: Data from **Salary.com**; Data for Investment banking from **http://www.forbes.com/ sites/kenrapoza/2013/03/13/how-much-do-wall-streeters-really-earn/**)

investment management fields. Many of these jobs have an investments focus, but not all do. Keep in mind that there is substantial variation around these averages. Larger firms and firms in areas with higher costs of living tend to pay more. For entry-level positions, an individual's salary might be higher or lower than the average reported here based on the candidate's undergraduate major, grade point average, extracurricular activities, or simply how they handle a job interview. Salaries reported in Table 1.5 also do not include bonuses, which can be considerable in certain industries (such as investment banking). Bonuses tend to account for a larger fraction of total pay in jobs that require more experience. Still, the table conveys the idea that job opportunities in finance are quite attractive.

CONCEPTS IN REVIEW

Answers available at
http://www.pearsonhighered
.com/smart

1.20 Why is an understanding of investment principles important to a senior manager working in corporate finance?

1.21 Why do insurance companies need employees with advanced training in investments?

MyFinanceLab

Here is what you should know after reading this chapter. MyFinanceLab will help you identify what you know and where to go when you need to practice.

What You Should Know	Key Terms	Where to Practice
NOTE The end-of-chapter summaries restate the chapter's Learning Goals and review the key points of information related to each goal.	**NOTE** A list of Key Terms gathers in one place the new vocabulary presented in each chapter.	
LG 1 Understand the meaning of the term *investment* and list the attributes that distinguish one investment from another. An investment is any asset into which investors can place funds with the expectation of generating positive income and/or increasing their value. The returns from investing are received either as income or as increased value. Some of the attributes that distinguish one type of investment from another include whether the investment is a security or property; direct or indirect; debt, equity, or derivative; low risk or high risk; short-term or long-term; and domestic or foreign.	debt, *p. 4* derivative securities, *p. 4* direct investment, *p. 3* domestic investments, *p. 5* equity, *p. 4* foreign investments, *p. 5* indirect investment, *p. 3* investment, *p. 2* liquidity, *p. 2* long-term investments, *p. 5* portfolio, *p. 2* property, *p. 3* returns, *p. 2* risk, *p. 4* securities, *p. 2* short-term investments, *p. 5*	MyFinanceLab Study Plan 1.1

What You Should Know	Key Terms	Where to Practice
LG2 **Describe the investment process and types of investors.** Financial institutions and financial markets bring together suppliers and demanders of funds. The dominant U.S. financial market is the securities market for stocks, bonds, and other securities. The participants in the investment process are government, business, and individuals. Only individuals are net suppliers of funds. Investors can be either individual investors or institutional investors.	diversification, *p. 4* financial institutions, *p. 5* financial markets, *p. 5* individual investors, *p. 6* institutional investors, *p. 6*	MyFinanceLab Study Plan 1.2
LG3 **Discuss the principal types of investments.** Short-term investments have low risk. They are used to earn a return on temporarily idle funds, to serve as a primary investment for conservative investors, and to provide liquidity. Common stocks offer dividends and capital gains. Fixed-income securities—bonds, convertible securities, and preferred stock—offer fixed periodic returns with some potential for gain in value. Mutual funds allow investors to buy or sell interests in a professionally managed, diversified group of securities. Exchange-traded funds are similar to mutual funds except that they can be bought and sold on an exchange during the trading day. Hedge funds are also similar to mutual funds except that they are open only to relatively wealthy investors, they tend to make riskier investments, and they are subject to less regulation than mutual funds. Derivative securities such as options and futures are high-risk investments. Options offer an opportunity to buy or sell another security at a specified price over a given period of time. Futures are contracts between a seller and a buyer for delivery of a specified commodity or financial instrument, at a specified future date, at an agreed-on price. Other popular investments include tax-advantaged investments, real estate, and tangibles.	bonds, *p. 9* capital gains, *p. 8* common stock, *p. 8* convertible security, *p. 9* dividends, *p. 8* exchange-traded funds (ETF), *p. 11* fixed-income securities, *p. 9* futures, *p. 13* hedge funds, *p. 12* money funds, *p. 11* money market mutual funds, *p. 11* mutual fund, *p. 10* options, *p. 12* preferred stock, *p. 10* real estate, *p. 13* tangibles, *p. 13* tax-advantaged investments, *p. 13*	MyFinanceLab Study Plan 1.3
LG4 **Describe the purpose and content of an investment policy statement, review fundamental tax considerations, and discuss investing over the life cycle.** Investing should be driven by well-developed plans established to achieve specific goals. A good place to begin an investment plan is to create a written investment policy statement. Investors must also consider the tax consequences associated with various investments and strategies. The key dimensions are ordinary income, capital gains and losses, tax planning, and tax-advantaged retirement plans. The investments selected are affected by the investor's stage in the life cycle and by economic cycles. Younger investors tend to prefer growth-oriented investments that stress capital gains. As they age, investors move to less risky securities. As they approach retirement, they become even more conservative. Some investments, such as stocks, behave as leading indicators of the state of the economy.	capital loss, *p. 18* investment goals, *p. 14* net losses, *p. 19* tax planning, *p. 19*	MyFinanceLab Study Plan 1.4 Video Learning Aid for Problems P1.1, P1.2

What You Should Know	Key Terms	Where to Practice
LG5 Describe the most common types of short-term investments. Liquidity needs can be met by investing in various short-term investments, which can earn interest at a stated rate or on a discount basis. They typically have low risk. Banks, the government, and brokerage firms offer numerous short-term investments. Their suitability depends on the investor's attitude toward availability, safety, liquidity, and rate of return.	discount basis, *p. 23*	MyFinanceLab Study Plan 1.5
LG6 Describe some of the main careers open to people with financial expertise and the role that investments play in each. Exciting and rewarding career opportunities in finance are available in many fields such as commercial banking, corporate finance, financial planning, insurance, investment banking, and money management.		MyFinanceLab Study Plan 1.6

Log into MyFinanceLab, take a chapter test, and get a personalized Study Plan that tells you which concepts you understand and which ones you need to review. From there, MyFinanceLab will give you further practice, tutorials, animations, videos, and guided solutions.

Log into **http://www.myfinancelab.com**

Discussion Questions

NOTE The Discussion Questions at the end of the chapter ask you to analyze and synthesize information presented in the. These questions, like all other end-of-chapter assignment materials, are keyed to the chapter's learning goals.

LG4 **Q1.1** Assume that you are 35 years old, are married with two young children, are renting a condo, and have an annual income of $90,000. Use the following questions to guide your preparation of a rough investment plan consistent with these facts.

a. What are your key investment goals?

b. How might personal taxes affect your investment plans? Use current tax rates to assess their impact.

c. How might your stage in the life cycle affect the types of risks you might take?

LG5 **Q1.2.** What role, if any, will short-term investments play in your portfolio? Why? Complete the following table for the short-term investments listed. Find their current yields online, and explain which, if any, you would include in your investment portfolio.

Type of Investment	Minimum Balance	Interest Rate	Federal Insurance	Method and Ease of Withdrawing Funds
a. Passbook savings account	None		Yes	In person or through teller machines; very easy
b. NOW account				Unlimited check-writing privileges
c. Money market deposit account (MMDA)				

Type of Investment	Minimum Balance	Interest Rate	Federal Insurance	Method and Ease of Withdrawing Funds
d. Asset manage-ment account				
e. Series I savings bond	Virtually none			
f. U.S. Treasury bill				
g. Certificate of deposit (CD)				
h. Commercial paper				
i. Banker's accep-tance				
j. Money market mutual fund (money fund)				

Problems

All problems are available on http://www.myfinancelab.com

NOTE The problems at the end of the chapter offer opportunities to perform calculations using the tools and techniques learned in the chapter.

LG4 **P1.1** Stefani German, a 40-year-old woman, plans to retire at age 65, and she wants to accumulate $500,000 over the next 25 years to supplement the retirement programs that are being funded by the federal government and her employer. She expects to earn an average annual return of about 5% by investing in a low-risk portfolio containing about 20% short-term securities, 30% common stock, and 50% bonds.

Stefani currently has $44,300 that at a 5% annual rate of return will grow to about $150,000 by her 65th birthday (the $150,000 figure is found using time value of money techniques, Chapter 4 appendix). Stefani consults a financial advisor to determine how much money she should save each year to meet her retirement savings objective. The advisor tells Stefani that if she saves about $20.95 each year, she will accumulate $1,000 by age 65. Saving 5 times that amount each year, $104.75, allows Stefani to accumulate roughly $5,000 by age 65.

  a. How much additional money does Stefani need to accumulate over time to reach her goal of $500,000?

  b. How much must Stefani save to accumulate the sum calculated in part **a** over the next 25 years?

LG5 **P1.2** During 2015, the Smiths and the Joneses both filed joint tax returns. For the tax year ended December 31, 2015, the Smiths' taxable income was $130,000, and the Joneses had total taxable income of $65,000.

  a. Using the federal tax rates given in Table 1.2 for married couples filing joint returns, calculate the taxes for both the Smiths and the Joneses.

  b. Calculate and compare the ratio of the Smiths' to the Joneses' taxable income and the ratio of the Smiths' to the Joneses' taxes. What does this demonstrate about the federal income tax structure?

LG6 **P1.3** Jason and Kerri Consalvo, both in their 50s, have $50,000 to invest and plan to retire in 10 years. They are considering two investments. The first is a utility company common stock that costs $50 per share and pays dividends of $2 per share per year. Note that these dividends will be taxed at the same rates that apply to long-term capital gains. The Consalvos do not expect the value of this stock to increase. The other investment under consideration is a highly rated corporate bond that currently sells for $1,000 and pays annual interest at a rate of 5%, or $50 per $1,000 invested. After 10 years, these bonds will be repaid at par, or $1,000 per $1,000 invested. Assume that the Consalvos keep the income from their investments but do not reinvest it (they keep the cash in a non-interest-bearing bank account). They will, however, need to pay income taxes on their investment income. If they buy the stock, they will sell it after 10 years. If they buy the bonds, in 10 years they will get back the amount they invested. The Consalvos are in the 33% tax bracket.

a. How many shares of the stock can the Consalvos buy?

b. How much will they receive after taxes each year in dividend income if they buy the stock?

c. What is the total amount they would have from their original $50,000 if they purchased the stock and all went as planned?

d. How much will they receive after taxes each year in interest if they purchase the bonds?

e. What is the total amount they would have from their original $50,000 if they purchased the bonds and all went as planned?

f. Based only on your calculations and ignoring other risk factors, should they buy the stock or the bonds?

LG4   **P1.4**   Mike and Julie Bedard are a working couple. They will file a joint income tax return. This year, they have the following taxable income:

1. $125,000 from salary and wages (ordinary income)
2. $1,000 in interest income
3. $3,000 in dividend income
4. $2,000 in profit from sale of a stock they purchased two years ago
5. $2,000 in profit from a stock they purchased this year and sold this year

Use the federal income tax rates given in Table 1.2 to work this problem.

a. How much will Mike and Julie pay in federal income taxes on item **2** above?

b. How much will Mike and Julie pay in federal income taxes on item **3** above? (*Note:* Remember that dividend income and ordinary income are taxed differently.)

c. How much will Mike and Julie pay in federal income taxes on item **4** above?

d. How much will Mike and Julie pay in federal income taxes on item **5** above?

P1.5   Kim and Kanye have been dating for years and are now thinking about getting married. As a financially sophisticated couple, they want to think through the tax implications of their potential union.

a. Suppose Kim and Kanye both earn $70,000 (so their combined income is $140,000). Using the tax bracket information in Table 1.2 (or the Excel file available on MyFinanceLab with the same information), calculate the combined tax bill that they would pay if they remain single, and compare that to the taxes they would pay if they were married and filed a joint return.

b. Now suppose that Kim and Kanye both earn $100,000 (so their combined income is $200,000). Calculate the combined tax bill that they would pay if they remain single, and compare that to the taxes that they would pay if they were married and filed a joint return.

c. What differences do you find in parts (a) and (b)? What is the cause of these differences?

NOTE Two Case Problems appear at the end of every chapter. They ask you to apply what you have learned in the chapter to a hypothetical investment situation.

Visit **http://www.myfinancelab.com** for web exercises, spreadsheets, and other online resources.

Case Problem 1.1   Investments or Golf?

LG1 LG2 LG3   Judd Read and Judi Todd, senior accounting majors at a large midwestern university, have been good friends since high school. Each has already found a job that will begin after graduation. Judd has accepted a position as an internal auditor in a medium-size manufacturing firm. Judi will be working for one of the major public accounting firms. Each is looking forward to the challenge of a new career and to the prospect of achieving success both professionally and financially.

Judd and Judi are preparing to register for their final semester. Each has one free elective to select. Judd is considering taking a golf course offered by the physical education department, which he says will help him socialize in his business career. Judi is planning to take a basic investments course and has been trying to convince Judd to take investments instead of golf. Judd believes he doesn't need to take investments because he already knows what common stock is. He believes that whenever he has accumulated excess funds, he can invest in the stock of a company that is doing well. Judi argues that there is much more to it than simply choosing common stock. She thinks that exposure to the field of investments would be more beneficial than learning to play golf.

Questions

a. Explain to Judd the structure of the investment process and the economic importance of investing.

b. List and discuss the other types of investments with which Judd is apparently unfamiliar.

c. Assuming that Judd already gets plenty of exercise, what arguments would you give to convince Judd to take investments rather than golf?

Case Problem 1.2   Preparing Carolyn Bowen's Investment Plan

LG4 LG5 Carolyn Bowen, who just turned 55, is employed as an administrative assistant for the Xcon Corporation, where she has worked for the past 20 years. She is in good health, lives alone, and has two grown children. A few months ago her husband died, leaving her with only their home and the proceeds from a $75,000 life insurance policy. After she paid medical and funeral expenses, $60,000 of the life insurance proceeds remained. In addition to the life insurance proceeds, Carolyn has $37,500 in a savings account, which she had accumulated over the past 10 years. Recognizing that she is within 10 years of retirement, Carolyn wishes to invest her limited resources so she will be able to live comfortably once she retires.

Carolyn is quite superstitious. After consulting with a number of psychics and studying her family tree, she is certain she will not live past 80. She plans to retire at either 62 or 65, whichever will allow her to meet her long-run financial goals. After talking with a number of knowledgeable individuals—including, of course, the psychics—Carolyn estimates that to live comfortably in retirement, she will need $45,000 per year before taxes. This amount will be required annually for 18 years if she retires at 62 or for 15 years if she retires at 65. As part of her financial plan, Carolyn intends to sell her home at retirement and rent an apartment. She has estimated that she will net $112,500 if she sells the house when she is 62 and $127,500 if she sells it when she is 65. Carolyn has no financial dependents and is not concerned about leaving a sizable estate to her heirs.

If Carolyn retires at age 62, she will receive from Social Security and an employer-sponsored pension plan a total of $1,359 per month ($16,308 annually); if she waits until age 65 to retire, her total retirement income will be $1,688 per month ($20,256 annually). For convenience, Carolyn has already decided to convert all her assets at the time of retirement into a stream of annual income and she will at that time purchase an annuity by paying a single premium. The annuity will have a life just equal to the number of years remaining until her 80th birthday. If Carolyn retires at age 62 and buys an annuity at that time, for each $1,000 that she puts into the annuity she will receive an annual benefit equal to $79 for the subsequent 18 years. If she waits until age 65 to retire, each $1,000 invested in the annuity will produce an annual benefit of $89.94 for the 15 years.

Carolyn plans to place any funds currently available into a savings account paying 6% compounded annually until retirement. She does not expect to be able to save or invest any additional funds between now and retirement. For every dollar that Carolyn invests today, she will have $1.50 by age 62; if she leaves the money invested until age 65, she will have $1.79 for each dollar invested today.

Questions

a. Assume that Carolyn places currently available funds in the savings account. Determine the amount of money Carolyn will have available at retirement once she sells her house if she retires at (1) age 62 and (2) age 65.

b. Using the results from item **a**, determine the level of annual income that will be provided to Carolyn through purchase of an annuity at (1) age 62 and (2) age 65.

c. With the results found in the preceding questions, determine the total annual retirement income Carolyn will have if she retires at (1) age 62 and (2) age 65.

d. From your findings, do you think Carolyn will be able to achieve her long-run financial goal by retiring at (1) age 62 or (2) age 65? Explain.

e. Evaluate Carolyn's investment plan in terms of her use of a savings account and an annuity rather than other investments. Comment on the risk and return characteristics of her plan. What recommendations might you offer Carolyn? Be specific.

Excel@Investing

Excel@Investing

In the following chapters of this text, you will be asked to solve spreadsheet problems using Microsoft Excel. While each person's skill and experience with Excel will vary, we assume that you understand its basics. This includes entering text and numbers, copying or moving a cell, moving and copying using the drag-and-drop function, inserting and deleting rows and columns, and performing basic algebraic functions. The review in this chapter focuses on entering and editing data in the worksheet.

To complete the spreadsheet review, go to http://www.myfinancelab.com and to Student Resources. Click on Spreadsheet Review. There you will be asked to create a spreadsheet and perform the following tasks.

Questions

a. Add and subtract data with a formula.

b. Multiply and divide data with a formula.

c. Total cells using the sum function and calculate an average.

d. Use the average function.

e. Copy a formula using the drag-and-drop method.

2 | Securities Markets and Transactions

LEARNING GOALS

After studying this chapter, you should be able to:

LG1 Identify the basic types of securities markets and describe their characteristics.

LG2 Explain the initial public offering (IPO) process.

LG3 Describe broker markets and dealer markets, and discuss how they differ from alternative trading systems.

LG4 Review the key aspects of the globalization of securities markets and discuss the importance of international markets.

LG5 Discuss trading hours and the regulation of securities markets.

LG6 Explain long purchases, margin transactions, and short sales.

"Wall Street" is an early 17th-century testament to the global beginnings of U.S. financial markets. Wall Street was originally the northern boundary of a Dutch colonial settlement founded in 1625 called New Amsterdam, which after coming under English rule in 1664 became New York City. The U.S. financial markets that we know today began to take shape in the late 18th century as stockbrokers and speculators informally gathered on Wall Street under a buttonwood tree to trade. In 1792 twenty-four stockbrokers signed the Buttonwood Agreement, agreeing to trade securities on a commission basis, thus becoming the first organized American securities exchange. In 1817 the Buttonwood organization renamed itself the New York Stock & Exchange Board (and later became known simply as "The Big Board") and rented rooms on Wall Street to establish the first centralized exchange location of what in 1863 became known as the New York Stock Exchange (NYSE). Jumping ahead 144 years, NYSE Euronext was formed in 2007 through a merger of NYSE Group, Inc., and Euronext N.V., thus creating the first global stock exchange. Euronext brought a consortium of European exchanges to the merger, including the Paris, Brussels, Lisbon, and Amsterdam stock exchanges and the London-based electronic derivatives market Euronext.liffe, which is known now as NYSE Liffe. In 2008 NYSE Liffe U.S. was launched, offering a wide range of U.S. derivatives contracts. Further expansion occurred in 2008 when NYSE Euronext acquired the American Stock Exchange. As a result of the acquisition, more than 500 Amex-listed companies joined NYSE Euronext. Through a series of acquisitions and mergers, the Buttonwood Agreement had become the world's largest and most liquid exchange group.

In November 2013 the Atlanta-based Intercontinental Exchange, Inc., acquired NYSE Euronext, paying NYSE Euronext shareholders stock in cash worth about $11 billion. The combined entity controlled 11 exchanges that traded common stocks as well as more exotic securities such as options, interest rate and credit derivatives, foreign exchange, and futures contracts on commodities and financial contracts. The transaction reflected the growing importance of derivatives trading (an Intercontinental Exchange specialty) and the declining influence of the 220-year-old Big Board. For years NYSE Euronext's share of trading volume had been on the decline, squeezing its profit margins.

From trading under a buttonwood tree in a Dutch colonial settlement in 1792 to the combination of NYSE Euronext with Intercontinental Exchange, Wall Street remains a truly global marketplace.

(Sources: "Who We Are," http://www.nyx.com, accessed April 12, 2012; "Wall Street," http://en.wikipedia.org/wiki/Wall_street, accessed April 12, 2012; "NYSE Group and Euronext N.V. Agree to a Merger of Equals," NYSE press release, June 2, 2006, http://www.euronext.com/fic/000/001/891/18919.pdf, accessed April 12, 2012; and "Intercontinental Exchange Completes Acquisition of NYSE Euronext," NYSE press release, November 13, 2013, http://www1.nyse.com/press/1388665271901.html, accessed February 27, 2015)

Securities Markets

LG1 LG2 LG3   **Securities markets** are markets that allow buyers and sellers of securities to make financial transactions. Their goal is to permit such transactions to be made quickly and at a fair price. In this section we will look at the various types of securities markets and their general characteristics.

Types of Securities Markets

In general, securities markets are broadly classified as either **money markets** or **capital markets**. The money market is the market where *short-term* debt securities (with maturities less than one year) are bought and sold. Investors use the money market for short-term borrowing and lending. Investors turn to the capital market to buy and sell *long-term* securities (with maturities of more than one year), such as stocks and bonds. In this text we will devote most of our attention to the capital market. There investors can make transactions in a wide variety of financial securities, including stocks, bonds, mutual funds, exchange-traded funds, options, and futures. Capital markets are classified as either *primary* or *secondary*, depending on whether securities are being sold initially to investors by the issuer (primary market) or resold among investors (secondary market).

Before offering its securities for public sale, the issuer must register them with and obtain approval from the **Securities and Exchange Commission (SEC)**. This federal regulatory agency must confirm both the adequacy and the accuracy of the information provided to potential investors. In addition, the SEC regulates the securities markets.

The Primary Market   The market in which *new issues* of securities are sold to investors is the **primary market**. In the primary market, the issuer of the equity or debt securities receives the proceeds of sales. The most significant transaction in the primary market is the **initial public offering (IPO)**, which marks the first public sale of a company's stock and results in the company's taking on a public status. The primary markets also provide a forum for the sale of additional stock, called *seasoned equity issues*, by already public companies.

Table 2.1 shows that only 21 operating companies sold stock to the public for the first time in the primary market in the United States during 2008, the first full year of the Great Recession, a period considered by many economists to be the worst economic downturn since the Great Depression of the 1930s. That number is less than one-twentieth the number of IPOs in 1999, the end of the technology-stock-driven bull market. When recovery from the Great Recession began in 2009, the number of IPOs per year also began to rebound, producing nearly twice as many IPOs relative to the previous year. Over the next five years, as the economy continued to rebound, so did IPO volume, reaching 206 IPOs in 2014. Seasoned equity offerings (SEOs) follow a similar pattern. The low point for SEO volume also occurred in 2008, though SEO deals have picked up since then.

Hear about Shake
Shack's IPO

To sell its securities in the primary market, a firm has three choices. It may make (1) a **public offering**, in which the firm offers its securities for sale to public investors; (2) a **rights offering**, in which the firm offers shares to existing stockholders on a pro rata basis (each outstanding share gets an equal proportion of new shares); or (3) a **private placement**, in which the firm sells securities directly without SEC registration to select groups of private investors such as insurance companies, investment management funds, and pension funds.

Going Public: The IPO Process Most companies that go public are small, fast-growing companies that require additional capital to continue expanding. For example, Shake Shack, a company that originated from a hot dog cart setup in 2001 to support the rejuvenation of New York City's Madison Square Park, raised about $98 million when it went public on January 30, 2015, at $21 per share. But not every IPO fits the typical start-up profile. Large companies may decide to spin off a unit into a separate public corporation. The media and entertainment company Time Warner did this when it spun off its magazine business, Time, Inc., in June 2014.

When a company decides to go public, it first must obtain the approval of its current shareholders, the investors who own its privately issued stock. Next, the company's auditors and lawyers must certify that all financial disclosure documents for the company are legitimate. The company then finds an investment bank willing to *underwrite* the offering. This bank is the lead underwriter and is responsible for promoting the company's stock and facilitating the sale of the company's IPO shares. The lead underwriter often brings in other investment banking firms to help underwrite and market the company's stock. We'll discuss the role of the investment banker in more detail in the next section.

The underwriter also assists the company in filing a registration statement with the SEC. One portion of this statement is the **prospectus**. It describes the key aspects of the securities to be issued, the issuer's management, and the issuer's financial position. Once a firm files a prospectus with the SEC, a *quiet period* begins, during which the firm faces a variety of restrictions on what it can communicate to investors. While waiting for the registration statement's SEC approval, prospective investors may receive a preliminary prospectus. This preliminary version is called a **red herring** because a notice printed in red on the front cover indicates the tentative nature of the offer. The purpose of the quiet period is to make sure that all potential investors have access to the same information about the company—that which is presented in the preliminary prospectus—but not to any unpublished data that might provide an unfair advantage. The quiet period ends when the SEC declares the firm's prospectus to be effective. The cover of the preliminary prospectus describing the 2015 stock issue of Shake Shack, Inc., appears in Figure 2.1. Notice that the preliminary prospectus has a blank where the offering price of the stock should be, just under the header that has the company name. Note also the warning, often referred to as the red herring, printed across the top of the front page.

During the registration period and before the IPO date, the investment bankers and company executives promote the company's stock offering through a *road show*, which consists of a series of presentations to potential investors—typically institutional investors—around the country and sometimes overseas. In addition to providing investors with information about the new issue, road shows help the investment bankers gauge the demand for the offering and set an expected price range. Once all of the issue terms have been set, including the price, the SEC must approve the offering before the IPO can take place.

Table 2.1 highlights several interesting features of the IPO market over the last 16 years. First, the table shows the number of IPOs each year. As mentioned earlier, the number of IPOs per year moves dramatically as economic conditions change and as the stock market moves up and down. Generally speaking, more companies go public when the economy is strong and stock prices are rising. Second, the table shows the average *first-day return* for IPOs each year. An IPO's first-day return is simply the percentage change from the price of the IPO in the prospectus to the closing price of the stock on its first day of trading. For example, when the details of Shake Shack's IPO were finalized, shares were offered to investors in the final prospectus at $21 per share.

FIGURE 2.1

Cover of a Preliminary Prospectus for a Stock Issue

Some of the key factors related to the 2015 common stock issue by Shake Shack Inc., are summarized on the cover of the prospectus. The disclaimer statement across the top of the page is normally printed in red, which explains its name, "red herring."

(Source: Shake Shack Inc., "Form S-1 Registration Statement," December 29, 2014, p. 2.)

The information in this preliminary prospectus is not complete and may be changed. We may not sell these securities until the registration statement filed with the Securities and Exchange Commission is effective. This preliminary prospectus is not an offer to sell these securities and it is not soliciting an offer to buy these securities in any state where the offer or sale is not permitted.

Subject to completion, dated December 29, 2014

PRELIMINARY PROSPECTUS

Shares

Class A Common Stock

This is an initial public offering of Shake Shack Inc. We anticipate that the initial public offering price will be between $ and $ per share of our Class A common stock.

Prior to this offering, there has been no public market for our Class A common stock. We have applied to have our Class A common stock listed on the New York Stock Exchange under the symbol "SHAK."

We will use the net proceeds that we receive from this offering to purchase from SSE Holdings, LLC, which we refer to as "SSE Holdings," newly-issued common membership interests of SSE Holdings, which we refer to as the "LLC Interests." There is no public market for the LLC Interests. The purchase price for the newly-issued LLC Interests will be equal to the public offering price of our Class A common stock, less the underwriting discount referred to below. We intend to cause SSE Holdings to use the net proceeds it receives from us in connection with this offering as described in "Use of Proceeds." In connection with the closing of this offering, certain of the holders of LLC Interests received in exchange for existing membership interests in SSE Holdings, whom we refer to as "Former SSE Equity Owners," will exchange their indirect ownership of LLC Interests for shares of Class A common stock and certain other holders of LLC Interests received in exchange for existing membership interests in SSE Holdings, whom we refer to as "Continuing SSE Equity Owners," will continue to own their LLC Interests. In addition, certain individuals who hold existing awards under our Unit Appreciation Rights Plan, whom we refer to as the "Former UAR Plan Participants," will receive shares of Class A common stock in settlement of their awards.

We will have two classes of common stock outstanding after this offering: Class A common stock and Class B common stock. Each share of Class A common stock and Class B common stock entitles its holder to one vote on all matters presented to our stockholders generally. All of our Class B common stock will be held by the Continuing SSE Equity Owners, on a one-to-one basis with the number of LLC Interests they own. Immediately following this offering, the holders of our Class A common stock issued in this offering collectively will hold   % of the economic interests in us and   % of the voting power in us, the Former SSE Equity Owners and the Former UAR Plan Participants, through their ownership of Class A common stock, collectively will hold   % of the economic interests in us and   % of the voting power in us, and the Continuing SSE Equity Owners, through their ownership of all of the outstanding Class B common stock, collectively will hold no economic interest in us and the remaining   % of the voting power in us. We will be a holding company, and upon consummation of this offering and the application of proceeds therefrom, our principal asset will be the LLC Interests we purchase from SSE Holdings and acquire from the Former SSE Equity Owners, representing an aggregate   % economic interest in SSE Holdings. The remaining   % economic interest in SSE Holdings will be owned by the Continuing SSE Equity Owners through their ownership of LLC Interests.

Although we will have a minority economic interest in SSE Holdings, because we will be the sole managing member of SSE Holdings, we will operate and control all of the business and affairs of SSE Holdings and, through SSE Holdings and its subsidiaries, conduct our business.

Following this offering, we will be a "controlled company" within the meaning of the corporate governance rules of the New York Stock Exchange. See "The Transactions" and "Management—Corporate Governance."

We are an "emerging growth company," as defined in Section 2(a) of the Securities Act of 1933, as amended, and will be subject to reduced public reporting requirements. This prospectus complies with the requirements that apply to an issuer that is an emerging growth company.

Investing in our Class A common stock involves risks. See "Risk Factors" beginning on page 22.

	Per Share	Total
Initial public offering price	$	$
Underwriting discounts and commissions(1)	$	$
Proceeds to us, before expenses	$	$

(1)   See "Underwriting (Conflicts of Interest)" for additional information regarding underwriting compensation.

We have granted the underwriters an option for a period of 30 days to purchase up to an additional   shares of Class A common stock solely to cover over-allotments.

Neither the Securities and Exchange Commission nor any other regulatory body has approved or disapproved of these securities or passed upon the accuracy or adequacy of this prospectus. Any representation to the contrary is a criminal offense.

Delivery of the shares will be made on or about

J.P. Morgan   Morgan Stanley

Goldman,
Sachs & Co.

Barclays   **Jefferies**
William Blair   **Stifel**

The date of this prospectus is   , 2015.

At the end of the stock's first trading day, its price had risen to $45.90, a one-day return of 118%! You can see in Table 2.1 that the average first-day return for all IPOs is positive in every year from 1999 to 2014, ranging from 6.4% in 2008 to 71.1% in 1999. Because IPO shares typically go up in value as soon as they start trading, we say that IPOs are *underpriced* on average. IPO shares are underpriced if they are sold to investors at a price that is lower than what the market will bear. In the Shake Shack offering, investors were apparently willing to pay $45.90 per share (based on the value of the shares once trading began), but shares were initially offered at just $21. We could say then that Shake Shack shares (say that three times fast) were underpriced by $24.90. Table 2.1 indicates that the average first-day return is closely connected to the number of IPOs. Average first-day returns are higher in years when many firms choose to go public (as in 1999), and first-day returns are lower in years when few firms conduct IPOs (as in 2008).

Shake Shack sold 5.75 million shares in its IPO for $21 per share, so the *gross proceeds* from the offer were $120.7 million, which equals 5.75 million shares times $21 per share. This is the third feature of the IPO market highlighted in Table 2.1. Total gross proceeds from IPOs ranged from $9.5 billion in 2003 to $65 billion in 1999. The last column in Table 2.1 lists total "money left on the table." *Money left on the table* represents a cost that companies bear when they go public if their shares are underpriced (as most IPOs are). For example, Shake Shack underpriced its offering by $143.2 million, which comes from multiplying 5.75 million shares sold times $24.90 underpricing per share. It shouldn't be a surprise that in the IPO market, aggregate money left on the table peaked at the same time that underpricing did. In 1999 the 477 companies that went public left $37.1 billion on the table by underpricing their shares. Given that the gross proceeds of IPOs that year (i.e., the total money paid by investors in the primary market to acquire IPO shares) were $65 billion, it seems that companies left more than half as much money on the table as they raised by going public in the first place. Put differently, if shares had not been underpriced at all in 1999, companies would have raised $102.1 billion rather than $65.0 billion, a difference of 57%.

Investing in IPOs is risky business, particularly for individual investors who can't easily acquire shares at the offering price. Most of those shares go to institutional investors and brokerage firms' best clients. Although news stories may chronicle huge first-day gains, IPO stocks are not necessarily good long-term investments.

The Investment Banker's Role   Most public offerings are made with the assistance of an investment banker. The **investment banker** is a financial intermediary that specializes in assisting companies issuing new securities and advising firms with regard to major financial transactions. In the context of IPOs, the main activity of the investment banker is **underwriting**. This process involves purchasing the securities from the issuing firm at an agreed-on price and bearing the risk of reselling them to the public. The investment banker also provides the issuer with advice about pricing and other important aspects of the issue.

In the case of large security issues, the lead or originating investment banker brings in other bankers as partners to form an **underwriting syndicate**. The syndicate shares the financial risk associated with buying the entire issue from the issuer and reselling the new securities to the public. The lead investment banker and the syndicate members put together a **selling group**, normally made up of themselves and a large number of brokerage firms. Each member of the selling group is responsible for selling a certain portion of the issue and is paid a commission on the securities it sells. The selling process for a large security issue is depicted in Figure 2.2.

TABLE 2.1   U.S. ANNUAL IPO DATA, 1999–2014

Year	Number of IPOs	Average First-Day Return	Aggregate Gross Proceeds (billions)	Aggregate Money Left on the Table (billions)
1999	477	71.1%	$65.0	$37.1
2000	381	56.3%	$64.9	$29.8
2001	79	14.2%	$34.2	$ 3.0
2002	66	9.1%	$22.0	$ 1.1
2003	63	11.7%	$ 9.5	$ 1.0
2004	173	12.3%	$31.2	$ 3.9
2005	159	10.3%	$28.2	$ 2.6
2006	157	12.1%	$30.5	$ 4.0
2007	159	14.0%	$35.7	$ 5.0
2008	21	6.4%	$22.8	$ 5.7
2009	41	9.8%	$13.2	$ 1.5
2010	91	9.4%	$29.8	$ 1.8
2011	81	13.3%	$ 27.0	$ 3.2
2012	93	17.9%	$31.1	$ 2.8
2013	157	21.1%	$38.8	$ 8.6
2014	206	15.5%	$42.2	$ 5.4

(Source: "Initial Public Offerings: Updated Statistics," **http://bear.warrington.ufl.edu/ritter/ IPOs2014Statistics.pdf**, Table 1, accessed February 26, 2015.)

The relationships among the participants in this process can also be seen on the cover of the December 29, 2014, preliminary prospectus for the common stock offering for Shake Shack, Inc., in Figure 2.1. The layout of the prospectus cover indicates the roles of the various participating firms. Placement and larger typefaces differentiate the originating underwriters (J.P. Morgan and Morgan Stanley) from the underwriting syndicate members (Goldman, Sachs & Co., Barclays, Jefferies, William Blair, and Stifel), whose names appear in a smaller font below. J.P. Morgan and Morgan Stanley are acting as joint-lead investment banks for Shake Shack's IPO.

Compensation for underwriting and selling services typically comes in the form of a discount on the sale price of the securities. For example, in the Shake Shack IPO, the investment bank, acting as a lead underwriter (say J.P. Morgan), might pay Shake Shack $19.50 for stock that investors will ultimately purchase for $21. Having guaranteed the issuer $19.50 per share, the lead underwriter may then sell the shares to the underwriting syndicate members for $19.75 per share. The additional 25 cents per share represents the lead underwriter's management fee. Next the underwriting syndicate members sell the shares to members of the selling group for 85 cents more, or $20.60 per share. That 85 cent difference represents the underwriters' discount, which is their profit per share. Finally, members of the selling group earn a selling concession of 40 cents per share when they sell shares to investors at $21 per share. The $1.50 difference between the price per share paid to Shake Shack ($19.50) and that paid by the investor ($21) is the *gross spread*, which comprises the lead underwriter's management fee ($0.25), the syndicate underwriters' discounts ($0.85), and the selling group's selling concession ($0.40). Although the issuer places (or sells) some primary security offerings directly, the majority of new issues are sold through public offering via the process just described.

FIGURE 2.2   **The Selling Process for a Large Security Issue**

The lead investment banker hired by the issuing firm may form an underwriting syndicate. The underwriting syndicate buys the entire security issue from the issuing corporation at an agreed-on discount to the public offering price. The investment banks in the underwriting syndicate then bear the risk of reselling the issue to the public at a public offering price. The investment banks' profit is the difference between the price they guaranteed the issuer and the public offering price. Both the lead investment bank and the other syndicate members put together a selling group to sell the issue on a commission basis to investors.

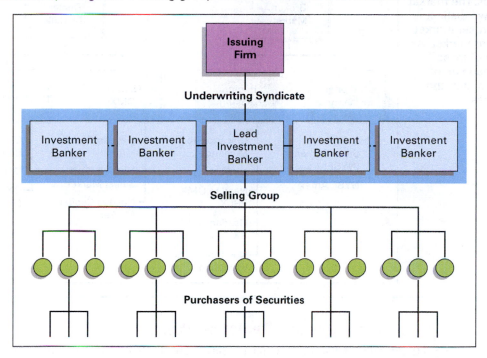

The Secondary Market

The **secondary market**, or the *aftermarket*, is the market in which securities are traded *after they have been issued*. Unlike the primary market, secondary-market transactions do not involve the corporation that issued the securities. Instead, the secondary market permits an investor to sell his or her holdings to another investor. The secondary market provides an environment for continuous pricing of securities that helps to ensure that security prices reflect the securities' true values on the basis of the best available information at any time. The ability to make securities transactions quickly and at a fair price in the secondary market provides securities traders with *liquidity*.

One major segment of the secondary market consists of various *national securities exchanges*, which are markets, registered with the SEC, in which the buyers and sellers of *listed securities* come together to execute trades. There are 18 national securities exchanges registered with the SEC under Section 6(a) of the Exchange Act. The **over-the-counter (OTC) market**, which involves trading in smaller, *unlisted securities*, represents the other major segment of the secondary market. The Financial Industry Regulatory Authority (FINRA) regulates securities transactions in the OTC market. FINRA is the largest independent regulator of securities firms doing business in the United States. FINRA's mission is to protect investors by making sure that the thousands of brokerage firms, tens of thousands of branch offices, and hundreds of thousands of registered securities representatives it oversees operate fairly and honestly.

FIGURE 2.3

Broker and Dealer Markets

On a typical trading day, the secondary market is a beehive of activity, where literally billions of shares change hands. The market consists of two distinct parts—the broker market and the dealer market. As shown, each of these markets is made up of various exchanges and trading venues.

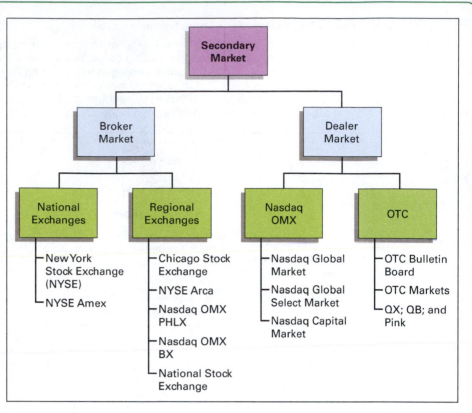

Broker Markets and Dealer Markets

Historically, the secondary market has been divided into two segments on the basis of how securities are traded: broker markets and dealer markets. Figure 2.3 depicts the makeup of the secondary market in terms of broker or dealer markets. As you can see, the **broker market** consists of national and regional securities exchanges, whereas the **dealer market** is made up of the Nasdaq OMX and OTC trading venues.

Before we look at these markets in more detail, it's important to understand that probably the biggest difference in the two markets is a technical point dealing with the way trades are executed. That is, when a trade occurs in a broker market, the two sides to the transaction, the buyer and the seller, are brought together—the seller sells his or her securities directly to the buyer. With the help of a *broker*, the securities effectively change hands on the floor of the exchange.

In contrast, when trades are made in a dealer market, buyers' orders and sellers' orders are never brought together directly. Instead, their buy/sell orders are executed by **market makers**, who are *securities dealers* that "make markets" by offering to buy or sell a certain amount of securities at stated prices. Essentially, two separate trades are made: The seller sells his or her securities (for example, in Intel Corp.) to a dealer, and the buyer buys his or her securities (in Intel Corp.) from another, or possibly even the same, dealer. Thus, there is always a dealer (*market maker*) on one side of a dealer-market transaction.

As the secondary market continues to evolve, the distinction between broker and dealer markets continues to fade. In fact, since the 21st century began there has been unprecedented consolidation of trading venues and their respective trading technologies to the point where most exchanges in existence today function as broker-dealer markets. Broker-dealer markets seamlessly facilitate both broker and dealer functions as necessary to provide liquidity for investors in the secondary market.

Broker Markets If you're like most people, when you think of the stock market, the first thing that comes to mind is the New York Stock Exchange (NYSE), which is a national securities exchange. Known as "the Big Board," the NYSE is, in fact, the largest stock exchange in the world. In 2015 more than 2,400 firms with an aggregate market value of greater than $19 trillion listed on the NYSE. Actually, the NYSE has historically been the dominant broker market. Also included in broker markets are the NYSE Amex (formally the American Stock Exchange), another national securities exchange, and several so-called regional exchanges. Regional exchanges are actually national securities exchanges, but they reside outside New York City. The number of securities listed on each of these exchanges is typically in the range of 100 to 500 companies. As a group, they handle a very small fraction (and a declining fraction) of the shares traded on organized exchanges. The best known of these are the Chicago Stock Exchange, NYSE Arca (formally the Pacific Stock Exchange), Nasdaq OMX PHLX (formally the Philadelphia Stock Exchange), Nasdaq OMX BX (formally the Boston Stock Exchange), and National Stock Exchange. These exchanges deal primarily in securities with local and regional appeal. Most are modeled after the NYSE, but their membership and listing requirements are considerably more lenient. To enhance their trading activity, regional exchanges often list securities that are also listed on the NYSE.

Other broker markets include foreign stock exchanges that list and trade shares of firms in their own foreign markets (we'll say more about these exchanges later in this chapter). Also, separate domestic exchanges exist for trading in options and in futures. Next we consider the basic structure, rules, and operations of each of the major exchanges in the broker markets.

The New York Stock Exchange Most organized securities exchanges were originally modeled after the New York Stock Exchange. Before the NYSE became a for-profit, publicly traded company in 2006, an individual or firm had to own or lease 1 of the 1,366 "seats" on the exchange to become a member of the exchange. The word *seat* comes from the fact that until the 1870s, members sat in chairs while trading. On December 30, 2005, in anticipation of becoming a publicly held company, the NYSE ceased having member seats. Now part of the NYSE Euronext group of exchanges, the NYSE sells one-year trading licenses to trade directly on the exchange. As of January 1, 2015, a one-year trading license cost $40,000 per license for the first two licenses and $25,000 per additional license held by a member organization. Investment banks and brokerage firms comprise the majority of trading license holders, and each typically holds more than one trading license.

See the NYSE's iPad App

Firms such as Merrill Lynch designate officers to hold trading licenses. Only such designated individuals can make transactions on the floor of the exchange. The two main types of floor broker are the commission broker and the independent broker. *Commission brokers* execute orders for their firm's customers. An *independent broker* works for herself and handles orders on a fee basis, typically for smaller brokerage firms or large firms that are too busy to handle their own orders.

Trading Activity The floor of the NYSE is an area about the size of a football field. It was once a hub of trading activity, and in some respects it looks the same today as it did years ago. The NYSE floor has trading posts, and certain stocks trade at each post.

Electronic gear around the perimeter transmits buy and sell orders from brokers' offices to the exchange floor and back again after members execute the orders. Transactions on the floor of the exchange occur through an auction process that takes place at the post where the particular security trades. Members interested in purchasing a given security publicly negotiate a transaction with members interested in selling that security. The job of the **designated market maker (DMM)**—an exchange member who specializes in making transactions in one or more stocks—is to manage the auction process. The DMM buys or sells (at specified prices) to provide a continuous, fair, and orderly market in those securities assigned to her. Despite the activity that still occurs on the NYSE trading floor, the trades that happen there account for a tiny fraction of trading volume. Most trading now occurs through electronic networks off the floor.

Listing Policies   To list its shares on a stock exchange, a domestic firm must file an application and meet minimum listing requirements. Some firms have **dual listings**, or listings on more than one exchange. Listing requirements have evolved over time, and as the NYSE has come under competitive pressure, it has relaxed many of its listing standards. Companies that sought a listing on the NYSE were once required to have millions in pretax earnings. Today, the NYSE will list companies with $750,000 in pretax earnings, or in some cases, with no pretax earnings at all. The NYSE does require that a listed firm have a minimum stock price of $2 to $3, and usually the market value of a company's public float (the value of shares available for trading on the exchange) must be $15 million or more. Still, an NYSE listing does not have the prestige that it once did.

Regional Stock Exchanges   Most regional exchanges are modeled after the NYSE, but their membership and listing requirements are more lenient. Trading costs are also lower. The majority of securities listed on regional exchanges are also listed on the NYSE. About 100 million NYSE shares pass through one of the regional exchanges on a typical trading day. This dual listing may enhance a security's trading activity.

Options Exchanges   *Options* allow their holders to sell or to buy another security at a specified price over a given period of time. The dominant options exchange is the Chicago Board Options Exchange (CBOE). Options are also traded on the NYSE, on Nasdaq OMX BX, NYSE Arca, and Nasdaq OMX PHLX exchanges, and on the International Securities Exchange (ISE). Usually an option to sell or buy a given security is listed on many of the exchanges.

Futures Exchanges   *Futures* are contracts that guarantee the delivery of a specified commodity or financial instrument at a specific future date at an agreed-on price. The dominant player in the futures trading business is the CME Group, a company comprised of four exchanges (CME, CBOT, NYMEX, and COMEX) known as designated contract markets. Some futures exchanges specialize in certain commodities and financial instruments rather than handling the broad spectrum of products.

Dealer Markets   One of the key features of the *dealer market* is that it has no centralized trading floors. Instead it is made up of a large number of market makers who are linked via a mass electronic network. Each market maker is actually a securities dealer who makes a market in one or more securities by offering to buy or sell them at stated bid/ask prices. The **bid price** and **ask price** represent, respectively, the highest price offered to purchase a given security and the lowest price offered to sell a given security. An investor pays the ask price when *buying* securities and receives the bid price when *selling* them. The dealer market is made up of both the Nasdaq OMX and the OTC markets. As an aside, the *primary market* is also a dealer market because all new issues—IPOs and **secondary distributions,** which involve the public sale of large blocks of previously issued securities held by large investors—are sold to the investing public by securities dealers acting on behalf of the investment banker.

Nasdaq The largest dealer market is made up of a large list of stocks that are listed and traded on the National Association of Securities Dealers Automated Quotation System, typically referred to as Nasdaq. Founded in 1971, Nasdaq had its origins in the OTC market but is today considered a totally separate entity that's no longer a part of the OTC market. In fact, in 2006 Nasdaq was formally recognized by the SEC as a national securities exchange, giving it pretty much the same stature and prestige as the NYSE.

To be traded on Nasdaq, all stocks must have at least two market makers, although the bigger, more actively traded stocks, like Cisco Systems, have many more than that. These dealers electronically post all their bid/ask prices so that when investors place market orders, they are immediately filled at the best available price.

The Nasdaq listing standards vary depending on the Nasdaq listing market. The 1,200 or so stocks traded on the Nasdaq Global Select Market meet the world's highest listing standards. Created in 2006, the Global Select Market is reserved for the biggest and the "bluest"—highest quality—of the Nasdaq stocks. In 2012 Facebook elected to list on Nasdaq Global Select rather than on the NYSE, further cementing Nasdaq's position as the preferred listing exchange for leading technology companies.

The listing requirements are also fairly comprehensive for the roughly 1,450 stocks traded on the Nasdaq Global Market. Stocks included on these two markets are all widely quoted, actively traded, and, in general, have a national following. The big-name stocks traded on the Nasdaq Global Select Market, and to some extent, on the Nasdaq Global Market, receive as much national visibility and are as liquid as those traded on the NYSE. As a result, just as the NYSE has its list of big-name players (e.g., ExxonMobil, GE, Citigroup, Walmart, Pfizer, IBM, Procter & Gamble, Coca-Cola, Home Depot, and UPS), so too does Nasdaq. Its list includes companies like Microsoft, Intel, Cisco Systems, eBay, Google, Yahoo!, Apple, Starbucks, and Staples. Make no mistake: Nasdaq competes head-to-head with the NYSE for listings. In 2015, 13 companies with a combined market capitalization of $82 billion moved their listings from the NYSE to Nasdaq. Some well-known companies that moved to Nasdaq include Viacom, Kraft Foods, and Texas Instruments. The Nasdaq Capital Market is still another Nasdaq market; it makes a market in about 600 or 700 stocks that, for one reason or another, are not eligible for the Nasdaq Global Market. In total, 48 countries are represented by approximately 3,000 securities listed on Nasdaq as of 2015.

The Over-the-Counter Market The other part of the dealer market is made up of securities that trade in the over-the-counter (OTC) market. These non-Nasdaq issues include mostly small companies that either cannot or do not wish to comply with Nasdaq's listing requirements. They trade on either the OTC Bulletin Board (OTCBB) or OTC Markets Group. The OTCBB is an electronic quotation system that links the market makers who trade the shares of small companies. The OTCBB provides access to more than 3,300 securities, includes more than 230 participating market makers, and electronically transmits real-time quote, price, and volume information in traded securities. The Bulletin Board is regulated by the FINRA, which, among other things, requires all companies traded on this market to file audited financial statements and comply with federal securities law.

The OTC Markets is an unregulated segment of the market, where the companies are not even required to file with the SEC. This market is broken into three tiers. The biggest is OTC Pink, which is populated by many small and often questionable companies that provide little or no information about their operations. Securities in the OTC QB tier must provide SEC, bank, or insurance reporting and be current in their disclosures. The top tier, OTC QX, albeit the smallest, is reserved for companies that choose to provide audited financial statements and other required information. If a security has been the subject of promotional activities and adequate current information concerning the issuer is not publicly available, OTC Markets will label the security "Caveat Emptor" (buyers beware). Promotional activities, whether they are published by the issuer or a third party, may include spam e-mail or unsolicited faxes or news releases.

Alternative Trading Systems

Some individual and institutional traders now make direct transactions outside of the broker and dealer markets in the third and fourth markets. The **third market** consists of over-the-counter transactions made in securities listed on the NYSE, the NYSE Amex, or one of the other exchanges. These transactions are typically handled by market makers that are not members of a securities exchange. They charge lower commissions than the exchanges and bring together large buyers and sellers. Institutional investors, such as mutual funds, pension funds, and life insurance companies, are thus often able to realize sizable savings in brokerage commissions and to have minimal impact on the price of the transaction.

The **fourth market** consists of transactions made through a computer network, rather than on an exchange, directly between large institutional buyers and sellers of securities. Unlike third-market transactions, fourth-market transactions bypass the market maker. **Electronic communications networks** (**ECNs**) are at the heart of the fourth market. Archipelago (part of the NYSE Arca), Bloomberg Tradebook, Island, Instinet, and MarketXT are some of the many ECNs that handle these trades. As with the exchanges, ECNs have undergone much consolidation. For example, in 2002 Island was merged with Instinet, and then in 2005 Instinet was acquired by Nasdaq.

ECNs are most effective for high-volume, actively traded securities, and they play a key role in after-hours trading, discussed later in this chapter. They automatically match buy and sell orders that customers place electronically. If there is no immediate match, the ECN, acting like a broker, posts its request under its own name on an exchange or with a market maker. The trade will be executed if another trader is willing to make the transaction at the posted price.

ECNs can save customers money because they charge only a transaction fee, either per share or based on order size. For this reason, money managers and institutions such as pension funds and mutual funds with large amounts of money to invest favor ECNs. Many also use ECNs or trade directly with each other to find the best prices for their clients.

General Market Conditions: Bull or Bear

Conditions in the securities markets are commonly classified as "bull" or "bear," depending on whether securities prices are rising or falling over time. Changing market conditions generally stem from changes in investor attitudes, changes in economic activity, and government actions aimed at stimulating or slowing down economic activity. **Bull markets** are normally associated with rising prices, investor optimism, economic recovery, and government stimulus. **Bear markets** are normally associated with falling prices, investor pessimism, economic slowdown, and government restraint. The beginning of 2003 marked the start of a generally bullish market cycle that peaked before turning sharply bearish in October 2007. The bearish market bottomed out in March 2009 and was generally bullish for the next several years. Since posting a return of almost –37% in 2008, the Standard and Poor's 500 Stock Index earned a positive return in each year from 2009 to 2014.

In general, investors experience higher (or positive) returns on common stock investments during a bull market. However, some securities perform well in a bear market and fare poorly in a bull market. Market conditions are notoriously difficult to predict, and it is nearly impossible to identify the bottom of a bear market or the top of a bull market until months after the fact.

CONCEPTS IN REVIEW
Answers available at
http://www.pearsonhighered.com/smart

2.1 Differentiate between each of the following pairs of terms.

    a. *Money market* and *capital market*
    b. *Primary market* and *secondary market*
    c. *Broker market* and *dealer market*

2.2 Briefly describe the IPO process and the role of the investment banker in underwriting a public offering. Differentiate among the terms *public offering*, *rights offering*, and *private placement*.

2.3 For each of the items in the left-hand column, select the most appropriate item in the right-hand column.

a. Prospectus	1. Trades unlisted securities
b. Underwriting	2. Buying securities from firms and reselling them to investors
c. NYSE	3. Conditions a firm must meet before its stock can be traded on an exchange
d. Nasdaq OMX BX	4. A regional stock exchange
e. Listing requirements	5. Describes the key aspects of a security offering
f . OTC	6. The largest stock exchange in the world

2.4 Explain how the dealer market works. Be sure to mention market makers, bid and ask prices, the Nasdaq market, and the OTC market. What role does the dealer market play in initial public offerings (IPOs) and secondary distributions?

2.5 What are the third and fourth markets?

2.6 Differentiate between a bull market and a bear market.

Globalization of Securities Markets

 LG4 Today investors, issuers of securities, and securities firms look beyond the markets of their home countries to find the best returns, lowest costs, and best international business opportunities. The basic goal of most investors is to earn the highest return with the lowest risk. This outcome is achieved through **diversification**—the inclusion of a number of different securities in a portfolio to increase returns and reduce risk. An investor can greatly increase the potential for diversification by holding (1) a wider range of industries and securities, (2) securities traded in a larger number of markets, and (3) securities denominated in different currencies, and the diversification is even greater if the investor does these things for a mix of domestic and foreign securities. The smaller and less diversified an investor's home market is, the greater the potential benefit

from prudent international diversification. However, even investors in the United States and other highly developed markets can benefit from global diversification.

In short, globalization of the securities markets enables investors to seek out opportunities to profit from rapidly expanding economies throughout the world. Here we consider the growing importance of international markets, international investment performance, ways to invest in foreign securities, and the risks of investing internationally.

Growing Importance of International Markets

Securities exchanges now operate in over 100 countries worldwide. Both large (Tokyo Stock Exchange) and small (South Pacific Stock Exchange), they are located not only in the major industrialized nations such as Japan, Great Britain, Canada, and Germany but also in emerging economies such as Brazil, Chile, India, South Korea, Malaysia, Mexico, Poland, Russia, and Thailand. The top four securities markets worldwide (based on dollar volume) are the NYSE, Nasdaq, London Stock Exchange, and Tokyo Stock Exchange. Other important foreign exchanges include the Shanghai Stock Exchange, Osaka Securities Exchange, Toronto Stock Exchange, Montreal Exchange, Australian Securities Exchange, Hong Kong Exchanges and Clearing Ltd., Swiss Exchange, and Taiwan Stock Exchange Corp.

The economic integration of the European Monetary Union (EMU), along with pressure from financial institutions that want an efficient process for trading shares across borders, is changing the European securities market environment. Instead of many small national exchanges, countries are banding together to create cross-border markets and to compete more effectively in the pan-European equity-trading markets. The Paris, Amsterdam, Brussels, and Lisbon exchanges, plus a derivatives exchange in London, merged to form Euronext, and the Scandinavian markets formed Norex. In mid-2006 Euronext and the NYSE Group—the NYSE parent—signed an agreement to combine their businesses in a merger of equals. Some stock exchanges—for example, Tokyo and Australian—are forming cooperative agreements. Others are discussing forming a 24-hour global market alliance, trading the stocks of selected large international companies via an electronic order-matching system. Nasdaq, with joint ventures in Japan, Hong Kong, Canada, and Australia, plans to expand into Latin America and the Middle East. The increasing number of mergers and cooperative arrangements represent steps toward a worldwide stock exchange.

Bond markets, too, have become global, and more investors than ever before regularly purchase government and corporate fixed-income securities in foreign markets. The United States dominates the international government bond market, followed by Japan, Germany, and Great Britain.

International Investment Performance

A motive for investing overseas is the lure of high returns. In fact, only once since 1980 did the United States stock market post the world's highest rate of return. For example, in 2014, a good year for U.S stocks, investors would have earned higher returns in many foreign markets. During that year the Standard and Poor's Global Index reported returns (translated into U.S. dollars) of 32% in India, 26% in Egypt, 20% in Indonesia, and 14% in Turkey. By comparison, the U.S. stock price index increased about 11%. Of course, foreign securities markets tend to be riskier than U.S. markets. A market with high returns in one year may not do so well in the next. However, even in 2008, one of the worst years on record for stock market investors, more than a dozen foreign exchanges earned returns higher than the NYSE Euronext.

Investors can compare activity on U.S. and foreign exchanges by following market indexes that track the performance of those exchanges. For instance, the Dow Jones averages and the Standard & Poor's indexes are popular measures of the U.S. markets, and indexes for dozens of different stock markets are available.

Ways to Invest in Foreign Securities

Investors can make foreign security transactions either indirectly or directly. One form of *indirect* investment is to purchase shares of a U.S.-based multinational corporation with substantial foreign operations. Many U.S.-based multinational firms, such as Accenture, Facebook, Google, IBM, Intel, McDonald's, Dow Chemical, Coca-Cola, and Nike, receive more than 50% of their revenues from overseas operations. By investing in the securities of such firms, an investor can achieve a degree of international diversification. Purchasing shares in a mutual fund or exchange-traded fund that invests primarily in foreign securities is another way to invest indirectly. Investors can make both of these indirect foreign securities investment transactions through a stockbroker.

To make *direct* investments in foreign companies, investors have three options. They can purchase securities on foreign exchanges, buy securities of foreign companies that trade on U.S. exchanges, or buy American Depositary Shares (ADSs).

The first way—purchasing securities on foreign exchanges—involves additional risks because foreign securities do not trade in U.S. dollars and, thus, investors must cope with currency fluctuations. This approach is not for the timid or inexperienced investor. Investors also encounter different securities exchange rules, transaction procedures, accounting standards, and tax laws in different countries. Direct transactions are best handled either through brokers at major Wall Street firms with large international operations or through major banks, such as JPMorgan Chase and Citibank, that have special units to handle foreign securities transactions. Alternatively, investors can deal with foreign broker-dealers, but such an approach is more complicated and riskier.

The second form of direct investment is to buy the securities of foreign companies that trade on both organized and over-the-counter U.S. exchanges. Transactions in foreign securities that trade on U.S. exchanges are handled in the same way as exchange-traded domestic securities. These securities are issued by large, well-known foreign companies. Stocks of companies such as Barrick Gold Corporation (Canada), General Steel Holdings (China), Cosan Ltd. (Brazil), Paragon Shipping (Greece), Manchester United (United Kingdom), and Tyco International (Switzerland) trade directly on U.S. exchanges. In addition, **Yankee bonds**, U.S. dollar–denominated debt securities issued by foreign governments or corporations and traded in U.S. securities markets, trade in both broker and dealer markets.

Finally, foreign stocks also trade on U.S. exchanges in the form of **American depositary shares (ADSs)**. These securities have been created to permit U.S. investors to hold shares of non-U.S. companies and trade them on U.S. stock exchanges. They are backed by **American depositary receipts (ADRs)**, which are U.S dollar–denominated receipts for the stocks of foreign companies that are held in the vaults of banks in the companies' home countries. Today more than 3,700 ADRs representing more than 100 home countries are traded on U.S. exchanges. About one-fourth of them are actively traded. Included are well-known companies such as Daimler, Fujitsu, LG Electronics, Mitsubishi, Nestle, and Royal Dutch Shell.

Risks of Investing Internationally

Investing abroad is not without pitfalls. In addition to the usual risks involved in any security transaction, investors must consider the risks of doing business in a particular foreign country. Changes in trade policies, labor laws, and taxation may affect operating conditions for the country's firms. The government itself may not be stable. You must track similar environmental factors in each foreign market in which you invest. This is clearly more difficult than following your home market.

U.S. securities markets are generally viewed as highly regulated and reliable. Foreign markets, on the other hand, may lag substantially behind the United States in both operations and regulation. Additionally, some countries place various restrictions on foreign investment. Saudi Arabia and China only recently opened their stock markets to foreign investors, and even then only to a limited extent. Mexico has a two-tier market, with certain securities restricted from foreigners. Some countries make it difficult for foreigners to get their funds out, and many impose taxes on dividends. For example, Swiss taxes are about 35% on dividends paid to foreigners. Other difficulties include illiquid markets and an inability to obtain reliable investment information because of a lack of reporting requirements.

Furthermore, accounting standards vary from country to country. Differences in accounting practices can affect a company's apparent profitability, conceal assets (such as the hidden reserves and undervalued assets that are permitted in many countries), and facilitate failure to disclose other risks. As a result, it is difficult to compare the financial performance of firms operating in different countries. Although the accounting profession has agreed on a set of international accounting standards, it will be years until all countries have adopted them and even longer until all companies apply them.

Another concern stems from the fact that international investing involves securities denominated in foreign currencies. Trading profits and losses are affected not only by a security's price changes but also by fluctuations in currency values. The price of one currency in terms of another is called the **currency exchange rate**. The values of the world's major currencies fluctuate with respect to each other daily, and these price movements can have a significant positive or negative impact on the return that you earn on an investment in foreign securities.

For example, on January 2, 2015, the exchange rate for the European Monetary Union euro (€) and the U.S. dollar (US$) was expressed as follows:

$$US\$ = €0.8324 \qquad € = US\$1.2013$$

This means that 1 U.S. dollar was worth 0.8324 euros, or equivalently, 1 euro was worth 1.2013 U.S. dollars. On that day, if you had purchased 100 shares of Heineken, which was trading for €57.72 per share on Euronext Amsterdam, it would have cost you $6,933.90 (i.e., 100 × 57.72 × 1.2013).

Four months later, the value of the euro had fallen relative to the dollar. On April 14, 2015, the euro/US$ exchange rate was 0.9386, which meant that during the first four months of 2015, the euro *depreciated* relative to the dollar (and therefore the dollar *appreciated* relative to the euro). On April 14 it took more euros to buy $1 (€0.9386 in April versus €0.8324 in January), so each euro was worth less in dollar terms (one euro was worth $1.0654 in April versus $1.2013 in January). Had the European Monetary Union euro instead *appreciated* (and the dollar *depreciated* relative to the euro), each euro would have been worth more in dollar terms.

Currency exchange risk is the risk caused by the varying exchange rates between the currencies of two countries. For example, assume that on April 14, 2015, you sold your 100 shares of Heineken, which was trading for €75.82 per share on Euronext Amsterdam; sale proceeds would have been $8,077.86 (i.e., 75.82 × 100 × 1.0654).

In this example you had a win-lose outcome. The price of Heineken stock rose 31.4% (from €57.72 to €75.82), but the value of the euro declined 11.3% (falling from 1.2013 to 1.0654). You made money on the investment in Heineken, but to purchase Heineken shares, you also had to purchase euros. Because the euro depreciated from January to April, you lost money on that part of the transaction. On net you realized a gain of 16.5% because you invested $6,933.90 in January and you received $8,077.86 in April. Put another way, the increase in the value of Heineken shares more than offset the currency loss that you experienced, so your overall return was positive. If the depreciation in the euro had been greater, it could have swamped the increase in Heineken shares, resulting in an overall negative rate of return. Similarly, if the euro had appreciated, that would have magnified the return on Heineken stock. Investors in foreign securities must be aware that the value of the foreign currency in relation to the dollar can have a profound effect on returns from foreign security transactions.

CONCEPTS IN REVIEW

Answers available at http://www .pearsonhighered.com/smart

2.7 Why is globalization of securities markets an important issue today? How have international investments performed in recent years?

2.8 Describe how foreign security investments can be made, both indirectly and directly.

2.9 Describe the risks of investing internationally, particularly currency exchange risk.

Trading Hours and Regulation of Securities Markets

LG5 Understanding the structure of domestic and international securities markets is an important foundation for developing a sound investment program. We'll begin with an overview of the trading hours and regulations that apply to U.S. securities markets.

WATCH YOUR BEHAVIOR

Overreacting to News A recent study found that when the prices of exchange-traded funds (ETFs) moved sharply during normal trading hours, those movements were often quickly reversed, suggesting that the initial move might have been caused by investors overreacting to news. During after-hours trading, the same pattern was not evident, suggesting that the traders who buy and sell after regular trading hours are less prone to overreaction.

MyFinanceLab

Trading Hours of Securities Markets

Traditionally, the regular trading session for organized U.S. exchanges ran from 9:30 A.M. to 4:00 P.M. eastern time. However, trading is no longer limited to these hours. Most securities exchanges and ECNs offer extended trading sessions before and after regular hours. Most of the after-hours markets are **crossing markets**, in which orders are filled only if they can be matched. That is, buy and sell orders are filled only if they can be matched with identical opposing sell and buy orders at the desired price. If an investor submits an order to buy shares but no matching sell order is posted, then the buy order is not filled. As you might expect, the liquidity of the market during extended hours is less than it is during the day. On the other hand, extended hours allow traders to respond to information that they receive after the official 4:00 P.M. market close. Extended hours allow U.S. securities markets to compete more effectively with foreign securities markets, in which investors can execute trades when U.S. markets are closed. ECNs were off limits to individual investors until 2003, but now both individuals and institutions can trade shares outside the traditional 9:30 to 4:00 trading day. For example, Nasdaq has its own extended-hours electronic-trading sessions from 4:00 A.M. to 9:30 A.M. and from 4:00 P.M. to 8:00 P.M.

Regulation of Securities Markets

U.S. securities laws protect investors and participants in the financial marketplace. A number of state and federal laws require that investors receive adequate and accurate disclosure of information. Such laws also regulate the activities of participants in the securities markets. State laws that control the sale of securities within state borders are

TABLE 2.2   IMPORTANT FEDERAL SECURITIES LAWS

Act	Brief Description
Securities Act of 1933	Passed to ensure full disclosure of information about new security issues. Requires the issuer of a new security to file a registration statement with the Securities and Exchange Commission (SEC) containing information about the new issue. The firm cannot sell the security until the SEC approves the registration statement, which usually takes about 20 days. Approval of the registration statement by the SEC merely indicates that the facts presented in the statement appear to reflect the firm's true position.
Securities Exchange Act of 1934	Formally established the SEC as the agency in charge of administering federal securities laws. The act gave the SEC the power to regulate the organized exchanges and the OTC market; their members, brokers, and dealers; and the securities traded in these markets.
Maloney Act of 1938	An amendment to the Securities Exchange Act of 1934, it provided for the establishment of trade associations to self-regulate the securities industry and led to the creation of the National Association of Securities Dealers (NASD). Today the Financial Industry Regulatory Authority (FINRA) has replaced the NASD as the industry's only self-regulatory body.
Investment Company Act of 1940	Established rules and regulations for investment companies (e.g., mutual funds) and authorized the SEC to regulate their practices. It required investment companies to register with the SEC and to fulfill certain disclosure requirements.
Investment Advisors Act of 1940	Requires investment advisors, persons hired by investors to advise them about security investments, to disclose all relevant information about their backgrounds, conflicts of interest, and any investments they recommend. Advisors must register and file periodic reports with the SEC.
Securities Acts Amendments of 1975	Requires the SEC and the securities industry to develop a competitive national system for trading securities. First, the SEC abolished fixed-commission schedules, thereby providing for negotiated commissions. Second, it established the Intermarket Trading System (ITS), an electronic communications network linking 9 markets and trading over 4,000 eligible issues, which allowed trades to be made across these markets wherever the network shows a better price for a given issue.
Insider Trading and Act of 1988	Established penalties for insider trading. Insiders include anyone who obtains nonpublic information, typically a company's directors, officers, major shareholders, bankers, investment bankers, accountants, and attorneys. The SEC requires corporate insiders to file monthly reports detailing all transactions made in the company's stock. Recent legislation substantially increased the penalties for insider trading and gave the SEC greater power to investigate and prosecute claims of illegal insider-trading activity.
Regulation Fair Disclosure (2000)	Reg FD required companies to disclosure material information to all investors at the same time.
Sarbanes-Oxley Act of 2002	Passed to protect investors against corporate fraud, particularly accounting fraud. It created an oversight board to monitor the accounting industry, tightened audit regulations and controls, toughened penalties against executives who commit corporate fraud, strengthened accounting disclosure requirements and ethical guidelines for financial officers, established corporate board structure and membership guidelines, established guidelines for analyst conflicts of interest, and increased the SEC's authority and budgets for auditors and investigators. The act also mandated instant disclosure of stock sales by corporate executives.
Dodd-Frank Wall Street Reform and Consumer Protection Act of 2010	Passed in the wake of the 2007–2008 financial crisis. Its stated aim was to promote the financial stability of the United States by improving accountability and transparency. It created the Bureau of Consumer Financial Protection and other new agencies.

commonly called *blue sky laws* because they are intended to prevent investors from being sold nothing but "blue sky." These laws typically establish procedures for regulating both security issues and sellers of securities doing business within the state. Most states have a regulatory body, such as a state securities commission, that is charged with enforcing the related state statutes. Table 2.2 summarizes the most important securities laws enacted by the federal government (listed in chronological order).

The intent of these federal securities laws is to protect investors. Most of these laws were passed in response to some type of crisis or scandal in the financial markets. In recent decades, Congress passed two major laws in response to public concern over corporate financial scandals: The *Sarbanes-Oxley Act of 2002* focuses on eliminating corporate fraud related to accounting and other information releases. The Dodd-Frank Wall Street Reform and Consumer Protection Act was passed in the wake of the 2007–2008 financial crisis. It sought to improve the financial stability of the U.S. economy through improved accountability and transparency in the financial system. The act created new financial regulatory agencies and merged or eliminated some existing agencies. Both of these acts heightened the public's awareness of **ethics**—standards of conduct or moral judgment—in business. The government and the financial community are continuing to develop and enforce ethical standards that will motivate market participants to adhere to laws and regulations. Ensuring that market participants adhere to ethical standards, whether through law enforcement or incentives, remains an ongoing challenge.

CONCEPTS IN REVIEW

Answers available at
http://www.pearsonhighered
.com/smart

2.10 How are after-hours trades typically handled? What is the outlook for after-hours trading?

2.11 Briefly describe the key requirements of the following federal securities laws:

  a. Securities Act of 1933
  b. Investment Company Act of 1940
  c. Investment Advisors Act of 1940
  d. Insider Trading and Fraud Act of 1988
  e. Regulation Fair Disclosure (2000)
  f. Sarbanes-Oxley Act of 2002
  g. Dodd-Frank Wall Street Reform and Consumer Protection Act of 2010

Basic Types of Securities Transactions

An investor can make a number of basic types of security transactions. Each type is available to those who meet the requirements established by government agencies as well as by brokerage firms. Although investors can use the various types of transactions in a number of ways to meet investment objectives, we describe only the most popular use of each transaction here, as we consider the long purchase, margin trading, and short selling.

Long Purchase

The **long purchase** is a transaction in which investors buy securities, usually in the hope that they will increase in value and can be sold at a later date for profit. The object, then, is to *buy low and sell high*. A long purchase is the most common type of transaction. Because investors generally expect the price of a security to rise over the period of time they plan to hold it, their return comes from any dividends or interest received during the ownership period, plus the difference (capital gain or loss) between the purchase and selling prices. Transaction costs, of course, reduce this return.

Ignoring dividends and transaction costs, we can illustrate the long purchase by a simple example. After studying Varner Industries, you are convinced that its common stock, which currently sells for $20 per share, will increase in value over the next few years. You expect the stock price to rise to $30 per share within two years. You place an order and buy 100 shares of Varner for $20 per share. If the stock price rises to, say, $40 per share, you will profit from your long purchase. If it drops below $20 per share, you will experience a loss on the transaction. Obviously, one of the major motivating factors in making a long purchase is an expected rise in the price of the security.

Margin Trading

Security purchases do not have to be made on a cash basis; investors can use funds borrowed from brokerage firms instead. This activity is referred to as **margin trading**. It is used for one basic reason: to magnify returns. As peculiar as it may sound, the term *margin* refers to the amount of equity (stated as a percentage) in an investment, or the amount that is *not* borrowed. If an investor uses 75% margin, for example, it means that 75% of the investment position is being financed with the person's own funds and the balance (25%) with borrowed money.

The Federal Reserve Board (the "Fed") sets the **margin requirement**, specifying the minimum amount of equity that must be the margin investor's own funds. The margin requirement for stocks has been at 50% for some time. By raising and lowering the margin requirement, the Fed can depress or stimulate activity in the securities markets. Brokers must approve margin purchases. The brokerage firm then lends the purchaser the needed funds and retains the purchased securities as collateral. It is important to recognize that margin purchasers must pay interest on the amount they borrow.

With the use of margin, you can purchase more securities than you could afford on a strictly cash basis and, thus, magnify your returns. However, the use of margin also presents substantial risks. Margin trading can only magnify returns, not produce them. One of the biggest risks is that the security may not perform as expected. If the security's return is negative, margin trading magnifies the loss. Because the security being margined is always the ultimate source of return, choosing the right securities is critical to this trading strategy. In the next section, we will look at how margin trading can magnify returns and losses.

Essentials of Margin Trading Investors can use margin trading with most kinds of securities. They regularly use it, for example, to buy common and preferred stocks, most types of bonds, options, warrants, and futures. It is not normally used with tax-exempt municipal bonds because the interest paid on such margin loans is not deductible for income tax purposes. It is also possible to use margin on certain foreign stocks and bonds that meet prescribed criteria. Foreign stocks eligible for margin trading must trade on an exchange located in a FTSE Global Index recognized country (there are roughly 50 such countries), and the companies issuing the shares must have a market capitalization of at least $500 million. These stocks must have daily price quotations that are made available to a U.S. broker continuously via an electronic quote system, and they must have median daily trading volume of 100,000 shares or $500,000.

Magnified Profits and Losses The idea of margin trading is to employ **financial leverage**—the use of debt financing to magnify investment returns. Here is how it works: Suppose you have $5,000 to invest and are considering the purchase of 100 shares of stock at $50 per share. If you do not margin, you can buy exactly 100 shares of the

AN ADVISOR'S PERSPECTIVE

Ryan McKeown
Senior VP—Financial Advisor, **Wealth Enhancement Group**

"Margin trading allows an investor to leverage up their investments."

MyFinanceLab

TABLE 2.3   THE EFFECT OF MARGIN TRADING ON SECURITY RETURNS

	Without Margin (100% Equity)	With Margins of		
		80%	65%	50%
Number of $50 shares purchased	100	100	100	100
Cost of investment	$5,000	$5,000	$5,000	$5,000
Less: Borrowed money	–$ 0	–$1,000	–$1,750	–$2,500
Equity in investment	$5,000	$4,000	$3,250	$2,500
A. Investor's position if price rises by $30 to $80/share				
Value of stock	$8,000	$8,000	$8,000	$8,000
Less: Cost of investment	–$5,000	–$5,000	–$5,000	–$5,000
Capital gain	$3,000	$3,000	$3,000	$3,000
Return on investor's equity (capital gain/equity in investment)	60%	75%	92.3%	120%
B. Investor's position if price falls by $30 to $20/share				
Value of stock	$2,000	$2,000	$2,000	$2,000
Less: Cost of investment	–$5,000	–$5,000	–$5,000	–$5,000
Capital loss*	–$3,000	–$3,000	–$3,000	–$3,000
Return on investor's equity (capital loss/equity in investment)*	(60%)	(75%)	(92.3%)	(120%)

*Both the capital loss and the return on investor's equity are negative, as noted by the parentheses.

stock (ignoring brokerage commissions). If you margin the transaction—for example, at 50%—you can acquire the same $5,000 position with only $2,500 of your own money. This leaves you with $2,500 to use for other investments or to buy on margin another 100 shares of the same stock. Either way, by margining you will reap greater benefits from the stock's price appreciation.

Table 2.3 illustrates the concept of margin trading. It shows a nonmargined (100% equity) transaction, along with the same transaction using various margins. For simplicity, we assume here that the investor pays no interest on borrowed funds, but in reality investors do pay interest, and that would lower returns throughout Table 2.3. Remember that the margin rates indicate the investor's equity in the investment. When the investment is not margined and the price of the stock goes up by $30 per share (see Table 2.3, part A), the investor enjoys a very respectable 60% rate of return. However, observe how the rate of return goes up when margin is used. For example, consider an investor who buys 100 shares using 80% margin. This means that to pay for the $5,000 cost of the shares, the investor uses 80% of her own money ($4,000) and borrows 20% ($1,000) to pay for the rest. Now suppose that the stock price rises from $50 to $80 per share. The shares are worth $8,000, so the investor earns a $3,000 capital gain. The gain, relative to the investor's initial investment of $4,000, represents a 75% rate of return. In other words, margin allowed the investor to earn 75% when the underlying stock only increased by 60%. It is in this sense that margin magnifies an investor's rate of return. In part A of Table 2.3, the rate of return ranges from 75% to 120%, depending on the amount of equity in the investment. The more the investor borrows, the greater her rate of return. This occurs because the dollar gain is the same ($3,000) *regardless of how the investor finances the transaction.* Clearly, as the investor's equity in the investment declines (with lower margins), the rate of return increases accordingly. Given this example, you might ask why an investor would ever buy a stock without borrowing money. The answer is that trading on margin also magnifies losses. Look at part B of Table 2.3. Suppose the investor uses 80% margin to buy 100 shares of the stock at $50 per share, but then the price of the stock falls to $20. In that case, the investor experiences a $3,000 capital loss. Relative to the initial $4,000 investment, the investor earns a −75% rate of return, whereas the decline in the stock price was just 60%.

Three important lessons about margin trading emerge from the table:

- Movements in the stock's price are not influenced by the method used to purchase the stock.

- The lower the amount of the investor's equity in the position, the *greater the rate of return* the investor will enjoy when the price of the security rises.

- The *loss is also magnified* when the price of the security falls (see Table 2.3, part B).

Note that Table 2.3 has an Excel@Investing icon. Throughout the text, tables with this icon indicate that the spreadsheet is available on http://www.myfinancelab.com. The use of electronic spreadsheets in finance and investments, as well as in all functional areas of business, is pervasive. We use spreadsheets from time to time throughout the text to demonstrate how the content has been constructed or calculated. As you know, we include Excel spreadsheet exercises at the end of most chapters to give you practice with spreadsheets and help you develop the ability to clearly set out the logic needed to solve investment problems.

Advantages and Disadvantages of Margin Trading   A magnified return is the major advantage of margin trading. The size of the magnified return depends on both the price behavior of the security and the amount of margin used. Another, more modest benefit of margin trading is that it allows for greater diversification of security holdings because investors can spread their limited capital over a larger number of investments.

The major disadvantage of margin trading, of course, is the potential for magnified losses if the price of the security falls. Another disadvantage is the cost of the margin loans themselves. A **margin loan** is the official vehicle through which the borrowed funds are made available in a margin transaction. All margin loans are made at a stated interest rate, which depends on prevailing market rates and the amount of money being borrowed. This rate is usually 1% to 3% above the **prime rate**—the interest rate charged to creditworthy business borrowers. For large accounts, the margin loan rate may be at the prime rate. The loan cost, which investors pay, will increase daily, reducing the level of profits (or increasing losses) accordingly.

Making Margin Transactions   To execute a margin transaction, an investor must establish a **margin account** with a minimum of $2,000 in equity or 100% of the purchase price, whichever is less, in the form of either cash or securities. The broker will retain any securities purchased on margin as collateral for the loan.

The margin requirement established by the Federal Reserve Board sets the minimum amount of equity for margin transactions. Investors need not execute all margin transactions by using exactly the minimum amount of margin; they can use more than the minimum if they wish. Moreover, it is not unusual for brokerage firms and the major exchanges to establish their own margin requirements, which are more restrictive than those of the Federal Reserve. Brokerage firms also may have their own lists of especially volatile stocks for which the margin requirements are higher. There are basically two types of margin requirement: initial margin and maintenance margin.

TABLE 2.4	INITIAL MARGIN REQUIREMENTS FOR VARIOUS TYPES OF SECURITIES
Security	Minimum Initial Margin (Equity) Required
Listed common and preferred stock	50%
Nasdaq OMX stocks	50%
Convertible bonds	50%
Corporate bonds	30%
U.S. government bills, notes, and bonds	10% of principal
U.S. government agencies	24% of principal
Options	Option premium plus 20% of market value of underlying stock
Futures	2% to 10% of the value of the contract

Initial Margin The minimum amount of equity that must be provided by the investor at the time of purchase is the **initial margin**. Because margin refers to the amount of equity in a trade, establishing a minimum margin requirement is equivalent to establishing a maximum borrowing limit. Initial margin requirements therefore place some restraint on how much risk investors can take through margin trading. All securities that can be margined have specific initial requirements, which the governing authorities can change at their discretion. Table 2.4 shows initial margin requirements for various types of securities. The more stable investments, such as U.S. government issues, generally have substantially lower margin requirements and thus offer greater opportunities to magnify returns. Stocks traded on the Nasdaq OMX markets can be margined like listed securities.

As long as the margin in an account remains at a level equal to or higher than prevailing initial requirements, the investor may use the account in any way he or she wants. However, if the value of the investor's holdings declines, the margin in his or her account will also drop. In this case, the investor will have what is known as a **restricted account**, one whose equity is less than the initial margin requirement. It does not mean that the investor must put up additional cash or equity. However, as long as the account is restricted, the investor may not make further margin purchases and must bring the margin back to the initial level when securities are sold.

Maintenance Margin The absolute minimum amount of margin (equity) that an investor must maintain in the margin account at all times is the **maintenance margin**. When an insufficient amount of maintenance margin exists, an investor will receive a **margin call**. This call gives the investor a short period of time, ranging from a few hours to a few days, to bring the equity up above the maintenance margin. If this doesn't happen, the broker is authorized to sell enough of the investor's margined holdings to bring the equity in the account up to this standard.

Margin investors can be in for a surprise if markets are volatile. When the Nasdaq stock market fell 14% in one day in early April 2000, brokerages made many more margin calls than usual. Investors rushed to sell shares, often at a loss, to cover their margin calls—only to watch the market bounce back a few days later.

The maintenance margin protects both the brokerage house and investors. Brokers avoid having to absorb excessive investor losses, and investors avoid being wiped out. The maintenance margin on equity securities is currently 25%. It rarely changes, although it is often set slightly higher by brokerage firms for the added protection of brokers and customers. For straight debt securities such as government bonds, there is no official maintenance margin except that set by the brokerage firms themselves.

The Basic Margin Formula The amount of margin is always measured in terms of its relative amount of equity, which is considered the investor's collateral. A simple formula can be used with all types of long purchases to determine the amount of margin in the transaction at any given time. Basically, only two pieces of information are required: (1) the prevailing market value of the securities being margined and (2) the **debit balance**, which is the amount of money being borrowed in the margin loan. Given this information, we can compute margin according to Equation 2.1.

Equation 2.1
$$\text{Margin} = \frac{\text{Value of securities} - \text{Debit balance}}{\text{Value of securities}}$$

Equation 2.1a
$$= \frac{V - D}{V}$$

To illustrate, consider the following example. Assume you want to purchase 100 shares of stock at $40 per share at a time when the initial margin requirement is 70%. Because 70% of the transaction must be financed with equity, you can finance the (30%) balance with a margin loan. Therefore, you will borrow $0.30 \times \$4,000$, or $1,200. This amount, of course, is the *debit balance*. The remaining $2,800 needed to buy the securities represents your equity in the transaction. In other words, equity is represented by the numerator $(V - D)$ in the margin formula.

What happens to the margin as the value of the security changes? If over time the price of the stock moves to $65, the margin is then

$$\text{Margin} = \frac{V - D}{V} = \frac{\$6,500 - \$1,200}{\$6,500} = 0.815 = \underline{81.5\%}$$

Note that the margin (equity) in this investment position has risen from 70% to 81.5%. *When the price of the security goes up, your margin also increases.*

On the other hand, *when the price of the security goes down, so does the amount of margin.* For instance, if the price of the stock in our illustration drops to $30 per share, the new margin is only 60% [i.e., ($3,000 − $1,200) ÷ $3,000]. In that case, we would be dealing with a *restricted account* because the margin level would have dropped below the prevailing initial margin of 70%.

Finally, note that although our discussion has been couched largely in terms of individual transactions, the same margin formula applies to margin accounts. The only difference is that we would be dealing with input that applies to the account *as a whole*—the value of all securities held in the account and the total amount of margin loans.

Return on Invested Capital When assessing the return on margin transactions, you must take into account the fact that you put up only part of the funds. Therefore, you are concerned with the *rate of return* earned on only the portion of the funds that you provided. Using both current income received from dividends or interest and total interest paid on the margin loan, we can apply Equation 2.2 to determine the return on invested capital from a margin transaction.

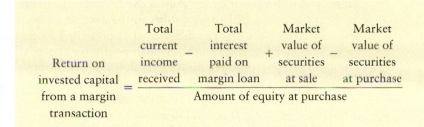

Equation 2.2

$$\text{Return on invested capital from a margin transaction} = \frac{\begin{array}{c}\text{Total} \\ \text{current} \\ \text{income} \\ \text{received}\end{array} - \begin{array}{c}\text{Total} \\ \text{interest} \\ \text{paid on} \\ \text{margin loan}\end{array} + \begin{array}{c}\text{Market} \\ \text{value of} \\ \text{securities} \\ \text{at sale}\end{array} - \begin{array}{c}\text{Market} \\ \text{value of} \\ \text{securities} \\ \text{at purchase}\end{array}}{\text{Amount of equity at purchase}}$$

We can use this equation to compute either the expected or the actual return from a margin transaction. To illustrate: Assume you want to buy 100 shares of stock at $50 per share because you feel it will rise to $75 within six months. The stock pays $2 per share in annual dividends, and during your 6-month holding period, you will receive half of that amount, or $1 per share. You are going to buy the stock with 50% margin and will pay 10% interest on the margin loan. Therefore, you are going to put up $2,500 equity to buy $5,000 worth of stock that you hope will increase to $7,500 in six months. Because you will have a $2,500 margin loan outstanding at 10% for six months, the interest cost that you will pay is calculated as $2,500 × 0.10 × 6 ÷ 12 which is $125. We can substitute this information into Equation 2.2 to find the expected return on invested capital from this margin transaction:

$$\text{Return on invested capital from a margin transaction} = \frac{\$100 - \$125 + \$7,500 - \$5,000}{\$2,500} = \frac{\$2,475}{\$2,500} = 0.99 = \underline{\underline{99\%}}$$

Keep in mind that the 99% figure represents the rate of return earned over a 6-month holding period. If you wanted to compare this rate of return to other investment opportunities, you could determine the transaction's annualized rate of return by multiplying by 2 (the number of six-month periods in a year). This would amount to an annual rate of return of 198% (i.e., 99 × 2 = 198).

Uses of Margin Trading Investors most often use margin trading in one of two ways. As we have seen, one of its uses is to magnify transaction returns. The other major margin tactic is called pyramiding, which takes the concept of magnified returns to its limits. **Pyramiding** uses the paper profits in margin accounts to partly or fully finance the acquisition of additional securities. This allows investors to make such transactions at margins below prevailing initial margin levels, sometimes substantially so. In fact, with this technique it is even possible to buy securities with no new cash at all. Rather, they can all be financed entirely with margin loans. The reason is that the paper profits in the account lead to **excess margin**—more equity in the account than required. For instance, if a margin account holds $60,000 worth of securities and has a debit balance of $20,000, it is at a margin level of 66.6% [i.e., ($60,000 − $20,000) ÷ $60,000]. This account would hold a substantial amount of excess margin if the prevailing initial margin requirement were only 50%.

The principle of pyramiding is to use the excess margin in the account to purchase additional securities. The only constraint—and the key to pyramiding—is that when the additional securities are purchased, your margin account must be at or above the prevailing required initial margin level. Remember that it is the account, not the individual transactions, that must meet the minimum standards. If the account has excess margin, you can use it to build up security holdings. Pyramiding can continue as long as there are additional paper profits in the margin account and as long as the margin level exceeds the initial requirement that prevailed when purchases were made. The tactic is somewhat complex but is also profitable, especially because it minimizes the amount of new capital required in the investor's account.

In general, margin trading is simple, but it is also risky. Risk is primarily associated with possible price declines in the margined securities. A decline in prices can result in a restricted account. If prices fall enough to cause the actual margin to drop below the maintenance margin, the resulting margin call will force you to deposit additional equity into the account almost immediately. In addition, losses (resulting from the price decline) are magnified in a fashion similar to that demonstrated in Table 2.3, part B. Clearly, the chance of a margin call and the magnification of losses make margin trading riskier than nonmargined transactions. Only investors who fully understand its operation and appreciate its pitfalls should use margin.

Short Selling

In most cases, investors buy stock hoping that the price will rise. What if you expect the price of a particular security to fall? By using short selling, you may be able to profit from falling security prices. Almost any type of security can be "shorted," including common and preferred stocks, all types of bonds, convertible securities, listed mutual funds, options, and warrants. In practice, though, the short-selling activities of most investors are limited almost exclusively to common stocks and to options. (However, investors are prohibited from using short-selling securities that they already own to defer taxes, a strategy called *shorting-against-the-box*.)

The Basics of Short Selling Explained

Essentials of Short Selling Short selling is generally defined as the practice of selling borrowed securities. Unusual as it may sound, selling borrowed securities is (in most cases) legal and quite common. Short sales start when an investor borrows securities from a broker and sells these securities in the marketplace. Later, when the price of the issue has declined, the short seller buys back the securities and then returns them to the lender. A short seller must make an initial equity deposit with the broker, subject to rules similar to those for margin trading. The deposit plus the proceeds from sale of the borrowed shares assure the broker that sufficient funds are available to buy back the shorted securities at a later date, even if their price increases. Short sales, like margin transactions, require investors to work through a broker.

Making Money When Prices Fall Making money when security prices fall is what short selling is all about. Like their colleagues in the rest of the investment world, short sellers are trying to make money by buying low and selling high. The only difference is that they reverse the investment process: *They start the transaction with a sale and end it with a purchase.*

Table 2.5 shows how a short sale works and how investors can profit from such transactions. (For simplicity, we ignore transaction costs.) The transaction results in a net profit of $2,000 as a result of an initial sale of 100 shares of stock at $50 per share (step 1) and subsequent covering (purchase) of the 100 shares for $30 per share (step 2). The amount of profit or loss generated in a short sale depends on the price at which the short seller can buy back the stock. Short sellers earn profits when the proceeds from the sale of the stock are higher than the cost of buying it back.

Who Lends the Securities? Acting through their brokers, short sellers obtain securities from the brokerage firm or from other investors. (Brokers are the principal source of

Excel@Investing

TABLE 2.5 THE MECHANICS OF A SHORT SALE	
Step 1. Short sale initiated	
100 shares of borrowed stock are sold at $50/share:	
Proceeds from sale to investor	$5,000
Step 2. Short sale covered	
Later, 100 shares of the stock are purchased at $30/share and returned to broker from whom stock was borrowed:	
Cost to investor	−$3,000
Net profit	$2,000

borrowed securities.) As a service to their customers, brokers lend securities held in their portfolios or in *street-name* accounts. It is important to recognize that when the brokerage firm lends street-name securities, it is lending the short seller the securities of other investors. Individual investors typically do not pay fees to the broker for the privilege of borrowing the shares; in exchange, investors do not earn interest on the funds they leave on deposit with the broker.

Margin Requirements and Short Selling To make a short sale, the investor must make a deposit with the broker that is equal to the initial margin requirement (currently 50%) applied to the short-sale proceeds. In addition, the broker retains the proceeds from the short sale.

To demonstrate, assume that you sell short 100 shares of Smart, Inc., at $50 per share at a time when the initial margin requirement is 50% and the maintenance margin on short sales is 30%. The values in lines 1 through 4 in column A in Table 2.6 indicate that your broker would hold a total deposit of $7,500 on this transaction. Note in columns B and C that regardless of subsequent changes in Smart's stock price, your deposit with the broker would remain at $7,500 (line 4).

By subtracting the cost of buying back the shorted stock at the given share price (line 5), you can find your equity in the account (line 6) for the current (column A) and two subsequent share prices (columns B and C). We see that at the initial short sale price of $50 per share, your equity would equal $2,500 (column A). If the share price subsequently drops to $30, your equity would rise to $4,500 (column B). If the share price subsequently rises to $70, your equity would fall to $500 (column C). Dividing these account equity values (line 6) by the then-current cost of buying back the stock

FAMOUS FAILURES IN FINANCE

Short Sellers Tip 60 Minutes

On March 1, 2015, the television news program, *60 Minutes*, ran a story alleging that Lumber Liquidators, a retail purveyor of home flooring products, was selling Chinese-made flooring that contained formaldehyde in concentrations that were up to 20 times greater than the legal limit in California. The day after the story was aired, Lumber Liquidators stock fell by 25%. Where did the producers at *60 Minutes* get the idea to investigate

Lumber Liquidators? Apparently Whitney Tilson, manager of the hedge fund Kase Capital, approached *60 Minutes* after he had conducted his own investigation and concluded that Lumber Liquidators was indeed selling flooring products that did not meet regulatory standards. Prior to giving *60 Minutes* the idea for the story, Tilson shorted 44,676 shares of Lumber Liquidators. Within days of the *60 Minutes* program being aired, Tilson had earned a profit on his short sale of $1.4 million.

TABLE 2.6   MARGIN POSITIONS ON SHORT SALES

Line	Item	A Initial Short Sale Price	B Subsequent Share Prices	C Subsequent Share Prices
1	Price per share	$ 50	$ 30	$ 70
2	Proceeds from initial short sale [(1) × 100 shares]	$5,000		
3	Initial margin deposit [0.50 × (2)]	$2,500		
4	Total deposit with broker [(2) + (3)]	$7,500	$ 7,500	$7,500
5	Current cost of buying back stock [(1) × 100 shares]	$5,000	$3,000	$7,000
6	Account equity [(4) − (5)]	$2,500	$4,500	$ 500
7	Actual margin [(6) ÷ (5)]	50%	150%	7.14%
8	Maintenance margin position [(7) > 30%?]	OK	OK	Margin call*

*Investor must either (a) deposit at least an additional $1,600 with the broker to bring the total deposit to $9,100 (i.e., $7,500 + $1,600), which would equal the current value of the 100 shares of $7,000 plus a 30% maintenance margin deposit of $2,100 (i.e., 0.30 × $7,000) or (b) buy back the 100 shares of stock and return them to the broker.

(line 5), we can calculate the actual margins at each share price (line 7). We see that at the current $50 price the actual margin is 50%, whereas at the $30 share price it is 150%, and at the $70 share price it is 7.14%.

As indicated in line 8, given the 30% maintenance margin requirement, your margin would be okay at the current price of $50 (column A) or lower (column B). But at the $70 share price, the 7.14% actual margin would be below the 30% maintenance margin, thereby resulting in a margin call. In that case (or whenever the actual margin on a short sale falls below the maintenance margin), you must respond to the margin call either by depositing additional funds with the broker or by buying the stock and covering (i.e., closing out) the short position.

If you wished to maintain the short position when the share price has risen to $70, you would have to deposit an additional $1,600 with the broker. Those funds would increase your total deposit to $9,100 (i.e., $7,500 + $1,600)—an amount equal to the $7,000 value of the shorted stock plus the 30% maintenance margin, or $2,100. Buying back the stock to cover the short position would cost $7,000, thereby resulting in the return of the $500 of equity in your account from your broker. Clearly, margin requirements tend to complicate the short-sale transaction and the impact of an increase in the shorted stock's share price on required deposits with the broker.

Advantages and Disadvantages The major advantage of selling short is, of course, the chance to profit from a price decline. The key disadvantage of many short-sale transactions is that the investor faces limited return opportunities along with high-risk exposure. The price of a security can fall only so far (to zero or near zero), yet there is really no limit to how far such securities can rise in price. (Remember, a short seller is hoping for a price decline; when a security goes up in price, a short seller loses.) For example, note in Table 2.5 that the stock in question cannot possibly fall by more than $50, yet who is to say how high its price can go?

A less serious disadvantage is that short sellers never earn dividend (or interest) income. In fact, short sellers owe the lender of the shorted security any dividends (or interest) paid while the transaction is outstanding. That is, if a dividend is paid during the course of a short-sale transaction, the short seller must pay an equal amount to the lender of the stock. (The mechanics of these payments are taken care of automatically by the short seller's broker.)

Uses of Short Selling Investors sell short primarily to seek speculative profits when they expect the price of a security to drop. Because the short seller is betting against the market, this approach is subject to a considerable amount of risk. The actual procedure works as demonstrated in Table 2.5. Note that had you been able to sell the stock at $50 per share and later repurchase it at $30 per share, you would have generated a profit of $2,000 (ignoring dividends and brokerage commissions). However, if the market had instead moved against you, all or most of your $5,000 investment could have been lost.

CONCEPTS IN REVIEW

Answers available at

http://www.pearsonhighered.com/smart

2.12 What is a long purchase? What expectation underlies such a purchase? What is margin trading, and what is the key reason why investors sometimes use it as part of a long purchase?

2.13 How does margin trading magnify profits and losses? What are the key advantages and disadvantages of margin trading?

2.14 Describe the procedures and regulations associated with margin trading. Be sure to explain restricted accounts, the maintenance margin, and the margin call. Define the term *debit balance*, and describe the common uses of margin trading.

2.15 What is the primary motive for short selling? Describe the basic short-sale procedure. Why must the short seller make an initial equity deposit?

2.16 What relevance do margin requirements have in the short-selling process? What would have to happen to experience a margin call on a short-sale transaction? What two actions could be used to remedy such a call?

2.17 Describe the key advantages and disadvantages of short selling. How are short sales used to earn speculative profits?

MyFinanceLab

Here is what you should know after reading this chapter. MyFinanceLab will help you identify what you know and where to go when you need to practice.

What You Should Know	Key Terms	Where to Practice
LG1 Identify the basic types of securities markets and describe their characteristics. Short-term investments trade in the money market; longer-term securities, such as stocks and bonds, trade in the capital market. New security issues are sold in the primary market. Investors buy and sell existing securities in the secondary markets.	ask price, *p. 46* bear markets, *p. 48* bid price, *p. 46* broker market, *p. 44* bull markets, *p. 48* capital market, *p. 38* dealer market, *p. 44* designated market maker (DMM), *p. 46* dual listing, *p. 46* electronic communications network (ECN), *p. 48* fourth market, *p. 48* initial public offering (IPO), *p. 38* investment banker, *p. 41* market makers, *p. 44* money market, *p. 38*	MyFinanceLab Study Plan 2.1

What You Should Know	Key Terms	Where to Practice
LG2 **Explain the initial public offering process.** The first public issue of a company's common stock is an IPO. The company selects an investment banker to sell the IPO. The lead investment banker may form a syndicate with other investment bankers and then create a selling group to sell the issue. The IPO process includes filing a registration statement with the Securities and Exchange Commission, getting SEC approval, promoting the offering to investors, pricing the issue, and selling the shares.		MyFinanceLab Study Plan 2.2
LG3 **Describe broker markets and dealer markets, and discuss how they differ from alternative trading systems.** In dealer markets, buy/sell orders are executed by market makers. The market makers are securities dealers who "make markets" by offering to buy or sell certain securities at stated bid/ask prices. Dealer markets also serve as primary markets for both IPOs and secondary distributions. Over-the-counter transactions in listed securities take place in the third market. Direct transactions between buyers and sellers are made in the fourth market. Market conditions are commonly classified as "bull" or "bear," depending on whether securities prices are generally rising or falling. Broker markets bring together buyers and sellers to make trades. Included are the New York Stock Exchange, the NYSE Amex, regional stock exchanges, foreign stock exchanges, options exchanges, and futures exchanges. In these markets the forces of supply and demand drive transactions and determine prices. These securities exchanges are secondary markets where existing securities trade.	over-the-counter (OTC) market, *p. 43* primary market, *p. 38* private placement, *p. 38* prospectus, *p. 39* public offering, *p. 38* red herring, *p. 39* rights offering, *p. 38* secondary distributions, *p. 47* secondary market, *p. 43* Securities and Exchange Commission (SEC), *p. 38* securities markets, *p. 38* selling group, *p. 41* third market, *p. 48* underwriting, *p. 41* underwriting syndicate, *p. 41*	MyFinanceLab Study Plan 2.3
LG4 **Review the key aspects of the globalization of securities markets, and discuss the importance of international markets.** Securities exchanges operate in over 100 countries—both large and small. Foreign security investments can be made indirectly by buying shares of a U.S.-based multinational with substantial foreign operations or by purchasing shares of a mutual fund that invests primarily in foreign securities. Direct foreign investment can be achieved by purchasing securities on foreign exchanges, by buying securities of foreign companies that are traded on U.S. exchanges, or by buying American depositary shares. International investments can enhance returns, but they entail added risk, particularly currency exchange risk.	American depositary receipts (ADRs), *p. 51* American depositary shares (ADSs), *p. 51* currency exchange rate, *p. 52* currency exchange risk, *p. 52* diversification, *p. 49* Yankee bonds, *p. 51*	MyFinanceLab Study Plan 2.4 Video Learning Aid for Problem P2.3

What You Should Know	Key Terms	Where to Practice
LG5 **Discuss trading hours and the regulation of securities markets.** Investors now can trade securities outside regular market hours (9:30 A.M. to 4:00 P.M., eastern time). Most after-hours markets are crossing markets, in which orders are filled only if they can be matched. Trading activity during these sessions can be quite risky. The securities markets are regulated by the federal Securities and Exchange Commission and by state commissions. The key federal laws regulating the securities industry are the Securities Act of 1933, the Securities Exchange Act of 1934, the Maloney Act of 1938, the Investment Company Act of 1940, the Investment Advisors Act of 1940, the Securities Acts Amendments of 1975, the Insider Trading and Fraud Act of 1988, the Sarbanes-Oxley Act of 2002, and the Dodd-Frank Wall Street Reform and Consumer Protection Act of 2010.	crossing markets, *p. 53* ethics, *p. 55* insider trading, *p. 54*	MyFinanceLab Study Plan 2.5
LG6 **Explain long purchases, margin transactions, and short sales.** Most investors make long purchases—that is, they buy securities—in expectation of price increases. Many investors establish margin accounts to use borrowed funds to enhance their buying power. The Federal Reserve Board establishes the margin requirement—the minimum investor equity in a margin transaction. The return on capital in a margin transaction is magnified for both positive returns and negative returns. Paper profits can be used to pyramid a margin account by investing its excess margin. The risks of margin trading are the chance of a restricted account or margin call and the consequences of magnified losses due to price declines. Short selling is used when a decline in security prices is anticipated. It involves selling securities, typically borrowed from the broker, to earn a profit by repurchasing them at a lower price in the future. The short seller makes an initial equity deposit with the broker. If the price of a shorted stock rises, the investor may receive a margin call and must then either increase the deposit with the broker or buy back the stock to cover the short position. The major advantage of selling short is the chance to profit from a price decline. The disadvantages of selling short are the unlimited potential for loss and the fact that short sellers never earn dividend (or interest) income. Short selling is used primarily to seek speculative profits.	debit balance, *p. 60* excess margin, *p. 61* financial leverage, *p. 56* initial margin, *p. 59* maintenance margin, *p. 59* long purchase, *p. 55* margin account, *p. 58* margin call, *p. 59* margin loan, *p. 58* margin requirement, *p. 56* margin trading, *p. 56* prime rate, *p. 58* pyramiding, *p. 61* restricted account, *p. 59* short selling, *p. 62*	MyFinanceLab Study Plan 2.6 Excel Tables 2.3, 2.5 Video Learning Aid for Problem P2.19

Log into MyFinanceLab, take a chapter test, and get a personalized Study Plan
that tells you which concepts you understand and which ones you need to
review. From there, MyFinanceLab will give you further practice, tutorials,
animations, videos, and guided solutions.

Log into **http://www.myfinancelab.com**

Discussion Questions

LG2 **Q2.1** From 1999 to 2014, the average IPO rose by 19% in its first day of trading. In 1999, 117 deals doubled in price on the first day. What factors might contribute to the huge first-day returns on IPOs? Some critics of the current IPO system claim that underwriters may knowingly underprice an issue. Why might they do this? Why might issuing companies accept lower IPO prices? What impact do institutional investors have on IPO pricing?

LG1 LG3 **Q2.2** Why do you think some large, well-known companies such as Cisco Systems, Intel, and Microsoft prefer to trade on the Nasdaq OMX markets rather than on an organized securities exchange such as the NYSE (for which they easily meet the listing requirements)? Discuss the pros and cons of listing on an organized securities exchange.

LG1 LG2 LG4 **Q2.3** On the basis of the current structure of the world's financial markets and your knowledge of the NYSE and Nasdaq OMX markets, describe the key features, functions, and problems that would be faced by a single global market (exchange) on which transactions can be made in all securities of all of the world's major companies. Discuss the likelihood of such a market developing.

LG5 **Q2.4** Critics of longer trading hours believe that expanded trading sessions turn the stock market into a casino and place the emphasis more on short-term gains than on long-term investment. Do you agree? Why or why not? Is it important to have a "breathing period" to reflect on the day's market activity? Why are smaller brokerages and ECNs, more than the NYSE and Nasdaq, pushing for longer trading hours?

LG6 **Q2.5** Describe how, if at all, conservative and aggressive investors might use each of the following types of transactions as part of their investment programs. Contrast these two types of investors in view of these preferences.
a. Long purchase
b. Margin trading
c. Short selling

Problems

All problems are available on **http://www.myfinancelab.com**

LG4 **P2.1** The current exchange rate between the U.S. dollar and the Japanese yen is 120 (yen/$). That is, 1 dollar can buy 120 yen. How many dollars would you get for 1,000 Japanese yen?

LG4 **P2.2** An investor recently sold some stock in a European company that was worth 20,000 euros. The U.S.$/euro exchange rate is currently 1.300, meaning that 1 euro buys 1.3 dollars. How many U.S. dollars will the investor receive?

LG4 **P2.3** In each of the following cases, calculate the price of one share of the foreign stock measured in United States dollars (US$).
a. A Belgian stock priced at 103.2 euros (€) when the exchange rate is 0.93€/US$.
b. A Swiss stock priced at 93.3 Swiss francs (Sf) when the exchange rate is 0.96Sf/US$.
c. A Japanese stock priced at 1,350 yen (¥) when the exchange rate is 110¥/US$.

LG4 **P2.4** Erin McQueen purchased 50 shares of BMW, a German stock traded on the Frankfurt Exchange, for €64.5 (euros) per share exactly one year ago when the exchange rate was €0.67/US$1. Today the stock is trading at €71.8 per share, and the exchange rate is €0.75/US$1.

a. Did the € depreciate or appreciate relative to the US$ during the past year? Explain.

b. How much in US$ did Erin pay for her 50 shares of BMW when she purchased them a year ago?

c. For how much in US$ can Erin sell her BMW shares today?

d. Ignoring brokerage fees and taxes, how much profit (or loss) in US$ will Erin realize on her BMW stock if she sells it today?

LG4 P2.5 Harold Perto purchased 100 shares of Barclays, a U.K. financial services firm, when they were trading for £260 (pounds sterling) and the exchange rate between British pounds and U.S. dollars was $1.50 per pound. A few months later, Harold sold his Barclays shares at a price of £280, converting the proceeds back into dollars at an exchange rate of $1.25 per pound. How much money did Harold spend (in U.S. dollars) to purchase the shares, and how much did he receive when he sold them?

LG5 P2.6 An investor believes that the U.S. dollar will rise in value relative to the Japanese yen. The same investor is considering two investments with identical risk and return characteristics: One is a Japanese yen investment and the other is a U.S. dollar investment. Should the investor purchase the Japanese yen investment?

LG6 P2.7 Elmo Inc.'s stock is currently selling at $60 per share. For each of the following situations (ignoring brokerage commissions), calculate the gain or loss that Courtney Schinke realizes if she makes a 100-share transaction.

a. She sells short and repurchases the borrowed shares at $70 per share.

b. She takes a long position and sells the stock at $75 per share.

c. She sells short and repurchases the borrowed shares at $45 per share.

d. She takes a long position and sells the stock at $60 per share.

LG6 P2.8 Assume that an investor buys 100 shares of stock at $50 per share, putting up a 60% margin.

a. What is the debit balance in this transaction?

b. How much equity capital must the investor provide to make this margin transaction?

LG6 P2.9 Assume that an investor buys 100 shares of stock at $50 per share, putting up a 60% margin. If the stock rises to $60 per share, what is the investor's new margin position?

LG6 P2.10 Assume that an investor buys 100 shares of stock at $35 per share, putting up a 75% margin.

a. What is the debit balance in this transaction?

b. How much equity funds must the investor provide to make this margin transaction?

c. If the stock rises to $55 per share, what is the investor's new margin position?

LG6 P2.11 Miguel Torres purchased 100 shares of CantWin.com.com for $50 per share, using as little of his own money as he could. His broker has a 50% initial margin requirement and a 30% maintenance margin requirement. The price of the stock falls to $30 per share. What does Miguel need to do?

LG6 P2.12 Jerri Kingston bought 100 shares of stock at $80 per share using an initial margin of 50%. Given a maintenance margin of 25%, how far does the stock have to drop before Jerri faces a margin call? (Assume that there are no other securities in the margin account.)

LG6 P2.13 An investor buys 200 shares of stock selling at $80 per share using a margin of 60%. The stock pays annual dividends of $1 per share. A margin loan can be obtained at an annual interest cost of 8%. Determine what return on invested capital the investor will realize if the price of the stock increases to $104 within six months. What is the annualized rate of return on this transaction?

LG6 **P2.14** Marlene Bellamy purchased 300 shares of Writeline Communications stock at $55 per share using the prevailing minimum initial margin requirement of 50%. She held the stock for exactly four months and sold it without brokerage costs at the end of that period. During the 4-month holding period, the stock paid $1.50 per share in cash dividends. Marlene was charged 9% annual interest on the margin loan. The minimum maintenance margin was 25%.

    a. Calculate the initial value of the transaction, the debit balance, and the equity position on Marlene's transaction.

    b. For each of the following share prices, calculate the actual margin percentage, and indicate whether Marlene's margin account would have excess equity, would be restricted, or would be subject to a margin call.

       1. $45

       2. $70

       3. $35

    c. Calculate the dollar amount of (1) dividends received and (2) interest paid on the margin loan during the 4-month holding period.

    d. Use each of the following sale prices at the end of the 4-month holding period to calculate Marlene's annualized rate of return on the Writeline Communications stock transaction.

       1. $50

       2. $60

       3. $70

LG6 **P2.15** Not long ago, Jack Edwards bought 200 shares of Almost Anything Inc. at $45 per share; he bought the stock on margin of 60%. The stock is now trading at $60 per share, and the Federal Reserve has recently lowered *initial margin* requirements to 50%. Jack now wants to do a little pyramiding and buy another 300 shares of the stock. What is the minimum amount of equity that he'll have to put up in this transaction?

LG6 **P2.16** An investor short sells 100 shares of a stock for $20 per share. The initial margin is 50%. How much equity will be required in the account to complete this transaction?

LG6 **P2.17** An investor short sells 100 shares of a stock for $20 per share. The initial margin is 50%. Ignoring transaction costs, how much will be in the investor's account after this transaction if this is the only transaction the investor has undertaken and the investor has deposited only the required amount?

LG6 **P2.18** An investor short sells 100 shares of a stock for $20 per share. The initial margin is 50%, and the maintenance margin is 30%. The price of the stock falls to $12 per share. What is the margin, and will there be a *margin call*?

LG6 **P2.19** An investor short sells 100 shares of a stock for $20 per share. The *initial margin* is 50%, and the maintenance margin is 30%. The price of the stock rises to $28 per share. What is the margin, and will there be a margin call?

LG6 **P2.20** Calculate the profit or loss per share realized on each of the following short-sale transactions.

Transaction	Stock Sold Short at Price/Share	Stock Purchased to Cover Short at Price/Share
A	$75	$83
B	$30	$24
C	$18	$15
D	$27	$32
E	$53	$45

LG6 **P2.21** Charlene Hickman expected the price of Bio International shares to drop in the near future in response to the expected failure of its new drug to pass FDA tests. As a result, she sold short 200 shares of Bio International at $27.50. How much would Charlene earn or lose on this transaction if she repurchased the 200 shares four months later at each of the following prices per share?
a. $24.75
b. $25.13
c. $31.25
d. $27.00

Visit **http://www.myfinancelab.com** for web exercises, spreadsheets, and other online resources.

Case Problem 2.1   Dara's Dilemma: What to Buy?

LG6 Dara Simmons, a 40-year-old financial analyst and divorced mother of two teenage children, considers herself a savvy investor. She has increased her investment portfolio considerably over the past five years. Although she has been fairly conservative with her investments, she now feels more confident in her investment knowledge and would like to branch out into some new areas that could bring higher returns. She has between $20,000 and $25,000 to invest.

Attracted to the hot market for technology stocks, Dara was interested in purchasing a tech IPO stock and identified NewestHighTech.com, a company that makes sophisticated computer chips for wireless Internet connections, as a likely prospect. The 1-year-old company had received some favorable press when it got early-stage financing and again when its chip was accepted by a major cell phone manufacturer.

Dara also was considering an investment in 400 shares of Casinos International common stock, currently selling for $54 per share. After a discussion with a friend who is an economist with a major commercial bank, Dara believes that the long-running bull market is due to cool off and that economic activity will slow down. With the aid of her stockbroker, Dara researches Casinos International's current financial situation and finds that the future success of the company may hinge on the outcome of pending court proceedings on the firm's application to open a new floating casino on a nearby river. If the permit is granted, it seems likely that the firm's stock will experience a rapid increase in value, regardless of economic conditions. On the other hand, if the company fails to get the permit, the falling stock price will make it a good candidate for a short sale.

Dara felt that the following alternatives were open to her:

Alternative 1: Invest $20,000 in NewestHighTech.com when it goes public.

Alternative 2: Buy Casinos International now at $54 per share and follow the company closely.

Alternative 3: Sell Casinos short at $54 in anticipation that the company's fortunes will change for the worse.

Alternative 4: Wait to see what happens with the casino permit and then decide whether to buy or short sell the Casinos International stock.

Questions

a. Evaluate each of these alternatives. On the basis of the limited information presented, recommend the one you feel is best.

b. If Casinos International's stock price rises to $60, what will happen under alternatives 2 and 3? Evaluate the pros and cons of these outcomes.

c. If the stock price drops to $45, what will happen under alternatives 2 and 3? Evaluate the pros and cons of these outcomes.

Case Problem 2.2   Ravi Dumar's High-Flying Margin Account

Ravi Dumar is a stockbroker who lives with his wife, Sasha, and their five children in Milwaukee, Wisconsin. Ravi firmly believes that the only way to make money in the market is to follow an aggressive investment posture—for example, to use margin trading. In fact, Ravi has built himself a substantial margin account over the years. He currently holds $75,000 worth of stock in his margin account, though the debit balance in the account amounts to only $30,000. Recently Ravi uncovered a stock that, on the basis of extensive analysis, he feels is about to take off. The stock, Running Shoes (RS), currently trades at $20 per share. Ravi feels it should soar to at least $50 within a year. RS pays no dividends, the prevailing initial margin requirement is 50%, and margin loans are now carrying an annual interest charge of 10%. Because Ravi feels so strongly about RS, he wants to do some pyramiding by using his margin account to purchase 1,000 shares of the stock.

Questions

a. Discuss the concept of pyramiding as it applies to this investment situation.

b. What is the present margin position (in percent) of Ravi's account?

c. Ravi buys the 1,000 shares of RS through his margin account (bear in mind that this is a $20,000 transaction).

   1. What will the margin position of the account be after the RS transaction if Ravi follows the prevailing initial margin (50%) and uses $10,000 of his money to buy the stock?

   2. What if he uses only $2,500 equity and obtains a margin loan for the balance ($17,500)?

   3. How do you explain the fact that the stock can be purchased with only 12.5% margin when the prevailing initial margin requirement is 50%?

d. Assume that Ravi buys 1,000 shares of RS stock at $20 per share with a minimum cash investment of $2,500 and that the stock does take off and its price rises to $40 per share in one year.

   1. What is the return on invested capital for this transaction?

   2. What return would Ravi have earned if he had bought the stock without margin—that is, if he had used all his own money?

e. What do you think of Ravi's idea to pyramid? What are the risks and rewards of this strategy?

Excel@Investing

Excel@Investing

You have just learned about the mechanics of margin trading and want to take advantage of the potential benefits of financial leverage. You have decided to open a margin account with your broker and to secure a margin loan. The specifics of the account are as follows:

- Initial margin requirement is 70%.

- Maintenance margin is 30%.

- You are informed that if the value of your account falls below the maintenance margin, your account will be subject to a margin call.

You have been following the price movements of a stock over the past year and believe that it is currently undervalued and that the price will rise in the near future. You feel that opening a margin account is a good investment strategy. You have decided to purchase three round lots (i.e., 300 shares) of the stock at its current price of $25 per share.

Create a spreadsheet similar to the spreadsheet for Table 2.3, which can be viewed at http://www.myfinancelab.com, to model and analyze the following market transactions.

Questions

a. Calculate the value of your investment in the stock if you did not make use of margin trading. In other words, how much must you invest if you fund your purchase with 100% cash equity?

b. Calculate the debit balance and the cash equity in the investment at the time of opening a margin account, adhering to the initial margin requirement.

c. If you use margin and the price of the stock rises by $15 to $40/share, calculate the capital gain earned and the return on investor's equity.

d. What is the current margin percentage based on item c?

e. If you use margin and the price of the stock falls by $15 to $10/share, calculate the capital loss and the respective return on investor's equity.

f. What is the new margin percentage based on item e, and what is the implication for you, the investor?

3

Investment Information and Securities Transactions

LEARNING GOALS

After studying this chapter, you should be able to:

LG1 Discuss the growth in online investing and the pros and cons of using the Internet as an investment tool.

LG2 Identify the major types and sources of investment information.

LG3 Explain the key aspects of the commonly cited stock and bond market averages and indexes.

LG4 Review the role of stockbrokers, including the services they provide, selection of a stockbroker, opening an account, and transaction basics.

LG5 Describe the basic types of orders, online transactions, transaction costs, and the legal aspects of investor protection.

LG6 Discuss the roles of investment advisors and investment clubs.

F ew events in the stock market generated more anticipation than the Facebook IPO. In the weeks leading up to Facebook's stock offering, most commentators expected strong demand for the social networking company's shares. Facebook seemed to confirm those expectations just a few days before the IPO when it raised the offer price for its shares to $38. These signs led many experts to predict that Facebook's share price would skyrocket when it became available for trading in the secondary market. Many investors wondered if the Facebook IPO would signal a return to the "dot-com bubble" of the late 1990s when IPOs of Internet-related companies often rose 100% or more on the first trading day.

The anticipated jump in Facebook's stock led some experts to warn investors against submitting *market orders* to buy shares. When an investor submits a market order, that order is executed as soon as possible at the prevailing market price. Therefore, an investor who placed a market order to buy Facebook stock on the first day it began trading risked paying a very high price if Facebook shares began trading well above its $38 offer price. Instead, some advisors recommended that investors use *limit orders* to buy Facebook stock. When an investor submits a limit order, the order specifies that the investor will buy the stock at or below a specific price. If the market price is higher than the price specified in the limit order, then no trade takes place. In this way, a limit order protects an investor from paying a higher-than-expected price.

On its opening day, Facebook stock quickly rose to $45 per share, with 110 million shares changing hands in the first seven minutes of trading. However, by that afternoon the stock had fallen below $40, closing the day at $38.23. Thus, investors who placed market orders to buy shares that morning probably endured significant one-day losses. Those who placed limit orders may have fared better, depending on the price specified in their orders. In this chapter, you'll learn about the many sources of information that can guide your investment decisions, and you'll see how different methods of buying and selling shares can affect your investment returns.

(Sources: "Why did Facebook's shares fall after its initial public offering?," by Samantha Nielson, *Market Realist*, January 14, 2014; "Here's How Facebook Doubled Its IPO Price," by Victor Luckerson, **Time.com**, July 24, 2014.)

Investment Research and Planning

LG1

Facebook's IPO Frenzy

Not too long ago, when investors wanted to buy or sell securities or to conduct research on different investment options, they called their full-service stockbrokers. Those brokers charged relatively high (by today's standards) commissions for processing customers' orders, but they also had access to a great deal of information that was either very expensive or completely impossible for individual investors to acquire. The fees that customers paid compensated their brokers not only for executing trades but also for providing access to information and research.

Today the Internet is a major force in the investing environment. It offers an extremely low-cost means for executing trades and provides access to tools formerly restricted to professionals. With these tools you can find and process a wealth of information and trade many types of securities. This information ranges from real-time stock prices to securities analysts' research reports to techniques for investment analysis. The time and money savings from online investing are huge. Instead of wading through reams of paper, you can quickly sort through vast databases to determine appropriate investments, make securities transactions to acquire your investments, and monitor the progress of your investments—all without leaving your computer. In this section, we introduce the wide range of options that you have for conducting investment research.

Getting Started in Investment Research

Although exceedingly valuable, the vast quantity of investment information available can be overwhelming and intimidating. The good news is that this chapter can help you begin to work through the maze of information and become a more informed investor. Educational sites are a good place to start. By mastering the basic concepts presented by these sites, you will be better prepared to identify the types of information that you will need to improve your investment decision-making skills.

Investment Education Sites The Internet offers many articles, tutorials, and online classes to educate the novice investor. Even experienced investors can find sites that will expand their investing knowledge. Here are a few good sites that feature investing fundamentals.

- *Investing Online Resource Center* (**http://www.investingonline.org**) provides abundant information for those getting started online as well as those already investing. It includes an online quiz that, based on your answers, will categorize your readiness for trading. There is even an investment simulator that creates an interactive learning experience that allows the user to "test drive" online trading.

- *InvestorGuide.com* (**http://www.investorguide.com**) offers InvestorGuide University, which is a collection of educational articles about investing and personal finance. In addition, the site provides access to quotes and charts, portfolio tracking software, research, news and commentary, and an extensive glossary of investment-related terms.

- *The Motley Fool* (**http://www.fool.com**) has sections on investing basics, mutual fund investing, choosing a broker, and investment strategies and styles, as well as lively discussion boards and more.

- *Investopedia* (**http://www.investopedia.com**) features tutorials on numerous basic and advanced investing and personal finance topics, a dictionary of investing terms, and other useful investment aids.

- *WSJ.com* (**http://www.wsj.com**), a free site from the *Wall Street Journal*, is an excellent starting place to learn what the Internet can offer investors.
- *Nasdaq* (**http://www.nasdaq.com**) has both an Investing and a Personal Finance section that provide links to a number of investment education resources.

Other good educational resources include leading personal finance magazines such as *Money*, *Kiplinger's Personal Finance Magazine*, and *Smart Money*.

Investment Tools Once you are familiar with investing basics, you can begin to develop financial plans and set investment goals, find securities that meet your objectives, analyze possible investments, and organize your portfolio. Many tools once used only by professional investment advisors are now free online. You can find financial calculators and worksheets, screening and charting tools, and stock quotes and portfolio trackers at general financial sites and at the sites of larger brokerage firms. You can even set up a personal calendar that notifies you of forthcoming earnings announcements and can receive alerts when one of your stocks has hit a predetermined price target.

Planning Online calculators and worksheets help you find answers to your financial planning and investing questions. Using them, you can determine how much to save each month for a particular goal, such as the down payment for your first home, a college education for your children, or a comfortable retirement at age 65. For example, the brokerage firm Fidelity has a number of planning tools: college planning, retirement planning, and research tools. One of the best sites for financial calculators is the Financial Industry Regulatory Authority (FINRA). It includes numerous tools that enable investors to perform tasks such as evaluating mutual funds, determining how much money to save for college expenses or retirement, or calculating the monthly payment on a loan. Figure 3.1 shows the Tools & Calculators page of FINRA's website. For example, if you click the Loan Calculator link, the site will ask you to submit a loan amount, an interest rate, and a term for the loan (in months), and then you simply click the CALCULATE button to find the monthly loan payment.

Screening With screening tools, you can quickly sort through huge databases of stocks, bonds, and mutual funds to find those that have specific characteristics. For stocks, you can select stocks based on their price-to-earnings ratios, market capitalizations, dividend yields, revenue growth rates, debt-to-equity ratios, and many other characteristics. For bonds, you can create screens based on the bond issuer's industry, as well as the bond's maturity date or yield. For mutual funds, you might identify funds based on the required minimum investment, a particular industry or geographic sector, or the fees that a fund investor must pay. For example, one tool asks you to specify the type of stock or fund, performance criteria, cost parameters, or other characteristics and then it provides a list of securities that meet your investment criteria. Each screening tool uses a different method to sort. If necessary you can do additional research on the individual stocks, bonds, or mutual funds to determine which ones best meet your investment objectives.

Zacks Investment Research provides some of the best free tools on its website. Figure 3.2 shows the opening page of Zacks "Stock Screener" and some of the ways you can sort stocks based on their characteristics. For example, you could identify a set of very large, dividend-paying companies by using the "Market Cap" item to select only those companies with a market capitalization (price per share times number of shares outstanding) greater than $100 billion and the "Div. Yield %" item

FIGURE 3.1

FINRA Tools & Calculators

At sites like **http://www.finra.org** you'll find many tools and calculators that you can use to solve specific investment problems. Below is the Tools & Calculators screen from the Financial Industry Regulatory Authority's website that offers several investment-related calculators.

(Source: ©2015 FINRA. All rights reserved. FINRA is a registered trademark of the Financial Industry Regulatory Authority, Inc. Reprinted with permission from FINRA.)

FIGURE 3.2

Zacks Stock Screener

Search for stocks based on a wide variety of characteristics such as a stock's market capitalization, price/earnings ratio, and dividend yield. Zacks's stock-screening tool will give you a list of stocks that meet your specifications.

(Source: Zacks, http://www.zacks.com. ©Zacks Investment Research, Inc. Reprinted with permission.)

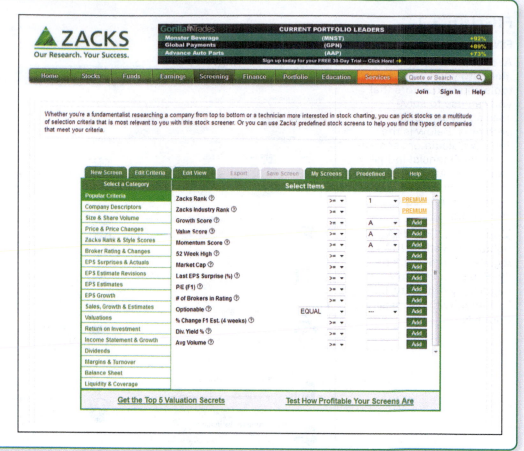

to include only those companies with a dividend yield greater than some small figure (say 0.25%). Google also offers a stock screener that allows you to select stocks based on dozens of characteristics and includes a graphic interface that shows the distribution of each characteristic (for example, the price/earnings ratio) across all of the stocks in Google's database. You can search by entering numerical values for particular characteristics or selecting an upper or lower boundary from the distribution. Yahoo! Finance and Morningstar offer screening tools for stocks, mutual funds, and bonds.

Charting Charting is a technique that plots the performance of securities over a specified time period, from a single day to a decade or longer. By creating charts, you can compare one company's price performance to that of other companies, industries, sectors, or market indexes, over almost any time period. Several good sites are Yahoo! Finance (**http://finance.yahoo.com**), Barchart (**http://barchart .com**), BigCharts (**http://bigcharts.marketwatch.com**), and Stock Charts (**http:// stockcharts.com**).

Stock Quotes and Portfolio Tracking Almost every investment-related website includes stock quotations and portfolio-tracking tools. Simply enter the stock symbol to get the price, either in real time or delayed several minutes. Once you create a portfolio of stocks in a portfolio tracker, the tracker automatically updates your portfolio's value every time you check. Usually, you can even link to more detailed information about each stock; many sites let you set up multiple portfolios. The features, quality, and ease of use of stock and portfolio trackers vary, so check several to find the one that meets your needs. Yahoo! Finance, MSN Money, and Morningstar have portfolio trackers that are easy to set up and customize.

Pros and Cons of the Internet as an Investment Tool

The power of the Internet as an investing tool is alluring. Do-it-yourself investing is readily available to the average investor, even to novices who have never before bought and sold securities. However, always remember that investing involves risk. Trading on the Internet requires that investors exercise the same caution as they would if they were getting information from and placing orders with a human broker. In fact, more caution is better because you don't have the safety net of a live broker suggesting that you rethink your trade. The ease of point-and-click investing may tempt inexperienced investors to trade too often, thereby driving up their transaction costs. Drawn by stories of others who have made lots of money, many novice investors take the plunge before they acquire an understanding of both the risks and the rewards of investing—sometimes with disastrous results.

The basic rules for smart investing are the same whether you trade online or through a broker. Do your homework to be sure that you understand the risks of any investment that you make. Be skeptical. If an investment sounds too good to be true, it probably is. Always do your own research; don't accept someone else's word that a security is a good buy. Perform your own analysis before you buy, using the skills you will develop as you work through this text.

Here is some additional advice:

- Don't let the speed and ease of making transactions blind you to the realities of online trading. More frequent trades mean higher total transaction costs. Although some brokers advertise costs as low as $3 per trade, the average online transaction fee is higher (generally about $10 to $15). If you trade often, it will take longer to recoup your costs. Studies reveal that the more often you trade, the harder it is to beat the market. In addition, on short-term trades of less than one year, you'll pay taxes on profits at the higher, ordinary income tax rates, not the lower capital gains rate.

- Don't believe everything you read. It's easy to be impressed with a screen full of data touting a stock's prospects or to act on a hot tip you read on a discussion board or see on an investment-oriented television show. Ask yourself, what do I know about the person who is recommending this investment? When conducting your research, stick to the sites of major brokerage firms, mutual funds, academic institutions, and well-known business and finance publications.

- If you get bitten by the online buying bug, don't be tempted to use margin debt to increase your stock holdings. As noted in Chapter 2, you may instead magnify your losses.

We will return to the subject of online investment fraud and scams and will discuss guidelines for online transactions in subsequent sections of this chapter.

3.1   Discuss the impact of the Internet on the individual investor and summarize the types of resources it provides.

3.2   Identify the four main types of online investment tools. How can they help you become a better investor?

3.3   What are the pros and cons of using the Internet to choose and manage your investments?

Types and Sources of Investment Information

LG2   As you learned in Chapter 1, becoming a successful investor starts with developing investment plans and meeting your liquidity needs. Once you have done that, you can search for the right investments to implement your investment plan and monitor your progress toward your goals. Whether you use the Internet or print sources, you should examine various kinds of investment information to formulate expectations of the risk and return behaviors of possible investments. This section describes the key types and sources of investment information.

Investment information can be either descriptive or analytical. **Descriptive information** presents factual data on the past behavior of the economy, the market, the industry, the company, or a given investment. **Analytical information** presents projections and recommendations about possible investments based on current data. The sample page from Yahoo! Finance included in Figure 3.3 provides descriptive and analytical information on McDonald's Corporation. The figure highlights that McDonald's is a very large company, with a market capitalization of nearly $93 billion (as of April 15, 2015), revenues in excess of $27 billion, and net income available to common stockholders (i.e., net profits) of $4.76 billion. Notice that McDonald's stock has a beta of 0.76, which is less than the average stock's beta of 1.0. Beta is an important measure of risk, specifically systematic or market risk, that we will discuss how to develop and use later in this text, but until then it is nice to know that various financial websites provide security betas online.

Some forms of investment information are free; others must be purchased individually or by annual subscription. You'll find free information on the Internet, in newspapers, in magazines, at brokerage firms, and at public, university, and brokerage firm libraries. Alternatively, you can subscribe to free and paid services that provide periodic reports summarizing the investment outlook and recommending certain actions. Many Internet sites now offer free e-mail newsletters and alerts. You can even set up your own personalized home page at many financial websites so that stock quotes, portfolio tracking, current business news, and other information on stocks of interest to you appear whenever you visit the site or are sent automatically to you via e-mail. Other sites charge for premium content, such as brokerage research reports, whether in print or online.

Although free information is more widely available today than ever before, it may still make sense to pay for services that save you time and money by gathering and processing relevant investment information for you. But first consider the value of information: For example, paying $40 for information that increases your return by $27 would not be economically sound. The larger your investment portfolio, the easier it is to justify information purchases because they are usually applicable to a number of investments.

FIGURE 3.3

A Report Containing Descriptive Information

The Yahoo! Finance report on McDonald's Corporation from April 15, 2015, contains descriptive information drawn from the company's financial statements as well as the stock's price performance.

(Source: Courtesy of Yahoo! Inc.)

McDonald's Corp. (MCD) - NYSE ★ Watchlist   ✚ Add to Portfolio

96.44 ↓1.14(1.17%) 4:00PM EDT

After Hours : **96.44** 0.00 (0.00%) 6:59PM EDT

Key Statistics

Get Key Statistics for: [GO]

Data provided by Capital IQ, except where noted.

Valuation Measures	
Market Cap (intraday)[5]:	92.69B
Enterprise Value (Apr 15, 2015)[3]:	106.91B
Trailing P/E (ttm, intraday):	20.01
Forward P/E (fye Dec 31, 2016)[1]:	18.16
PEG Ratio (5 yr expected)[1]:	3.27
Price/Sales (ttm):	3.42
Price/Book (mrq):	7.31
Enterprise Value/Revenue (ttm)[3]:	3.90
Enterprise Value/EBITDA (ttm)[6]:	11.12

Financial Highlights	
Fiscal Year	
Fiscal Year Ends:	Dec 31
Most Recent Quarter (mrq):	Dec 31, 2014
Profitability	
Profit Margin (ttm):	17.34%
Operating Margin (ttm):	29.04%
Management Effectiveness	
Return on Assets (ttm):	14.05%
Return on Equity (ttm):	32.97%
Income Statement	
Revenue (ttm):	27.44B
Revenue Per Share (ttm):	27.99
Qtrly Revenue Growth (yoy):	-7.30%
Gross Profit (ttm):	10.46B
EBITDA (ttm)[6]:	9.61B
Net Income Avl to Common (ttm):	4.76B
Diluted EPS (ttm):	4.82
Qtrly Earnings Growth (yoy):	-21.40%
Balance Sheet	
Total Cash (mrq):	2.08B
Total Cash Per Share (mrq):	2.17
Total Debt (mrq):	15.00B
Total Debt/Equity (mrq):	116.68
Current Ratio (mrq):	1.52
Book Value Per Share (mrq):	13.35
Cash Flow Statement	
Operating Cash Flow (ttm):	6.73B
Levered Free Cash Flow (ttm):	3.52B

Trading Information	
Stock Price History	
Beta:	0.76
52-Week Change[3]:	-3.22%
S&P500 52-Week Change[3]:	12.54%
52-Week High (May 14, 2014)[3]:	103.78
52-Week Low (Dec 16, 2014)[3]:	87.62
50-Day Moving Average[3]:	97.43
200-Day Moving Average[3]:	94.42
Share Statistics	
Avg Vol (3 month)[3]:	7,441,780
Avg Vol (10 day)[3]:	4,802,830
Shares Outstanding[5]:	961.12M
Float:	960.27M
% Held by Insiders[1]:	0.04%
% Held by Institutions[1]:	65.30%
Shares Short (as of Mar 31, 2015)[3]:	16.30M
Short Ratio (as of Mar 31, 2015)[3]:	2.20
Short % of Float (as of Mar 31, 2015)[3]:	N/A
Shares Short (prior month)[3]:	15.77M
Dividends & Splits	
Forward Annual Dividend Rate[4]:	3.40
Forward Annual Dividend Yield[4]:	3.50%
Trailing Annual Dividend Yield[3]:	3.32
Trailing Annual Dividend Yield[3]:	3.40%
5 Year Average Dividend Yield[4]:	3.30%
Payout Ratio[4]:	68.00%
Dividend Date[3]:	Mar 16, 2015
Ex-Dividend Date[4]:	Feb 26, 2015
Last Split Factor (new per old)[2]:	2:1
Last Split Date[3]:	Mar 8, 1999

View Financials
Income Statement - Balance Sheet - Cash Flow

See Key Statistics Help for definitions of terms used.

Abbreviation Guide: K = Thousands; M = Millions; B = Billions
mrq = Most Recent Quarter (as of Dec 31, 2014)
ttm = Trailing Twelve Months (as of Dec 31, 2014)
yoy = Year Over Year (as of Dec 31, 2014)
lfy = Last Fiscal Year (as of Dec 31, 2014)
fye = Fiscal Year Ending
[1] Data provided by Thomson Reuters
[2] Data provided by EDGAR Online
[3] Data derived from multiple sources or calculated by Yahoo! Finance
[4] Data provided by Morningstar, Inc.
[5] Shares outstanding is taken from the most recently filed quarterly or annual report and Market Cap is calculated using shares outstanding.
[6] EBITDA is calculated by Capital IQ using methodology that may differ from that used by a company in its reporting

Currency in USD.

Types of Information

Investment information can be divided into five types, each concerned with an important aspect of the investment process.

- *Economic and current event information* includes background and forecast data related to economic, political, and social trends on both domestic and global scales. Such information provides a basis for assessing the environment in which decisions are made.

- *Industry and company information* includes background and forecast data on specific industries and companies. Investors use such information to assess the outlook for a given industry or a specific company. Because of its company orientation, it is most relevant to stock, bond, or options investments.

- *Information on alternative investments* includes background and forecast data for securities other than stocks, bonds, and cash, such as real estate, private equity, and commodities.

- *Price information* includes price quotations on investment securities. These quotations are commonly accompanied by statistics on the recent price behavior of the security.

- *Information on personal investment strategies* includes recommendations on investment strategies or specific purchase or sale recommendations. In general, this information tends to be educational or analytical rather than descriptive.

Sources of Information

The discussion in this section focuses on the most common online and traditional sources of information on economic and current events, industries and companies, and prices, as well as other online sources. Beyond the discussion in this section, however, there are countless sources of investment information available to investors.

Economic and Current Event Information Investors who are aware of current economic, political, and business events tend to make better investment decisions. Popular sources of economic and current event information include financial journals, general newspapers, institutional news, business periodicals, government publications, and special subscription services. These are available in print and online versions; often the online versions are free but may have limited content. Most offer free searchable archives and charge a nominal fee for each article downloaded.

Financial Journals The **Wall Street Journal** is the most popular source of financial news. Published daily Monday through Saturday in U.S., European, and Asian editions, the *Journal* also has an online version called *WSJ Online*, which is updated frequently throughout the day including the weekends. In addition to giving daily price quotations on thousands of investment securities, the *Journal* reports world, national, regional, and corporate news. Both the published and online versions of the *WSJ* contain a column called "Heard on the Street" that focuses on specific market and company events both in the United States and abroad. The *WSJ* also includes articles that address personal finance issues in the Family Finances section. *WSJ Online* includes features such as quotes and news that provide stock and mutual fund charting, company profiles, financials, and analyst ratings, article searches, special online-only articles, and access to the Dow Jones article archives.

A second popular source of financial news is *Barron's,* which is published weekly. *Barron's* generally offers lengthier articles on a variety of topics of interest to individual investors. Probably the most popular column in *Barron's* is "Up & Down Wall Street," which provides a critical, and often humorous, assessment of major developments affecting the stock market and business. *Barron's* also includes current price quotations and a summary of statistics on a range of investment securities. Subscribers to *WSJ Online* also have access to *Barron's* online edition because both are published by Dow Jones & Company (a subsidiary of Rupert Murdoch's News Corporation).

Investor's Business Daily is a third national business newspaper published Monday through Friday. It is similar to the *Wall Street Journal* but contains more detailed price and market data. Its website has limited free content. Another source of financial news is the *Financial Times,* with U.S., U.K., European, and Asian editions.

General Newspapers Major metropolitan newspapers such as the *New York Times, Washington Post, Los Angeles Times,* and *Chicago Tribune* provide investors with a wealth of financial information in their print and online editions. Most major newspapers contain stock price quotations for major exchanges, price quotations on stocks of local interest, and a summary of the major stock market averages and indexes. Local newspapers are another convenient source of financial news. In most large cities, the daily newspaper devotes at least a few pages to financial and business news.

Another popular source of financial news is *USA Today,* the national newspaper published daily Monday through Friday. It is available in print and online versions. Each issue contains a "Money" section devoted to business and personal financial news and to current security price quotations and summary statistics. On Mondays the "Money" section publishes an interesting graphic showing the performance of different industry groups against the S&P 500 index.

Institutional News The monthly economic letters of the nation's leading banks, such as Bank of America (based in Charlotte, North Carolina), Northern Trust (Chicago), and Wells Fargo (San Francisco), provide useful economic information. Wire services such as Dow Jones, Bloomberg Financial Services, AP (Associated Press), and UPI (United Press International) provide economic and business news feeds to brokerages, other financial institutions, and websites that subscribe to them. Bloomberg has its own comprehensive site. Websites specializing in financial news include CNNMoney and MarketWatch.

Business Periodicals Business periodicals vary in scope. Some present general business and economic articles, others cover securities markets and related topics, and still others focus solely on specific industries. Regardless of the subject matter, most business periodicals present descriptive information, and some also include analytical information. They rarely offer recommendations.

The business sections of general-interest periodicals such as *Newsweek, Time,* and *U.S. News & World Report* cover business and economic news. Strictly business- and finance-oriented periodicals, including *Business Week, Fortune,* and *The Economist,* provide more in-depth articles. These magazines also have investing and personal finance articles.

Some financial periodicals specialize in securities and marketplace articles. The most basic, commonsense articles appear in *Forbes, Kiplinger's Personal Finance, Money, Smart Money,* and *Worth.* Published every two weeks, *Forbes* is the most

INVESTOR FACTS

Beware the Spin Companies sometimes hire outside investor relations (IR) firms to help generate media coverage of their press releases. A recent study found that IR firms tend to "spin" company news by generating more media coverage when companies disclose favorable information, and that the spin created by IR firms increased the stock prices of their clients on days when press releases occurred. However, when these same IR clients released their earnings, a type of hard, quantitative news that is hard to spin, their stock returns were worse than those of companies that did not hire IR firms to help disseminate information.

(Source: "Selective Publicity and Stock Prices," *Journal of Finance,* Vol. 67, Issue 2, pp. 599–638.)

investment oriented. *Kiplinger's Personal Finance, Money, Smart Money,* and *Worth* are published monthly and contain articles on managing personal finances and on investments.

All these business and personal finance magazines have websites with free access to recent, if not all, content. Most include a number of other features. For example, *Smart Money* has interactive investment tools, including a color-coded "Market Map 1000" that gives an aerial view of 1,000 U.S. and international stocks so that you can see the sectors and stocks whose prices are rising (or falling).

Government Publications   A number of government agencies publish economic data and reports useful to investors. The annual *Economic Report of the President,* which can be found at the U.S. Government Printing Office, provides a broad view of the current and expected state of the economy. This document reviews and summarizes economic policy and conditions and includes data on important aspects of the economy.

The *Federal Reserve Bulletin,* published monthly by the Board of Governors of the Federal Reserve System, and periodic reports published by each of the 12 Federal Reserve District Banks provide articles and data on various aspects of economic and business activity. Visit **http://www.federalreserve.gov** to read many of these publications.

A useful Department of Commerce publication is the *Survey of Current Business.* Published monthly, it includes indicators and data related to economic and business conditions. A good source of financial statement information on all manufacturers, broken down by industry and asset size, is the *Quarterly Financial Report for U.S. Manufacturing, Mining, and Wholesale Trade Corporations* published by the Department of Commerce.

Special Subscription Services   Investors who want additional insights into business and economic conditions can subscribe to special services. These reports include business and economic forecasts and give notice of new government policies, union plans and tactics, taxes, prices, wages, and so on. One popular service is the *Kiplinger Washington Letter,* a weekly publication that provides a wealth of economic information and analyses.

Industry and Company Information   Of special interest to investors is information on particular industries and companies. Many trade magazines provide in-depth coverage of business trends in just one industry. Trade publications such as *Chemical Week, American Banker, Computerworld, Industry Week, Oil and Gas Journal,* and *Public Utilities Fortnightly* provide highly focused industry and company information. For example, *Red Herring, CIO Magazine, Business 2.0,* and *Fast Company* are magazines that can help you keep up with the high-tech world; all have good websites. Often, after choosing an industry in which to invest, an investor will want to analyze specific companies. General business periodicals such as *Business Week, Forbes,* the *Wall Street Journal,* and *Fortune* carry articles on the activities of specific industries and individual companies. In addition, company websites typically offer a wealth of information about the company—investor information, annual reports, filings, and financial releases, press releases, and more. Table 3.1 presents several free and subscription resources that emphasize industry and company information.

Fair Disclosure Rules   In August 2000 the SEC passed the **fair disclosure rule,** known as **Regulation FD,** requiring senior executives to disclose material information such as earnings forecasts and news of mergers and new products simultaneously to investment professionals and the public via press releases or SEC filings. Companies may choose to limit contact with professional stock analysts if they are unsure whether the particular

TABLE 3.1   ONLINE SOURCES FOR INDUSTRY AND COMPANY INFORMATION

Website	Description	Cost
Hoover's Online (**http://www.hoovers.com**)	Reports and news on public and private companies with in-depth coverage of 43,000 of the world's top firms.	Varies according to level of service
CNET (**http://news.cnet.com**)	One of the best sites for high-tech news, analysis, and breaking news. Has great search capabilities and links.	Free
Yahoo! Finance (**http://finance.yahoo.com**)	Provides information on companies gathered from around the web: stock quotes, news, investment ideas, research, financials, analyst ratings, insider trades, and more.	Free
Market Watch (**http://www .marketwatch.com**)	Latest news from various wire services. Searchable by market or industry. Good for earnings announcements and company news.	Free

information requires a press release. However, Regulation FD does not apply to communications with journalists and securities ratings firms like Moody's Investors Service and Standard & Poor's. In other words, firms may disclose information to members of the media without simultaneously disclosing it publicly via a press release. The law takes the view that the media has a mission to disclose the information that they learn from companies, not to trade on that information as analysts might. Violations of the rule carry injunctions and fines but are not considered fraud.

Stockholders' Reports An excellent source of data on an individual firm is the **stockholders' report**, or **annual report**, published yearly by publicly held corporations. These reports contain a wide range of information, including financial statements for the most recent period of operation, along with summarized statements for several prior years. These reports are free and are usually also available on a company's website. An excerpt from AT&T's 2014 Annual Report appears in Figure 3.4. These pages show AT&T's growth rates and revenues for their different lines of business, and detailed financial statements are also available elsewhere in this report. If you don't want to search for annual reports one company at a time, AnnualReports.com boasts having "the most complete and up-to-date listing of annual reports on the Internet."

Tesla Motors 2014 Annual Meeting

In addition to the stockholders' report, many serious investors review a company's **Form 10-K**, which is a statement that firms with securities listed on a securities exchange or traded in the OTC market must file annually with the SEC. Finding 10-K and other SEC filings is now a simple task, thanks to SEC/EDGAR (Electronic Data Gathering and Analysis Retrieval), which has reports filed by all companies traded on a major exchange. You can read them free either at the SEC's website or at EDGAR's FreeEdgar site.

Comparative Data Sources Sources of comparative data, typically broken down by industry and firm size, are a good tool for analyzing the financial condition of companies. Among these sources are Dun & Bradstreet's *Key Business Ratios*, RMA's *Annual Statement Studies*, the *Quarterly Financial Report for U.S. Manufacturing, Mining, and Wholesale Trade Corporations* (cited earlier), and the *Almanac of Business & Industrial*

FIGURE 3.4 **Pages from AT&T's Stockholders' Report**

The excerpt from AT&T's 2014 Annual Report quickly acquaints the investor with some key information on the firm's operations over the past year. (Source: AT&T annual report, **http://www.att.com/gen/investor-relations?pid=9186**, April 15, 2015.)

Financial Highlights

RAMPING REVENUE GROWTH

AT&T's full-year consolidated revenues grew more than 3 percent, adjusting for the sale of Connecticut wireline properties

2014 ADJUSTED REVENUES

$131.6B ▲**3.1%**

2013: $127.6B   Adjusted YOY Growth

SOLID BUSINESS REVENUE GROWTH

Total 2014 revenues from business customers, including wireless and wireline, were $71.9 billion and grew 4.0 percent, with fourth-quarter revenues up 5.8 percent

BUSINESS SOLUTIONS REVENUES

$71.9B ▲**4.0%**

2013: $69.1B   YOY Growth

WIRELINE GROWTH DRIVERS TOP MORE THAN $25 BILLION IN ANNUALIZED REVENUES

AT&T U-verse and strategic business services combined for more than $25 billion in annualized revenues by the end of 2014, and both are growing in the double digits, adjusting for the sale of our Connecticut wireline properties

U-VERSE

$14.5B ▲**24.8%**

Total Adjusted Revenues   Adjusted YOY Growth

STRATEGIC BUSINESS SERVICES

$9.7B ▲**14.4%**

Total Adjusted Revenues   Adjusted YOY Growth

FIGURE 3.4 *continued*

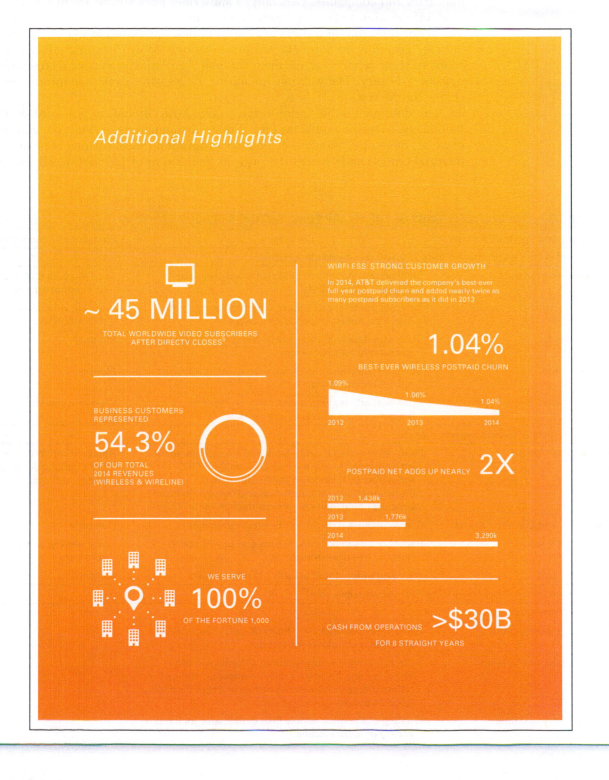

Additional Highlights

~ 45 MILLION

TOTAL WORLDWIDE VIDEO SUBSCRIBERS
AFTER DIRECTV CLOSES[3]

BUSINESS CUSTOMERS
REPRESENTED

54.3%

OF OUR TOTAL
2014 REVENUES
(WIRELESS & WIRELINE)

WE SERVE
100%
OF THE FORTUNE 1,000

WIRELESS STRONG CUSTOMER GROWTH

In 2014, AT&T delivered the company's best-ever
full-year postpaid churn and added nearly twice as
many postpaid subscribers as it did in 2013

1.04%

BEST-EVER WIRELESS POSTPAID CHURN

1.09%

1.06%

1.04%

2012   2013   2014

POSTPAID NET ADDS UP NEARLY   2X

2012   1,438k
2013   1,776k
2014   3,290k

CASH FROM OPERATIONS   >$30B

FOR 8 STRAIGHT YEARS

Financial Ratios. These sources, which are typically available in public and university libraries, provide useful benchmarks for evaluating a company's financial condition.

Subscription Services A variety of subscription services provide data on specific industries and companies. Generally, a subscriber pays a basic fee to access the service's information and can also purchase premium services for greater depth or range. The major subscription services provide both descriptive and analytical information, but they generally do not make recommendations. Most investors, rather than subscribe to these services, access them through their stockbrokers or a large public or university library. The websites for most services offer some free information and charge for the rest.

The dominant subscription services are those offered by Standard & Poor's, Bloomberg, Mergent, and Value Line. Table 3.2 summarizes the most popular services of these companies. **Standard & Poor's Corporation (S&P)** offers a large number of financial reports and services. Through its acquisition of *Business Week*, Bloomberg

TABLE 3.2   POPULAR OFFERINGS OF THE MAJOR SUBSCRIPTION SERVICES

Subscription Service/Offerings	Coverage	Frequency of Publication
Standard & Poor's Corporation (http:// www.standardandpoors.com)		
Corporation Records	Detailed descriptions of publicly traded securities of public corporations.	Annually with updates throughout the year
Stock Reports	Summary of financial history, current finances, and future prospects of public companies.	Annually with updates throughout the year
Stock Guide	Statistical data and analytical rankings of investment desirability for major stocks.	Monthly
Bond Guide	Statistical data and analytical rankings of investment desirability of bonds.	Monthly
The Outlook	Analytical articles with investment advice on the economy, market, and investments.	Weekly magazine
Mergent (http:// www.mergent.com)		
Mergent's Manuals	Eight reference manuals—Bank and Finance, Industrial, International, Municipal and Government, OTC Industrial, OTC Unlisted, Public Utility, and Transportation—with historical and current financial, organizational, and operational data on major firms.	Annually with monthly print updates (weekly online updates)
Handbook of Common Stocks	Common stock data on NYSE-listed companies.	Quarterly
Dividend Record	Recent dividend announcements and payments on publicly listed securities.	Twice weekly, with annual summary
Bond Record	Price and interest rate behavior of bond issues.	Monthly
Value Line Investment Survey **(http:// www.valueline.com)**		
Includes three reports:		Weekly
Ratings and Reports	Full-page report including financial data, descriptions, analyses, and ratings for stocks.	
Selection and Opinion	A 12- to 16-page report featuring a discussion of the U.S. economy and the stock market, sample portfolios for different types of investors, and an in-depth analysis of selected stocks.	
Summary and Index	A listing of the most widely held stocks. Also includes a variety of stock screens.	

offers an excellent resource for individual investors to complement its products for institutional investors. Although basic news and market commentary is free, *Business Week* subscribers obtain access to premium online services. **Mergent** (formerly Moody's Financial Information Services Division) also publishes a variety of material, including its equity and bond portraits, corporate research, well-known reference manuals on eight industries, and numerous other products. The *Value Line Investment Survey* is one of the most popular subscription services used by individual investors. It is available at most libraries and provides online access to additional services including data, graphing, portfolio tracking, and technical indicators.

Brokerage Reports Brokerage firms often make available to their clients reports from the various subscription services and research reports from their own securities analysts. They also provide clients with prospectuses for new security issues and *back-office research reports*. As noted in Chapter 2, a *prospectus* is a document that describes in detail the key aspects of the issue, the issuer, and its management and financial position. The cover of the preliminary prospectus describing the 2015 stock issue of Shake Shack is shown in Figure 2.1. **Back-office research reports** include the brokerage firm's analyses of and recommendations on prospects for the securities markets, specific industries, or specific securities. Usually a brokerage firm publishes lists of securities classified by its research staff as "buy," "hold," or "sell." Brokerage research reports are available on request at no cost to existing and prospective clients.

Securities analysts' reports are now available on the web, either from brokerage sites or from sites that consolidate research from many brokerages. At Reuters.com, a leading research site, analysts' reports on companies and industries from most brokerage and research firms are available. Investors can use Zacks's Investment Research to find and purchase analyst reports on widely followed stocks or to read free brokerage report abstracts with earnings revisions and recommendations.

Investment Letters Investment letters are newsletters that provide, on a subscription basis, the analyses, conclusions, and recommendations of experts in securities investment. Some letters concentrate on specific types of securities; others are concerned solely with assessing the economy or securities markets. Among the more popular investment letters are *Blue Chip Advisor*, *Dick Davis Digest*, *The Dines Letter*, *Dow Theory Letters*, and *The Prudent Speculator*. Most investment letters come out weekly or monthly. Advertisements for many of these investment letters can be found in *Barron's* and in various business periodicals. *The Hulbert Financial Digest* monitors the performance of investment letters. It is an excellent source of objective information on investment letters and a good place to check out those that interest you.

Price Information Price information about various types of securities is contained in their **quotations**, which include current price data and statistics on recent price behavior. The web makes it easy to find price quotes for actively traded securities. Most of these sites ask you to locate a stock by entering its ticker symbol. Table 3.3 lists the ticker symbols for some well-known companies.

Investors can easily find the prior day's security price quotations in the published news media, both nonfinancial and financial. They also can find delayed or real-time quotations for free at numerous websites, including *financial portals* (described below), most business periodical websites, and brokerage sites. The website for CNBC TV has real-time stock quotes, as do sites that subscribe to their news feed.

Other Online Investment Information Sources Many other excellent websites provide information of all sorts to increase your investment knowledge and skills. Let's now

TABLE 3.3   SYMBOLS FOR SOME WELL-KNOWN COMPANIES

Company	Symbol	Company	Symbol
Amazon.com	AMZN	Lucent Technologies	LU
Apple	AAPL	McDonald's Corporation	MCD
AT&T	T	Microsoft	MSFT
Bank of America	BAC	Nike	NKE
Cisco Systems	CSCO	Oracle	ORCL
The Coca-Cola Company	KO	PepsiCo, Inc.	PEP
Dell	DELL	Ralph Lauren	RL
Estee Lauder Companies	EL	Sears Holdings	SHLD
ExxonMobil	XOM	Starbucks	SBUX
FedEx	FDX	Target	TGT
General Electric	GE	Texas Instruments	TXN
Google	GOOG	Time Warner	TWX
Hewlett-Packard	HPQ	United Parcel Service	UPS
Intel	INTC	Walmart Stores	WMT
Int'l. Business Machines	IBM	Yahoo!	YHOO

look at financial portals, sites for bonds and mutual funds, international sites, and investment discussion forums. Table 3.4 lists some of the most popular financial portals, bond sites, and mutual fund sites. We'll look at online brokerage and investment advisor sites later in the chapter.

Financial Portals Financial portals are supersites that bring together a wide range of investing features, such as real-time quotes, stock and mutual fund screens, portfolio trackers, news, research, and transaction capabilities, along with other personal finance features. These sites want to be your investing home page.

Some financial portals are general sites, such as Yahoo! Finance and Google Finance, that offer a full range of investing features along with their other services, or they may be investing-oriented sites. You should check out several to see which suits your needs because their strengths and features vary greatly. Some portals, to motivate you to stay at their site, offer customization options so that your start page includes the data you want. Although finding one site where you can manage your investments is indeed appealing, you may not be able to find the best of what you need at one portal. You'll want to explore several sites to find the ones that meet your needs. Table 3.4 summarizes the features of several popular financial portals.

Bond Sites Although many general investment sites include bond and mutual fund information, you can also visit sites that specialize in these investments. Because individuals generally do not trade bonds as actively as they trade stocks, there are fewer resources focused on bonds for individuals. Some brokerage firms are starting to allow clients access to bond information that formerly was restricted to investment professionals. In addition to the sites listed in Table 3.4, other good sites for bond and interest rate information include Bloomberg and the *Wall Street Journal*.

The sites of the major bond ratings agencies—Moody's, Standard & Poor's, and Fitch—provide ratings lists, recent ratings changes, and information about how they determine ratings.

TABLE 3.4   POPULAR INVESTMENT WEBSITES

The following websites are just a few of the thousands of sites that provide investing information. Unless otherwise mentioned, all are free.

Website	Description
Financial Portals	
Daily Finance (**http://dailyfinance.com**)	Includes investing and personal finance areas containing business news, market and stock quotes, stocks, mutual funds, investment research, retirement, saving and planning, credit and debt, banking and loans, and more.
MSN Money (**http://www.money.msn.com**)	More editorial content than many sites; good research and interactive tools. Can consolidate accounts in portfolio tracker.
Motley Fool (**http://www.fool.com**)	Comprehensive and entertaining site with educational features, research, news, and message boards. Model portfolios cover a variety of investment strategies. Free but offers premium services such as its Stock Advisor monthly newsletter for a fee.
Yahoo! Finance (**http://finance.yahoo.com**)	Simple design, content-rich; easy to find information quickly. Includes financial news, price quotes, portfolio trackers, bill paying, personalized home page, and a directory of other major sites.
Yodlee (**http://www.yodlee.com**)	Aggregation site that collects financial account data from banking, credit card, brokerage, mutual fund, mileage, and other sites. One-click access saves time and enables users to manage and interact with their accounts. Offers e-mail accounts; easy to set up and track finances. Security issues concern potential users; few analytical tools.
Bond Sites	
Investing in Bonds (**http://www.investinginbonds.com**)	Developed by the Securities Industry and Financial Markets Association; good for novice investors. Bond education, research reports, historical data, and links to other sites. Searchable database.
BondsOnline (**http://www.bondsonline.com**)	Comprehensive site for news, education, free research, ratings, and other bond information. Searchable database. Some charges for newsletters and research.
CNN Money (**http://www.money.cnn.com**)	Individual investors can search for bond-related news, market data, and bond offerings.
Bureau of the Public Debt Online (**http://www.publicdebt.treas.gov**)	Run by U.S. Treasury Department. Information about U.S. savings bonds and Treasury securities. Can buy Treasury securities online through Treasury Direct program.
Mutual Fund Sites	
Morningstar (**http://www.morningstar.com**)	Profiles mutual funds with ratings; screening tools, portfolio analysis and management; fund manager interviews, e-mail newsletters; educational sections. Advanced screening and analysis tools are available for a fee.
Mutual Fund Investor's Center (**http://www.mfea.com**)	Not-for-profit, easy-to-navigate site from the Mutual Fund Education Alliance with investor education, search feature, and links to profiles of funds, calculators for retirement, asset allocation, and college planning.
Mutual Fund Observer (**http://mutualfundobserver.com**)	A free, independent site offering information and analysis of mutual funds and the fund industry.
MAXfunds (**http://www.maxfunds.com**)	Offers several custom metrics and data points to help find the best funds and give investors tools other than past performance to choose funds. Covers more funds than any other on- or offline publication. MAXadvisor Powerfund Portfolios, a premium advisory service, is available for a fee.
IndexFunds.com (**http://www.indexfunds.com**)	Comprehensive site covering only index funds.
Personal Fund (**http://www.personalfund.com**)	Especially popular for its Mutual Fund Cost Calculator that shows the true cost of ownership, after fees, brokerage commissions, and taxes. Suggests lower-cost alternatives with similar investment objectives.

Mutual Fund Sites With thousands of mutual funds, how do you find the ones that match your investment goals? The Internet makes this task much easier, offering many sites not tied to specific fund companies with screening tools and worksheets. Every major mutual fund family has its own site as well. Some allow visitors to hear interviews or participate in chats with fund managers. Fidelity has one of the most comprehensive sites, with educational articles, fund selection tools, fund profiles, and more. Portals and brokerage sites also offer these tools. Table 3.4 includes some independent mutual fund sites that are worth checking out.

International Sites The international reach of the Internet makes it a natural resource to help investors sort out the complexity of global investing, from country research to foreign currency exchange. Site-By-Site! International Investment Portal & Research Center is a comprehensive portal just for international investing. Free daily market data, news, economic insights, research, and analysis and commentary covering numerous countries and investment vehicles are among this site's features. For more localized coverage, check out Euroland.com, UK-Invest.com, Latin-Focus.com, and similar sites for other countries and regions. J P. Morgan provides a site devoted exclusively to American Depositary Receipts (ADRs), one of the most popular ways for investors to diversify their portfolios internationally. For global business news, the *Financial Times* gets high marks. Dow Jones's MarketWatch has good technology and telecommunications news, as well as coverage of global markets.

Investment Discussion Forums Investors can exchange opinions about their favorite stocks and investing strategies at the *online discussion forums* (message boards and chat rooms) found at most major financial websites. However, remember that the key word here is *opinion*. You don't really know much about the qualifications of the person posting the information. *Always do your own research before acting on any hot tips!* The Motley Fool's discussion boards are among the most popular, and Fool employees monitor the discussions. Message boards at Yahoo! Finance are among the largest online, although many feel that the quality is not as good as at other sites. The Raging Bull includes news and other links along with its discussion groups. Technology investors flock to Silicon Investor, a portal site whose high-tech boards are considered among the best.

Avoiding Scams The ease with which information is available to all investors today makes it easier for scam artists and others to spread false news and manipulate information. Anyone can sound like an investment expert online, posting stock tips with no underlying substance. As mentioned earlier, you may not know the identity of the person touting or panning a stock on the message boards. The person panning a stock could be a disgruntled former employee or a short seller. For example, the ousted former chief executive of San Diego's Avanir Pharmaceuticals posted negative remarks on stock message boards, adversely affecting the firm's share price. The company sued and won a court order prohibiting him from ever posting derogatory statements about the company.

In the fast-paced online environment, two types of scams turn up frequently: "pump-and-dump" and "get-rich-quick" scams. In *pump-and-dump* scams, perpetrators buy select stocks and then falsely promote or hype the stocks to the public. The false promotion tends to push up the stock price, at which point the scam artist dumps the stock at an inflated price. In *get-rich-quick* scams, promoters sell worthless investments to naïve buyers.

One well-publicized pump-and-dump scam demonstrates how easy it is to use the Internet to promote stocks. In December 2011 the SEC charged Daniel Ruettiger, the man who inspired the film *Rudy*, in a pump-and-dump scam involving his company, Rudy Nutrition. Ruettiger's company promoted a sports drink called "Rudy," which was designed to compete with Gatorade. The SEC alleged that Ruettiger sent false e-mails claiming that his sports drink outperformed Gatorade and Powerade by a 2-to-1 margin in taste tests. The SEC further alleged that Ruettiger engaged in manipulative trading to artificially inflate his company's stock price while selling unregistered securities to investors.

To crack down on cyber-fraud, in 1998 the SEC formed the Office of Internet Enforcement, which was merged into the Office of Market Intelligence in 2010. Its staff members quickly investigate reports of suspected hoaxes and prosecute the offenders. At **http://www.sec.gov**, you can find specific instructions about how to spot and avoid Internet investment scams. Among other pieces of advice, the SEC recommends that you ask the following five key questions before making any investment.

- *Is the seller licensed?* Do some research on the background of the person recommending an investment to you. For example, you can investigate a broker's background at FINRA.

- *Is the investment registered?* You can learn whether an investment is registered by searching the SEC's EDGAR database.

- *How do the risks compare with the potential rewards?* Investment opportunities pitched as offering high potential returns without much risk are likely to be frauds.

- *Do you understand the investment?* A good rule of thumb, one followed even by sophisticated investors such as Warren Buffett, is to never invest in something that you do not understand.

- *Where can you turn for help?* The SEC urges investors to conduct investment research on the SEC's website, as well as sites provided by FINRA and state securities regulators.

Asking these questions cannot ensure that you will never fall victim to an investment scam, but it tilts the odds in your favor.

CONCEPTS IN REVIEW

Answers available at
www.pearsonhighered.com/smart

3.4 Differentiate between descriptive information and analytical information. How might one logically assess whether the acquisition of investment information or advice is economically justified?

3.5 What popular financial business periodicals would you use to follow the financial news? General news? Business news? Would you prefer to get your news from print sources or online, and why?

3.6 Briefly describe the types of information that the following resources provide.

a. Stockholders' report
b. Comparative data sources
c. Standard & Poor's Corporation
d. Mergent
e. *Value Line Investment Survey*

3.7 How would you access each of the following types of information, and how would the content help you make investment decisions?

a. Prospectuses
b. Back-office research reports
c. Investment letters
d. Price quotations

3.8 Briefly describe several types of information that are especially well suited to publication on the Internet. What are the differences between the online and print versions, and when would you use each?

Understanding Market Averages and Indexes

LG3 The investment information we have discussed in this chapter helps investors understand when the economy is moving up or down and how individual investments have performed. You can use this and other information to formulate expectations about future investment performance. It is also important to know whether market behavior is favorable or unfavorable. The ability to interpret various market measures should help you to select and time investment actions.

A widely used way to assess the behavior of securities markets is to study the performance of market averages and indexes. These measures allow you to conveniently (1) gauge general market conditions; (2) compare your portfolio's performance to that of a large, diversified (market) portfolio; and (3) study the market's historical performance and use that as a guide to understand future market behavior. Here we discuss key measures of stock and bond market activity. In later chapters, we will discuss averages and indexes associated with other investment securities. Like price quotations, measures of market performance are available at many websites.

Stock Market Averages and Indexes

Stock market averages and indexes measure the general behavior of stock prices over time. Although the terms *average* and *index* tend to be used interchangeably when people discuss market behavior, technically they are different types of measures. **Averages** reflect the arithmetic average price behavior of a representative group of stocks at a given point in time. **Indexes** measure the current price behavior of a representative group of stocks in relation to a base value set at an earlier point in time.

Averages and indexes provide a convenient method of capturing the general mood of the market. Investors can also compare these measures at different points in time to assess the relative strength or weakness of the market. Current and recent values of the key averages and indexes are quoted daily on financial websites, in the financial news, in most local newspapers, and on many radio and television news programs.

The Dow Jones Averages The S&P Dow Jones Indices prepares four different stock averages and several stock indexes. The most well known of these is the **Dow Jones Industrial Average (DJIA)**. This average is made up of 30 stocks, most of which are issued by large, well-respected companies with long operating histories. The DJIA represents a broad sample of the U.S. economy and includes stocks from sectors such as technology, transportation, banking, energy, health care, consumer products, and many others. The DJIA is a *price-weighted* index, meaning that stocks with higher prices get more weight in the index than do stocks with lower prices.

Occasionally, a merger or bankruptcy causes a change in the makeup of the average. For example, Kraft Foods replaced American International Group (AIG) in September 2008 after AIG experienced a liquidity crisis and required an $85 billion credit facility from the U.S. Federal Reserve. Kraft was replaced in 2012 by UnitedHealth Group after Kraft announced plans to spin off its North American Grocery Business. Changes to the 30 stocks also occur when Dow Jones believes that the average does not reflect the broader market. In 2015, AT&T was dropped from the average in favor of Apple. In part this change reflected Apple's tremendous growth. By 2015, Apple had become the largest U.S. company measured by its market capitalization. But Apple's addition to the index was also influenced by the company's decision in 2014 to split its stock 7-for-1. After the split, Apple's stock price was roughly one-seventh of what it had been before the split when its shares traded for roughly $600 each. Because the

Dow is a price-weighted index, a stock with a price as high as $600 would have a disproportionate influence on the index, so the index almost never includes companies with extremely high stock prices. When a new stock is added to the Dow, the average is adjusted so that it continues to behave in a manner consistent with the immediate past.

The value of the DJIA is calculated each business day by substituting the closing share prices of each of the 30 stocks in the DJIA into the following equation:

Equation 3.1

$$\text{DJIA} = \frac{\begin{array}{c}\text{Closing share price} \\ \text{of stock 1}\end{array} + \begin{array}{c}\text{Closing share price} \\ \text{of stock 2}\end{array} + \cdots + \begin{array}{c}\text{Closing share price} \\ \text{of stock 30}\end{array}}{\text{DJIA divisor}}$$

The value of the DJIA is merely the sum of the closing share prices of the 30 stocks included the Dow, divided by a "divisor." The purpose of the divisor is to adjust for stock splits, company changes, or other events that have occurred over time. Without the divisor, whose calculation is very complex, the DJIA value would be totally distorted. The divisor makes it possible to use the DJIA to track the performance of the 30 stocks on a consistent basis over time. On April 15, 2015, the DJIA divisor was 0.14985889030177, and the sum of the closing prices of the Dow 30 stocks that day was 2,702.96. Using Equation 3.1, you can divide the sum of the closing prices of the 30 industrials by the DJIA divisor and arrive at that day's DJIA closing value of 18,036.70.

Because the DJIA results from summing the prices of the 30 stocks, higher-priced stocks tend to affect the index more than do lower-priced stocks. For example, a 5% change in the price of a $50 stock (i.e., $2.50) has less impact on the index than a 5% change in a $100 stock (i.e., $5.00) or a 5% change in a $600 stock (i.e., $30). Many experts argue that because the Dow is price weighted, it is not a particularly good indicator of the direction of the overall stock market. In spite of this and other criticisms leveled at the DJIA, it remains the most widely cited stock market indicator.

The actual value of the DJIA is meaningful only when compared to earlier values. For example, the DJIA on April 15, 2015, closed at 18,112.61. This value is meaningful only when compared to the previous day's closing value of 18,036.70, a change of about 0.42%. Many people mistakenly believe that one DJIA "point" equals $1 in the value of an average share. Actually, 1 point currently translates into about 0.25 cents in average share value, but that figure varies widely over time.

Three other widely cited Dow Jones averages are the transportation, utilities, and composite. The *Dow Jones Transportation Average* is based on 20 stocks, including railroads, airlines, freight forwarders, and mixed transportation companies. The *Dow Jones Utilities Average* is computed using 15 public-utility stocks. The *Dow Jones Composite Average* is made up of the 30 industrials, the 20 transportations, and the 15 utilities. Like the DJIA, each of the other Dow Jones averages is calculated using a divisor to allow for continuity of the average over time. The transportation, utilities, and 65-stock composite are often cited along with the DJIA.

Dow Jones also publishes numerous indexes including the U.S. Total Stock Market Index, which tracks the performance of all equities with readily available prices. Dow Jones also publishes indexes for various sectors based on company size (e.g., large cap, mid cap, small cap) or industry. Dow Jones's index products are not limited to U.S. markets. The company provides indexes that track the global equities market, developed and emerging stock markets, and regional markets in Asia, Europe, the Americas, the Middle East, and Africa.

Standard & Poor's Indexes Standard & Poor's Corporation, another leading financial publisher, publishes six major common stock indexes. One oft-cited S&P index is the **S&P 500 Stock Index**, which is calculated each business day by substituting the *closing market value of each stock* (closing price × number of shares outstanding) into the following equation:

Equation 3.2

$$\text{S \& P 500 Index} = \frac{\begin{array}{c}\text{Current closing} \\ \text{market value} \\ \text{of stock 1}\end{array} + \begin{array}{c}\text{Current closing} \\ \text{market value} \\ \text{of stock 2}\end{array} + \cdots + \begin{array}{c}\text{Current closing} \\ \text{market value} \\ \text{of last stock}\end{array}}{\text{Divisor}}$$

INVESTOR FACTS

Google Not "All in" S&P 500
Standard & Poor's does not count all of a company's shares as part of the S&P 500 Index if some shares are not publicly traded. For example, Google has a class of shares (Class B) with special voting rights that is not publicly traded and is held by the company's founders, Sergey Brin and Larry Page. These shares are not counted in the S&P 500 Index calculation, so Google's weight in the index is actually less than its true market capitalization.

The value of the S&P 500 Index is found by dividing the sum of the market values of all stocks included in the index by a divisor. The divisor is a number that serves two functions. First, it provides a scaling factor to make the index value easier to work with. The scaling factor works by measuring the current market value of stocks in the index relative to a base period value (for the S&P 500, the base period is 1941–1943). For example, the total market value of all stocks in the S&P 500 Index is several trillion dollars. No one wants to work with an index in the trillions, so the divisor brings the index value down to a more manageable value (for example, the S&P 500 Index value was 2,106.63 on April 15, 2015). The divisor's second function is to adjust the index to account for changes in the composition of the S&P 500 stocks, such as when a company in the index is deleted due to a merger or bankruptcy and another company is added in its place. In these instances, the index value should not "jump" simply because the list of companies in the index changed. Likewise, certain corporate events such as new share issues or share repurchases can change the market value of a firm in the index. The divisor is calculated in a manner such that these events by themselves do not cause movement in the S&P 500 Index.

Certain of the S&P indexes contain many more shares than the Dow averages do, and all of them are based on the *market values* (shares outstanding × price per share) of the companies in the indexes rather than the *share prices*. Therefore, many investors feel that the S&P indexes provide a more broad-based and representative measure of general market conditions than do the Dow averages. Although some technical computational problems exist with these indexes, they are widely used—frequently as a basis for estimating the "market return," an important concept that we introduce later.

Some of the widely followed stock indexes published by Standard & Poor's are the following:

- The *S&P 500 Index* comprises 500 large companies (but not necessarily the largest 500).

- The *S&P 100 Index* comprises 100 large companies, each of which must have stock options available for investors to trade.

- The *S&P 400 MidCap Index* comprises 400 medium-sized companies, accounting for about 7% of the U.S. equity market.

- The *S&P 600 SmallCap Index* comprises 600 small-sized companies, accounting for about 3% of the U.S. equity market.

FIGURE 3.5

The DJIA Average Compared to the S&P 500 Index from April 16, 2013, to April 15, 2015

During this period, both indexes followed a rising trend, with the DJIA gaining about 23% and the S&P 500 gaining about 34%.

(Source: Yahoo! Finance screenshot, http://www.finance. yahoo.com.)

- The *S&P Total Market Index* comprises all stocks listed on the NYSE (including NYSE Arca and NYSE MKT) and Nasdaq (including NASDAQ Global Select Market, the NASDAQ Global Market, and the NASDAQ Capital Market).

Although the Dow Jones averages and S&P indexes tend to behave in a similar fashion over time, their day-to-day magnitude and even direction (up or down) can differ significantly because of the differences in how the indexes are constructed. Figure 3.5 plots the performance of the DJIA and the S&P 500 from April 16, 2013, to April 15, 2015. During this period, both indexes followed a rising trend, with the DJIA gaining about 23% while the S&P 500 gained about 34%. This figure highlights that the two indexes do not move perfectly in sync, but they experience similar movements more often than not.

NYSE, NYSE MKT, and Nasdaq Indexes Three indexes measure the daily results of the New York Stock Exchange (NYSE), the NYSE MKT Exchange (formally the American Stock Exchange), and the National Association of Securities Dealers Automated Quotation (Nasdaq) system. Each reflects the movement of stocks listed on its exchange.

FAMOUS FAILURES IN FINANCE

PIIGS Feast on Wall Street

In the summer of 2011 an economic crisis gripped Europe, particularly Portugal, Italy, Ireland, Greece, and Spain, the so-called PIIGS nations. Their fiscal problems made investors doubt that governments would be able to repay their debts without massive cuts in government spending, and investors feared that deep budget cuts might trigger a recession that might sweep across the globe. The DJIA fell by nearly 15% in less than two weeks before a series of rescue packages from the European Union nations reassured investors, at least temporarily. That story repeated itself on a smaller scale in October 2014 when the Dow fell 5.2% over a span of less than two weeks.

The **NYSE Composite Index** includes about 1,900 or so stocks listed on the "Big Board." In addition to the composite index, the NYSE publishes indexes for financial and other subgroups. The behavior of the NYSE composite index is normally similar to that of the DJIA and the S&P 500 indexes. The NYSE MKT Composite Index reflects the price of all shares traded on the NYSE MKT Exchange. Although it does not always closely follow the S&P and NYSE indexes, the NYSE MKT index tends to move in the general direction they do.

The **Nasdaq Stock Market indexes** reflect Nasdaq stock market activity. The most comprehensive of the Nasdaq indexes is the *composite index*, which is calculated using the almost 3,000 common stocks traded on the Nasdaq stock market. The index includes other types of securities such as real estate investment trusts (REITs) and American Depositary Receipts. Also important is the *Nasdaq 100*, which includes 100 of the largest domestic and international nonfinancial companies listed on Nasdaq. The other two commonly quoted Nasdaq indexes are the *biotech* and *computer indexes*. The Nasdaq indexes tend to move in the same direction at the same time as the other major indexes, but movements in Nasdaq indexes are often sharper than those of the other major indexes. The companies listed on the Nasdaq tend to be smaller and operate in riskier industries (such as technology) than those included in indexes such as the DJIA and the S&P 500.

Value Line Indexes Value Line publishes a number of stock indexes constructed by equally weighting the price of each stock included. This is accomplished by considering only the percentage changes in stock prices. This approach eliminates the effects of varying market price and total market value on the relative importance of each stock in the index. The **Value Line Composite Index** includes the nearly 1,700 stocks in the *Value Line Investment Survey* that are traded on the NYSE, NYSE MKT, and OTC markets. In addition to its composite index, Value Line publishes other specialized indexes.

Other Averages and Indexes A number of other indexes are available. Frank Russell Company, a pension advisory firm, publishes three primary indexes. The *Russell 1000* includes the 1,000 largest companies, the most widely quoted *Russell 2000* includes 2,000 small to medium-sized companies, and the *Russell 3000* includes all 3,000 companies in the Russell 1000 and 2000.

In addition, the *Wall Street Journal* publishes a number of global and foreign stock market indexes. Included are Dow Jones indexes for countries in the Americas, Europe, Africa, Asia, and the Pacific region. About 35 foreign stock market indexes are also given for major countries, including a *World Index* and the *Europe/Australia/Far East (EAFE MSCI) Index*. Like the purely domestic averages and indexes, these international averages and indexes measure the general price behavior of the stocks that are listed and traded in the given market. Useful comparisons of the market averages and indexes over time and across markets are often made to assess both trends and relative strengths of foreign markets throughout the world.

Bond Market Indicators

A number of indicators are available for assessing the general behavior of the bond markets. However, there are fewer indicators of overall bond market behavior than of stock market behavior. In part this is because many bonds do not trade as actively as stocks do. Even so, it is not hard to find several useful measures related to bond-market performance. The key measures of overall U.S. bond market behavior are bond yields and bond indexes.

FAMOUS FAILURES IN FINANCE

Bond Yields Hit Historic Lows

Concerns about disappointing retail sales in the U.S economy pushed the yield on the 30-year U.S. Treasury bond to a record low of 2.395% in January 2015. Investors who purchased Treasury bonds at these yields earned almost nothing, so why would they invest? One answer is safety. Investors have long viewed U.S. Treasury bonds as the safest investment in the world, so when fears of a recession or other economic crisis grip the market,

investors will buy Treasury bonds even if the return that they offer is barely above zero. Monetary policy may also push interest rates down when policy makers want to encourage investors to hold riskier assets. An extreme example of this occurred in the spring of 2015 when government bonds in countries such as Switzerland, Germany, and Denmark were sold with *negative* yields. Investors who bought these bonds were paying the government for the privilege to hold their bonds.

Bond Yields   A **bond yield** is the return an investor would receive on a bond if it were purchased and held to maturity. Bond yields are reported as annual rates of return, and they reflect both the interest payments that bond investors receive as well as any gain or loss in the bond's value from the date the bond is purchased until it is redeemed. For example, a bond with a yield of 5.50% would provide its owner with a total return (including interest and capital gains or losses) that would be equivalent to a 5.50% annual rate of earnings on the amount invested (i.e., the bond's purchase price), if the bond were purchased and held to maturity.

Typically, bond yields are quoted for a group of bonds that are similar with respect to type and quality. For example, *Barron's* quotes the yields on the Dow Jones bond averages of 10 high-grade corporate bonds, 10 medium-grade corporate bonds, and a confidence index that is calculated as a ratio of the high-grade to medium-grade indexes. In addition, like the *Wall Street Journal*, it quotes numerous other bond indexes and yields, including those for Treasury and municipal bonds. Similar bond yield data are available from S&P, Moody's, and the Federal Reserve. Like stock market averages and indexes, bond yield data are especially useful when viewed over time.

Bond Indexes   There is a variety of bond indexes. The **Dow Jones Corporate Bond Index**, which is an equal-weighted index of U.S.-issued corporate bonds, includes 96 bonds—48 industrial, 36 financial, and 12 utility bonds. It reflects the simple mathematical average of the *closing prices* for the bonds. Dow Jones's stated objective for the index is to represent the market performance, on a total-return basis, of investment-grade bonds issued by leading U.S. companies and to minimize the pricing and liquidity problems associated with most corporate bond indexes. The index is published daily in the *Wall Street Journal* and summarized weekly in *Barron's*.

CONCEPTS IN REVIEW

Answers available at
http://www.pearsonhighered.com/smart

3.9 Describe the basic philosophy and use of stock market averages and indexes. Explain how the behavior of an average or index can be used to classify general market conditions as bull or bear.

3.10 List each of the major averages or indexes prepared by (a) Dow Jones & Company and (b) Standard & Poor's Corporation. Indicate the number and source of the securities used in calculating each average or index.

3.11 Briefly describe the composition and general thrust of each of the following indexes.

a. NYSE Composite Index
b. NYSE MKT Composite Index
c. Nasdaq Stock Market indexes
d. Value Line Composite Index

3.12 Discuss each of the following as they are related to assessing bond market behavior.

a. Bond yields
b. Bond indexes

Making Securities Transactions

LG4 LG5 Now that you know how to find information to help you locate attractive security investments, you need to understand how to make securities transactions. Whether you decide to start a self-directed online investment program or to use a traditional stockbroker, you must first open an account with a brokerage service. In this section, we will look at the role stockbrokers play and how that role has changed in recent years. We will also explain the basic types of orders you can place, the procedures required to make regular and online securities transactions, the costs of investment transactions, and investor protection.

The Role of Stockbrokers

Stockbrokers—also called *account executives, investment executives,* and *financial consultants*—act as intermediaries between buyers and sellers of securities. They typically charge a commission to facilitate these securities transactions. Stockbrokers must be licensed by both the SEC and the securities exchanges, and they must follow the ethical guidelines of those bodies.

Although the procedures for executing orders in different stock markets may vary, stock trades often start the same way: An investor places an order with his or her stockbroker. The broker works for a brokerage firm that maintains memberships on the securities exchanges, and members of the securities exchange execute orders that the brokers in the firm's various sales offices transmit to them. For example, one of the largest U.S. brokerage firms, Bank of America's Merrill Lynch, transmits orders for listed securities from its offices in most major cities throughout the country to the main office of Merrill Lynch and then to the floor of an exchange, such as the NYSE, where Merrill Lynch exchange members execute the orders. Confirmation of the order goes back to the broker placing the order, who relays it to the customer. This process can take a matter of seconds with the use of sophisticated telecommunications networks and Internet trading.

For securities transactions in markets such as Nasdaq, brokerage firms typically transmit orders to *market makers*. Normally, these transactions are executed rapidly, since there is considerable competition among dealers for the opportunity to execute brokerage orders. The revenue that market makers generate from executing orders is offset by the cost of maintaining inventories of the securities in which they deal.

Brokerage Services The primary activity of stockbrokers is to route clients' buy and sell orders to the markets where they will be executed at the best possible price. The speed with which brokers can get clients' orders executed is enhanced by the fact that brokerage firms typically hold their clients' security certificates for safekeeping.

Securities kept by the firm in this manner are held in **street name**. Because the brokerage house issues the securities in its own name and holds them in trust for the client (rather than issuing them in the client's name), the firm can transfer the securities at the time of sale without the client's signature. Street name is actually a common way of buying securities because most investors do not want to be bothered with the handling and safekeeping of stock certificates. In such cases, the brokerage firm records the details of the client's transaction and keeps track of his or her investments through a series of bookkeeping entries. Dividends and notices received by the broker are forwarded to the client who owns the securities.

In addition to order routing and certificate storage, stockbrokers offer clients a variety of other services. For example, the brokerage firm normally provides free information about investments. Quite often, the firm has a research staff that periodically issues reports on economic, market, industry, or company behavior and makes recommendations to buy, sell, or hold certain securities. Clients also receive a statement describing their transactions for the month and showing commission and interest charges, dividends and interest received, and detailed listings of their current holdings.

Today most brokerage firms invest surplus cash left in a client's account in a money market mutual fund, allowing the client to earn a reasonable rate of interest on these balances. Such arrangements help the investor earn as much as possible on temporarily idle funds.

Types of Brokerage Firms Just a few years ago, there were three distinct types of brokerage firm: full-service, premium discount, and basic discount. No longer are the lines between these categories clear-cut. Most brokerage firms, even the most traditional ones, now offer online services. And many discount brokers now offer services, like research reports for clients, that were once available only from a full-service broker.

The traditional broker, or **full-service broker**, in addition to executing clients' transactions, offers investors a full array of brokerage services: providing investment advice and information, holding securities in street name, offering online brokerage services, and extending margin loans.

Investors who wish merely to make transactions and are not interested in taking advantage of other services should consider either a premium or basic discount broker.

Premium discount brokers focus primarily on making transactions for customers. They charge low commissions and provide limited free research information and investment advice. The investor visits the broker's office, calls a toll-free number, or accesses the broker's website to initiate a transaction. The broker confirms the transaction in person or by phone, e-mail, or regular mail. Premium discount brokers like Charles Schwab, the first discount broker, now offer many of the same services that you'd find at a full-service broker. Other premium discounters are similar.

Basic discount brokers, also called *online brokers* or *electronic brokers*, are typically deep-discount brokers through whom investors can execute trades electronically online via a commercial service, on the Internet, or by phone. The investor accesses the basic discount broker's website to open an account, review the commission schedule, or see a demonstration of the available transactional services and procedures. Confirmation of online trades can take mere seconds, and most trades occur within one minute. Most basic discount brokers operate primarily online but also provide telephone and live broker backup in case there are problems with the website or the customer is away from his or her computer. In response to the rapid growth of online investors, most brokerage firms now offer online trading. These firms usually charge higher commissions when live broker assistance is required.

TABLE 3.5	SELECT FULL-SERVICE, PREMIUM DISCOUNT, AND BASIC DISCOUNT BROKERS	
Full-Service Broker	Premium Discount Broker	Basic Discount Broker
Morgan Stanley	Bank of America	Firstrade
Merrill Lynch	Charles Schwab	Scottrade
UBS Financial Services	E*Trade	Thinkorswim
Wells Fargo	Fidelity.com	TradeKing
	TD Ameritrade	Wall Street*E
	Wells Trade	

The rapidly growing volume of business done by both premium and basic discount brokers attests to their success. Today, many full-service brokers, banks, and savings institutions are making discount and online brokerage services available to their customers and depositors who wish to buy stocks, bonds, mutual funds, and other investment securities. Some of the full-service, premium discount, and basic discount brokers are listed in Table 3.5. (Brokerage Review (**http://brokerage-review.com**) is a good online source for finding the right brokerage service to fit your needs.)

The SEC's Advice on Selecting a Broker

Selecting a Stockbroker If you decide to start your investing activities with the assistance of either a full-service or premium discount stockbroker, select the person you believe best understands your investment goals. Choosing a broker whose disposition toward investing is similar to yours is the best way to establish a solid working relationship. Your broker should also make you aware of investment possibilities that are consistent with your objectives and attitude toward risk.

You should also consider the cost and types of services available from the firm with which the broker is affiliated, in order to receive the best service at the lowest possible cost to you. The premium discount brokerage service is primarily transactional, and the basic discount brokerage service is *purely* transactional. Contact with a broker for advice or research assistance is generally only available at a higher price. Investors must weigh the added commissions they pay a full-service broker against the value of the advice they receive because the amount of available advice is the only major difference among the three types of brokers.

Referrals from friends or business associates are a good way to begin your search for a stockbroker. (Don't forget to consider the investing style and goals of the person making the recommendation.) However, it is not important—and often not even advisable—to know your stockbroker personally. In this age of online brokers, you may never meet your broker face to face. A strictly business relationship eliminates the possibility that personal concerns will interfere with the achievement of your investment goals. For an example of how a stockbroker got into trouble through a personal relationship with a friend, see the following Famous Failures in Finance feature.

Your broker's main interest should not be commissions. Responsible brokers do not engage in **churning**—that is, causing excessive trading of their clients' accounts to increase commissions. Churning is both illegal and unethical under SEC and exchange rules, although it is often difficult to prove.

Opening an Account To open an account, you will fill out various forms that establish a legal relationship between you and the brokerage firm. The stockbroker should have

FAMOUS FAILURES IN FINANCE

Hello, I Am Tim, an Insider Trader

In May 2012 the SEC charged stockbroker Timothy McGee with using inside information to buy shares in Philadelphia Consolidated Holding Corporation (PHLY) just before the company was acquired by Tokio Marine. McGee purchased 10,250 shares of PHLY for less than $39 per share. One day later, after Tokio announced its plan to buy the company, PHLY's stock price jumped to almost $60, leaving Mr. McGee with a profit of more than $200,000. In addition, federal prosecutors alleged that McGee passed along information about the acquisition to a friend, who also bought Philadelphia Consolidated stock.

McGee learned about the impending takeover after attending an Alcoholics Anonymous meeting with a friend who was an executive at PHLY. In its indictment, the SEC claimed that McGee owed the executive "fiduciary and other duties of trust and confidence" stemming from their long friendship through Alcoholics Anonymous. To obtain an insider trading conviction,

the government would have to prove that the person conveying the information and the person receiving it had a history of maintaining confidentiality regarding other personal or professional matters. This point is crucial because it is not illegal to trade based on material, nonpublic information unless doing so involves a breach of fiduciary duty to someone or a breach of trust and confidence. For the first time, the government hoped to prove that such a breach had occurred based on a shared membership in Alcoholics Anonymous.

(Source: Based on Alan Farnham, "Insider Trading Case Involves Secrets Shared Among AA Members," March 15, 2012, http://abcnews.com.)

Critical Thinking Question Suppose you are on an airplane and you overhear two executives of a company talking about a merger that is about to take place. If you buy stock based on what you overheard, are you committing insider trading?

a reasonable understanding of your personal financial situation to assess your investment goals—and to be sure that you can pay for the securities purchased. You also provide the broker with instructions regarding the transfer and custody of securities. Customers who wish to borrow money to make transactions must establish a margin account (described following). If you are acting as a custodian, a trustee, an executor, or a corporation, the brokerage firm will require additional documents.

Investors may have accounts with more than one stockbroker. Many investors establish accounts at different types of firms to obtain the benefit and opinions of a diverse group of brokers and to reduce their overall cost of making buy and sell transactions.

Next you must select the type of account best suited to your needs. We will briefly consider several of the more popular types.

Single or Joint A brokerage account may be either single or joint. Joint accounts are most common between husband and wife or parent and child. The account of a minor (a person younger than 18 years) is a **custodial account,** in which a parent or guardian must be part of all transactions. Regardless of the form of the account, the name(s) of the account holder(s) and an account number are used to identify it.

Cash or Margin A **cash account,** the more common type, is one in which the customer can make only cash transactions. Customers can initiate cash transactions via phone or online and are given three business days in which to transmit the cash to the brokerage firm. The firm is likewise given three business days in which to deposit the proceeds from the sale of securities in the customer's cash account.

A **margin account** is an account in which the brokerage firm extends borrowing privileges to a creditworthy customer. By leaving securities with the firm as collateral, the customer can borrow a prespecified proportion of the securities' purchase price. The brokerage firm will, of course, charge the customer a stated rate of interest on borrowings.

Wrap The **wrap account** (also called a *managed account*) allows brokerage customers with large portfolios (generally $100,000 or more) to shift stock selection decisions conveniently to a professional money manager, either in-house or independent. In return for a flat annual fee, commonly between 1% and 3% of the portfolio's total asset value, the brokerage firm helps the investor select a money manager, pays the manager's fee, and executes the money manager's trades. Initially the investor, broker, and/or manager discuss the client's overall goals.

Wrap accounts are appealing for a number of reasons other than convenience. The annual fee in most cases covers commissions on all trades, virtually eliminating the chance of the broker churning the account. In addition, the broker monitors the manager's performance and provides the investor with detailed reports, typically quarterly.

Odd-Lot and Round-Lot Transactions   Investors can buy stock in either odd or round lots. An **odd lot** consists of fewer than 100 shares of a stock. A **round lot** is a 100-share unit. You would be dealing in an odd lot if you bought, say, 25 shares of stock, but in round lots if you bought 200 shares. A trade of 225 shares would be a combination of one odd lot and two round lots.

Transactions in odd lots once required either additional processing by the brokerage firm or the assistance of a specialist, but now computerized trading systems make trading odd lots much easier. As a result, trading odd lots usually does not trigger higher fees, as was once the case. Small investors in the early stages of their investment programs are primarily responsible for odd-lot transactions since they often lack the financial resources to purchase round lots.

Basic Types of Orders

Investors can use different types of orders to make security transactions. The type placed normally depends on the investor's goals and expectations. The three basic types of orders are the market order, the limit order, and the stop-loss order.

Market Order   An order to buy or sell stock at the best price available at the time the investor places the order is a **market order**. It is generally the quickest way to fill orders because market orders are usually executed as soon as they reach the exchange floor or are received by the market maker. Because of the speed with which market orders are executed, the buyer or seller of a security can be sure that the price at which the order is transacted will be very close to the market price prevailing at the time the order was placed.

Limit Order   A **limit order** is an order to buy at or below a specified price (a limit buy order) or to sell at or above a specified price (a limit sell order). When the investor places a limit order, the broker transmits it to a market maker dealing in the security. The market maker notes the number of shares and price of the limit order in his or her book and executes the order as soon as the specified limit price (or better) exists. The market maker must first satisfy all other orders with precedence—similar orders received earlier, buy orders at a higher specified price, or sell orders at a lower specified price. Investors can place a limit order in one of the following forms:

- A *fill-or-kill order*, which is canceled if not immediately executed.

- A *day order*, which if not executed is automatically canceled at the end of the day.

- A *good-'til-canceled (GTC) order*, which generally remains in effect for 30 to 90 days unless executed, canceled, or renewed.

Example

> Suppose that you place a limit order to buy, at a limit price of $30, 100 shares of a stock currently selling at $30.50. Once the specialist clears all similar orders received before yours, and once the market price of the stock falls to $30 or lower, he or she executes your order. It is possible, of course, that your order might expire before the stock price drops to $30.

Although a limit order can be quite effective, it can also keep you from making a transaction. If, for instance, you wish to buy at $30 or less and the stock price moves from its current $30.50 price to $42 while you are waiting, you have missed the opportunity to make a profit of $11.50 per share. If you had placed a *market order* to buy at the best available price of $30.50, the profit of $11.50 would have been yours. Limit orders for the sale of a stock are also disadvantageous when the stock price closely approaches but does not attain the minimum sale price limit before dropping substantially. Generally speaking, limit orders are most effective when the price of a stock fluctuates greatly because there is then a better chance that the order will be executed.

Stop-Loss Order When an investor places a **stop-loss order**, or **stop order**, the broker tells the market maker to sell a stock when its market price reaches or drops below a specified level. Stop-loss orders are *suspended orders* placed on stocks; they are activated when and if the stock reaches a certain price. The stop-loss order is placed on the market maker's book and becomes active once the stock reaches the stop price. Like limit orders, stop-loss orders are typically day or GTC orders. When activated, the stop order becomes a *market order* to sell the security at the best price available. Thus it is possible for the actual price at which the sale is made to be well below the price at which the stop was initiated. Investors use these orders to protect themselves against the adverse effects of a rapid decline in share price.

Example

> Assume you own 100 shares of Ballard Industries, which is currently selling for $35 per share. Because you believe the stock price could decline rapidly at any time, you place a stop order to sell at $30. If the stock price does in fact drop to $30, the market maker will sell the 100 shares at the best price available at that time. If the market price declines to $28 by the time your stop-loss order comes up, you will receive less than $30 per share. Of course, if the market price stays above $30 per share, you will have lost nothing as a result of placing the order because the stop order will never be initiated. Often investors raise the level of the stop as the price of the stock rises. Such action helps to lock in a higher profit when the price is increasing.

Investors can also place stop orders to *buy* a stock, although buy orders are far less common than sell orders. For example, you may place a stop order to buy 100 shares of MJ Enterprises, currently selling for $70 per share, once its price rises to, say, $75 (the stop price). These orders are commonly used either to limit losses on short sales (discussed in Chapter 2) or to buy a stock just as its price begins to rise.

To avoid the risk of the market moving against you when your stop order becomes a market order, you can place a *stop-limit order* rather than a plain stop order. This is an order to buy or sell stock at a given or better price once a stipulated stop price has been met. For example, in the Ballard Industries example, had a stop-limit order been in effect, then when the market price of Ballard dropped to $30, the broker would have entered a limit order to sell your 100 shares at $30 a share or *better*. Thus you would have run no risk of getting less than $30 a share for your stock—unless the price of the stock kept right on falling. In that case, as is true for any limit order, you might miss the market altogether and end up with stock worth much less than $30. Even though the stop order to sell was triggered (at $30), the stock will not be sold, with a stop-limit order, if it keeps falling in price.

Online Transactions

The competition for your online business increases daily as more players enter an already crowded arena. Brokerage firms are encouraging customers to trade online and offering a variety of incentives to get their business, including free trades! However, low cost is not the only reason to choose a brokerage firm. As with any financial decision, you must consider your needs and find the firm that matches them. One investor may want timely information, research, and quick, reliable trades from a full-service broker like Bank of America or a premium discounter like Charles Schwab or TD Ameritrade. Another, who is an active trader, will focus on cost and fast trades rather than research and so will sign up with a basic discounter like Firstrade or Wall Street*E. Ease of site navigation is a major factor in finding a basic discount broker to use in executing online transactions. Some online brokers also offer online trading of bonds and mutual funds.

Day Trading For some investors, online stock trading is so compelling that they become day traders. The opposite of buy-and-hold investors with a long-term perspective, **day traders** buy and sell stocks quickly throughout the day. They hope that their stocks will continue to rise in value for the very short time they own them—sometimes just seconds or minutes—so they can make quick profits. Some also sell short, looking for small price decreases. True day traders do not own stocks overnight—hence the term "day trader"—because they believe that the extreme risk of prices changing radically from day to day will lead to large losses.

Day trading is not illegal or unethical, but it is highly risky. To compound their risk, day traders usually buy on margin in order to leverage their potential profits. But as we already know, margin trading also increases the risk of large losses.

Because the Internet makes investment information and transactions accessible to the masses, day trading has grown in popularity. It's a very difficult task—essentially a very stressful, full-time job. Although sales pitches for day trading make it seem like an easy route to quick riches, quite the reverse is more generally true. About twice as many day traders lose money as make money. In addition, they have high expenses for brokerage commissions, training, and computer equipment. They must earn sizable trading profits annually to break even on fees and commissions alone. Some never achieve profitability.

Technical and Service Problems As the number of online investors increases, so do the problems that beset brokerage firms and their customers. During the past few years most brokerage firms have upgraded their systems to reduce the number of service outages. But the potential problems go beyond the brokerage sites. Once an investor places a trade at a firm's website, it goes through several other parties to be executed. Most online brokers don't have their own trading desks and have agreements with other trading firms to execute their orders on the New York Stock Exchange or Nasdaq Stock Market. Slowdowns at any point in the process can create problems confirming trades. Investors, thinking that their trades had not gone through, might place the order again—only to discover later that they have bought the same stock twice. Online investors who don't get immediate trade execution and confirmation use the telephone when they can't get through online or to solve other problems with their accounts, and they often face long waiting times on hold.

Tips for Successful Online Trades Successful online investors take additional precautions before submitting their orders. Here are some tips to help you avoid some common problems:

- *Know how to place and confirm your order before you begin trading.* This simple step can keep you from having problems later.

- *Verify the stock symbol of the security you wish to buy.* Two very different companies can have similar symbols. Some investors have bought the wrong stock because they didn't check before placing their order.

- *Use limit orders.* The price you see on your computer screen may not be the one you get. With a limit order, you avoid getting burned in fast-moving markets. Although limit orders cost more, they can save you thousands of dollars. For example, it is not uncommon for customers eager to get shares of a hot IPO stock to place market orders. Instead of buying the stock near the offering price in the IPO prospectus, these customers may be shocked to find that their orders are filled at much higher prices during the stock's first trading day. Investors who learn of the price run-up and try to cancel orders may not always be able to get through to brokers. Because of this, some brokers accept only limit orders for online IPO purchases on the first day of trading.

- *Don't ignore the online reminders that ask you to check and recheck.* It's easy to make a typo that adds an extra digit to a purchase amount.

- *Don't get carried away.* It's easy to churn your own account. In fact, new online investors trade about twice as much as they did before they went online. To control impulse trading, have a strategy and stick to it.

- *Open accounts with two brokers.* This protects you if your online brokerage's computer system crashes. It also gives you an alternative if one brokerage is blocked with heavy trading volume.

- *Double-check orders for accuracy.* Make sure each trade was completed according to your instructions. It's very easy to make typos or use the wrong stock symbol, so review the confirmation notice to verify that the right number of shares was bought or sold and that the price and commissions or fees are as quoted. Check your account for "unauthorized" trades.

Transaction Costs

Making transactions through brokers or market makers is considerably easier for investors than it would be to negotiate directly, trying to find someone who wants to buy what you want to sell (or vice versa). To compensate the broker for executing the transaction, investors pay transaction costs, which are usually levied on both the purchase and the sale of securities. When making investment decisions, you must consider the structure and magnitude of transaction costs because they affect returns.

Since the passage of the *Securities Acts Amendments of 1975*, brokers have been permitted to charge whatever brokerage commissions they deem appropriate. Most firms have established **fixed commissions** that apply to small transactions, the ones most often made by individual investors. On large institutional transactions, the client and broker may arrange a **negotiated commission**—a commission to which both parties agree. Negotiated commissions are also available to individual investors who maintain large accounts, typically above $50,000. The commission structure varies with the type of security and the type of broker. In subsequent chapters we'll describe the basic commission structures for various types of securities.

Because of the way brokerage firms charge commissions on stock trades, it is difficult to compare prices precisely. Traditional brokers generally charge on the basis of number of shares and the price of the stock at the time of the transaction. Internet brokers usually charge flat rates, often for transactions up to 1,000 shares, with additional fees for larger or more complicated orders. However, many traditional brokerage firms have reduced their commissions on broker-assisted trades and have instituted annual flat fees (on wrap accounts) set as a specified percentage of the value of the assets in the account. Unless you are a very active trader, you are probably better off paying commissions on a per-transaction basis.

Obviously, premium and basic discount brokers charge substantially less than full-service brokers for the same transaction. However, some discounters charge a minimum fee to discourage small orders. The savings from the discounter can be substantial. Depending on the size and type of transaction, premium and basic discount brokers can typically save investors between 30% and 80% of the commission charged by the full-service broker.

Investor Protection: SIPC and Arbitration

Although most investment transactions take place safely, it is important to know what protection you have if things don't go smoothly. As a client, you are protected against the loss of the securities or cash held by your broker. The **Securities Investor Protection Corporation (SIPC)**, a nonprofit membership corporation, was authorized by the *Securities Investor Protection Act of 1970* to protect customer accounts against the consequences of financial failure of the brokerage firm. The SIPC currently insures each customer's account for up to $500,000, with claims for cash limited to $250,000 per customer. Note that SIPC insurance does not guarantee that the investor will recover the dollar value of the securities. It guarantees only that the securities themselves will be returned. Some brokerage firms also insure certain customer accounts for amounts in excess of $500,000. Certainly, in light of the diversity and quality of services available among brokerage firms, this may be an additional service you should consider when you select a firm and an individual broker.

The SIPC provides protection in case your brokerage firm fails. But what happens if your broker gave you bad advice and, as a result, you lost a lot of money on an investment? Or what if you feel your broker is churning your account? In either case, the SIPC won't help. It's not intended to insure you against bad investment advice or churning. Instead, if you have a dispute with your broker, the first thing you should do is discuss the situation with the managing officer at the branch where you do business. If that doesn't resolve the problem, then contact the firm's compliance officer and the securities regulator in your home state.

If you still don't get any satisfaction, you can use litigation (judicial methods in the courts) to resolve the dispute. Alternative dispute-resolution processes that may avoid litigation include mediation and arbitration. **Mediation** is an informal, voluntary approach in which you and the broker agree to a professional mediator, who facilitates negotiations between the two of you to resolve the case. The mediator does not impose a solution on you and the broker. The Financial Industry Regulatory Authority and securities-related organizations encourage investors to mediate disputes rather than arbitrate them because mediation can reduce costs and time for both investors and brokers.

If mediation is not pursued or if it fails, you may have no choice but to take the case to **arbitration**, a formal process whereby you and your broker present the two sides of the argument before an arbitration panel. The panel then decides the case. Many brokerage firms require you to resolve disputes by *binding arbitration*; in this case, you don't have the option to sue. You must accept the arbitrator's decision, and in most cases you cannot go to court to resolve your case. Before you open an account, check whether the brokerage agreement contains a binding-arbitration clause.

Mediation and arbitration proceedings typically cost less and are resolved more quickly than litigation. Recent legislation has given many investors the option of using either securities industry panels or independent arbitration panels such as those sponsored by the American Arbitration Association (AAA). Independent panels are considered more sympathetic toward investors. In addition, only one of the three arbitrators on a panel can be connected with the securities industry. On its website, FINRA reports that in 2014 it brought 1,397 disciplinary actions against registered brokers and firms, levied $134 million in fines, and ordered $32.3 million in restitution to harmed investors.

Probably the best thing you can do to avoid the need to mediate, arbitrate, or litigate is to select your broker carefully, understand the financial risks involved in the broker's recommendations, thoroughly evaluate the advice he or she offers, and continuously monitor the volume of transactions that he or she recommends and executes. Clearly, it is much less costly to choose the right broker initially than to incur later the financial and emotional costs of having chosen a bad one.

If you have a problem with an online trade, immediately file a written—not e-mail—complaint with the broker. Cite dates, times, and amounts of trades, and include all supporting documentation. File a copy with the Financial Industry Regulatory Authority (**http://www.finra.org**) and with your state securities regulator. If you can't resolve the problems with the broker, you can try mediation and then resort to arbitration, with litigation being the last resort.

CONCEPTS IN REVIEW

Answers available at
http://www.pearsonhighered
.com/smart

3.13 Describe the types of services offered by brokerage firms, and discuss the criteria for selecting a suitable stockbroker.

3.14 Briefly differentiate among the following types of brokerage accounts:

a. Single or joint
b. Custodial
c. Cash
d. Margin
e. Wrap

3.15 Differentiate among market orders, limit orders, and stop-loss orders. What is the rationale for using a stop-loss order rather than a limit order?

3.16 Differentiate between the services and costs associated with full-service, premium discount, and basic discount brokers. Be sure to discuss online transactions.

3.17 What is day trading, and why is it risky? How can you avoid problems as an online trader?

3.18 In what two ways, based on the number of shares transacted, do brokers typically charge for executing transactions? How are online transaction fees structured relative to the degree of broker involvement?

3.19 What protection does the Securities Investor Protection Corporation (SIPC) provide for securities investors? How are mediation and arbitration procedures used to settle disputes between investors and their brokers?

Investment Advisors and Investment Clubs

 Many investors feel that they have neither the time nor the expertise to analyze financial information and make decisions on their own. Instead, they turn to an **investment advisor,** an individual or firm that provides investment advice, typically for a fee. Alternatively, some small investors join **investment clubs.** Here we will discuss using an investment advisor and then briefly cover the key aspects of investment clubs.

Using an Investment Advisor

The "product" provided by an investment advisor ranges from broad, general advice to detailed, specific analyses and recommendations. The most general form of advice is a newsletter published by the advisor. These letters comment on the economy, current events, market behavior, and specific securities. Investment advisors also provide complete individualized investment evaluation, recommendation, and management services.

Regulation of Advisors
The *Investment Advisors Act of 1940* ensures that investment advisors make full disclosure of information about their backgrounds, conflicts of interest, and so on. The act requires professional advisors to register and file periodic reports with the SEC. A 1960 amendment permits the SEC to inspect the records of investment advisors and to revoke the registration of those who violate the act's provisions. However, financial planners, stockbrokers, bankers, lawyers, and accountants who provide investment advice in addition to their main professional activity are not regulated by the act. Many states have also passed similar legislation, requiring investment advisors to register and to abide by the guidelines established by the state law.

Be aware that the federal and state laws regulating the activities of professional investment advisors do not guarantee competence. Rather, they are intended to protect the investor against fraudulent and unethical practices. It is important to recognize that, at present, no law or regulatory body controls entrance into the field. Therefore, investment advisors range from highly informed professionals to totally incompetent amateurs. Advisors who possess a professional designation are usually preferred because they have completed academic courses in areas directly or peripherally related to the investment process. Such designations include CFA (Chartered Financial Analyst), CIMA (Certified Investment Management Analyst), CIC (Chartered Investment Counselor), CFP® (Certified Financial Planner™), ChFC (Chartered Financial Consultant), CLU (Chartered Life Underwriter), and CPA (Certified Public Accountant).

INVESTOR FACTS

You can lead a horse to water, but you can't make it drink In an interesting experiment, a large German brokerage house offered free, unbiased (i.e., unrelated to the brokerage's monetary incentives) financial advice to a pool of more than 8,000 randomly selected clients. Only 5% of the firm's clients accepted the offer, and on average they were wealthier than clients who didn't accept the offer. In other words, it appears that the investors who most needed financial advice were least likely to accept it.

(Source: "Is Unbiased Financial Advice to Retail Investors Sufficient? Answers from a Large Field Study," *Review of Financial Studies*, Vol. 25, Issue 4, pp. 975–1032.)

Online Investment Advice You can also find investment advice online. Whether it's a retirement planning tool or advice on how to diversify your assets, automated investment advisors may be able to help you. If your needs are specific rather than comprehensive, you can find good advice at other sites. For example, T. Rowe Price has an excellent college planning section (**http://www.troweprice.com/college**). Financial Engines (**http://www.financialengines.com**), AdviceAmerica (**http://www.adviceamerica.com**), and DirectAdvice (**http://www.directadvice.com**) are among several independent advice sites that offer broader planning capabilities. Many mutual fund websites have online financial advisors. For example, The Vanguard Group (**http://www.vanguard.com**) has a personal investors section that helps you choose funds for specific investment objectives, such as retirement or financing a college education.

The Cost and Use of Investment Advice The annual costs of obtaining professional investment advice typically run between 0.25% and 3% of the dollar amount of money being managed. For large portfolios, the fee is typically in the range of 0.25% to 0.75%. For small portfolios (less than $100,000), an annual fee ranging from 2% to 3% of the dollar amount of funds managed would not be unusual. These fees generally cover complete management of a client's money. The cost of periodic investment advice not provided as part of a subscription service could be based on a fixed-fee schedule or quoted as an hourly charge for consultation. Online advisors are much less expensive; they either are free or charge an annual fee.

Whether you choose a traditional investment advisory service or decide to try an online service, some are better than others. More expensive services do not necessarily provide better advice. It is best to study carefully the track record and overall reputation of an investment advisor before purchasing his or her services. Not only should the advisor have a good performance record, but he or she also should be responsive to your personal goals.

How good is the advice from online advisors? It's very hard to judge. Their suggested plans are only as good as the input. Beginning investors may not have sufficient knowledge to make wise assumptions on future savings, tax, or inflation rates or to analyze results thoroughly. A good face-to-face personal financial planner will ask lots of questions to assess your investing expertise and explain what you don't know. Automated tools for these early-stage questions may take too narrow a focus and not consider other parts of your investment portfolio. For many investors, online advisors lack what leads them to get help in the first place—the human touch. They want personal guidance, expertise, and encouragement to follow through on their plans.

Investment Clubs

Another way to obtain investment advice and experience is to join an investment club. This route can be especially useful for those of moderate means who do not want to incur the cost of an investment advisor. An investment club is a legal partnership binding a group of investors (partners) to a specified organizational structure, operating procedure, and purpose. The goal of most clubs is to earn favorable long-term returns by making investments in accordance with the group's investment objectives.

Individuals with similar goals usually form investment clubs to pool their knowledge and money in a jointly owned and managed portfolio. Certain members are responsible for obtaining and analyzing data on a specific investment strategy. At periodic meetings, the members present their findings for discussion and further analysis by the members. Once discussed, the group decides whether to pursue the proposed strategy. Most clubs require members to make scheduled contributions to the club's treasury, thereby regularly increasing the pool of investable funds. Although most clubs concentrate on investments in stocks and bonds, some may concentrate on specialized investments such as options or futures. Membership in an investment club provides an excellent way for the novice investor to learn the key aspects of portfolio construction and investment management while (one hopes) earning a favorable return on his or her funds.

As you might expect, investment clubs have also joined the online investing movement. By tapping into the Internet, clubs are freed from geographical restrictions. Now investors around the world, many who have never met, can form a club and discuss investing strategies and stock picks just as easily as if they gathered in person. Finding a time or place to meet is no longer an issue. Some clubs are formed by friends. Other clubs are made up of people who have similar investing philosophies and may have met online. Online clubs conduct business via e-mail or set up a private website. Members of the *Better Investing Community*, a not-for-profit organization, have access to educational materials, investment tools, and other investment features.

Better Investing, which has over 200,000 individual and club investors and over 16,000 investment clubs, publishes a variety of useful materials and also sponsors regional and national meetings. To learn how to start an investment club, visit the Better Investing website.

CONCEPTS IN REVIEW

Answers available at http://www.pearsonhighered.com/smart

3.20 Describe the services that professional investment advisors perform, how they are regulated, online investment advisors, and the cost of investment advice.

3.21 What benefits does an investment club offer the small investor? Would you prefer to join a regular or an online club, and why?

MyFinanceLab

Here is what you should know after reading this chapter. MyFinanceLab will help you identify what you know and where to go when you need to practice.

What You Should Know	Key Terms	Wheat to Practice
LG1 Discuss the growth in online investing and the pros and cons of using the Internet as an investment tool. The Internet has empowered individual investors by providing information and tools formerly available only to investing professionals and by simplifying the investing process. The time and money it saves are huge. Investors get the most current information, including real-time stock price quotes, market activity data, research reports, educational articles, and discussion forums. Tools such as financial planning calculators, stock-screening programs, charting, stock quotes, and portfolio tracking are free at many sites. Buying and selling securities online is convenient, relatively simple, inexpensive, and fast.		MyFinanceLab Study Plan 3.1

What You Should Know	Key Terms	Wheat to Practice
LG2 Identify the major types and sources of invest-ment information. Investment information, descriptive or analytical, includes information about the economy and current events, industries and companies, and alternative investment vehicles, as well as price information and personal investment strategies. It can be obtained from financial journals, general newspapers, institutional news, business periodicals, government publications, special subscription services, stockholders' reports, comparative data sources, subscription services, brokerage reports, investment letters, price quotations, and electronic and online sources. Most print publications also have websites with access to all or part of their content. Financial portals bring together a variety of financial information online. Investors will also find specialized sites for bond, mutual fund, and international information, as well as discussion forums that discuss individual securities and investment strategies. Because it is hard to know the qualifications of those who make postings on message boards, participants must do their own homework before acting on an online tip.	analytical information, *p. 80* back-office research reports, *p. 89* *Barron's, p. 83* descriptive information, *p. 80* fair disclosure rule (Regulation FD), *p. 84* financial portals, *p. 90* Form 10-K, *p. 85* investment letters, *p. 89* Mergent, *p. 89* quotations, *p. 89* Standard & Poor's Corporation (S&P), *p. 88* stockholders' (annual) report, *p. 85* *Value Line Investment Survey, p. 89* *Wall Street Journal, p. 82*	MyFinanceLab Study Plan 3.2
LG3 Explain the key aspects of the commonly cited stock and bond market averages and indexes. Investors commonly rely on stock market averages and indexes to stay abreast of market behavior. The most often cited are the Dow Jones averages, which include the Dow Jones Industrial Average (DJIA). Also widely followed are the Standard & Poor's indexes, the NYSE Composite Index, the NYSE MKT Composite Index, the Nasdaq Stock Market indexes, and the Value Line indexes. Numerous other averages and indexes, including a number of global and foreign market indexes, are regularly reported in financial publications. Bond market indicators are most often reported in terms of bond yields and bond indexes. The Dow Jones Corporate Bond Index is among the most popular. Yield and price index data are also available for various types of bonds and various domestic and foreign markets. Both stock and bond market statistics are published daily in the *Wall Street Journal* and summarized weekly in *Barron's*.	averages, *p. 94* bond yield, *p. 99* Dow Jones Corporate Bond Index, *p. 99* Dow Jones Industrial Average (DJIA), *p. 94* indexes, *p. 94* Nasdaq Stock Market indexes, *p. 98* NYSE Composite Index, *p. 98* Standard & Poor's 500 Stock Index, *p. 96* Value Line Composite Index, *p. 98*	MyFinanceLab Study Plan 3.3 Video Learning Aid for Problem P3.2

What You Should Know	Key Terms	Wheat to Practice
LG4 Review the role of stockbrokers, including the services they provide, selection of a stockbroker, opening an account, and transaction basics. Stockbrokers facilitate buying and selling of securities, and provide other client services. An investor should select a stockbroker who has a compatible disposition toward investing and whose firm offers the desired services at competitive costs. Today the distinctions among full-service, premium discount, and basic discount (online) brokers are blurring. Most brokers now offer online trading capabilities, and many no-frills brokers are expanding their services to include research and advice. Investors can open a variety of types of brokerage accounts, such as single, joint, custodial, cash, margin, and wrap. Transactions take place in odd lots (less than 100 shares) or round lots (100 shares or multiples thereof).	basic discount broker, p. 101 cash account, p. 103 churning, p. 102 custodial account, p. 103 full-service broker, p. 101 margin account, p. 103 odd lot, p. 104 premium discount broker, p. 101 round lot, p. 104 stockbrokers, p. 100 street name, p. 101 wrap account, p. 104	MyFinanceLab Study Plan 3.4
LG5 Describe the basic types of orders, online transactions, transaction costs, and the legal aspects of investor protection. A market order is an order to buy or sell stock at the best price available. A limit order is an order to buy at a specified price or below, or to sell at a specified price or above. Stop-loss orders become market orders as soon as the minimum sell price or the maximum buy price is hit. Limit and stop-loss orders can be placed as fill-or-kill orders, day orders, or good-'til-canceled (GTC) orders. On small transactions, most brokers have fixed commission schedules; on larger transactions, they will negotiate commissions. Commissions also vary by type of security and type of broker. The Securities Investor Protection Corporation (SIPC) insures customers' accounts against the brokerage firm's failure. Mediation and arbitration procedures are frequently employed to resolve disputes. These disputes typically concern the investor's belief that the broker either gave bad advice or churned the account.	arbitration, p. 109 day trader, p. 106 fixed commissions, p. 108 limit order, p. 104 market order, p. 104 mediation, p. 109 negotiated commissions, p. 108 Securities Investor Protection Corporation (SIPC), p. 108 stop-loss (stop) order, p. 105	MyFinanceLab Study Plan 3.5 Video Learning Aid for Problem P3.10
LG6 Discuss the roles of investment advisors and investment clubs. Investment advisors charge an annual fee ranging from 0.25% to 3% of the dollar amount being managed and are often regulated by federal and state law. Websites that provide investment advice are now available as well. Investment clubs provide individual investors with investment advice and help them gain investing experience. Online clubs have members in various geographical areas and conduct business via e-mail or at a private website.	investment advisor, p. 110 investment club, p. 110	MyFinanceLab Study Plan 3.6

Log into MyFinanceLab, take a chapter test, and get a personalized Study Plan that tells you which concepts you understand and which ones you need to review. From there, MyFinanceLab will give you further practice, tutorials, animations, videos, and guided solutions.

Log into **http://www.myfinancelab.com**

Discussion Questions

LG2 **Q3.1** Thomas Weisel, chief executive of a securities firm that bears his name, believes that individual investors already have too much information. "Many lose money by trading excessively on stray data," he says. Other industry professionals oppose the SEC's fair disclosure rule (Regulation FD) for the same reason. The Securities Industry Association's general counsel expressed concern that the rule restricts rather than encourages the flow of information. Other securities professionals argue that individual investors aren't really capable of interpreting much of the information now available to them. Explain why you agree or disagree with these opinions.

LG2 **Q3.2** From its roots as an online bookseller, Amazon.com has expanded into other retail categories. Gather appropriate information from relevant sources to assess the following with an eye toward investing in Amazon.com.
   a. Economic conditions and the key current events during the past 12 months
   b. Information on the status and growth (past and future) of the retail industry and specific information on Amazon.com and its major competitors
   c. Brokerage reports and analysts' recommendations with respect to Amazon.com
   d. A history of the past and recent dividends and price behavior of Amazon.com, which is traded on the Nasdaq National Market
   e. A recommendation with regard to the advisability of investing in Amazon.com

LG2 LG6 **Q3.3** Visit four financial portals or other financial information websites listed in Table 3.4. Compare them in terms of ease of use, investment information, investment tools, advisory services, and links to other services. Also catalog the costs, if any, of obtaining these services. Which would you recommend, and why?

LG3 **Q3.4** Gather and evaluate relevant market averages and indexes over the past six months to assess recent stock and bond market conditions. Describe the conditions in each of these markets. Using recent history, coupled with relevant economic and current event data, forecast near-term market conditions. On the basis of your assessment of market conditions, would you recommend investing in stocks, in bonds, or in neither at this time? Explain the reasoning underlying your recommendation.

LG4 **Q3.5** Prepare a checklist of questions and issues you would use when shopping for a stockbroker. Describe both the ideal broker and the ideal brokerage firm, given your investment goals and disposition. Discuss the pros and cons of using a full-service rather than a premium discount or basic discount broker. If you plan to trade online, what additional questions would you ask?

LG4 **Q3.6** Find and visit the sites of two basic discount brokerages listed in Table 3.5 or any others you know. After exploring the sites, compare them for ease of use, quality of information, availability of investing tools, reliability, other services, and any other criteria important to you. Summarize your findings and explain which you would choose if you were to open an account, and why.

LG5 **Q3.7** Describe how, if at all, a conservative and an aggressive investor might use each of the following types of orders as part of their investment programs. Contrast these two types of investors in view of these preferences.
   a. Market
   b. Limit
   c. Stop-loss

LG5 **Q3.8** Visit three websites devoted to investor protection: **http://www.finra.org**, **http://www.investorprotection.org**, and **http://www.sipc.org**. What do these sites have in common?

Are there common lessons that you can learn about becoming a wise investor at all three sites? How are the sites different?

LG6 **Q3.9** Differentiate between the financial advice you would receive from a traditional investment advisor and one of the new online planning and advice sites. Which would you prefer to use, and why? How could membership in an investment club serve as an alternative to a paid investment advisor?

Problems

All problems are available on http://www.myfinancelab.com

P3.1 Chris LeBlanc estimates that if he does five hours of research using data that will cost $75, there is a good chance that he can improve his expected return on a $10,000, 1-year investment from 8% to 10%. Chris feels that he must earn at least $20 per hour on the time he devotes to his research.
a. Find the cost of Chris's research.
b. By how much (in dollars) will Chris's return increase as a result of the research?
c. On a strict economic basis, should Chris perform the proposed research?

LG3 **P3.2** Imagine that the Mini-Dow Average (MDA) is based on the closing prices of five stocks. The divisor used in the calculation of the MDA is currently 0.765. The closing prices for each of the five stocks in the MDA today and exactly one year ago, when the divisor was 0.780, are given in the accompanying table.
a. Calculate the MDA today and that of a year ago.
b. Compare the values of the MDA calculated in part **a** and describe the apparent market behavior over the last year. Was it a bull or a bear market?

Stock	Today	1 Year Ago
Ace Computers	$ 74	$65
Coburn Motor Company	$ 39	$34
National Soap & Cosmetics	$112	$95
Ronto Foods	$ 71	$72
Wings Aircraft	$ 97	$88

LG3 **P3.3** The SP-6 Index (a fictitious index) is used by many investors to monitor the general behavior of the stock market. It has a base value set equal to 100 at January 1, 1978. In the accompanying table, the closing market values for each of the six stocks included in the index are given for three dates.
a. Calculate the value of the SP-6 index on both January 1, 2016, and June 30, 2016, using the data presented here.
b. Compare the values of the SP-6 Index calculated in part **a** and relate them to the base index value. Would you describe the general market condition during the 6-month period January 1 to June 30, 2016, as a bull or a bear market?

Stock	Closing Market Value of Stock ($Thousands)		
	June 30, 2016	January 1, 2016	January 1, 1978
1	$ 430	$ 460	$240
2	$1,150	$1,120	$630
3	$ 980	$ 990	$450
4	$ 360	$ 420	$150
5	$ 650	$ 700	$320
6	$ 290	$ 320	$ 80

LG3 **P3.4** Deepa Chungi wishes to develop an average, or index, that can be used to measure the general behavior of stock prices over time. She has decided to include six closely followed, high-quality stocks in the average or index. She plans to use August 15, 1987, her birthday, as the base and is interested in measuring the value of the average or index on August 15, 2013, and August 15, 2016. She has found the closing prices for each of the six stocks, A through F, at each of the three dates and has calculated a divisor that can be used to adjust for any stock splits, company changes, and so on that have occurred since the base year, which has a divisor equal to 1.00.

a. Using the data given in the table, calculate the market average, using the same methodology used to calculate the Dow averages, at each of the dates—August 15, 1987, 2013, and 2016.

b. Using the data given in the table and assuming a base index value of 10 on August 15, 1987, calculate the market index, using the same methodology used to calculate the S&P indexes, at each of the dates.

Stock	Closing Stock Prices		
	August 15, 2016	August 15, 2013	August 15, 1987
A	$46	$40	$50
B	$37	$36	$10
C	$20	$23	$ 7
D	$59	$61	$26
E	$82	$70	$45
F	$32	$30	$32
Divisor	0.70	0.72	1.00

Note: The number of shares of each stock outstanding has been the same on these dates. Therefore, the closing stock prices will behave identically to the closing market values.

c. Use your findings in parts **a** and **b** to describe the general market condition—bull or bear—that existed between August 15, 2013, and August 15, 2016.

d. Calculate the percentage changes in the average and index values between August 15, 2013, and August 15, 2016. Why do they differ?

LG5 **P3.5** Al Cromwell places a market order to buy a round lot of Thomas, Inc., common stock, which is traded on the NYSE and is currently quoted at $50 per share. Ignoring brokerage commissions, determine how much money Cromwell will probably have to pay. If he had placed a market order to sell, how much money will he probably receive? Explain.

LG5 **P3.6** Imagine that you have placed a limit order to buy 100 shares of Sallisaw Tool at a price of $38, although the stock is currently selling for $41. Discuss the consequences, if any, of each of the following situations.

a. The stock price drops to $39 per share two months before cancellation of the limit order.

b. The stock price drops to $38 per share.

c. The minimum stock price achieved before cancellation of the limit order was $38.50. When the limit order was canceled, the stock was selling for $47.50 per share.

LG5 **P3.7** If you place a stop-loss order to sell at $23 on a stock currently selling for $26.50 per share, what is likely to be the minimum loss you will experience on 50 shares if the stock price rapidly declines to $20.50 per share? Explain. What if you had placed a stop-limit order to sell at $23, and the stock price tumbled to $20.50?

LG5 **P3.8** You sell 200 shares of a stock short for $60 per share. You want to limit your loss on this transaction to no more than $1,400. What order should you place?

LG5 **P3.9** You have been researching a stock that you like, which is currently trading at $50 per share. You would like to buy the stock if it were a little less expensive—say, $47 per share. You believe that the stock price will go to $70 by year-end and then level off or decline. You decide to place a limit order to buy 100 shares of the stock at $47 and a limit order to sell it at $70. It turns out that you were right about the direction of the stock price, and it goes straight to $75. What is your current position?

LG5 **P3.10** You own 500 shares of Ups&Downs, Inc., stock. It is currently priced at $50. You are going on vacation, and you realize that the company will be reporting earnings while you are away. To protect yourself against a rapid drop in the price, you place a stop-limit order to sell 500 shares at $40. It turns out the earnings report was not so good, and the stock price fell to $30 right after the announcement. It did, however, bounce back, and by the end of the day it was back to $42. What happened in your account?

LG5 **P3.11** You have $5,000 in a 50% margin account. You have been following a stock that you think you want to buy. The stock is priced at $52. You decide that if the stock falls to $50, you would like to buy it. You place a limit order to buy 300 shares at $50. The stock falls to $50. What happens?

Visit **http://www.myfinancelab.com** for web exercises, spreadsheets, and other online resources.

Case Problem 3.1   The Perezes' Good Fortune

LG2 **LG4** **LG6**   Angel and Marie Perez own a small pool hall located in southern New Jersey. They enjoy running the business, which they have owned for nearly three years. Angel, a retired professional pool shooter, saved for nearly 10 years to buy this business, which he and his wife own free and clear. The income from the pool hall is adequate to allow Angel, Marie, and their children, Mary (age 10) and José (age 4), to live comfortably. Although he lacks formal education beyond the 10th grade, Angel has become an avid reader. He enjoys reading about current events and personal finance, particularly investing. He especially likes *Money* magazine, from which he has gained numerous ideas for better managing the family's finances. Because of the long hours required to run the business, Angel can devote 3 to 4 hours a day (on the job) to reading.

Recently Angel and Marie were notified that Marie's uncle had died and left them a portfolio of stocks and bonds with a current market value of $300,000. They were elated to learn of their good fortune but decided it would be best not to change their lifestyle as a result of this inheritance. Instead, they want their newfound wealth to provide for their children's college educations as well as their own retirement. They decided that, like their uncle, they would keep these funds invested in stocks and bonds.

Angel felt that in view of this plan, he needed to acquaint himself with the securities currently in the portfolio. He knew that to manage the portfolio himself, he would have to stay abreast of the securities markets as well as the economy in general. He also realized that he would need to follow each security in the portfolio and continuously evaluate possible alternative securities that could be substituted as conditions warranted. Because Angel enjoyed using his spare time to follow the market, he strongly believed that with proper information, he could manage the portfolio. Given the amount of money involved, Angel was not too concerned with the information costs; rather, he wanted the best information he could get at a reasonable price.

Questions

a. Explain what role the *Wall Street Journal* and/or *Barron's* might play in meeting Angel's needs. What other general sources of economic and current event information would you recommend to Angel? Explain.

b. How might Angel be able to use the services of Standard & Poor's Corporation, Mergent, and the *Value Line Investment Survey* to learn about the securities in the portfolio? Indicate which, if any, of these services you would recommend, and why.

c. Recommend some specific online investment information sources and tools to help Angel and Marie manage their investments.

d. Explain to Angel the need to find a good stockbroker and the role the stockbroker could play in providing information and advice. Should he consider hiring a financial advisor to manage the portfolio?

e. Give Angel a summary prescription for obtaining information and advice that will help to ensure the preservation and growth of the family's newfound wealth.

Case Problem 3.2   Paul and Deborah's Choices of Brokers and Advisors

LG4 LG5 LG6 Paul Chang and Deborah Barry, friends who work for a large software company, decided to leave the relative security of their employer and join the staff of OnlineSpeed, Inc., a 2-year-old company working on new fiber-optic technology for fast Internet access. Paul will be a vice president for new-product development; Deborah will be treasurer. Although they are excited about the potential their new jobs offer, they recognize the need to consider the financial implications of the move. Of immediate concern are their 401(k) retirement plans. On leaving their current employer, each of them will receive a lump-sum settlement of about $75,000 that they must roll over into self-directed, tax-deferred retirement accounts. The friends met over lunch to discuss their options for investing these funds.

Paul is 30 years old and single, with a bachelor's degree in computer science. He rents an apartment and would like to buy a condominium fairly soon but is in no rush. For now, he is happy using his money on the luxuries of life. He considers himself a bit of a risk taker and has dabbled in the stock market from time to time, using his technology expertise to invest in software and Internet companies.

Deborah's undergraduate degree was in English, followed by an M.B.A. in finance. She is 32, is married, and hopes to start a family very soon. Her husband is a physician in private practice.

Paul is very computer-savvy and likes to pick stocks on the basis of his own Internet research. Although Deborah's finance background gives her a solid understanding of investing fundamentals, she is more conservative and has thus far stayed with blue-chip stocks and mutual funds. Among the topics that come up during their lunchtime conversation are stockbrokers and financial planners. Paul is leaning toward a bare-bones basic discount broker with low cost per online trade that is offering free trades for a limited time. Deborah is also cost-conscious but warns Paul that the low costs can be deceptive if you have to pay for other services or find yourself trading more often. She also thinks Paul is too focused on the technology sector and encourages him to seek financial advice to balance his portfolio. They agree to research a number of brokerage firms and investment advisors and meet again to compare notes.

Questions

a. Research at least two different full-service, premium discount, and basic discount stock brokerage firms, and compare the services and costs. What brokers would suit Paul's needs best, and why? What brokers would suit Deborah's needs best, and why? What are some key questions each should ask when interviewing potential brokers?

b. What factors should Paul and Deborah consider before deciding to use a particular broker? Compare the pros and cons of getting the personal attention of a full-service broker with the services provided by the discount brokers.

c. Do you think that a broker that assists in making transactions and focuses on personal attention would be a good choice for either Paul or Deborah?

d. Paul mentioned to Deborah that he had read an article about day trading and wanted to try it. What would you advise Paul about the risks and rewards of this strategy?

e. Prepare a brief overview of the traditional and online sources of investment advice that could help Paul and Deborah create suitable portfolios. Which type of advisor would you recommend for Paul? For Deborah? Explain your reasoning.

Excel@Investing

Peter Tanaka is interested in starting a stock portfolio. He has heard many financial reporters talk about the Dow Jones Industrial Average as being a proxy for the overall stock market. From visiting various online investment sites, Peter is able to track the variability in the DIJA. Peter would like to develop an average or index that will measure the price performance of his selected portfolio over time. He has decided to create a price-weighted index, similar to the Dow, where the stocks are held in proportion to their share prices. He wishes to form an index based on the following 10 high-quality stocks and has designated October 13, 1980, as the base year. The number of shares outstanding has remained constant over the time period 1980 through 2016. The implication is that the closing stock prices will behave just like the closing market values. Given the data below, create a spreadsheet to model and analyze the use of an index.

	Prices		
	10/13/2016	10/13/2012	10/13/1980
A	$45	$50	$55
B	$12	$ 9	$15
C	$37	$37	$37
D	$65	$66	$67
E	$36	$42	$48
F	$26	$35	$43
G	$75	$68	$59
H	$35	$38	$30
I	$67	$74	$81
J	$84	$88	$92

Questions

a. The divisor is 1 on October 13, 1980, 0.75 on October 13, 2012, and 0.85 on October 13, 2016. Using this information and the data supplied above, calculate the market average, using the same methodology used to calculate the Dow averages, on each of the three dates—October 13, 1980, 2012, and 2016.

b. The DJIA is the most widely cited stock market indicator, yet there are criticisms of the model. One criticism is that the higher-priced stocks in the portfolio will impact the Dow more than the relatively lower-priced stocks. Assume that Stock J increases by 10%. Recalculate the market averages on each of the three dates.

c. Next, assume Stock J is back to its original level and Stock B increases by 10%. Recalculate the market averages on each of the three dates. Compare your findings in all three scenarios. Do you find support for the criticism of the Dow? Explain.

4

Return and Risk

LEARNING GOALS

After studying this chapter, you should be able to:

LG1 Review the concept of return, its components, the forces that affect the level of return, and historical returns.

LG2 Discuss the role of the time value of money in measuring return and defining a satisfactory investment.

LG3 Describe real, risk-free, and required returns and the calculation and application of holding period return.

LG4 Explain the concept and the calculation of an internal rate of return and how to find growth rates.

LG5 Discuss the key sources of risk that might affect potential investments.

LG6 Understand the risk of a single asset, risk assessment, and the steps that combine return and risk.

An old saying often attributed to Mark Twain advises, "Buy land—they're not making it anymore." That bit of folk wisdom gained enormous popularity during the U.S. real estate boom. According to the S&P/Case-Shiller Index, which tracks home prices in 20 large cities, U.S. homeowners saw their property values increase more than 100% from 2000 to 2005. Over the same six years, the U.S. stock market (as measured by the S&P 500 Index) lost more than 7% of its value.

Moreover, the tantalizing returns on real estate seemed to come without much risk. The average home price rose every single month from July 1996 to May 2006. No wonder, then, that investing in real estate became fashionable, as evidenced by the introduction of television shows such as A&E's *Flip This House*. It seemed that no one could lose money by investing in residential real estate.

Unfortunately, home prices began to decline in late summer 2006, and their fall continued through March 2012. Over that period, average home prices dropped 34% and millions of properties were lost to foreclosure, reminding homeowners that investing in real estate has both rewards and risks. After hitting bottom in March 2012 the S&P/Case-Shiller Index rose 29% by the end of 2014; however, this rebound lagged behind the S&P 500 Index return of 46% over the same period.

The boom and bust cycles in both the housing and stock markets over the last decade provide great examples of the almost inextricable link between risk and return. Some investments may deliver high returns for several consecutive years, just as housing did in the mid 2000s, but high returns tend to be associated with high risks, as investors in housing learned after 2006. This chapter and the next discuss tools that will help you quantify the tradeoff between risk and return.

(Source: S&P/Case-Shiller price indexes downloaded from http://www.standardandpoors.com and http://www.realtytrac.com/, "Year-End 2014 U.S. Foreclosure Market Report.")

The Concept of Return

LG1 LG2 People are motivated to invest in a given asset by its expected return. The **return** is the level of profit from an investment—that is, the reward for investing. Suppose you have $1,000 in an insured savings account paying 2% annual interest, and a business associate asks you to lend her that much money. If you lend her the money for one year, at the end of which she pays you back, your return will depend on the amount of interest you charge. If you make an interest-free loan, your return will be 0. If you charge 2% interest, your return will be $20 (i.e., 0.02 × $1,000). Because you are already earning a safe 2% on the $1,000, it seems clear that to equal that return you should charge your associate a minimum of 2% interest.

Some investments guarantee a return, but most do not. The return on a bank deposit insured by the federal government is virtually certain. The return earned on a loan to your business associate might be less certain. The size and the certainty of the expected return are important factors in choosing a suitable investment.

Components of Return

The return on an investment comes from two sources. One source is periodic payments, such as dividends and interest. The other source is the change in the investment's price. We call these two components of an investment's return *current income* and *capital gains* (or *capital losses*), respectively.

Income Income may take the form of dividends from stocks or mutual funds or interest received on bonds. For our purposes, an investment's **income** is the cash that investors periodically receive as a result of owning the investment.

Using the data in Table 4.1, we can calculate the income from investments A and B, both purchased for $1,000, over a one-year period of ownership. Investment A provides income of $80, and investment B pays $120. Solely on the basis of the income received over the one year, investment B seems preferable.

Capital Gains (or Losses) The second dimension of return focuses on the change in an investment's market value. As noted in Chapter 1, the amount by which the proceeds from the sale of an investment exceed its original purchase price is a *capital gain*. If an investment sells for less than its original purchase price, a *capital loss* results.

TABLE 4.1   PROFILES OF TWO INVESTMENTS

	Investment	
	A	B
Purchase price (beginning of year)	$1,000	$1,000
Cash received		
1st quarter	$ 10	$ 0
2nd quarter	$ 20	$ 0
3rd quarter	$ 20	$ 0
4th quarter	$ 30	$ 120
Total income (for year)	$ 80	$ 120
Sale price (end of year)	$1,100	$ 960

TABLE 4.2	TOTAL RETURNS OF TWO INVESTMENTS	
	Investment	
Return	A	B
Income	$ 80	$120
Capital gain (loss)	$100	$(40)
Total return	$180	$ 80

We can calculate the capital gain or loss of the investments shown in Table 4.1. Investment A experiences a capital gain of $100 (i.e., $1,100 sale price −$1,000 purchase price) over the one-year period. Investment B, on the other hand, earned a $40 capital loss because the sale price of $960 is $40 less than the $1,000 purchase price.

Combining the capital gain (or loss) with the income (calculated in the preceding section) gives the **total return**. Table 4.2 shows the total return for investments A and B over the year. Investment A earns a $180 total return, compared to just $80 earned by investment B.

It is generally preferable to use *percentage returns* rather than dollar returns. Percentages allow direct comparison of different sizes and types of investments. Investment A earned an 18% return, which equals $180 divided by $1,000; B produced only an 8% return (i.e., $80 ÷ $1,000). At this point investment A appears preferable, but as we'll see, differences in risk might cause some investors to prefer B.

Why Return Is Important

An asset's return is a key variable in the investment decision because it indicates how rapidly an investor can build wealth. Naturally, because most people prefer to have more wealth rather than less, they prefer investments that offer high returns rather than low returns if all else is equal. However, we've already said that the returns on most investments are uncertain, so how do investors distinguish assets that offer high returns from those likely to produce low returns? One way to make this kind of assessment is to examine the returns that different types of investments have produced in the past.

Historical Performance Most people recognize that future performance is not guaranteed by past performance, but past data often provide a meaningful basis for future expectations. A common practice in the investment world is to look closely at the historical record when formulating expectations about the future.

Consider the data for ExxonMobil Corporation presented in Table 4.3. ExxonMobil paid dividends every year from 2005 through 2014. ExxonMobil's stock price generally rose during this decade, starting at $51.26 and ending at $92.45. Despite the overall upward trend, the company's stock price fell in 2008 and 2009 (largely due to the Great Recession and the corresponding drop in oil prices), and it declined again in 2014 (largely due to a rapid increase in the supply of oil and shrinking worldwide demand for oil).

Two aspects of these data are important. First, we can determine the *annual total return* generated by this investment over the past 10 years. The average annual total return earned by ExxonMobil's shareholders (column 6) over this period was 9.6%, performance that put ExxonMobil ahead of

TABLE 4.3   HISTORICAL INVESTMENT DATA FOR EXXONMOBIL CORP. (XOM)

Year	(1) Dividend Income	Market Value (Price) (2) Beginning of Year	(3) End of Year	(4) (3) − (2) Capital Gain	Yearly Total Return (5) (1) + (4)	(6) (5) ÷ (2)
2005	$1.14	$ 51.26	$ 56.17	$ 4.91	$ 6.05	11.8%
2006	$1.28	$ 56.17	$ 76.63	$20.46	$ 21.74	38.7%
2007	$1.37	$ 76.63	$ 93.69	$17.06	$18.43	24.1%
2008	$1.55	$ 93.69	$ 79.83	−$13.86	−$12.31	−13.1%
2009	$1.66	$ 79.83	$ 68.19	−$11.64	−$ 9.98	−12.5%
2010	$1.74	$ 68.19	$ 73.12	$ 4.93	$ 6.67	9.8%
2011	$1.85	$ 73.12	$ 84.76	$11.64	$13.49	18.4%
2012	$2.18	$ 84.76	$ 86.55	$ 1.79	$ 3.97	4.7%
2013	$2.46	$ 86.55	$101.20	$14.65	$ 17.11	19.8%
2014	$2.70	$101.20	$ 92.45	−$ 8.75	−$ 6.05	−6.0%
Average	$1.79			$ 4.12	$ 5.91	9.6%

(Source: Dividends and end-of-year closing prices were obtained from Yahoo! Finance.)

Excel@Investing

many other stocks for the same period. Second, observe that there was considerable variation in ExxonMobil's return from one year to the next. The firm's best year was 2006, during which its investors earned a total return of 38.7%. But in 2008, ExxonMobil's worst year, shareholders lost 13.1%.

Expected Return In the final analysis, of course, it's the future that matters when we make investment decisions. Therefore an investment's **expected return** is a vital measure of its performance. It's what you think the investment will earn in the future that determines what you should be willing to pay for it.

To demonstrate, let's return to the data in Table 4.3. A naive investor might estimate ExxonMobil's expected return to be the same as its average return from the prior decade, 9.6%. That's not necessarily a bad starting point, but it would be wise to ask, "What contributed to ExxonMobil's past returns, and is it likely that the same factors will occur in the future?" Central to ExxonMobil's success in the recent past was a generally upward trend in oil prices. In early 2005, crude oil traded for around $58 per barrel, but prices rose steadily until they peaked around $140 per barrel in June 2008. Even though prices fell sharply for a brief period during the recession, the price of oil did not fall below $70 at any point from June 2009 to October 2014, so this was a very favorable period for ExxonMobil. This suggests that the historical returns shown in Table 4.3 might represent a better-than-average period for the company. An investor who believed that oil prices would not continue to move up indefinitely, but rather would stabilize, might estimate ExxonMobil's expected return by looking at its historical performance during a period of relatively stable oil prices.

Level of Return

The level of return achieved or expected from an investment will depend on a variety of factors. The key factors are internal characteristics and external forces.

Fears of Deflation Worry Investors

For most of your lifetime, prices of most goods and services have been rising. There are important exceptions, such as the prices of consumer electronics and computers, but from one year to the next, the overall price level rose continuously in the United States from 1955 through 2007. However, as the recession deepened in 2008, consumer prices in the United States began to decline, falling in each of the last five months that year. Countries in the European Union experienced a brief deflationary period around the same time. The news raised fears among some investors that the recession might turn into a depression like the one that had brought about a price decline of −27% from November 1929 to March 1933. Although prices began to rise again, fears of deflation resurfaced again in late 2014 and early 2015. Prices in the United States were flat or down in the first three months of 2015, while countries in the European Union experienced falling prices for four consecutive months starting in December 2015.

Critical Thinking Question   Suppose you own an investment that pays a fixed return in dollars year after year. How do you think inflation (rising prices) or deflation (falling prices) would influence the value of this type of investment?

Internal Characteristics   Certain characteristics of an investment affect its return. For investments issued by companies, the important characteristics include things such as the type of investment (e.g., stocks or bonds), the quality of the firm's management, and whether the firm finances its operations with debt or equity. For example, investors might expect a different return on the common stock of a large, well-managed, completely equity-financed plastics manufacturer than they would anticipate from the common stock of a small, poorly managed, largely debt-financed clothing manufacturer. As we will see in later chapters, assessing internal factors and their impact on return is one important step in analyzing possible investments.

What Is Inflation?

External Forces   External forces such as Federal Reserve actions, recessions, wars, and political events may also affect an investment's return. None of these are under the control of the issuer of the investment, and investments react differently to these forces. For example, if investors expect oil prices to rise, they may raise their expected return for ExxonMobil stock and lower it for the stock of an automobile manufacturer that produces gas guzzlers. Likewise, the economies of various countries respond to external forces in different ways.

Another external force is the *general level of price changes*, either up—**inflation**—or down—**deflation**. How inflation (or deflation) affects investment returns is complex, but it depends in part on whether investors correctly anticipate the rate of inflation. Generally speaking, when investors expect inflation to occur, they will demand higher returns. For example, when we look back through history, we see that interest rates on bonds were usually higher in periods when inflation was higher. However, when investors are caught off guard and the rate of inflation is higher or lower than they expected, returns on investments may rise or fall in response. The way that investment returns respond to unexpected changes in inflation will vary from one type of investment to another, and that response can be influenced by investors' beliefs about how policymakers will react to changing inflation. For example, if inflation unexpectedly rises, investors might anticipate that the Federal Reserve will take action to slow economic growth to bring inflation back down. In that case, returns on some investments might fall even as inflation is accelerating.

TABLE 4.4   HISTORICAL RETURNS FOR MAJOR ASSET CLASSES (1900–2014)

	Average Annual Return			
	Stocks	Long-Term Government Bonds	Short-Term Government Bills	Inflation
Australia	11.4%	5.6%	4.5%	3.8%
Belgium	7.9%	5.5%	4.8%	5.1%
Canada	8.9%	5.3%	4.5%	3.0%
Denmark	9.3%	7.2%	6.0%	3.8%
Finland	12.9%	7.3%	6.6%	7.1%
France	10.4%	7.2%	4.0%	7.0%
Germany	8.4%	3.2%	2.2%	4.7%
Ireland	8.5%	5.8%	4.8%	4.1%
Italy	10.3%	7.0%	4.4%	8.2%
Japan	11.2%	5.8%	4.8%	6.8%
Netherlands	8.0%	4.7%	3.5%	2.9%
New Zealand	10.0%	5.8%	5.4%	3.7%
Norway	8.0%	5.6%	4.8%	3.7%
South Africa	12.7%	6.9%	6.0%	4.9%
Spain	9.5%	7.6%	6.0%	5.7%
Sweden	9.4%	6.3%	5.3%	3.4%
Switzerland	6.8%	4.6%	3.0%	2.2%
United Kingdom	9.4%	5.5%	4.8%	3.9%
United States	9.6%	5.0%	3.8%	2.9%

(Source: Data from *Credit Suisse Global Investment Returns Yearbook 2015*.)

Historical Returns

Returns vary both over time and among types of investments. By averaging historical yearly returns over a long period of time, it is possible to observe the differences in annual returns earned by various types of investments. Table 4.4 shows the average annual rates of return for three major asset classes (stocks, treasury bonds, and treasury bills) in 19 countries over the 115-year period from 1900 to 2014. With more than 100 years of data to draw on, some clear patterns emerge. You can see that significant differences exist among the average annual rates of return realized on stocks, long-term government bonds, and short-term government bills. In all 19 countries, stocks earn higher returns than government bonds, which in turn earn higher average returns than short-term government bills. Later in this chapter, we will see how we can link these differences in return to differences in the risk of each of these investments.

We now turn our attention to the role that time value of money principles play in determining investment returns.

The Time Value of Money and Returns

The phrase *the time value of money* refers to the fact that it is generally better to receive cash sooner rather than later. For example, consider two investments, A and B. Investment A will pay you $100 next year and $100 the year after that. Investment B pays you $200 in two years. Assume that neither investment has any risk, meaning that you are certain that you will receive these cash payments. Clearly both investments pay $200 over two years, but investment A is preferable because you can reinvest the $100 you receive in the first year to earn more interest the second year. You should always consider time value of money principles when making investment decisions.

We now review the key computational aids for streamlining time value of money calculations, and then we demonstrate the application of time value of money techniques to determine an acceptable investment.

Computational Aids for Use in Time Value of Money Calculations The once time-consuming calculations involved in applying time value of money techniques can be simplified with a number of computational aids. Throughout this text we will demonstrate the use of hand-held financial calculators and electronic spreadsheets. Financial calculators include numerous preprogrammed financial routines. To demonstrate the calculator keystrokes for various financial computations, we show a keypad, with the keys defined below.

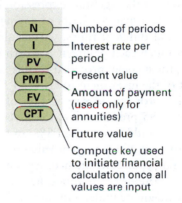

Electronic spreadsheet use has become a prime skill for today's investors. Like financial calculators, spreadsheets have built-in routines that simplify time value of money calculations. For most time value of money calculations in the text, we show spreadsheet solutions with clearly identified cell entries.

Determining a Satisfactory Investment You can use time value of money techniques to determine whether an investment's return is satisfactory given the investment's cost. Ignoring risk at this point, a **satisfactory investment** would be one for which the present value of benefits (discounted at the appropriate discount rate) equals or exceeds its cost. The three possible cost–benefit relationships and their interpretations follow:

1. If the present value of the benefits equals the cost, you would earn a rate of return equal to the discount rate.

2. If the present value of benefits exceeds the cost, you would earn a rate of return greater than the discount rate.

3. If the present value of benefits is less than the cost, you would earn a rate of return less than the discount rate.

You would prefer only those investments for which the present value of benefits equals or exceeds its cost—situations 1 and 2. In these cases, the rate of return would be equal to or greater than the discount rate.

Excel@Investing

TABLE 4.5 PRESENT VALUE APPLIED TO AN INVESTMENT

End of Year	(1) Income	(2) Present Value Calculation at 8%	(3) Present Value at 8%
1	$ 90	$ 90/(1.08)^1	$ 83.33
2	$ 100	$ 100/(1.08)^2	$ 85.73
3	$ 110	$ 110/(1.08)^3	$ 87.32
4	$ 120	$ 120/(1.08)^4	$ 88.20
5	$ 100	$ 100/(1.08)^5	$ 68.06
6	$ 100	$ 100/(1.08)^6	$ 63.02
7	$1,200	$1,200/(1.08)^7	$ 700.19
		Total Present Value	$1,175.85

Time Is Money

The information in Table 4.5 demonstrates the application of present value to investment decision making. (*Note:* You can use a financial calculator or an Excel spreadsheet to convert the algebraic expression in column 2 to the numeric value in column 3.) This investment makes a series of payments over the next seven years. Because the payments arrive at different times, we calculate the present value of each payment to determine how much each payment is worth in today's dollars. The present value of the benefits (i.e., the income) provided by this investment over its seven-year life is $1,175.85. If the cost of the investment today is $1,175.85 or less, then the investment is acceptable, and an investor would earn a rate of return equal to at least 8%. At a cost above the $1,175.85 present value, the investment would not be acceptable because the rate of return would be less than 8%. In that case it would be preferable to find an alternative investment with a present value of benefits that equals or exceeds its cost.

For your convenience, Appendix 4A provides a complete review of the key time value of money techniques. Be sure to review it before reading ahead, to make sure you have adequate understanding of this important financial concept.

CONCEPTS IN REVIEW

Answers available at
http://www.pearsonhighered
.com/smart

4.1 Explain what is meant by the return on an investment. Differentiate between the two components of return—income and capital gains (or losses).

4.2 What role do historical performance data play in estimating an investment's expected return? Discuss the key factors affecting investment returns—internal characteristics and external forces.

4.3 What is a satisfactory investment? When the present value of benefits exceeds the cost of an investment, what can you conclude about the rate of return earned by the investor relative to the discount rate?

Measuring Return

LG3 LG4 Thus far, we have discussed the concept of return in terms of its two components (income and capital gains) and the key factors that affect the level of return (internal characteristics and external forces). These discussions intentionally oversimplified the computations involved in determining the historical or expected return. To compare returns from different investments, we need to incorporate time value of money concepts that explicitly consider differences in the timing of investment income and capital gains. We must also be able to calculate the present value of future benefits. Here we will look at several measures that enable us to compare alternative investments. First, we must define and consider the relationships among various rates of return.

Real, Risk-Free, and Required Returns

Inflation and Returns Glance back at Table 4.4, which reports that in the United States the average annual return on a short-term government Treasury bill was 3.8% between 1900 and 2014. The table also shows that the average annual inflation rate was 2.9%. It's no coincidence that the T-bill rate of return exceeds the inflation rate because investors want to earn returns that exceed the inflation rate. Inflation erodes the purchasing power of money. For example, if prices of most goods and services rise by 3% in a year, $1 buys about 3% fewer goods and services at the end of the year than at the beginning. Thus, if investors seek to increase their purchasing power over time, they must earn returns that exceed the inflation rate.

The **nominal rate of return** on an investment is the return that the investment earns expressed in current dollars. For example, if you put $50 into an investment that promises to pay 3% interest, at the end of the year you will have $51.50 (the initial $50 plus a $1.50 return). Your nominal return is 3%, but this does not necessarily mean that you are better off financially at the end of the year because the nominal return does not take into account the effects of inflation.

To continue the example, assume that at the beginning of the year, one bag of groceries costs $50. During the year, suppose grocery prices rise by 3%. This means that by the end of the year one bag of groceries costs $51.50. In other words, at the beginning of the year you could have used your $50 either to buy one bag of groceries or to make the investment that promised a 3% return. If you invested your money rather than spending it on groceries, by the end of the year you would have had $51.50, still just enough to buy one bag of groceries. In other words, your purchasing power did not increase at all during the year. The **real rate of return** on an investment measures the increase in purchasing power that the investment provides. In our continuing example, the real rate of return is 0% even though the nominal rate of return is 3%. In dollar terms, by investing $50 you increased your wealth by 3% to $51.50, but in terms of purchasing power you are no better off because you can only buy the same amount of goods that you could have bought before you made the investment. In mathematical terms, the real rate of return is approximately equal to the nominal rate of return minus the inflation rate.

Example

Suppose you have $50 today and are trying to decide whether to invest that money or spend it. If you invest it, you believe that you can earn a nominal return of 10%, so after one year your money will grow to $55. If you spend the money today, you plan to feed your caffeine habit by purchasing 20 lattes at your favorite coffee shop at $2.50 each. You decide to save and invest your money, so a year later you have $55. How many more lattes can you buy because you chose to invest your money rather than spend it right away? Unfortunately, during the year inflation caused the price of a latte to increase by 4.8% from $2.50 to $2.62. At the new price, you can just about afford to buy 21 lattes (i.e., 21 × $2.62 = $55.02). That extra latte represents an increase in your purchasing power of 5% (21 is 5% more than 20), so your real return on the investment is 5% because it enabled you to buy 5% more than you could before you invested. Notice that the real return is approximately equal to the difference between the investment's nominal return (10%) and the inflation rate (4.8%):

$$\text{Real return} \approx \text{Nominal return} - \text{Inflation rate}$$
$$5\% \approx 10\% - 4.8\%$$

Risk and Returns Investors are generally *risk averse*, meaning that they do not like risk and will only take risk when they expect compensation for doing so. The greater the risk associated with any particular investment, the greater the return that investors will require to make that investment. The rate of return that fully compensates for an investment's risk is called the **required return**. Note that the required return is a kind of forecast. If an investor expects an investment to earn a return equal to or greater than the required return, the investor will want to buy the investment. However, the return that an investment actually earns can be quite different from the investor's required return.

The required return on any investment *j* consists of three components: the real rate of return, an expected inflation premium, and a risk premium, as noted in Equation 4.1.

Equation 4.1

$$\text{Required return on investment } j = \text{Real rate of return} + \text{Expected inflation premium} + \text{Risk premium for investment } j$$

Equation 4.1a

$$r_j = r^* + IP + RP_j$$

The **expected inflation premium** represents the rate of inflation expected over an investment's life. Although the historical average inflation rate in the United States has been close to 3.0%, investors' expectations may deviate from the historical norm for many reasons. For instance, most inflation forecasts for 2016 projected very low inflation due to the lingering effects of the global recession. By adding the first two terms in Equation 4.1, we obtain the **risk-free rate**. This is the rate of return that can be earned on a risk-free investment, such as a short-term U.S. Treasury bill. The formula for this rate appears in Equation 4.2.

Equation 4.2

$$\text{Risk-free rate} = \text{Real rate of return} + \text{Expected inflation premium}$$

Equation 4.2a

$$r_f = r^* + IP$$

The required return can be found by adding to the risk-free rate a **risk premium**, which varies depending on specific issue and issuer characteristics. *Issue characteristics* are the type of investment (stock, bond, etc.), its maturity (two years, five years, infinity, etc.), and its features (voting/nonvoting, callable/noncallable, etc.). *Issuer characteristics* are industry and company factors such as the line of business and financial condition of the issuer. Together, the issue and issuer factors contribute to the overall risk of an investment and cause investors to require a risk premium above the risk-free rate.

Substituting the risk-free rate, r_f, from Equation 4.2a into Equation 4.1a for the first two terms to the right of the equal signs ($r^* + IP$), we get Equation 4.3.

Equation 4.3

$$\text{Required return on investment } j = \text{Risk-free rate} + \text{Risk premium for investment } j$$

Equation 4.3a

$$r_j = r_f + RP_j$$

For example, if the required return on Nike common stock is 7% when the risk-free rate is 2%, investors require a 5% risk premium as compensation for the risk associated with common stock (the issue) and Nike (the issuer). Notice also that if investors expect 1% inflation, then the real required rate on Nike is approximately 6%. Later, we will explore further the relationship between the risk premium and required returns.

Next, we consider the specifics of return measurement. We look at two return measures—one used primarily for short-term investments and the other for longer-term investments.

Holding Period Return

The return to a *saver* is the amount of interest earned on a given deposit. Of course, the amount "invested" in a savings account does not change in value, as does the amount invested in stocks, bonds, and mutual funds. Because we are concerned with a broad range of investments, we need a measure of return that captures both periodic income and changes in value. One such measure is the *holding period return*.

The **holding period** is the period of time over which one wishes to measure the return on an investment. When comparing returns, be sure to use holding periods of the same length. For example, comparing the return on a stock over a six-month period with the return on a bond over a one-year period could result in a poor investment decision. To avoid this problem, be sure you define the holding period. It is common practice to annualize the holding period and use that as a standard.

Understanding Return Components Earlier in this chapter we identified the two components of investment return: income and capital gains (or losses). The income received by the investor during the investment period is a **realized return**. Capital gains and losses, on the other hand, are realized only when the investor sells an asset at the end of the investment period. Until the sale occurs, the capital gain or loss is called a **paper return** or an unrealized return.

For example, the capital gain return on an investment that increases in market value from $50 to $70 during a year is $20. For that capital gain to be realized, you would sell the investment for $70 at the end of that year. An investor who purchased the same investment but plans to hold it for another three years would also experience the $20 capital gain return during the first year, but he or she would not have realized the gain by collecting the $20 profit in cash. However, even if the capital gain is not realized, it must be included in the total return calculation.

A second point to recognize about returns is that both the income and the capital gains components can have a negative value. Occasionally, an investment may have negative income. That is, you may be required to pay out cash to meet certain obligations. (This situation is most likely to occur in various types of property investments that require periodic maintenance.) A capital loss can occur on any investment. Stocks, bonds, mutual funds, options, futures, real estate, and gold can all decline in value.

Computing the Holding Period Return The **holding period return** (HPR) is the total return earned from holding an investment for a specified time (the holding period). Analysts typically use the HPR with holding periods of one year or less. (We'll explain why later.) It represents the sum of income and capital gains (or losses) achieved over the holding period, divided by the beginning investment value (market price). The annual total returns in Table 4.3 are calculated in this fashion. The equation for HPR is

Equation 4.4

$$\text{Holding period return} = \frac{\text{Income during period} + \text{Capital gain (or loss) during period}}{\text{Beginning investment value}}$$

Equation 4.4a

$$\text{HPR} = \frac{\text{Inc} + \text{CG}}{V_0}$$

where

Equation 4.5

$$\frac{\text{Capital gain (or loss)}}{\text{during period}} = \frac{\text{Ending}}{\text{investment value}} - \frac{\text{Beginning}}{\text{investment value}}$$

Equation 4.5a

$$\text{CG} = V_n - V_0$$

The HPR equation provides a convenient method for either measuring the total return earned or estimating the total return expected. For example, Table 4.6 summarizes the key financial variables for four investments over the past year. The total income and capital gain or loss during the investment period appear in the lines labeled (1) and (3), respectively. The total return over the year is calculated, as shown in line (4), by adding these two sources of return. Dividing the total return value [line (4)] by the beginning-of-year investment value [line (2)], we find the holding period return, given in line (5). Over the one-year holding period the common stock had the highest HPR (12.25%). The savings account had the lowest (6%).

As these calculations show, to find the HPR we need the beginning-of-period and end-of-period investment values, along with income received during the period. Note that if the current income and capital gain (or loss) values in lines (1) and (3) of Table 4.6 had been drawn from a 6-month rather than a one-year period, the HPR values calculated in line (5) would have been the same.

Excel@Investing

TABLE 4.6   KEY FINANCIAL VARIABLES FOR FOUR INVESTMENTS

	Investment			
	Savings Account	Common Stock	Bond	Real Estate
Cash Received				
1st quarter	$ 15	$ 10	$ 0	$ 0
2nd quarter	$ 15	$ 10	$ 70	$ 0
3rd quarter	$ 15	$ 10	$ 0	$ 0
4th quarter	$ 15	$ 15	$ 70	$ 0
(1) Total current income	$ 60	$ 45	$ 140	$ 0
Investment Value				
End-of-year	$ 1,000	$2,200	$ 970	$3,300
(2) Beginning-of-year	–$ 1,000	–$2,000	–$ 1,000	–$3,000
(3) Capital gain (loss)	$ 0	$ 200	–$ 30	$ 300
(4) Total return [(1) + (3)]	$ 60	$ 245	$ 110	$ 300
(5) Holding period return [(4) ÷ (2)]	6.00%	12.25%	11.00%	10.00%

An investment's holding period return can be negative or positive. You can use Equation 4.4 to calculate HPRs using either historical data (as in the preceding example) or forecast data.

Using the HPR in Investment Decisions The holding period return is easy to use in making investment decisions. It measures an investment's return (including both the income and capital gains components) relative to the investment's initial cost, and in so doing makes it easier to compare the performance of investments that may differ greatly in terms of the amount of money required from an investor.

If we look only at the total returns in dollars calculated for each of the investments in Table 4.6 [line (4)], the real estate investment appears best because it has the highest total return. However, the real estate investment would require the largest dollar outlay ($3,000). The holding period return (or total return expressed as a percentage of the investment's cost) offers a *relative comparison*, by dividing the total return by the amount of the investment. Comparing HPRs [line (5)], we find that common stock is the investment alternative with the highest return per invested dollar at 12.25%. Because the return per invested dollar reflects the efficiency of the investment, the HPR provides a logical method for evaluating and comparing investment returns, particularly for holding periods of one year or less.

The Internal Rate of Return

For investments with holding periods greater than one year, an alternative way to define a satisfactory investment is in terms of the annual rate of return it earns. Why do we need an alternative to the HPR? Because the HPR calculation fails to fully account for the time value of money, and the HPRs for competing investments are not always comparable. Instead, sophisticated investors prefer to use a present value–based measure, called the **internal rate of return** (**IRR**), to determine the annual rate of return earned on investments held for longer than one year. An investment's IRR is the discount rate that equates the investment's cost to the present value of the benefits that it provides for the investor.

Once you know the IRR, you can decide whether an investment is acceptable. If the IRR on an investment is equal to or greater than the required return, then the investment is acceptable. An investment with an IRR below the required return is unacceptable.

The IRR on an investment providing a single future cash flow is relatively easy to calculate. The IRR on an investment providing a stream of future cash flows generally involves more complex calculations. Hand-held financial calculators or Excel spreadsheets simplify these calculations.

IRR for a Single Cash Flow Some investments, such as U.S. savings bonds, stocks paying no dividends, and zero-coupon bonds, provide no periodic income. Instead, investors pay a lump sum up front to purchase these investments, and in return investors expect to receive a single, future cash flow when they sell the investment or when the investment matures. The IRR on such an investment is easy to calculate using a financial calculator or an Excel spreadsheet.

CALCULATOR USE Assume you wish to find the IRR on an investment that costs $1,000 today and will pay you $1,400 in five years. To compute the IRR for this investment on a financial calculator, you treat the investment's cost as a present value, PV, and the investment's payoff as a future value, FV. (*Note:* Most calculators require you to enter either the PV or FV as a negative number to calculate an unknown IRR. Generally, the PV is entered as a negative value since it represents the initial cost of an investment.) Using the inputs shown at the left, you can verify that the IRR is 6.96%.

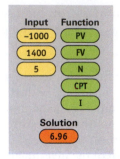

SPREADSHEET USE You can calculate the IRR for the single cash flow as shown on the following Excel spreadsheet.

	A	B
1	**IRR FOR A SINGLE CASH FLOW**	
2	Investment	Cash Flow
3	Cost (PV)	-$1,000
4	Payoff (FV)	$1,400
5	Number of Years	5
6	IRR	6.96%
7	Entry in Cell B6 is =Rate(B5,0,B3,B4,0). The minus sign appears before the $1,000 in B3 because the cost of the investment is treated as a cash outflow.	

Excel@Investing

IRR for a Stream of Income Investments such as income-oriented stocks and bonds typically provide the investor with an income stream. The IRR on an investment that pays income periodically is the discount rate that equates the present value of the investment's cash flows to its current price.

Example

Consider once more the investment presented in Table 4.5. The table illustrates that the present value of the investment's cash flows given a discount rate of 8% is $1,175.85. If the market price of the investment is also $1,175.85 (equal to the present value), then 8% is its internal rate of return, because at that discount rate the present value and the market price are the same. Suppose that the price of this investment falls to $1,100. At that price, what IRR does the investment offer? Table 4.7 uses a trial-and-error approach in an attempt to find the answer. If we discount the investment's cash flows at 9%, the present value of those cash flows is $1,117.75. That's above the investment's market price, so the IRR must be above 9%. Table 4.7 shows that at a 10% discount rate, the present value of the cash flows is $1,063.40, so the investment's IRR must be below 10%. Therefore, you need to keep searching for the exact discount rate at which the investment's cash flows equal $1,100. You can do that using a financial calculator or an Excel spreadsheet.

Excel@Investing

TABLE 4.7   PRESENT VALUE APPLIED TO AN INVESTMENT

End of Year	(1) Income	(2) Present Value Calculation at 9%	(3) Present Value at 9%	(4) Present Value Calculation at 10%	(5) Present Value at 10%
1	$ 90	$ 90/(1 + 0.09)^1	$ 82.57	$ 90/(1 + 0.1)^1	$ 81.82
2	$ 100	$ 100/(1 + 0.09)^2	$ 84.17	$ 100/(1 + 0.1)^2	$ 82.64
3	$ 110	$ 110/(1 + 0.09)^3	$ 84.94	$ 110/(1 + 0.1)^3	$ 82.64
4	$ 120	$ 120/(1 + 0.09)^4	$ 85.01	$ 120/(1 + 0.1)^4	$ 81.96
5	$ 100	$ 100/(1 + 0.09)^5	$ 64.99	$ 100/(1 + 0.1)^5	$ 62.09
6	$ 100	$ 100/(1 + 0.09)^6	$ 59.63	$ 100/(1 + 0.1)^6	$ 56.45
7	$1,200	$1,200/(1 + 0.09)^7	$ 656.44	$1,200/(1 + 0.1)^7	$ 615.79
Total Present Value			$1,117.75		$1,063.40

CALCULATOR USE Using a financial calculator to find an investment's IRR typically involves three steps: (1) Enter the cost of the investment (typically referred to as the *cash outflow* at time 0). (2) Enter all of the income expected each period (typically referred to as the *cash inflow* in year *x*). (3) Calculate the IRR.

SPREADSHEET USE We can also calculate the IRR for a stream of income as shown on the following Excel spreadsheet.

Excel@Investing

	A	B
1	IRR FOR A STREAM OF INCOME	
2	Year	Cash Flow
3	0	-$1,100
4	1	$90
5	2	$100
6	3	$110
7	4	$120
8	5	$100
9	6	$100
10	7	$1,200
11	IRR	9.32%
12	Entry in Cell B11 is =IRR(B3:B10). The minus sign appears before the $1,100 in B3 because the cost of the investment is treated as a cash outflow.	

Interest on Interest: The Critical Assumption The IRR is a measure of the return that an investment provides, but the IRR calculation contains a subtle assumption. That assumption is that the investor can reinvest all of the income that the investment provides, and that the return earned on reinvested income equals the return on the original investment. This concept can best be illustrated with a simple example. Suppose you buy a $1,000 U.S. Treasury bond that pays 8% annual interest ($80) over its 20-year life. Each year you receive $80, and at maturity you get the $1,000 principal back. To earn an 8% IRR on this investment, you must be able to reinvest the $80 annual interest income for the remaining 20-year life at the same annual rate of return of 8%.

Figure 4.1 shows the elements of return on this investment to demonstrate the point. If you don't *reinvest* the interest income of $80 per year, you'll end up earning an IRR of about 4.9%. You'll have $2,600—the $1,000 principal plus $1,600 in interest ($80 per year for 20 years)—at the end of 20 years. (The IRR on a single cash flow of $1,000 today that will be worth $2,600 in 20 years is about 4.9%.) Alternatively, if you reinvest each $80 annual interest payment, and if those reinvestment payments earn an 8% return from the time that they are received until the end of the bond's 20-year life, then at the end of 20 years you'll have $4,661—the $1,000 principal plus the $3,661 future value of the $80 interest payments reinvested at 8%. (The IRR on a single cash flow of $1,000 today that will be worth $4,661 in 20 years is 8%.) Figure 4.1 shows that this investment's future value is $2,061 greater ($4,661 −$2,600) with interest payments reinvested compared to the case when interest payments are not reinvested.

It should be clear to you that if you buy an investment that makes periodic cash payments, and if you want an 8% return on that investment, you must earn that same 8% rate of return when reinvesting your income to earn the full IRR. The rate of

FIGURE 4.1

Earning Interest on Interest

If you invested in a $1,000, 20-year bond with an annual interest rate of 8%, you would have only $2,600 at the end of 20 years if you did not reinvest the $80 annual interest payments. That is roughly equivalent to investing $1,000 today and letting it grow at 5% for 20 years.

 If you reinvested the interest payments at 8%, you would have $4,661 at the end of 20 years. That's the same amount that you would have by investing $1,000 today and letting that grow at 8% per year for 20 years. To achieve the calculated IRR of 8%, you must therefore be able to earn interest on interest at that same 8% rate.

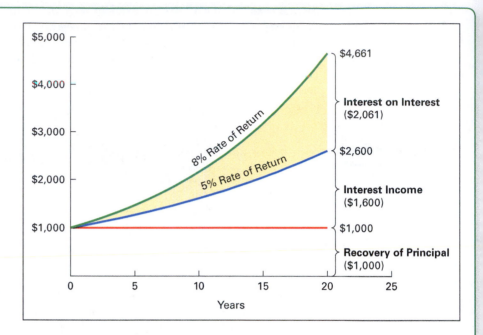

return you start with is the required, or minimum, **reinvestment rate**. This is the rate of return earned on interest or other income received over the relevant investment horizon. By putting your income to work at this rate, you'll earn the rate of return you set out to earn. If you must reinvest income at a lower rate, your return will decline accordingly.

Because the IRR calculation assumes that you can earn interest on the periodic income that you receive, financial experts say that the IRR is a **fully compounded rate of return**. That simply means that the IRR calculation accounts for the fact that you earn a higher return on an investment when you can reinvest its cash flows.

Interest on interest is a particularly important element of return for investment programs that involve a lot of income. You must actively reinvest income. (With capital gains, the money is automatically reinvested unless you sell the asset to realize the gain.) It follows, therefore, that for investment programs that lean toward income-oriented securities, the continued reinvestment of income plays an important role in investment success.

Finding Growth Rates

In addition to finding compound annual rates of return, we frequently need to find the **rate of growth**. This is the compound annual *rate of change* in some financial quantity, such as the price of a stock or the size of its dividend. Here we use an example to demonstrate a simple technique for estimating growth rates using a financial calculator and an Excel spreadsheet.

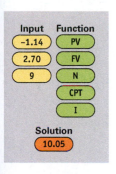

CALCULATOR USE Imagine that you wish to determine the rate at which ExxonMobil Corp. dividends grew from 2005 to 2014. Exxon's dividends appear in Table 4.3. The table presents 10 years of dividend payments, which means that the dividend had 9 years to grow from its 2005 value through 2014.

To use a financial calculator to find the growth rate for ExxonMobil dividends shown in Table 4.3, you treat the earliest (2005) value as a present value, PV, and the latest (2014) value as a future value, FV. (*Note:* Most calculators require you to key in either the PV or the FV as a negative number to calculate an unknown growth rate.) As noted above, although 10 years of dividends appear in Table 4.3, there are only nine years of growth ($N = 9$) because the earliest year (2005) must be defined as the base year (year 0). Using the inputs shown at the left, we calculate the growth rate to be 10.05%.

Excel@Investing

SPREADSHEET USE You can also calculate the growth rate using an Excel spreadsheet as shown below. Like the calculator, the spreadsheet equation simply calculates the annualized rate of change from the first dividend paid in 2005 to the last dividend paid in 2014. (Notice that only the first and last dividends and the nine years between them were necessary to find the annual growth rate.)

	A	B
1	**GROWTH RATE FOR A DIVIDEND STREAM**	
2	Year	Dividend
3	2005	$1.14
4	2006	$1.28
5	2007	$1.37
6	2008	$1.55
7	2009	$1.66
8	2010	$1.74
9	2011	$1.85
10	2012	$2.18
11	2013	$2.46
12	2014	$2.70
13	Annual Growth Rate	10.05%
14	Entry in Cell B13 is =RATE((A12-A3),0,-B3,B12,0). The expression (A12-A3) in the entry calculates the number of years of growth. The minus sign appears before B3 because the dividend in 2002 is treated as a cash outflow.	

4.4 Define the following terms and explain how they are used to find the risk-free rate of return and the required rate of return for a given investment.

     a. *Real rate of return*
     b. *Expected inflation premium*
     c. *Risk premium* for a given investment

4.5 What is meant by the holding period, and why is it advisable to use holding periods of equal length when comparing alternative investments? Define the *holding period return*, and explain for what length holding periods it is typically used.

4.6 Define *internal rate of return.* When is it appropriate to use IRR rather than the HPR to measure the return on an investment?

4.7 Explain why you must earn 10% on all income received from an investment during its holding period in order for its IRR actually to equal the 10% value you've calculated.

4.8 Explain how either the present value (of benefits versus cost) or the IRR measure can be used to find a satisfactory investment. Given the following data, indicate which, if any, of these investments is acceptable. Explain your findings.

	Investment		
	A	B	C
Cost	$200	$160	$500
Required return	7%	10%	9%
Present value of income	—	$150	—
IRR	8%	—	8%

Risk: The Other Side of the Coin

LG5 LG6 Thus far, our primary concern in this chapter has been the return on an investment. However, we cannot consider return without also looking at risk. *Risk* is the uncertainty surrounding the actual return that an investment will generate.

    The risk associated with a given investment is directly related to its expected return. In general, the greater the investment's risk, the higher the expected return it must offer to attract investors. Riskier investments should provide higher returns. Otherwise, what incentive is there for an investor to risk his or her money?

    This relationship between risk and return is called the **risk-return tradeoff**. In general, investors want to obtain the highest possible return for the level of risk that they are willing to take. To introduce this concept, we begin by examining the key sources of risk. We then consider the measurement and assessment of risk: the risk of a single asset, the assessment of risk associated with a potential investment, and the steps by which return and risk can be combined in the decision process.

How Are Risk and Return Related?

Sources of Risk

The risk associated with an investment may come from many different sources. A prudent investor considers how the major sources of risk might affect potential investments. The combined effect of different risks will be reflected in the investment's *risk premium.* As discussed earlier and shown in Equation 4.3, you can find the required return on an investment by adding its risk premium to the risk-free rate. This premium in a broad sense results from the sources of risk, which derive from characteristics of both the investment and the entity issuing the investment.

Business Risk In general, **business risk** is the degree of uncertainty associated with an investment's earnings and the investment's ability to pay the returns (interest, principal, dividends) that investors expect. For example, business owners may receive no return if the firm's earnings are not adequate to meet obligations. Debt holders, on the other hand, are likely to receive some (but not necessarily all) of the amount owed them because of the preferential treatment legally accorded to debt.

The business risk associated with an investment is tied to the firm's industry. For example, the business risk in a public utility common stock differs from the risk in the stock of a high-fashion clothing manufacturer or an Internet start-up. Generally, investments in similar kinds of firms have similar business risk, although differences in management, costs, and location can cause varying risk levels.

Financial Risk Many firms raise money both by issuing common stock to investors and by borrowing money. When firms borrow money, they commit themselves to make future interest and principal payments, and those payments are generally not linked to a firm's profits but are instead fixed according to a contract between the firm and its lender. Therefore, when business conditions are good and profits are high, shareholders benefit from the use of debt because payments to lenders do not rise with profits, leaving more for shareholders. All other things being equal, a firm that uses debt will generate higher profits for its shareholders compared to a firm that uses no debt, but only when business conditions are good. When business conditions are poor, firms must repay their debts even if they are not making a profit. In that case, debt magnifies the losses that shareholders must endure, so in bad times a firm that uses debt will experience greater losses compared to a firm that has no debt. If a firm using debt has higher profits in good times and steeper losses in bad times (compared to a firm that borrows no money), we can say that debt magnifies a firm's business risk. Firms in all industries are subject to the ups and downs that we refer to as business risk, but firms that use debt take even more risk. That is why debt is also referred to as *leverage*. The increased uncertainty that results when a firm borrows money is called **financial risk**. The more debt used to finance a firm, the greater its financial risk.

Purchasing Power Risk The chance that unanticipated changes in price levels (inflation or deflation) will adversely affect investment returns is **purchasing power risk**. Specifically, this risk is the chance that an unexpected increase in prices (inflation) will reduce purchasing power (the goods and services that can be purchased with a dollar).

In general, investments whose values move with general price levels have low purchasing power risk and are most profitable during periods of rising prices. Those that provide fixed returns have high purchasing power risk, and they are most profitable during periods of low inflation or declining price levels. The returns on stocks of durable-goods manufacturers, for example, tend to move with the general price level, whereas returns from deposit accounts and bonds do not, at least in the short run.

Interest Rate Risk Securities are especially affected by interest rate risk. This is particularly true for those securities that offer purchasers a fixed periodic return. **Interest rate risk** is the chance that changes in interest rates will adversely affect a security's value. The interest rate changes themselves result from changes in the general relationship between the supply of and the demand for money.

As interest rates change, the prices of many securities fluctuate. The prices of fixed-income securities (bonds and preferred stock) typically drop when interest rates rise. As interest rates rise, new securities become available in the market, and those new securities pay the new, higher rates. Securities that are already outstanding make cash payments that reflect lower market rates from the past, so they are not competitive in the higher rate environment. Investors sell them, and their prices fall. The opposite occurs when interest rates fall. Prices of outstanding securities that make cash payments above the current market rate become more attractive, and their prices rise.

A second, more subtle aspect of interest rate risk is associated with reinvestment of income. When interest rates rise, bond prices fall, but bondholders have the opportunity to reinvest interest payments that they receive at a new, higher rate. This opportunity boosts the compound rate of return that investors earn on their bonds. In other words, a rise in interest rates causes bond returns to drop because bond prices fall, but income reinvested at the new higher interest rate partially offsets that effect. This offsetting effect is larger for bonds that make higher interest payments, and it is entirely absent for zero-coupon bonds.

A final aspect of interest rate risk is related to investing in short-term securities such as U.S. Treasury bills and certificates of deposit. Investors face the risk that when short-term securities mature, they may have to invest those proceeds in lower-yielding, new short-term securities. By initially making a long-term investment, you can lock in a return for a period of years rather than face the risk of declines in short-term interest rates. Clearly, when interest rates are declining, the returns from investing in short-term securities are adversely affected. (On the other hand, interest rate increases have a positive impact on such a strategy.) The chance that interest rates will decline is therefore the interest rate risk of a strategy of investing in short-term securities.

Most investments are subject to interest rate risk. Although interest rate movements most directly affect fixed-income securities, they also affect other long-term investments such as common stock and mutual funds. Holding other factors constant, the higher the interest rate, the lower the value of an investment, and vice versa.

Liquidity Risk The risk of not being able to sell (or liquidate) an investment quickly without reducing its price is called **liquidity risk**. One can generally sell an investment by significantly cutting its price. However, a liquid investment is one that investors can sell quickly without having an adverse impact on its price. For example, a security recently purchased for $1,000 would not be viewed as highly liquid if it could be quickly sold only at a greatly reduced price, such as $500.

An investment's liquidity is an important consideration. In general, investments traded in thin markets, where transaction volume is low, tend to be less liquid than those traded in broad markets. Assets such as stocks issued by large companies and bonds issued by the U.S. Treasury are generally highly liquid; others, such as artwork and antique furniture, are relatively illiquid.

Tax Risk The chance that Congress will make unfavorable changes in tax laws is known as **tax risk**. The greater the chance that such changes will drive down the after-tax returns and market values of certain investments, the greater the tax risk. Unfavorable changes in tax laws include elimination of tax exemptions, limitation of deductions, and increases in tax rates. For example, a new tax on investment income went into effect on January 1, 2013, as part of the Affordable Care Act. That tax requires certain high-income taxpayers to pay an additional 3.8% tax on their net investment income.

Event Risk Event risk occurs when something happens to a company that has a sudden and substantial impact on its financial condition. Event risk goes beyond business and financial risk. It does not necessarily mean the company or market is doing poorly. Instead, it involves an unexpected event that has a significant and usually immediate effect on the underlying value of an investment. An example of event risk is the May 2015 death of the president of American Express. On the day he died returning on a plane from a business trip to New York, the market value of American Express stock fell by about $400 million.

Event risk can take many forms and can affect all types of investments. Fortunately, its impact tends to be isolated in most cases.

Market Risk Market risk is the risk that investment returns will decline because of factors that affect the broader market, not just one company or one investment. Examples include political, economic, and social events, as well as changes in investor tastes and preferences. Market risk actually embodies a number of different risks including purchasing power risk, interest rate risk, and tax risk.

The impact of market factors on investment returns is not uniform. Both the degree and the direction of change in return differ among investments. For example, a rapid economic boom would likely increase the value of companies that produce luxury goods, while it might have a more muted positive effect (or even a slight negative effect) on companies like Walmart and Dollar General that focus on selling goods at bargain prices. Essentially, market risk is reflected in a stock's sensitivity to these broad market forces. In other words, if a stock tends to move up or down sharply when the overall market moves, that stock has a high degree of market risk.

Risk of a Single Asset

Most people have at some time in their lives asked themselves how risky some anticipated course of action is. In such cases, the answer is usually a subjective judgment. In finance, we seek to quantify risk because doing so improves comparisons between investments and enhances decision making.

We can use statistical concepts to measure the risk of both single assets and portfolios of assets. First, we focus solely on the risk of single assets, and we show how the concept of standard deviation provides insights regarding an investment's risk. We will consider the risk and return of portfolios of assets later.

Standard Deviation: An Absolute Measure of Risk One indicator of an asset's risk is the **standard deviation, s**. It measures the dispersion (variation) of returns around an asset's average or expected return. The formula is

Equation 4.6

$$\text{Standard deviation} = \sqrt{\frac{\sum_{t=1}^{n}\left(\begin{array}{c}\text{Return for} \\ \text{outcome } t\end{array} - \begin{array}{c}\text{Average or} \\ \text{expected return}\end{array}\right)^2}{\begin{array}{c}\text{Total number} \\ \text{of outcomes}\end{array} - 1}}$$

Equation 4.6a

$$s = \sqrt{\frac{\sum_{t=1}^{n}(r_t - \bar{r})^2}{n-1}}$$

Consider two competing investments—shares of stock in Target Corporation (TGT) and American Eagle Outfitters, Inc. (AEO)—described in Table 4.8. From 2005 to 2014, Target earned an average return of 7.7%, but American Eagle Outfitters achieved a superior average return of 12.4%. Looking at the returns each year, you can see that American Eagle Outfitters returns fluctuated over a much wider range (from −53.5% to 105.8%) than did Target returns (from −30.0% to 42.5%).

The standard deviation provides a quantitative tool for comparing investment risk. Table 4.9 demonstrates the standard deviation calculations for Target and American Eagle Outfitters. (Note: Values in column 4 may not appear to equal the square of values in column 3, but that is simply due to rounding. See the available Excel file for the exact calculations.) We can see that the standard deviation of 21.5% for the returns on Target is, not surprisingly, considerably below the standard deviation of 51.9% for American Eagle Outfitters. The fact that American Eagle Outfitters stock returns fluctuate over a very wide range is reflected in its larger standard deviation and indicates that American Eagle Outfitters is a more volatile investment than Target. Of course, these figures are based on historical data. There is no assurance that the risks of these two investments will remain the same in the future.

AN ADVISOR'S PERSPECTIVE

Carol Schmidlin
President, Franklin
Planning

"I describe standard deviation to my clients in simple terms."

MyFinanceLab

Historical Returns and Risk We can now use the standard deviation as a measure of risk to assess the historical (1900–2014) investment return data in Table 4.4. Table 4.10 reports the average return and the standard deviation associated with stocks, bonds, and bills in many countries. Within each country, a close relationship exists between the average return and the standard deviation of different types of investments. Stocks earn higher returns than bonds, and bonds earn higher returns than bills. Similarly, stock returns are more volatile than bond returns, with bill returns displaying the least volatility (i.e., the lowest standard deviation). Regardless of the country, the general pattern is clear: Investments with higher average returns

Excel@Investing

TABLE 4.8	HISTORICAL ANNUAL RETURNS FOR TARGET AND AMERICAN EAGLE OUTFITTERS	
	Annual Rate of Return* (r_t)%	
Year (t)	Target	American Eagle Outfitters
2005	6.6%	−1.4%
2006	4.7%	105.8%
2007	−11.6%	−32.4%
2008	−30.0%	−53.6%
2009	42.5%	86.5%
2010	26.3%	−8.4%
2011	−13.0%	8.0%
2012	18.2%	47.5%
2013	9.5%	−28.1%
2014	23.8%	0.3%
Average ($\bar{r}$)	**7.7%**	**12.4%**

*Annual rate of return is calculated based on end-of-year closing prices.

(Source: End-of-year closing prices are obtained from Yahoo! Finance and are adjusted for dividends and stock splits.)

TABLE 4.9 CALCULATION OF STANDARD DEVIATIONS OF RETURNS FOR TARGET AND AMERICAN EAGLE OUTFITTERS

	Target			
Year (t)	(1) Return r_t	(2) Average Return $\bar{r}$	(3) (1) − (2) $r_t − \bar{r}$	(4) (3)^2 $(r_t − \bar{r})^2$
2005	6.6%	7.7%	−1.1%	1.2%^{2}
2006	4.7%	7.7%	−3.0%	9.2%^{2}
2007	−11.6%	7.7%	−19.3%	371.4%^{2}
2008	−30.0%	7.7%	−37.7%	1421.3%^{2}
2009	42.5%	7.7%	34.8%	1208.6%^{2}
2010	26.3%	7.7%	18.6%	347.0%^{2}
2011	−13.0%	7.7%	−20.7%	427.6%^{2}
2012	18.2%	7.7%	10.5%	109.6%^{2}
2013	9.5%	7.7%	1.8%	3.2%^{2}
2014	23.8%	7.7%	16.1%	260.3%^{2}
			Sum	4159.5%^{2}
		Variance %^{2}	$S^2_{TGT} =$	462.2%^{2}
		Standard deviation %	$S_{TGT} =$	21.5%

$$S_{TGT} = \sqrt{\frac{\sum_{t=1}^{10}(r_t - \bar{r})^2}{n-1}} = \sqrt{\frac{4{,}159.5}{10-1}} = \sqrt{462.2} = 21.5\%$$

	American Eagle Outfitters			
Year (t)	(1) Return r_t	(2) Average Return $\bar{r}$	(3) (1) − (2) $r_t − \bar{r}$	(4) (3)2 $(r_t − \bar{r})^2$
2005	−1.4%	12.4%	−13.8%	190.0%^{2}
2006	105.8%	12.4%	93.4%	8,718.2%^{2}
2007	−32.4%	12.4%	−44.8%	2,010.1%^{2}
2008	−53.6%	12.4%	−66.0%	4,355.4%^{2}
2009	86.5%	12.4%	74.0%	5,482.4%^{2}
2010	−8.4%	12.4%	−20.8%	433.8%^{2}
2011	8.0%	12.4%	−4.4%	19.5%^{2}
2012	47.5%	12.4%	35.1%	1,229.6%^{2}
2013	−28.1%	12.4%	−40.5%	1,639.2%^{2}
2014	0.3%	12.4%	−12.1%	147.2%^{2}
			Sum	24,225.5%^{2}
		Variance %^{2}	$s^2_{AOE} =$	2,691.7%^{2}
		Standard deviation %	$s_{AEO} =$	51.9%

$$S_{AEO} = \sqrt{\frac{\sum_{t=1}^{10}(r_t - \bar{r})^2}{n-1}} = \sqrt{\frac{24{,}225.5}{10-1}} = \sqrt{2{,}691.7} = 51.9\%$$

Excel@Investing

have higher standard deviations. Because higher standard deviations are associated with greater risk, the historical data confirm the existence of a positive relationship between risk and return. That relationship reflects the fact that market participants require higher returns as compensation for greater risk.

TABLE 4.10   HISTORICAL RETURNS AND STANDARD DEVIATIONS FOR SELECT ASSET CLASSES (1900–2014)

	Stocks		Long-Term Government Bonds		Short-Term Government Bills	
	Average Annual Return	Standard Deviation of Returns	Average Annual Return	Standard Deviation of Returns	Average Annual Return	Standard Deviation of Returns
Australia	11.4%	18.3%	5.6%	11.5%	4.5%	3.9%
Belgium	7.9%	24.5%	5.5%	10.1%	4.8%	3.0%
Canada	8.9%	17.0%	5.3%	8.9%	4.5%	3.6%
Denmark	9.3%	22.0%	7.2%	10.5%	6.0%	3.5%
Finland	12.9%	31.2%	7.3%	6.1%	6.6%	3.4%
France	10.4%	25.1%	7.2%	8.8%	4.0%	2.4%
Germany	8.4%	33.6%	3.2%	13.7%	2.2%	9.5%
Ireland	8.5%	23.1%	5.8%	13.0%	4.8%	4.0%
Italy	10.3%	33.3%	7.0%	10.1%	4.4%	3.3%
Japan	11.2%	29.2%	5.8%	14.1%	4.8%	2.5%
Netherlands	8.0%	22.9%	4.7%	8.3%	3.5%	2.4%
New Zealand	10.0%	20.4%	5.8%	8.2%	5.4%	4.2%
Norway	8.0%	28.0%	5.6%	8.9%	4.8%	3.5%
South Africa	12.7%	22.9%	6.9%	9.6%	6.0%	5.5%
Spain	9.5%	22.8%	7.6%	11.2%	6.0%	4.1%
Sweden	9.4%	21.8%	6.3%	9.7%	5.3%	3.2%
Switzerland	6.8%	18.9%	4.6%	6.0%	3.0%	1.8%
United Kingdom	9.4%	21.4%	5.5%	12.0%	4.8%	3.8%
United States	9.6%	19.8%	5.0%	9.1%	3.8%	2.8%

(Source: Data from Elroy Dimson, Paul Marsh, and Mike Staunton, *Credit Suisse Global Investment Returns Sourcebook 2015*.)

Assessing Risk

Techniques for quantifying the risk of an investment are quite useful. However, they will be of little value if you are unaware of your feelings toward risk. Individual investors typically seek answers to these questions: "Is the amount of perceived risk worth taking to get the expected return?" "Can I get a higher return for the same level of risk, or can I earn the same return while taking less risk?" A look at the general risk-return characteristics of alternative investments and at the question of an acceptable level of risk will shed light on how to evaluate risk.

Risk-Return Characteristics of Alternative Investments A very rough generalization of the risk-return characteristics of the major types of investments appears in Figure 4.2. Of course, within each category, specific investments can vary dramatically in terms of their risk and return characteristics. For instance, some common stocks offer low returns and low risk, while others offer high returns and high risk. In other words, once you have selected the appropriate type of investment, you must decide which specific security to acquire.

An Acceptable Level of Risk Individuals differ in the amount of risk that they are willing to bear and the return that they require as compensation for bearing that risk. Broadly speaking, we can talk about investors' attitudes toward risk by defining three distinct categories of investors whose preferences regarding risk vary in fundamental

FIGURE 4.2

Risk-Return Tradeoffs for Various Investments

A risk-return tradeoff exists such that for a higher risk one expects a higher return, and vice versa. In general, low-risk/low-return investments include U.S. government securities and deposit accounts. High-risk/high-return investments include real estate and other tangible investments, common stocks, options, and futures.

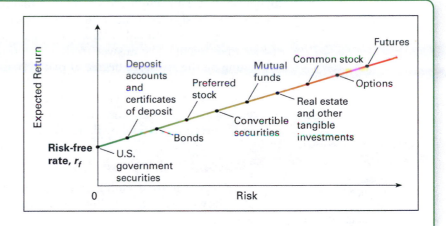

ways, as depicted in Figure 4.3. The figure shows how the required return on an investment is related to risk for investors with different preferences. The three categories are risk-indifferent, risk-averse, and risk-seeking investors.

- For **risk-indifferent** (or risk-neutral) investors, the required return does not change as risk changes. For example, in Figure 4.3, the horizontal blue line indicates that the risk-indifferent investor will accept the same return even if an investment's risk increases from x_1 to x_2.

- For **risk-averse** investors, the required return increases with risk. Because they do not like risk, these investors require higher expected returns to compensate them for taking greater risk. In Figure 4.3, the preferences of risk-averse investors are depicted by the upward sloping green line.

- For the **risk-seeking** investor, the required return decreases as risk increases. These investors simply enjoy the thrill of taking a risk, so they willingly give up some return to take more risk, as indicated by the downward sloping red line in Figure 4.3.

We have already seen historical data on the risk and return of different investments from all over the world, and that data indicate that riskier investments tend to pay

FIGURE 4.3

Risk Preferences

The risk-indifferent investor requires no change in return for a given increase in risk. The risk-averse investor requires an increase in return for a given risk increase. The risk-seeking investor gives up some return for more risk. The majority of investors are risk averse.

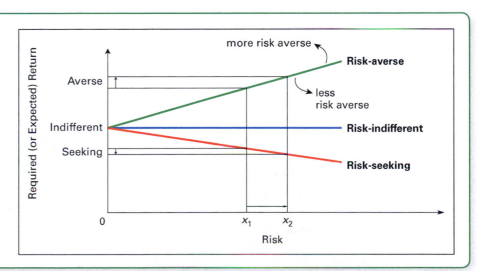

higher returns. This simply reflects the fact that most investors are risk averse, so riskier investments must offer higher returns to attract buyers.

How much additional return is required to convince an investor to purchase a riskier investment? The answer to that question varies from one person to another depending on the investor's degree of risk aversion. A very risk-averse investor requires a great deal of compensation to take on additional risk, meaning that the green line in Figure 4.3 would be very steep for such a person. Someone who is less risk averse does not require as much compensation to be persuaded to accept risk, so for that sort of person the green line would be flatter (but still upward sloping).

Steps in the Decision Process: Combining Return and Risk

When you are deciding among alternative investments, you should take the following steps to combine return and risk.

- Using historical or projected return data, estimate the expected return over a given holding period. Be sure that your estimate of an investment's expected return takes into account the time value of money.

- Using historical or projected return data, assess the risk associated with the investment. You can assess an investment's risk by making a subjective judgment, by calculating the standard deviation of an investment's returns, or by using one of the more sophisticated methods that we discuss elsewhere.

- Evaluate the risk-return characteristics of each investment option to make sure that the return that you expect is reasonable given the risk that you are taking. If other investments with lower levels of risk provide equal or greater expected returns, or if other investments with the same level of risk provide higher returns, the investment is not acceptable.

- Select the investments that offer the highest returns associated with the level of risk you are willing to take. As long as you get the highest expected return for your acceptable level of risk, you have made a "good investment."

Probably the most difficult step in this process is assessing risk. Aside from return and risk considerations, other factors such as taxes and liquidity affect the investment decision. You will learn more about assessing these other factors in subsequent chapters.

CONCEPTS IN REVIEW

Answers available at
http://www.pearsonhighered.com/smart

4.9 Define *risk*. Explain what we mean by the *risk-return tradeoff*. What happens to the required return as risk increases? Explain.

4.10 Define and briefly discuss each of the following sources of risk.
   a. Business risk
   b. Financial risk
   c. Purchasing power risk
   d. Interest rate risk
   e. Liquidity risky
   f. Tax risk
   g. Event risk
   h. Market risk

4.11 Briefly describe standard deviation as a measure of risk or variability.

4.12 Differentiate among the three basic risk preferences: risk-indifferent, risk-averse, and risk-seeking. Which of these attitudes toward risk best describes most investors?

4.13 Describe the steps involved in the investment decision process. Be sure to mention how returns and risks can be evaluated together to determine acceptable investments.

MyFinanceLab

Here is what you should know after reading this chapter. MyFinanceLab will help you identify what you know and where to go when you need to practice.

What You Should Know	Key Terms	Where to Practice
LG1 **Review the concept of return, its components, the forces that affect the level of return, and historical returns.** Return is the reward for investing. The total return provided by an investment includes income and capital gains (or losses). Return is commonly calculated on a historical basis and then used to project expected returns. The level of return depends on internal characteristics and external forces, which include the general level of price changes. Significant differences exist among the average annual rates of return realized over time on various types of security investments.	deflation, *p. 125* expected return, *p. 124* income, *p. 122* inflation, *p. 125* return, *p. 122* total return, *p. 123*	MyFinanceLab Study Plan 4.1 Excel Table 4.3
LG2 **Discuss the role of time value of money in measuring return and defining a satisfactory investment.** Because investors have opportunities to earn interest on their funds, money has a time value. Time value of money concepts should be considered when making investment decisions. Financial calculators and electronic spreadsheets can be used to streamline time value of money calculations. A satisfactory investment is one for which the present value of its benefits equals or exceeds the present value of its costs.	satisfactory investment, *p. 127*	MyFinanceLab Study Plan 4.2 Excel Table 4.5
LG3 **Describe real, risk-free, and required returns and the calculation and application of holding period return.** The required return is the rate of return an investor must earn to be fully compensated for an investment's risk. It represents the sum of the real rate of return and the expected inflation premium (which together represent the risk-free rate), plus the risk premium. The risk premium varies depending on issue and issuer characteristics. The holding period return (HPR) is the return earned over a specified period of time. It is frequently used to compare returns earned in periods of 1 year or less.	expected inflation premium, *p. 130* holding period, *p. 131* holding period return (HPR), *p. 131* nominal rate of return, *p. 129* paper return, *p. 131* real rate of return, *p. 129* realized return, *p. 131* required return, *p. 130* risk-free rate, *p. 130* risk premium, *p. 130*	MyFinanceLab Study Plan 4.3 Excel Table 4.6 Video Learning Aid for Problem P4.10

What You Should Know	Key Terms	Where to Practice
LG4 **Explain the concept and the calculation of IRR and how to find growth rates.** Internal rate of return is the compound annual rate of return earned on investments held for more than 1 year. If the IRR is greater than or equal to the required return, the investment is acceptable. The concept of IRR assumes that the investor will be able to earn interest at the calculated IRR on all income from the investment. Present value techniques can be used to find a rate of growth, which is the compound annual rate of change in the value of a stream of income, particularly dividends or earnings.	fully compounded rate of return, *p. 136* rate of growth, *p. 137* reinvestment rate, *p. 136* internal rate of return, *p. 133*	MyFinanceLab Study Plan 4.4 Excel Table 4.7
LG5 **Discuss the key sources of risk that might affect potential investments.** Risk is uncertainty surrounding the actual return that an investment will generate. Risk results from a combination of sources: business, financial, purchasing power, interest rate, liquidity, tax, market, and event risk. These risks have varying effects on different types of investments. The combined impact of any of the sources of risk in a given investment would be reflected in its risk premium.	business risk, *p. 139* event risk, *p. 141* financial risk, *p. 139* interest rate risk, *p. 139* liquidity risk, *p. 140* market risk, *p. 141* purchasing power risk, *p. 139* risk-return tradeoff, *p. 138* tax risk, *p. 140*	MyFinanceLab Study Plan 4.5
LG6 **Understand the risk of a single asset, risk assessment, and the steps that combine return and risk.** The standard deviation measures the volatility of both single assets and portfolios of assets. Investors require higher returns as compensation for greater risk. Generally, each type of investment displays certain risk-return characteristics. Most investors are risk averse: For a given increase in risk, they require an increase in expected return. Investors estimate the return and risk of each alternative and then select investments that offer the highest returns for the level of acceptable risk.	risk-averse, *p. 145* risk-indifferent, *p. 145* risk-seeking, *p. 145* standard deviation, *s, p. 141*	MyFinanceLab Study Plan 4.6 Excel Table 4.9

Log into MyFinanceLab, take a chapter test, and get a personalized Study Plan that tells you which concepts you understand and which ones you need to review. From there, MyFinanceLab will give you further practice, tutorials, animations, videos, and guided solutions.
Log into **http://www.myfinancelab.com**

Discussion Questions

LG1 **Q4.1** Choose a publicly traded company that has been listed on a major exchange or in the over-the-counter market for at least five years. Use any data source of your choice to find the annual cash dividend, if any, paid by the company in each of the past five calendar years. Also find the closing price of the stock at the end of each of the preceding six years.
a. Calculate the return for each of the five one-year periods.
b. Create a graph that shows the return that the investment earned on the y-axis and the year in which the return was earn on the x-axis.
c. On the basis of the graph in part **b**, estimate the return for the coming year, and explain your answer.

LG2 **Q4.2** Two investments offer a series of cash payments over the next four years, as shown in the following table.

Investment	Year 1	Year 2	Year 3	Year 4
1	$100	$200	$300	$400
2	$250	$250	$250	$250

a. What is the total amount of money paid by each investment over the four years?
b. From a time value of money perspective, which of these investments is more attractive?
c. Can you think of a reason why investors might prefer Investment 1?

LG4 **Q4.3** Access appropriate estimates of the expected inflation rate over the next year, and the current yield on one-year, risk-free securities (the yield on these securities is referred to as the *nominal* rate of interest). Use the data to estimate the current risk-free *real* rate of interest.

LG3 **LG6** **Q4.4** Choose three NYSE-listed stocks and maintain a record of their dividend payments, if any, and closing prices each week over the next six weeks.
a. At the end of the six-week period, calculate the one-week HPRs for each stock for each of the six weeks.
b. For each stock, average the six weekly HPRs calculated in part **a** and compare them.
c. Use the averages you computed in part **b** and compute the standard deviation of the six HPRs for each stock. Discuss the stocks' relative risk and return behavior. Did the stocks with the highest risk earn the greatest return?

Problems

All problems are available on **http://www.myfinancelab.com**

LG1 **P4.1** How much would an investor earn on a stock purchased one year ago for $45 if it paid an annual cash dividend of $2.25 and had just been sold for $52.50? Would the investor have experienced a capital gain? Explain.

LG1 **P4.2** An investor buys a bond for $10,000. The bond pays $200 interest every 6 months. After 18 months, the investor sells the bond for $9,500. Describe the types of income and/or loss the investor had.

LG1 **P4.3** Assuming you purchased a share of stock for $50 one year ago, sold it today for $60, and during the year received three dividend payments totaling $2.70, calculate the following.
a. Income
b. Capital gain (or loss)
c. Total return
(1) In dollars
(2) As a percentage of the initial investment

LG1   **P4.4**   Assume you purchased a bond for $9,500. The bond pays $300 interest every 6 months. You sell the bond after 18 months for $10,000. Calculate the following.
a. Income
b. Capital gain or loss
c. Total return in dollars and as a percentage of the original investment

LG1   **P4.5**   Consider the historical data for an investment given in the accompanying table.
a. Calculate the total return (in dollars) for each year.
b. Indicate the level of return you would expect in 2018 and in 2019.
c. Comment on your forecast.

		Market Value	
Year	Income	Beginning	Ending
2013	$1.00	$30.00	$32.50
2014	$1.20	$32.50	$35.00
2015	$1.30	$35.00	$33.00
2016	$1.60	$33.00	$40.00
2017	$1.75	$40.00	$45.00

LG1   **P4.6**   Refer to the table in Problem 4.5. What is the total return in dollars and as a percentage of your original investment if you purchased 100 shares of the investment at the beginning of 2013 and sold it at the end of 2015?

LG3   **P4.7**   Given a real rate of interest of 2%, an expected inflation premium of 3%, and risk premiums for investments A and B of 4% and 6%, respectively, find the following.
a. The risk-free rate of return, r_f
b. The required returns for investments A and B

LG3   **P4.8**   The risk-free rate is 3%, and expected inflation is 1.5%. If inflation expectations change such that future expected inflation rises to 2.5%, what will the new risk-free rate be?

LG3   **P4.9**   Calculate a one-year holding period return for the following two investment alternatives. Which investment would you prefer, assuming they are of equal risk? Explain.

	Investment	
	X	Y
Cash received		
1st quarter	$ 1.00	$ 0.00
2nd quarter	$ 1.20	$ 0.00
3rd quarter	$ 0.00	$ 0.00
4th quarter	$ 2.30	$ 2.00
Investment value		
Beginning of year	$30.00	$50.00
End of year	$29.00	$56.00

LG3   **P4.10**   You are considering two investment alternatives. The first is a stock that pays quarterly dividends of $0.25 per share and is trading at $20 per share; you expect to sell the stock in six months for $24. The second is a stock that pays quarterly dividends of $0.50 per share and is trading at $27 per share; you expect to sell the stock in one year for $30. Which stock will provide the better annualized holding period return?

LG3   **P4.11**   You are considering purchasing a bond that pays annual interest of $50 per $1,000 of par value. The bond matures in one year, and at that time you will collect the par value and the interest payment. If you can purchase this bond for $950, what is the holding period return?

LG4 **P4.12** Assume you invest $4,000 today in an investment that promises to return $9,000 in **P4.1** exactly 10 years.
  a. Use the present value technique to estimate the IRR on this investment.
  b. If a minimum annual return of 9% is required, would you recommend this investment?

LG4 **P4.13** You invest $7,000 in stock and receive dividends of $65, $70, $70, and $65 over the following four years. At the end of the four years, you sell the stock for $7,900. What was the IRR on this investment?

LG4 **P4.14** Your friend asks you to invest $10,000 in a business venture. Based on your estimates, you would receive nothing for three years, at the end of year four you would receive $4,900, and at the end of year five you would receive $14,500. If your estimates are correct, what would be the IRR on this investment?

LG4 **P4.15** Use a financial calculator or an Excel spreadsheet to estimate the IRR each of the following investments.

Investment	Initial Investment	Future Value	End of Year
A	$ 1,000	$ 1,200	5
B	$10,000	$20,000	7
C	$ 400	$ 2,000	20
D	$ 3,000	$ 4,000	6
E	$ 5,500	$25,000	30

LG4 **P4.16** Sara Holliday must earn a return of 10% on an investment that requires an initial outlay of $2,500 and promises to return $6,000 in eight years.
  a. Use present value techniques to estimate the IRR on this investment.
  b. On the basis of your finding in part a, should Sara make the proposed investment? Explain.

LG4 **P4.17** Use a financial calculator or an Excel spreadsheet to estimate the IRR for each of the following investments.

	Investment	
	A	B
Initial Investment	$8,500	$9,500
End of Year	Income	
1	$2,500	$2,000
2	$2,500	$2,500
3	$2,500	$3,000
4	$2,500	$3,500
5	$2,500	$4,000

LG4 **P4.18** Elliott Dumack must earn a minimum rate of return of 11% to be adequately compensated for the risk of the following investment.

Initial Investment	$14,000
End of Year	Income
1	$6,000
2	$3,000
3	$5,000
4	$2,000
5	$2,100

a. Use present value techniques to estimate the IRR on this investment.
b. On the basis of your finding in part a, should Elliott make the proposed investment? Explain.

IG4 **P4.19** Assume that an investment generates the following income stream and can be purchased at the beginning of 2017 for $1,000 and sold at the end of 2020 for $1,200. Estimate the IRR for this investment. If a minimum return of 9% is required, would you recommend this investment? Explain.

End of Year	Income Stream
2017	$140
2018	$120
2019	$100
2020	$ 80
2021	$ 60
2022	$ 40
2023	$ 20

IG4 **P4.20** For each of the following streams of dividends, estimate the compound annual rate of growth between the earliest year for which a value is given and 2017.

	Dividend Stream		
Year	A	B	C
2008		$1.50	
2009		$1.55	
2010		$1.61	
2011		$1.68	$2.50
2012		$1.76	$2.60
2013	$5.10	$1.85	$2.65
2014	$5.60	$1.95	$2.65
2015	$6.40	$2.06	$2.80
2016	$7.20	$2.17	$2.85
2017	$7.90	$2.28	$2.90

IG4 **P4.21** A company paid dividends of $1.00 per share in 2009 and just announced that it will pay $2.21 in 2016. Estimate the compound annual growth rate of the dividends.

IG4 **P4.22** A company reported net income in 2012 of $350 million. In 2016 the company expects net income to be $446.9 million. Estimate the annual compound growth rate of net income.

IG4 **P4.23** The historical returns for two investments—A and B—are summarized in the following table for the period 2013 to 2017. Use the data to answer the questions that follow.

	A	B
Year	Rate of Return	
2013	19%	8%
2014	1%	10%
2015	10%	12%
2016	26%	14%
2017	4%	16%
Average	12%	12%

a. On the basis of a review of the return data, which investment appears to be more risky? Why?

b. Calculate the standard deviation for each investment's returns.

c. On the basis of your calculations in part **b**, which investment is more risky? Compare this conclusion to your observation in part **a**.

Visit **http://www.myfinancelab.com** for web exercises, spreadsheets, and other online resources.

Case Problem 4.1   Coates's Decision

LG2 LG4   On January 1, 2017, Dave Coates, a 23-year-old mathematics teacher at Xavier High School, received a tax refund of $1,100. Because Dave didn't need this money for his current living expenses, he decided to make a long-term investment. After surveying a number of alternative investments costing no more than $1,100, Dave isolated two that seemed most suitable to his needs.

Each of the investments cost $1,050 and was expected to provide income over a 10-year period. Investment A provided a relatively certain stream of income. Dave was a little less certain of the income provided by investment B. From his search for suitable alternatives, Dave found that the appropriate discount rate for a relatively certain investment was 4%. Because he felt a bit uncomfortable with an investment like B, he estimated that such an investment would have to provide a return at least 4% higher than investment A. Although Dave planned to reinvest funds returned from the investments in other vehicles providing similar returns, he wished to keep the extra $50 ($1,100 − $1,050) invested for the full 10 years in a savings account paying 3% interest compounded annually.

As he makes his investment decision, Dave has asked for your help in answering the questions that follow the expected return data for these investments.

End of Year	Expected Returns	
	A	B
2017	$ 50	$ 0
2018	$ 50	$150
2019	$ 50	$150
2020	$ 50	$150
2021	$ 50	$200
2022	$ 50	$250
2023	$ 50	$200
2024	$ 50	$150
2025	$ 50	$100
2026	$1,050	$ 50

Questions

a. Assuming that investments A and B are equally risky and using the 4% discount rate, apply the present value technique to assess the acceptability of each investment and to determine the preferred investment. Explain your findings.

b. Recognizing that investment B is more risky than investment A, reassess the two alternatives, adding the 4% risk premium to the 4% discount rate for investment A and therefore applying a 8% discount rate to investment B. Compare your findings relative to acceptability and preference to those found for question a.

c. From your findings in questions **a** and **b**, indicate whether the IRR for investment A is above or below 4% and whether that for investment B is above or below 8%. Explain.

d. Use the present value technique to estimate the IRR on each investment. Compare your findings and contrast them with your response to question **c**.

e. From the information given, which, if either, of the two investments would you recommend that Dave make? Explain your answer.

f. Indicate to Dave how much money the extra $50 will have grown to by the end of 2026, assuming he makes no withdrawals from the savings account.

Case Problem 4.2   The Risk-Return Tradeoff: Molly O'Rourke's Stock Purchase Decision

LG3 LG6   Over the past 10 years, Molly O'Rourke has slowly built a diversified portfolio of common stock. Currently her portfolio includes 20 different common stock issues and has a total market value of $82,500.

Molly is at present considering the addition of 50 shares of either of two common stock issues—X or Y. To assess the return and risk of each of these issues, she has gathered dividend income and share price data for both over the last 10 years (2007–2016). Molly's investigation of the outlook for these issues suggests that each will, on average, tend to behave in the future just as it has in the past. She therefore believes that the expected return can be estimated by finding the average HPR over the past 10 years for each of the stocks. The historical dividend income and stock price data collected by Molly are given in the accompanying table.

| | Stock X | | | Stock Y | | |
| | Dividend | Share Price | | Dividend | Share Price | |
Year	Income	Beginning	Ending	Income	Beginning	Ending
2007	$1.00	$20.00	$22.00	$1.50	$20.00	$20.00
2008	$1.50	$22.00	$21.00	$1.60	$20.00	$20.00
2009	$1.40	$21.00	$24.00	$1.70	$20.00	$21.00
2010	$1.70	$24.00	$22.00	$1.80	$21.00	$21.00
2011	$1.90	$22.00	$23.00	$1.90	$21.00	$22.00
2012	$1.60	$23.00	$26.00	$2.00	$22.00	$23.00
2013	$1.70	$26.00	$25.00	$2.10	$23.00	$23.00
2014	$2.00	$25.00	$24.00	$2.20	$23.00	$24.00
2015	$2.10	$24.00	$27.00	$2.30	$24.00	$25.00
2016	$2.20	$27.00	$30.00	$2.40	$25.00	$25.00

Questions

a. Determine the HPR for each stock in each of the preceding 10 years. Find the expected return for each stock, using the approach specified by Molly.

b. Use the HPRs and expected return calculated in question **a** to find the standard deviation of the HPRs for each stock over the 10-year period.

c. Use your findings to evaluate and discuss the return and risk associated with stocks X and Y. Which stock seems preferable? Explain.

d. Ignoring her existing portfolio, what recommendations would you give Molly with regard to stocks X and Y?

Excel@Investing

Excel@Investing

From her Investment Analysis class, Laura has been given an assignment to evaluate several securities on a risk-return tradeoff basis. The specific securities to be researched are International Business Machines, Helmerich & Payne, Inc., and the S&P 500 Index. The respective ticker symbols for the stocks are IBM and HP. She finds the following data on the securities in question.

Year	2009	2010	2011	2012	2013	2014
Price$_{IBM}$	$130.90	$146.76	$183.88	$191.55	$187.57	$160.44
Dividend$_{IBM}$	$ 2.15	$ 2.50	$ 2.90	$ 3.30	$ 3.70	$ 4.25
Price$_{HP}$	$ 39.88	$ 48.48	$ 58.36	$ 56.01	$ 84.08	$ 67.42
Dividend$_{HP}$	$ 0.20	$ 0.22	$ 0.26	$ 0.28	$ 1.30	$ 2.63
Value$_{S\&P}$	1115.10	1257.64	1257.60	1426.19	1848.36	2058.90

Note: The value of the S&P 500 Index includes dividends.

Questions

Part One

a. Use the data that Laura has found on the three securities and create a spreadsheet to calculate the holding period return for each year and the average return over a five-year period. Specifically, the HPR will be based upon five unique one-year periods (i.e., 2009 to 2010, 2010 to 2011, 2011 to 2012, 2012 to 2013, 2013 to 2014). Use the following formula:

$$HPR = [Inc + (V_n - V_0)]/V_0$$

where

Inc = income during period

V_n = ending investment value

V_0 = beginning investment value

Part Two

Create a spreadsheet similar to the spreadsheet for Table 4.9, which can be viewed at http://www.myfinancelab.com, in order to evaluate the risk-return tradeoff.

b. Calculate the standard deviations of the returns for IBM, HP, and the S&P 500 Index.

c. What industries are associated with IBM and HP?

d. Based on your answer in part c and your results for the average return and the standard deviation, what conclusions can Laura make about investing in either IBM or HP?

Chapter-Opening Problem

The table below shows the annual change in the average U.S. home price from 2005 to 2014 according to the S&P/Case-Shiller Index. Calculate the average annual return and its standard deviation. Compare this to the average return and standard deviation for Target Corporation and American Eagle Outfitters, Inc., shown in Table 4.9. In terms of average return and standard deviation, how does residential real estate compare as an investment relative to those two common stocks?

Year	% Change
2005	15.5%
2006	0.7%
2007	− 9.0%
2008	− 18.6%
2009	− 3.1%
2010	− 2.4%
2011	− 4.1%
2012	6.9%
2013	13.4%
2014	4.5%

Appendix
The Time Value of Money

Imagine that at age 25 you begin making annual deposits of $1,000 into a savings account that pays 5% annual interest. After 40 years, at age 65, you will have made deposits totaling $40,000 (i.e., 40 years × $1,000 per year). Assuming you made no withdrawals, what do you think your account balance will be—$50,000? $75,000? $100,000? The answer is none of the above. Your $40,000 will have grown to nearly $121,000! Why? Because the deposits earn interest, and that interest also earns interest over the 40 years. The **time value of money** refers to the idea that as long as an opportunity exists to earn interest, the value of money depends on when it is received and a dollar received today is worth more than a dollar in the future.

Interest: The Basic Return to Savers

A savings account at a bank is one of the most basic investments. The saver receives interest in exchange for placing idle funds in an account. **Interest** can be viewed as the "rent" paid by a borrower for use of the lender's money. The saver will experience neither a capital gain nor a capital loss because the value of the investment (the initial deposit) will change only by the amount of interest earned. For the saver, the interest earned over a given time frame is that period's income.

Simple Interest

The income earned on investments that pay interest (such as CDs and bonds) is sometimes calculated using **simple interest**—interest paid only on the initial investment for each period of time it is invested. For example, if you made a $100 initial deposit in an account paying 6% simple interest, you would earn $6 in interest in each year that you left the money on deposit. After one year your account balance would grow to $106, after two years it would grow to $112, and so on. The account value goes up $6 each year because you earn interest only on the initial deposit.

Compound Interest

Compound interest is interest paid not only on the initial deposit but also on any interest accumulated from one period to the next. This is the method typically used by savings institutions. When interest compounds, the rate of return on an investment increases, and it increases more when interest compounds more frequently. Once again, suppose that you invest $100 in an account that earns 6% per year, but this time assume that interest compounds once each year. After one year, your account balance is $106, just as was the case with simple interest. However, in the second year you earn $6.36 in interest (0.06 × $106), and the account balance grows to $112.36. As long as all of the money is left on deposit, interest payments increase year after year.

Example

Suppose that on January 1, 2016, you place $1,000 into an account that earns 5% interest and interest compounds each year. You plan to withdraw $300 at the beginning of 2017, but you will invest another $1,000 at the beginning of 2018. What will be the account balance at the end of 2018?

The data in Table 4A.1 provides a solution to this problem. During 2016, you earn $50 in interest. The $50 of interest earned on the $1,000 initial deposit during 2016 becomes part of the beginning (initial) balance on which interest is paid in 2017, and so on. After three years, at the end of 2018, the balance in your account is $1,876.88.

Excel@Investing

TABLE 4A.1 SAVINGS ACCOUNT BALANCE DATA (5% INTEREST COMPOUNDED ANNUALLY)

Date	(1) Deposit (Withdrawal)	(2) Beginning Account Balance	(3) 0.05 × (2) Interest for Year	(4) (2) + (3) Ending Account Balance
1/1/2016	$1,000	$1,000.00	$50.00	$1,050.00
1/1/2017	$ (300)	$ 750.00	$ 37.50	$ 787.50
1/1/2018	$1,000	$ 1,787.50	$89.38	$1,876.88

In our examples so far, we allowed interest to compound just once each year. In fact, interest on many investments compounds more frequently than that. In general, the more frequently interest compounds, the higher the true rate of interest. The **true rate of interest** is the rate at which money grows over time after accounting for the effects of compounding. In contrast, the *stated rate of interest* is simply the rate used to calculate interest earnings in each period.

Example

Once again, suppose that on January 1, 2016, you invest $1,000 in an account that pays 5% interest. As before, you have plans to withdraw $300 after one year and to deposit and additional $1,000 after two years. However, in this case, let's assume that interest is paid and compounded twice each year (i.e., semiannually). Does this change the rate at which money accumulates in your account?

The relevant calculations appear in Table 4A.2. To find the interest for each six-month period, multiply the beginning (initial) balance for the six months by half of the stated 5% interest rate (see column 3 of Table 4A.2). You can see that larger returns are associated with more frequent compounding. Compare the end-of-2018 account balance at 5% compounded annually with the end-of-2018 account balance at 5% compounded semiannually. The semiannual compounding results in a higher balance ($1,879.19 versus $1,876.88). Clearly, with semiannual compounding, you are effectively earning a higher rate of interest than when interest compounds just once per year. In other words, the true rate of interest is greater than the 5% stated rate.

Table 4A.3 shows the true rates of interest associated with a 5% stated rate and various compounding frequencies.

Continuous compounding calculates interest by compounding over the smallest possible interval of time. Continuous compounding maximizes the true rate of interest

TABLE 4A.2 SAVINGS ACCOUNT BALANCE DATA (5% INTEREST COMPOUNDED SEMIANNUALLY)

Date	(1) Deposit (Withdrawal)	(2) Beginning Account Balance	(3) 0.05 × 1/2 × (2) Interest for 6 Months	(4) (2) + (3) Ending Account Balance
1/1/2016	$1,000	$1,000.00	$25.00	$1,025.00
7/1/2016		$1,025.00	$25.63	$1,050.63
1/1/2017	$(300)	$ 750.63	$18.77	$ 769.40
7/1/2017		$ 769.40	$19.24	$ 788.64
1/1/2018	$1,000	$1,788.64	$44.72	$1,833.36
7/1/2018		$1,833.36	$45.83	$1,879.19

TABLE 4A.3 TRUE RATE OF INTEREST FOR VARIOUS COMPOUNDING FREQUENCIES (5% STATED RATE OF INTEREST)

Compounding Frequency	True Rate of Interest	Compounding Frequency	True Rate of Interest
Annually	5.000%	Monthly	5.120%
Semiannually	5.063%	Weekly	5.125%
Quarterly	5.094%	Continuously	5.127%

for a given stated interest rate. Table 4A.3 shows that the more frequently interest compounds, the higher the true rate of interest. Because of the impact that differences in compounding frequencies have on return, you should evaluate the true rate of interest associated with various alternatives before making a deposit.

Computational Aids for Use in Time Value Calculations

In most situations, proper investment analysis requires computations that take into account the time value of money, and these computations can be quite tedious to perform by hand. Although you should understand the concepts and mathematics underlying these calculations, you can streamline the application of time value of money techniques by using financial calculators and spreadsheets as we demonstrate below.

Financial Calculators

Financial calculators include numerous preprogrammed financial routines. Throughout this book, we show the keystrokes for various financial computations. We focus primarily on the keys pictured and defined in Figure 4A.1. We typically use 4 of the 5 keys in the left column, plus the compute (CPT) key. One of the keys represents the unknown value being calculated. (Occasionally, we use all of the keys, with one representing the unknown value.) The keystrokes on some of the more sophisticated calculators are menu-driven. After you select the appropriate routine, the calculator prompts you to input each value. On these calculators, a compute key is not needed to obtain a solution. Regardless, you can use any calculator with the basic time value of money

FIGURE 4A.1

Calculator Keys

Important financial keys on the typical calculator.

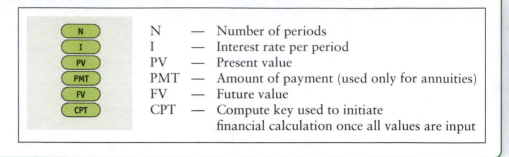

N	—	Number of periods
I	—	Interest rate per period
PV	—	Present value
PMT	—	Amount of payment (used only for annuities)
FV	—	Future value
CPT	—	Compute key used to initiate financial calculation once all values are input

functions in lieu of manual computations. The keystrokes for other financial calculators are explained in the reference guides that accompany them.

Once you understand the basic underlying concepts, you probably will want to use a calculator to streamline routine financial calculations. With a little practice, you can increase both the speed and the accuracy of your financial computations. Remember that conceptual understanding of the material is the objective. An ability to solve problems with the aid of a calculator does not necessarily reflect such an understanding, so don't just settle for answers. Work with the material until you are sure you also understand the concepts.

Computers and Spreadsheets

The ability to use spreadsheets has become a prime skill for today's investors. Like financial calculators, computers and spreadsheets have built-in routines that simplify time value of money calculations. We provide in the text a number of spreadsheet solutions that identify the cell entries for calculating time value of money results. The value for each variable is entered in a cell in the spreadsheet, and the calculation is programmed using an equation that links the individual cells. If you change values of the variables, the solution automatically changes. In the spreadsheet solutions in this book, we show at the bottom of the spreadsheet the equation that determines the calculation.

We now turn to the key time value of money concepts, beginning with future value.

Future Value: An Extension of Compounding

Future value is the amount to which a current deposit will grow over time when it is placed in an account paying compound interest. Consider a deposit of $1,000 that is earning 8% (0.08 in decimal form) compounded annually. The formula below calculates the future value of this deposit at the end of one year.

Equation 4A.1

$$\text{Future value at end of year} = \$1{,}000 \times (1 + 0.08) = \$1{,}080$$

If the money stayed on deposit for another year, the $1,080 balance would earn 8% interest again. Thus, at the end of the second year, there would be $1,166.40 in the account. This amount would represent the beginning-of-year balance of $1,080 plus 8% of the $1,080 ($86.40) in interest. The future value at the end of the second year would be calculated as follows.

Equation 4A.2

$$\text{Future value at end of year 2} = \$1,080 \times (1 + 0.08) = \$1,166.40$$

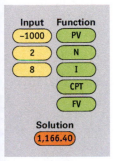

To find the future value of the $1,000 at the end of year n, the procedure illustrated above would be repeated n times. Future values can be determined either mathematically or by using a financial calculator or a spreadsheet. Here we demonstrate use of a calculator and an Excel spreadsheet.

CALCULATOR USE You can use a financial calculator to calculate the future value directly.* First enter −1,000 and depress PV; next enter 2 and depress N; then enter 8 and depress I.** Finally, to calculate the future value, depress CPT and then FV. The future value of $1,166.40 should appear on the calculator display, as shown in the illustration at the left.

Excel@Investing

SPREADSHEET USE You can also calculate the future value as shown on the following Excel spreadsheet.

◇	A	B
1	FUTURE VALUE OF A SINGLE AMOUNT	
2	Present value	− $1,000
3	Annual rate of interest	8.0%
4	Number of years	2
5	Future value	$1,166.40
6	Entry in Cell B5 is =FV(B3,B4,0,B2,0). The minus sign appears before the 1,000 in B2 because the cost of the investment is treated as a cash outflow.	

---

* Many calculators allow the user to set the number of payments per year. Most of these calculators are preset for monthly payments—12 payments per year. Because we work primarily with annual payments—1 payment per year—it is important to be sure that your calculator is set for1 payment per year. And although most calculators are preset to recognize that all payments occur at the end of the period, it is important to make sure that your calculator is correctly set on the END mode. Consult the reference guide that accompanies your calculator for instructions for setting these values. To avoid including previous data in current calculations, always clear all registers of your calculator before inputting values and making each computation.

** You can enter the known values into the calculator in any order. The calculator differentiates inflows from outflows with a negative sign. For example, in the problem just demonstrated, the −1,000 present value (PV), because it was keyed as a negative number (1000), is considered an investment cash outflow or cost. Therefore, the calculated future value (FV) of 1,166.40 is a positive value to show that it is the resulting investment cash inflow, or payoff. If you key in the $1,000 present value as a positive number (e.g., 1,000), the calculator will display the future value of $1,166.40 as a negative number (e.g., −1,166.40). Simply stated, present value and future value cash flows will have opposite signs.

Future Value of an Annuity

An **annuity** is a stream of equal cash flows that occur at equal intervals over time. The cash flows can be *outflows* of funds invested to earn future returns or *inflows* of returns earned from an investment. Investing $1,000 per year at the end of each of the next eight years is an example of an annuity.

Investors often want to calculate the future value of an annuity. A typical annuity, called an **ordinary annuity**, is one for which the cash flows occur at the end of each period. You can quickly find the future value of an ordinary annuity by using a financial calculator or an Excel spreadsheet.

CALCULATOR USE When you use a financial calculator to find the future value of an annuity, key in the annuity cash flow using the PMT key. The PMT key tells the calculator that a stream of N (the number of years input) end-of-year deposits in the amount of PMT dollars represents the annuity stream.

Using the calculator inputs shown at the left, you can verify that the future value of the $1,000 annuity (notice that the $1,000 annuity cash flow is entered as a negative value to indicate that it is a cash outflow) is $10,636.63.

SPREADSHEET USE You also can calculate the future value of the ordinary annuity as shown on the following Excel spreadsheet.

Input	Function
−1000	PMT
8	N
8	I
	CPT
	FV

Solution
10,636.63

Excel@Investing

	A	B
1	FUTURE VALUE OF AN ORDINARY ANNUITY	
2	Annual annuity payment	− $1,000
3	Annual rate of interest	8.0%
4	Number of years	8
5	Future value	$10,636.63
6	Entry in Cell B5 is =FV(B3,B4,B2,0,0). The minus sign appears before the 1,000 in B2 because the annuity cash flow is a cash outflow.	

Present Value: An Extension of Future Value

Present value is the inverse of future value. As you have seen, future value calculations determine how much money will accumulate over time based on some investment that you make today. **Present value** calculations, on the other hand, determine the value today of a cash flow or stream of cash flows that an investment may provide in the future. Present value calculations help investors decide how much they should be willing to pay today for an investment that promises cash payments later on.

Calculating the present value of a lump sum is equivalent to answering this question: If an investor wants to accumulate a specific lump sum, *n* years in the future, how much money must the investor set aside today, assuming that the investment earns *i*% interest? The interest rate used to calculate present values is commonly called the **discount rate** (or *opportunity cost*). It represents the rate of return that the investor requires given the risk of the investment.

Imagine that you can buy an investment that will pay $1,000 one year from today. If you could earn 8% on similar types of investments, what is the most you would pay for this investment today? In other words, what is the present value of the $1,000 that you will receive one year from now, using a discount rate of 8%? Letting x equal the present value, we can use Equation 4A.3 to describe this situation.

Equation 4A.3

$$x \times (1 + 0.08) = \$1,000$$

Solving Equation 4A.3 for x, we get

Equation 4A.4

$$x = \frac{\$1,000}{(1 + 0.08)} = \$925.93$$

Thus, the present value of $1,000 to be received one year from now, discounted at 8%, is $925.93. In other words, if you deposited $925.93 today into an account paying 8% interest, your money will grow to $1,000 in one year.

The calculations required to find the present value of a sum that arrives in the distant future are more complex than those for a one-year investment. We can use a financial calculator or an Excel spreadsheet to reexamine the previous example assuming the $1,000 will be received seven years from now.

CALCULATOR USE Using the financial calculator inputs shown at the left, we find that the present value of $1,000 to be received seven years from now, discounted at 8%, is $583.49.

SPREADSHEET USE You can also calculate the present value of the $1,000 payment as shown on the following Excel spreadsheet.

Input	Function
1000	FV
7	N
8	I
	CPT
	PV

Solution
−583.49

Excel@Investing

◇	A	B
1	**PRESENT VALUE OF A SINGLE AMOUNT**	
2	Future value	$1,000
3	Annual rate of interest	8.0%
4	Number of years	7
5	Present value	−$583.49
6	Entry in Cell B5 is =PV(B3,B4,0,B2,0). The negative sign in cell B5 indicates that the value is a cash outflow, or the cost of the investment.	

Present Value of a Stream of Returns

In the preceding paragraphs we illustrated the technique for finding the present value of a single sum that will be paid on some future date. Because most investments pay out cash at various future dates rather than as a single lump sum, we also need to calculate the present value of a stream of cash payments.

A stream of payments can be viewed as a package of individual lump sum payments. A **mixed stream** is a series of payments that exhibits no special pattern (unlike an annuity that makes equal payments each period). Table 4A.4 illustrates both a mixed stream and an annuity that make five end-of-year cash payments from 2017 to 2021. To find the present value of each of these streams (measured at the beginning of 2017), we must calculate the present value of each payment and then add them up.

TABLE 4A.4   MIXED AND ANNUITY RETURN STREAMS

	Returns	
End of Year	Mixed Stream	Annuity
2017	$30	$50
2018	$40	$50
2019	$50	$50
2020	$60	$50
2021	$70	$50

Present Value of a Mixed Stream

Table 4A.5 shows the present value calculations for each cash flow in the mixed stream using an 8% discount rate. Once we find all of the individual present values, we sum them to find that the present value of all the future cash flows is $193.51. We can streamline the calculation of the present value of a mixed stream using a financial calculator or an Excel spreadsheet.

Excel@Investing

TABLE 4A.5   MIXED STREAM PRESENT VALUE CALCULATION

Year	End of Year	(1) Income	(2) Present Value Calculation at 8%	(3) Present Value at 8%
2017	1	$30	$30/(1 + 0.08)^1$	$ 27.78
2018	2	$40	$40/(1 + 0.08)^2$	$ 34.29
2019	3	$50	$50/(1 + 0.08)^3$	$ 39.69
2020	4	$60	$60/(1 + 0.08)^4$	$ 44.10
2021	5	$70	$70/(1 + 0.08)^5$	$ 47.64
			Total Present Value	$193.51

CALCULATOR USE You can use a financial calculator to find the present value of individual cash flows, as demonstrated previously. You then sum the individual present values to get the present value of the mixed stream. However, most financial calculators have a function that allows you to enter all cash flows, specify the discount rate, and then directly calculate the net present value of the entire return stream using the NPV function on the calculator.

SPREADSHEET USE The present value of the mixed stream also can be calculated as shown on the following Excel spreadsheet.

Excel@Investing

◇	A	B
1	PRESENT VALUE OF A MIXED STREAM	
2	Year	Cash flow
3	1	$30
4	2	$40
5	3	$50
6	4	$60
7	5	$70
8	Annual discount rate	8.0%
9	Present value	−$193.51
10	Entry in Cell B5 is =-NPV(B8,B3:B7). A negative sign can be inserted in front of the NPV function in B9 to indicate that the value is a cash outflow or the investment cost.	

Present Value of an Annuity

We can find the present value of an annuity in the same way that we find the present value of a mixed stream—find and sum the individual present values. However, both the financial calculator and an Excel spreadsheet have a built-in function to simultaneously handle all of the annuity cash flows.

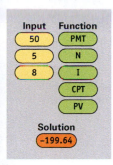

Input	Function
50	PMT
5	N
8	I
	CPT
	PV

Solution
−199.64

CALCULATOR USE Using the calculator inputs shown at the left, we find that the present value of the $50, five-year ordinary annuity is $199.64 when the discount rate is 8%. Recall that the minus sign in the calculator solution indicates a cash outflow relative to the $50 cash inflows.

SPREADSHEET USE The present value of the annuity also can be calculated as shown on the following Excel spreadsheet.

Excel@Investing

	A	B
1	PRESENT VALUE OF A SINGLE AMOUNT	
2	Annual annuity payment	$50
3	Annual rate of interest	8.0%
4	Number of years	5
5	Present value	−$199.64
6	Entry in Cell B5 is =PV(B3,B4,B2,0,0). The parentheses around the present value result indicate that the value is a cash outflow or the investment cost.	

4A.1 What is the time value of money? Explain why an investor should be able to earn a positive return.

4A.2 Define, discuss, and contrast the following terms.

    a. Interest   b. Simple interest
    c. Compound interest   d. True rate of interest (or return)

4A.3 When interest is compounded more frequently than annually, what happens to the true rate of interest? Under what condition would the stated and true rates of interest be equal? What is continuous compounding?

4A.4 Describe, compare, and contrast the concepts of future value and present value. Explain the role of the discount rate in calculating present value.

4A.5 What is an annuity? How can calculation of the future value of an annuity be simplified? What about the present value of an annuity?

4A.6 What is a mixed stream of returns? Describe the procedure used to find the present value of such a stream.

MyFinanceLab

Here is what you should know after reading this appendix. MyFinanceLab will help you identify what you know and where to go when you need to practice.

What You Should Know	Key Terms	Where to Practice
Because investors have opportunities to earn interest on their funds, money has a time value. Interest can be applied using either simple interest or compound interest. The more frequently interest is compounded at a stated rate, the higher the true rate of interest. Financial calculators and spreadsheets can be used to streamline time value of money calculations. The future value of a present sum or an annuity can be found using compound interest concepts. The present value of a future sum is the amount that would have to be deposited today into an account earning interest at a given rate to accumulate the specified future sum. The present value of streams of future returns can be found by adding the present values of the individual returns. When the stream is an annuity, its present value can be more simply calculated.	annuity, *p. 162* compound interest, *p. 157* continuous compounding, *p. 158* discount rate, *p. 162* future value, *p. 160* interest, *p. 157* mixed stream, *p. 163* ordinary annuity, *p. 162* present value, *p. 162* simple interest, *p. 157* time value of money, *p. 157* true rate of interest, *p. 158*	Excel Tables 4A.1, 4A.2, 4A.4, 4A.5 Video Learning Aid for Problem P4A.12

Log into MyFinanceLab, take the appendix test, and get a personalized Study Plan that tells you which concepts you understand and which ones you need to review. From there, MyFinanceLab will give you further practice, tutorials, animations, videos, and guided solutions. Log into **http://www.myfinancelab.com**

Problems

All problems are available on **http://www.myfinancelab.com**

P4A.1 The accompanying table shows a series of transactions in a savings account. The account pays 6% simple interest, and the account owner withdraws interest as soon as it is paid. Create a new table that shows (a) the account balance at the end of each year and (b) the interest earned each year. What is the true rate of interest that the investor earns in this account?

Date	Deposit (Withdrawal)	Date	Deposit (Withdrawal)
1/1/17	$ 5,000	1/1/19	$2,000
1/1/18	$(4,000)	1/1/20	$3,000

P4A.2 Using a financial calculator or spreadsheet, calculate the following.
   a. The future value of a $350 deposit left in an account paying 6% annual interest for 10 years.
   b. The future value at the end of five years of a $700 annual end-of-year deposit into an account paying 8% annual interest.

P4A.3 For each of the following initial investment amounts, calculate the future value at the end of the investment period if interest compounds annually.

Investment	Investment Amount	Rate of Return	Investment Period (yr)
A	$ 200	5%	20
B	$ 4,500	8%	7
C	$10,000	9%	10
D	$25,000	10%	12
E	$37,000	11%	5

P4A.4 Using a financial calculator or spreadsheet, calculate the future value in seven years of $10,000 invested today in an account that pays a stated annual interest rate of 6%, compounded monthly.

P4A.5 The following table describes the characteristics of five annuities. Calculate the future value of each annuity given its characteristics.

Deposit	Annual Annuity Payment	Interest Rate	Annuity Length (yr)
A	$ 2,500	8%	10
B	$ 500	12%	6
C	$ 1,000	20%	5
D	$12,000	16%	8
E	$ 4,000	14%	30

P4A.6 If you deposit $1,000 into an account at the end of each of the next 10 years and the account pays an annual interest rate of 2%, how much will be in the account after 10 years?

P4A.7 Assume you can earn 9% on the investments described below. How much money would each investment provide for you after six years?
a. Invest $5,000 as a lump sum today.
b. Invest $2,000 at the end of each of the next six years.
c. Invest a lump sum of $3,000 today and $1,000 at the end of each of the next six years.
d. Invest $900 at the end of years 1, 3, and 5.

P4A.8 The following table lists the lump sum payout, the timing of that payout, and the discount rate associated with five different investments. Calculate the present value of each investment.

Investment	Future Sum	Discount Rate	Payout at End of Year
A	$ 7,000	7%	4
B	$ 28,000	3%	20
C	$ 10,000	9%	12
D	$150,000	6%	6
E	$ 45,000	15%	8

P4A.9 A Florida state savings bond pays $1,000 when it matures seven years from now. If the state bonds are to be competitive with U.S. savings bonds, which pay 2% interest compounded annually, at what price will the state's bonds sell?

P4A.10 Referring to Problem 4A.9, at what price would the bond sell if U.S. savings bonds were paying 4% interest compounded annually? Compare your answer to your answer to the preceding problem.

P4A.11 How much should you be willing to pay for a lump sum of $10,000 five years from now if you can earn 3% every six months on other similar investments?

P4A.12 Find the present value of each of the following streams of income, assuming a 12% discount rate.

A		B		C	
End of Year	Income	End of Year	Income	End of Year	Income
1	$2,200	1	$10,000	1–5	$10,000/yr
2	$3,000	2–5	$5,000/yr	6–10	$ 8,000/yr
3	$4,000	6	$7,000		
4	$6,000				
5	$8,000				

P4A.13 Consider the streams of income given in the following table.
a. Find the present value of each income stream, using a 1% discount rate., then repeat those calculations using an 8% discount rate.
b. Compare the present values and discuss them in light of the fact that the undiscounted total income amounts to $10,000 in each case.

	Income Stream	
End of Year	A	B
1	$ 4,000	$ 1,000
2	$ 3,000	$ 2,000
3	$ 2,000	$ 3,000
4	$ 1,000	$ 4,000
Total	$10,000	$10,000

P4A.14 For each of the investments below, calculate the present value of the annual end-of-year payments at the specified discount rate over the given period.

Investment	Annual Payments	Discount Rate	Period (yr)
A	$ 1,200	7%	3
B	$ 5,500	12%	15
C	$ 700	20%	9
D	$14,000	5%	7
E	$ 2,200	10%	5

P4A.15 Congratulations! You have won the lottery! Would you rather have $1 million at the end of each of the next 20 years or $15 million today? (Assume an 8% discount rate.)

P4A.16 Using a financial calculator or an Excel spreadsheet, calculate the following.
a. The present value of $500 to be received four years from now, using an 11% discount rate.
b. The present value of the following end-of-year income streams, using a 9% discount rate and assuming it is now the beginning of 2018.

End of Year	Income Stream A	Income Stream B
2018	$80	$140
2019	$80	$120
2020	$80	$100
2021	$80	$ 80
2022	$80	$ 60
2023	$80	$ 40
2024	$80	$ 20

P4A.17 Terri Allessandro has an opportunity to make any of the following investments. The purchase price, the lump-sum future value, and the year of receipt are given below for each investment. Terri can earn a 10% rate of return on investments similar to those currently under consideration. Evaluate each investment to determine whether it is satisfactory and make an investment recommendation to Terri.

Investment	Purchase Price	Future Value	Year of Receipt
A	$18,000	$30,000	5
B	$ 600	$ 3,000	20
C	$ 3,500	$10,000	10
D	$ 1,000	$15,000	40

P4A.18 Kent Weitz wishes to assess whether the following investments are satisfactory. Use his required return (discount rate) of 17% to evaluate each investment. Make an investment recommendation to Kent.

	Investment ($)	
	A	B
Purchase Price	$13,000	$8,500
End of Year	Income Stream	
1	$2,500	$4,000
2	$3,500	$3,500
3	$4,500	$3,000
4	$5,000	$1,000
5	$5,500	$ 500

P4A.19 You purchased a car using some cash and borrowing $15,000 (the present value) for 50 months at 12% per year. Calculate the monthly payment (annuity).

P4A.20 Referring to Problem 4A.19, assume you have made 10 payments. What is the balance (present value) of your loan?

5

Modern Portfolio Concepts

LEARNING GOALS

After studying this chapter, you should be able to:

LG1 Understand portfolio objectives and the procedures used to calculate portfolio return and standard deviation.

LG2 Discuss the concepts of correlation and diversification and the key aspects of international diversification.

LG3 Describe the components of risk and the use of beta to measure risk.

LG4 Explain the capital asset pricing model (CAPM) conceptually, mathematically, and graphically.

LG5 Review the traditional and modern approaches to portfolio management.

LG6 Describe portfolio betas, the risk-return tradeoff, and reconciliation of the two approaches to portfolio management.

nited Rentals Inc. (URI) rents construction and industrial equipment to contractors, businesses, governments, and individuals. The company specializes in heavy equipment such as earth-moving machines and forklifts. During the recession that began in 2007, many companies found that they did not have enough work to do to keep the machines they already owned running, so naturally the demand for rental equipment suffered. URI stock reached a 2007 peak of over $35 per share in May, but after that began a long slide, hitting bottom at $2.52 in March 2009.

That spring, the economy began to show signs of life, and URI stock surged, rising nearly 200% from its low point by August 2009. Heiko Ihle, a stock analyst for the Gabelli & Co. money management firm, issued a "buy" rating on URI despite the fact that the company had high leverage (meaning that it borrowed a lot of money to finance its operations). Ihle noted that URI stock had a high beta, meaning that it moved sharply when the broader market shifted.

Mr. Ihle's recommendation proved to be a good one. From the end of August 2009 to the end of August 2014, the value of URI stock climbed almost 1,200% and was trading above $119 per share. Over that same period of time, the S&P 500 Index, a widely used indicator of the overall stock market, rose by a less dramatic 95%.

In this chapter we continue to explore the tradeoff between risk and return, and we'll see that a stock's beta—its sensitivity to movements in the overall stock market—has a big effect on both the stock's risk and the return that it offers investors.

(Sources: Yahoo! Finance; "U.S. Hot Stocks: Legg Mason, JDA Software Active in Late Trading," July 20, 2009; The Wall Street Journal Digital Network, http://online.wsj.com/article/BT-CO-20090720-713541.html.)

Principles of Portfolio Planning

LG1 LG2 Investors benefit from holding portfolios of investments rather than single investments. Without necessarily sacrificing returns, investors who hold portfolios can reduce risk. Surprisingly, the volatility of a portfolio may be less than the volatilities of the individual assets that make up the portfolio. In other words, when it comes to portfolios and risk, the whole is less than the sum of its parts!

A *portfolio* is a collection of investments assembled to meet one or more investment goals. Of course, different investors have different objectives for their portfolios. The primary goal of a **growth-oriented portfolio** is long-term price appreciation. An **income-oriented portfolio** is designed to produce regular dividends and interest payments.

Portfolio Objectives

Setting portfolio objectives involves definite tradeoffs, such as the tradeoff between risk and return or between potential price appreciation and income. How investors evaluate these tradeoffs will depend on their tax bracket, current income needs, and ability to bear risk. The key point is that portfolio objectives must be established *before* one begins to invest.

The ultimate goal of an investor is an **efficient portfolio**, one that provides the highest return for a given risk level. Efficient portfolios aren't necessarily easy to identify. Investors usually must search out investment alternatives to get the best combinations of risk and return.

Portfolio Return and Standard Deviation

The first step in forming a portfolio is to analyze the characteristics of the securities that an investor might include in the portfolio. Two of the most important characteristics to examine are the returns that each asset might be expected to earn and the uncertainty surrounding that expected return. As a starting point, we will examine historical data to see what returns stocks have earned in the past and how much those returns have fluctuated to get a feel for what the future might hold.

The portfolio return is calculated as a weighted average of returns on the assets (i.e., the investments) that make up the portfolio. You can calculate the portfolio return, r_p, by using Equation 5.1. The portfolio return depends on the returns of each asset in the portfolio and on the fraction invested in each asset, w_j.

Equation 5.1

$$\text{Portfolio Return} = \left(\begin{array}{c} \text{Proportion of} \\ \text{portfolio's total} \\ \text{dollar value} \\ \text{invested in} \\ \text{asset 1} \end{array} \times \begin{array}{c} \text{Return} \\ \text{on asset} \\ 1 \end{array} \right) + \left(\begin{array}{c} \text{Proportion of} \\ \text{portfolio's total} \\ \text{dollar value} \\ \text{invested in} \\ \text{asset 2} \end{array} \times \begin{array}{c} \text{Return} \\ \text{on asset} \\ 2 \end{array} \right) + \cdots +$$

$$\left(\begin{array}{c} \text{Proportion of} \\ \text{portfolio's total} \\ \text{dollar value} \\ \text{invested in} \\ \text{asset } n \end{array} \times \begin{array}{c} \text{Return} \\ \text{on asset} \\ n \end{array} \right) = \sum_{j=1}^{n} \left(\begin{array}{c} \text{Proportion of} \\ \text{portfolio's total} \\ \text{dollar value} \\ \text{invested in} \\ \text{asset } j \end{array} \times \begin{array}{c} \text{Return} \\ \text{on asset} \\ j \end{array} \right)$$

Equation 5.1a

$$r_p = (w_1 \times r_1) + (w_2 \times r_2) + \cdots + (w_n \times r_n) = \sum_{j=1}^{n} (w_j \times r_j)$$

The fraction invested in each asset, w_j, is also known as a portfolio weight because it indicates the weight that each asset receives in the portfolio. Of course, $\sum_{j=1}^{n} w_j = 1$, which means that the sum of the portfolio weights must equal 100%. In other words, when you add up the fractions invested in all of the assets, that sum must equal 1.0.

Panel A of Table 5.1 shows the historical annual returns on two stocks, International Business Machines Corp. (IBM) and Celgene Corp. (CELG), from 2005 through 2014. Over that period, IBM earned an average annual return of 9.0%, which is close to the average annual return on the U.S. stock market during the past century. In contrast, Celgene Corp. earned a spectacular 40.7% average annual return. Although Celgene may not repeat that kind of performance over the next decade, it is still instructive to examine the historical figures.

Excel@Investing

TABLE 5.1 INDIVIDUAL AND PORTFOLIO RETURNS AND STANDARD DEVIATION OF RETURNS FOR INTERNATIONAL BUSINESS MACHINES (IBM) AND CELGENE (CELG)

A. Individual and Portfolio Returns

	(1)		(3)		(4)
	Historical Returns*		Portfolio Weights		Portfolio Return
Year (t)	r_{IBM}	r_{CELG}	$W_{IBM} = 0.86$	$W_{CELG} = 0.14$	r_p
2005	−15.8%	144.3%	$(0.86 \times -15.8\%) + (0.14 \times 144.3\%) =$		6.6%
2006	19.8%	77.5%	$(0.86 \times 19.8\%) + (0.14 \times 77.5\%) =$		27.9%
2007	12.8%	−19.7%	$(0.86 \times 12.8\%) + (0.14 \times -19.7\%) =$		8.3%
2008	−20.8%	19.7%	$(0.86 \times -20.8\%) + (0.14 \times 19.7\%) =$		−15.1%
2009	58.6%	0.7%	$(0.86 \times 58.6\%) + (0.14 \times 0.7\%) =$		50.5%
2010	14.3%	6.2%	$(0.86 \times 14.3\%) + (0.14 \times 6.2\%) =$		13.1%
2011	27.4%	14.3%	$(0.86 \times 27.4\%) + (0.14 \times 14.3\%) =$		25.6%
2012	5.9%	16.1%	$(0.86 \times 5.9\%) + (0.14 \times 16.1\%) =$		7.3%
2013	−0.2%	115.3%	$(0.86 \times -0.2\%) + (0.14 \times 115.3\%) =$		16.0%
2014	−12.4%	32.4%	$(0.86 \times -12.4\%) + (0.14 \times 32.4\%) =$		−6.1%
Average Return	9.0%	40.7%			13.4%

B. Individual and Portfolio Standard Deviations

Standard Deviation Calculation for IBM:

$$s_{IBM} = \sqrt{\frac{\sum_{t=1}^{10}(r_t - \bar{r})^2}{n-1}} = \sqrt{\frac{(-15.8\% - 9.0\%)^2 + \ldots + (-12.4\% - 9.0\%)^2}{10 - 1}} = \sqrt{\frac{5015.4\%^2}{10 - 1}} = 23.6\%$$

Standard Deviation Calculation for CELG:

$$s_{CELG} = \sqrt{\frac{\sum_{t=1}^{10}(r_t - \bar{r})^2}{n-1}} = \sqrt{\frac{(144.3\% - 40.7\%)^2 + \ldots + (32.4\% - 40.7\%)^2}{10 - 1}} = \sqrt{\frac{2,5913.3\%^2}{10 - 1}} = 53.7\%$$

Standard Deviation Calculation for Portfolio:

$$s_p = \sqrt{\frac{\sum_{t=1}^{10}(r_t - \bar{r})^2}{n-1}} = \sqrt{\frac{(6.6\% - 13.4\%)^2 + \ldots + (-6.1\% - 13.4\%)^2}{10 - 1}} = \sqrt{\frac{3045.8\%^2}{10 - 1}} = 18.4\%$$

*Annual rate of return is calculated based on end-of-year closing prices.

Source: End-of-year closing prices are obtained from Yahoo Finance and are adjusted for dividends and stock splits.

Suppose we want to calculate the return on a portfolio containing investments in both IBM and Celgene. The first step in that calculation is to determine how much of each stock to hold. In other words, we must to decide what weight each stock should receive in the portfolio. Let's assume that we want to invest 86% of our money in IBM and 14% in CELG. What kind of return would such a portfolio earn?

We know that over this period, Celgene earned much higher returns than IBM, so intuitively we might expect that a portfolio containing both stocks would earn a return higher than IBM's but lower than Celgene's. Furthermore, because most (i.e., 86%) of the portfolio is invested in IBM, you might guess that the portfolio's return would be closer to IBM's than to Celgene's.

Columns 3 and 4 in Panel A show the portfolio's return each year. The average annual return on this portfolio was 13.4% and as expected it is higher than the return on IBM and lower than the return on Celgene. By investing a little in Celgene, an investor could earn a higher return than would be possible by holding IBM stock in isolation.

What about the portfolio's risk? To examine the risk of this portfolio, start by measuring the risk of the stocks in the portfolio. Recall that one measure of an investment's risk is the standard deviation of its returns. Panel B of Table 5.1 applies the formula for standard deviation that we introduced earlier to calculate the standard deviation of returns on IBM and Celgene stock. Or, if you prefer, rather than using the formulas in Table 5.1 to find the standard deviation of returns for IBM and CELG, you can construct an Excel spreadsheet to do the calculations, as shown below. The standard deviation of IBM's returns is 23.6%, and for Celgene's stock returns the standard deviation is 53.7%. Here again we see evidence of the tradeoff between risk and return. Celgene's stock earned much higher returns than IBM's stock, but Celgene returns fluctuate a great deal more as well.

	A	B	C	D
1	STANDARD DEVIATION OF RETURNS FOR IBM, CELG, AND PORTFOLIO			
2	Year (t)	r_{IBM}	r_{CELG}	r_p
3	2005	-15.8%	144.3%	6.6%
4	2006	19.8%	77.5%	27.9%
5	2007	12.8%	-19.7%	8.3%
6	2008	-20.8%	19.7%	-15.1%
7	2009	58.6%	0.7%	50.5%
8	2010	14.3%	6.2%	13.1%
9	2011	27.4%	14.3%	25.6%
10	2012	5.9%	16.1%	7.3%
11	2013	-0.2%	115.3%	16.0%
12	2014	-12.4%	32.4%	-6.1%
13	Standard deviation	23.6%	53.7%	18.4%
14	Entries in Cells B13, C13, and D13 are =STDEV(B3:B12), =STDEV(C3:C12), and			
15	=STDEV(D3:D12), respectively.			

Because Celgene's returns are more volatile than IBM's, you might expect that a portfolio containing both stocks would have a standard deviation that is higher than IBM's but lower than Celgene's. In fact, that's not what happens. The final calculation in Panel B inserts the IBM-Celgene portfolio return data from column 4 in Panel A into the standard deviation formula to calculate the portfolio's standard deviation. Panel B shows the surprising result that the portfolio's returns are less volatile than are the returns of either stock in the portfolio! The portfolio's standard deviation is just 18.4%. This is great news for investors. An investor who held only IBM shares would have earned an average return of only 9.0%, but to achieve that return the investor would have had to endure IBM's 23.6% standard deviation. By selling a few IBM shares and using the proceeds to buy a few Celgene shares (resulting in the 0.86 and 0.14 portfolio weights shown in Table 5.1), an investor could have simultaneously increased his or her return to 13.4% and reduced the standard deviation to 18.4%. In other words, the investor could have had more return and less risk at the same time. This means that an investor who owns nothing but IBM shares holds an inefficient portfolio—an alternative portfolio exists that has a better return-to-risk tradeoff. That's the power of diversification. Next, we will see that the key factor in making this possible is a low correlation between IBM and Celgene returns.

Correlation and Diversification

Diversification involves the inclusion of a number of different investments in a portfolio, and it is an important aspect of creating an efficient portfolio. Underlying the intuitive appeal of diversification is the statistical concept of correlation. Effective portfolio planning requires an understanding of how correlation and diversification influence a portfolio's risk.

Correlation   **Correlation** is a statistical measure of the relationship between two series of numbers. If two series tend to move in the same direction, they are **positively correlated**. For instance, if each day we record the number of hours of sunshine and the average daily temperature, we would expect those two series to display positive correlation. Days with more sunshine tend to be days with higher temperatures. If the series tend to move in opposite directions, they are **negatively correlated**. For example, if each day we record the number of hours of sunshine and the amount of rainfall, we would expect those two series to display negative correlation because, on average, rainfall is lower on days with lots of sunshine. Finally, if two series bear no relationship to each other, then they are **uncorrelated**. For example, we would probably expect no correlation between the number of hours of sunshine on a particular day and the change in the value of the U.S. dollar against other world currencies on the same day. There is no obvious connection between sunshine and world currency markets.

The degree of correlation—whether positive or negative—is measured by the **correlation coefficient**, which is usually represented by the Greek symbol rho (ρ). It's easy to use Excel to calculate the correlation coefficient between IBM and Celgene stock returns, as shown in the following spreadsheet.

	A	B	C
1	CORRELATION COEFFICIENT OF RETURNS FOR IBM AND CELG		
2	Year (t)	r_{IBM}	r_{CELG}
3	2005	-15.8%	144.3%
4	2006	19.8%	77.5%
5	2007	12.8%	-19.7%
6	2008	-20.8%	19.7%
7	2009	58.6%	0.7%
8	2010	14.3%	6.2%
9	2011	27.4%	14.3%
10	2012	5.9%	16.1%
11	2013	-0.2%	115.3%
12	2014	-12.4%	32.4%
13		Correlation coefficient	-0.43
14		Entry in Cell B13 is	
15		=CORREL(B3:B12,C3:C12).	

Excel will quickly tell you that the correlation coefficient between IBM and Celgene during the 2005–2014 period was −0.43. The negative figure means that there was a tendency over this period for the two stocks to move in opposite directions. In other words, years in which IBM's return was better than average tended to be years in which Celgene's return was worse than average, and vice versa. A negative correlation between two stocks is somewhat unusual because most stocks are affected in the same way by large, macroeconomic forces. In other words, most stocks tend to move in the same direction as the overall economy, which means that most stocks will display at least some positive correlation with each other.

Because IBM is a major provider of information technology services and Celgene is a biopharmaceutical manufacturer, it is not too surprising that the correlation between these two stocks is not strongly positive. The companies compete in entirely different industries, have different customers and suppliers, and operate within very different regulatory constraints; however, the relatively large (i.e., −0.43) magnitude of their negative correlation raises concerns and should cause us to question the validity of basing investment decisions on this correlation measure. Perhaps the sample period we are using to estimate this correlation is too short or is not truly representative of the investment performance of these two stocks. The 2005 to 2014 period that we are focusing on consists of just 10 yearly return observations, and during this particular period there were no fewer than three strong systematic market-wide events (i.e., a financial crisis, a Great Recession, and an economic recovery). Those sharp macroeconomic fluctuations tended to drive most securities' returns up and down at the same time, which in turn leads to a positive correlation between most pairs of stocks, even when those stocks are drawn from different industries. Ten yearly observations is without question a small sample size, and it may be too small, at least in this case, to accurately capture a meaningful measure of correlation between IBM and Celgene. One way to address this concern is to increase the period of time over which the correlation is being measured and in this way increase the number of yearly observations. Alternatively, one could use monthly returns over the same 10-year period, thereby increasing the number of observations by a factor of 12.

For any pair of investments that we might want to study, the correlation coefficient ranges from +1.0 for **perfectly positively correlated** series to −1.0 for **perfectly negatively correlated** series. Figure 5.1 illustrates these two extremes for two pairs of

What's the Correlation?

FIGURE 5.1

The Correlations of Returns between Investments M and P and Investments M and N.

Investments M and P produce returns that are perfectly positively correlated and move exactly together. On the other hand, returns on investments M and N move in exactly opposite directions and are perfectly negatively correlated. In most cases, the correlation between any two investments will fall between these two extremes.

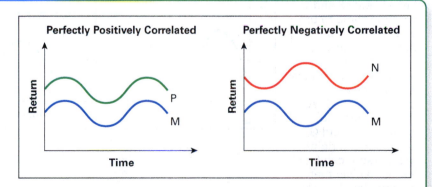

investments: M and P, and M and N. M and P represent the returns on two investments that move perfectly in sync, so they are perfectly positively correlated. In the real world it is extremely rare to find two investments that are perfectly correlated like this, but you could think of M and P as representing two companies that operate in the same industry, or even two mutual funds that invest in the same types of stocks. In contrast, returns on investments M and N move in exactly opposite directions and are perfectly negatively correlated. While these two extreme cases can be illustrative, the correlations between most asset returns exhibit some degree (ranging from high to low) of positive correlation. Negative correlation is the exception.

Diversification   As a general rule, the lower the correlation between any two assets, the greater the risk reduction that investors can achieve by combining those assets in a portfolio. Figure 5.2 shows negatively correlated assets F and G, both having the same average return, $\bar{r}$. The portfolio that contains both F and G has the same return, $\bar{r}$, but has less risk (variability) than either of the individual assets because some of the fluctuations in asset F cancel out fluctuations in G. As a result, the combination of F and G is less volatile than either F or G alone. Even if assets are not negatively correlated, the lower the positive correlation between them, the lower the resulting risk.

Table 5.2 shows the average return and the standard deviation of returns for many combinations of IBM and Celgene stock. Columns 1 and 2 show the percentage of the portfolio invested in IBM and Celgene, respectively, and columns 3 and 4 show the portfolio average return and standard deviation. Notice that as you move from the top of the table to the bottom (i.e., from investing the entire portfolio in IBM to investing all of it in Celgene), the portfolio return goes up. That makes sense because as you move from top to bottom, the percentage invested in Celgene increases, and Celgene's average return is higher than IBM's. The general conclusion from column 3 is that when a portfolio contains two stocks, with one having a higher average return than the other, the portfolio's return rises the more you invest in the stock with the higher return.

FIGURE 5.2

Combining Negatively Correlated Assets to Diversify Risk

Investments F and G earn the same return on average, $\bar{r}$, but they are negatively correlated, so movements in F sometimes partially offset movements in G. As a result, a portfolio containing F and G (shown in the rightmost graph) exhibits less variability than the individual assets display on their own while earning the same return.

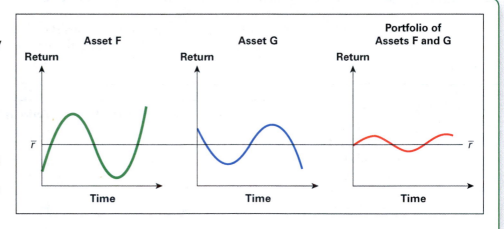

Excel@Investing

TABLE 5.2 PORTFOLIO RETURNS AND STANDARD DEVIATIONS FOR INTERNATIONAL BUSINESS MACHINES (IBM) AND CELGENE (CELG)

(1)		(3)		(4)
Portfolio Weights		**Portfolio Return**		**Portfolio Standard Deviation**
W_{IBM}	W_{CELG}	$\overline{r}_{IBM} = 9.0\%$	$\overline{r}_{CELG} = 40.7\%$	
1.0	0.0	$(1.0 \times 9.0\%) + (0.0 \times 40.7\%) = 9.0\%$		23.6%
0.9	0.1	$(0.9 \times 9.0\%) + (0.1 \times 40.7\%) = 12.1\%$		19.6%
0.8	0.2	$(0.8 \times 9.0\%) + (0.2 \times 40.7\%) = 15.3\%$		17.3%
0.7	0.3	$(0.7 \times 9.0\%) + (0.3 \times 40.7\%) = 18.5\%$		17.5%
0.6	0.4	$(0.6 \times 9.0\%) + (0.4 \times 40.7\%) = 21.7\%$		20.0%
0.5	0.5	$(0.5 \times 9.0\%) + (0.5 \times 40.7\%) = 24.8\%$		24.3%
0.4	0.6	$(0.4 \times 9.0\%) + (0.6 \times 40.7\%) = 28.0\%$		29.4%
0.3	0.7	$(0.3 \times 9.0\%) + (0.7 \times 40.7\%) = 31.2\%$		35.1%
0.2	0.8	$(0.2 \times 9.0\%) + (0.8 \times 40.7\%) = 34.3\%$		41.1%
0.1	0.9	$(0.1 \times 9.0\%) + (0.9 \times 40.7\%) = 37.5\%$		47.3%
0.0	1.0	$(0.0 \times 9.0\%) + (1.0 \times 40.7\%) = 40.7\%$		53.7%

Example: Calculation of the Standard Deviation for the Equally Weighted Portfolio

$s_{IBM} = 23.6\%$

$s_{CELG} = 53.7\%$

$\rho_{IBM,\,CELG} = -0.43$

$s_p = \sqrt{w_i^2 s_i^2 + w_j^2 s_j^2 + 2w_i w_j \rho_{i,j} s_i s_j}$

$s_p = \sqrt{0.5^2 \times 23.6\%^2 + 0.5^2 \times 53.7\%^2 + 2(0.5 \times 0.5 \times -0.43 \times 23.6\% \times 53.7\%)} = 24.3\%$

Column 4 shows the standard deviation of returns for different portfolios of IBM and Celgene. Here again we see a surprising result. A portfolio invested entirely in IBM has a standard deviation of 23.6%. Intuitively, it might seem that reducing the investment in IBM slightly and increasing the investment in Celgene would increase the portfolio's standard deviation because Celgene stock is so much more volatile than IBM stock. However, the opposite is true, at least up to a point. The portfolio standard deviation initially falls as the percentage invested in Celgene rises. Eventually, however, increasing the amount invested in Celgene does increase the portfolio's standard deviation. So the general conclusion from column 4 is that when a portfolio contains two stocks, with one having a higher standard deviation than the other, the portfolio's standard deviation may rise or fall the more you invest in the stock with the higher standard deviation.

Figure 5.3 illustrates the two lessons emerging from Table 5.2. The curve plots the return (*y*-axis) and standard deviation (*x*-axis) for each portfolio listed in Table 5.2. As the portfolio composition moves from 100% IBM to a mix of IBM and Celgene, the portfolio return rises, but the standard deviation initially falls. Therefore, portfolios of IBM and Celgene trace out a backward-bending arc. Clearly no investor should place all of his or her money in IBM because the investor could earn a higher return with a lower standard deviation by holding at least some stock in Celgene. However, investors who want to earn the highest possible returns, and who therefore will invest heavily in Celgene, have to accept a higher standard deviation.

FIGURE 5.3

Portfolios of IBM and Celgene

Because the returns of IBM and Celgene are not highly correlated, investors who hold only IBM shares can simultaneously increase the portfolio return and reduce its standard deviation by holding at least some Celgene shares. At some point, however, investing more in Celgene does increase the portfolio volatility while also increasing its expected return.

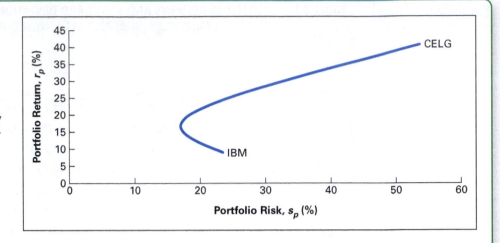

Excel@Investing

The relationship between IBM and Celgene is obviously a special case, so let's look at the more general patterns that investors encounter in the markets. Table 5.3 presents the projected returns from three assets—X, Y, and Z—in each of the next five years (2018–2022). Table 5.3 also shows the average return that we expect each asset to earn over the five-year period and the standard deviation of each asset's returns. Asset X has an average return of 12% and a standard deviation of 3.2%. Assets Y and Z each have an average return of 16% and a standard deviation of 6.3%. Thus, we can view asset X as having a low-return, low-risk profile while assets Y and Z are high-return, high-risk stocks. The returns of assets X and Y are perfectly negatively correlated—they move in exactly opposite directions over time. The returns of assets X and Z are perfectly positively correlated—they move in precisely the same direction.

Portfolio XY (shown in Table 5.3) is constructed by investing $\frac{2}{3}$ in asset X and $\frac{1}{3}$ in asset Y. The average return on this portfolio, 13.3%, is a weighted average of the average returns of assets X and Y $\left(\frac{2}{3} \times 12\% + \frac{1}{3} \times 16\%\right)$. To calculate the portfolio's standard deviation, use the equation shown in Table 5.2 with a value of −1.0 for the correlation between X and Y. Notice that portfolio XY generates a predictable 13.3% return every year. In other words, the portfolio is risk-free and has a standard deviation of 0.

Now consider portfolio XZ, which is created by investing $\frac{2}{3}$ in asset X and $\frac{1}{3}$ in asset Z. Like portfolio XY, portfolio XZ has an expected return of 13.3%. Notice, however, that portfolio XZ does not provide a risk-free return. Its return fluctuates from year to year, and its standard deviation is 4.2%.

To summarize, the two portfolios, XY and XZ, have identical average returns, but they differ in terms of risk. The reason for that difference is correlation. Movements in X are offset by movements in Y, so by combining the two assets in a portfolio, the investor can reduce or eliminate risk. Assets X

TABLE 5.3   EXPECTED RETURNS AND STANDARD DEVIATIONS FOR ASSETS X, Y, AND Z AND PORTFOLIOS XY AND XZ

Year (t)	Asset's Projected Returns			Portfolio's Projected Returns	
				$E(r_{xy})$	$E(r_{xz})$
	$E(r_X)$	$E(r_Y)$	$E(r_Z)$	$[2/3 \times E(r_X) + 1/3 \times E(r_Y)]$	$[2/3 \times E(r_X) + 1/3 \times E(r_Z)]$
2018	8.0%	24.0%	8.0%	13.3%	8.0%
2019	10.0%	20.0%	12.0%	13.3%	10.7%
2020	12.0%	16.0%	16.0%	13.3%	13.3%
2021	14.0%	12.0%	20.0%	13.3%	16.0%
2022	16.0%	8.0%	24.0%	13.3%	18.7%
Average Return	12.0%	16.0%	16.0%	13.3%	13.3%
Standard Deviation	3.2%	6.3%	6.3%	0.0%	4.2%

Excel@Investing

and Z move together, so movements in one cannot offset movements in the other, and the standard deviation of portfolio XZ cannot be reduced below the standard deviation of asset X.

Figure 5.4 illustrates how the relation between a portfolio's expected return and standard deviation depends on the correlation between the assets in the portfolio. The black line illustrates a case like portfolio XY where the correlation coefficient is −1.0. In that case, it is possible to combine two risky assets in just the right proportions so that the portfolio return is completely predictable (i.e., has no risk). Notice that in this situation, it would be very unwise for an investor to hold an undiversified position in the least risky asset. By holding a portfolio of assets rather than just one, the investor moves up and to the left along the black line to earn a higher return while taking less risk. Beyond some point, however, increasing the investment in the more risky asset pushes both the portfolio return and risk higher, so the investor's portfolio moves up and to the right along the second segment of the black line.

The red line in Figure 5.4 illustrates a situation like portfolio XZ in which the correlation coefficient is +1.0. In that instance, when an investor decreases his or her investment in the low-risk asset to hold more of the high-risk asset, the portfolio's expected return rises, but so does its standard deviation. The investor moves up and to

FIGURE 5.4

Risk and Return for Combinations of Two Assets with Various Correlation Coefficients

This graph illustrates how a low-return, low-risk asset can be combined with a high-return, high-risk asset in a portfolio, and how the performance of that portfolio depends on the correlation between the two assets. In general, as an investor shifts the portfolio weight from the low-return to the high-return investment, the portfolio return will rise. But the portfolio's standard deviation may rise or fall depending on the correlation. In general, the lower the correlation, the greater the risk reduction that can be achieved through diversification.

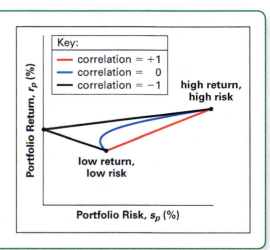

the right along the red line. An investor might choose to invest in both assets, but making that decision is a matter of one's risk tolerance, and not all investors will make that choice. In other words, when the correlation between two assets is −1.0, diversifying is definitely the right move, but when the correlation is +1.0, whether to diversify or not is less obvious.

The blue line in Figure 5.4 illustrates an intermediate case in which the correlation coefficient is between −1.0 and +1.0. This is what investors encounter in real markets most of the time—assets are neither perfectly negatively correlated nor perfectly positively correlated. When the correlation coefficient is between the extremes, portfolios of two assets lie along an arc (i.e., the blue line). When two assets have very low correlation, that arc may bend back upon itself, as was the case with IBM and Celgene. When the correlation is higher, but still below 1.0, the arc merely curves up and to the right. Even then, the benefits of diversification are better than when the correlation is 1.0, meaning that portfolios along the blue arc earn higher returns for the same risk compared to portfolios along the red line.

International Diversification

Diversification is clearly a primary consideration when constructing an investment portfolio. As noted earlier, many opportunities for international diversification are now available. Here we consider three aspects of international diversification: effectiveness, methods, and costs.

INVESTOR FACTS

Culture and Correlation In finance we usually think about economic factors that cause the returns of different stocks to be more or less correlated. But a recent study suggests cultural influences matter too. In some cultures, behavioral norms are stronger and society's tolerance for deviations in those norms tends to be low. Researchers found that in these countries, stock returns were more highly correlated than those in countries with less rigid social norms. The study's authors suggest that in "tighter" cultures, investors are more likely to buy or sell the same stocks at the same time, and that leads to highly correlated stock returns.

(Source: Cheol S. Eun, Lingling Wang, and Steven C. Xiao, "Culture and R²," *Journal of Financial Economics*, 2015, Vol. 115, pp. 283–303.)

Effectiveness of International Diversification Investing internationally offers greater diversification than investing only domestically. That is true for U.S. investors as well as for investors in countries with capital markets that offer much more limited diversification opportunities than are available in the United States. Broadly speaking, the diversification benefits from investing internationally come from two sources. The first source is that returns in different markets around the world do not move exactly in sync. In other words, the correlation between markets is less than +1.0. As you have already seen, the lower the correlation is between investments, the larger are the benefits from diversification. Unfortunately, as globalization has brought about greater integration of markets (both financial markets and markets for goods and services) around the world, the correlation in returns across national markets has risen. This trend reduces the benefit of international diversification.

However, the second source of the benefits of international diversification has been on the rise for many years. Over time, the number of stock markets around the world has been increasing. For example, at the beginning of the 20th century fewer than 40 countries in the world had active stock markets, but by the end of the century the number of stock markets had more than doubled. Just as someone who invests only in domestic stocks will generally have a more diversified portfolio if there are more stocks in the portfolio, so it is for investors who can diversify across many stock markets around the world rather than just a few.

On net, there is little question that it benefits investors to diversify internationally, even if the rising correlation across markets (especially the larger, more developed markets) limits these benefits to an extent. Next, we discuss how investors can access international markets to diversify their portfolios.

Methods of International Diversification Later in this text we will examine a wide range of alternatives for international portfolio diversification. We will see that investors can make investments in bonds and other debt instruments in U.S. dollars or in foreign currencies—either directly or via foreign mutual funds. Foreign currency investment, however, brings currency exchange risk. Investors can hedge this risk with contracts such as currency forwards, futures, and options. Even if there is little or no currency exchange risk, investing abroad is generally less convenient, more expensive, and riskier than investing domestically. When making direct investments abroad, you must know what you're doing. You should have a clear idea of the benefits being sought and enough time to monitor foreign markets.

U.S. investors can capture at least some of the benefits of international diversification without having to send money abroad. Investors can buy stock of foreign companies listed on U.S. exchanges. Many foreign issuers, both corporate and government, sell their bonds (called *Yankee bonds*) in the United States. The stocks of more than 2,000 foreign companies, from more than 60 countries, trade in the United States in the form of American depositary shares (ADSs). Finally, international mutual funds provide foreign investment opportunities.

You might wonder whether it is possible to achieve the benefits of international diversification by investing in a portfolio of U.S.-based multinational corporations. The answer is yes and no. Yes, a portfolio of U.S. multinationals is more diversified than a portfolio of wholly domestic firms. Multinationals generate revenues, costs, and profits in many markets and currencies, so when one part of the world is doing poorly, another part may be doing well.

Investors who invest only in U.S.-based multinationals will still not enjoy the full benefits of international diversification. That's because a disproportionate share of the revenues and costs generated by these firms *is* still in the United States. Thus, to fully realize the benefits of international diversification, it is necessary to invest in firms located outside the United States.

Costs of International Diversification You can find greater returns overseas than in the United States, and you can reduce a portfolio's risk by including foreign investments. Still, you should not jump to the conclusion that it is wise to invest all of your money in overseas assets. A successful global investment strategy depends on many things, just as a purely domestic strategy does. The percentage of your portfolio that you should allocate to foreign investments depends on your overall investment goals and risk preferences. Many investment advisers suggest allocations to foreign investments of about 20% to 30%, with two-thirds of this allocation in established foreign markets and the other one-third in emerging markets.

In general, investing directly in foreign-currency-denominated instruments is very costly. Unless you have hundreds of thousands of dollars to invest, the transaction costs of buying securities directly on foreign markets will tend to be high. A less costly approach to international diversification is to invest in international mutual funds, which offer diversified foreign investments and the professional expertise of fund managers. You could also purchase ADSs to make foreign investments in individual stocks. With either mutual funds or ADSs, you can obtain international diversification along with low cost, convenience, transactions in U.S. dollars, and protection under U.S. security laws.

5.1   What is an efficient portfolio, and what role should such a portfolio play in investing?

5.2   How do you calculate the return and standard deviation of a portfolio? Compare the calculation of a portfolio's standard deviation to that for a single asset.

5.3   What is correlation, and why is it important with respect to portfolio returns? Describe the characteristics of returns that are (a) positively correlated, (b) negatively correlated, and (c) uncorrelated. Differentiate between perfect positive correlation and perfect negative correlation.

5.4   What is diversification? How does the diversification of risk affect the risk of the portfolio compared to the risk of the individual assets it contains?

5.5   Discuss how the correlation between asset returns affects the risk and return behavior of the resulting portfolio. Describe the potential range of risk and return when the correlation between two assets is (a) perfectly positive, (b) uncorrelated, and (c) perfectly negative.

5.6   What benefit, if any, does international diversification offer the individual investor? Compare and contrast the methods of achieving international diversification by investing abroad versus investing domestically.

The Capital Asset Pricing Model

LG3 LG4   Intuitively we would expect that any risky investment should offer a return that exceeds what investors can earn on a risk-free investment. In other words, the return that investors expect to earn on a risky asset equals the risk-free rate plus a risk premium. But what determines the magnitude of the risk premium? In the previous section we learned that investors can reduce or eliminate many types of risk simply by diversifying their portfolios, a process that is neither particularly time consuming nor expensive. However, diversification can't eliminate risk entirely. Therefore, from an investor's perspective, the most worrisome risk is *undiversifiable risk*—the risk that can't be eliminated through diversification. The more undiversifiable risk that a particular investment entails, the higher the risk premium it must offer to attract investors.

That logic provides the underpinning for a theory that links return and risk for all assets. The theory is called the *capital asset pricing model*, or the *CAPM*. The CAPM says that the expected return on a risky asset equals the risk-free rate plus a risk premium, and the risk premium depends on how much of the asset's risk is undiversifiable. In this section, we introduce the concept of undiversifiable risk, and we explain how the CAPM quantifies that risk and links it to investment returns.

Components of Risk

The risk of an investment consists of two components: diversifiable and undiversifiable risk. **Diversifiable risk,** sometimes called **unsystematic risk,** results from factors that are firm-specific, such as whether a new product succeeds or fails, the performance of senior managers, or a firm's relationships with its customers and suppliers. Unsystematic risk is the portion of an investment's risk that can be eliminated through diversification. **Undiversifiable risk,** also called **systematic risk** or **market risk,** is the inescapable portion of an investment's risk. In other words, it's the risk that remains even if a portfolio is well diversified. Systematic risk is associated with broad forces such as economic growth, inflation, interest rates, and political events that affect all investments and therefore are not unique to any single investment. The sum of undiversifiable risk and diversifiable risk is called **total risk.**

Equation 5.2

Total risk = Diversifiable risk + Undiversifiable risk

Any careful investor can reduce or virtually eliminate diversifiable risk by holding a diversified portfolio of securities. Studies have shown that investors can eliminate most diversifiable risk by carefully selecting a portfolio of as few as two or three dozen securities, and most investors hold many more securities than that through investments such as mutual funds and pension funds. Because it is relatively easy to eliminate unsystematic risk through diversification, there is no reason for investors to expect a reward (i.e., higher returns) for bearing this kind of risk. Investors who fail to diversify are simply bearing more risk than they have to without getting a reward for doing so.

But no matter how many securities are in a portfolio, some systematic risk will remain. Remember, undiversifiable risk refers to the broad forces that tend to affect most stocks simultaneously, such as whether the economy is booming or in recession. Some stocks are more sensitive to these forces than others. For example, companies that produce luxury goods tend to do very well when the economy is surging, but when a recession hits, these companies struggle to find customers. On the other hand, some stocks are relatively insulated from swings in the business cycle. Companies that produce food and other basic necessities do not see their revenues and profits rise and fall sharply with the ups and downs of the economy.

This discussion implies that systematic risk varies from one stock to another, and stocks with greater systematic risk must offer higher returns to attract investors. To identify these stocks, we need a way to measure the undiversifiable risk associated with any particular stock. The CAPM provides just such a measure called the stock's *beta*.

Beta: A Measure of Undiversifiable Risk

During the past 50 years, the finance discipline has developed much theory on the measurement of risk and its use in assessing returns. The two key components of this theory are beta, which is a measure of systematic risk, and the capital asset pricing model, which links an investment's beta to its return.

First we will look at **beta,** a number that quantifies undiversifiable risk. A security's beta indicates how the security's return responds to fluctuations in market returns, which is why market risk is synonymous with undiversifiable risk. The more sensitive the return of a security is to changes in market returns, the higher that security's beta. When we speak of returns on the overall market, what we have in mind is something like the return on a broad portfolio of stocks or on a stock index. Analysts commonly use changes in the value of the Standard & Poor's 500 Index or some other broad stock index to measure market returns. To calculate a security's beta, you gather historical returns on the security and on the overall market to see how they relate to each other. You don't have to calculate betas yourself; you can easily obtain them for actively traded securities from a variety of published and online sources. But you should understand how betas are derived, how to interpret them, and how to apply them to portfolios.

Deriving Beta We can demonstrate graphically the relationship between a security's return and the market return. Figure 5.5 plots the relationship between the returns of two securities, United Parcel Service, Inc. (UPS) and FedEx Corporation (FDX), and the market return measured as the return on the S&P 500 (GSPC). The return data necessary to plot the relationships shown in Figure 5.5 are easily obtained from numerous online financial websites. In this case, we obtained historical closing prices from Yahoo! Finance by entering the security ticker symbols and downloading the end-of-year historical prices to a spreadsheet. In a spreadsheet, we used the end-of-year

FIGURE 5.5

Graphical Derivation of Beta for Securities C and D

Betas can be derived graphically by plotting the coordinates for the market return and security return at various points in time and using statistical techniques to fit the "characteristic line" to the data points. The slope of the characteristic line is beta. For FedEx the beta is about 1.12, and for UPS the beta is about 0.76.

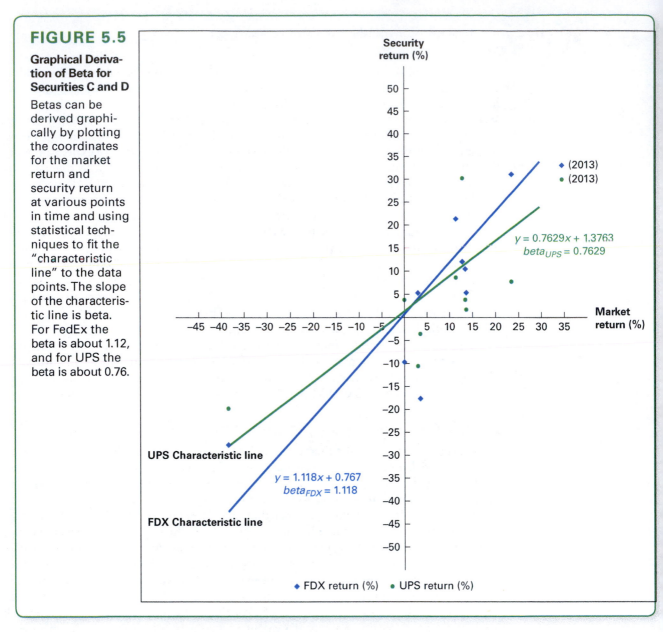

security prices to calculate the following annual returns (in the case of the S&P 500, we calculated annual returns based on the index level):

	A	B	C	D	E	F	G
1	Year	December month-ending index level	S&P 500 return	December month-ending price	UPS return	December month-ending price	FDX return
2	2004	1211.9		$64.93		$93.50	
3	2005	1248.3	3.0%	$58.10	-10.5%	$98.49	5.3%
4	2006	1418.3	13.6%	$59.12	1.8%	$103.80	5.4%
5	2007	1468.4	3.5%	$57.05	-3.5%	$85.53	-17.6%
6	2008	903.3	-38.5%	$45.79	-19.7%	$61.86	-27.7%
7	2009	1115.1	23.5%	$49.35	7.8%	$81.12	31.1%
8	2010	1257.6	12.8%	$64.28	30.3%	$90.92	12.1%
9	2011	1257.6	0.0%	$66.75	3.8%	$82.14	-9.7%
10	2012	1426.2	13.4%	$69.32	3.9%	$90.79	10.5%
11	2013	1848.4	29.6%	$101.57	46.5%	$143.06	57.6%
12	2014	2058.9	11.4%	$110.38	8.7%	$173.66	21.4%

We calculated annual returns by dividing the current year-end price by the previous year-end price and subtracting 1. (Note: the prices we are using here have been adjusted in a way that accounts for dividends, meaning that the percentage price change includes both the stock's capital gain or loss as well as its dividend payments.) For example, the annual return of 30.3% for UPS in 2010 is ($64.28 ÷ $49.35) − 1. Notice that we are simply letting the previous year's closing price be the present value, the current year's closing price be the future value, the one-year time interval be the number of periods, and then solving for the interest rate.

In Figure 5.5 we plot coordinates showing the annual return on each stock (on the *y*-axis) and the S&P 500 (on the *x*-axis) in each year. Each green circle shows the return earned by UPS and the S&P 500 in a particular year, and each blue diamond shows the return on FedEx and the S&P 500 in a particular year. For example, the blue diamond and the green circle diamond in the upper right quadrant of the figure show that in 2013 FedEx earned a return of about 60%, UPS earned a return of roughly 45%, and the overall market's return was about 30% (you can verify these numbers in the previous table).

With the data points plotted, we used Excel to insert a trendline (also called the *characteristic line*) that best fit the coordinates for each stock. The green line in Figure 5.5 goes through the middle of the green circles (the coordinates for UPS and S&P 500 returns), so it shows the general relation between the return on the S&P 500 and the return on UPS. Similarly, the blue line is the line that best fits the blue diamonds (the coordinates for FedEx and S&P 500 returns), and it shows the relation between FedEx and S&P 500 returns. Remember that the equation for any straight line takes the form $y = mx + b$, where m represents the slope of the line, or the relation between x and y. Figure 5.5 shows the equation for each trendline, and the slope for each line is the beta for that stock. For UPS, the equation for the characteristic line is $y = 0.7629x + 1.3763$, so the beta of UPS stock is 0.7639. The beta for FedEx is higher at 1.118. Because FedEx has a higher beta than UPS, we would say that FedEx stock is more sensitive to movements in the overall market. This also means that FedEx has more systematic risk, so overall we conclude the FedEx is a riskier investment than UPS.

Interpreting Beta By definition, the beta for the overall market is equal to 1.0 (i.e., the market moves in a one-to-one relationship with itself). That also implies that the beta of the "average" stock is 1.0. All other betas are viewed in relation to this value. Table 5.4 shows some selected beta values and their associated interpretations. As you can see, an investment's beta can, in principle, be positive or negative, although nearly all investments have positive betas. The positive or negative sign preceding the beta number merely indicates whether the stock's return moves in the same direction as the general market (*positive beta*) or in the opposite direction (*negative beta*).

TABLE 5.4   SELECTED BETAS AND ASSOCIATED INTERPRETATIONS

Beta	Comment	Interpretation
2.0	Move in same direction as the market	Twice as responsive as the market
1.0		Same response as the market
0.5		One half as responsive as the market
0.0		Unaffected by market movement
−0.5	Move in opposite direction of the market	One-half as responsive as the market
−1.0		Same response as the market
−2.0		Twice as responsive as the market

Most stocks have betas that fall between 0.50 and 1.75. The return of a stock that is half as responsive as the market ($b = 0.5$) will, on average, change by ½ of 1% for each 1% change in the return of the market portfolio. A stock that is twice as responsive as the market ($b = 2$) will, on average, experience a 2% change in its return for each 1% change in the return of the market portfolio. Listed here, for illustration purposes, are the actual betas for some popular stocks, as reported on Yahoo! Finance on February 27, 2015:

Stock	Beta	Stock	Beta
Amazon.com Inc.	1.27	Int'l Business Machines Corp.	0.88
Molson Coors Brewing Co.	1.45	Goldman Sachs Inc.	1.64
Bank of America Corp.	1.33	Microsoft Corp.	0.79
Procter & Gamble Co.	0.93	Nike Inc.	0.51
Walt Disney Co.	1.02	Celgene Corp.	1.84
eBay Inc.	0.82	Qualcomm Inc.	1.2
ExxonMobil Corp.	1.16	Sempra Energy	0.39
The Gap Inc.	1.63	Walmart Stores Inc.	0.29
Ford Motor Co.	0.76	Xerox Corp.	1.34
INTEL Corp.	0.95	YAHOO! Inc.	1.27

How to Estimate a Beta

Applying Beta Individual investors will find beta useful. It can help in assessing the risk of a particular investment and in understanding the impact the market can have on the return expected from a share of stock. In short, beta reveals how a security responds to market forces. For example, if the market is expected to experience a 10% increase in its rate of return over the next period, we would expect a stock with a beta of 1.5 to experience an increase in return of about 15% ($1.5 \times 10\%$).

For stocks with positive betas, increases in market returns result in increases in security returns. Unfortunately, decreases in market returns are translated into decreasing security returns. In the preceding example, if the market is expected to experience a 10% decrease in its rate of return, then a stock with a beta of 1.5 should experience a 15% decrease in its return. Because the stock has a beta greater than 1.0, it is riskier than an average stock and will tend to experience dramatic swings when the overall market moves.

Stocks that have betas less than 1.0 are, of course, less responsive to changing returns in the market and are therefore less risky. For example, a stock with a beta of 0.50 will increase or decrease its return by about half that of the market as a whole. Thus, if the market return went down by 8%, such a stock's return would probably experience only about a 4% ($0.50 \times 8\%$) decline.

Here are some important points to remember about beta:

- Beta measures the undiversifiable (or market) risk of a security.

- The beta for the market as a whole, and for the average stock, is 1.0.

- In theory, stocks may have positive or negative betas, but most stocks have positive betas.

- Stocks with betas greater than 1.0 are more responsive than average to market fluctuations and therefore are more risky than average. Stocks with betas less than 1.0 are less risky than the average stock.

FAMOUS FAILURES IN FINANCE

Bulging Betas

Ford Motor Company has always been considered a cyclical stock whose fortunes rise and fall with the state of the economy. Ford's beta was as high as 2.80 during the financial crisis, which hit auto manufacturers particularly hard and resulted in the bankruptcy of Ford's major competitor, General Motors. Bank of America, another firm in an industry hit hard by the recession, had a beta of 1.96 during the crisis, indicating that it too was extremely sensitive to movements in the overall economy. Notice that both Ford and Bank of America have lower betas now than they did during the last recession.

The CAPM: Using Beta to Estimate Return

Intuitively, we expect riskier investments to provide higher returns than less risky investments. If beta measures the risk of a stock, then stocks with higher betas should earn higher returns, on average, than stocks with lower betas. About 50 years ago, finance professors William F. Sharpe and John Lintner developed a model that uses beta to formally link the notions of risk and return. Called the **capital asset pricing model (CAPM)**, it attempts to quantify the relation between risk and return for different investments. It also provides a mechanism whereby investors can assess the impact of a proposed security investment on their portfolio's risk and return. The CAPM predicts that a stock's expected return depends on three things: the risk-free rate, the expected return on the overall market, and the stock's beta.

The Equation With beta, *b*, as the measure of undiversifiable risk, the capital asset pricing model defines the expected return on an investment as follows.

Equation 5.3

$$\text{Expected return on investment } j = \text{Risk-free rate} + \left[\text{Beta for investment } j \times \left(\text{Expected market return} - \text{Risk-free rate} \right) \right]$$

Equation 5.3a

$$r_j = r_{rf} + \left[b_j \times (r_m - r_{rf}) \right]$$

where

r_j = the expected return on investment j, given its risk as measured by beta
r_{rf} = the risk-free rate of return; the return that can be earned on a risk-free investment
b_j = beta coefficient, or index of undiversifiable risk for investment j
r_m = the expected market return; the average return on all securities (typically measured by the average return on all securities in the Standard & Poor's 500 Composite Index or some other broad stock market index)

The CAPM can be divided into two parts: (1) the risk-free rate of return, r_{rf}, and (2) the *risk premium*, $b_j \times (r_m - r_{rf})$. The risk premium is the return investors require beyond the risk-free rate to compensate for the investment's undiversifiable risk as measured by beta. The equation shows that as beta increases, the stock's risk premium increases, thereby causing the expected return to increase.[1]

---

[1] Note that we are using the terms *expected return* and *required return* interchangeably here. Investors require investments to earn a return that is sufficient compensation based on the investment's risk, and in equilibrium, the return that they require and the return that they expect to earn are the same.

Example

We can demonstrate use of the CAPM with the following example. Assume you are thinking about investing in Bank of America stock, which has a beta of 1.33. At the time you are making your investment decision, the risk-free rate (r_{rf}) is 2% and the expected market return (r_m) is 8%. Substituting these data into the CAPM equation, Equation 5.3a, we get:

$$r = 2\% + 1.33(8\% - 2\%) = 10\%$$

You should therefore expect—indeed, require—a 10% return on this investment as compensation for the risk you have to assume, given the security's beta of 1.33.

If the beta were lower, say, 1.0, the required return would be lower. In fact, in this case the required return on the stock is the same as the expected (or required) return on the market.

$$r = 2\% + 1.0(8\% - 2\%) = 8\%$$

If the beta were higher, say 2.0, the required return would be higher:

$$r = 2\% + 2.0(8\% - 2\%) = 14\%$$

Clearly, the CAPM reflects the positive tradeoff between risk and return: The higher the risk (beta), the higher the risk premium, and therefore the higher the required return.

The Graph: The Security Market Line Figure 5.6 depicts the CAPM graphically. The line in the figure is called the **security market line** (SML), and it shows the expected return (y-axis) for any security given its beta (x-axis). For each level of undiversifiable risk (beta), the SML shows the return that the investor should expect to earn in the marketplace.

We can plot the CAPM by simply calculating the required return for a variety of betas. For example, as we saw earlier, using a 2% risk-free rate and an 8% market return, the required return is 10% when the beta is 1.33. Increase the beta to 2.0, and the required return equals 14% [2% + 2.0(8% − 2%)]. Similarly, we can find the required return for a number of betas and end up with the following combinations of risk (beta) and required return.

Risk (beta)	Required Return
0.0	2%
0.5	5%
1.0	8%
1.5	11%
2.0	14%
2.5	17%

Plotting these values on a graph (with beta on the horizontal axis and required return on the vertical axis) would yield a straight line like the one in Figure 5.6. It is clear from the SML that as risk (beta) increases, so do the risk premium and required return, and vice versa.

Some Closing Comments The capital asset pricing model generally relies on historical data in the sense that the value of beta used in the model is typically based on calculations using historical returns. A company's risk profile may change at any time as the company moves in and out of different lines of business, issues or retires debt, or takes

FIGURE 5.6

The Security Market Line (SML)

The security market line clearly depicts the tradeoff between risk and return. At a beta of 0, the required return is the risk-free rate of 2%. At a beta of 1.0, the required return is the market return of 8%. Given these data, the required return on an investment with a beta of 2.0 is 14% and its risk premium is 12% (14% − 2%).

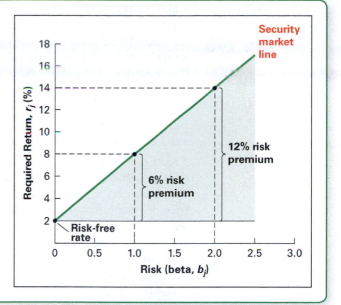

other actions that affect the risk of its common stock. Therefore, betas estimated from historical data may or may not accurately reflect how the company's stock will perform relative to the overall market in the future. Therefore, the required returns specified by the model can be viewed only as rough approximations. Analysts who use betas commonly make subjective adjustments to the historically determined betas based on other information that they possess.

Despite its limitations, the CAPM provides a useful conceptual framework for evaluating and linking risk and return. Its simplicity and practical appeal cause beta and CAPM to remain important tools for investors who seek to measure risk and link it to required returns in security markets. The CAPM also sees widespread use in corporate finance. Before they spend large sums of money on big investment projects, companies need to know what returns their shareholders require. Many surveys show that the primary method that companies use to determine the required rate of return on their stock is the CAPM.

CONCEPTS IN REVIEW

Answers available at
http://www.pearsonhighered.com/smart

5.7 Briefly define and give examples of each of the following components of total risk. Which type of risk matters, and why?

   a. Diversifiable risk
   b. Undiversifiable risk

5.8 Explain what is meant by beta. What type of risk does beta measure? What is the market return? How is the interpretation of beta related to the market return?

5.9 What range of values does beta typically exhibit? Are positive or negative betas more common? Explain.

5.10 What is the capital asset pricing model (CAPM)? What role does beta play in the model? What is the risk premium? How is the security market line (SML) related to the CAPM?

5.11 Is the CAPM a predictive model? Why do beta and the CAPM remain important to investors?

Traditional Versus Modern Portfolio Management

LG5 LG6 Individual and institutional investors currently use two approaches to plan and construct their portfolios. The traditional approach refers to the less quantitative methods that investors have been using since the evolution of the public securities markets. Modern portfolio theory (MPT) is a more mathematical approach that relies on quantitative analysis to guide investment decisions.

The Traditional Approach

Traditional portfolio management emphasizes balancing the portfolio by assembling a wide variety of stocks and/or bonds. The typical emphasis is *interindustry diversification*. This produces a portfolio with securities of companies from a broad range of industries. Investors construct traditional portfolios using security analysis techniques that we will discuss later.

Table 5.5 presents some of the industry groupings and the percentages invested in them by a typical mutual fund that is managed by professionals using the traditional approach. This fund, American Funds' Growth Fund of America (AGTHX), is an open-end mutual fund with a net asset value of $145.2 billion as of December 31, 2014. Its objective is to invest in a wide range of companies that appear to offer superior opportunities for growth of capital. The Growth Fund of America holds shares of more than 280 different companies and short-term securities issued from a wide range of industries. The AGTHX fund is most heavily invested in information technology, representing 21.7% of the portfolio. The consumer discretionary and health care industries represent 17.9% and 17.8% of the fund's investment, respectively.

TABLE 5.5   THE GROWTH FUND OF AMERICA (AGTHX) INVESTMENTS IN SELECT INDUSTRY GROUPS AS OF DECEMBER 31, 2014

The Growth Fund of America appears to adhere to the traditional approach to portfolio management. Its total portfolio value is $145.2 billion, of which 80.8% ($117.3 billion) is U.S. equities, 10.2% ($14.8 billion) is non-U.S. equities, 0.2% ($290.4 million) is U.S. bonds, and 8.8% ($12.8 billion) is cash & equivalents.

Sector Breakdown	Percentage
Information technology	21.7%
Consumer discretionary	17.9%
Health care	17.8%
Industrials	9.6%
Financials	8.2%
Energy	7.7%
Consumer staples	4.6%
Materials	2.8%
Telecommunication services	0.6%
Utilities	0.1%

(Source: Data from The Growth Fund of America, Class A Shares, Quarterly Fund Fact Sheet, December 31, 2014.)

Analyzing the stock position of the Growth Fund of America, which accounts for 91% of the fund's assets, we observe the traditional approach to portfolio management at work. This fund holds numerous stocks from a broad cross-section of the universe of available stocks. The stocks are a mix of large and small companies. The fund's largest individual holding is Amazon.com Inc., which accounts for 3.7% of the portfolio. Google Inc., the world's do-everything search engine, ranks second, at 3.3%. The third largest holding, 2.3%, is Gilead Sciences. Although many of the fund's stocks are those of large, recognizable companies, its portfolio does include stocks of smaller, less recognizable firms.

Those who manage traditional portfolios tend to invest in well-known companies for three reasons. First, fund managers and investors may believe that investing in well-known companies is less risky than investing in lesser-known firms. Second, the securities of large firms are more liquid and are available in large quantities. Third, institutional investors prefer successful, well-known companies because it is easier to convince clients to invest in them. Called *window dressing*, this practice of loading up a portfolio with successful, well-known stocks makes it easier for institutional investors to sell their services.

One tendency often attributed to institutional investors during recent years is that of "herding"—investing in securities similar to those held by their competitors. These institutional investors effectively mimic the actions of their competitors. In the case of The Growth Fund of America, for example, its managers would buy stocks in companies that are held by other large, growth-oriented mutual funds. While we don't know for certain why The Growth Fund of America's managers bought specific stocks, it is clear that most funds with similar objectives hold many of the same well-known stocks.

Modern Portfolio Theory

During the 1950s, Harry Markowitz, a trained mathematician, first developed the theories that form the basis of modern portfolio theory. In the years since Markowitz's pioneering work, many other scholars and investment experts have contributed to the theory. **Modern portfolio theory (MPT)** uses several basic statistical measures to develop a portfolio plan. Portfolios formed using MPT principles estimate the average returns, standard deviations, and correlations among many combinations of investments to find an optimal portfolio. According to MPT, the maximum benefits of diversification occur when investors find securities that are relatively uncorrelated and put those securities together in a portfolio. Two important aspects of MPT are the efficient frontier and portfolio betas.

The Efficient Frontier At any point in time, you are faced with hundreds of investments from which to choose. You can form any number of possible portfolios. In fact, using only a few different assets, you could create an unlimited number of portfolios by changing the proportion of each asset in the portfolio.

If we were to create all possible portfolios, calculate the return and risk of each, and plot each risk-return combination on a graph, we would have the *feasible*, or *attainable*, *set* of possible portfolios. This set is represented by the shaded area in Figure 5.7. It is the area bounded by ABYOZCDEF. As defined earlier, an *efficient portfolio* is a portfolio that provides the highest return for

FIGURE 5.7

The Feasible, or Attainable, Set and the Efficient Frontier

The feasible, or attainable, set (shaded area) represents the risk-return combinations attainable with all possible portfolios; the efficient frontier is the locus of all efficient portfolios. The point O, where the investor's highest possible indifference curve is tangent to the efficient frontier, is the optimal portfolio. It represents the highest level of satisfaction the investor can achieve given the available set of portfolios.

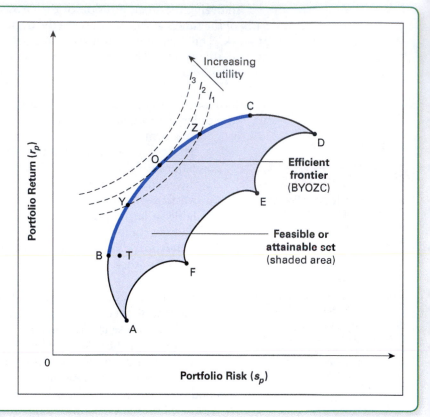

a given level of risk. For example, let's compare portfolio T to portfolios B and Y shown in Figure 5.7. Portfolio Y appears preferable to portfolio T because it has a higher return for the same level of risk. Portfolio B also "dominates" portfolio T because it has lower risk for the same level of return.

The boundary BYOZC of the feasible set of portfolios represents all efficient portfolios—those portfolios that provide the best tradeoff between risk and return. This boundary is the **efficient frontier**. All portfolios on the efficient frontier are preferable to all other portfolios in the feasible set. Any portfolios that would fall to the left of the efficient frontier are not available for investment because they fall outside of the attainable set. For example, anyone would love to buy an investment with an extremely high return and no risk at all, but no such investment exists. Portfolios that fall to the right of the efficient frontier are not desirable because their risk-return tradeoffs are inferior to those of portfolios on the efficient frontier.

We can, in theory, use the efficient frontier to find the highest level of satisfaction the investor can achieve given the available set of portfolios. To do this, we would plot on the graph an *investor's indifference curves*. These curves indicate, for a given level of utility (satisfaction), the set of risk-return combinations about which an investor would be indifferent. These curves, labeled I_1, I_2, and I_3 in Figure 5.7, reflect increasing satisfaction as we move from I_1 to I_2 to I_3. The optimal portfolio, O, is the point at which indifference curve I_2 meets the efficient frontier. The investor cannot achieve the higher utility provided by I_3 because there is no investment available that offers a combination of risk and return falling on the curve I_3.

If we introduced a risk-free investment-paying return r_f into Figure 5.7, we could eventually derive the equation for the capital asset pricing model introduced previously. Rather than focus further on theory, let's shift our attention to the more practical aspects of the efficient frontier and its extensions.

Portfolio Betas As we have noted, investors strive to diversify their portfolios by including a variety of noncomplementary investments that allow investors to reduce risk while meeting their return objectives. Remember that investments embody two basic types of risk: (1) diversifiable risk, the risk unique to a particular investment, and (2) undiversifiable risk, the risk possessed, at least to some degree, by every investment.

A great deal of research has been conducted on the topic of risk as it relates to security investments. The results show that, in general, to earn a higher return, you must bear more risk. Just as important, however, are research results showing that the positive relation between risk and return holds only for undiversifiable risk. High levels of diversifiable risk do not result in correspondingly high levels of return. Because there is no reward for bearing diversifiable risk, investors should minimize this form of risk by diversifying the portfolio so that only undiversifiable risk remains.

Risk Diversification As we've seen, diversification minimizes diversifiable risk by offsetting the below-average return on one investment with the above-average return on another. Minimizing diversifiable risk through careful selection of investments requires that the investments chosen for the portfolio come from a wide range of industries.

To better understand how diversification benefits investors, let's examine what happens when we begin with a single asset (security) in a portfolio and then expand the portfolio by randomly selecting additional securities. Using the standard deviation, s_p, to measure the portfolio's total risk, we can depict the behavior of the total portfolio risk as more securities are added in Figure 5.8. As we add securities to the portfolio (*x*-axis), the total portfolio risk (*y*-axis) declines because of the effects of diversification, but there is a limit to how much risk reduction investors can achieve.

FIGURE 5.8

Portfolio Risk and Diversification

As more securities are combined to create a portfolio, the total risk of the portfolio (measured by its standard deviation, s_p) declines. The portion of the risk eliminated is the diversifiable risk; the remaining portion is the undiversifiable, or relevant, risk.

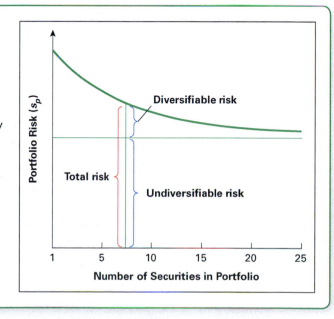

On average, most of the risk-reduction benefits of diversification can be gained by forming portfolios containing two or three dozen carefully selected securities, but our recommendation is to hold 40 or more securities to achieve efficient diversification. This suggestion tends to support the popularity of investment in mutual funds.

Because any investor can create a portfolio of assets that will eliminate virtually all diversifiable risk, the only **relevant risk** is that which is undiversifiable. You must therefore be concerned solely with undiversifiable risk. The measurement of undiversifiable risk is thus of primary importance.

Calculating Portfolio Betas As we saw earlier, beta measures the undiversifiable, or relevant, risk of a security. The beta for the market is equal to 1.0. Securities with betas greater than 1.0 are more risky than the market, and those with betas less than 1.0 are less risky than the market. The beta for the risk-free asset is 0.

The **portfolio beta**, b_p, is merely the weighted average of the betas of the individual assets in the portfolio. You can easily calculate a portfolio's beta by using the betas of the component assets. To find the portfolio beta, b_p, calculate a weighted average of the betas of the individual stocks in the portfolio, where the weights represent the percentage of the portfolio's value invested in each security, as shown in Equation 5.4.

Equation 5.4

$$\text{Portfolio beta} = \left(\begin{array}{c}\text{Proportion of}\\ \text{portfolio's total}\\ \text{dollar value}\\ \text{in asset 1}\end{array} \times \begin{array}{c}\text{Beta}\\ \text{for}\\ \text{asset 1}\end{array}\right) + \left(\begin{array}{c}\text{Proportion of}\\ \text{portfolio's total}\\ \text{dollar value}\\ \text{in asset 2}\end{array} \times \begin{array}{c}\text{Beta}\\ \text{for}\\ \text{asset 2}\end{array}\right) + \cdots +$$

$$\left(\begin{array}{c}\text{Proportion of}\\ \text{portfolio's total}\\ \text{dollar value}\\ \text{in asset } n\end{array} \times \begin{array}{c}\text{Beta}\\ \text{for}\\ \text{asset } n\end{array}\right) = \sum_{j=1}^{n}\left(\begin{array}{c}\text{Proportion of}\\ \text{portfolio's total}\\ \text{dollar value}\\ \text{in asset } j\end{array} \times \begin{array}{c}\text{Beta}\\ \text{for}\\ \text{asset } j\end{array}\right)$$

Equation 5.4a

$$b_p = (w_1 \times b_1) + (w_2 \times b_2) + \cdots + (w_n \times b_n) = \sum_{j=1}^{n}(w_j \times b_j)$$

Of course, $\sum_{j=1}^{n} w_j = 1$, which means that 100% of the portfolio's assets must be included in this computation.

Portfolio betas are interpreted in exactly the same way as individual asset betas. They indicate the degree of responsiveness of the portfolio's return to changes in the market return. For example, when the market return increases by 10%, a portfolio with a beta of 0.75 will experience a 7.5% increase in its return $(0.75 \times 10\%)$. A portfolio with a beta of 1.25 will experience a 12.5% increase in its return $(1.25 \times 10\%)$. Low-beta portfolios are less responsive, and therefore less risky, than high-beta portfolios.

To demonstrate, consider the Austin Fund, a large investment company that wishes to assess the risk of two portfolios, V and W. Both portfolios contain five assets, with the proportions and betas shown in Table 5.6. We can calculate the betas for portfolios V and W, b_v and b_w, by substituting the appropriate data from the table into Equation 5.4, as follows:

TABLE 5.6   AUSTIN FUND'S PORTFOLIOS V AND W

Asset	Portfolio V Proportion	Portfolio V Beta	Portfolio W Proportion	Portfolio W Beta
1	0.10	1.65	0.10	0.80
2	0.30	1.00	0.10	1.00
3	0.20	1.30	0.20	0.65
4	0.20	1.10	0.10	0.75
5	0.20	1.25	0.50	1.05
Total	1.00		1.00	

$$b_v = (0.10 \times 1.65) + (0.30 \times 1.00) + (0.20 \times 1.30) + (0.20 \times 1.10) + (0.20 \times 1.25)$$
$$= 0.165 + 0.300 + 0.260 + 0.220 + 0.250 = 1.195 \approx \underline{1.20}$$
$$b_w = (0.10 \times 0.80) + (0.10 \times 1.00) + (0.20 \times 0.65) + (0.10 \times 0.75) + (0.50 \times 1.05)$$
$$= 0.080 + 0.100 + 0.130 + 0.075 + 0.525 = \underline{0.91}$$

Portfolio V's beta is 1.20, and portfolio W's is 0.91. These values make sense because portfolio V contains relatively high-beta assets and portfolio W contains relatively low-beta assets. Clearly, portfolio V's returns are more responsive to changes in market returns—and therefore more risky—than portfolio W's.

Interpreting Portfolio Betas If a portfolio has a beta of 1.0, the portfolio experiences changes in its rate of return equal to changes in the market's rate of return. The 1.0 beta portfolio would tend to experience a 10% increase in return if the stock market as a whole experienced a 10% increase in return. Conversely, if the market return fell by 6%, the return on the 1.0 beta portfolio would also fall by 6%.

Table 5.7 lists the expected returns for three portfolio betas in two situations: an increase in market return of 10% and a decrease in market return of 10%. The portfolio with a beta of 2.0 moves twice as much (on average) as the market does. When the market return increases by 10%, the portfolio return increases by 20%. When the market return declines by 10%, the portfolio's return will fall by 20%. This portfolio would be considered a high-risk, high-return portfolio.

The middle, 0.5 beta portfolio is considered a low-risk, low-return portfolio. This would be a conservative portfolio for investors who wish to maintain a low-risk investment posture. The 0.5 beta portfolio is half as volatile as the market.

A portfolio with a beta of −1.0 moves in the opposite direction from the market. A bearish investor would probably want to own a negative-beta portfolio because this

TABLE 5.7   PORTFOLIO BETAS AND ASSOCIATED CHANGES IN RETURNS

Portfolio Beta	Changes in Market Return (%)	Change in Expected Portfolio Return (%)
+ 2.0	+ 10.0%	+ 20.0%
	− 10.0%	− 20.0%
+ 0.5	+ 10.0%	+ 5.0%
	− 10.0%	− 5.0%
− 1.0	+ 10.0%	− 10.0%
	− 10.0%	+ 10.0%

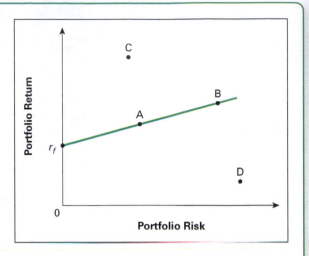

FIGURE 5.9

The Portfolio Risk-Return Tradeoff

As the risk of an investment portfolio increases from 0, the return provided should increase above the risk-free rate, r_f. Portfolios A and B offer returns commensurate with their risk, portfolio C provides a high return at a low-risk level, and portfolio D provides a low return for high risk. Portfolio C is highly desirable; portfolio D should be avoided.

type of investment tends to rise in value when the stock market declines, and vice versa. Finding securities with negative betas is difficult, however. Most securities have positive betas because they tend to experience return movements in the same direction as changes in the stock market.

The Risk-Return Tradeoff: Some Closing Comments Another valuable outgrowth of modern portfolio theory is the specific link between undiversifiable risk and investment returns. The basic premise is that an investor must have a portfolio of relatively risky investments to earn a relatively high rate of return. That relationship is illustrated in Figure 5.9. The upward-sloping line shows the **risk-return tradeoff**. The point where the risk-return line crosses the return axis is called the **risk-free rate**, r_f. This is the return an investor can earn on a risk-free investment such as a U.S. Treasury bill or an insured money market deposit account.

As we proceed upward along the risk-return tradeoff line, portfolios of risky investments appear, as depicted by four investment portfolios, A through D. Portfolios A and B are investment opportunities that provide a level of return commensurate with their respective risk levels. Portfolio C provides a high return at a relatively low risk level—and therefore would be an excellent investment. Portfolio D, in contrast, offers high risk but low return—an investment to avoid.

Reconciling the Traditional Approach and MPT

We have reviewed two fairly different approaches to portfolio management: the traditional approach and MPT. The question that naturally arises is which technique should you use? There is no definite answer; the question must be resolved by the judgment of each investor. However, we can offer a few useful ideas.

The average individual investor does not have the resources and the mathematical acumen to implement a total MPT portfolio strategy. But most individual investors can extract and use ideas from both the traditional and MPT approaches. The traditional approach stresses security selection, which we will discuss later in this text. It also emphasizes diversification of the portfolio across industry lines. MPT stresses reducing correlations between securities within the portfolio. This approach calls for diversification to minimize diversifiable risk. Thus, diversification must be accomplished to ensure satisfactory performance with either strategy. Also, beta is a useful tool for determining the level of a portfolio's undiversifiable risk and should be part of the decision-making process.

We recommend the following portfolio management policy, which uses aspects of both approaches:

- Determine how much risk you are willing to bear.

- Seek diversification among types of securities and across industry lines, and pay attention to how the return from one security is related to that from another.

- Consider how a security responds to the market, and use beta in diversifying your portfolio to keep the portfolio in line with your acceptable risk level.

- Evaluate alternative portfolios to make sure that the portfolio selected provides the highest return for the acceptable level of risk.

CONCEPTS IN REVIEW

Answers available at http://www.pearsonhighered.com/smart

5.12 Describe traditional portfolio management. Give three reasons why traditional portfolio managers like to invest in well-established companies.

5.13 What is modern portfolio theory (MPT)? What is the feasible or attainable set of all possible portfolios? How is it derived for a given group of investments?

5.14 What is the efficient frontier? How is it related to the attainable set of all possible portfolios? How can it be used with an investor's utility function to find the optimal portfolio?

5.15 Define and differentiate among the diversifiable, undiversifiable, and total risk of a portfolio. Which is considered the relevant risk? How is it measured?

5.16 Define beta. How can you find the beta of a portfolio when you know the beta for each of the assets included within it?

5.17 Explain how you can reconcile the traditional and modern portfolio approaches.

MyFinanceLab

Here is what you should know after reading this chapter. MyFinanceLab will help you identify what you know and where to go when you need to practice.

What You Should Know	Key Terms	Where to Practice
LG1 Understand portfolio objectives and the procedures used to calculate portfolio return and standard deviation. A portfolio is a collection of investments assembled to achieve one or more investment goals. It produces potential price appreciation and current income, subject to a tradeoff between risk and return. The return on a portfolio is calculated as a weighted average of the returns of the assets from which it is formed. The standard deviation of a portfolio's returns is found by applying the same formula that is used to find the standard deviation of a single asset.	efficient portfolio, *p. 171* growth-oriented portfolio, *p. 171* income-oriented portfolio, *p. 171*	MyFinanceLab Study Plan 5.1 Excel Table 5.1 Video Learning Aid for Problem P5.5

What You Should Know	Key Terms	Where to Practice
LG2 Discuss the concepts of correlation and diversification and the key aspects of international diversification. Correlation is a statistic used to measure the relationship between the returns on assets. To diversify, it is best to add assets with negatively correlated returns. In general, the less positive and more negative the correlation between asset returns, the more effectively a portfolio can be diversified to reduce its risk. Diversification can reduce the risk (standard deviation) of a portfolio below the risk of the least risky asset (sometimes to 0). The return of the resulting portfolio will be no lower than the smallest return of its component assets. For any two-asset portfolio, the ability to reduce risk depends on both the degree of correlation and the proportion of each asset in the portfolio. International diversification may allow an investor to reduce portfolio risk without necessarily imposing a corresponding reduction in return. It can be achieved by investing abroad or through domestic investment in foreign companies or funds, but it typically cannot be achieved by investing in U.S. multinationals. The preferred method of international diversification for individual investors is the use of ADSs or international mutual funds available in the United States. Although opportunities to earn "excess" returns in international investments are diminishing over time, international investments continue to provide an effective way to diversify.	correlation, *p. 174* correlation coefficient, *p. 174* negatively correlated, *p. 174* perfectly negatively correlated, *p. 175* perfectly positively correlated, *p. 175* positively correlated, *p. 174* uncorrelated, *p. 174*	MyFinanceLab Study Plan 5.2 Excel Tables 5.2, 5.3
LG3 Describe the components of risk and the use of beta to measure risk. The two basic components of total risk are diversifiable (unsystematic) and undiversifiable (systematic) risk. Undiversifiable risk is the relevant risk. Beta measures the undiversifiable, or market, risk associated with a security investment. It is derived from the historical relationship between a security's return and the market return.	beta, *p. 183* diversifiable (unsystematic) risk, *p. 182* market risk, *p. 182* undiversifiable (systematic) risk, *p. 182* total risk, *p. 183*	MyFinanceLab Study Plan 5.3 Video Learning Aid for Problem P5.22
LG4 Explain the capital asset pricing model conceptually, mathematically, and graphically. The CAPM relates risk (as measured by beta) to return. It can be divided into (1) the risk-free rate of return, r_{rf}, and (2) the risk premium, $b \times (r_m - r_{rf})$. The graphic depiction of the CAPM is the security market line (SML). The CAPM reflects increasing required returns for increasing risk.	capital asset pricing model (CAPM), *p. 187* security market line (SML), *p. 188*	MyFinanceLab Study Plan 5.4
LG5 Review the traditional and modern approaches to portfolio management. The traditional approach constructs portfolios by combining a large number of securities issued by companies from a broad cross-section of industries. Modern portfolio theory (MPT) uses statistical diversification to develop efficient portfolios. To determine the optimal portfolio, MPT finds the efficient frontier and couples it with an investor's risk-indifference curves.	efficient frontier, *p. 192* modern portfolio theory (MPT), *p. 191* portfolio beta, b_p, *p. 194* relevant risk, *p. 194* risk-return tradeoff, *p. 196* risk-free rate, r_{rf}, *p. 196* traditional portfolio management, *p. 190*	MyFinanceLab Study Plan 5.5

What You Should Know	Key Terms	Where to Practice
LG6 Describe portfolio betas, the risk-return tradeoff, and reconciliation of the two approaches to portfolio management. Portfolio betas can be used to develop efficient portfolios consistent with the investor's risk-return preferences. Portfolio betas are merely a weighted average of the betas of the individual assets in the portfolio. Generally, investors use elements of both the traditional approach and MPT to create portfolios. This approach involves determining how much risk you are willing to bear, seeking diversification, using beta to diversify your portfolio, and evaluating alternative portfolios to select the one that offers the highest return for an acceptable level of risk.		MyFinanceLab Study Plan 5.6 Video Learning Aid for Problem P5.22

Log into MyFinanceLab, take a chapter test, and get a personalized Study Plan that tells you which concepts you understand and which ones you need to review. From there, MyFinanceLab will give you further practice, tutorials, animations, videos, and guided solutions.
Log into **http://www.myfinancelab.com**

Discussion Questions

LG1 **Q5.1** State your portfolio objectives. Then construct a 10-stock portfolio that you feel is consistent with your objectives. (Use companies that have been public for at least five years.) Obtain annual dividend and price data for each of the past five years.
  a. Calculate the historical return for each stock for each year.
  b. Using your findings in part **a**, calculate the historical portfolio return for each of the five years.
  c. Use your findings in part **b** to calculate the average portfolio return over the five years.
  d. Use your findings in parts **b** and **c** to find the standard deviation of the portfolio's returns over the five-year period.
  e. Use the historical average return from part **c** and the standard deviation from part **d** to evaluate the portfolio's return and risk in light of your stated portfolio objectives.

LG2 **Q5.2** Using the following guidelines, choose the stocks—A, B, and C—of three firms that have been public for at least 10 years. Stock A should be one you are interested in buying. Stock B should be a stock, possibly in the same line of business or industry, that you feel will have the highest possible return correlation with stock A. Stock C should be one you feel will have the lowest possible return correlation with stock A.
  a. Calculate the annual rates of return for each of the past 10 years for each stock.
  b. Plot the 10 annual return values for each stock on the same set of axes, where the x-axis is the year and the y-axis is the annual return in percentage terms.
  c. Join the points for the returns for each stock on the graph. Evaluate and describe the returns of stocks A and B in the graph. Do they exhibit the expected positive correlation? Why or why not?
  d. Evaluate and describe the relationship between the returns of stocks A and C in the graph. Do they exhibit negative correlation? Why or why not?
  e. Compare and contrast your findings in parts **c** and **d** to the expected relationships among stocks A, B, and C. Discuss your findings.

LG2   **Q5.3**   From the *Wall Street Journal*, a website such as Yahoo! Finance, or some other source, obtain a current estimate of the risk-free rate (use a 10-year Treasury bond). Use the *Value Line Investment Survey* or Yahoo! Finance to obtain the beta for each of the following stocks:

Ford (autos)
Dell (computers)
Sempra Energy (utilities)
Kroger (groceries)
Bank of America (financial services)

Use the information you gathered along with the market risk premium on large stocks given in the chapter to find the required return for each stock with the capital asset pricing model.

LG3 LG4   **Q5.4**   From the *Wall Street Journal*, a website such as Yahoo! Finance, or some other source, obtain a current estimate of the risk-free rate (use a 10-year Treasury bond). Use the *Value Line Investment Survey* or Yahoo! Finance to obtain the beta for each of the companies listed on page 186.
a. Compare the current betas to the February 27, 2015 betas given in the chapter for each of the companies.
b. What might cause betas to change over time, even in a stable economic environment?
c. Use the current betas, along with a market risk premium on stocks of 8.5%, to find the required return for each stock with the CAPM.
d. Compare and discuss your findings in part c with regard to the specific business of each company.

LG2 LG5 LG6   **Q5.5**   Obtain a prospectus and an annual report for a major mutual fund that includes some international securities. Carefully read the prospectus and annual report and study the portfolio's composition in light of the fund's stated objectives.
a. Evaluate the amount of diversification and the types of industries and companies held. Is the portfolio well diversified?
b. Discuss the additional risks faced by an investor in this fund compared to an investor in a domestic stock portfolio such as the S&P 500.

LG6   **Q5.6**   Use Yahoo! Finance or some other source to select four stocks with betas ranging from about 0.50 to 1.50. Record the current market prices of each of these stocks. Assume you wish to create a portfolio that combines all four stocks in such a way that the resulting portfolio beta is about 1.10.
a. Through trial and error, use all four stocks to create a portfolio with the target beta of 1.10.
b. If you have $100,000 to invest in this portfolio, on the basis of the weightings determined in part a, what dollar amounts would you invest in each stock?
c. Approximately how many shares of each of the four stocks would you buy given the dollar amounts calculated in part b?
d. Repeat parts a, b, and c with a different set of weightings that still result in a portfolio beta of 1.10. Can only one unique portfolio with a given beta be created from a given set of stocks?

Problems

All problems are available on **http://www.myfinancelab.com**

LG1   **P5.1**   Your portfolio had the values in the following table for the four years listed. There were no withdrawals or contributions of new funds to the portfolio. Calculate your average return over the four-year period.

Year	Beginning Value	Ending Value
2013	$50,000	$55,000
2014	$55,000	$58,000
2015	$58,000	$65,000
2016	$65,000	$70,000

LG1   **P5.2** Using your data from Problem 5.1, calculate the portfolio standard deviation.

LG1 LG2   **P5.3** Assume you are considering a portfolio containing two assets, L and M. Asset L will represent 40% of the dollar value of the portfolio, and asset M will account for the other 60%. The projected returns over the next six years, 2018–2023, for each of these assets are summarized in the following table.

	Projected Return	
Year	Asset L	Asset M
2018	14%	20%
2019	14%	18%
2020	16%	16%
2021	17%	14%
2022	17%	12%
2023	19%	10%

a. Use an Excel spreadsheet to calculate the projected portfolio return, $\bar{r}_p$, for each of the six years.
b. Use an Excel spreadsheet to calculate the average portfolio return, $\bar{r}_p$, over the six-year period.
c. Use an Excel spreadsheet to calculate the standard deviation of expected portfolio returns, s_p, over the six-year period.
d. How would you characterize the correlation of returns of the assets L and M?
e. Discuss any benefits of diversification achieved through creation of the portfolio.

LG1 LG2   **P5.4** Refer to Problem 5.3. Assume that asset L represents 60% of the portfolio and asset M is 40%. Calculate the average return and standard deviation of this portfolio's returns over the six-year period. Compare your answers to the answers from Problem 5.3.

LG1 LG2   **P5.5** You have been given the following return data on three assets—F, G, and H—over the period 2018–2021.

	Expected Return		
Year	Asset F	Asset G	Asset H
2018	16%	17%	14%
2019	17%	16%	15%
2020	18%	15%	16%
2021	19%	14%	17%

Using these assets, you have isolated three investment alternatives:

Alternative	Investment
1	100% of asset F
2	50% of asset F and 50% of asset G
3	50% of asset F and 50% of asset H

a. Calculate the portfolio return over the four-year period for each of the three alternatives.

b. Calculate the standard deviation of returns over the four-year period for each of the three alternatives.

c. On the basis of your findings in parts a and b, which of the three investment alternatives would you recommend? Why?

LG1 LG2   **P5.6**   You have been asked for your advice in selecting a portfolio of assets and have been supplied with the following data.

	Projected Return		
Year	Asset A	Asset B	Asset C
2018	12%	16%	12%
2019	14%	14%	14%
2020	16%	12%	16%

You have been told that you can create two portfolios—one consisting of assets A and B and the other consisting of assets A and C—by investing equal proportions (50%) in each of the two component assets.

a. What is the average return, $\bar{r}$, for each asset over the three-year period?

b. What is the standard deviation, s, for each asset's return?

c. What is the average return, $\bar{r}_p$, for each of the portfolios?

d. How would you characterize the correlations of returns of the two assets in each of the portfolios identified in part c?

e. What is the standard deviation of expected returns, s_p, for each portfolio?

f. Which portfolio do you recommend? Why?

LG1 LG2   **P5.7**   Referring to Problem 5.6, what would happen if you constructed a portfolio consisting of assets A, B, and C, equally weighted? Would this reduce risk or enhance return?

LG1 LG2   **P5.8**   Assume you wish to evaluate the risk and return behaviors associated with various combinations of assets V and W under three assumed degrees of correlation: perfect positive, uncorrelated, and perfect negative. The following average return and risk values were calculated for these assets.

Asset	Average Return, $\bar{r}$	Risk (Standard Asset Deviation), s
V	8%	5%
W	13%	10%

a. If the returns of assets V and W are perfectly positively correlated (correlation coefficient = +1), describe the range of (1) return and (2) risk associated with all possible portfolio combinations.

b. If the returns of assets V and W are uncorrelated (correlation coefficient = 0), describe the approximate range of (1) return and (2) risk associated with all possible portfolio combinations.

c. If the returns of assets V and W are perfectly negatively correlated (correlation coefficient = −1), describe the range of (1) return and (2) risk associated with all possible portfolio combinations.

LG1   **P5.9**   The following table contains annual returns for the stocks of Home Depot (HD) and Lowe's (LOW). The returns are calculated using end-of-year prices (adjusted for dividends and stock splits) retrieved from **http://www.finance.yahoo.com/**. Use Excel to create a spreadsheet that calculates annual portfolio returns for an equally weighted portfolio of HD and LOW. Also, calculate the average annual return for both stocks and the portfolio.

Year	HD Returns	LOW Returns
2005	−4.3%	16.1%
2006	1.0%	−6.1%
2007	−31.1%	−26.8%
2008	−11.4%	−3.3%
2009	30.5%	10.6%
2010	25.0%	9.2%
2011	23.5%	3.4%
2012	50.3%	42.9%
2013	35.9%	41.8%
2014	30.2%	41.2%

LG1 LG2 **P5.10** Use the table of annual returns in Problem 5.9 for Home Depot (HD) and Lowe's (LOW) to create an Excel spreadsheet that calculates the standard deviation of annual returns for HD, LOW, and the equally weighted portfolio of HD and LOW.

LG1 LG2 **P5.11** Use the table of annual returns in Problem 5.9 for Home Depot (HD) and Lowe's (LOW) to create an Excel spreadsheet that calculates the correlation coefficient for HD and LOW annual returns.

LG1 LG2 **P5.12** Use the table of annual returns in Problem 5.9 for Home Depot (HD) and Lowe's (LOW) to create an Excel spreadsheet that calculates returns for portfolios that comprise HD and LOW using the following, respective, weightings: (1.0, 0.0), (0.9, 0.1), (0.8, 0.2), (0.7, 0.3), (0.6, 0.4), (0.5, 0.5), (0.4, 0.6), (0.3, 0.7), (0.2, 0.8), (0.1, 0.9), and (0.0, 1.0). Also, calculate the portfolio standard deviation associated with each portfolio composition. You will need to use the standard deviations found previously for HD and LOW and their correlation coefficient.

LG1 LG2 **P5.13** Create an Excel spreadsheet that graphs the portfolio return and standard deviation combinations found in Problem 5.12 for Home Depot and Lowe's.

LG1 LG2 **P5.14** The following table contains annual returns for the stocks of M and N. Use Excel to create a spreadsheet that calculates the average, standard deviation, and correlation coefficient for the two annual return series. Next, use the averages, standard deviations, and correlation coefficient along with the portfolios shown in the lower table to calculate a range of portfolio return and risk combinations. Finally, graph the range of return and risk combinations. (Hint: Review Figure 5.3)

Year	M Returns	N Returns
2015	40.6%	7.6%
2016	−37.9%	−30.0%
2017	18.1%	63.2%
2018	4.8%	20.9%
2019	−18.2%	50.0%
2020	17.4%	80.3%
2021	10.4%	−17.0%
2022	−23.2%	22.3%
2023	56.2%	13.6%
2024	11.9%	8.9%

Portfolio Weights	
w_M	w_N
1.0	0.0
0.9	0.1
0.8	0.2
0.7	0.3
0.6	0.4
0.5	0.5
0.4	0.6
0.3	0.7
0.2	0.8
0.1	0.9
0.0	1.0

LG3 **P5.15** Imagine you wish to estimate the betas for two investments, A and B. You have gathered the following return data for the market and for each of the investments over the past 10 years, 2008–2017.

	Historical Returns		
		Investment	
Year	Market	A	B
2008	6%	11%	16%
2009	2%	8%	11%
2010	−13%	−4%	10%
2011	−4%	3%	3%
2012	−8%	0%	3%
2013	16%	19%	30%
2014	10%	14%	22%
2015	15%	18%	29%
2016	8%	12%	19%
2017	13%	17%	26%

a. On a set of market return (*x*-axis)–investment return (*y*-axis) axes, use the data to draw the characteristic lines for investments A and B on the same graph.
b. Use the characteristic lines from part **a** to estimate the betas for investments A and B.
c. Use the betas found in part **b** to comment on the relative risks of investments A and B.

LG3 **P5.16** You are evaluating two possible stock investments, Buyme Co. and Getit Corp. Buyme Co. has an expected return of 14% and a beta of 1.0. Getit Corp. has an expected return of 14% and a beta of 1.2. Based only on this data, which stock should you buy and why?

LG3 **P5.17** Referring to Problem 5.16, if you expected a significant market rally, would your decision be altered? Explain.

LG3 **P5.18** A security has a beta of 1.2. Is this security more or less risky than the market? Explain. Assess the impact on the required return of this security in each of the following cases.
a. The market return increases by 15%.
b. The market return decreases by 8%.
c. The market return remains unchanged.

LG3 **P5.19** Assume the betas for securities A, B, and C are as shown here.

Security	Beta
A	1.4
B	0.8
C	−0.9

a. Calculate the change in return for each security if the market experiences an increase in its rate of return of 13.2% over the next period.
b. Calculate the change in return for each security if the market experiences a decrease in its rate of return of 10.8% over the next period.
c. Rank and discuss the relative risk of each security on the basis of your findings. Which security might perform best during an economic downturn? Explain.

LG3 LG6 **P5.20** Referring to Problem 5.19, assume you have a portfolio with $20,000 invested in each of investments A, B, and C. What is your portfolio beta?

LG3 LG6 **P5.21** Referring to Problem 5.20, using the portfolio beta, what would you expect the value of your portfolio to be if the market rallied 20%? Declined 20%?

LG2 **P5.22** Use the capital asset pricing model to find the required return for each of the following securities in light of the data given.

Security	Risk-Free Rate	Market Return	Beta
A	5%	8%	1.3
B	8%	13%	0.9
C	9%	12%	0.2
D	10%	15%	1.0
E	6%	10%	0.6

LG4 **P5.23** Jay is reviewing his portfolio of investments, which include certain stocks and bonds. He has a large amount tied up in U.S. Treasury bills paying 3%. He is considering moving some of his funds from the T-bills into a stock. The stock has a beta of 1.25. If Jay expects a return of 14% from the stock (a little better than the current market return of 13%), should he buy the stock or leave his funds in the T-bill?

LG4 **P5.24** The risk-free rate is currently 3%, and the market return is 10%. Assume you are considering the following investments.

Investment	Beta
A	1.5
B	1.0
C	0.75
D	0.0
E	2.0

a. Which investment is most risky? Least risky?
b. Use the capital asset pricing model to find the required return on each of the investments.
c. Using your findings in part b, draw the security market line.
d. On the basis of your findings in part c, what relationship exists between risk and return? Explain.

LG5 LG6 **P5.25** Portfolios A through J, which are listed in the following table along with their returns (r_p) and risk (measured by the standard deviation, s_p), represent all currently available portfolios in the feasible or attainable set.

Portfolio	Return, r_p	Risk, s_p
A	9%	8%
B	3%	3%
C	14%	10%
D	12%	14%
E	7%	11%
F	11%	6%
G	10%	12%
H	16%	16%
I	5%	7%
J	8%	4%

a. Plot the feasible, or attainable, set represented by these data on a graph showing portfolio risk, s_p (x-axis), and portfolio return, r_p (y-axis).
b. Draw the efficient frontier on the graph in part **a.**
c. Which portfolios lie on the efficient frontier? Why do these portfolios dominate all others in the feasible set?
d. How would an investor's utility function or risk-indifference curves be used with the efficient frontier to find the optimal portfolio?

LG5 LG6 **P5.26** For his portfolio, Jack Cashman randomly selected securities from all those listed on the New York Stock Exchange. He began with one security and added securities one by one until a total of 20 securities were held in the portfolio. After each security was added, Jack calculated the portfolio standard deviation, s_p. The calculated values follow.

Number of Securities	Portfolio Risk, s_p	Number of Securities	Portfolio Risk, s_p
1	14.5%	11	7.00%
2	13.3%	12	6.80%
3	12.2%	13	6.70%
4	11.2%	14	6.65%
5	10.3%	15	6.60%
6	9.5%	16	6.56%
7	8.8%	17	6.52%
8	8.2%	18	6.5%
9	7.7%	19	6.48%
10	7.3%	20	6.47%

a. On a graph showing the number of securities in the portfolio (x-axis) and portfolio risk, s_p (y-axis), plot the portfolio risk given the data in the preceding table.
b. Divide the portfolio risk in the graph into its undiversifiable and diversifiable risk components, and label each of these on the graph.
c. Describe which of the two risk components is the relevant risk, and explain why it is relevant. How much of this risk exists in Jack Cashman's portfolio?

LG3 LG6 **P5.27** If portfolio A has a beta of 1.5 and portfolio Z has a beta of −1.5, what do the two values indicate? If the return on the market rises by 20%, what impact, if any, would this have on the returns from portfolios A and Z? Explain.

LG3 LG6 **P5.28** Stock A has a beta of 0.8, stock B has a beta of 1.4, and stock C has a beta of −0.3.
  a. Rank these stocks from the most risky to the least risky.
  b. If the return on the market portfolio increases by 12%, what change in the return for each of the stocks would you expect?
  c. If the return on the market portfolio declines by 5%, what change in the return for each of the stocks would you expect?
  d. If you felt the stock market was about to experience a significant decline, which stock would you be most likely to add to your portfolio? Why?
  e. If you anticipated a major stock market rally, which stock would you be most likely to add to your portfolio? Why?

LG6 **P5.29** Jeanne Lewis is attempting to evaluate two possible portfolios consisting of the same five assets but held in different proportions. She is particularly interested in using beta to compare the risk of the portfolios and, in this regard, has gathered the following data.

| | | Portfolio Weights | |
Asset	Asset Beta	Portfolio A	Portfolio B
1	1.3	10%	30%
2	0.7	30%	10%
3	1.25	10%	20%
4	1.1	10%	20%
5	0.9	40%	20%
Total		100%	100%

  a. Calculate the betas for portfolios A and B.
  b. Compare the risk of each portfolio to the market as well as to each other. Which portfolio is more risky?

LG4 **P5.30** Referring to Problem 5.29, if the risk-free rate is 2% and the market return is 7%, calculate the required return for each portfolio using the CAPM.

LG5 LG6 **P5.31** Referring to Problem 5.30, assume that you believe that each of the five assets will earn the return shown in the table below. Based on these figures and the weights in Problem 5.29, what returns do you believe that Portfolios A and B will earn. Which portfolio would you invest in and why?

Asset	Returns
1	16.5%
2	12.0%
3	15.0%
4	13.0%
5	7.0%

Visit **http://www.myfinancelab.com** for web exercises, spreadsheets, and other online resources.

Case Problem 5.1   Traditional Versus Modern Portfolio Theory: Who's Right?

LG5 LG6 Walt Davies and Shane O'Brien are district managers for Lee, Inc. Over the years, as they moved through the firm's sales organization, they became (and still remain) close friends. Walt, who is 33 years old, currently lives in Princeton, New Jersey. Shane, who is 35, lives in Houston, Texas.

Recently, at the national sales meeting, they were discussing various company matters, as well as bringing each other up to date on their families, when the subject of investments came up. Each had always been fascinated by the stock market, and now that they had achieved some degree of financial success, they had begun actively investing.

As they discussed their investments, Walt said he thought the only way an individual who does not have hundreds of thousands of dollars can invest safely is to buy mutual fund shares. He emphasized that to be safe, a person needs to hold a broadly diversified portfolio and that only those with a lot of money and time can achieve independently the diversification that can be readily obtained by purchasing mutual fund shares.

Shane totally disagreed. He said, "Diversification! Who needs it?" He thought that what one must do is look carefully at stocks possessing desired risk-return characteristics and then invest all one's money in the single best stock. Walt told him he was crazy. He said, "There is no way to measure risk conveniently—you're just gambling." Shane disagreed. He explained how his stockbroker had acquainted him with beta, which is a measure of risk. Shane said that the higher the beta, the more risky the stock, and therefore the higher its return. By looking up the betas for potential stock investments on the Internet, he can pick stocks that have an acceptable risk level for him. Shane explained that with beta, one does not need to diversify; one merely needs to be willing to accept the risk reflected by beta and then hope for the best.

The conversation continued, with Walt indicating that although he knew nothing about beta, he didn't believe one could safely invest in a single stock. Shane continued to argue that his broker had explained to him that betas can be calculated not just for a single stock but also for a portfolio of stocks, such as a mutual fund. He said, "What's the difference between a stock with a beta of, say, 1.2 and a mutual fund with a beta of 1.2? They have the same risk and should therefore provide similar returns."

As Walt and Shane continued to discuss their differing opinions relative to investment strategy, they began to get angry with each other. Neither was able to convince the other that he was right. The level of their voices now raised, they attracted the attention of the company's vice president of finance, Elinor Green, who was standing nearby. She came over and indicated she had overheard their argument about investments and thought that, given her expertise on financial matters, she might be able to resolve their disagreement. She asked them to explain the crux of their disagreement, and each reviewed his own viewpoint. After hearing their views, Elinor responded, "I have some good news and some bad news for each of you. There is some validity to what each of you says, but there also are some errors in each of your explanations. Walt tends to support the traditional approach to portfolio management. Shane's views are more supportive of modern portfolio theory." Just then, the company president interrupted them, needing to talk to Elinor immediately. Elinor apologized for having to leave and offered to continue their discussion later that evening.

Questions

a. Analyze Walt's argument and explain why a mutual fund investment may be overdiversified. Also explain why one does not necessarily have to have hundreds of thousands of dollars to diversify adequately.

b. Analyze Shane's argument and explain the major error in his logic relative to the use of beta as a substitute for diversification. Explain the key assumption underlying the use of beta as a risk measure.

c. Briefly describe the traditional approach to portfolio management and relate it to the approaches supported by Walt and Shane.

d. Briefly describe modern portfolio theory and relate it to the approaches supported by Walt and Shane. Be sure to mention diversifiable risk, undiversifiable risk, and total risk, along with the role of beta.

e. Explain how the traditional approach and modern portfolio theory can be blended into an approach to portfolio management that might prove useful to the individual investor. Relate this to reconciling Walt's and Shane's differing points of view.

Case Problem 5.2   Susan Lussier's Inherited Portfolio: Does It Meet Her Needs?

LG3 LG4
LG5 LG6

Susan Lussier is 35 years old and employed as a tax accountant for a major oil and gas explora-
tion company. She earns nearly $135,000 a year from her salary and from participation in the
company's drilling activities. An expert on oil and gas taxation, she is not worried about job
security—she is content with her income and finds it adequate to allow her to buy and do whatever she wishes. Her current philosophy is to live each day to its fullest, not concerning herself
with retirement, which is too far in the future to require her current attention.

A month ago, Susan's only surviving parent, her father, was killed in a sailing accident. He
had retired in La Jolla, California, two years earlier and had spent most of his time sailing. Prior
to retirement, he managed a children's clothing manufacturing firm in South Carolina. Upon
retirement he sold his stock in the firm and invested the proceeds in a security portfolio that
provided him with supplemental retirement income of over $30,000 per year. In his will, he left
his entire estate to Susan. The estate was structured in such a way that in addition to a few family
heirlooms, Susan received a security portfolio having a market value of nearly $350,000 and
about $10,000 in cash.

Susan's father's portfolio contained 10 securities: 5 bonds, 2 common stocks, and 3 mutual
funds. The following table lists the securities and their key characteristics. The common stocks
were issued by large, mature, well-known firms that had exhibited continuing patterns of dividend payment over the past five years. The stocks offered only moderate growth potential—
probably no more than 2% to 3% appreciation per year. The mutual funds in the portfolio were
income funds invested in diversified portfolios of income-oriented stocks and bonds. They provided stable streams of dividend income but offered little opportunity for capital appreciation.

The Securities Portfolio That Susan Lussier Inherited

		Bonds				
Par Value	Issue	S&P Rating	Interest Income	Quoted Price	Total Cost	Current Yield
$40,000	Delta Power and Light 10.125% due 2029	AA	$4,050	$ 98	$39,200	10.33%
$30,000	Mountain Water 9.750% due 2021	A	$2,925	$102	$30,600	9.56%
$50,000	California Gas 9.500% due 2016	AAA	$4,750	$ 97	$48,500	9.79%
$20,000	Trans-Pacific Gas 10.000% due 2027	AAA	$2,000	$ 99	$19,800	10.10%
$20,000	Public Service 9.875% due 2017	AA	$1,975	$100	$20,000	9.88%

		Common Stocks				
Number of Shares	Company	Dividend per Share	Dividend Income	Price per Share	Total Cost	Beta	Dividend Yield
2,000	International Supply	$2.40	$4,800	$22	$44,900	0.97	10.91%
3,000	Black Motor	$1.50	$4,500	$17	$52,000	0.85	8.82%

Number of Shares	Fund	Dividend per Share Income	Dividend Income	Price per Share	Total Cost	Beta	Dividend Yield
		Mutual Funds					
2,000	International Capital Income A Fund	$0.80	$1,600	$10	$20,000	1.02	8.00%
1,000	Grimner Special Income Fund	$2.00	$2,000	$15	$15,000	1.10	7.50%
4,000	Ellis Diversified Income Fund	$1.20	$4,800	$12	$48,000	0.90	10.00%
	Total annual income: $33,400		Portfolio value: $338,000			Portfolio current yield: 9.88%	

Now that Susan owns the portfolio, she wishes to determine whether it is suitable for her situation. She realizes that the high level of income provided by the portfolio will be taxed at a rate (federal plus state) of about 40%. Because she does not currently need it, Susan plans to invest the after-tax income primarily in common stocks offering high capital gain potential. During the coming years she clearly needs to avoid generating taxable income. (Susan is already paying out a sizable portion of her income in taxes.) She feels fortunate to have received the portfolio and wants to make certain it provides her with the maximum benefits, given her financial situation. The $10,000 cash left to her will be especially useful in paying brokers' commissions associated with making portfolio adjustments.

Questions

a. Briefly assess Susan's financial situation and develop a portfolio objective for her that is consistent with her needs.

b. Evaluate the portfolio left to Susan by her father. Assess its apparent objective and evaluate how well it may be doing in fulfilling this objective. Use the total cost values to describe the asset allocation scheme reflected in the portfolio. Comment on the risk, return, and tax implications of this portfolio.

c. If Susan decided to invest in a security portfolio consistent with her needs—indicated in response to question **a**—describe the nature and mix, if any, of securities you would recommend she purchase. Discuss the risk, return, and tax implications of such a portfolio.

d. From the response to question **b**, compare the nature of the security portfolio inherited by Susan with what you believe would be an appropriate security portfolio for her, based on the response to question **c**.

e. What recommendations would you give Susan about the inherited portfolio? Explain the steps she should take to adjust the portfolio to her needs.

Excel@Investing

Excel@Investing

Katie plans to form a portfolio consisting of two securities, Intel (INTC) and Procter & Gamble (PG), and she wonders how the portfolio's return will depend on the amount that she invests in each stock. Katie's professor suggests that she use the capital asset pricing model to define the required returns for the two companies. (Refer to Equations 5.3 and 5.3a.)

$$r_j = r_{rf} + [b_j \times (r_m - r_{rf})]$$

Katie measures r_{rf} using the current long-term Treasury bond return of 5%. Katie determines that the average return on the S&P 500 Index over the last several years is 6.1%, so she uses that figure to measure r_m. She researches a source for the beta information and follows these steps:

- Go to http://money.msn.com
- In the Get Quote box, type INTC and press Get Quote.

- On the next page, look for the stock's beta.
- Repeat the steps for the PG stock.

Questions

a. What are the beta values for INTC and PG? Using the CAPM, create a spreadsheet to determine the required rates of return for both INTC and PG.

b. Katie has decided that the portfolio will be distributed between INTC and PG in a 60% and 40% split, respectively. Hence, a weighted average can be calculated for both the returns and betas of the portfolio. This concept is shown in the spreadsheet for Table 5.2, which can be viewed at **http://www.myfinancelab.com**. Create a spreadsheet using the following models for the calculations:

$$war = (w_i \times r_i) + (w_j \times r_j)$$

where

    war = weighted average required rate of return for the portfolio

    w_i = weight of security i in the portfolio

    r_i = required return of security i in the portfolio

    w_j = weight of security j in the portfolio

    r_j = required return of security j in the portfolio

$$wab = (w_i \times b_i) + (w_j \times b_j)$$

where

    wab = weighted average beta for the portfolio

    w_i = weight of security i in the portfolio

    b_i = beta for security i

    w_j = weight of security j in the portfolio

    b_j = beta for security j

Chapter-Opening Problem

In this problem we will visit United Rentals Inc. (URI), which was introduced at the beginning of the chapter. The following table shows the monthly return on URI stock and on the S&P 500 stock index from January 2009 to December 2014.

Month/Year	S&P 500 Return	United Rentals Return	Month/Year	S&P 500 Return	United Rentals Return
1/2/2009	−8.6%	−38.8%	10/1/2009	−2.0%	−7.9%
2/2/2009	−11.0%	−27.4%	11/2/2009	5.7%	−2.8%
3/2/2009	8.5%	4.0%	12/1/2009	1.8%	6.4%
4/1/2009	9.4%	43.9%	1/4/2010	−3.7%	−18.3%
5/1/2009	5.3%	−21.6%	2/1/2010	2.9%	−5.7%
6/1/2009	0.0%	36.6%	3/1/2010	5.9%	24.2%
7/1/2009	7.4%	15.1%	4/1/2010	1.5%	53.1%
8/3/2009	3.4%	23.0%	5/3/2010	−8.2%	−15.4%
9/1/2009	3.6%	12.1%	6/1/2010	−5.4%	−23.3%

Month/Year	S&P 500 Return	United Rentals Return	Month/Year	S&P 500 Return	United Rentals Return
7/1/2010	6.9%	41.4%	10/1/2012	−2.0%	24.3%
8/2/2010	−4.7%	−14.6%	11/1/2012	0.3%	2.1%
9/1/2010	8.8%	31.9%	12/3/2012	0.7%	9.6%
10/1/2010	3.7%	26.6%	1/2/2013	5.0%	11.2%
11/1/2010	−0.2%	4.4%	2/1/2013	1.1%	5.5%
12/1/2010	6.5%	16.0%	3/1/2013	3.6%	2.9%
1/3/2011	2.3%	17.1%	4/1/2013	1.8%	−4.3%
2/1/2011	3.2%	16.2%	5/1/2013	2.1%	8.0%
3/1/2011	−0.1%	7.4%	6/3/2013	−1.5%	−12.2%
4/1/2011	2.8%	−11.6%	7/1/2013	4.9%	14.8%
5/2/2011	−1.4%	−7.1%	8/1/2013	−3.1%	−4.4%
6/1/2011	−1.8%	−7.1%	9/3/2013	3.0%	6.4%
7/1/2011	−2.1%	−9.4%	10/1/2013	4.5%	10.8%
8/1/2011	−5.7%	−27.5%	11/1/2013	2.8%	6.4%
9/1/2011	−7.2%	1.0%	12/2/2013	2.4%	13.4%
10/3/2011	10.8%	39.0%	1/2/2014	−3.6%	3.8%
11/1/2011	−0.5%	20.2%	2/3/2014	4.3%	9.1%
12/1/2011	0.9%	5.0%	3/3/2014	0.7%	7.5%
1/3/2012	4.4%	29.4%	4/1/2014	0.6%	−1.2%
2/1/2012	4.1%	9.0%	5/1/2014	2.1%	7.7%
3/1/2012	3.1%	2.9%	6/2/2014	1.9%	3.6%
4/2/2012	−0.7%	8.8%	7/1/2014	−1.5%	1.1%
5/1/2012	−6.3%	−26.0%	8/1/2014	3.8%	11.1%
6/1/2012	4.0%	−1.5%	9/2/2014	−1.6%	−5.6%
7/2/2012	1.3%	−15.1%	10/1/2014	2.3%	−0.9%
8/1/2012	2.0%	11.8%	11/3/2014	2.5%	3.0%
9/4/2012	2.4%	1.2%	12/1/2014	−0.4%	−10.0%

Questions

a. Using an Excel spreadsheet calculate the average monthly return on URI stock and on the S&P 500.

b. Using an Excel spreadsheet calculate the standard deviation of monthly returns for URI and the S&P 500. What do your answers tell you about diversifiable risk, undiversifiable risk, and total risk?

c. Using an Excel spreadsheet plot the returns of URI on the vertical axis and the returns of the S&P 500 on the horizontal axis of a graph. Does it appear that URI and the S&P 500 are correlated? If so, are they correlated positively or negatively?

d. Using an Excel spreadsheet add a trend line that best fits the scatterplot of points that you created in part c. What is the slope of this line? How can you interpret the slope? What does it say about the risk of URI compared to the risk of the S&P 500?

Being certified as a Chartered Financial Analyst (CFA) is globally recognized as the highest professional designation you can receive in the field of professional money management. The CFA charter is awarded to those candidates who successfully pass a series of three levels of exams, with each exam lasting six hours and covering a full range of investment topics. The CFA program is administered by the CFA Institute in Charlottesville, VA. (For more information about the CFA program, go to http://www.cfainstitute.org.)

Starting with this Part (2) of the text, and at the end of each part hereafter, you will find a small sample of questions similar to those that you might encounter on the Level I exam.

The Investment Environment and Conceptual Tools

Following is a sample of questions similar to ones that you might find on the CFA exam, Level 1. These questions deal with many of the topics covered in Parts 1 and 2 of this text, including the time value of money, measures of risk and return, securities markets, and portfolio management. (When answering the questions, give yourself 1½ minutes for each question; the objective is to correctly answer 8 of the 11 questions in 16½ minutes.)

1. Liquidity is best described as
   a. wanting a portfolio to grow over time in real terms to meet future needs.
   b. converting an asset into cash without much of a price concession.
   c. wanting to minimize the risk of loss and maintain purchasing power.

2. A portfolio consists of 75% invested in Security A with an expected return of 35% and 25% invested in Security B with an expected return of 7%. Compute the expected return on the portfolio.

3. Stocks A and B have standard deviations of 8% and 15%, respectively. The correlation between the two stocks' returns has historically been 0.35. What is the standard deviation of a portfolio consisting of 60% invested in Stock A and 40% invested in Stock B?

4. Which of the following portfolios would be off the efficient frontier?

Portfolio	Expected Return	Risk
A	13%	17%
B	12%	18%
C	18%	30%

5. As the correlation coefficient between two securities changes in a portfolio,
   a. both expected return and risk change.
   b. neither expected return nor risk changes.
   c. only risk changes.

6. Portfolio risk is
   a. equal to the sum of the standard deviations of each of the securities in the portfolio.
   b. not dependent on the relative weights of the securities in the portfolio.
   c. not equal to the weighted average of the risks of the individual securities in the portfolio.

7. Faced with an efficient set of portfolios, an investor would
   a. choose the one with the highest expected return.
   b. always select portfolios on the left end of the efficient frontier.
   c. choose the portfolio at the point of tangency between the investor's highest indifference curve and the efficient frontier.

8. Both Portfolio Y and Portfolio Z are well diversified. The risk-free rate is 6%, the expected return on the market is 15%, and the portfolios have these characteristics:

Portfolio	Expected Return	Beta
Y	17%	1.20
Z	14%	1.00

Which of the following best characterizes the valuations of Portfolio Y and Portfolio Z?

	Portfolio Y	Portfolio Z
a.	Undervalued	Correctly valued
b.	Correctly valued	Overvalued
c.	Undervalued	Overvalued

9. For a stock with a margin requirement of 40%, how much cash is required, expressed as a percentage of the purchase cost?
   a. 0%
   b. 40%
   c. 50%

10. Which of the following is not a weighting scheme commonly used in creating equity market indexes?
   a. Price-weighted
   b. Industry-weighted
   c. Value-weighted

11. iCorporation has a relative systematic risk level that is 40% greater than the overall market. The expected return on the market is 16%, and the risk-free rate is 7%. Using the CAPM, the required rate of return for iCorporation is closest to
   a. 16.0%
   b. 19.6%
   c. 22.4%

Answers: 1. b; 2. 28%; 3. approximately 8.9%; 4. Portfolio B; 5. c; 6. c; 7. c; 8. c; 9. b; 10. b; 11. b

6

Common Stocks

LEARNING GOALS

After studying this chapter, you should be able to:

LG1 Explain the investment appeal of common stocks and why individuals like to invest in them.

LG2 Describe stock returns from a historical perspective and understand how current returns measure up to historical standards of performance.

LG3 Discuss the basic features of common stocks, including issue characteristics, stock quotations, and transaction costs.

LG4 Understand the different kinds of common stock values.

LG5 Discuss common stock dividends, types of dividends, and dividend reinvestment plans.

LG6 Describe various types of common stocks, including foreign stocks, and note how stocks can be used as investment vehicles.

O ver the last 15 years, stock markets in the United States and around the world have been extremely volatile. U.S. stocks, as indicated by the S&P 500 Index, roared into the new millennium achieving a new all-time high value in March 2000. Over the next two years, the market swooned, falling to levels not seen since mid 1997. From September 2002 to October 2007, the S&P500 rallied again, gaining 90% in roughly five years. However, from October 2007 to March 2009, U.S. stocks lost more than half their value, and in many markets around the world, the results were even worse. Those declining stock values mirrored the state of the world economy, as country after country slipped into a deep recession. U.S. firms responded by cutting dividends. Standard and Poor's reported that a record number of firms cut their dividend payment in the first quarter of 2009, and a record low number announced plans to increase their dividends.

Fortunately, from its March 2009 low, the U.S. stock market nearly doubled over the next two years, hitting a post-recession peak in April 2011. The run-up in stock prices coincided with an increase in dividend payouts. Of the 500 firms included in the S&P 500 stock index, 154 increased their dividend payment in 2010 or 2011, compared to just three firms who cut payments over the same period. Even so, the good news for stocks didn't last very long. In the spring of 2011, concern about a looming economic crisis in Europe sent U.S. stocks lower again. The S&P 500 Index fell by more than 17% from April to September in 2011. The roller coaster ride wasn't over because from September 2011 to May 2015 the U.S. stock market, with a few more rough spots along the way, increased in value 88% to achieve yet another all-time high.

Throughout this volatile period, some companies managed to increase their dividends each year. Standard and Poor's tracks the performance of a portfolio of firms that it calls "dividend aristocrats" because these firms have managed to increase their dividends for at least 25 consecutive years. Including household names such as Johnson & Johnson, Exxon Mobil, and AFLAC, the dividend aristocrat index displays ups and downs that mirror those of the overall market, but at least investors in these firms have enjoyed consistently rising dividends.

(Sources: Stephen Bernard, "S&P: Record Number of Firms Cut Dividends in 1st Quarter," *Pittsburgh Post Gazette*, April 7, 2009; "S&P 500 Dividend Payers Rose to Dozen Year High," May 1, 2012, http://seekingalpha.com/article/545451-s-p-500-dividend-payers-rise-to-dozen-year-high; http://www.standardandpoors.com/indices/sp-500-dividend-aristocrats/en/us/?indexId=spusa-500dusdff--p-us----&ffFix=yes); Oliver Renick, "S&P 500 Sets New Record High Close," *Bloomberg Business*, May 14, 2015, http://www.bloomberg.com/news/articles/2015-05-14/u-s-stock-index-futures-gain-as-s-p-500-heads-for-weekly-loss.)

What Stocks Have to Offer

LG1 LG2 Common stock enables you to participate in the profits of a firm. Every shareholder is a part owner of the firm and, as such, has a claim on the wealth created by the company. This claim is not without limitations, however, because common stockholders are really the **residual owners** of the company. That is, their claim is subordinate to the claims of other investors, such as lenders, so for stockholders to get rich, the firm must first meet all its other financial obligations. Accordingly, as residual owners, holders of common stock have no guarantee that they will receive any return on their investment.

The Appeal of Common Stocks

Even in spite of the steep declines in the U.S. stock market in 2002 and 2008, common stocks remain a popular investment choice among both individual and institutional investors. For most investors, the allure of common stocks is the prospect that they will increase in value over time and generate significant capital gains. Many stocks also pay dividends, thereby providing investors with a periodic income stream. For most stocks, however, the dividends paid in any particular year pale in comparison to the capital gains (and capital losses) that are the natural consequence of stock price fluctuations.

Putting Stock Price Behavior in Perspective

Given the nature of common stocks, when the market is strong, you can generally expect to benefit from price appreciation. A good example is the performance that took place in 2013, when the market, as measured by the Dow Jones Industrial Average (DJIA), went up by more than 26%. Unfortunately, when markets falter, so do investor returns. Just look at what happened in 2008, when the market (again, as measured by the DJIA) fell by almost 34%. Excluding dividends, that means a $100,000 investment declined in value to a little more than $66,000. That hurts!

The market does have its bad days, and sometimes those bad days seem to go on for months. Even though it may not always appear to be so, bad days are the exception rather than the rule. That is certainly the case over the 118-year period from 1897 through 2014, when the DJIA went down (for the year) just 40 times—about one-third of the time. The other two-thirds of the time, the market was up—anywhere from less than 1% on the year to nearly 82%. True, there is some risk and price volatility (even in good markets), but that's the price you pay for all the upside potential. For example, from the end of 1987 to early 2000, in one of the longest bull markets in history, the DJIA grew more than 500% over a 12-year period at an average annual rate of nearly 17%. Yet, even in this market, there were some off days, and even a few off years. But, clearly, they were the exception rather than the rule.

From Stock Prices to Stock Returns

Our discussion so far has centered on stock prices. However, more important than stock prices are *stock returns*, which take into account both price behavior and dividend income. Table 6.1 uses the Standard and Poor's 500 Index (S&P 500) to illustrate how the U.S. stock market has performed since 1930. Like the DJIA, the S&P 500 is a barometer of the overall stock market. As its name implies, the S&P 500 tracks 500 companies (most of which are large firms), so most experts consider it a better indicator of the market's overall performance than the DJIA, which tracks just 30 industrial firms. In addition to total returns, the table breaks market performance down into the two basic sources of return: dividends and capital gains. These figures, of

<table>
<tr><td>**FAMOUS FAILURES IN FINANCE**</td><td>**Beware of the Lumbering Bear**</td></tr>
</table>

FAMOUS FAILURES IN FINANCE

Beware of the Lumbering Bear

Bear markets occur when stock prices are falling. But not all falling markets end up as bears. A drop of 5% or more in one of the major market indexes, like the Dow Jones Industrial Average, is called a "routine decline." Such declines are considered routine because they typically occur several times a year. A "correction" is a drop of 10% or more in an index, whereas the term *bear market* is reserved for severe market declines of 20% or more. Bear markets occur every three to four years on average, although that pattern does not make it easy to predict bear markets. For example, the 1990s were totally bear-free. The most recent bear market began in October 2007 when the S&P 500 peaked a little shy of 1,600. The next 20 months witnessed one of the worst bear markets in U.S. history, with the S&P 500 falling almost 57% by March 2009.

course, reflect the general behavior of the market as a whole, not necessarily that of individual stocks. Think of them as the return behavior on a well-balanced portfolio of common stocks.

The table shows several interesting patterns. First, the returns from capital gains range from an average of 16.5% during the booming 1990s to −1.4% in the 1930s. Returns from dividends vary too, but not nearly as much, ranging from 5.8% in the 1940s to 1.8% in the 2000–2009 period. Breaking down the returns into dividends and capital gains reveals, not surprisingly, that the big returns (or losses) come from capital gains.

Second, stocks generally earn positive total returns over long time periods. From 1930 to 2014, the average annual total return on the S&P 500 was 11.4% per year. At that rate, you could double your money every six or seven years. To look at the figures another way, if you had invested $10,000 in the S&P 500 at the beginning of 1930,

Excel@Investing

TABLE 6.1 HISTORICAL AVERAGE ANNUAL RETURNS ON THE STANDARD AND POOR'S 500, 1930–2014

	Rate of Return from Dividends	Rate of Return from Capital Gains	Average Annual Total Return
1930s	5.7%	−1.4%	4.3%
1940s	5.8%	3.8%	9.6%
1950s	4.7%	16.2%	20.9%
1960s	3.2%	5.4%	8.6%
1970s	4.2%	3.3%	7.5%
1980s	4.1%	13.8%	17.9%
1990s	2.4%	16.5%	18.9%
2000–2009	1.8%	−0.7%	1.1%
1900–2014	3.9%	7.5%	11.4%

Note: The S&P 500 annual total returns come from Damodaran Online and the S&P 500 annual dividend returns come from multpl.com. The S&P 500 annual capital gain returns are approximations, imputed by the authors by subtracting the annual dividend return from the annual total return.

(Sources: Data from http://pages.stern.nyu.edu/~adamodar/New_Home_Page/datafile/histretSP.html and http://www.multpl.com)

then based on the yearly annual returns, your investment would have grown to more than $21.9 million over the next 85 years. You can get rich by investing in the stock market, as long as you are patient!

Third, investing in stocks is clearly not without risk. Although during the first seven decades shown in Table 6.1 the average annual return on stocks was 12.5%, the beginning of the 21st century witnessed several years with double-digit negative returns. In 2008 alone, the S&P 500 lost roughly 36% of its value. From 2000 through 2009, the U.S. stock market's average annual return was only 1.1% per year! If you had invested $10,000 in stocks in 1930, your portfolio would have grown to more than $16 million by the end of 2007, but one year later your portfolio would have fallen to approximately $10 million, before rising again to just over $26 million by the end of 2014. These figures suggest that stocks may be a very good investment in the long run, but that was little consolation to investors who saw their wealth fall dramatically in the early years of the 21st century.

Now keep in mind that the numbers here represent market performance. Individual stocks can and often do perform quite differently. But at least the averages give us a benchmark against which we can assess current stock returns and our own expectations. For example, if a return of about 11% can be considered a good long-term estimate for stocks, then sustained returns of 16% to 18% should definitely be viewed as extraordinary. (These higher returns are possible, of course, but to get them, you very likely will have to take on more risk.) Likewise, long-run stock returns of only 4% to 6% should probably be viewed as substandard. If that's the best you think you can do, then you may want to consider sticking with bonds, where you'll earn almost as much, but with less risk.

A Real Estate Bubble Goes Bust and So Does the Market

An old investment tip is, "Buy land because they aren't making any more of it." For many years, it appeared that this advice applied to housing in the United States, as home prices enjoyed a long, upward march. According to the Standard and Poor's Case-Shiller Home Price Index, a measure of the average value of a single-family home in the United States, the average home price peaked in July 2006. Over the next three years, home prices fell sharply, falling 31% by the summer of 2009. As prices fell, some homeowners realized that they owed more on their mortgages than their homes were worth, and mortgage defaults began to rise. Unfortunately, some of the biggest investors in home mortgages were U.S. commercial and investment banks. As homeowners fell behind on their mortgage payments, the stock prices of financial institutions began to drop, raising serious concerns about the health of the entire U.S. financial system. Those fears seemed to have been realized when a top-tier investment bank, Lehman Brothers, filed for bankruptcy in September 2008. That event sparked a free fall in the stock market.

The House Price Puzzle

Figure 6.1 shows that U.S. stocks rose along with housing prices for many years, but when weakness in the housing sector spilled over into banking, stock prices plummeted. Over the same three-year period the S&P 500 Index lost 28% of its value, and the U.S. economy fell into a deep recession. In the spring of 2009 the stock and housing markets signaled that a recovery might be on the horizon. Indeed, the recession officially ended in June 2009, but by historical standards the economic recovery was somewhat anemic and the housing market continued to languish for another three years. In early 2012 the housing market began a sustained recovery and by the end of 2014 values had climbed back to 84% of their peak values.

FIGURE 6.1   A Snapshot of U.S. Stock and Housing Indexes (2003 through 2014)

From the start of 2003 until the summer of 2006, U.S. stocks rose along with housing prices, but when crumbling U.S. housing prices began to spill over into banking, stock prices plummeted, wiping out all the gains accumulated over the prior six years. Three years after the stock market hit bottom, it had still not reached its precrisis peak, nor had house prices rebounded from their crisis lows to any significant degree. In the summer of 2012 the housing market began a sustained appreciation, and in early 2013 the stock market surged past its precrisis peak.
(Source: Data from S&P Dow Jones Indices LLC.)

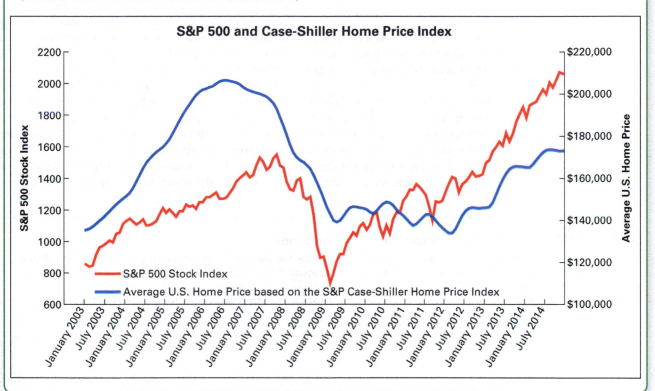

The Pros and Cons of Stock Ownership

Investors own stocks for all sorts of reasons. Some buy stock for the potential for capital gains, while others seek dividend income. Still others appreciate the high degree of liquidity in the stock market. But as with any investment, there are pros and cons to these securities.

The Advantages of Stock Ownership One reason stocks are so appealing is the possibility for substantial returns that they offer. As we just saw, stocks generally provide relatively high returns over the long haul. Indeed, common stock returns compare very favorably to other investments such as long-term corporate bonds and U.S. Treasury securities. For example, over the last century, high-grade corporate bonds earned annual returns that were about half as large as the returns on common stocks. Although long-term bonds outperform stocks in some years, the opposite is true more often than not. Stocks typically outperform bonds, and usually by a wide margin. Stocks also provide protection from inflation because over time their returns exceed the inflation rate. In other words, by purchasing stocks, you gradually increase your purchasing power.

Stocks offer other benefits as well. They are easy to buy and sell, and the costs associated with trading stocks are modest. Moreover, information about stock prices and the stock market is widely disseminated in the news and financial media. A final advantage is that the unit cost of a share of common stock is typically fairly low. Unlike bonds, which normally carry minimum denominations of at least $1,000, and some mutual funds that have fairly hefty minimum investments, common stocks don't have such minimums. Instead, most stocks today are priced at less than $50 or $60 a share—and you can buy any number of shares that you want.

The Disadvantages of Stock Ownership   There are also some disadvantages to common stock ownership. Risk is perhaps the most significant. Stocks are subject to various types of risk, including business and financial risk, purchasing power risk, market risk, and event risk. All of these can adversely affect a stock's earnings and dividends, its price appreciation, and, of course, the rate of return that you earn. Even the best of stocks possess elements of risk that are difficult to eliminate because company earnings are subject to many factors, including government control and regulation, foreign competition, and the state of the economy. Because such factors affect sales and profits, they also affect stock prices and (to a lesser degree) dividend payments.

All of this leads to another disadvantage. Stock returns are highly volatile and very hard to predict, so it is difficult to consistently select top performers. The stock

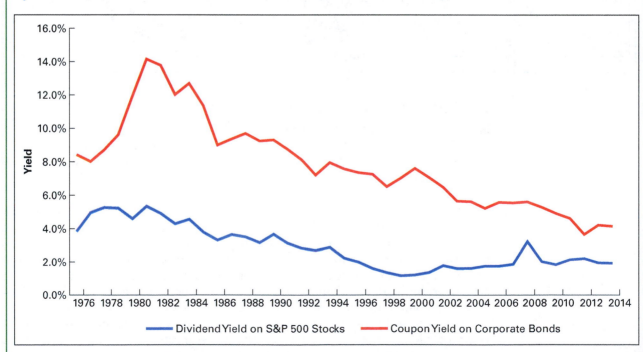

FIGURE 6.2   **The Current Income of Stocks and Bonds**
The current income (dividends) paid to stockholders falls far short of interest income paid to bondholders. The dividend yield is the average dividend yield for stocks in the S&P 500 Index, and the bond yield is for high-quality corporate bonds.
(Source: Data from Federal Reserve Board of Governors and http://www.multpl.com/s-p-500-dividend-yield/table.)

selection process is complex because so many elements affect how a company will perform. In addition, the price of a company's stock today reflects investors' expectations about how the company will perform. In other words, identifying a stock that will earn high returns requires that you not only identify a company that will exhibit strong future financial performance (in terms of sales and earnings) but also that you can spot that opportunity before other investors do and bid up the stock price.

A final disadvantage is that stocks generally distribute less current income than some other investments. Several types of investments—bonds, for instance—pay more current income and do so with much greater certainty. Figure 6.2 compares the dividend yield on common stocks with the coupon yield on high-grade corporate bonds. It shows the degree of sacrifice common stock investors make in terms of current income. Clearly, even though the yield gap has narrowed a great deal in the past few years, common stocks still have a long way to go before they catch up with the current income levels available from bonds and most other types of fixed-income securities.

6.1 What is a common stock? What is meant by the statement that holders of common stock are the residual owners of the firm?

6.2 What are two or three of the major investment attributes of common stocks?

6.3 Briefly describe the behavior of the U.S. stock market over the last half of the 20th century and the early part of the 21st century.

6.4 How important are dividends as a source of return to common stock? What about capital gains? Which is more important to total return? Which causes wider swings in total return?

6.5 What are some of the advantages and disadvantages of owning common stock? What are the major types of risks to which stockholders are exposed?

Basic Characteristics of Common Stock

LG3 LG4 Each share of common stock represents an equity (or ownership) position in a company. It's this equity position that explains why common stocks are often referred to as *equity securities* or **equity capital**. Every share entitles the holder to an equal ownership position and participation in the corporation's earnings and dividends, an equal vote (usually), and an equal voice in management. Together the common stockholders own the company. The more shares an investor owns, the bigger his or her ownership position. Common stock has no maturity date—it remains outstanding indefinitely.

Common Stock as a Corporate Security

All corporations issue common stock of one type or another. But the shares of many, if not most, corporations are never traded because the firms either are too small or are family controlled. The stocks of interest to us in this book are **publicly traded issues**—the shares that are readily available to the general public and that are bought and sold in the open market. The firms issuing such shares range from giants like Apple Inc. and Exxon Mobil Corporation to much smaller regional and local firms. The market for publicly traded stocks is enormous. According to the World Federation of Exchanges, the value of all U.S. stocks in early 2015 was more than $26.6 trillion.

Issuing New Shares Companies can issue shares of common stock in several ways. The most widely used procedure is the **public offering**. When using this procedure, the corporation offers the investing public a certain number of shares of its stock at a certain price. Figure 6.3 shows an announcement for such an offering. In this case Box is offering 12,500,000 shares of its Class A stock at a price of $14 per share. At $14 per share, the offering will raise $175 million and after underwriting fees Box will receive $162.75 million. Notice that each of the newly issued shares of Class A stock sold by the company to public investors will be entitled to one vote, whereas the Class B shares that remain in the hands of the Box's founders have 10 votes per share. The result of this dual-class stock structure is that following the IPO the new investors will control fewer than 2% of the votes compared to the founders, who will control more than 98% of the votes.

Companies also can issue new shares of stock using what is known as a **rights offering**. In a rights offering, existing stockholders are given the first opportunity to buy the new issue. In essence, a stock right gives a shareholder the right (but not the obligation) to purchase new shares of the company's stock in proportion to his or her current ownership position.

For instance, if a stockholder currently owns 1% of a firm's stock and the firm issues 10,000 additional shares, the rights offering will give that stockholder the opportunity to purchase 1% (100 shares) of the new issue. If the investor does not want to use the rights, he or she can sell them to someone who does. The net result of a rights offering is the same as that of a public offering. The firm ends up with more equity in its capital structure, and the number of shares outstanding increases.

Stock Spin-Offs Perhaps one of the most creative ways of bringing a new issue to the market is through a **stock spin-off**. Basically, a spin-off occurs when a company gets rid of one of its subsidiaries or divisions. For example, Time Warner did this when it spun off its Time Inc. subsidiary in June 2014. The company doesn't just sell the subsidiary to some other firm. Rather, it creates a new stand-alone company and then distributes stock in that company to its existing stockholders. Thus, every Time Warner shareholder received 1 share in the newly created, and now publicly traded, Time Inc. for every 8 shares of Time Warner stock that he or she held.

There have been hundreds of stock spin-offs in the last 10 to 15 years. Some of the more notable recent ones are the spin-off of Land's End by Sears Holdings, News Corporation by 21st Century Fox, and TripAdvisor by Expedia. Normally, companies execute stock spin-offs if they believe the subsidiary is no longer a good fit or if they feel they've become too diversified and want to focus on their core products. The good news is that such spin-offs often work very well for investors, too.

Stock Splits Companies can also increase the number of shares outstanding by executing a **stock split**. In declaring a split, a firm merely announces that it will increase the number of shares outstanding by exchanging a specified number of new shares for each outstanding share of stock. For example, in a two-for-one stock split, two new shares of stock are exchanged for each old share. In a three-for-two split, three new shares are exchanged for every two old shares outstanding. Thus, a stockholder who owned 200 shares of stock before a two-for-one split becomes the owner of 400 shares; the same investor would hold 300 shares if there had been a three-for-two split.

A company uses a stock split when it wants to enhance its stock's trading appeal by lowering its market price. Normally, the price of the stock falls roughly in proportion to the terms of the split (unless the stock split is accompanied by a big increase in the level of dividends). For example, using the ratio of the number of old shares to new, we

FIGURE 6.3 An Announcement of a New Stock Issue

This announcement indicates that the company—Box—is issuing 12,500,000 shares of stock at a price of $14 per share. For this cloud-based file-sharing and document-management company, the new issue will mean $162.75 million in fresh capital.
(Source: *Box Inc.*, Initial Public Offer prospectus, http://www.nasdaq.com/markets/ipos/filing.ashx?filingid=9961051.)

PROSPECTUS

12,500,000 Shares

CLASS A COMMON STOCK

Box, Inc. is offering 12,500,000 shares of its Class A common stock. This is our initial public offering and no public market currently exists for shares of our Class A common stock. The initial public offering price is $14.00 per share.

Following this offering, we will have two classes of authorized common stock, Class A common stock and Class B common stock. The rights of the holders of our Class A common stock and Class B common stock will be identical, except with respect to voting and conversion rights. Each share of our Class A common stock will be entitled to one vote. Each share of our Class B common stock will be entitled to 10 votes and will be convertible at any time into one share of our Class A common stock. The holders of our outstanding Class B common stock will hold approximately 98.8% of the voting power of our outstanding capital stock following this offering.

Our Class A common stock has been approved for listing on the New York Stock Exchange under the symbol "BOX."

We are an "emerging growth company" as defined under the federal securities laws and, as such, may elect to comply with certain reduced public company reporting requirements for future filings. Investing in our Class A common stock involves risks. See "**Risk Factors**" beginning on page 16.

Price $14.00 A Share

	Price to Public	Underwriting Discounts and Commissions [1]	Proceeds to Box, Inc.
Per Share	$14.00	$0.98	$13.02
Total	$175,000,000	$12,250,000	$162,750,000

(1) See the section titled "Underwriters" for a description of the compensation payable to the underwriters.

We have granted the underwriters the right to purchase up to an additional 1,875,000 shares of our Class A common stock to cover over-allotments.

Entities affiliated with Coatue Management, L.L.C. (Coatue Entities), an affiliate of certain of our existing stockholders, may purchase less than 1,250,000 shares of our Class A common stock in this offering at the initial public offering price. The Coatue Entities may ultimately elect not to purchase shares in this offering or the underwriters may elect not to sell any shares in this offering to the Coatue Entities. The underwriters will receive the same discount from any shares sold to the Coatue Entities as they will from any other shares sold to the public in this offering.

The Securities and Exchange Commission and state securities regulators have not approved or disapproved of these securities, or determined if this prospectus is truthful or complete. Any representation to the contrary is a criminal offense.

The underwriters expect to deliver the shares of our Class A common stock to purchasers on January 28, 2015.

Morgan Stanley   **Credit Suisse**   **J.P. Morgan**

BMO Capital Markets

Canaccord Genuity   **Pacific Crest Securities**   **Raymond James**   **Wells Fargo Securities**

January 22, 2015

can expect a $100 stock to trade at or close to $50 a share after a two-for-one split. Specifically, we divide the original price per share by the ratio of new shares to old. That same $100 stock would trade at about $67 after a three-for-two split—that is, $100 \div 3/2 = \$100 \div 1.5 = \$67$.

Example

> On April 9, 2015, Starbucks Corporation split its shares two-for-one. On the day before the split, Starbucks shares closed at $95.23. Theoretically, after the split the stock price should fall by half to $47.62. In fact, once the split went into effect on April 9th, the opening price of 1 Starbucks share fell to $47.65.

Treasury Stock   Instead of increasing the number of outstanding shares, corporations sometimes find it desirable to reduce the number of shares by buying back their own stock. Firms may repurchase their own stock when they view it as undervalued in the marketplace. When that happens, the company's own stock becomes an attractive investment candidate. Firms also repurchase shares as an alternative to paying dividends. Paying dividends may force some shareholders to pay taxes on the income they receive, while repurchasing shares may have different tax consequences for shareholders.

Firms usually purchase their stock in the open market, like any other individual or institution. When acquired, these shares become known as **treasury stock**. Technically, treasury stocks are simply shares of stock that have been issued and subsequently repurchased by the issuing firm. Treasury stocks are kept by the corporation and can be used at a later date for several purposes. For example, they could be used to pay for mergers and acquisitions, to meet employee stock option plans, or as a means of paying stock dividends. Or the shares can simply be held in treasury for an indefinite time.

The short-term impact of these share repurchases—or *buybacks*, as they're sometimes called—is generally positive, meaning that stock prices generally go up when firms announce their intentions to conduct share repurchases. The long-term impact is less settled, with some research indicating that share repurchases are followed by periods of above-average stock returns and other research contesting that conclusion.

Classified Common Stock   For the most part, all the stockholders in a corporation enjoy the same benefits of ownership. Occasionally, however, a company will issue different classes of common stock, each of which entitles holders to different privileges and benefits. These issues are known as **classified common stock**. Hundreds of publicly traded firms, including well-known tech companies such as Google and Facebook, have created such stock classes. Although issued by the same company, each class of common stock may have unique characteristics.

Firms that issue multiple classes of stock usually do so to grant different voting rights to different groups of investors. For instance, when Facebook conducted its 2012 IPO, it issued Class A and Class B shares. The Class A shares, available for purchase by the public, were entitled to 1 vote per share. Class B shares, held by Facebook CEO and founder Mark Zuckerberg (and other Facebook insiders) were entitled to 10 votes per share. This ensured that Zuckerberg would have voting control of the company even if Facebook issued many more Class A shares over time in subsequent stock offerings. On rare occasions firms may use classified stock to grant different dividend rights to different investors.

Regardless of the specifics, whenever there is more than one class of common stock outstanding, you should take the time to determine the privileges, benefits, and limitations of each class.

Buying and Selling Stocks

To be an informed stock trader, you need a basic awareness of how to read stock-price quotes. You also need to understand the transaction costs associated with buying and selling stock. Certainly, keeping track of current prices is an essential element in buy-and-sell decisions. Prices help you monitor the market performance of your security holdings. Similarly, transaction costs are important because of the impact they have on investment returns. Indeed, the costs of executing stock transactions can sometimes consume most (or all) of the profits from an investment. You should not take these costs lightly.

Reading the Quotes Investors in the stock market have come to rely on a highly efficient information system that quickly disseminates market prices to the public. The stock quotes that appear daily in the financial press and online are a vital part of that information system. To see how to read and interpret stock price quotations, consider the quotes that appear at Yahoo! Finance. These quotes give not only the most recent price of each stock but also a great deal of additional information.

Figure 6.4 illustrates a basic quote for Abercrombie & Fitch Co. stock, which trades under the ticker symbol ANF. The quote was taken after trading hours on Friday, May 15, 2015. On that day, the price of Abercrombie common stock closed at $21.42 per share, up $0.17 (or 0.8%) from the previous day's close of $21.25. Notice that the stock opened on Friday at $21.27, reaching an intraday high of $21.55 and an intraday low of $21.17 (see "Day's Range"). Figure 6.4 also reveals that during the preceding 52 weeks Abercrombie stock traded as high as $45.50 and as low as $19.34 (see "52wk Range"). Trading volume for the stock on May 15 was 1.245 million shares, considerably less than the average daily volume over the previous three months of just under three million shares.

A few other items from Figure 6.4 are noteworthy. Abercrombie's stock has a beta of 2.2, meaning that it is more than twice as risky (i.e., has more than twice as much systematic risk) as the average stock in the market (as the very wide trading range over the past year would also indicate). Abercrombie's total *market capitalization* (or market cap) is $1.49 billion. Remember, a company's market cap is simply its share price times

FIGURE 6.4 **A Stock Quote for Abercrombie & Fitch**

This figure shows a stock quote for Abercrombie & Fitch on May 15, 2015. (Source: Yahoo! Finance, **http://finance.yahoo.com/q?uhb=uh3_finance_vert&fr=&type=2button&s=anf**.)

the number of shares outstanding. In its most recent reporting period, the company earned $0.71 per share, and given the closing price of $21.42, the price-to-earnings ratio of Abercrombie stock was just over 30.

Transaction Costs Investors can buy and sell common stock in round or odd lots. A *round lot* is 100 shares of stock or multiples thereof. An *odd lot* is a transaction involving fewer than 100 shares. For example, the sale of 400 shares of stock would be a round-lot transaction, and the sale of 75 shares would be an odd-lot transaction. Trading 250 shares of stock would involve a combination of two round lots and an odd lot.

An investor incurs certain transaction costs when buying or selling stock. In addition to some modest transfer fees and taxes paid by the seller, the major cost is the brokerage fee paid—by both buyer and seller—at the time of the transaction. As a rule, brokerage fees can amount to just a fraction of 1% to as much as 2% or more, depending on whether you use the services of a discount broker or full-service broker. But they can go even higher, particularly for very small trades. Historically, transactions involving odd lots required a specialist called an *odd-lot dealer* and triggered an extra cost called an *odd-lot differential*. Today, electronic trading systems make it easier to process odd-lot transactions, so these trades do not increase trading costs as much as they once did. Not surprisingly, odd-lot trades have become more common in recent years. For example, roughly one-third of all trades of Google shares involve odd lots.

Another type of transaction cost is the *bid-ask spread*, the difference between the bid and ask prices for a stock. In Figure 6.4, you can see that the last quoted ask price for Abercrombie stock was $21.42 and the bid price was $21.41, so the spread between these two prices was $0.01. Remember that the ask price represents what you would pay to buy the stock and the bid price is what you receive if you sell the stock, so the difference between them is a kind of transaction cost that you incur when you make a roundtrip (i.e., a purchase and then later a sale) trade. Of course, these prices change throughout the trading day, as does the spread between them, but the current bid-ask spread gives you at least a rough idea of the transaction cost that you pay to the market maker or dealer who makes a living buying and selling shares every day.

AN ADVISOR'S PERSPECTIVE

Steve Wright
Managing Member, The Wright Legacy Group

"Over the past 20 years, the costs for an average individual to buy and sell stocks have gone down dramatically."

MyFinanceLab

Common Stock Values

The worth of a share of common stock can be described in a number of ways. Terms such as *par value*, *book value*, *market value*, and *investment value* are all found in the financial media. Each designates some accounting, investment, or monetary attribute of a stock.

Par Value A stock's **par value** is an arbitrary amount assigned to the stock when it is first issued. It has nothing to do with the stock's market price, but instead represents a minimum value below which the corporate charter does not allow a company to sell shares. Because par value establishes a kind of floor for the value of a stock, companies set par values very low. For example, in Facebook's IPO, the par value of its shares was set at $0.000006. Except for accounting purposes, par value is of little consequence. Par value is a throwback to the early days of corporate law, when it was used as a basis for assessing the extent of a stockholder's legal liability. Because the term has little or no significance for investors, many stocks today are issued without a par value.

Book Value Another accounting measure, **book value** is the stockholders' equity in the firm as reported on the balance sheet (and sometimes expressed on a per share basis). Remember that on the balance sheet, stockholders' equity is just the difference between the value of the firm's assets and its liabilities (less any preferred stock). The book value represents the amount of capital that shareholders contributed to the firm when it initially sold shares as well as any profits that have been reinvested in the company over time.

Example

> Social Networks Incorporated (SNI) lists assets worth $100 million on its balance sheet along with $60 million in liabilities. There is no preferred stock, but the company has 10 million common shares outstanding. The book value of SNI's stockholders' equity is $40 million, or $4 per common share. Of the $40 million in stockholders' equity, $30 million was raised in the company's initial public offering of common stock and the other $10 million represents profits that the company earned and reinvested in the business since its IPO.

A stock's book value is inherently a backward-looking estimate of its value because it focuses on things that happened in the past (like the original sale of stock and profits earned and reinvested in earlier periods). In contrast, a stock's market value is forward-looking and reflects investors' expectations about how the company will perform in the future.

Market Value A stock's **market value** is simply its prevailing market price. It reflects what investors are willing to pay to acquire the company today, and it is essentially independent of the book value. In fact, stocks usually trade at market prices that exceed their book values, sometimes to a very great degree.

As you have already learned, by multiplying the market price of the stock by the number of shares outstanding, you can calculate a firm's market capitalization, which represents the total market value of claims held by shareholders. A firm's market capitalization is somewhat analogous to the stockholders' equity figure on the balance sheet, except that the market capitalization represents what the firm's equity is actually worth in today's market, whereas the stockholders' equity balance is a backward-looking assessment of shareholders' claims.

Example

> Investors believe that prospects for Social Networks Incorporated are very bright and that the company will rapidly increase its revenues and earnings for the next several years. As a result, investors have bid up the market price of SNI's stock to $20, which is five times greater than the company's book value per share. With 10 million common shares outstanding, SNI's market capitalization is $200 million compared to the book value of stockholders' equity of just $40 million.

When a stock's market value drops below its book value, it is usually because the firm is dealing with some kind of financial distress and does not have good prospects for growth. Some investors like to seek out stocks that are trading below book value in the hope that the stocks will recover and earn very high returns in the process. While such a strategy may offer the prospect of high returns, it also entails significant risks.

Investment Value Investment value is probably the most important measure for a stockholder. It indicates the worth investors place on the stock—in effect, what they think the stock should be trading for. Determining a security's investment value is a complex process based on expectations of the return and risk characteristics of a stock. Any stock has two potential sources of return: dividend payments and capital gains. In establishing investment value, investors try to determine how much money they will make from these two sources. They then use those estimates as the basis for formulating the return potential of the stock. At the same time, they try to assess the amount of risk to which they will be exposed by holding the stock. Such return and risk information helps them place an investment value on the stock. This value represents the maximum price an investor should be willing to pay for the issue.

CONCEPTS IN REVIEW

Answers available at
http://www.pearsonhighered.com/smart

6.6 What is a stock split? How does a stock split affect the market value of a share of stock? Do you think it would make any difference (in price behavior) if the company also changed the dividend rate on the stock? Explain.

6.7 What is a stock spin-off? In very general terms, explain how a stock spin-off works. Are these spin-offs of any value to investors? Explain.

6.8 Define and differentiate between the following pairs of terms.

    a. Treasury stock versus classified stock
    b. Round lot versus odd lot
    c. Par value versus market value
    d. Book value versus investment value

6.9 What is an odd-lot differential? How can you avoid odd-lot differentials? Which of the following transactions would involve an odd-lot differential?

    a. Buy 90 shares of stock
    b. Sell 200 shares of stock
    c. Sell 125 shares of stock

Common Stock Dividends

LG5 In 2014, U.S. corporations paid out billions in dividends. Counting only the companies included in the S&P 500 stock index, dividends that year totaled more than $375 billion. Yet, in spite of these numbers, dividends still don't get much attention. Many investors, particularly younger ones, often put very little value on dividends. To a large extent, that's because capital gains provide a much bigger source of return than dividends—at least over the long haul.

But attitudes toward dividends are changing. The protracted bear market of 2007 through 2009 revealed just how uncertain capital gains can be and, indeed, that all those potential profits can turn into substantial capital losses. Dividend payments do not fluctuate as much as stock prices do. Plus, dividends provide a nice cushion when the market stumbles (or falls flat on its face). Moreover, current tax laws put dividends on the same plane as capital gains. Both now are taxed at the same tax rate. Dividends are tax-free for taxpayers in the 10% and 15% brackets, taxed at a 15% rate for the 25% to 35% tax brackets, and taxed at a 20% rate for taxpayers whose income surpasses the 35% tax bracket. Single taxpayers with modified adjusted gross income of $200,000 and married couples exceeding $250,000 are also subject to a 3.8% Medicare surtax on investment income, including dividend income.

The Dividend Decision

By paying out dividends, typically on a quarterly basis, companies share some of their profits with stockholders. Actually, a firm's board of directors decides how much to pay in dividends. The directors evaluate the firm's operating results and financial condition to determine whether dividends should be paid and, if so, in what amount. They also consider whether the firm should distribute some of its cash to investors by paying a dividend or by repurchasing some of the firm's outstanding stock. If the directors decide to pay dividends, they also establish several important payment dates. In this section we'll look at the corporate and market factors that go into the dividend decision. Then we'll briefly examine some of the key payment dates.

Corporate versus Market Factors When the board of directors assembles to consider the question of paying dividends, it weighs a variety of factors. First, the board looks at the firm's earnings. Even though a company does not have to show a profit to pay dividends, profits are still considered a vital link in the dividend decision.

With common stocks, the annual earnings of a firm are usually measured and reported in terms of **earnings per share (EPS)**. Basically, EPS translates aggregate corporate profits into profits per share. It provides a convenient measure of the amount of earnings available to stockholders. Earnings per share is found by using the following formula.

Equation 6.1

$$EPS = \frac{\begin{array}{c} \text{Net profit} \\ \text{after taxes} \end{array} - \text{Preferred dividends}}{\begin{array}{c} \text{Number of shares of} \\ \text{common stock outstanding} \end{array}}$$

For example, if a firm reports a net profit of \$1.25 million, pays \$250,000 in dividends to preferred stockholders, and has 500,000 shares of common stock outstanding, it has an EPS of \$2 ((\$1,250,000 − \$250,000)/500,000). Note in Equation 6.1 that preferred dividends are subtracted from profits because they must be paid before any funds can be made available to common stockholders.

While assessing profits, the board also looks at the firm's growth prospects. It's very likely that the firm will need some of its earnings for investment purposes and to help finance future growth. In addition, the board will take a close look at the firm's cash position, making sure that paying dividends will not lead to a cash shortfall. Furthermore, the firm may be subject to a loan agreement that legally limits the amount of dividends it can pay.

After looking at internal matters, the board will consider certain market effects and responses. Most investors feel that if a company is going to retain earnings rather than pay them out in dividends, it should reinvest those funds to achieve faster growth and higher profits. If the company retains earnings but cannot reinvest them at a favorable rate of return, investors begin to clamor for the firm to distribute those earnings through dividends.

Moreover, to the extent that different types of investors tend to be attracted to different types of firms, the board must make every effort to meet the dividend expectations of its shareholders. For example, income-oriented investors are attracted to firms that generally pay high dividends. Failure to meet those expectations might prompt some investors to sell their shares, putting downward pressure on the stock price. In addition, some institutional investors (e.g., certain mutual funds and pension funds) are restricted to investing only in companies that pay a dividend. This is a factor in some companies' decisions to initiate a dividend payment.

Some Important Dates Let's assume the directors decide to declare a dividend. Once that's done, they must indicate the date of payment and other important dates associated with the dividend. Three dates are particularly important to the stockholders: date of record, payment date, and ex-dividend date. The **date of record** is the date on which the investor must be a registered shareholder of the firm to be entitled to a dividend. All investors who are official stockholders as of the close of business on that date will receive the dividends that have just been declared. These stockholders are often referred to as *holders of record*. The **payment date**, also set by the board of directors, generally follows the date of record by a week or two. It is the actual date on which the company will mail dividend checks to holders of record (and is also known as the *payable date*).

Because of the time needed to make bookkeeping entries after a stock is traded, the stock will sell without the dividend (ex-dividend) for three business days up to and including the date of record. The **ex-dividend date** will dictate whether you were an official shareholder and therefore eligible to receive the declared dividend. If you sell a stock on or after the ex-dividend date, you receive the dividend. The reason is that the buyer of the stock (the new shareholder) will not have held the stock on the date of record. Instead, you (the seller) will still be the holder of record. Just the opposite will occur if you sell the stock before the ex-dividend date. In this case, the new shareholder (the buyer of the stock) will receive the dividend because he or she will be the holder of record.

To see how this works, consider the following sequence of events. On June 3, the board of directors of Cash Cow, Inc., declares a quarterly dividend of 50 cents per share to holders of record on June 18. Checks will be mailed out on the payment date, June 30. The calendar below shows these dividend dates. In this case, if you bought 200 shares of the stock on June 15, you would receive a check in the mail sometime after June 30 in the amount of $100. On the other hand, if you purchased the stock on June 16, the seller of the stock would receive the check because he or she, not you, would be recognized as the holder of record.

June

S	M	T	W	T	F	S	
	1	2	**3**	4	5	6	— Declaration date
7	8	9	10	11	12	13	
14	15	**16**	17	**18**	19	20	— Date of record
21	22	23	24	25	26	27	— Ex-dividend date
28	29	**30**					— Payment date

Types of Dividends

Normally, companies pay dividends in the form of cash. Sometimes they pay dividends by issuing additional shares of stock. The first type of distribution is known as a **cash dividend,** and the second is a **stock dividend.** Occasionally, companies pay dividends in other forms, such as a stock spin-off (discussed earlier) or perhaps even samples of the company's products. But these other forms of dividend payments are relatively rare compared to cash dividends.

Cash Dividends More firms pay cash dividends than any other type of dividend. A nice feature of cash dividends is that they tend to increase over time, as companies' earnings grow. In fact, for companies that pay cash dividends, the average annual increase in dividends is around 3% to 5%. This trend represents good news for investors because a steadily increasing stream of dividends tends to shore up stock returns in soft markets.

A convenient way of assessing the amount of dividends received is to measure the stock's **dividend yield**. Basically, this is a measure of dividends on a relative (percentage) basis rather than on an absolute (dollar) basis. A stock's dividend yield measures its current income as a percentage of its price. The dividend yield is computed as follows:

Equation 6.2

$$\text{Dividend yield} = \frac{\text{Annual dividends received per share}}{\text{Current market price of the stock}}$$

Thus, a company that annually pays $2 per share in dividends to its stockholders, and whose stock is trading at $40, has a dividend yield of 5%.

> **Example**
>
> In May 2015 Nordic American Tankers (NAT) paid its quarterly dividend of $0.38 per share, which translates into an annual dividend of $1.52. At that time, NAT's share price was $11.40, so its dividend yield was 13.3% ($1.52 ÷ $11.40), which is an unusually high level for common stock.

Firms generally do not pay out all of their earnings as dividends. Instead, they distribute some of their earnings as dividends and retain some to reinvest in the business. The **dividend payout ratio** measures the percentage of earnings that a firm pays in dividends. It is computed as follows:

Equation 6.3

$$\text{Dividend payout ratio} = \frac{\text{Dividends per share}}{\text{Earnings per share}}$$

A company would have a payout ratio of 50% if it had earnings of $4 a share and paid annual dividends of $2 a share. Although stockholders like to receive dividends, they normally do not like to see extremely high payout ratios. Such high payout ratios are difficult to maintain and may lead the company into trouble.

> **Example**
>
> In the 12 months ending in May 2015, Pepsico Inc. paid dividends of $2.81 per share to investors. Over the same period, the company's earnings per share were $4.30, so Pepsico's dividend payout ratio was about 65%. In other words, Pepsico used almost two-thirds of its earnings to pay dividends and it reinvested the other third.

The appeal of cash dividends took a giant leap forward in 2003 when the federal tax code changed to reduce the tax on dividends. Prior to this time, cash dividends were taxed as ordinary income, meaning at that time they could be taxed at rates as high as 35%. For that reason, many investors viewed cash dividends as a relatively unattractive source of income, especially because capital gains (when realized) were taxed at much lower preferential rates. After 2003 both dividends and capital gains were taxed at the same rate. That, of course, makes dividend-paying stocks far more attractive, even to investors in higher tax brackets. Firms responded to the tax change in two ways. First, firms that already paid dividends increased them. Total dividends paid by U.S. companies increased by 30% from 2003 to 2005. Second, many firms that had never paid dividends began paying them. In the year leading up to the tax cut, about four firms per quarter announced plans to initiate dividend payments. In the following year, the number of firms initiating dividends surged to 29 companies per quarter, an increase of roughly 700%! The dividend paying trend resumed as the economy began to recover from the most recent recession. In 2010 U.S. companies paid out $197 billion worth of dividends and for 2013 the amount grew to $302 billion, a 50% increase. Paying dividends is fashionable not only in the United States but around the world as well. In 2013 publicly traded companies worldwide paid over $1 trillion in dividends for the first time and between 2009 and 2013 companies world-wide paid about $4.4 trillion in cash dividends.

Stock Dividends Occasionally, a firm may declare a stock dividend. A stock dividend simply means that the firm pays its dividend by distributing additional shares of stock. For instance, if the board declares a 10% stock dividend, then you will receive 1 new share of stock for each 10 shares that you currently own.

Stock dividends are similar to stock splits in the sense that when you receive a stock dividend, you receive no cash. As the number of shares outstanding increases due to the dividend, the share price falls, leaving the total value of your holdings in the company basically unchanged. As with a stock split, a stock dividend represents primarily a cosmetic change because the market responds to such dividends by adjusting share prices downward according to the terms of the stock dividend. Thus, in the example above, a 10% stock dividend normally leads to a decline of around 10% in the stock's share price. If you owned 200 shares of stock that were trading at $100 per share, the total market value of your investment would be $20,000. After a 10% stock dividend, you would own 220 shares of stock (i.e., 200 shares × 1.10), but each share would be worth about $90.91. You would own more shares, but they would be trading at lower prices, so the total market value of your investment would remain about the same (i.e., 220 × $90.91 = $20,000.20). There is, however, one bright spot in all this. Unlike cash dividends, stock dividends are not taxed until you actually sell the stocks.

Dividend Reinvestment Plans

For investors who plan to reinvest any dividends that they receive, a **dividend reinvestment plan (DRIP)** may be attractive. In these corporate-sponsored programs, shareholders can have their cash dividends automatically reinvested into additional shares of the company's common stock. (Similar reinvestment programs are offered by mutual funds and by some brokerage houses such as Bank of America and Fidelity.) The basic investment philosophy is that *if the company is good enough to invest in, it's good enough to reinvest in.* As Table 6.2 demonstrates, such an approach can have a tremendous impact on your investment position over time.

Today more than 1,000 companies (including most major corporations) offer dividend reinvestment plans. These plans provide investors with a convenient and inexpensive way to accumulate capital. Stocks in most DRIPs are acquired free of brokerage commissions, and most plans allow partial participation. That is, participants may specify a portion of their shares for dividend reinvestment and receive cash dividends

TABLE 6.2 CASH OR REINVESTED DIVIDENDS?

Situation: You buy 100 shares of stock at $25 a share (total investment, $2,500); the stock currently pays $1 a share in annual dividends. The price of the stock increases at 8% per year; dividends grow at 5% per year.

Investment Period (yr.)	Number of Shares Held	Market Value of Stock Holdings ($)	Total Cash Dividends Received ($)
Take Dividends in Cash			
5	100	$ 3,672	$ 552
10	100	$ 5,397	$1,258
15	100	$ 7,930	$2,158
20	100	$11,652	$3,307
Full Participation in Dividend Reinvestment Plan **(100% of cash dividends reinvested)**			
5	115.59	$ 4,245	0
10	135.66	$ 7,322	0
15	155.92	$12,364	0
20	176.00	$20,508	0

on the rest. Some plans even sell stocks to their DRIP investors at below-market prices—often at discounts of 3% to 5%. In addition, most plans will credit fractional shares to the investor's account, and many will even allow investors to buy additional shares of the company's stock. For example, once enrolled in the General Mills plan, investors can purchase up to $3,000 worth of the company's stock each quarter, free of commissions.

Shareholders can join dividend reinvestment plans by simply sending a completed authorization form to the company. Once you're enrolled, the number of shares you hold will begin to grow with each dividend. There is a catch, however. Even though these dividends take the form of additional shares of stock, you must still pay taxes on them as though they were cash dividends. Don't confuse these dividends with stock dividends—reinvested dividends are treated as taxable income in the year they're received, just as though they had been received in cash. But as long as the preferential tax rate on dividends remains in effect, paying taxes on stock dividends, will be much less of a burden than it used to be.

CONCEPTS IN REVIEW

Answers available at http://www.pearsonhighered.com/smart

6.10 Briefly explain how the dividend decision is made. What corporate and market factors are important in deciding whether, and in what amount, to pay dividends?

6.11 Why is the ex-dividend date important to stockholders? If a stock is sold on the ex-dividend date, who receives the dividend—the buyer or the seller? Explain.

6.12 What is the difference between a cash dividend and a stock dividend? Which would be more valuable to you? How does a stock dividend compare to a stock split? Is a 200% stock dividend the same as a two-for-one stock split? Explain.

6.13 What are dividend reinvestment plans, and what benefits do they offer to investors? Are there any disadvantages?

Types and Uses of Common Stock

 6 Common stocks appeal to investors because they offer the potential for everything from current income and stability of capital to attractive capital gains. The market contains a wide range of stocks, from the most conservative to the highly speculative. Generally, the kinds of stocks that investors seek depend on their investment objectives and investment programs. We will examine several of the more popular types of common stocks here, as well as the various ways such securities can be used in different types of investment programs.

Types of Stocks

Not all stocks are alike, and the risk and return profile of each stock depends on the characteristics of the company that issued it. Some of the characteristics include whether the company pays a dividend, the company's size, how rapidly the company is growing, and how susceptible its earnings are to changes in the business cycle. Over time, investors have developed a classification scheme that helps them place a particular stock into one of several categories. Investors use these categories to help design their portfolios to achieve a good balance of risk and return. Some of the categories that you hear about most often are blue chip stocks, income stocks, growth stocks, tech stocks, cyclical stocks, defensive stocks, large-cap stocks, mid-cap stocks, and small-cap stocks.

Blue-Chip Stocks Blue chips are the cream of the common stock crop. They are stocks issued by companies that have a long track record of earning profits and paying dividends. **Blue-chip stocks** are issued by large, well-established firms that have impeccable financial credentials. These companies are often the leaders in their industries.

Not all blue chips are alike, however. Some provide consistently high dividend yields; others are more growth-oriented. Good examples of blue-chip growth stocks are Nike, Procter & Gamble, Home Depot, Walgreen's, Lowe's Companies, and United Parcel Service. Figure 6.5 shows some basic operating and market information about P&G's stock, as obtained from the introductory part of a typical Zacks Investment Research report. Notice that in addition to a real-time quotation and hold recommendation, the Zacks report provides a company summary, price chart, consensus recommendations, EPS information, and more for P&G. Examples of high-yielding blue chips include such companies as AT&T, Chevron, Merck, Johnson & Johnson, McDonald's, and Pfizer.

While blue-chip stocks are not immune from bear markets, they are less risky than most stocks. They tend to appeal to investors who are looking for quality, dividend-paying investments with some growth potential. Blue chips appeal to investors who want to earn higher returns than bonds typically offer without taking a great deal of risk.

Income Stocks Some stocks are appealing simply because of the dividends they pay. This is the case with **income stocks**. These issues have a long history of regularly paying higher-than-average dividends. Income stocks are ideal for those who seek a relatively safe and high level of current income from their investment capital. Holders of income stocks (unlike bonds and preferred stocks) can expect the dividends they receive to increase regularly over time. Thus, a company that paid, say, $1.00 a share in dividends in 2000 would be paying just over $1.80 a share in 2015, if dividends had been

FIGURE 6.5   A Blue-Chip Stock

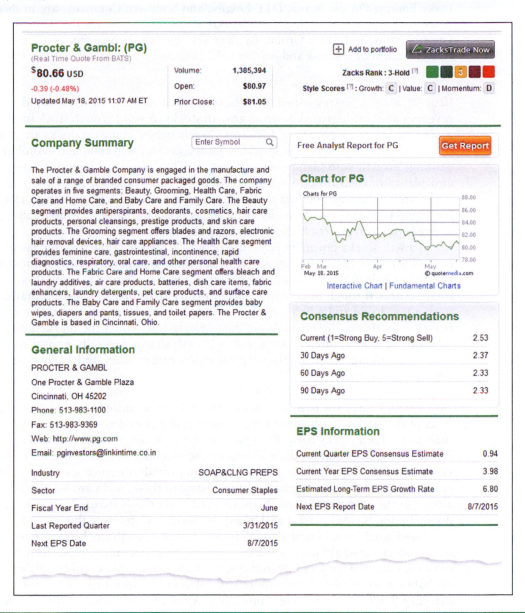

growing at around 4% per year. Dividends that grow over time provide investors with some protection from the effects of inflation.

The major disadvantage of income stocks is that some of them may be paying high dividends because of limited growth potential. Indeed, it's not unusual for income securities to exhibit relatively low earnings growth. This does not mean that such firms are unprofitable or lack future prospects. Quite the contrary: Most firms whose shares qualify as income stocks are highly profitable organizations with excellent prospects. A number of income stocks are among the giants of U.S. industry, and many are also classified as quality blue chips. Many public utilities, such as American Electric Power, Duke Energy, Oneok, Scana, DTE Energy, and Southern Company, are in this group. Also in this group are selected industrial and financial issues like Conagra Foods, General Mills, and Altria Group. By their very nature, income stocks are not exposed to a great deal of business and market risk. They are, however, subject to a fair amount of interest rate risk.

Growth Stocks Shares issued by companies that are experiencing rapid growth in revenues and earnings are known as **growth stocks**. A good growth stock might exhibit a sustained earnings growth of 15% to 18% when most common stocks are growing at 6% to 8% per year. Generally speaking, established growth companies combine steady earnings growth with high returns on equity. They also have high operating margins and plenty of cash flow to service their debt. Amazon.com, Apple, Google, eBay, Berkshire Hathaway, and Starbucks are all prime examples of growth stocks. As this list suggests, some growth stocks also rate as blue chips and provide quality growth, whereas others represent higher levels of speculation.

Growth stocks normally pay little or no dividends. Their payout ratios seldom exceed 10% to 15% of earnings. Instead, these companies reinvest most of their profits to help finance additional growth. Thus, investors in growth stocks earn their returns through price appreciation rather than dividends—and that can have both a good side and a bad side. When the economy is strong and the stock market is generally rising, these stocks are particularly hot. When the markets turn down, so do these stocks, often in a big way. Growth shares generally appeal to investors who are looking for attractive capital gains rather than dividends and who are willing to bear more risk.

Tech Stocks Over the past 20 years or so, tech stocks have become such a dominant force in the market (both positive and negative) that they deserve to be put in a class all their own. **Tech stocks** basically represent the technology sector of the market. They include companies that produce computers, semiconductors, data storage devices, and software. They also include companies that provide Internet services, networking equipment, and wireless communications. Some of these stocks are listed on the NYSE, although the vast majority of them are traded on the Nasdaq. Tech stocks, in fact, dominate the Nasdaq market and, thus, the Nasdaq Composite Index.

These stocks would probably fall into either the growth stock category or the speculative stock class, although some of them are legitimate blue chips. Tech stocks may offer the potential for very high returns, but they also involve considerable risk and are probably most suitable for the more risk-tolerant investor. Included in the tech-stock category you'll find some big names, like Apple, Cisco Systems, Google, and Intel. You'll also find many not-so-big names, like NVIDIA, Marvell Technology, LinkedIn, SanDisk, Advantest, L-3 Communications, and Electronic Arts.

Speculative Stocks Shares that lack sustained records of success but still offer the potential for substantial price appreciation are known as **speculative stocks**. Perhaps investors' hopes are spurred by a new management team that has taken over a troubled company or by the introduction of a promising new product. Other times, it's the hint that some new information, discovery, or production technique will favorably affect the growth prospects of the firm. Speculative stocks are a special breed of securities, and they enjoy a wide following, particularly when the market is bullish.

Generally speaking, the earnings of speculative stocks are uncertain and highly unstable. These stocks are subject to wide swings in price, and they usually pay little or nothing in dividends. On the plus side, speculative stocks such as Sirius XM Radio, Bona Film Group, Destination Maternity, Global Power Equipment Group, and Iridium Communications offer attractive growth prospects and the chance to "hit it big" in the market. To be successful, however, an investor has to identify the big-money winners before the rest of the market does. Speculative stocks are highly risky; they require not only a strong stomach but also a considerable amount of investor know-how. They are used to seek capital gains, and investors will often aggressively trade in and out of these securities as the situation demands.

Cyclical Stocks **Cyclical stocks** are issued by companies whose earnings are closely linked to the overall economy. They tend to move up and down with the business cycle. Companies that serve markets tied to capital equipment spending by business or to consumer spending for big-ticket, durable items like houses and cars typically head the list of cyclical stocks. Examples include Alcoa, Caterpillar, Genuine Parts, Lennar, Brunswick, and Timken.

Cyclical stocks generally do well when the economy is moving ahead, but they tend to do especially well when the country is in the early stages of economic recovery. Likewise, they perform poorly when the economy begins to weaken. Cyclical stocks are probably most suitable for investors who are willing to trade in and out of these stocks as the economic outlook dictates and who can tolerate the accompanying exposure to risk.

Defensive Stocks Sometimes it is possible to find stocks whose prices remain stable or even increase when general economic activity is tapering off. These securities are known as **defensive stocks**. They tend to be less susceptible to downswings in the business cycle than the average stock.

Defensive stocks include the shares of many public utilities, as well as industrial and consumer goods companies that produce or market such staples as beverages, foods, and drugs. An excellent example of a defensive stock is Walmart. This recession-resistant company is the world's leading retailer. Other examples are Checkpoint Systems, a manufacturer of antitheft clothing security clips, WD-40, the maker of that famous all-purpose lubricant, and Extendicare, a leading provider of long-term care and assisted-living facilities. Defensive shares are commonly used by more aggressive investors, who tend to "park" their funds temporarily in defensive stocks while the economy remains soft or until the investment atmosphere improves.

Market-Cap Stocks A stock's size is based on its market value—or, more commonly, its market capitalization. This value is calculated as the market price of the stock times the number of shares outstanding. Generally speaking, the U.S. stock market can be broken into three segments, as measured by a stock's market cap:

Small-cap	less than $2 billion
Mid-cap	$2 billion up to $10 billion
Large-cap	more than $10 billion

The **large-cap stocks** are the corporate giants such as Walmart, Exxon Mobil, and Apple. Although large-cap stocks are few in number, these companies account for more than 75% of the market value of all U.S. equities. But as the saying goes, bigger isn't necessarily better. Nowhere is that statement more accurate than in the stock market. On average, small-cap stocks tend to earn higher returns than do large-caps.

Mid-cap stocks offer investors some attractive return opportunities. They provide much of the sizzle of small-stock returns, without as much price volatility. At the same time, because mid-caps are fairly good-sized companies and many of them have been around for a long time, they offer some of the safety of the big, established stocks. Among the ranks of the mid-caps are such well-known companies as Dick's Sporting Goods, Hasbro, Wendy's, and Williams-Sonoma. Although these securities offer a nice alternative to large stocks without the uncertainties of small-caps, they probably are most appropriate for investors who are willing to tolerate a bit more risk and price volatility than large-caps have.

One type of mid-cap stock of particular interest is the so-called baby blue chip. Also known as "baby blues," these companies have all the characteristics of a regular blue chip except size. Like their larger counterparts, baby blues have rock-solid balance sheets, modest levels of debt, and several years of steady profit growth. Baby blues normally pay a modest level of dividends, but like most mid-caps, they tend to emphasize growth. Thus, they're considered ideal for investors seeking quality long-term growth. Some well-known baby blues are Logitech, American Eagle Outfitters, and Garmin Ltd.

Some investors consider small companies to be in a class by themselves in terms of attractive return opportunities. In many cases, this has turned out to be true. Known as **small-cap stocks**, these companies generally have annual revenues of less than $250 million. But because of their size, spurts of growth can have dramatic effects on their earnings and stock prices. Callaway Golf, MannKind, and Shoe Carnival are some of the better-known small-cap stocks.

Although some small-caps are solid companies with equally solid financials, that's not the case with most of them. Indeed, because many of these companies are so small, they don't have a lot of stock outstanding, and their shares are not widely traded. In addition, small-cap stocks have a tendency to be "here today and gone tomorrow." Although some of these stocks may hold the potential for high returns, investors should also be aware of the very high-risk exposure that comes with many of them.

A special category of small-cap stocks is the initial public offering (IPO). Most IPOs are small, relatively new companies that are going public for the first time. (Prior to their public offering, these stocks were privately held and not publicly traded.) Like other small-company stocks, IPOs are attractive because of the substantial capital gains that investors can earn. Of course, there's a catch: To stand a chance of buying some of the better, more attractive IPOs, you need to be either an active trader or a preferred client of the broker. Otherwise, the only IPOs you're likely to hear of will be the ones these investors don't want. Without a doubt, IPOs are high-risk investments, with the odds stacked against the investor. Because there's no market record to rely on, only investors who know what to look for in a company and who can tolerate substantial risk should buy these stocks.

Investing in Foreign Stocks

One of the most dramatic changes to occur in U.S. financial markets in the past 25 years was the trend toward globalization. Indeed, globalization became the buzzword of the 1990s, and nowhere was that more evident than in the world's equity markets. Consider, for example, that in 1970 the U.S. stock market accounted for fully two-thirds of the world market. In essence, the U.S. stock market was twice as big as all the rest of the world's stock markets combined. That's no longer true: According to the World Federation of Exchanges in 2015, the U.S. share of the world equity market value had dropped to 40%.

Today the world equity markets are dominated by just six markets, which together account for about 75% of the global total. The United States, by far, has the biggest equity market, which in 2015 had a total value approaching $27 trillion. China is in second place with nearly $8 trillion in total equity market value, and if you include the Hong Kong Exchanges, then China's total is more than $11 trillion. Japan is in third place with nearly $5 trillion and is followed by Euronext, which includes exchanges in Belgium, France, the Netherlands, Portugal, and the United Kingdom. The last of the markets valued above $3 trillion is India with its two major exchanges. Other equity markets worth more than $1 trillion can be found in Canada, Germany, Switzerland, Australia, and Korea.

Comparative Returns The United States still dominates the world equity markets in terms of sheer size. But that leaves unanswered an important question: How has the U.S. equity market performed in comparison to the rest of the world's major stock markets? In 2014, which was generally a good year for stock returns, the U.S. market earned more than 13.5% (as measured by the S&P 500 Index). One year is probably not the best way to judge the performance of a country's stock market, so Figure 6.6 plots the average annual return on stocks from 1900 to 2014 for 19 countries. Over that period the U.S. stock market earned an average annual return of 9.6%, a performance equal to the average for the countries listed. In other words, over a long period of time, stock returns in the United States have been unremarkable relative to stock

FIGURE 6.6

Average Annual Stock Returns around the World (1900 to 2014)

(Source: Elroy Dimson, Paul Marsh, and Mike Staunton, Credit Suisse Global Investment Returns Sourcebook 2015, https://www.credit-suisse.com/investment_banking/doc/cs_global_investment_returns_yearbook.pdf.)

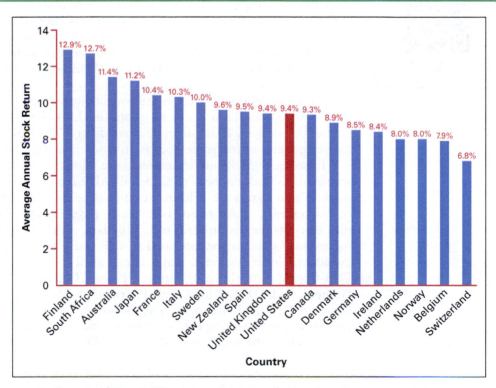

returns in other markets around the world. If we looked on a year-by-year basis, we would see that U.S. stocks rarely earn the highest returns in any given year. Translated, that means there definitely are attractive returns awaiting those investors who are willing to venture beyond our borders.

Going Global: Direct Investments Basically, there are two ways to invest in foreign stocks: through direct investments or through ADRs.

Without a doubt, the most adventuresome way is to buy shares directly in foreign markets. Investing directly is *not* for the uninitiated, however. You have to know what you're doing and be prepared to tolerate a good deal of market risk. Although most major U.S. brokerage houses are set up to accommodate investors interested in buying foreign securities, there are still many logistical problems to face. To begin with, you have to cope with currency fluctuations that can have a dramatic impact on your returns. But that's just the start. You also have to deal with different regulatory and accounting standards. The fact is that most foreign markets, even the bigger ones, are not as closely regulated as U.S. exchanges. Investors in foreign markets, therefore, may have to put up with insider trading and other practices that can create disadvantages for foreign investors. Finally, there are the obvious language barriers, tax issues, and general "red tape" that all too often plague international transactions. The returns from direct foreign investments can be substantial, but so can the obstacles.

How Do ADRs Work?

Going Global with ADRs Fortunately, there is an easier way to invest in foreign stocks, and that is to buy American Depositary Receipts (ADRs). ADRs are dollar-denominated instruments (or certificates) that represent ownership interest in American Depositary Shares (ADSs). ADSs, in turn, represent a certain number of shares in a non-U.S. company that have been deposited with a U.S. bank (the number of shares can range from a fraction of a share to 20 shares or more). The first ADR was created in 1927 by a U.S. bank to allow U.S. investors to invest in shares of a British department store. ADRs are great for investors who want to own foreign stocks but don't want the hassles that often come with them. For example, because ADRs trade in U.S. dollars and are cleared through U.S. settlement system, ADR holders avoid having to transact in a foreign currency.

American depositary receipts are bought and sold on U.S. markets just like stocks in U.S. companies. Their prices are quoted in U.S. dollars. Furthermore, dividends are paid in U.S. dollars. Today, there are more than 3,700 ADRs available in the U.S. representing shares of companies located in more than 100 countries around the world.

To see how ADRs are structured, take a look at BP, the British oil and gas firm whose ADRs trade on the NYSE. Each BP ADR represents ownership of 6 shares of BP stock. These shares are held in a custodial account by a U.S. bank (or its foreign correspondent), which receives dividends, pays any foreign withholding taxes, and then converts the net proceeds to U.S. dollars, which it passes on to investors. Other foreign stocks that can be purchased as ADRs include Sony (Japan), Ericsson Telephone (Sweden), Nokia (Finland), Royal Dutch Shell (Netherlands), Nestle (Switzerland), Elan Corporation (Ireland), Suntech Power (China), BASF (Germany), Hutchison Wampoa, Ltd. (Hong Kong), Teva Pharmaceuticals (Israel), Norsk Hydro (Norway), Diageo (U.K.), and Grupo Televisa (Mexico). You can even buy ADRs on Russian companies, such as Vimpel-Communications, a Moscow-based cellular phone company whose shares trade (as ADRs) on the NYSE.

Putting Global Returns in Perspective Whether you buy foreign stocks directly or through ADRs, the whole process of global investing is a bit more complicated and more risky than domestic investing. When investing globally, you have to pick both the right stock and the right market. Basically, foreign stocks are valued much the same way as U.S. stocks. Indeed, the same variables that drive U.S. share prices (earnings, dividends, and so on) also drive stock values in foreign markets. On top of this, each market reacts to its own set of economic forces (inflation, interest rates, level of economic activity), which set the tone of the market. At any given time, some markets are performing better than others. The challenge facing global investors is to be in the right market at the right time.

As with U.S. stocks, foreign shares produce the same two basic sources of returns: dividends and capital gains (or losses). But with global investing, there is a third variable—currency exchange rates—that affects returns to U.S. investors. In particular, as the U.S. dollar weakens or strengthens relative to a foreign currency, the returns to U.S. investors from foreign stocks increase or decrease accordingly. In a global context, total return to U.S. investors in foreign securities is defined as follows:

Equation 6.4
$$\begin{array}{c} \text{Total returns} \\ (\text{in U.S. dollars}) \end{array} = \begin{array}{c} \text{Current income} \\ (\text{dividends}) \end{array} + \begin{array}{c} \text{Capital gains} \\ (\text{or losses}) \end{array} \pm \begin{array}{c} \text{Changes in currency} \\ \text{exchange rates} \end{array}$$

Because current income and capital gains are in the "local currency" (the currency in which the foreign stock is denominated, such as the euro or the Japanese yen), we can shorten the total return formula to:

Equation 6.5
$$\begin{array}{c} \text{Total return} \\ (\text{in U.S. dollars}) \end{array} = \begin{array}{c} \text{Returns from current} \\ \text{income and capital gains} \\ (\text{in local currency}) \end{array} \pm \begin{array}{c} \text{Returns from} \\ \text{changes in currency} \\ \text{exchange rates} \end{array}$$

Thus, the two basic components of total return are those generated by the stocks themselves (dividends plus change in share prices) and those derived from movements in currency exchange rates.

Measuring Global Returns Employing the same two basic components noted in Equation 6.5, we can compute total return in U.S. dollars by using the following holding period return (HPR) formula, as modified for changes in currency exchange rates.

Equation 6.6
$$\begin{array}{c} \text{Total return} \\ (\text{in U.S. dollars}) \end{array} = \left[\frac{\begin{array}{c} \text{Ending value of} \\ \text{stock in foreign} \\ \text{currency} \end{array} + \begin{array}{c} \text{Amount of dividends} \\ \text{received in} \\ \text{foreign currency} \end{array}}{\begin{array}{c} \text{Beginning value of stock} \\ \text{in foreign currency} \end{array}} \times \frac{\begin{array}{c} \text{Exchange rate} \\ \text{at end of} \\ \text{holding period} \end{array}}{\begin{array}{c} \text{Exchange rate} \\ \text{at beginning of} \\ \text{holding period} \end{array}} \right] - 1$$

In Equation 6.6, the "exchange rate" represents the value of the foreign currency in U.S. dollars—that is, how much one unit of the foreign currency is worth in U.S. money.

This modified HPR formula is best used over investment periods of one year or less. Essentially, the first component of Equation 6.6 provides returns on the stock in local currency, and the second element accounts for the impact of changes in currency exchange rates.

To see how this formula works, consider a U.S. investor who buys several hundred shares of Siemens AG, the German electrical engineering and electronics company that trades on the Frankfurt Stock Exchange. Since Germany is part of the European Community (EC), its currency is the euro. Let's assume that the investor paid a price per share of 90.48 euros for the stock, at a time when the exchange rate between the U.S. dollar and the euro (US$/€) was $0.945, meaning one euro was worth almost 95 (U.S.) cents. The stock paid annual dividends of 5 euros per share. Twelve months later, the stock was trading at 94.00 euros, when the US$/€ exchange rate was $1.083. Clearly, the stock went up in price and so did the euro, so the investor must have done all right. To find out just what kind of return this investment generated (in U.S. dollars), we'll have to use Equation 6.6.

$$\begin{aligned}\text{Total return} \atop \text{(in U.S. dollars)} &= \left[\frac{€94.00 + €5.00}{€90.48} \times \frac{\$1.083}{\$0.945}\right] - 1 \\ &= [1.0942 \times 1.1460] - 1 \\ &= [1.2540] - 1 \\ &= 25.4\% \end{aligned}$$

With a return of 25.4%, the investor obviously did quite well. However, most of this return was due to currency movements, not to the behavior of the stock. Look at just the first part of the equation, which shows the return (in local currency) earned on the stock from dividends and capital gains: $1.0942 - 1 = 9.42\%$. Thus, the stock itself produced a return of less than 9.50%. All the rest of the return—about 16% (i.e., $25.40\% - 9.42\%$)—came from the change in currency values. In this case, the value of the U.S. dollar went down relative to the euro and thus added to the return.

Currency Exchange Rates As we've just seen, exchange rates can have a dramatic impact on investor returns. They can convert mediocre returns or even losses into very attractive returns—and vice versa. Only one thing determines whether the so-called currency effect is going to be positive or negative: the behavior of the U.S. dollar relative to the currency in which the security is denominated. In essence, a stronger dollar has a negative impact on total returns to U.S. investors, and a weaker dollar has a positive impact. Thus, other things being equal, the best time to be in foreign securities is when the dollar is falling.

Of course, the greater the amount of fluctuation in the currency exchange rate, the greater the impact on total returns. The challenge facing global investors is to find not only the best-performing foreign stock(s) but also the best-performing foreign currencies. You want the value of both the foreign stock and the foreign currency to go up over your investment horizon. And note that this rule applies both to direct investment in foreign stocks and to the purchase of ADRs. (Even though ADRs are denominated in dollars, their quoted prices vary with ongoing changes in currency exchange rates.)

Alternative Investment Strategies

Basically, common stocks can be used as (1) a "storehouse" of value, (2) a way to accumulate capital, and (3) a source of income. Storage of value is important to all investors, as nobody likes to lose money. However, some investors are more concerned than others about losses. They rank safety of principal as their most important stock selection criterion. These investors are more quality-conscious and tend to gravitate toward blue chips and other nonspeculative shares.

Accumulation of capital, in contrast, is generally an important goal to those with long-term investment horizons. These investors use the capital gains and/or dividends that stocks provide to build up their wealth. Some use growth stocks for this purpose, while others do it with income shares, and still others use a little of both.

Finally, some investors use stocks as a source of income. To them, a dependable flow of dividends is essential. High-yielding, good-quality income shares are usually their preferred investment vehicle.

Individual investors can use various investment strategies to reach their investment goals. These include buy-and-hold, current income, quality long-term growth, aggressive stock management, and speculation and short-term trading. The first three strategies appeal to investors who consider storage of value important. Depending on the temperament of the investor and the time he or she has to devote to an investment program, any of these strategies might be used to accumulate capital. In contrast, the current-income strategy is the logical choice for those using stocks as a source of income.

We discuss these strategies in more detail below. You should understand these strategies so that you can choose which one suits your needs.

Buy-and-Hold Buy-and-hold is the most basic of all investment strategies and certainly one of the most conservative. The objective is to place money in a secure investment (safety of principal is vital) and watch it grow over time. In this strategy, investors select high-quality stocks that offer attractive current income and/or capital gains and hold them for extended periods—perhaps as long as 10 to 15 years. This strategy is often used to finance retirement funds, to meet the educational needs of children, or simply to accumulate capital over the long haul. Generally, investors pick a portfolio of good stocks and invest in them on a regular basis for long periods of time—until either the investment climate or corporate conditions change dramatically.

Buy-and-hold investors regularly add fresh capital to their portfolios (many treat them like savings plans). Most also plow the income from annual dividends back into the portfolio and reinvest in additional shares (often through dividend reinvestment plans). Long popular with so-called value-oriented investors, this approach is used by quality-conscious individuals who are looking for competitive returns over the long haul.

Current Income Some investors use common stocks to seek high current income. Common stocks are desirable for this purpose, not so much for their high dividend yields but because their dividends tend to increase over time. In this strategy, safety of principal and stability of income are vital; capital gains are of secondary importance. Quality income shares are the obvious choice for this strategy. Some investors adopt it simply as a way of earning high (and relatively safe) returns on their investment capital. More often, however, the current-income strategy is used by those who are trying to supplement their income. Indeed, many of these investors plan to use the added income for consumption purposes, such as a retired couple supplementing their retirement benefits.

Quality Long-Term Growth This strategy is less conservative than either of the first two in that it seeks capital gains as the primary source of return. A fair amount of trading takes place with this approach. Most of the trading is confined to quality growth stocks (including some of the better tech stocks, as well as baby blues and other mid-caps). These stocks offer attractive growth prospects and the chance for considerable price appreciation. Although a number of growth stocks also pay dividends, this strategy emphasizes capital gains as the principal way to earn big returns.

This approach involves greater risk because of its heavy reliance on capital gains. Therefore, a good deal of diversification is often used. Long-term accumulation of capital is the most common reason for using this approach, but compared to the buy-and-hold tactic, the investor aggressively seeks a bigger payoff by doing considerably more trading and assuming more market risk.

A variation of this investment strategy combines quality long-term growth with high income. This is the total-return approach to investing. Although solidly anchored in long-term growth, this approach also considers dividend income as a source of return. Investors who use the total-return approach seek attractive long-term returns from both dividend income and capital gains by holding both income stocks and growth stocks in their portfolios. Or they may hold stocks that provide both dividends and capital gains. In the latter case, the investor doesn't necessarily look for high-yielding stocks but for stocks that offer the potential for high rates of growth in their dividend streams.

Total-return investors are very concerned about quality. Indeed, about the only thing that separates them from current-income and quality long-term growth investors is that total-return investors care more about the amount of return than about the source of return. For this reason, total-return investors seek the most attractive returns wherever they can find them, be it from a growing stream of dividends or from appreciation in the price of a stock.

Aggressive Stock Management Aggressive stock management also seeks attractive rates of return through a fully managed portfolio. An investor using this strategy aggressively trades in and out of stocks to achieve eye-catching returns, primarily from capital gains. Blue chips, growth stocks, big-name tech stocks, mid-caps, and cyclical issues are the primary investments. More aggressive investors might even consider small-cap stocks, including some of the more speculative tech stocks, foreign shares, and ADRs.

This approach is similar to the quality long-term growth strategy. However, it involves considerably more trading, and the investment horizon is generally much shorter. For example, rather than waiting 2 or 3 years for a stock to move, an aggressive stock trader would go after the same investment payoff in 6 to 12 months. Timing security transactions and turning investment capital over fairly rapidly are both key elements of this strategy. These investors try to stay fully invested in stocks when the market is bullish. When the market weakens, they put a big chunk of their money into defensive stocks or even into cash and other short-term debt instruments.

This aggressive strategy has substantial risks and trading costs. It also places real demands on the individual's time and investment skills. But the rewards can be substantial.

Speculation and Short-Term Trading Speculation and short-term trading characterize the least conservative of all investment strategies. The sole objective of this strategy is capital gains. The shorter the time in which the objective can be achieved, the better. Although investors who use this strategy confine most of their attention to speculative or small-cap stocks and tech stocks, they are not averse to using foreign shares (especially those in so-called emerging markets) or other forms of common stock if they offer attractive short-term opportunities. Many speculators feel that information about the industry or company is less important than market psychology or the general tone of the market. It is a process of constantly switching from one position to another, as new opportunities appear.

Because the strategy involves so much risk, many transactions yield little or no profit, or even substantial losses. The hope is, of course, that when one does hit, it will be in a big way, and returns will be more than sufficient to offset losses. This strategy obviously requires considerable knowledge and time. Perhaps most important, it also requires the psychological and financial fortitude to withstand the shock of financial losses.

<table>
<tr><td>

CONCEPTS IN REVIEW

Answers available at http://www.pearsonhighered.com/smart

</td><td>

6.14 Define and briefly discuss the investment merits of each of the following.

a. Blue chips	b. Income stocks
c. Mid-cap stocks	d. American depositary receipts
e. IPOs	f. Tech stocks

6.15 Why do most income stocks offer only limited capital gains potential? Does this mean the outlook for continued profitability is also limited? Explain.

6.16 With all the securities available in the United States, why would a U.S. investor want to buy foreign stocks? Describe the two ways in which a U.S. investor can buy stocks in a foreign company. As a U.S. investor, which approach would you prefer? Explain.

6.17 Which investment approach (or approaches) do you feel would be most appropriate for a quality-conscious investor? What kind of investment approach do you think you'd be most comfortable with? Explain.

</td></tr>
</table>

MyFinanceLab

Here is what you should know after reading this chapter. MyFinanceLab will help you identify what you know and where to go when you need to practice.

What You Should Know	Key Terms	Where to Practice
LG1 Explain the investment appeal of common stocks and why individuals like to invest in them. Common stocks have long been a popular investment vehicle, largely because of the attractive return opportunities they provide. From current income to capital gains, there are common stocks available to fit any investment need.	residual owners, *p. 216*	MyFinanceLab Study Plan 6.1
LG2 Describe stock returns from a historical perspective and understand how current returns measure up to historical standards of performance. Stock returns consist of both dividends and capital gains, although price appreciation is the key component. Over the long run, stocks have provided investors with annual returns of around 10% to 12%. The decade of the 1990s was especially rewarding, as stocks generated returns of anywhere from around 20% (on the Dow) to nearly 30% in the tech-heavy Nasdaq market. That situation changed in early 2000, when one of the biggest bull markets in history came to an abrupt end. From 2000 through late 2002, the S&P 500 fell nearly 50%, but it moved to an all-time high in October 2007. With the onset of the financial crises and economic recession the S&P 500 again lost half of its value between 2007 and 2009, nearly doubling over the next two years to a post-recession high in early 2011. After giving back 17% during 2011, the market surged in value 88% to set a new all-time high in early 2015.		MyFinanceLab Study Plan 6.2

What You Should Know	Key Terms	Where to Practice
LG3 Discuss the basic features of common stocks, including issue characteristics, stock quotations, and transaction costs. Common stocks are a form of equity capital, with each share representing partial ownership of a company. Publicly traded stock can be issued via a public offering or through a rights offering to existing stockholders. Companies can also increase the number of shares outstanding through a stock split. To reduce the number of shares in circulation, companies can buy back shares, which are then held as treasury stock. Occasionally, a company issues different classes of common stock, known as classified common stock.	classified common stock, *p. 224* equity capital, *p. 221* public offering, *p. 222* publicly traded issues, *p. 221* rights offering, *p. 222* stock spin-off, *p. 222* stock split, *p. 222* treasury stock, *p. 224*	MyFinanceLab Study Plan 6.3 Video Learning Aid for Problem P6.1
LG4 Understand the different kinds of common stock values. There are several ways to calculate the value of a share of stock. Book value represents accounting value. Market value is a security's prevailing market price. Investment value is the amount that investors think the stock should be worth.	book value, *p. 227* investment value, *p. 227* market value, *p. 227* par value, *p. 226*	MyFinanceLab Study Plan 6.4
LG5 Discuss common stock dividends, types of dividends, and dividend reinvestment plans. Companies often share their profits by paying out cash dividends to stockholders. Companies pay dividends only after carefully considering a variety of corporate and market factors. Sometimes companies declare stock dividends rather than, or in addition to, cash dividends. Many firms that pay cash dividends have dividend reinvestment plans, through which shareholders can automatically reinvest cash dividends in the company's stock.	cash dividend, *p. 230* date of record, *p. 230* dividend payout ratio, *p. 231* dividend reinvestment plan (DRIP), *p. 232* dividend yield, *p. 231* earnings per share (EPS), *p. 229* ex-dividend date, *p. 230* payment date, *p. 230* stock dividend, *p. 230*	MyFinanceLab Study Plan 6.5
LG6 Describe various types of common stocks, including foreign stocks, and note how stocks can be used as investment vehicles. Depending on their needs and preferences, investors can choose blue chips, income stocks, growth stocks, tech stocks, speculative issues, cyclicals, defensive shares, large-cap, mid-cap stocks, small-cap stocks, and initial public offerings. Also, U.S. investors can buy common stock of foreign companies either directly on foreign exchanges or on U.S. markets as American depositary Receipts (ADRs). Generally, common stocks can be used as a storehouse of value, as a way to accumulate capital, or as a source of income. Investors can follow different investment strategies (buy-and-hold, current income, quality long-term growth, aggressive stock management, and speculation and short-term trading) to achieve these objectives.	blue-chip stocks, *p. 234* cyclical stocks, *p. 237* defensive stocks, *p. 237* growth stocks, *p. 236* income stocks, *p. 234* mid-cap stocks, *p. 238* small-cap stocks, *p. 238* speculative stocks, *p. 236* tech stocks, *p. 236*	MyFinanceLab Study Plan 6.6 Video Learning Aid for Problem P6.14

Log into MyFinanceLab, take a chapter test, and get a personalized Study Plan that tells you which concepts you understand and which ones you need to review. From there, MyFinanceLab will give you further practice, tutorials, animations, videos, and guided solutions.
Log into **http://www.myfinancelab.com**

Discussion Questions

LG1 **Q6.1** Look at the record of stock returns in Table 6.1.
a. How would you compare the average annual returns for the various decades?
b. Considering the average annual returns that have been generated over holding periods of 10 years or more, what rate of return do you feel is typical for the stock market in general? Is it unreasonable to expect this kind of return, on average, in the future? Explain.

LG2 **Q6.2** Given the information in Figure 6.4, answer the following questions for Abercrombie & Fitch Co.
a. On what day did the trading activity occur?
b. At what price did the stock sell when the market closed?
c. What is the firm's price-to-earnings ratio? What does that indicate?
d. What is the first price at which the stock traded on the date quoted?
e. What was the dividend paid per share for the previous year?
f. What are the highest and lowest prices at which the stock traded during the latest 52-week period?
g. How many shares of stock were traded on the day quoted?
h. How much, if any, of a change in price took place between the day quoted and the immediately preceding day? At what price did the stock close on the immediately preceding day?

LG4 **Q6.3** Listed below are three pairs of stocks. Look at each pair and select the security you would like to own, given that you want to select the one that's worth more money. Then, after you make all three of your selections, use the *Wall Street Journal* or some other source to find the latest market value of the securities in each pair.
a. 50 shares of Berkshire Hathaway (stock symbol BRKA) or 150 shares of Coca-Cola (stock symbol KO). (Both are listed on the NYSE.)
b. 100 shares of WD-40 (symbol WDFC—a Nasdaq National Market issue) or 100 shares of Nike (symbol NKE—a NYSE stock).
c. 150 shares of Walmart (symbol WMT) or 50 shares of Sprint Nextel Corp. (symbol S). (Both are listed on the NYSE.)
How many times did you pick the one that was worth more money? Did the price of any of these stocks surprise you? If so, which one(s)? Does the price of a stock represent its value? Explain.

LG6 **Q6.4** Assume that a wealthy woman comes to you looking for some investment advice. She is in her early forties and has $250,000 to put into stocks. She wants to build up as much capital as she can over a 15-year period and is willing to tolerate a "fair amount" of risk.
a. What types of stocks do you think would be most suitable for this investor? Come up with at least three types of stocks, and briefly explain the rationale for each.
b. Would your recommendations change if you were dealing with a smaller amount of money—say, $50,000? What if the investor were more risk-averse? Explain.

LG6 **Q6.5** Identify and briefly describe the three sources of return to U.S. investors in foreign stocks. How important are currency exchange rates? With regard to currency exchange rates, when is the best time to be in foreign securities?
a. Listed below are exchange rates (for the beginning and end of a hypothetical one-year investment horizon) for the British pound (B£), the Australian dollar (A$), and the Mexican peso (Mp).

	Currency Exchange Rates	
Currency	Beginning of Investment Horizon	End of 1-Year Investment Horizon
British pound (B£)	1.55 U.S.$ per B£	1.75 U.S.$ per B£
Australian dollar (A$)	1.35 A$ per U.S.$	1.25 A$ per U.S.$
Mexican peso (Mp)	0.10 U.S.$ per Mp	0.08 U.S.$ per Mp

From the perspective of a U.S. investor holding a foreign (British, Australian, or Mexican) stock, which of the above changes in currency exchange rates would have a positive effect on returns (in U.S. dollars)? Which would have a negative effect?

b. ADRs are denominated in U.S. dollars. Are their returns affected by currency exchange rates? Explain.

LG6 **Q6.6** Briefly define each of the following types of investment programs and note the kinds of stock (blue chips, speculative stocks, etc.) that would best fit with each.

a. A buy-and-hold strategy
b. A current-income portfolio
c. Long-term total return
d. Aggressive stock management

Problems

All problems are available on http://www.myfinancelab.com

LG3 **P6.1** An investor owns some stock in Harry's Pottery Inc. The stock recently underwent a 5-for-3 stock split. If the stock was trading at $40 per share just before the split, how much is each share most likely selling for after the split? If the investor owned 200 shares of the stock before the split, how many shares would she own afterward?

LG3 **P6.2** An investor deposits $20,000 into a new brokerage account. The investor buys 1,000 shares of Tipco stock for $19 per share. Two weeks later, the investor sells the Tipco stock for $20 per share. When the investor receives his brokerage account statement, he sees that there is a balance of $20,900 in his account:

Item	Number of Shares	Price per Share ($)	Total Transaction ($)	Account Balance ($)
1. Deposit			$20,000	$20,000
2. Tipco purchase	1,000	$19	($19,000)	$20,000
3. Tipco sale	1,000	$20	$20,000	$21,000
4.				
5. Balance				$20,900

What belongs in item 4 on this statement?

LG4 **P6.3** Ron's Rodents Co. has total assets of $5 million, total short- and long-term debt of $2.8 million, and $400,000 worth of 8% preferred stock outstanding. What is the firm's total book value? What would its book value per share be if the firm had 50,000 shares of common stock outstanding?

LG4 **P6.4** Lockhart's Bookstores is trading at $45 per share. There are 280 million shares outstanding. What is the market capitalization of this company?

LG5 **P6.5** The MedTech Company recently reported net profits after taxes of $15.8 million. It has 2.5 million shares of common stock outstanding and pays preferred dividends of $1 million per year.

    a. Compute the firm's earnings per share (EPS).

    b. Assuming that the stock currently trades at $60 per share, determine what the firm's dividend yield would be if it paid $2 per share to common stockholders.

    c. What would the firm's dividend payout ratio be if it paid $2 per share in dividends?

LG5 **P6.6** On January 1, 2013, an investor bought 200 shares of Gottahavit, Inc., for $50 per share. On January 3, 2014, the investor sold the stock for $55 per share. The stock paid a quarterly dividend of $0.25 per share. How much (in $) did the investor earn on this investment and, assuming the investor is in the 33% tax bracket, how much will she pay in income taxes on this transaction?

LG4 **LG5** **P6.7** Consider the following information about Truly Good Coffee, Inc.

Total assets	$240 million
Total debt	$115 million
Preferred stock	$ 25 million
Common stockholders' equity	$100 million
Net profits after taxes	$22.5 million
Number of preferred stock outstanding	1 million shares
Number of common stock outstanding	10 million shares
Preferred dividends paid	$2 per share
Common dividends paid	$0.75 per share
Market price of the preferred stock	$30.75 per share
Market price of the common stock	$25.00 per share

Use the information above to find the following.

    a. The company's book value

    b. Its book value per share

    c. The stock's earnings per share (EPS)

    d. The dividend payout ratio

    e. The dividend yield on the common stock

    f. The dividend yield on the preferred stock

LG5 **P6.8** East Coast Utilities is currently trading at $28 per share. The company pays a quarterly dividend of $0.28 per share. What is the dividend yield?

LG5 **P6.9** West Coast Utilities had a net profit of $900 million. It has 900 million shares outstanding and paid annual dividends of $0.90 per share. What is the dividend payout ratio?

LG5 **P6.10** Wilfred Nadeau owns 200 shares of Consolidated Glue. The company's board of directors recently declared a cash dividend of 50 cents a share payable April 18 (a Wednesday) to shareholders of record on March 22 (a Thursday).

    a. How much in dividends, if any, will Wilfred receive if he sells his stock on March 20?

    b. Assume Wilfred decides to hold on to the stock rather than sell it. If he belongs to the company's dividend reinvestment plan, how many new shares of stock will he receive if the stock is currently trading at $40 and the plan offers a 5% discount on the share price of the stock? (Assume that all of Wilfred's dividends are diverted to the plan.) Will Wilfred have to pay any taxes on these dividends, given that he is taking them in stock rather than cash?

LG5 P6.11 Southern Cities Trucking Company has the following five-year record of earnings per share.

Year	EPS
2012	$1.40
2013	$2.10
2014	$1.00
2015	$3.25
2016	$0.80

Which of the following procedures would produce higher dividends to stockholders over this five-year period?

a. Paying out dividends at a fixed ratio of 40% of EPS

b. Paying out dividends at a fixed rate of $1 per share

LG4 LG5 P6.12 Using the resources at your campus or public library or on the Internet, select any three common stocks you like and determine the latest book value per share, earnings per share, dividend payout ratio, and dividend yield for each. (Show all your calculations.)

LG4 LG5 P6.13 In January 2012 an investor purchased 800 shares of Engulf & Devour, a rapidly growing high-tech conglomerate. From 2012 through 2016, the stock turned in the following dividend and share price performance.

Year	Share Price Beginning of Year	Dividends Paid during Year	Share Price End of Year
2012	$42.50*	$0.82	$ 54.00
2013	$54.00	$1.28	$ 74.25
2014	$74.25	$1.64	$ 81.00
2015	$81.00	$1.91	$ 91.25
2016	$91.25	$2.30	$128.75

*Investor purchased stock in 2012 at this price.

On the basis of this information, find the annual holding period returns for 2012 through 2016.

LG4 P6.14 George Robbins considers himself an aggressive investor. He's thinking about investing in some foreign securities and is looking at stocks in (1) Bayer AG, the big German chemical and health-care firm, and (2) Swisscom AG, the Swiss telecommunications company.

Bayer AG, which trades on the Frankfurt Exchange, is currently priced at 53.25 euros per share. It pays annual dividends of 1.50 euros per share. Robbins expects the stock to climb to 60.00 euros per share over the next 12 months. The current exchange rate is 0.9025€/US$, but that's expected to rise to 1.015€/US$. The other company, Swisscom, trades on the Zurich Exchange and is currently priced at 71.5 Swiss francs (Sf) per share. The stock pays annual dividends of 1.5 Sf per share. Its share price is expected to go up to 76.0 Sf within a year. At current exchange rates, 1 Sf is worth $0.75 U.S., but that's expected to go to $0.85 by the end of the one-year holding period.

a. Ignoring the currency effect, which of the two stocks promises the higher total return (in its local currency)? Based on this information, which looks like the better investment?

b. Which of the two stocks has the better total return in U.S. dollars? Did currency exchange rates affect their returns in any way? Do you still want to stick with the same stock you selected in part a? Explain.

LG6 **P6.15** Bruce buys $25,000 of UH-OH Corporation stock. Unfortunately, a major newspaper reveals the very next day that the company is being investigated for accounting fraud, and the stock price falls by 50%. What is the percentage increase now required for Bruce to get back to $25,000 of value?

Visit **http://www.myfinancelab.com** for web exercises, spreadsheets, and other online resources.

Case Problem 6.1   Sara Decides to Take the Plunge

LG1 LG6 Sara Thomas is a child psychologist who has built a thriving practice in her hometown of Boise, Idaho. Over the past several years she has been able to accumulate a substantial sum of money. She has worked long and hard to be successful, but she never imagined anything like this. Even so, success has not spoiled Sara. Still single, she keeps to her old circle of friends. One of her closest friends is Terry Jenkins, who happens to be a stockbroker and who acts as Sara's financial advisor.

Not long ago Sara attended a seminar on investing in the stock market, and since then she's been doing some reading about the market. She has concluded that keeping all of her money in low-yielding savings accounts doesn't make sense. As a result, Sara has decided to move part of her money to stocks. One evening, Sara told Terry about her decision and explained that she had found several stocks that she thought looked "sort of interesting." She described them as follows:

• *North Atlantic Swim Suit Company.* This highly speculative stock pays no dividends. Although the earnings of NASS have been a bit erratic, Sara feels that its growth prospects have never been brighter—"what with more people than ever going to the beaches the way they are these days," she says.

• *Town and Country Computer.* This is a long-established computer firm that pays a modest dividend yield (of about 1.50%). It is considered a quality growth stock. From one of the stock reports she read, Sara understands that T&C offers excellent long-term growth and capital gains potential.

• *Southeastern Public Utility Company.* This income stock pays a dividend yield of around 5%. Although it's a solid company, it has limited growth prospects because of its location.

• *International Gold Mines, Inc.* This stock has performed quite well in the past, especially when inflation has become a problem. Sara feels that if it can do so well in inflationary times, it will do even better in a strong economy. Unfortunately, the stock has experienced wide price swings in the past. It pays almost no dividends.

Questions

a. What do you think of the idea of Sara keeping "substantial sums" of money in savings accounts? Would common stocks make better investments for her than savings accounts? Explain.

b. What is your opinion of the four stocks Sara has described? Do you think they are suitable for her investment needs? Explain.

c. What kind of common stock investment program would you recommend for Sara? What investment objectives do you think she should set for herself, and how can common stocks help her achieve her goals?

Case Problem 6.2   Wally Wonders Whether There's a Place for Dividends

LG5 LG6   Wally Wilson is a commercial artist who makes a good living by doing freelance work—mostly layouts and illustrations—for local ad agencies and major institutional clients (such as large department stores). Wally has been investing in the stock market for some time, buying mostly high-quality growth stocks as a way to achieve long-term growth and capital appreciation. He feels that with the limited time he has to devote to his security holdings, high-quality issues are his best bet. He has become a bit perplexed lately with the market, disturbed that some of his growth stocks aren't doing even as well as many good-grade income shares. He therefore decides to have a chat with his broker, Al Fried.

During their conversation, it becomes clear that both Al and Wally are thinking along the same lines. Al points out that dividend yields on income shares are indeed way up and that, because of the state of the economy, the outlook for growth stocks is not particularly bright. He suggests that Wally seriously consider putting some of his money into income shares to capture the high dividend yields that are available. After all, as Al says, "the bottom line is not so much where the payoff comes from as how much it amounts to!" They then talk about a high-yield public utility stock, Hydro-Electric Light and Power. Al digs up some forecast information about Hydro-Electric and presents it to Wally for his consideration:

Year	Expected EPS ($)	Expected Dividend Payout Ratio (%)
2016	$3.25	40%
2017	$3.40	40%
2018	$3.90	45%
2019	$4.40	45%
2020	$5.00	45%

The stock currently trades at $60 per share. Al thinks that within five years it should be trading at $75 to $80 a share. Wally realizes that to buy the Hydro-Electric stock, he will have to sell his holdings of CapCo Industries—a highly regarded growth stock that Wally is disenchanted with because of recent substandard performance.

Questions

a. How would you describe Wally's present investment program? How do you think it fits him and his investment objectives?

b. Consider the Hydro-Electric stock.

1. Determine the amount of annual dividends Hydro-Electric can be expected to pay over the years 2016 to 2020.
2. Compute the total dollar return that Wally will make from Hydro-Electric if he invests $6,000 in the stock and all the dividend and price expectations are realized.
3. If Wally participates in the company's dividend reinvestment plan, how many shares of stock will he have by the end of 2020? What will they be worth if the stock trades at $80 on December 31, 2020? Assume that the stock can be purchased through the dividend reinvestment plan at a net price of $50 a share in 2016, $55 in 2017, $60 in 2018, $65 in 2019, and $70 in 2020. Use fractional shares, to 2 decimals, in your computations. Also, assume that, as in part **b**, Wally starts with 100 shares of stock and all dividend expectations are realized.

c. Would Wally be going to a different investment strategy if he decided to buy shares in Hydro-Electric? If the switch is made, how would you describe his new investment program? What do you think of this new approach? Is it likely to lead to more trading on Wally's behalf? If so, can you reconcile that with the limited amount of time he has to devote to his portfolio?

Excel@Investing

Excel@Investing | Build a spreadsheet containing the following quoted information. Based on the information given, what is the firm's current market cap? What was the firm's net income?

(Source: Courtesy of Yahoo! Finance.)

Analyzing Common Stocks

LEARNING GOALS

After studying this chapter, you should be able to:

LG1 Discuss the security analysis process, including its goals and functions.

LG2 Understand the purpose and contributions of economic analysis.

LG3 Describe industry analysis and note how investors use it.

LG4 Demonstrate a basic appreciation of fundamental analysis and why it is used.

LG5 Calculate a variety of financial ratios and describe how analysts use financial statement analysis to gauge the financial vitality of a company.

LG6 Use various financial measures to assess a company's performance, and explain how the insights derived form the basic input for the valuation process.

A March 2015 analyst report from the European investment bank, UBS, offered a pessimistic assessment of the semiconductor manufacturer, Advanced Micro Devices (AMD). The analyst report cited overall lackluster macroeconomic performance as well as political turmoil as contributors to slowing sales of AMD's chips designed for personal computers (PCs). The report noted that sales of desktop and laptop computers had been dwindling, both in the United States and overseas, as consumers showed an increasing preference for smaller mobile devices such as smartphones and tablets. The higher cost of PCs relative to tablets was a particular deterrent to consumer purchases in emerging markets where consumers had less disposable income to buy consumer electronics goods. AMD's problems weren't just temporary either. A respected market research group forecasted that global PC shipments would fall from 2015 to 2019. AMD competed head-to-head with its larger rival, Intel, but the analyst's report suggested that AMD would suffer more from declining PC sales because it focused more heavily on the consumer market, which had been cannibalized by tablets, whereas Intel's revenues were more heavily weighted toward business customers. The report concluded by predicting that AMD's stock would underperform the broader market, and that prediction sent the stock tumbling 5.7%.

The report issued by UBS is typical of those produced by professional securities analysts every day. In forming their recommendations to clients, stock analysts have to consider broad macroeconomic trends, industry factors, and specific attributes of individual firms. This chapter, the first of two on security analysis, introduces some of the techniques and procedures you can use to evaluate the future of the economy, of industries, and of specific companies, such as AMD or Intel.

(Source: "Advanced Micro Tumbles 5.7% on Analyst Downgrade to Sell," March 26, 2015, http://www.zacks.com/stock/news/169063/advanced-micro-tumbles-57-on-analyst-downgrade-to-sell.)

Security Analysis

LG1 The obvious motivation for investing in stocks is to watch your money grow. Consider, for example, the case of Google, the hugely successful search engine and software company. If you had purchased $10,000 worth of Google stock when the company had its initial public offering (IPO) on August 19, 2004, 10 years later, in August 2014, that stock would have had a market value of $113,653. That works out to an average annual return of 27.5%; compare that with the 5.9% annual return generated over the same period by the S&P 500. Unfortunately, for every story of great success in the market, there are others that don't end so well.

More often than not, most of those investment flops can be traced to bad timing, poor planning, or failure to use common sense in making investment decisions. Although these chapters on stock investments cannot offer magic keys to sudden wealth, they do provide sound principles for formulating a successful long-range investment program. The techniques described are proven methods that have been used by millions of successful investors.

Principles of Security Analysis

Security analysis consists of gathering information, organizing it into a logical framework, and then using the information to determine the intrinsic value of common stock. That is, given a rate of return that's compatible with the amount of risk involved in a proposed transaction, **intrinsic value** provides a measure of the underlying worth of a share of stock. It provides a standard to help you judge whether a particular stock is undervalued, fairly priced, or overvalued. The entire concept of stock valuation is based on the idea that all securities possess an intrinsic value that their market value will approach over time.

In investments, the question of value centers on return. That is, a satisfactory investment is one that offers a level of expected return proportionate to the amount of risk involved. As a result, not only must an investment be profitable, but it also must be sufficiently profitable—in the sense that you'd expect it to generate a return that's high enough to offset the perceived exposure to risk.

The problem, of course, is that returns on securities are difficult to predict. One approach is to buy whatever strikes your fancy. A more rational approach is to use security analysis to look for promising candidates. Security analysis addresses the question of what to buy by determining what a stock ought to be worth and comparing that value to the stock's market price. Presumably, an investor will buy a stock only if its prevailing market price does not exceed its worth—its intrinsic value. Ultimately, intrinsic value depends on several factors:

1. Estimates of the stock's future cash flows (e.g., the amount of dividends you expect to receive over the holding period and the estimated price of the stock at time of sale)

2. The discount rate used to translate those future cash flows into a present value

3. The risk associated with future performance, which helps define the appropriate discount rate

The Top-Down Approach to Security Analysis Traditional security analysis often takes a top-down approach. It begins with economic analysis, moves to industry analysis, and then arrives at a fundamental analysis of a specific company. *Economic*

analysis assesses the general state of the economy and its potential effects on businesses. For example, the UBS research report on Advanced Micro Devices pointed out that a weak economy caused consumers to be more price-sensitive when they shopped, so they purchased less expensive tablets or laptops rather than desktop PCs. *Industry analysis* deals with the industry within which a particular company operates. It looks at the overall outlook for that industry and at how companies compete in that industry. In the case of the computer chip industry, UBS noted that the increasing price sensitivity of consumers favored companies such as Intel, which focused more on business customers than general consumers. *Fundamental analysis* looks at the financial condition and operating results of a specific company. The fundamentals include the company's investment decisions, the liquidity of its assets, its use of debt, its profit margins, and its earnings growth. In its fundamental analysis of AMD, the UBS report highlighted AMD's excessive inventory, but it also noted that the company was trying to design new custom chips for customers that Intel did not serve. Once an analyst, or an investor, has synthesized all of the information from the economic, industry, and fundamental analyses, the analyst uses that information to estimate the intrinsic value of a company's stock and then compares that intrinsic value to the actual market value of the stock. When the intrinsic value is greater than the market price, an analyst will recommend that clients purchase the stock, and when the opposite is true, the analyst may issue a recommendation to sell. If the market price and intrinsic value are approximately the same, the analyst may issue a "neutral" or "hold" recommendation. In the case of AMD, the UBS report suggested that AMD's intrinsic value was just $2.40, whereas its market price was $2.79. Hence, UBS expected the stock to underperform, and they did not recommend it to their clients.

Fundamental analysis is closely linked to the notion of intrinsic value because it provides the basis for projecting a stock's future cash flows. A key part of this analytical process is *company analysis*, which takes a close look at the actual financial performance of the company. Such analysis is not meant simply to provide interesting tidbits of information about how the company has performed in the past. Rather, company analysis helps investors formulate expectations about the company's future performance. But to understand the future prospects of the firm, investors should have a good handle on the company's current condition and its ability to produce earnings. That's what company analysis does. It helps investors predict the future by looking at the past and determining how well the company is situated to meet the challenges that lie ahead.

Who Needs Security Analysis in an Efficient Market?

The concept of security analysis in general, and fundamental analysis in particular, is based on the assumption that at least some investors are capable of identifying stocks whose intrinsic values differ from their market values. Fundamental analysis operates on the broad premise that some securities may be mispriced in the marketplace at least some of the time. If securities are occasionally mispriced, and if investors can identify mispriced securities, then fundamental analysis may be a worthwhile and profitable pursuit.

To many, those two premises seem reasonable. However, there are others who do not accept the assumptions of fundamental analysis. Instead, they believe that the market is so efficient in processing new information that securities trade very close to their correct values at all times and that even when securities are mispriced, it is nearly impossible for investors to determine which stocks are overvalued and which are

FAMOUS FAILURES IN FINANCE

Staying on Top a Challenge for Fund Managers

Research conducted by Standard & Poor's asked whether the performance of top mutual funds was due to the skill of fund managers or random luck. The study started with 2,862 actively managed stock mutual funds, and it selected the top 25% from that group based on their 12-month returns starting from March 2009 (the start of the latest bull market). Researchers wanted to know how many of these top-performing funds would remain in the top quartile for each of the next four years. The surprising answer was that only two funds achieved that feat, and neither of those achieved top-quartile performance in the study's most recent year, 2015. While this study doesn't prove that it is impossible for a fund manager to deliver market-beating performance year after year, it does seem that very few funds are able to do so.

(Source: "How Many Mutual Funds Routinely Rout the Market? Zero," Jeff Sommer, March 14, 2015, *The New York Times*, http://www.nytimes.com/2015/03/15/your-money/how-many-mutual-funds-routinely-rout-the-market-zero.html?smid=nytcore-iphone-share&smprod=nytcore-iphone&_r=0.)

undervalued. Thus, they argue, it is virtually impossible to consistently outperform the market. In its strongest form, the *efficient market hypothesis* asserts the following:

1. Securities are rarely, if ever, substantially mispriced in the marketplace.

2. No security analysis, however detailed, is capable of consistently identifying mispriced securities with a frequency greater than that which might be expected by random chance alone.

Is the efficient market hypothesis correct? Is there a place for fundamental analysis in modern investment theory? Interestingly, most financial theorists and practitioners would answer "yes" to both questions.

The solution to this apparent paradox is quite simple. Basically, fundamental analysis is of value in the selection of alternative investments for two important reasons. First, financial markets are as efficient as they are because a large number of people and financial institutions invest a great deal of time and money analyzing the fundamentals of most widely held investments. In other words, markets tend to be efficient and securities tend to trade at or near their intrinsic values simply because a great many people have done the research to determine what their intrinsic values should be.

Second, although the financial markets are generally quite efficient, they are by no means perfectly efficient. Pricing errors are inevitable. Those individuals who have conducted the most thorough studies of the fundamentals of a given security are the most likely to profit when errors do occur. We will study the ideas and implications of efficient markets in some detail later in this text. For now, however, we will adopt the view that traditional security analysis may be useful in identifying attractive equity investments.

CONCEPTS IN REVIEW

Answers available at
http://www.pearsonhighered.com/smart

7.1 Identify the three major parts of security analysis and explain why security analysis is important to the stock selection process.

7.2 What is intrinsic value? How does it fit into the security analysis process?

7.3 How would you describe a satisfactory investment? How does security analysis help in identifying investment candidates?

7.4 Would there be any need for security analysis if we operated in an efficient market environment? Explain.

Economic Analysis

LG2 Stock prices are heavily influenced by the state of the economy and by economic events. As a rule, stock prices tend to move up when the economy is strong, and they retreat when the economy starts to weaken. Figure 7.1 illustrates this pattern. The vertical gray bars in the figure indicate periods when the economy was in recession (i.e., when total output of the economy was shrinking rather than growing), and the blue line shows the level of the S&P 500 stock index. In general, the index falls during the early stages of a recession, and it tends to rebound sometime before the economy does (i.e., sometime before the recession ends). It's not a perfect relationship, but it is a fairly powerful one.

The reason that the economy is so important to the market is simple. The overall performance of the economy has a significant bearing on the performance and profitability of most companies. As firms' fortunes change with economic conditions, so do the prices of their stocks. Of course, not all stocks are affected in the same way or to the same extent. Some sectors of the economy, like food retailing, may be only mildly affected by the economy. Others, like the construction and auto industries, are often hard hit when times get rough.

Economic analysis consists of a general study of the prevailing economic environment, often on both a global and a domestic basis (although here we'll concentrate, for the most part, on the domestic economy). Such analysis is meant to help investors gain insight into the underlying condition of the economy and the impact it might have on the behavior of share prices. It can go so far as to include a detailed examination of

FIGURE 7.1 The Economy and the Stock Market

The figure shows that during recessions (indicated by the vertical gray bars) the stock market tends to fall, though the stock market usually begins to rebound before the recession ends.

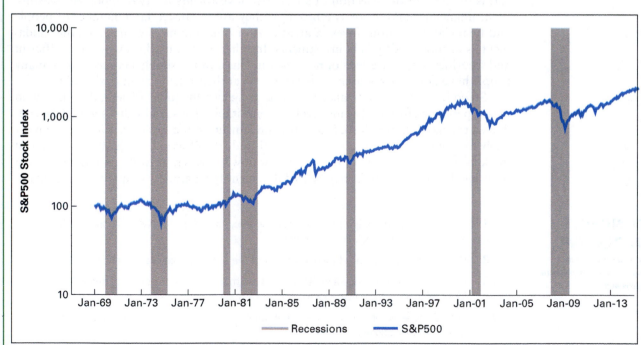

each sector of the economy, or it may be done on a very informal basis. However, from a security analysis perspective, its purpose is always the same: to establish a sound foundation for the valuation of common stock.

Economic Analysis and the Business Cycle

Economic analysis is the first step in the top-down approach. It sets the tone for the entire security analysis process. Thus, if the economic future looks bleak, you can probably expect most stock returns to be equally dismal. If the economy looks strong, stocks should do well. The behavior of the economy is captured in the **business cycle**, a series of alternating contractions and expansions, which reflects changes in total economic activity over time.

Two widely followed measures of the business cycle are gross domestic product and industrial production. *Gross domestic product* (GDP) is the market value of all goods and services produced in a country over a given period. When economists say that the economy is in recession, this means that GDP has been contracting for at least two consecutive quarters. On the other hand, an economic expansion generally refers to a period when GDP is growing. *Industrial production* is an indicator of the output produced by industrial companies. Normally, GDP and the index of industrial production move up and down with the business cycle.

Key Economic Factors

The state of the economy is affected by a wide range of factors, from the consumption, saving, and investment decisions made independently by millions of households to major government policy decisions. Some of the most important factors that analysts examine when conducting a broad economic analysis include:

Government fiscal policy
  Taxes
  Government spending
  Debt management

Monetary policy
  Money supply
  Interest rates

Other factors
  Inflation
  Consumer spending
  Business investments
  Foreign trade and foreign exchange rates

Government fiscal policies can influence how fast the economy grows through a variety of channels. When the government increases spending or reduces taxes, it is pursuing an expansionary fiscal policy. Examples of this type of policy are the American Recovery and Reinvestment Act of 2009, a $787 billion stimulus bill, and the Tax Relief, Unemployment Insurance Reauthorization, and Job Creation Act of 2010, an $858 billion stimulus bill, passed by Congress and signed by President Barack Obama. Similarly, monetary policy is said to be expansive when interest rates are relatively low and money is readily available. An expanding economy is also characterized by growing spending by consumers and businesses. These same variables moving in a

reverse direction can have a contractionary (recessionary) impact on the economy, for example, when taxes and interest rates increase or when spending by consumers and businesses falls off.

The impact of these major forces filters through the system and affects several key dimensions of the economy. The most important of these are industrial production, corporate profits, retail sales, personal income, the unemployment rate, and inflation. For example, a strong economy exists when industrial production, corporate profits, retail sales, and personal income are moving up and unemployment is down.

Thus, when conducting an economic analysis, investors should keep an eye on fiscal and monetary policies, consumer and business spending, and foreign trade for the impact they might have on the economy. At the same time, they must stay abreast of the level of industrial production, corporate profits, retail sales, personal income, unemployment, and inflation in order to assess the current state of the business cycle.

Table 7.1 provides a brief description of some key economic measures that would typically be part of a broad analysis of the macroeconomy. These economic statistics are compiled by various government agencies and are widely reported in the financial media. Most of the reports are released monthly. Investors and analysts invest a lot of time to carefully read about the various economic measures and reports cited in Table 7.1. Over time, they develop an understanding of how each statistical series behaves over the business cycle and how the stock market reacts to movements in these series.

Developing an Economic Outlook

Conducting an economic analysis involves studying fiscal and monetary policies, inflationary expectations, consumer and business spending, and the state of the business cycle. Often, investors do this on a fairly informal basis. As they form their economic judgments, many rely on one or more of the popular published sources (e.g., the *Wall Street Journal*, *Barron's*, *Fortune*, and *Business Week*) as well as on periodic reports from major brokerage houses. These sources provide a convenient summary of economic activity and give investors a general feel for the condition of the economy.

Once an investor has developed a general economic outlook, he or she can use the information in one of two ways. One approach is to use the information in the economic outlook to determine where it leads in terms of possible areas for further analysis. For example, suppose an investor uncovers information that strongly suggests the outlook for business spending is very positive. On the basis of such an analysis, the investor might look more closely at capital goods producers, such as office equipment manufacturers. Similarly, if an analyst feels that because of sweeping changes in world politics, U.S. government defense spending is likely to drop off, the analyst might guide clients to avoid the stocks of major defense contractors.

A second way to use information about the economy is to consider specific industries or companies and ask, "How will they be affected by expected developments in the economy?" Suppose that an investor has an interest in *business equipment stocks*. This industry category includes companies involved in the production of everything from business machines and electronic systems to work lockers and high-fashion office furnishings. This industry includes companies like Pitney Bowes, Diebold, Herman Miller, and Steelcase. These stocks are highly susceptible to changing economic conditions. That's because when the economy starts slowing down, companies can put off purchases of durable equipment and fixtures. Especially important to this industry, therefore, is the outlook for corporate profits and business investments. As long as these economic factors look good, the prospects for business equipment stocks should be positive.

TABLE 7.1 KEEPING TRACK OF THE ECONOMY

To help you sort out the confusing array of figures that flow almost daily from Washington, DC, and keep track of what's happening in the economy, here are some of the most important economic measures and reports to watch.

- **Gross domestic product (GDP).** This is the broadest measure of the economy's performance. Measured every three months by the Commerce Department, GDP is an estimate of the total dollar value of all the goods and services produced in this country. In particular, watch the annual rate of growth or decline in "real" or "constant" dollars. This number eliminates the effects of inflation and thus measures the actual volume of production. Remember, though, that frequent revisions of GDP figures sometimes change the picture of the economy.

- **Industrial production.** Issued monthly by the Federal Reserve Board, this index shows changes in the physical output of U.S. factories, mines, and electric and gas utilities. The index tends to move in the same direction as the economy, so it is a good guide to business conditions between reports on GDP. Detailed breakdowns of the index give a reading on how individual industries are faring.

- **The leading economic index** This boils down to one number, which summarizes the movement of a dozen statistics that tend to predict—or "lead"—changes in the GDP. This monthly index, issued by the Conference Board, includes such things as average weekly hours worked by employees of manufacturing firms, initial weekly claims for unemployment insurance, stock prices, and consumer expectations. If the index moves in the same direction for several months, it's a fairly good sign that total output will move the same way in the near future.

- **Personal income.** A monthly report from the Commerce Department, this shows the before-tax income received in the form of wages and salaries, interest and dividends, rents, and other payments, such as Social Security, unemployment compensation, and pensions. As a measure of individuals' spending power, the report helps explain trends in consumer buying habits, a major part of GDP. When personal income rises, people often increase their buying.

- **Retail sales.** The Commerce Department's monthly estimate of total retail sales includes everything from cars to groceries. Based on a sample of retail establishments, the figure gives a rough clue to consumer attitudes.

- **Money supply.** The amount of money in circulation as reported weekly by the Federal Reserve is known as the money supply. Actually, there are several measures of the money supply. M1, which is designed to measure the most liquid forms of money, is basically currency, demand deposits, and NOW accounts. M2, the most widely followed measure, equals M1 plus savings deposits, money market deposit accounts, and money market mutual funds. An expanding economy is generally associated with a rising money supply, although when the money supply increases too fast, inflation may result. A reduction in the money supply is often associated with recessions.

- **Consumer prices.** Issued monthly by the Labor Department, the Consumer Price Index (CPI) shows changes in prices for a fixed market basket of goods and services. The CPI is the most widely watched indicator of inflation.

- **Producer prices.** The Labor Department's monthly Producer Price Index (PPI) shows price changes of goods at various stages of production, from crude materials such as raw cotton to finished goods like clothing and furniture. An upward surge may mean higher consumer prices later. However, the index can miss discounts and may exaggerate rising price trends. Watch particularly changes in the prices of finished goods. These do not fluctuate as widely as the prices of crude materials and thus are a better measure of inflationary pressures.

- **Employment.** The percentage of the workforce that is involuntarily out of work (unemployment) is a broad indicator of economic health. But another monthly figure issued by the Labor Department—the number of payroll jobs—may be better for spotting changes in business. A decreasing number of jobs is a sign that firms are cutting production.

- **Housing starts.** A pickup in the pace of housing starts usually follows an easing in the availability and cost of money and is an indicator of improving economic health. This monthly report from the Commerce Department also includes the number of new building permits issued across the country, an even earlier indicator of the pace of future construction.

Assessing the Potential Impact on Share Prices How does an economic outlook translate into a prediction about where stock prices are headed? Suppose that an investor has assessed the current state of the business cycle. Using that insight, he could then formulate some expectations about the future of the economy and the potential impact it holds for the stock market in general and business equipment stocks in particular. Table 7.2 shows how some of the more important economic variables can affect the behavior of the stock market.

To see how this might be done, let's assume that the economy has just gone through a year-long recession and is now in the recovery stage of the business cycle: Employment

TABLE 7.2 ECONOMIC VARIABLES AND THE STOCK MARKET

Economic Variable	Potential Effect on the Stock Market
Real growth in GDP	Positive impact—it's good for the market.
Industrial production	Continued increases are a sign of strength, which is good for the market.
Inflation	Detrimental to stock prices when running high. High inflation leads to higher interest rates and lower price-to-earnings multiples, and generally makes equity securities less attractive.
Corporate profits	Strong corporate earnings are good for the market.
Unemployment	A downer—an increase in unemployment means business is starting to slow down.
Federal budget	Budget surpluses during strong economic times are generally positive, but modest deficits are usually not cause for alarm. Larger deficits during downturns may stimulate the market.
Weak dollar	Has a complex impact on the market. A weak dollar may increase the value of U.S. firms' overseas earnings, while at the same time making U.S. investments less attractive to foreigners.
Interest rates	Another downer—rising rates tend to have a negative effect on the market for stocks.
Money supply	Moderate growth can have a positive impact on the economy and the market. Rapid growth, however, is inflationary and therefore detrimental to the stock market.

is starting to pick up. Inflation and interest rates are low. Both GDP and industrial production have experienced sharp increases in the past two quarters. Also, Congress is putting the finishing touches on a major piece of legislation that will lead to reduced taxes. More important, although the economy is now in the early stages of a recovery, things are expected to get even better in the future. The economy is definitely starting to build steam, and all indications are that both corporate profits and business spending should undergo a sharp increase. All of these predictions should be good news for the producers of business equipment and office furnishings, as a good deal of their sales and an even larger portion of their profits depend on the level of corporate profits and business spending. In short, our investor sees an economy that's in good shape and set to become even stronger—the consequences of which are favorable not only for the market but for business equipment stocks as well.

Note that these conclusions could have been reached by relying on sources such as *Barron's* or *Business Week*. In fact, about the only "special thing" this investor would have to do is pay careful attention to those economic forces that are particularly important to the business equipment industry (e.g., corporate profits and capital spending). The economic portion of the analysis has set the stage for further evaluation by indicating the type of economic environment to expect in the near future. The next step is to narrow the focus a bit and conduct the industry phase of the analysis.

The Market as a Leading Indicator Before we continue our analysis, it is vital to clarify the relationship that normally exists between the stock market and the economy. As we just saw, investors use the economic outlook to get a handle on the market and to identify developing industry sectors. Yet it is important to note that changes in stock prices normally occur before the actual forecasted changes become apparent in the economy. Indeed, the current trend of stock prices is frequently used to help predict the course of the economy itself.

The apparent conflict here can be resolved somewhat by noting that because of this relationship, it is even more important to derive a reliable economic outlook and to be sensitive to underlying economic changes that may mean the current outlook is becoming dated. Investors in the stock market tend to look into the future to justify the purchase or sale of stock. If their perception of the future is changing, stock prices are also likely to be changing. Therefore, watching the course of stock prices as well as the course of the general economy can make for more accurate investment forecasting.

CONCEPTS IN REVIEW
Answers available at
http://www.pearsonhighered.com/smart
	7.5 Describe the general concept of economic analysis. Is this type of analysis necessary, and can it really help the individual investor make a decision about a stock? Explain.
	
	7.6 Why is the business cycle so important to economic analysis? Does the business cycle have any bearing on the stock market?
	
	7.7 Briefly describe each of the following:
	  a. Gross domestic product b. Leading indicators
	  c. Money supply d. Producer prices
	
	7.8 What effect, if any, does inflation have on common stocks?

Industry Analysis

LG3 Once an investor has developed an outlook for the overall course of the economy, a logical next step is to begin focusing the analysis on particular industries such as energy, autos, chemicals, consumer products, or technology. Looking at securities in terms of industry groupings is common practice among both individual and institutional investors. This approach makes a lot of sense because stock prices are influenced, to one degree or another, by industry conditions. Indeed, various industry forces, including the level of demand within an industry, can have a real impact on individual companies.

Industry analysis, in effect, sets the stage for a more thorough analysis of individual companies and securities. Clearly, if the outlook is good for an industry, then the prospects are likely to be favorable for many of the companies that make up that industry. In addition, industry analysis also helps the investor assess the riskiness of a company and therefore define the appropriate risk-adjusted rate of return to use in setting a value on the company's stock. That's true because there are always at least some similarities in the riskiness of the companies that make up an industry, so if you can gain an understanding of the risks inherent in an industry, you'll gain valuable insights about the risks inherent in individual companies and their securities.

Key Issues

Because all industries do not perform the same, the first step in **industry analysis** is to establish the competitive position of a particular industry in relation to others. The next step is to identify companies within the industry that hold particular promise. Analyzing an industry means looking at such things as its makeup and basic characteristics, the key economic and operating variables that drive industry performance, and the outlook for the industry. You will also want to keep an eye out for specific companies that appear well situated to take advantage of industry conditions. Companies with strong market positions should be favored over those with less secure positions. Such dominance indicates an ability to maintain pricing leadership and suggests that the firm will be in a position to enjoy economies of scale and low-cost production. Market dominance also enables a company to support a strong research and development effort, thereby helping it secure its leadership position for the future.

Normally, you can gain valuable insight about an industry by seeking answers to the following questions.

1. *What is the nature of the industry?* Is it monopolistic or are there many competitors? Do a few set the trend for the rest, and if so, who are those few?

2. *Is the industry regulated?* If so, how and by what agency is it regulated? How "friendly" are the regulatory bodies?

3. *What role does labor play in the industry?* How important are labor unions? Are there good labor relations within the industry? When is the next round of contract talks?

4. *How important are technological developments?* Are any new developments taking place? What impact are potential breakthroughs likely to have?

5. *Which economic forces are especially important to the industry?* Is demand for the industry's goods and services related to key economic variables? If so, what is the outlook for those variables? How important is foreign competition to the health of the industry?

6. *What are the important financial and operating considerations?* Is there an adequate supply of labor, material, and capital? What are the capital spending plans and needs of the industry?

The Industry Growth Cycle Questions like these can sometimes be answered in terms of an industry's **growth cycle**, which reflects the vitality of the industry over time. In the first stage—*initial development*—investment opportunities are usually not available to most investors. The industry is new and untried, and the risks are very high. The second stage is *rapid expansion*, during which product acceptance is spreading and investors can see the industry's future more clearly. At this stage, economic and financial variables have little to do with the industry's overall performance. Investors will be interested in investing almost regardless of the economic climate. This is the phase that is of substantial interest to investors, and a good deal of work is done to find such opportunities.

Unfortunately, most industries do not experience rapid growth for long. Instead, they eventually slip into the next category in the growth cycle, *mature growth*, which is the one most influenced by economic developments. In this stage, expansion comes from growth of the economy. It is a slower source of overall growth than that experienced in stage two. In stage three, the long-term nature of the industry becomes apparent. Industries in this category include defensive ones, like food and apparel, and cyclical ones, like autos and heavy equipment.

The last stage is either *stability* or *decline*. In the decline phase, demand for the industry's products is diminishing, and companies are leaving the industry. Investment opportunities at this stage are almost nonexistent, unless you are seeking only dividend income. Certainly, growth-oriented investors will want to stay away from industries at the decline stage of the cycle. Other investors may be able to find some investment opportunities here, especially if the industry (like, say, tobacco) is locked in the mature, stable phase. The fact is, however, that very few really good companies ever reach this final stage because they continually bring new products to the market and, in so doing, remain at least in the mature growth phase.

Developing an Industry Outlook

Individual investors can conduct industry analysis themselves. Or, as is more often the case, it can be done with the help of published industry reports, such as the popular *S&P Industry Surveys*. These surveys cover all the important economic, market, and financial aspects of an industry, providing commentary as well as vital statistics. Other widely used sources of industry information include brokerage house reports and articles in the popular financial media, as well as industry information from well-known sources of financial analysis such as Morningstar, Value Line, and Mergent. There also are scores of websites (like yahoo.com, zacks.com, businessweek.com, and bigcharts.com) that provide all sorts of useful information about various industries and subindustries.

Let's resume our example of the investor who is thinking about buying business equipment stocks. Recall from our prior discussion that the economic phase of the analysis suggested a strong economy for the foreseeable future—one in which corporate profits and business spending will be expanding. Now the investor is ready to focus on the industry. A logical starting point is to assess the expected industry response to forecasted economic developments. Demand for the product and industry sales would be especially important. The industry is made up of many large and small competitors, and although it is labor-intensive, labor unions are not an important force. Thus, our investor may want to look closely at the potential effect of these factors on the industry's cost structure. Also worth a look is the work being done in research and development (R&D) and in industrial design within the industry. Our investor would also want to know which firms are coming out with the new products and fresh ideas because these firms are likely to be the industry leaders.

Industry analysis yields an understanding of the nature and operating characteristics of an industry, which can then be used to form judgments about the prospects for industry growth. Let's assume that our investor, by using various types of published and online reports, has examined the key elements of the office equipment industry and has concluded that the industry, particularly the office furnishings segment, is well positioned to take advantage of the rapidly improving economy. Many new and exciting products have come out in the last several years, and more are in the R&D stage. Even more compelling is the current emphasis on new products that will contribute to long-term business productivity. Thus, the demand for office furniture and fixtures should increase, and although profit margins may tighten a bit, the level of profits should move up smartly, providing a healthy outlook for growth.

In the course of researching the industry, the investor has noticed several companies that stand out, but one looks particularly attractive: Universal Office Furnishings. Long regarded as one of the top design firms in the industry, Universal designs, manufactures, and sells a full line of high-end office furniture and fixtures (desks, chairs, credenzas, modular workstations, filing systems, etc.). In addition, the company produces and distributes state-of-the-art computer furniture and a specialized line of institutional furniture for the hospitality, health care, and educational markets. The company was founded over 50 years ago, and its stock has been trading since the late 1970s. Universal would be considered a mid-cap stock, with total market capitalization of around $2 or $3 billion. The company experienced rapid growth in the last decade, as it expanded its product line. Looking ahead, the general consensus is that the company should benefit nicely from the strong economic environment now in place. Everything about the economy and the industry looks good for the stock, so our investor decides to take a closer look at Universal Office Furnishings.

We now turn our attention to fundamental analysis, which will occupy the rest of this chapter.

7.9   What is industry analysis, and why is it important?

7.10   Identify and briefly discuss several aspects of an industry that are important to its behavior and operating characteristics. Note especially how economic issues fit into industry analysis.

7.11   What are the four stages of an industry's growth cycle? Which of these stages offers the biggest payoff to investors? Which stage is most influenced by forces in the economy?

Fundamental Analysis

LG4 LG5 LG6   **Fundamental analysis** is the study of the financial affairs of a business for the purpose of understanding the company that issued the common stock. First, we will deal with several aspects of fundamental analysis. We will examine the general concept of fundamental analysis and introduce several types of financial statements that provide the raw material for this type of analysis. We will then describe some key financial ratios that are widely used in company analysis and will conclude with an interpretation of those financial ratios. It's important to understand that this represents the more traditional approach to security analysis. This approach is commonly used in any situation where investors rely on financial statements and other databases to at least partially form an investment decision.

The Concept

Fundamental analysis rests on the belief that the value of a stock is influenced by the performance of the company that issued the stock. If a company's prospects look strong, the market price of its stock is likely to reflect that and be bid up. However, the value of a security depends not only on the return it promises but also on its risk exposure. Fundamental analysis captures these dimensions (risk and return) and incorporates them into the valuation process. It begins with a historical analysis of the financial strength of a firm: the *company analysis* phase. Using the insights obtained, along with economic and industry analyses, an investor can then formulate expectations about the growth and profitability of a company.

In the company analysis phase, the investor studies the financial statements of the firm to learn its strengths and weaknesses, identify any underlying trends and developments, evaluate operating efficiencies, and gain a general understanding of the nature and operating characteristics of the firm. The following points are of particular interest.

- The competitive position of the company

- The types of assets owned by the company and the growth rate of sales

- Profit margins and the dynamics of company earnings

- The composition and liquidity of corporate resources (the company's asset mix)
- The company's capital structure (its financing mix)

This phase is in many respects the most demanding and time-consuming. Because most investors have neither the time nor the inclination to conduct such an extensive study, they rely on published reports and financial websites for the background material. Fortunately, individual investors have a variety of sources to choose from. These include the reports and recommendations of major brokerage houses, the popular financial media, and financial subscription services like S&P and Value Line. Also available is a whole array of online financial sources, such as wsj.com, finance.yahoo.com, morningstar.com, money.msn.com, wsj.com, money.cnn.com, and smartmoney.com. These are all valuable sources of information, and the paragraphs that follow are not meant to replace them. Nevertheless, to be an intelligent investor you should have at least a basic understanding of financial reports and financial statement analysis, for ultimately you will be drawing your own conclusions about a company and its stock.

Financial Statements

Financial statements are a vital part of company analysis. They enable investors to develop an opinion about the operating results and financial condition of a firm. Investors use three financial statements in company analysis: the balance sheet, the income statement, and the statement of cash flows. The first two statements are essential to carrying out basic financial analysis because they contain the data needed to compute many of the financial ratios. The statement of cash flows is used primarily to assess the cash/liquidity position of the firm.

Companies prepare financial statements quarterly (abbreviated statements compiled for each three-month period of operation) and at the end of each calendar year or fiscal year. (The fiscal year is the 12-month period the company has defined as its operating year, which may or may not end on December 31.) Companies must hire independent certified public accountants (CPAs) to audit their financial statements to confirm that firms prepared those statements in accordance with generally accepted accounting principles. Companies must also file their financial statements with the U.S. Securities and Exchange Commission (SEC). Once filed at the SEC, these documents are available to any investor through the SEC's Edgar website (http://www.sec.gov/edgar.shtml).

By themselves, corporate financial statements are an important source of information to the investor. When used with financial ratios, and in conjunction with fundamental analysis, they become even more powerful. But to get the most from financial ratios, you must have a good understanding of the uses and limitations of the financial statements themselves.

The Balance Sheet The **balance sheet** is a statement of what a company owns and what it owes at a specific time. A balance sheet lists a company's assets, liabilities, and stockholders' equity. The *assets* represent the resources of the company (the things the company owns). The *liabilities* are debts owed to various creditors that have lent money to the firm. A firm's creditors may include suppliers, banks, or bondholders. *Stockholders' equity* is the difference between a firm's assets and its liabilities, and as such it represents the claim held by the firm's stockholders. As the term *balance sheet* implies, a firm's total assets must equal the sum of its liabilities and equity.

A typical balance sheet appears in Table 7.3. It shows the comparative 2015–2016 figures for Universal Office Furnishings. Tables 7.3, 7.4, and 7.5 illustrate the three main financial statements produced by Universal Office Furnishings. Those statements will be the basis for a fundamental analysis of the company.

The Income Statement The **income statement** provides a financial summary of the operating results of the firm over a period of time such as a quarter or year. It shows the revenues generated during the period, the costs and expenses incurred, and the company's profits (the difference between revenues and costs). Income statements generally list revenues (i.e., sales) first, followed by various types of expenses, and ending

Excel@Investing

TABLE 7.3   CORPORATE BALANCE SHEET

Universal Office Furnishings, Inc. Comparative Balance Sheets December 31 ($ millions)

	2016	2015
Assets		
Current assets		
Cash and equivalents	$ 95.8	$ 80.0
Receivables	$ 227.2	$192.4
Inventories	$103.7	$ 107.5
Other current assets	$ 73.6	$ 45.2
Total current assets	$500.3	$425.1
Noncurrent assets		
Property, plant, & equipment, gross	$771.2	$696.6
Accumulated depreciation	($372.5)	($379.9)
Property, plant, & equipment, net	$398.7	$316.7
Other noncurrent assets	$ 42.2	$ 19.7
Total noncurrent assets	$440.9	$336.4
Total assets	**$941.2**	**$761.5**
Liabilities and stockholders' equity		
Current liabilities		
Accounts payable	$ 114.2	$ 82.4
Short-term debt	$174.3	$ 79.3
Other current liabilities	$ 85.5	$ 89.6
Total current liabilities	$374.0	$251.3
Noncurrent liabilities		
Long-term debt	$177.8	$190.9
Other noncurrent liabilities	$ 94.9	$ 110.2
Total noncurrent liabilities	$272.7	$301.1
Total liabilities	**$646.7**	**$552.4**
Stockholders' equity		
Common shares	$ 92.6	$137.6
Retained earnings	$ 201.9	$ 71.5
Total stockholders' equity	**$294.5**	**$209.1**
Total liabilities and stockholders' equity	**$941.2**	**$761.5**

TABLE 7.4   CORPORATE INCOME STATEMENT

Universal Office Furnishings, Inc. Income Statements Fiscal Year Ended December 31 ($ millions)

	2016	2015
Sales revenue	$1,938.0	$1,766.2
Cost of goods sold	$1,128.5	$1,034.5
Gross profit	**$ 809.5**	**$ 731.7**
Selling, general, and administrative, and other operating expenses	$ 496.7	$ 419.5
Depreciation & amortization	$ 77.1	$ 62.1
Other expenses	$ 0.5	$ 12.9
Total operating expenses	**$ 574.3**	**$ 494.5**
Earnings before interest & taxes (EBIT)	**$ 235.2**	**$ 237.2**
Interest expense	$ 13.4	$ 7.3
Earnings before taxes	$ 221.8	$ 229.9
Income taxes	$ 82.1	$ 88.1
Net profit after taxes	**$ 139.7**	**$ 141.8**
Dividends paid per share	$ 0.15	$ 0.13
Earnings per share (EPS)	$ 2.26	$ 2.17
Number of common shares outstanding (in millions)	61.80	65.30

WATCH YOUR BEHAVIOR

Not Counting the Days Some firms define their fiscal quarters as 13-week periods, resulting in a fiscal year of exactly 52 weeks (364 days). These firms must add a "catch-up week" to 1 quarter every five or six years. Recent research indicates that professional stock analysts and investors fail to account for the extra week, meaning that during a 14-week quarter, firms tend to report higher-than-expected earnings, and stock returns are unusually high during these periods.

(Source: Rick Johnson, Andrew J. Leone, Sundaresh Ramnath, Ya-wen Yang, "14-Week Quarters," *Journal of Accounting and Economics*, Vol. 53, pp. 271–289.)

with profits or net income. In contrast to a balance sheet, which shows a firm's financial position at a single point in time, the income statement describes what happens over a period of time.

Table 7.4 shows the income statements for Universal Office Furnishings for 2015 and 2016. Note that these annual statements cover operations for the 12-month period ending on December 31, which corresponds to the date of the balance sheet. The income statement indicates how successful the firm has been in using the assets listed on the balance sheet. That is, management's success in operating the firm is reflected in the profit or loss the company generates during the year.

The Statement of Cash Flows The **statement of cash flows** provides a summary of the firm's cash flow and other events that caused changes in its cash position. This statement essentially brings together items from both the balance sheet and the income statement to show how the company obtained its cash and how it used this valuable liquid resource.

Unfortunately, because of certain accounting conventions (the *accrual concept* being chief among them), a company's reported earnings may bear little resemblance to its cash flow. That is, whereas profits are simply the difference between revenues and the accounting costs that have been charged against them, *cash flow* is the amount of money a company actually takes in as a result of doing business. For example, if a firm spends $1 billion in cash to build a new factory, the cash flow statement will show a $1 billion cash outflow for this expenditure. However, there will be no corresponding $1 billion expense on the income statement. Accounting rules dictate that when a firm invests in an asset that will provide benefits over many years, the cost of that asset must be spread over many years. Even though a firm might spend $1 billion in cash to build a factory this year, it will only deduct a portion of that as a *depreciation* expense on this year's income statement (perhaps $100 million). Additional depreciation deductions will appear on income statements over the next several years until the entire $1 billion cost has been deducted. In other words, the cost of the new factory will not be fully accounted for on a firm's income statement until several years have passed, even if the firm paid cash for the factory in the year that it was built.

What this means is that the cash flow statement is highly valued because it helps investors determine how much cash a firm actually spent and received in a particular year. This is important because a firm that shows positive profits on its income statement may in fact be spending more cash than it is taking in, and that could lead to financial distress. In addition, accounting rules give managers a great deal of flexibility in how they report certain revenue and expense items. For example, a firm that spends $1 billion to build a new factory can calculate depreciation expenses using several methods. Depending on the method that managers choose, the cost of the factory may be spread equally over many years or the firm's income statements may show depreciation charges that are very high at first but gradually decline over time. Items on the cash flow statement may also be affected to an extent by these types of accounting choices but not to the same degree as the income statement. We should emphasize here that in our discussion so far, we are emphasizing the *legal discretion* that accounting rules allow managers when reporting revenues and expenses. (Nevertheless, accounting fraud can occur, as discussed in the Famous Failures in Finance box. As suggested there, audits are an important aspect of a company's financial statements.)

Table 7.5 presents the 2015 and 2016 statement of cash flows for Universal Office Furnishings. The statement is broken into three parts. The most important part is the first one, labeled "Cash from operating activities." It captures *the net cash flow from operating activities*—the line highlighted on the statement. This is what people typically mean when they say "cash flow"—the amount of cash generated by the company and available for investment and financing activities.

Note that Universal's 2016 cash flow from operating activities was $195.6 million, down slightly from the year before. This amount was more than enough to cover the company's investing activities ($97.1 million) and its financing activities ($82.7 million). Thus, Universal's actual cash position—see the line near the bottom of the statement, labeled "Net increase (decrease) in cash"—increased by some $15.8 million. That result was a big improvement over the year before, when the firm's cash position fell by more than $35 million. A high (and preferably increasing) cash flow means the company has enough money to service debt, finance growth, and pay dividends. In addition, investors like to see the firm's cash position increase over time because of the positive impact that it has on the company's liquidity and its ability to meet operating needs in a prompt and timely fashion.

Financial Ratios

To see what accounting statements really have to say about the financial condition and operating results of a firm, we have to turn to *financial ratios*. Such ratios provide a different perspective on the financial affairs of the firm—particularly with regard to the balance sheet and income statement—and thus expand the information content of the company's financial statements. Simply stated, **ratio analysis** is the study of the relationships between various financial statement accounts. Each

How Depreciation Works

TABLE 7.5   STATEMENT OF CASH FLOWS

Universal Office Furnishings, Inc. Statements of Cash Flows Fiscal Year Ended December 31 ($ millions)

	2016	2015
Cash from operating activities		
Net earnings	$139.7	$ 141.8
Depreciation and amortization	$ 77.1	$ 62.1
Other noncash charges	$ 84.5	$ 16.7
Decrease (increase) in noncash current assets	($ 59.4)	$ 14.1
Increase (decrease) in current liabilities	$122.7	($ 29.1)
Net cash flow from operating activities	**$195.6**	**$205.6**
Cash from investing activities		
Acquisitions of property, plant, and equipment—net	($ 74.6)	($ 90.6)
Acquisitions of other noncurrent assets	($ 22.5)	($ 0.0)
Net cash flow from investing activities	**($ 97.1)**	**($ 90.6)**
Cash from financing activities		
Proceeds from long-term borrowing	$ 0.0	$ 79.1
Reduction in long-term debt	($ 28.4)	($ 211.1)
Net repurchase of capital stock	($ 45.0)	($ 26.8)
Payment of dividends on common stock	($ 9.3)	($ 8.5)
Net cash flow from financing activities	**($ 82.7)**	**($150.3)**
Net increase (decrease) in cash	**$ 15.8**	**($ 35.3)**
Cash and equivalents at beginning of period	$ 80.0	$ 115.3
Cash and equivalents at end of period	$ 95.8	$ 80.0

FAMOUS FAILURES IN FINANCE

Cooking the Books: What Were They Thinking?

Recent scandals involving fraudulent accounting practices have resulted in public outrage, not only in the United States but around the world as well. In December 2013, the SEC charged Fifth Third Bank of Cincinnati and its former chief financial officer, Daniel Poston, with improper accounting for commercial real estate loans during the financial crisis. Fifth Third was forced to pay a $6.5 million fine to settle the case, and Poston agreed never to work as an accountant for a publicly traded company, effectively ending his professional career. In February 2012, the San Francisco–based maker of products such as Kettle Chips and Pop Secret Popcorn, Diamond Foods, fired its CEO and CFO after discovering $80 million in payments to walnut growers that had been accounted for improperly. Diamond's stock fell nearly 40% in a single day on news of the accounting fraud, which led to a $5 million fine from the SEC in 2014.

These were hardly the first cases of accounting fraud leading to financial ruin. Unscrupulous executives used a number of accounting tricks to deceive the public including capitalizing operating expenses on the balance sheet, recognizing fictitious or premature revenues, creating off-balance-sheet liabilities, using off-balance-sheet derivative transactions to understate risk, and writing off goodwill as extraordinary loss rather than amortizing it over time to manipulate future earnings growth.

Critical Thinking Question One of the steps to strengthen corporate reporting is to separate internal and external audits of a company by not permitting an auditor to provide both internal and external audits to the same client. Will this regulation be able to eliminate conflict of interest? Discuss.

measure relates an item on the balance sheet (or income statement) to another or, as is more often the case, a balance sheet account to an operating (income statement) item. In this way, we can look not so much at the absolute size of the financial statement accounts but rather at what they indicate about the liquidity, activity, or profitability of the firm.

What Ratios Have to Offer Investors use financial ratios to evaluate the financial condition and operating results of the company and to compare those results to historical or industry standards. When using historical standards, investors compare the company's ratios from one year to the next. When using industry standards, investors compare a particular company's ratios to those of other companies in the same line of business.

Remember, the reason we use ratios is to develop information about the past that can be used to get a handle on the future. It's only from an understanding of a company's past performance that you can forecast its future with some degree of confidence. For example, even if sales have been expanding rapidly over the past few years, you must carefully assess the reasons for the growth, rather than naively assuming that past growth-rate trends will continue into the future. Such insights are obtained from financial ratios and financial statement analysis.

Financial ratios can be divided into five groups: (1) liquidity, (2) activity, (3) leverage, (4) profitability, and (5) common-stock, or market, measures. Using the 2016 figures from the Universal financial statements (Tables 7.3 and 7.4), we will now identify and briefly discuss some of the more widely used ratios in each of these categories.

Liquidity Ratios **Liquidity ratios** focus on the firm's ability to meet its day-to-day operating expenses and satisfy its short-term obligations as they come due. Of major concern is whether a company has adequate cash and other liquid assets on hand to service its debt and operating needs in a prompt and timely fashion. Three ratios that investors use to assess a firm's liquidity position are the current ratio, the quick ratio, and the working capital ratio.

Current Ratio One of the most commonly cited of all financial ratios is the *current ratio*. The current ratio measures a company's ability to meet its short-term liabilities with its short-term assets and is one of the best measures of a company's financial health.

Equation 7.1

$$\text{Current ratio} = \frac{\text{Current assets}}{\text{Current liabilities}}$$

$$\text{For Universal} = \frac{\$500.3}{\$374.0} = \underline{1.34}$$

This figure indicates that Universal had $1.34 in short-term resources to service every dollar of current debt. That's a fairly good number and, by most standards today, suggests that the company is carrying an adequate level of liquid assets to satisfy the current period's obligations.

Quick Ratio Of all the current assets listed on a firm's balance sheet, the least liquid is often the firm's inventory balance. Particularly when a firm is going through a period of declining sales, it can have difficulty selling its inventory and converting it into cash. For this reason, many investors like to subtract out inventory from the current assets total when assessing whether a firm has sufficient liquidity to meet its near-term obligations. Thus, the quick ratio is similar to the current ratio but it excludes inventory in the numerator.

Equation 7.2

$$\text{Quick ratio} = \frac{\text{Current assets} - \text{inventory}}{\text{Current liabilities}}$$

$$\text{For Universal} = \frac{\$500.3 - 103.7}{\$374.0} = \underline{1.06}$$

Even excluding its inventory holdings, Universal appears to have sufficient liquidity.

Net Working Capital Although technically not a ratio, *net working capital* is often viewed as such. Actually, net working capital is an absolute measure, which indicates the dollar amount of equity in the working capital position of the firm. It is the difference between current assets and current liabilities. For 2016, the net working capital position for Universal amounted to the following.

Equation 7.3

$$\text{Net working capital} = \text{Current assets} - \text{Current liabilities}$$

$$\text{For Universal} = \$500.3 - \$374.0 = \underline{\$126.3 \text{ million}}$$

A net working capital figure that exceeds $125,000,000 is indeed substantial (especially for a firm this size). It reinforces our contention that the liquidity position of this firm is good—so long as it is not made up of slow-moving, obsolete inventories and/or past-due accounts receivable.

How much liquidity is enough? What are the desirable ranges for measures such as the current ratio and quick ratio? The answer depends on many factors and will vary across industries. When a company's business is more volatile, having extra liquidity is more important, so investors would like to see higher values for these ratios for firms in turbulent industries. On the other hand, it is possible to have too much liquidity. Consider a firm that holds vast cash reserves, like Apple Inc. In the quarter ending on March 28, 2015, Apple's balance sheet indicated that the company held more than $33 billion in cash and marketable securities plus another $160 billion in cash invested in long-term securities. Those cash balances earned a very low rate of return, so investors put pressure on Apple to distribute some of its cash through dividends. In general, investors want firms to maintain enough liquidity to cover their short-term obligations, but they do not want firms to hold excessive amounts of liquid assets because doing so depresses the rate of return that the company earns on its overall asset portfolio.

Activity Ratios Measuring general liquidity is only the beginning of the analysis. We must also assess the composition and underlying liquidity of key current assets and evaluate how effectively the company is managing these resources. **Activity ratios** (also called efficiency ratios) compare company sales to various asset categories in order to measure how well the company is using its assets. Three of the most widely used activity ratios deal with accounts receivable, inventory, and total assets. Other things being equal, high or increasing ratio values indicate that a firm is managing its assets efficiently, though there may be instances when activity ratios can be too high, as was the case with liquidity ratios.

Accounts Receivable Turnover A glance at most financial statements will reveal that the asset side of the balance sheet is dominated by just a few accounts that make up 80% to 90%, or even more, of total resources. Certainly, this is the case with Universal Office Furnishings, where, as you can see in Table 7.3, three entries (accounts receivable, inventory, and net property, plant, and equipment) accounted for nearly 80% of total assets in 2016. Like Universal, most firms hold a significant accounts receivable balance, and for this reason firms want to monitor their receivables closely. Remember, receivables represent credit that a firm grants to its customers. Other things being equal, firms would like to collect from their customers as quickly as possible, and the sooner the firm's customers pay their bills, the lower will be the accounts receivable balance. On the other hand, if a firm gives its customers a long time to pay their bills, the receivables balance will be relatively high, but giving customers more time to pay might generate more sales. Therefore, determining the optimal approach to collecting from customers represents a balance between collecting faster (and therefore taking advantage of the time value of money) and using more generous credit terms to attract customers. The *accounts receivable turnover ratio* captures the relationship between a firm's receivables balance and its sales. It is computed as follows:

Equation 7.4

$$\text{Accounts receivable turnover} = \frac{\text{Sales revenue}}{\text{Accounts receivable}}$$

$$\text{For Universal} = \frac{\$1,938.0}{\$227.2} = \underline{8.53}$$

A firm that has a high receivables turnover generates its sales without having to extend customers credit for long periods. In 2016 Universal was turning its receivables about 8.5 times a year. That excellent turnover rate suggests a very strong credit and collection policy. Investors would generally be pleased with this performance as long as they did not believe that Universal's rapid collection policy did not discourage customers from buying Universal products. The 8.53 turnover ratio means that each dollar invested in receivables was supporting, or generating, $8.53 in sales.

Inventory Turnover Another important corporate resource—and one that requires a considerable amount of management attention—is inventory. Control of inventory is important to the well-being of a company and is commonly assessed with the *inventory turnover measure.*

Equation 7.5

$$\text{Inventory turnover} = \frac{\text{Sales revenue}}{\text{Inventory}}$$

$$\text{For Universal} = \frac{\$1,938.0}{\$103.7} = \underline{18.69}$$

In most cases, firms would rather sell their products quickly than hold them in stock as inventory. Some items, such as perishable goods and consumer electronics, lose value the longer they sit on shelves. Besides, a firm cannot make a profit on an item that it has produced until the item sells. All of this means that firms have great incentives to increase inventory turnover. Universal's 2016 turnover of almost 19 times a year means that the firm is holding inventory for less than a month—actually, for about 20 days $(365/18.69 = 19.5)$. A turnover ratio that high indicates that the firm is doing an excellent job managing its inventory.

Keep in mind that the inventory turnover ratio will be higher if the inventory balance is lower, holding the sales level constant. This suggests that firms could improve their turnover ratio simply by holding less inventory. Here again there is a tradeoff that firms have to manage. If firms are too aggressive at trimming their inventory levels, then they may not be able to fill customers' orders on time, or they could experience production delays due to raw materials shortages. In general, investors like to see rapid inventory turnover as long as it is not accompanied by any of the problems associated with inventory levels that are too lean.

Note that, rather than sales, some analysts prefer to use *cost of goods sold* in the numerator of Equation 7.5, on the premise that the inventory account on the balance sheet is more directly related to cost of goods sold from the income statement. Because cost of goods sold is less than sales, using it will, of course, lead to a lower inventory turnover figure—for Universal in 2016: $1,128.5/$103.7 = 10.88$, versus 18.69 when sales is used. Regardless of whether you use sales (which we'll continue to do here) or cost of goods sold, for analytical purposes you'd still use the measure in the same way.

Total Asset Turnover *Total asset turnover* indicates how efficiently a firm uses its assets to support sales. It is calculated as follows:

Equation 7.6

$$\text{Total asset turnover} = \frac{\text{Sales revenue}}{\text{Total assets}}$$

$$\text{For Universal} = \frac{\$1,938.0}{\$941.2} = \underline{2.06}$$

Note in this case that Universal is generating more than $2 in revenues from every dollar invested in assets. This is a fairly high number and is important because it has a direct bearing on corporate profitability. The principle at work here is simple: Earning $100 from a $1,000 investment is far more desirable than earning $100 from a $2,000 investment. A high total asset turnover figure suggests that corporate resources are being well managed and that the firm is able to realize a high level of sales (and, ultimately, profits) from its asset investments.

Leverage Ratios Leverage ratios (sometimes called solvency ratios) look at the firm's financial structure. They indicate the amount of debt being used to support the resources and operations of the company. The amount of indebtedness within the financial structure and the ability of the firm to service its debt are major concerns to potential investors. There are three widely used leverage ratios. The first two, the debt-equity ratio and the equity multiplier, measure the amount of debt that a company uses. The third, times interest earned, assesses how well the company can service its debt.

Debt-Equity Ratio The *debt-equity ratio* measures the relative amount of funds provided by lenders and owners. It is computed as follows:

Equation 7.7

$$\text{Debt-equity ratio} = \frac{\text{Long-term debt}}{\text{Stockholders' equity}}$$

$$\text{For Universal} = \frac{\$177.8}{\$294.5} = \underline{0.60}$$

Because highly leveraged firms (those that use large amounts of debt) run an increased risk of defaulting on their loans, this ratio is particularly helpful in assessing a stock's risk exposure. The 2016 debt-equity ratio for Universal is reasonably low (at 0.60) and shows that most of the company's capital comes from its owners. Stated another way, there was only 60 cents of long-term debt in the capital structure for every dollar of equity. Unlike the other measures we've looked at so far, a low or declining debt-equity ratio indicates lower risk exposure, as that would suggest the firm has a more reasonable debt load.

Equity Multiplier The *equity multiplier* (also known as the *financial leverage ratio*) provides an alternative measure of a firm's debt usage. The formula for the equity multiplier appears below.

Equation 7.8

$$\text{Equity multiplier} = \frac{\text{Total assets}}{\text{Stockholders' equity}}$$

$$\text{For Universal} = \frac{\$941.2}{\$294.5} = \underline{3.20}$$

It may seem odd to say that the equity multiplier measures a firm's use of debt because debt does not appear directly in Equation 7.8, but keep in mind that total assets is the sum of liabilities and equity. For a firm that has no liabilities (i.e., no debt) at all, assets will equal stockholders' equity, and the equity multiplier will be 1.0. Holding equity fixed, the more debt the firm uses, the higher will be its total assets, and the higher will be the equity multiplier. For Universal, the equity multiplier of 3.2 suggests that there is $3.20 of assets for every $1 of equity. Because assets is the sum of debt and equity, an equity multiplier of 3.2 says that Universal has $2.20 of debt (debt of all types, not just long-term debt) for each $1 of equity.

Times Interest Earned *Times interest earned* is called a coverage ratio. It measures the ability of the firm to meet ("cover") its fixed interest payments. It is calculated as follows:

Equation 7.9

$$\text{Times interest earned} = \frac{\text{Earnings before interest and taxes}}{\text{Interest expense}}$$

$$\text{For Universal} = \frac{\$235.2}{\$13.4} = \underline{17.55}$$

The ability of the company to meet its interest payments (which, with bonds, are fixed contractual obligations) in a timely fashion is an important consideration in evaluating risk exposure. Universal's times interest earned ratio indicates that the firm has about $17.55 of EBIT available to cover every dollar of interest expense. That's a very high coverage ratio—way above average. As a rule, a ratio eight to nine times earnings is considered strong. To put this number in perspective, there's usually little concern until times interest earned drops to something less than two or three times earnings.

It has recently become popular to use an alternative earnings figure in the numerator for the times interest earned ratio. In particular, some analysts are adding back depreciation and amortization expenses to earnings and are using what is known as *earnings before interest, taxes, depreciation, and amortization* (EBITDA). Their argument is that because depreciation and amortization are both noncash expenditures (i.e., they're little more than bookkeeping entries), they should be added back to earnings to provide a more realistic "cash-based" figure. The problem is that EBITDA figures invariably end up putting performance in a far more favorable light. (Indeed, many argue that this is the principal motivation behind their use.) As a result, EBITDA tends to sharply increase ratios such as times interest earned. For example, in the case of Universal, adding depreciation and amortization (2016: $77.1 million) to EBIT (2016: $235.2 million) results in a coverage ratio of $312.3/$13.4 = 23.31—versus 17.5 when this ratio is computed in the conventional way (with EBIT).

Profitability Ratios **Profitability** is a relative measure of success. Each of the various profitability measures relates the returns (profits) of a company to its sales, assets, or equity. There are three widely used profitability measures: net profit margin, return on assets, and return on equity. Clearly, the more profitable the company, the better—thus, other things being equal, higher or increasing measures of profitability are what you'd like to see.

Net Profit Margin This is the "bottom line" of operations. *Net profit margin* indicates the rate of profit being earned from sales and other revenues. It is computed as follows:

Equation 7.10

$$\text{Net profit margin} = \frac{\text{Net profit after taxes}}{\text{Sales revenue}}$$

$$\text{For Universal} = \frac{\$139.7}{\$1,938.0} = 0.072 = \underline{\underline{7.2\%}}$$

The net profit margin looks at profits as a percentage of sales (and other revenues). Note that Universal had a net profit margin of 7.2% in 2016. That is, for every dollar of revenue that the company generated, it earned a profit of a little more than seven cents. That may be about average for large U.S. companies, but it is well above average for firms in the business equipment industry.

Return on Assets As a profitability measure, *return on assets (ROA)* looks at the amount of resources needed to support operations. Return on assets reveals management's effectiveness in generating profits from the assets it has available, and it is perhaps the most important measure of return. ROA is computed as follows:

Equation 7.11

$$ROA = \frac{\text{Net profit after taxes}}{\text{Total assets}}$$

$$\text{For Universal} = \frac{\$139.7}{\$941.2} = 0.148 = \underline{14.8\%}$$

AN ADVISOR'S PERSPECTIVE

Ryan McKeown *Senior VP–Financial Advsior,* **Wealth Enhancement Group**

"A simple method that I use is looking at the ROE."

MyFinanceLab

In the case of Universal Office Furnishings, the company earned almost 15% on its asset investments in 2016. That is a very healthy return, and well above average. As a rule, you'd like to see a company maintain as high an ROA as possible. The higher the ROA, the more profitable the company.

Return on Equity A measure of the overall profitability of the firm, *return on equity (ROE)* is closely watched by investors because of its direct link to the profits, growth, and dividends of the company. Return on equity—or return on investment (ROI), as it's sometimes called—measures the return to the firm's stockholders by relating profits to shareholder equity.

Equation 7.12

$$ROE = \frac{\text{Net profit after taxes}}{\text{Stockholders' equity}}$$

$$\text{For Universal} = \frac{\$139.7}{\$294.5} = 0.474 = \underline{47.4\%}$$

ROE shows the annual profit earned by the firm as a percentage of the equity that stockholders have invested in the firm. For Universal, that amounts to about 47 cents for every dollar of equity. That, too, is an outstanding measure of performance and suggests that the company is doing its best to maximize shareholder value. Generally speaking, look out for a falling ROE, as it could mean trouble later on.

Breaking Down ROA and ROE ROA and ROE are both important measures of corporate profitability. But to get the most from these two measures, we have to break them down into their component parts. ROA, for example, is made up of two key components: the firm's net profit margin and its total asset turnover. Thus, rather than using Equation 7.11 to find ROA, we can use the net profit margin and total asset turnover figures that we computed earlier (Equations 7.10 and 7.6, respectively). Using this expanded format, we can find Universal's 2016 ROA.

Equation 7.13

$$ROA = \text{Net profit margin} \times \text{Total asset turnover}$$

$$\text{For Universal} = 7.2\% \times 2.06 = \underline{14.8\%}$$

Note that we end up with the same figure as that found with Equation 7.11. So why would you want to use the expanded version of ROA? The major reason is that it shows you what's driving company profits. As an investor, you want to know if ROA is moving up (or down) because of improvement (or deterioration) in the company's profit margin and/or its total asset turnover. Ideally, you'd like to see ROA moving up (or staying high) because the company is doing a good job in managing both its profits and its assets.

Going from ROA to ROE Just as ROA can be broken into its component parts, so too can the return on equity (ROE) measure. Actually, ROE is nothing more than an extension of ROA. It brings the company's financing decisions into the assessment of profitability. That is, the expanded ROE measure indicates the extent to which financial leverage (i.e., how much debt the firm uses) can increase return to stockholders. The use of debt in the capital structure, in effect, means that ROE will always be greater than ROA. The question is how much greater. Rather than using the abbreviated version of ROE in Equation 7.12, we can compute ROE as follows.

Equation 7.14

$$\text{ROE} = \text{ROA} \times \text{Equity multiplier}$$

To find ROE according to Equation 7.14, recall first that Universal's equity multiplier was 3.2.

We can now find the 2016 ROE for Universal as follows:

$$\text{ROE} = 14.8 \times 3.20 = \underline{47.4}\%$$

Here we can see that the use of debt (the equity multiplier) has magnified—in this case, tripled—returns to stockholders.

An Expanded ROE Equation Alternatively, we can expand Equation 7.14 still further by breaking ROA into its component parts. In this case, we could compute ROE as

Equation 7.15

$$\text{ROE} = \text{ROA} \times \text{Equity multiplier}$$
$$= (\text{Net profit margin} \times \text{Total asset turnover}) \times \text{Equity multiplier}$$

For Universal $= 7.2\% \times 2.06 \times 3.20 = \underline{47.4}\%$

This expanded version of ROE is especially helpful because it enables investors to assess the company's profitability in terms of three key components: net profit margin, total asset turnover, and financial leverage. In this way, you can determine whether ROE is moving up simply because the firm is employing more debt, which isn't necessarily beneficial, or because of how the firm is managing its assets and operations, which certainly does have positive long-term implications. To stockholders, ROE is a critical measure of performance. A high ROE means that the firm is currently very profitable, and if some of those profits are reinvested in the business, the firm may grow rapidly.

Common-Stock Ratios Finally, there are a number of **common-stock ratios** (sometimes called valuation ratios) that convert key bits of information about the company to a per-share basis. Also called **market ratios**, they tell the investor exactly what portion of total profits, dividends, and equity is allocated to each share of stock. Popular common-stock ratios include earnings per share, price-to-earnings ratio, dividends per share, dividend yield, payout ratio, and book value per share. We examined two of these measures (earnings per share and dividend yield) earlier in this text. Let's look now at the other four.

Price-to-Earnings Ratio This measure, an extension of the earnings per share ratio, is used to determine how the market is pricing the company's common stock. The *price-to-earnings (P/E) ratio* relates the company's earnings per share (EPS) to the market price of its stock. To compute the P/E ratio, it is necessary to first know the stock's EPS. Using the earnings per share equation, we see that the EPS for Universal in 2016 was

$$EPS = \frac{\text{Net profit after taxes } - \text{ Preferred dividends}}{\text{Number of common shares outstanding}}$$

$$\text{For Universal} = \frac{\$139.7 - \$0}{61.8} = \underline{\$2.26}$$

In this case, the company's profits of $139.7 million translate into earnings of $2.26 for each share of outstanding common stock. (Note in this case that dividends are shown as $0 because the company has no preferred stock outstanding.) Given this EPS figure and the stock's current market price (assume it is currently trading at $41.50), we can use Equation 7.16 to determine the P/E ratio for Universal.

Equation 7.16

$$P/E = \frac{\text{Price of common stock}}{EPS}$$

$$\text{For Universal} = \frac{\$41.50}{\$2.26} = \underline{18.36}$$

INVESTOR FACTS

Record P/E Ratio Signals Bear Market In addition to calculating a P/E ratio for a single stock, you can do the same calculation for a group of stocks such as the S&P 500. In April 1999 the P/E ratio for the S&P 500 reached an all-time high of almost 43. Stocks at the time were valued at nearly 43 times current earnings. About a year later, the S&P 500 began a long slide, losing more than 40% of its value over the next two years. It took more than a decade for the index to recover.

(Source: Robert Shiller, http://www.econ.yale.edu/~shiller/data.htm)

In effect, the stock is currently selling at a multiple of about 18 times its 2016 earnings.

Price-to-earnings multiples are widely quoted in the financial press and are an essential part of many stock valuation models. Other things being equal, you would like to find stocks with rising P/E ratios because higher P/E multiples usually translate into higher future stock prices and better returns to stockholders. But even though you'd like to see them going up, you also want to watch out for P/E ratios that become too high (relative either to the market or to what the stock has done in the past). When this multiple gets too high, it may be a signal that the stock is becoming overvalued (and may be due for a fall).

One way to assess the P/E ratio is to compare it to the company's rate of growth in earnings. The market has developed a measure of this comparison called the **PEG ratio**. Basically, it looks at the latest P/E relative to the three- to five-year rate of growth in earnings. (The earnings growth rate can be all historical—the last three to five years—or perhaps part historical and part forecasted.) The PEG ratio is computed as:

Equation 7.17

$$\text{PEG ratio} = \frac{\text{Stock's P/E ratio}}{\text{3- to 5-year growth rate in earnings}}$$

As we saw earlier, Universal Office Furnishings had a P/E ratio of 18.36 times earnings in 2016. If corporate earnings for the past five years had been growing at an average annual rate of, say, 15%, then its PEG ratio would be:

$$\text{For Universal} = \frac{18.36}{15.0} = \underline{1.22}$$

A PEG ratio this close to 1.0 is certainly reasonable. It suggests that the company's P/E is not out of line with the earnings growth of the firm. In fact, the idea is to look for stocks that have PEG ratios that are equal to or less than 1. In contrast, a high PEG means the stock's P/E has outpaced its growth in earnings and, if anything, the stock is probably "fully valued." Some investors, in fact, won't even look at stocks if their PEGs are too high—say, more than 1.5 or 2.0. At the minimum, PEG is probably something you would want to look at because it certainly is not unreasonable to expect some correlation between a stock's P/E and its rate of growth in earnings.

Dividends per Share The principle here is the same as for EPS: to translate total common dividends paid by the company into a per-share figure. (*Note:* If not shown on the income statement, the amount of dividends paid to common stockholders can usually be found on the statement of cash flows—see Table 7.5.) Dividends per share is measured as follows:

Equation 7.18

$$\text{Dividends per share} = \frac{\text{Annual dividends paid to common stock}}{\text{Number of common shares outstanding}}$$

$$\text{For Universal} = \frac{\$9.3}{61.8} = \underline{\$0.15}$$

For fiscal 2016, Universal paid out dividends of $0.15 per share—at a quarterly rate of about 3.75 cents per share.

As we saw earlier in this text, we can relate dividends per share to the market price of the stock to determine its *dividend yield*: i.e., $0.15 ÷ $41.50 = 0.004, or 0.4%. Clearly, you won't find Universal Office Furnishings within the income sector of the market. It pays very little in annual dividends and has a dividend yield of less than one-half of 1%.

Payout Ratio Another important dividend measure is the dividend *payout ratio*. It indicates how much of its earnings a company pays out to stockholders in the form of dividends. Well-managed companies try to maintain target payout ratios. If earnings are going up over time, so will the company's dividends. The payout ratio is calculated as follows:

Equation 7.19

$$\text{Dividend payout ratio} = \frac{\text{Dividends per share}}{\text{Earnings per share}}$$

$$\text{For Universal} = \frac{\$0.15}{\$2.26} = \underline{0.07}$$

For Universal in 2016, dividends accounted for about 7% of earnings. Traditionally, most companies that pay dividends tend to pay out somewhere between 30% and 50% of earnings. By that standard, Universal's payout, like its dividend yield, is quite low. But that's not necessarily bad, as it indicates that the company is retaining most of its earnings to, at least in part, internally finance the firm's rapid growth. Indeed, it is quite common for growth-oriented companies to have low payout ratios. Some of the better-known growth companies, like Genentech, Boston Scientific, EchoStar Communications, and Starbucks, all retain 100% of their earnings. (In other words, they have dividend payout ratios of zero.)

Companies that pay dividends are generally reluctant to cut them, so when earnings fall, dividends usually do not fall right away. This suggests that a rising dividend payout ratio may, counterintuitively, signal trouble. A rising dividend payout is often a sign that a company's earnings are falling rather than a sign that the company is doing well and increasing its dividend payments. For example, at the end of the last recession, the average dividend payout ratio among companies in the S&P 500 was nearly twice as high as it was when the recession began, so clearly in that period rising payouts signaled bad rather than good times. Once the payout ratio reaches 70% to 80% of earnings, you should take extra care. A payout ratio that high is often an indication that the company may not be able to maintain its current level of dividends. That generally means that dividends will have to be cut back to more reasonable levels unless earnings grow rapidly. And if there's one thing the market doesn't like, it's cuts in dividends; they're usually associated with big cuts in share prices.

Book Value per Share The last common-stock ratio is *book value per share*, a measure that deals with stockholders' equity. Actually, *book value* is simply another term for equity (or net worth). It represents the difference between total assets and total liabilities. Note that in this case we're defining equity as common stockholders' equity, which would exclude preferred stock. That is, common stockholders' equity = total equity − preferred stocks. (Universal has no preferred outstanding, so its total equity equals its common stockholders' equity.) Book value per share is computed as follows:

Equation 7.20

$$\text{Book value per share} = \frac{\text{Stockholders' equity}}{\text{Number of common shares outstanding}}$$

$$\text{For Universal} = \frac{\$294.5}{61.8} = \underline{\$4.76}$$

Presumably, a stock should sell for more than its book value (as Universal does). If not, it could be an indication that something is seriously wrong with the company's outlook and profitability.

A convenient way to relate the book value of a company to the market price of its stock is to compute the *price-to-book-value ratio*.

Equation 7.21

$$\text{Price-to-book-value} = \frac{\text{Market price of common stock}}{\text{Book value per share}}$$

$$\text{For Universal} = \frac{\$41.50}{\$4.76} = \underline{8.72}$$

Widely used by investors, this ratio shows how aggressively the stock is being priced. Most stocks have a price-to-book-value ratio of more than 1.0—which simply indicates that the stock is selling for more than its book value. In fact, in strong bull markets, it is not uncommon to find stocks trading at 4 or 5 times their book values, or even more. Universal's price-to-book ratio of 8.7 times is definitely on the high side. That is something to evaluate closely. It may indicate that the stock is already fully priced, or perhaps even overpriced. Or it could result from nothing more than a relatively low book value per share.

Interpreting the Numbers

Rather than compute all the financial ratios themselves, most investors rely on published reports for such information. Many large brokerage houses and a variety of financial services firms publish such reports. An example is given in Figure 7.2. These reports provide a good deal of vital information in a convenient and easy-to-read format. Best of all, they relieve investors of the chore of computing the financial ratios themselves. (Similar information is also available from a number of online services, as well as from various software providers.) Even so, as an investor, you must be able to evaluate this published information. To do so, you need not only a basic understanding of financial ratios but also some performance standard, or benchmark, against which you can assess trends in company performance.

Basically, financial statement analysis uses two types of performance standards: historical and industry. With historical standards, various financial ratios and measures are run on the company for a period of three to five years (or longer). You would use these to assess developing trends in the company's operations and financial condition. That is, are they improving or deteriorating, and where do the company's strengths and weaknesses lie? In contrast, industry standards enable you to compare the financial ratios of the company with comparable firms or with the average results for the industry as a whole. Here, we focus on determining the relative strengths of the firm with respect to its competitors. Using Universal Office Furnishings, we'll see how to use both of these standards of performance to evaluate and interpret financial ratios.

Using Historical and Industry Standards   Look at Table 7.6. It provides a summary of historical data and average industry figures (for the latest year) for most of the ratios we have discussed. (Industry averages, such as those used in Table 7.6, are readily available from such sources as S&P, Moody's, and many industry-specific publications.) By carefully evaluating these ratios, we should be able to draw some basic conclusions about the financial condition, operating results, and general financial health of the company. By comparing the financial ratios contained in Table 7.6, we can make the following observations about the company:

1. Universal's *liquidity position* is a bit below average. This doesn't seem to be a source of major concern, however, especially when you consider its receivables and inventory positions. That is, based on its respective turnover ratios (see item 2 below), both of these current assets appear to turn faster than the industry average, which means that Universal holds lower receivables and inventory balances relative to sales than other firms do. This could explain the relatively low current ratio of this company. That is, the current ratio is a bit below average not because the firm has a lot of current liabilities but because it is doing such a good job in controlling current assets.

2. Universal's *activity measures* are all way above average. This company consistently has very high turnover measures, which in turn make significant contributions not only to the firm's liquidity position but also to its profitability. Clearly, the company has been able to get a lot more from its assets than the industry as a whole.

3. The company's *leverage position* seems well controlled. It tends to use a lot less debt in its financial structure than the average firm in the office equipment industry. The payoff for this judicious use of debt comes in the form of a coverage ratio that's well above average.

FIGURE 7.2

An Example of a Published Report with Financial Statistics

This and similar reports are widely available to investors and play an important part in the security analysis process. (Source: *Mergent*, May 17, 2015. © 2015. Used with permission.)

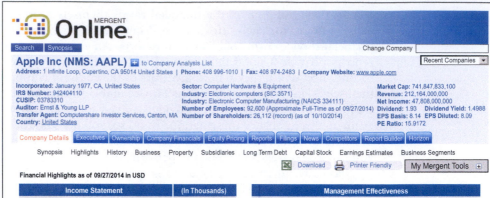

Apple Inc (NMS: AAPL) ➕ to Company Analysis List
Address: 1 Infinite Loop, Cupertino, CA 95014 United States | Phone: 408 996-1010 | Fax: 408 974-2483 | Company Website: www.apple.com

Incorporated: January 1977, CA, United States
IRS Number: 942404110
CUSIP: 03783310
Auditor: Ernst & Young LLP
Transfer Agent: Computershare Investor Services, Canton, MA
Country: United States

Sector: Computer Hardware & Equipment
Industry: Electronic computers (SIC 3571)
Industry: Electronic Computer Manufacturing (NAICS 334111)
Number of Employees: 92,600 (Approximate Full-Time as of 09/27/2014)
Number of Shareholders: 26,112 (record) (as of 10/10/2014)

Market Cap: 741,847,833,100
Revenue: 212,164,000,000
Net Income: 47,808,000,000
Dividend: 1.93   Dividend Yield: 1.4988
EPS Basis: 8.14   EPS Diluted: 8.09
PE Ratio: 15.9172

Company Details | Executives | Ownership | Company Financials | Equity Pricing | Reports | Filings | News | Competitors | Report Builder | Horizon

Synopsis   Highlights   History   Business   Property   Subsidiaries   Long Term Debt   Capital Stock   Earnings Estimates   Business Segments

Download   Printer Friendly   My Mergent Tools ➕

Financial Highlights as of 09/27/2014 in USD

Income Statement	(In Thousands)
Total Revenue	182,795,000
EBITDA	60,018,000
Operating Income	52,503,000
Net Income	39,510,000
Revenue per Share	30.12
EPS from Continuing Operations	6.45
EPS - Net Income - Diluted	6.45
Share Outstanding	5,866,161
Weighted Average Shares Outstanding - Basic	6,085,572
Weighted Average Shares Outstanding - Diluted	6,122,663
Earnings per Share - Basic	6.49

Balance Sheet	(In Thousands)
Total Assets	231,839,000
Current Assets	68,531,000
Total Liabilities	120,292,000
Long Term Debt	28,987,000
Stockholders' Equity	111,547,000
Total Assets per Share	39.52
Current Liabilities	63,448,000
Net Assets per Share	19.02

Cash Flow Statement	(In Thousands)
Cash from Operations	59,713,000
Cash from Investing	(22,579,000)
Cash from Financing	(37,549,000)
Capital Expenditures	9,571,000
Cash Flow per Share	9.75
Cash & Cash Equivalents, Beginning of Year	14,259,000
Cash & Cash Equivalents, End of Year	13,844,000

Stock Price and Valuation (Data as of 05/15/2015)	
Market Cap(mil)	741,848
Share Outstanding(000's)	5,761,030
PE Ratio	15.9172
Dividend Per Share(TTM)	1.93
Earning Per Share(TTM)	8.14
Last Closing Price	128.77
Previous Trading Day Range	128.21 - 129.49
52 Week Range	84.12 - 133.00
7 Day Average Closing Price	127.26
30 Day Average Closing Price	127.61
200 Day Average Closing Price	119.41
Beta	1.65
High Price Last 3 Mos.	133.00
Low Price Last 3 Mos.	122.24
Avg Daily Volume Last 3 Mos.	51,133,536.71

Management Effectiveness	
Revenue per Employee	1,889,662
Net Income per Employee	408,439
ROA % (Net)	18.06
ROE % (Net)	33.70
ROI % (Operating)	36.64

Profitability Ratios	
Gross Margin	38.59
Operating Margin	28.72
EBITDA Margin %	32.83
Calculated Tax Rate %	26.13
Profit Margin (TTM)	21.61

Valuation Ratios	
Price/Earnings (TTM)	15.48
Price/Book (TTM)	5.30
Price/Cash Flow (TTM)	10.24

Asset Management	
Total Asset Turnover	0.84
Receivables Turnover	7.66
Inventory Turnover	57.94
Property Plant & Equip Turnover	9.85
Cash & Equivalents Turnover	13.04

Debt Management	
Long Term Debt/Equity	0.26
Long Term Debt as % of Invested Capital	19.74
Total Debt/Equity	0.32
Accounts Payable Turnover	6.97
Accrued Expenses Turnover	23.94

Liquidity Indicators	
Quick Ratio	0.82
Current Ratio	1.08
Net Current Assets as % of Total Assets	2.19
Free Cash Flow per Share	8.26
Revenue to Assets	0.79

Consensus Estimates	2015Ae	2015Q2e	2015Q3e
Earnings per Share	8.96	1.73	1.83
Revenue	231,122.00	47,990.00	50,611.50
EBITDA	79,929.90	15,730.60	16,197.82

TABLE 7.6   COMPARATIVE HISTORICAL AND INDUSTRY RATIOS

	Historical Figures for Universal Office Furnishings, Inc.				Office Equipment Industry Average in 2016
	2013	2014	2015	2016	
Liquidity measures					
Current ratio	1.55	1.29	1.69	1.34	1.45
Quick ratio	1.21	1.02	1.26	1.06	1.15
Activity measures					
Receivables turnover	9.22	8.87	9.18	8.53	5.7
Inventory turnover	15.25	17.17	16.43	18.69	7.8
Total asset turnover	1.85	1.98	2.32	2.06	0.85
Leverage measures					
Debt-equity ratio	0.7	0.79	0.91	0.6	1.58
Equity multiplier	3.32	3.45	3.64	3.20	6.52
Times interest earned	15.37	26.22	32.49	17.55	5.6
Profitability measures					
Net profit margin	6.60%	7.50%	8.00%	7.20%	4.60%
Return on assets	9.80%	16.40%	18.60%	14.80%	3.90%
Return on equity	25.90%	55.50%	67.80%	47.40%	17.30%
Common stock measures					
Earnings per share	$ 1.92	$ 2.00	$ 2.17	$ 2.26	N/A
Price-to-earnings ratio	16.2	13.9	15.8	18.4	16.2
Dividend yield	0.30%	0.40%	0.40%	0.40%	1.10%
Payout ratio	5.20%	5.50%	6.00%	6.60%	24.80%
Price-to-book-value ratio	7.73	10.73	10.71	8.72	3.54

Ratio Analysis Overview

4. The *profitability picture* for Universal is equally attractive. The profit margin, return on assets, and ROE are all well above the industry norms. Clearly, the company is doing an outstanding job in managing its profits and is getting good results from its sales, assets, and equity.

In summary, our analysis shows that this firm is very well managed and highly profitable. The results of this are reflected in common-stock ratios that are consistently equal or superior to industry averages. Universal does not pay out a lot in dividends, but that's only because it uses those valuable resources to finance its growth and to reward its investors with consistently high ROEs.

Looking at the Competition In addition to analyzing a company historically and relative to the average performance of the industry, it's useful to evaluate the firm relative to two or three of its major competitors. A lot can be gained from seeing how a company stacks up against its competitors and by determining whether it is, in fact, well positioned to take advantage of unfolding developments. Table 7.7 offers an array of comparative financial statistics for Universal and three of its major competitors. One is about the same size (Cascade Industries), one is much smaller (Colwyn Furniture), and one is much larger (High Design, Inc.).

As the data in Table 7.7 show, Universal can hold its own against other leading producers in the industry. Indeed, in virtually every category, Universal's numbers are

TABLE 7.7   COMPARATIVE FINANCIAL STATISTICS: UNIVERSAL OFFICE FURNISHINGS AND ITS MAJOR COMPETITORS (All figures are for year-end 2016 or for the 5-year period ending in 2016; $ in millions)

Financial Measure	Universal Office Furnishings	Cascade Industries	Colwyn Furniture	High Design, Inc.
Total assets	$ 941.20	$ 906.70	$342.70	$ 3,037.60
Long-term debt	$ 177.80	$ 124.20	$ 73.90	$ 257.80
Stockholders' equity	$ 294.50	$ 501.30	$183.90	$1,562.20
Stockholders' equity as a % of total assets	31.30%	55.30%	53.70%	51.40%
Total revenues	$1,938.00	$1,789.30	$642.20	$3,316.10
Net earnings	$ 139.70	$ 87.40	$ 38.50	$ 184.20
Net profit margin	7.20%	4.90%	6.00%	5.50%
5-year growth rates in:				
Total assets	14.4%	19.4%	17.3%	17.7%
Total revenues	15.0%	17.8%	15.9%	15.8%
EPS	56.7%	38.9%	21.1%	24.7%
Dividends	1.5%	11.1%	N/A	12.0%
Total asset turnover	2.06	1.97	1.88	1.09
Debt-equity ratio	0.60	0.43	1.46	0.17
Times interest earned	17.55	13.38	8.35	14.36
ROA	14.80%	9.50%	6.70%	6.70%
ROE	47.40%	18.80%	21.80%	13.00%
P/E ratio	18.4	14.4	13.3	12.4
PEG ratio	1.2	2.4	2.0	1.1
Payout ratio	6.60%	26.20%	N/A	32.40%
Dividend yield	0.40%	1.80%	N/A	2.60%
Price-to-book-value ratio	8.7	2.7	2.9	1.6

about equal or superior to those of its three major competitors. It may not be the biggest (or the smallest), but it outperforms them all in profit margins and growth rates (in revenues and earnings). Equally important, it has the highest asset turnover, ROE, and price-to-earnings ratio. Tables 7.6 and 7.7 clearly show that Universal Office Furnishings is a solid, up-and-coming business that's been able to make a name for itself in a highly competitive industry. The company has done well in the past and appears to be well managed today. Our major concern at this point is whether Universal can continue to produce above-average returns for investors.

CONCEPTS IN REVIEW

Answers available at
http://www.pearsonhighered.com/smart

7.12 What is fundamental analysis? Does the performance of a company have any bearing on the value of its stock? Explain.

7.13 Why do investors bother to look at the historical performance of a company when future behavior is what really counts? Explain.

7.14 What is ratio analysis? Describe the contribution of ratio analysis to the study of a company's financial condition and operating results.

7.15 Contrast historical standards of performance with industry standards. Briefly note the role of each in analyzing the financial condition and operating results of a company.

MyFinanceLab

Here is what you should know after reading this chapter. MyFinanceLab will help you identify what you know and where to go when you need to practice.

What You Should Know	Key Terms	Where to Practice
LG1 **Discuss the security analysis process, including its goals and functions.** Success in buying common stocks is largely a matter of careful security selection and investment timing. Security analysis helps the investor make the selection decision by gauging the intrinsic value (underlying worth) of a stock.	intrinsic value, *p. 255* security analysis, *p. 255*	MyFinanceLab Study Plan 7.1
LG2 **Understand the purpose and contributions of economic analysis.** Economic analysis evaluates the general state of the economy and its potential effects on security returns. Its purpose is to characterize the future economic environment the investor is likely to face, and to set the tone for the security analysis process.	business cycle, *p. 259* economic analysis, *p. 258*	MyFinanceLab Study Plan 7.2
LG3 **Describe industry analysis and note how investors use it.** In industry analysis, the investor focuses on the activities of one or more industries. Especially important are how the competitive position of a particular industry stacks up against others and which companies within an industry hold special promise.	growth cycle, *p. 264* industry analysis, *p. 263*	MyFinanceLab Study Plan 7.3
LG4 **Demonstrate a basic appreciation of fundamental analysis and why it is used.** Fundamental analysis looks closely at the financial and operating characteristics of the company—at its competitive position, its sales and profit margins, its asset mix, its capital structure, and, eventually, its future prospects. A key aspect of this analytical process is company analysis, which involves an in-depth study of the financial condition and operating results of the company.	balance sheet, *p. 267* fundamental analysis, *p. 266* income statement, *p. 268* statement of cash flows, *p. 269*	MyFinanceLab Study Plan 7.4
LG5 **Calculate a variety of financial ratios and describe how financial statement analysis is used to gauge the financial vitality of a company.** The company's balance sheet, income statement, and statement of cash flows are all used in company analysis. An essential part of this analysis is financial ratios, which expand the perspective and information content of financial statements. There are five broad categories of financial ratios—liquidity, activity, leverage, profitability, and common-stock (market) ratios. All involve the study of relationships between financial statement accounts.	activity ratios, *p. 273* common-stock (market) ratios, *p. 279* leverage ratios, *p. 275* liquidity ratios, *p. 272* PEG ratio, *p. 280* profitability, *p. 277* ratio analysis, *p. 271*	MyFinanceLab Study Plan 7.5 Video Learning Aid for Problems P7.7, P7.15
LG6 **Use various financial measures to assess a company's performance, and explain how the insights derived form the basic input for the valuation process.** To evaluate financial ratios properly, it is necessary to base the analysis on historical and industry standards of performance. Historical standards are used to assess developing trends in the company. Industry benchmarks enable the investor to see how the firm stacks up against its competitors. Together they provide insight into how well the company is situated to take advantage of unfolding market conditions and opportunities.		MyFinanceLab Study Plan 7.6 Excel Table 7.6

Log into MyFinanceLab, take a chapter test, and get a personalized Study Plan that tells you which concepts you understand and which ones you need to review. From there, MyFinanceLab will give you further practice, tutorials, animations, videos, and guided solutions.
Log into **http://www.myfinancelab.com**

Discussion Questions

LG2 Q7.1 Economic analysis is generally viewed as an integral part of the top-down approach to security analysis. In this context, identify each of the following and note how each would probably behave in a strong economy.
  a. Fiscal policy
  b. Interest rates
  c. Industrial production
  d. Retail sales
  e. Producer prices

LG1 LG2 Q7.2 As an investor, what kind(s) of economic information would you look for if you were thinking about investing in the following?
  a. An airline stock
  b. A cyclical stock
  c. An electrical utility stock
  d. A building materials stock
  e. An aerospace firm, with heavy exposure in the defense industry

LG5 Q7.3 Match the specific ratios in the left-hand column with the category in the right-hand column to which it belongs.
  a. Inventory turnover   1. Profitability ratios
  b. Debt-equity ratio   2. Activity ratios
  c. Current ratio   3. Liquidity ratios
  d. Net profit margin   4. Leverage ratios
  e. Return on assets   5. Common-stock ratios
  f. Total asset turnover
  g. Price-to-earnings ratio
  h. Times interest earned
  i. Price-to-book-value ratio
  j. Payout ratio

Problems

All problems are available on http://www.myfinancelab.com

LG5 P7.1 Assume you are given the following abbreviated financial statement.

	($ in millions)
Current assets	$150.0
Fixed and other assets	$200.0
Total assets	$350.0
Current liabilities	$100.0
Long-term debt	$ 50.0
Stockholders' equity	$200.0
Total liabilities and equities	$350.0
Common shares outstanding	10 million shares
Total revenues	$500.0
Total operating costs and expenses	$435.0
Interest expense	$ 10.0
Income taxes	$ 20.0
Net profits	$ 35.0
Dividends paid to common stockholders	$ 10.0

On the basis of this information, calculate as many liquidity, activity, leverage, profitability, and common stock measures as you can. (*Note:* Assume the current market price of the common stock is $75 per share.)

LG5 **P7.2** A firm has 1 million shares of common stock outstanding with a book value of $15 per share. The firm also has total assets with a book value of $20 million. There is no preferred stock. What are the firm's total liabilities?

LG5 **P7.3** A firm has $750 million in total assets, no preferred stock, and total liabilities of $300 million. There are 300 million shares of common stock outstanding. The stock is selling for $5.25 per share. What is the price-to-book ratio?

LG5 **P7.4** The Amherst Company has net profits of $10 million, sales of $150 million, and 2.5 million shares of common stock outstanding. The company has total assets of $75 million and total stockholders' equity of $45 million. It pays $1 per share in common dividends, and the stock trades at $20 per share. Given this information, determine the following:
a. Amherst's EPS
b. Amherst's book value per share and price-to-book-value ratio
c. The firm's P/E ratio
d. The company's net profit margin
e. The stock's dividend payout ratio and its dividend yield
f. The stock's PEG ratio, given that the company's earnings have been growing at an average annual rate of 7.5%

LG5 **P7.5** ZIPBIT common stock is selling at a P/E of 10 times trailing earnings. The stock price is $23.50. What were the firm's earnings per share?

LG5 **P7.6** PEGCOR has a P/E ratio of 15. Earnings per share are $2.00, and the expected EPS five years from today is $3.22. Calculate the PEG ratio.

LG5 **P7.7** Highgate Computer Company produces $1.8 million in profits from $27 million in sales. It has total assets of $15 million.
a. Calculate Highgate's total asset turnover and its net profit margin.
b. Find the company's ROA, ROE, and book value per share, given that it has a total net worth of $6 million and 500,000 shares of common stock outstanding.

P7.8 The following data have been gathered from the financial statements of HiFly Corporation:

	2015	2016
Operating profit	$550,000,000	$600,000,000
Interest expense	$200,000,000	$250,000,000
Taxes	$126,000,000	$126,000,000
Net profit	$224,000,000	$224,000,000

Calculate the times interest earned ratios for 2015 and 2016. Is the company more or less able to meet its interest payments in 2016 when measured this way?

LG5 **LG6** **P7.9** Financial Learning Systems has 2.5 million shares of common stock outstanding and 100,000 shares of preferred stock. (The preferred pays annual cash dividends of $5 a share, and the common pays annual cash dividends of 25 cents a share.) Last year, the company generated net profits (after taxes) of $6,850,000. The company's balance sheet shows total assets of $78 million, total liabilities of $32 million, and $5 million in preferred stock. The firm's common stock is currently trading in the market at $45 a share.

a. Given the preceding information, find the EPS, P/E ratio, and book value per share.
b. What will happen to the price of the stock if EPS rises to $3.75 and the P/E ratio stays where it is? What will happen if EPS drops to $1.50 and the P/E doesn't change?
c. What will happen to the price of the stock if EPS rises to $3.75 and the P/E jumps to 25 times earnings?
d. What will happen if both EPS and the P/E ratio drop—to $1.50 and 10 times earnings, respectively?
e. Comment on the effect that EPS and the P/E ratio have on the market price of the stock.

LG5 **P7.10** The Buffalo Manufacturing Company has total assets of $12 million, an asset turnover of 2.2 times, and a net profit margin of 14%.
a. What is Buffalo's return on assets?
b. Find Buffalo's ROE, given that 40% of the assets are financed with stockholders' equity.

LG5 **P7.11** Find the EPS, P/E ratio, and dividend yield of a company that has five million shares of common stock outstanding (the shares trade in the market at $25), earns 10% after taxes on annual sales of $150 million, and has a dividend payout ratio of 35%. At what rate would the company's net earnings be growing if the stock had a PEG ratio of 2.0?

LG5 **P7.12** P. Deen Enterprises Inc. has a total asset turnover ratio of 3.0 and a net profit margin of 9%. What is the company's return on assets?

LG5 **P7.13** Stroud Sporting Gear Inc. has a net profit margin of 9%, a total asset turnover of 2.4, total assets of $225 million, and total equity of $120 million. What is the company's return on equity?

LG5 **P7.14** Snapgram Corporation has a net profit margin of 8%, a total asset turnover of 2.0 times, total assets of $1 billion, and total equity of $500 million. What were the company's sales and net profit?

LG5 **P7.15** Using the resources available at your campus or public library (or on the Internet), select any common stock you like and determine as many of the profitability, activity, liquidity, leverage, and market ratios covered in this and the preceding chapter as you can. Compute the ratios for the latest available fiscal year. (*Note:* Show your work for all calculations.)

LG2 **LG5** **LG5** **P7.16** Listed below are six pairs of stocks. Pick one of these pairs and then, using the resources available at your campus or public library (or on the Internet), comparatively analyze the two stocks. Which is fundamentally stronger and holds more promise for the future? Compute (or obtain) as many ratios as you see fit. As part of your analysis, obtain the latest S&P and/or Value Line reports on both stocks, and use them for added insights about the firms and their stocks.
a. Walmart versus Target
b. General Mills versus Campbell Soup
c. Texas Instruments versus Intel
d. Marriott International versus Intercontinental Hotels Group
e. Columbia Sportswear versus Under Armour
f. General Dynamics versus Boeing

LG2 **LG5** **LG5** **P7.17** The following table lists the 2015 and 2016 financial statements for Otago Bay Marine Motors, a major manufacturer of top-of-the-line outboard motors.

Otago Bay Marine Motors Balance Sheets ($ in thousands)

	As of December 31	
	2016	2015
Assets		
Current assets		
Cash and cash equivalents	$ 56,203	$ 88,942
Accounts receivable, net of allowances	$ 20,656	$ 12,889
Inventories	$ 29,294	$ 24,845
Prepaid expenses	$ 5,761	$ 6,536
Total current assets	$ 111,914	$ 133,212
Property, plant, and equipment, at cost	$ 137,273	$ 85,024
Less: Accumulated depreciation and amortization	($ 50,574)	($ 44,767)
Net fixed assets	$ 86,699	$ 40,257
Other assets	$ 105,327	$ 51,001
Total assets	$ 303,940	$ 224,470
Liabilities and shareholders' equity		
Current liabilities		
Notes and accounts payable	$ 28,860	$ 4,927
Dividends payable	$ 1,026	$ 791
Accrued liabilities	$ 20,976	$ 16,780
Total current liabilities	$ 50,862	$ 22,498
Noncurrent liabilities		
Long-term debt	$ 40,735	$ 20,268
Shareholders' equity		
Common stock	$ 7,315	$ 7,103
Capital in excess of par value	$ 111,108	$ 86,162
Retained earnings	$ 93,920	$ 88,439
Total shareholders' equity	$ 212,343	$ 181,704
Total liabilities and equity	$ 303,940	$ 224,470
Average number of common shares outstanding	10,848,000	10,848,000

Otago Bay Marine Motors income statements ($ in thousands)

	For the Year Ended December 31	
	2016	2015
Sales revenue	$ 259,593	$245,424
Cost of goods sold	$ 133,978	$ 127,123
Gross profit margin	$ 125,615	$ 118,301
Operating expenses	$ 72,098	$ 70,368
Earnings from operations	$ 53,517	$ 47,933
Other income (expense), net	$ 4,193	$ 3,989
Earnings before income taxes	$ 57,710	$ 51,922
Provision for income taxes	$ 22,268	$ 19,890
Net earnings	$ 35,442	$ 32,032
Cash dividends ($0.35 and $0.27 per share)	$ 3,769	$ 2,947
Average price per share of common stock (in the fourth quarter of the year)	$ 74.25	$ 80.75

a. On the basis of the information provided, calculate the following financial ratios for 2015 and 2016.

	Otago Bay Marine Motors		Industry Average (for 2016)
	2016	2015	
Current ratio			2.36
Total asset turnover			1.27
Debt-equity ratio			10.00
Net profit margin			9.30
ROA			15.87
ROE			19.21
EPS			1.59
P/E ratio			19.87
Dividend yield			.44
Payout ratio			.26
Price-to-book-value ratio			6.65

b. Considering the financial ratios you computed, along with the industry averages, how would you characterize the financial condition of Otago Bay Marine Motors? Explain.

LG5 LG6 **P7.18** The following summary financial statistics were obtained from the 2015 Otago Bay Marine Motors (OBMM) annual report.

	2015 ($ in millions)
Sales revenue	$179.3
Total assets	$136.3
Net earnings	$ 20.2
Shareholders' equity	$109.6

a. Use the profit margin and asset turnover to compute the 2015 ROA for OBMM. Now introduce the equity multiplier to find ROE.
b. Use the summary financial information from the 2016 OBMM financial statements (see Problem 7.17) to compute the 2016 ROA and ROE. Use the same procedures to calculate these measures as you did in part a.
c. On the basis of your calculations, describe how each of the three components (profit margin, asset turnover, and leverage) contributed to the change in OBMM's ROA and ROE between 2015 and 2016. Which component(s) contributed the most to the change in ROA? Which contributed the most to the change in ROE?
d. Generally speaking, do you think that these changes are fundamentally healthy for the company?

Visit **http://www.myfinancelab.com** for web exercises, spreadsheets, and other online resources.

Case Problem 7.1   Some Financial Ratios Are Real Eye-Openers

LG5 LG6 Jack Arnold is a resident of Lubbock, Texas, where he is a prosperous rancher and businessman. He has also built up a sizable portfolio of common stock, which, he believes, is due to the fact that he thoroughly evaluates each stock he invests in. As Jack says, "You can't be too careful about these things! Anytime I plan to invest in a stock, you can bet I'm going to learn as much as I can about the company." Jack prefers to compute his own ratios even though he could easily obtain analytical reports from his broker at no cost. (In fact, Bob Smith, his broker, has been volunteering such services for years.)

Recently Jack has been keeping an eye on a small chemical stock. The firm, South Plains Chemical Company, is big in the fertilizer business—which is something Jack knows a lot about. Not long ago, he received a copy of the firm's latest financial statements (summarized here) and decided to take a closer look at the company.

South Plains Chemical Company Balance Sheet ($ thousands)

Cash	$ 1,250		
Accounts receivable	$ 8,000	Current liabilities	$10,000
Inventory	$12,000	Long-term debt	$ 8,000
Current assets	$21,250	Stockholders' equity	$12,000
Fixed and other assets	$ 8,750	Total liabilities and	
Total assets	$30,000	stockholders' equity	$30,000

South Plains Chemical Company Income Statement ($ thousands)

Sales	$50,000
Cost of goods sold	$25,000
Operating expenses	$15,000
Operating profit	$10,000
Interest expense	$ 2,500
Taxes	$ 2,500
Net profit	$ 5,000
Dividends paid to common stockholders ($ in thousands)	$ 1,250
Number of common shares outstanding	5 million
Recent market price of the common stock	$ 25

Questions

a. Using the South Plains Chemical Company figures, compute the following ratios.

	Latest Industry Averages		Latest Industry Averages
Liquidity		*Profitability*	
a. Net working capital	N/A	h. Net profit margin	8.5%
b. Current ratio	1.95	i. Return on assets	22.5%
Activity		j. ROE	32.2%
c. Receivables turnover	5.95	*Common-Stock Ratios*	
d. Inventory turnover	4.50	k. Earnings per share	$2.00
e. Total asset turnover	2.65	l. Price-to-earnings ratio	20.0
Leverage		m. Dividends per share	$1.00
f. Debt-equity ratio	0.45	n. Dividend yield	2.5%
g. Times interest earned	6.75	o. Payout ratio	50.0%
		p. Book value per share	$6.25
		q. Price-to-book-value ratio	6.4

b. Compare the company ratios you prepared to the industry figures given in part **a**. What are the company's strengths? What are its weaknesses?

c. What is your overall assessment of South Plains Chemical? Do you think Jack should continue with his evaluation of the stock? Explain.

Case Problem 7.2   Doris Looks at an Auto Issue

LG2 LG3 LG5   Doris Wise is a young career woman. She lives in Phoenix, Arizona, where she owns and operates a highly successful modeling agency. Doris manages her modest but rapidly growing investment portfolio, made up mostly of high-grade common stocks. Because she's young and single and has no pressing family requirements, Doris has invested primarily in stocks that offer the potential for attractive capital gains. Her broker recently recommended an auto company stock and sent her some literature and analytical reports to study. One report, prepared by the brokerage house she deals with, provided an up-to-date look at the economy, an extensive study of the auto industry, and an equally extensive review of several auto companies (including the one her broker recommended). She feels strongly about the merits of security analysis and believes it is important to spend time studying a stock before making an investment decision.

Questions

a. Doris tries to stay informed about the economy on a regular basis. At the present time, most economists agree that the economy is getting stronger. What information about the economy do you think Doris would find helpful in evaluating an auto stock? Prepare a list—and be specific. Which three items of economic information (from your list) do you feel are most important? Explain.

b. In relation to a study of the auto industry, briefly note the importance of each of the following.
   1. Auto imports
   2. The United Auto Workers union
   3. Interest rates
   4. The price of a gallon of gas

c. A variety of financial ratios and measures are provided about one of the auto companies and its stock. These are incomplete, however, so some additional information will have to be computed. Specifically, we know the following:

Net profit margin	15%
Total assets	$25 billion
Earnings per share	$3.00
Total asset turnover	1.5
Net working capital	$3.4 billion
Payout ratio	40%
Current liabilities	$5 billion
Price-to-earnings ratio	12.5

Given this information, calculate the following:
   1. Sales
   2. Net profits after taxes
   3. Current ratio
   4. Market price of the stock
   5. Dividend yield

Excel@Investing

Excel@Investing

You have been asked to analyze the financial statements of the Dayton Corporation for the two years ending 2015 and 2016.

◇	A	B	C	D	E
1	Dayton Corporation				
2	Financial Data				
3		2015	2016		
4	Net sales	$47,715	$40,363		
5	Cost sales	$27,842	$21,485		
6	SG & A expenses	$ 8,090	$ 7,708		
7	Depreciation expense	$ 628	$ 555		
8	Interest expense	$ 754	$ 792		
9	Tax expense	$ 3,120	$ 3,002		
10	Cash & equivalents	$ 2,144	$ 2,536		
11	Receivables	$ 5,215	$ 5,017		
12	Inventory	$ 3,579	$ 3,021		
13	Other current assets	$ 2,022	$ 2,777		
14	Plant & equipment	$18,956	$16,707		
15	Accumulated depreciation	$ 5,853	$ 5,225		
16	Intangible assets	$ 7,746	$ 7,374		
17	Other non-current assets	$10,465	$ 7,700		
18	Payables	$ 5,108	$ 4,361		
19	Short-term notes payable	$ 4,066	$ 3,319		
20	Other current liabilities	$ 2,369	$ 2,029		
21	Long-term debt	$ 4,798	$ 3,600		
22	Other non-current liabilities	$ 4,837	$ 5,020		
23	Common stock	$ 6,776	$ 6,746		
24	Retained earnings	$16,050	$14,832		
25	Common shares outstanding	$ 2,300	$ 2,300		
26	Current market price of stock	$ 45	$ 45		

Questions

a. Create a comparative balance sheet for the years 2016 and 2015, similar to the spreadsheet for Table 7.3, which can be viewed at http://www.myfinancelab.com.

b. Create a comparative income statement for the years 2016 and 2015, similar to the spreadsheet for Table 7.4, which can be viewed at http://www.myfinancelab.com.

c. Create a spreadsheet to calculate the listed financial ratios for both 2016 and 2015, similar to the spreadsheet for Table 7.6, which can be viewed at http://www.myfinancelab.com.

Ratios	2015	2016
Current ratio		
Quick ratio		
Accounts receivable turnover		
Inventory turnover		
Total asset turnover		
Debt-equity		
Times interest earned		
Net profit margin		
Return on equity (ROE)		
Earnings per share		
Price-to-earnings		
Book value per share		
Price-to-book-value		

Chapter-Opening Problem

At the beginning of the chapter you read about an analyst's report on Advanced Micro Devices. Use an online source such as Yahoo! Finance or AMD's own website to look up the company's income statement for the fiscal year ending in early 2016. What was AMD's net profit margin in 2015 and 2016? Did the profit margin improve or deteriorate in the face of competition from Intel?

8

Stock Valuation

LEARNING GOALS

After studying this chapter, you should be able to:

LG1 Explain the role that a company's future plays in the stock valuation process.

LG2 Develop a forecast of a stock's expected cash flow, starting with corporate sales and earnings, and then moving to expected dividends and share price.

LG3 Discuss the concepts of intrinsic value and required rates of return, and note how they are used.

LG4 Determine the underlying value of a stock using the zero-growth, constant-growth, and variable-growth dividend valuation models.

LG5 Use other types of present value–based models to derive the value of a stock, as well as alternative price-relative procedures.

LG6 Understand the procedures used to value different types of stocks, from traditional dividend-paying shares to more growth-oriented stocks.

What drives a stock's value? Many factors come into play, including how much profit the company earns, how its new products fare in the marketplace, and the overall state of the economy. But what matters most is what investors believe about the company's future.

Nothing illustrates this principle better than the stock of the oil driller, Helmerich & Payne (ticker symbol HP). The company announced its financial results for the first quarter of its fiscal year on January 29, 2015, reporting earnings per share of $1.85 with total revenue of $1.06 billion. Wall Street stock analysts had been expecting the company to earn just $1.55 per share with $977 million in total revenue, so the company's performance was much better than expected. Even so, HP's stock price slid nearly 5% in response to the earnings news. Why would investors drive down the stock price of a company that was outperforming expectations? The answer had to do with the company's future rather than its past earnings. In its earnings report, HP warned investors that its earnings for the rest of 2015 would likely be hit by falling oil prices. Indeed, in early 2015 oil prices were lower than they had been in six years, and many analysts believed that the market had not yet hit bottom. Stock analysts who followed HP acknowledged that the company had experienced solid revenue growth and used a reasonable amount of debt. Nevertheless, these analysts advised investors who did not already own HP to stay away from the stock because of the company's poor return on equity and lackluster growth in earnings per share.

How do investors determine a stock's true value? This chapter explains how to determine a stock's intrinsic value by using dividends, free cash flow, price/earnings, and other valuation models.

(Source: Richard Saintvilus, "Helmerich & Payne Stock Falls on Outlook Despite Earnings Beat," http://www.thestreet.com/story/13027986/1/helmerich-payne-stock-falls-on-outlook-despite-earnings-beat.html, accessed on May 27, 2015.)

Valuation: Obtaining a Standard of Performance

LG1 **LG2** **LG3** Obtaining an estimate of a stock's intrinsic value that investors can use to judge the merits of a share of stock is the underlying purpose of **stock valuation**. Investors attempt to resolve the question of whether and to what extent a stock is under- or over-valued by comparing its current market price to its intrinsic value. At any given time, the price of a share of stock depends on investors' expectations about the future performance of the company. When the outlook for the company improves, its stock price will probably go up. If investors' expectations become less rosy, the price of the stock will probably go down.

Valuing a Company Based on Its Future Performance

Thus far we have examined several aspects of security analysis including macroeconomic factors, industry factors, and company-specific factors. But as we've said, for stock valuation the future matters more than the past. The primary reason for looking at past performance is to gain insight about the firm's future direction. Although past performance provides no guarantees about what the future holds, it can give us a good idea of a company's strengths and weaknesses. For example, history can tell us how well the company's products have done in the marketplace, how the company's fiscal health shapes up, and how management tends to respond to difficult situations. In short, the past can reveal how well the company is positioned to take advantage of the things that may occur in the future.

Because the value of a share of stock depends on the company's future performance, an investor's task is to use historical data to project key financial variables into the future. In this way, he or she can judge whether a stock's market price aligns well with the company's prospects.

AN ADVISOR'S PERSPECTIVE

Rod Holloway
Equity Portfolio Manager, CFCI

"The best way to analyze a stock is to determine what you expect its sales numbers to be."

MyFinanceLab

Forecasted Sales and Profits The key to the forecast is, of course, the company's future performance, and the most important aspects to consider in this regard are the outlook for sales and profits. One way to develop a sales forecast is to assume that the company will continue to perform as it has in the past and simply extend the historical trend. For example, if a firm's sales have been growing at a rate of 10% per year, then investors might assume sales will continue at that rate. Of course, if there is some evidence about the economy, industry, or company that hints at a faster or slower rate of growth, investors would want to adjust the forecast accordingly. Often, this "naive" approach will be about as effective as more complex techniques.

Once they have produced a sales forecast, investors shift their attention to the net profit margin. We want to know what profit the firm will earn on the sales that it achieves. One of the best ways of doing that is to use what is known as a **common-size income statement**. Basically, a common-size statement takes every entry found on an ordinary income statement or balance sheet and converts it to a percentage. To create a common-size income statement, divide every item on the statement by *sales*—which, in effect, is the common denominator. An example of this appears in Table 8.1, which shows the 2016 dollar-based and common-size income statements for Universal Office Furnishings. (This is the same income statement that we first saw in Table 7.4.)

Excel@Investing

**TABLE 8.1   COMPARATIVE DOLLAR-BASED AND COMMON-SIZE INCOME STATEMENT
UNIVERSAL OFFICE FURNISHINGS, INC. 2016 INCOME STATEMENT**

	($ millions)	(Common-Size)*
Net Sales	$1,938.0	100.0%
Cost of goods sold	$1,128.5	58.2%
Gross operating Profit	**$ 809.5**	**41.8%**
Selling, general, & administrative expenses	$ 496.7	25.6%
Depreciation & amortization	$ 77.1	4.0%
Other expenses	$ 0.5	0.0%
Total operating expenses	**$ 574.3**	**29.6%**
Earnings before interest & taxes (EBIT)	**$ 235.2**	**12.1%**
Interest Expense	$ 13.4	0.7%
Income taxes	$ 82.1	4.2%
Net profit after taxes	**$ 139.7**	**7.2%**

*Common-size figures are found by using 'Net Sales" as the common denominator, and then dividing all
entries by net sales. For example, cost of goods sold = $1,128.5 ÷ $1,938.0 = 58.2%; EBIT = $235.2 ÷
$1,938.0 = 12.1%.

Example

To understand how to construct these statements, let's use the gross profit
margin (41.8%) as an illustration. In this case, divide the gross operating profit
of $809.5 million by sales of $1,938.0 million:

$$\$809.5 \div \$1,938.0 = 0.4177 = 41.8\%$$

Use the same procedure for every other entry on the income statement. Note
that a common-size statement adds up, just like its dollar-based counterpart. For
example, sales of 100.0% minus costs of goods sold of 58.2% equals a gross
profit margin of 41.8%. (You can also work up common-size balance sheets,
using total assets as the common denominator.)

Securities analysts and investors use common-size income statements to compare
operating results from one year to the next. The common-size format helps investors
identify changes in profit margins and highlights possible causes of those changes. For
example, a common-size income statement can quickly reveal whether a decline in a
firm's net profit margin is caused by a reduction in the gross profit margin or a rise in
other expenses. That information also helps analysts make projections of future profits.
For example, analysts might use the most recent common-size statement (or perhaps an
average of the statements that have prevailed for the past few years) combined with a
sales forecast to create a forecasted income statement a year or two ahead. Analysts
can make adjustments to specific line items to sharpen their projections. For example,
if analysts know that a firm has accumulated an unusually large amount of inventory
this year, it is likely that the firm will cut prices next year to reduce its inventory holdings, and that will put downward pressure on profit margins. Adjustments like these
(hopefully) improve the accuracy of forecasts of profits.

Given a satisfactory sales forecast and estimate of the future net profit margin, we
can combine these two pieces of information to arrive at future earnings (i.e., profits).

Equation 8.1

$$\begin{array}{ccc} \text{Future after-tax} \\ \text{earnings in year } t \end{array} = \begin{array}{c} \text{Estimated sales} \\ \text{in year } t \end{array} \times \begin{array}{c} \text{Net profit margin} \\ \text{expected in year } t \end{array}$$

The *year t* notation in this equation simply denotes a future calendar or fiscal year. Suppose that in the year just completed, a company reported sales of $100 million. Based on the company's past growth rate and on industry trends, you estimate that revenues will grow at an 8% annual rate, and you think that the net profit margin will be about 6%. Thus, the forecast for next year's sales is $108 million (i.e., $100 million ×1.08), and next year's profits will be $6.5 million:

$$\text{Future after-tax earnings next year} = \$108 \text{ million} \times 0.06 = \underline{\underline{\$6.5 \text{ million}}}$$

Using this same process, investors could estimate sales and earnings for other years in the forecast period.

Forecasted Dividends and Prices At this point the forecast provides some insights into the company's future earnings. The next step is to evaluate how these results will influence the company's stock price. Given a corporate earnings forecast, investors need three additional pieces of information:

- An estimate of future dividend payout ratios
- The number of common shares that will be outstanding over the forecast period
- A future price-to-earnings (P/E) ratio

For the first two pieces of information, lacking evidence to the contrary, investors can simply project the firm's recent experience into the future. Except during economic downturns, payout ratios are usually fairly stable, so recent experience is a fairly good indicator of what the future will bring. Similarly, the number of shares outstanding does not usually change a great deal from one year to the next, so using the current number in a forecast will usually not lead to significant errors. Even when shares outstanding do change, companies usually announce their intentions to issue new shares or repurchase outstanding shares, so investors can incorporate this information into their forecasts.

Getting a Handle on the P/E Ratio The most difficult issue in this process is coming up with an estimate of the future P/E ratio—a figure that has considerable bearing on the stock's future price behavior. Generally speaking, the P/E ratio (also called the P/E multiple) is a function of several variables, including the following:

- The growth rate in earnings
- The general state of the market
- The amount of debt in a company's capital structure
- The current and projected rate of inflation
- The level of dividends

As a rule, higher P/E ratios are associated with higher rates of growth in earnings, an optimistic market outlook, and lower debt levels (less debt means less financial risk).

The link between the inflation rate and P/E multiples, however, is a bit more complex. Generally speaking, as inflation rates rise, so do the interest rates offered by bonds. As returns on bonds increase, investors demand higher returns on stocks because they are riskier than bonds. Future returns on stocks can increase if companies earn higher profits and pay higher dividends, but if earnings and profits remain fixed, investors will only earn higher future returns if stock prices are lower today. Thus, inflation often puts downward pressure on stock prices and P/E multiples. On the other hand, declining

What Is a P/E Ratio?

inflation (and interest) rates normally have a positive effect on the economy, and that translates into higher P/E ratios and stock prices. Holding all other factors constant, a higher dividend payout ratio leads to a higher P/E ratio. In practice, however, most companies with high P/E ratios have *low* dividend payouts because firms that have the opportunity to grow rapidly tend to reinvest most of their earnings. In that case, the prospect of earnings growth drives up the P/E, more than offsetting the low dividend payout ratio.

A Relative Price-to-Earnings Multiple A useful starting point for evaluating the P/E ratio is the *average market multiple*. This is simply the average P/E ratio of all the stocks in a given market index, like the S&P 500 or the DJIA. The average market multiple indicates the general state of the market. It gives us an idea of how aggressively the market, in general, is pricing stocks. Other things being equal, the higher the P/E ratio, the more optimistic the market, though there are exceptions to that general rule. Figure 8.1 plots the S&P 500 price-to-earnings multiple from 1901 to 2015. This figure calculates the market P/E ratio by dividing prices at the beginning of the year by earnings over the previous 12 months. The figure shows that market multiples move over a fairly wide range. For example, in 2009, the market P/E ratio was at an all-time high of more than 70, but just one year later the ratio had fallen to just under 21. It is worth noting that the extremely high P/E ratio in 2009 was not primarily the result of stock prices hitting all-time highs. Instead, the P/E ratio at the time was high because earnings over the preceding 12 months had been extraordinarily low due to a severe recession. This illustrates that you must be cautious when interpreting P/E ratios as a sign of the health of individual stocks or of the overall market.

FIGURE 8.1   Average P/E Ratio of S&P 500 Stocks

The average price-to-earnings ratio for stocks in the S&P 500 Index fluctuated around a mean of 13 from 1940 to 1990 before starting an upward climb. Increases in the P/E ratio do not necessarily indicate a bull market. The P/E ratio spiked in 2009 not because prices were high, but because earnings were very low due to the recession. (Source: **Data from http://www.multpl.com**.)

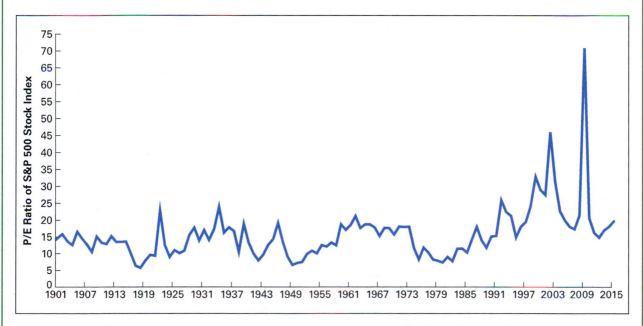

P/E Ratios Can Be Misleading

The most recent spike in the S&P 500 P/E ratio cannot be explained by a booming economy or a rising stock market. Recall that in 2008 stock prices fell dramatically, with the overall market declining by more than 30%. Yet, as 2009 began the average P/E ratio stood at an extraordinarily high level. The reason is that with the deep recession of 2008, corporate earnings declined even more sharply than stock prices did. So, in the market P/E ratio, the denominator (last year's earnings) declined more rapidly than the numerator (prices), and the overall P/E ratio jumped. In fact, in mid-2009 the average S&P 500 P/E ratio reached an all-time high of 144!

Looking at Figure 8.1, you can see that the market's P/E ratio has increased in recent years. From 1900 to 1990, the market P/E averaged about 13, but since then its average value has been above 24 (or more than 22 if you exclude the peak in 2009). At least during the 1990s, that upward trend could easily be explained by the very favorable state of the economy. Business was booming and new technologies were emerging at a rapid pace. There were no recessions from 1991 to 2000. If investors believed that the good times would continue indefinitely, then it's easy to understand why they might be willing to pay higher and higher P/E ratios over time.

With the market multiple as a benchmark, investors can evaluate a stock's P/E performance relative to the market. That is, investors can calculate a **relative P/E multiple** by dividing a stock's P/E by a market multiple. For example, if a stock currently has a P/E of 35 and the market multiple for the S&P 500 is, say, 25, the stock's relative P/E is $35 \div 25 = 1.4$. Looking at the relative P/E, investors can quickly get a feel for how aggressively the stock has been priced in the market and what kind of relative P/E is normal for the stock.

Other things being equal, a high relative P/E is desirable—up to a point, at least. For just as abnormally high P/Es can spell trouble (i.e., the stock may be overpriced and headed for a fall), so too can abnormally high relative P/Es. Given that caveat, it follows that the higher the relative P/E measure, the higher the stock will be priced in the market. But watch out for the downside: High relative P/E multiples can also mean lots of price volatility, which means that both large gains and large losses are possible. (Similarly, investors use average industry multiples to get a feel for the kind of P/E multiples that are standard for a given industry. They use that information, along with market multiples, to assess or project the P/E for a particular stock.)

The next step is to generate a forecast of the stock's future P/E over the anticipated *investment horizon* (the period of time over which an investor expects to hold the stock). For example, with the existing P/E multiple as a base, an increase might be justified if investors believe the market multiple will increase (as the market becomes more bullish) even if they do not expect the relative P/E to change. Of course, if investors believe the stock's relative P/E will increase as well, that would result in an even more bullish forecast.

Estimating Earnings per Share So far we've been able to come up with an estimate for the dividend payout ratio, the number of shares outstanding, and the price-to-earnings multiple. Now we are ready to forecast the stock's future earnings per share (EPS) as follows:

Equation 8.2

$$\text{Estimated EPS in year } t = \frac{\text{Future after-tax earnings in year } t}{\text{Number of shares of common stock outstanding in year } t}$$

Earnings per share is a critical part of the valuation process. Investors can combine an EPS forecast with (1) the dividend payout ratio to obtain (future) dividends per share and (2) the price-to-earnings multiple to project the (future) price of the stock.

Equation 8.2 simply converts total corporate earnings to a per-share basis by dividing forecasted company profits by the expected number of shares outstanding. Although this approach works quite effectively, some investors may want to analyze earnings per share from a slightly different perspective. One way to do this begins by measuring a firm's ROE. For example, rather than using Equation 8.2 to calculate EPS, investors could use Equation 8.3 as follows:

Equation 8.3

$$\text{EPS} = \frac{\text{After-tax earnings}}{\text{Book value of equity}} \times \frac{\text{Book value of equity}}{\text{Shares outstanding}} = \text{ROE} \times \text{Book value per share}$$

This formula will produce the same results as Equation 8.2. The major advantage of this form of the equation is that it highlights how much a firm earns relative to the book value of its equity. As we've already seen, earnings divided by book equity is the firm's ROE. Return on equity is a key financial measure because it captures the amount of success the firm is having in managing its assets, operations, and capital structure. And as we see here, ROE is not only important in defining overall corporate profitability, but it also plays a crucial role in defining a stock's EPS.

To produce an estimated EPS using Equation 8.3, investors would go directly to the two basic components of the formula and try to estimate how those components might change in the future. In particular, what kind of growth in the firm's book value per share is reasonable to expect, and what's likely to happen to the company's ROE? In the vast majority of cases, ROE is really the driving force, so it's important to produce a good estimate of that variable. Investors often do that by breaking ROE into its component parts— net profit margin, total asset turnover, and the equity multiplier (see Equation 7.15).

With a forecast of ROE and book value per share in place, investors can plug these figures into Equation 8.3 to produce estimated EPS. The bottom line is that, one way or another (using the approach reflected in Equation 8.2 or that in Equation 8.3), investors have to arrive at a forecasted EPS number that they are comfortable with. After that, it's a simple matter to use the forecasted payout ratio to estimate dividends per share:

Equation 8.4

$$\frac{\text{Estimated dividends}}{\text{per share in year } t} = \frac{\text{Estimated EPS}}{\text{for year } t} \times \frac{\text{Estimated}}{\text{payout ratio}}$$

Finally, estimate the future value of the stock by multiplying expected earnings times the expected P/E ratio:

Equation 8.5

$$\frac{\text{Estimated share price}}{\text{at end of year } t} = \frac{\text{Estimated EPS}}{\text{in year } t} \times \frac{\text{Estimated P/E}}{\text{ratio}}$$

Pulling It All Together Now, to see how all of these components fit together, let's continue with the example we started above. Using the aggregate sales and earnings approach, if the company had two million shares of common stock outstanding and investors expected that to remain constant, then given the estimated earnings of $6.5 million obtained from Equation 8.1, the firm should generate earnings per share next year of

$$\frac{\text{Estimated EPS}}{\text{next year}} = \frac{\$6.5 \text{ million}}{2 \text{ million}} = \underline{\$3.25}$$

An investor could obtain the same figure using forecasts of the firm's ROE and its book value per share. For instance, suppose we estimate that the firm will have an ROE of 15% and a book value per share of $21.67. According to Equation 8.3, those conditions would also produce an estimated EPS of $3.25 (i.e., $0.15 \times \$21.67$). Using this EPS figure, along with an estimated payout ratio of 40%, dividends per share next year should equal

$$\frac{\text{Estimated dividends}}{\text{per share next year}} = \$3.25 \times .40 = \underline{\$1.30}$$

Keep in mind that firms don't always adjust dividends in lockstep with earnings. A firm might pay the same dividend for many years if managers are not confident that an increase in earnings can be sustained over time. In a case like this, when a firm has a history of adjusting dividends slowly if at all, it may be that past dividends are a better guide to future dividends than projected earnings are. Finally, if it has been estimated that the stock should sell at 17.5 times earnings, then a share of stock in this company should be trading at $56.88 by the end of next year.

$$\frac{\text{Estimated share price}}{\text{at the end of next year}} = \$3.25 \times 17.5 = \underline{\$56.88}$$

Actually, an investor would be most interested in the price of the stock at the end of the anticipated investment horizon. Thus, the $56.88 figure would be appropriate for an investor who had a one-year horizon. However, for an investor with a three-year holding period, extending the EPS figure for two more years and repeating these calculations with the new data would be a better approach. The bottom line is that the estimated share price is important because it has embedded in it the capital gains portion of the stock's total return.

Developing a Forecast of Universal's Financial Performance

Using information obtained from Universal Office Furnishings (UVRS), we can illustrate the forecasting procedures we discussed above. Recall that our earlier assessment of the economy and the office equipment industry was positive and that the company's operating results and financial condition looked strong, both historically and relative to industry standards. Because everything looks favorable for Universal, we decide to take a look at the future prospects of the company and its stock.

Let's assume that an investor considering Universal common stock has a three-year investment horizon. Perhaps the investor believes (based on earlier studies of economic and industry factors) that the economy and the market for office equipment stocks will start running out of steam near the end of 2019 or early 2020. Or perhaps the investor plans to sell any Universal common stock purchased today to finance a major expenditure in three years. Regardless of the reason behind the investor's three-year horizon, we will focus on estimating Universal's performance for 2017, 2018, and 2019.

TABLE 8.2   SELECTED HISTORICAL FINANCIAL DATA, UNIVERSAL OFFICE FURNISHINGS

	2012	2013	2014	2015	2016
Total assets (millions)	$554.20	$ 694.90	$ 755.60	$ 761.50	$ 941.20
Total asset turnover	1.72	1.85	1.98	2.32	2.06
Sales revenue (millions)	$953.20	$1,283.90	$1,495.90	$1,766.20	$1,938.00
Annual rate of growth in sales*	−1.07%	34.69%	16.51%	18.07%	9.73%
Net profit margin	4.20%	6.60%	7.50%	8.00%	7.20%
Payout ratio	6.80%	5.20%	5.50%	6.00%	6.60%
Price/earnings ratio	13.5	16.2	13.9	15.8	18.4
Number of common shares outstanding (millions)	77.7	78.0	72.8	65.3	61.8

*To find the annual rate of growth in sales divide sales in one year by sales in the previous year and then subtract one. For example, the annual rate of growth in sales for 2016 = ($1,938.00 − $1,766.20) ÷ $1,766.20 − 1 = 9.73%.

Table 8.2 provides selected historical financial data for the company, covering a five-year period (ending with the latest fiscal year) and provides the basis for much of our forecast. The data reveal that, with one or two exceptions, the company has performed at a fairly steady pace and has been able to maintain a very attractive rate of growth. Our previous economic analysis suggested that the economy is about to pick up, and our research indicated that the industry and company are well situated to take advantage of the upswing. Therefore, we conclude that the rate of growth in sales should pick up from the 9.7% rate in 2016, attaining a growth rate of over 20% in 2017—a little higher than the firm's five-year average. After a modest amount of pent-up demand is worked off, the rate of growth in sales should drop to about 19% in 2018 and to 15% in 2019.

The essential elements of the financial forecast for 2017 through 2019 appear in Table 8.3. Highlights of the key assumptions and the reasoning behind them are as follows:

- *Net profit margin.* Various published industry and company reports suggest a comfortable improvement in earnings, so we decide to use a profit margin of 8.0% in 2017 (up a bit from the latest margin of 7.2% recorded in 2016). We're projecting even better profit margins (8.5%) in 2018 and 2019, as Universal implements some cost improvements.

- *Common shares outstanding.* We believe the company will continue to pursue its share buyback program, but at a substantially slower pace than in the 2013–2016 period. From a current level of 61.8 million shares, we project that the number of shares outstanding will drop to 61.5 million in 2017, to 60.5 million in 2018, and to 59.0 million in 2019.

- *Payout ratio.* We assume that the dividend payout ratio will hold at a steady 6% of earnings.

- *P/E ratio.* Primarily on the basis of expectations for improved growth in revenues and earnings, we are projecting a P/E multiple that will rise from its present level of 18.4 times earnings to roughly 20 times earnings in 2017. Although this is a fairly conservative increase in the P/E, when it is coupled with the hefty growth in EPS, the net effect will be a big jump in the projected price of Universal stock.

TABLE 8.3 SUMMARY FORECAST STATISTICS, UNIVERSAL OFFICE FURNISHINGS

	Latest Actual Figure (Fiscal 2016)	Weighted Average in Recent Years (2012–2016)	Forecasted Figures**		
			2017	2018	2019
Annual rate of growth in sales	9.7%	15.0%	22.0%	19.0%	15.0%
Net sales (millions)	$1,938.0	N/A*	$2,364.4	$2,813.6	$3,235.6
× Net profit margin	7.2%	5.6%	8.0%	8.5%	8.5%
= Net after-tax earnings (millions)	$ 139.7	N/A	$ 189.1	$ 239.2	$ 275.0
÷ Common shares outstanding (millions)	61.8	71.1	61.5	60.5	59.0
= Earnings per share	$ 2.26	N/A	$ 3.08	$ 3.95	$ 4.66
× Payout ratio	6.6%	6.2%	6.0%	6.0%	6.0%
= Dividends per share	$ 0.15	$0.08	$ 0.18	$ 0.24	$ 0.28
Earnings per share	$ 2.26	N/A	$ 3.08	$ 3.95	$ 4.66
× P/E ratio	18.4	16.8	20.0	20.0	20.0
= Share price at year end	$ 41.58	N/A	$ 61.51	$ 79.06	$ 93.23

*N/A: Not applicable.

**Forecasted sales figures: Sales from preceding year × (1 + growth rate in sales) = forecasted sales.
For example, for 2017: $1,938.0 × (1 + 0.22) = $2,364.4.

Excel@Investing

Table 8.3 also shows the sequence involved in arriving at forecasted dividends and share price behavior; that is:

1. The company dimensions of the forecast are handled first. These include sales and revenue estimates, net profit margins, net earnings, and the number of shares of common stock outstanding.

2. Next we estimate earnings per share by dividing expected earnings by shares outstanding.

3. The bottom line of the forecast is, of course, the returns in the form of dividends and capital gains expected from a share of Universal stock, given that the assumptions about sales, profit margins, earnings per share, and so forth hold up. We see in Table 8.3 that dividends should go up to 28 cents per share, which is a big jump from where they are now (15 cents per share). Even with a big dividend increase, it's clear that dividends still won't account for much of the stock's return. In fact, our projections indicate that the dividend yield in 2019 will fall to just 0.3% (divide the expected $0.28 dividend by the anticipated $93.23 price to get a yield of just 0.3%). Clearly, our forecast implies that the returns from this stock are going to come from capital gains, not dividends. That's obvious when we look at year-end share prices, which we expect to more than double over the next three years. That is, if our projections are valid, the price of a share of stock should rise from around $41.50 to more than $93.00 by year-end 2019.

We now have an idea of what the future cash flows of the investment are likely to be. We can now use that information to establish an intrinsic value for Universal Office Furnishings stock.

The Valuation Process

Valuation is a process by which an investor determines the worth of a security keeping in mind the tradeoff between risk and return. This process can be applied to any asset that produces a stream of cash—a share of stock, a bond, a piece of real estate, or an oil well. To establish the value of an asset, the investor must determine certain key inputs, including the amount of future cash flows, the timing of these cash flows, and the rate of return required on the investment.

In terms of common stock, the essence of valuation is to determine what the stock ought to be worth, given estimated cash flows to stockholders (future dividends and capital gains) and the amount of risk. Toward that end we employ various types of stock valuation models, the end product of which represents the elusive intrinsic value we have been seeking. That is, the stock valuation models determine either an expected rate of return or the intrinsic worth of a share of stock, which in effect represents the stock's "justified price." In this way, we obtain a standard of performance, based on forecasted stock behavior, which we can use to judge the investment merits of a particular security.

Either of two conditions would make us consider a stock a worthwhile investment candidate: (1) the expected rate of return equals or exceeds the return we feel is warranted given the stock's risk, or (2) the justified price (intrinsic worth) is equal to or greater than the current market price. In other words, a security is a good investment if its expected return is at least as high as the return that an investor demands based on the security's risk or if its intrinsic value equals or exceeds the current market price of the security. There is nothing irrational about purchasing a security in those circumstances. In either case, the security meets our minimum standards to the extent that it is giving investors the rate of return they wanted.

Remember this, however, about the valuation process: Even though valuation plays an important part in the investment process, there is absolutely no assurance that the actual outcome will be even remotely similar to the projections. The stock is still subject to economic, industry, company, and market risks, any one of which could negate *all* of the assumptions about the future. Security analysis and stock valuation models are used not to guarantee success but to help investors better understand the return and risk dimensions of a potential transaction.

Required Rate of Return   One of the key ingredients in the stock valuation process is the **required rate of return**. Generally speaking, the return that an investor requires should be related to the investment's risk. In essence, the required return establishes a level of compensation compatible with the amount of risk involved. Such a standard helps determine whether the expected return on a stock (or any other security) is satisfactory. Because investors don't know for sure what the cash flow of an investment will be, they should expect to earn a rate of return that reflects this uncertainty. Thus, the greater the perceived risk, the more investors should expect to earn. This is basically the notion behind the capital asset pricing model (CAPM).

Recall that using the CAPM, we can define a stock's required return as

Equation 8.6

$$\text{Required rate of return} = \text{Risk-free rate} + \left[\text{Stock's beta} \times \left(\text{Market return} - \text{Risk-free rate} \right) \right]$$

Two of the required inputs for this equation are readily available. You can obtain a stock's beta from many online sites or print sources. The risk-free rate is the current return provided by a risk-free investment such as a Treasury bill or a Treasury bond.

Estimating the expected return on the overall stock market is not as straightforward. A simple way to calculate the market's expected return is to use a long-run average return on the stock market. This average return may, of course, have to be adjusted up or down a bit based on what investors expect the market to do over the next year or so.

In the CAPM, the risk of a stock is captured by its beta. For that reason, the required return on a stock increases (or decreases) with increases (or decreases) in its beta. As an illustration of the CAPM at work, consider Universal's stock, which we'll assume has a beta of 1.30. If the risk-free rate is 3.5% and the expected market return is 10%, according to the CAPM model, this stock would have a required return of

$$\text{Required return} = 3.5\% + [1.30 \times (10.0\% - 3.5\%)] = \underline{11.95\%}$$

This return—let's round it to 12%—can now be used in a stock valuation model to assess the investment merits of a share of stock. To accept a lower return means you'll fail to be fully compensated for the risk you must assume.

8.1 What is the purpose of stock valuation? What role does intrinsic value play in the stock valuation process?

8.2 Are the expected future earnings of the firm important in determining a stock's investment suitability? Discuss how these and other future estimates fit into the stock valuation framework.

8.3 Can the growth prospects of a company affect its price-to-earnings multiple? Explain. How about the amount of debt a firm uses? Are there any other variables that affect the level of a firm's P/E ratio?

8.4 What is the market multiple and how can it help in evaluating a stock's P/E ratio? Is a stock's relative P/E the same thing as the market multiple? Explain.

8.5 In the stock valuation framework, how can you tell whether a particular security is a worthwhile investment candidate? What roles does the required rate of return play in this process? Would you invest in a stock if all you could earn was a rate of return that just equaled your required return? Explain.

Stock Valuation Models

LG4 LG5 LG6   Investors employ several stock valuation models. Although they are usually aimed at a security's future cash flows, their approaches to valuation are nonetheless considerably different. Some models, for example, focus heavily on the dividends that a stock will pay over time. Other models emphasize the cash flow that a firm generates, focusing less attention on whether the company pays that cash out as dividends, uses it to repurchase shares, or simply holds it in reserve.

There are still other stock valuation models in use—models that employ such variables as dividend yield, abnormally low P/E multiples, relative price performance over time, and even company size or market cap as key elements in the decision-making process. For purposes of our discussion, we'll focus on several stock valuation models that derive value from the fundamental performance of the company. We'll look first at stocks that pay dividends and at a procedure known as the dividend valuation model. From there, we'll look at several valuation procedures that can be used with companies that pay little or nothing in dividends. Finally, we'll move on to procedures that set the price of a stock based on how it behaves relative to earnings, cash flow, sales, or book value. The stock valuation procedures that we'll examine in this chapter are the same as those used by many professional security analysts and are, in fact, found throughout the "Equity Investments" portion of the CFA exam, especially at Level-I. And, of course, an understanding of these valuation models will enable you to better evaluate analysts' recommendations.

The Dividend Valuation Model

In the valuation process, the intrinsic value of any investment equals the present value of its expected cash benefits. For common stock, this amounts to the cash dividends received each year plus the future sale price of the stock. One way to view the cash flow benefits from common stock is to assume that the dividends will be received over an infinite time horizon—an assumption that is appropriate as long as the firm is considered a "going concern." Seen from this perspective, the value of a share of stock is equal to the present value of all the future dividends it is expected to provide over an infinite time horizon.

When an investor sells a stock, from a strictly theoretical point of view, what he or she is really selling is the right to all future dividends. Thus, just as the current value of a share of stock is a function of future dividends, the future price of the stock is also a function of future dividends. In this framework, the future price of the stock will rise or fall as the outlook for dividends (and the required rate of return) changes. This approach, which holds that the value of a share of stock is a function of its future dividends, is known as **dividend valuation model (DVM)**.

There are three versions of the dividend valuation model, each based on different assumptions about the future rate of growth in dividends:

1. *The zero-growth model* assumes that dividends will not grow over time.

2. *The constant-growth model* assumes that dividends will grow by a constant rate over time.

3. *The variable-growth model* assumes that the rate of growth in dividends will vary over time.

In one form or another, the DVM is widely used in practice to solve many kinds of valuation problems.

Zero Growth   The simplest way to picture the dividend valuation model is to assume the stock has a fixed stream of dividends. In other words, dividends stay the same year in and year out, and they're expected to do so in the future. Under such conditions, the value of a zero-growth stock is simply the present value of its annual dividends. To find the present value, just divide annual dividends by the required rate of return:

Equation 8.7

$$\text{Value of a share of stock} = \frac{\text{Annual dividends}}{\text{Required rate of return}}$$

FAMOUS FAILURES IN FINANCE

Ethical Conflicts Faced by Stock Analysts: Don't Always Believe the Hype

Buy, sell, or hold? Unfortunately, many investors have learned the hard way not to trust analysts' recommendations.

Consider the late 1990s stock market bubble. As the market began to fall in 2000, 95% of publicly traded stocks were free of sell recommendations, according to investment research firm Zacks, and 5% of stocks that did have a sell rating had exactly that: one sell rating from a single analyst. When the market began its climb back up, analysts missed the boat again. From 2000 to 2004, stocks that analysts told investors to sell rose 19% per annum on average, while their "buys" and "holds" rose just 7%.

Why were the all-star analysts wrong so often? Conflict of interest is one explanation. Analysts often work for investment banks who have business relationships with the companies that analysts follow. Analysts may feel pressure to make positive comments to please current or prospective investment banking clients. Also, analysts' buy recommendations may induce investors to trade, and those trades generate commissions for the analysts' employers.

Analyst hype is a real problem for both Wall Street and Main Street, and the securities industry has taken steps to correct it. The SEC's Regulation Fair Disclosure requires that all company information be released to the public rather than quietly disseminated to analysts. Some brokerages ban analysts from owning stocks they cover. In 2003 the SEC ruled that compensation for analyst research must be separated from investment banking fees, so that the analyst's job is to research stock rather than solicit clients.

Most important, investors must learn how to read between the lines of analysts' reports. In early 2014

there were nearly eight times as many "buy" recommendations for stocks in the S&P 500 as there were "sell" recommendations. If analysts were really unbiased, it seems very unlikely that their recommendations would be so heavily tilted toward the buy side. What should investors do? To start, they should probably lower analysts' ratings by one notch. A strong buy could be interpreted as a buy or a buy as a hold, and a hold or neutral as a sell. Also, investors should give more weight to negative ratings than to positive ones. A recent study found that sell recommendations were followed by an immediate drop of 3% in the price of downgraded stocks, whereas buy recommendations had either a more muted effect or no effect at all. Downgrades and those rare sell recommendations may signal future problems. Investors should also pay attention to forecasts in which a ratings change is accompanied by an earnings forecast revision in the same direction. That is, if an analyst moves a stock from sell to buy and simultaneously raises the earnings forecast for the stock, that is more credible than a report that simply changes the rating to "buy." Finally, when in doubt, investors should do their own homework, using the techniques taught in this text.

Critical Thinking Question Why do you think sell ratings tend to cause stock prices to fall, while buy ratings do not lead to stock price increases?

(Sources: Jack Hough, "How to Make Money off Analysts' Stock Recommendations," *Smart Money*, January 19, 2012, http://www.smartmoney.com/invest/stocks/how-to-make-money-off-analysts-stock-recommendations-1326759491635/; Rich Smith, "Analysts Running Scared," *The Motley Fool*, April 5, 2006, http://www.fool.com.)

Example

Suppose a stock pays a dividend of $3 per share each year, and you don't expect that dividend to change. If you want a 10% return on your investment, how much should you be willing to pay for the stock?

Value of stock = $3 ÷ 0.10 = $30

If you paid a higher price, you would earn a rate of return less than 10%, and likewise if you could acquire the stock for less, your rate of return would exceed 10%.

As you can see, the only cash flow variable that's used in this model is the fixed annual dividend. Given that the annual dividend on this stock never changes, does that mean the price of the stock never changes? Absolutely not! For as the required rate of return (capitalization rate) changes, so will the price of the stock. Thus, if the required rate of return goes up to 15%, the price of the stock will fall to $20 ($3 ÷ 0.15). Although this may be a very simplified view of the valuation model, it's actually not as far-fetched as it may appear, for this is basically the procedure used to price preferred stocks in the marketplace.

Constant Growth The zero-growth model is a good beginning, but it does not take into account a growing stream of dividends. The standard and more widely recognized version of the dividend valuation model assumes that dividends will grow over time at a specified rate. In this version, the value of a share of stock is still considered to be a function of its future dividends, but such dividends are expected to grow forever at a constant rate of growth, g. Accordingly, we can find the value of a share of stock as follows:

Equation 8.8

$$\text{Value of a share of stock} = \frac{\text{Next year's dividends}}{\text{Required rate of return} - \text{Dividend growth rate}}$$

Equation 8.8a

$$V = \frac{D_1}{r - g}$$

where

D_1 = annual dividend expected next year (the first year in the forecast period)
r = the required rate of return on the stock
g = the annual rate of growth in dividends, which must be less than r

Even though this version of the model assumes that dividends will grow at a constant rate forever, it is important to understand that doesn't mean we assume the investor will hold the stock forever. Indeed, the dividend valuation model makes no assumptions about how long the investor will hold the stock, for the simple reason that the investment horizon has no bearing on the computed value of a stock. Thus, with the constant-growth DVM, it is irrelevant whether the investor has a one-year, five-year, or ten-year expected holding period. The computed value of the stock will be the same under all circumstances. So long as the input assumptions (r, g, and D_1) are the same, the value of the stock will be the same regardless of the intended holding period.

Note that this model succinctly captures the essence of stock valuation. Increase the cash flow (through D or g) or decrease the required rate of return (r), and the stock value will increase. We know that, in practice, there are potentially two components that make up the total return to a stockholder: dividends and capital gains. This model captures both components. If you solve Equation 8.8a for r, you will find that $r = D_1/V + g$. The first term in this sum, D_1/V, represents the dividend expected next year relative to the stock's current price. In other words, D_1/V is the stock's expected dividend yield. The second term, g, is the expected dividend growth rate. But if dividends grow at rate g, the stock price will grow at that rate too, so g also represents the capital gain component of the stock's total return. Therefore, the stock's total return is the sum of its dividend yield and its capital gain.

The constant-growth model should not be used with just any stock. Rather, it is best suited to the valuation of mature, dividend-paying companies that have a long track record of increasing dividends. These are probably large-cap (or perhaps even some mature mid-cap) companies that have demonstrated an ability to generate steady—although perhaps not spectacular—rates of growth year in and year out. The growth rates may not be identical from year to year, but they tend to move within a relatively narrow range. These are companies that have established dividend policies and fairly predictable growth rates in earnings and dividends.

INVESTOR FACTS

Steady Stream of Dividends The Canadian company Power Financial Corp. paid a $0.35 dividend for 27 consecutive quarters from December 2008 to December 2014. After receiving the same dividend for so long, did investors value Power Financial based on the assumption that it would pay $1.40 per year ($0.35 per quarter 4 times per year) forever? If we assume that investors required an 8% return on the stock, then under the assumption of constant dividends, the stock would sell for $17.50 per share (i.e., 1.40 ÷ 0.08). In fact, the stock traded in the $30 range in December 2014. Therefore, we can surmise that investors either required a return that was lower than 8% or they expected dividends to rise. In fact, the company did announce a dividend increase a few months later in March 2015.

Example

In the 25 years between 1990 and 2015, the food company General Mills increased its dividend payments by about 7% per year. The food industry is not one where we would expect explosive growth. Food consumption is closely tied to population growth, so profits in this business should grow relatively slowly over time. In April 2015 General Mills was paying an annual dividend of $1.76 per share, so for 2016 investors were expecting a modest increase in General Mills dividends over the coming year to $1.88 per share (7% more than the 2015 dividend). If the required return on General Mills stock is 10%, then investors should have been willing to pay $62.67 for the stock ($1.88 ÷ (0.10 − 0.07)) in 2015. In fact, General Mills stock was trading in a range between $55 and $57 at the time, so our application of the constant growth model suggests that General Mills was slightly undervalued. That is, its intrinsic value ($62.67) was a little higher than the stock's market price. Of course, our estimate of intrinsic value might be too high if the required return on General Mills shares is higher than 10% or if the long-run growth rate in dividends in less than 7%. Indeed, one drawback to the constant growth model is that the estimate of value that it produces is very sensitive to the assumptions one makes about the required return and the dividend growth rate. For example, if we assumed that the required return on General Mills stock was 11% rather than 10%, our estimate of intrinsic value would fall from $62.67 to $47!

Analysts sometimes use the constant-growth DVM to estimate the required return on a stock based on the assumption that the stock's market price is equal to its intrinsic value. In other words, analysts plug the stock's market price and an estimate of the dividend growth rate into Equation 8.8a and solve for r rather than solving for V. For General Mills, if the stock's market price is $56, the next dividend is $1.88, and the dividend growth rate is 7%, we can estimate the required return on General Mills' stock as follows:

$$\$56 = \$1.88 \div (r - 0.07)$$

Solving this equation for r, we find that the required return on General Mills' stock is about 10.36%.

Estimating the Dividend Growth Rate Use of the constant-growth DVM requires some basic information about the stock's required rate of return, its current level of dividends, and the expected rate of growth in dividends. A fairly simple, albeit naïve, way to find the dividend growth rate, g, is to look at the historical behavior of dividends. If they are growing at a relatively constant rate, you can assume they will continue to grow at (or near) that average rate in the future. You can get historical dividend data in a company's annual report or from various online sources

With the help of a calculator or spreadsheet, we can use basic present value arithmetic to find the growth rate embedded in a stream of dividends. For example, compare the dividend that a company is paying today to the dividend it paid several years ago. If dividends have been growing steadily, dividends today will be higher than they were in the past. Next, use your calculator to find the discount rate that equates the present value of today's dividend to the dividend paid several years earlier. When you find that rate, you've found the dividend growth rate. In this case, the discount rate is the average rate of growth in dividends. (See Chapter 4 for a detailed discussion of how to calculate growth rates.)

Example

In 2015 General Mills paid an annual dividend of $1.76 per share. The company had been increasing dividends steadily since 1990, when the annual dividend was just $0.32 per share. The table below shows the present value of the 2015 dividend, discounted back 25 years at various interest rates. You can see that when the discount rate is 7%, the present value of the 2015 dividend is approximately equal to the dividend paid in 1990, so 7% is the growth rate in dividends from 1990 to 2015.

Discount rate	PV of 2015 dividend ($1.76)
5%	$0.52
6%	$0.41
7%	$0.32 (matches actual 1990 dividend)
8%	$0.26

Growth Rate Calculator

Once you've determined the dividend growth rate, you can find next year's dividend, D_1, as $D_0 \times (1 + g)$, where D_0 equals the current dividend. In 2015 General Mills was paying dividends at an annual rate of $1.76 per share. If you expect those dividends to grow at the rate of 7% a year, you can find the expected 2016 dividend as follows: $D_1 = D_0(1 + g) = \$1.76(1 + 0.07) = \$1.88$. The only other information you need is the required rate of return (capitalization rate), r. (Note that r must be greater than g for the constant-growth model to be mathematically operative.) As we have already seen, if we assume that the required return on General Mills stock is 10%, that assumption, combined with an expected dividend next year of $1.88 and a projected dividend growth rate of 7%, produces an estimate of General Mills' stock value of $62.67.

Stock-Price Behavior over Time The constant-growth model implies that a stock's price will grow over time at the same rate that dividends grow, g, and that the growth rate plus the dividend yield equals the required return. To see how this works, consider the following example.

Suppose that today's date is January 2, 2016, and a stock just paid (on January 1) its annual dividend of $2.00 per share. Suppose too that investors expect this dividend to grow at 5% per year, so they believe that next year's dividend (which will be paid on January 1, 2017) will be $2.10, which is 5% more than the previous year's dividend. Finally, assume that investors require a 9% return on the stock. Based on those assumptions, we can estimate the price of the stock on January 2, 2016, as follows:

$$\text{Price on January 2, 2016} = \text{Dividend on January 1, 2017} \div (r - g)$$
$$\text{Price} = \$2.10 \div (0.09 - 0.05) = \$52.50.$$

Imagine that an investor purchases this stock for $52.50 on January 2 and holds it for one year. The investor receives the next dividend on January 1, 2017, and then sells the stock a day later on January 2, 2017. To estimate the expected return on this purchase, we must calculate the expected stock price that the investor will receive when she sells the stock on January 2, 2017.

$$\text{Price on January 2, 2017} = \text{Dividend on January 1, 2018} \div (r - g)$$
$$\text{Price} = \$2.10(1 + 0.05) \div (0.09 - 0.05)$$
$$\text{Price} = \$2.205 \div (0.09 - 0.05) = \$55.125$$

Now let's look at the investor's expected return during the calendar year 2016. She purchases the stock for $52.50 at the beginning of the year. One year later on January 1, 2017, she receives a dividend of $2.10 per share, and then she sells the stock for $55.125. Her total return equals the dividend plus the capital gain, divided by the original purchase price.

$$\text{Total return} = (\text{dividend} + \text{capital gain}) \div \text{purchase price}$$
$$\text{Total return} = (\$2.10 + \$55.125 - \$52.50) \div \$52.50 = 0.09 = 9.0\%$$

The investor expects to earn 9% over the year, which is exactly the required return on the stock. Notice that during the year the stock price increased by 5% from $52.50 to $55.125. So the stock price increased at the same rate that the dividend payment did. Furthermore, the dividend yield that the investor earned was 4% ($2.10 /$52.50). Therefore the 9% total return consists of a 5% capital gain and a 4% dividend yield.

Repeating this process allows you to estimate the stock price on January 2 of any succeeding year. As the table below shows, each and every year the stock price increases by 5%, and the stock's dividend yield is 4%. Therefore, an investor in this stock earns exactly the 9% required return year after year.

Year	Dividend paid on January 1	Stock price on January 2*
2016	$2.000	$52.50
2017	$2.100	$55.125
2018	$2.205	$57.881
2019	$2.315	$60.775

*As determined by the dividend valuation mode, given $g = 0.05$ and $r = 0.09$.

Variable Growth Although the constant-growth dividend valuation model is an improvement over the zero-growth model, it still has some shortcomings. The most obvious deficiency is that the model does not allow for changes in expected growth rates. To overcome this problem, we can use a form of the DVM that allows for variable rates of growth over time. Essentially, the variable-growth dividend valuation model calculates a stock price in two stages. In the first stage, dividends grow rapidly but not necessarily at a single rate. The dividend growth rate can rise or fall during this initial stage. In the second stage, the company matures and dividend growth settles down to some long-run, sustainable rate. At that point, it is possible to value the stock using the constant-growth version of the DVM. The variable-growth version of the model finds the value of a share of stock as follows:

Equation 8.9

$$\begin{array}{c}\text{Value of a share} \\ \text{of stock}\end{array} = \begin{array}{c}\text{Present value of} \\ \text{future dividends} \\ \text{during the initial} \\ \text{variable-growth period}\end{array} + \begin{array}{c}\text{Present value of the price} \\ \text{of the stock at the end of} \\ \text{the variable-growth period}\end{array}$$

Equation 8.9a

$$V = \frac{D_1}{(1 + r)^1} + \frac{D_2}{(1 + r)^2} + \cdots + \frac{D_v}{(1 + r)^v} + \frac{\dfrac{D_v(1 + g)}{(r - g)}}{(1 + r)^v}$$

where

D_1, D_2, etc. = future annual dividends

v = number of years in the initial variable-growth period

Note that the last element in this equation is the standard constant-growth dividend valuation model, which is used to find the price of the stock at the end of the initial variable-growth period, discounted back v periods.

This form of the DVM is appropriate for companies that are expected to experience rapid or variable rates of growth for a period of time—perhaps for the first three to five years—and then settle down to a more stable growth rate thereafter. This, in fact, is the growth pattern of many companies, so the model has considerable application in practice. It also overcomes one of the operational shortcomings of the constant-growth DVM in that r does not have to be greater than g during the initial stage. That is, during the variable-growth period, the rate of growth, g, can be greater than the required rate of return, r, and the model will still be fully operational.

Finding the value of a stock using Equation 8.9 is actually a lot easier than it looks. To do so, follow these steps:

1. Estimate annual dividends during the initial variable-growth period and then specify the constant rate, g, at which dividends will grow after the initial period.

2. Find the present value of the dividends expected during the initial variable-growth period.

3. Using the constant-growth DVM, find the price of the stock at the end of the initial growth period.

4. Find the present value of the price of the stock (as determined in step 3). Note that the price of the stock is discounted for the same length of time as the last dividend payment in the initial growth period because the stock is being priced (per step 3) at the end of this initial period.

5. Add the two present value components (from steps 2 and 4) to find the value of a stock.

Applying the Variable-Growth DVM To see how this works, let's apply the variable-growth model to Sweatmore Industries (SI). Let's assume that dividends will grow at a variable rate for the first three years (2016, 2017, and 2018). After that, the annual dividend growth rate will settle down to 3% and stay there indefinitely. Starting with the latest (2015) annual dividend of $2.21 a share, we estimate that Sweatmore's dividends should grow by 20% next year (in 2016), by 16% in 2017, and then by 13% in 2018 before dropping to a 3% rate. Finally, suppose that SI's investors require an 11% rate of return.

Using these growth rates, we project that dividends in 2016 will be $2.65 a share ($2.21 × 1.20) and will rise to $3.08 ($2.65 × 1.16) in 2017 and to $3.48 ($3.08 × 1.13) in 2018. Dividing 2019's $3.58 dividend by 8% ($r - g$) gives us the present value in 2018 of all dividends paid in 2019 and beyond. We now have all the inputs we need to put a value on Sweatmore Industries. Table 8.4 shows the variable-growth DVM in action. The value of Sweatmore stock, according to the variable-growth DVM, is $40.19 a share. In essence, that's the maximum price an investor should be willing to pay for the stock to earn an 11% rate of return.

Defining the Expected Growth Rate Mechanically, application of the DVM is really quite simple. It relies on just three key pieces of information: future dividends, future

TABLE 8.4 USING THE VARIABLE-GROWTH DVM TO VALUE SWEATMORE STOCK

Step

1. Projected annual dividends:

Most recent dividend	2015	$2.21
Future dividends	2016	$2.65
	2017	$3.08
	2018	$3.48

Estimated annual rate of growth in dividends, g, for 2019 and beyond: 3%

2. Present value of dividends, using a required rate of return, r, of 11%, during the initial variable-growth period:

Year	Dividends	Present Value
2016	$2.65	$2.39
2017	$3.08	$2.50
2018	$3.48	$2.54
	Total	$7.43 (to step 5)

3. Price of the stock at the end of the initial growth period:

$$P_{2018} = \frac{D_{2019}}{r-g} = \frac{D_{2018} \times (1-g)}{r-g} = \frac{\$3.48 \times (1.03)}{0.11 - 0.03} = \frac{\$3.58}{0.08} = \$44.81$$

4. Discount the price of the stock (as computed above) back to its present value, at r, of 11%:

$$\$44.81 \div (1.11)^3 = \$32.76 \text{ (to step 5)}$$

5. Add the present value of the initial dividend stream (step 2) to the present value of the price of the stock at the end of the initial growth period (step 4):

Value of Sweatmore stock: 7.43 + $32.76 = $40.19

growth in dividends, and a required rate of return. But this model is not without its difficulties. One of the most difficult (and most important) aspects of the DVM is specifying the appropriate growth rate, g, over an extended period of time. Whether you are using the constant-growth or the variable-growth version of the dividend valuation model, the growth rate, g, has an enormous impact on the value derived from the model. As a result, in practice analysts spend a good deal of time trying to come up with a good way to estimate a company's dividend growth rate.

As we saw earlier, we can estimate the growth rate by looking at a company's historical dividend growth. While that approach might work in some cases, it does have some serious shortcomings. What's needed is a procedure that looks at the key forces that actually drive the growth rate. Fortunately, there is such an approach that is widely used in practice. This approach assumes that future dividend growth depends on the rate of return that a firm earns and the fraction of earnings that managers reinvest in the company. Equation 8.10 illustrates this idea:

Equation 8.10 $g = \text{ROE} \times \text{The firm's retention rate, } rr$

where

Equation 8.10a $rr = 1 - \text{Dividend payout ratio}$

Both variables in Equation 8.10 (ROE and *rr*) are directly related to the firm's future growth rate. The retention rate represents the percentage of its profits that the firm plows back into the company. Thus, if the firm pays out 35% of its earnings in dividends (i.e., it has a dividend payout ratio of 35%), then it has a retention rate of 65%: *rr* = 1 − 0.35 = 0.65. The retention rate indicates the amount of capital that is flowing back into the company to finance growth. Other things being equal, the more money managers reinvest in the company, the higher the growth rate.

The other component of Equation 8.10 is the familiar return on equity (ROE). Clearly, the more the company can earn on its retained capital, the higher the growth rate. Remember that ROE is the product of three things: the net profit margin, total asset turnover, and the equity multiplier (see Equation 7.13).

Example

> Consider a situation where a company retains, on average, about 80% of its earnings and generates an ROE of around 18%. (Driving the firm's ROE is a net profit margin of 7.5%, a total asset turnover of 1.20, and an equity multiplier of 2.0.) Under these circumstances, we would expect the firm to have a growth rate of 14.4%:
>
> $$g = \text{ROE} \times rr = 0.18 \times 0.80 = 14.4\%$$

This firm might even achieve faster growth if it raises more capital through a stock offering or borrows more money and thereby increases its equity multiplier. If the firm chooses not to do any of those things, Equation 8.10 gives you a good idea of what growth the company might be able to achieve. To further refine your estimate of a company's growth rate, consider the two key components of the formula (ROE and *rr*) to see whether they're likely to undergo major changes in the future. If so, then what impact is the change in ROE or *rr* likely to have on the growth rate? The idea is to take the time to study the forces (ROE and *rr*) that drive the growth rate because the DVM itself is so sensitive to the rate of growth being used. Employ a growth rate that's too high and you'll end up with an intrinsic value that's way too high also. The downside, of course, is that you may end up buying a stock that you really shouldn't.

Other Approaches to Stock Valuation

In addition to the DVM, the market has developed other ways of valuing stock. One motivation for using these approaches is to find techniques that allow investors to estimate the values of non-dividend-paying stocks. In addition, for a variety of reasons, some investors prefer to use procedures that don't rely on corporate earnings as the basis of valuation. For these investors, it's not earnings that matter, but instead things like cash flow, sales, or book value.

One approach that many investors use is the *free cash flow to equity method* (or simply *the flow to equity method*), which estimates the cash flow that a firm generates for common stockholders, whether it pays those out as dividends or not. Another is the *P/E approach*, which builds the stock valuation process around the stock's price-to-earnings ratio. One of the major advantages of these procedures is that they don't rely on dividends as the primary input. Accordingly, investors can use these methods to value stocks that are more growth-oriented and that pay little or nothing in dividends. Let's take a closer look at both of these approaches, as well as a technique that arrives at the expected return on the stock (in percentage terms) rather than a (dollar-based) "justified price."

Free Cash Flow to Equity As we saw earlier, the value of a share of stock is a function of the amount and timing of future cash flows that stockholders receive and the risk associated with those cash flows. The **free cash flow to equity method** estimates the cash flow that a company generates over time for its shareholders and discounts that to the present to determine the company's total equity value. The model does not consider whether a firm distributes free cash flow by paying dividends or repurchasing shares or whether it merely retains free cash flow. Instead, the model simply accounts for the cash that "flows to equity," meaning that it is the residual cash flow produced by the firm that is not needed to pay bills or fund new investments. The model begins by estimating the free cash flow that a company is expected to generate over time.

Free cash flow to equity is the cash flow that remains after a firm pays all of its expenses and makes necessary investments in working capital and fixed assets. It includes a company's after-tax earnings, plus any noncash expenses like depreciation, minus new investments in working capital and fixed assets. Using the flow-to-equity method requires forecasts of the cash flow going to equity far out into the future, just as the dividend valuation model requires long-term dividend forecasts. With cash flow forecasts in hand, analysts calculate the stock's intrinsic value by taking the present value of free cash flow going to equity and dividing by the number of shares outstanding. We can summarize the flow-to-equity model with the following equations:

Equation 8.11

$$\text{Value of a share of stock} = \frac{\text{present value of future free cash flows going to equity}}{\text{shares outstanding}}$$

$$\text{Free cash flow} = \text{after-tax earnings} + \text{depreciation}$$
$$- \text{ investments in working capital} - \text{investments in fixed assets}$$

Equation 8.11a

$$V = \frac{\dfrac{FCF_1}{(1 + r)^1} + \dfrac{FCF_2}{(1 + r)^2} + \cdots}{N}$$

where

$FCF_t = $ free cash flow in year t
$N = $ number of common shares outstanding

Note that there are similarities here to the dividend-growth model. Equation 8.11a is a present-value calculation, except that we are discounting future free cash flows rather than future dividends. As in the dividend-growth model, we may assume that free cash flows remain constant over time, grow at a constant rate, or grow at a rate that varies over time.

Zero Growth in Free Cash Flow Victor's Secret Sauce is a specialty retail company that sells a variety of bottled sauces for home cooks. Last year (2015) the company generated $2.2 million in after-tax earnings. Victor's took depreciation charges against its fixed assets equal to $250,000, and it invested $50,000 in new working capital and $40,000 in new fixed assets. Thus, the company's free cash flow last year was:

Victor's Secret Sauce free cash flow (2015) = $2,200,000 + $250,000 −
$50,000 − $40,000 = $2,360,000

Victor's had four million common shares outstanding, and the firm's shareholders expected a 9% rate of return on their investment. Suppose you believe that Victor's would continue to generate $2.36 million in free cash flow indefinitely, without additional growth. In other words, you would treat Victor's free cash flow like a perpetuity, so the present value of all of the company's future cash flows would equal:

$$\text{PV of future cash flows} = \$2,360,000 \div 0.09 = \$26,222,222$$

Given that the company has four million outstanding shares, the intrinsic value of the company's stock would be:

$$\text{Value of Victor's common shares} = \$26,222,222 \div 4,000,000 \text{ shares} = \$6.56 \text{ per share}$$

Our calculation here is analogous to the approach we took in dividend valuation model when dividends were not expected to grow. In this case, however, we are discounting free cash flow rather than dividends, and we take no stand on whether the firm will actually pay this cash out as a dividend in the current year or not.

Constant Growth in Free Cash Flow Now suppose that you expect Victor's free cash flow to grow over time at a constant rate of 2%. This implies that the company will generate cash flow next year (in 2016) that is 2% higher than last year's cash flow. Clearly, with a growing cash flow, Victor's shares should be more valuable than in the no-growth case, and indeed, that is what we find.

$$\text{PV (in 2015) of future cash flows} = \text{Cash flow (in 2016)} \div (r - g)$$
$$\text{PV of future cash flows} = \$2,360,000\,(1 + 0.02) \div (0.09 - 0.02)$$
$$= \$34,388,571$$
$$\text{Value of common shares} = \$34,388,571 \div 4,000,000 = \$8.60 \text{ per share}$$

Notice that we obtained the present value of Victor's future cash flows in the same way that we did in the constant-growth version of the dividend valuation model. We divided the cash flow expected next year, which is 2% greater than the previous year's free cash flow, by the difference between the required return on the stock and the expected growth rate in cash flow.

Variable Growth in Free Cash Flow Finally, suppose that you expected Victor's Secret Sauce to experience rapid growth in free cash flow for the next couple of years. To be specific, suppose that Victor's cash flow grows 20% next year, 10% the year after that, and then 2% per year for all subsequent years. To value the company's stock, we follow the same method that we used when valuing a company whose dividends grew at a variable rate.

First, calculate the expected free cash flow for 2016 and 2017. If last year's cash flow was \$2.36 million, then next year's cash flow will be 20% higher, or \$2,832,000 (i.e., \$2,360,000 × 1.20). The year after, Victor's cash flow rises another 10% to \$3,115,200 (i.e., \$2,832,000 × 1.10). Using the required return of 9%, we can calculate the present value of the cash flow generated in the next two years.

Year	Cash Flow	Present Value
2016	\$2,832,000	\$2,832,000 ÷ 1.09 = \$2,598,165
2017	\$3,115,200	\$3,115,200 ÷ 1.09^2 = \$2,622,002

Next, calculate the present value as of 2017 of all the cash flows that Victor's will generate in years 2018 in beyond. In 2018, the company will generate 2% more in cash flow than it did the prior year, and from that point forward, cash flows grow at the constant 2% rate. We can calculate the present value (as of 2017) of all cash flows generated in years 2018 and beyond as follows:

$$PV_{2017} = FCF_{2018} \div (r - g) = FCF_{2017}(1 + g) \div (r - g)$$
$$PV_{2017} = \$3,115,200\,(1 + 0.02) \div (0.09 - 0.02) = \$45,392,914$$

As of 2017, the present value of all free cash flow that Victor's generates in 2018 and beyond is almost $45.4 million. As an additional step, we need to discount this figure two more years, so we have the present value as of 2015.

$$PV_{2015} = \$45,392,914 \div 1.09^2 = \$38,206,308$$

Now we are ready to calculate the present value of all future free cash flows generated by the company, including the cash flows produced during the rapid growth stage (2016 and 2017) and the cash flows earned during the constant-growth phase (2018 and beyond). Dividing that total by 4,000,000 shares outstanding gives us an estimate of Victor's intrinsic value.

PV of all future cash flows = $2,598,165 + $2,622,002 + $38,206,308

$$= \$43,426,474$$

Value of common shares = $43,426,474 ÷ 4,000,000 = $10.86 per share

To summarize, our estimate of the value of Victor's is $6.56 when we expect no growth in cash flow, $8.60 when we expect steady 2% growth, and $10.86 when we expect rapid growth for two years followed by constant 2% growth. Because the free cash flow to equity method does not focus on the timing and amount of dividends that a company pays, but instead emphasizes the cash flow that the firm generates for its stockholders, it is well suited for valuing younger companies that have not yet established a dividend-paying history.

Using IRR to Solve for the Expected Return Sometimes investors find it more convenient to think about what a stock's expected return will be, given its current market price, rather than try to estimate the stock's intrinsic value. This is no problem, nor is it necessary to sacrifice the present value dimension of the stock valuation model to achieve such an end. You can find the expected return by using a trial-and-error approach to find the discount rate that equates the present value of a company's future free cash flows going to equity (or its future dividends if the firm pays dividends) to the current market value of the firm's common stock. Having estimated the stock's expected return, an investor would then decide whether that return is sufficient to justify buying the stock given its risk.

To see how to estimate a stock's expected return, look once again at the variable growth scenario for Victor's Secret Sauce. Recall that as of the end of 2015, we had the following projections for Victor's free cash flow going to equity:

2016	$2,832,000
2017	$3,115,200

Remember that cash flow in 2018 is 2% higher than in 2017 and that cash flow will continue to grow at 2% indefinitely starting in 2018. This means that as of 2017, the present value of all cash flow that Victor's will generate for stockholders from 2018 and beyond can be calculated as:

$$PV_{2017} = \frac{3,115,200\,(1.02)}{(r - 0.02)} = \frac{3,177,504}{(r - 0.02)}$$

Therefore, if we wanted to calculate the present value in 2015 of Victor's cash flow going to equity, we could use this equation:

$$PV = \frac{2,832,000}{(1 + r)} + \frac{3,115,200}{(1 + r)^2} + \frac{3,177,504 \div (r - 0.02)}{(1 + r)^2}$$

Suppose we know that in 2015 the price of Victor's common stock is $12 per share. With four million common shares outstanding, the total value of Victor's common equity is $48 million. What does that value imply about the expected return on Victor's shares? Just plug $48 million into the equation above as the present value of Victor's free cash flow going to equity, and then use a trial and error method to solve for r. If you do this, you will find that the value of r that solves the equation is roughly 8.34%. Again, this means that given the cash flow forecast for Victor's and given the company's current stock price, its expected return is 8.34%. An investor who believed that Victor's stock ought to pay a 9% return based on its risk would not see Victor's as an attractive stock at its current $12 per share market price.

The Price-to-Earnings (P/E) Approach One of the problems with the stock valuation procedures we've looked at so far is that they require long-term forecasts of either dividends or free cash flows. They involve a good deal of "number crunching," and naturally the valuations that these models produce are only as good as the forecasts that go into them. Fortunately, there is a simpler approach. That alternative is the **price-to-earnings (P/E) approach** to stock valuation.

The P/E approach is a favorite of professional security analysts and is widely used in practice. It's relatively simple to use. It's based on the standard P/E formula first introduced previously. We showed that a stock's P/E ratio is equal to its market price divided by the stock's EPS. Using this equation and solving for the market price of the stock, we have

Equation 8.12

$$\text{Stock price} = \text{EPS} \times \text{P/E ratio}$$

Equation 8.12 basically captures the P/E approach to stock valuation. That is, given an estimated EPS figure, you decide on a P/E ratio that you feel is appropriate for the stock. Then you use it in Equation 8.12 to see what kind of price you come up with and how that compares to the stock's current price.

Actually, this approach is no different from what's used in the market every day. Look at the stock quotes in the *Wall Street Journal* or online at Yahoo! Finance. They include the stock's P/E ratio and show what investors are willing to pay for each dollar of earnings. Essentially, this ratio relates the company's earnings per share for the last 12 months (known as *trailing earnings*) to the latest price of the stock. In practice, however, investors buy stocks not for their past earnings but for their expected future earnings. Thus, in Equation 8.12, it's customary to use forecasted EPS for next year—that is, to use projected earnings one year out.

The first thing you have to do to implement the P/E approach is to come up with an expected EPS figure for next year. In the early part of this chapter, we saw how this might be done (see, for instance, Equations 8.2 and 8.3 on pages 302 and 303). Given the forecasted EPS, the next step is to evaluate the variables that drive the P/E ratio. Most of that assessment is intuitive. For example, you might look at the stock's expected rate of growth in earnings, any potential major changes in the firm's capital structure or dividends, and any other factors such as relative market or industry P/E multiples that might affect the stock's multiple. You could use such inputs to come up with a base P/E ratio. Then adjust that base, as necessary, to account for the perceived state of the market and/or anticipated changes in the rate of inflation.

Along with estimated EPS, we now have the P/E ratio we need to compute (via Equation 8.12) the price at which the stock should be trading. Take, for example, a stock that's currently trading at $37.80. One year from now, it's estimated that this stock should have an EPS of $2.25 a share. If you feel that the stock should be trading at a P/E ratio of 20 times projected earnings, then it should be valued at $45 a share (i.e., $2.25 × 20). By comparing this targeted price to the current market price of the stock, you can decide whether the stock is a good buy. In this case, you would consider the stock undervalued and therefore a good buy, since the computed price of the stock of $45 is more than its market price of $37.80.

Other Price-Relative Procedures

As we saw with the P/E approach, price-relative procedures base their valuations on the assumptions that the value of a share of stock should be directly linked to a given performance characteristic of the firm, such as earnings per share. These procedures involve a good deal of judgment and intuition, and they rely heavily on the market expertise of the analysts. Besides the P/E approach, there are several other price-relative procedures that are used by investors who, for one reason or another, want to use some measure other than earnings to value stocks. They include:

- The price-to-cash-flow (P/CF) ratio

- The price-to-sales (P/S) ratio

- The price-to-book-value (P/BV) ratio

Like the P/E multiple, these procedures determine the value of a stock by relating share price to cash flow, sales, or book value. Let's look at each of these in turn to see how they're used in stock valuation.

A Price-to-Cash-Flow (P/CF) Procedure

This measure has long been popular with investors who believe that cash flow provides a more accurate picture of a company's true value than do net earnings. When used in stock valuation, the procedure is almost identical to the P/E approach. That is, analysts use a P/CF ratio along with projected cash flow per share to estimate the stock's value.

Although it is quite straightforward, this procedure nonetheless has one problem—defining the appropriate cash flow measure. While some investors use cash flow from operating activities, as obtained from the statement of cash flows, others use free cash flow. The one measure that seems to be the most popular with professional analysts is EBITDA (earnings before interest, taxes, depreciation, and amortization), which we'll use here. EBITDA represents "pretax cash earnings" to the extent that the major noncash expenditures (depreciation and amortization) are added back to operating earnings (EBIT).

The price-to-cash-flow ratio is computed as follows:

Equation 8.13

$$\text{P/CF ratio} = \frac{\text{Market price of common stock}}{\text{Cash flow per share}}$$

where cash flow per share = EBITDA ÷ number of common shares outstanding.

Before you can use the P/CF procedure to assess the current market price of a stock, you first have to come up with a forecasted cash flow per share one year out and then define an appropriate P/CF multiple to use. For most firms, it is very likely that the cash flow (EBITDA) figure will be larger than net earnings available to stockholders. As a result, the cash flow multiple will probably be lower than the P/E multiple. In any event, once you determine an appropriate P/CF multiple (subjectively and with the help of any historical market information), simply multiply it by the expected cash flow per share one year from now to find the price at which the stock should be trading. That is, the computed price of a share of stock = cash flow per share × P/CF ratio.

> **Example**
>
> Assume a company currently is generating an EBITDA of $325 million, which is expected to increase by some 12% to around $364 million (i.e., $325 million × 1.12) over the course of the next 12 months. Suppose the company has 56 million shares of stock outstanding. The company's projected cash flow per share is $6.50. If we feel this stock should be trading at about eight times its projected cash flow per share, then it should be valued at around $52 a share. Thus, if it is currently trading in the market at $45.50 (or at seven times its projected cash flow per share), we can conclude, once again, that the stock is undervalued and, therefore, should be considered a viable investment candidate.

Price-to-Sales (P/S) and Price-to-Book-Value (P/BV) Ratios Some companies, like high-tech startups, have little, if any, earnings. Or if they do have earnings, they tend to be quite volatile and therefore highly unpredictable. In these cases, valuation procedures based on earnings (and even cash flows) aren't much help. So investors turn to other procedures—those based on sales or book value, for example. While companies may not have much in the way of profits, they almost always have sales and, ideally, some book value.

Investors use the P/S and P/BV ratios exactly like the P/E and P/CF procedures. Recall that we defined the P/BV ratio in Equation 7.21 (on page 282) as follows:

$$\text{P/BV ratio} = \frac{\text{Market price of common stock}}{\text{Book value per share}}$$

We can define the P/S ratio in a similar fashion:

Equation 8.14

$$\text{P/S ratio} = \frac{\text{Market price of common stock}}{\text{Sales per share}}$$

where sales per share equals net annual sales (or revenues) divided by the number of common shares outstanding.

Many bargain-hunting investors look for stocks with P/S ratios of 2.0 or less. They believe that these securities offer the most potential for future price appreciation. Especially attractive to these investors are very low P/S multiples of 1.0 or less. Think about it: With a P/S ratio of, say, 0.9, you can buy $1 in sales for only 90 cents! As long as the company can convert some of the sales into cash flow and earnings for shareholders, such low P/S multiples may well be worth pursuing.

Keep in mind that while the emphasis may be on low multiples, high P/S ratios aren't necessarily bad. To determine if a high multiple—more than 3.0 or 4.0, for example—is justified, look at the company's net profit margin. Companies that can consistently generate high net profit margins often have high P/S ratios. Here's a valuation rule to remember: High profit margins should go hand-in-hand with high P/S multiples. That makes sense because a company with a high profit margin brings more of its sales down to the bottom line in the form of profits.

INVESTOR FACTS

Crafty Investors Spot Problem with Etsy's IPO In April 2015, Etsy, Inc., the online marketplace for hand-crafted goods, became a public company by issuing shares to the public in an IPO. Initially priced at $16 per share, Etsy's common stock doubled on its first trading day. That runup put Etsy's price-to-sales ratio into double digits, several times higher than the P/S of the S&P 500, and even higher than some of the most rapidly growing tech stocks. Etsy's inflated P/S ratio was a sign of trouble to come, as the stock lost more than 40% of its value in its first two months of trading.

WATCH YOUR BEHAVIOR

Short-Lived Growth So-called value stocks are stocks that have low price-to-book ratios, and growth stocks are stocks that have relatively high price-to-book ratios. Many studies demonstrate that value stocks outperform growth stocks, perhaps because investors overestimate the odds that a firm that has grown rapidly in the past will continue to do so.

You would also expect the price-to-book-value measure to be low, but probably not as low as the P/S ratio. Indeed, unless the market becomes grossly overvalued (think about what happened in 1999 and 2000), most stocks are likely to trade at multiples of less than three to five times their book values. And in this case, unlike with the P/S multiple, there's usually little justification for abnormally high price-to-book-value ratios—except perhaps for firms that have abnormally low levels of equity in their capital structures. Other than that, high P/BV multiples are almost always caused by "excess exuberance." As a rule, when stocks start trading at seven or eight times their book values, or more, they are becoming overvalued.

CONCEPTS IN REVIEW

Answers available at
http://www.pearsonhighered.com/smart

8.6 Briefly describe the dividend valuation model and the three versions of this model. Explain how CAPM fits into the DVM.

8.7 What is the difference between the variable-growth dividend valuation model and the free cash flow to equity approach to stock valuation? Which procedure would work better if you were trying to value a growth stock that pays little or no dividends? Explain.

8.8 How would you go about finding the expected return on a stock? Note how such information would be used in the stock selection process.

8.9 Briefly describe the P/E approach to stock valuation and note how this approach differs from the variable-growth DVM. Describe the P/CF approach and note how it is used in the stock valuation process. Compare the P/CF approach to the P/E approach, noting the relative strengths and weaknesses of each.

8.10 Briefly describe the price-to-sales ratio and explain how it is used to value stocks. Why not just use the P/E multiple? How does the P/S ratio differ from the P/BV measure?

MyFinanceLab

Here is what you should know after reading this chapter. MyFinanceLab will help you identify what you know and where to go when you need to practice.

What You Should Know	Key Terms	Where to Practice
LG1 **Explain the role that a company's future plays in the stock valuation process.** The final phase of security analysis involves an assessment of the investment merits of a specific company and its stock. The focus here is on formulating expectations about the company's prospects and the risk and return behavior of the stock. In particular, we would want some idea of the stock's future earnings, dividends, and share prices, which are ultimately the basis of return.	common-size income statement, *p. 298* relative P/E multiple, *p. 302* stock valuation, *p. 298* target price, *p. 304*	MyFinanceLab Study Plan 8.1 Excel Table 8.1

What You Should Know	Key Terms	Where to Practice
LG2 Develop a forecast of a stock's expected cash flow, starting with corporate sales and earnings, and then moving to expected dividends and share price. Because the value of a share of stock is a function of its future returns, investors must formulate expectations about what the future holds for the company. Look first at the company's projected sales and earnings, and then translate those data into forecasted dividends and share prices. These variables define an investment's future cash flow and, therefore, investor returns.	valuation, *p. 307*	MyFinanceLab Study Plan 8.2 Excel Table 8.3
LG3 Discuss the concepts of intrinsic value and required rates of return, and note how they are used. Information such as projected sales, forecasted earnings, and estimated dividends are important in establishing intrinsic value. This is a measure, based on expected return and risk exposure, of what the stock ought to be worth. A key element is the investor's required rate of return, which is used to define the amount of return that should be earned given the stock's perceived exposure to risk.	required rate of return, *p. 307*	MyFinanceLab Study Plan 8.3 Video Learning Aid for Problem P8.18
LG4 Determine the underlying value of a stock using the zero-growth, constant-growth, and variable-growth dividend valuation models. The dividend valuation model derives the value of a share of stock from the stock's future growth in dividends. There are three versions of the DVM. Zero-growth valuation assumes that dividends are fixed and won't change. Constant-growth valuation assumes that dividends will grow at a constant rate into the future. Variable-growth valuation assumes that dividends will initially grow at varying (or abnormally high) rates before eventually settling down to a constant rate of growth.	dividend valuation model (DVM), *p. 309*	MyFinanceLab Study Plan 8.4 Excel Table 8.4 Video Learning Aid for Problem P8.9
LG5 Use other types of present value-based models to derive the value of a stock, as well as alternative price-relative procedures. The DVM works well with some types of stocks but not so well with others. Investors may turn to other stock-valuation approaches, including the free cash flow to equity approach, as well as certain price-relative procedures, like the P/E, P/CF, P/S, and P/BV methods. The free cash flow to equity model projects the free cash flows that a firm will generate over time, discounts them to the present, and divides by the number of shares outstanding to estimate a common stock's intrinsic value. Several price-relative procedures exist as well, such as the price-to-earnings approach, which uses projected EPS and the stock's P/E ratio to determine whether a stock is fairly valued.	free cash flow to equity method, *p. 318* free cash flow, *p. 318* price-to-earnings (P/E) approach, *p. 321*	MyFinanceLab Study Plan 8.5 Video Learning Aid for Problem P8.18

What You Should Know	Key Terms	Where to Practice
LG6 Understand the procedures used to value different types of stocks, from traditional dividend-paying shares to more growth-oriented stocks. All sorts of stock valuation models are used in the market; this chapter examined several widely used procedures. One thing that becomes apparent in stock evaluation is that one approach definitely does not fit all situations. Some approaches (e.g., the DVM) work well with mature, dividend-paying companies. Others (e.g., the P/E and P/CF approaches) are more suited to growth-oriented firms, which may not pay dividends. Other price-relative procedures (e.g., P/S and P/BV) are often used to value companies that have little or nothing in earnings or whose earnings records are sporadic.		MyFinanceLab Study Plan 8.6

Log into MyFinanceLab, take a chapter test, and get a personalized Study Plan that tells you which concepts you understand and which ones you need to review. From there, MyFinanceLab will give you further practice, tutorials, animations, videos, and guided solutions.
Log into **http://www.myfinancelab.com**

Discussion Questions

LG1 **Q8.1** Select a company from *Yahoo! Finance* or another online source that would be of interest to you. (*Hint*: Pick a company that's been publicly traded for at least 10 years and avoid public utilities, banks, and other financial institutions.) Using the historical and forecasted data reported in the source you select, along with one of the valuation techniques described in this chapter, calculate the maximum (i.e., justified) price you'd be willing to pay for this stock. Use the CAPM to find the required rate of return on your stock. (For this problem, use a market rate of return of 10%, and for the risk-free rate, use the latest three-month Treasury bill rate.)
   a. How does the justified price you computed compare to the latest market price of the stock?
   b. Would you consider this stock to be a worthwhile investment candidate? Explain.

LG5 **LG6** **Q8.2** In this chapter, we examined nine stock valuation procedures:
   * Zero-growth DVM
   * Constant-growth DVM
   * Variable-growth DVM
   * Free cash flow to equity approach
   * Expected return (IRR) approach
   * P/E approach
   * Price-to-cash-flow ratio
   * Price-to-sales ratio
   * Price-to-book-value ratio

a. Which one (or more) of these procedures would be appropriate when trying to put a value on:
   1. A growth stock that pays little or nothing in dividends?
   2. The S&P 500?
   3. A relatively new company that has only a brief history of earnings?
   4. A large, mature, dividend-paying company?
   5. A preferred stock that pays a fixed dividend?
   6. A company that has a large amount of depreciation and amortization?
b. Of the nine procedures listed above, which three do you think are the best? Explain.
c. If you had to choose just one procedure to use in practice, which would it be? Explain. (*Note:* Confine your selection to the list above.)

LG1 LG3 **Q8.3** Explain the role that the future plays in the stock valuation process. Why not just base the valuation on historical information? Explain how the intrinsic value of a stock is related to its required rate of return. Illustrate what happens to the value of a stock when the required rate of return increases.

LG4 **Q8.4** Assume an investor uses the constant-growth DVM to value a stock. Listed below are various situations that could affect the computed value of a stock. Look at each one of these individually and indicate whether it would cause the computed value of a stock to go up, go down, or stay the same. Briefly explain your answers.
a. Dividend payout ratio goes up.
b. Stock's beta rises.
c. Equity multiplier goes down.
d. T-bill rates fall.
e. Net profit margin goes up.
f. Total asset turnover falls.
g. Market return increases.

Assume throughout that the current dividend (D_0) remains the same and that all other variables in the model are unchanged.

Problems

All problems are available on http://www.myfinancelab.com

LG1 **P8.1** An investor estimates that next year's sales for Dursley's Hotels, Inc., should amount to about $100 million. The company has five million shares outstanding, generates a net profit margin of about 10%, and has a payout ratio of 50%. All figures are expected to hold for next year. Given this information, compute the following.
a. Estimated net earnings for next year
b. Next year's dividends per share
c. The expected price of the stock (assuming the P/E ratio is 24.5 times earnings)
d. The expected holding period return (latest stock price: $40 per share)

LG2 **P8.2** GrowthCo had sales of $55 million in 2016 and is expected to have sales of $83,650,000 for 2017. The company's net profit margin was 5% in 2016 and is expected to increase to 8% by 2017. Estimate the company's net profit for 2017.

LG2 **P8.3** Granger Toothpaste Corp. has total equity of $600 million and 125 million shares outstanding. Its ROE is 18%. Calculate the company's EPS.

LG2 **P8.4** Goodstuff Corporation has total equity of $500 million and 100 million shares outstanding. Its ROE is 15%. The dividend payout ratio is 33.3%. Calculate the company's dividends per share (round to the nearest penny).

LG2 **P8.5** HighTeck has an ROE of 15%. Its earnings per share are $2.00, and its dividends per share are $0.20. Estimate HighTeck's growth rate.

LG2 **P8.6** Last year, InDebt Company paid $75 million of interest expense, and its average rate of interest for the year was 10%. The company's ROE is 15%, and it pays no dividends. Estimate next year's interest expense assuming that interest rates will fall by 25% and the company keeps a constant equity multiplier of 20%.

LG2 **P8.7** From 2010 to 2015 Steller Strollers, Inc., has paid dividends of $1.06, $1.13, $1.21, $1.25, $1.31, and $1.38. Use an Excel spreadsheet like the template below to find Steller's historical dividend growth rate.

	A	B
1	**GROWTH RATE FOR A DIVIDEND STREAM**	
2	Year	Dividend
3		
4		
5		
6		
7		
8		
9	Annual Growth Rate	=RATE((A8-A3),0,-B3,B8,0)
10	Entry in Cell B9 is =RATE((A8-A3),0,-B3,B8,0). The expression (A8-A3) in the entry calculates the number of years of growth. The minus sign appears before B3 because the dividend in 2002 is treated as a cash outflow.	

LG2 **P8.8** Melissa Popp is thinking about buying some shares of R. H. Lawncare Equipment, at $48 per share. She expects the price of the stock to rise to $60 over the next three years. During that time she also expects to receive annual dividends of $4 per share.
   a. What is the intrinsic worth of this stock, given a 12% required rate of return?
   b. What is its expected return?

LG4 **P8.9** Investors expect that Amalgamated Aircraft Parts, Inc., will pay a dividend of $2.50 in the coming year. Investors require a 12% rate of return on the company's shares, and they expect dividends to grow at 7% per year. Using the dividend valuation model, find the intrinsic value of the company's common shares.

LG4 **P8.10** Danny is considering a stock purchase. The stock pays a constant annual dividend of $2.00 per share and is currently trading at $20. Danny's required rate of return for this stock is 12%. Should he buy this stock?

LG4 **LG5** **P8.11** Larry and Curley are brothers. They're both serious investors, but they have different approaches to valuing stocks. Larry, the older brother, likes to use the dividend valuation model. Curley prefers the free cash flow to equity valuation model.
   As it turns out, right now, both of them are looking at the same stock—American Home Care Products, Inc. (AHCP). The company has been listed on the NYSE for over 50 years and is widely regarded as a mature, rock-solid, dividend-paying stock. The brothers have gathered the following information about AHCP's stock:

Current dividend (D_0) = $2.50/share

Current free cash flow (FCF_0) = $1 million

Expected growth rate of dividends and cash flows (g) = 5.0%

Required rate of return (r) = 12.0%

Shares outstanding = 400,000

How would Larry and Curley each value this stock?

LG5 P8.12 Assume you've generated the following information about the stock of Bufford's Burger Barns: The company's latest dividends of $4 a share are expected to grow to $4.32 next year, to $4.67 the year after that, and to $5.04 in three years. After that, you think dividends will grow at a constant 6% rate.

　　a. Use the variable growth version of the dividend valuation model and a required return of 15% to find the value of the stock.

　　b. Suppose you plan to hold the stock for three years, selling it immediately after receiving the $5.04 dividend. What is the stock's expected selling price at that time? As in part (a), assume a required return of 15%.

　　c. Imagine that you buy the stock today paying a price equal to the value that you calculated in part (a). You hold the stock for three years, receiving the dividends as described above. Immediately after receiving the third dividend, you sell the stock at the price calculated in part **b**. Use the IRR approach to calculate the expected return on the stock over three years. Could you have guessed what the answer would be before doing the calculation?

　　d. Suppose the stock's current market price is actually $44.65. Based on your analysis from part **a**, is the stock overvalued or undervalued?

　　e. A friend of yours agrees with your projections of Bufford's future dividends, but he believes that in three years, just after the company pays the $5.04 dividend, the stock will be selling in the market for $53.42. Given that belief, along with the stock's current market price from part **d**, calculate the return that your friend expects to earn on this stock over the next three years.

LG6 P8.13 Let's assume that you're thinking about buying stock in West Coast Electronics. So far in your analysis, you've uncovered the following information: The stock pays annual dividends of $5.00 a share indefinitely. It trades at a P/E of 10 times earnings and has a beta of 1.2. In addition, you plan on using a risk-free rate of 3% in the CAPM, along with a market return of 10%. You would like to hold the stock for three years, at the end of which time you think EPS will be $7 a share. Given that the stock currently trades at $62, use the IRR approach to find this security's expected return. Now use the dividend valuation model (with constant dividends) to put a price on this stock. Does this look like a good investment to you? Explain.

LG6 P8.14 The price of Myrtle's Plumbing Supply Co. is now $80. The company pays no dividends. Ms. Bossard expects the price three years from now to be $110 per share. Should she buy Myrtle's Plumbing stock if she desires a 10% rate of return? Explain.

LG5 P8.15 This year, Shoreline Light and Gas (SL&G) paid its stockholders an annual dividend of $3 a share. A major brokerage firm recently put out a report on SL&G predicting that the company's annual dividends would grow at the rate of 10% per year for each of the next five years and then level off and grow at 6% thereafter.

　　a. Use the variable-growth DVM and a required rate of return of 12% to find the maximum price you should be willing to pay for this stock.

　　b. Redo the SL&G problem in part **a**, this time assuming that after year 5, dividends stop growing altogether (for year 6 and beyond, g = 0). Use all the other information given to find the stock's intrinsic value.

　　c. Contrast your two answers and comment on your findings. How important is growth to this valuation model?

LG5   **P8.16**   Assume there are three companies that in the past year paid exactly the same annual dividend of $2.25 a share. In addition, the future annual rate of growth in dividends for each of the three companies has been estimated as follows:

Buggies-Are-Us	Steady Freddie, Inc.	Gang Buster Group	
$g = 0$	$g = 6\%$	Year 1	$2.53
(i.e., dividends	(for the	2	$2.85
are expected to	foreseeable	3	$3.20
remain at	future)	4	$3.60
$2.25/share)		Year 5 and beyond: $g = 6\%$	

Assume also that as the result of a strange set of circumstances, these three companies all have the same required rate of return ($r = 10\%$).
   a.   Use the appropriate DVM to value each of these companies.
   b.   Comment briefly on the comparative values of these three companies. What is the major cause of the differences among these valuations?

LG5   **P8.17**   New Millennium Company earned $2.5 million in net income last year. It took depreciation deductions of $300,000 and made new investments in working capital and fixed assets of $100,000 and $350,000, respectively.
   a.   What was New Millennium's free cash flow last year?
   b.   Suppose that the company's free cash flow is expected to grow at 5% per year forever. If investor's require an 8% return on Millennium stock, what is the present value of Millennium's future free cash flows?
   c.   New Millennium has 3.5 million shares of common stock outstanding. What is the per-share value of the company's common stock?
   d.   What is the company's P/E ratio based on last year's earnings (i.e., trailing earnings)?
   e.   What is the company's P/E ratio based on next year's earnings (assume that earnings grow at the same rate as free cash flow).

LG6   **P8.18**   A particular company currently has sales of $250 million; sales are expected to grow by 20% next year (year 1). For the year after next (year 2), the growth rate in sales is expected to equal 10%. Over each of the next two years, the company is expected to have a net profit margin of 8% and a payout ratio of 50% and to maintain the common stock outstanding at 15 million shares. The stock always trades at a P/E of 15 times earnings, and the investor has a required rate of return of 20%. Given this information,
   a.   Find the stock's intrinsic value (its justified price).
   b.   Use the IRR approach to determine the stock's expected return, given that it is currently trading at $15 per share.
   c.   Find the holding period returns for this stock for year 1 and for year 2.

LG3   **LG5**   **P8.19**   Assume a major investment service has just given Oasis Electronics its highest investment rating, along with a strong buy recommendation. As a result, you decide to take a look for yourself and to place a value on the company's stock. Here's what you find: This year Oasis paid its stockholders an annual dividend of $3 a share, but because of its high rate of growth in earnings, its dividends are expected to grow at the rate of 12% a year for the next four years and then to level out at 9% a year. So far, you've learned that the stock has a beta of 1.80, the risk-free rate of return is 5%, and the expected return on the market is 11%. Using the CAPM to find the required rate of return, put a value on this stock.

LG5   **P8.20**   Consolidated Software doesn't currently pay any dividends but is expected to start doing so in four years. That is, Consolidated will go three more years without paying dividends and then is expected to pay its first dividend (of $3 per share) in the fourth year. Once the company starts paying dividends, it's expected to continue to do so. The company is expected to have a dividend payout ratio of 40% and to maintain a return on equity of

20%. Based on the DVM, and given a required rate of return of 15%, what is the maximum price you should be willing to pay for this stock today?

LG5 **P8.21** Assume you obtain the following information about a certain company:

Total assets	$50,000,000
Total equity	$25,000,000
Net income	$3,750,000
EPS	$5.00 per share
Dividend payout ratio	40%
Required return	12%

Use the constant-growth DVM to place a value on this company's stock.

LG6 **P8.22** You're thinking about buying some stock in Affiliated Computer Corporation and want to use the P/E approach to value the shares. You've estimated that next year's earnings should come in at about $4.00 a share. In addition, although the stock normally trades at a relative P/E of 1.15 times the market, you believe that the relative P/E will rise to 1.25, whereas the market P/E should be around 18.5 times earnings. Given this information, what is the maximum price you should be willing to pay for this stock? If you buy this stock today at $87.50, what rate of return will you earn over the next 12 months if the price of the stock rises to $110.00 by the end of the year? (Assume that the stock doesn't pay dividends.)

LG5 **P8.23** AviBank Plastics generated an EPS of $2.75 over the last 12 months. The company's earnings are expected to grow by 25% next year, and because there will be no significant change in the number of shares outstanding, EPS should grow at about the same rate. You feel the stock should trade at a P/E of around 30 times earnings. Use the P/E approach to set a value on this stock.

LG6 **P8.24** Newco is a young company that has yet to make a profit. You are trying to place a value on the stock, but it pays no dividends and you obviously cannot calculate a P/E ratio. As a result, you decide to look at other stocks in the same industry as Newco to see if you can find a way to value this company. You find the following information:

	Per-Share Data ($)			
	Newco	Adolescentco	Middle-Ageco	Oldco
Sales	$10	$200	$800	$800
Profit	–$10	$ 10	$ 60	$ 80
Book value	–$ 2	$ 2	$ 5	$ 8
Market value	?	$ 20	$ 80	$ 75

Estimate a market value for Newco. Discuss how your estimate could change if Newco was expected to grow much faster than the other companies.

LG4 **P8.25** World Wide Web Wares (4W, for short) is an online retailer of small kitchen appliances and utensils. The firm has been around for a few years and has created a nice market niche for itself. In fact, it actually turned a profit last year, albeit a fairly small one. After doing some basic research on the company, you've decided to take a closer look. You plan to use the price-to-sales ratio to value the stock, and you have collected P/S multiples on the following Internet retailer stocks:

Company	P/S Multiples
Amazing.com	4.5
ReallyCooking.com	4.1
Fixtures & Appliances Online	3.8

Find the average P/S ratio for these three firms. Given that 4W is expected to generate $40 million in sales next year and will have 10 million shares of stock outstanding, use the average P/S ratio you computed above to put a value on 4W's stock.

Visit **http://www.myfinancelab.com** for web exercises, spreadsheets, and other online resources

Case Problem 8.1   Chris Looks for a Way to Invest His Wealth

LG1 LG2 LG4   Chris Norton is a young Hollywood writer who is well on his way to television superstardom. After writing several successful television specials, he was recently named the head writer for one of TV's top-rated sitcoms. Chris fully realizes that his business is a fickle one, and on the advice of his dad and manager, he has decided to set up an investment program. Chris will earn about a half-million dollars this year. Because of his age, income level, and desire to get as big a bang as possible from his investment dollars, he has decided to invest in speculative, high-growth stocks.

Chris is currently working with a respected Beverly Hills broker and is in the process of building up a diversified portfolio of speculative stocks. The broker recently sent him information on a hot new issue. She advised Chris to study the numbers and, if he likes them, to buy as many as 1,000 shares of the stock. Among other things, corporate sales for the next three years have been forecasted as follows:

Year	Sales ($ millions)
1	$22.5
2	$35.0
3	$50.0

The firm has 2.5 million shares of common stock outstanding. They are currently being traded at $70 a share and pay no dividends. The company has a net profit rate of 20%, and its stock has been trading at a P/E of around 40 times earnings. All these operating characteristics are expected to hold in the future.

Questions

a. Looking first at the stock:
   1. Compute the company's net profits and EPS for each of the next 3 years.
   2. Compute the price of the stock three years from now.
   3. Assuming that all expectations hold up and that Chris buys the stock at $70, determine his expected return on this investment.
   4. What risks is he facing by buying this stock? Be specific.
   5. Should he consider the stock a worthwhile investment candidate? Explain.

b. Looking at Chris's investment program in general:
   1. What do you think of his investment program? What do you see as its strengths and weaknesses?
   2. Are there any suggestions you would make?
   3. Do you think Chris should consider adding foreign stocks to his portfolio? Explain.

Case Problem 8.2   An Analysis of a High-Flying Stock

LG2 LG6   Marc Dodier is a recent university graduate and a security analyst with the Kansas City brokerage firm of Lippman, Brickbats, and Shaft. Marc has been following one of the hottest issues on Wall Street, C&I Medical Supplies, a company that has turned in an outstanding performance lately and, even more important, has exhibited excellent growth potential. It has five million shares outstanding and pays a nominal annual dividend of $0.05 per share. Marc has decided to take a closer look at C&I to assess its investment potential. Assume the company's sales for the past five years have been as follows:

Year	Sales ($ millions)
2012	$10.0
2013	$12.5
2014	$16.2
2015	$22.0
2016	$28.5

Marc is concerned with the future prospects of the company, not its past. As a result, he pores over the numbers and generates the following estimates of future performance:

Expected net profit margin	12%
Estimated annual dividends per share	5¢
Number of common shares outstanding	No change
P/E ratio at the end of 2017	35
P/E ratio at the end of 2018	50

Questions

a. Determine the average annual rate of growth in sales over the past five years. (Assume sales in 2011 amounted to $7.5 million.)

1. Use this average growth rate to forecast revenues for next year (2017) and the year after that (2018).

2. Now determine the company's net earnings and EPS for each of the next two years (2017 and 2018).

3. Finally, determine the expected future price of the stock at the end of this two-year period.

b. Because of several intrinsic and market factors, Marc feels that 25% is a viable figure to use for a desired rate of return.

1. Using the 25% rate of return and the forecasted figures you came up with in question a, compute the stock's justified price.

2. If C&I is currently trading at $32.50 per share, should Marc consider the stock a worthwhile investment candidate? Explain.

Excel@Investing

Excel@Investing   Fundamental to the valuation process is the determination of the intrinsic value of a security, where an investor calculates the present value of the expected future cash benefits of the investment. Specifically, in the case of common stock, these future cash flows are defined by expected future dividend payments and future potential price appreciation. A simple but useful way to view stock value is that it is equal to the present value of all expected future dividends it may provide over an infinite time horizon.

Based on this latter concept, the dividend valuation model (DVM) has evolved. It can take on any one of three versions—the zero-growth model, the constant-growth model, and the variable-growth model.

Create a spreadsheet that applies the variable-growth model to predict the intrinsic value of the Rhyhorn Company common stock. Assume that dividends will grow at a variable rate for the next three years (2016, 2017, and 2018). After that, the annual rate of growth in dividends is expected to be 7% and stay there for the foreseeable future. Starting with the latest (2015) annual dividend of $2.00 per share, Rhyhorn's earnings and dividends are estimated to grow by 18% in 2016, by 14% in 2017, and by 9% in 2018 before dropping to a 7% rate. Given the risk profile of the firm, assume a minimum required rate of return of at least 12%. The spreadsheet for Table 8.4, which you can view on http://www.myfinance.lab.com, is a good reference for solving this problem.

Questions

a. Calculate the projected annual dividends over the years 2016, 2017, and 2018.

b. Determine the present value of dividends during the initial variable-growth period.

c. What do you believe the price of Rhyhorn stock will be at the end of the initial growth period (2018)?

d. Having determined the expected future price of Rhyhorn stock in part c, discount the price of the stock back to its present value.

e. Determine the total intrinsic value of Rhyhorn stock based on your calculations above.

Chapter-Opening Problem

At the beginning of this chapter you read about a 2015 earnings announcement from HP in which earnings per share were reported as $1.85 for the quarter. Let's make a simple assumption and say that earnings for the year were four times as much, or $7.40 per share. At the time of that announcement, the average P/E for stocks in the U.S. was close to 15.

a. If you use the market's P/E and HP's current earnings to estimate the stock's intrinsic value, what value do you obtain?

b. The actual price of HP after the earnings announcement was about $73. What does this tell you about your answer to part a?

c. Suppose HP paid out all of its earnings as a dividend. Suppose also that investors expected the firm to continue doing that forever, and because the company was not reinvesting any earnings, investors expected no growth in dividends. If the required return on HP stock is 9%, what is the stock price?

d. Comment on your answer to part c in light of HP's market price at the time.

9

Market Efficiency and Behavioral Finance

LEARNING GOALS

After studying this chapter, you should be able to:

LG1 Describe the characteristics of an efficient market, explain what market anomalies are, and note some of the challenges that investors face when markets are efficient.

LG2 Summarize the evidence which indicates that the stock market is efficient.

LG3 List four "decision traps" that may lead investors to make systematic errors in their investment decisions.

LG4 Explain how behavioral finance links market anomalies to investors' cognitive biases.

LG5 Describe some of the approaches to technical analysis, including, among others, moving averages, charting, and various indicators of the technical condition of the market.

LG6 Compute and use technical trading rules for individual stocks and the market as a whole.

In 2013 the Nobel Prize in economics was awarded to three co-recipients: Eugene Fama, Robert Shiller, and Lars Peter Hanson. In giving a shared award to Fama and Shiller, the committee appeared to display a sense of humor because those two scholars are best known for holding opposing views on the efficiency of financial markets. Eugene Fama was among the first to define the term "efficient markets" in his landmark study that concluded that stock prices moved almost at random and that any attempt to earn better-than-average returns by identifying winners and losers in the stock market was a fool's errand. Fama argued that competition among rational investors resulted in stock prices that accurately reflected all information available to market participants. If market prices reflected all available information, then no single investor could consistently identify overvalued or undervalued stocks, and therefore no investor could earn a return that consistently beat the market average (on a risk-adjusted basis).

Shiller, on the other hand, gained popular notoriety through his book, *Irrational Exuberance*, which argued that the stock market had become grossly overvalued in the late 1990s due to irrational behavior by investors. Indeed, Shiller's book was published just before a stock market crash in 2000. Shiller's message was that the stock market was anything but efficient, and that smart investors could identify times when it would be wiser to sit on the sidelines than to invest in stocks. Less than a decade later, Shiller made headlines again through his warnings that the housing market was becoming overheated, a prediction that the subsequent collapse in housing prices and related financial crisis seemed to confirm.

For many years, academics and investment professionals were on opposite sides of this debate. A broad consensus existed among academics that the market was very efficient and that neither amateur nor professional investors were likely to earn better-than-average returns over time. The professional investment community mostly disagreed with this view, arguing that well-trained investors with access to sophisticated information and trading systems could deliver superior returns to their clients. Over time, the two sides have moved closer together. A growing body of academic research, generally referred to as *behavioral finance*, has found evidence that the market is not as efficient as scholars once believed and that human cognitive biases place a limit on how efficient the market can be. At the same time, members of the investment community have acknowledged that consistently identifying overvalued or undervalued securities is extremely difficult and that many investors will be better off buying and holding a diversified portfolio of securities rather than paying experts to identify mispriced stocks. Among practitioners, this view has led to the growth in low-cost investment options such as index funds and exchange-traded funds.

Efficient Markets

LG1 LG2 To some observers, the stock market is little more than a form of legalized gambling. They argue that movements in the stock market have no real connection to what is happening in the economy or to the financial results produced by specific companies. In the eyes of people who hold this view, large swings in the market are driven by emotions like greed and fear rather than by business fundamentals. In this chapter we study the connection between prices in the stock market (and other financial markets) and real business conditions, and we ask whether and how stock prices might be affected by human emotions.

To begin, consider Figure 9.1, which shows quarterly revenues reported by Walmart from 2000 to mid 2015. A quick glance at the figure reveals two obvious patterns. First, Walmart's revenues have grown over time. In early 2015 the company reported quarterly revenues of $132 billion, more than double the quarterly revenues that they had generated in early 2000. Perhaps an even more striking pattern is that there is clearly one quarter each year in which Walmart earns higher revenues than any other quarter. Those peaks, marked by red dots in Figure 9.1, occur in Walmart's first quarter, which ends on January 31st each year. In other words, in every year since 2000, Walmart has sold more goods in November, December, and January than in any other quarter, a remarkably stable pattern. When you think about this pattern a little, it should come as no surprise. Nearly every retail company in the United States sells more near the end of the year because of the Christmas season, and Walmart is no exception. Although Figure 9.1 plots Walmart's revenues, a plot of the company's net income would show similar patterns.

Walmart is a huge corporation, and roughly 11% of U.S. retail sales (not counting automobiles) occur in Walmart stores. Partly because it is so large and partly because much of its business focuses on life's necessities, Walmart's financial results are not terribly difficult to predict. This is another lesson from Figure 9.1. The persistence of the patterns in Walmart's revenues over a long period of time suggests that forecasts of

FIGURE 9.1

Walmart Quarterly Revenues

From 2000 to mid 2015 Walmart steadily increased its quarterly revenues from $43 billion to more than $132 billion. The long-term upward trend is marked by a distinct seasonal pattern in which Walmart's revenues peak in the first quarter each year, marked by red dots in the figure. The peak in revenues is due to the Christmas shopping season and is common in retail companies.

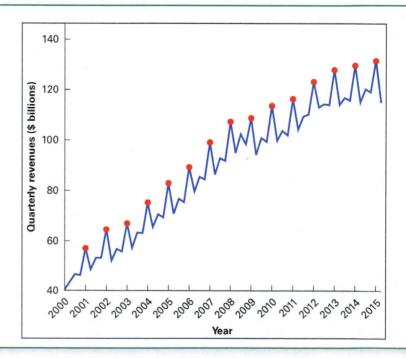

FIGURE 9.2

Walmart's Stock Price

From 2000 to mid 2015, Walmart's stock price rose, but it did not follow a predictable trend. Furthermore, the seasonal pattern in Walmart's revenues does not appear in its stock price. The stock price in the first quarter of each year is marked by a red dot, and those red dots show no discernible pattern over the past 15 years.

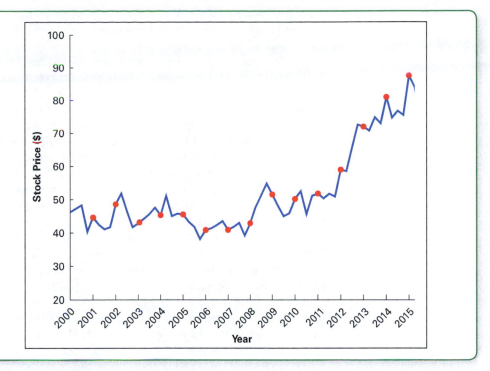

Walmart's future performance, at least in the not-too-distant future, are likely to be fairly accurate. Is Walmart's stock price just as predictable?

Figure 9.2 plots Walmart's stock price at the end of each quarter from 2000 to mid 2015, the same period covered in Figure 9.1. Like the company's revenues, Walmart's stock price was higher in 2015 than it was in 2000, but it hardly followed the relatively smooth upward trend that revenues did. The striking difference between Figures 9.1 and 9.2 is the seemingly random movements in Walmart's stock price, which stand in sharp contrast to the predictable movements in Walmart's revenues. Clearly there was no tendency for Walmart's stock to peak at the same time that its revenues did (i.e., at the end of the first quarter each year, marked by the red dots in Figure 9.2). Does this mean that there is no connection between Walmart's financial performance and the behavior of its stock?

Naturally our answer to that question is a firm no. To understand why, it may be helpful to think about what would happen if Walmart's stock price moved in sync with its revenues, showing a seasonal peak at the end of each year. Suppose that over many years, Walmart stock displayed a regular, predictable tendency to shoot up every year in the fourth quarter. If that pattern persisted and investors came to expect the pattern to continue, what would they do? Smart investors would buy Walmart's stock in the third quarter each year, hoping to profit from the fourth quarter runup. But if investors rushed to buy Walmart shares in the third quarter each year, their actions would put upward pressure on the stock price in the third quarter rather than the fourth. In other words, the pattern of fourth-quarter peaks in the stock price would change to a pattern of third-quarter peaks. Pretty soon, investors would see that pattern and begin buying even sooner, perhaps in the second quarter each year. Eventually, the actions of investors trying to buy ahead of any peak in the stock price would cause the seasonal pattern to disappear. So the lesson here is that even if a company's financial results follow a highly predictable pattern, its stock price will not follow the same pattern (or perhaps even any pattern). If stock prices do exhibit predictable patterns, the actions of investors will tend to eliminate those patterns over time.

A second line of argument helps explain why the seemingly random behavior of Walmart's stock price (or any stock price) does not imply that the stock market and Walmart's financial performance are unconnected. Remember that you previously learned that a stock's price depends on investors' expectations about the future performance of the company that issued the stock. Prices move up when investors' expectations become brighter, and prices move down when the opposite occurs. Investors who bought Walmart's stock way back in 2000 probably expected that over the next 15 years the company's revenues would grow and that they would peak in the fourth quarter every year. After all, by the year 2000, Walmart had already established a long history of growth, and the seasonal pattern in revenues was well known to the investment community. In other words, much of the performance displayed in Figure 9.1 would not have surprised investors and therefore would not have moved Walmart's stock a great deal. What would cause a sudden and potentially large change in Walmart's stock price is any sign that the firm's future financial performance would deviate from what investors expected. For example, suppose that in 2015 Walmart's revenues were not only high in the first quarter (as usual) but that they were even higher than investors had anticipated they would be. In that case, investors would likely raise their expectations about Walmart's future performance, and the company's stock price would go up as a result. If Walmart reported financial results that failed to match investors' expectations, then its stock price would probably fall as investors revised their views about how the company would perform in the future.

The main point here is that stock prices respond to *new* information. By definition, new information is something that people do not already know and that they do not anticipate. That Walmart's revenues peak at the end of each year is not new information, so when the peak occurs each year it does not tend to boost the company's stock price. Only if fourth-quarter revenues are surprising (better or worse than expected) would Walmart's stock price respond. Because new information is unpredictable, stock price movements are also largely unpredictable. This is the central idea of the **random walk hypothesis**, which says that predicting stock price movements is very difficult, if not impossible. We must emphasize here that if stock prices move at random, it is not a sign that the stock market is a casino that lacks any connection to the real business world. Just the opposite is true. The seemingly random behavior of stock prices is a sign that the stock market is processing information quickly and efficiently. In fact, economists say that a market that rapidly and fully incorporates all new information is an **efficient market**.

AN ADVISOR'S PERSPECTIVE

Bob Grace
President, Grace Tax Advisory Group

"There is absolutely no connection between what happened yesterday and what will happen tomorrow."

MyFinanceLab

The Efficient Markets Hypothesis

The notion that stock prices (and prices in other financial markets) rapidly incorporate new information is known formally as the **efficient markets hypothesis (EMH)**. An implication of this idea is that it is very difficult for investors, even professional investors, to earn abnormally high returns by identifying undervalued stocks and buying them (or identifying overvalued stocks and selling them). Spotting bargains in the stock market is difficult because if the market is indeed efficient, by the time you have processed the information that leads you to believe that a stock is a good buy, the market has already incorporated that information, and the information is reflected in the stock's price.

The EMH says that investors should not expect to earn abnormal returns consistently. What constitutes an abnormal return? Previously you learned that there is a positive relation between risk and return. Investments that tend to earn higher returns also tend to be riskier. Therefore, an investment's expected return is directly related to its risk. An **abnormal return** (also known as **alpha**) is the difference between an investment's actual return and its expected return (i.e., the return that it should earn given its risk).

Equation 9.1

Abnormal return (or alpha) = Actual return − Expected return

One way that investors can estimate the expected return on a stock is to use the capital asset pricing model, or CAPM. Recall that the CAPM says that the expected return on a stock ($E(r_j)$) is equal to the risk-free rate (r_{rf}) plus the product of the stock's beta (b_j) and the risk premium on the overall market ($r_m - r_{rf}$).

Equation 9.2

$$E(r_j) = r_{rf} + b_j(r_m - r_{rf})$$

Example

Suppose that a particular stock has a beta of 1.0. This means that the stock has average risk and should earn a return that is on average equal to the return on the overall market. Suppose that in a particular year the risk-free rate is 2% and the return on the overall stock market is 10%. Equation 9.2 tells us that the return that we should expect on this stock is 10%:

$$E(r) = 2\% + 1.0(10\% - 2\%) = 10\%$$

Suppose instead that the stock earned a 12% return. In this case it earns an abnormal positive return (alpha) of 2%:

$$\text{Abnormal return} = \text{Actual return} - \text{Expected return}$$

$$= 12\% - 10\%$$

$$= 2\%$$

The EMH says that spotting stocks like this (i.e., stocks that earn positive abnormal returns) on a consistent basis over time is nearly impossible, even for highly sophisticated investors with extensive training.

The efficient markets hypothesis focuses on the extent to which markets incorporate information into prices. The more information that is incorporated into stock prices and the more rapidly that information becomes incorporated into prices, the more efficient the market becomes. One way of characterizing the extent to which markets are efficient is to define different levels of efficiency corresponding to different types of information that prices may reflect. These levels of market efficiency are known as the weak form, the semi-strong form, and the strong form.

Weak Form   The **weak form** of the EMH holds that stock prices fully reflect any relevant information that can be obtained from an analysis of past price movements. If investors study the historical record of stock prices and spot some kind of pattern that seems to repeat, their attempts to exploit that pattern through trading will cause the pattern to disappear over time. We have already described this idea to explain why Walmart's stock price does not exhibit predictable patterns, even though its revenues show distinct seasonal peaks. In short, the weak form of the EMH says that past data on stock prices are of no use in predicting future price changes. According to this hypothesis, prices follow a random walk, meaning that tomorrow's price change is unrelated to today's or yesterday's price, or that of any other day.

WATCH YOUR BEHAVIOR

Investors' Expectations vs. Expected Returns When investors are asked about their future expectations for stock market returns, those expectations are positively correlated with recent market returns. Since we know actual market returns do not have this kind of correlation, it suggests that investors beliefs are not fully rational. In fact, research shows that investors' expectations are negatively correlated with the predictions of sophisticated financial models.

(Source: Robin Greenwood and Andrei Shleifer, "Expectations of Returns and Expected Returns," *The Review of Financial Studies RFS*, 2014, Vol. 27, Iissue 3, pp. 714–746.)

The earliest research on the weak form of market efficiency appeared to confirm the prediction that prices moved at random. Using databases that contained the past prices of listed stocks in the United States, researchers constructed a variety of "trading rules," such as buying a stock when it hit a 52-week low, and then tested these rules using historical information to see what returns investors following these rules might have earned. The results were encouraging to theorists but not to traders—none of the trading rules earned abnormal returns, but they did generate significant transactions costs. The researchers concluded that investors would do better by purchasing a diversified portfolio and holding it.

Semi-Strong Form The **semi-strong form of the EMH** asserts that stock prices fully reflect all relevant information that investors can obtain from any public source. This means that investors cannot consistently earn abnormally high returns using publicly available information such as annual reports and other required filings, analyst recommendations, product reviews, and so on. To illustrate the idea, suppose that you see that a particular firm has just posted its latest financial results online. You read the report and see that the company reported an unexpected surge in profits in the most recent quarter. Should you call your broker and buy some shares? The semi-strong form of the EMH says that by the time you download the annual report, read it, and call your broker, the market price of the stock will have already increased, reflecting the company's latest good news.

Figure 9.3 comes from a recent research study that tested this form of the EMH. The researchers gathered data on a large number of earnings announcements by

FIGURE 9.3 **Daily Stock Price Reactions Surrounding Positive Earnings News**
The figure shows that for a group of companies reporting favorable earnings, abnormal returns are close to 0 leading up to the announcement and beyond 2 days after the announcement. The market responds fully to the new information in 1 or at most 2 days. (Source: Modified from Andreas Neuhierl, Anna Scherbina, and Bernd Schlusche, "Market Reaction to Corporate Press Releases," *Journal of Financial and Quantitative Analysis*, August 2013.)

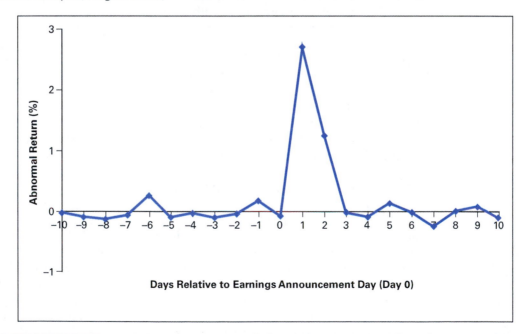

different companies and tracked the companies' stock price behavior before and after the announcements. The common factor in all of these announcements was that the companies were reporting good news that their earnings were higher than analysts had expected. In a sense, the question that the researchers were asking was, is it smart to buy the stock of a company that announces this kind of good news?

The horizontal axis of Figure 9.3 measures time relative to the earnings announcement day. The earnings announcement day is day 0, so day −1 is one day before the announcement and day +1 is one day after the announcement. Keep in mind that many firms release their financial information after the market has closed. This means that the first opportunity for the stock market to incorporate the new information occurs the day after the announcement, on day +1. The vertical axis in the figure measures the average abnormal return exhibited by companies in the sample. The behavior of stock prices exhibited in Figure 9.3 is very close to what the semi-strong form of the EMH would predict. Observe that leading up to the earnings announcements, the companies in the sample earn returns that are essentially normal (i.e., the abnormal return is 0, so the actual return matches the expected return). However, from day 0 to day +1, the average company in the sample earned an abnormal return of about 2.5%, with an additional 1% abnormal return occurring from day +1 to day +2. Beyond that point, however, abnormal returns quickly revert to 0%. In other words, the market quickly (in a day or at most two days) incorporates the good news from earnings announcements.

Many tests of semi-strong efficiency have examined how stock prices respond before and after particular types of news. One study looked at four companies that were major contractors in the space shuttle program. When the shuttle *Challenger* exploded shortly after liftoff in 1986, the stock prices of all four companies fell, but the one that fell the most was Morton Thiokol. That company made the booster rockets that lifted the shuttle into orbit, and months after the accident occurred, an investigation concluded that a problem with the O-rings in these rockets had caused the accident. In other words, the market's initial reaction within minutes of the accident seemed to point to the same conclusion as the subsequent investigation.

Numerous studies have examined the investment performance of professional investors such as mutual fund managers. Some people argue that although the stock market may be efficient enough to prevent individual investors from earning abnormally high returns, surely professional investors who have advanced training in investments and who spend their entire professional lives thinking about investments can perform better. The conclusions from research in this area are not unanimous, but most studies find that even professional investors struggle to earn abnormal returns on a consistent basis. On average, mutual fund managers do not earn returns that beat the market average by a sufficient degree to cover the fees that they charge investors. Furthermore, there is not much persistence in mutual fund returns. In other words, fund managers who have above-average returns one year do not have a very high likelihood of generating above-average returns the next year.

The overwhelming evidence indicates that stock prices react very rapidly to any important new information, which makes it very hard for investors (individuals or professionals) to "beat the market." Unless you hear about an event almost as soon as it happens, the stock price will adjust to the news before you can trade the stock.

Strong Form The **strong form of the EMH** holds that the stock market can rapidly incorporate new information even if it is not disseminated through public sources. It states that stock prices rapidly adjust to any information, even if it isn't available to every investor.

INVESTOR FACTS

Robots and Efficient Markets Professional investors have to work even harder these days to trade on information before prices react. For example, the hedge fund Two Sigma Investments, LLC, uses computer programs to sift through real-time data from sources like Twitter to identify emerging news about stocks and execute trades within seconds.

One type of private information is the kind obtained by corporate insiders, such as officers and directors of a corporation. They have access to valuable information about major strategic and tactical decisions the company makes. They also have detailed information about the financial state of the firm that may not be available to other shareholders. Insiders are generally prohibited from trading the shares of their employers prior to major news releases. However, at other times corporate insiders may legally trade shares of stock in their company, if they report the transactions to the Securities and Exchange Commission (SEC). When insiders file the required forms with the SEC, they are quickly made available to the public via the Internet. Several studies of corporate insiders find that their trades are particularly well timed, meaning that they tend to buy before significant price increases and sell prior to big declines. This, of course, is contrary to what you'd expect to find if the strong form of the EMH were true.

Insiders and other market participants occasionally have inside—nonpublic—information that they obtained or traded on illegally. With this information, they can gain an unfair advantage that permits them to earn an abnormal return. Clearly, those who violate the law when they trade have an unfair advantage. Empirical research has confirmed that those with such inside information do indeed have an opportunity to earn an abnormal return—but there might be an awfully high price attached, such as spending time in prison, if they're caught.

Arbitrage and Efficient Markets Closely linked to the notion of efficient markets is the concept of arbitrage. **Arbitrage** is a type of transaction in which an investor simultaneously buys and sells the same asset at different prices to earn an instant, risk-free profit. Let us give a simple example to illustrate the concept of arbitrage before examining the concept more closely.

Example

Suppose that banks in New York City will convert dollars into euros (or vice versa) at an exchange rate of one dollar per euro. In London, however, banks are exchanging dollars and euros at the rate of $1.25 dollars per euro. Notice that given these exchange rates, one euro is more valuable in London than in New York. Another way to say this is that euros are relatively cheap in New York and relatively expensive in London. This means that we have the identical asset (the euro) trading in different markets at different prices, so we would say that this presents an arbitrage opportunity. A trader could exploit this opportunity by buying cheap euros in New York and selling them in London as follows:

1. At a New York bank, use $1 million to buy €1 million. Remember, in New York, €1 is worth $1. Of course, if many traders begin buying euros in New York, the price of the euro will tend to rise in this market.

2. At a bank in London, sell the €1 million in exchange for $1.25 million at the prevailing exchange rate of $1.25 dollars per euro. Again, if many investors begin selling euros on the London market, then the price of the euro should begin to fall there.

3. Simply by purchasing euros in New York and selling them in London, the trader makes an instant profit of $250,000. But as the price of the euro rises in New York and falls in London, the opportunity to profit from these transactions will shrink, and ultimately vanish.

Consider how the definition of arbitrage applies to this example. First, arbitrage occurs when an investor simultaneously buys and sells the same asset. In this example, the underlying asset is just a currency, so the investor is buying euros in New York and selling them in London. The underlying asset is literally the same thing in each market. Furthermore, the purchase in New York and the sale in London can occur simultaneously through electronic transactions. The second part of the definition says that the purchase and sale must occur at different prices, and clearly that is the case here. In New York, €1 is worth $1, but in London it is worth $1.25. Finally, the definition of arbitrage says that the profit earned must be instantaneous and free of risk. Again, this example seems to satisfy those conditions because the trader earns the profit as soon as the currency trades take place, and because they take place essentially at the same time, there would appear to be no risk involved.

In the real world, naturally, we do not see large differences in currency prices in different markets. The price quoted in New York and in London will be virtually the same. If that were not true, arbitragers would exploit the price differences and, through their buying and selling transactions, push the prices closer together until no arbitrage opportunity remained. Economists refer to this as the "no arbitrage" condition, which simply means that prices in financial markets will quickly adjust to eliminate arbitrage opportunities.

Believers in efficient markets often cite arbitrage as a key mechanism that makes markets efficient. For example, suppose that the true intrinsic value of Pepsi stock is $100 per share but for some reason investors have been irrationally pessimistic about the company and have driven its price down to $80. To efficient markets advocates, this represents a kind of arbitrage opportunity. Smart investors will buy the under-valued shares of Pepsi and to hedge their bets they will simultaneously sell shares in another similar company, like Coca-Cola, for example. The buying pressure will cause Pepsi shares to move back toward their intrinsic value of $100, so in the end the market price and the intrinsic value of Pepsi are equal.

Arbitrage is a powerful force, and it plays a very important role in setting the prices of many types of securities, but there are limits to arbitrage. In the Pepsi example, the arbitrage process involves not only buying Pepsi shares but also selling something else that is very similar to Pepsi. Although Pepsi and Coca-Cola are similar stocks, one cannot really argue that they are identical investments. They are imperfect substitutes for one another, so even if Pepsi is mispriced, buying Pepsi and selling Coca-Cola may be risky. In addition, making these trades is costly, especially for an investor who wants to sell Coca-Cola but does not own any shares. That investor must engage in a short sale, which means that the investor must borrow Coca-Cola shares from someone else before selling them. Short sales often carry high transactions costs, and at times, shorting a particular stock is just not possible because there is no one willing to lend the required shares.

Another risk associated with arbitrage has to do with what created the apparent arbitrage opportunity in the first place. We presumed that some investors were irratio-nally pessimistic about Pepsi, and their pessimism caused Pepsi to be undervalued. It may be true that some smart investors can spot this situation, but what if other traders continue to be pessimistic or become even more pessimistic about Pepsi? In that case, there is no absolute guarantee that the actions of smart traders (who are buying Pepsi) will swamp the trades of irrational traders (who continue to sell Pepsi) and thereby move Pepsi's stock price toward its intrinsic value. Instead, Pepsi could become more undervalued, which would cause losses for the "smart" traders conducting the arbitrage trades.

To sum up, there is considerable evidence suggesting that the stock market is relatively efficient, and there are compelling reasons to expect that to be the case. Nevertheless, some contrary evidence exists, and it is to that evidence that we now turn.

Market Anomalies

Despite considerable evidence in support of the EMH, researchers have uncovered some patterns that seem inconsistent with the theory. Collectively, this body of puzzling evidence is known as **market anomalies**, a name that itself suggests that there is less evidence contradicting the EMH than there is in support of it. What all of these anomalies have in common is that they reveal patterns or trading strategies that, at least in hindsight, earned higher returns than would be expected in efficient markets.

Calendar Effects   One widely cited anomaly is the *calendar effect*, which holds that stock returns may be closely tied to the time of the year or the time of the week. That is, certain months or days of the week may produce better investment results than others. The most famous of the calendar anomalies is the *January effect*, which is a tendency for small-cap stocks to outperform large-cap stocks by an unusually wide margin in the month of January. One possible explanation for this pattern has to do with taxes. Under certain conditions, investors can deduct investment losses when calculating their federal income taxes. Thus, there is an incentive for investors to sell stocks that have gone down in value during the year, and investors who recognize that incentive are particularly likely to sell in December as the tax year comes to a close. Think about what happens to the market capitalization of a firm when its stock falls during the year—the market cap gets smaller. Thus, if investors have a tax incentive to sell their loser stocks in December, and if these stocks by definition tend to be smaller than average, then their prices may be temporarily depressed due to December tax selling, and they may rebound in January. As plausible as this explanation may sound, there is at best mixed evidence that it can account for the puzzling behavior of small stocks in January.

Small-Firm Effect   Another anomaly is the *small-firm effect*, or *size effect*, which states that small firms tend to earn positive abnormal returns of as much as 5% to 6% per year. Indeed, several studies have shown that small firms (or small-cap stocks) earn higher returns than large firms (or large-cap stocks), even after taking into account the higher betas typical of most small firms. This tendency has been documented in the United States as well as in many stock markets around the world and is not confined to the month of January.

Post Earnings Announcement Drift (or Momentum)   Another market anomaly has to do with how stock prices react to earnings announcements. In Figure 9.3 we showed the results of a study that tracked stock returns around earnings announcements. In that study, stocks reporting good earnings exhibited abnormal returns for a day or two, but those abnormal returns quickly dissipated. However, several older studies reported a tendency for stocks to "drift" after earnings announcements in the same direction as the initial reaction. In other words, when companies reported better-than-expected earnings, their stock prices jumped immediately, earning positive abnormal returns. But surprisingly, these firms' stock prices continued to earn positive abnormal returns for weeks or even months after the earnings announcements. Similarly, firms reporting bad earnings earned negative abnormal returns that continued for several months beyond the initial announcement. This seems to indicate that investors *underreact* to the information in earnings announcements. When firms report good news, investors don't realize just how good the news is, and similarly, when bad news comes, investors don't fully appreciate how bad the news is, so stock prices take a long time to fully adjust to a new level. This pattern seems to create an opportunity for investors to earn abnormal returns by purchasing stocks that have recently issued good earnings news or by short selling stocks that have recently delivered poor earnings results.

Figure 9.4 illustrates the post earnings announcement drift pattern. The horizontal axis marks time measured in weeks relative to an earnings announcement, and the vertical axis measures the cumulative abnormal return from 52 weeks prior to the earnings announcement to 52 weeks after the announcement. The earnings announcement occurs at week 0. Two types of companies are tracked in the figure—companies that announce better-than-expected earnings and companies that announce worse-than-expected earnings. The blue line in the figure plots cumulative abnormal returns (i.e., the abnormal return over the entire period) earned by the sample of "good news" stocks, and the red line tracks abnormal returns for the "bad news" stocks. Notice that when firms announce good news, their stock prices react quickly, as indicated by the jump in the blue line at week 0. Similarly, when firms reveal that their earnings are below investors' expectations, their stock prices move down almost immediately, as shown by the drop in the red line at week 0. That rapid initial reaction is exactly the pattern that an efficient market should produce.

However, it appears that investors underreact to the news contained in earnings announcements. Observe that after the initial reaction to the earnings announcement,

FIGURE 9.4

Post Earnings Announcement Drift

When firms announce better-than-expected earnings, their stock prices jump quickly, as the EMH would predict, but contrary to the EMH, stock prices continue to drift upward at an abnormally rapid clip over the next year or so. The same thing happens in reverse when firms announce poor earnings.

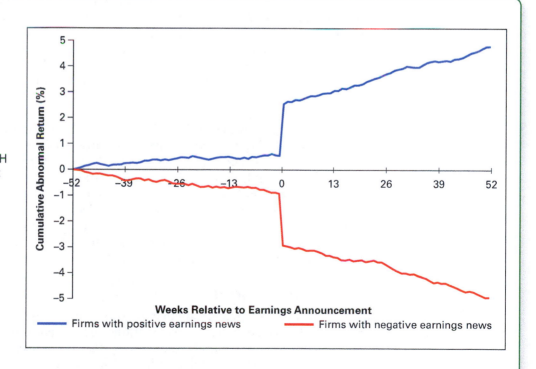

both the blue and red lines exhibit trends, with the blue line slowly rising and the red line slowly falling. This means that the initial reaction to the earnings announcement was not large enough, and stock prices are adjusting slowly to the information contained in the earnings announcement. The slow adjustment process creates an opportunity for investors. For example, after a company announces positive earnings news (i.e., investors do not have to anticipate what the content of the announcement will be), investors who buy the stock earn significant abnormal returns. Looking at the blue line in Figure 9.4, you can see that the amount of drift is roughly 2% over the 52 weeks following the earnings announcement. In other words, Figure 9.4 suggests that investors who closely monitor earnings announcements and buy stocks after firms announce better-than-expected returns will earn a return that is about 2% above normal (i.e., 2% greater than one would expect given the risk of the stocks being purchased). Investors can also make money by short selling the shares of companies that announce poor earnings results. The drift in stock prices following the earnings announcement is not consistent with the predictions of the EMH.

A slight variation on this story is known as the momentum anomaly. In physics, *momentum* refers to the tendency of an object in motion to continue moving or the tendency of an object at rest to remain at rest. Applied to stocks, momentum refers to the tendency for stocks that have gone up recently to keep going up or the tendency for stocks that have gone down recently to continue going down. The connection to earnings announcement drift is easy to see. When a company has a particularly good quarter, it is common for some of the good news to leak out into the market before the official earnings announcement. So leading up to the earnings release, it is common to see the stock price moving up, just as the blue line in Figure 9.4 rises ahead of the earnings news. As we've already discussed, when the firm releases the news that it has had a very strong quarter, the price goes up more, but then it continues to drift up for weeks. Taking the entire pattern into account, we observe that before a company releases very good earnings news, its stock price has gone up, and then it keeps going up after the earnings announcement. Hence, these stocks display positive momentum. The same thing happens in reverse for companies that have particularly bad quarters. Some of the bad news leaks out early, and the stock goes down (see the red line in Figure 9.4), but then the stock continues to go down after the announcement.

The Value Effect According to the *value effect*, the best way to make money in the market is to buy stocks that have relatively low prices relative to some measure of fundamental value such as book value or earnings. An investor following a value strategy might calculate the P/E ratio or the ratio of market value to book value for many stocks, and then buy the stocks with the lowest ratios (and perhaps short sell the stocks with high P/E or market-to-book ratios). Studies have shown that, on average, value stocks outperform stocks with high P/E or market-to-book ratios (so-called growth stocks). This pattern has repeated itself decade after decade in the United States and in most stock markets around the world.

Possible Explanations

Each new discovery of an anomaly that appears to violate the EMH prompts a flurry of research that offers rational explanations for the pattern observed. The most common explanation for market anomalies is that the stocks that earn abnormally high returns are simply riskier than other stocks, so the higher returns reflect a risk premium rather than mispricing by the market. For example, most academics and practitioners would agree that small firms are riskier than large firms, so it is not surprising that small stocks earn higher returns. The real question is, how much riskier are small firms, and how large should the risk premium be on those securities? According to the CAPM, if a small stock has a beta of 2.0 and a large stock has a beta of 1.0, the small stock should earn roughly twice the risk premium (over Treasury bills) that the large stock earns. The reason that the small-firm effect is known as an anomaly is that small stocks seem to earn higher returns than their betas can justify. Believers in the EMH argue that beta is an imperfect measure of risk and that if a better risk measure were available, the difference in returns between small and large stocks could be fully attributed to differences in risk.

Another explanation for market anomalies is that even in an efficient market where prices move essentially at random, some trading rules may appear to earn abnormally high returns simply as a matter of chance. For example, one of the more amusing market anomalies is known as the Super Bowl anomaly. This anomaly says that if the team winning the Super Bowl in a particular year is one of the original National Football League teams (prior to the merger with the old American Football League), then the stock market will rise. Otherwise, the stock market will fall. This "trading rule" correctly predicted the direction of the market more than 80% of the time in the last 48 years. But should investors rely on it in the future? Most people would agree that the connection between the Super Bowl winner and the stock market is purely a matter of chance and is unlikely to exhibit a similar track record in the next 48 years. Some EMH advocates believe that most market anomalies are similarly just an artifact of random chance. However, this explanation is less persuasive in the face of evidence that anomalies such as the small-firm effect, momentum, and the value effect appear in most markets around the world.

The discovery of these and other anomalies led to the development of an entirely new way of viewing the workings of financial markets that has come to be known as **behavioral finance**. In contrast to traditional finance, which starts with the assumption that investors, managers, and other actors in financial markets are rational, behavioral finance posits that market participants make systematic mistakes and that those mistakes are inextricably linked to cognitive biases that are hard-wired into human nature. We now turn to a discussion of the basic tenets of behavioral finance and how they may help explain market anomalies.

CONCEPTS IN REVIEW

Answers available at
http://www.pearsonhighered.com/smart

9.1 What is the random walk hypothesis, and how does it apply to stocks? What is an efficient market? How can a market be efficient if its prices behave in a random fashion?

9.2 Explain why it is difficult, if not impossible, to consistently outperform an efficient market.

a. Does this mean that high rates of return are not available in the stock market?
b. How can an investor earn a high rate of return in an efficient market?

9.3 What are market anomalies and how do they come about? Do they support or refute the EMH? Briefly describe each of the following:

a. The January effect
b. The size effect
c. The value effect

Behavioral Finance: A Challenge to the Efficient Markets Hypothesis

LG3 **LG4** For more than 40 years, the efficient markets hypothesis has been an influential force in financial markets. The notion that asset prices fully reflect all available information is supported by a large body of academic research. In practitioner circles, supporters of market efficiency include John Bogle of Vanguard, who helped pioneer the development of a special type of mutual fund known as an index fund. Managers of index funds don't try to pick individual stocks or bonds because they assume that the market is efficient. They recognize that any time and energy spent researching individual securities will merely serve to increase the fund's expenses, which will drag down investors' returns.

Although considerable evidence supports the concept of market efficiency, an increasing number of academic studies have begun to cast doubt on the EMH. This research documents various anomalies and draws from research on cognitive psychology to offer explanations for the anomalies. One notable event that acknowledged the importance of this field was the awarding of the 2002 Nobel Prize in economics to Daniel Kahneman, whose work integrated insights from psychology and economics. In addition to academic studies, some professional money managers are also incorporating concepts from behavioral finance into their construction and management of portfolios.

INVESTOR FACTS

Behavioral Funds Underperform Too A recent study tracked the performance of 22 U.S. mutual funds that claimed to use the findings from behavioral finance to guide their stock selections. From 2007 to 2013, these funds as a group performed slightly worse than average, generating negative abnormal returns of less than 0.20% per month.

(Source: Nikolaos Philippas, "Did Behavioral Funds Exploit Market Inefficiencies during or after the Financial Crisis?" *Multinational Finance Journal* 2014, Vol. 18, Iss.1/2, pp. 85–138.)

Investor Behavior and Security Prices

Researchers in behavioral finance believe that investors' decisions are affected by a number of psychological biases that lead investors to make systematic, predictable mistakes in certain decision-making situations. These mistakes, in turn, may lead to predictable patterns in stock prices that create opportunities for other investors to earn abnormally high profits without accepting abnormally high risk. Let's now take a look at some of the behavioral factors that might influence the actions of investors.

Overconfidence and Self-Attribution Bias Research in psychology provides overwhelming evidence that, on average, people tend to exhibit **overconfidence**, putting too much faith in their own ability to perform complex tasks. Try this experiment. The next time you are in a large group, ask people to indicate whether they believe they have above average, average, or below average skill in driving a car. What you will probably find is that a majority of the group believes that they have above-average ability, and almost no one will lay claim to having below-average skill. But simply by the definition of average, some people have to be above average and some must be below average. Therefore, at least some people in the group are overconfident in their driving ability.

Closely linked to overconfidence is a phenomenon known as self-attribution bias. **Self-attribution bias** roughly means that when something good happens, individuals attribute that outcome to actions that they have taken, but when something bad happens, they attribute it to bad luck or external factors beyond their control. The connection to overconfidence is straightforward. An individual takes an action or makes a decision that leads to a favorable outcome. Self-attribution bias causes the individual to discount the role that chance may have played in determining the outcome and to put too much emphasis on his or her actions as the cause. This causes the individual to become overconfident.

What effects do overconfidence and self-attribution bias have in the investments realm? Consider an individual investor, or even a professional money manager, who analyzes stocks to determine which ones are overvalued and which are bargains. Suppose in a particular year the investor's portfolio earns very high returns. Perhaps the high returns are largely due to a booming stock market, but perhaps in addition the investor's stock picks performed even better than the overall market. Is this the result of good fortune or good analysis? It's not easy to separate the roles of skill and luck, but most investors would probably attribute the favorable outcome to their own investing prowess. What is the consequence if investors mistakenly attribute investment success to their own skill? One study found that investors whose portfolios had outperformed the market in the past subsequently increased their trading activity. After beating the overall market average by 2% per year for several years, these investors increased their trading activity more than 70%. The increase in trading led to much higher transactions costs and much lower returns. The same group of investors trailed the market by 3% per year after increasing their trading activity.

This tendency is not confined to individual investors. A recent study found that CEOs exhibit similar behavior when they undertake acquisitions of other firms. When a CEO acquires a firm and the acquisition target performs well, the CEO is more likely to acquire a second firm. The CEO is also more likely to buy more shares in his or her employer's stock prior to the next acquisition. But these second acquisitions actually destroy shareholder value on average. In other words, it appears that CEOs become overconfident regarding their ability to acquire other firms and run them profitably.

Loss Aversion Here's an interesting series of questions. Suppose you have just won $8,500 in a game of chance. You can walk away with your winnings or you can risk them. If you take the risk, there is a 90% chance that you will win an additional $1,500, but there is a 10% chance that you will lose everything. Would you walk away or gamble? Most people who are asked this question say that they would take the $8,500—the sure thing. They say this even though the expected value from the additional gamble is $500. That is,

Expected value = (Probability of gain) × (Amount of gain) − (Probability of loss)

$$\times (\text{Amount of loss}) = 0.90 \times \$1,500 - 0.10 \times \$8,500 = \underline{\$500}$$

In this case, the decision to take the $8,500 indicates that the individual making that choice is risk averse. The risk of losing $8,500 isn't worth the expected $500 gain.

However, if we reframe the question, most people respond differently. Suppose you have already lost $8,500 in a game of chance. You can walk away and cut your losses or you can gamble again. If you gamble, there is a 90% chance that you will lose $1,500 more, but there is a 10% chance that you will win $8,500, thus entirely reversing your initial loss. When confronted with this choice, most people say that they will take the risk to try to "get even," even though the expected value of this gamble is −$500.

$$\text{Expected value} = 0.10 \times \$8,500 - 0.90 \times \$1,500 = \underline{-\$500}$$

In this case, people are exhibiting risk-seeking behavior. They are accepting a risk that they do not have to take, and it is a risk that has a negative expected return.

FAMOUS FAILURES IN FINANCE

Loss Aversion and Trading Volume

When people are loss averse, they are reluctant to sell investments that have lost value because doing so forces them to realize the loss. But if investors are reluctant to sell when prices are falling, trading activity can dry up. That was a finding from a study of residential real estate activity over several market cycles in Boston. Researchers found that when market prices were rising, homeowners were generally willing to sell their properties at market value. But when price declines left homeowners in a position such that the market

value of their home was less than what they had paid for it, homeowners exhibited a tendency to set asking prices above the true market value. For these homeowners, selling at the current market price would mean recognizing a loss, something homeowners were very averse to do. As a consequence, overpriced homes sat on the market month after month, with very few transactions taking place.

(Source: David Genesove and Christopher Mayer, "Loss Aversion and Seller Behavior: Evidence from the Housing Market," *Quarterly Journal of Economics*, 2001, Vol. 116, No. 4, pp. 1233–1260.)

In behavioral finance, the tendency to exhibit risk-averse behavior when confronting gains and risk-seeking behavior when confronting losses is called **loss aversion**. Loss aversion simply means that people feel the pain of loss more acutely than the pleasure of gain. In an investments context, loss aversion can lead people to hold onto investments that have lost money longer than they should. In fact, numerous studies have documented that when investors want to sell a stock in their portfolio, they are much more likely to sell a stock that has gone up in value than one that has fallen. Other studies have documented a tendency for the stocks that investors sell (i.e., stocks that have gone up) to perform better than the stocks that they choose to hold (i.e., stocks that have lost value).

Representativeness

Overreaction In an interesting experiment, six people were asked to flip a coin 20 times and count the number of heads that came up. Six others were asked to imagine flipping a coin 20 times and write down the sequence of heads and tails that might occur. The table below shows the results reported by each group.

Group	Subject	Number of Heads	Group	Subject	Number of Heads
A	1	10	B	1	6
	2	10		2	13
	3	8		3	7
	4	10		4	11
	5	10		5	8
	6	10		6	14
	Average	9.7		Average	9.8

Looking at the responses from individuals in each group, which group do you think actually flipped coins, and which imagined doing so?

The answer is that Group A only imagined flipping coins. Notice that almost everyone in the group said they expected to obtain 10 heads in 20 flips, but in the group that actually tossed the coins, the number of heads varied widely, from 6 to 14. What accounts for the differences between the two groups?

Representativeness refers to cognitive biases that occur because people have difficulty thinking about randomness in outcomes. Subjects in Group A assume (correctly) that the probability of obtaining a heads on any single flip of a coin is 50%, but they also assume (incorrectly) that this means that in 20 flips of a coin, it is very likely that heads will come up exactly 10 times. It is true that 10 is the average number of heads that one should expect, and notice that the average number of heads flipped by both groups was about 10. However, individual results vary quite a bit around that average. As the results of Group B's coin flips clearly show, it is rather unusual to obtain exactly 10 heads in 20 flips. Lots of other outcomes are quite likely.

Consider this analogy. Suppose picking stocks is like flipping coins in the sense that if markets are efficient, when you buy a stock there is about a 50% chance that it will do better than average (let's call that outcome heads) and a 50% chance that it will do worse than average (call that tails). Investors in Group A would appear to believe that if one buys 20 stocks, it is very likely that the outcome of that portfolio will be average because 10 stocks will do better than average and 10 will perform worse than average. However, we know from Group B that it is quite likely that a portfolio of 20 stocks could perform much better (more than 10 heads) or much worse (fewer than 10 heads) than average. In other words, even in an efficient market, some portfolios will do very well while others will lag behind.

Subjects in this experiment were also asked to report whether they obtained a "string" of five heads or five tails in a row in the course of flipping a coin 20 times. Here are their answers to that question.

Group	Subject	Five Heads or Tails in a Row?	Group	Subject	Five Heads or Tails in a Row
A	1	no	B	1	yes
	2	no		2	yes
	3	no		3	no
	4	no		4	yes
	5	no		5	no
	6	no		6	yes

Notice that among the subjects in Group B, those who actually flipped coins 20 times, obtaining a string of five flips in a row with the same outcome (either five heads or five tails in a row) was relatively common. But subjects in Group A did not imagine that they would see a string of five consecutive identical outcomes. Why not? These subjects know that there is a 50% chance of getting heads (or tails) in every flip, so they imagine that on a series of flips they will see a kind of oscillation in outcomes. That is, they appear to believe that a sequence of alternating heads and tails is more likely than a sequence that has several heads (or tails) in a row. This is representativeness at work again. Subjects in Group A dramatically underestimate the likelihood of getting the coin to come up heads or tails several times in a row because they think a 50-50 gamble is much more likely to result in alternating heads and tails.

Now consider how this feature of representativeness can influence the behavior of investors. Think about investors who are trying to decide which mutual fund to invest in. The EMH says that for a mutual fund to earn an above-average return is more a matter of luck than of skill, so any particular fund manager has roughly a

50% chance of beating the market in a particular year. There are thousands of mutual funds to choose from, so even if mutual fund performance is as much due to luck as it is to skill, there will be some fund managers who "beat the market" several years in a row, just as there were several coin flippers in Group B who flipped five heads in a row. However, if investors misinterpret randomness like the subjects in Group A did, they will believe that it is very unlikely for a fund manager to have a string of several good years in a row if the market is efficient. Put another way, these investors will interpret a string of good years as a sign that the market is not efficient, at least not for the fund manager achieving that string of good performance. Therefore, when investors see a manager who has delivered better-than-average returns for several years in a row, they may mistakenly attribute that record to skill. Research shows that investors overreact to a string of good performance and pour money into successful funds, enriching the fund managers but not necessarily themselves. Apparently, many investors see a string of good performance and overestimate the likelihood that the trend will continue. Investors overreact to the past performance of funds, even though there is little objective evidence that past performance is a good predictor of future success.

This logic may provide a behavioral explanation for the value phenomenon cited earlier. Recall that value stocks are stocks that have low prices relative to earnings or book value. These stocks generally display rather poor past performance—several years of declining prices is what puts these stocks in the value category. Similarly,

growth stocks, stocks with high prices relative to earnings or book value, generally have very good past performance. One of the earliest studies of the value effect studied the results of a very simple trading rule. Each year, researchers sorted all stocks based on their cumulative performance in the previous three years. The trading rule was to buy the stocks that had performed worst (the value stocks) and sell short the stocks that had performed best (the growth stocks). Researchers discovered that this strategy earned returns that beat the market by 8% per year! Why would such a simple trading rule that anyone could follow work so well?

The researchers argued that it was due to representativeness. To be specific, they proposed that investors who watched particular stocks decline in value for three years in a row overreacted to those events by deciding that the trend would continue indefinitely, so they bid the prices of these stocks below their true values. Similarly, after watching other stocks do very well several years in a row, investors overreacted to that trend by naively assuming that this excellent performance would continue, and they bid up the prices of these stocks above their true values. Over time, the firms that had been performing poorly surprised investors by rebounding, and the firms that had been earning spectacular returns failed to sustain that performance. As a result, past price trends reversed themselves, and value investors made money.

Individual investors are not the only participants in markets likely to be affected by representativeness. Consider a firm that is looking to make an acquisition. What makes an acquisition target attractive? One criterion might be recent increases in sales and earnings. Would acquirers be wise to pay a premium to acquire a firm that has been growing faster than its competitors in recent years? The research evidence says no. There is almost no correlation between how fast firms have grown in the past and how fast they will grow in the future. In fact, that is a fundamental prediction of basic economic theory. When one firm enjoys great success in a particular market, other firms will enter the industry. Competition makes it more difficult for firms to sustain the high growth that

FAMOUS FAILURES IN FINANCE

Buying High and Selling Low

Research by the Federal Reserve and the University of Michigan suggests that individual investors, particularly those with lower incomes and wealth, displayed particularly poor timing with their investment decisions before, during, and after the sharp market downturn in 2008. Data from the Fed's triennial Survey of Consumer Finance shows that as the stock market rose from 2004 to 2007, the percentage of lower-income households who owned stocks climbed. However, from 2007 to 2010, a period containing a steep drop in stock values, the percentage of households owning stocks dropped, and that drop was steepest among households with lower incomes and wealth. The percentage of lower-income households owning stocks continued to fall from 2010 to 2013, while the stock market boomed. In contrast, the percentage of households with higher incomes and greater wealth who owned stocks rose from 2010 to 2013. In other words, the rich got richer, in part because the slump in stocks in 2008 did not deter them from continuing to invest in the market. Less wealthy households bought stocks when market values were high, sold them when the market crashed, and failed to benefit from the subsequent stock market recovery.

(Source: Josh Zumbrun, "Bad Stock-Market Timing Fueled Wealth Disparity," http://www.wsj.com/articles/bad-stock-market-timing-fueled-wealth-disparity-1414355341, accessed 6/26/2015.)

---

attracted new entrants in the first place. Yet there is ample evidence that managers do pay a larger premium when they acquire firms that experienced rapid growth prior to the acquisition, even though the prospect of sustaining the growth is low.

Underreaction   In certain instances, representativeness can cause investors to underreact to new information. Consider this problem from statistics. On a table are 100 sacks, each of which contains 1,000 poker chips. Forty-five of these sacks contain 70% black chips and 30% red chips. The other 55 bags hold 70% red chips and 30% black chips. If you pick one bag at random, what is the likelihood that it will contain mostly black chips?

Most people get this answer right. If 45 out of 100 bags contain mostly black chips, then the probability of picking a bag at random that has mostly black chips is 45%. Here is a much harder problem. Suppose you choose one bag at random and then take out 12 chips, without looking at the others. Of the 12 chips that you pull out, 8 are black and 4 are red. What is the probability that the bag you picked contains mostly black chips?

Intuitively, people know that if the sample of 12 chips taken from the bag has a majority of black chips, then that means the probability that the bag has mostly black chips is higher than in the first problem where we select a bag at random and learn nothing more about it. But how much higher? Few people come close to guessing that the probability is over 95%! In other words, people tend to underreact to the new information they obtain in the second version of the question.

Let's make an analogy between drawing poker chips out of a bag and reading firms' earnings announcements. Earnings announcements contain a mix of good and bad news that varies over time. When a company announces particularly good (or bad) news, representativeness may cause investors to underreact to the new information. That is, investors may not appreciate that very good earnings news this quarter probably means the likelihood of good news next quarter has gone up (and vice versa for bad news this quarter). When the firm announces the next quarter's earnings, investors are surprised by how positive the news is, and the firm's stock price goes up again. That could explain the post earnings announcement drift (or momentum) phenomenon discussed earlier.

WATCH YOUR BEHAVIOR

Who Underreacts to News?   A recent study found that it is primarily individual investors who underreact to information such as earnings announcements. For example, after firms release good earnings news, individuals tend to sell their shares too quickly before prices have risen high enough to incorporate the new information. Who's buying these shares from individuals? Professional investors like mutual fund managers.

A careful reader may object that we have asserted that representativeness can lead to both overreaction (in the case of value stocks) and underreaction (in the case of momentum). Keep in mind that there are important differences in the nature of the information that investors are reacting to in each case. In the value phenomenon, investors see a common string of information—several good years or several bad years in a row. This causes them to discount the role of chance in the outcome and *overreact to the series of events*. In the case of earnings announcement drift, investors are responding to a single new piece of information that is extreme—particularly good or particularly bad. In that case, representativeness may lead investors to *underreact to the new information* they've received.

Narrow Framing Many people tend to analyze a situation in isolation, while ignoring the larger context. This behavior is called **narrow framing**. A common example in investments relates to the asset allocation decisions that investors make in their retirement plans. The table below summarizes the retirement savings plans offered to employees of two firms. Firm A offers its employees two options for investing retirement savings—a stock fund and a bond fund. Firm B also offer two options—a stock fund and a blended fund that holds 50% stocks and 50% bonds.

Fund Offered	Company A	Company B
Stock fund (100% stocks)	Yes	Yes
Bond fund (100% bonds)	Yes	Not available
Blended fund (50% stocks, 50% bonds)	Not available	Yes

Research shows that many investors view this decision through the narrow frame of two choices, and they follow a simple guideline—put 50% into one fund and 50% into the other. It is as if investors know that they should diversify, so they divide their investments equally between the available options. However, investors seemingly fail to recognize how the asset allocation of the individual funds influences the resulting composition of their overall portfolios. The narrow frame (splitting money evenly between two funds) combined with the options offered by each company produces an odd outcome. Employees of Company A who divide their money between the stock fund and the bond fund will wind up with portfolios containing 50% stocks and 50% bonds. Employees of Company B also divide their money equally between the two funds, but in this case the two funds are the stock fund and the blended fund. Splitting money equally between those options results in an overall portfolio allocation of 75% stocks and 25% bonds. The retirement portfolios held by employees of Company B are much riskier than those held by workers at Company A, but not necessarily because Company B's employees prefer to take more risk. Instead, framing influences the risk of their portfolios.

Belief Perseverance People typically ignore information that conflicts with their existing beliefs, a phenomenon called **belief perseverance**. If they believe a stock is good and purchase it, for example, they later tend to discount any signs of trouble. In many cases, they even avoid gathering new information for fear it will contradict their initial opinion. It would be better to view each stock owned as a "new" stock when periodically reviewing a portfolio and to ask whether the information available at that time would cause you to buy or sell the stock.

Anchoring Anchoring refers to a phenomenon in which individuals attempting to predict or estimate some unknown quantity place too much weight on information that they have at hand, even when that information is not particularly relevant. For example, it is reasonably well known that a firm's past rate of growth in revenues is a very poor predictor of its future growth rate. Even so, when individuals are ask to predict the sales growth rate for a firm, if they are given information about the firm's past growth rate, that information appears to influence their projections. Specifically, individuals tend to predict faster (slower) sales growth when they know that a firm's past growth rate has been high (low).

A key component of the capital asset pricing model is the expected return on the market. To use the CAPM, an investor must form an expectation for the market's future return. How do investors estimate future returns? It appears in part that they anchor on the market's recent past returns. More specifically, surveys of investors reveal that when the previous year's stock market return was high, investor's expect a higher return in the subsequent year compared to cases in which the previous market return was low. In fact, high past returns are generally not a reliable signal for high future returns, so when investors based their forecast on recent past returns (i.e., when they anchor on last year's market return), they were overestimating the market's return, and that in turn would lead them to overestimate returns on specific stocks via the CAPM.

Familiarity Bias In this text we have discussed a number of analytical methods that investors can use to decide whether they want to purchase a particular investment. It turns out that in many cases people simply invest in things that are familiar to them, a behavior called **familiarity bias**. Research has shown that investors tend to invest in stocks located close to their homes. Even professional investors are not immune to this bias. A recent study found that mutual fund managers tend to invest more heavily in stocks located in their home states.

Investing something familiar is not necessarily a bad thing. Perhaps being more familiar with a company helps investors determine whether that company's stock is a good buy. However, if familiarity helps give investors an information edge, then investors should earn higher returns on the investments that they make based on familiarity (e.g., investments in companies located nearby). Even among professional investors, the evidence on this question is mixed. One study found that mutual fund managers earned unusually high returns on their investments in nearby firms, but other studies found that investing in companies based on familiarity influenced fund managers to form portfolios that were not fully diversified. As a result, those funds did not earn higher returns, but they did experience higher risk.

Investing heavily in familiar stocks does have one serious potential drawback. Industries are often concentrated in specific geographic areas. Think of the concentration of high-tech firms in Silicon Valley, for example. If investors in northern California invest mostly in companies from that region, they will form portfolios that are heavily weighted in tech firms, neglecting other sectors of the economy. Thus, familiarity bias may lead investors to hold underdiversified portfolios. Investors who do not take full advantage of diversification opportunities bear more risk than they need to without necessarily earning higher returns.

Implications of Behavioral Finance for Security Analysis

Our discussion of the psychological factors that affect financial decisions suggests that behavioral finance can play an important role in investing. Naturally, the debate on the efficiency of markets rages on and will continue to do so for many years. The

TABLE 9.1   USING BEHAVIORAL FINANCE TO IMPROVE INVESTMENT RESULTS

Studies have documented a number of behavioral factors that appear to influence investors' decisions and adversely affect their returns. By following some simple guidelines, you can avoid making mistakes and improve your portfolio's performance. A little common sense goes a long way in the financial markets!

- **Don't hesitate to sell a losing stock.** If you buy a stock at $20 and its price drops to $10, ask yourself whether you would buy that same stock if you came into the market today with $10 in cash. If the answer is yes, then hang onto it. If not, sell the stock and buy something else.
- **Don't chase performance.** The evidence suggests that past performance is at best a very noisy guide to future performance. For example, the best performing mutual funds in the last year or even the last five years are not especially likely to perform best in subsequent years. Don't buy last year's hottest mutual fund based solely on its performance. Always keep your personal investment objectives and constraints in mind.
- **Be humble and open-minded.** Many investment professionals, some of whom are extremely well paid, are frequently wrong in their predictions. Admit your mistakes and don't be afraid to take corrective action. The fact is, reviewing your mistakes can be a very rewarding exercise—all investors make mistakes, but the smart ones learn from them. Winning in the market is often about not losing, and one way to avoid loss is to learn from your mistakes.
- **Review the performance of your investments on a periodic basis.** Remember the old saying, "Out of sight, out of mind." Don't be afraid to face the music and to make changes as your situation changes. Nothing runs on "autopilot" forever—including investment portfolios.
- **Don't trade too much.** Investment returns are uncertain, but transaction costs are guaranteed. Considerable evidence indicates that investors who trade frequently perform poorly.

contribution of behavioral finance is to identify psychological factors that can lead investors to make systematic mistakes and to determine whether those mistakes may contribute to predictable patterns in stock prices. If that's the case, the mistakes of some investors may be the profit opportunities for others. See Table 9.1 for our advice on how to keep your own mistakes to a minimum.

CONCEPTS IN REVIEW

Answers available at
http://www.pearsonhighered.com/smart

9.4 How can behavioral finance have any bearing on investor returns? Do supporters of behavioral finance believe in efficient markets? Explain.

9.5 Briefly explain how behavioral finance can affect each of the following:

a. The trading activity of investors
b. The tendency of value stocks to outperform growth stocks
a. The tendency of stock prices to drift up (down) after unusually good (bad) earnings news

Technical Analysis

LG5 LG6 In the first section of this chapter we introduced the idea of market efficiency and suggested that there are many good reasons to believe that stock prices (and prices in other financial markets) are inherently unpredictable. The second section presented the behavioral finance challenge to market efficiency and discussed the evidence that there is at least some predictability in stock returns. In this section we introduce **technical analysis**, which is the practice of searching the historical record of stock prices and returns for patterns. If these patterns repeat, investors who know about them and can spot them early may have an opportunity to earn better-than-average returns.

Because it focuses on using past price movements to predict future returns, technical analysis is fundamentally at odds with even the weak form of market efficiency. For this reason, the practice of technical analysis remains controversial. For some investors, it's another piece of information to use when deciding whether to buy, hold, or sell a stock. For others, it's the only input they use in their investment decisions. Still others regard technical analysis as a waste of time.

Analyzing market behavior dates back to the 1800s, when there was no such thing as industry or company analysis. Detailed financial information about individual companies simply was not made available to stockholders, let alone the general public. About the only thing investors could study was the market itself. Some investors used detailed charts to monitor what large market operators were doing. These charts were intended to show when major buyers were moving into or out of particular stocks and to provide information useful for profitable buy-and-sell decisions. The charts centered on stock price movements. These movements were said to produce certain "formations," indicating when the time was right to buy or sell a particular stock. The same principle is still applied today. Technical analysts argue that internal market factors, such as trading volume and price movements, often reveal the market's future direction long before it is evident in financial statistics.

Measuring the Market

If using technical analysis to assess the overall market is a worthwhile endeavor, then we need some sort of tool or measure to do it. Charts are popular with many investors because they provide a visual summary of the behavior of the market and the price movements of individual stocks. As an alternative or supplement to charting, some investors prefer to study various market statistics. They might look at trends in market indexes or track other aspects of market behavior such as trading volume, short selling, or trading behavior of small investors (e.g., odd-lot transactions).

Technical analysis addresses those factors in the marketplace that can (or may) have an effect on the price movements of stocks in general. The idea is to understand the general condition (or "tone") of the market and to gain some insights into where the market may be headed over the next few months. Several approaches try to do just that, and we summarize some of the more common approaches below.

The Confidence Index One measure that attempts to capture the tone of the market is the **confidence index,** which deals not with the stock market but with bond returns. Computed and published by *Barron's*, the confidence index is a ratio that reflects the spread between the average yield on high-grade corporate bonds relative to the yield on average- or intermediate-grade corporate bonds. Technically, the index is computed by relating the average yield on 10 high-grade corporate bonds to the yield on 10 intermediate-grade bonds. The formula is as follows:

Equation 9.3

$$\frac{\text{Confidence}}{\text{index}} = \frac{\text{Average yield on 10 high-grade corporate bonds}}{\text{Average yield on 10 intermediate-grade bonds}}$$

Thus, the index measures the yield spread between high-grade bonds and intermediate-grade bonds. Because the yield on high-grade bonds should always be lower than the average yield on a sample of intermediate-grade bonds, the confidence index should never exceed 1.0. Indeed, as the measure approaches 1.0 (or 100%), the spread between the two sets of bonds will get smaller and smaller, which, according to the theory, is a positive sign. The idea is that as investors become more confident about the economy, they will be willing to invest in riskier bonds, driving down their yields and pushing up the confidence index. Those who follow the confidence index interpret a rise in the index as a positive sign for future stock returns.

Consider, for example, a point in time where high-grade bonds are yielding 4.50%, while intermediate-grade bonds, on average, are yielding 5.15%. This would amount to a yield spread of 65 "basis points," or 65/100 of 1% (i.e., 5.15% − 4.50% = 0.65%), and a confidence index of 4.50 ÷ 5.15 = 87.38%. Now, look what happens when yields (and yield spreads) fall or rise:

	Yields (Yield Spreads)	
	Fall	Rise
Yields on high-grade bonds	4.25%	5.25%
Yields on average bonds	4.50%	6.35%
Yield spread	0.25%	1.10%
Confidence index	94.44%	82.68%

Lower-yield spreads, in effect, lead to higher confidence indexes. These, in turn, indicate that investors are demanding a lower premium in yield for the lower-rated (riskier) bonds and in so doing are showing more confidence in the economy. This theory implies that the trend of "smart money" is usually revealed in the bond market before it shows up in the stock market, meaning that a rise in the confidence index today foreshadows a rise in the stock market.

Market Volume Market volume is an obvious reflection of the amount of investor interest in stocks. As a rule, technical analysts who follow market volume say that increasing volume during a rising market is a positive sign that the upward movement in stocks will continue. On the other hand, when stocks are falling, a decline in volume may suggest that the decline in stock prices is approaching an end. In a similar vein, when stocks have been moving up and volume begins to drop off, that may signal the end of the bull market. Numerous financial periodicals and websites report total market volume daily, so it is an easy statistic to track.

Breadth of the Market Each trading day, some stocks go up in price and others go down. In market terminology, some stocks advance and others decline. Breadth of the market deals with these advances and declines. The principle behind this indicator is that the number of advances and declines reflects the underlying sentiment of investors.

Analysts who use market breadth to help guide their investment decisions interpret the numbers as follows. As long as the number of stocks that advance in price on a given day exceeds the number that decline, the market is strong. The extent of that strength depends on the spread between the number of advances and declines. For example, if the spread narrows (the number of declines starts to approach the number of advances), market strength deteriorates. Similarly, the market is weak when the number of declines repeatedly exceeds the number of advances. When the mood is optimistic, advances outnumber declines. Again, data on advances and declines

WATCH YOUR BEHAVIOR

Plane Crashes and Sentiment
Investor sentiment is a tricky thing to define, and it's even harder to quantify. One study looked at how major airline disasters affected investor sentiment and stock returns. The author of the study found that the average one-day return on the U.S. stock market is about 4 basis points (0.04%), but the average return on a day with a major airline disaster was negative 32 basis points (−0.32%). That one-day dip represented an aggregate market value loss of $60 billion per airline disaster, but over the next two weeks as sentiment returned to normal, the market recovered most of its losses.

(Source: Guy Kaplanski, "Sentiment and Stock Prices: The Case of Aviation Disasters," *Journal of Financial Economics*, 2010, Vol. 95, pp. 174–201.)

FIGURE 9.5

Basic Market Statistics

Here is an example of the kind of information on market volume, advances, and declines that is easily accessible on the web. (Source: **http://finance.yahoo.com/advances**, accessed August 12, 2015.)

Advances & Declines	NYSE	AMEX	NASDAQ	BB
Advancing Issues	922 (28%)	448 (30%)	781 (27%)	100 (37%)
Declining Issues	2,216 (68%)	976 (66%)	1,997 (70%)	112 (42%)
Unchanged Issues	121 (4%)	65 (4%)	91 (3%)	57 (21%)
Total Issues	**3,259**	**1,489**	**2,869**	**269**
New Highs	**76**	**17**	**132**	**11**
New Lows	**39**	**25**	**41**	**25**
Up Volume	645,655,898 (21%)	204,871,316 (40%)	435,985,588 (27%)	322,898,146 (66%)
Down Volume	2,342,076,687 (77%)	290,403,641 (57%)	1,162,111,459 (72%)	130,996,046 (27%)
Unchanged Volume	68,657,120 (2%)	11,132,061 (2%)	19,031,533 (1%)	38,445,283 (8%)
Total Volume	**3,056,389,705**[1]	**506,407,018**[1]	**1,617,128,580**[1]	**492,339,475**[1]

[1]Volume totals include pre-market and regional exchanges. Advancers & Decliners calculations are delayed 15 minutes.

are widely available. Figure 9.5 illustrates data on market volume, advances, and declines taken from Yahoo! Finance.

Short Interest When investors anticipate a market decline, they sometimes sell a stock short. That is, they sell borrowed stock. The number of shares of stocks sold short in the market at any point in time is known as the **short interest**. The more stocks that are sold short, the higher the short interest. Because all short sales must eventually be "covered" (the borrowed shares must be returned), a short sale in effect ensures future demand for the stock. Thus, the market is viewed optimistically when the level of short interest becomes relatively high by historical standards. The logic is that as shares are bought back to cover outstanding short sales, the additional demand will push stock prices up. The amount of short interest on the NYSE, the Amex, and Nasdaq's National Market is published in the *Wall Street Journal*, *Barron's*, and other sources.

Keeping track of the level of short interest can indicate future market demand, but it can also reveal present market optimism or pessimism. Knowledgeable investors usually do short selling, and a significant buildup or decline in the level of short interest hints at the sentiment of sophisticated investors about the current state of the market or a company. For example, a significant shift upward in short interest might indicate pessimism concerning the current state of the market, even though it may signal optimism with regard to future levels of demand.

Odd-Lot Trading A rather cynical saying on Wall Street suggests that the best thing to do is just the opposite of whatever the small investor is doing. The reasoning behind this is that as a group, small investors exhibit notoriously bad timing. The investing public usually does not come into the market in force until after a bull market has pretty much run its course, and it does not get out until late in a bear market. Although its validity is debatable, this is the premise behind a widely followed technical indicator and is the basis for the **theory of contrary opinion**. This theory uses the amount and type of odd-lot trading as an indicator of the current state of the market and pending changes.

Because many individual investors deal in transactions of fewer than 100 shares, their combined sentiments are supposedly captured in odd-lot figures. The idea is to see what odd-lot investors "on balance" are doing. So long as there is little or no difference in the spread between the volume of odd-lot purchases and sales, the theory of contrary opinion holds that the market will probably continue along its current line (either up or down). A dramatic change in the balance of odd-lot purchases and sales may be a signal that a bull or bear market is about to end. For example, if the amount of odd-lot purchases starts to exceed odd-lot sales by an ever-widening margin, speculation on the part of small investors may be starting to get out of control—an ominous signal that the final stages of a bull market may be at hand.

Two trends have diminished the usefulness of odd-lot trading as a market indicator. First, transactions costs have fallen dramatically in recent decades, so the cost advantage of trading in round lots rather than odd lots has diminished. Second, it has become more common for larger traders to break their orders into smaller parts to disguise their activities. For both of these reasons, it is less clear today than it used to be that an individual investor is behind an odd-lot trade. If the purpose of watching odd-lot trades is to assess the trading behavior of individuals rather than professionals, that purpose is harder to achieve today than it once was.

Trading Rules and Measures

Market technicians—analysts who believe it is chiefly (or solely) supply and demand that drive stock prices—use a variety of mathematical equations and measures to assess the underlying condition of the market. These analysts often use computers to produce the measures, plotting them on a daily basis. They then use those measures as indicators of when to get into or out of the market or a particular stock. In essence, they develop trading rules based on these market measures. Technical analysts almost always use several of these market measures, rather than just one (or two), because one measure rarely works the same way for all stocks. Moreover, they generally look for confirmation of one measure by another. In other words, market analysts like to see three or four of these ratios and measures all pointing in the same direction.

Although dozens of these market measures and trading rules exist, we'll confine our discussion here to some of the more widely used technical indicators: (1) advance-decline lines, (2) new highs and lows, (3) the Arms index, (4) the mutual fund cash ratio, (5) on-balance volume, and (6) the relative strength index (RSI).

Advance-Decline Line   Each trading day, the NYSE, Amex, and Nasdaq publish statistics on how many of their stocks closed higher on the day (i.e., advanced in price) and how many closed lower (declined in price). The *advance-decline (A/D) line* is simply the difference between these two numbers. To calculate it, you take the number of stocks that have risen in price and subtract the number that have declined, usually for the previous day. For example, if 1,000 issues advanced on a day when 450 issues declined, the day's net number would be 550 (i.e., 1,000 − 450). If 450 advanced and 1,000 declined, the net number would be −550. Each day's net number is then added to (or subtracted from) the running total, and the results are plotted on a graph.

If the graph is rising, the advancing issues are dominating the declining issues, and the technical analysts conclude that the market is strong. When declining issues start to dominate, the graph will turn down as the market begins to soften. Technicians use the A/D line as a signal for when to buy or sell stocks.

New Highs–New Lows This measure is similar to the advance-decline line but looks at price movements over a longer period of time. A stock is defined as reaching a "new high" if its current price is at the highest level it has been over the past year (sometimes referred to as the "52-week high"). Conversely, a stock reaches a "new low" if its current price is at the lowest level it has been over the past year.

The *new highs–new lows (NH-NL) indicator* equals the number of stocks reaching new 52-week highs minus the number reaching new lows. Thus, you end up with a net number, which can be either positive (when new highs dominate) or negative (when new lows exceed new highs), just like with the advance-decline line. To smooth out the daily fluctuations, the net number is often added to (or subtracted from) a 10-day moving average and then plotted on a graph.

As you might have guessed, a graph that's increasing over time indicates a strong market, where new highs are dominating. A declining graph indicates a weak market, where new lows are more common than new highs. Technicians following a momentum-based strategy will buy stocks when new highs dominate and sell them when there are more new lows than new highs. Alternatively, they might use the indicator to rotate money into stocks when the market looks strong and to rotate money out of stocks and into cash or bonds when the market looks weak.

The Arms Index This indicator, also known as the TRIN, for *trading index*, builds on the advance-decline line by considering the volume in advancing and declining stocks in addition to the number of stocks rising or falling in price. The formula is

Equation 9.4
$$\text{TRIN} = \frac{\text{Number of up stocks}}{\text{Number of down stocks}} \div \frac{\text{Volume in up stocks}}{\text{Volume in down stocks}}$$

For example, suppose we are analyzing the S&P 500. Assume on a given day 300 of these stocks rose in price and 200 fell in price. Also assume that the total trading volume in the rising ("up") stocks was 400 million shares, and the total trading volume in the falling ("down") stocks was 800 million shares. The value of the TRIN for the day would be

$$\text{TRIN} = \frac{300}{200} \div \frac{400 \text{ million}}{800 \text{ million}} = 3.0$$

Alternatively, suppose the volume in up stocks was 700 million shares, and the volume in down stocks was 300 million. The value of the TRIN then would be

$$\text{TRIN} = \frac{300}{200} \div \frac{700 \text{ million}}{300 \text{ million}} = 0.64$$

Higher TRIN values are interpreted as being bad for the market because even though more stocks rose than fell, the trading volume in the falling stocks was much greater. The underlying idea is that a strong market is characterized by more stocks rising in price than falling, along with greater volume in the rising stocks than in the falling ones, as in the second example.

Mutual Fund Cash Ratio This indicator looks at the cash position of mutual funds as an indicator of future market performance. The *mutual fund cash ratio (MFCR)* measures the percentage of mutual fund assets that are held in cash. It is computed as follows:

Equation 9.5
$$\text{MFCR} = \text{Mutual fund cash position} \div \text{Total assets under management}$$

The assumption is that the higher the MFCR, the stronger the market. Indeed, the ratio is considered very bullish when it moves to abnormally high levels (i.e., when mutual fund cash exceeds 10% to 12% of assets). It is seen as bearish when the ratio drops to very low levels (e.g., less than 5% of assets). The logic goes as follows: When fund managers hold a lot of cash (when the MFCR is high), that's good news for the market because they will eventually have to invest that cash, buying stocks and causing prices to rise. If fund managers hold very little cash, investors might be concerned for two reasons. First, there is less demand for stocks if most of the cash is already invested. Second, if the market takes a downturn, investors might want to withdraw their money. Fund managers will then have to sell some of their stocks to accommodate these redemptions (because they don't have much accumulated cash), putting additional downward pressure on prices.

On-Balance Volume Technical analysts usually consider stock prices to be the key measure of market activity. However, they also consider trading volume as a secondary indicator. *On-balance volume (OBV)* is a momentum indicator that relates volume to price change. It uses trading volume in addition to price and tracks trading volume as a running total. In this way, OBV indicates whether volume is flowing into or out of a security. When the security closes higher than its previous close, all the day's volume is considered "up-volume," all of which is added to the running total. In contrast, when a stock closes lower, all the day's volume is considered "down-volume," which is then subtracted from the running total.

The OBV indicator is used to confirm price trends. According to this measure, you want to see a lot of volume when a stock's price is rising because that would suggest that the stock will go even higher. On the other hand, if prices are rising but OBV is falling, technical analysts would describe the situation as a divergence and interpret it as a sign of possible weakness.

When analyzing OBV, it is the direction or trend that is important, not the actual value. To begin the computation of OBV, you can start with an arbitrary number, such as 50,000. Suppose you are calculating the OBV for a stock that closed yesterday at a price of $50 per share, and you start with an OBV value of 50,000. Assume that the stock trades 80,000 shares today and closes at $49. Because the stock declined in price, we would subtract the full 80,000 shares from the previous balance (our starting point of 50,000); now the OBV is 50,000 − 80,000 = −30,000 (Note that the OBV is simply the trading volume running total.) If the stock trades 120,000 shares on the following day and closes up at $52 per share, we would then add all of those 120,000 shares to the previous day's OBV: −30,000 + 120,000 = +90,000. This process would continue day after day. The normal procedure is to plot these daily OBVs on a graph. As long as the graph is moving up, it's bullish; when the graph starts moving down, it's bearish.

Relative Strength One of the most widely used technical indicators is the *relative strength index (RSI)*, an index measuring a security's strength of advances and declines over time. The RSI indicates a security's momentum and gives the best results when used for short trading periods. It also helps identify market extremes, signaling that a security is approaching its price top or bottom and may soon reverse trend. The RSI is the ratio of average price change on "up days" to the average price change on "down days" during the same period. The index formula is

Equation 9.6
$$RSI = 100 - \left[100 \div \left(1 + \frac{\text{Average price change on up days}}{\text{Average price change on down days}} \right) \right]$$

The average price change in this formula is usually calculated over a 9-, 14-, or 25-day period. In the RSI calculation, both price increases and price decreases are treated as positive values. In other words, if a stock fell by $0.05 for 14 days in a row, then the average price change on down days would be 0.05, and the same would hold if a stock rose by $0.05 for 14 days in a row.

The RSI ranges between 0 and 100, with most RSIs falling between 30 and 70. Generally, values above 70 or 80 indicate an *overbought* condition (more and stronger buying than fundamentals would justify). RSI values below 30 indicate a possible *oversold* condition (more selling than fundamentals may indicate). When the RSI crosses these points, it signals a possible trend reversal. The wider 80–20 range is often used with the 9-day RSI, which tends to be more volatile than longer-period RSIs. In bull markets, 80 may be a better upper indicator than 70; in bear markets, 20 is a more accurate lower level. Different sectors and industries may have varying RSI threshold levels.

To use the RSI in their own trading, investors set buy and sell ranges—such as sell when the RSI crosses above 70 and buy when it moves below 30. Another strategy is to compare RSIs with stock charts. Most of the time both move in the same direction, but a divergence between RSI and a price chart can be a strong predictor of a changing trend.

Charting

Charting is perhaps the best-known activity of the technical analyst. Indeed, technical analysts use various types of charts to plot the behavior of everything from the Dow Jones Industrial Average and share price movements of individual stocks to moving averages (see below) and advance-decline lines. In fact, as noted above, just about every type of technical indicator is charted in one form or another.

Practice Your Charting Skills

Charts are popular because they provide a visual summary of activity over time. Perhaps more important (in the eyes of technicians, at least), they contain valuable information about developing trends and the future behavior of the market or individual stocks. Chartists believe price patterns evolve into chart formations that provide signals about the future course of the market or a stock.

Chart Formations A chart by itself tells you little more than where the market or a stock has been. But to chartists, those price patterns yield formations that tell them what to expect in the future. Chartists believe that history repeats itself, so they study the historical reactions of stocks (or the market) to various formations, and they devise trading rules based on these observations. It makes no difference to chartists whether they are following the market or an individual stock. It is the formation that matters, not the issue being plotted. Chartists believe that they can see formations building and recognize buy and sell signals. These chart formations are often given exotic names, such as *head and shoulders*, *falling wedge*, *scallop and saucer*, *ascending triangle*, and *island reversal*, to name just a few.

Figure 9.6 shows six of these formations. The patterns form "support levels" and "resistance lines" that when combined with the basic formations, yield buy and sell signals. Panel A is an example of a buy signal that occurs when prices break out above a resistance line in a particular pattern. In contrast, when prices break out below a support level, as they do at the end of the formation in panel B, a sell signal is said to occur. Supposedly, a sell signal means everything is in place for a major drop in the market (or in the price of a share of stock). A buy signal indicates that the opposite is about to occur.

FIGURE 9.6

Some Popular Chart Formations

To chartists, each of these formations has meaning about the future course of events.

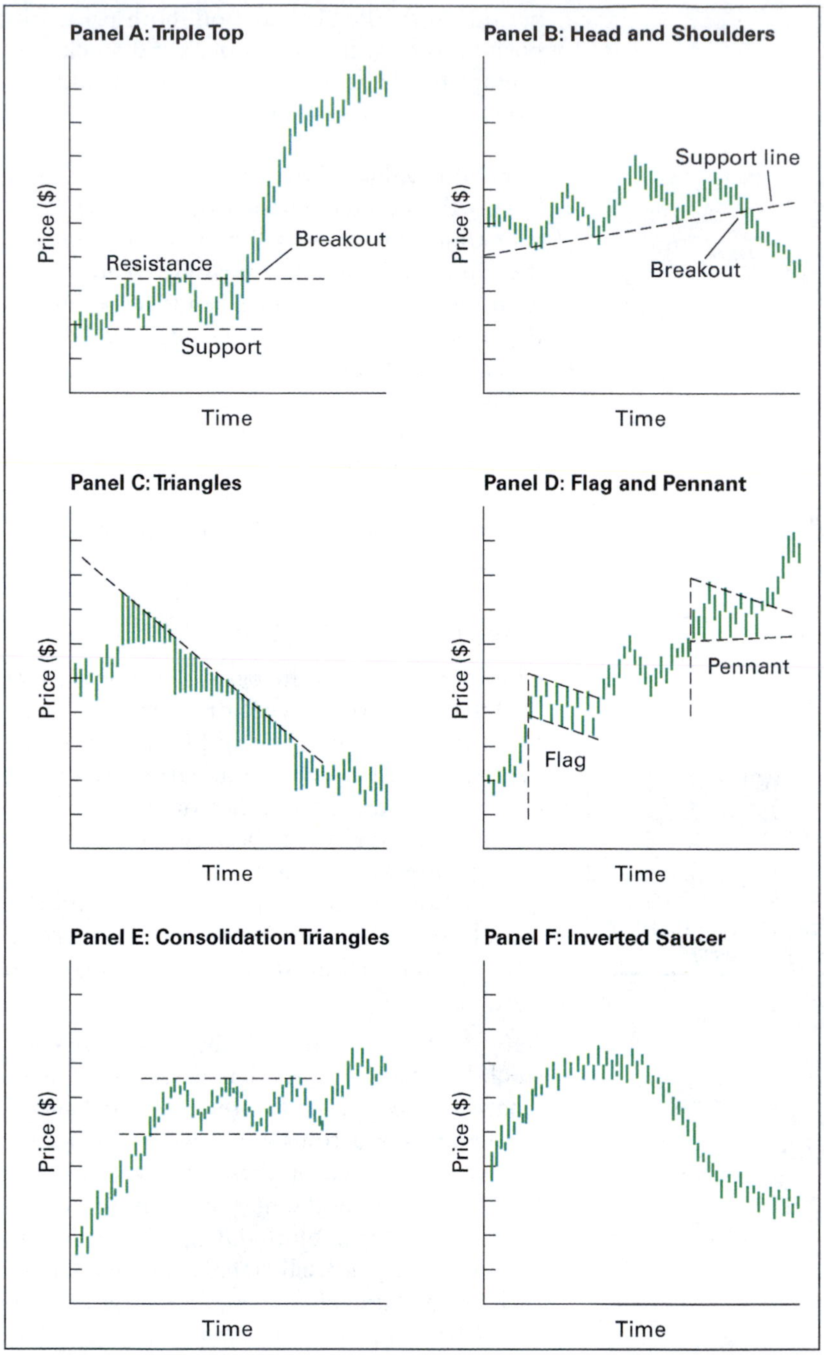

Panel A: Triple Top
Price ($)
Time
Resistance
Breakout
Support
Panel B: Head and Shoulders
Price ($)
Time
Support line
Breakout
Panel C: Triangles
Price ($)
Time
Panel D: Flag and Pennant
Price ($)
Time
Pennant
Flag
Panel E: Consolidation Triangles
Price ($)
Time
Panel F: Inverted Saucer
Price ($)
Time

Unfortunately, one of the major problems with charting is that the formations rarely appear as neatly and cleanly as those in Figure 9.6. Rather, identifying and interpreting them often demands considerable imagination.

Moving Averages One problem with daily price charts is that they may contain a lot of short-term price swings that mask the overall trend in prices. As a result, technical analysts often use moving averages not only to eliminate those minor blips but also to highlight underlying trends. A **moving average** is a mathematical procedure that records the average value of a series of prices, or other data, over time. Because they incorporate a stream of these average values, moving averages will smooth out a data series and make it easier to spot trends. The moving average is one of the oldest and most popular technical indicators. It can, in fact, be used not only with share prices but also with market indexes and even other technical measures.

Moving averages are computed over time periods ranging from 10 to 200 days—meaning that from 10 to 200 data points are used in each calculation. For example, a series of 15 data points is used in a 15-day moving average. The length of the time period has a bearing on how the MA will behave. Shorter periods (10 to 30 days) are more sensitive and tend to more closely track actual daily behavior. Longer periods (say, 100 to 200 days) are smoother and only pick up the major trends. Several types of moving averages exist, with the most common (and the one we'll use here) being the *simple average*, which gives equal weight to each observation. In contrast, there are other procedures that give more weight to the most recent data points (e.g., the "exponential" and "weighted" averages) or apply more weight to the middle of the time period (e.g., "triangular" averages).

Using closing share prices as the basis of discussion, we can calculate the simple moving average by adding up the closing prices over a given time period (e.g., 10 days) and then dividing this total by the length of the time period. Thus, the simple moving average is nothing more than the arithmetic mean. To illustrate, consider the following stream of closing share prices:

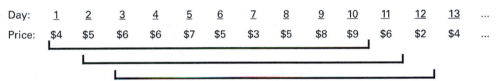

Day:	1	2	3	4	5	6	7	8	9	10	11	12	13	...
Price:	$4	$5	$6	$6	$7	$5	$3	$5	$8	$9	$6	$2	$4	...

Using a 10-day moving average, we add up the closing prices for days 1 through 10 ($4 + $5 + \cdots + $8 + $9 = $58) and then divide this total by 10 ($58 ÷ 10 = $5.8). Thus, the average closing price for this 10-day period was $5.80. The next day, the process is repeated once again for days 2 through 11; that turns out to be $60 ÷ 10 = $6.00. This procedure is repeated each day, so that over time we have a series of these individual averages that, when linked together, form a moving-average line. This line is then plotted on a chart, either by itself or along with other market information.

Figure 9.7 shows a 100-day moving average (i.e., the red line) plotted against the daily closing prices for Facebook (i.e., the blue line) starting with its May 2012 IPO and continuing through June 2015. In contrast to the actual closing prices, the moving average provides a much smoother line, without all the short-term fluctuations; it clearly reveals the general trend in prices for this stock.

Technicians often use charts like the one in Figure 9.7 to help them make buy and sell decisions about a stock. Specifically, if the security's price starts moving above the moving average, they read that situation as a good time to buy because prices should be drifting up (e.g., see the buy signal). In contrast, a sell signal occurs when the security's price moves below the moving-average line (e.g., see the sell signal). A problem arises when volatility in the stock price leads to repeated buy and sell signals. For example, for Facebook, the red and blue lines cross 11 times between April 4, 2014 and May 6, 2014, resulting in six sell signals and five buy signals all within a single month. Trading based on the moving-average indicator during that period would result in a lot of transactions costs, but not much profit.

FIGURE 9.7

Daily Closing Prices and 100-Day Moving-Average Line for Facebook

Moving-average lines are often plotted along with the actual daily closing prices for a stock. They're also widely used with market indexes, such as the S&P 500, and with a variety of technical indicators, including the advance-decline line.

CONCEPTS IN REVIEW

Answers available at http://www.pearsonhighered.com/smart

9.6 What is the purpose of technical analysis? Explain how and why it is used by technicians; note how it can be helpful in timing investment decisions.

9.7 Can the market really have a measurable effect on the price behavior of individual securities? Explain.

9.8 Describe the confidence index, and note the feature that makes it unique.

9.9 Briefly describe each of the following and explain how it is used in technical analysis:
   a. Breadth of the market
   b. Short interest
   c. Odd-lot trading

9.10 Briefly describe each of the following and note how it is computed and how it is used by technicians:
   a. Advance-decline lines
   b. Arms index
   c. On-balance volume
   d. Relative strength index
   e. Moving averages

9.11 What is a stock chart? What kind of information can be put on charts, and what is the purpose of charting?

MyFinanceLab

Here is what you should know after reading this chapter. MyFinanceLab will help you identify what you know and where to go when you need to practice.

What You Should Know	Key Terms	Where to Practice
LG1 **Describe the characteristics of an efficient market, explain what market anomalies are, and note some of the challenges that investors face when markets are efficient.** An efficient market is one in which prices fully reflect all available information; in an efficient market, price movements are nearly random. If markets are efficient, then investors should not expect to earn above-average returns consistently by using either technical or fundamental analysis.	abnormal return, *p. 339* alpha, *p. 339* arbitrage, *p. 342* behavioral finance, *p. 347* efficient market, *p. 338* efficient markets hypothesis (EMH), *p. 338* market anomalies, *p. 344* random walk hypothesis, *p. 338* semi-strong form (EMH), *p. 340* strong form (EMH), *p. 341* weak form (EMH), *p. 339*	MyFinanceLab Study Plan 9.1
LG2 **Summarize the evidence which suggests that the stock market is efficient.** Early research on the market efficiency question found that stock prices were essentially unpredictable and moved at random. Other studies found that even professional investors did not consistently earn returns that beat market averages.		MyFinanceLab Study Plan 9.2
LG3 **List four "decision traps" that may lead investors to make systematic errors in their investment decisions.** Behavioral finance asserts that investors are subject to a variety of decision traps, which include overconfidence, loss aversion, representativeness, narrow framing, and belief perseverance. If investors do indeed make systematic errors in their investment decisions, then those errors may influence prices in financial markets.	anchoring, *p. 355* belief perseverance, *p. 354* familiarity bias, *p. 355* loss aversion, *p. 349* narrow framing, *p. 354* overconfidence, *p. 348* representativeness, *p. 351* self-attribution bias, *p. 348*	MyFinanceLab Study Plan 9.3
LG4 **Explain how behavioral finance links market anomalies to investors' cognitive biases.** A market anomaly represents a pattern in stock prices that would appear to present investors with an opportunity to earn above-average returns without taking above-average risk. Behavioral finance suggests that some market anomalies exist because investors make systematic errors, such as undervaluing stocks that have performed poorly in recent years.		MyFinanceLab Study Plan 9.4
LG5 **Describe some of the approaches to technical analysis, including, among others, moving averages, charting, and various indicators of the technical condition of the market.** Market analysts look at those factors in the marketplace that can affect the price behavior of stocks in general. This analysis can be done by assessing the overall condition of the market, by informally or formally studying various internal market statistics (e.g., short interest or advance-decline lines), or by charting various aspects of the market (including the use of moving averages).	confidence index, *p. 357* market technician, *p. 360* short interest, *p. 359* technical analysis, *p. 356* theory of contrary opinion, *p. 360*	MyFinanceLab Study Plan 9.5 Video Learning Aid for Problems P9.2, P9.6

What You Should Know	Key Terms	Where to Practice
LG6 **Compute and use technical trading rules for individual stocks and the market as a whole.** Technical analysts use a number of mathematical equations and measures to gauge the direction of the market, including advance-decline lines, new highs and lows, the trading index, the mutual fund cash ratio, on-balance volume, and the relative strength index. They test different indicators using historical price data to find those that generate profitable trading strategies, which then are developed into trading rules used to guide buy and sell decisions.	charting, *p. 363* moving average (MA), *p. 365*	MyFinanceLab Study Plan 9.6

Log into MyFinanceLab, take a chapter test, and get a personalized Study Plan
that tells you which concepts you understand and which ones you need to
review. From there, MyFinanceLab will give you further practice, tutorials,
animations, videos, and guided solutions.
Log into **http://www.myfinancelab.com**

Discussion Questions

LG1 Q9.1 Much has been written about the concept of an efficient market. It's probably safe to say that some of your classmates believe the markets are efficient and others believe they are not. Have a debate to see whether you can resolve this issue (at least among you and your classmates). Pick a side, either for or against efficient markets, and then develop your "ammunition." Be prepared to discuss these three aspects:
 a. What is an efficient market? Do such markets really exist?
 b. Are stock prices always (or nearly always) correctly set in the market? If so, does that mean little opportunity exists to find undervalued stocks?
 c. Can you cite any reasons to use fundamental or technical analysis in your stock selection process? If not, how would you go about selecting stocks?

LG1 LG2 Q9.2 Each year financial periodicals like the *Wall Street Journal* and *Money Magazine* publish a list of the top performing mutual fund managers. And every year there are some fund managers who earn much higher returns than the market average, and in some cases they do so without taking above-average risk. Is this inconsistent with the efficient markets hypothesis?

LG3 LG4 Q9.3 Briefly define each of the following terms and describe how it can affect investors' decisions.
 a. Loss aversion
 b. Representativeness
 c. Narrow framing
 d. Overconfidence
 e. Biased self-attribution

LG3 LG4 Q9.4 Describe how representativeness may lead to biases in stock valuation.

LG5 Q9.5 Briefly describe how technical analysis is used as part of the stock valuation process. What role does it play in an investor's decision to buy or sell a stock?

LG5 **Q9.6** Describe each of the following approaches to technical analysis and note how it would be used by investors.

a. Confidence index

b. Arms index

c. Odd-lot trading

d. Charting

e. Moving averages

f. On-balance volume

Which of these approaches is likely to involve some type of mathematical equation or ratio?

LG5 **Q9.7** Briefly define each of the following and note the conditions that would suggest the market is technically strong.

a. Breadth of the market

b. Short interest

c. Relative strength index

d. Theory of contrary opinion

e. Head and shoulders

Problems

All problems are available on http://www.myfinancelab.com

LG5 **LG6** **P9.1** Compute the Arms index for the S&P 500 over the following three days:

Day	Number of Stocks **Rising** in Price	Number of Stocks **Falling** in Price	Volume for Stocks **Rising** in Price	Volume for Stocks **Falling** in Price
1	350	150	850 million shares	420 million shares
2	275	225	450 million shares	725 million shares
3	260	240	850 million shares	420 million shares

Which of the three days would be considered the most bullish? Explain why.

LG5 **LG6** **P9.2** Listed below are data that pertain to the corporate bond market. (*Note:* Each "period" below covers a span of six months.)

	Period 1	Period 2	Period 3	Period 4
Average yield on 10 high-grade corporate bonds	5.30%	5.70%	5.10%	?
Yield on the Dow Jones average of 40 corporate bonds	6.50%	?	6.00%	4.90%
Yield spread (in basis points)	?	155	?	25
Confidence index				

a. Compute the confidence index for each of the four periods listed above.

b. Assume that the latest confidence index (for period 0, in effect) amounts to 86.83%, while the yield spread between high- and average-grade corporate bonds is 85 basis points. Based on your calculations, what's happening to bond yield spreads and the confidence index over the period of time covered in the problem (i.e., from period 0 through period 4)?

c. Based on the confidence index measures you computed, what would be your overall assessment of the stock market? In which one or more of the periods (1 through 4) is the confidence index bullish? In which one(s) is it bearish?

LG5 LG6 **P9.3** Compute the level of on-balance volume (OBV) for the following three-day period for a stock, if the beginning level of OBV is 50,000 and the stock closed yesterday at $25.

Day	Closing Price	Trading Volume (shares)
1	$27	70,000
2	$26	45,000
3	$29	120,000

Does the movement in OBV appear to confirm the rising trend in prices? Explain.

LG5 LG6 **P9.4** Below are figures representing the number of stocks making new highs and new lows for each month over a six-month period:

Month	New Highs	New Lows
July	117	22
August	95	34
September	84	41
October	64	79
November	53	98
December	19	101

Would a technical analyst consider the trend to be bullish or bearish over this period? Explain.

LG5 LG6 **P9.5** You hear a market analyst on television say that the advance/decline ratio for the session was 1.2. What does that mean?

LG5 LG6 **P9.6** At the end of a trading day you find that on the NYSE 2,200 stocks advanced and 1,000 stocks declined. What is the value of the advance-decline line for that day?

LG5 LG6 **P9.7** You are given the following information for the number of stocks making new highs and new lows for each day:

Day	New Highs	New Lows
1 (yesterday)	117	22
2	95	34
3	84	41
4	64	79
5	53	98
6	19	101
7	19	105
8	18	110
9	19	90
10	22	88

a. Calculate the 10-day moving-average NH-NL indicator.
b. If there are 120 new highs and 20 new lows today, what is the new 10-day moving-average NH-NL indicator?

LG5 LG6 **P9.8** You have collected the following NH-NL indicator data:

Day	NH-NL Indicator
1 (yesterday)	100
2	95
3	61
4	43
5	−15
6	−45
7	−82
8	−86
9	−92
10	−71

If you are a technician following a momentum-based strategy, are you buying or selling today?

LG5 LG6 **P9.9** You are presented with the following data:

Week	Mutual Fund Cash Position	Mutual Fund Total Assets
Most recent	$281,478,000	$2,345,650,000
2	$258,500,000	$2,350,000,000
3	$234,800,000	$2,348,000,000
4	$211,950,000	$2,355,000,000
5	$188,480,000	$2,356,000,000

Calculate the MFCR for each week. Based on the result, are you bullish or bearish?

LG5 LG6 **P9.10** You find the closing prices for a stock you own. You want to use a 10-day moving average to monitor the stock. Calculate the 10-day moving average for days 11 through 20. Based on the data in the table below, are there any signals you should act on? Explain.

Day	Closing Price	Day	Closing Price
1	$25.25	11	$30.00
2	$26.00	12	$30.00
3	$27.00	13	$31.00
4	$28.00	14	$31.50
5	$27.00	15	$31.00
6	$28.00	16	$32.00
7	$27.50	17	$29.00
8	$29.00	18	$29.00
9	$27.00	19	$28.00
10	$28.00	20	$27.00

LG5 LG6   **P9.11**   Data on a stock's closing price and its price change for the last 14 trading days appears below.

Day	Closing Price	Price Change	Price Increase	Price Decrease
1	$22.50	+$0.14	$0.14	
2	$22.28	−$0.22		$0.22
3	$22.32	+$0.04	$0.04	
4	$23.01	+$0.69	$0.69	
5	$22.82	−$0.19		$0.19
6	$23.41	+$0.59	$0.59	
7	$23.83	+$0.42	$0.42	
8	$23.67	−$0.16		$0.16
9	$24.02	+$0.35	$0.35	
10	$24.14	+$0.12	$0.12	
11	$23.99	−$0.15		$0.15
12	$24.54	+$0.55	$0.55	
13	$25.17	+$0.63	$0.63	
14	$25.01	−$0.16		$0.16

a. Over this 14-day period what is the average gain on up days? (*Note:* to calculate the average, divide the sum of all gains by 14, not by the number of days on which the stock went up.)

b. Over this 14-day period, what is the average loss on down days?

c. What is the RSI?

d. Is the RSI sending a strong buy or sell signal?

Visit **http://www.myfinancelab.com** for web exercises, spreadsheets, and other online resources.

Case Problem 9.1   Brett Runs Some Technical Measures on a Stock

LG5   Brett Daly is an active stock trader and an avid market technician. He got into technical analysis about 10 years ago, and although he now uses the Internet for much of his analytical work, he still enjoys running some of the numbers and doing some of the charting himself. Brett likes to describe himself as a serious stock trader who relies on technical analysis for some—but certainly not all—of the information he uses to make an investment decision; unlike some market technicians, he does not totally ignore a stock's fundamentals. Right now he's got his eye on a stock that he's been tracking for the past three or four months.

The stock is Nautilus Navigation, a mid-sized high-tech company that's been around for a number of years and has a demonstrated ability to generate profits year-in and year-out. The problem is that the earnings are a bit erratic, tending to bounce up and down from year to year, which causes the price of the stock to be a bit erratic as well. And that's exactly why Brett likes the stock—the volatile prices enable him, as a trader, to move in and out of the stock over relatively short (three- to six-month) periods of time.

Brett has already determined that the stock has "decent" fundamentals, so he does not worry about its basic soundness. Hence, he can concentrate on the technical side of the stock. In particular, he wants to run some technical measures on the market price behavior of the security. He's obtained recent closing prices on the stock, which are shown in the table below.

Recent Price Behavior: Nautilus Navigation			
$14 (8/15/16)	$18.55	$20	$17.50
$14.25	$17.50	$20.21	$18.55
$14.79	$17.50	$20.25	$19.80
$15.50	$17.25	$20.16	$19.50
$16	$17	$20	$19.25
$16	$16.75	$20.25	$20
$16.50	$16.50	$20.50	$20.90
$17	$16.55	$20.80	$21
$17.25	$16.15	$20	$21.75
$17.20	$16.80	$20	$22.50
$18	$17.15	$20.25	$23.25
$18 (9/30/16)	$17.22	$20	$24
$18.55	$17.31 (10/31/16)	$19.45	$24.25
$18.65	$17.77	$19.20	$24.15
$18.80	$18.23	$18.25 (11/30/16)	$24.75
$19	$19.22	$17.50	$25
$19.10	$20.51	$16.75	$25.50
$18.92	$20.15	$17	$25.55 (12/31/16)

Nautilus shares are actively traded on the Nasdaq Global Market and enjoy considerable market interest.

Questions

a. Use the closing share prices in the table above to compute the stock's relative strength index for (1) the 20-day period from 9/30/16 to 10/31/16; and (2) the 22-day period from 11/30/16 to 12/31/16. [*Hint:* Use a simple (unweighted) average to compute the numerator (average price change on up days) and denominator (average price change on down days) of the RSI formula.]
   1. Contrast the two RSI measures you computed. Is the index getting bigger or smaller, and is that good or bad?
   2. Is the latest RSI measure giving a buy or a sell signal? Explain.

b. Based on the above closing share prices, prepare a moving-average line covering the period shown in the table; use a 10-day time frame to calculate the individual average values.
   1. Plot the daily closing prices for Nautilus from 8/15/16 through 12/31/16 on a graph/chart.
   2. On the same graph/chart, plot a moving-average line using the individual average values computed earlier. Identify any buy or sell signals.
   3. As of 12/31/16, was the moving-average line giving a buy, hold, or sell signal? Explain. How does that result compare to what you found with the RSI in part a? Explain.

c. Based on the technical measures and charts you've prepared, what course of action would you recommend that Brett take with regard to Nautilus Navigation? Explain.

Case Problem 9.2   Deb Takes Measure of the Market

LG5   Several months ago, Deb Forrester received a substantial sum of money from the estate of her late aunt. Deb initially placed the money in a savings account because she was not sure what to do with it. Since then, however, she has taken a course in investments at the local university. The textbook for the course was, in fact, this one, and the class just completed this chapter. Excited about what she has learned in class, Deb has decided that she definitely wants to invest in stocks. But before she does, she wants to use her newfound knowledge in technical analysis to determine whether now would be a good time to enter the market.

Deb has decided to use all of the following measures to help her determine if now is, indeed, a good time to start putting money into the stock market:

- Advance-decline line
- New highs-new lows indicator (Assume the current 10-day moving average is 0 and the last 10 periods were each 0.)
- Arms index
- Mutual fund cash ratio

Deb goes to the Internet and, after considerable effort, is able to put together the accompanying table of data.

Questions

a. Based on the data presented in the table, calculate a value (where appropriate) for periods 1 through 5, for each of the four measures listed above. Chart your results, where applicable.

b. Discuss each measure individually and note what it indicates for the market, as it now stands. Taken collectively, what do these four measures indicate about the current state of the market? According to these measures, is this a good time for Deb to consider getting into the market, or should she wait a while? Explain.

c. Comment on the time periods used in the table, which are not defined here. What if they were relatively long intervals of time? What if they were relatively short? Explain how the length of the time periods can affect the measures.

	Period 1	Period 2	Period 3	Period 4	Period 5
Dow Jones Industrial Average	8,300	7,250	8,000	9,000	9,400
Dow Transportation Average	2,375	2,000	2,000	2,850	3,250
New highs	$ 68	$ 85	$ 85	$ 120	$ 200
New lows	$ 75	$ 60	$ 80	$ 75	$ 20
Volume up	600,000,000	836,254,123	275,637,497	875,365,980	1,159,534,297
Volume down	600,000,000	263,745,877	824,362,503	424,634,020	313,365,599
Mutual fund cash (trillions of dollars)	$0.31	$0.32	$0.47	$0.61	$0.74
Total assets managed (trillions of dollars)	$6.94	$6.40	$6.78	$6.73	$7.42
Advancing issues (NYSE)	1,120	1,278	1,270	1,916	1,929
Declining issues (NYSE)	2,130	1,972	1,980	1,334	1,321

Excel@Investing

Excel@Investing

Technical analysis looks at the demand and supply for securities based on trading volumes and price studies. Charting is a common method used to identify and project price trends in a security. A well-known technical indicator is the Bollinger Band. It creates two bands, one above and one below the price performance of a stock. The upper band is a resistance level and represents the level above which the stock is unlikely to rise. The bottom forms a support level and shows the price that a stock is unlikely to fall below.

According to technicians, if you see a significant "break" in the upper band, the expectation is that the stock price will fall in the immediate future. A "break" in the lower band signals that the security is about to rise in value. Either of these occurrences will dictate a unique investment strategy.

Replicate the following technical analysis for Amazon.com (AMZN)

- Go to http://www.finance.yahoo.com

- Symbol(s): **AMZN**

- In the left-hand column, click on Interactive Chart.

- Select a 5-year chart.

- Click on Indicator.

- Choose Bollinger Bands.

- The price performance graph for Amazon stock with an upper and lower Bollinger Band should appear.

- Make sure that the graph covers, at a minimum, the first six months of 2015.

Questions

    a. On approximately April 20, 2015, what happened to the upper band (resistance level) of Amazon stock?

    b. During the following nine days, how did the price of the stock behave?

    c. Is this in line with what a technician would predict?

    d. What strategy would a technician have undertaken on April 20?

    e. At around the same time, what happened to the lower band (support level) of Amazon stock?

    f. How did the stock behave through the month of May 2015?

CFA Exam Questions

Investing in Common Stocks

Following is a sample of 11 Level-I CFA exam questions that deal with many topics covered in Chapters 6, 7, 8, and 9 of this text, including the use of financial ratios, various stock valuation models, and efficient market concepts. (*Note*: When answering some of the questions, remember: "Forward P/E" is the same as a P/E based on estimated earnings one year out.) When answering the questions, give yourself 1½ minutes for each question; the objective is to correctly answer 8 of the 11 questions in a period of 16½ minutes.

1. Holding constant all other variables and excluding any interactions among the determinants of value, which of the following would most likely increase a firm's price-to-earnings multiple?
   a. The risk premium increases.
   b. The retention rate increases.
   c. The beta of the stock increases.

2. A rationale for the use of the price-to-sales (P/S) approach is:
   a. Sales are more volatile than earnings.
   b. P/S ratios assess cost structures accurately.
   c. Revenues are less subject to accounting manipulation than earnings.

3. A cyclical company tends to
   a. have earnings that track the overall economy.
   b. have a high price-to-earnings ratio.
   c. have less volatile earnings than the overall market.

4. Consider a company that earned $4.00 per share last year and paid a dividend of $1.00. The firm has maintained a consistent payout ratio over the years and analysts expect this to continue. The firm is expected to earn $4.40 per share next year, and the stock is expected to sell for $30.00. The required rate of return is 12%. What is the best estimate of the stock's current value?
   a. $44.00
   b. $22.67
   c. $27.77

5. A stock's current dividend is $1 and its expected dividend is $1.10 next year. If the investor's required rate of return is 15% and the stock is currently trading at $20.00, what is the implied expected price in one year?
   a. $21.90
   b. $22.00
   c. $23.00

6. A firm has total revenues of $187,500, net income of $15,000, total current liabilities of $50,000, total common equity of $75,000, and total assets of $150,000. What is the firm's ROE?
   a. 15%
   b. 20%
   c. 24%

7. A stock currently pays a dividend of $2.00 per share. Expected dividend growth is 20% for the next three years and then is expected to revert to 7% thereafter indefinitely. The required rate of return on this stock is 15%. The stock's current intrinsic value is
   a. $6.54
   b. $165.63
   c. $36.93

8. The required rate of return used in equity valuation is influenced most by which of the following?
   a. Expected inflation
   b. Actual inflation
   c. The ability to sell short

9. Confirmation bias is the tendency for investors to
   a. focus on information that confirms prior opinions and actions.
   b. be overconfident in forecasting future growth.
   c. feel responsible for poor investments and do even worse.

10. Which of the following would provide the most compelling evidence contradicting the semi-strong form of the efficient markets hypothesis?
    a. Transactions costs are high.
    b. Low P/E stocks have positive long-term abnormal returns.
    c. Approximately half of professionally managed funds outperform the overall market.

11. The strong-form efficient market hypothesis
    a. assumes that no one has an informational advantage.
    b. assumes that certain groups have access to privileged information.
    c. directly challenges the methods of technical analysis.

Answers: 1. b; 2. c; 3. a; 4. c; 5. a; 6. b; 7. c; 8. a; 9. a; 10. b; 11. a.

Fixed-Income Securities

LEARNING GOALS

After studying this chapter, you should be able to:

LG1 Explain the basic investment attributes of bonds and their use as investment vehicles.

LG2 Describe the essential features of a bond, note the role that bond ratings play in the market, and distinguish among different types of call, refunding, and sinking-fund provisions.

LG3 Explain how bond prices are quoted in the market and why some bonds are more volatile than others.

LG4 Identify the different types of bonds and the kinds of investment objectives these securities can fulfill.

LG5 Discuss the global nature of the bond market and the difference between dollar-denominated and non-dollar-denominated foreign bonds.

LG6 Describe the basic features and characteristics of convertible securities and measure the value of a convertible security.

When investors lend money to corporations or governments by purchasing bonds, they are very focused on the likelihood that their loans will be paid back. One way to assess that likelihood is to examine a borrower's credit rating. On April 10, 2014, the credit rating arm of Standard & Poor's downgraded Automated Data Processing (ADP) from the top triple-A (AAA) credit rating to double-A (AA). This move was significant not only because ADP had held the AAA rating for years but also because it left only three U.S. companies holding the coveted AAA rating: Johnson & Johnson, Microsoft, and Exxon-Mobil. As recently as 1980, the AAA rating was held by 60 U.S. firms, but that number had been dwindling for years. ADP joined the likes of General Electric and Pfizer, who also lost their AAA ratings after the recession.

Despite some high-profile downgrades, as the world economy slowly recovered from the 2008 recession, fewer companies received downgrades and more earned upgrades. It wasn't until 2014 that upgrades outnumbered downgrades on a global basis, and even then the margin was slim, with roughly nine companies receiving a downgrade for every ten companies whose credit ratings were upgraded. Still, the improving economy meant that most firms were more likely to generate the cash that would enable them to repay their debts, so credit ratings were on the rise.

Before you invest in debt securities, whether issued by corporations or countries, it is important that you consider credit quality, interest rates, maturity, and other relevant factors. Chapters 10 and 11 will provide the background you need to make wise choices in the bond market.

(Sources: "Fitch: Corporate Downgrades Trailed Upgrades in 2014," Reuters, March 16, 2015, http://www.reuters.com/article/2015/03/16/idUSFit91529120150316; "ADP Downgraded by Moody's, S&P after Spin-off News," MarketWatch, April 10, 2014, http://www.marketwatch.com/story/adp-downgraded-by-moodys-sp-after-spin-off-news-2014-04-10.)

Why Invest in Bonds?

LG1 In contrast to stocks, bonds are liabilities—publicly traded IOUs where the bond-holders are actually lending money to the issuer. **Bonds are publicly traded, long-term debt securities.** They are issued in various denominations, by a variety of borrowing organizations, including the U.S. Treasury, agencies of the U.S. government, state and local governments, and corporations. Bonds are often referred to as *fixed-income securities* because the payments made by bond issuers are usually fixed. That is, in most cases the issuing organization agrees to pay a fixed amount of interest periodically and to repay a fixed amount of principal at maturity.

Like stocks, bonds can provide two kinds of income: (1) current income and (2) capital gains. The current income comes from the periodic interest payments paid over the bond's life. The capital gains component is a little different. Because the companies issuing bonds promise to repay a fixed amount when the bonds mature, the interest payments that bonds make do not typically rise in step with a firm's profits the way that stock dividends often do, which is another reason bonds are known as fixed-income securities. By the same token, a company's stock price tends to rise and fall dramatically with changes in the firm's financial performance, but bond prices are less sensitive to changes in a company's profits. However, bond prices do rise and fall as market interest rates change. A basic relationship that you must keep in mind is that interest rates and bond prices move in opposite directions. When interest rates rise, bond prices fall, and when rates drop, bond prices move up. We'll have more to say about this relation later in the chapter, but here's the intuition behind it. Imagine that you buy a brand-new bond, issued by a company like GE, paying 5% interest. Suppose that a month later market rates have risen, and new bonds pay investors 6% interest. If you want to sell your GE bond, you're likely to experience a capital loss because investors will not want to buy a bond paying 5% interest when the going rate in the market is 6%. With fewer buyers interested in them, GE bonds will decline in value. Happily, the opposite outcome can occur if market rates fall. When the going rate on bonds is 4%, your GE bond paying 5% would command a premium in the market. Taken together, the current income and capital gains earned from bonds can lead to attractive returns.

A wide variety of bonds are available in the market, from relatively safe issues (e.g., General Electric bonds) sought by conservative investors to highly speculative securities (e.g., Sirius XM bonds) appropriate for investors who can tolerate a great deal of risk. In addition, the risks and returns offered by all types of bonds depend in part upon the volatility of interest rates. Because interest rate movements cause bond prices to change, higher interest rate volatility makes bond returns less predictable.

Other bonds have special features designed to appeal to certain types of investors. Investors in high tax brackets who want to shelter income from taxes find tax-exempt bonds appealing. Bonds issued by state and local government entities, called municipal bonds, pay interest that is not subject to federal income taxation, so these bonds have special appeal to investors in high tax brackets. Interest on U.S. Treasury bonds is exempt from state income tax, so taxpayers from states with high income tax rates may have particular interest in these bonds. Despite the term *fixed income*, some bonds make interest payments that vary through time according to a formula. In a sense, the term *fixed income* is still appropriate for these bonds because the formula that determines their interest payments is contractually fixed. For example, governments in the United States and many other countries issue inflation-indexed bonds with interest payments that rise with inflation. As the inflation rate changes, the payments on these bonds will change, but investors know in advance exactly how the interest payments will adjust as inflation occurs. Those bonds appeal to investors who want some protection from the risk of rising inflation.

A Brief History of Bond Prices, Returns, and Interest Rates

Interest rates drive the bond market. In fact, the behavior of interest rates is the most important influence on bond returns. Interest rates determine not only the current income investors will receive but also the capital gains (or losses) they will incur. It's not surprising, therefore, that bond-market participants follow interest rates closely. When commentators in the news media describe how the market has performed on a particular day, they usually speak in terms of what happened to bond yields (i.e., what happened to interest rates) that day rather than what happened to bond prices.

Figure 10.1 provides a look at interest rates on bonds issued by U.S. corporations and the U.S. government from 1963 through 2014. It shows that rates on both types of bonds rose steadily through the 1960s and 1970s, peaking in 1982 at more than three times their 1963 levels. Rates then began a long downward slide, and by 2014 the rates were not that different from their 1963 levels. Keep in mind that rising interest rates lead to falling bond prices, so prior to the 1980s investors who held bonds that had been issued in the 60s and 70s realized capital losses if they sold their bonds after

FIGURE 10.1

The Behavior of Interest Rates over Time, 1963 through 2014

Interest rates rose dramatically from 1963 to 1982 before starting a long-term decline that continued through 2014. Rates on corporate bonds tend to mirror rates on government bonds, although corporate rates are higher due to the risk of default by the issuing corporation. Note that the gap, or "spread," between U.S. corporate bond and U.S. Treasury bond yields has been particularly wide following the 2008 financial crisis. (Source: Board of Governors of the Federal Reserve System (US), Moody's Seasoned Aaa Corporate Bond Yield© [AAA], retrieved from FRED, Federal Reserve Bank of St. Louis **https://research .stlouisfed.org/fred2/series/AAA/**, May 20, 2015. Board of Governors of the Federal Reserve System (US), 10-Year Treasury Constant Maturity Rate [DGS10], retrieved from FRED, Federal Reserve Bank of St. Louis **https://research.stlouisfed.org/fred2/series/DGS10/**, May 20, 2015.)

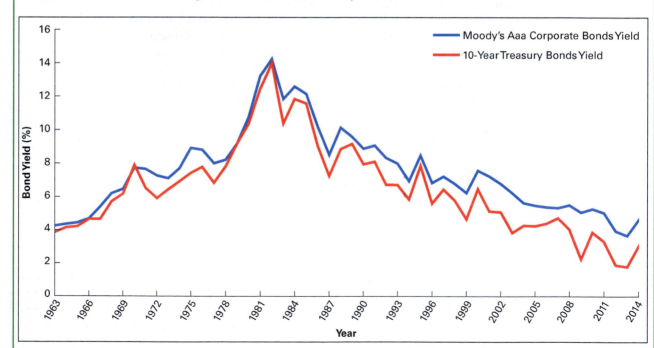

interest rates had risen. By the same token, investors who purchased bonds when interest rates were high earned capital gains from selling their bonds after market interest rates had declined.

Figure 10.1 shows that rates on corporate and government bonds tend to move together, but corporate bond rates are higher. Higher rates on corporate bonds provide compensation for the risk that corporations might default on their debts. The difference between the rate on corporate bonds and the rate on government bonds is called the *yield spread*, or the *credit spread*. When the risk of defaults on corporate bonds increases, the yield spread widens, as it did in 2008. The average annual yield spread for triple-A corporate bonds over the 52 years shown in Figure 10.1 was about 1%, the average from 1987 through 2014 was nearly 1.4%, and the average from 2008 through 2014 was 1.8%. Because changes in the credit spread are tied to the risk of default on corporate bonds, prices of these bonds are not completely insensitive to a company's financial performance. When a company's performance improves, investors recognize the default risk is falling, so the credit spread falls and the company's bond prices rise. When a firm's financial results deteriorate, default risk rises, the credit spread increases, and the company's bond prices fall. Even so, bond prices are nowhere near as sensitive to a firm's financial results as are stock prices.

Historical Returns As with stocks, total returns in the bond market are made up of both current income from the bond's interest payments and capital gains (or losses) from changes in the bond's value. Table 10.1 lists beginning-of-year and end-of-year bond yields and the total returns for 10-year U.S. government bonds from 1963 through 2014. The beginning-of-year yield represents the return that investors buying 10-year Treasury bonds require at the start of each year, and likewise the end-of-year yield represents the interest rate required by purchasers of 10-year bonds at the end of the year. Note how different the beginning-of-year yields can be from the end-of-year yields. For example, the year 2009 began with 10-year bond investors requiring a 2.3% return, but by the end of that year the required return on 10-year bonds had gone up to 3.9%. Notice the effect that this increase in interest rates had on the total return that investors earned on 10-year bonds in 2009. An investor who purchased a bond in January of 2009 received interest payments based on the bond's 2.3% yield, but they also experienced a capital loss during the year because 10-year bond yields increased (remember, bond prices go down when interest rates go up). The total return on 10-year bond in 2009 was −10.8%, which simply means that the capital loss on bonds that year far exceed the 2.3% in interest income that bondholders received.

During a period of rising rates, total returns on bonds include capital losses that can sometimes exceed the bonds' current interest income, resulting in a negative total return. Total returns on U.S. Treasury bonds were negative in 10 out of 52 years, and as Table 10.1 shows, the years with negative total returns on bonds were years in which bond yields rose: That is, the end-of-year yield was higher than the beginning-of-year yield.

Fortunately the inverse relationship between bond prices and yields can work in favor of investors too. Consider 2008. At the beginning of that year, the required return on bonds was 4.0%, but by the end of the year the required return had fallen to 2.3%. Notice that the total return earned by bond investors that year was 19.9%. In other words, bondholders earned about 4% in interest income, but they also earned a large capital gain (almost 16%) because interest rates fell during the year. As Table 10.1 shows, the years with the highest total returns on bonds are almost always years in which bond yields fell during the year.

TABLE 10.1   HISTORICAL ANNUAL YIELDS AND TOTAL RETURNS FOR TREASURY BONDS

Year	Beginning-of-Year T-Bond Yield	End-of-Year T-Bond Yield	T-Bond Total Return	Year	Beginning-of-Year T-Bond Yield	End-of-Year T-Bond Yield	T-Bond Total Return
1963	3.9%	4.1%	1.5%	1989	9.1%	7.9%	17.3%
1964	4.1%	4.2%	3.6%	1990	7.9%	8.1%	6.9%
1965	4.2%	4.7%	0.8%	1991	8.1%	6.7%	17.8%
1966	4.7%	4.6%	4.7%	1992	6.7%	6.7%	6.8%
1967	4.6%	5.7%	−3.3%	1993	6.7%	5.8%	13.2%
1968	5.7%	6.2%	2.3%	1994	5.8%	7.8%	−7.8%
1969	6.2%	7.9%	−5.4%	1995	7.8%	5.6%	24.8%
1970	7.9%	6.5%	17.8%	1996	5.6%	6.4%	−0.6%
1971	6.5%	5.9%	11.0%	1997	6.4%	5.8%	11.5%
1972	5.9%	6.4%	2.1%	1998	5.8%	4.7%	14.4%
1973	6.4%	6.9%	3.0%	1999	4.7%	6.5%	−8.3%
1974	6.9%	7.4%	3.5%	2000	6.5%	5.1%	16.7%
1975	7.4%	7.8%	5.0%	2001	5.1%	5.1%	5.5%
1976	7.8%	6.8%	14.5%	2002	5.1%	3.8%	15.2%
1977	6.8%	7.8%	0.2%	2003	3.8%	4.3%	0.3%
1978	7.8%	9.2%	−1.0%	2004	4.3%	4.2%	4.5%
1979	9.2%	10.3%	2.0%	2005	4.2%	4.4%	3.0%
1980	10.3%	12.4%	−1.3%	2006	4.4%	4.7%	1.9%
1981	12.4%	14.0%	4.3%	2007	4.7%	4.0%	10.1%
1982	14.0%	10.4%	35.9%	2008	4.0%	2.3%	19.9%
1983	10.4%	11.8%	2.0%	2009	2.3%	3.9%	−10.8%
1984	11.8%	11.6%	13.4%	2010	3.9%	3.3%	8.5%
1985	11.6%	9.0%	27.9%	2011	3.3%	1.9%	16.0%
1986	9.0%	7.2%	21.3%	2012	1.9%	1.8%	2.9%
1987	7.2%	8.8%	−3.1%	2013	1.8%	3.0%	−8.9%
1988	8.8%	9.1%	6.9%	2014	3.0%	2.2%	10.8%

(Source: Board of Governors of the Federal Reserve System (US), 10-Year Treasury Constant Maturity Rate [DGS10], retrieved from FRED, Federal Reserve Bank of St. Louis **https://research.stlouisfed.org/fred2/series/DGS10/**, May 20, 2015.)

We can use the return data from Table 10.1 to look at average bond returns over different periods, as shown below:

Period	Average Annual Total Returns
5 years: 2010–2014	5.9%
10 years: 2005–2014	5.3%
20 years: 1995–2014	6.9%
30 years: 1985–2014	8.5%

These figures show that the last 30 years were generally good to bond investors. This was mostly due to the fact that the U.S. economy was in a sustained period of declining interest rates, which in turn produced hefty capital gains and above-average returns. In fact, in 14 of the last 30 years, bonds earned double-digit total returns. Whether market interest rates will (or even can) continue on that path is, of course, the big question. Given the current record low yields, most market observers expect yields to begin rising over the next several years, leading to capital losses and below-average returns on bonds.

Bonds versus Stocks Compared to stocks, bonds are generally less risky and provide higher current income. Bonds, like stocks, are issued by a wide range of companies as well as various governmental bodies, so investors can construct well-diversified portfolios with bonds, just as they do with stocks. On the other hand, compared to stocks, the potential for very high returns on bonds is much more limited, even though the last two decades have been exceptional for bonds.

Figure 10.2 illustrates some of the performance differences between stocks and bonds by showing how a $10,000 investment in either stocks or bonds would have grown from 1990 through 2014. Although the investment in bonds slightly outpaced stocks in the early 1990s, investors in stocks were far better off in the late 1990s as the equity market boomed. Stocks peaked in August 2000 and then fell sharply. Stocks fell even more after the terrorist attacks on September 11, 2001, and they eventually hit bottom in September 2002. By the end of 2002, the bond investment was back in front, but only for a brief time. Stocks quickly recovered much of the ground that they had lost, peaking again in October 2007, only to have the U.S. housing bubble burst and the financial crisis begin. With the stock market in free fall in 2008 the bond market investment again took over the lead, and it would remain there for more than four years. After the financial crisis began to ease, stocks began a rocky rebound, and by the end of 2014, the $10,000 investment in stocks had grown to more than $60,000, whereas the money invested in bonds had grown to just over $48,000.

Figure 10.2 illustrates that over the last 25 years, stocks have outperformed bonds, but it also illustrates that stock returns are much more volatile than bond returns. If stocks are riskier, then investors should, on average, earn higher returns on stocks than on bonds, and we know from the historical evidence that stocks have outperformed bonds over long horizons. Still, Figure 10.2 shows that bonds can outperform stocks for a long time. For example, the cumulative returns on bonds far outpaced returns on stocks from July 2000 all the way through 2014. An investor who purchased $10,000 in bonds in July 2000 would have accumulated more than $21,200 by the end of 2014, whereas a $10,000 investment in stocks would have grown to just $13,900 over the same period.

The biggest differences in returns between stocks and bonds usually come during bear markets when stock returns are negative. In part, this reflects a phenomenon called "flight to quality" in which investors pull their funds out of the stock market to invest in less risky securities such as bonds. For example, while Figure 10.2 shows that investors in stocks lost roughly 40% of their money in 2008, Table 10.1 shows that government bond investors made about 20% that year.

Many investors argue that even if bonds earn lower returns than stocks on average, that's a low price to pay for the stability that bonds bring to a portfolio. The fact is, bond returns are far more stable than stock returns, plus they possess excellent portfolio diversification properties. As a general rule, adding bonds to a portfolio will, up to a point, reduce the portfolio's risk without dramatically reducing its return. Investors don't buy bonds for their high returns, except when they think interest rates are heading down. Rather, investors buy them for their current income and for the stability they bring to a portfolio.

FIGURE 10.2

Comparative Performance of Stocks and Bonds, 1990 through 2014

This graph shows what happened to $10,000 invested in bonds and $10,000 invested in stocks over the 25-year period from January 1990 through December 2014. Clearly, while stocks held a commanding lead going into the 21st century, the ensuing bear market more than erased that advantage. That pattern repeated itself as stocks outperformed bonds from early 2003 to late 2007, only to fall sharply through the end of 2008. From early 2009 through the end of 2012, stocks took a bumpy path toward rebounding, and from there stocks continued to climb at a rapid pace through 2014.

Note: Performance figures and graphs are based on rates of return and include reinvested current income (dividends and interest) as well as capital gains (or losses); taxes have been ignored in all calculations.

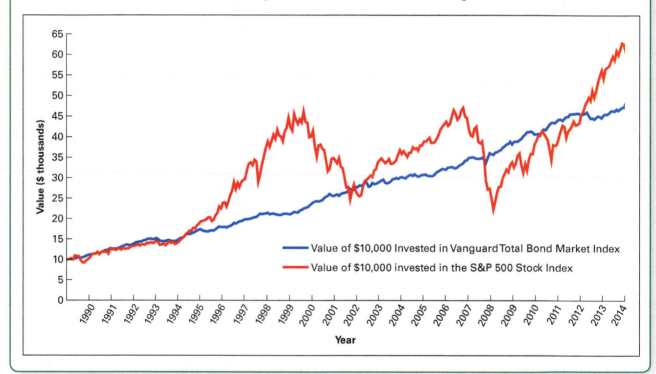

Exposure to Risk

Like all other investments, bonds are subject to a variety of risks. Generally speaking, bonds are exposed to five major types of risk: interest rate risk, purchasing power risk, business/financial risk, liquidity risk, and call risk.

- *Interest Rate Risk.* Interest rate risk is the most important risk that fixed-income investors face because it's the major cause of price volatility in the bond market. For bonds, interest rate risk translates into market risk, meaning that the behavior of interest rates affects nearly all bonds and cuts across all sectors of the market, even the U.S. Treasury market. When market interest rates rise, bond prices fall, and vice versa. As interest rates become more volatile, so do bond prices.

- *Purchasing Power Risk.* Inflation erodes the purchasing power of money, and that creates purchasing power risk. Naturally, investors are aware of this, so market interest rates on bonds compensate investors for the rate of inflation that they expect over a bond's life. When inflation is low and predictable, bonds do pretty well because their returns exceed the inflation rate by an amount sufficient to provide investors with a positive return, even after accounting for inflation's effect on purchasing power. When inflation takes off unexpectedly, as it did in the late 1970s, bond yields start to lag behind inflation rates, and the interest payments made by bonds fail to keep up. The end result is that the purchasing power of the money that bond investors receive falls faster than they anticipated. That's what the term *purchasing power risk* means. Of course, risk cuts both ways, so when the inflation rate falls unexpectedly, bonds do exceptionally well.

- *Business/Financial Risk.* This is basically the risk that the issuer will default on interest or principal payments. Also known as *credit risk*, or *default risk*, business/financial risk has to do with the quality and financial health of the issuer. The stronger the financial position of the issuer, the less business/financial risk there is to worry about. Default risk is negligible for some securities. Historically, investors have viewed U.S. Treasury securities as being free of default risk, although the growing debt of the United States has raised some concern about the potential for a default. For other types of bonds, such as corporate and municipal bonds, default risk is a much more important consideration.

- *Liquidity Risk.* Liquidity risk is the risk that a bond will be difficult to sell quickly without cutting the price if the investor wants to sell it. In some market sectors, this can be a big problem. Even though the bond market is enormous, many bonds do not trade actively once they are issued. U.S. Treasury bonds are the exception to the rule, but most corporate and municipal bonds are relatively illiquid.

- *Call Risk.* Call risk, or *prepayment risk*, is the risk that a bond will be "called" (retired) long before its scheduled maturity date. Issuers often prepay their bonds when interest rates fall. (We'll examine call features later.) When issuers call their bonds, the bondholders get their cash back and have to find another place for their funds, but because rates have fallen, bondholders have to reinvest their money at lower rates. Thus, investors have to replace high-yielding bonds with much lower-yielding bonds.

The returns on bonds are, of course, related to risk. Other things being equal, the more risk embedded in a bond, the greater the expected return. The risks of investing in bonds depend upon the characteristics of the bond and the entity that issued it. For example, as we'll see later in the chapter, there's more interest rate risk with a long-term bond than with a short-term bond. In addition, for particular bonds, the characteristics that affect risk may have offsetting effects, and that makes risk comparisons of bonds difficult. That is, one issue could have more interest rate and call risk but less credit and liquidity risk than another issue. We'll examine the various features that affect a bond's risk exposure as we work our way through this chapter.

CONCEPTS IN REVIEW

Answers available at
http://www.pearsonhighered.com/smart

10.1 What appeal do bonds hold for investors? Give several reasons why bonds make attractive investment outlets.

10.2 How would you describe the behavior of market interest rates and bond returns over the last 50 years? Do swings in market interest rates have any bearing on bond returns? Explain.

10.3 Identify and briefly describe the five types of risk to which bonds are exposed. What is the most important source of risk for bonds in general? Explain.

Essential Features of a Bond

LG2 **LG3** A bond is a long-term debt instrument that carries certain obligations (the payment of interest and the repayment of principal) on the part of the issuer. Bondholders are lenders, not owners, so they are not entitled to any of the rights and privileges associated with common stock, such as the right to vote at shareholders' meetings. But bondholders do have a number of well-defined rights and obligations that together define the essential features of a bond. We'll now take a look at some of these features. When it comes to bonds, it's especially important for investors to know what they're getting into, for many seemingly insignificant features can have dramatic effects on a bond's return.

Bond Interest and Principal

Bonds make periodic interest and principal payments. Most bonds pay interest every six months, although some make monthly interest payments, and some pay interest annually. A bond's **coupon** is the annual interest income that the issuer will pay to the bondholder, and its **par value, principal,** or **face value** is the amount of capital that the borrower must repay at maturity. For instance, if a bond with a par value of $1,000 pays $60 in interest each year, we say that $60 is the coupon. The **coupon rate** is the dollar coupon divided by the bond's par value, and it simply expresses the interest payment that the bond issuer makes as a percentage of the bond's par value. In the case of the $1,000 par value bond paying an annual $60 coupon, the coupon rate is 6% (i.e., $60 ÷ $1,000). If the bond makes semiannual payments, there would be a $30 interest payment every six months. Likewise, if the bond made monthly payments, the $60 coupon would be paid as 12 equal monthly interest payments of $5. The bond's **current yield** measures the interest component of a bond's return relative to the bond's market price. The current yield equals the annual coupon divided by the bond's current market price.

Example

> Suppose that a 6% bond with a $1,000 par value is currently priced in the market at $950. You can calculate the bond's current yield as follows:
>
> $$\frac{\$1,000 \times 0.06}{\$950} = 0.0632 = 6.32\%$$
>
> Notice that the 6.32% current yield is greater than the bond's coupon rate. That's because the bond's market price is below its par value. Note that a bond's market price need not, and usually does not, equal its par value. As we have discussed, bond prices fluctuate as interest rates move, yet a bond's par value remains fixed over its life.

Maturity Date

Unlike common stock, all debt securities have limited lives and will mature on some future date, the issue's **maturity date**. Whereas bond issuers may make interest payments annually or semiannually over the life of the issue, they repay principal only at maturity. The maturity date on a bond is fixed. It not only defines the life of a new issue but also denotes the amount of time remaining for older, outstanding bonds. Such a life span is known as an issue's *term to maturity*. For example, a new issue may come out as a 25-year bond; five years later, it will have 20 years remaining to maturity.

We can distinguish two types of bond offerings based on the issuer's plans to mature the debt: term and serial bond issues. A **term bond** issue has a single, fairly lengthy maturity date for all of the bonds being issued and is the most common type of bond issue. A **serial bond** issue, in contrast, has a series of bonds with different maturity dates, perhaps as many as 15 or 20, within a single bond offering. For example, in an offering of 20-year term bonds issued in 2015, all the bonds have a single maturity date of 2035. If the bonds were offered as serial bonds, they might have different maturity dates, extending from 2016 through 2035. At each of these maturity dates, a certain portion of the issue (i.e., a certain number of bonds) would mature.

Debt instruments with different maturities go by different names. A debt security that's originally issued with a maturity of 2 to 10 years is known as a **note**, whereas a bond technically has an initial term to maturity of more than 10 years. In practice, notes are often issued with maturities of 5 to 7 years, whereas bonds normally carry maturities of 20 to 30 years, or more.

Principles of Bond Price Behavior

Practice Pricing Bonds

The price of a bond is a function of the bond's coupon, its maturity, and the level of market interest rates. Figure 10.3 captures the relationship of bond prices to market interest rates. Basically, the graph reinforces the *inverse relationship* that exists between bond prices and market rates: Lower rates lead to higher bond prices.

Figure 10.3 also shows the difference between premium and discount bonds. A **premium bond** is one that sells for more than its par value. A premium results when market interest rates drop below the bond's coupon rate. A **discount bond**, in contrast, sells for less than par value. The discount is the result of market interest rates being greater than the issue's coupon rate. Thus, the 10% bond in Figure 10.3 trades at a premium when the market requires 8% but at a discount when the market rate is 12%.

When a bond is first issued, it usually sells at a price that equals or is very close to par value because bond issuers generally set the coupon rate equal or close to the market's required interest rate at the time of the issue. Likewise, when the bond matures—some 15, 20, or 30 years later—it will once again be priced at its par value. What happens to the price of the bond in between is of considerable interest to most bond investors. In this regard, the extent to which bond prices move depends not only on the direction of change in market interest rates but also on the magnitude of such change. The greater the moves in interest rates, the greater the swings in bond prices.

However, bond price volatility also varies according to an issue's coupon and maturity. Bonds with lower coupons and/or longer maturities have more price volatility and are more responsive to changes in market interest rates. (Note in Figure 10.3 that for a given change in interest rates—for example, from 10% to 8%—the largest change in price occurs when the bond has the greatest number of years to maturity.) Therefore, if investors expect a decline in interest rates, they should buy bonds with lower coupons and longer maturities to maximize capital gains. When interest rates move up, they should do just the opposite: Purchase bonds with high coupons and short maturities. This choice will minimize the price decline and act to preserve as much capital as possible.

The maturity of an issue has a greater impact on price volatility than the coupon does. For example, suppose there are two bonds that both pay an 8% coupon rate and currently sell at par value. One bond matures in 5 years while the other matures in 25 years. Look what happens to the bond prices when market rates change:

	Percentage Change in the Price of an 8% Coupon Bond When Market Interest Rates Change					
Interest Rate Change	−3%	−2%	−1%	+1%	+2%	+3%
Bond Maturity (yr)						
5	13.0%	8.4%	4.1%	−3.9%	−7.6%	−11.1%
25	42.3%	25.6%	11.7%	−9.8%	−18.2%	−25.3%

The prices of both bonds rise when interest rates fall, but the effect is much larger for the 25-year bond. Similarly, both bonds fall in value when rates rise, but the 25-year bond falls a lot more than the 5-year bond does. Such behavior is universal with all fixed-income securities and is very important. It means that if investors want to reduce their exposure to capital losses or, more to the point, to lower the price volatility in their bond holdings, then they should buy bonds with shorter maturities.

FIGURE 10.3

The Price Behavior of a Bond

A bond will sell at its par value so long as the prevailing market interest rate remains the same as the bond's coupon—in this case, 10%. However, even when the market rate does not equal the coupon rate, as a bond approaches its maturity, the price of the issue moves toward its par value.

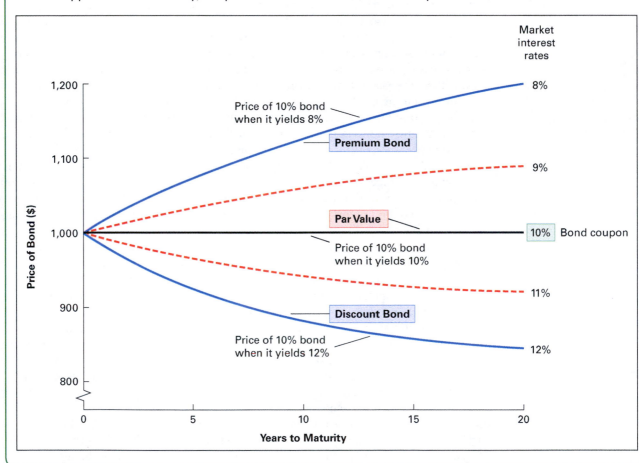

Quoting Bond Prices

Unlike stocks, the vast majority of bonds—especially corporate and municipal bonds—rarely change hands in the secondary markets. As a result, with the exception of U.S. Treasury and some agency issues, bonds are not widely quoted in the financial press, not even in the *Wall Street Journal*. Prices of all types of bonds are usually expressed as a percent of par, meaning that a quote of, say, 85 translates into a price of 85% of the bond's par value or $850 for a bond with a $1,000 par value (most corporate and municipal bonds have $1,000 par values). Also, the price of any bond depends on its coupon and maturity, so those two features are always a part of any price quote.

In the corporate and municipal markets, bond prices are expressed in decimals, using three places to the right of the decimal. Thus, a quote of 87.562, as a percent of a $1,000 par bond, converts to a price of $875.62. Similarly, a quote of 121.683 translates into a price of $1,216.83. In contrast, U.S. Treasury and agency bond quotes are stated in thirty-seconds of a point (where 1 point equals $10). For example, a website might list the price of a T-bond at 94:16. Translated, that means the bond is priced at 94 16/32, or 94.5% of par—in other words, at $945.00. With government bonds, the figures to the right of the colon show the number of thirty-seconds embedded in the price. Consider another bond that's trading at 141:08. This bond is being priced at 141 8/32, or 141.25% of par. Thus, the price of this bond in dollars is $1,412.50.

Call Features—Let the Buyer Beware!

Consider the following situation: You've just made an investment in a newly issued 25-year bond with a high coupon rate. Now you can sit back and let the cash flow in, right? Well, perhaps. Certainly, that will happen for the first several years. But if market interest rates drop, it's also likely that you'll receive a notice from the issuer that the bond is being called—that the issue is being retired before its maturity date. There's really nothing you can do but turn in the bond and invest your money elsewhere. Every bond is issued with a **call feature**, which stipulates whether and under what conditions a bond can be called in for retirement prior to maturity.

Basically, there are three types of call features:

1. A bond can be *freely callable*, which means the issuer can prematurely retire the bond at any time.

2. A bond can be *noncallable*, which means the issuer is prohibited from retiring the bond prior to maturity.

3. The issue could carry a *deferred call*, which means the issue cannot be called until after a certain length of time has passed from the date of issue. In essence, the issue is noncallable during the deferment period and then becomes freely callable thereafter.

Call features allow bond issuers to take advantage of declines in market interest rates. Companies usually call outstanding bonds paying high rates and then reissue new bonds at lower rates. In other words, call features work for the benefit of the issuers. When a bond is called, the net result is that the investor is left with a much lower rate of return than would be the case if the bond could not be called.

Investors who find their bonds called away from them often receive a small amount of extra compensation called the **call premium**. If the issue is called, the issuer will pay the call premium to investors, along with the issue's par value. The sum of the par value plus the call premium represents the issue's **call price**. This is the amount the issuer must pay to retire the bond prematurely. Call premiums often amount to as much as a year's worth of interest payments, at least if the bond is called at the earliest possible date. As the bond gets closer to maturity, the call premium gets smaller. Using this rule, the initial call price of a 5% bond could be as high as $1,050, where $50 represents the call premium.

In addition to call features, some bonds may carry **refunding provisions**. These are much like call features except that they prohibit the premature retirement of an issue from the proceeds of a lower-coupon bond. For example, a bond could come out as freely callable but nonrefundable for five years. In this case, brokers would probably sell the bond as a *deferred refunding issue*, with little or nothing said about its call feature. The distinction between nonrefundable and noncallable is important. A nonrefundable bond can still be called at any time as long as the money that the company uses to retire the bond prematurely comes from a source other than a new, lower-coupon bond issue.

Sinking Funds

Another provision that's important to investors is the **sinking fund,** which stipulates how the issuer will pay off the bond over time. This provision applies only to term bonds, of course, because serial issues already have a predetermined repayment schedule. Not all (term) bonds have sinking-fund requirements, but for those that do, the sinking fund specifies the annual repayment schedule that will be used to pay off the issue. It indicates how much principal will be retired each year.

Sinking-fund requirements generally begin one to five years after the date of issue and continue annually thereafter until all or most of the issue is paid off. Any amount not repaid (which might equal 10% to 25% of the issue) would then be retired with a single "balloon" payment at maturity. Unlike a call or refunding provision, the issuer generally does not have to pay a call premium with sinking-fund calls. Instead, the bonds are normally called at par for sinking-fund purposes.

There's another difference between sinking-fund provisions and call or refunding features. That is, whereas a call or refunding provision gives the issuer the right to retire a bond prematurely, a sinking-fund provision obligates the issuer to pay off the bond systematically over time. The issuer has no choice. It must make sinking-fund payments in a prompt and timely fashion or run the risk of being in default.

Secured or Unsecured Debt

A single issuer may have a number of different bonds outstanding at any given time. In addition to coupon and maturity, one bond can be differentiated from another by the type of collateral behind the issue. Bonds can be either junior or senior. **Senior bonds** are secured obligations, which are backed by a legal claim on some specific property of the issuer. Such issues include the following:

- **Mortgage bonds,** which are secured by real estate

- **Collateral trust bonds,** which are backed by financial assets owned by the issuer but held in trust by a third party

- **Equipment trust certificates,** which are secured by specific pieces of equipment (e.g., boxcars and airplanes) and are popular with railroads and airlines

- **First and refunding bonds,** which are basically a combination of first mortgage and junior lien bonds (i.e., the bonds are secured in part by a first mortgage on some of the issuer's property and in part by second or third mortgages on other properties).

Note that first and refunding bonds are less secure than, and should not be confused with, straight first-mortgage bonds.

Junior bonds, on the other hand, are backed only by the promise of the issuer to pay interest and principal on a timely basis. There are several classes of unsecured bonds, the most popular of which is a **debenture.** For example, a major company like Hewlett-Packard could issue $500 million worth of 20-year debenture bonds. Being a debenture, the bond would be totally unsecured, meaning there is no collateral backing up the obligation, other than the good name of the issuer. For that reason, highly regarded firms have no trouble selling billion-dollar debenture bond issues at competitive rates.

Subordinated debentures can also be found in the market. These issues have a claim on income secondary to other debenture bonds. **Income bonds,** the most junior of all bonds, are unsecured debts requiring that interest be paid only after a certain amount of income is earned. With these bonds, there is no legally binding requirement to meet interest payments on a timely or regular basis so long as a specified amount of income has not been earned. These issues are similar in many respects to revenue bonds found in the municipal market.

Bond Ratings

To many investors, an issue's *agency rating* is just as important in defining the characteristics of a bond as are its coupon, maturity, and call features. **Bond rating agencies** are institutions that perform extensive financial analysis on companies issuing bonds to assess the credit risk associated with a particular bond issue. The ratings that these agencies publish indicate the amount of credit risk embedded in a bond, and they are widely used by fixed-income investors. **Bond ratings** are essentially the grades that rating agencies give to new bond issues, where the letter grade corresponds to a certain level of credit risk. Ratings are an important part of the municipal and corporate bond markets, where issues are regularly evaluated and rated by one or more of the rating agencies. The three largest and best-known rating agencies are Moody's, Standard & Poor's, and Fitch.

How Ratings Work When a new bond issue comes to the market, a staff of professional credit analysts from the rating agencies estimates the likelihood that the bond issuer will default on its obligations to pay principal and interest. The rating agency studies the financial records of the issuing organization and assesses its prospects. As you might expect, the firm's financial strength and stability are very important in determining the appropriate bond rating. Although there is far more to setting a rating than cranking out a few financial ratios, a strong relationship does exist between the operating results and financial condition of the firm and the rating its bonds receive. Generally, higher ratings are associated with more profitable companies that rely less on debt as a form of financing, are more liquid, have stronger cash flows, and have no trouble servicing their debt in a prompt and timely fashion.

Table 10.2 lists the various ratings assigned to bonds by two of the three major services. In addition to the standard rating categories noted in the table, Moody's uses numerical modifiers (1, 2, or 3) on bonds rated Aa to Caa, while S&P uses plus (+) and minus (−) signs on the same rating classes to show relative standing within a major

TABLE 10.2   BOND RATINGS

Moody's	S&P	Definition
Aaa	AAA	High-grade investment bonds. The highest rating assigned, denoting extremely strong capacity to pay principal and interest. Often called "gilt-edge" securities.
Aa	AA	High-grade investment bonds. High quality but rated lower primarily because the margins of protection are not quite as strong as AAA bonds.
A	A	Medium-grade investment bonds. Many favorable investment attributes, but elements may be present that suggest susceptibility to adverse economic changes.
Baa	BBB	Medium-grade investment bonds. Adequate capacity to pay principal and interest but possibly lacking certain protective elements against adverse economic conditions.
Ba	BB	Speculative issues. Only moderate protection of principal and interest in varied economic times.
B	B	Speculative issues. Generally lacking desirable characteristics of investment bonds. Assurance of principal and interest may be small.
Caa	CCC	Default. Poor-quality issues that may be in default or in danger of default.
Ca	CC	Default. Highly speculative issues, often in default or possessing other market shortcomings.
C		Default. These issues may be regarded as extremely poor in investment quality.
	C	Default. Rating given to income bonds on which no interest is paid.
	D	Default. Issues actually in default, with principal or interest in arrears.

(Source: Moody's Investors Service and Standard & Poor's Ratings Services.)

rating category. For example, A+ (or A1) means a strong, high A rating, whereas A− (or A3) indicates that the issue is on the low end of the A rating scale.

Note that the top four ratings (Aaa through Baa, or AAA through BBB) designate **investment-grade bonds**. Such ratings are highly coveted by issuers because they indicate financially strong, well-run companies. Companies and governmental bodies that want to raise money by issuing bonds save money if they have an investment-grade rating because investors will accept lower yields on these bonds. Bonds with below-investment-grade ratings are called **high-yield bonds**, or **junk bonds**. The issuers of these bonds generally lack the financial strength that backs investment-grade issues. Most of the time, when the rating agencies assign ratings to a particular bond issue, their ratings agree. Sometimes, however, an issue carries different ratings from different rating agencies, and in that case the bond issue is said to have a **split rating**. For example, an issue might be rated Aa by Moody's but A or A+ by S&P. These split ratings are viewed simply as "shading" the quality of an issue one way or another.

Also, just because a bond receives a certain rating at the time of issue doesn't mean it will keep that rating for the rest of its life. Ratings change as the financial condition of the issuer changes, as the example involving Automated Data Processing at the start of this chapter illustrates. In fact, all rated issues are reviewed regularly to ensure that the assigned rating is still valid. Many issues do carry a single rating to maturity, but it is not uncommon for ratings to be revised up or down, and the market responds to rating revisions by adjusting bond yields accordingly. For example, an upward revision (e.g., from A to AA) causes the market yield on the bond to drop, reflecting the bond's improved quality. By the same token, if a company's financial condition deteriorates, ratings on its bonds may be downgraded. In fact, there is a special name given to junk bonds that once had investment-grade ratings—fallen angels. Although it may appear that the firm is receiving the rating, it is actually the issue that receives it. As a result, a firm's different issues can have different ratings. The senior securities, for example, might carry one rating and the junior issues another, lower rating.

What Ratings Mean Investors pay close attention to agency ratings because ratings are tied to bond yields. Specifically, the higher the rating the lower the yield, other things being equal. For example, whereas an A-rated bond might offer a 6.5% yield, a comparable AAA issue would probably yield something like 6%. Furthermore, a bond's rating has an impact on how sensitive its price is to interest rate movements as well as to changes in the company's financial performance. Junk bond prices tend to respond more when a company's financial position improves (or deteriorates) than prices of investment-grade bonds do.

Perhaps most important, bond ratings serve to relieve individual investors of the drudgery of evaluating the investment quality of an issue on their own. Large institutional investors often have their own staff of credit analysts who independently assess the creditworthiness of various corporate and municipal issuers. Individual investors, in contrast, have little if anything to gain from conducting their own credit analysis. After all, credit analysis is time-consuming and costly, and it demands a good deal more expertise than the average individual investor possesses. Two words of caution are in order, however. First, bear in mind that bond ratings are intended to measure only an issue's default risk, which has no bearing whatsoever on an issue's exposure to interest rate risk. Thus, if interest rates increase, even the highest-quality issues go down in price, subjecting investors to capital losses. Second, ratings agencies do make mistakes, and during the recent financial crisis, their mistakes made headlines.

FAMOUS FAILURES IN FINANCE

Rating Agencies Miss a Big One

Mortgage-backed securities, essentially debt instruments with returns that depended upon payments on an underlying pool of residential real estate mortgages, played a central role in the financial crisis that began in 2007 and the Great Recession that followed. Moody's and Standard & Poor's provided ratings on these instruments, just as they did with corporate bonds. Rating these securities was much more complex than rating corporate bonds for a variety of reasons, among them the fact that rating agencies knew relatively little about the creditworthiness of the individual homeowners whose mortgages were in the pool. The rating agencies gave many mortgage-backed securities investment-grade ratings, and those ratings prompted investors of all kinds, including large financial institutions, to pour money into those assets. As real estate prices began to decline, the values of "toxic" mortgage-backed securities plummeted. That led to the failure of Lehman Brothers and bailouts of other large financial institutions.

10.4 Can issue characteristics (such as coupon and call features) affect the yield and price behavior of bonds? Explain.

10.5 What is the difference between a call feature and a sinking-fund provision? Briefly describe the three types of call features. Can a bond be freely callable but nonrefundable?

10.6 What is the difference between a premium bond and a discount bond? What three attributes are most important in determining an issue's price volatility?

10.7 Bonds are said to be quoted "as a percent of par." What does that mean? What is one point worth in the bond market?

10.8 What are bond ratings, and how can they affect investor returns? What are split ratings?

10.9 From the perspective of an individual investor, what good are bond ratings? Do bond ratings indicate the amount of market risk embedded in a bond? Explain.

The Market for Debt Securities

LG4 **LG5** Thus far, our discussion has dealt with basic bond features. We now shift our attention to a review of the market in which these securities are traded. To begin with, the bond market is chiefly over-the-counter in nature, as listed bonds represent only a small portion of total outstanding obligations. In addition, this market is far more stable than the stock market. Indeed, although interest rates—and therefore bond prices—do move up and down over time, when bond price activity is measured daily, it is remarkably stable. Two other things that stand out about the bond market are its size and its growth rate. From a $250 billion market in 1950, it has grown to the point where, at the end of 2014, the amount of bonds outstanding in the United States totaled $39 trillion! That makes the U.S. bond market quite a bit larger than the size of the U.S. stock market.

Here's what the U.S. bond market looked like at the end of 2014:

	Amount Outstanding ($ trillions)
Treasury bonds	12.5
Agency bonds	2.0
Municipal bonds	3.7
Corporate bonds	7.8
Mortgage-backed bonds	8.7
Asset-backed bonds	1.3
Other	2.9
Total	39.0

(Source: Securities Industry and Financial Markets Association, "U.S. Bond Market Issuance and Outstanding," 2014.)

Major Market Segments

There are bonds available in today's market to meet almost any investment objective and to suit just about any type of investor. As a matter of convenience, the domestic bond market is normally separated into four major segments, according to type of

More about
Treasury Bills

issuer: Treasury, agency, municipal, and corporate. As we shall see, each sector has developed its own features, as well as its own trading characteristics.

Treasury Bonds "Treasuries" (or "governments," as they are sometimes called) are a dominant force in the fixed-income market. If not the most popular type of bond, they certainly are the best known. In addition to T-bills (a popular short-term debt security), the U.S. Treasury issues notes and bonds. It also issues *inflation-indexed securities.*

All Treasury obligations are of the highest quality because they are all backed by the "full faith and credit" of the U.S. government. This backing, along with their liquidity, makes them very popular with individual and institutional investors both in the United States and abroad. Indeed, U.S. Treasury securities are traded in all the major markets of the world, from New York to London to Sydney and Tokyo.

Treasury notes are issued with maturities of 2, 3, 5, 7, and 10 years, whereas **Treasury bonds** carry 30-year maturities. All Treasury notes and bonds pay interest semiannually. Interest income from these securities is subject to normal federal income tax but is exempt from state and local taxes. The Treasury today issues only noncallable securities; the last time it issued callable debt was in 1984. It issues its securities at regularly scheduled auctions, the results of which are widely reported by the financial media (see Figure 10.4). The Treasury establishes the initial yields and coupons on the securities it issues through this auction process.

Investors participating in an auction have a choice of two bidding options—competitive and noncompetitive. Investors who place competitive bids specify the yield that they are willing to accept (and hence, the price that they are willing to pay). Investors submitting competitive bids may be allocated securities in any given auction depending on how their bids compare to bids submitted by others. In a noncompetitive bid, investors agree to accept securities at the yield established in the auction. To conduct an auction, the Treasury first accepts all noncompetitive bids and then accepts competitive bids in ascending order in terms of their yield (i.e., descending order in terms of price) until the quantity of accepted bids reaches the full offering amount. All bidders receive the same yield as the highest accepted bid.

FIGURE 10.4

Auction Results for a 30-Year Treasury Bond

Treasury auctions are closely followed by the financial media. The number of competitive bids submitted generally far exceeds the number accepted; in this case only 45% of the competitive bids were accepted and issued bonds. (Source: Department of the Treasury, Bureau of Public Debt, Washington, DC 20239, May 14, 2015.)

U.S. Treasury Auction Results February 15, 2012	
Type of security	30-Year Bond
Interest rate	3%
High yield[1]	3.044%
Price	99.138514
Competitive	$15,980,095,000
Total	**$35,551,052,800**

[1] All tenders at lower yields were accepted in full.

Yield Spreads Approach Records

One interesting indicator of the state of the economy is the yield spread between low-risk government bonds and high-risk junk bonds issued by corporations. During the 1990–1991 recession, this yield spread set a record of 10.5%. That means that if investors require a 3% interest rate on government bonds, then they will demand a 13.5% rate on the most risky corporate bonds. In 2008 the junk bond credit spread widened again, reaching a new high of 14.68%, eclipsing the 1990s record. Interestingly, both of these episodes corresponded with a major crisis in the investment banking industry.

In 1990 it was the failure of Drexel Burnham Lambert and the fall of junk-bond king Michael Milken that led to wide spreads on junk bonds. In 2008 the yield spreads reflected investors' concerns following the 2007 failure of Lehman Brothers and bailouts of several other large financial institutions. In part due to the growing crisis in Europe, junk bond credit spreads began climbing again in 2011. Although the spread topped 7% in October of 2011, as of early 2015 it has remained below this level.

(Source: New York University Salomon Center and FRED Economic Data, St. Louis Fed.)

Inflation-Protected Securities The newest form of Treasury security (first issued in 1997) is the **Treasury Inflation-Protected Securities**, also known as **TIPS**. They are issued with 5-, 10-, and 30-year maturities, and they pay interest semiannually. They offer investors the opportunity to stay ahead of inflation by periodically adjusting their returns for any inflation that has occurred. The adjustment occurs through the bond's principal or par value. That is, the par value rises over time at a pace that matches the inflation rate. Coupon payments rise, too, because the coupon rate is paid on the inflation-adjusted principal.

Example

Suppose you purchased a 30-year TIPS with a par value of $1,000 and a 2% coupon rate. If there is no inflation, you expect to receive $20 in interest per year (i.e., $1,000 × 0.020), paid in two $10 semiannual installments. However, one year after you purchased the bond, inflation has caused the prices of goods and services to increase by 3%. The par value of your bond will increase by 3% to $1,030, and your interest payments will rise to $20.60 per year (i.e., $1,030 × 0.02). Notice that your interest payments have increased by 3%, thus compensating you for the inflation that occurred while you held the bond.

Because this type of bond offers payments that automatically adjust with inflation, investors do not have to guess what the inflation rate will be over the bond's life. In other words, TIPS eliminate purchasing power risk. Because they are less risky than ordinary bonds, TIPS generally offer lower returns than ordinary Treasury bonds do.

Agency Bonds **Agency bonds** are debt securities issued by various agencies and organizations of the U.S. government, such as the Federal Home Loan Bank, the Federal Farm Credit Systems, the Small Business Administration, the Student Loan Marketing Association, and the Federal National Mortgage Association. Although these securities are the closest things to Treasuries, they are not obligations of the U.S. Treasury and technically should not be considered the same as Treasury bonds. Even so, they are very high-quality securities that have almost no risk of default. In spite of the similar default risk, however, these securities usually provide yields that are slightly above the market rates for Treasuries. Thus, they offer a way to increase returns with little or no real difference in risk.

Implicit Guarantee Becomes Explicit

Debt securities issued by agencies such as the Federal National Mortgage Association (Fannie Mae) and the Federal Home Loan Mortgage Corporation (Freddie Mac) have generally had an implicit guarantee from the federal government, meaning that investors believed that the government would not allow a default on any of these instruments even if they were not "officially" backed by the full faith and credit of the U.S. government as Treasury bills, notes, and bonds are. In 2007 as residential mortgage defaults began to rise, Fannie Mae and Freddie Mac came under severe financial distress. On September 7, 2008, the federal government effectively took over these institutions, injecting $100 billion of new capital into each to stabilize them and to reassure investors that these giants of the mortgage industry, who held or guaranteed about $5.5 trillion in residential mortgage debt, would not disappear. Although the capital infusion helped initially, investor confidence in the two government-sponsored enterprises was rocked again on August 8, 2011, when their credit ratings were downgraded. Standard & Poor's said that the downgrade reflected their "direct reliance on the U.S. government," which had seen its own credit rating downgraded three days earlier.

There are basically two types of agency issues: government-sponsored and federal agencies. Six government-sponsored organizations and more than two dozen federal agencies offer agency bonds. To overcome some of the problems in the marketing of many relatively small federal agency securities, Congress established the Federal Financing Bank to consolidate the financing activities of all federal agencies. (As a rule, the generic term *agency* is used to denote both government-sponsored and federal agency obligations.)

Table 10.3 presents selected characteristics of some of the more popular agency bonds. As the list of issuers shows, most of the government agencies support either agriculture or housing. Although agency issues are not direct liabilities of the U.S. government, a few of them do carry government guarantees and therefore represent the full faith and credit of the U.S. Treasury. Even those issues that do not carry such guarantees are viewed as moral obligations of the U.S. government, implying it's highly unlikely that Congress would allow one of them to default. Agency issues are normally noncallable or carry lengthy call deferment features.

Municipal Bonds **Municipal bonds** (also called munis) are issued by states, counties, cities, and other political subdivisions (such as school districts and water and sewer districts). This is a $3.7 trillion market today, and it's the only segment of the bond market where the individual investor plays a major role: More than 40% of municipal bonds are directly held by individuals. These bonds are often issued as *serial obligations*, which means the issue is broken into a series of smaller bonds, each with its own maturity date and coupon.

Municipal bonds ("munis") are brought to the market as either general obligation or revenue bonds. **General obligation bonds** are backed by the full faith, credit, and taxing power of the issuer. **Revenue bonds,** in contrast, are serviced by the income generated from specific income-producing projects (e.g., toll roads). The vast majority of munis today come out as revenue bonds, accounting for about 75% to 80% of the new-issue volume. Municipal bonds are customarily issued in $5,000 denominations.

The distinction between a general obligation bond and a revenue bond is important because the issuer of a revenue bond is obligated to pay principal and interest only if a sufficient level of revenue is generated. If the funds aren't there, the issuer does not have to make payment on the bond. General obligation bonds, however, must be

TABLE 10.3 CHARACTERISTICS OF SOME POPULAR AGENCY ISSUES

Type of Issue	Minimum Denomination	Initial Maturity	Tax Status* Federal	State	Local
Federal Farm Credit System	$ 1,000	13 months to 15 years	T	E	E
Federal Home Loan Bank	$10,000	1 to 20 years	T	E	E
Federal Land Banks	$ 1,000	1 to 10 years	T	E	E
Farmers Home Administration	$25,000	1 to 25 years	T	T	T
Federal Housing Administration	$50,000	1 to 40 years	T	T	T
Federal Home Loan Mortgage Corp.** ("Freddie Mac")	$25,000	18 to 30 years	T	T	T
Federal National Mortgage Association** ("Fannie Mae")	$25,000	1 to 30 years	T	T	T
Government National Mortgage Association** (GNMA— "Ginnie Mae")	$25,000	12 to 40 years	T	T	T
Student Loan Marketing Association ("Sallie Mae")	$10,000	3 to 10 years	T	E	E
Tennessee Valley Authority (TVA)	$ 1,000	5 to 50 years	T	E	E
U.S. Postal Service	$10,000	25 years	T	E	E
Federal Financing Corp.	$ 1,000	1 to 20 years	T	E	E

*T = taxable; E = tax-exempt.
**Mortgage-backed securities.

serviced in a timely fashion irrespective of the level of tax income generated by the municipality. Obviously, revenue bonds involve more risk than general obligations, and because of that, they provide higher yields.

Some municipal bonds are backed by **municipal bond guarantees**, though these have become much less common than they once were. With these guarantees, a party other than the issuer assures the bondholder that payments will be made in a timely manner. The third party, in essence, provides an additional source of collateral in the form of insurance, placed on the bond at the date of issue, which is nonrevocable over the life of the obligation. This additional collateral improves the quality of the bond. The three principal insurers are the Assured Guaranty Corp., Municipal Bond Investors Assurance Corporation, and the American Municipal Bond Assurance Corporation. These guarantors will normally insure any general obligation or revenue bond as long as it carries an S&P rating of BBB or better. Municipal bond insurance results in higher ratings and improved liquidity for these bonds, which are generally more actively traded in the secondary markets. Insured bonds are more common in the revenue market, where the insurance markedly boosts their attractiveness. That is, whereas an uninsured revenue bond lacks certainty of payment, a guaranteed issue is very much like a general obligation bond because the investor knows that principal and interest payments will be made on time.

Tax Advantages The most important unique feature of municipal securities is that, in most cases, their interest income is exempt from federal income taxes. That's why these issues are known as tax-free, or tax-exempt, bonds.

Normally, municipal bonds are also exempt from state and local taxes in the state in which they were issued. For example, a California issue is free of California tax if the bondholder lives in California, but its interest income is subject to state tax if the investor resides in Arizona. Note that capital gains on municipal bonds are not exempt from taxes.

Individual investors are the biggest buyers of municipal bonds, and the tax-free interest that these bonds offer is a major draw. When investors think about buying municipal bonds, they compare the tax-free yield offered by the municipal bond and compare it to the after-tax yield that they could earn on a similar taxable bond.

Example

Suppose you are in the 25% tax bracket, so each dollar of interest that you earn triggers $0.25 in taxes, allowing you to keep $0.75. Suppose a tax-free municipal bond offers a yield of 6%. What yield would a taxable bond have to offer to give you the same 6% return after taxes that you could earn on the municipal bond? The after-tax yield on a taxable bond is just the stated yield times one minus the tax rate:

$$\text{After-tax yield} = \text{Yield on taxable bond} \times (1 - \text{tax rate})$$

If you desire an after-tax yield of 6% (because that's what the municipal bond offers) and your tax rate is 25%, then we can calculate the yield that you would need to earn on a taxable bond as follows:

$$0.06 = \text{Yield on taxable bond} \times (1 - 0.25)$$
$$\text{Yield on taxable bond} = 0.06 \div (1 - 0.25)$$
$$= 0.08$$

If the taxable bond offers 8% and the municipal bond offers 6%, then you are essentially indifferent to the choice between the two securities as long as they are similar in terms of risk (and not counting any tax benefit on your state income taxes). Notice that this value is highlighted in Table 10.4.

Table 10.4 shows how the yield that a taxable bond would have to offer to remain competitive with a municipal bond depends on the investor's *marginal tax rate*. Intuitively, the tax break that municipal bonds offer is more appealing to investors in higher tax brackets who face higher marginal tax rates. For these investors, taxable bonds are not very attractive unless their yields are much higher than the yields on municipal bonds. To put it another way, investors facing high tax rates will gladly purchase municipal bonds even if they offer yields that are somewhat lower than yields on taxable bonds. For example, Table 10.4 shows that an investor in the 10% tax bracket would be indifferent to the choice between a municipal bond offering a 6% yield and a taxable bond offering a slightly higher 6.67% yield. In contrast, an investor in the 35% tax bracket would prefer the 6% municipal bond unless the yield on the taxable bond was much higher at 9.23%. Not surprisingly, investors subject to high tax rates are the main purchasers of municipal bonds. Individuals in lower tax brackets generally do not

Excel@Investing

TABLE 10.4   TAXABLE EQUIVALENT YIELDS FOR VARIOUS TAX-EXEMPT RETURNS

Federal Tax Bracket	Tax-Free Yield					
	5%	6%	7%	8%	9%	10%
10%	5.56%	6.67%	7.78%	8.89%	10.00%	11.11%
15%	5.88%	7.06%	8.24%	9.41%	10.59%	11.76%
25%	6.67%	8.00%	9.33%	10.67%	12.00%	13.33%
28%	6.94%	8.33%	9.72%	11.11%	12.50%	13.89%
33%	7.46%	8.96%	10.45%	11.94%	13.43%	14.93%
35%	7.69%	9.23%	10.77%	12.31%	13.85%	15.38%
39.6%	8.28%	9.93%	11.59%	13.25%	14.90%	16.56%

invest as heavily in municipal bonds because for them, the higher yield on taxable bonds more than offsets the benefit of earning tax-free income. The favorable tax status given to municipal bonds allows state and local governments to borrow money at lower rates than they would otherwise be able to obtain in the market.

Taxable Equivalent Yields   As you can see from the previous example and from Table 10.4, it is possible to determine the return that a fully taxable bond would have to provide in order to match the return provided by a tax-free bond. The taxable yield that is equivalent to a municipal bond's lower, tax-free yield is called the municipal's **taxable equivalent yield**. The taxable equivalent yield allows an investor to quickly compare the yield on a municipal bond with the yield offered by any number of taxable issues. The following formula shows how to calculate the taxable equivalent yield given the yield on the municipal bond and the investor's tax rate.

Equation 10.1

$$\text{Taxable equivalent yield} = \frac{\text{Yield on municipal bond}}{1 - \text{Marginal federal tax rate}}$$

For example, if a municipal offered a yield of 6.5%, then an individual in the 35% tax bracket would have to find a fully taxable bond with a yield of 10.0% (i.e., $6.5\% \div (1 - 0.35) = 10.0\%$) to reap the same after-tax returns as the municipal.

Note, however, that Equation 10.1 considers federal income taxes only. As a result, the computed taxable equivalent yield applies only to certain situations: (1) to states that have no state income tax; (2) to the investor who is looking at an out-of-state bond (which would be taxable by the investor's state of residence); or (3) to the investor who is comparing a municipal bond to a Treasury (or agency) bond—in which case both the Treasury and the municipal bonds are free from state income tax; (4) to taxpayers with income levels low enough such that they are not subject to the 3.8% tax on net investment income that was passed as part of the Affordable Care Act. Under any of these conditions, the only tax that's relevant is federal income tax, so using Equation 10.1 is appropriate.

But what if you are comparing an in-state bond to a corporate bond? In this case, the in-state bond would be free from both federal and state taxes, but the corporate bond would not. As a result, Equation 10.1 would not calculate the correct taxable equivalent yield. Instead, you should use a form of the equivalent yield formula that considers both federal and state income taxes:

Equation 10.2

$$\text{Taxable equivalent yield for both federal and state taxes} = \frac{\text{Municipal bond yield}}{1 - [\text{Federal tax rate} + \text{State tax rate} (1 - \text{Federal tax rate})]}$$

Notice that the inclusion of state taxes means that the denominator of Equation 10.2 is slightly smaller than the denominator of Equation 10.1, which in turn means that the taxable equivalent yield will be higher with state taxes as part of the analysis. Intuitively this makes sense because if municipal bonds offer tax advantages at both the federal and state levels, then taxable yields must be even higher to remain competitive.

Example

Suppose your marginal federal tax rate is 35% and your state income tax rate is 3%. There is a municipal bond issued by your state that offers a yield of 6.305%. According to Equation 10.2, the taxable-equivalent yield is 10%:

$$\frac{0.06305}{1 - [0.35 + 0.03(1 - 0.35)]} = 0.10$$

Just to confirm that this is correct, suppose you purchased a $1,000 bond paying a 10% coupon rate. In the first year, you would receive $100 in interest income that is fully taxable at both the state and federal levels. Remember that taxes paid to state governments may be deducted from income before you pay federal taxes. How much of the $100 coupon payment will you have to pay in combined federal and state taxes?

Income	$100.00
State taxes (3%)	−$3.00
Taxable income (federal)	$97.00
Federal taxes (35%)	−$33.95
Net	$ 63.05

After paying $3 in state taxes and $33.95 in federal taxes, you get to keep $63.05 of the bond's $100 coupon payment. Given that you paid $1,000 for the bond, your return is 6.305%. In other words, as you found by using Equation 10.2, a 6.305% yield on a tax-free bond is equivalent to a 10% yield on a taxable bond.

Notice that if there had been no state tax in this example, the taxable equivalent yield would have been 9.7%. That's not a huge difference, but the difference would be higher for a higher state tax rate, and some U.S. states have tax rates as high as 11%.

Corporate Bonds   Corporations are the major nongovernmental issuers of bonds. The market for corporate bonds is customarily subdivided into four segments based on the types of companies that issue bonds: *industrials* (the most diverse of the groups), *public utilities* (the dominant group in terms of volume of new issues), *transportation*, and *financial services* (e.g., banks, finance companies). In the corporate sector of the bond market investors can find bonds from high-quality AAA-rated issues to junk bonds in or near default, and there is also a wide assortment of bonds with many different features. These range from first-mortgage obligations to convertible bonds (which we'll examine later in this chapter), debentures, subordinated debentures, senior subordinated issues, capital notes (a type of unsecured debt issued by banks and other financial institutions), and income bonds. Companies pay interest on corporate bonds semiannually, and sinking funds are fairly common. The bonds usually come in $1,000 denominations and are issued on a term basis with a single maturity date of 10 years or more. Many corporate bonds, especially the longer ones, carry call deferment provisions that prohibit prepayment for the first 5 to 10 years. Corporate issues are popular with individuals because of the steady, predictable income that they provide.

While most corporate issues fit the general description above, one that does not is the *equipment trust certificate*, a security issued by railroads, airlines, and other transportation concerns. The proceeds from equipment trust certificates are used to purchase equipment (e.g., jumbo jets and railroad engines) that serves as the collateral for the issue. These bonds are usually issued in serial form and carry uniform annual installments throughout. They normally carry maturities that range up to about 15 years, with the maturity reflecting the useful life of the equipment. Despite a near-perfect payment record that dates back to pre-Depression days, these issues generally offer above-average yields to investors.

Specialty Issues

In addition to the basic bonds described above, investors can choose from a number of specialty issues—bonds that possess unusual issue characteristics. These bonds have coupon or repayment provisions that are out of the ordinary. Most of them are issued by corporations, although they are being used increasingly by other issuers as well. Four of the most actively traded specialty issues today are zero-coupon bonds, mortgage-backed securities, asset-backed securities, and high-yield junk bonds. All of these rank as some of the more popular bonds on Wall Street.

Zero-Coupon Bonds   As the name implies, **zero-coupon bonds** have no coupons. Rather, these securities are sold at a discount from their par values and then increase in value over time at a compound rate of return. Thus, at maturity, they are worth more than their initial cost, and this difference represents the bond's return. Other things being equal, the cheaper the zero-coupon bond, the greater the return an investor can earn: For example, a bond with a 6% yield might cost $420, but one with a 10% yield might cost only $240.

Because they do not have coupons, these bonds do not pay interest semiannually. In fact, they pay nothing at all until the issue matures. As strange as it might seem, this feature is the main attraction of zero-coupon bonds. Because there are no coupon payments, there is no need to worry about reinvesting interest income twice a year. Instead, the rate of return on a zero-coupon bond is virtually guaranteed to be the yield that existed at the time of purchase as long as the investor holds the bond to maturity. For example, in mid-2015, U.S. Treasury zero-coupon bonds with 10-year maturities were available at yields of around 2.5%. For around $780, investors could buy a bond that would be worth $1,000 at maturity in 10 years. That 2.5% yield is a rate of return that's locked in for the life of the issue.

The foregoing advantages notwithstanding, zeros do have some serious disadvantages. One is that if market interest rates move up, investors won't be able to participate in the higher return. (They'll have no interest income to reinvest.) In addition, zero-coupon bonds are subject to tremendous price volatility. If market rates climb, investors will experience a sizable capital loss as the prices of zero-coupons plunge. (Of course, if interest rates drop, investors who hold long-term zeros will reap enormous capital gains.) A final disadvantage is that the IRS has ruled that zero-coupon bondholders must pay tax on interest as it accrues, even though investors holding these bonds don't actually receive interest payments.

Zeros are issued by corporations, municipalities, and federal agencies. Actually, the Treasury does not issue zero-coupon bonds. Instead, it allows government securities dealers to sell regular coupon-bearing notes and bonds in the form of zero-coupon securities known as **Treasury strips**. Essentially, the interest and principal payments are stripped from a Treasury bond and then sold separately as zero-coupon bonds. For example, a 10-year Treasury note has 20 semiannual interest payments, plus 1 principal payment. These 21 cash flows can be sold as 21 different zero-coupon securities, with maturities that range from 6 months to 10 years. The minimum par value needed to strip a Treasury note or bond is $100 and any par value to be stripped above $100 must be in a multiple of $100. Treasury strips with the same maturity are often bundled and sold in minimum denominations (par values) of $10,000. Because there's an active secondary market for Treasury strips, investors can get in and out of these securities with ease just about anytime they want. Strips offer the maximum in issue quality, a wide array of maturities, and an active secondary market—all of which explains why they are so popular.

Mortgage-Backed Securities Simply put, a **mortgage-backed bond** is a debt issue that is secured by a pool of residential mortgages. An issuer, such as the Government National Mortgage Association (GNMA), puts together a pool of home mortgages and then issues securities in the amount of the total mortgage pool. These securities, also known as *pass-through securities* or *participation certificates*, are usually sold in minimum denominations of $25,000. Although their maturities can go out as far as 30 years, the average life is generally much shorter (perhaps as short as 8 years) because many of the mortgages are paid off early.

As an investor in one of these securities, you hold an undivided interest in the pool of mortgages. When a homeowner makes a monthly mortgage payment, that payment is essentially passed through to you, the bondholder, to pay off the mortgage-backed bond you hold. Although these securities come with normal coupons, the interest is paid monthly rather than semiannually. Actually, the monthly payments received by bondholders are, like mortgage payments, made up of both principal and interest. Because the principal portion of the payment represents return of capital, it is considered tax-free. The interest portion, however, is subject to ordinary state and federal income taxes.

Mortgage-backed securities (MBSs) are issued primarily by three federal agencies. Although there are some state and private issuers (mainly big banks and S&Ls), agency issues dominate the market and account for 90% to 95% of the activity. The major agency issuers of mortgage-backed securities (MBSs) are:

- *Government National Mortgage Association (GNMA)*. Known as Ginnie Mae, it is the oldest and largest issuer of MBSs.

- *Federal Home Loan Mortgage Corporation (FHLMC)*. Known as Freddie Mac, it was the first to issue pools containing conventional mortgages.

- *Federal National Mortgage Association (FNMA)*. Known as Fannie Mae, it's the leader in marketing seasoned/older mortgages.

One feature of mortgage-backed securities is that they are self-liquidating investments; that is, a portion of the monthly cash flow to the investor is repayment of principal. Thus, investors are always receiving back part of the original investment capital, so that at maturity, there is no big principal payment. To counter this effect, a number of mutual funds invest in mortgage-backed securities but automatically reinvest the capital/principal portion of the cash flows. Mutual fund investors therefore receive only the interest from their investments and their capital remains fully invested.

Collateralized Mortgage Obligations Loan prepayments are another problem with mortgage-backed securities. In fact, it was in part an effort to diffuse some of the prepayment uncertainty in standard mortgage-backed securities that led to the creation of **collateralized mortgage obligations (CMOs)**. Normally, as pooled mortgages are prepaid, all bondholders receive a prorated share of the prepayments. The net effect is to sharply reduce the life of the bond. A CMO, in contrast, divides investors into classes (called *tranches*, which is French for "slice"), depending on whether they want a short-, intermediate-, or long-term investment. Although interest is paid to all bondholders, all principal payments go first to the shortest tranche until it is fully retired. Then the next class in the sequence becomes the sole recipient of principal, and so on, until the last tranche is retired.

Basically, CMOs are *derivative securities* created from traditional mortgage-backed bonds, which are placed in a trust. Participation in this trust is then sold to the investing public in the form of CMOs. The net effect of this transformation is that CMOs look and behave very much like any other bond. They offer predictable interest payments and have (relatively) predictable maturities. However, although they carry the same AAA ratings and implicit U.S. government backing as the mortgage-backed bonds that underlie them, CMOs represent a quantum leap in complexity. Some types of CMOs can be as simple and safe as Treasury bonds. Others can be far more volatile—and risky—than the standard MBSs they're made from. That's because when putting CMOs together, Wall Street performs the financial equivalent of gene splicing. Investment bankers isolate the interest and principal payments from the underlying MBSs and rechannel them to the different tranches. It's not issue quality or risk of default that's the problem here, but rather prepayment, or call, risk. Even if all of the bonds are ultimately paid off, investors don't know exactly when those payments will arrive. Different types of CMO tranches have different levels of prepayment risk. The overall risk in a CMO cannot, of course, exceed that of the underlying mortgage-backed bonds, so in order for there to be some tranches with very little (or no) prepayment risk, others have to endure a lot more. The net effect is that while some CMO tranches are low in risk, others are loaded with it.

Investors discovered just how complex and how risky these securities could be as the financial crisis unfolded in 2007 and 2008. As homeowner defaults on residential mortgages began to rise, the values of CMOs plummeted. Trading in the secondary market dried up, so it was difficult to know what the underlying values of some CMOs really were. Investment and commercial banks that had invested heavily in these securities came under intense pressure as doubts about their solvency grew into a near panic. Everyone wanted to know which institutions held these "toxic assets" on their balance sheets and how large their losses were on these instruments. Lehman Brothers, Bear Stearns, Merrill Lynch, and many other financial institutions went bankrupt or were acquired under distress by other institutions, and the federal government poured hundreds of billions of dollars into the banking system to try to prevent total collapse.

Asset-Backed Securities The creation of mortgage-backed securities and CMOs quickly led to the development of a new market technology—the process of **securitization**, whereby various lending vehicles are transformed into marketable securities, much like a mortgage-backed security. In recent years, investment bankers sold billions of dollars' worth of pass-through securities, known as **asset-backed securities (ABS)**, which are backed by pools of auto loans, credit card bills, and home equity lines of credit (three of the principal types of collateral), as well as computer leases, hospital receivables, small business loans, truck rentals, and even royalty fees.

These securities, first introduced in the mid-1980s, are created when an investment bank bundles some type of debt-linked asset (such as loans or receivables) and then sells to investors—via asset-backed securities—the right to receive all or part of the future payments made on that debt. For example, GMAC, the financing arm of General Motors, is a regular issuer of collateralized auto loan securities. When it wants to get some of its car loans off its books, GMAC takes the monthly cash flow from a pool of auto loans and pledges them to a new issue of bonds, which are then sold to investors. In similar fashion, credit card receivables are regularly used as collateral for these bonds (indeed, they represent the biggest segment of the ABS market), as are home equity loans, the second-biggest type of ABS.

Investors are drawn to ABSs for a number of reasons. These securities offer relatively high yields, and they typically have short maturities, which often extend out no more than five years. A third reason that investors like ABSs is the monthly, rather than semiannual, principal/interest payments that accompany many of these securities. Also important to investors is their high credit quality. That's due to the fact that most of these deals are backed by generous credit protection. For example, the securities are often overcollateralized: the pool of assets backing the bonds may be 25% to 50% larger than the bond issue itself. A large fraction of ABSs receive the highest credit rating possible (AAA) from the leading rating agencies.

Junk Bonds Junk bonds (or high-yield bonds, as they're also called) are highly speculative securities that have received low, sub-investment-grade ratings (typically Ba or B). These bonds are issued primarily by corporations and also by municipalities. Junk bonds often take the form of *subordinated debentures*, which means the debt is unsecured and has a low claim on assets. These bonds are called "junk" because of their high risk of default. The companies that issue them generally have excessive amounts of debt in their capital structures and their ability to service that debt is subject to considerable doubt.

Probably the most unusual type of junk bond is something called a **PIK bond**. PIK stands for *payment in kind* and means that rather than paying the bond's coupon in cash, the issuer can make annual interest payments in the form of additional debt. This "financial printing press" usually goes on for five or six years, after which time the issuer is supposed to start making interest payments in real money.

Why would any rational investor be drawn to junk bonds? The answer is simple: They offer very high yields. Indeed, in a typical market, relative to investment-grade bonds, investors can expect to pick up anywhere from two to five percentage points in added yield. For example, in June of 2015, investors were getting roughly 6.5% yields on junk bonds, compared to just under 4% on investment-grade corporates. Obviously, such yields are available only because of the correspondingly higher exposure to risk. Junk bonds are subject to a good deal of risk, and their prices are unstable. Indeed, unlike investment-grade bonds, whose prices are closely linked to the behavior of market interest rates, junk bonds tend to behave more like stocks. As a result, the returns are highly unpredictable. Accordingly, only investors who are thoroughly familiar with the risks involved, and who are comfortable with such risk exposure, should purchase these securities.

A Global View of the Bond Market

Globalization has hit the bond market, just as it has the stock market. Foreign bonds have caught on with U.S. investors because of their high yields and attractive returns. There are risks with foreign bonds, of course, but high risk of default is not always one of them. Instead, the big risk with foreign bonds has to do with the impact that currency fluctuations can have on returns in U.S. dollars.

The United States has the world's biggest bond market, accounting for a little less than half of the global market. Following the United States is Japan, China, and several countries in the European Union (principally Germany, Italy, and France). Together these countries account for more than 90% of the world bond market. Worldwide, various forms of government bonds (e.g., Treasuries, agencies, and munis) dominate the market.

U.S.-Pay versus Foreign-Pay Bonds There are several ways to invest in foreign bonds. From the perspective of a U.S. investor, we can divide foreign bonds into two broad categories on the basis of the currency in which the bond is denominated: *U.S.-pay* (or dollar-denominated) bonds and *foreign-pay* (or non-dollar-denominated) bonds. All the cash flows—including purchase price, maturity value, and coupon income—from dollar-denominated foreign bonds are in U.S. dollars. The cash flows from non-dollar bonds are designated in a foreign currency, such as the euro, British pound, or Swiss franc.

Dollar-Denominated Bonds Dollar-denominated foreign bonds are of two types: Yankee bonds and Eurodollar bonds. **Yankee bonds** are issued by foreign governments or corporations or by so-called supranational agencies, like the World Bank and the InterAmerican Bank. These bonds are issued and traded in the United States; they're registered with the SEC, and all transactions are in U.S. dollars. Not surprisingly, Canadian issuers dominate the Yankee-bond market. Buying a Yankee bond is really no different from buying any other U.S. bond. These bonds are traded on U.S. exchanges and the OTC market, and because everything is in dollars, there's no currency exchange risk to deal with. The bonds are generally very high in quality (which is not surprising, given the quality of the issuers) and offer highly competitive yields to investors.

Eurodollar bonds, in contrast, are issued and traded outside the United States. They are denominated in U.S. dollars, but they are not registered with the SEC, which means underwriters are legally prohibited from selling new issues to the U.S. public. (Only "seasoned" Eurodollar issues can be sold in this country.) The Eurodollar market today is dominated by foreign-based investors (though that is changing) and is primarily aimed at institutional investors.

Foreign-Pay Bonds From the standpoint of U.S. investors, foreign-pay international bonds encompass all those issues denominated in a currency other than dollars. These bonds are issued and traded overseas and are not registered with the SEC. Examples are

German government bonds, which are payable in euros; Japanese bonds, issued in yen; and so forth. When investors speak of foreign bonds, it's this segment of the market that most of them have in mind.

Foreign-pay bonds are subject to changes in currency exchange rates, which can dramatically affect total returns to U.S. investors. The returns on foreign-pay bonds depend on three things: (1) the level of coupon (interest) income earned on the bonds; (2) the change in market interest rates, which determines the level of capital gains (or losses); and (3) the behavior of currency exchange rates. The first two variables are the same as those that drive U.S. bond returns. They are, of course, just as important to foreign bonds as they are to domestic bonds. Thus, if individuals are investing overseas, they still want to know what the yields are today and where they're headed. It's the third variable that separates the return behavior of dollar-denominated from foreign-pay bonds.

We can assess returns from foreign-pay bonds by employing the following equation:

Equation 10.3

$$\text{Total return (in U.S. dollars)} = \left[\frac{\substack{\text{Ending value of} \\ \text{bond in foreign} \\ \text{currency}} + \substack{\text{Amount of interest} \\ \text{received in} \\ \text{foreign currency}}}{\substack{\text{Beginning value of bond} \\ \text{in foreign currency}}} \times \frac{\substack{\text{Exchange rate} \\ \text{at end of} \\ \text{holding period}}}{\substack{\text{Exchange rate} \\ \text{at beginning of} \\ \text{holding period}}}\right] - 1.00$$

For example, assume a U.S. investor purchased a Swedish government bond, in large part because of the attractive 7.5% coupon it carried. If the bond was bought at par and market rates fell over the course of the year, the security itself would have provided a return in excess of 7.5% (because the decline in rates would provide some capital gains). However, if the Swedish krona (SEK) fell relative to the dollar, the total return (in U.S. dollars) could have actually ended up at a lot less than 7.5%, depending on what happened to the U.S.$/SEK exchange rate. To find out exactly how this investment performed, you could use the equation above. Like foreign stocks, foreign-pay bonds can pay off from both the behavior of the security and the behavior of the currency. That combination, in many cases, means superior returns to U.S. investors. Knowledgeable investors find these bonds attractive not only because of their competitive returns but also because of the positive diversification effects they have on bond portfolios.

CONCEPTS IN REVIEW

Answers available at
http://www.pearsonhighered.com/smart

10.10 Briefly describe each of the following types of bonds: (a) Treasury bonds, (b) agency issues, (c) municipal securities, and (d) corporate bonds. Note some of the major advantages and disadvantages of each.

10.11 Briefly define each of the following and note how they might be used by fixed-income investors: (a) zero-coupon bonds, (b) CMOs, (c) junk bonds, and (d) Yankee bonds.

10.12 What are the special tax features of (a) Treasury securities, (b) agency issues, and (c) municipal bonds?

10.13 Describe an asset-backed security (ABS) and identify some forms of collateral used with these issues. Briefly note how an ABS differs from an MBS. What is the central idea behind securitization?

10.14 What's the difference between dollar-denominated and non-dollar-denominated (foreign-pay) bonds? Briefly describe the two major types of U.S.-pay bonds. Can currency exchange rates affect the total return of U.S.-pay bonds? Of foreign-pay bonds? Explain.

Convertible Securities

In addition to the many types of bonds covered in the preceding material, there is still another type of fixed-income security that merits discussion at this point—namely, **convertible bonds**. Issued only by corporations, convertibles are different from most other types of corporate debt because even though these securities may start out as bonds, they usually end up as shares of common stock. That is, while these securities are originally issued as bonds (or even preferred stock), they contain a provision that gives investors the option to convert their bonds into shares of the issuing firm's stock. Convertibles are *hybrid securities* because they contain attributes of both debt and equity. But even though they possess the features and performance characteristics of both fixed-income and equity securities, convertibles should be viewed primarily as a form of equity. That's because most investors commit their capital to such obligations not for the yields they provide but rather for the potential price performance of the stock side of the issue. In fact, it is always a good idea to determine whether a corporation has convertible issues outstanding whenever you are considering a common stock investment. In some circumstances, the convertible may be a better investment than the firm's common stock. (Preferred stocks represent another type of hybrid security because they too have features and characteristics of both equity and fixed-income securities.)

Convertibles as Investment Outlets

Convertible securities are popular with investors because of their **equity kicker**—the right to convert these bonds into shares of the company's common stock. Because of this feature, the market price of a convertible has a tendency to behave very much like the price of its underlying common stock. Convertibles are used by all types of companies and are issued either as convertible bonds (by far the most common type) or as convertible *preferreds*. Convertibles enable firms to raise equity capital at fairly attractive prices. That is, when a company issues stock in the normal way (by selling more shares in the company), it does so by setting a price on the stock that's slightly below prevailing market prices. For example, it might be able to get $25 for a stock that's currently priced in the market at, say, $27 a share. In contrast, when it issues the stock indirectly through a convertible issue, the firm can set a price that's above the prevailing market—for example, it might be able to get $35 for the same stock. In this case, convertible bond investors will only choose to convert their bonds into shares if the market price of the shares subsequently increases above $35. As a result, the company can raise the same amount of money by issuing a lot less stock. Thus, companies issue convertibles not as a way of raising debt capital but as a way of raising equity. Because they are eventually converted into shares of the issuing company's common stock, convertibles are usually viewed as a form of **deferred equity**.

Convertible bonds and convertible preferreds are both linked to the equity position of the firm, so they are usually considered interchangeable for investment purposes. Except for a few peculiarities (e.g., preferreds pay dividends rather than interest and do so quarterly rather than semiannually), convertible bonds and convertible preferreds are evaluated in much the same way. Because of their similarities, the discussion that follows will be couched largely in terms of bonds, but the information and implications apply equally well to convertible preferreds.

Convertible Notes and Bonds   Firms usually issue convertible bonds as subordinated debentures attached with the provision that within a stipulated time period, the bond may be converted into a certain number of shares of the issuing company's common stock. Convertible notes are just like convertible bonds except that the debt portion of the security carries a shorter maturity—usually of 5 to 10 years. Other than the life of the debt, there is no real difference between the convertible notes and bonds. They're both unsecured debt obligations, and they're usually subordinated to other forms of debt.

Generally speaking, little or no cash is exchanged between investors and issuing firms at the time of conversion. Convertible bondholders merely trade in the convertible bond (or note) for a stipulated number of shares of common stock. For example, assume that a certain convertible security recently came to the market, and it carried the provision that each $1,000 note could be converted into shares of the issuing company's stock at $50 a share. Thus, regardless of what happens to the market price of the stock, investors can redeem each note for 20 shares of the company's stock ($1,000 ÷ $50 = 20 shares). So, if the company's stock is trading in the market at, say, $65 a share at the time of conversion, then an investor could convert a $1,000 debt obligation into $1,300 worth of stock (20 × $65 = $1,300). Not surprisingly, this conversion privilege comes at a price: the low coupon (or dividend) that convertibles usually carry. That is, when new convertible issues come to the market, their coupons are normally just a fraction of those on comparable straight (nonconvertible) bonds. Indeed, the more attractive the conversion feature, the lower the coupon.

Actually, while it's the bondholder who has the right to convert the bond at any time, more often than not, the issuing firm initiates conversion by calling the bonds—a practice known as **forced conversion**. To provide the corporation with the flexibility to retire the debt and force conversion, most convertibles come out as freely callable issues, or they carry very short call deferment periods. To force conversion, the corporation would call for the retirement of the bond and give the bondholder two options: Either convert the bond into common stock or redeem it for cash at the stipulated call price (which, in the case of convertibles, contains very little call premium). As long as the convertible is called when the market value of the stock exceeds the call price of the bond (which is almost always the case), seasoned investors would never choose the second option. Instead, they would opt to convert the bond, as the firm wants them to. Then they can hold the stocks if they want to or they can sell their new shares in the market (and end up with more cash than they would have received by taking the call price). After the conversion is complete, the bonds no longer exist; instead, there is additional common stock in their place.

Conversion Privilege   The key element of any convertible is its **conversion privilege**, which stipulates the conditions and specific nature of the conversion feature. To begin with, it states exactly when the debenture can be converted. With some issues, there may be an initial waiting period of six months to perhaps two years after the date of issue, during which time the security cannot be converted. The **conversion period** then begins, and the issue can be converted at any time. The conversion period typically extends for the remaining life of the debenture, but in some instances, it may exist for only a certain number of years. This is done to give the issuing firm more control over its capital structure. If the issue has not been converted by the end of its conversion period, it reverts to a straight-debt issue with no conversion privileges.

From the investor's point of view, the most important piece of information is the conversion price or the conversion ratio. These terms are used interchangeably and specify, either directly or indirectly, the number of shares of stock into which the bond can be converted. The **conversion ratio** denotes the number of common shares into which the bond can be converted. The **conversion price** indicates the stated value per share at which the common stock will be delivered to the investor in exchange for the bond. When you stop to think about these two measures, it becomes clear that a given conversion ratio implies a certain conversion price, and vice versa.

Example

> Suppose that a certain $1,000 convertible bond stipulates a conversion ratio of 40, which means that the bond can be converted into 40 shares of common stock. In effect, if you give up your $1,000 bond in exchange for 40 shares, you are essentially buying 40 shares of stock for $1,000, or $25 per share. In other words, the conversation ratio of 40 is equivalent to a conversion price of $25. (One basic difference between a convertible debenture and a convertible preferred relates to conversion ratio: The conversion ratio of a debenture generally deals with large multiples of common stock, such as 15, 20, or 30 shares. In contrast, the conversion ratio of a preferred is generally very small, often less than one share of common and seldom more than three or four shares.)

The conversion ratio is normally adjusted for stock splits and significant stock dividends. As a result, if a firm declares, say, a 2-for-1 stock split, the conversion ratio of any of its outstanding convertible issues also doubles. And when the conversion ratio includes a fraction, such as 33.5 shares of common, the conversion privilege specifies how any fractional shares are to be handled. Usually, the investor can either put up the additional funds necessary to purchase another full share of stock at the conversion price or receive the cash equivalent of the fractional share (at the conversion price).

LYONs Leave it to Wall Street to take a basic investment product and turn it into a sophisticated investment vehicle. That's the story behind LYONs, which some refer to as "zeros on steroids." Start with a zero-coupon bond, throw in a conversion feature and a put option, and you have a **LYON** (the acronym stands for **liquid yield option note**). LYONs are zero-coupon convertible bonds that are convertible, at a fixed conversion ratio, for the life of the issue. Thus, they offer the built-in increase in value over time that accompanies any zero-coupon bond (as it moves toward its par value at maturity), plus full participation in the equity side of the issue via the equity kicker. Unlike most convertibles, there's no current income with a LYON (because it is a zero-coupon bond). On the other hand, however, it does carry an option feature that enables investors to "put" or sell the bonds back to the issuer (at specified values). That is, the put option gives investors the right to redeem their bonds periodically at prespecified prices. Thus, investors know they can get out of these securities, at set prices, if they want to.

Although LYONs may appear to provide the best of all worlds, they do have some negative aspects. It is true that LYONs provide downside protection (via the put option feature) and full participation in the equity kicker. But like all zero-coupon bonds, they don't generate current income. And investors have to watch out for the put option. Depending on the type of put option, the payout does not have to be in cash—it can be in stocks or bonds. One other important issue to be aware of is that because the conversion ratio on the LYON is fixed, the conversion price on the stock increases over time. This occurs because the value of the zero-coupon bond increases as it reaches maturity. Thus, the market price of the stock had better go up by more than the bond's rate of appreciation or investors will never be able to convert their LYONs.

Sources of Value

Because convertibles are fixed-income securities linked to the equity position of the firm, they are normally valued in terms of both the stock and the bond dimensions of the issue. Thus, it is important to both analyze the underlying common stock and formulate interest rate expectations when considering convertibles as an investment outlet. Let's look first at the stock dimension.

Convertible securities trade much like common stock whenever the market price of the stock starts getting close to (or exceeds) the stated conversion price. When that happens, the convertible will exhibit price behavior that closely matches that of the underlying common stock. If the stock goes up in price, so does the convertible, and vice versa. In fact, the absolute price change of the convertible will exceed that of the common because of the conversion ratio, which will define the convertible's rate of change in price. For example, if a convertible carries a conversion ratio of, say, 20, then for every dollar the common stock goes up (or down) in price, the price of the convertible will move in the same direction by roughly that same multiple (in this case, $20). In essence, whenever a convertible trades as a stock, its market price will approximate a multiple of the share price of the common, with the size of the multiple being defined by the conversion ratio.

When the market price of the common is well below the conversion price, the convertible loses its tie to the underlying common stock and begins to trade as a bond. When that happens, the convertible becomes linked to prevailing bond yields, and investors focus their attention on market rates of interest. However, because of the equity kicker and their relatively low agency ratings, convertibles generally do not possess high interest rate sensitivity. Gaining more than a rough idea of what the prevailing yield of a convertible obligation ought to be is often difficult. For example, if the issue is rated Baa and the market rate for this quality range is 9%, then the convertible should be priced to yield something around 9%, plus or minus perhaps half a percentage point. Because of the interest and principal payments that they offer, convertible bonds essentially have a price floor, meaning that convertible values generally cannot drop as much as the underlying stock can. If a company experiences financial problems that cause its stock price to drop dramatically, the firm's convertible bonds will retain much of their value because investors are still entitled to receive interest and principal payments. That is, the price of the convertible will not fall to much less than its price floor because at that point, the issue's bond value will kick in.

Measuring the Value of a Convertible

In order to evaluate the investment merits of convertible securities, investors should consider both the bond and the stock dimensions of the issue. Fundamental security analysis of the equity position is, of course, especially important in light of the key role the equity kicker plays in defining the price behavior of a convertible. In contrast, market yields and agency ratings are used in evaluating the bond side of the issue. But there's more: In addition to analyzing the bond and stock dimensions of the issue, it is essential to evaluate the conversion feature itself. The two critical areas in this regard are conversion value and investment value. These measures have a vital bearing on a convertible's price behavior and therefore can have a dramatic effect on an issue's holding period return.

Conversion Value In essence, **conversion value** indicates what a convertible issue would trade for if it were priced to sell on the basis of its stock value. Conversion value is easy to find:

Equation 10.4

Conversion value = Conversion ratio × Current market price of the stock

Example

Suppose that a particular convertible bond has a conversion ratio of 20. If the price of the company's stock is $60 per share, then the conversion value of the bond is $1,200 (i.e., 20 × $60).

Sometimes analysts use an alternative measure that computes the **conversion equivalent,** also known as **conversion parity.** The conversion equivalent indicates the price at which the common stock would have to sell in order to make the convertible security worth its present market price. The conversion equivalent is calculated as follows:

Equation 10.5

$$\text{Conversion equivalent} = \frac{\text{Current market price of the convertible bond}}{\text{Conversion ratio}}$$

Example

If a convertible bond has a current market price of $1,400 and a conversion ratio of 20, the conversion equivalent of the common stock would be $70 per share (i.e., $1,400 ÷ 20). Although convertible bonds can trade above par value simply because of a decline in interest rates, as a practical matter, it would be unusual for a bond to trade as high as $1,400 based only on an interest rate drop. Accordingly, you would expect the current market price of the common stock in this example to be at or near $70 per share in order to support a convertible trading at $1,400.

Conversion Premium   Convertible issues seldom trade precisely at their conversion values. Rather, they usually trade at prices that exceed the bond's underlying conversion value. The extent to which the market price of the convertible exceeds its conversion value is known as the *conversion premium*. The absolute size of an issue's conversion premium is found by taking the difference between the convertible's market price and its conversion value (per Equation 10.4). To place the premium on a relative basis, simply divide the dollar amount of the conversion premium by the issue's conversion value. That is,

Equation 10.6

$$\text{Conversion premium (in \$)} = \frac{\text{Current market price}}{\text{of the convertible bond}} - \frac{\text{Conversion}}{\text{value}}$$

where conversion value is found according to Equation 10.4.
Then

Equation 10.7

$$\text{Conversion premium (in \%)} = \frac{\text{Conversion premium (in \$)}}{\text{Conversion value}}$$

Example

Suppose that a convertible bond trades at $1,400 and its conversion value equals $1,200. This bond has a conversion premium of $200 (i.e., $1,400 − $1,200). That $200 represents a conversion premium of 16.7% relative to the bond's conversion value.

Conversion premiums are common in the market and can often amount to 30% to 40% (or more) of an issue's conversion value. Investors are willing to pay a premium because of the added current income that a convertible provides relative to the underlying common stock and because of the convertible's upside potential. An investor can recover this premium either through the added current income or by selling the issue at a premium equal to or greater than that which existed at the time of purchase. Unfortunately, the latter source of recovery is tough to come by because conversion premiums tend to fade away as the price of the convertible goes up. That means that if an investor purchases a convertible for its potential price appreciation, then he must accept the fact that all or a major portion of the price premium is very likely to disappear as the convertible appreciates over time and moves closer to its true conversion value. Thus, if he hopes to recover any conversion premium, it will probably have to come from the added current income that the convertible provides.

Payback Period The size of the conversion premium can obviously have a major impact on investor return. When picking convertibles, one of the major questions investors should ask is whether the premium is justified. One way to assess conversion premium is to compute the issue's **payback period**, a measure of the length of time it will take to recover the conversion premium from the extra interest income earned on the convertible. Because this added income is a principal reason for the conversion premium, it makes sense to use it to assess the premium. The payback period can be found as follows:

Equation 10.8

$$\text{Payback period} = \frac{\text{Conversion premium (in \$)}}{\substack{\text{Annual interest} \\ \text{income from the} \\ \text{convertible bond}} - \substack{\text{Annual dividend} \\ \text{income from the} \\ \text{underlying common stock}}}$$

In this equation, annual dividends are found by multiplying the stock's latest annual dividends per share by the bond's conversion ratio.

Example

In the previous example, the bond had a conversion premium of $200. Assume this bond (which carries a conversion ratio of 20) has an 8.5% coupon ($85 per year), and the underlying stock paid dividends this past year of 50 cents a share. Given this information, you can use Equation 10.8 to find the payback period.

$$\text{Payback period} = \frac{\$200}{\$85 - (20 \times \$0.50)}$$
$$= \frac{\$200}{\$85 - (\$10.00)} = 2.7 \text{ years}$$

In essence, you would recover the premium in 2.7 years (a fairly short payback period).

As a rule, everything else being equal, the shorter the payback period, the better. Also, watch out for excessively high premiums (of 50% or more). Indeed, to avoid such premiums, which are difficult to recover, most experts recommend that investors look for convertibles that have payback periods of five to seven years, or less. Be careful when using this measure, however. Some convertibles will have very high payback periods simply because they carry very low coupons (of 1% to 2%, or less).

Investment Value The price floor of a convertible is defined by its bond properties and is the focus of the investment value measure. It's the point within the valuation process where we focus on current and expected market interest rates. **Investment value** is the price at which the bond would trade if it were nonconvertible and if it were priced at or near the prevailing market yields of comparable nonconvertible bonds.

We will cover the mechanics of bond pricing in more detail later, but suffice it to say at this point that the investment value of a convertible is found by discounting the issue's coupon stream and its par value back to the present, using a discount rate equal to the prevailing yield on comparable nonconvertible issues. In other words, using the yields on comparable nonconvertible bonds as the discount rate, find the present value of the convertible's coupon stream, add that to the present value of its par value, and you have the issue's investment value. In practice, because the convertible's coupon and maturity are known, the only additional piece of information needed is the market yield of comparably rated issues.

For example, if comparable nonconvertible bonds were trading at 9% yields, we could use that 9% return as the discount rate in finding the present value (i.e., "investment value") of a convertible. Thus, if a particular 20-year, $1,000 par value convertible bond carried a 6% annual coupon rate, its investment value (using a 9% discount rate) can be found using a financial calculator as shown in the margin.

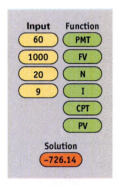

Input	Function
60	PMT
1000	FV
20	N
9	I
	CPT
	PV

Solution
−726.14

CALCULATOR USE Based on the information given, $60 is entered as the interest payment amount, PMT; the $1,000 par value is entered as the future value, FV; the time till maturity, 20 years, is entered, N; and the yield of 9% is entered for the discount rate, I. Push the compute key, CPT, and then the present value key, PV, to find that the resulting value of the convertible would be about $726. This figure indicates how far the convertible will have to fall before it hits its price floor and begins trading as a straight-debt instrument.

Other things being equal, the greater the distance between the current market price of a convertible and its investment value, the farther the issue can fall in price and, as a result, the greater the downside risk exposure.

CONCEPTS IN REVIEW

Answers available at
http://www.pearsonhighered.com/smart

10.15 What is a convertible debenture? How does a convertible bond differ from a convertible preferred?

10.16 Identify the equity kicker of a convertible security and explain how it affects the value and price behavior of convertibles.

10.17 Explain why it is necessary to examine both the bond and stock properties of a convertible debenture when determining its investment appeal.

10.18 What is the difference between conversion parity and conversion value? How would you describe the payback period on a convertible? What is the investment value of a convertible, and what does it reveal?

MyFinanceLab

Here is what you should know after reading this chapter. MyFinanceLab will help you identify what you know and where to go when you need to practice.

What You Should Know	Key Terms	Where to Practice
LG1 Explain the basic investment attributes of bonds and their use as investment vehicles. Bonds are publicly traded debt securities that provide investors with 2 basic sources of return: (1) current income and (2) capital gains. Current income is derived from the coupon (interest) payments received over the life of the issue. Capital gains can be earned whenever market interest rates fall. Bonds also can be used to shelter income from taxes and for the preservation and long-term accumulation of capital. The diversification properties of bonds are such that they can greatly enhance portfolio stability.	bonds, *p. 379*	MyFinanceLab Study Plan 10.1
LG2 Describe the essential features of a bond, note the role that bond ratings play in the market, and distinguish among different types of call, refunding, and sinking-fund provisions. All bonds carry some type of coupon, which specifies the annual rate of interest the issuer will pay. Bonds also have predetermined maturity dates: Term bonds carry a single maturity date, and serial bonds have a series of maturity dates. Municipal and corporate issues are rated for bond quality by independent rating agencies. These ratings indicate a bond's risk of default: The lower the rating, the higher the risk and the higher the expected return. Every bond is issued with some type of call feature, be it freely callable, noncallable, or deferred callable. Call features spell out whether an issue can be prematurely retired and, if so, when. Some bonds (temporarily) prohibit the issuer from paying off one bond with the proceeds from another by including a refunding provision. Others are issued with sinking-fund provisions, which specify how a bond is to be paid off over time.	bond ratings, *p. 391* bond rating agencies, *p. 391* call feature, *p. 389* call premium, *p. 389* call price, *p. 389* collateral trust bonds, *p. 390* coupon, *p. 386* coupon rate, *p. 386* current yield, *p. 386* debenture, *p. 391* discount bond, *p. 387* equipment trust certificates, *p. 390* face value, *p. 396* first and refunding bonds, *p. 390* high-yield bonds, *p. 392* income bonds, *p. 391* investment-grade bonds, *p. 392* junior bonds, *p. 391* junk bonds, *p. 392* maturity date, *p. 386* mortgage bonds, *p. 390* note, *p. 387* par value, *p. 386* premium bond, *p. 387* principal, *p. 386* refunding provisions, *p. 390* senior bonds, *p. 390* serial bond, *p. 387* sinking fund, *p. 390* split ratings, *p. 392* subordinated debentures, *p. 391* term bond, *p. 387*	MyFinanceLab Study Plan 10.2 Video Learning Aid for Problem P10.8

What You Should Know	Key Terms	Where to Practice
LG3 **Explain how bond prices are quoted in the market and why some bonds are more volatile than others.** In the bond market prices are quoted as a percentage of par and are driven by the issue's coupon and maturity, along with prevailing market yields. When interest rates go down, bond prices go up, and vice versa. The extent to which bond prices move up or down depends on the coupon and maturity of an issue. Bonds with lower coupons and/or longer maturities generate larger price swings.		MyFinanceLab Study Plan 10.3
LG4 **Identify the different types of bonds and the kinds of investment objectives these securities can fulfill.** The bond market is divided into four major segments: Treasuries, agencies, municipals, and corporates. Treasury bonds are issued by the U.S. Treasury and are virtually default-free. Agency bonds are issued by various subdivisions of the U.S. government and make up an increasingly important segment of the bond market. Municipal bonds are issued by state and local governments in the form of either general obligation or revenue bonds. Corporate bonds make up the major nongovernment sector of the market and are backed by the assets and profitability of the issuing companies. Generally speaking, Treasuries are attractive because of their high quality; agencies and corporates, because of the added returns they provide; and munis, because of the tax shelter they offer.	agency bonds, *p. 396* asset-backed securities (ABS), *p. 405* collateralized mortgage obligation (CMO), *p. 404* Eurodollar bonds, *p. 406* general obligation bonds, *p. 397* mortgage-backed bond, *p. 403* municipal bond guarantees, *p. 398* municipal bonds, *p. 397* PIK bond, *p. 405* revenue bonds, *p. 397* securitization, *p. 405* taxable equivalent yield, *p. 400* Treasury bonds, *p. 395* Treasury Inflation-Protected Securities (TIPS), *p. 396* Treasury notes, *p. 395* Treasury strips, *p. 403* Yankee bonds, *p. 406* zero-coupon bonds, *p. 402*	MyFinanceLab Study Plan 10.4
LG5 **Discuss the global nature of the bond market and the difference between dollar-denominated and non-dollar-denominated foreign bonds.** Foreign bonds, particularly foreign-pay securities, offer highly competitive yields and returns. Foreign-pay bonds cover all issues that are denominated in some currency other than U.S. dollars. These bonds have an added source of return: currency exchange rates. In addition, there are dollar-denominated foreign bonds—Yankee bonds and Eurodollar bonds—which have no currency exchange risk because they are issued in U.S. dollars.		MyFinanceLab Study Plan 10.5

What You Should Know	Key Terms	Where to Practice
LG6 Describe the basic features and characteristics of convertible securities, and measure the value of a convertible. Convertible securities are initially issued as bonds (or preferreds) but can subsequently be converted into shares of common stock. These securities offer investors a stream of fixed income (annual coupon payments) plus an equity kicker (a conversion feature). The value of a convertible is driven by the price behavior of the underlying common stock (when the stock price is at or above its conversion price) or by market interest rates and the behavior of bonds (when the stock's price is well below its conversion price). The key values of a convertible are (1) its conversion (stock) value and (2) its investment (bond) value.	conversion equivalent (conversion parity), *p. 412* conversion period, *p. 409* conversion price, *p. 409* conversion privilege, *p. 409* conversion ratio, *p. 409* conversion value, *p. 411* convertible bonds, *p. 408* deferred equity, *p. 408* equity kicker, *p. 408* forced conversion, *p. 409* investment value, *p. 414* LYON (liquid yield option note), *p. 410* payback period, *p. 413*	MyFinanceLab Study Plan 10.6 Video Learning Aid for Problem P10.20

Log into MyFinanceLab, take a chapter test, and get a personalized Study Plan that tells you which concepts you understand and which ones you need to review. From there, MyFinanceLab will give you further practice, tutorials, animations, videos, and guided solutions.

Log into **http://www.myfinancelab.com**

Discussion Questions

LG1   **Q10.1** Using the bond returns in Table 10.1 as a basis of discussion:
     a. Compare the total returns on Treasury bonds during the 1970s to those produced in the 1980s. How do you explain the differences?
     b. How did the bond market do in the 1990s? How does the performance in this decade compare to that in the 1980s? Explain.
     c. What do you think would be a reasonable rate of return from bonds in the future? Explain.
     d. Assume that you're out of school and hold a promising, well-paying job. How much of your portfolio (in percentage terms) would you want to hold in bonds? Explain. What role do you see bonds playing in your portfolio, particularly as you go farther and farther into the future?

LG4 **LG5**   **Q10.2** Identify and briefly describe each of the following types of bonds.
     a. Agency bonds
     b. Municipal bonds
     c. Zero-coupon bonds
     d. Junk bonds
     e. Foreign bonds
     f. Collateralized mortgage obligations (CMOs)

     What type of investor do you think would be most attracted to each?

LG1 **LG4**   **Q10.3** "Treasury securities are guaranteed by the U.S. government. Therefore, there is no risk in the ownership of such bonds." Briefly discuss the wisdom (or folly) of this statement.

LG4 LG5 **Q10.4** Select the security in the left-hand column that best fits the investor's desire described in the right-hand column.

a. 5-year Treasury note	1. Lock in a high-coupon yield
b. A bond with a low coupon and a long maturity	2. Accumulate capital over a long period of time
c. Yankee bond	3. Generate a monthly income
d. Insured revenue bond	4. Avoid a lot of price volatility
e. Long-term Treasury strips	5. Generate tax-free income
f. Noncallable bond	6. Invest in a foreign bond
g. CMO	7. Go for the highest yield available
h. Junk bond	8. Invest in a pool of credit card receivables
i. ABS receivables	9. Go for maximum price appreciation

LG6 **Q10.5** Why do companies like to issue convertible securities? What's in it for them?

LG6 **Q10.6** Describe LYONs, and note how they differ from conventional convertible securities. Are there any similarities between LYONs and conventional convertibles? Explain.

LG6 **Q10.7** Using the resources at your campus or public library or on the Internet, find the information requested below.
a. Select any two convertible debentures (notes or bonds) and determine the conversion ratio, conversion parity, conversion value, conversion premium, and payback period for each.
b. Select any two convertible preferreds and determine the conversion ratio, conversion parity, conversion value, conversion premium, and payback period for each.
c. In what way(s) are the two convertible bonds and the two convertible preferreds you selected similar? Are there any differences? Explain.

Problems

All problems are available on **http://www.myfinancelab.com**

LG2 **P10.1** A 9%, 20-year bond is callable in 12 years at a call price of $1,090. The bond is currently priced in the market at $923.68. What is the issue's current yield?

LG2 **P10.2** A certain bond has a current yield of 6.5% and a market price of $846.15. What is the bond's coupon rate?

LG2 **P10.3** Buck buys a 7.5% corporate bond with a current yield of 4.8%. How much did he pay for the bond?

LG4 **P10.4** An investor is in the 28% tax bracket and lives in a state with no income tax. He is trying to decide which of two bonds to purchase. One is a 7.5% corporate bond that is selling at par. The other is a municipal bond with a 5.25% coupon that is also selling at par. If all other features of these bonds are comparable, which should the investor select? Why? Would your answer change if this were an in-state municipal bond and the investor lived in a place with high state income taxes? Explain.

LG4 **P10.5** An investor lives in a state with a 3% income tax rate. Her federal income tax bracket is 35%. She wants to invest in one of two bonds that are similar in terms of risk (and both bonds currently sell at par value). The first bond is fully taxable and offers a yield of 10%. The second bond is exempt from both state and federal taxes and offers a yield of 7%. In which bond should she invest?

LG4 **P10.6** Maria Lopez is a wealthy investor who's looking for a tax shelter. Maria is in the maximum (35%) federal tax bracket and lives in a state with a very high state income tax. (She pays the maximum of 11½% in state income tax.) Maria is currently looking at two municipal bonds, both of which are selling at par. One is a AA-rated, in-state bond that carries a coupon of 6⅜%. The other is a AA-rated, out-of-state bond that carries a 7⅛% coupon. Her broker has informed her that comparable fully taxable corporate bonds are currently available with yields of 9¾%. Alternatively, long Treasuries are now available at yields of 9%. She has $100,000 to invest, and because all the bonds are high-quality issues, she wants to select the one that will give her maximum after-tax returns.
  a. Which one of the four bonds should she buy?
  b. Rank the four bonds (from best to worst) in terms of their taxable equivalent yields.

LG4 **P10.7** Sara Nixon is looking for a fixed-income investment. She is considering two bond issues:
  a. A Treasury with a yield of 5%
  b. An in-state municipal bond with a yield of 4%
  Sara is in the 33% federal tax bracket and the 8% state tax bracket. Which bond would provide Sara with a higher tax-adjusted yield?

LG2 **P10.8** Which of the following bonds offers the highest current yield?
  a. A 9½%, 20-year bond quoted at 97¾
  b. A 16%, 15-year bond quoted at 164⅝
  c. A 5¼%, 18-year bond quoted at 54

LG2 **P10.9** Assume that you pay $850 for a long-term bond that carries a 7½% coupon. Over the course of the next 12 months, interest rates drop sharply. As a result, you sell the bond at a price of $962.50.
  a. Find the current yield that existed on this bond at the beginning of the year. What was it by the end of the 1-year holding period?
  b. Determine the holding period return on this investment. (See Chapter 5 for the HPR formula.)

LG3 **P10.10** Caleb buys an 8.75% corporate bond with a current yield of 5.6%. When he sells the bond 1 year later, the current yield on the bond is 6.6%. How much did Caleb make on this investment?

LG1 **P10.11** In early January 2010, you purchased $30,000 worth of some high-grade corporate bonds. The bonds carried a coupon of 8⅛% and mature in 2024. You paid a price of 94.125 when you bought the bonds. Over the five years from 2010 through 2014, the bonds were priced in the market as follows:

	Quoted Prices (% of $1,000 par value)	
Year	Beginning of the Year	End of the Year
2010	94.125	100.625
2011	100.625	102.000
2012	102.000	104.625
2013	104.625	110.125
2014	110.125	121.250

Coupon payments were made on schedule throughout the five-year period.
  a. Find the annual holding period returns for 2010 through 2014. (See Chapter 5 for the HPR formula.)
  b. Use the return information in Table 10.1 to evaluate the investment performance of this bond. How do you think it stacks up against the market? Explain.

LG4 P10.12 Rhett purchased a 13%, zero-coupon bond with a 15-year maturity and a $20,000 par value 15 years ago. The bond matures tomorrow. How much will Rhett receive in total from this investment, assuming all payments were made on these bonds as expected?

LG4 P10.13 Nate purchased an interest-bearing security last year, planning to hold it until maturity. He received interest payments and, to his surprise, a sizable amount of the principal was paid back in the first year. This happened again in year two. What type of security did Nate purchase?

LG5 P10.14 Letticia Garcia, an aggressive bond investor, is currently thinking about investing in a foreign (non-dollar-denominated) government bond. In particular, she's looking at a Swiss government bond that matures in 15 years and carries a 9½% coupon. The bond has a par value of 10,000 Swiss francs (CHF) and is currently trading at 110 (i.e., at 110% of par).

Letticia plans to hold the bond for one year, at which time she thinks it will be trading at 117½—she's anticipating a sharp decline in Swiss interest rates, which explains why she expects bond prices to move up. The current exchange rate is 1.58 CHF/U.S.$, but she expects that to fall to 1.25 CHF/U.S.$. Use the foreign investment total return formula (Equation 10.3) to find the following information.

a. Ignoring the currency effect, find the bond's total return (in its local currency).
b. Now find the total return on this bond in U.S. dollars. Did currency exchange rates affect the return in any way? Do you think this bond would make a good investment? Explain.

LG5 P10.15 Red Electrica España SA (E.REE) is refinancing its bank loans by issuing Eurobonds to investors. You are considering buying $10,000 of these bonds, which will yield 6%. You are also looking at a U.S. bond with similar risk that will yield 5%. You expect that interest rates will not change over the course of the next year, after which time you will sell the bonds you purchase.

a. How much will you make on each bond if you buy it, hold it for one year, and then sell it for $10,000 (or the Eurodollar equivalent)?
b. Assume the dollar/euro exchange rate goes from 1.11 to 0.98. How much will this currency change affect the proceeds from the Eurobond? (Assume you receive annual interest at the same time you sell the Eurobond.)

LG6 P10.16 A certain convertible bond has a conversion ratio of 21 and a conversion premium of 20%. The current market price of the underlying common stock is $40. What is the bond's conversion equivalent?

LG6 P10.17 You are considering investing $800 in Higgs B. Technology Inc. You can buy common stock at $25 per share; this stock pays no dividends. You can also buy a convertible bond ($1,000 par value) that is currently trading at $790 and has a conversion ratio of 30. It pays $40 per year in interest. If you expect the price of the stock to rise to $33 per share in one year, which instrument should you purchase?

LG6 P10.18 A certain 6% annual coupon rate convertible bond (maturing in 20 years) is convertible at the holder's option into 20 shares of common stock. The bond is currently trading at $800. The stock (which pays 75¢ a share in annual dividends) is currently priced in the market at $35 a share.

a. What is the bond's conversion price?
b. What is its conversion ratio?
c. What is the conversion value of this issue? What is its conversion parity?
d. What is the conversion premium, in dollars and as a percentage?
e. What is the bond's payback period?
f. If comparably rated nonconvertible bonds sell to yield 8%, what is the investment value of the convertible?

LG6 **P10.19** An 8% convertible bond carries a par value of $1,000 and a conversion ratio of 20. Assume that an investor has $5,000 to invest and that the convertible sells at a price of $1,000 (which includes a 25% conversion premium). How much total income (coupon plus capital gains) will this investment offer if, over the course of the next 12 months, the price of the stock moves to $75 per share and the convertible trades at a price that includes a conversion premium of 10%? What is the holding period return on this investment? Finally, given the information in the problem, determine what the underlying common stock is currently selling for.

LG6 **P10.20** Assume you just paid $1,200 for a convertible bond that carries a 7½% coupon and has 15 years to maturity. The bond can be converted into 24 shares of stock, which are now trading at $50 a share. Find the bond investment value of this issue, given that comparable nonconvertible bonds are currently selling to yield 9%.

LG1 **P10.21** Find the conversion value of a convertible preferred stock that carries a conversion ratio of 1.8, given that the market price of the underlying common stock is $40 a share. Would there be any conversion premium if the convertible preferred were selling at $90 a share? If so, how much (in dollar and percentage terms)? Also, explain the concept of conversion parity, and then find the conversion parity of this issue, given that the preferred trades at $90 per share.

Visit **http://www.myfinancelab.com** for web exercises, spreadsheets, and other online resources.

Case Problem 10.1   Max and Veronica Develop a Bond Investment Program

LG1 **LG4**   Max and Veronica Shuman, along with their teenage sons, Terry and Thomas, live in Portland, Oregon. Max is a sales rep for a major medical firm, and Veronica is a personnel officer at a local bank. Together they earn an annual income of around $100,000. Max has just learned that his recently departed rich uncle has named him in his will to the tune of some $250,000 after taxes. Needless to say, the family is elated. Max intends to spend $50,000 of his inheritance on a number of long-overdue family items (like some badly needed remodeling of their kitchen and family room, the down payment on a new Porsche Boxster, and braces to correct Tom's overbite). Max wants to invest the remaining $200,000 in various types of fixed-income securities.

Max and Veronica have no unusual income requirements or health problems. Their only investment objectives are that they want to achieve some capital appreciation, and they want to keep their funds fully invested for at least 20 years. They would rather not have to rely on their investments as a source of current income but want to maintain some liquidity in their portfolio just in case.

Questions

a. Describe the type of bond investment program you think the Shuman family should follow. In answering this question, give appropriate consideration to both return and risk factors.

b. List several types of bonds that you would recommend for their portfolio and briefly indicate why you would recommend each.

c. Using a recent issue of the *Wall Street Journal*, *Barron's*, or an online source, construct a $200,000 bond portfolio for the Shuman family. Use real securities and select any bonds (or notes) you like, given the following ground rules:

1. The portfolio must include at least one Treasury, one agency, and one corporate bond; also, in total, the portfolio must hold at least five but no more than eight bonds or notes.
2. No more than 5% of the portfolio can be in short-term U.S. Treasury bills (but note that if you hold a T-bill, that limits your selections to just seven other notes/bonds).
3. Ignore all transaction costs (i.e., invest the full $200,000) and assume all securities have par values of $1,000 (although they can be trading in the market at something other than par).
4. Use the latest available quotes to determine how many bonds/notes/bills you can buy.

d. Prepare a schedule listing all the securities in your recommended portfolio. Use a form like the one shown below and include the information it calls for on each security in the portfolio.

e. In one brief paragraph, note the key investment attributes of your recommended portfolio and the investment objectives you hope to achieve with it.

Security Issuer-Coupon-Maturity	Latest Quoted Price	Number of Bonds Purchased	Amount Invested	Annual Coupon Income	Current Yield
Example: U.S. Treas - 8½%-'18	$146^8/_{32}$	15	$21,937.50	$1,275	5.81%
1.					
2.					
3.					
4.					
5.					
6.					
7.					
8.					
Totals	—		$200,000.00	$	%

Case Problem 10.2 The Case of the Missing Bond Ratings

LG2

It's probably safe to say that there's nothing more important in determining a bond's rating than the underlying financial condition and operating results of the company issuing the bond. Just as financial ratios can be used in the analysis of common stocks, they can also be used in the analysis of bonds—a process we refer to as credit analysis. In credit analysis, attention is directed toward the basic liquidity and profitability of the firm, the extent to which the firm employs debt, and the ability of the firm to service its debt.

A TABLE OF FINANCIAL RATIOS
(All ratios are real and pertain to real companies.)

Financial Ratio	Company 1	Company 2	Company 3	Company 4	Company 5	Company 6
1. Current ratio	1.13	1.39	1.78	1.32	1.03	1.41
2. Quick ratio	0.48	0.84	0.93	0.33	0.50	0.75
3. Net profit margin	4.6%	12.9%	14.5%	2.8%	5.9%	10.0%
4. Return on total capital	15.0%	25.9%	29.4%	11.5%	16.8%	28.4%
5. Long-term debt to total capital	63.3%	52.7%	23.9%	97.0%	88.6%	42.1%

(Continued)

A TABLE OF FINANCIAL RATIOS (*Continued*)
(All ratios are real and pertain to real companies.)

Financial Ratio	Company 1	Company 2	Company 3	Company 4	Company 5	Company 6
6. Owners' equity ratio	18.6%	18.9%	44.1%	1.5%	5.1%	21.2%
7. Pretax interest coverage	2.3	4.5	8.9	1.7	2.4	6.4
8. Cash flow to total debt	34.7%	48.8%	71.2%	20.4%	30.2%	42.7%

Notes:
1. Current ratio = current assets / current liabilities
2. Quick ratio = (current assets − inventory) / current liabilities
3. Net profit margin = net profit / sales
4. Return on total capital = pretax income / (equity + long-term debt)
5. Long-term debt to total capital = long-term debt / (long-term debt + equity)
6. Owner's equity ratio = stockholders' equity / total assets
7. Pretax interest coverage = earnings before interest and taxes / interest expense
8. Cash flow to total debt = (net profit + depreciation) / total liabilities

The financial ratios shown in the preceding table are often helpful in carrying out such analysis. The first two ratios measure the liquidity of the firm; the next two, its profitability; the following two, the debt load; and the final two, the ability of the firm to service its debt load. (For ratio 5, the lower the ratio, the better. For all the others, the higher the ratio, the better.) The table lists each of these ratios for six companies.

Questions

a. Three of these companies have bonds that carry investment-grade ratings. The other three companies carry junk-bond ratings. Judging by the information in the table, which three companies have the investment-grade bonds and which three have the junk bonds? Briefly explain your selections.

b. One of these six companies is an AAA-rated firm and one is B-rated. Identify those companies. Briefly explain your selections.

c. Of the remaining four companies, one carries an AA rating, one carries an A rating, and two have BB ratings. Which companies are they?

Excel@Investing

The cash flow component of bond investments is made up of the annual interest payments and the future redemption value or its par value. Just like other time-value-of-money considerations, the bond cash flows are discounted back in order to determine their present value.

In comparing bonds to stocks, many investors look at the respective returns. The total returns in the bond market are made up of both current income and capital gains. Bond investment analysis should include the determination of the current yield as well as a specific holding period return.

On January 13, 2016, you gather the following information on three corporate bonds issued by the General Pineapple Corporation (GPC). Remember that corporate bonds are quoted as a percentage of their par value. Assume the par value of each bond to be $1,000. These debentures are quoted in eighths of a point. Create a spreadsheet that will model and answer the following bond investment problems.

Bonds	Current Yield	Volume	Close
GPC 5.3 13	?	25	$105^{7}/_{8}$
GPC 6.65s 20	?	45	103
GPC 7.4 22	?	37	$104^{6}/_{8}$

Questions

a. Calculate the current yields for these 3 GPC corporate debentures.

b. Calculate the holding period returns under the following scenarios.
   1. Purchased the 5.3 bonds for $990 on January 13, 2015
   2. Purchased the 6.65s for $988 on January 13, 2015
   3. Purchased the 7.4 bonds for $985 on January 13, 2013

c. As of January 13, 2016, GPC common stock had a close price of $26.20. The price of GPC stock in January 2013 was $25.25. The stock paid a 2013 dividend of $0.46, a 2014 dividend of $0.46, and a 2015 dividend of $0.46.
   1. Calculate the current (January 13, 2016) dividend yield for this security.
   2. Assuming you purchased the stock in January 2013, what is the holding period return as of January 2015?

Chapter-Opening Problem

The chart shows the number of global corporate bond issues for which Standard & Poor's issued ratings upgrades or downgrades every year from 1981 to 2014.

a. What is the trend in the number of ratings changes (both upgrades and downgrades) over time? Why?

b. Which type of ratings change, upgrade or downgrade, is most common in most years? Why do you think that is so?

c. In what years does the ratio of downgrades/upgrades appear to be particularly high? Why?

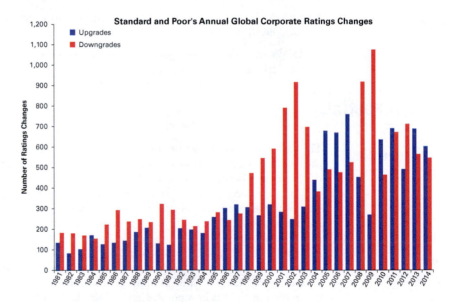

11

Bond Valuation

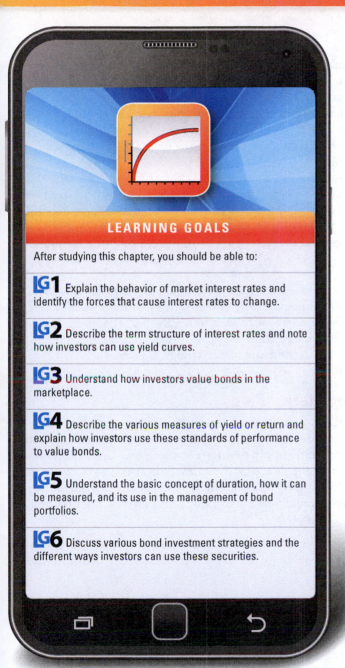

LEARNING GOALS

After studying this chapter, you should be able to:

LG1 Explain the behavior of market interest rates and identify the forces that cause interest rates to change.

LG2 Describe the term structure of interest rates and note how investors can use yield curves.

LG3 Understand how investors value bonds in the marketplace.

LG4 Describe the various measures of yield or return and explain how investors use these standards of performance to value bonds.

LG5 Understand the basic concept of duration, how it can be measured, and its use in the management of bond portfolios.

LG6 Discuss various bond investment strategies and the different ways investors can use these securities.

Money market investors made very little money during the Great Recession due to historically low interest rates on the short-term debt securities that comprise the U.S. money market. At the start of 2007, U.S. Treasury bills with 6-month maturities were earning yields slightly better than 5%. Over the next few years, Treasury bill yields tumbled to record lows. By the end of 2009, investors who purchased a 6-month bill at the Treasury auction earned only one-fifth of 1 percent (0.20%) on their money. Even worse, by September of 2014, investors in 6-month bills received a yield of just 3 basis points (0.03%).

Investors in other parts of the world faced even lower, unprecedented rates. In April 2015 Switzerland issued 10-year government bonds that offered investors a yield of −5 basis points (−0.05%). In other words, investors who purchased these bonds were actually paying the Swiss government for that privilege. That marked the first time in history that any 10-year bond was successfully sold with a negative yield. Presumably hoping to take advantage of historically low interest rates in Europe, Mexico issued its own bonds, denominated in euros. What made Mexico's bonds unique was their maturity—100 years. Prior to Mexico's bond issue, no one had ever issued 100-year bonds in euros.

The low interest rates were a result of actions by the U.S. Federal Reserve, the European Central Bank, and other authorities around the world who were trying to stimulate their economies to help pull out of (or prevent) a recession. The resulting low rates around the world sparked a borrowing binge.

In this chapter we'll learn about the forces that move market interest rates up and down and how those movements affect bonds and the investors who buy them.

(Source: Emese Bartha, Chiara Albanese, and Anthony Harp, "New Era in Bonds: Zero Yield, or Less," *The Wall Street Journal*, April 9, 2015, p. 1.)

The Behavior of Market Interest Rates

LG1 LG2 Recall from earlier discussions that rational investors try to earn a return that fully compensates them for risk. In the case of bondholders, that required return (r_i) has three components: the real rate of return (r^*), an expected inflation premium (IP), and a risk premium (RP). Thus, the required return on a bond can be expressed by the following equation:

Equation 11.1

$$r_i = r^* + IP + RP$$

The real rate of return and inflation premium are external economic factors, which together equal the risk-free rate (r_f). To find the required return, we need to consider the unique features and properties of the bond issue itself that influence its risk. After we do this, we add a risk premium to the risk-free rate to obtain the required rate of return. A bond's risk premium (RP) will take into account key issue and issuer characteristics, including such variables as the type of bond, the issue's term to maturity, its call features, and its bond rating.

Together, the three components in Equation 11.1 (r^*, IP, and RP) drive the required return on a bond. Recall in the previous chapter that we identified five types of risks to which bonds are exposed. All of these risks are embedded in a bond's required rate of return. That is, the bond's risk premium addresses, among other things, the business and financial (credit) risk characteristics of an issue, along with its liquidity and call risks, whereas the risk-free rate (r_f) takes into account interest rate and purchasing power risks.

Because these interest rates have a significant bearing on bond prices and yields, investors watch them closely. For example, more conservative investors watch interest rates because one of their major objectives is to lock in high yields. Aggressive traders also have a stake in interest rates because their investment programs are often built on the capital gains opportunities that accompany major swings in rates.

Keeping Tabs on Market Interest Rates

The bond market is not a single market. Rather, it consists of many different sectors. Similarly, there is no single interest rate that applies to all segments of the bond market. Instead, different interest rates apply to different segments. Granted, the various rates do tend to drift in the same direction over time, but it is also common for **yield spreads** (interest rate differentials) to exist among the various market sectors. Some important factors to keep in mind when you think about interest rates on bonds are as follows:

- Municipal bonds usually offer the lowest market rates because of their tax-exempt feature. As a rule, their market yields are about 20% to 30% lower than corporate bond yields.

- In the municipal sector, revenue bonds pay higher rates than general obligation bonds.

- In the taxable sector, Treasury securities have the lowest yields (because they have the least risk), followed by agency bonds and then corporate bonds, which provide the highest returns.

Signs of a Recession

When short-term interest rates on treasury bills exceed the rates on long-term treasury bonds, watch out. That is often the precursor to a recession. This "inversion" in the relationship between short-term and long-term rates has occurred prior to each of the last five U.S. recessions. Just as important, this indicator has rarely issued a false recession warning signal.

- Issues that normally carry bond ratings (e.g., municipals or corporates) generally display the same behavior: the lower the rating, the higher the yield.

- Most of the time, bonds with long maturities provide higher yields than short-term issues. However, this rule does not always hold. When short-term bond yields exceed yields on longer-term bonds, as they did in February 2006, that may be an early signal that a recession is coming.

- Bonds that are freely callable generally pay the highest interest rates, at least at date of issue. These are followed by deferred call obligations and then by noncallable bonds, which offer lower yields.

As an investor, you should pay close attention to interest rates and yield spreads. Try to stay abreast of both the current state of the market and the future direction of market rates. Thus, if you are a conservative (income-oriented) investor and think that rates have just about peaked, that should be a signal to try to lock in the prevailing high yields with some form of call protection. (For example, buy bonds, such as Treasuries or AA-rated utilities that are noncallable or still have lengthy call deferments.) In contrast, if you're an aggressive bond trader who thinks rates have peaked (and are about to drop), that should be a clue to buy bonds that offer maximum price appreciation potential (low-coupon bonds that still have a long time before they mature).

But how do you formulate such expectations? Unless you have considerable training in economics, you will probably need to rely on various published sources. Fortunately, a wealth of such information is available. Your broker is an excellent source for such reports, as are investor services like Moody's and Standard & Poor's. Also, of course, there are numerous online sources. Finally, there are widely circulated business and financial publications (like the *Wall Street Journal*, *Forbes*, *Business Week*, and *Fortune*) that regularly address the current state and future direction of market interest rates. Predicting the direction of interest rates is not easy. However, by taking the time to read some of these publications and reports regularly and carefully, you can at least get a sense of what experts predict is likely to occur in the near future.

WATCH YOUR BEHAVIOR

Anchoring on Credit Spreads The credit spread is the difference in yield between a risky bond and a safe bond. In theory, credit spreads are determined by forward-looking economic fundamentals that measure a borrower's capacity to repay its debts. A recent study found that borrowers and lenders appear to focus excessively (i.e., to anchor) on past deal terms when setting spreads for a new bond issue. The study found that when a firm's most recent past debt issue had a credit spread that was higher than an upcoming issue, the interest rate on the upcoming deal was higher than fundamentals could justify. In other words, both the firm and its lenders were anchored to the older, higher interest rate.

(Source: Casey Dougal, Joseph Engelberg, Christopher A. Parsons, & Edward D. Van Wesep, "Anchoring on Credit Spreads," *Journal of Finance*, June 2015.)

What Causes Rates to Move?

Although the determination of interest rates is a complex economic issue, we do know that certain forces are especially important in influencing rate movements. Serious bond investors should make it a point to become familiar with the major determinants of interest rates and try to monitor those variables, at least informally.

In that regard, perhaps no variable is more important than inflation. Changes in the inflation rate, or to be more precise, changes in the expected inflation rate, have a direct and profound effect on market interest rates. When investors expect inflation to slow down, market interest rates generally fall as well. To gain an appreciation of the extent to which interest rates are linked to inflation, look at Figure 11.1. The figure plots the behavior of the interest rate on a 10-year U.S. Treasury bond and the inflation rate from 1963 to 2014. The blue line in the figure tracks the actual inflation rate over time, although as we have already noted, the expected inflation rate has a more direct effect on interest rates. Even so, there is a clear link between actual inflation and interest rates. Note that, in general, as inflation drifts up, so do interest rates. On the other hand, a decline in inflation is matched by a similar decline in interest rates. Most of the time, the rate on the 10-year bond exceeded the inflation rate, which is exactly what you should expect. When that was not the case, such as in the 1970s and more recently in 2012, investors in the 10-year Treasury bond did not earn enough interest to keep up with inflation. Notice that in 2009 as the U.S. struggled to recover from the Great Recession, the inflation rate was negative and the Treasury yields dropped sharply. On average, the 10-year Treasury yield exceeded the inflation rate by about 2.4 percentage points per year.

FIGURE 11.1 **The Impact of Inflation on the Behavior of Interest Rates**

The behavior of interest rates has always been closely tied to the movements in the rate of inflation. Since 1963 the average spread between the U.S. 10-year Treasury rate and inflation is 2.4 percentage points. This spread fluctuates quite a bit over time. Some extreme examples occurred in 1974 when the rate of inflation exceeded the 10-year Treasury rate by 4.1 percentage points and in 1985 when 10-year Treasury rates outpaced inflation by 8 percentage points.

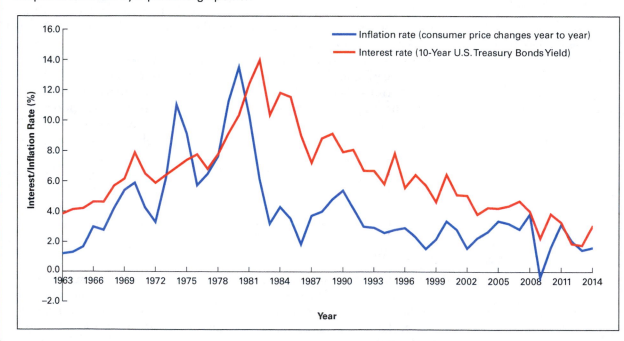

In addition to inflation, five other important economic variables can significantly affect the level of interest rates:

- *Changes in the money supply.* An increase in the money supply pushes rates down (as it makes more funds available for loans), and vice versa. This is true only up to a point, however. If the growth in the money supply becomes excessive, it can lead to inflation, which, of course, means higher interest rates.

- *The size of the federal budget deficit.* When the U.S. Treasury has to borrow large amounts to cover the budget deficit, the increased demand for funds exerts an upward pressure on interest rates. That's why bond market participants become so concerned when the budget deficit gets bigger and bigger—other things being equal, that means more upward pressure on market interest rates.

- *The level of economic activity.* Businesses need more capital when the economy expands. This need increases the demand for funds, and rates tend to rise. During a recession, economic activity contracts, and rates typically fall.

- *Policies of the Federal Reserve.* Actions of the Federal Reserve to control inflation also have a major effect on market interest rates. When the Fed wants to slow actual (or anticipated) inflation, it usually does so by driving up interest rates, as it did repeatedly in the mid- and late 1970s. Unfortunately, such actions sometimes have the side effect of slowing down business activity as well. Likewise, when the Federal Reserve wants to stimulate the economy, it takes action to push interest rates down, as it did repeatedly during and after the 2008-2009 recession.

- *The level of interest rates in major foreign markets.* Today investors look beyond national borders for investment opportunities. Rising rates in major foreign markets put pressure on rates in the United States to rise as well; if U.S. rates don't keep pace, foreign investors may be tempted to dump their dollars to buy higher-yielding foreign securities.

The Term Structure of Interest Rates and Yield Curves

Living Yield Curve

Bonds having different maturities typically have different interest rates. The relationship between interest rates (yield) and time to maturity for any class of similar-risk securities is called the **term structure of interest rates**. This relationship can be depicted graphically by a **yield curve**, which shows the relation between time to maturity and yield to maturity for a group of bonds having similar risk. The yield curve constantly changes as market forces push bond yields at different maturities up and down.

Types of Yield Curves   Two types of yield curves are illustrated in Figure 11.2. By far, the most common type is curve 1, the red upward-sloping curve. It indicates that yields tend to increase with longer maturities. That's partly because the longer a bond has to maturity, the greater the potential for price volatility. Investors, therefore, require higher-risk premiums to induce them to buy the longer, riskier bonds. Long-term rates may also exceed short-term rates if investors believe short-term rates will rise. In that case, rates on long-term bonds might have to be higher than short-term rates to attract investors. That is, if investors think short-term rates are rising, they will not want to tie up their money for long at today's lower rates. Instead, they would prefer to invest in a short-term security so that they can reinvest that money quickly after rates have risen. To induce investors to purchase a long-term bond, the bond must offer a higher rate than investors think they could earn by buying a series of short-term bonds, with each new bond in that series offering a higher rate than the one before.

FIGURE 11.2

Two Types of Yield Curves

A yield curve plots the relation between term to maturity and yield to maturity for a series of bonds that are similar in terms of risk. Although yield curves come in many shapes and forms, the most common is the upward-sloping curve. It shows that yields increase with longer maturities.

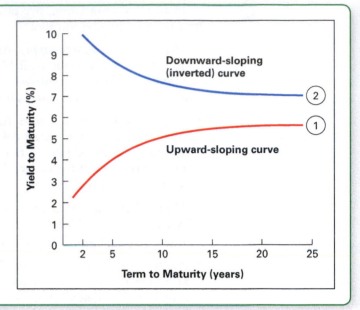

Occasionally, the yield curve becomes inverted, or downward sloping, as shown in curve 2, which occurs when short-term rates are higher than long-term rates. This curve sometimes results from actions by the Federal Reserve to curtail inflation by driving short-term interest rates up. An inverted yield curve may also occur when firms are very hesitant to borrow long-term (such as when they expect a recession). With very low demand for long-term loans, long-term interest rates fall. In addition to these two common yield curves, two other types appear from time to time: the *flat* yield curve, when rates for short- and long-term debt are essentially the same, and the *humped* yield curve, when intermediate-term rates are the highest.

Plotting Your Own Curves   Yield curves are constructed by plotting the yields for a group of bonds that are similar in all respects but maturity. Treasury securities (bills, notes, and bonds) are typically used to construct yield curves. There are several reasons for this. Treasury securities have no risk of default. They are actively traded, so their prices and yields are easy to observe, and they are relatively homogeneous with regard to quality and other issue characteristics. Investors can also construct yield curves for other classes of debt securities, such as A-rated municipal bonds, Aa-rated corporate bonds, and even certificates of deposit.

Figure 11.3 shows the yield curves for Treasury securities on March 7, 2007, and March 16, 2015. To draw these curves, you need Treasury quotes from the U.S. Department of the Treasury or some other similar source. (Note that actual quoted yields for curve 1 are highlighted in yellow in the table below the graph.) Given the required quotes, select the yields for the Treasury bills, notes, and bonds maturing in approximately 1 month, 3 months, 6 months, and 1, 2, 3, 5, 7, 10, 20, and 30 years. That covers the full range of Treasury issues' maturities. Next, plot the points on a graph whose horizontal (x) axis represents time to maturity in years and whose vertical (y) axis represents yield to maturity. Now, just connect the points to create the curves shown in Figure 11.3. You'll notice that curve 1 is upward sloping, while curve 2 is downward sloping. Downward-sloping yield curves are less common,

Historical Yield Curves

FIGURE 11.3

Yield Curves on U.S. Treasury Issues
Here we see two yield curves constructed from actual market data obtained from the U.S. Department of the Treasury. Curve 2 shows a less common downward-sloping yield curve. The yields that make up the more common upward-sloping curve 1 are near U.S. record low levels.

(Source: U.S. Department of the Treasury, June 4, 2015.)

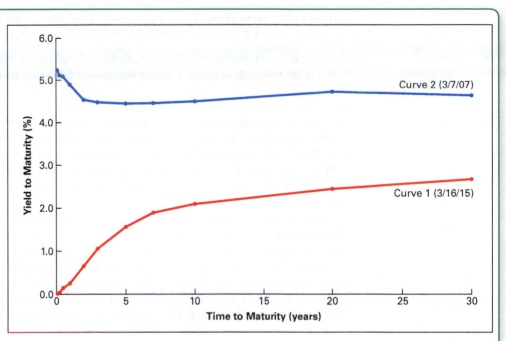

Date	1 mo	3 mo	6 mo	1 yr	2 yr	3 yr	5 yr	7 yr	10 yr	20 yr	30 yr
03/02/15	0.02	0.02	0.08	0.22	0.66	1.06	1.57	1.89	2.08	2.46	2.68
03/03/15	0.01	0.02	0.08	0.26	0.68	1.09	1.61	1.94	2.12	2.49	2.71
03/04/15	0.01	0.01	0.08	0.26	0.66	1.07	1.6	1.93	2.12	2.49	2.72
03/05/15	0.02	0.02	0.08	0.25	0.65	1.05	1.57	1.9	2.11	2.49	2.71
03/06/15	0.02	0.01	0.08	0.27	0.73	1.16	1.7	2.04	2.24	2.63	2.83
03/09/15	0.01	0.02	0.1	0.27	0.7	1.13	1.66	1.99	2.2	2.58	2.8
03/10/15	0.03	0.02	0.1	0.25	0.7	1.1	1.62	1.94	2.14	2.51	2.73
03/11/15	0.03	0.03	0.1	0.25	0.7	1.09	1.6	1.92	2.11	2.47	2.69
03/12/15	0.03	0.03	0.1	0.24	0.67	1.06	1.59	1.91	2.1	2.47	2.69
03/13/15	0.03	0.03	0.11	0.24	0.68	1.07	1.6	1.93	2.13	2.48	2.7
03/16/15	0.02	0.05	0.15	0.26	0.66	1.06	1.57	1.9	2.1	2.45	2.67

thankfully so because they often signal an upcoming recession. For example, the downward-sloping yield curve shown in Figure 11.3 signaled the Great Recession that officially ran from December 2007 to June of 2009. While curve 1 is the more typical upward-sloping yield curve, it nonetheless reflects the historically low interest rates that prevailed as the U.S. economy recovered from a deep recession.

Explanations of the Term Structure of Interest Rates   As we noted earlier, the shape of the yield curve can change over time. Three commonly cited theories—the expectations hypothesis, the liquidity preference theory, and the market segmentation theory—explain more fully the reasons for the general shape of the yield curve.

Expectations Hypothesis The **expectations hypothesis** suggests that the yield curve reflects investor expectations about the future behavior of interest rates. This theory argues that the relationship between short-term and long-term interest rates today reflects investors' expectations about how interest rates will change in the future. When the yield curve slopes upward, and long-term rates are higher than short-term rates, the expectations hypothesis interprets this as a sign that investors expect short-term rates to rise. That's why long-term bonds pay a premium compared to short-term bonds. People will not lock their money away in a long-term investment when they think interest rates are going to rise unless the rate on the long-term investment is higher than the current rate on short-term investments.

For example, suppose the current interest rate on a 1-year Treasury bill is 5%, and the current rate on a 2-year Treasury note is 6%. The expectations hypothesis says that this pattern of interest rates reveals that investors believe that the rate on a 1-year Treasury bill will go up to 7% next year. Why? That's the rate that makes investors today indifferent between locking their money away for 2 years and earning 6% on the 2-year note versus investing in the 1-year T-bill today at 5% and then next year reinvesting the money from that instrument into another 1-year T-bill paying 7%.

Investment Strategy	(1) Rate Earned This Year	(2) Rate Earned Next Year	(3) Return over 2 Years [(1) + (2)]
Buy 2-year note today	6%	6%	12%
Buy 1-year T-bill, then reinvest in another T-bill next year	5%	7%	12%

Only if the rate on a 1-year T-bill rises from 5% this year to 7% next year will investors be indifferent between these 2 strategies. Thus, according to the expectations hypothesis, an upward-sloping yield curve means that investors expect interest rates to rise, and a downward-sloping yield curve means that investors expect interest rates to fall.

Example

Suppose the yield curve is inverted, and 1-year bonds offer a 5% yield while 2-year bonds pay a 4.5% yield. According to the expectations hypothesis, what do investors expect the 1-year bond yield to be 1 year from now? Remember that the expectations hypothesis says today's short-term and long-term interest rates are set at a level which makes investors indifferent between short-term and long-term bonds, given their beliefs about where interest rates are headed. Therefore, to determine the expected 1-year bond yield next year, you must determine what return in the second year would make investors just as happy to buy two 1-year bonds as they are to buy one 2-year bond.

$$\text{Return on a 2-year bond} = 4.5\% + 4.5\%$$
$$\text{Return on two 1-year bonds} = 5.0\% + x$$

The x in the second equation represents the expected rate on the 1-year bond next year. The top equation shows that an investor earns 9% over 2 years by purchasing a 2-year bond, so to achieve the same return on a series of two 1-year bonds, the return in the second year must be 4%.

Liquidity Preference Theory   More often than not, yield curves have an upward slope. The expectations hypothesis would interpret this as a sign that investors *usually* expect rates to rise. That seems somewhat illogical. Why would investors expect interest rates to rise more often than they expect rates to fall? Put differently, why would investors expect interest rates to trend up over time? There is certainly no historical pattern to lead one to hold that view. One explanation for the frequency of upward-sloping yield curves is the **liquidity preference theory**. This theory states that long-term bond rates should be higher than short-term rates because of the added risks involved with the longer maturities. In other words, because of the risk differential between long- and short-term debt securities, rational investors will prefer the less risky, short-term obligations unless they can be motivated, via higher interest rates, to invest in longer-term bonds. Even if investors do not expect short-term rates to rise, long-term bonds will still have to offer higher yields to attract investors.

Actually, there are a number of reasons why rational investors should prefer short-term securities. To begin with, they are more liquid (more easily converted to cash) and less sensitive to changing market rates, which means there is less price volatility. For a given change in market rates, the prices of longer-term bonds will show considerably more movement than the prices of short-term bonds. In addition, just as investors tend to require a premium for tying up funds for longer periods, borrowers will also pay a premium in order to obtain long-term funds. Borrowers thus assure themselves that funds will be available, and they avoid having to roll over short-term debt at unknown and possibly unfavorable rates. All of these preferences explain why higher rates of interest should be associated with longer maturities and why it's perfectly rational to expect upward-sloping yield curves.

Market Segmentation Theory   Another often-cited theory, the **market segmentation theory**, suggests that the market for debt is segmented on the basis of the maturity preferences of different financial institutions and investors. According to this theory, the yield curve changes as the supply and demand for funds within each maturity segment determines its prevailing interest rate. The equilibrium between the financial institutions that supply the funds for short-term maturities (e.g., banks) and the borrowers of those short-term funds (e.g., businesses with seasonal loan requirements) establishes interest rates in the short-term markets. Similarly, the equilibrium between suppliers and demanders in such long-term markets as life insurance and real estate determines the prevailing long-term interest rates.

The shape of the yield curve can slope either upward or downward, as determined by the general relationship between rates in each market segment. When supply outstrips demand for short-term loans, short-term rates are relatively low. If, at the same time, the demand for long-term loans is higher than the available supply of funds, then long-term rates will move up, and the yield curve will have an upward slope. If supply and demand conditions are reversed—with excess demand for borrowing in the short-term market and an excess supply of funds in the long-term market—the yield curve could slope down.

Which Theory Is Right?   All three theories of the term structure have at least some merit in explaining the shape of the yield curve. These theories tell us that, at any time, the slope of the yield curve is affected by the interaction of (1) expectations regarding future interest rates, (2) liquidity preferences, and (3) the supply and demand conditions in the short- and long-term market segments. Upward-sloping yield curves result from expectations of rising interest rates, lender preferences for shorter-maturity loans, and a greater supply of short- than of long-term loans relative to the respective demand in each market segment. The opposite conditions lead to a downward-sloping yield curve.

Using the Yield Curve in Investment Decisions   Bond investors often use yield curves in making investment decisions. Analyzing the changes in yield curves provides investors with information about future interest rate movements, which in turn affect the prices and returns on different types of bonds. For example, if the entire yield curve begins to move upward, it usually means that inflation is starting to heat up or is expected to do so in the near future. In that case, investors can expect that interest rates, too, will rise. Under these conditions, most seasoned bond investors will turn to short or intermediate (three to five years) maturities, which provide reasonable returns and at the same time minimize exposure to capital loss when interest rates go up. A downward-sloping yield curve signals that rates have peaked and are about to fall and that the economy is slowing down.

Another factor to consider is the difference in yields on different maturities—the "steepness" of the curve. For example, a steep yield curve is one where long-term rates are much higher than short-term rates. This shape is often seen as an indication that the spread between long-term and short-term rates is about to fall, either because long-term rates will fall or short-term rates will rise. Steep yield curves are generally viewed as a bullish sign. For aggressive bond investors, they could be the signal to start moving into long-term securities. Flatter yield curves, on the other hand, sharply reduce the incentive for going long-term since the difference in yield between the 5- and 30-year maturities can be quite small. Under these conditions, investors would be well advised to just stick with the 5- to 10-year maturities, which will generate about the same yield as long bonds but without the risks.

More about the Yield Curve

CONCEPTS IN REVIEW

Answers available at
http://www.pearsonhighered
.com/smart

11.1 Is there a single market rate of interest applicable to all segments of the bond market, or is there a series of market yields? Explain and note the investment implications of such a market environment.

11.2 Explain why interest rates are important to both conservative and aggressive bond investors. What causes interest rates to move, and how can you monitor such movements?

11.3 What is the term structure of interest rates and how is it related to the yield curve? What information is required to plot a yield curve? Describe an upward-sloping yield curve and explain what it has to say about the behavior of interest rates. Do the same for a flat yield curve.

11.4 How might you, as a bond investor, use information about the term structure of interest rates and yield curves when making investment decisions?

The Pricing of Bonds

LG3   No matter who the issuer is, what kind of bond it is, or whether it's fully taxable or tax-free, all bonds are priced using similar principles. That is, all bonds (including notes with maturities of more than one year) are priced according to the present value of their future cash flow streams. Indeed, once the prevailing or expected market yield is known, the whole process becomes rather mechanical.

Market yields largely determine bond prices. That's because in the marketplace, investors first decide what yield is appropriate for a particular bond, given its risk, and then they use that yield to find the bond's price (or market value). As we saw earlier, the appropriate yield on a bond is a function of certain market and economic forces (e.g., the risk-free rate of return and inflation), as well as key issue and issuer characteristics (like years to maturity and the issue's bond rating). Together these forces combine to form the required rate of return, which is the rate of return the investor would like to earn in order to justify an investment in a given fixed-income security. The required return defines the yield at which the bond should be trading and serves as the discount rate in the bond valuation process.

The Basic Bond Valuation Model

Generally speaking, when you buy a bond you receive two distinct types of cash flow: (1) periodic interest income (i.e., coupon payments) and (2) the principal (or par value) at the end of the bond's life. Thus, in valuing a bond, you're dealing with an annuity of coupon payments for a specified number of periods plus a large single cash flow at maturity. You can use these cash flows, along with the required rate of return on the investment, in a present value-based bond valuation model to find the dollar value, or price, of a bond. Using annual compounding, you can calculate the price of a particular bond (BPi) using the following equation:

Equation 11.2

$$BP_i = \sum_{t=1}^{N} \frac{C}{(1 + r_i)^t} + \frac{PV_N}{(1 + r_i)^N}$$

$$= \quad \begin{array}{c} \text{Present value of} \\ \text{coupon payments} \end{array} + \begin{array}{c} \text{Present value of} \\ \text{bond's par value} \end{array}$$

where

$$
\begin{aligned}
BP_i &= \text{current price (or value) of a particular bond } i \\
C &= \text{annual coupon (interest) payment} \\
PV_N &= \text{par value of the bond, at maturity} \\
N &= \text{number of years to maturity} \\
r_i &= \text{prevailing market yield, or required annual return on bonds similar to bond } i
\end{aligned}
$$

In this form, you can compute the bond's current value, or what you would be willing to pay for it, given that you want to generate a certain rate of return, as defined by r_i. Alternatively, if you already know the bond's price, you can solve for r_i in the equation, in which case you'd be looking for the yield to maturity embedded in the current market price of the bond.

In the discussion that follows, we will demonstrate the bond valuation process in two ways. First, we'll use annual compounding—that is, because of its computational simplicity, we'll assume we are dealing with coupons that are paid once a year. Second, we'll examine bond valuation under conditions of semiannual compounding, which is the way most bonds actually pay their interest.

Annual Compounding

You need the following information to value a bond: (1) the annual coupon payment, (2) the par value (usually $1,000), and (3) the number of years (i.e., time periods) remaining to maturity. You then use the prevailing market yield, r_i, as the discount rate to compute the bond's price, as follows:

Equation 11.3

$$\text{Bond price} = \frac{\text{Present value of}}{\text{coupon payments}} + \frac{\text{Present value of}}{\text{bond's par value}}$$

Equation 11.3a

$$BP_i = \frac{C}{(1 + r_i)^1} + \frac{C}{(1 + r_i)^2} + \cdots + \frac{C}{(1 + r_i)^N} + \frac{\$1,000}{(1 + r_i)^N}$$

where again

C = annual coupon payment
N = number of years to maturity

Example

A 20-year, 4.5% bond is priced to yield 5%. That is, the bond pays an annual coupon of 4.5% (or $45), has 20 years left to maturity, and has a yield to maturity of 5%, which is the current market rate on bonds of this type. We can use Equation 11.3 to find the bond's price.

$$BP_i = \frac{\$45}{(1 + 0.05)^1} + \frac{\$45}{(1 + 0.05)^2} + \cdots + \frac{\$45}{(1 + 0.05)^{20}} + \frac{\$1,000}{(1 + 0.05)^{20}} = \$937.69$$

Note that because this is a coupon-bearing bond, we have an annuity of coupon payments of $45 a year for 20 years, plus a single cash flow of $1,000 that occurs at the end of year 20. Thus, we find the present value of the coupon annuity and then add that amount to the present value of the recovery of principal at maturity. In this particular case, you should be willing to pay almost $938 for this bond, as long as you're satisfied with earning 5% on your money.

Notice that this bond trades at a discount of $62.31 ($1,000 − $937.69). It trades at a discount because its coupon rate (4.5%) is below the market's required return (5%). You can directly link the size of the discount on this bond to the present value of the difference between the coupons that it pays ($45) and the coupons that would be required if the bond matched the market's 5% required return ($50). In other words, this bond's coupon payment is $5 less than what the market requires, so if you take the present value of that difference over the bond's life, you will calculate the size of the bond's discount:

$$\frac{\$5}{(1 + 0.05)^1} + \frac{\$5}{(1 + 0.05)^2} + \cdots + \frac{\$5}{(1 + 0.05)^{20}} = \$62.31$$

In a similar vein, for a bond that trades at a premium, the size of that premium equals the present value of the difference between the coupon that the bond pays and the (lower) coupon that the market requires.

Bonds initially sell for a price close to par value because bond issuers generally set the bond's coupon rate equal or close to the market's required return at the time the bonds are issued. If market interest rates change during the life of the bond, then the bond's price will adjust up or down to reflect any differences between the bond's coupon rate and the market interest rate. Although bonds can sell at premiums or discounts over their lives, as the maturity date arrives, bond prices will converge to par value. This happens because as time passes and a bond's maturity date approaches, there are fewer interest payments remaining (so any premium or discount is diminishing) and the principal to be repaid at maturity is becoming an ever bigger portion of the bond's price since the periods over which it is being discounted are disappearing.

CALCULATOR USE For annual compounding, to price a 20-year, 4.5% bond to yield 5%, use the keystrokes shown in the margin, where:

$$N = \text{number of years to maturity}$$
$$I = \text{required annual return on the bond (what the bond is being priced to yield)}$$
$$PMT = \text{annual coupon payment}$$
$$FV = \text{par value of the bond}$$
$$PV = \text{computed price of the bond}$$

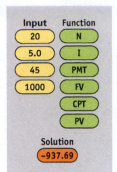

Recall that the calculator result shows the bond's price as a negative value, which indicates that the price is a cash outflow for an investor when buying the bond's cash flows.

SPREADSHEET USE The bond's price can also be calculated as shown on the following Excel spreadsheet.

Financial Calculator
Tutorials

	A	B
1	**Bond's Price**	
2	Par value	$1,000
3	Annual coupon rate	4.5%
4	Annual coupon payment	$45
5	Number of years to maturity	20
6	Required annual return	5.0%
7	Bond's price	-$937.69
8	Entry in Cell B7 is =PV(B6,B5,B4,B2,0). The minus sign appears before the $937.69 in B7 because the price of the bond is treated as a cash outflow.	

Semiannual Compounding

Although using annual compounding simplifies the valuation process a bit, it's not the way most bonds are actually valued in the marketplace. In practice, most bonds pay interest every six months, so it is appropriate to use semiannual compounding to value bonds. Fortunately, it's relatively easy to go from annual to semiannual compounding: All you need to do is cut the annual interest income and the required rate of return in half and double the number of periods until maturity. In other words, rather than one compounding and payment interval per year, there are two (i.e., two 6-month periods per year). Given these changes, finding the price of a bond under conditions of semiannual compounding is much like pricing a bond using annual compounding. That is:

Equation 11.4

$$\begin{array}{ccc} \text{Bond price (with semi-} & = & \text{Present value of the annuity of} \\ \text{annual compounding)} & & \text{semiannual coupon payments} \end{array} + \begin{array}{c} \text{Present value of the} \\ \text{bond's par value} \end{array}$$

Equation 11.4a

$$BP_i = \frac{C/2}{\left(1 + \dfrac{r_i}{2}\right)^1} + \frac{C/2}{\left(1 + \dfrac{r_i}{2}\right)^2} + \cdots + \frac{C/2}{\left(1 + \dfrac{r_i}{2}\right)^{2N}} + \frac{\$1,000}{\left(1 + \dfrac{r_i}{2}\right)^{2N}}$$

where, in this case,

$$C/2 = \text{semiannual coupon payment, or the amount of interest paid every 6 months}$$
$$r_i/2 = \text{the required rate of return per 6-month period}$$

Example

In the previous bond-pricing example, you priced a 20-year bond to yield 5%, assuming annual interest payments of $45. Suppose the bond makes semiannual interest payments instead. With semiannual payments of $22.50, you adjust the semiannual return to 2.5% and the number of periods to 40. Using Equation 11.4, you'd have:

$$BP_i = \frac{\$45/2}{\left(1+\dfrac{0.05}{2}\right)^1} + \frac{\$45/2}{\left(1+\dfrac{0.05}{2}\right)^2} + \cdots + \frac{\$45/2}{\left(1+\dfrac{0.05}{2}\right)^{40}} + \frac{1{,}000}{\left(1+\dfrac{0.05}{2}\right)^{40}} = \$937.24$$

The price of the bond in this case ($937.24) is slightly less than the price we obtained with annual compounding ($937.69).

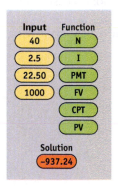

CALCULATOR USE For *semiannual compounding*, to price a 20-year, 4.5% semiannual-pay bond to yield 5%, use the keystrokes shown in the margin, where:

N = number of 6-month periods to maturity ($20 \times 2 = 40$)
I = yield on the bond, adjusted for semiannual compounding ($5\% \div 2 = 2.5\%$)
PMT = semiannual coupon payment ($\$45.00 \div 2 = \$22.50$)
FV = par value of the bond
PV = computed price of the bond

SPREADSHEET USE You can calculate the bond's price with semiannual coupon payments as shown on the following Excel spreadsheet. Notice that in cell B8 the required annual return is divided by coupon payment frequency to find the required rate of return per 6-month period, and the number of years to maturity is multiplied times the coupon payment frequency to find the total number of 6-month periods remaining until maturity.

	A	B
1	**Bond's Price**	
2	Par value	$1,000
3	Coupon rate	4.5%
4	Coupon payment frequency	2
5	Coupon payment	$22.50
6	Number of years to maturity	20
7	Required annual return	5.0%
8	Bond's price	-$937.24
9	Entry in Cell B8 is =PV(B7/B4,B6*B4,B5,B2,0). The minus sign appears before the $937.24 in B8 because the price of the bond is treated as a cash outflow.	

Accrued Interest

Most bonds pay interest every six months, but you can trade them any time that the market is open. Suppose you own a bond that makes interest payments on January 15 and July 15 each year. What happens if you sell this bond at some time between the scheduled coupon payment dates? For example, suppose you sell the bond on October 15, a date that is roughly halfway between two payment dates. Fortunately, interest accrues on bonds between coupon payments, so selling the bond prior to a coupon payment does not mean that you sacrifice any interest that you earned. **Accrued interest** is the amount of interest earned on a bond since the last coupon payment. When you sell a bond in between coupon dates, the bond buyer adds accrued interest to the bond's price (the price calculated using Equation 11.3 or 11.4 depending on whether coupons arrive annually or semiannually).

> **Example**
>
> Suppose you purchase a $1,000 par value bond that pays a 6% coupon in semi-annual installments of $30. You received a coupon payment two months ago, and now you are ready to sell the bond. Contacting a broker, you learn that the bond's current market price is $1,010. If you sell the bond, you will receive not only the market price, but also accrued interest. Because you are about one-third of the way between the last coupon payment and the next one, you receive accrued interest of $10 (i.e., 1/3 × $30), so the total cash that you receive in exchange for your bond is $1,020.

Traders in the bond market sometimes refer to the price of a bond as being either clean or dirty. The **clean price** of a bond equals the present value of its cash flows, as in Equations 11.3 and 11.4. As a matter of practice, bond price quotations that you may find in financial periodicals or online are nearly always clean prices. The **dirty price** of a bond is the clean price plus accrued interest. In the example above, the clean price is $1,010, and the dirty price is $1,020.

CONCEPTS IN REVIEW

Answers available at http://www.pearsonhighered .com/smart

11.5 Explain how market yield affects the price of a bond. Could you price a bond without knowing its market yield? Explain.

11.6 Why are bonds generally priced using semiannual compounding? Does it make much difference if you use annual compounding?

Measures of Yield and Return

In the bond market, investors focus as much on a bond's yield to maturity as on its price. As you have seen, the yield to maturity helps determine the price at which a bond trades, but it also measures the rate of return on the bond. When you can observe the price of a bond that is trading in the market, you can simply reverse the bond valuation process described above to solve for the bond's yield to maturity rather than its price. That gives you a pretty good idea of the return that you might earn if you purchased the bond at its current market price. Actually, there are three widely used metrics to assess the return on a bond: the current yield, the yield to maturity, and the yield to call (for bonds that are callable). We'll look at all three measures here, along with a concept known as the *expected return*, which measures the expected (or actual) rate of return earned over a specific holding period.

Current Yield

The **current yield** is the simplest of all bond return measures, but it also has the most limited application. This measure looks at just one source of return: a bond's annual interest income. In particular, it indicates the amount of current income a bond provides relative to its prevailing market price. The current yield equals:

Equation 11.5

$$\text{Current yield} = \frac{\text{Annual interest income}}{\text{Current market price of the bond}}$$

> An 8% bond would pay $80 per year in interest for every $1,000 of principal. However, if the bond was currently priced at $800, it would have a current yield of $80 ÷ $800 = 0.10 = 10%. The current yield measures a bond's annual interest income, so it is of interest primarily to investors seeking high levels of current income, such as endowments or retirees.

Yield to Maturity

The **yield to maturity** (**YTM**) is the most important and most widely used measure of the return provided by a bond. It evaluates the bond's interest income and any gain or loss that results from differences between the price that an investor pays for a bond and the par value that the investor receives at maturity. The YTM takes into account all of the cash flow received over a bond's life. Also known as the **promised yield**, the YTM shows the rate of return earned by an investor, given that the bond is held to maturity and all principal and interest payments are made in a prompt and timely fashion. In addition, the YTM calculation implicitly assumes that the investor can reinvest all the coupon payments at an interest rate equal to the bond's yield to maturity. This "reinvestment assumption" plays a vital role in the YTM, which we will discuss in more detail later in this chapter (see the section entitled Yield Properties).

The yield to maturity is used not only to gauge the return on a single issue but also to track the behavior of the market in general. In other words, market interest rates are basically a reflection of the average promised yields that exist in a given segment of the market. The yield to maturity provides valuable insights into an issue's investment merits that investors can use to assess the attractiveness of different bonds. Other things being equal, the higher the promised yield of an issue, the more attractive it is.

Although there are a couple of ways to compute the YTM, the best and most accurate procedure is derived directly from the bond valuation model described above. That is, you can use Equations 11.3 and 11.4 to determine the YTM for a bond. The difference is that now instead of trying to determine the price of the bond, you know its price and are trying to find the discount rate that will equate the present value of the bond's cash flow (coupon and principal payments) to its current market price. This procedure may sound familiar. It's just like the internal rate of return measure described earlier in the text. Indeed, the YTM is basically the internal rate of return on a bond. When you find that, you have the bond's yield to maturity.

Using Annual Compounding Finding yield to maturity is a matter of trial and error. In other words, you try different values for YTM until you find the one that solves the equation. Let's say you want to find the YTM for a 7.5% ($1,000 par value) annual-coupon-paying bond that has 15 years remaining to maturity and is currently trading in the market at $809.50. From Equation 11.3, we know that

$$BP_i = \$809.50 = \frac{\$75}{(1 + r_i)^1} + \frac{\$75}{(1 + r_i)^2} + \cdots + \frac{\$75}{(1 + r_i)^{15}} + \frac{\$1,000}{(1 + r_i)^{15}}$$

Notice that this bond sells below par (i.e., it sells at a discount). What do we know about the relationship between the required return on a bond and its coupon rate when the bond sells at a discount? Bonds sell at a discount when the required return (or yield to maturity) is higher than the coupon rate, so the yield to maturity on this bond must be higher than 7.5%.

Through trial and error, we might initially try a discount rate of 8% or 9% (or, since it sells at a discount, any value above the bond's coupon). Sooner or later, we'll try a discount rate of 10%, and at that discount rate, the present value of the bond's cash flows is $809.85 (use Equation 11.3 to verify this), which is very close to the bond's market price.

Because the computed price of $809.85 is reasonably close to the bond's current market price of $809.50, we can say that 10% represents the approximate yield to maturity on this bond. That is, 10% is the discount rate that leads to a computed bond price that's equal (or very close) to the bond's current market price. In this case, if you were to pay $809.50 for the bond and hold it to maturity, you would expect to earn a YTM very close to 10.0%. Doing trial and error by hand can be time consuming, so you can use a handheld calculator or computer software to calculate the YTM.

CALCULATOR USE For annual compounding, to find the YTM of a 15-year, 7.5% bond that is currently priced in the market at $809.50, use the keystrokes shown in the margin. The present value (*PV*) key represents the current market price of the bond, and all other keystrokes are as defined earlier.

Input	Function
15	N
–809.50	PV
75	PMT
1000	FV
	CPT
	I

Solution
10.0

SPREADSHEET USE The bond's YTM can also be calculated as shown on the following Excel spreadsheet.

	A	B
1	**Bond's YTM**	
2	Par value	$1,000
3	Annual coupon rate	7.5%
4	Annual coupon payment	$75
5	Number of years to maturity	15
6	Bond's price	-$809.50
7	Bond's YTM	10.0%
8	Entry in Cell B7 is =RATE(B5,B4,B6,B2,0). The minus sign appears before the $809.50 in B6 because the price of the bond is treated as a cash outflow.	

Using Semiannual Compounding Given some fairly simple modifications, it's also possible to find the YTM using semiannual compounding. To do so, we cut the annual coupon and discount rate in half and double the number of periods to maturity. Returning to the 7.5%, 15-year bond, let's see what happens when you use Equation 11.4 and try an initial discount rate of 10%.

$$BP_i = \frac{\$75.00/2}{\left(1 + \frac{0.10}{2}\right)^1} \quad \frac{\$75.00/2}{\left(1 + \frac{0.10}{2}\right)^2} + \cdots + \frac{\$75.00/2}{\left(1 + \frac{0.10}{2}\right)^{30}} + \frac{\$1,000}{\left(1 + \frac{0.10}{2}\right)^{30}} = \$807.85$$

As you can see, a semiannual discount rate of 5% results in a computed bond value that's well short of the market price of $809.50. Given the inverse relationship between price and yield, it follows that if you need a higher price, you have to try a lower YTM (discount rate). Therefore, you know the semiannual yield on this bond has to be something less than 5%. By trial and error, you would determine that the yield to maturity on this bond is just a shade under 5% per half year—approximately 4.99%. Remember that this is the yield expressed over a 6-month period. The market convention is to simply state the annual yield as twice the semiannual yield. This practice produces what the market refers to as the **bond equivalent yield**. Returning to the YTM problem started above, you know that the issue has a semiannual yield of about 4.99%.

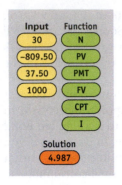

Input	Function
30	N
–809.50	PV
37.50	PMT
1000	FV
	CPT
	I

Solution

4.987

According to the bond equivalent yield convention, you double the semiannual rate to obtain the annual rate of return on this bond. Doing this results in an annualized yield to maturity (or promised yield) of approximately $4.99\% \times 2 = 9.98\%$. This is the annual rate of return you will earn on the bond if you hold it to maturity.

CALCULATOR USE For semiannual compounding, to find the YTM of a 15-year, 7.5% bond that is currently priced in the market at $809.50, use the keystrokes shown here. As before, the *PV* key is the current market price of the bond, and all other keystrokes are as defined earlier. Remember that to find the bond equivalent yield, you must double the computed value of *I*, 4.987%. That is $4.987\% \times 2 = 9.97\%$. The difference between our answer here, 9.97%, and the 9.98% figure in the previous paragraph is simply due to the calculator's more precise rounding.

SPREADSHEET USE A semiannual bond's YTM and bond equivalent yield can also be calculated as shown on the following Excel spreadsheet.

	A	B
1	**Bond's YTM**	
2	Par value	$1,000
3	Coupon rate	7.5%
4	Coupon payment frequency	2
5	Coupon payment	$37.50
6	Number of years to maturity	15
7	Bond's price	–$809.50
8	Bond's YTM	4.99%
9	Bond-equivalent yield	9.97%
10	Entry in Cell B8 is =RATE(B6*B4,B5,B7,B2,0). The minus sign appears before the $809.50 in B7 because the price of the bond is treated as a cash outflow.	

Yield Properties Actually, in addition to holding the bond to maturity, there are several other critical assumptions embedded in any yield to maturity figure. The promised yield measure—whether computed with annual or semiannual compounding—is based on present value concepts and therefore contains important reinvestment assumptions. To be specific, the YTM calculation assumes that when each coupon payment arrives, you can reinvest it for the remainder of the bond's life at a rate that is equal to the YTM. When this assumption holds, the return that you earn over a bond's life is in fact equal to the YTM. In essence, the calculated yield to maturity figure is the return "promised" only as long as the issuer meets all interest and principal obligations on a timely basis and the investor reinvests all interest income at a rate equal to the computed promised yield. In our example above, you would need to reinvest each of the coupon payments and earn a 10% return on those reinvested funds. Failure to do so would result in a realized yield of less than the 10% YTM. If you made no attempt to reinvest the coupons, you would earn a realized yield over the 15-year investment horizon of just over 6.5%—far short of the 10% promised return. On the other hand, if you could reinvest coupons at a rate that exceeded 10%, the actual yield on your bond over the 15 years would be higher than its 10% YTM. The bottom line is that unless you are dealing with a zero-coupon bond, a significant portion of the bond's total return over time comes from reinvested coupons.

When we use present value-based measures of return, such as the YTM, there are actually three components of return: (1) coupon/interest income, (2) capital gains (or losses), and (3) interest on interest. Whereas current income and capital gains make up the profits from an investment, interest on interest is a measure of what you do with those profits. In the context of a bond's yield to maturity, the computed YTM defines the required, or minimum, reinvestment rate. Put your investment profits (i.e., interest income) to work at this rate and you'll earn a rate of return equal to YTM. This rule applies to any coupon-bearing bond—as long as there's an annual or semiannual flow of interest income, the reinvestment of that income and interest on interest are matters that you must deal with. Also, keep in mind that the bigger the coupon and/or the longer the maturity, the more important the reinvestment assumption. Indeed, for many long-term, high-coupon bond investments, interest on interest alone can account for well over half the cash flow.

Finding the Yield on a Zero   You can also use the procedures described above (Equation 11.3 with annual compounding or Equation 11.4 with semiannual compounding) to find the yield to maturity on a zero-coupon bond. The only difference is that you can ignore the coupon portion of the equation because it will, of course, equal zero. All you need to do to find the promised yield on a zero-coupon bond is to solve the following expression:

$$\text{Yield} = \left(\frac{\$1,000}{\text{Price}}\right)^{\frac{1}{N}} - 1$$

Example

Suppose that today you could buy a 15-year zero-coupon bond for $315. If you purchase the bond at that price and hold it to maturity, what is your YTM?

$$\text{Yield} = \left(\frac{\$1,000}{\$315}\right)^{\frac{1}{15}} - 1 = 0.08 = 8\%$$

The zero-coupon bond pays an annual compound return of 8%. Had we been using semiannual compounding, we'd use the same equation except we'd substitute 30 for 15 (because there are 30 semiannual periods in 15 years). The yield would change to 3.93% per half year, or 7.86% per year.

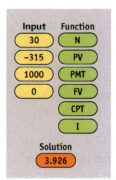

Input	Function
30	N
−315	PV
1000	PMT
0	FV
	CPT
	I

Solution
3.926

CALCULATOR USE   For semiannual compounding, to find the YTM of a 15-year zero-coupon bond that is currently priced in the market at $315, use the keystrokes shown in the margin. *PV* is the current market price of the bond, and all other keystrokes are as defined earlier. To find the bond equivalent yield, double the computed value of *I*, 3.926%. That is, 3.926% × 2 = 7.85%.

SPREADSHEET USE   A semiannual bond's YTM and bond equivalent yield can also be calculated as shown on the following Excel spreadsheet. Notice that the spreadsheet also shows 7.85% for the bond equivalent yield.

	A	B
1	**Bond's YTM**	
2	Par value	$1,000
3	Coupon rate	0.0%
4	Coupon payment frequency	2
5	Coupon payment	$0.00
6	Number of years to maturity	15
7	Bond's price	−$315.00
8	Bond's YTM	3.93%
9	Bond-equivalent yield	7.85%
10	Entry in Cell B8 is =RATE(B6*B4,B5,B7,B2,0). The minus sign appears before the $315.00 in B7 because the price of the bond is treated as a cash outflow.	

Yield to Call

Bonds can be either noncallable or callable. Recall that a noncallable bond prohibits the issuer from calling the bond prior to maturity. Because such issues will remain outstanding to maturity, you can value them by using the standard yield to maturity measure. In contrast, a callable bond gives the issuer the right to retire the bond before its maturity date, so the issue may not remain outstanding to maturity. As a result, the YTM may not always provide a good measure of the return that you can expect if you purchase a callable bond. Instead, you should consider the impact of the bond being called away prior to maturity. A common way to do that is to use a measure known as the **yield to call (YTC)**, which shows the yield on a bond if the issue remains outstanding not to maturity but rather until its first (or some other specified) call date.

The YTC is commonly used with bonds that carry deferred-call provisions. Remember that such issues start out as noncallable bonds and then, after a call deferment period (of 5 to 10 years), become freely callable. Under these conditions, the YTC would measure the expected yield on a deferred-call bond assuming that the issue is retired at the end of the call deferment period (that is, when the bond first becomes freely callable). You can find the YTC by making two simple modifications to the standard YTM equation (Equation 11.3 or 11.4). First, define the length of the investment horizon (N) as the number of years to the first call date, not the number of years to maturity. Second, instead of using the bond's par value ($1,000), use the bond's call price (which is stated in the indenture and is frequently greater than the bond's par value).

For example, assume you want to find the YTC on a 20-year, 10.5% deferred-call bond that is currently trading in the market at $1,204 but has five years to go to first call (that is, before it becomes freely callable), at which time it can be called in at a price of $1,085. Rather than using the bond's maturity of 20 years in the valuation equation (Equation 11.3 or 11.4), you use the number of years to first call (five years), and rather than the bond's par value, $1,000, you use the issue's call price, $1,085. Note, however, you still use the bond's coupon (10.5%) and its current market price ($1,204). Thus, for annual compounding, you would have:

Equation 11.6

$$BP_i = \$1,204 = \frac{\$105}{(1+r_i)^1} + \frac{\$105}{(1+r_i)^2} + \frac{\$105}{(1+r_i)^3} + \frac{\$105}{(1+r_i)^4} + \frac{\$105}{(1+r_i)^5} + \frac{\$1,085}{(1+r_i)^5}$$

Through trial and error, you could determine that at a discount rate of 7%, the present value of the future cash flows (coupons over the next five years, plus call price) will exactly (or very nearly) equal the bond's current market price of $1,204.

Thus, the YTC on this bond is 7%. In contrast, the bond's YTM is 8.37%. In practice, bond investors normally compute both YTM and YTC for deferred-call bonds that are trading at a premium. They do this to find which yield is lower; the market convention is *to use the lower, more conservative measure of yield (YTM or YTC) as the appropriate indicator of the bond's return.* As a result, the premium bond in our example would be valued relative to its yield to call. The assumption is that because interest rates have dropped so much (the YTM is two percentage points below the coupon rate), it will be called in the first chance the issuer gets. However, the situation is totally different when this or any bond trades at a discount. Why? Because the YTM on any discount bond, whether callable or not, will always be less than the YTC. Thus, the YTC is a totally irrelevant measure for discount bonds—it's used only with premium bonds.

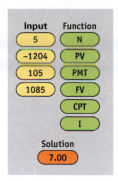

Input	Function
5	N
−1204	PV
105	PMT
1085	FV
CPT
I

Solution
7.00

CALCULATOR USE For annual compounding, to find the YTC of a 20-year, 10.5% bond that is currently trading at $1,204 but can be called in five years at a call price of $1,085, use the keystrokes shown in the margin. In this computation, N is the number of years to first call date, and FV represents the bond's call price. All other keystrokes are as defined earlier.

SPREADSHEET USE A callable bond's YTC can also be calculated as shown on the following Excel spreadsheet.

	A	B
1	Bond's YTC	
2	Par value	$1,000
3	Annual coupon rate	10.5%
4	Annual coupon payment	$105
5	Number of years to maturity	5
6	Call price	$1,085.00
7	Bond's price	-$1,204.00
8	Bond's YTM	7.0%
9	Entry in Cell B8 is =RATE(B5,B4,B7,B6,0). The minus sign appears before the $1,204.00 in B7 because the price of the bond is treated as a cash outflow.	

Expected Return

Rather than just buying and holding bonds, some investors prefer to actively trade in and out of these securities over fairly short investment horizons. As a result, measures such as yield to maturity and yield to call have relatively little meaning, other than as indicators of the rate of return used to price the bond. These investors obviously need an alternative measure of return that they can use to assess the investment appeal of those bonds they intend to trade. Such an alternative measure is the **expected return**. It indicates the rate of return an investor can expect to earn by holding a bond over a period of time that's less than the life of the issue. (Expected return is also known as **realized yield** because it shows the return an investor would realize by trading in and out of bonds over short holding periods.)

The expected return lacks the precision of the yield to maturity (and YTC) because the major cash flow variables are largely the product of investor estimates. In particular, going into the investment, both the length of the holding period and the future selling price of the bond are pure estimates and therefore subject to uncertainty. Even so, you can use essentially the same procedure to find a bond's realized yield as you did to find the promised yield. That is, with some simple modifications to the standard bond-pricing formula, you can use the following equation to find the expected return on a bond.

Equation 11.7

$$\text{Bond price} = \begin{array}{c}\text{Present value of the bond's}\\\text{annual coupon payments}\\\text{over the holding period}\end{array} + \begin{array}{c}\text{Present value of the bond's}\\\text{future price at the end}\\\text{of the holding period}\end{array}$$

Equation 11.7a

$$BP_i = \frac{C}{(1 + r_i)^1} + \frac{C}{(1 + r_i)^2} + \cdots + \frac{C}{(1 + r_i)^N} + \frac{FV}{(1 + r_i)^N}$$

where this time *N* represents the length of the holding period (not years to maturity), and *FV* is the expected future price of the bond.

As indicated above, you must determine the future price of the bond when computing its expected return. This is done by using the standard bond price formula, as described earlier. The most difficult part of deriving a reliable future price is, of course, coming up with future market interest rates that you feel will exist when the bond is sold. By evaluating current and expected market interest rate conditions, you can estimate the YTM that you expect the issue to provide at the date of sale and then use that yield to calculate the bond's future price.

To illustrate, take one more look at our 7.5%, 15-year bond. This time, let's assume that you feel the price of the bond, which is now trading at a discount, will rise sharply as interest rates fall over the next few years. In particular, assume the bond is currently priced at $809.50 (to yield 10%) and you anticipate holding the bond for three years. Over that time, you expect market rates to drop to 8%. With that assumption in place, and recognizing that three years from now the bond will have 12 remaining coupon payments, you can use Equation 11.3 to estimate that the bond's price will be approximately $960 in three years. Thus, you are assuming that you will buy the bond today at a market price of $809.50 and sell it three years later—after interest rates have declined to 8%—at a price of $960. Given these assumptions, the expected return (realized yield) on this bond is 14.6%, which is the discount rate in the following equation that will produce a current market price of $809.50.

$$BP_i = \$809.50 = \frac{\$75}{(1 + r_i)^1} + \frac{\$75}{(1 + r_i)^2} + \frac{\$75}{(1 + r_i)^3} + \frac{\$960}{(1 + r_i)^3}$$

where $r_i = 0.146 = 14.6\%$.

The return on this investment is fairly substantial, but keep in mind that this is only an estimate. It is, of course, subject to variation if things do not turn out as anticipated, particularly with regard to the market yield expected at the end of the holding period. This example uses annual compounding, but you could just as easily have used semiannual compounding, which, everything else being the same, would have resulted in an expected yield of 14.4% rather than the 14.6% found with annual compounding.

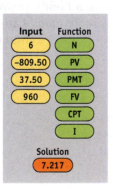

CALCULATOR USE For semiannual compounding, to find the expected return on a 7.5% bond that is currently priced in the market at $809.50 but is expected to rise to $960 within a three-year holding period, use the keystrokes shown in the margin. In this computation, *PV* is the current price of the bond, and *FV* is the expected price of the bond at the end of the (three-year) holding period. All other keystrokes are as defined earlier. To find the bond equivalent yield, double the computed value of *I*, 7.217%. That is 7.217% × 2 = 14.43%.

SPREADSHEET USE The expected return for semiannual compounding can also be calculated as shown on the following Excel spreadsheet. Notice that the spreadsheet shows 14.43% for the bond equivalent yield.

	A	B
1	**Bond's YTM**	
2	Par value	$1,000
3	Coupon rate	7.5%
4	Coupon payment frequency	2
5	Coupon payment	$37.50
6	Holding period in years	3
7	Bond's current price	-$809.50
8	Bond's future price	$960.00
9	Bond's YTM	7.22%
10	Bond-equivalent yield	14.43%
11	Entry in Cell B9 is =RATE(B6*B4,B5,B7,B8,0). The minus sign appears before the $809.50 in B7 because the price of the bond is treated as a cash outflow.	

Valuing a Bond

Depending on their objectives, investors can estimate the return that they will earn on a bond by calculating either its yield to maturity or its expected return. Conservative, income-oriented investors focus on the YTM. Earning interest income over extended periods of time is their primary objective, above earning a quick capital gain if interest rates fall. Because these investors intend to hold most of the bonds that they buy to maturity, the YTM (or the YTC) is a reliable measure of the returns that they can expect over time—assuming, of course, the reinvestment assumptions embedded in the yield measure are reasonable. More aggressive bond traders, who hope to profit from swings in market interest rates, calculate the expected return to estimate the return that they will earn on a bond. Earning capital gains by purchasing and selling bonds over relatively short holding periods is their chief concern, so the expected return is more important to them than the YTM.

In either case, the promised or expected yield provides a measure of return that investors can use to determine the relative attractiveness of fixed-income securities. But to evaluate the merits of different bonds, we must evaluate their returns and their risks. Bonds are no different from stocks in that the return (promised or expected) that they provide should be sufficient to compensate investors for the risks that they take. Thus, the greater the risk, the greater the return the bond should generate.

11.7 What's the difference between current yield and yield to maturity? Between promised yield and realized yield? How does YTC differ from YTM?

11.8 Briefly describe the term *bond equivalent yield*. Is there any difference between promised yield and bond equivalent yield? Explain.

11.9 Why is the reinvestment of interest income so important to bond investors?

Duration and Immunization

LG5 One of the problems with the yield to maturity is that it assumes you can reinvest the bond's periodic coupon payments at the same rate over time. If you reinvest this interest income at a lower rate (or if you spend it), your actual return will be lower than the YTM. Another flaw is that YTM assumes the investor will hold the bond to maturity. If you sell a bond prior to its maturity, the price that you receive will reflect prevailing interest rates, which means that the return that you will earn will probably differ from the YTM. If rates have moved up since you purchased the bond, the bond will sell at a discount, and your return will be less than the YTM. If interest rates have dropped, the opposite will happen.

The problem with yield to maturity, then, is that it fails to take into account the effects of reinvestment risk and price (or market) risk. To see how reinvestment and price risks behave relative to one another, consider a situation in which market interest rates have undergone a sharp decline. Under such conditions, bond prices will rise. You might be tempted to cash out your holdings and take some gains (i.e., do a little "profit taking"). Indeed, selling before maturity is the only way to take advantage of falling interest rates because a bond will pay its par value at maturity, regardless of prevailing interest rates. That's the good news about falling rates, but there is a downside. When interest rates fall, so do the opportunities to reinvest at high rates. Therefore, although you gain on the price side, you lose on the reinvestment side. Even if you don't sell out, you are faced with decreased reinvestment opportunities. To earn the YTM promised on your bonds, you must reinvest each coupon payment at the same YTM rate. Obviously, as rates fall, you'll find it increasingly difficult to reinvest the stream of coupon payments at that rate. When market rates rise, just the opposite happens. The price of the bond falls, but your reinvestment opportunities improve.

Bond investors need a measure that helps them judge just how significant these risks are for a particular bond. Such a yardstick is provided by something called **duration**. It captures in a single measure the extent to which the price of a bond will react to different interest rate environments. Because duration gauges the price volatility of a bond, it gives you a better idea of how likely you are to earn the return (YTM) you expect. That, in turn, will help you tailor your holdings to your expectations of interest rate movements.

The Concept of Duration

The concept of duration was first developed in 1938 by actuary Frederick Macaulay to help insurance companies match their cash inflows with payments. When applied to bonds, duration recognizes that the amount and frequency of interest payments, the yield to maturity, and the term to maturity all affect the interest rate risk of a particular bond. Term to maturity is important because it influences how much a bond's price will rise or fall as interest rates change. In general, when rates move, bonds with longer maturities fluctuate more than shorter issues. On the other hand, while the amount of price risk embedded in a bond is related to the issue's term to maturity, the amount of reinvestment risk is directly related to the size of a bond's coupon. Bonds that pay high coupons have greater reinvestment risk simply because there's more to reinvest.

As it turns out, both price and reinvestment risk are related in one way or another to interest rates, and therein lies the conflict. Any change in interest rates (whether up or down) will cause price risk and reinvestment risk to push and pull bonds in opposite directions. An increase in rates will produce a drop in price but will increase reinvestment opportunities. Declining rates, in contrast, will boost prices but decrease reinvestment opportunities. At some point in time, these two forces should exactly offset each other. That point in time is a bond's duration.

In general, bond duration possesses the following properties:

- Higher *coupons* result in shorter durations.

- Longer *maturities* mean longer durations.

- Higher *yields* (YTMs) lead to shorter durations.

Together these variables—coupon, maturity, and yield—interact to determine an issue's duration. Knowing a bond's duration is helpful because it captures the bond's underlying price volatility. That is, since a bond's duration and volatility are directly related, it follows that the shorter the duration, the less volatility in bond prices—and vice versa, of course.

Measuring Duration

Duration is a measure of the average maturity of a fixed-income security. The term *average maturity* may be confusing because bonds have only one final maturity date. An alternative definition of average maturity might be that it captures the average timing of the bond's cash payments. For a zero-coupon bond that makes only one cash payment on the final maturity date, the bond's duration equals its maturity. But because coupon-paying bonds make periodic interest payments, the average timing of these payments (i.e., the average maturity) is different from the actual maturity date. For instance, a 10-year bond that pays a 5% coupon each year distributes a small cash flow in year 1, in year 2, and so on up until the last and largest cash flow in year 10. Duration is a measure that puts some weight on these intermediate payments, so that the "average maturity" is a little less than 10 years.

You can think of duration as the *weighted-average life of a bond*, where the weights are the fractions of the bond's total value accounted for by each cash payment that the bond makes over its life. Mathematically, we can find the duration of a bond as follows:

Equation 11.8

$$\text{Duration} = \sum_{t=1}^{N} \left[\frac{PV(C_t)}{BP} \times t \right]$$

where

$$PV(C_t) = \text{present value of a future coupon or principal payment}$$
$$BP = \text{current market price of the bond}$$
$$t = \text{year in which the cash flow (coupon or principal) payment is received}$$
$$N = \text{number of years to maturity}$$

The duration measure obtained from Equation 11.8 is commonly referred to as *Macaulay duration*—named after the actuary who developed the concept.

Although duration is often computed using semiannual compounding, Equation 11.8 uses annual coupons and annual compounding to keep the ensuing discussion and calculations as simple as possible. Even so, the formula looks more formidable than it really is. If you follow the basic steps noted below, you'll find that duration is not tough to calculate.

Step 1. Find the present value of each annual coupon or principal payment [$PV(C_t)$]. Use the prevailing YTM on the bond as the discount rate.

Step 2. Divide this present value by the current market price of the bond (*BP*). This is the weight, or the fraction of the bond's total value accounted for by each individual payment. Because a bond's value is just the sum of the present values of its cash payments, these weights must sum to 1.0.

Step 3. Multiply this weight by the year in which the cash flow is to be received (*t*).

Step 4. Repeat steps 1 through 3 for each year in the life of the bond, and then add up the values computed in step 3.

TABLE 11.1   DURATION CALCULATION FOR A 7.5%, 15-YEAR BOND PRICED TO YIELD 8%

(1)	(2)	(3)	(4)	(5)
Year t	Annual Cash Flow C_t	Present Value at 8% of Annual Cash Flow $(2) \div (1.08)^t$	Present Value of Annual Cash Flow Divided by Price of the Bond $(3) \div \$957.20$	Time-Weighted Relative Cash Flow $(1) \times (4)$
1	$ 75	$ 69.44	0.0725	0.0725
2	$ 75	$ 64.30	0.0672	0.1344
3	$ 75	$ 59.54	0.0622	0.1866
4	$ 75	$ 55.13	0.0576	0.2304
5	$ 75	$ 51.04	0.0533	0.2666
6	$ 75	$ 47.26	0.0494	0.2963
7	$ 75	$ 43.76	0.0457	0.3200
8	$ 75	$ 40.52	0.0423	0.3387
9	$ 75	$ 37.52	0.0392	0.3528
10	$ 75	$ 34.74	0.0363	0.3629
11	$ 75	$ 32.17	0.0336	0.3696
12	$ 75	$ 29.78	0.0311	0.3734
13	$ 75	$ 27.58	0.0288	0.3745
14	$ 75	$ 25.53	0.0267	0.3735
15	$1,075	$338.88	0.3540	5.3106
	Price of Bond: $957.20		1.00	**Duration: 9.36 yr**

Excel@Investing

Duration for a Single Bond   Table 11.1 illustrates the four-step procedure for calculating the duration of a 7.5%, 15-year bond priced at $957.20 to yield 8%. Table 11.1 provides the basic input data: Column (1) shows the year t in which each cash flow arrives. Column (2) provides the dollar amount of each annual cash flow (C_t) (coupons and principal) made by the bond. Column (3) lists the present value of each annual cash flow in year t at an 8% discount rate (which is equal to the prevailing YTM on the bond). For example, in row 1 of Table 11.1, we see that in year 1 the bond makes a $75 coupon payment, and discounting that to the present at 8% reveals that the first coupon payment has a present value of $69.44. If we sum the present value of the annual cash flows in column (3), we find that the current market price of the bond is $957.20.

Next, in column 4 we divide the present value in column 3 by the current market price of the bond. If the present value of this bond's first coupon payment is $69.45 and the total price of the bond is $957.20, then that first payment accounts for 7.25% of the bond's total value (i.e., $69.45 ÷ $957.20 = 0.0725) Therefore, 7.25% is the "weight" given to the cash payment made in year 1. If you sum the weights in column 4, you will see that they add to 1.0. Multiplying the weights from column 4 by the year t in which the cash flow arrives results in a time-weighted value for each of the annual cash flow streams shown in column 5. Adding up all the values in column 5 yields the duration of the bond. As you can see, the duration of this bond is a lot less than its maturity. In addition, keep in mind that the duration on any bond will change over time as YTM and term to maturity change. For example, the duration on this 7.5%, 15-year bond will fall as the bond nears maturity and/or as the market yield (YTM) on the bond increases.

INVESTOR FACTS

Different Bonds, Same Durations Sometimes, you really can't judge a book—or a bond, for that matter—by its cover. Here are three bonds that, on the surface, appear to be totally different:

- An 8-year, zero-coupon bond priced to yield 6%
- A 12-year, 8.5% bond that trades at a yield of 8%
- An 18-year, 10.5% bond priced to yield 13%

Although these bonds have different coupons and different maturities, they have one thing in common: they all have identical durations of eight years. Thus, if interest rates went up or down by 50 to 100 basis points, the market prices of these bonds would all behave pretty much the same!

Duration for a Portfolio of Bonds   The concept of duration is not confined to individual bonds only. It can also be applied to whole portfolios of fixed-income securities. The duration of an entire portfolio is fairly easy to calculate. All we need are the durations of the individual securities in the portfolio and their weights (i.e., the proportion that each security contributes to the overall value of the portfolio). Given this, the duration of a portfolio is the weighted average of the durations of the individual securities in the portfolio. Actually, this weighted-average approach provides only an approximate measure of duration. But it is a reasonably close approximation and, as such, is widely used in practice—so we'll use it, too.

To see how to measure duration using this approach, consider the following five-bond portfolio:

Bond	Amount Invested*	Weight	×	Bond Duration	=	Portfolio Duration
Government bonds	$ 270,000	0.15		6.25		0.9375
Aaa corporates	$ 180,000	0.10		8.90		0.8900
Aa utilities	$ 450,000	0.25		10.61		2.6525
Agency issues	$ 360,000	0.20		11.03		2.2060
Baa industrials	$ 540,000	0.30		12.55		3.7650
	$1,800.000	1.00				10.4510

*Amount invested = Current market price × Par value of the bonds. That is, if the government bonds are quoted at 90 and the investor holds $300,000 in these bonds, then 0.90 × $300,000 = $270,000.

In this case, the $1.8 million bond portfolio has an average duration of approximately 10.5 years.

If you want to change the duration of the portfolio, you can do so by (1) changing the asset mix of the portfolio (shift the weight of the portfolio to longer- or shorter-duration bonds, as desired) and/or (2) adding new bonds to the portfolio with the desired duration characteristics. As we will see below, this approach is often used in a bond portfolio strategy known as *bond immunization*.

Bond Duration and Price Volatility

A bond's price volatility is, in part, a function of its term to maturity and, in part, a function of its coupon. Unfortunately, there is no exact relationship between bond maturities and bond price volatilities with respect to interest rate changes. There is, however, a fairly close relationship between bond duration and price volatility—as long as the market doesn't experience wide swings in interest rates. A bond's duration can be used as a viable predictor of its price volatility only as long as the yield swings are relatively small (no more than 50 to 100 basis points or so). That's because as interest rates change, bond prices change in a nonlinear (convex) fashion. For example, when interest rates fall, bond prices rise at an increasing rate. When interest rates rise, bond prices fall at a decreasing rate. The duration measure essentially predicts that as interest rates change, bond prices will move in the opposite direction in a linear fashion. This means that when interest rates fall, bond prices will rise a bit faster than the duration measure would predict, and when interest rates rise, bond prices will fall at a slightly slower rate than the duration measure would predict. The bottom line is that the duration measure helps investors understand how bond prices will respond to changes in market rates, as long as those changes are not too large.

The mathematical link between changes in interest rates and changes in bond prices involves the concept of *modified duration*. To find modified duration, we simply take the (Macaulay) duration for a bond (as found from Equation 11.8) and divide it by the bond's yield to maturity.

Equation 11.9

$$\text{Modified duration} = \frac{(\text{Macaulay}) \text{ Duration in years}}{1 + \text{Yield to maturity}}$$

Thus, the modified duration for the 15-year bond discussed above is

$$\text{Modified duration} = \frac{9.36}{1 + 0.08} = \underline{\underline{8.67}}$$

Note that here we use the bond's computed (Macaulay) duration of 9.36 years and the same YTM we used to compute duration in Equation 11.8; in this case, the bond was priced to yield 8%, so we use a yield to maturity of 8%.

To determine, in percentage terms, how much the price of this bond would change as market interest rates increased by 50 basis points from 8% to 8.5%, we multiply the modified duration value calculated above first by −1 (because of the inverse relationship between bond prices and interest rates) and then by the change in market interest rates. That is,

Equation 11.10

$$\begin{aligned}\text{Percent change} \atop \text{in bond price} &= -1 \times \text{Modified duration} \times \text{Change in interest rates} \\ &= -1 \times 8.67 \times 0.5\% = \underline{-4.33}\end{aligned}$$

Thus, a 50-basis-point (or ½ of 1%) increase in market interest rates will lead to an approximate 4.33% drop in the price of this 15-year bond. Such information is useful to bond investors seeking—or trying to avoid—price volatility.

Effective Duration

One problem with the duration measures that we've studied so far is that they do not always work well for bonds that may be called or converted before they mature. That is, the duration measures we've been using assume that the bond's future cash flows are paid as originally scheduled through maturity, but that may not be the case with callable or convertible bonds. An alternative duration measure that is used for these types of bonds is the effective duration. To calculate effective duration (ED), you use Equation 11.11:

Equation 11.11

$$ED = \frac{BP(r_i \downarrow) - BP(r_i \uparrow)}{2 \times BP \times \Delta r_i}$$

where

$$\begin{aligned} BP(r_i \uparrow) &= \text{the new price of the bond if market interest rates go up} \\ BP(r_i \downarrow) &= \text{the new price of the bond if market interest rates go down} \\ BP &= \text{the original price of the bond} \\ \Delta r_i &= \text{the change in market interest rates} \end{aligned}$$

> **Example**
>
> Suppose you want to know the effective duration of a 25-year bond that pays a 6% coupon semiannually. The bond is currently priced at $882.72 for a yield of 7%. Now suppose the bond's yield goes up by 0.5% to 7.5%. At that yield the new price would be $831.74 (using a calculator, N = 50, I = 3.75, PMT = 30, and PV = 1,000). What if the yield drops by 0.5% to 6.5%? In that case, the price rises to $938.62 (N = 50, I = 3.25, PMT = 30, PV = 1,000). Now we can use Equation 11.11 to calculate the bond's effective duration.
>
> Effective duration = ($938.62 − $831.74) ÷ (2 × $882.72 × 0.005) = 12.11

This means that if interest rates rise or fall by a full percentage point, the price of the bond would fall or rise by approximately 12.11%. Note that you can use effective duration in place of modified duration in Equation 11.10 to find the percent change in the price of a bond when interest rates move by more or less than 1.0%. When calculating the effective duration of a callable bond, one modification may be necessary. If the calculated price of the bond when interest rates fall is greater than the bond's call price, then use the call price in the equation rather than $BP(r_i\downarrow)$ and proceed as before.

Uses of Bond Duration Measures

You can use duration analysis in many ways to guide your decisions about investing in bonds. For example, as we saw earlier, you can use modified duration or effective duration to measure the potential price volatility of a particular issue. Another equally important use of duration is in the structuring of bond portfolios. That is, if you thought that interest rates were about to increase, you could reduce the overall duration of the portfolio by selling higher-duration bonds and buying shorter-duration bonds. Such a strategy could prove useful because shorter-duration bonds do not decline in value to the same degree as longer-duration bonds. On the other hand, if you felt that interest rates were about to decline, the opposite strategy would be appropriate.

Active, short-term investors frequently use duration analysis in their day-to-day operations. Longer-term investors also employ it in planning their investment decisions. Indeed, a strategy known as *bond portfolio immunization* represents one of the most important uses of duration.

Bond Immunization   Some investors hold portfolios of bonds not for the purpose of "beating the market," but rather to accumulate a specified level of wealth by the end of a given investment horizon. For these investors, bond portfolio **immunization** often proves to be of great value. Immunization allows you to derive a specified rate of return from bond investments over a given investment interval regardless of what happens to market interest rates over the course of the holding period. In essence, you are able to "immunize" your portfolio from the effects of changes in market interest rates over a given investment horizon.

To understand how and why bond portfolio immunization is possible, you will recall from our earlier discussion that changes in market interest rates will lead to two distinct and opposite changes in bond valuation. The first effect is known as the *price effect*, and the second is known as the *reinvestment effect*. Whereas an increase in rates has a negative effect on a bond's price, it has a positive effect on the reinvestment of coupons. Therefore, when interest rate changes do occur, the price and reinvestment effects work against each other from the standpoint of the investor's wealth.

TABLE 11.2   BOND IMMUNIZATION

Year t	Cash Flow from Bond					Terminal Value of Reinvested Cash Flow
1	$ 80	$\times$	$(1.08)^4$	$\times$	$(1.06)^3$ =	$ 129.63
2	$ 80	$\times$	$(1.08)^3$	$\times$	$(1.06)^3$ =	$ 120.03
3	$ 80	$\times$	$(1.08)^2$	$\times$	$(1.06)^3$ =	$ 111.14
4	$ 80	$\times$	(1.08)	$\times$	$(1.06)^3$ =	$ 102.90
5	$ 80	$\times$	$(1.06)^3$		=	$ 95.28
6	$ 80	$\times$	$(1.06)^2$		=	$ 89.89
7	$ 80	$\times$	(1.06)		=	$ 84.80
8	$ 80				=	$ 80.00
8	$1,036.67					$1,036.67
			Total			$1,850.33
			Investor's required wealth at 8%			$1,850.93
			Difference			$ 0.60

When the average duration of the portfolio just equals the investment horizon, these counteracting effects offset each other and leave your position unchanged. This should not come as much of a surprise because such a property is already embedded in the duration measure. If that relationship applies to a single bond, it should also apply to the weighted-average duration of a whole bond portfolio. When such a condition (of offsetting price and reinvestment effects) exists, a bond portfolio is immunized. More specifically, your wealth is immunized from the effects of interest rate changes when the weighted-average duration of the bond portfolio exactly equals your desired investment horizon. Table 11.2 provides an example of bond immunization using a 10-year, 8% coupon bond with a duration of 8 years. Here, we assume that your desired investment horizon is also 8 years.

The example in Table 11.2 assumes that you originally purchased the 8% coupon bond at par. It further assumes that market interest rates for bonds of this quality drop from 8% to 6% at the end of the fifth year. Because you had an investment horizon of exactly 8 years and desire to lock in an interest rate return of exactly 8%, it follows that you expect to accumulate cash totaling $1,850.93 [i.e., $1,000 invested at 8% for 8 years = $1,000 \times (1.08)^8 = $1,850.93], regardless of interest rate changes in the interim. As you can see from the results in Table 11.2, the immunization strategy netted you a total of $1,850.33—just 60 cents short of your desired goal. Note that in this case, although reinvestment opportunities declined in years 5, 6, and 7 (when market interest rates dropped to 6%), that same lower rate led to a higher market price for the bond. That higher price, in turn, provided enough capital gains to offset the loss in reinvested income. This remarkable result clearly demonstrates the power of bond immunization and the versatility of bond duration. And note that even though the table uses a single bond for purposes of illustration, the same results can be obtained from a bond portfolio that is maintained at the proper weighted-average duration.

Maintaining a fully immunized portfolio (of more than one bond) requires continual portfolio rebalancing. Indeed, every time interest rates change, the duration of a portfolio changes. Because effective immunization requires that the portfolio have a duration value equal in length to the remaining investment horizon, the composition of the portfolio must be rebalanced each time interest rates change. Further, even in the absence of interest rate changes, a bond's duration declines more slowly than its term to maturity. This, of course, means that the mere passage of time will dictate changes in portfolio composition. Such changes will ensure that the duration of the portfolio continues to match the remaining time in the investment horizon. In summary, portfolio immunization strategies can be extremely effective, but immunization is not a passive strategy and is not without potential problems, the most notable of which are associated with portfolio rebalancing.

11.10 What does the term *duration* mean to bond investors and how does the duration of a bond differ from its maturity? What is modified duration, and how is it used? What is effective duration, and how does it differ from modified duration?

11.11 Describe the process of bond portfolio immunization, and explain why an investor would want to immunize a portfolio. Would you consider portfolio immunization a passive investment strategy comparable to, say, a buy-and-hold approach? Explain.

Bond Investment Strategies

Generally speaking, bond investors tend to follow one of three kinds of investment programs. First, there are those who live off the income. They are conservative, quality-conscious, income-oriented investors who seek to maximize current income. Second, there are the speculators (bond traders). Their investment objective is to maximize capital gains, often within a short time span. Finally, there are the long-term investors. Their objective is to maximize total return—from both current income and capital gains—over fairly long holding periods.

In order to achieve the objectives of any of these programs, you need to adopt a strategy that is compatible with your goals. Professional money managers use a variety of techniques to manage the multimillion- (or multibillion-) dollar bond portfolios under their direction. These range from passive approaches, to semiactive strategies, to active, fully managed strategies using interest rate forecasting and yield spread analysis. Most of these strategies are fairly complex and require substantial computer support. Even so, we can look briefly at some of the more basic strategies to gain an appreciation of the different ways in which you can use fixed-income securities to reach different investment objectives.

Passive Strategies

The bond immunization strategies we discussed earlier are considered to be primarily passive in nature. Investors using these tools typically are not attempting to beat the market but to lock in specified rates of return that they deem acceptable, given the risks involved. As a rule, passive investment strategies are characterized by a lack of input regarding investor expectations of changes in interest rates and/or bond prices. Further, these strategies typically do not generate significant transaction costs. A buy-and-hold strategy is perhaps the most passive of all investment strategies. All that is required is that the investor replace bonds that have deteriorating credit ratings, have matured, or have been called. Although buy-and-hold investors restrict their ability to earn above-average returns, they also minimize the losses that transaction costs represent.

One popular approach that is a bit more active than buy-and-hold is the use of **bond ladders**. In this strategy, equal amounts are invested in a series of bonds with staggered maturities. Here's how a bond ladder works. Suppose you want to confine your investing to fixed-income securities with maturities of 10 years or less. Given that maturity constraint, you could set up a ladder by investing (roughly) equal amounts in, say, 3-, 5-, 7-, and 10-year issues. When the 3-year issue matures, you would put the money from it (along with any new capital) into a new 10-year note. You would continue this rolling-over process so that eventually you would hold a full ladder of staggered 10-year notes. By rolling into new 10-year issues every 2 or 3 years, the interest income on your portfolio will be an average of the rates available over time. The laddered approach is a safe, simple, and almost automatic way of investing for the long haul. A key ingredient of this or any other passive strategy is, of course, the use of high-quality investments that possess attractive features, maturities, and yields.

Trading on Forecasted Interest Rate Behavior

In contrast to passive strategies, a more risky approach to bond investing is the *forecasted interest rate* approach. Here, investors seek attractive capital gains when they expect interest rates to decline and preservation of capital when they anticipate an increase in interest rates. This strategy is risky because it relies on the imperfect forecast of future interest rates. The idea is to increase the return on a bond portfolio by making strategic moves in anticipation of interest rate changes. Such a strategy is essentially *market timing*. An unusual feature of this tactic is that most of the trading is done with investment-grade securities because these securities are the most sensitive to interest rate movements, and that sensitivity is what active traders hope to profit from.

This strategy brings together interest rate forecasts and the concept of duration. For example, when a decline in rates is anticipated, aggressive bond investors often seek to lengthen the duration of their bonds (or bond portfolios) because bonds with longer durations (e.g., long-term bonds) rise more in price than do bonds with shorter durations. At the same time, investors look for low-coupon and/or moderately discounted bonds because these bonds have higher durations, and their prices will rise more when interest rates fall. Interest rate swings may be short-lived, so bond traders try to earn as much as possible in as short a time as possible. When rates start to level off and move up, these investors begin to shift their money out of long, discounted bonds and into high-yielding issues with short maturities. In other words, they do a complete reversal and look for bonds with shorter durations. During those periods when bond prices are dropping, investors are more concerned about preservation of capital, so they take steps to protect their money from capital losses. Thus, they tend to use such short-term obligations as Treasury bills, money funds, short-term (two- to five-year) notes, or even variable-rate notes.

Bond Swaps

In a **bond swap**, an investor simultaneously liquidates one position and buys a different issue to take its place. Swaps can be executed to increase current yield or yield to maturity, to take advantage of shifts in interest rates, to improve the quality of a portfolio, or for tax purposes. Although some swaps are highly sophisticated, most are fairly simple transactions. They go by a variety of colorful names, such as "profit takeout," "substitution swap," and "tax swap," but they are all used for one basic reason: portfolio improvement. We will briefly review two types of bond swaps that are fairly simple and hold considerable appeal: the yield pickup swap and the tax swap.

In a **yield pickup swap**, an investor switches out of a low-coupon bond into a comparable higher-coupon issue in order to realize an instantaneous pickup of current yield and yield to maturity. For example, you would be executing a yield pickup swap if you sold 20-year, A-rated, 6.5% bonds (which were yielding 8% at the time) and replaced them with an equal amount of 20-year, A-rated, 7% bonds that were priced to yield 8.5%. By executing the swap, you would improve your current yield (your interest income would increase from $65 a year to $70 a year) as well as your yield to maturity (from 8% to 8.5%). Such swap opportunities arise because of the yield spreads that normally exist between different types of bonds. You can execute such swaps simply by watching for swap candidates and asking your broker to do so. In fact, the only thing you must be careful of is that transaction costs do not eat up all the profits.

Another popular type of swap is the **tax swap**, which is also relatively simple and involves few risks. You can use this technique whenever you have a substantial tax liability as a result of selling some security holdings at a profit. The objective is to execute a swap to eliminate or substantially reduce the tax liability accompanying the capital gains. This is done by selling an issue that has undergone a capital loss and replacing it with a comparable obligation.

For example, assume that you had $10,000 worth of corporate bonds that you sold (in the current year) for $15,000, resulting in a capital gain of $5,000. You can eliminate the tax liability accompanying the capital gain by selling securities that have capital losses of $5,000. Let's assume you find you hold a 20-year, 4.75% municipal bond that has undergone a $5,000 drop in value. Thus, you have the required tax shield in your portfolio. Now you need to find a viable swap candidate. Suppose you find a comparable 20-year, 5% municipal issue currently trading at about the same price as the issue being sold. By selling the 4.75s and simultaneously buying a comparable amount of the 5s, you will not only increase your tax-free yields (from 4.75% to 5%) but will also eliminate the capital gains tax liability.

The only precaution in doing tax swaps is that you cannot use identical issues in the swap transactions. The IRS would consider that a "wash sale" and disallow the loss. Moreover, the capital loss must occur in the same taxable year as the capital gain. Typically, at year-end, tax loss sales and tax swaps multiply as knowledgeable investors hurry to establish capital losses.

CONCEPTS IN REVIEW

Answers available at
http://www.pearsonhighered
.com/smart

11.12 Briefly describe a bond ladder and note how and why an investor would use this investment strategy. What is a tax swap and why would it be used?

11.13 What strategy would you expect an aggressive bond investor (someone who's looking for capital gains) to employ?

11.14 Why is interest sensitivity important to bond speculators? Does the need for interest sensitivity explain why active bond traders tend to use high-grade issues? Explain.

MyFinanceLab

Here is what you should know after reading this chapter. MyFinanceLab will help you identify what you know and where to go when you need to practice.

What You Should Know	Key Terms	Where to Practice
LG1 **Explain the behavior of market interest rates and identify the forces that cause interest rates to change.** The behavior of interest rates is the most important force in the bond market. It determines not only the amount of current income an investor will receive but also the investor's capital gains (or losses). Changes in market interest rates can have a dramatic impact on the total returns obtained from bonds over time.	yield spreads, *p. 426*	MyFinanceLab Study Plan 11.1
LG2 **Describe the term structure of interest rates and note how investors can use yield curves.** Many forces drive the behavior of interest rates over time, including inflation, the cost and availability of funds, and the level of interest rates in major foreign markets. One particularly important force is the term structure of interest rates, which relates yield to maturity to term to maturity. Yield curves essentially plot the term structure and are often used by investors as a way to get a handle on the future behavior of interest rates.	expectations hypothesis, *p. 432* liquidity preference theory, *p. 433* market segmentation theory, *p. 433* term structure of interest rates, *p. 429* yield curve, *p. 429*	MyFinanceLab Study Plan 11.2
LG3 **Understand how investors value bonds in the marketplace.** Bonds are valued (priced) in the marketplace on the basis of their required rates of return (or market yields). The process of pricing a bond begins with the yield it should provide. Once that piece of information is known (or estimated), a standard, present value-based model is used to find the dollar price of a bond.	accrued interest, *p. 438* clean price, *p. 439* dirty price, *p. 439*	MyFinanceLab Study Plan 11.3 Video Learning Aid for Problems P11.1, P11.2
LG4 **Describe the various measures of yield and return and explain how investors use these standards of performance to value bonds.** Four types of yields are important to investors: current yield, promised yield, yield to call, and expected yield (or return). Promised yield (yield to maturity) is the most widely used bond valuation measure. It captures both the current income and the price appreciation of an issue. Yield to call, which assumes the bond will be outstanding only until its first (or some other) call date, also captures both current income and price appreciation. The expected return, in contrast, is a valuation measure used by aggressive bond traders to show the total return that can be earned from trading in and out of a bond long before it matures.	bond equivalent yield, *p. 441* current yield, *p. 439* expected return, *p. 445* promised yield, *p. 440* realized yield, *p. 445* yield to call (YTC), *p. 444* yield to maturity (YTM), *p. 440*	MyFinanceLab Study Plan 11.4

What You Should Know	Key Terms	Where to Practice
LG5 Understand the basic concept of duration, how it **can be measured, and its use in the management of bond portfolios.** Bond duration takes into account the effects of both reinvestment and price (or market) risks. It captures in a single measure the extent to which the price of a bond will react to different interest rate environments. Equally important, duration can be used to immunize whole bond portfolios from the often-devastating forces of changing market interest rates.	duration, *p. 448* immunization, *p. 453*	MyFinanceLab Study Plan 11.5 Excel Tables 11.1, 11.2
LG6 Discuss various bond investment strategies and **the different ways investors can use these securi- ties.** Bonds can be used as a source of income, as a way to seek capital gains by speculating on interest rate movement, or as a way to earn long-term returns. Investors often employ one or more of the following strategies: passive strategies such as buy-and-hold, bond ladders, and portfolio immunization; bond trading based on forecasted interest rate behavior; and bond swaps.	bond ladders, *p. 456* bond swap, *p. 456* tax swap, *p. 457* yield pickup swap, *p. 457*	MyFinanceLab Study Plan 11.6

Log into MyFinanceLab, take a chapter test, and get a personalized Study Plan that tells you which concepts you understand and which ones you need to review. From there, MyFinanceLab will give you further practice, tutorials, animations, videos, and guided solutions.
Log into **http://www.myfinancelab.com**

Discussion Questions

LG1 **Q11.1** Briefly describe each of the following theories of the term structure of interest rates.
  a. Expectations hypothesis
  b. Liquidity preference theory
  c. Market segmentation theory

According to these theories, what conditions would result in a downward-sloping yield curve? What conditions would result in an upward-sloping yield curve? Which theory do you think is most valid, and why?

LG2 **Q11.2** Using the *Wall Street Journal*, *Barron's*, or an online source, find the bond yields for Treasury securities with the following maturities: 3 months, 6 months, 1 year, 3 years, 5 years, 10 years, 15 years, and 20 years. Construct a yield curve based on these reported yields, putting term to maturity on the horizontal (*x*) axis and yield to maturity on the vertical (*y*) axis. Briefly discuss the general shape of your yield curve. What conclusions might you draw about future interest rate movements from this yield curve?

LG5 **Q11.3** Briefly explain what will happen to a bond's duration measure if each of the following events occur.
  a. The yield to maturity on the bond falls from 8.5% to 8%.
  b. The bond gets 1 year closer to its maturity.

c. Market interest rates go from 8% to 9%.

d. The bond's modified duration falls by half a year.

LG6   **Q11.4**   Assume that an investor comes to you looking for advice. She has $200,000 to invest and wants to put it all into bonds.

a. If she considers herself a fairly aggressive investor who is willing to take the risks necessary to generate the big returns, what kind of investment strategy (or strategies) would you suggest? Be specific.

b. What kind of investment strategies would you recommend if your client were a very conservative investor who could not tolerate market losses?

c. What kind of investor do you think is most likely to use

   1. an immunized bond portfolio?

   2. a yield pickup swap?

   3. a bond ladder?

   4. a long-term, zero-coupon bond when interest rates fall?

LG4 LG5   **Q11.5**   Using the resources at your campus or public library (or on the Internet), select any six bonds you like, consisting of two Treasury bonds, two corporate bonds, and two agency issues. Determine the latest current yield and promised yield for each. (For promised yield, use annual compounding.) In addition, find the duration and modified duration for each bond.

a. Assuming that you put an equal amount of money into each of the six bonds you selected, find the duration for this six-bond portfolio.

b. What would happen to your bond portfolio if market interest rates fell by 100 basis points?

c. Assuming that you have $100,000 to invest, use at least four of these bonds to develop a bond portfolio that emphasizes either the potential for capital gains or the preservation of capital. Briefly explain your logic.

Problems

All problems are available on http://www.myfinancelab.com

LG3   **P11.1**   You are considering the purchase of a $1,000 par value bond with an 6.5% coupon rate (with interest paid semiannually) that matures in 12 years. If the bond is priced to provide a required return of 8%, what is the bond's current price?

LG3   **P11.2**   Two bonds have par values of $1,000. One is a 5%, 15-year bond priced to yield 8%. The other is a 7.5%, 20-year bond priced to yield 6%. Which of these has the lower price? (Assume annual compounding in both cases.)

LG3   **P11.3**   Using semiannual compounding, find the prices of the following bonds.

a. A 10.5%, 15-year bond priced to yield 8%

b. A 7%, 10-year bond priced to yield 8%

c. A 12%, 20-year bond priced at 10%

Repeat the problem using annual compounding. Then comment on the differences you found in the prices of the bonds.

LG3   **P11.4**   You have the opportunity to purchase a 25-year, $1,000 par value bond that has an annual coupon rate of 9%. If you require a YTM of 7.6%, how much is the bond worth to you?

LG3   **P11.5**   A $1,000 par value bond has a current price of $800 and a maturity value of $1,000 and matures in five years. If interest is paid semiannually and the bond is priced to yield 8%, what is the bond's annual coupon rate?

LG3   **P11.6**   A 20-year bond has a coupon of 10% and is priced to yield 8%. Calculate the price per $1,000 par value using semiannual compounding. If an investor purchases this bond two months before a scheduled coupon payment, how much accrued interest must be paid to the seller?

LG4 **P11.7** Three years ago you purchased a 10% coupon bond that pays semiannual coupon payments for $975. What would be your bond equivalent yield if you sold the bond for current market price of $1,050?

LG4 **P11.8** A bond is priced in the market at $1,150 and has a coupon of 8%. Calculate the bond's current yield.

LG4 **P11.9** A $1,000 par value bond with a 7.25% coupon rate (semiannual interest) matures in seven years and currently sells for $987. What is the bond's yield to maturity and bond equivalent yield?

LG4 **P11.10** What is the current yield for a $1,000 par value bond that pays interest semiannually, has nine years to maturity, and is currently selling for $937 with a bond equivalent yield of 12%?

LG3 **P11.11** An investor is considering the purchase of an 8%, 18-year corporate bond that's being priced to yield 10%. She thinks that in a year, this bond will be priced in the market to yield 9%. Using annual compounding, find the price of the bond today and in one year. Next, find the holding period return on this investment, assuming that the investor's expectations are borne out.

LG4 **P11.12** You notice in the WSJ a bond that is currently selling in the market for $1,070 with a coupon of 11% and a 20-year maturity. Using annual compounding, calculate the promised yield on this bond.

LG4 **P11.13** A bond is currently selling in the market for $1,098.62. It has a coupon of 9% and a 20-year maturity. Using annual compounding, calculate the yield to maturity on this bond.

LG4 **P11.14** Compute the current yield of a 10%, 25-year bond that is currently priced in the market at $1,200. Use annual compounding to find the promised yield on this bond. Repeat the promised yield calculation, but this time use semiannual compounding to find yield to maturity.

LG4 **P11.15** You are evaluating an outstanding issue of $1,000 par value bonds with an 8.75% coupon rate that mature in 25 years and make quarterly interest payments. If the current market price for the bonds is $865, what is the quoted annual yield to maturity for the bonds?

LG4 **P11.16** A 10%, 25-year bond has a par value of $1,000 and a call price of $1,075. (The bond's first call date is in five years.) Coupon payments are made semiannually (so use semiannual compounding where appropriate).
  a. Find the current yield, YTM, and YTC on this issue, given that it is currently being priced in the market at $1,200. Which of these three yields is the highest? Which is the lowest? Which yield would you use to value this bond? Explain.
  b. Repeat the three calculations above, given that the bond is being priced at $850. Now which yield is the highest? Which is the lowest? Which yield would you use to value this bond? Explain.

LG4 **P11.17** Assume that an investor is looking at two bonds: Bond A is a 20-year, 9% (semiannual pay) bond that is priced to yield 10.5%. Bond B is a 20-year, 8% (annual pay) bond that is priced to yield 7.5%. Both bonds carry 5-year call deferments and call prices (in 5 years) of $1,050.
  a. Which bond has the higher current yield?
  b. Which bond has the higher YTM?
  c. Which bond has the higher YTC?

LG4 **P11.18** A zero-coupon bond that matures in 15 years is currently selling for $209 per $1,000 par value. What is the promised yield on this bond?

LG4 **P11.19** What is the price of a zero-coupon ($1,000 par value) bond that matures in 20 years and has a promised yield of 9.5%?

LG4 **P11.20** A 25-year, zero-coupon bond was recently being quoted at 11.625% of par. Find the current yield and the promised yield of this issue, given that the bond has a par value of $1,000. Using semiannual compounding, determine how much an investor would have to pay for this bond if it were priced to yield 12%.

LG4   **P11.21** Assume that an investor pays $800 for a long-term bond that carries an 8% coupon. In three years, he hopes to sell the issue for $950. If his expectations come true, what yield will this investor realize? (Use annual compounding.) What would the holding period return be if he were able to sell the bond (at $950) after only nine months?

LG4   **P11.22** Using annual compounding, find the yield to maturity for each of the following bonds.
a. A 9.5%, 20-year bond priced at $957.43
b. A 16%, 15-year bond priced at $1,684.76
c. A 5.5%, 18-year bond priced at $510.65

Now assume that each of the above bonds is callable as follows: Bond **a** is callable in seven years at a call price of $1,095; bond **b** is callable in five years at $1,250; and bond **c** is callable in three years at $1,050. Use annual compounding to find the yield to call for each bond.

LG5   **P11.23** A bond has a Macaulay duration equal to 9.5 and a yield to maturity of 7.5%. What is the modified duration of this bond?

LG5   **P11.24** A bond has a Macaulay duration of 8.62 and is priced to yield 8%. If interest rates go up so that the yield goes to 8.5%, what will be the percentage change in the price of the bond? Now, if the yield on this bond goes down to 7.5%, what will be the bond's percentage change in price? Comment on your findings.

LG5   **P11.25** An investor wants to find the duration of a 25-year, 6% semiannual-pay, noncallable bond that's currently priced in the market at $882.72, to yield 7%. Using a 50 basis point change in yield, find the effective duration of this bond. (Hint: Use Equation 11.11.)

LG5   **P11.26** Find the Macaulay duration and the modified duration of a 20-year, 10% corporate bond priced to yield 8%. According to the modified duration of this bond, how much of a price change would this bond incur if market yields rose to 9%? Using annual compounding, calculate the price of this bond in one year if rates do rise to 9%. How does this price change compare to that predicted by the modified duration? Explain the difference.

LG5   **P11.27** Which one of the following bonds would you select if you thought market interest rates were going to fall by 50 basis points over the next six months?
a. A bond with a Macaulay duration of 8.46 years that's currently being priced to yield 7.5%
b. A bond with a Macaulay duration of 9.30 years that's priced to yield 10%
c. A bond with a Macaulay duration of 8.75 years that's priced to yield 5.75%

LG5 LG6   **P11.28** Stacy Picone is an aggressive bond trader who likes to speculate on interest rate swings. Market interest rates are currently at 9%, but she expects them to fall to 7% within a year. As a result, Stacy is thinking about buying either a 25-year, zero-coupon bond or a 20-year, 7.5% bond. (Both bonds have $1,000 par values and carry the same agency rating.) Assuming that Stacy wants to maximize capital gains, which of the two issues should she select? What if she wants to maximize the total return (interest income and capital gains) from her investment? Why did one issue provide better capital gains than the other? Based on the duration of each bond, which one should be more price volatile?

LG5 LG6   **P11.29** Elliot Karlin is a 35-year-old bank executive who has just inherited a large sum of money. Having spent several years in the bank's investments department, he's well aware of the concept of duration and decides to apply it to his bond portfolio. In particular, Elliot intends to use $1 million of his inheritance to purchase four U.S. Treasury bonds:
a. An 8.5%, 13-year bond that's priced at $1,083.84 to yield 7.47%
b. A 7.875%, 15-year bond that's priced at $1,024.12 to yield 7.60%
c. A 20-year stripped Treasury that's priced at $205.99 to yield 8.22%
d. A 24-year, 7.5% bond that's priced at $957.53 to yield 7.90%
   1. Find the duration and the modified duration of each bond.
   2. Find the duration of the whole bond portfolio if Elliot puts $250,000 into each of the four U.S. Treasury bonds.
   3. Find the duration of the portfolio if Elliot puts $360,000 each into bonds a and c and $140,000 each into bonds b and d.

4. Which portfolio—**b** or **c**—should Elliot select if he thinks rates are about to head up and he wants to avoid as much price volatility as possible? Explain. From which portfolio does he stand to make more in annual interest income? Which portfolio would you recommend, and why?

Visit **http://www.myfinancelab.com** for web exercises, spreadsheets, and other online resources.

Case Problem 11.1 The Bond Investment Decisions of Dave and Marlene Carter

LG3 LG4 LG6 Dave and Marlene Carter live in the Boston area, where Dave has a successful orthodontics practice. Dave and Marlene have built up a sizable investment portfolio and have always had a major portion of their investments in fixed-income securities. They adhere to a fairly aggressive investment posture and actively go after both attractive current income and substantial capital gains. Assume that it is now 2016 and Marlene is currently evaluating two investment decisions: one involves an addition to their portfolio, the other a revision to it.

The Carters' first investment decision involves a short-term trading opportunity. In particular, Marlene has a chance to buy a 7.5%, 25-year bond that is currently priced at $852 to yield 9%; she feels that in two years the promised yield of the issue should drop to 8%.

The second is a bond swap. The Carters hold some Beta Corporation 7%, 2029 bonds that are currently priced at $785. They want to improve both current income and yield to maturity and are considering one of three issues as a possible swap candidate: (a) Dental Floss, Inc., 7.5%, 2041, currently priced at $780; (b) Root Canal Products of America, 6.5%, 2029, selling at $885; and (c) Kansas City Dental Insurance, 8%, 2030, priced at $950. All of the swap candidates are of comparable quality and have comparable issue characteristics.

Questions

a. Regarding the short-term trading opportunity:

1. What basic trading principle is involved in this situation?

2. If Marlene's expectations are correct, what will the price of this bond be in two years?

3. What is the expected return on this investment?

4. Should this investment be made? Why?

b. Regarding the bond swap opportunity:

1. Compute the current yield and the promised yield (use semiannual compounding) for the bond the Carters currently hold and for each of the three swap candidates.

2. Do any of the swap candidates provide better current income and/or current yield than the Beta Corporation bonds the Carters now hold? If so, which one(s)?

3. Do you see any reason why Marlene should switch from her present bond holding into one of the other issues? If so, which swap candidate would be the best choice? Why?

Case Problem 11.2 Grace Decides to Immunize Her Portfolio

LG4 LG5 LG6 Grace Hesketh is the owner of an extremely successful dress boutique in downtown Chicago. Although high fashion is Grace's first love, she's also interested in investments, particularly bonds and other fixed-income securities. She actively manages her own investments and over time has built up a substantial portfolio of securities. She's well versed on the latest investment techniques and is not afraid to apply those procedures to her own investments.

Grace has been playing with the idea of trying to immunize a big chunk of her bond portfolio. She'd like to cash out this part of her portfolio in seven years and use the proceeds to buy a vacation home in her home state of Oregon. To do this, she intends to use the $200,000 she now has invested in the following four corporate bonds (she currently has $50,000 invested in each one).

1. A 12-year, 7.5% bond that's currently priced at $895
2. A 10-year, zero-coupon bond priced at $405
3. A 10-year, 10% bond priced at $1,080
4. A 15-year, 9.25% bond priced at $980

(*Note:* These are all noncallable, investment-grade, nonconvertible/straight bonds.)

Questions

a. Given the information provided, find the current yield and the promised yield for each bond in the portfolio. (Use annual compounding.)

b. Calculate the Macaulay and modified durations of each bond in the portfolio and indicate how the price of each bond would change if interest rates were to rise by 75 basis points. How would the price change if interest rates were to fall by 75 basis points?

c. Find the duration of the current four-bond portfolio. Given the seven-year target that Grace has set, would you consider this an immunized portfolio? Explain.

d. How could you lengthen or shorten the duration of this portfolio? What's the shortest portfolio duration you can achieve? What's the longest?

e. Using one or more of the four bonds described above, is it possible to come up with a $200,000 bond portfolio that will exhibit the duration characteristics Grace is looking for? Explain.

f. Using one or more of the four bonds, put together a $200,000 immunized portfolio for Grace. Because this portfolio will now be immunized, will Grace be able to treat it as a buy-and-hold portfolio-one she can put away and forget about? Explain.

Excel@Investing

Excel@Investing

All bonds are priced according to the present value of their future cash flow streams. The key components of bond valuation are par value, coupon interest rate, term to maturity, and market yield. It is market yield that drives bond prices. In the market for bonds, the appropriate yield at which the bond should sell is determined first, and then that yield is used to find the market value of the bond. The market yield can also be referred to as the required rate of return. It implies that this is the rate of return that a rational investor requires before he or she will invest in a given fixed-income security.

Create a spreadsheet to model and answer the following bond valuation questions.

Questions

a. One of the bond issues outstanding by H&W Corporation has an annual-pay coupon of 5.625% plus a par value of $1,000 at maturity. This bond has a remaining maturity of 23 years. The required rate of return on securities of similar-risk grade is 6.76%. What is the value of this corporate bond today?

b. What is the current yield for the H&W bond?

c. In the case of the H&W bond issue from question **a**, if the coupon interest payment is compounded on a semiannual basis, what would be the value of this security today?

d. How would the price of the H&W bond react to changing market interest rates? To find out, determine how the price of the issue reacts to changes in the bond's yield to maturity. Find the value of the security when the YTM is (1) 5.625%, (2) 8.0%, and (3) 4.5%. Label your findings as being a premium, par, or discount bond. Comment on your findings.

e. The Jay & Austin Company has a bond issue outstanding with the following characteristics: par of $1,000, a semiannual-pay coupon of 6.5%, remaining maturity of 22 years, and a current price of $878.74. What is the bond's YTM?

CFA Exam Questions

Investing in Fixed-Income Securities

Following is a sample of 10 Level-I CFA exam questions that deal with many of the topics covered in Chapters 10 and 11 of this text, including bond prices and yields, interest rates and risks, bond price volatility, and bond redemption provisions. (When answering the questions, give yourself 1½ minutes for each question; the objective is to correctly answer 7 of the 10 questions in 15 minutes.)

1. Sinking funds are most likely to
   a. reduce credit risk (default risk).
   b. never allow issuers to retire more than the sinking fund requirement.
   c. always reduce the outstanding balance of the bond issue to 0 prior to maturity.

2. An analyst stated that a callable bond has less reinvestment risk and more price appreciation potential than an otherwise identical noncallable bond. The analyst's statement most likely is
   a. incorrect with respect to both reinvestment risk and price appreciation potential.
   b. incorrect with respect to reinvestment risk but correct with respect to price appreciation potential.
   c. correct with respect to reinvestment risk but incorrect with respect to price appreciation potential.

3. A bond portfolio manager gathered the following information about a bond issue:

Par value	$10,000,000
Current market value	$9,850,000
Duration	4.8

   If yields are expected to decline by 75 basis points, which of the following would provide the most appropriate estimate of the price change for the bond issue?
   a. 3.6% of $9,850,000
   b. 3.6% of $10,000,000
   c. 4.8% of $9,850,000

4. Treasury STRIPS are securities created by stripping the coupon and principal payments made by an ordinary bond and selling them as individual securities. A U.S. Treasury note with exactly 4 years to maturity most likely can be broken into as many as
   a. 4 Treasury STRIPS.
   b. 8 Treasury STRIPS.
   c. 9 Treasury STRIPS.

5. Frieda Wannamaker is a taxable investor who is currently in the 28% income-tax bracket. She is considering purchasing a tax-exempt bond with a yield of 3.75%. The taxable equivalent yield on this bond is closest to
   a. 1.46%.
   b. 5.21%.
   c. 7.47%.

6. The present value of a $1,000 par value, zero-coupon bond with a three-year maturity assuming an annual discount rate of 6% compounded semiannually is closest to
   a. $837.48.
   b. $839.62.
   c. $943.40.

7. A bond with 14 years to maturity and a coupon rate of 6.375% has a yield to maturity of 4.5%. Assuming the bond's YTM remains constant, the bond's value as it approaches maturity will most likely
   a. increase.
   b. decrease.
   c. remain constant.

8. A coupon-bearing bond purchased when issued at par value was held until maturity during which time interest rates rose. The ex-post realized return of the bond investment most likely was
   a. above the YTM at the time of issue.
   b. below the YTM at the time of issue.
   c. equal to the YTM at the time of issue because the bond was held until maturity.

9. An analyst accurately calculates that the price of an ordinary, noncallable bond with a 9% coupon would experience a 12% change if market yields increase 100 basis points. If market yields decrease 100 basis points, the bond's price would most likely
   a. increase by 12%.
   b. increase by less than 12%.
   c. increase by more than 12%.

10. A bond with a par value of $1,000 has a duration of 6.2. If the yield on the bond is expected to change from 8.80% to 8.95%, the estimated new price for the bond following the expected change in yield is best described as being
   a. 0.93% lower than the bond's current price.
   b. 1.70% lower than the bond's current price.
   c. 10.57% lower than the bond's current price.

Answers: 1. a; 2. a; 3. a; 4. c; 5. b; 6. a; 7. b; 8. a; 9. c; 10. a.

Mutual Funds and Exchange-Traded Funds

LEARNING GOALS

After studying this chapter, you should be able to:

LG1 Describe the basic features of mutual funds and note what they have to offer as investments.

LG2 Distinguish between open- and closed-end funds, exchange-traded funds, and other types of professionally managed investment companies, and discuss the various types of fund loads, fees, and charges.

LG3 Discuss the types of funds available and the variety of investment objectives these funds seek to fulfill.

LG4 Discuss the investor services offered by mutual funds and how these services can fit into an investment program.

LG5 Describe the investor uses of mutual funds along with the variables to consider when assessing and selecting funds for investment purposes.

LG6 Identify the sources of return and compute the rate of return earned on a mutual fund investment.

In 1976 John Bogle, founder of the Vanguard Group, had a radical idea to create a mutual fund that would hold only stocks included in the Standard & Poor's 500 Stock Index. Unlike other mutual funds, the goal of the Vanguard 500 Index fund—originally called the First Index Investment Trust—would not be to outperform the equities market but to keep pace with the returns offered by the S&P 500 Index. Vanguard's index fund held down costs in two ways. First, because the fund simply purchased whatever stocks were included in the S&P 500 stock index, there was no need for Vanguard to pay employees to conduct analysis to determine which stocks they should buy and sell. Second, because the composition of the S&P 500 Index is relatively stable over time, mimicking the index did not require Vanguard to trade excessively, so the fund's transactions costs were low.

Today the Vanguard 500 Index fund is one of the largest mutual funds in the world, with net assets exceeding $213 billion. The fund garnered a major endorsement when Warren Buffet, perhaps the world's most famous investor, suggested that when he died the trustees of his estate should put 90% of his wealth in the S&P 500 Index fund. Vanguard's philosophy of providing investors with low-cost funds made it the largest U.S. mutual fund company, and its popularity shows no signs of slowing. In 2014 investors poured $216 billion into Vanguard, a record inflow of funds for any mutual fund company, and assets under management at the company swelled to more than $3 trillion. Vanguard's emphasis on limited stock turnover has kept its operating expenses low. For every $1,000 an investor places in Vanguard's funds, Vanguard extracts just $1.80 per year for operating costs, less than one-fifth of the industry average of $10.20 annually per $1,000 invested. Vanguard's S&P 500 fund has earned an average annual return of approximately 11% over the past 39 years, outperforming almost 90% of the other stock mutual funds that were also in business way back in 1976.

In 1993, State Street Global Advisors improved on the idea of index funds by creating the first exchange-traded fund (ETF). An ETF is created by placing a large portfolio of securities in a trust and then selling shares that represent claims against that trust. The first ETF was known as the Standard & Poor's Depositary Receipt (SPDR), a.k.a. the "spider." Like the Vanguard index fund, the spider tracks movements in the S&P 500 Index, but has an important advantage. Investors who want to buy or sell shares in mutual funds must wait until the stock market closes each day, but investors in ETFs can buy or sell shares at any time during the trading day.

(Sources: Rick Ferri, "Index Fund Returns Get Better with Age," http://www .forbes.com/sites/rickferri/2013/04/04/index-fund-returns-get-better-with- age/2/, accessed July 1, 2015; Kristen Grind, "Vanguard Sets Record Funds Inflow," http://www.wsj.com/articles/vanguard-sets-record-funds-inflow- 1420430643, accessed July 1, 2015.)

The Mutual Fund Concept

LG1 LG2 Questions of which stock or bond to select, how best to build a diversified portfolio, and how to manage the costs of building a portfolio have challenged investors for as long as there have been organized securities markets. These concerns lie at the very heart of the mutual fund concept and in large part explain the growth that mutual funds have experienced. Many investors lack the know-how, time, or commitment to manage their own portfolios. Furthermore, many investors do not have sufficient funds to create a well-diversified portfolio, so instead they turn to professional money managers and allow them to decide which securities to buy and sell. More often than not, when investors look for professional help, they look to mutual funds.

Basically, a **mutual fund** (also called an investment company) is a type of financial services organization that receives money from a group of investors and then uses those funds to purchase a portfolio of securities. When investors send money to a mutual fund, they receive shares in the fund and become part owners of a portfolio of securities. That is, the investment company builds and manages a portfolio of securities and sells ownership interests—shares—in that portfolio through a vehicle known as a mutual fund.

Portfolio management deals with both asset allocation and security selection decisions. By investing in mutual funds, investors delegate some, if not all, of the security selection decisions to professional money managers. As a result, investors can concentrate on key asset allocation decisions—which, of course, play a vital role in determining long-term portfolio returns. Indeed, it's for this reason that many investors consider mutual funds the ultimate asset allocation vehicle. All that investors have to do is decide in which fund they want to invest—and then let the professional money managers at the mutual funds do the rest.

An Overview of Mutual Funds

Mutual funds have been a part of the investment landscape in the United States for 91 years. The first one started in Boston in 1924 and is still in business. By 1940 the number of mutual funds had grown to 68, and by 2015 there were more than 9,300 of them. To put that number in perspective, there are more mutual funds in existence today than there are stocks listed on all the major U.S. stock exchanges combined. As the number of fund offerings has increased, so have the assets managed by these funds, rising from about $135 billion in 1980 to $15.8 trillion by the end of 2014. Compared to less than 6% in 1980, 43% of U.S. households (90 million people) owned mutual funds in 2014. The mutual fund industry has grown so much, in fact, that it is now the largest financial intermediary in this country—even ahead of banks.

Mutual funds are big business in the United States and, indeed, all over the world. Worldwide there were more than 79,000 mutual funds in operation in 2014, which collectively held $31.4 trillion in assets. U.S. mutual funds held roughly half of those assets. Measured by the number of funds or by assets under management, U.S. stock funds hold the largest share of mutual fund assets. Figure 12.1 shows the major types of mutual funds and their share of total assets under management. Funds that invest primarily in U.S. stocks (domestic equity) managed 42% of assets held by mutual funds in 2014, and funds investing in foreign stocks held another 14% of industry assets. The share of mutual fund assets invested in domestic and world stocks has been rising in recent years, while the share of assets invested in fixed-income securities such as bonds and money market instruments has fallen. The decline in assets invested in fixed-income instruments reflects the historically low interest rates that have prevailed in the market in recent years.

FIGURE 12.1   U.S. Mutual Fund Assets under Management by Type of Fund

The chart shows the distribution of mutual fund assets under management by type of fund. Funds that invested in either domestic or foreign stocks managed 56% of industry assets, while funds that invested in fixed-income assets such as bonds and money market instruments managed 36% of industry assets. Just three years earlier, equity and fixed-income funds held roughly an equal share of industry assets, but with interest rates stuck at historically low levels, investors have been moving out of bonds and into stocks. (Source: Data from the *2015 Investment Company Institute Factbook*, **https://www.ici.org/pdf/2015_factbook.pdf**.)

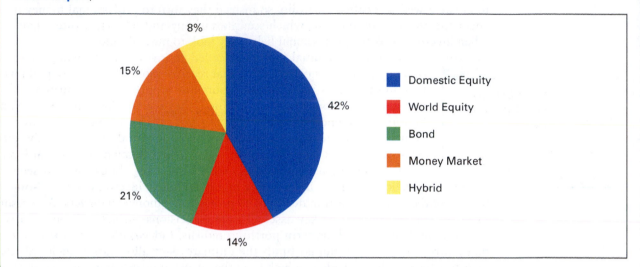

How Mutual Funds Get Started

Mutual funds appeal to investors from all walks of life and all income levels. Both inexperienced and highly experienced investors hold mutual funds in their portfolios. All of these investors have a common view: Each has decided, for one reason or another, to turn over at least a part of his or her investment management activities to professionals.

Pooled Diversification   The mutual fund concept is based on the simple idea of combining money from a group of people with similar investment goals and investing that money in a diversified portfolio. This idea is called **pooled diversification**. Mutual funds make it easy for investors to hold well-diversified portfolios, even if the amount of money that they can invest is relatively small. It's not uncommon for a single mutual fund to hold hundreds of different stocks or bonds. For example, as of March 2015 Fidelity Contrafund held 335 different securities, while the Dreyfus GNMA fund held 830 securities. That's far more diversification than most individual investors could ever hope to attain by purchasing individual securities on their own. Yet each investor who owns shares in a fund is, in effect, a part owner of that fund's diversified portfolio of securities.

No matter what the size of the fund, as the securities it holds move up and down in price, the market value of the mutual fund shares moves accordingly. When the fund receives dividend and interest payments, they too are passed on to the mutual fund shareholders and distributed on the basis of prorated ownership. Thus, if you own 1,000 shares in a mutual fund and that represents 1% of shares outstanding, you will receive 1% of the dividends paid by the fund. When the fund sells a security for a profit, it also passes the capital gain on to fund shareholders on a prorated basis.

Active versus Passive Management   Broadly speaking, mutual funds fall into one of two categories based on how they decide which securities to buy. In an **actively managed fund**, a professional portfolio manager conducts an analysis to determine which securities are likely to exhibit above-average future performance. The portfolio manager might conduct fundamental analysis by combing through companies' financial reports and developing complex valuation models to estimate the intrinsic value of many different securities. The manager would then invest in those securities whose intrinsic values were greater than their market prices. Alternatively, the manager might use technical analysis to try to spot trends that predict the direction in which securities prices will move in the near future. In either case, the manager's goal is to identify and invest in securities that will achieve superior performance.

Comparing the portfolio's performance to a benchmark assesses whether the manager succeeds or fails in that task. The benchmark to which a particular fund is compared should have a similar risk profile as the fund. For example, if a particular fund's objective is to invest in large, blue-chip companies, that fund's benchmark might be the S&P 500 stock index. The fund manager's goal is to generate higher returns, after fees, than the S&P 500 Index. On the other hand, if a particular fund focuses on investing in small-cap stocks, the S&P 500 would be a poor benchmark because small-cap stocks are riskier than the large-cap firms in that index. Instead, an index like the Russell 2000 Index would be an appropriate benchmark.

Consider the consequences of setting an inappropriate benchmark for a fund. Suppose a fund investing in small-cap stocks sets the S&P 500 as its benchmark. Because stocks in the S&P 500 are less risky than small-cap stocks, over time we would expect returns on the S&P 500 to be lower than returns on a small-cap portfolio. In other words, a small-cap fund should outperform the S&P 500, not because the fund manager is skillful, but because the fund invests in riskier assets. To the extent that fund managers are judged based on their ability to earn a return above some benchmark, there will be at least some incentive for the fund to compare its performance to a less risky benchmark.

In a **passively managed fund**, managers make no attempt to select a portfolio that will outperform a benchmark. Instead, passively managed funds are designed to mimic the performance of a particular benchmark or stock index. The Vanguard S&P 500 Index fund described at the beginning of this chapter is a perfect example of a passively managed fund. In these funds, the manager's goal is to track the performance of the index as closely as possible while keeping expenses as low as possible. Indeed, the management fees charged by passively managed funds are, on average, a small fraction of the fees charged by actively managed funds. Purveyors of passively managed funds appeal to investors by arguing that actively managed funds offer only the possibility of earning superior returns, but their higher expenses are a certainty.

> **WATCH YOUR BEHAVIOR**
>
> **Beating the Benchmarks**
> Investment companies that offer a variety of mutual funds often advertise that a high fraction of their funds outperform their benchmarks. Investors should be wary of these claims. Mutual fund families often close funds that trail their benchmarks (or merge them into other funds outperforming the benchmark). This "survivorship bias" artificially raises the percentage of mutual funds in a particular family outperforming a benchmark. Numerous studies have shown that without the benefit of survivorship bias, most mutual funds trail their benchmarks.

Attractions and Drawbacks of Mutual Fund Ownership   Among the many reasons for owning mutual funds, one of the most important is the portfolio diversification that they can offer. As we saw above, fund shareholders can achieve diversification benefits by spreading fund holdings over a wide variety of industries and companies, thus reducing risk. Because they buy and sell large quantities of securities, mutual funds generally pay lower transactions costs than individual investors would pay to trade the same securities. Another appeal of mutual funds is full-time professional management. In the case of actively managed funds, investors delegate the task of selecting securities to a highly trained fund manager, but even in a passively managed fund, there are record-keeping chores and other routine tasks that fund managers can perform more efficiently than can individual investors. Still another advantage is that most mutual fund investments can be started with a modest amount of investment capital. With a few thousand dollars an investor can purchase a claim on a portfolio containing hundreds of different securities. The services that mutual funds offer also make them appealing to many investors. These services include automatic reinvestment of dividends and capital gains, record keeping for taxes, and exchange privileges. Finally, mutual funds offer convenience. They are relatively easy to buy and sell, and investors can easily find up-to-date information about a fund's price and its recent performance.

There are, of course, some costs associated with mutual fund ownership. Mutual funds charge a variety of fees which, in some cases, can be quite significant. Some funds carry a "sales load," which is an up-front fee that investors pay to acquire shares in the fund (like a commission). Funds charge other fees to cover the expenses of running the fund. These expenses include the compensation of the portfolio manager and staff, advertising expenses, and other administrative and operating costs. Collectively, these fees (excluding the separate sales load) are known as the fund's **expense ratio**. The expense ratio is a charge, expressed as a percentage of assets managed by a fund, that fund investors pay each year. Investors pay these expenses each year regardless of whether the fund has a good year or a bad year. Expense ratios vary a great deal from one fund to another. The expense ratio for the median (mean) actively managed fund was 1.25% (0.86%) in 2014. If you invest $10,000 in a fund charging a 1.25% expense ratio, you will pay $125 per year in fees regardless of how the fund's investments perform. The expense ratios charged by passively managed funds are typically much lower. The median (mean) expense ratio for passive funds was 0.44% (0.11%) in 2014. Some mutual funds justify higher fees by claiming that their managers will generate superior returns, but investors should be wary of those claims. There is not much evidence that mutual funds on average earn above-average returns. There are some notable exceptions, of course, but most actively managed funds do little more than keep up with the market. In many cases, they don't even do that. For example, 82% of actively managed large-cap equity funds trailed their benchmark over the 10-year period ending in 2014. The spotty performance record and relatively high fees of actively managed funds have drawn more and more investors to passively managed funds over time.

Performance of Mutual Funds For an actively managed fund, the goal is to earn a return that exceeds the fund's benchmark by more than enough to cover the fund's fees. But how successful are professional fund managers at achieving this goal? Figure 12.2 provides some evidence on that question. The figure shows the percentage of mutual funds in various categories that were outperformed by their benchmark over a five-year period from 2009 to 2014. The figure focuses on a five-year investment horizon in part to smooth out the volatility of year-to-year performance but also because investors want to know whether actively managed funds can deliver superior performance consistently. Unfortunately, the news in Figure 12.2 is not good for portfolio managers. Across a wide variety of funds, a majority of portfolio managers trail their benchmark. Looking at all U.S. equity funds, 74% of managers failed to earn a higher five-year return than their benchmark. Bond fund managers fared worse, with 85% of junk bond funds and 96% of long-term bond funds trailing their benchmarks. The only group in which a majority of fund managers beat their benchmark was the short-term bond category, and even there 49% of funds trailed the

FIGURE 12.2   **Percentage of Mutual Funds Outperformed by Their Benchmarks from 2009 to 2014**

Even with the services of professional money managers, it's tough to outperform the market. In this case, only one fund category had a majority of funds that succeeded in beating the market during the five-year period from 2009 to 2014. (Source: SPIVA U.S Scorecard, mid-year 2014, http://www.spindices.com/documents/spiva/spiva-us-mid-year-2014.pdf)

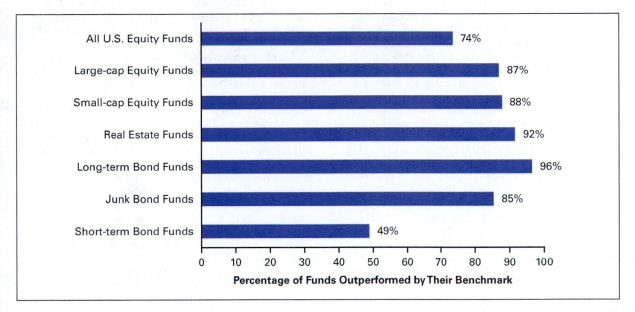

benchmark while 51% exceeded it. The message is clear: Consistently beating the market is no easy task, even for professional money managers. Although a handful of funds have given investors above-average and even spectacular rates of return, most mutual funds simply do not meet those levels of performance. This is not to say that the long-term returns from mutual funds are substandard or that they fail to equal what you could achieve by putting your money in, say, a savings account or some other risk-free investment outlet. Quite the contrary. The long-term returns from mutual funds have been substantial (and perhaps even better than what many individual investors could have achieved on their own), but a good deal of those returns can be traced to strong market conditions and/or to the reinvestment of dividends and capital gains.

How Mutual Funds Are Organized and Run   Athough it's tempting to think of a mutual fund as a single large entity, that view is not really accurate. Funds split their various functions—investing, record keeping, safekeeping, and others—among two or more companies. To begin with, there's the fund itself, which is organized as a separate corporation or trust. It is owned by the shareholders, not by the firm that runs it. In addition, there are several other major players:

- A *management company* runs the fund's daily operations. Management companies are the firms we know as Fidelity, Vanguard, T. Rowe Price, American

FAMOUS FAILURES IN FINANCE

When Mutual Funds Behaved Badly

For the 90 million Americans who own them, mutual funds are a convenient and relatively safe place to invest money. So it came as a big shock to investors in September 2003 when New York Attorney General Eliot Spitzer shook the mutual fund industry with allegations of illegal after-hours trading, special deals for large institutional investors, market timing in flagrant violation of funds' written policies, and other abuses. Nearly 20 companies, including several large brokerages, were dragged into scandals.

Some of the abuses stemmed from market timing, a practice in which short-term traders seek to exploit differences between hours of operations of various global markets. An example best illustrates this practice. Suppose a U.S. mutual funds holds Japanese stocks. The Japanese market closes approximately 14 hours before the U.S. market does, but the net asset value of the mutual fund will be calculated at 4:00 p.m. when the U.S. market closes. Suppose on a Monday the U.S. market has a strong rally. Investors know that this means it is very likely that stocks will open higher on Tuesday morning in Japan, but by purchasing shares in the mutual fund, they can essentially buy Japanese stocks at prices that are "stale," meaning that the prices do not reflect the good news that the U.S market rallied on Monday. Instead, the fund's net asset value reflects the prices in Japan 14 hours earlier. By purchasing shares in the mutual fund on days when the U.S. market goes up and selling them on days when the U.S. market goes down, traders can earn profits that are far above normal. Most funds prohibit this kind of activity, yet exceptions were made for large institutional investors who traded millions of dollars' worth of fund shares. According to the regulators, this practice resembles betting on a winning horse after the horse race is over.

More recently, investigations have uncovered abuses having to do with a mutual fund known as a "funds of funds." Some large investment companies that offer many different funds give investors the option of investing in a fund that only holds shares of the investment company's other funds. The manager of such a fund does not select individual securities, but instead decides how to allocate investors' dollars across different mutual funds operated by the same fund family. Suppose that one of the investment company's funds is hit by an unexpected, large request for withdrawals. Such an event could force the fund to conduct a fire sale, selling securities at discount prices to raise cash and lowering the fund's return as a result. In steps the fund of funds manager. She simply reallocates some of the dollars under her control by purchasing shares in the fund hit with withdrawals and selling shares in other funds not facing pressure to distribute cash to shareholders. This practice benefits the fund family as a whole but not the shareholders in the fund of funds. They are effectively providing liquidity to other funds in the family hit by redemption requests without being compensated for doing so.

Critical Thinking Question How are shareholders in a "fund of funds" harmed if their fund manager purchases shares in another fund that has been hit by unexpected investor withdrawals?

Century, and Dreyfus. They are the ones that create the funds in the first place. Usually, the management firm also serves as investment advisor.

- An *investment advisor* buys and sells stocks or bonds and otherwise oversees the portfolio. Usually, three parties participate in this phase of the operation: (1) *the money manager*, who actually runs the portfolio and makes the buy and sell decisions; (2) *securities analysts*, who analyze securities and look for viable investment candidates; and (3) *traders*, who buy and sell big blocks of securities at the best possible price.

- A *distributor* sells the fund shares, either directly to the public or through authorized dealers (like major brokerage houses and commercial banks). When you request a prospectus and sales literature, you deal with the distributor.

- A *custodian* physically safeguards the securities and other assets of the fund, without taking a role in the investment decisions. To discourage foul play, an independent party (usually a bank) serves in this capacity.

- A *transfer agent* keeps track of purchase and redemption requests from shareholders and maintains other shareholder records.

This separation of duties is designed to protect mutual fund shareholders. You can lose money as a mutual fund investor (if your fund's stock or bond holdings go down in value), but that's usually the only risk of loss you face with a mutual fund. Here's why: In addition to the separation of duties noted above, one of the provisions of the contract between the mutual fund and the company that manages it is that the fund's assets— stocks, bonds, cash, or other securities in the portfolio—can never be in the hands of the management company. As still another safeguard, each fund must have a board of directors, or trustees, who are elected by shareholders and are charged with keeping tabs on the management company. Nevertheless, as the Famous Failures in Finance box nearby explains, some mutual funds have engaged in some improper trading, which imposed losses on their investors.

Open- or Closed-End Funds Some mutual funds, known as **open-end funds**, regularly receive new infusions of cash from investors, and the funds use that money to purchase a portfolio of securities. When investors send money to an open-end fund, they receive new shares in the fund. There is no limit to the number of shares that the mutual fund can issue, and as long as new money flows in from investors, the portfolio of securities grows. Of course, investors are free to withdraw their money from the fund, and when that happens the fund manager redeems investors' shares in cash. Sometimes, withdrawal requests by fund shareholders may force the fund manager to sell securities (thus reducing the size of the portfolio) to obtain the cash to distribute to investors. In extreme cases, when investor withdrawals are unexpectedly large and the securities held by the fund are illiquid, the fund may have to conduct a **fire sale**. A fire sale occurs when a fund must sell illiquid assets quickly to raise cash to meet investors' withdrawal requests. In a fire sale, the fund may have to substantially reduce the price of the securities it wants to sell to attract buyers. In such an instance, the buyers are essentially providing liquidity to the fund, and the discounted price that buyers receive on the securities that they purchase from the fund is effectively a form of compensation that they earn for providing that liquidity. To avoid having to sell securities at fire-sale prices and to reward investors who leave their money in the fund for a long time, some funds charge redemption fees. A **redemption fee** is a charge that investors pay if they sell shares in the fund only a short time after buying them. Unlike other fees that mutual funds charge, the redemption fees are reinvested into the fund and do not go to the investment company. All open-end mutual funds stand behind their shares and buy them back when investors decide to sell. There is never any trading of shares between individuals. The vast majority of mutual funds in the United States are open-end funds.

When investors buy and sell shares of an open-end fund, those transactions are carried out at prices based on the current market value of all the securities held in the fund's portfolio and the number of shares the fund has issued. These transactions occur at a price known as the fund's **net asset value** (**NAV**). The NAV equals the total market value of securities held in the fund divided by the fund's outstanding shares. Open-end funds usually calculate their NAVs at the end of each day, and it is at that price that withdrawals from or contributions to the fund take place. Of course, a fund's NAV changes throughout the day as the prices of the securities that the fund holds change. Nevertheless, transactions between open-end funds and their customers generally occur at the end-of-day NAV.

Example

> If the market value of all the assets held by XYZ mutual fund at the end of a given day equaled $10 million, and if XYZ on that particular day had 500,000 shares outstanding, the fund's net asset value per share would be $20 ($10,000,000 ÷ 500,000). Investors who want to put new money into the fund obtain one new share for every $20 that they invest. Similarly, investors who want to liquidate their investment in the fund receive $20 for each share of the fund that they own.

An Introduction
to Closed-End Funds

Closed-End Investment Companies An alternative mutual fund structure is the closed-end fund. **Closed-end funds** operate with a fixed number of shares outstanding and do not regularly issue new shares of stock. The term *closed* means that the fund is closed to new investors. At its inception, the fund raises money by issuing shares to investors, and then it invests that pool of money in securities. No new investments in the fund are permitted, nor are withdrawals allowed. So how do investors acquire shares in closed-end funds, and how do they liquidate their investments in closed-end funds? Shares in closed-end investment companies, like those of any other common stock, are actively traded in the secondary market. Unlike open-end funds, all trading in closed-end funds is done between investors in the open market and not between investors and the fund itself. In other words, when an investor in a closed-end fund wants to redeem shares, he or she does not return them to the fund company for cash, as would be the case with an open-end fund. Instead, the investor simply sells the shares on the open market to another individual who wants to invest in the fund. In this respect, buying and selling shares in closed-end funds is just like trading the shares of a company like Apple or ExxonMobil. Investors who want to acquire shares in a particular fund must buy them from other investors who already own them.

An important difference between closed-end and open-end funds arises because investors in closed-end funds buy and sell their shares in the secondary market. For both open- and closed-end funds, the NAV equals the market value of assets held by the fund divided by the fund's outstanding shares. However, whereas investors in open-end funds can buy or sell shares at the NAV at the end of each day, closed-end fund investors trade their shares during the trading day at the fund's current market price. Importantly, in closed-end funds, the price of shares in the secondary market may or may not (in fact, usually does not) equal the fund's NAV. When a closed-end fund's share price is below its NAV, the fund is said to be trading at a discount, and when the share price exceeds the fund's NAV, the fund is trading at a premium. We will have more to say later about how closed-end fund discounts and premiums can affect investors' returns.

Because closed-end funds do not need to deal with daily inflows and outflows of cash from investors, the capital at their disposal is fixed. Managers of these funds don't need to keep cash on hand to satisfy redemption requests from investors, nor must they constantly search for new investment opportunities simply because more investors want to be part of the fund.

Most closed-end investment companies are traded on the New York Stock Exchange, although a few are traded on other exchanges. As of 2014, the 568 closed-end funds operating in the United States managed $289 billion in assets, and 60% of the assets in closed-end funds were held in bond funds.

Exchange-Traded Funds

A relatively new form of investment company called an exchange-traded fund, or ETF for short, combines some of the operating characteristics of an open-end fund with some of the trading characteristics of a closed-end fund. An *exchange-traded fund (ETF)* is a type of open-end fund that trades as a listed security on one of the stock exchanges. Exchange-traded funds are also sometimes referred to as exchange-traded portfolios, or ETPs. As the beginning of the chapter described, the first ETF was created in 1993, and it was designed to track the movements of the S&P 500 stock index. Nearly all ETFs were structured as index funds up until 2008 when the SEC cleared the way for actively managed ETFs, which, like actively managed mutual funds, create a unique mix of investments to meet a specific investment objective.

In terms of how shares are created and redeemed, ETFs function in essentially the opposite way that mutual funds do. Mutual funds receive cash from investors, and then they invest that cash in a portfolio of securities. An ETF is created when a portfolio of securities is purchased and placed in a trust, and then shares are issued that represent claims against that trust.

To be more precise, suppose a company called Smart Investors wants to create an ETF. Smart Investors, the *ETF sponsor*, decides that it wants its ETF to track the S&P 500 stock index. Smart Investors contacts an entity known as an authorized participant (AP), which is usually a large institutional investor of some kind. The essential trait of an AP is that it has the ability to acquire a large quantity of shares relatively quickly. The AP acquires a portfolio of shares in which all of the companies in the S&P 500 Index are represented (and in proportions that match those of the index) and delivers those shares to Smart Investors, who then places the shares in a trust. In exchange, Smart Investors gives the AP a block of equally valued shares in the ETF. This block of shares is called a *creation unit*. The number of ETF shares in one creation unit may vary, but 50,000 shares per creation unit is a common structure. Therefore, each ETF share represents a 1/50,000th claim against the shares held in trust by Smart Investors. The AP takes the shares that it receives and sells them to investors so the shares can begin trading freely on the secondary market. Figure 12.3 illustrates the relationships of the ETF, the authorized participant, and investors.

Example

> An authorized participant has acquired a portfolio of stocks that includes all stocks in the S&P 500 Index. The total market value of these stocks is $100 million. The AP transfers these shares to Smart Investors, who in turn issues 100 creation units containing 50,000 ETF shares each to the AP. Therefore, the AP holds a total of 5,000,000 ETF shares. The AP sells the shares to investors at a price of $20 each, so the total value of ETF shares outstanding equals the value of the shares held in trust. Each day the ETF share price will move in sync with changes in the value of the securities held in the trust.

ETFs provide liquidity to investors just as closed-end funds do. That is, investors in ETFs can buy or sell their shares at any time during trading hours. But unlike closed-end funds, an ETF does not necessarily have a fixed number of shares. Going back to our example of the Smart Investors ETF that tracks the S&P 500 Index, if investor demand for this ETF is strong, then Smart Investors can work with the authorized participant to purchase a larger block of shares, creating additional creation units and

FIGURE 12.3 How an ETF Works

An ETF is created when an authorized participant delivers a portfolio of securities to the ETF sponsor, which in turn delivers ETF shares to the authorized participant. Those shares are then sold to investors and traded on an exchange.

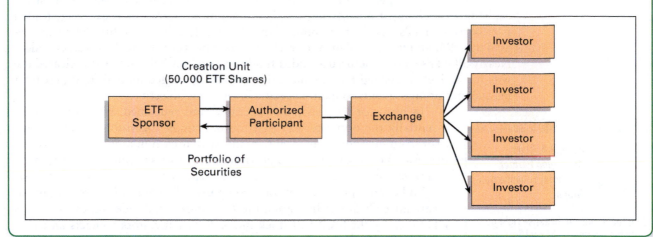

issuing new ETF shares. The process can also work in reverse. If at some point in time interest in the S&P 500 ETF wanes, the authorized participant can buy up 50,000 ETF shares in the open market and then sell those shares back to Smart Investors in exchange for some of the shares held in trust (remember, 50,000 ETF shares equals 1 creation unit). So the number of outstanding ETF shares may ebb and flow over time, unlike a closed-end fund's fixed number of shares.

Because authorized participants can create new ETF shares or redeem outstanding shares, the ETF share price generally matches the NAV of shares held in trust. In other words, ETFs generally do not trade at a premium or a discount as closed-end funds do. For example, suppose at a particular point in time the share price of an S&P 500 ETF is trading below the NAV (i.e., below the value of the shares held in trust). In this case, the authorized participant can simply buy up ETF shares on the open market, deliver them back to the sponsor (e.g., Smart Investors) who created the ETF, and reclaim the shares from the trust. The authorized participant would make a profit on this transaction because the value of the ETF shares that they purchased was less than the value of the shares that they received. Of course, as the authorized participants begin buying up ETF shares to execute this transaction, they would put upward pressure on the ETF price. In short, the actions of authorized participants help to ensure that ETF prices closely, if not perfectly, match the NAVs of the securities held in trust.

Investors seem to be pleased with the advantages that ETFs provide. Figure 12.4 documents the explosive growth in ETFs since 1995. Starting from less than $1 billion in 1994, assets invested in ETFs totaled almost $2 trillion in 2014, a compound annual growth rate of roughly 50%! As you would expect, the variety of ETFs has dramatically increased as well. In 1995 there were just two ETFs available on U.S. markets, but by 2014 that number had skyrocketed to 1,411 ETFs. Of these, the vast majority were index ETFs. With so many index ETFs available, it is not surprising that investors can find an ETF to track almost any imaginable sector

A Behavioral Difference between ETFs and Mutual Funds

FIGURE 12.4   Assets Invested in Exchange-Traded Funds

Assets invested in exchange-traded funds grew from roughly $1 billion to $2 trillion from 1995 to 2014. (Source: Data from *2015 Investment Company Institute Factbook*, p. 10, http://www.icifactbook.org/2012_factbook.pdf.)

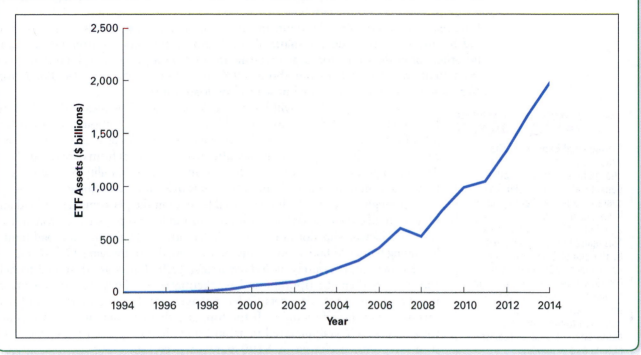

of the stock market including technology stocks, utilities, and many others. There are also ETFs that focus on other asset classes such as bonds, commodities, real estate, and currencies. By far the most common type of ETF is one that focuses on large-cap U.S. stocks.

ETFs combine many of the advantages of closed-end funds with those of traditional (open-end) funds. As with closed-end funds, you can buy and sell ETFs at any time of the day by placing an order through your broker (and paying a standard commission, just as you would with any other stock). In contrast, you cannot trade a traditional open-end fund on an intraday basis; all buy and sell orders for those funds are filled at the end of the trading day, at closing prices. ETFs can also be bought on margin, and they can be sold short. Moreover, because index ETFs are passively managed, they offer many of the advantages of any index fund, including low costs and low taxes. In fact, the fund's tax liability is kept very low because ETFs rarely distribute any capital gains to shareholders.

Thus, you could hold index ETFs for decades and never pay a dime in capital gains taxes (at least not until you sell the shares).

Some Important Considerations

When you buy or sell shares in a closed-end investment company (or in ETFs, for that matter), you pay a commission, just as you would with any other listed or OTC stock. This is not the case with open-end mutual funds. The cost of investing in an open-end fund depends on the fees and load charges that the fund levies on its investors.

Load and No-Load Funds The load charge on an open-end fund is the commission you pay when you buy shares in a fund. Generally speaking, the term **load fund** describes a mutual fund that charges a commission when shares are bought. (Such charges are also known as *front-end loads*.) A **no-load fund** levies no sales charges. Although load charges have fallen over time, they can still be fairly substantial. The average front load charge in an equity fund has fallen from 7.9% in 1980 to around 5.4% in 2014. However, many funds offer discounts on their sales loads. Some funds charge no sales load for investments made automatically each month through a retirement account, and others offer discounts for large investments. On average, the sales load that investors actually pay has fallen from about 3.9% in 1990 to 0.9% in 2014. Funds that offer these types of discounts are known as **low-load funds**.

Occasionally, a fund will have a **back-end load**. This means that the fund levies commissions when shares are sold. These loads may amount to as much as 5% of the value of the shares sold, although back-end loads tend to decline over time and usually disappear altogether after five or six years from date of purchase. The stated purpose of back-end loads is to enhance fund stability by discouraging investors from trading in and out of the funds over short investment horizons.

Although there may be little or no difference in the performance of load and no-load funds, the cost savings with no-load funds tend to give investors a head start in achieving superior rates of return. Unfortunately, the true no-load fund is becoming harder to find, as more and more no-loads are charging *12(b)-1 fees*.

Known appropriately as *hidden loads*, **12(b)-1 fees** are designed to help funds cover their distribution and marketing costs. They can amount to as much as 1% per year of assets under management. In good markets and bad, investors pay these fees right off the top, and that can take its toll. Consider, for instance, $10,000 invested in a fund that charges a 1% 12(b)-1 fee. That translates into a charge of $100 per year—certainly not an insignificant amount of money. The 12(b)-1 fee is included with a fund's other operational fees as part of the fund's expense ratio.

To try to bring some semblance of order to fund charges and fees, the Financial Industry Regulatory Authority (FINRA) instituted a series of caps on mutual fund fees. According to the latest regulations, a mutual fund cannot charge more than 8.5% in total sales charges and fees, including front- and back-end loads as well as 12(b)-1 fees. Thus, if a fund charges a 5% front-end load and a 1% 12(b)-1 fee, it can charge a maximum of only 2.5% in back-end load charges without violating the 8.5% cap. In addition, FINRA set a 1% cap on annual 12(b)-1 fees and, perhaps more significantly, stated that true no-load funds cannot charge more than 0.25% in annual 12(b)-1 fees. If they do, they must drop the no-load label in their sales and promotional material.

Other Fees and Costs Another cost of owning mutual funds is the management fee. This is the compensation paid to the professional managers who administer the fund's portfolio. You must pay this fee regardless of whether a fund is load or no-load and whether it is an open- or closed-end fund or an exchange-traded fund. Unlike load charges, which are one-time costs, investment companies levy management and 12(b)-1 fees annually, regardless of the fund's performance. In addition, there are the administrative costs of operating the fund. These are fairly modest and represent the normal cost of doing business (e.g., the commissions paid when the fund buys and sells securities). The various fees that funds charge generally range from less than 0.2% to as much as 2% of average assets under management. In addition to these management fees, some funds charge an exchange fee, assessed whenever you transfer money from one fund to another within the same fund family, or an annual maintenance fee, to help defer the costs of providing service to low-balance accounts.

The SEC requires the mutual funds themselves to fully disclose all of their fees and expenses in a standardized, easy-to-understand format. Every fund profile or prospectus must contain, up front, a fairly detailed fee table, much like the one illustrated in Table 12.1. This table has three parts. The first specifies all shareholder transaction costs. This tells you what it's going to cost to buy and sell shares in the mutual fund. The next section lists the annual operating expenses of the fund. Showing these expenses as a percentage of average net assets, the fund must break out management fees, 12(b)-1 fees, and any other expenses. The third section provides a rundown of the total cost over time of buying, selling, and owning the fund. This part of the table contains both transaction and operating expenses and shows what the total costs would be over hypothetical 1-, 3-, 5-, and 10-year holding periods. To ensure consistency and comparability, the funds must follow a rigid set of guidelines when constructing the illustrative costs.

Other Types of Investment Companies

In addition to open-end, closed-end, and exchange-traded funds, other types of investment companies are (1) real estate investment trusts, (2) hedge funds, (3) unit investment trusts, and (4) annuities. Unit investment trusts, annuities, and hedge funds are similar to mutual funds to the extent that they, too, invest primarily in marketable securities, such as stocks and bonds. Real estate investment trusts, in contrast, invest primarily in various types of real estate–related investments, like mortgages. We'll look at real estate investment trusts and hedge funds in this section.

TABLE 12.1 MUTUAL FUND FEE TABLE (REQUIRED BY FEDERAL LAW)

The following table describes the fees and expenses that are incurred when you buy, hold, or sell shares of the fund.

Shareholder Fees (Paid by the Investor Directly)

Maximum sales charge (load) on purchases (as a % of offering price)	3%
Sales charge (load) on reinvested distributions	None
Deferred sales charge (load) on redemptions	None
Exchange fees	None
Annual account maintenance fee (for accounts under $2,500)	$12.00

Annual Fund Operating Expenses (Paid from Fund Assets)

Management fee	0.45%
Distribution and service 12(b)-1 fee	None
Other expenses	0.20%
Total Annual Fund Operating Expenses	0.65%

Example

This example is intended to help an investor compare the cost of investing in different funds. The example assumes a $10,000 investment in the fund for 1, 3, 5, and 10 years and then redemption of all fund shares at the end of those periods. The example also assumes that an investment returns 5% each year and that the fund's operating expenses remain the same. Although actual costs may be higher or lower, based on these assumptions an investor's costs would be:

1 year	$ 364
3 years	$ 502
5 years	$ 651
10 years	$1,086

Real Estate Investment Trusts   A real estate investment trust (REIT) is a type of closed-end investment company that invests money in mortgages and various types of real estate investments. A REIT is like a mutual fund in that it sells shares of stock to the investing public and uses the proceeds, along with borrowed funds, to invest in a portfolio of real estate investments. The investor, therefore, owns a part of the real estate portfolio held by the real estate investment trust. The basic appeal of REITs is that they enable investors to receive both the capital appreciation and the current income from real estate ownership without all the headaches of property management. REITs are also popular with income-oriented investors because of the very attractive dividend yields they provide.

There are three basic types of REIT. First is the *property REIT* or *equity REIT*. These are REITs that invest in physical structures such as shopping centers, hotels, apartments, and office buildings. The second type is called a *mortgage REIT*, so called because they invest in mortgages, and the third type is the hybrid REIT, which may invest in both properties and mortgages. Mortgage REITs tend to be more income-oriented. They emphasize their high current yields, which is to be expected from a security that basically invests in debt. In contrast, while equity REITs may promote their attractive current yields, most of them also offer the potential for earning varying amounts of capital gains (as their property holdings appreciate in value). In early 2015 there were 177 equity REITs, which together held $846 billion in various real estate assets. Equity REITs dominated the market. There were only 39 mortgage REITs with assets valued at $61 billion, and hybrid REITs had all but disappeared from the market.

REITs must abide by the Real Estate Investment Trust Act of 1960, which established requirements for forming a REIT, as well as rules and procedures for making investments and distributing income. Because they are required to pay out nearly all their earnings to the owners, REITs do quite a bit of borrowing to obtain funds for their investments. A number of insurance companies, mortgage bankers, and commercial banks have formed REITs, many of which are traded on the major securities exchanges. The income earned by a REIT is not taxed, but the income distributed to the owners is designated and taxed as ordinary income. REITs have become very popular in the past five to ten years, in large part because of the very attractive returns they offer. Comparative average annual returns are listed below; clearly, REITs have at least held their own against common stocks over time:

Period	REITs*	S&P 500	Nasdaq Composite
5-yr. (2009–2014)	16.6%	15.4%	15.8%
10-yr. (2002–2012)	7.5%	7.7%	8.1%

(*Source: National Association of Real Estate Investment Trusts, REIT Watch, January 2015, **https://www.reit.com/sites/default/files/reitwatch/RW1501.pdf**)

In addition to their highly competitive returns, REITs offer desirable portfolio diversification properties and very attractive dividend yields (around 4.0%), which are generally well above the yields on common stock.

Hedge Funds   First of all, in spite of the name similarities, it is important to understand that hedge funds are not mutual funds. They are totally different types of investment products! **Hedge funds** are set up as private entities, usually in the form of limited partnerships and, as such, are largely unregulated. The general partner runs the fund and directly participates in the fund's profits—often taking a "performance fee" of 10% to 20%

What Is a Hedge Fund?

of the profits, in addition to a base fee of 1% to 2% of assets under management. The limited partners are the investors and consist mainly of institutions, such as pension funds, endowments, and private banks, as well as high-income individual investors. Because hedge funds are unregulated, they can be sold only to "accredited investors," meaning the individual investor must have a net worth in excess of $1 million and/or an annual income (from qualified sources) of at least $200,000. Many hedge funds are, by choice, even more restrictive, and limit their investors to only very-high-net-worth individuals. In addition, some hedge funds limit the number of investors they'll let in (often to no more than 100 investors).

These practices, of course, stand in stark contrast to the way mutual funds operate. While hedge funds are largely unregulated, mutual funds are very highly regulated and monitored. Individuals do not need to qualify or be accredited to invest in mutual funds. Although some mutual funds do have minimum investments of $50,000 to $100,000 or more, they are the exception rather than the rule. Not so with hedge funds—many of them have minimum investments that can run into the millions of dollars. Also, mutual fund performance is open for all to see, whereas hedge funds simply do not divulge such information, at least not to the general public. Mutual funds are required by law to provide certain periodic and standardized pricing and valuation information to investors, as well as to the general public, whereas hedge funds are totally free from such requirements. The world of hedge funds is very secretive and about as non-transparent as you can get.

Hedge funds and mutual funds are similar in one respect, however: Both are pooled investment vehicles that accept investors' money and invest those funds on a collective basis. Put another way, both sell shares (or participation) in a professionally managed portfolio of securities. Most hedge funds structure their portfolios so as to reduce volatility and risk while trying to preserve capital (i.e., "hedge" against market downturns) and still deliver positive returns under different market conditions. They do so by taking often very complex market positions that involve both long and short positions, the use of various arbitrage strategies (to lock in profits), as well as the use of options, futures, and other derivative securities. Indeed, hedge funds will invest in almost any opportunity in almost any market as long as impressive gains are believed to be available at reasonable levels of risk. Thus, these funds are anything but low-risk, fairly stable investment vehicles.

CONCEPTS IN REVIEW

Answers available at
http://www.pearsonhighered.com/smart

12.1 What is a mutual fund? Discuss the mutual fund concept, including the importance of diversification and professional management.

12.2 What are the advantages and disadvantages of mutual fund ownership?

12.3 Briefly describe how a mutual fund is organized. Who are the key players in a typical mutual fund organization?

12.4 Define each of the following:

a. Open-end investment companies   b. Closed-end investment companies
c. Exchange-traded funds   d. Real estate investment trusts
e. Hedge funds

12.5 What is the difference between a load fund and a no-load fund? What are the advantages of each type? What is a 12(b)-1 fund? Can such a fund operate as a no-load fund?

12.6 Describe a back-end load, a low load, and a hidden load. How can you tell what kinds of fees and charges a fund has?

Types of Funds and Services

LG3 **LG4** Some mutual funds specialize in stocks, others in bonds. Some have maximum capital gains as an investment objective; some have high current income. Some funds appeal to speculators, others to income-oriented investors. Every fund has a particular investment objective, and each fund is expected to conform to its stated investment policy and objective. Categorizing funds according to their investment policies and objectives is a common practice in the mutual fund industry. The categories indicate similarities in how the funds manage their money and also their risk and return characteristics. Some of the more popular types of mutual funds are growth, aggressive growth, value, equity-income, balanced, growth-and-income, bond, money market, index, sector, socially responsible, asset allocation, and international funds.

Of course, it's also possible to define fund categories based on something other than stated investment objectives. For example, Morningstar, the industry's leading research and reporting service, has developed a classification system based on a fund's actual portfolio position. Essentially, it carefully evaluates the makeup of a fund's portfolio to determine where its security holdings are concentrated. It then uses that information to classify funds on the basis of investment style (growth, value, or blend), market segment (small-, mid-, or large-cap), or other factors. Such information helps mutual fund investors make informed asset allocation decisions when structuring or rebalancing their own portfolios. That benefit notwithstanding, let's stick with the investment-objective classification system noted above and examine the various types of mutual funds to see what they are and how they operate.

Types of Mutual Funds

Growth Funds The objective of a **growth fund** is simple: capital appreciation. They invest principally in well-established large- or mid-cap companies that have above-average growth potential. They offer little (if anything) in the way of dividends because the companies whose shares they buy reinvest their earnings rather than pay them out. Growth funds invest in stocks that have greater than average risk.

Aggressive-Growth Funds Aggressive-growth funds are the so-called performance funds that tend to increase in popularity when markets heat up. **Aggressive-growth funds** are highly speculative with portfolios that consist mainly of "high-flying" common stocks. These funds often buy stocks of small, unseasoned companies, and stocks with relatively high price/earnings multiples. They often invest in companies that are recovering from a period of very poor financial performance, and they may even use leverage in their portfolios (i.e., buy stocks on margin). Aggressive-growth funds are among the most volatile of all mutual funds. When the markets are good, aggressive-growth funds do well; conversely, when the markets are bad, these funds often experience substantial losses.

Value Funds **Value funds** confine their investing to stocks considered to be undervalued by the market. That is, the funds look for stocks whose prices are trading below intrinsic value. In stark contrast to growth funds, value funds look for stocks with relatively low price-to-earnings ratios, high dividend yields, and moderate amounts of financial leverage.

Value investing is not easy. It involves extensive evaluation of corporate financial statements and any other documents that will help fund managers estimate stocks' intrinsic values. The track record of value investing is quite good. Even though value investing is regarded by many as less risky than growth investing, the long-term return to investors in value funds is competitive with that from growth funds and even aggressive-growth funds. Thus, value funds are often viewed as a viable investment alternative for relatively conservative investors who are looking for the attractive returns that common stocks have to offer without taking too much risk.

Equity-Income Funds **Equity-income funds** purchase stocks with high dividend yields. Capital preservation is also an important goal of these funds, which invest heavily in high-grade common stocks, some convertible securities and preferred stocks, and occasionally even junk bonds or certain types of high-grade foreign bonds. As far as their stock holdings are concerned, they lean heavily toward blue chips, public utilities, and financial shares. In general, because of their emphasis on dividends and current income, these funds tend to hold higher-quality securities that are subject to less price volatility than the market as a whole. They're generally viewed as a fairly low-risk way of investing in stocks.

Balanced Funds **Balanced funds** tend to hold a balanced portfolio of both stocks and bonds for the purpose of generating a balanced return of both current income and long-term capital gains. They're much like equity-income funds, but balanced funds usually put more into fixed-income securities. The bonds are used principally to provide current income, and stocks are selected mainly for their long-term growth potential. Balanced funds tend to be less risky than funds that invest exclusively in common stocks.

Growth-and-Income Funds **Growth-and-income funds** also seek a balanced return made up of both current income and long-term capital gains, but they place a greater emphasis on growth of capital. Unlike balanced funds, growth-and-income funds put most of their money into equities. In fact, it's not unusual for these funds to have 80% to 90% of their capital in common stocks. They tend to confine most of their investing to quality issues, so growth-oriented blue-chip stocks appear in their portfolios, along with a fair amount of high-quality income stocks. Part of the appeal of these funds is the fairly substantial returns many have generated over the long haul. These funds involve a fair amount of risk, if for no other reason than the emphasis they place on stocks and capital gains. Thus, growth-and-income funds are most suitable for those investors who can tolerate the risk and price volatility.

Bond Funds As the name implies, **bond funds** invest exclusively in various types and grades of bonds—from Treasury and agency bonds to corporate and municipal bonds and other debt securities such as mortgage-backed securities. Income from the bonds' interest payments is the primary investment objective.

There are three important advantages to buying shares in bond funds rather than investing directly in bonds. First, the bond funds are generally more liquid than direct investments in bonds. Second, they offer a cost-effective way of achieving a high degree of diversification in an otherwise expensive asset class. (Most bonds carry minimum denominations of $1,000 to $5,000.) Third, bond funds will automatically reinvest interest and other income, thereby allowing you to earn fully compounded rates of return.

Bond funds are generally considered to be a fairly conservative form of investment, but they are not without risk. The prices of the bonds held in the fund's portfolio fluctuate with changing interest rates. In today's market, investors can find everything from high-grade government bond funds to highly speculative funds that invest in nothing but junk bonds or even in highly volatile derivative securities. Here's a list of the different types of domestic bond funds available to investors and their chief investment types.

- *Government bond funds* invest in U.S. Treasury and agency securities.

- *High-grade corporate bond funds* invest chiefly in investment-grade securities rated BBB or better.

- *High-yield corporate bond funds* are risky investments that buy junk bonds for the yields they offer.

- *Municipal bond funds* invest in tax-exempt securities. These are suitable for investors who seek tax-free income. Like their corporate counterparts, municipal bond funds can be packaged as either high-grade or high-yield funds. A special type of municipal bond fund is the so-called single-state fund, which invests in the municipal issues of only one state, thus producing (for residents of that state) interest income that is exempt from both federal and state taxes (and possibly even local/city taxes as well).

- *Mortgage-backed bond funds* put their money into various types of mortgage-backed securities of the U.S. government (e.g., GNMA issues). These funds appeal to investors for several reasons: (1) They provide diversification; (2) they are an affordable way to get into mortgage-backed securities; and (3) they allow investors to reinvest the principal portion of the monthly cash flow, thereby enabling them to preserve their capital.

- *Convertible bond funds* invest primarily in securities that can be converted or exchanged into common stocks. These funds offer investors some of the price stability of bonds, along with the capital appreciation potential of stocks.

- *Intermediate-term bond funds* invest in bonds with maturities of 10 years or less and offer not only attractive yields but relatively low price volatility as well. Shorter (two- to five-year) funds are also available; these shorter-term funds are often used as substitutes for money market investments by investors looking for higher returns on their money, especially when short-term rates are way down.

Clearly, no matter what you're looking for in a fixed-income security, you're likely to find a bond fund that fits the bill. According to the *2015 Investment Company Fact Book*, bond funds account for approximately 21% of U.S. mutual fund and exchange-traded fund assets.

Money Market Funds **Money market mutual funds,** or **money funds** for short, apply the mutual fund concept to the buying and selling of short-term money market instruments—bank certificates of deposit, U.S. Treasury bills, and the like. These funds offer investors with modest amounts of capital access to the high-yielding money market, where many instruments require minimum investments of $100,000 or more. At the close of 2014, money market funds held approximately 15% of U.S. mutual fund assets, a figure that had been shrinking for several years due to the extraordinarily low interest rates on short-term securities available since the 2008 recession.

There are several kinds of money market mutual funds:

- *General-purpose money funds* invest in any and all types of money market investment vehicles, from Treasury bills and bank CDs to corporate commercial paper. The vast majority of money funds are of this type.

FAMOUS FAILURES IN FINANCE

Breaking the Buck

Traditionally, investors have viewed money market mutual funds as the safest type of mutual fund because they generally invest in low-risk, short-term debt securities. These funds generally maintain their share price at $1, and they distribute the interest they earn on short-term securities to investors. The very first money market mutual fund, The Reserve Fund, was formed in 1971. Unfortunately, when Lehman Brothers filed for bankruptcy on September 15, 2008, the Reserve Fund was caught holding $785 million in short-term loans to Lehman. Those holdings were suddenly worthless, and that caused The Reserve Fund's share price to "break the buck" by falling to $0.97. Investors in the fund became worried about the fund's other holdings, and a flood of redemption requests poured in. Ultimately, the fund could not satisfy all of the redemption requests that it received, so the fund ceased operations and liquidated its assets. In response to this event and others during the financial crisis, the SEC imposed new restrictions on money market funds, forcing them to hold securities with higher credit ratings and greater liquidity than had been required in the past.

- *Government securities money funds* effectively eliminate any risk of default by confining their investments to Treasury bills and other short-term securities of the U.S. government or its agencies.

- *Tax-exempt money funds* limit their investing to very short (30- to 90-day) tax-exempt municipal securities. Because their income is free from federal income taxes, they appeal predominantly to investors in high tax brackets.

Just about every major brokerage firm has at least four or five money funds of its own, and hundreds more are sold by independent fund distributors. Because the maximum average maturity of their holdings cannot exceed 90 days, money funds are highly liquid investment vehicles, although their returns do move up and down with interest-rate conditions. They're also nearly immune to capital loss because at least 95% of the fund's assets must be invested in top-rated/prime-grade securities. In fact, with the check-writing privileges they offer, money funds are just as liquid as checking or savings accounts. Many investors view these funds as a convenient, safe, and (reasonably) profitable way to accumulate capital and temporarily store idle funds.

Index Funds "If you can't beat 'em, join 'em." That saying pretty much describes the idea behind index funds. Essentially, an **index fund** buys and holds a portfolio of stocks (or bonds) equivalent to those in a market index like the S&P 500. Rather than try to beat the market, as most actively managed funds do, index funds simply try to match the market. They do this through low-cost investment management. In fact, in most cases, a computer that matches the fund's holdings with those of the targeted index runs the whole portfolio almost entirely.

The approach of index funds is strictly buy-and-hold. Indeed, about the only time an index-fund portfolio changes is when the targeted market index alters its "market basket" of securities. A pleasant by-product of this buy-and-hold approach is that the funds have extremely low portfolio turnover rates and, therefore, very little in realized capital gains. As a result, aside from a modest amount of dividend income, these funds produce very little taxable income from year to year, which leads many high-income investors to view them as a type of tax-sheltered investment. Index funds have grown in popularity over the years. Since 1999, equity index funds have increased their market share (relative to all equity mutual funds) from 9.4% to 20.2%. In other words, for every $5 that investors place in stock mutual funds, they invest $1 in indexed funds. The most popular index funds are those tied to the S&P 500, accounting for roughly 33% of all assets held in indexed mutual funds.

Sector Funds A **sector fund** is a mutual fund that restricts its investments to a particular sector (or segment) of the market. For example, a health care sector fund would focus on stocks issued by drug companies, hospital management firms, medical suppliers, and biotech concerns. Among the more popular sector funds are those that concentrate in technology, financial services, real estate (REITs), natural resources, telecommunications, and health care. The overriding investment objective of a sector fund is usually capital gains. A sector fund is generally similar to a growth fund and should be considered speculative, particularly because it is not well diversified.

Socially Responsible Funds For some, investing is far more than just cranking out financial ratios and calculating investment returns. To these investors, the security selection process also includes the active, explicit consideration of moral, ethical, and environmental issues. The idea is that social concerns should play just as big a role in investment decisions as do financial matters. Not surprisingly, a number of funds cater to such investors. Known as **socially responsible funds,** they actively and directly incorporate ethics and morality into the investment decision. Their investment decisions, in effect, revolve around both morality and profitability.

Socially responsible funds consider only certain companies for inclusion in their portfolios. If a company does not meet the fund's moral, ethical, or environmental tests, fund managers simply will not buy the stock, no matter how good the bottom line looks. These funds refrain from investing in companies that derive revenues from tobacco, alcohol, gambling, weapons, or fossil fuels. In addition, the funds tend to favor firms that produce "responsible" products or services, that have strong employee relations and positive environmental records, and that are socially responsive to the communities in which they operate.

Asset Allocation Funds Studies have shown that the most important decision an investor can make is how to allocate assets among different types of investments (e.g., between stocks and bonds). Asset allocation deals in broad terms (types of securities) and does not focus on individual security selection. Because many individual investors have a tough time making asset allocation decisions, the mutual fund industry has created a product to do the job for them. Known as **asset allocation funds**, these funds spread investors' money across different types of asset classes. Whereas most mutual funds concentrate on one type of investment—whether stocks, bonds, or money market securities—asset allocation funds put money into all these assets. Many of them also include foreign securities, and some even include inflation-resistant investments, such as gold, real estate, and inflation-indexed bonds.

These funds are designed for people who want to hire fund managers not only to select individual securities but also to allocate money among the various markets. Here's how a typical asset allocation fund works. The money manager establishes a desired allocation mix for the fund, which might look something like this: 50% to U.S. stocks, 30% to bonds, 10% to foreign securities, and 10% to money market securities. The manager purchases securities in these proportions, and the overall portfolio maintains the desired mix. As market conditions change over time, the asset allocation mix changes as well.

For example, if the U.S. stock market starts to soften, the fund may reduce the (domestic) stock portion of the portfolio to, say, 35%, and simultaneously increase the foreign securities portion to 25%. There's no assurance, of course, that the money manager will make the right moves at the right time.

One special type of asset allocation fund is known as a target date fund. A **target date fund** follows an asset allocation plan tied to a specific target date. In the beginning, the fund's asset allocation is heavily tilted toward stocks, but as time passes and the fund's target date approaches, the portfolio becomes more conservative with the allocation shifting away from stocks toward bonds. These funds appeal to investors who want to save money for retirement. For example, a 25-year-old worker might choose a fund with a target date of 2055, whereas a 45-year-old might select a fund with a target date of 2035. By choosing target dates that correspond (at least roughly) to their expected retirement dates, both investors can be assured that the fund managers will gradually lower the risk profile of their investments as retirement approaches.

International Funds In their search for more diversification and better returns, U.S. investors have shown a growing interest in foreign securities. Sensing an opportunity, the mutual fund industry has been quick to respond with **international funds**—mutual funds that do all or most of their investing in foreign securities. A lot of people would like to invest in foreign securities but simply do not have the know-how to do so. International funds may be just the vehicle for such investors, provided they have at least a fundamental understanding of international economics issues and how they can affect fund returns.

Technically, the term *international fund* describes a type of fund that invests exclusively in foreign securities. Such funds often confine their activities to specific geographic regions (e.g., Mexico, Australia, Europe, or the Pacific Rim). In contrast, *global funds* invest in both foreign securities and U.S. companies—usually multinational firms. Regardless of whether they're global or international (we'll use the term *international* to apply to both), you can find just about any type of fund you could possibly want. There are international stock funds, international bond funds, and even international money market funds. There are aggressive-growth funds, balanced funds, long-term growth funds, and high-grade bond funds. There are funds that confine their investing to large, established markets (like Japan, Germany, and Australia) and others that stick to emerging markets (such as Thailand, Mexico, Chile, and even former Communist countries like Poland). In 2014 about 25% of all assets invested in stock mutual funds were invested in international funds.

Investor Services

Investors obviously buy shares in mutual funds to make money, but there are other important reasons for investing in mutual funds, not the least of which are the valuable services they provide. Some of the most sought-after mutual fund services are automatic investment and reinvestment plans, regular income programs, conversion privileges, and retirement programs.

Automatic Investment Plans It takes money to make money. For an investor, that means being able to accumulate the capital to put into the market. Mutual funds have come up with a program that makes savings and capital accumulation as painless as possible. The program is the **automatic investment plan**. This service allows fund shareholders to automatically funnel fixed amounts of money from their paychecks or bank accounts into a mutual fund. It's much like a payroll deduction plan.

This fund service has become very popular because it enables shareholders to invest on a regular basis without having to think about it. Just about every fund group offers some kind of automatic investment plan for virtually all of its stock and bond funds. To enroll, you simply fill out a form authorizing the fund to siphon a set amount (usually a minimum of $25 to $100 per period) from your bank account at regular intervals. Once enrolled, you'll be buying more shares on a regular basis. Of course, if it's a load fund, you'll still have to pay normal sales charges on your periodic investments, though many load funds reduce or eliminate the sales charge for investors participating in automatic investment plans. You can get out of the program at any time, without penalty, by simply calling the fund. Although convenience is perhaps the chief advantage of automatic investment plans, they also make solid investment sense. One of the best ways of building up a sizable amount of capital is to add funds to your investment program systematically over time. The importance of making regular contributions to your investment portfolio cannot be overstated. It ranks right up there with compound interest.

Automatic Reinvestment Plans   An automatic reinvestment plan is another of the real draws of mutual funds and is offered by just about every open-end fund. Whereas automatic investment plans deal with money you are putting into a fund, automatic reinvestment plans deal with the dividends the funds pay to their shareholders. The **automatic reinvestment plans** of mutual funds enable you to keep your capital fully employed by using dividend and/or capital gains income to buy additional shares in the fund. Most funds do not charge commissions for purchases made with reinvested funds. Keep in mind, however, that even though you may reinvest all dividends and capital gains distributions, the IRS still treats them as cash receipts and taxes them as investment income in the year in which you received them.

Automatic reinvestment plans enable you to earn fully compounded rates of return. By plowing back profits, you can put them to work in generating even more earnings. Indeed, the effects of these plans on total accumulated capital over the long run can be substantial. Figure 12.5 shows the long-term impact of reinvested dividend and capital gain income for the S&P 500 Index. In the illustration, we assume that the investor starts with $10,000 in January 1988. The upper line shows how much money accumulates if the investor keeps reinvesting dividends as they arrive, and the lower line shows what happens if the investor fails to do so. Over time, the difference in these two approaches becomes quite large. With reinvested dividends, the investor would have had a portfolio worth $149,223 by July 2015, but if the investor had failed to reinvest dividends, the portfolio value would have reached just $80,787.

Regular Income   Automatic investment and reinvestment plans are great for the long-term investor. But what about the investor who's looking for a steady stream of income? Once again, mutual funds have a service to meet this need. Called a **systematic withdrawal plan,** it's offered by most open-end funds. Once enrolled, an investor automatically receives a predetermined amount of money every month or quarter. Most funds require a minimum investment of $5,000 or more to participate, and the size of the minimum payment normally must be $50 or more per period (with no limit on the maximum). The funds will pay out the monthly or quarterly income first from dividends and realized capital gains. If this source proves to be inadequate and the shareholder so authorizes, the fund can then tap the principal or original paid-in capital to meet the required periodic payments.

Conversion Privileges   Sometimes investors find it necessary to switch out of one fund and into another. For example, your objectives or the investment climate itself may have changed. **Conversion** (or **exchange**) **privileges** were devised to meet such needs

FIGURE 12.5   The Effects of Reinvesting Dividends

Reinvesting dividends can have a tremendous impact on one's investment position. This graph shows the results of investing $10,000 in the S&P 500 in January 1988 with and without reinvestment of dividends. (Source: Author's calculations and Yahoo!Finance.)

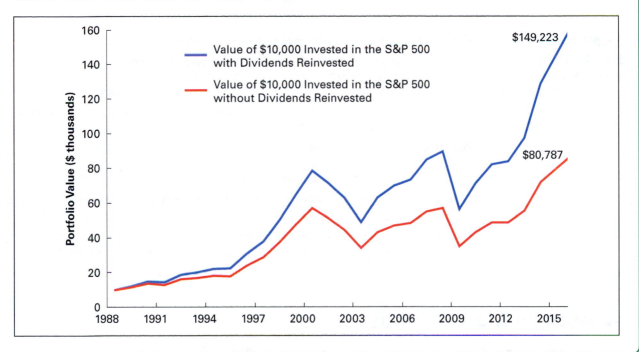

conveniently and economically. Investment management companies that offer a number of different funds—known as **fund families**—often provide conversion privileges that enable shareholders to move money from one fund to another, either by phone or via the Internet. The only constraint is that the switches must be confined to the same family of funds. For example, you can switch from a Dreyfus growth fund to a Dreyfus money fund, or any other fund managed by Dreyfus.

Conversion privileges are usually considered beneficial because they allow you to meet ever-changing long-term goals, and they also permit you to manage your mutual fund holdings more aggressively by moving in and out of funds as the investment environment changes. Unfortunately, there is one major drawback. For tax purposes, the exchange of shares from one fund to another is regarded as a sale transaction followed by a subsequent purchase of a new security. As a result, if any capital gains exist at the time of the exchange, you are liable for the taxes on that profit, even though the holdings were not truly "liquidated."

Retirement Programs As a result of government legislation, self-employed individuals are permitted to divert a portion of their pretax income into self-directed retirement plans (SEPs). Also, U.S. workers are allowed to establish individual retirement arrangements (IRAs). Indeed, with legislation passed in 1997, qualified investors can now choose between deductible and nondeductible (Roth) IRAs. Even those who make too much to qualify for one of these programs can set up special nondeductible IRAs. Today all mutual funds provide a service that allows individuals to set up tax-deferred retirement programs as either IRA or Keogh accounts—or, through their place of employment, to participate in a tax-sheltered retirement plan, such as a 401(k). The funds set up the plans and handle all the administrative details so that the shareholder can easily take full advantage of available tax savings.

CONCEPTS IN REVIEW

Answers available at
http://www.pearsonhighered.com/smart

12.7 Briefly describe each of the following types of mutual funds:

a. Aggressive-growth funds
b. Equity-income funds
c. Growth-and-income funds
d. Bond funds
e. Sector funds
f. Socially responsible funds

12.8 What is an asset allocation fund and how does it differ from other types of mutual funds? How does a target date fund work?

12.9 If growth, income, and capital preservation are the primary objectives of mutual funds, why do we bother to categorize funds by type? Do you think such classifications are helpful in the fund selection process? Explain.

12.10 What are fund families? What advantages do fund families offer investors? Are there any disadvantages?

12.11 Briefly describe some of the investor services provided by mutual funds. What are automatic reinvestment plans, and how do they differ from automatic investment plans?

Investing in Mutual Funds

LG5 LG6 Suppose you are confronted with the following situation. You have money to invest and are trying to select the right place to put it. You obviously want to pick a security that meets your idea of acceptable risk and will generate an attractive rate of return. The problem is that you must make the selection from a list containing thousands of securities. That's basically what you're facing when trying to select a suitable mutual fund. However, if you approach the problem systematically, it may not be so formidable a task. First, it might be helpful to examine more closely the various investor uses of mutual funds. With this background, we can then look at the selection process and at several measures of return that you can use to assess performance. As we will see, it is possible to whittle down the list of alternatives by matching your investment needs with the investment objectives of the funds.

Investor Uses of Mutual Funds

Mutual funds can be used in a variety of ways. For instance, performance funds can serve as a vehicle for capital appreciation, whereas bond funds can provide current income. Regardless of the kind of income a mutual fund provides, investors tend to use these securities as (1) a way to accumulate wealth, (2) a storehouse of value, or (3) a speculative vehicle for achieving high rates of return.

Accumulation of Wealth This is probably the most common reason for using mutual funds. Basically, the investor uses mutual funds over the long haul to build up investment capital. Depending on your goals, a modest amount of risk may be acceptable, but usually preservation of capital and capital stability are considered important. The whole idea is to form a "partnership" with the mutual fund in building up as big a pool of capital as possible. You provide the capital by systematically investing and reinvesting in the fund and the fund provides the return by doing its best to invest your resources wisely.

Storehouse of Value Investors also use mutual funds as a storehouse of value. The idea is to find a place where investment capital can be fairly secure and relatively free from deterioration yet still generate a relatively attractive rate of return. Short- and intermediate-term bond funds are logical choices for such purposes, and so are money funds. Capital preservation and income over the long term are very important to some investors. Others might seek storage of value only for the short term, using, for example, money funds as a place to "sit it out" until a more attractive opportunity comes along.

Speculation and Short-Term Trading Although speculation is becoming more common, it is still not widely used by most mutual fund investors. The reason, of course, is that most mutual funds are long-term in nature and thus not meant to be used as aggressive trading vehicles. However, a growing number of funds (e.g., sector funds) now cater to speculators. Some investors have found that mutual funds are, in fact, attractive for speculation and short-term trading.

One way to do this is to aggressively trade in and out of funds as the investment climate changes. Load charges can be avoided (or reduced) by dealing in families of funds offering low-cost conversion privileges and/or by dealing only in no-load funds. Other investors might choose mutual funds as a long-term investment but seek high rates of return by investing in funds that follow very aggressive trading strategies. These are usually the fairly specialized, smaller funds such as leverage funds, option funds, emerging-market funds, small-cap aggressive-growth funds, and sector funds. In essence, investors in such funds are simply letting professional money managers handle their accounts in a way they would like to see them handled: aggressively.

The Selection Process

When it comes to mutual funds, there is one question every investor has to answer right up front. Why invest in a mutual fund to begin with—why not "go it alone" by buying individual stocks and bonds directly? For beginning investors and investors with little capital, the answer is simple: With mutual funds, you are able to achieve far more diversification than you could ever obtain on your own. Plus, you get the help of professional money managers at a very reasonable cost. For more seasoned investors, the answers are probably more involved. Certainly, diversification and professional money management come into play, but there are other reasons as well. The competitive returns mutual funds offer are a factor, as are the services they provide. Many seasoned investors simply have decided they can get better returns by carefully selecting mutual funds than by investing on their own. Some of these investors use part of their capital to buy and sell individual securities on their own and use the rest to buy mutual funds that invest in areas they don't fully understand or don't feel well informed about. For example, they'll use mutual funds to get into foreign markets or buy mortgage-backed securities.

Once you have decided to use mutual funds, you must decide which fund(s) to buy. The selection process involves putting into action all you know about mutual funds in order to gain as much return as possible from an acceptable level of risk. It begins with an assessment of your investment needs. Obviously, you want to select from those thousands of funds the one or two (or six or eight) that will best meet your total investment needs.

Objectives and Motives for Using Funds The place to start is with your investment objectives. Why do you want to invest in a mutual fund, and what are you looking for in a fund? Obviously, an attractive rate of return would be desirable, but there is also the matter of a tolerable amount of risk exposure. Probably, when you look at your own risk temperament in relation to the various types of mutual funds available, you will discover that certain types of funds are more appealing to you than others. For instance, aggressive-growth or sector funds are usually not attractive to individuals who wish to avoid high exposure to risk.

Another important factor is the intended use of the mutual fund. Do you want to invest in mutual funds as a means of accumulating wealth, as a storehouse of value, or to speculate for high rates of return? This information puts into clearer focus the question of what you want to do with your investment dollars. Finally, there is the matter of the services provided by the fund. If you are particularly interested in certain services, be sure to look for them in the funds you select.

What the Funds Offer Just as each individual has a set of investment needs, each fund has its own investment objective, its own manner of operation, and its own range of services. These elements are useful in helping you to assess investment alternatives. Where do you find such information? One obvious place is the fund's profile, or its prospectus. Publications such as the *Wall Street Journal*, *Barron's*, *Money*, *Fortune*, and *Forbes* also provide a wealth of operating and performance statistics.

There are also a number of reporting services that provide background information and assessments on funds. Among the best in this category are *Morningstar Mutual Funds* and *Value Line Mutual Fund Survey* (which produces a mutual fund report similar to its stock report). There also are all sorts of performance statistics available on the Internet. For example, there are scores of free finance websites, like Yahoo! Finance, where you can obtain historical information on a fund's performance, security holdings, risk profile, load charges, and purchase information.

Whittling Down the Alternatives At this point, fund selection becomes a process of elimination. You can eliminate a large number of funds from consideration simply because they fail to meet your specified needs. Some funds may be too risky; others may be unsuitable as a storehouse of value. Thus, rather than try to evaluate thousands of different funds, you can narrow down the list to two or three types of funds that match your investment needs. From here, you can whittle down the list a bit more by introducing other constraints. For example, because of cost considerations, you may want to consider only no-load or low-load funds (more on this topic below). Or you may be seeking certain services that are important to your investment goals.

Another attribute of a fund that you may want to consider is its *tax efficiency*. As a rule, funds that have low dividends and low asset turnover do not expose their shareholders to high taxes and therefore have higher tax-efficiency ratings. And while you're looking at performance, check out the fund's fee structure. Be on guard for funds that charge abnormally high management fees.

Another important consideration is how well a particular fund fits into your portfolio. If you're trying to follow a certain asset allocation strategy, then be sure to take that into account when you're thinking about adding a fund to your portfolio. In other words, evaluate any particular fund in the context of your overall portfolio.

Finally, how much weight should you give to a fund's past performance when deciding whether you want to invest? Although it may seem intuitive that funds with good past performance should make better investments, remember superior past performance is no guarantee of future success. In fact, we would make the stronger statement that past performance has almost no correlation with future performance. Accordingly, we recommend that you place more weight on other factors such as the fund's investment objective and its costs when making your investment decisions.

Stick with No-Loads or Low-Loads There's a long-standing "debate" in the mutual fund industry regarding load funds and no-load funds. Do load funds add value? If not, why pay the load charges? As it turns out, empirical results generally do not support the idea that load funds provide added value. Load-fund returns, on average, do not seem to be any better than the returns from no-load funds. In fact, in many cases, the funds with abnormally high loads and 12(b)-1 charges often produce returns that are far less than what you can get from no-load funds. In addition, because of compounding, the differential returns tend to widen with longer holding periods. These results should come as no surprise because big load charges and/or 12(b)-1 fees reduce your investable capital—and therefore the amount of money you have working for you. In fact, the only way a load fund can overcome this handicap is to produce superior returns, which is no easy thing to do year in and year out. Granted, a handful of load funds have produced very attractive returns over extended periods of time, but they are the exception rather than the rule.

Obviously, it's in your best interest to pay close attention to load charges (and other fees). As a rule, to maximize returns, you should seriously consider sticking to no-load funds or to low-loads (funds that have total load charges, including 12(b)-1 fees, of 3% or less). There may well be times when the higher costs are justified, but far more often than not, you're better off trying to minimize load charges. That should not be difficult to do because there are thousands of no-load and low-load funds from which to choose. What's more, most of the top-performing funds are found in the universe of no-loads or low-loads. So why would you even want to look anywhere else?

Investing in Closed-End Funds

The assets of closed-end funds (CEFs) represent just over 1.5% of the $18 trillion invested in open-end mutual funds. Like open-end funds, CEFs come in a variety of types and styles, including funds that specialize in municipal bonds, taxable bonds, various types of equity securities, and international securities, as well as regional and single-country funds. Historically, unlike the open-end market, bond funds have accounted for the larger share of assets in closed-end funds. In 2014 there was $170 billion worth of bond CEFs assets, or 59% of CEFs assets. Equity CEFs totaled $119 billion in assets for 2014.

Some Key Differences between Closed-End and Open-End Funds Because closed-end funds trade like stocks, you must deal with a broker to buy or sell shares, and the usual brokerage commissions apply. Open-end funds, in contrast, are bought from and sold to the fund operators themselves. Another difference between open- and closed-end funds is their liquidity. You can buy and sell relatively large dollar amounts of an open-end mutual fund at its net asset value (NAV) without worrying about affecting the price. However, a relatively large buy or sell order for a CEF could easily bump its price up or down. Like open-end funds, most CEFs offer dividend reinvestment plans, but in many cases, that's about it. CEFs simply don't provide the full range of services that mutual fund investors are accustomed to.

All things considered, probably the most important difference is the way these funds are priced in the marketplace. As we discussed earlier in the chapter, CEFs have two values—a market value (or stock price) and an NAV. They are rarely the same because CEFs typically trade at either a premium or a discount. A *premium* occurs when a fund's shares trade for more than its NAV; a *discount* occurs when the fund's shares trade for less than its NAV. As a rule, CEFs trade at discounts. Exactly why CEFs trade at a discount is not fully understood, and financial experts sometimes refer to this tendency as the closed-end fund puzzle. The puzzle is that closed-end fund share prices are priced lower than the corresponding NAVs. It's as if when you buy shares in a CEF, you are buying the underlying stocks in the fund at a discount. Some of the possible reasons that CEFs trade at a discount include the following.

- Investors anticipate that the fund's future performance may be poor, so they pay less for shares in the fund up front.

- Shares held by the fund are illiquid, so if they are ever sold, they will sell for less than their current market prices.

- Shares held by the fund have built-in unrealized capital gains, and because investors will eventually be required to pay taxes on those gains, they are unwilling to pay the full NAV when they purchase fund shares.

- Investor sentiment may cause fund prices to deviate from NAVs; when sentiment is positive, fund shares trade at a premium, but when investors are more pessimistic, fund shares trade at a discount.

Information about CEFs is widely available in print and online sources. Figure 12.6 illustrates some of the free CEF information that you can find at Morningstar's website. In addition to each fund's name, you can quickly determine whether it currently trades at a discount or a premium relative to NAV. Morningstar also provides the year-to-date return based on the performance of the fund's share price as well as the return based on the fund's NAV.

The premium or discount on CEFs is calculated as follows:

Equation 12.1

$$\text{Premium (or discount)} = (\text{Share price} - \text{NAV}) \div \text{NAV}$$

Example

Suppose Fund A has an NAV of $10. If its share price is $8, it sells at a 20% discount. That is,

$$\text{Premium (or discount)} = (\$8 - \$10)/\$10$$
$$= -\$2/\$10 = -0.20 = 20\%$$

This negative value indicates that the fund is trading at a discount (or below its NAV). On the other hand, if this same fund were priced at $12 per share, it would be trading at a premium of 20%—that is, ($12 − $10)/$10 = $2/$10 = 0.20.

FIGURE 12.6 Selected Performance of CEFs

The figure demonstrates information about closed-end funds available at no cost from the Morningstar website. (Source: http://news.morningstar.com/CELists/CEReturns.html, accessed July 4, 2015. Courtesy of Morningstar, Inc. Used with permission.)

Closed End Funds: Overview								
Fund Name	Premiums/ Discounts	Market Return YTD	NAV Return YTD	3 Year Avg Standard Deviation	Morningstar Star Rating	Avg Daily Volume Shares	Net Assets $mil	Manager Tenure
Tekla Life Sciences Investors (HQL)	-1.93	18.97	19.91	15.31	Not Rated	86,318	562	12.5
Japan Smaller Capitalization (JOF)	-10.69	21.85	19.28	11.74	Not Rated	53,026	347	7.9
MS China A Share (CAF)	-19.55	8.66	18.21	23.16	★★★★	273,806	898	8.8
Tekla Healthcare Investors (HQH)	-0.11	17.89	17.87	14.06	Not Rated	141,640	1,306	9.4
Aberdeen Japan Equity Fund (JEQ)	-8.47	22.90	15.65	12.99	Not Rated	29,855	124	1.3
Asia Pacific Fund (APB)	-11.53	13.65	15.46	13.68	Not Rated	12,681	150	3.0
BlackRock Health Sciences (BME)	-0.32	4.04	15.43	9.90	Not Rated	18,853	340	10.3
JPMorgan China Region (JFC)	-15.00	10.88	13.77	14.59	★★★	9,724	142	9.8
Aberdeen Israel (ISL)	-14.48	12.10	12.57	9.98	★★★★	5,353	89	6.0
China Fund Inc (CHN)	-14.10	9.60	12.53	12.70	★★★★	45,656	365	4.1
New Ireland Fund (IRL)	-13.70	13.53	11.76	12.64	★★	10,926	80	4.0
New Germany Fund (GF)	-8.16	10.77	10.29	13.82	★★★★	35,090	254	3.5
Columbia Seligman Premium Tech Growth (STK)	0.86	3.94	10.28	11.26	Not Rated	73,376	284	4.8
Gabelli Health & Wellness (GRX)	-10.79	11.23	10.17	10.29	Not Rated	65,475	253	6.1
PIMCO Global StocksPLUS & Income (PGP)	36.35	-3.30	9.87	10.68	★★★★★	75,784	137	10.2
Templeton Russia & East Europe (TRF)	-10.30	11.22	9.84	21.55	★★	44,949	59	18.3
Templeton Dragon Fund (TDF)	-14.64	2.58	9.64	13.74	★★★	63,773	1,043	17.7
Taiwan Fund (TWN)	-8.42	9.72	9.50	11.99	★★	9,186	161	3.8
MS India Investment (IIF)	-11.75	5.02	9.44	20.67	Not Rated	48,687	496	10.4
Korea Fund (KF)	-7.19	11.54	9.02	13.07	★	12,002	345	17.8

What to Look for in a Closed-End Fund If you know what to look for and your timing and selection are good, you may find that some deeply discounted CEFs provide a great way to earn attractive returns. For example, if a fund trades at a 20% discount, you pay only 80 cents for each dollar's worth of assets. If you can buy a fund at an abnormally wide discount (say, more than 10%) and then sell it when the discount narrows or turns to a premium, you can enhance your overall return. In fact, even if the discount does not narrow, your return will be improved because the yield on your investment is higher than it would be with an otherwise equivalent open-end fund.

Example

> Suppose a CEF trades at $8, a 20% discount from its NAV of $10. If the fund distributed $1 in dividends for the year, it would yield 12.5% ($1 divided by its $8 price). However, if it was a no-load, open-end fund, it would be trading at its higher NAV and therefore would yield only 10% ($1 divided by its $10 NAV).

Thus, when investing in CEFs, pay special attention to the size of the premium and discount. In particular, keep your eyes open for funds trading at deep discounts because that feature alone can enhance returns. One final point to keep in mind about closed-end funds. Stay clear of new issues (IPOs) of closed-end funds and funds that sell at steep premiums. Never buy new CEFs when they are brought to the market as IPOs. Why? Because IPOs are nearly always brought to the market at hefty premiums, which are necessary to cover the underwriter spread. Thus, you face the almost inevitable fate of losing money as the shares fall to a discount, or at the minimum, to their NAVs within a month or two.

For the most part, except for the premium or discount, you should analyze a CEF just like any other mutual fund. That is, check out the fund's expense ratio, portfolio turnover rate, past performance, cash position, and so on. In addition, study the history of the discount. Also, keep in mind that with CEFs, you probably will not get a prospectus (as you might with an open-end fund) because they do not continuously offer new shares to investors.

Measuring Performance

As in any investment decision, return performance is a part of the mutual fund selection process. The level of dividends paid by the fund, its capital gains, and its growth in capital are all-important aspects of return. Such return information enables you to judge the investment behavior of a fund and to appraise its performance in relation to other funds and investments. Here, we will look at different measures that investors can use to assess mutual fund returns. Also, because risk is so important in defining the investment behavior of a fund, we will examine mutual fund risk as well.

Sources of Return An open-end mutual fund has three potential sources of return: (1) dividend income, (2) capital gains distribution, and (3) change in the price (or net asset value) of the fund. Depending on the type of fund, some mutual funds derive more income from one source than from another. For example, we would normally expect income-oriented funds to have much higher dividend income than capital gains distributions.

Open-end mutual funds regularly publish reports that recap investment performance. One such report is the *Summary of Income and Capital Changes*, an example of which appears in Table 12.2. This statement, found in the fund's profile or prospectus,

TABLE 12.2 A REPORT OF MUTUAL FUND INCOME AND CAPITAL CHANGES (FOR A SHARE OUTSTANDING THROUGHOUT THE YEAR)

		2016	2015	2014
1.	**Net asset value, beginning of period**	$24.47	$27.03	$24.26
2.	**Income from investment operations**			
3.	Net investment income	$ 0.60	$ 0.66	$ 0.50
4.	Net gains on securities (realized and unrealized)	6.37	(1.74)	3.79
5.	Total from investment operations	$ 6.97	($ 1.08)	$ 4.29
6.	**Less distributions:**			
7.	Dividends from net investment income	($ 0.55)	($ 0.64)	($ 0.50)
8.	Distributions from realized gains	(1.75)	(0.84)	(1.02)
9.	Total distributions	($ 2.30)	($ 1.48)	($ 1.52)
10.	**Net asset value, end of period**	$29.14	$ 24.47	$ 27.03
11.	**Total return**	28.48%	(4.00%)	17.68%
12.	**Ratios/supplemental data**			
13.	Net assets, end of period ($000)	$307,951	$153,378	$108,904
14.	Ratio of expenses to average net assets	1.04%	0.85%	0.94%
15.	Ratio of net investment income to average net assets	1.47%	2.56%	2.39%
16.	Portfolio turnover rate[*]	85%	144%	74%

*Portfolio turnover rate relates the number of shares bought and sold by the fund to the total number of shares held in the fund's portfolio. A high turnover rate (in excess of 100%) means the fund has been doing a lot of trading.

gives a brief overview of the fund's investment activity, including expense ratios and portfolio turnover rates. Of interest to us here is the top part of the report (which runs from "Net asset value, beginning of period" to "Net asset value, end of period"—lines 1 to 10). This part reveals the amount of dividend income and capital gains distributed to the shareholders, along with any change in the fund's net asset value.

Dividend income (see line 7 of Table 12.2) is derived from the dividend and interest income earned on the security holdings of the mutual fund. It is paid out of the net investment income that's left after the fund has met all operating expenses. When the fund receives dividend or interest payments, it passes these on to shareholders in the form of dividend payments. The fund accumulates all of the current income for the period and then pays it out on a prorated basis. Thus, if a fund earned, say, $2 million in dividends and interest in a given year and if that fund had one million shares outstanding, each share would receive an annual dividend payment of $2. Because the mutual fund itself is tax exempt, any taxes due on dividend earnings are payable by the individual investor. For funds that are not held in tax-deferred accounts, like IRAs or 401(k)s, the amount of taxes due on dividends will depend on the source of such dividends. That is, if these distributions are derived from dividends earned on the fund's common stock holdings, then they are subject to a preferential tax rate of 15%, or less. However, if these distributions are derived from interest earnings on bonds, dividends from REITs, or dividends from most types of preferred stocks, then such dividends do not qualify for the preferential tax treatment, and instead are taxed as ordinary income.

Capital gains distributions (see line 8) work on the same principle, except that these payments are derived from the capital gains actually earned by the fund. It works like this: Suppose the fund bought some stock a year ago for $50 and sold that stock in the current period for $75 per share. Clearly, the fund has achieved capital gains of $25 per share. If it held 50,000 shares of this stock, it would have realized a total capital gain of $1,250,000 (i.e., $25 × 50,000 = $1,250,000). Given that the fund has one million shares outstanding, each share is entitled to $1.25 in the form of a capital gains distribution. (From a tax perspective, if the capital gains are long-term, then they qualify for the preferential tax rate of 15% or less; if not, then they're treated as ordinary income.) Note that these (capital gains) distributions apply only to realized capital gains (that is, the security holdings were actually sold and the capital gains actually earned).

Unrealized capital gain (or paper profits) are what make up the third and final element of a mutual fund's return. When the fund's holdings go up or down in price, the net asset value of the fund moves accordingly. Suppose an investor buys into a fund at $10 per share and sometime later the fund's NAV is quoted at $12.50. The difference of $2.50 per share is the unrealized capital gain. It represents the profit that shareholders would receive (and are entitled to) if the fund were to sell its holdings. (Actually, as Table 12.2 shows, some of the change in net asset value can also be made up of undistributed income.)

For closed-end investment companies, the return is derived from the same three sources as that for open-end funds, and from a fourth source as well: changes in price discounts or premiums. But because the discount or premium is already embedded in the share price of a fund, for a closed-end fund, the third element of return—change in share price—is made up not only of change in net asset value but also of change in price discount or premium.

Measures of Return A simple but effective measure of performance is to describe mutual fund returns in terms of the three major sources noted above: dividends earned, capital gains distributions received, and change in price. When dealing with investment horizons of one year or less, we can convert these fund payoffs into a return figure by using the standard holding period return (HPR) formula. The computations are illustrated here using the 2016 figures from Table 12.2. In 2016 this hypothetical no-load, open-end fund paid 55 cents per share in dividends and another $1.75 in capital gains distributions. It had a price at the beginning of the year of $24.47 that rose to $29.14 by the end of the year. Thus, summarizing this investment performance, we have

Price (NAV) at the beginning of the year (line 1)	$24.47
Price (NAV) at the end of the year (line 10)	$29.14
Net increase	$ 4.67
Return for the year:	
Dividends received (line 7)	$ 0.55
Capital gains distributions (line 8)	$ 1.75
Net increase in price (NAV)	$ 4.67
Total return	$ 6.97
Holding period return (HPR) (Total return/beginning price)	**28.48%**

This HPR measure is comparable to the procedure used by the fund industry to report annual returns: This same value can be seen in Table 12.2, line 11, which shows the fund's "Total return." It not only captures all the important elements of mutual fund return but also provides a handy indication of yield. Note that the fund had a total dollar return of $6.97, and on the basis of a beginning investment of $24.47, the fund produced an annual return of nearly 28.5%.

HPR with Reinvested Dividends and Capital Gains Many mutual fund investors have their dividends and/or capital gains distributions reinvested in the fund. How do you measure return when you receive your (dividend/capital gains) payout in additional shares of stock rather than cash? With slight modifications, you can continue to use holding period return. The only difference is that you must keep track of the number of shares acquired through reinvestment.

To illustrate, let's continue with the example above. Assume that you initially bought 200 shares in the mutual fund and also that you were able to acquire shares through the fund's reinvestment program at an average price of $26.50 a share. Thus, the $460 in dividends and capital gains distributions $[(\$0.55 + \$1.75) \times 200]$ provided you with another 17.36 shares in the fund (i.e., $460/$26.50). The holding period return under these circumstances would relate the market value of the stock holdings at the beginning of the period with the holdings at the end.

Equation 12.2

$$\text{Holding period return} = \frac{\left(\begin{array}{c}\text{Number of}\\\text{shares at end}\\\text{of period}\end{array} \times \begin{array}{c}\text{Ending}\\\text{price}\end{array}\right) - \left(\begin{array}{c}\text{Number of}\\\text{shares at beginning}\\\text{of period}\end{array} \times \begin{array}{c}\text{Initial}\\\text{price}\end{array}\right)}{\left(\begin{array}{c}\text{Number of shares}\\\text{at beginning of}\\\text{period}\end{array} \times \begin{array}{c}\text{Initial}\\\text{price}\end{array}\right)}$$

Thus, the holding period return on this investment would be

$$\text{Holding period return} = \frac{(217.36 \times \$29.14) - (200 \times \$24.47)}{(200 \times \$24.47)}$$

$$= \frac{(\$6,333.87) - (\$4,894.00)}{(\$4,894.00)} = \underline{29.4\%}$$

This holding period return, like the preceding one, provides a rate-of-return measure that you can use to compare the performance of this fund to those of other funds and investment vehicles.

Measuring Long-Term Returns Rather than use one-year holding periods, it is sometimes necessary to assess the performance of mutual funds over extended periods of time. In these cases, using the holding period return as a measure of performance would be inappropriate because it ignores the time value of money. Instead, when faced with multiple-year investment horizons, we can use the present value–based internal rate of return (IRR) procedure to determine the fund's average annual compound rate of return.

To illustrate, refer once again to Table 12.2. Assume that this time we want to find the annual rate of return over the full three-year period (2014 through 2016). We see that the mutual fund had the following annual dividends and capital gains distributions:

Item	2016	2015	2014
Annual dividends paid	$0.55	$0.64	$0.50
Annual capital gains distributed	$1.75	$0.84	$1.02
Total distributions	$2.30	$1.48	$1.52

Given that the fund had a price of $24.26 at the beginning of the period (1/1/14) and was trading at $29.14 at the end of 2016 (three years later), we have the following time line of cash flows.

Initial Cash Flow	Subsequent Cash Flows		
	Year 1	Year 2	Year 3
$24.26	$1.52	$1.48	$2.30 + $29.14
(Beginning Price)	(Distributions)	(Distributions)	(Distributions + Ending Price)

We want to find the discount rate that will equate the annual dividends/capital gains distributions and the ending price in year 3 to the beginning (2014) price of the fund ($24.26).

Using standard present value calculations, we find that the mutual fund in Table 12.2 provided an annual rate of return of 13.1% over the three-year period. That is, at 13.1%, the present value of the cash flows in years 1, 2, and 3 equals the beginning price of the fund ($24.26). Such information helps us assess fund performance and compare the return performance of various investments.

According to SEC regulations, if mutual funds report historical returns, they must do so in a standardized format that employs fully compounded, total-return figures similar to those obtained from the above present value–based calculations. The funds are not required to report such information, but if they do cite performance in their promotional material, they must follow a full-disclosure manner of presentation that takes into account not only dividends and capital gains distributions but also any increases or decreases in the fund's NAV that have occurred over the preceding 1-, 3-, 5-, and 10-year periods.

Returns on Closed-End Funds The returns of CEFs have traditionally been reported on the basis of their NAVs. That is, price premiums and discounts were ignored when computing return measures. However, it is becoming increasingly common to see return performance expressed in terms of actual market prices, a practice that captures the impact of changing market premiums or discounts on holding period returns. As you might expect, the greater the premiums or discounts and the greater the changes in these values over time, the greater their impact on reported returns. It's not at all uncommon for CEFs to have different market-based and NAV-based holding period returns. Using NAVs, you find the returns on CEFs in exactly the same way as you do the returns on open-end funds. In contrast, when using actual market prices to measure return, all you need do is substitute the market price of the fund (with its embedded premium or discount) for the corresponding NAV in the holding period or internal rate of return measures.

Some CEF investors like to run both NAV-based and market-based measures of return to see how changing premiums (or discounts) have affected the returns on their mutual fund holdings. Even so, as a rule, NAV-based return numbers are generally viewed as the preferred measures of performance. Because fund managers often have little or no control over changes in premiums or discounts, NAV-based measures are felt to give a truer picture of the performance of the fund itself.

The Matter of Risk Because most mutual funds are so diversified, their investors are largely immune to the unsystematic risks normally present with individual securities. Even with extensive diversification, however, most funds are still exposed to a considerable amount of systematic risk or market risk. In fact, because mutual fund portfolios are so well diversified, they often tend to perform very much like the market—or like the segment of the market that the fund targets. Although a few funds, like gold funds, tend to be defensive (countercyclical), market risk is still an important ingredient for most types of mutual funds, both open- and closed-end. You should be aware of the effect the general market has on the investment performance of a mutual fund. For example, if the market is trending downward and you anticipate that trend to continue, it might be best to place any new investment capital into something like a money fund until the market trend reverses.

Another important risk consideration revolves around the management practices of the fund itself. If the portfolio is managed conservatively, the risk of a loss in capital is likely to be much less than that for aggressively managed funds. Alternatively, the more speculative are the investment goals of the fund, the greater the risk of instability in the net asset value. But, a conservatively managed portfolio does not eliminate all price volatility. The securities in the portfolio are still subject to inflation, interest rate, and general market risks. However, these risks are generally less with funds whose investment objectives and portfolio management practices are more conservative.

CONCEPTS IN REVIEW

Answers available at
http://www.pearsonhighered.com/smart

12.12 How important is the general behavior of the market in affecting the price performance of mutual funds? Explain. Does the future behavior of the market matter in the selection process? Explain.

12.13 What is the major/dominant type of closed-end fund? How do CEFs differ from open-end funds?

12.14 Identify three potential sources of return to mutual fund investors and briefly discuss how each could affect total return to shareholders. Explain how the discount or premium of a closed-end fund can also be treated as a return to investors.

12.15 Discuss the various types of risk to which mutual fund shareholders are exposed. What is the major risk exposure of mutual funds? Are all funds subject to the same level of risk? Explain.

MyFinanceLab

Here is what you should know after reading this chapter. MyFinanceLab will help you identify what you know and where to go when you need to practice.

What You Should Know	Key Terms	Where to Practice
LG1 **Describe the basic features of mutual funds and note what they have to offer as investments.** Mutual fund shares represent ownership in a diversified, professionally managed portfolio of securities. Many investors who lack the time, know-how, or commitment to manage their own money turn to mutual funds. Mutual funds' shareholders benefit from a level of diversification and investment performance they might otherwise find difficult to achieve. They also can invest with a limited amount of capital and can obtain investor services not available elsewhere.	actively managed fund, *p. 471* expense ratio, *p. 472* mutual fund, *p. 469* passively managed fund, *p. 471* pooled diversification, *p. 470*	MyFinanceLab Study Plan 12.1
LG2 **Distinguish between open- and closed-end funds, ETFs, and other types of professionally managed investment companies, and discuss the various types of fund loads, fees, and charges.** Open-end funds have no limit on the number of shares they may issue. Closed-end funds have a fixed number of shares outstanding and trade in the secondary markets like shares of common stock. Exchange-traded funds (ETFs) possess characteristics of both open-end and closed-end funds. Other types of investment companies are unit investment trusts, hedge funds (private, unregulated investment vehicles available to institutional and high-net-worth individuals), REITs (which invest in various types of real estate), and variable annuities. Mutual fund investors face an array of loads, fees, and charges, including front-end loads, back-end loads, annual 12(b)-1 charges, and annual management fees. Some of these costs are one-time charges (e.g., front-end loads). Others are paid annually (e.g., 12(b)-1 and management fees). Investors should understand fund costs, which can drag down fund performance and return.	back-end load, *p. 480* closed-end fund, *p. 476* fire sale, *p. 475* hedge fund, *p. 482* load fund, *p. 480* low-load fund, *p. 480* net asset value (NAV), *p. 475* no-load fund, *p. 480* open-end fund, *p. 475* real estate investment trust (REIT), *p. 482* redemption fee 12(b)-1 fee, *p. 475*	MyFinanceLab Study Plan 12.2
LG3 **Discuss the types of funds available and the variety of investment objectives these funds seek to fulfill.** Each fund has an established investment objective that determines its investment policy and identifies it as a certain type of fund. Some popular types of funds are growth, aggressive-growth, value, equity-income, balanced, growth-and-income, asset allocation, index, bond, money, sector, socially responsible, and international funds. The different categories of funds have different risk-return characteristics.	aggressive-growth fund, *p. 484* asset allocation fund, *p. 488* automatic investment plan, *p. 489* automatic reinvestment plan, *p. 490* balanced fund, *p. 485* bond fund, *p. 485* conversion (exchange) privilege, *p. 490* equity-income fund, *p. 485* fund families, *p. 491*	MyFinanceLab Study Plan 12.3

What You Should Know	Key Terms	Where to Practice
LG4 **Discuss the investor services offered by mutual funds and how these services can fit into an investment program.** Mutual funds also offer special services, such as automatic investment and reinvestment plans, systematic withdrawal programs, low-cost conversion and phone-switching privileges, and retirement programs.	growth-and-income fund, *p. 485* growth fund, *p. 484* index fund, *p. 486* international fund, *p. 489* money market mutual fund (money fund), *p. 486* sector fund, *p. 488* socially responsible fund, *p. 488* systematic withdrawal plan, *p. 490* target date fund value fund, *p. 489* value fund, *p. 484*	MyFinanceLab Study Plan 12.4
LG5 **Describe the investor uses of mutual funds along with the variables to consider when assessing and selecting funds for investment purposes.** Investors can use mutual funds to accumulate wealth, as a storehouse of value, or as a vehicle for speculation and short-term trading. Fund selection generally starts by assessing the investor's needs and wants. The next step is to consider what the funds have to offer with regard to investment objectives, risk exposure, and investor services. The investor then narrows the alternatives by aligning his or her needs with the types of funds available and, from this short list of funds, applies the final selection tests: fund performance and cost.	capital gains distributions, *p. 499* dividend income, *p. 499*	MyFinanceLab Study Plan 12.5
LG6 **Identify the sources of return and compute the rate of return earned on a mutual fund investment.** The payoff from investing in a mutual fund includes dividend income, distribution of realized capital gains, growth in capital (unrealized capital gains), and—for closed-end funds—the change in premium or discount. Various measures of return recognize these elements and provide simple yet effective ways of gauging the annual rate of return from a mutual fund. Risk is also important to mutual fund investors. A fund's extensive diversification may protect investors from business and financial risks, but considerable market risk still remains because most funds tend to perform much like the market, or like that segment of the market in which they specialize.	unrealized capital gains (paper profits), *p. 499*	MyFinanceLab Study Plan 12.6 Video Learning Aid for Problems P12.11, P12.16

Log into MyFinanceLab, take a chapter test, and get a personalized Study Plan that tells you which concepts you understand and which ones you need to review. From there, MyFinanceLab will give you further practice, tutorials, animations, videos, and guided solutions.
Log into **http://www.myfinancelab.com**

Discussion Questions

LG1 LG2 **Q12.1** Contrast mutual fund ownership with direct investment in stocks and bonds. Assume your class is going to debate the merits of investing through mutual funds versus investing directly in stocks and bonds. Develop some arguments on each side of this debate and be prepared to discuss them in class. If you had to choose one side to be on, which would it be? Why?

LG2 **Q12.2** Describe the process of creating an ETF. How does it differ from the process by which an open-end fund is created?

LG3 **Q12.3** For each pair of funds listed below, select the one that is likely to be less risky. Briefly explain your answer.
  a. Growth versus growth-and-income funds
  b. Equity-income versus high-grade corporate bond funds
  c. Balanced versus sector funds
  d. Global versus value funds
  e. Intermediate-term bonds versus high-yield municipal bond funds
  f. Target date fund with a target date of 2020 vs. one with a target date of 2040.

LG2 LG3 **Q12.4** Describe an ETF and explain how these funds combine the characteristics of both open-end and closed-end funds. Consider the Vanguard family of funds. Which of its funds most closely resembles a "spider" (SPDR)? In what respects are the Vanguard fund (that you selected) and spiders the same? How are they different? If you could invest in only one of them, which would it be? Explain.

LG2 LG6 **Q12.5** In the absence of any load charges, open-end mutual funds are priced at (or very close to) their net asset values, whereas closed-end funds rarely trade at their NAVs. Explain why one type of fund would normally trade at its NAV while the other type (CEFs) usually does not. What are price premiums and discounts and in what segment of the mutual fund market will you usually find them? Look online at WSJ.com or another source and find five funds that trade at a discount and five funds that trade at a premium. List all of them, including the sizes of their respective discounts and premiums. What's the biggest price discount you could find? How about the biggest price premium? What would cause a fund to trade at a discount? At a premium?

LG3 LG5 **Q12.6** Imagine that you've just inherited $25,000. Now you're faced with the "problem" of how to spend it. You could make a down payment on a condo or on that sports car you've always wanted. Or you could build a mutual fund portfolio. After some soul searching, you decide to build a $25,000 mutual fund portfolio. Using actual mutual funds and actual quoted prices, come up with a plan to invest as much of the $25,000 as you can in a portfolio of mutual funds. (In addition to one or more open-end funds, include at least one CEF or ETF.) Be specific! Briefly describe your planned portfolio, including the investment objectives you are trying to achieve.

Problems

All problems are available on http://www.myfinancelab.com

LG6 **P12.1** A year ago, an investor bought 200 shares of a mutual fund at $8.50 per share. Over the past year, the fund has paid dividends of $0.90 per share and had a capital gains distribution of $0.75 per share.
  a. Find the investor's holding period return, given that this no-load fund now has a net asset value of $9.10.
  b. Find the holding period return, assuming all the dividends and capital gains distributions are reinvested into additional shares of the fund at an average price of $8.75 per share.

LG6 **P12.2** A year ago, the Really Big Growth Fund was being quoted at an NAV of $21.50 and an offer price of $23.35. Today, it's being quoted at $23.04 (NAV) and $25.04 (offer). What is the holding period return on this load fund, given that it was purchased a year ago and that its dividends and capital gains distributions over the year have totaled $1.05 per share? (*Hint:* You, as an investor, buy fund shares at the offer price and sell at the NAV.)

LG6 **P12.3** The All-State Mutual Fund has the following five-year record of performance:

	2016	2015	2014	2013	2012
Net investment income	$ 0.98	$ 0.85	$ 0.84	$ 0.75	$ 0.64
Dividends from net investment income	(0.95)	(0.85)	(0.85)	(0.75)	(0.60)
Net realized and unrealized gains (or losses) on security transactions	4.22	5.08	(2.18)	2.65	(1.05)
Distributions from realized gains	(1.06)	(1.00)	—	(1.00)	—
Net increase (decrease) in NAV	$ 3.19	$ 4.08	($ 2.19)	$ 1.65	($ 1.01)
NAV at beginning of year	$12.53	$ 8.45	$ 10.64	$ 8.99	$ 10.00
NAV at end of year	$15.72	$12.53	$ 8.45	$10.64	$ 8.99

Find this no-load fund's five-year (2012–2016) average annual compound rate of return. Also find its three-year (2014–2016) average annual compound rate of return. If an investor bought the fund in 2012 at $10.00 a share and sold it five years later (in 2016) at $15.72, how much total profit per share would she have made over the five-year holding period?

LG2 **LG6** **P12.4** You've uncovered the following per-share information about a certain mutual fund:

	2014	2015	2016
Ending share prices:			
Offer	$46.20	$64.68	$61.78
NAV	43.20	60.47	57.75
Dividend income	2.10	2.84	2.61
Capital gains distribution	1.83	6.26	4.32
Beginning share prices:			
Offer	55.00	46.20	64.68
NAV	51.42	43.20	60.47

On the basis of this information, find the fund's holding period return for 2014, 2015, and 2016. (In all three cases, assume you buy the fund at the beginning of the year and sell it at the end of each year.) In addition, find the fund's average annual compound rate of return over the three-year period 2014–2016. What would the 2015 holding period return have been if the investor had initially bought 500 shares of stock and reinvested both dividends and capital gains distributions into additional shares of the fund at an average price of $52.50 per share?

LG2 **LG6** **P12.5** Listed below is the 10-year, per-share performance record of Larry, Moe, & Curley's Growth Fund, as obtained from the fund's May 30, 2016, prospectus.

		2016	2015	2014	2013	2012	2011	2010	2009	2008	2007
1.	**Net asset value, beginning of period**	$ 58.60	$52.92	$44.10	$59.85	$55.34	$37.69	$35.21	$34.25	$19.68	$29.82
2.	**Income from investment operations:**										
3.	Net investment income	$ 1.39	$ 1.35	$ 1.09	$ 0.63	$ 0.42	$ 0.49	$ 0.79	$ 0.37	$ 0.33	$ 0.38
4.	Net gains on securities	$ 8.10	$ 9.39	$ 8.63	($6.64)	$ 11.39	$19.59	$ 5.75	$ 2.73	$ 15.80	(0.02)
5.	Total from investment	$ 9.49	$ 10.74	$ 9.72	$ (6.01)	$ 11.81	$20.08	$ 6.54	$ 3.10	$16.13	0.36
6.	**Less distributions:**										
7.	Dividends from net	($ 0.83)	($ 1.24)	($ 0.90)	($ 0.72)	($ 0.46)	($ 0.65)	($ 0.37)	($ 0.26)	($ 0.33)	($ 0.58)
8.	Distributions from realized gains	($2.42)	($3.82)	—	($9.02)	($6.84)	($1.78)	($3.69)	($1.88)	($1.23)	(9.92)
9.	Total distributions	($3.25)	($5.06)	($0.90)	($9.74)	($7.30)	($2.43)	($4.06)	($2.14)	($1.56)	(10.50)
10.	**Net asset value, end of period**	$64.84	$58.60	$52.92	$44.10	$59.85	$55.34	$37.69	$35.21	$34.25	$19.68

Use this information to find LM&C's holding period return in 2016 and 2013. Also find the fund's rate of return over the 5-year period 2012–2016, and the 10-year period 2007–2016. Finally, rework the four return figures, assuming the LM&C fund has a front-end load charge of 5% (of NAV). Comment on the impact of load charges on the return behavior of mutual funds.

LG3 LG6   P12.6 Using the resources at your campus or public library (or on the Internet), select five mutual funds—a growth fund, an equity-income fund, an international (stock) fund, an index fund, and a high-yield corporate bond fund—that you think would make good investments. Briefly explain why you selected these funds. List the funds' holding period returns for the past year and their annual compound rates of return for the past three years. (Use a schedule like the one in Table 12.2 to show relevant performance figures.)

LG6   P12.7 One year ago, Super Star Closed-End Fund had an NAV of $10.40 and was selling at an 18% discount. Today, its NAV is $11.69 and it is priced at a 4% premium. During the year, Super Star paid dividends of $0.40 and had a capital gains distribution of $0.95. On the basis of this information, calculate each of the following:
a. Super Star's NAV-based holding period return for the year.
b. Super Star's market-based holding period return for the year. Did the market premium/discount hurt or add value to the investor's return? Explain.
c. Repeat the market-based holding period return calculation, except this time assume the fund started the year at an 18% premium and ended it at a 4% discount. (Assume the beginning and ending NAVs remain at $10.40 and $11.69, respectively.) Is there any change in this measure of return? Why?

LG6   P12.8 The Well-Managed Closed-End Fund turned in the following performance for the year 2016.
a. Based on this information, what was the NAV-based HPR for the WMCEF in 2016?
b. Find the percentage (%) premium or discount at which the fund was trading at the beginning of the year and at the end of the year.
c. What was the market-based HPR for the fund in 2016? Did the market premium or discount add to or hurt the holding period return on this CEF? Explain.

Item	Beginning of the Year	End of the Year
NAV	$7.50	$9.25
Market price of the fund shares	$7.75	$9.00
Dividends paid over the year	—	$1.20
Capital gains distributed over the year	—	$0.90

LG6   P12.9 Three years ago, you invested in the Future Investco Mutual Fund by purchasing 1,000 shares of the fund at a net asset value of $20.00 per share. Because you did not need the

income, you elected to reinvest all dividends and capital gains distributions. Today, you sell your 1,100 shares in this fund for $22.91 per share. What is the compounded rate of return on this investment over the three-year period?

LG6 **P12.10** Refer to Problem 12.9. If there were a 3% load on this fund, assuming you purchased the same number of shares, what would your rate of return be?

LG6 **P12.11** You invested in the no-load OhYes Mutual Fund one year ago by purchasing 1,000 shares of the fund at the net asset value of $25.00 per share. The fund distributed dividends of $1.50 and capital gains of $2.00. Today, the NAV is $26. What was your holding period return?

LG6 **P12.12** Refer to Problem 12.11. If OhYes was a load fund with a 2% front-end load, what would be the HPR?

LG6 **P12.13** You are considering the purchase of shares in a closed-end mutual fund. The NAV is equal to $22.50 and the latest close is $20.00. Is this fund trading at a premium or a discount? How big is the premium or discount?

LG6 **P12.14** You purchased 1,000 shares of MutualMagic one year ago for $20.00 per share. During the year, you received $2.00 in dividends, half of which was from dividends on stock the fund held and half of which was from interest earned on bonds in the fund portfolio. Assuming your federal marginal tax rate is 25%, how much will you owe in federal taxes on the distributions you received this year? (Your answer should be in dollars.)

Visit **http://www.myfinancelab.com** for web exercises, spreadsheets, and other online resources.

Case Problem 12.1   Reverend Mark Thomas Ponders Mutual Funds

LG3 LG5 The Reverend Mark Thomas is the minister of a church in the San Diego area. He is married, has one young child, and earns a "modest income." Because religious organizations are not notorious for their generous retirement programs, the reverend has decided he should do some investing on his own. He would like to set up a program that enables him to supplement the church's retirement program and at the same time provide some funds for his child's college education (which is still some 12 years away). He is not out to break any investment records but wants some backup to provide for the long-run needs of his family.

Although he has a modest income, Mark Thomas believes that with careful planning, he can probably invest about $250 a quarter (and, with luck, increase this amount over time). He currently has about $15,000 in a savings account that he would be willing to use to begin this program. In view of his investment objectives, he is not interested in taking a lot of risk. Because his knowledge of investments extends to savings accounts, Series EE savings bonds, and a little bit about mutual funds, he approaches you for some investment advice.

Questions

a. In light of Mark's long-term investment goals, do you think mutual funds are an appropriate investment vehicle for him?

b. Do you think he should use his $15,000 savings to start a mutual fund investment program?

c. What type of mutual fund investment program would you set up for the reverend? Include in your answer some discussion of the types of funds you would consider, the investment objectives you would set, and any investment services (e.g., withdrawal plans) you would seek. Would taxes be an important consideration in your investment advice? Explain.

Case Problem 12.2   Calvin Jacobs Seeks the Good Life

LG3 LG4

Calvin Jacobs is a widower who recently retired after a long career with a major Midwestern manufacturer. Beginning as a skilled craftsman, he worked his way up to the level of shop supervisor over a period of more than 30 years with the firm. Calvin receives Social Security benefits and a generous company pension. Together, these amount to over $4,500 per month (part of which is tax-free). The Jacobses had no children, so he lives alone. Calvin owns a two-bedroom rental house that is next to his home, and the rental income from it covers the mortgage payments for both the rental house and his house.

Over the years, Calvin and his late wife, Allie, always tried to put a little money aside each month. The results have been nothing short of phenomenal. The value of Calvin's liquid investments (all held in bank CDs and savings accounts) runs well into the six figures. Up to now, Calvin has just let his money grow and has not used any of his savings to supplement his Social Security, pension, and rental income. But things are about to change. Calvin has decided, "What the heck, it's time I start living the good life!" Calvin wants to travel and, in effect, start reaping the benefits of his labors. He has therefore decided to move $100,000 from a savings account to one or two high-yielding mutual funds. He would like to receive $1,000 to $1,500 a month from the fund(s) for as long as possible because he plans to be around for a long time.

Questions

a. Given Calvin's financial resources and investment objectives, what kinds of mutual funds do you think he should consider?

b. What factors in Calvin's situation should be taken into consideration in the fund selection process? How might these affect Calvin's course of action?

c. What types of services do you think he should look for in a mutual fund?

d. Assume Calvin invests in a mutual fund that earns about 10% annually from dividend income and capital gains. Given that Calvin wants to receive $1,000 to $1,500 a month from his mutual fund, what would be the size of his investment account five years from now? How large would the account be if the fund earned 15% on average and everything else remained the same? How important is the fund's rate of return to Calvin's investment situation? Explain.

Excel@Investing

Excel@Investing

In the *Wall Street Journal*, open-end mutual funds are listed separately from other securities. They have their own quotation system where the primary data variables are the net asset value (NAV) and the year-to-date returns. The NAV represents the price you get when you sell shares, or what you pay when you buy no-load funds.

Create a spreadsheet model similar to the spreadsheet for Table 12.2, which you can view at http://www.myfinancelab.com, to analyze the following three years of data relating to the MoMoney Mutual Fund. It should report the amount of dividend income and capital gains distributed to the shareholders, along with any other changes in the fund's net asset value ($b = 0.50$).

A	B	C	D	E
1	**2016**	**2015**	**2014**	
2 NAV (beginning of period)	$ 35.24	$ 37.50	$ 36.25	
3 Net investment income	$ 0.65	$ 0.75	$ 0.60	
4 Net gains on securities	$ 5.25	$ 4.75	$ (3.75)	
5 Dividends from net investment income	$ 0.61	$ 0.57	$ 0.52	
6 Distributions from realized gains	$ 1.75	$ 2.01	$ 1.55	
7				

Questions

a. What is the total income from the investment operations?

b. What are the total distributions from the investment operations?

c. Calculate the net asset value for MoMoney Fund as of the end of the years 2016, 2015, and 2014.

d. Calculate the holding period returns for each of the years 2016, 2015, and 2014.

Chapter-Opening Problem

Go to Yahoo! Finance and look up data on the Vanguard 500 Index Investor fund (ticker symbol VFINX) and the Fidelity Magellan Fund (ticker symbol FMAGX). These are among the largest mutual funds in the United States. Pick one of these funds and click the Basic Chart link to see how it has performed over the last five years. With that chart open, enter the ticker symbol of the other fund into the box that allows you to plot another fund's performance on the same chart. Which of these two funds has performed better in recent years? Click the Holdings link to see the top 10 holdings of each fund. Do any of the same stocks appear in the top 10 lists of both funds?

13

Managing Your Own Portfolio

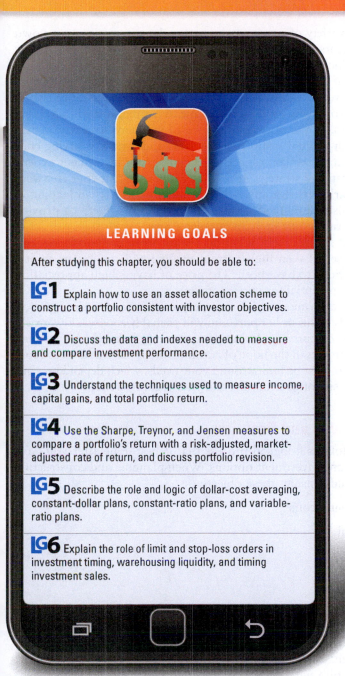

LEARNING GOALS

After studying this chapter, you should be able to:

LG1 Explain how to use an asset allocation scheme to construct a portfolio consistent with investor objectives.

LG2 Discuss the data and indexes needed to measure and compare investment performance.

LG3 Understand the techniques used to measure income, capital gains, and total portfolio return.

LG4 Use the Sharpe, Treynor, and Jensen measures to compare a portfolio's return with a risk-adjusted, market-adjusted rate of return, and discuss portfolio revision.

LG5 Describe the role and logic of dollar-cost averaging, constant-dollar plans, constant-ratio plans, and variable-ratio plans.

LG6 Explain the role of limit and stop-loss orders in investment timing, warehousing liquidity, and timing investment sales.

He's known as the "Oracle of Omaha" for his stock-picking prowess, and in 2015 he was ranked by Forbes as the third richest person in the world with an estimated net worth of $73 billion. As chairman of Berkshire Hathaway, Inc., Warren Buffett has seen his initial $7 per share investment in 1962 grow to a value of $206,000 per share in 2015. The Omaha-based corporation's 60 subsidiaries include insurance (GEICO), apparel (Fruit of the Loom), building products (Acme Brick Company and Johns Manville), food and gourmet retailers (International Dairy Queen, The Pampered Chef, and See's Candies), flight services (FlightSafety International), home furnishings (Star Furniture), and jewelry retailers (Ben Bridge Jeweler, Borsheims Fine Jewelry, and Helzberg Diamonds). In addition, Berkshire Hathaway is a public investment company with major holdings in companies that read like a veritable who's who of American business: Wells Fargo, IBM, Wal-Mart, ExxonMobil, American Express, Coca-Cola, Procter & Gamble, and many others.

What's the secret to Buffett's success? His long-term investing horizon and patience are legendary. His claim to fame has been his ability to buy businesses at prices far below what he calls their "intrinsic" value, which includes such intangibles as quality of management and the power of superior brand names. Buffett waits until a desired investment reaches his target price and won't buy until then. "We measure our success by the long-term progress of the companies rather than by the month-to-month movements of their stocks," he says.

Another secret that investors in Berkshire Hathaway are anxious to discover is the identity of the 85-year-old Buffett's successor. In early 2015 Buffett revealed that Berkshire Hathaway's board had chosen his successor, an unnamed person who was already working for the company. Hopefully for Berkshire's investors, Buffett can pick his successor as adeptly as he has picked his investments.

As you'll see in this chapter, which introduces the basics of portfolio management, investing is a process of analysis, followed by action, followed by still more analysis. You may not be the next Warren Buffett (or maybe you will!), but understanding these techniques for building and evaluating your own portfolio will put you on the right track.

(Source: "Warren Buffett on His Successor: We Have Our Man," http://fortune.com/2015/02/28/warren-buffett-successor/, accessed July 2015; historical data from http://www.finance.yahoo.com, accessed July 2015.)

Constructing a Portfolio Using an Asset Allocation Scheme

LG1 We begin by examining the criteria for constructing a portfolio and then use them to develop a plan for allocating assets in various investment categories. This plan provides a basic, useful framework for selecting individual investments for the portfolio. In attempting to weave the concepts of risk and diversification into a solid portfolio policy, we will rely on both traditional and modern approaches.

Investor Characteristics and Objectives

You should consider a wide variety of issues as you make plans to manage your own portfolio. Of course these factors include the risk and return characteristics of specific investments that you might include in your portfolio, but they also include personal issues. For example, the size of your income and the certainty of your employment are important. If you hold a secure, well-paying job, you can afford to take more risk in your investment portfolio. Also, as you earn more income over time, you will probably face higher marginal tax rates, so the tax ramifications of your investment program become more important. Your marital status is important, and certainly having children changes your savings and investment objectives. Finally, your investment experience also influences your investment strategy. It normally is best to "get your feet wet" in the investment market by slipping into it gradually rather than leaping in head first. A cautiously developed investment program is likely to provide more favorable long-run results than an impulsive one.

Now you should ask yourself, what do I want from my portfolio? You must generally choose between high current income and significant capital appreciation. It is difficult to have both. The price of having high appreciation potential is often low potential for current income.

Your needs may determine which avenue you choose. A retired person whose income depends on his or her portfolio will probably choose a lower-risk, current-income-oriented approach. A young investor may be much more willing to take on risky investments in the hope of accumulating wealth at a more rapid pace. Thus, a portfolio must be built around your needs, which depend on your income, your age, the size of your family, and your risk preferences.

Portfolio Objectives and Policies

Constructing a portfolio is a logical process that is best done after you have analyzed your needs and investment options. When planning and constructing a portfolio, you should consider these objectives:

- Generating current income
- Preserving capital
- Growing capital
- Reducing taxes
- Managing risk

All of these factors may play an influential role in defining the portfolio that is best for you. The first two items, current income and capital preservation, are consistent with a low-risk, conservative investment strategy. Normally, a portfolio with this orientation contains low-beta (low-risk)

---

securities. The third item, a capital growth objective, implies increased risk and a reduced level of current income. Higher-risk growth stocks, options, futures, and other more speculative investments may be suitable for you if you place a high value on the capital growth objective. The fourth item, your tax bracket, will also influence your investment strategy. If you are in a high tax bracket, you have a great incentive to defer taxes and earn investment returns in the form of capital gains. This implies a strategy of higher-risk investments and a longer holding period. If you are in a lower bracket, you will be less concerned with the form that your investment income takes, so you may be more willing to invest in higher-current-income securities. The most important item, finally, is risk. Investors should consider the risk-return tradeoff in all investment decisions.

Developing an Asset Allocation Scheme

How to Choose Your
Asset Allocation

Once you have translated your needs into specific portfolio objectives, you can construct a portfolio designed to achieve these goals. Before buying any investments, however, you must develop an asset allocation scheme. **Asset allocation** involves dividing your portfolio into various asset classes, such as U.S. stocks and bonds, foreign securities, short-term securities, and other assets like tangibles (e.g., gold) and real estate. Asset allocation and diversification are related but different ideas. Asset allocation focuses on investment in various asset classes. Spreading your wealth across different types of assets does help to diversify your portfolio, but then beyond that, you can diversify within an asset class by selecting individual securities that are not highly correlated with each other. For example, by allocating your assets between stocks and bonds you reap some diversification benefit, but within the stock portfolio, you want to select stocks that do not move together so that the stock portfolio itself is well diversified. The same could be said of the bonds in your portfolio. The second step in this process is called **security selection**—selecting the specific securities to be held within an asset class.

Asset allocation is based on the belief that the total return of a portfolio is influenced more by the division of investments into asset classes than by the actual investments within each asset class. In fact, studies have shown that as much as 90% of a portfolio's return comes from asset allocation. Therefore, less than 10% can be attributed to the actual security selection. Furthermore, researchers have found that asset allocation has a much greater impact on reducing total risk than does selecting the best investment in any single asset category.

Approaches to Asset Allocation   The basic approaches to asset allocation are (1) fixed weightings, (2) flexible weightings, and (3) tactical asset allocation. The first and second differ with respect to the proportions of each asset category maintained in the portfolio. The third is a more exotic technique used by institutional portfolio managers.

Fixed Weightings   The **fixed-weightings** approach allocates a fixed percentage of the portfolio to each of the asset categories (most individuals invest in three to five asset classes). Assuming four categories—common stock, bonds, foreign securities, and short-term securities—a fixed allocation might be as follows.

Category	Allocation
Common stock	30%
Bonds	50%
Foreign securities	15%
Short-term securities	5%
Total Portfolio	100%

Generally, the fixed weightings do not change over time. Because market values shift, you may have to adjust the portfolio annually or after major market moves to maintain the desired fixed-percentage allocations. For example, if the stock market booms, the percentage of the portfolio in stocks will rise, even without any new investments, so to maintain the fixed weightings, you would sell stocks and buy securities in the other asset classes.

Fixed weights may or may not represent equal percentage allocations to each category. One could, for example, allocate 25% to each of the four categories above. Research has shown that many investors choose to spread their money evenly across the investment options presented to them, a phenomenon called the "1/N heuristic." This behavior appears to be especially common in retirement accounts. For example, if a firm's retirement plan allows employees to allocate the retirement contributions among five mutual funds, many investors will choose to invest 1/5th (i.e., 1/N where N equals the number of choices) of their money to each fund. While this simple rule of thumb will probably result in a portfolio with a reasonable balance between risk and return, there is no guarantee that spreading assets equally among the available asset classes represents an optimal strategy.

Flexible Weightings The **flexible-weightings approach** involves periodic adjustment of the weights for each asset category on the basis of market analysis. The use of a flexible-weighting scheme is often called *strategic asset allocation.* For example, the initial and new allocation based on a flexible-weighting scheme may be as follows.

Category	Initial Allocation	New Allocation
Common stock	30%	45%
Bonds	40%	40%
Foreign securities	15%	10%
Short-term securities	15%	5%
Total portfolio	100%	100%

A change from the initial to the new allocation would be triggered by shifts in market conditions or expectations. For example, the new allocation shown above may have resulted from an anticipated improvement in domestic economic conditions. That improvement should result in increased domestic stock prices, producing higher returns on that asset class relative to foreign and short-term securities. The weightings were therefore changed to capture greater returns in a changing market.

Tactical Asset Allocation The third approach, **tactical asset allocation,** is a form of market timing that uses stock-index futures and bond futures, which we will discuss later, to change a portfolio's asset allocation. When investors expect lower returns on stocks than on bonds, this strategy would direct them to sell stock-index futures and buy bond futures. Conversely, when bonds are forecast to be less attractive than stocks, the strategy results in buying stock-index futures and selling bond futures. Because this sophisticated technique relies on a large portfolio and the use of quantitative models for market timing, it is generally appropriate only for large institutional investors.

Asset Allocation Alternatives Assuming the use of a fixed-weight asset allocation plan and using, just as an example, four asset categories, we can demonstrate three

Test Your Risk Tolerance

TABLE 13.1 ALTERNATIVE ASSET ALLOCATIONS

Category	Allocation Alternative		
	Conservative (low return/low risk)	Moderate (average return/average risk)	Aggressive (high return/high risk)
Common stock	15%	30%	40%
Bonds	45%	40%	30%
Foreign securities	5%	15%	25%
Short-term securities	35%	15%	5%
Total portfolio	100%	100%	100%

asset allocations. Table 13.1 shows allocations in each of four categories for conservative (low return/low risk), moderate (average return/average risk), and aggressive (high return/high risk) portfolios. The conservative allocation relies heavily on bonds and short-term securities to provide predictable returns. The moderate allocation consists largely of common stock and bonds and includes more foreign securities and fewer short-term securities than the conservative allocation. Its moderate risk-return behavior reflects a move away from safe, short-term securities to a larger dose of common stock and foreign securities. Finally, in the aggressive allocation, more dollars are invested in common stock, fewer in bonds, and more in foreign securities, thereby generally increasing the expected portfolio return and risk.

Applying Asset Allocation An asset allocation plan should consider the economic outlook, your savings and spending patterns, your tax situation, the returns expected from different asset classes, and your risk tolerance. You also must periodically revise the plan to reflect changing investment goals. Generally, to decide on the appropriate asset mix, you must evaluate each asset category in terms of current return, growth potential, safety, liquidity, transaction costs (brokerage fees), and potential tax savings.

Many investors use mutual funds as part of their asset allocation activities, to diversify within each asset category. Or, as an alternative to constructing your own portfolio, you can buy shares in an asset allocation fund—a mutual fund that seeks to reduce variability of returns by investing in the right assets at the right time. These funds, like all asset allocation schemes, emphasize diversification. They perform at a relatively consistent level by passing up the potential for spectacular gains in favor of predictability. Some asset allocation funds use fixed weightings, whereas others have flexible weights that change within prescribed limits. As a rule, investors with more than about $100,000 to invest and adequate time can justify do-it-yourself asset allocation. Those with between $25,000 and $100,000 and adequate time can use mutual funds to create a workable asset allocation. Those with less than $25,000 or with limited time may find asset allocation funds most attractive.

Most important, you should recognize that to be effective, an asset allocation scheme must be designed for the long haul. Develop an asset allocation scheme you can live with for at least seven years, and perhaps longer. Once you have it set, stick with it. The key to success is remaining faithful to your asset allocation and fighting the temptation to deviate from your plan.

13.1 What role, if any, do an investor's personal characteristics play in determining portfolio policy? Explain.

13.2 What role do an investor's portfolio objectives play in constructing a portfolio?

13.3 What is asset allocation? How does it differ from diversification? What role does asset allocation play in constructing an investment portfolio?

13.4 Briefly describe the basic approaches to asset allocation: (a) fixed weightings, (b) flexible weightings, and (c) tactical asset allocation.

13.5 What role could an asset allocation fund play? What makes an asset allocation scheme effective?

Evaluating the Performance of Individual Investments

LG2 Imagine that one of your most important personal goals is to have accumulated enough savings three years from now in order to make the down payment on your first house. You project that the desired house will cost $200,000 and that the $33,000 will be sufficient to make a 15% down payment and pay the associated closing costs. Your calculations indicate that you can achieve this goal by investing existing savings plus an additional $200 per month over the next three years in an investment earning 10% per year. Projections of your income and expenses over the three-year period indicate that you should just be able to set aside the needed $200 per month. You consult with an investment advisor, Cliff Orbit, who leads you to believe that under his management, the 10% return can be achieved.

It seems simple. Give Cliff your existing savings, send him $200 each month for the next 36 months, and at the end of that period, you will have the $33,000 needed to purchase the house. Unfortunately, there are many uncertainties involved. What if you don't set aside $200 each month? What if Cliff fails to earn the 10% annual return? What if in three years the desired house costs more than $200,000? Clearly, you must do more than simply devise what appears to be a feasible plan for achieving a goal. Rarely are there guarantees that your planned investment and portfolio outcomes will actually occur. Therefore, it is important to assess your progress toward your investment goals periodically.

As actual outcomes occur, you must compare them to the planned outcomes and make any necessary alterations in your plans—or in your goals. Knowing how to measure investment performance is therefore crucial. Here we will emphasize measures suitable for analyzing investment performance. We begin with sources of data.

Obtaining Data

The first step in analyzing investment returns is gathering data that reflect the actual performance of each investment. Many sources of investment information are available, both online and in print. The *Wall Street Journal*, WSJ.com, and Yahoo! Finance, for example, contain numerous items of information useful in assessing the performance of securities. You use the same type of information to evaluate investment performance that you use to make an investment decision. Two key areas to stay informed about are (1) returns on investments and (2) economic and market activity.

Return Data The basic ingredient in analyzing investment returns is current market information, such as daily price quotations for stocks and bonds. Investors often maintain logs or spreadsheets that contain the cost of each investment, as well as dividends, interest, and other sources of income received. By regularly recording price and return data, you can create an ongoing record of price fluctuations and cumulative returns. You should also monitor corporate earnings and dividends, which affect a company's stock price. These sources of investment return—current income and capital gains—must of course be combined to determine total return.

Economic and Market Activity Changes in the economy and market affect returns—both the level of current income and the market value of an investment. The astute investor keeps abreast of international, national, and local economic and market developments. By following economic and market changes, you should be able to assess their potential impact on returns. As economic and market conditions change, you must be prepared to make revisions in the portfolio. In essence, being a knowledgeable investor will improve your chances of generating a profit (or avoiding a loss).

Indexes of Investment Performance

In measuring investment performance, it is often worthwhile to compare your returns with broad-based market measures. Indexes useful for the analysis of common stock include the Dow Jones Industrial Average (DJIA), the Standard & Poor's 500 Stock Composite Index (S&P 500), and the Nasdaq Composite Index. Although the DJIA is widely cited by the news media, it is not the most appropriate comparative gauge of stock price movement because of its narrow coverage and because it is a price-weighted index. If your portfolio is composed of a broad range of common stocks, the S&P 500 Index is probably a more appropriate tool.

A number of indicators are also available for assessing the general behavior of the bond markets. These indicators consider either bond yield or bond price behavior. Bond yield data reflect the rate of return one would earn on a bond purchased today and held to maturity. Popular sources of these data include the *Wall Street Journal*, *Barron's*, Standard & Poor's, Mergent, Yahoo! Finance, and the Federal Reserve. The Dow Jones Corporate Bond Index, based on the closing prices of 32 industrial, 32 financial, and 32 utility/telecom bonds, is a popular measure of bond price behavior. It reflects the mathematical average of the closing prices of the bonds.

Indexes of bond prices and information about bond yields can be obtained for specific types of bonds (industrial, utility, and municipal), as well as on a composite basis. In addition, indexes reported in terms of total returns are available for both stocks and bonds. They combine dividend/interest income with price behavior (capital gain or loss) to reflect total return.

Investors frequently use the Lipper indexes to assess the general behavior of mutual funds. These indexes are available for various types of equity and bond funds. Unfortunately, for most other types of funds, no widely published index or average is available. A few other indexes cover listed options and futures.

Measuring the Performance of Investments

To monitor an investment portfolio, investors need reliable techniques for consistently measuring the performance of each investment in the portfolio. In particular, the holding period return (HPR) measure that we studied earlier can be used to determine actual return performance. HPR is an excellent way to assess actual return behavior because it captures total return performance. It is most appropriate for holding or assessment periods of one year or less. Total return, in this context, includes the periodic cash income from the investment as well as price appreciation (or loss), whether realized or unrealized. To calculate returns for periods of more than a year, you can use the internal rate of return, which recognizes the time value of money. Because the following discussions center on the annual assessment of return, we will use HPR as the measure of return.

The formula for HPR is restated in Equation 13.1.

Equation 13.1

$$\text{Holding period return} = \frac{\begin{matrix}\text{Current income} \\ \text{during period}\end{matrix} + \begin{matrix}\text{Capital gain (or loss)} \\ \text{during period}\end{matrix}}{\text{Beginning investment value}}$$

Equation 13.1a

$$\text{HPR} = \frac{C + CG}{V_0}$$

where

Equation 13.2

$$\begin{matrix}\text{Capital gain (or loss)} \\ \text{during period}\end{matrix} = \begin{matrix}\text{Ending} \\ \text{investment value}\end{matrix} - \begin{matrix}\text{Beginning} \\ \text{investment value}\end{matrix}$$

Equation 13.2a

$$CG = V_n - V_0$$

Stocks and Bonds There are several measures of investment return for stocks and bonds. *Dividend yield*, measures the current yearly dividend return earned from a stock investment. It is calculated by dividing a stock's yearly cash dividend by its price. The *current yield* and *yield to maturity* (promised yield) for bonds capture various components of return but do not always reflect actual total return. The holding period return method measures the total return (income plus change in value) actually earned on an investment over a given investment period. We will use HPR, with a holding period of approximately one year, in the illustrations that follow.

Stocks The HPR for common and preferred stocks includes both cash dividends received and any price change in the security during the period of ownership. Table 13.2 illustrates the HPR calculation as applied to the actual performance of a common stock. Assume you purchased 1,000 shares of Dallas National Corporation in May 2016 at a cost of $27,312 (including commissions). After holding the stock for just over one year, you sold it, reaping proceeds of $32,040. In addition to the $4,728 capital gain on the sale, you also received $2,000 in cash dividends. Thus, the calculated HPR is 24.63%.

This HPR was calculated without consideration for income taxes paid on the dividends and capital gain. Because many investors are concerned with both pretax and after-tax rates of return, it is useful to calculate an after-tax HPR. We assume, for simplicity, that you are in the 30% ordinary tax bracket (federal and state combined). We also assume that, for federal and state tax purposes, dividends and capital gains for holding periods of more than 12 months are taxed at a 15% rate. Thus, both your dividend and capital gain income are taxed at a 15% rate. Income taxes reduce the after-tax dividend income to $1,700 [i.e., $(1 - 0.15) \times \$2,000$] and the after-tax capital gain to $4,019 [i.e, $(1 - 0.15) \times (\$32,040 - \$27,312)$]. The after-tax HPR is therefore 20.94% or $(\$1,700 + \$4,019) \div \$27,312 = 0.2094$, a reduction of 3.69 percentage points. It should be clear that both pretax HPR and after-tax HPR are useful gauges of return.

TABLE 13.2   CALCULATION OF PRETAX HPR ON A COMMON STOCK

Security: Dallas National Corporation common stock

Date of purchase: May 1, 2016

Purchase cost: $27,312

Date of sale: May 7, 2017

Sale proceeds: $32,040

Dividends received (May 2016 to May 2017): $2,000

$$\text{Holding period return} = \frac{\$2,000 + \$32,040 - \$27,312}{\$27,312}$$

$$= 24.63\%$$

Bonds The HPR for a bond investment is similar to that for stocks. The calculation holds for both straight debt and convertible issues. It includes the two components of a bond investor's return: interest income and capital gain or loss.

Calculation of the HPR on a bond investment is illustrated in Table 13.3. Assume you purchased Phoenix Brewing Company bonds for $10,000, held them for just over one year, and then realized $9,704 at their sale. In addition, you earned $1,000 in interest during the year. The HPR of this investment is 7.04%. The HPR is lower than the bond's current yield of 10% (i.e., $1,000 interest ÷ $10,000 purchase price) because the bonds were sold at a capital loss. Assuming a 30% ordinary tax bracket and a 15% capital gains tax rate (because the bond has been held more than 12 months), the after-tax HPR is 4.48%: $\{[(1 - 0.30) \times \$1,000] + [(1 - 0.15) \times (\$9,704 - \$10,000)]\}$ ÷$10,000. This is 2.56% less than the pretax HPR.

TABLE 13.3   CALCULATION OF PRETAX HPR ON A BOND

Security: Phoenix Brewing Company 10% bonds

Date of purchase: June 2, 2016

Purchase cost: $10,000

Date of sale: June 5, 2017

Sale proceeds: $9,704

Interest earned (June 2016 to June 2017): $1,000

$$\text{Holding period return} = \frac{\$1,000 + (\$9,704 - \$10,000)}{\$10,000}$$

$$= 7.04\%$$

Mutual Funds The basic components of return from a mutual fund investment are dividend income (including any capital gains distribution) and change in value. The basic HPR equation for mutual funds is identical to that for stocks.

Table 13.4 presents a holding period return calculation for a no-load mutual fund. Assume you purchased 1,000 shares of the fund in July 2016 at a net asset value (NAV) of $10.40 per share. Because it is a no-load fund, no commission was charged, so your cost was $10,400. During the one-year period of ownership, the Pebble Falls Mutual Fund distributed investment income dividends totaling $270 and capital gains dividends of $320. You redeemed (sold) this fund at an NAV of $10.79 per share, thereby realizing $10,790. As seen in Table 13.4, the pretax holding period return on this investment is 9.42%. Assuming a 30% ordinary tax bracket and a 15% dividend and capital gains tax rate (because the fund has been held for more than 12 months),

TABLE 13.4 CALCULATION OF PRETAX HPR ON A MUTUAL FUND

Security: Pebble Falls Mutual Fund

Date of purchase: July 1, 2016

Purchase cost: $10,400

Date of redemption: July 3, 2017

Sale proceeds: $10,790

Distributions received (July 2016 to July 2017)

Investment income dividends: $270

Capital gains dividends: $320

$$\text{Holding period return} = \frac{(\$270 + \$320) + (\$10,790 - \$10,400)}{\$10,400}$$

$$= \underline{9.42\%}$$

the after-tax HPR for the fund is 8.01%: $\{[(1 - 0.15) \times (\$270 + \$320)] + [(1 - 0.15) \times (\$10,790 - \$10,400)]\} \div \$10,400$. This is 1.41% below the pretax return.

Options and Futures The only source of return on options and futures is capital gains. To calculate a holding period return for an investment in a call option, for instance, you use the basic HPR formula, but you would set current income equal to zero. If you purchased a call on 100 shares of Facebook for $325 and sold the contract for $385 after holding it for just over 12 months, the pretax holding period return would be 18.46%. This calculation simply takes the sales proceeds of $385, subtracts the initial cost of $325, and divides by the initial cost. Assuming the 15% capital gains tax rate applies, the after-tax HPR would be 15.69%, which is the after-tax gain of $51 [i.e., $(1 - 0.15) \times \$60$] divided by the initial cost of $325.

The HPRs of futures are calculated in a similar fashion. Because the return is in the form of capital gains only, the HPR analysis can be applied to any investment on a pretax or an after-tax basis. (The same basic procedure is used for securities that are sold short.)

Comparing Performance to Investment Goals

After computing an HPR (or yield) on an investment, you should compare it to your investment goal. Keeping track of an investment's performance will help you decide which investments you should continue to hold and which you might want to sell. Clearly, an investment would be a candidate for sale under any one of the following conditions: (1) The investment failed to perform up to expectations and no real change in performance is anticipated. (2) It has fulfilled the original investment objective. (3) Better investment outlets are currently available.

Balancing Risk and Return We have frequently discussed the basic tradeoff between investment risk and return. To earn more return, you must take more risk. In analyzing an investment, the key question is, am I getting the proper return for the amount of investment risk I am taking?

Nongovernment security investments are by nature riskier than U.S. government bonds or insured money market deposit accounts. This implies that a rational investor should invest in these riskier assets only when the expected rate of return exceeds what could have been earned from a low-risk investment. Thus, one benchmark against which to compare investment returns is the rate of return on low-risk investments. If one's risky investments are outperforming low-risk investments, they are obtaining extra return for taking extra risk. If they are not outperforming low-risk investments, you should carefully reexamine your investment strategy.

Isolating Problem Investments It is best to analyze each investment in a portfolio periodically. For each, you should consider two questions. First, has it performed in a manner that could reasonably be expected? Second, if you didn't currently own it, would you buy it today? If the answers to both are negative, then the investment probably should be sold. A negative answer to one of the questions qualifies the investment for the "problem list." A *problem investment* is one that has not lived up to expectations. It may be a loss situation or an investment that has provided a return less than you expected. Many investors try to forget about problem investments, hoping the problem will go away or the investment will turn itself around. This is a mistake. Problem investments require immediate attention, not neglect. In studying a problem investment, the key question is, "Should I take my loss and get out, or should I hang on and hope it turns around?"

CONCEPTS IN REVIEW

Answers available at
http://www.pearsonhighered
.com/smart

13.6   Why is it important to continuously manage and control your portfolio?

13.7   What role does current market information play in analyzing investment returns? How do changes in economic and market activity affect investment returns? Explain.

13.8   Which indexes can you use to compare your investment performance to general market returns? Briefly explain each of these indexes.

13.9   What are indicators of bond market behavior, and how are they different from stock market indicators? Name three sources of bond yield data.

13.10   Briefly discuss holding period return (HPR) and yield as measures of investment return. Are they equivalent? Explain.

13.11   Distinguish between the types of dividend distributions that mutual funds make. Are these dividends the only source of return for a mutual fund investor? Explain.

13.12   Under what three conditions would an investment holding be a candidate for sale? What must be true about the expected return on a risky investment, when compared with the return on a low-risk investment, to cause a rational investor to acquire the risky investment? Explain.

13.13   What is a problem investment? What questions should one consider when analyzing each investment in a portfolio?

Assessing Portfolio Performance

LG3 LG4   A portfolio can be passively or actively managed. A *passive* portfolio results from buying and holding a well-diversified portfolio over the given investment horizon. An active portfolio is built using the traditional and modern approaches presented earlier and is managed and controlled to achieve its stated objectives. Passive portfolios may at times outperform equally risky active portfolios. But **active portfolio management** can help you adjust your portfolio as your investment objectives change. Many of the ideas presented in this text are consistent with the belief that active portfolio management will help you achieve your investment goals.

Once you have built a portfolio, the first step in active portfolio management is to assess performance, perhaps after a few quarters or a year. Based on the information from your assessment, you may revise the portfolio, continuing to assess and revise the portfolio periodically as needed. Calculating the portfolio return can be tricky. The procedures used to assess portfolio performance are based on many of the concepts presented earlier in this chapter. Here we will demonstrate how to assess portfolio performance, using a hypothetical securities portfolio over a one-year holding period. We will examine three measures that you can use to compare a portfolio's return with a risk-adjusted, market-adjusted rate of return.

Measuring Portfolio Return

Table 13.5 presents the investment portfolio, as of January 1, 2017, of Bob Hathaway. He is a 50-year-old widower, whose children are married. His income is $60,000 per year. His primary investment objective is long-term growth with a moderate dividend return. He selects stocks with two criteria in mind: quality and growth potential. On January 1, 2017, his portfolio consisted of 10 stocks, all of good quality. Hathaway has been fortunate in his selection process. He has approximately $74,000 in unrealized price appreciation in his portfolio. During 2017 he decided to make a change in the portfolio. On May 7 he sold 1,000 shares of Dallas National Corporation for $32,040. The holding period return for that issue was discussed earlier (see Table 13.2). Using proceeds from the Dallas National sale, he acquired an additional 1,000 shares of Florida Southcoast Banks on May 10 because he liked the prospects for the Florida bank. Florida Southcoast is based in one of the fastest growing counties in the country.

Measuring the Amount Invested   Every investor would be well advised to list his or her holdings periodically, as is done in Table 13.5. The table shows number of shares, acquisition date, cost, and current value for each issue. These data aid in continually formulating strategy decisions. The cost data, for example, are used to determine the amount invested. Hathaway's portfolio does not use the leverage of a margin account. Were leverage present, all return calculations would be based on the investor's equity in

TABLE 13.5   BOB HATHAWAY'S PORTFOLIO (JANUARY 1, 2017)

Number of Shares	Company	Date Acquired	Total Cost (including commission)	Cost per Share	Current Price per Share	Current Value
1,000	Bancorp West, Inc.	1/16/12	$ 21,610	$21.61	$30	$ 30,000
1,000	Dallas National Corporation	5/01/13	$ 27,312	$27.31	$29	$ 29,000
1,000	Dator Companies, Inc.	4/13/08	$ 13,704	$13.70	$27	$ 27,000
500	Excelsior Industries	8/16/11	$ 40,571	$81.14	$54	$ 27,000
1,000	Florida Southcoast Banks	12/16/11	$ 17,460	$17.46	$30	$ 30,000
1,000	Maryland-Pacific	9/27/11	$ 22,540	$22.54	$26	$ 26,000
1,000	Moronson	2/27/11	$ 19,100	$19.10	$47	$ 47,000
500	Northwest Mining and Mfg.	4/17/12	$ 25,504	$51.00	$62	$ 31,000
1,000	Rawland Petroleum	3/12/12	$ 24,903	$24.90	$30	$ 30,000
1,000	Vornox	4/16/12	$ 37,120	$37.12	$47	$ 47,000
	Total		$249,824			$324,000

the account. Recall that an investor's equity in a margin account equals the total value of all the securities in the account minus any margin debt.

To measure Hathaway's return on his invested capital, we need to calculate the one-year holding period return. His invested capital as of January 1, 2017, is $324,000. He made no new additions of capital in the portfolio during 2017, although he sold one stock, Dallas National, and used the proceeds to buy another, Florida Southcoast Banks.

Measuring Income There are two sources of return from a portfolio of common stocks: income and capital gains. Current income is realized from dividends or, for bonds, is earned in the form of interest. Investors must report taxable dividends and interest on federal and state income tax returns. Companies are required to furnish income reports (Form 1099-DIV for dividends and Form 1099-INT for interest) to stockholders and bondholders. Many investors maintain logs to keep track of dividend and interest income as it is received.

Table 13.6 lists Hathaway's dividends for 2017. He received two quarterly dividends of $0.45 per share before he sold the Dallas National stock. He also received two $0.32-per-share quarterly dividends on the additional Florida Southcoast Banks shares he acquired. His total dividend income for 2017 was $10,935.

Measuring Capital Gains Table 13.7 shows the unrealized gains in value for each of the issues in the Hathaway portfolio. The January 1, 2017, and December 31, 2017, values are listed for each issue except the additional shares of Florida Southcoast Banks. The amounts listed for Florida Southcoast Banks reflect the fact that 1,000 additional shares of the stock were acquired on May 10, 2017, at a cost of $32,040. Hathaway's current holdings had beginning-of-the-year values of $327,040 (including the additional Florida Southcoast Banks shares at the date of purchase) and are worth $356,000 at year-end.

TABLE 13.6	DIVIDEND INCOME ON HATHAWAY'S PORTFOLIO (CALENDAR YEAR 2017)		
Number of Shares	Company	Annual Dividend per Share	Dividends Received
1,000	Bancorp West, Inc.	$1.20	$ 1,200
1,000	Dallas National Corporation*	$1.80	$ 900
1,000	Dator Companies, Inc.	$1.12	$ 1,120
500	Excelsior Industries	$2.00	$ 1,000
2,000	Florida Southcoast Banks**	$1.28	$ 1,920
1,000	Maryland-Pacific	$1.10	$ 1,100
1,000	Moronson	—	—
500	Northwest Mining and Mfg.	$2.05	$ 1,025
1,000	Rawland Petroleum	$1.20	$ 1,200
1,000	Vornox	$1.47	$ 1,470
	Total		$10,935

*Sold May 7, 2017.
**1,000 additional shares acquired on May 10, 2017.

TABLE 13.7 UNREALIZED GAINS IN VALUE OF HATHAWAY'S PORTFOLIO (JANUARY 1, 2017, TO DECEMBER 31, 2017)

Number of Shares	Company	Market Value (1/1/17)	Market Price (12/31/17)	Market Value (12/31/17)	Unrealized Gain (Loss)	Percentage Change
1,000	Bancorp West, Inc.	$ 30,000	$27	$ 27,000	($ 3,000)	–10.0%
1,000	Dator Companies, Inc.	$ 27,000	$36	$ 36,000	$ 9,000	33.3%
500	Excelsior Industries	$ 27,000	$66	$ 33,000	$ 6,000	22.2%
2,000	Florida Southcoast Banks*	$ 62,040	$35	$ 70,000	$ 7,960	12.8%
1,000	Maryland-Pacific	$ 26,000	$26	$ 26,000	—	—
1,000	Moronson	$ 47,000	$55	$ 55,000	$ 8,000	17.0%
500	Northwest Mining and Mfg.	$ 31,000	$60	$ 30,000	($ 1,000)	–3.2%
1,000	Rawland Petroleum	$ 30,000	$36	$ 36,000	$ 6,000	20.0%
1,000	Vornox	$ 47,000	$43	$ 43,000	($ 4,000)	–8.5%
	Total	$327,040**		$356,000	$28,960	8.9%

*1,000 additional shares acquired on May 10, 2017, at a cost of $32,040. The value listed is the cost plus the market value of the previously owned shares as of January 1, 2017.

**This total includes the $324,000 market value of the portfolio on January 1, 2017 (from Table 13.5) plus the $3,040 realized gain on the sale of the Dallas National Corporation stock on May 7, 2017. The inclusion of the realized gain in this total is necessary to calculate the unrealized gain on the portfolio during 2017.

During 2017 the portfolio increased in value by 8.9%, or $28,960, in unrealized capital gains. In addition, Hathaway realized a capital gain in 2017 by selling his Dallas National holding. From January 1, 2017, until its sale on May 7, 2017, the Dallas National holding rose in value from $29,000 to $32,040. This was the only sale in 2017, so the total *realized* gain was $3,040. During 2017 the portfolio had both a realized gain of $3,040 and an unrealized gain of $28,960. The total gain in value equals the sum of the two: $32,000. Put another way, Hathaway neither added nor withdrew capital over the year. Therefore, the total capital gain is simply the difference between the year-end market value (of $356,000, from Table 13.7) and the value on January 1 (of $324,000, from Table 13.5). This, of course, amounts to $32,000. Of that amount, for tax purposes, only $3,040 is considered realized.

Measuring the Portfolio's Holding Period Return We use the holding period return to measure the total return on the Hathaway portfolio during 2017. The basic one-year HPR formula for portfolios appears below.

Equation 13.3

$$\text{Holding period return for a portfolio} = \frac{\text{Dividends and interest received} + \text{Realized gain} + \text{Unrealized gain}}{\text{Initial equity investment} + \left(\text{New funds} \times \frac{\text{Number of months in portfolio}}{12}\right) - \left(\text{Withdrawn funds} \times \frac{\text{Number of months Withdrawn form portfolio}}{12}\right)}$$

Equation 13.3a

$$HPR_p = \frac{C + RG + UG}{E_0 + \left(NF \times \frac{ip}{12}\right) - \left(WF \times \frac{wp}{12}\right)}$$

TABLE 13.8   HOLDING PERIOD RETURN CALCULATION ON HATHAWAY'S PORTFOLIO (JANUARY 1, 2017, TO DECEMBER 31, 2017)

Data	Value
Portfolio value (1/1/17)	$324,000
Portfolio value (12/31/17)	$356,000
Realized appreciation (1/1/17 to 5/7/17 when Dallas National Corporation was sold)	$ 3,040
Unrealized appreciation (1/1/17 to 12/31/17)	$ 28,960
Dividends received	$ 10,935
New funds invested or withdrawn	None
Portfolio HPR Calculation	

$$HPR_p = \frac{\$10,935 + \$3,040 + \$28,960}{\$324,000 + \$0 + \$0}$$

$$= \underline{13.25\%}$$

This formula includes both the realized gains (income plus capital gains) and the unrealized yearly gains of the portfolio. Portfolio additions and deletions are time-weighted for the number of months they are in the portfolio.

Table 13.7 lays out in detail the portfolio's change in value: It lists all the stocks that are in the portfolio as of December 31, 2017, and calculates the unrealized gain during the year. The beginning and year-end values are included for comparison purposes. The crux of the analysis is the HPR calculation for the year, presented in Table 13.8. All the elements of a portfolio's return are included. Dividends total $10,935 (from Table 13.6). The realized gain of $3,040 represents the increment in value of the Dallas National holding from January 1, 2017, until its sale. During 2017 the portfolio had a $28,960 unrealized gain (from Table 13.7). There were no additions of funds, and no funds were withdrawn. Using Equation 13.3 for HPR, we find that the portfolio had a total return of 13.25% in 2017.

Comparison of Return with Overall Market Measures

Bob Hathaway can compare the HPR figure for his portfolio with market measures such as stock indexes. This comparison will show how his portfolio is doing in relation to the stock market as a whole. The S&P 500 Stock Composite Index and the Nasdaq Composite Index are acceptable indexes to represent the stock market as a whole. Assume that during 2017 the return on the S&P 500 Index was 10.75% (including both dividends and capital gains). The return from Hathaway's portfolio was 13.25%, which compares very favorably with the broadly based index. The Hathaway portfolio performed about 23% better than the broad indicator of stock market return.

Such a comparison factors out general market movements, but it fails to consider whether Hathaway's portfolio is more or less risky than the broad stock market indexes. That requires further analysis. A number of risk-adjusted, market-adjusted rate-of-return measures are available for use in assessing portfolio performance. Here we'll discuss the most popular—Sharpe's measure, Treynor's measure, and Jensen's measure—and demonstrate their application to Hathaway's portfolio.

Sharpe's Measure **Sharpe's measure** of portfolio performance, developed by William F. Sharpe, compares the risk premium on a portfolio to the portfolio's standard deviation of return. The risk premium on a portfolio is the total portfolio return minus the risk-free rate. Sharpe's measure can be expressed as the following formula:

Equation 13.4

$$\text{Sharpe's measure} = \frac{\text{Total portfolio return} - \text{Risk-free rate}}{\text{Standard deviation of portfolio return}}$$

Equation 13.4a

$$SM = \frac{r_p - r_f}{s_p}$$

This measure allows the investor to assess the risk premium per unit of total risk, which is measured by the portfolio standard deviation of return.

Assume the risk-free rate, r_f, is 7.50% and the standard deviation of return on Hathaway's portfolio, s_p, is 16%. The total portfolio return, r_p, which is the HPR for Hathaway's portfolio calculated in Table 13.8, is 13.25%. Substituting those values into Equation 13.4, we get Sharpe's measure, SM_p.

$$SM_p = \frac{13.25\% - 7.50\%}{16\%} = \frac{5.75\%}{16\%} = \underline{0.36}$$

Sharpe's measure is meaningful when compared either to other portfolios or to the market. In general, the higher the value of Sharpe's measure, the better—the higher the risk premium per unit of risk. If we assume that the market return, r_m, is currently 10.75% and the standard deviation of return for the market portfolio, s_{pm}, is 11.25%, Sharpe's measure for the market, SM_m, is

$$SM_m = \frac{10.75\% - 7.50\%}{11.25\%} = \frac{3.25\%}{11.25\%} = \underline{0.29}$$

Because Sharpe's measure of 0.36 for Hathaway's portfolio is greater than the measure of 0.29 for the market portfolio, Hathaway's portfolio exhibits superior performance. Its risk premium per unit of risk is above that of the market. Had Sharpe's measure for Hathaway's portfolio been below that of the market (below 0.29), the portfolio's performance would be considered inferior to the market performance.

Treynor's Measure Jack L. Treynor developed a portfolio performance measure similar to Sharpe's measure. **Treynor's measure** uses the portfolio beta to measure the portfolio's risk. Treynor therefore focuses only on nondiversifiable risk, assuming that the portfolio has been built in a manner that diversifies away all diversifiable risk. (In contrast, Sharpe focuses on total risk.) Treynor's measure is calculated as shown in Equation 13.5.

Equation 13.5

$$\text{Treynor's measure} = \frac{\text{Total portfolio return} - \text{Risk-free rate}}{\text{Portfolio beta}}$$

Equation 13.5a

$$TM = \frac{r_p - r_f}{b_p}$$

This measure gives the risk premium per unit of nondiversifiable risk, which is measured by the portfolio beta.

Using the data for the Hathaway portfolio presented earlier and assuming that the beta for Hathaway's portfolio, b_p, is 1.20, we can substitute into Equation 13.5 to get Treynor's measure, TM_p, for Hathaway's portfolio.

$$TM_p = \frac{13.25\% - 7.50\%}{1.20} = \frac{5.75\%}{1.20} = 4.79\%$$

Treynor's measure, like Sharpe's measure, is useful when compared either to other portfolios or to the market. Generally, the higher the value of Treynor's measure, the better—the greater the risk premium per unit of nondiversifiable risk. Again assuming that the market return, r_m, is 10.75% and recognizing that, by definition, the beta for the market portfolio, b_m, is 1.00, we can use Equation 13.5 to find Treynor's measure for the market, TM_m.

$$TM_m = \frac{10.75\% - 7.50\%}{1.00} = \frac{3.25\%}{1.00} = 3.25\%$$

The fact that Treynor's measure of 4.79% for Hathaway's portfolio is greater than the market portfolio measure of 3.25% indicates that Hathaway's portfolio exhibits superior performance. Its risk premium per unit of nondiversifiable risk is above that of the market. Had Treynor's measure for Hathaway's portfolio been below that of the market (below 3.25%), the portfolio's performance would be viewed as inferior to that of the market.

Jensen's Measure (Jensen's Alpha) Michael C. Jensen developed a portfolio performance measure that seems quite different from the measures of Sharpe and Treynor, yet is theoretically consistent with Treynor's measure. **Jensen's measure**, also called **Jensen's alpha**, is based on the capital asset pricing model (CAPM). It calculates the portfolio's *excess return*. Excess return is the amount by which the portfolio's actual return deviates from its required (or expected) return, which is determined using its beta and the CAPM. The value of the excess return may be positive, zero, or negative. Like Treynor's measure, Jensen's measure focuses only on the nondiversifiable, or relevant, risk by using beta and CAPM. It assumes that the portfolio has been adequately diversified. Jensen's measure is calculated as shown in Equation 13.6.

Equation 13.6

Jensen's measure = (Total portfolio return − Risk-free rate) − [Portfolio beta × (Market return − Risk-free rate)]

Equation 13.6a

$$JM = (r_p - r_f) - [b_p \times (r_m - r_f)]$$

Jensen's measure indicates the difference between the portfolio's actual return and its required return. Positive values indicate superior performance. They indicate that the portfolio earned a return in excess of its risk-adjusted, market-adjusted required return. A value of zero indicates that the portfolio earned exactly its required return. Negative values indicate the portfolio failed to earn its required return.

Using the data for Hathaway's portfolio presented earlier, we can substitute into Equation 13.6 to get Jensen's measure, JM_p, for Hathaway's portfolio.

$$JM_p = (13.25\% - 7.50) - [1.20 \times (10.75\% - 7.50)]$$

$$= 5.75\% - (1.20 \times 3.25) = 5.75\% - 3.90\% = 1.85\%$$

The 1.85% value for Jensen's measure indicates that Hathaway's portfolio earned an excess return that was 1.85 percentage points above its required return, given its nondiversifiable risk as measured by beta. Clearly, Hathaway's portfolio has outperformed the market on a risk-adjusted basis.

Note that unlike the Sharpe and Treynor measures, Jensen's measure, through its use of CAPM, automatically adjusts for the market return. Therefore, there is no need to make a separate market comparison. In general, the higher the value of Jensen's measure, the better the portfolio has performed. Only those portfolios with positive Jensen measures have outperformed the market on a risk-adjusted basis. Because of its computational simplicity, its reliance only on nondiversifiable risk, and its inclusion of both risk and market adjustments, Jensen's measure (alpha) tends to be preferred over those of Sharpe and Treynor for assessing portfolio performance.

Portfolio Revision

In the Hathaway portfolio we have been discussing, one transaction occurred during 2017. The reason for this transaction was that Hathaway believed the Florida Southcoast Banks stock had more return potential than the Dallas National stock. You should periodically analyze your portfolio with one basic question in mind. Does this portfolio continue to meet my needs? In other words, does the portfolio contain those issues that are best suited to your risk-return needs? Investors who systematically study the issues in their portfolios occasionally find a need to sell certain issues and purchase new securities to replace them. This process is commonly called **portfolio revision**. As the economy evolves, certain industries and stocks become either less or more attractive as investments, prompting investors to make adjustments to their portfolios.

Given the dynamics of the investment world, periodic reallocation and rebalancing of the portfolio are a necessity. Many circumstances require such changes. For example, as an investor nears retirement, the portfolio's emphasis normally evolves from a strategy that stresses growth and capital appreciation to one that seeks to preserve capital. Changing a portfolio's emphasis normally occurs as an evolutionary process rather than an overnight switch. Individual issues in the portfolio often change in risk-return characteristics. As this occurs, you would be wise to eliminate those issues that do not meet your objectives. In addition, the need for diversification is constant. As investments rise or fall in value, their diversification effect may be lessened. Thus, you may need portfolio revision to maintain diversification.

CONCEPTS IN REVIEW

Answers available at
http://www.pearsonhighered.com/smart

13.14 What is active portfolio management? Will it result in superior returns? Explain.

13.15 Describe the steps involved in measuring portfolio return. Explain the role of the portfolio's HPR in this process and explain why one must differentiate between realized and unrealized gains.

13.16 Why is comparing a portfolio's return to the return on a broad market index generally inadequate? Explain.

13.17 Briefly describe each of the following measures for assessing portfolio performance and explain how they are used.

a. Sharpe's measure
b. Treynor's measure
c. Jensen's measure (Jensen's alpha)

13.18 Why is Jensen's measure (alpha) generally preferred over the measures of Sharpe and Treynor for assessing portfolio performance? Explain.

13.19 Explain the role of portfolio revision in the process of managing a portfolio.

Timing Transactions

LG5 **LG6**   The essence of timing is to "buy low and sell high." This is the dream of all investors. Although there is no tried-and-true way to achieve such a goal, there are several methods you can use to time purchases and sales. First, there are formula plans, which we discuss next. Investors can also use limit and stop-loss orders as a timing aid. They can follow procedures for warehousing liquidity, and they can also take into consideration other aspects of timing when selling their investments.

Formula Plans

Formula plans are mechanical methods of portfolio management that try to take advantage of price changes that result from cyclical price movements. Formula plans are not set up to provide unusually high returns. Rather, they are conservative strategies employed by investors who do not wish to bear a high level of risk. We discuss four popular formula plans: dollar-cost averaging, the constant-dollar plan, the constant-ratio plan, and the variable-ratio plan.

Dollar-Cost Averaging   **Dollar-cost averaging** is a formula plan in which a fixed dollar amount is invested in a security at fixed time intervals. In this passive buy-and-hold strategy, the periodic dollar investment is held constant. To make the plan work, you must invest on a regular basis. The goal of a dollar-cost averaging program is growth in the value of the security to which the funds are allocated. The price of the investment security will probably fluctuate over time. If the price were to decline, you would purchase more shares per period. Conversely, if the price were to rise, you would purchase fewer shares per period.

Look at the example of dollar-cost averaging in Table 13.9. The table shows investment of $500 per month in the Wolverine Mutual Fund, a growth-oriented, no-load mutual fund. Assume that during one year's time you have placed $6,000 in the mutual fund shares. (Because this is a no-load fund, shares are purchased at net asset value.) You made purchases at NAVs ranging from a low of $24.16 to a high of $30.19. At year-end, the value of your holdings in the fund was slightly less than $6,900. Dollar-cost averaging is a passive strategy; other formula plans are more active.

Constant-Dollar Plan   A **constant-dollar plan** consists of a portfolio that is divided into two parts, speculative and conservative. The speculative portion consists of securities that have high promise of capital gains. The conservative portion consists of low-risk investments such as bonds or a money market account. The target dollar amount for the speculative portion is constant. You establish trigger points (upward or downward movement in the speculative portion) at which funds are removed from or added to that portion. The constant-dollar plan basically skims off profits from the speculative portion of the portfolio if it rises a certain percentage or amount in value and adds these funds to the conservative portion of the portfolio. If the speculative portion of the portfolio declines by a specific percentage or amount, you add funds to it from the conservative portion.

Assume that you have established the constant-dollar plan shown in Table 13.10. The beginning $20,000 portfolio consists of $10,000 invested in a high-beta, no-load mutual fund and $10,000 deposited in a money market account. You have decided to rebalance the portfolio every time the speculative portion is worth $2,000 more or $2,000 less than its initial value of $10,000. If the speculative portion of the portfolio

TABLE 13.9   DOLLAR-COST AVERAGING ($500 PER MONTH, WOLVERINE MUTUAL FUND SHARES)

Transactions

Month	Net Asset Value (NAV) Month-End	Number of Shares Purchased
January	$26.00	19.23
February	$27.46	18.21
March	$27.02	18.50
April	$24.19	20.67
May	$26.99	18.53
June	$25.63	19.51
July	$24.70	20.24
August	$24.16	20.70
September	$25.27	19.79
October	$26.15	19.12
November	$29.60	16.89
December	$30.19	16.56

Annual Summary

Total investment: $6,000.00
Total number of shares purchased: 227.95
Average cost per share: $26.32
Year-end portfolio value: $6,881.81

equals or exceeds $12,000, you sell sufficient shares of the fund to bring its value down to $10,000 and add the proceeds from the sale to the conservative portion. If the speculative portion declines in value to $8,000 or less, you use funds from the conservative portion to purchase sufficient shares to raise the value of the speculative portion to $10,000.

Two portfolio-rebalancing actions are taken in the time sequence illustrated in Table 13.10. Initially, $10,000 was allocated to each portion of the portfolio. When the mutual fund's net asset value rose to $12, the speculative portion was worth $12,000. At that point, you sold 166.67 shares valued at $2,000 and added the proceeds to the money market account. Later, the mutual fund's NAV declined to $9.50 per share, causing the value of the speculative portion to drop below $8,000. This change triggered the purchase of sufficient shares to raise the value of the speculative portion to $10,000. Over the long run, if the speculative investment of the constant-dollar plan rises in value, the conservative component of the portfolio will increase in dollar value as profits are transferred into it.

Constant-Ratio Plan The **constant-ratio plan** is similar to the constant-dollar plan except that it establishes a desired fixed ratio of the speculative portion to the conservative portion of the portfolio. When the actual ratio of the two differs by a predetermined amount from the desired ratio, rebalancing occurs. At that point, you make transactions to bring the actual ratio back to the desired ratio. To use the constant-ratio plan, you must decide on the appropriate apportionment of the portfolio between speculative and conservative investments. You must also choose the ratio trigger point at which transactions occur.

TABLE 13.10   CONSTANT-DOLLAR PLAN

Mutual Fund NAV	Value of Speculative Portion	Value of Conservative Portion	Total Portfolio Value	Transactions	Number of Shares in Speculative Portion
$10.00	$10,000.00	$10,000.00	$20,000.00		1,000.00
$11.00	$11,000.00	$10,000.00	$21,000.00		1,000.00
$12.00	$12,000.00	$10,000.00	$22,000.00		1,000.00
→ $12.00	$10,000.00	$12,000.00	$22,000.00	Sold 166.67 shares	833.33
$11.00	$ 9,166.63	$12,000.00	$21,166.63		833.33
$ 9.50	$ 7,916.64	$12,000.00	$19,916.64		833.33
→ $ 9.50	$10,000.00	$ 9,916.64	$19,916.64	Purchased 219.30 shares	1,052.63
$10.00	$10,526.30	$ 9,916.64	$20,442.94		1,052.63

To see how this works, assume that the constant-ratio plan illustrated in Table 13.11 is yours. The initial portfolio value is $20,000. You have decided to allocate 50% of the portfolio to the speculative, high-beta mutual fund and 50% to a money market account. You will rebalance the portfolio when the ratio of the speculative portion to the conservative portion is greater than or equal to 1.20 or less than or equal to 0.80. A sequence of changes in net asset value is listed in Table 13.11. Initially, $10,000 is allocated to each portion of the portfolio. When the fund NAV reaches $12, the 1.20 ratio triggers the sale of 83.33 shares. Then the portfolio is back to its desired 50:50 ratio. Later, the fund NAV declines to $9, lowering the value of the speculative portion to $8,250. The ratio of the speculative portion to the conservative portion is then 0.75, which is below the 0.80 trigger point. You purchase 152.78 shares to bring the desired ratio back up to the 50:50 level.

The long-run expectation under a constant-ratio plan is that the speculative securities will rise in value. When this occurs, you will sell securities to reapportion the

TABLE 13.11   CONSTANT-RATIO PLAN

Mutual Fund NAV	Value of Speculative Portion	Value of Conservative Portion	Total Portfolio Value	Ratio of Speculative Portion to Conservative Portion	Transactions	Number of Shares in Speculative Portion
$10.00	$10,000.00	$10,000.00	$20,000.00	1.000		1,000.00
$ 11.00	$11,000.00	$10,000.00	$21,000.00	1.100		1,000.00
$12.00	$12,000.00	$10,000.00	$22,000.00	1.200		1,000.00
→ $12.00	$11,000.00	$11,000.00	$22,000.00	1.000	Sold 83.33 shares	916.67
$ 11.00	$10,083.00	$11,000.00	$21,083.00	0.917		916.67
$10.00	$ 9,166.70	$11,000.00	$20,166.70	0.833		916.67
$ 9.00	$ 8,250.00	$11,000.00	$19,250.00	0.750		916.67
→ $ 9.00	$ 9,625.00	$ 9,625.00	$19,250.00	1.000	Purchased 152.78 shares	1,069.44
$10.00	$ 10,694.40	$ 9,625.00	$20,319.40	1.110		1,069.44

portfolio and increase the value of the conservative portion. This philosophy is similar to the constant-dollar plan, except that it uses a ratio as a trigger point.

Variable-Ratio Plan   The **variable-ratio plan** is the most aggressive of these four fairly passive formula plans. It attempts to turn stock market movements to the investor's advantage by timing the market. That is, it tries to "buy low and sell high." The ratio of the speculative portion to the total portfolio value varies depending on the movement in value of the speculative securities. When the ratio rises a certain predetermined amount, the amount committed to the speculative portion of the portfolio is reduced. Conversely, if the value of the speculative portion declines so that it drops significantly in proportion to the total portfolio value, the amount committed to the speculative portion of the portfolio is increased.

When implementing the variable-ratio plan, you have several decisions to make. First, you must determine the initial allocation between the speculative and conservative portions of the portfolio. Next, you must choose trigger points to initiate buy or sell activity. These points are a function of the ratio between the value of the speculative portion and the value of the total portfolio. Finally, you must set adjustments in that ratio at each trigger point.

Assume that you use the variable-ratio plan shown in Table 13.12. Initially, you divide the portfolio equally between the speculative and the conservative portions. The speculative portion consists of a high-beta (around 2.0) mutual fund. The conservative portion is a money market account. You decide that when the speculative portion reaches 60% of the total portfolio, you will reduce its proportion to 45%. If the speculative portion of the portfolio drops to 40% of the total portfolio, then you will raise its proportion to 55%. The logic behind this strategy is an attempt to time the cyclical movements in the mutual fund's value. When the fund moves up in value, you take profits, and you increase the proportion invested in the no-risk money market account. When the fund declines markedly in value, you increase the proportion of capital committed to the speculative portion.

A sequence of transactions is depicted in Table 13.12. When the fund net asset value climbs to $15, the 60% ratio trigger point is reached, and you sell 250 shares of the fund. You place the proceeds in the money market account, which causes the speculative portion then to represent 45% of the value of the portfolio. Later, the fund NAV declines to $10, causing the speculative portion of the portfolio to drop to 35%. This triggers a portfolio rebalancing, and you purchase 418.75 shares, moving the speculative portion to 55%. When the fund NAV then moves to $12, the total portfolio is

TABLE 13.12   VARIABLE-RATIO PLAN

Mutual Fund NAV	Value of Speculative Portion	Value of Conservative Portion	Total Portfolio Value	Ratio of Speculative Portion to Total Portfolio Value	Transactions	Number of Shares in Speculative Portions
$10.00	$10,000.00	$10,000.00	$20,000.00	0.50		1,000.00
$15.00	$15,000.00	$10,000.00	$25,000.00	0.60		1,000.00
→ $15.00	$ 11,250.00	$13,750.00	$25,000.00	0.45	Sold 250 shares	750.00
$10.00	$ 7,500.00	$13,750.00	$21,250.00	0.35		750.00
→ $10.00	$ 11,687.50	$ 9,562.50	$21,250.00	0.55	Purchased 418.75 shares	1,168.75
$12.00	$14,025.00	$ 9,562.50	$ 23,587.50	0.59		1,168.75

worth in excess of $23,500. In comparison, had the initial investment of $20,000 been allocated equally and had no rebalancing been done between the mutual fund and the money market account, the total portfolio value at this time would have been only $22,000 (i.e., $12 × 1,000 = $12,000 in the speculative portion plus $10,000 in the money market account).

Using Limit and Stop-Loss Orders

Earlier in this text we discussed the market order, the limit order, and the stop-loss order. Here we will see how you can use the limit and stop-loss orders to rebalance a portfolio. These types of security orders, if properly used, can increase return by lowering transaction costs.

Limit Orders   There are many ways investors can use limit orders when they buy or sell securities. For instance, if you have decided to add a stock to the portfolio, a limit order to buy will ensure that you buy only at or below the desired purchase price. A limit *good-'til-canceled* (GTC) order to buy instructs the broker to buy stock until the entire order is filled. The primary risk in using limit instead of market orders is that the order may not be executed. For example, if you placed a GTC order to buy 100 shares of State Oil of California at $27 per share and the stock never traded at $27 per share or less, the order would never be executed. Thus, you must weigh the need for immediate execution (market order) against the possibility of a better price with a limit order.

Limit orders, of course, can increase your return if they enable you to buy a security at a lower cost or sell it at a higher price. During a typical trading day, a stock's price will fluctuate up and down over a normal trading range. For example, suppose the common shares of Jama Motor traded 10 times in the following sequence: $36.00, $35.88, $35.75, $35.94, $35.50, $35.63, $35.82, $36.00, $36.13, and $36.00. A market order to sell could have been executed at somewhere between 35.50 (the low) and 36.13 (the high). A limit order to sell at 36.00 would have been executed at 36.00. Thus, $0.50 per share might have been gained by using a limit order.

Stop-Loss Orders   Stop-loss orders can be used to limit the downside loss exposure of an investment. For example, assume you purchase 500 shares of Easy Work at $26.00 and have set a specific goal to sell the stock if it reaches $32.00 or drops to $23.00. To implement this goal, you would enter a GTC stop order to sell with a price limit of $32.00 and another stop order at a price of $23.00. If the issue trades at $23.00 or less, the stop-loss order becomes a market order, and the broker sells the stock at the best price available. Or, if the issue trades at $32.00 or higher, the broker will sell the stock. In the first situation, you are trying to reduce your losses; in the second, you are attempting to protect a profit.

The principal risk in using stop-loss orders is **whipsawing**—a situation where a stock temporarily drops in price and then bounces back upward. If Easy Work dropped to $23.00, then $22.57, and then rallied back to $26.00, you would have been sold out at a price between $23.00 and $22.57. For this reason, limit orders, including stop-loss orders, require careful analysis before they are placed. You must consider the stock's probable fluctuations as well as the need to purchase or sell the stock when choosing among market, limit, and stop-loss orders.

Warehousing Liquidity

Investing in risky stocks or in options or futures offers probable returns in excess of those available with money market deposit accounts or bonds. However, stocks and options and futures are risky investments. One recommendation for an efficient portfolio is to keep a portion of it in a low-risk, highly liquid investment to protect against total loss. The low-risk asset acts as a buffer against possible investment losses. A second reason for maintaining funds in a low-risk asset is the possibility of future opportunities. When opportunity strikes, an investor who has extra cash available will be able to take advantage of the situation. If you have set aside funds in a highly liquid investment, you need not disturb the existing portfolio.

The primary media for warehousing liquidity are money market deposit accounts at financial institutions and money market mutual funds. The money market accounts at savings institutions provide relatively easy access to funds and furnish returns competitive with (but somewhat lower than) money market mutual funds. The products offered by financial institutions are becoming more competitive with those offered by mutual funds and stock brokerage firms.

Timing Investment Sales

Knowing when to sell a stock is as important as choosing which stock to buy. You should review your portfolio periodically and consider possible sales and new purchases. Here we discuss two issues relevant to the sale decision: tax consequences and achieving investment goals.

Tax Consequences Taxes affect nearly all investment actions. All investors can and should understand certain basics. The treatment of capital losses is important: A maximum of $3,000 of losses in excess of capital gains can be written off against other income in any one year. If you have a loss position in an investment and have concluded that it would be wise to sell it, the best time to sell is when you have a capital gain against which you can apply the loss. Clearly, one should carefully consider the tax consequences of investment sales prior to taking action.

Achieving Investment Goals Every investor would enjoy buying an investment at its lowest price and selling it at its top price. At a more realistic level, you should sell an investment when it no longer meets your needs. In particular, if an investment has become either more or less risky than is desired or if it has not met its return objective, it should be sold. The tax consequences mentioned above help to determine the appropriate time to sell. However, taxes are not the foremost consideration in a sale decision. The dual concepts of risk and return should be the overriding concerns.

Be sure to take the time periodically to examine each investment in light of its return performance and relative risk. You should sell any investment that no longer belongs in the portfolio and should buy investments that are more suitable. Finally, you should not hold out for every nickel of profit. Very often, those who hold out for the top price watch the value of their holdings plummet. If an investment looks ripe to sell, sell it, take the profit, reinvest it in an appropriate asset, and enjoy your good fortune.

CONCEPTS IN REVIEW

Answers available at http://www.pearsonhighered .com/smart

13.20 Explain the role that formula plans can play in the timing of security transactions. Describe the logic underlying the use of these plans.

13.21 Briefly describe each of the following plans and differentiate among them.

a. Dollar-cost averaging
b. Constant-dollar plan
c. Constant-ratio plan
d. Variable-ratio plan

13.22 Describe how a limit order can be used when securities are bought or sold. How can a stop-loss order be used to reduce losses? To protect profit?

13.23 Give two reasons why an investor might want to maintain funds in a low-risk, highly liquid investment.

13.24 Describe the two items an investor should consider before reaching a decision to sell an investment.

MyFinanceLab

Here is what you should know after reading this chapter. MyFinanceLab will help you identify what you know and where to go when you need to practice.

What You Should Know	Key Terms	Where to Practice
LG1 **Explain how to use an asset allocation scheme to construct a portfolio consistent with investor objectives.** To construct a portfolio, consider personal characteristics and establish consistent portfolio objectives such as current income, capital preservation, capital growth, tax considerations, and level of risk. Asset allocation, which is the key influence on portfolio return, involves dividing the portfolio into asset classes. Asset allocation aims to protect against negative developments while taking advantage of positive ones. The basic approaches to asset allocation involve the use of fixed weightings, flexible weightings, and tactical asset allocation. Asset allocation can be achieved on a do-it-yourself basis, with the use of mutual funds, or by merely buying shares in an asset allocation fund.	asset allocation, *p. 513* fixed-weightings approach, *p. 513* flexible-weightings approach, *p. 514* security selection, *p. 513* tactical asset allocation, *p. 514*	MyFinanceLab Study Plan 13.1
LG2 **Discuss the data and indexes needed to measure and compare investment performance.** To analyze the performance of individual investments, gather current market information and stay abreast of international, national, and local economic and market developments. Indexes of investment performance such as the Dow Jones Industrial Average (DJIA) and bond market indicators are available for use in assessing market behavior. The performance of individual investments can be measured on both a pretax and an after-tax basis by using the holding period return. HPR measures the total return (income plus change in value) earned on the investment during an investment period of one year or less. HPR can be compared to investment goals to assess whether the proper return is being earned for the risk involved and to isolate any problem investments.		MyFinanceLab Study Plan 13.2

What You Should Know	Key Terms	Where to Practice
LG3 **Understand the techniques used to measure income, capital gains, and total portfolio return.** To measure portfolio return, estimate the amount invested, the income earned, and any capital gains (both realized and unrealized) over the relevant current time period. Using these values, calculate the portfolio's holding period return by dividing the total returns by the amount of investment during the period. Comparison of the portfolio's HPR to overall market measures can provide some insight about the portfolio's performance relative to the market.	active portfolio management, *p. 521*	MyFinanceLab Study Plan 13.3 Video Learning Aid for Problem P13.3
LG4 **Use the Sharpe, Treynor, and Jensen measures to compare a portfolio's return with a risk-adjusted, market-adjusted rate of return, and discuss portfolio revision.** A risk-adjusted, market-adjusted evaluation of a portfolio's return can be made using Sharpe's measure, Treynor's measure, or Jensen's measure. Sharpe's and Treynor's measures find the risk premium per unit of risk, which can be compared with similar market measures to assess the portfolio's performance. Jensen's measure (alpha) calculates the portfolio's excess return using beta and CAPM. Jensen's measure tends to be preferred because it is relatively easy to calculate and directly makes both risk and market adjustments. Portfolio revision—selling certain issues and purchasing new ones to replace them—should take place when returns are unacceptable or when the portfolio fails to meet the investor's objectives.	Jensen's measure (Jensen's alpha), *p. 527* portfolio revision, *p. 528* Sharpe's measure, *p. 525* Treynor's measure, *p. 526*	MyFinanceLab Study Plan 13.4 Video Learning Aid for Problem P13.15
LG5 **Describe the role and logic of dollar-cost averaging, constant-dollar plans, constant-ratio plans, and variable-ratio plans.** Formula plans are used to time purchase and sale decisions to take advantage of price changes that result from cyclical price movements. The common formula plans are dollar-cost averaging, the constant-dollar plan, the constant-ratio plan, and the variable-ratio plan. All of them have certain decision rules or triggers that signal a purchase and/or sale action.	constant-dollar plan, *p. 529* constant-ratio plan, *p. 530* dollar-cost averaging, *p. 529* formula, *p. 529* variable-ratio plan, *p. 532*	MyFinanceLab Study Plan 13.5 Excel Table 13.9

What You Should Know	Key Terms	Where to Practice
LG6 Explain the role of limit and stop-loss orders in investment timing, warehousing liquidity, and timing investment sales. Limit and stop-loss orders can be used to trigger the rebalancing of a portfolio to contribute to improved portfolio returns. Low-risk, highly liquid investments such as money market deposit accounts and money market mutual funds can warehouse liquidity. Such liquidity can protect against total loss and allow you to seize any attractive opportunities. Investment sales should be timed to obtain maximum tax benefits (or minimum tax consequences) and to contribute to the achievement of the investor's goals.	whipsawing, p. 533	MyFinanceLab Study Plan 13.6

Log into MyFinanceLab, take a chapter test, and get a personalized Study Plan that tells you which concepts you understand and which ones you need to review. From there, MyFinanceLab will give you further practice, tutorials, animations, videos, and guided solutions.
Log into **http://www.myfinancelab.com**

Discussion Questions

LG1 **Q13.1** List your personal characteristics and then state your investment objectives in light of them. Use these objectives as a basis for developing your portfolio objectives and policies. Assume that you plan to create a portfolio aimed at achieving your stated objectives. The portfolio will be constructed by allocating your money to any of the following asset classes: common stock, bonds, foreign securities, and short-term securities.
   a. Determine and justify an asset allocation to these four classes in light of your stated portfolio objectives and policies.
   b. Describe the types of investments you would choose for each of the asset classes.
   c. Assume that after making the asset allocations specified in part a, you receive a sizable inheritance that causes your portfolio objectives to change to a much more aggressive posture. Describe the changes that you would make in your asset allocations.
   d. Describe other asset classes you might consider when developing your asset allocation scheme.

LG2 **LG3** **Q13.2** Choose an established local (or nearby) company whose stock is listed and actively traded on a major exchange. Find the stock's closing price at the end of each of the preceding six years and the amount of dividends paid in each of the preceding five years. Also, obtain the value of the Dow Jones Industrial Average at the end of each of the preceding six years.
   a. Use Equation 13.1 to calculate the pretax holding period return on the stock for each of the preceding five years.
   b. Study the international, national, and local economic and market developments that occurred during the preceding five years.
   c. Compare the stock's returns to the DJIA for each year over the five-year period of concern.
   d. Discuss the stock's returns in light of the economic and market developments noted in part **b** and the behavior of the DJIA as noted in part **c** over the five preceding years. How well did the stock perform in light of these factors?

LG2 LG3 **Q13.3** Assume that you are in the 35% ordinary tax bracket (federal and state combined) and that dividends and capital gains for holding periods of more than 12 months are taxed at a 15% rate. Select a major stock, bond, and mutual fund in which you are interested in investing. For each of them, gather data for each of the past three years on the annual dividends or interest paid and the capital gain (or loss) that would have resulted had they been purchased at the start of each year and sold at the end of each year. For the mutual fund, be sure to separate any dividends paid into investment income dividends and capital gains dividends.

a. For each of the three investments, calculate the pretax and after-tax HPR for each of the three years.

b. Use your annual HPR findings in part a to calculate the average after-tax HPR for each of the investments over the three-year period.

c. Compare the average returns found in part b for each of the investments. Discuss the relative risks in view of these returns and the characteristics of each investment.

LG2 LG3 **Q13.4** Choose six actively traded stocks for inclusion in your investment portfolio. Assume the portfolio was created three years ago by purchasing 200 shares of each of the six stocks. Find the acquisition price of each stock, the annual dividend paid by each stock, and the year-end prices for the three calendar years. Record for each stock its total cost, cost per share, current price per share, and total current value at the end of each of the three calendar years.

a. For each of the three years, find the amount invested in the portfolio.

b. For each of the three years, measure the annual income from the portfolio.

c. For each of the three years, determine the unrealized capital gains from the portfolio.

d. For each of the three years, calculate the portfolio's HPR, using the values in parts a, b, and c.

e. Use your findings in part d to calculate the average HPR for the portfolio over the three-year period. Discuss your finding.

LG4 **Q13.5** Find five actively traded stocks and record their prices at the start and the end of the most recent calendar year. Also, find the amount of dividends paid on each stock during that year and each stock's beta at the end of the year. Assume that the five stocks were held during the year in an equal-dollar-weighted portfolio (20% in each stock) created at the start of the year. Also find the current risk-free rate, r_f, and the market return, r_m, for the given year. Assume that the standard deviation for the portfolio of the five stocks is 14.25% and that the standard deviation for the market portfolio is 10.80%.

a. Use the following formula to find the portfolio return, r_p, for the year under consideration:

$$\begin{pmatrix} \text{Return} \\ \text{on} \\ \text{portfolio} \end{pmatrix} = \begin{pmatrix} \text{Proportion of} \\ \text{portfolio's total} \\ \text{dollar value} \\ \text{invested in} \\ \text{asset 1} \end{pmatrix} \times \begin{pmatrix} \text{Return} \\ \text{on asset} \\ 1 \end{pmatrix} + \begin{pmatrix} \text{Proportion of} \\ \text{portfolio's total} \\ \text{dollar value} \\ \text{invested in} \\ \text{asset 2} \end{pmatrix} \times \begin{pmatrix} \text{Return} \\ \text{on asset} \\ 2 \end{pmatrix} + \cdots +$$

$$\begin{pmatrix} \text{Proportion of} \\ \text{portfolio's total} \\ \text{dollar value} \\ \text{invested in} \\ \text{asset } n \end{pmatrix} \times \begin{pmatrix} \text{Return} \\ \text{on asset} \\ n \end{pmatrix} = \sum_{j=1}^{n} \begin{pmatrix} \text{Proportion of} \\ \text{portfolio's total} \\ \text{dollar value} \\ \text{invested in} \\ \text{asset } j \end{pmatrix} \times \begin{pmatrix} \text{Return} \\ \text{on asset} \\ j \end{pmatrix}$$

b. Calculate Sharpe's measure for both the portfolio and the market. Compare and discuss these values. On the basis of this measure, is the portfolio's performance inferior or superior? Explain.

c. Calculate Treynor's measure for both the portfolio and the market. Compare and discuss these values. On the basis of this measure, is the portfolio's performance inferior or superior? Explain.

    d. Calculate Jensen's measure (Jensen's alpha) for the portfolio. Discuss its value. On the basis of this measure, is the portfolio's performance inferior or superior? Explain.

    e. Compare, contrast, and discuss your analysis using the measures in parts **b, c**, and **d**. Evaluate the portfolio.

LG5 **Q13.6** Choose a high-growth mutual fund and a money market mutual fund. Find and record their closing net asset values at the end of each week for the immediate past year. Assume that you wish to invest $10,400.

    a. Assume you use dollar-cost averaging to buy shares in both the high-growth and the money market funds by purchasing $100 of each of them at the end of each week—a total investment of $10,400 (i.e., 52 weeks × $200/week). How many shares would you have purchased in each fund by year-end? What are the total number of shares, the average cost per share, and the year-end portfolio value of each fund? Total the year-end fund values and compare them to the total that would have resulted from investing $5,200 in each fund at the end of the first week.

    b. Assume you use a constant-dollar plan with 50% invested in the high-growth fund (speculative portion) and 50% invested in the money market fund (conservative portion). If the portfolio is rebalanced every time the speculative portion is worth $500 more or $500 less than its initial value of $5,200, what would be the total portfolio value and the number of shares in the speculative portion at year-end?

    c. Assume that, as in part **b**, you initially invest 50% in the speculative portion and 50% in the conservative portion. But in this case you use a constant-ratio plan under which rebalancing to the 50:50 mix occurs whenever the ratio of the speculative to the conservative portion is greater than or equal to 1.25 or less than or equal to 0.75. What would be the total portfolio value and the number of shares in the speculative portion at year-end?

    d. Compare and contrast the year-end values of the total portfolio under each of the plans in parts **a, b**, and **c**. Which plan would have been best in light of these findings? Explain.

Problems

All problems are available on http://www.myfinancelab.com

LG1 **P13.1** Refer to the table below:

	Fund A	Fund B
Beta	1.8	1.1
Investor A	20%	80%
Investor B	80%	20%

Between Investor A and Investor B, which is more likely to represent a retired couple? Why?

LG1 **P13.2** Portfolio A and Portfolio B had the same holding period return last year. Most of the returns from Portfolio A came from dividends, while most of the returns from Portfolio B came from capital gains. Which portfolio was likely owned by a single working person making a high salary, and which one was likely owned by a retired couple? Why?

LG1 **P13.3** John Reardon purchased 100 shares of Tomco Corporation in December 2016 at a total cost of $1,762. He held the shares for 15 months and then sold them, netting $2,500.

During the period he held the stock, the company paid him $3 per share in cash dividends. How much, if any, was the capital gain realized upon the sale of stock? Calculate John's pretax HPR.

LG3 **P13.4** Jeff Krause purchased 1,000 shares of a speculative stock on January 2 for $2.00 per share. Six months later on July 1, he sold them for $9.50 per share. He uses an online broker that charges him $10 per trade. What was Jeff's annualized HPR on this investment?

LG3 **P13.5** Jill Clark invested $25,000 in the bonds of Industrial Aromatics, Inc. She held them for 13 months, at the end of which she sold them for $26,746. During the period of ownership she received $2,000 interest. Calculate the pretax and after-tax HPR on Jill's investment. Assume that she is in the 31% ordinary tax bracket (federal and state combined) and pays a 15% capital gains rate on dividends and on capital gains for holding periods longer than 12 months.

LG3 **P13.6** Charlotte Smidt bought 2,000 shares of the balanced no-load LaJolla Fund exactly one year and two days ago for an NAV of $8.60 per share. During the year, the fund distributed investment income dividends of $0.32 per share and capital gains dividends of $0.38 per share. At the end of the year, Charlotte, who is in the 35% ordinary tax bracket (federal and state combined) and pays a 15% capital gains rate on dividends and on capital gains for holding periods longer than 12 months, realized $8.75 per share on the sale of all 2,000 shares. Calculate Charlotte's pretax and after-tax HPR on this transaction.

LG3 **P13.7** Linda Babeu, who is in a 33% ordinary tax bracket (federal and state combined) and pays a 15% capital gains rate on dividends and capital gains for holding periods longer than 12 months, purchased 10 options contracts for a total cost of $4,000 just over one year ago. Linda netted $4,700 upon the sale of the 10 contracts today. What are Linda's pretax and after-tax HPRs on this transaction?

LG3 **P13.8** Mom and Pop had a portfolio of long-term bonds that they purchased many years ago. The bonds pay 12% interest annually, and the face value is $100,000. If Mom and Pop are in the 25% tax bracket, what is their annual after-tax HPR on this investment? (Assume it trades at par.)

LG3 **P13.9** On January 1, 2017, Simon Love's portfolio of 15 common stocks had a market value of $264,000. At the end of May 2017, Simon sold one of the stocks, which had a beginning-of-year value of $26,300, for $31,500. He did not reinvest those or any other funds in the portfolio during the year. He received total dividends from stocks in his portfolio of $12,500 during the year. On December 31, 2017, Simon's portfolio had a market value of $250,000. Find the HPR on Simon's portfolio during the year ended December 31, 2017. (Measure the amount of withdrawn funds at their beginning-of-year value.)

LG3 **P13.10** Congratulations! Your portfolio returned 11% last year, 2% better than the market return of 9%. Your portfolio's return had a standard deviation equal to 18%, and the risk-free rate is 3%. Calculate Sharpe's measure for your portfolio. If the market's Sharpe's measure is 0.3, did you do better or worse than the market from a risk/return perspective?

LG4 **P13.11** Niki Malone's portfolio earned a return of 11.8% during the year just ended. The portfolio's standard deviation of return was 14.1%. The risk-free rate is currently 6.2%. During the year, the return on the market portfolio was 9.0% and its standard deviation was 9.4%.

a. Calculate Sharpe's measure for Niki Malone's portfolio for the year just ended.
b. Compare the performance of Niki's portfolio found in part **a** to that of Hector Smith's portfolio, which has a Sharpe's measure of 0.43. Which portfolio performed better? Why?
c. Calculate Sharpe's measure for the market portfolio for the year just ended.
d. Use your findings in parts **a** and **c** to discuss the performance of Niki's portfolio relative to the market during the year just ended.

LG4 **P13.12** Your portfolio has a beta equal to 1.3. It returned 12% last year. The market returned 10%; the risk-free rate is 2%. Calculate Treynor's measure for your portfolio and the market. Did you earn a better return than the market given the risk you took?

LG4 **P13.13** During the year just ended, Anna Schultz's portfolio, which has a beta of 0.90, earned a return of 8.6%. The risk-free rate is currently 3.3%, and the return on the market portfolio during the year just ended was 9.2%.
a. Calculate Treynor's measure for Anna's portfolio for the year just ended.
b. Compare the performance of Anna's portfolio found in part **a** to that of Stacey Quant's portfolio, which has a Treynor's measure of 1.25%. Which portfolio performed better? Explain.
c. Calculate Treynor's measure for the market portfolio for the year just ended.
d. Use your findings in parts **a** and **c** to discuss the performance of Anna's portfolio relative to the market during the year just ended.

LG4 **P13.14** Your portfolio returned 13% last year, with a beta equal to 1.5. The market return was 10%, and the risk-free rate 4%. Did you earn more or less than the required rate of return on your portfolio? (Use Jensen's measure.)

LG4 **P13.15** Chee Chew's portfolio has a beta of 1.3 and earned a return of 12.9% during the year just ended. The risk-free rate is currently 4.2%. The return on the market portfolio during the year just ended was 11.0%.
a. Calculate Jensen's measure (Jensen's alpha) for Chee's portfolio for the year just ended.
b. Compare the performance of Chee's portfolio found in part **a** to that of Carri Uhl's portfolio, which has a Jensen's measure of −0.24. Which portfolio performed better? Explain.
c. Use your findings in part **a** to discuss the performance of Chee's portfolio during the period just ended.

LG4 **P13.16** The risk-free rate is currently 8.1%. Use the data in the accompanying table for the Fio family's portfolio and the market portfolio during the year just ended to answer the questions that follow.

Data Item	Fios's Portfolio	Market Portfolio
Rate of return	12.8%	11.2%
Standard deviation of return	13.5%	9.6%
Beta	1.10	1.00

a. Calculate Sharpe's measure for the portfolio and the market. Compare the two measures, and assess the performance of the Fios's portfolio during the year just ended.
b. Calculate Treynor's measure for the portfolio and the market. Compare the two measures, and assess the performance of the Fios's portfolio during the year just ended.
c. Calculate Jensen's measure (Jensen's alpha). Use it to assess the performance of the Fios's portfolio during the year just ended.
d. On the basis of your findings in parts **a**, **b**, and **c**, assess the performance of the Fios's portfolio during the year just ended.

LG5 P13.17 Over the past two years, Jonas Cone has used a dollar-cost averaging formula to purchase $300 worth of FCI common stock each month. The price per share paid each month over the two years is given in the following table. Assume that Jonas paid no brokerage commissions on these transactions.

	Price per Share of FCI	
Month	Year 1	Year 2
January	$ 11.63	$ 11.38
February	$ 11.50	$ 11.75
March	$ 11.50	$12.00
April	$ 11.00	$12.00
May	$ 11.75	$12.13
June	$12.00	$12.50
July	$12.38	$12.75
August	$12.50	$13.00
September	$12.25	$13.25
October	$12.50	$13.00
November	$ 11.85	$13.38
December	$ 11.50	$13.50

a. How much was Jonas's total investment over the two-year period?
b. How many shares did Jonas purchase over the two-year period?
c. Use your findings in parts **a** and **b** to calculate Jonas's average cost per share of FCI.
d. What was the value of Jonas's holdings in FCI at the end of the second year?

LG5 P13.18 Using the data in the following table, assume you are using a constant-dollar plan with a rebalancing trigger of $1,500. The stock price represents your speculative portfolio, and the MM mutual fund represents your conservative portfolio. What action, if any, should you take in time period two? Be specific.

			MM Mutual	
Time Period	Stock Price	Shares	Fund NAV	Shares
1	$20.00	1,000	$20.00	1,000
2	$25.00		$21.00	

LG5 P13.19 Referring to Problem 13.18, assume you are using a constant-ratio plan with a rebalance trigger of speculative-to-conservative of 1.25. What action, if any, should you take in time period 2? Be specific.

LG5 P13.20 Using the data in the following table, assume you are using a variable-ratio plan. You have decided that when the speculative portfolio reaches 60% of the total, you will reduce its proportion to 45%. What action, if any, should you take in time period two? Be specific.

			MM Mutual	
Time Period	Stock Price	Shares	Fund NAV	Shares
1	$20.00	1,000	$20.00	1,000
2	$30.00	1,000	$19.00	1,000

Case Problem 13.1   Assessing the Stalchecks's Portfolio Performance

LG3 LG4   Mary and Nick Stalcheck have an investment portfolio containing four investments. It was developed to provide them with a balance between current income and capital appreciation. Rather than acquire mutual fund shares or diversify within a given class of investments, they developed their portfolio with the idea of diversifying across various asset classes. The portfolio currently contains common stock, industrial bonds, mutual fund shares, and options. They acquired each of these investments during the past three years, and they plan to purchase other investments sometime in the future.

Currently, the Stalchecks are interested in measuring the return on their investment and assessing how well they have done relative to the market. They hope that the return earned over the past calendar year is in excess of what they would have earned by investing in a portfolio consisting of the S&P 500 Stock Composite Index. Their research has indicated that the risk-free rate was 7.2% and that the (before-tax) return on the S&P 500 portfolio was 10.1% during the past year. With the aid of a friend, they have been able to estimate the beta of their portfolio, which was 1.20. In their analysis, they have planned to ignore taxes because they feel their earnings have been adequately sheltered. Because they did not make any portfolio transactions during the past year, all of the Stalchecks's investments have been held more than 12 months, and they would have to consider only unrealized capital gains, if any. To make the necessary calculations, the Stalchecks have gathered the following information on each investment in their portfolio.

Common stock. They own 400 shares of KJ Enterprises common stock. KJ is a diversified manufacturer of metal pipe and is known for its unbroken stream of dividends. Over the past few years, it has entered new markets and, as a result, has offered moderate capital appreciation potential. Its share price has risen from $17.25 at the start of the last calendar year to $18.75 at the end of the year. During the year, quarterly cash dividends of $0.20, $0.20, $0.25, and $0.25 were paid.

Industrial bonds. The Stalchecks own eight Cal Industries bonds. The bonds have a $1,000 par value, have a 9.250% coupon, and are due in 2027. They are A-rated by Moody's. The bonds were quoted at 97.000 at the beginning of the year and ended the calendar year at 96.375%.

Mutual fund. The Stalchecks hold 500 shares in the Holt Fund, a balanced, no-load mutual fund. The dividend distributions on the fund during the year consisted of $0.60 in investment income and $0.50 in capital gains. The fund's NAV at the beginning of the calendar year was $19.45, and it ended the year at $20.02.

Options. The Stalchecks own 100 options contracts on the stock of a company they follow. The value of these contracts totaled $26,000 at the beginning of the calendar year. At year-end the total value of the options contracts was $29,000.

Questions

a. Calculate the holding period return on a before-tax basis for each of these four investments.

b. Assuming that the Stalchecks's ordinary income is currently being taxed at a combined (federal and state) tax rate of 38% and that they would pay a 15% capital gains tax on dividends and capital gains for holding periods longer than 12 months, determine the after-tax HPR for each of their four investments.

c. Recognizing that all gains on the Stalchecks's investments were unrealized, calculate the before-tax portfolio HPR for their four-investment portfolio during the past calendar year. Evaluate this return relative to its current income and capital gain components.

d. Use the HPR calculated in question c to compute Jensen's measure (Jensen's alpha). Use that measure to analyze the performance of the Stalchecks's portfolio on a risk-adjusted, market-adjusted basis. Comment on your finding. Is it reasonable to use Jensen's measure to evaluate a four-investment portfolio? Why or why not?

e. On the basis of your analysis in questions **a**, **c**, and **d**, what, if any, recommendations might you offer the Stalchecks relative to the revision of their portfolio? Explain your recommendations.

Case Problem 13.2   Evaluating Formula Plans: Charles Spurge's Approach

LG5   Charles Spurge, a mathematician with Ansco Petroleum Company, wishes to develop a rational basis for timing his portfolio transactions. He currently holds a security portfolio with a market value of nearly $100,000, divided equally between a very conservative, low-beta common stock, ConCam United, and a highly speculative, high-beta stock, Fleck Enterprises. On the basis of his reading of the investments' literature, Charles does not believe it is necessary to diversify one's portfolio across 8 to 15 securities. His thinking, based on his independent mathematical analysis, is that one can achieve the same results by holding a two-security portfolio in which one security is very conservative and the other is highly speculative. His thinking on this point will not be altered. He plans to continue to hold such a two-security portfolio until he finds that his theory does not work. During the past several years, he has earned a rate of return in excess of the risk-adjusted, market-adjusted rate expected on such a portfolio.

Charles's current interest centers on possibly developing his own formula plan for timing portfolio transactions. The current stage of his analysis focuses on the evaluation of four common formula plans in order to isolate the desirable features of each. The plans he is considering are (1) dollar-cost averaging, (2) the constant-dollar plan, (3) the constant-ratio plan, and (4) the variable-ratio plan. Charles's analysis of the plans will involve two types of data. Dollar-cost averaging is a passive buy-and-hold strategy in which the periodic investment is held constant. The other plans are more active in that they involve periodic purchases and sales within the portfolio. Thus, differing data are needed to evaluate the plans.

For evaluating the dollar-cost averaging plan, Charles decided he would assume an investment of $500 at the end of each 45-day period. He chose 45-day time intervals to achieve certain brokerage fee savings that would be available by making larger transactions. The $500 per 45 days totaled $4,000 for the year and equaled the total amount Charles invested during the past year. (Note: For convenience, the returns earned on the portions of the $4,000 that remain uninvested during the year are ignored.) In evaluating this plan, he would assume that half ($250) was invested in the conservative stock (ConCam United) and the other half in the speculative stock (Fleck Enterprises). The share prices for each of the stocks at the end of the eight 45-day periods when purchases were to be made are given in the accompanying table.

	Price per Share	
Period	ConCam	Fleck
1	$22.13	$22.13
2	$21.88	$24.50
3	$21.88	$25.38
4	$22.00	$28.50
5	$22.25	$21.88
6	$22.13	$19.25
7	$22.00	$21.50
8	$22.25	$23.63

To evaluate the three other plans, Charles decided to begin with a $4,000 portfolio evenly split between the two stocks. He chose to use $4,000 because that amount would correspond to the total amount invested in the two stocks over one year using dollar-cost averaging. He planned to use the same eight points in time given earlier to assess the portfolio and make transfers within it if required. For each of the plans evaluated using these data, he established the following triggering points.

Constant-dollar plan. Each time the speculative portion of the portfolio is worth 13% more or less than its initial value of $2,000, the portfolio is rebalanced to bring the speculative portion back to its initial $2,000 value.

Constant-ratio plan. Each time the ratio of the value of the speculative portion of the portfolio to the value of the conservative portion is (1) greater than or equal to 1.15 or (2) less than or equal to 0.84, the portfolio is rebalanced through sale or purchase, respectively, to bring the ratio back to its initial value of 1.0.

Variable-ratio plan. Each time the value of the speculative portion of the portfolio rises above 54% of the total value of the portfolio, its proportion is reduced to 46%. Each time the value of the speculative portion of the portfolio drops below 38% of the total value of the portfolio, its proportion is raised to 50%.

Questions

a. Under the dollar-cost averaging plan, determine the total number of shares purchased, the average cost per share, and the year-end portfolio value expressed both in dollars and as a percentage of the amount invested for (1) the conservative stock, (2) the speculative stock, and (3) the total portfolio.

b. Using the constant-dollar plan, determine the year-end portfolio value expressed both in dollars and as a percentage of the amount initially invested for (1) the conservative portion, (2) the speculative portion, and (3) the total portfolio.

c. Repeat question **b** for the constant-ratio plan. Be sure to answer all parts.

d. Repeat question **b** for the variable-ratio plan. Be sure to answer all parts.

e. Compare and contrast your results from questions **a** through **d**. You may want to summarize them in tabular form. Which plan would appear to have been most beneficial in timing Charles's portfolio activities during the past year? Explain.

Excel@Investing

Excel@Investing

While most people believe that it is not possible to consistently time the market, there are several plans that allow investors to time purchases and sales of securities. These are referred to as formula plans—mechanical methods of managing a portfolio that attempt to take advantage of cyclical price movements. The objective is to mitigate the level of risk facing the investor. One such formula plan is dollar-cost averaging. Here, a fixed dollar amount is invested in a security at fixed intervals. One objective is to increase the value of the given security over time. If prices decline, more shares are purchased; when market prices increase, fewer shares are purchased per period. The essence is that an investor is more likely not to buy overvalued securities. Over the past 12 months, March 2016 through February 2017, Mrs. Paddock has used the dollar-cost averaging formula to purchase $1,000 worth of Neo common stock each month. The monthly price per share paid over the 12-month period is given in the following table. Assume that Mrs. Paddock paid no brokerage commissions on these transactions.

Create a spreadsheet model similar to the spreadsheet for Table 13.9, which you can view at http://www.myfinancelab.com, to analyze the following investment situation for Neo common stock through dollar-cost averaging.

Year	Month	Price Paid per Share
2016	March	$14.30
	April	$16.18
	May	$18.37
	June	$16.25
	July	$14.33
	August	$15.14
	September	$15.93
	October	$19.36
	November	$23.25
	December	$18.86
2017	January	$22.08
	February	$23.23

Questions

a. What is the total investment over the period from March 2016 through February 2017?

b. What is the total number of Neo shares purchased over the 12-month period?

c. What is the average cost per share?

d. What is the year-end (February 2017) portfolio value?

e. What is the profit or loss as of the end of February 2017?

f. What is the return on the portfolio after the 12-month period?

Portfolio Management

Following is a sample of eight Level-1 CFA exam questions that deal with many of the topics covered in Chapters 11, 12 and 13 of this text, including the structure of mutual funds, portfolio diversification, portfolio returns, and the administration of personal portfolios. (When answering the questions, give yourself 1½ minutes for each question; the objective is to correctly answer 6 of the 8 questions in 12 minutes.)

1. An analyst compared the performance of a hedge fund index with the performance of a major stock index over the past eight years. She noted that the hedge fund index (created from a database) had a higher average return, lower standard deviation, and higher Sharpe ratio than the stock index. All the successful funds that have been in the hedge fund database continued to accept new money over the eight-year period. Are the average return and the Sharpe ratio, respectively, for the hedge fund index most likely overstated or understated?

	Average return for the hedge fund index	Sharpe ratio for the hedge fund index
a.	Overstated	Overstated
b.	Overstated	Understated
c.	Understated	Overstated

2. In-kind redemption is a process available to investors participating in
   a. traditional mutual funds but not exchange-traded funds.
   b. exchange-traded funds but not traditional mutual funds.
   c. both traditional mutual funds and exchange-traded funds.

3. Does trading take place only once a day at closing market prices in the case of

	exchange-traded funds?	traditional mutual funds?
a.	No	No
b.	No	Yes
c.	Yes	No

4. Do funds that are likely to trade at substantial discounts from their net asset values include

	exchange-traded funds?	closed-end funds?
a.	No	No
b.	No	Yes
c.	Yes	No

5. Forms of real estate investment that typically involve issuing shares that are traded on the stock market include
   a. real estate investment trusts but not commingled funds.
   b. commingled funds but not real estate investment trusts.
   c. both real estate investment trusts and commingled funds.

6. An analyst gathered the following information:

Portfolio	Mean Return	Standard Deviation of Returns
1	9.8%	19.9%
2	10.5%	20.3%
3	13.3%	33.9%

If the risk-free rate of return is 3.0 percent, the portfolio that had the *best* risk-adjusted performance based on the Sharpe ratio is
a. Portfolio 1
b. Portfolio 2
c. Portfolio 3

7. An analyst gathered the following information about a portfolio's performance over the past 10 years:

Mean annual return	11.8%
Standard deviation of annual returns	15.7%
Portfolio beta	1.2

If the mean return on the risk-free asset over the same period was 5.0%, the Sharpe ratio for the portfolio is closest to

	Sharpe ratio
a.	0.23
b.	0.36
c.	0.43

8. Western Investments holds a fixed-income portfolio that comprise four bonds whose market values and durations are given in the following table.

	Bond A	Bond B	Bond C	Bond D
Market Value	$200,000	$300,000	$250,000	$550,000
Duration	4	6	7	8

The portfolio's duration is closest to
a. 6.06   b. 6.25   c. 6.73

Answers: 1. a; 2. b; 3. b; 4. b; 5. a; 6. b; 7. c; 8. c.

14

Options: Puts and Calls

LEARNING GOALS

After studying this chapter, you should be able to:

LG1 Discuss the basic nature of options in general and puts and calls in particular and understand how these investments work.

LG2 Describe the options market and note key options provisions, including strike prices and expiration dates.

LG3 Explain how put and call options are valued and the forces that drive option prices in the marketplace.

LG4 Describe the profit potential of puts and calls and note some popular put and call investment strategies.

LG5 Explain the profit potential and loss exposure from writing covered call options and discuss how writing options can be used as a strategy for enhancing investment returns.

LG6 Describe market index options, puts and calls on foreign currencies, and LEAPS and discuss how these securities can be used by investors.

Would you spend $229 million to keep a promise to your college roommate? That's what GoPro Inc. founder Nick Woodman did in May of 2015. Ten years earlier, Woodman made a promise to Neil Dana, his then-roommate at the University of California at San Diego, that he would pay Dana 10% of any proceeds that he received from the sale of GoPro shares. Later, Woodman and Dana struck a new agreement in which Dana would receive six million GoPro stock options rather than cash in the event that the company was sold. If Dana ever exercised those options, Woodman would have to repay GoPro by turning in some of his own shares to the company. When Dana exercised his stock options, he spent $3.6 million to acquire stock valued at $229 million. True to his word, Woodman turned in millions of his own shares to repay GoPro for their payout to his former roommate.

(Source: "GoPro's CEO Just Dropped $229 Million to Fulfill a Promise to His College Roommate," http://www.bloomberg.com/news/articles/2015-05-13/gopro-billionaire-returns-229-million-to-satisfy-10-year-vow, accessed July 6, 2015.)

Call and Put Options

LG1   **LG2**   When investors buy shares of common or preferred stock, they are entitled to all the rights and privileges of ownership such as receiving dividends or, in the case of common stock, having the right to vote at shareholder meetings. Investors who acquire bonds or convertible issues are also entitled to certain benefits of ownership such as receiving periodic interest payments. Stocks, bonds, and convertibles are all examples of *financial assets*. They represent financial claims on the issuing organization. In contrast, investors who buy options acquire nothing more than the right to subsequently buy or sell other, related securities. An **option** gives the holder the right to buy or sell an underlying asset (such as common stock) at a fixed price over a limited period of time.

Options are contractual instruments, whereby two parties enter into an agreement to exchange something of value. The option buyer has the right to buy or sell an underlying asset, and in exchange for this right the option buyer makes an up-front payment to the seller. The option seller receives the payment and then stands ready to buy or sell the underlying asset to the option holder according to the terms of the contract. In this chapter we'll look at two basic kinds of options: *calls and puts*.

Before we get into the details of call and put options, note that there are two other types of options: *rights* and *warrants*. Rights are issued by corporations to their existing shareholders, and they entitle shareholders to buy new shares that the company plans to issue in the near future, usually at a price that is slightly below the stock's market value. By using their rights to buy new shares, existing stockholders can avoid having their ownership stake diluted when the company issues new shares. If they do not wish to purchase new shares, existing stockholders can sell their rights on the open market. These rights typically expire within 30 to 60 days, so they hold very little investment appeal for the average individual investor.

In contrast, warrants are long-term options that grant the right to buy shares in a certain company for a given period of time (often fairly long—5 to 10 years or more). Warrants are usually created as "sweeteners" to bond issues and are used to make the issues more attractive to investors. That is, some bonds come with warrants attached, which gives bondholders the opportunity to earn higher returns if the underlying stock performs well. In essence, the buyer of one of these bonds also receives one or more warrants, and the additional upside potential that these bonds provide is called an *equity kicker*.

Basic Features of Calls and Puts

Stock options began trading on the Chicago Board Options Exchange in the early 1970s. Soon the interest in options spilled over to other kinds of financial assets. Today investors can trade puts and calls on common stock, stock indexes, exchange-traded funds, foreign currencies, debt instruments, and commodities and financial futures. For the most part, we will focus on options on common stock, though many of the principles that apply to stock options also apply to options on other kinds of financial assets.

As we will see, although the underlying financial assets may vary, the basic features of different types of options are very similar. Perhaps the most important feature to understand is that options allow investors to benefit from price changes in the underlying asset without investing much capital.

The Option Contract   Call and put options allow the holder to buy or sell an underlying security at a fixed price known as the *strike price* or *exercise price*. We'll focus our attention on calls and puts that grant the right to buy or sell shares of common stock.

A **call** enables the holder to buy the underlying stock at the strike price over a set period of time. A **put**, in contrast, gives the holder the right to sell the stock at the strike price within a set period of time. In most cases, calls and puts allow investors to buy or sell 100 shares of the underlying stock. Calls and puts are entitled to no voting rights, no privileges of ownership, and no interest or dividend income. Instead, calls and puts possess value to the extent that they allow the holder to benefit from price movements of the underlying asset.

Because call and put options derive their value from the price of some other underlying asset, they are known as **derivative securities**. In other words, call and put options derive their value from the price of the underlying asset. Rights and warrants, as well as futures contracts (which we'll study later), are also derivative securities. Although certain segments of the derivative market are for big institutional investors only, there's still ample room for the individual investor. Many of these securities—especially those listed on exchanges—are readily available for individuals to trade.

The price that an investor pays to buy an option is called the **option premium**. As we will see, an option's premium depends on the option's characteristics such as its strike price and expiration date and on the price and volatility of the underlying asset. However, don't let the word *premium* confuse you. It's just the market price of the option.

One of the key features of puts and calls is the attractive **leverage** opportunities they offer. Option buyers can invest a relatively small amount of capital, yet the potential return on that capital can be very large. To illustrate, consider a call on a common stock that gives an investor the right to buy a share of stock at a strike price of $45 a share. If that stock currently sells for $45, the call option would cost just a few dollars— for the sake of illustration, let's say $3 per option or $300 total since the option contract covers 100 shares. Next, suppose that a month or two later the underlying stock's price has increased by $10 to $55. At that point, the investor might exercise his right to buy 100 shares for $45 each. He pays $4,500 to acquire the shares and then immediately resells them at the market price for $5,500, pocketing a gain of $1,000. Thus, in a short period of time his $300 up-front investment grew to $1,000, a gain of 233%. The percentage increase in the stock over this period was just 22.2% ($10 ÷ $45), so the percentage gain on the option is much greater than the percentage gain on the stock. That's the benefit of the leverage the options provide.

Seller versus Buyer Puts and calls are a unique type of security because they are not issued by the organizations that issue the underlying stock. Instead, they are created by investors. It works like this. Suppose Abby wants to sell Carli the right to buy 100 shares of Fitbit common stock (i.e., Abby wants to sell a Fitbit call option to Carli). Abby does this by "writing a call." More generally, the individual (or institution) writing the option is known as the **option seller** or **option writer**. As the option writer, Abby sells the option in the market, so she is entitled to receive the price paid by Carli for the call option. However, Abby does have an obligation. If Carli later decides that she wants to exercise her right to buy Fitbit stock, Abby must sell those shares to her. If Abby does not already own Fitbit shares, she must go into the open market to buy them. Her obligation is legally binding, so she cannot walk away from the deal if it turns out to be a money loser for her. In contrast, Carli has no obligation. She has an option. She can buy Fitbit shares if she wants to, but she is under no obligation to do so. Puts work in much the same way. If Abby sold Carli a put option, then Carli would have the right to sell Fitbit shares to Abby, but she would not be obligated to do so. Abby, on the other hand, must stand behind her promise to buy Fitbit shares from Carli if Carli chooses to sell them. It is important to note that no matter what happens in these transactions between Abby and Carli, Fitbit Inc. is not affected. They do not receive any money, nor do they issue or retire any common shares.

Investors trade calls and puts with the help of securities brokers and dealers. In fact, options are as easy to buy and sell as common stocks. A simple phone call, or a few mouse clicks, is all it takes. Investors trade options for a variety of reasons, many of which we will explore in this chapter. At this point, suffice it to say that trading options can be a viable investment strategy.

How Calls and Puts Work Taking the buyer's point of view, we will briefly examine how calls and puts work and how they derive their value. To start, it is best to look at their profit-making potential. For example, consider the call described earlier that has a $45 strike price and sells for $3. A buyer of the call option hopes for a rise in the price of the underlying common stock. What is the profit potential from this transaction if the price of the stock does indeed move up to, say, $75 by the expiration date on the call?

The answer is that the buyer will earn $30 ($75 − $45) on each of the 100 shares of stock in the call, minus the original $300 cost of the option. In other words, the buyer earns a gross profit of $3,000 from the $300 investment. This is so because the buyer has the right to buy 100 shares of the stock, from the option seller, at a price of $45 each, and then immediately turn around and sell them in the market for $75 a share.

Could an investor have made the same gross profit ($3,000) by investing directly in the common stock? Yes, if the investor had purchased 100 shares of stock. Buying 100 shares of a $45 stock requires an initial investment of $4,500 compared to the $300 investment needed to buy the options. As a consequence, the rate of return from buying the shares is much less than the rate of return from buying the options. The return potential of common stocks and calls differs considerably. This difference attracts investors and speculators to calls whenever the price outlook for the underlying financial asset is positive. Such differential returns are, of course, the direct result of leverage, which is similar to buying a stock on margin. We learned earlier that buying stock on margin raises the potential return that an investor might earn, but it also increases the risk of the investment.

To see the downside of buying a call option, suppose that the stock price in the previous example did not increase to $75, but instead fell to $40.50. That represents just a 10% decline from the initial $45 stock price, but when the stock is worth $40.50, the call option will not be exercised. No investor would choose to pay the $45 strike price to buy the stock when they can simply purchase shares in the open market at a cheaper price. Therefore, if the option contract expires when the stock price is at $40.50, the option will be worthless, and the option buyer's $300 initial investment will be worth nothing. Another way to say this is that the option buyer earns a return of −100% even though the stock price fell just 10%. Clearly call options have a lot of upside potential, but the risk of a total loss is also very real.

A similar situation can be worked out for puts. Assume that for the same stock (which has a current price of $45) an investor could pay $250 to buy a put option, which gives the investor the right to sell 100 shares of the stock at a strike price of $45 each. As the buyer of a put, the investor wants the price of the stock to drop. Assume that the investor's expectations are correct and the price of the stock does indeed drop to $25 a share. The investor goes into the market and purchases 100 shares for $25 each, and then she immediately exercises her put option by selling those shares for $45 each (note: the person who sold the put option is obligated to buy these shares at $45 each). The investor makes a gross profit of $20 per share, or $2,000 total on her initial investment of $250. That represents a rate of return of 700%! Of course, put options are risky just as call options are. If the stock price had risen to $50 rather than falling to $25, the put option buyer's $250 investment would be totally lost.

In some cases, investors who buy calls and puts do not actually have to trade the underlying asset to realize their profits. Instead, investors can "cash settle" their options, meaning that they receive the profits from their option in cash. This arrangement is most common when the underlying asset is difficult to trade, as would be the case when the underlying asset is a stock index rather than stock of a single company. Though most options that have a single common stock as the underlying asset are settled by exchanging the stock, to keep things simple we will illustrate the cash settlement process for a basic stock option. For example, consider once more the call option that had a strike price of $45. Suppose the underlying stock price rises to $75, so on paper at least, the call option buyer has made a gross profit of $30 per share. Rather than pay the $45 exercise price, take delivery of the shares from the call writer, and then resell the shares in the open market for $75, the call buyer may simply receive a $30 per share or $3,000 total cash payment from the call seller in exchange for the option. Settling options in cash eliminates the need for the option buyer and seller to exchange the underlying shares and the need for the option buyer to sell shares in the open market to monetize his or her profit.

Investors can trade options in the secondary market, just as they can trade other securities such as stocks and bonds. The value of both calls and puts is directly linked to the market price of the underlying common stock. For example, the secondary market price of a call increases as the market price of the underlying stock rises. Likewise, the price of a put increases as the underlying common stock price declines. Thus, another way that investors can realize their profits on options is simply to sell them in the secondary market after they have increased in value.

Advantages and Disadvantages The major advantage of investing in puts and calls is the leverage they offer. This feature allows investors to earn large profits from relatively small movements in the underlying asset without investing a large amount of money up front. Another advantage is that options allow investors to profit whether the underlying stock price goes up or down. Investors who believe that the underlying stock price will go up can buy calls, and those who believe that the stock price will fall can buy puts.

A major disadvantage of calls and puts is that the holder enjoys neither interest or dividend income nor any other ownership benefits. Moreover, because options have limited lives, there is a limited time during which the underlying asset can move in the direction that makes the option profitable. Finally, while it is possible to buy calls and puts without investing a lot of money up front, the likelihood that an investor will lose 100% of the money that he or she does invest is much higher with options than with stocks. That's because if the underlying stock moves just a little in the wrong direction, a call or put option on that stock may be totally worthless when it expires.

Options Markets

Although the concept of options can be traced back to the writings of Aristotle, options trading in the United States did not begin until the late 1700s. Even then, up to the early 1970s, this market remained fairly small, largely unorganized, and the almost-private domain of a handful of specialists and traders. All of this changed, however, on April 26, 1973, when the Chicago Board Options Exchange (CBOE) opened.

Conventional Options Prior to the creation of the CBOE, options trading occurred in the over-the-counter market through a handful of specialized dealers. Investors who wished to purchase options contacted their own brokers, who contacted the options dealers. The dealers would find investors willing to write the options. If the buyer wished to exercise an option, he or she did so with the writer and no one else—a system that largely prohibited any secondary trading. Options were written on New York and American exchange stocks, as well as on regional and over-the-counter securities, for as short a time as 30 days and for as long as a year. Over-the-counter options, known today as **conventional options**, are not as widespread as they once were. Accordingly, our attention in this chapter will focus on listed markets, like the CBOE, where individual investors do most of their options trading.

Listed Options The creation of the CBOE signaled the birth of **listed options**, a term that describes options traded on organized exchanges. The CBOE launched trading in calls on just 16 firms. From these rather humble beginnings, there evolved in a relatively short time a large and active market for listed options. Today trading in listed options in the United States is done in both calls and puts and takes place on several exchanges, the most active of which are the CBOE, the International Securities Exchange (ISE), the BATS Exchange, and the Nasdaq PHLX. Collectively those four exchanges accounted for more than half of all options trading in 2015. In total, put and call options are now traded on thousands of different stocks, with many of those options listed on multiple exchanges. In addition to stocks, the options exchanges also offer listed options on stock indexes, exchange-traded funds, debt securities, foreign currencies, and even commodities and financial futures.

Listed options provide not only a convenient market for calls and puts but also standardized expiration dates and exercise prices. The listed options exchanges created a clearinghouse that eliminated direct ties between buyers and sellers of options and reduced the cost of executing put and call transactions. They also developed an active secondary market, with wide distribution of price information. As a result, it is now as easy to trade a listed option as a listed stock.

Stock Options

The advent of the CBOE and the other listed option exchanges had a dramatic impact on the trading volume of puts and calls. Today 4.3 billion listed options contracts are traded each year, most of which are stock options. In 2015 about 89% of listed options contracts were stock options.

Listed options exchanges have unquestionably added a new dimension to investing. In order to avoid serious (and possibly expensive) mistakes with these securities, however, investors must fully understand their basic features. In the sections that follow, we will look closely at the investment attributes of stock options and the trading strategies for using them. Later, we'll explore stock-index (and ETF) options and then briefly look at other types of calls and puts, including interest rate and currency options, and long-term options.

Stock Option Provisions Because of their low unit cost, stock options (or *equity options*, as they're also called) are very popular with individual investors. Except for the underlying financial asset, they are like any other type of call or put, subject to the same kinds of contract provisions and market forces. Two provisions are especially important for stock options: (1) the price—known as the *strike price*—at which the stock can be bought or sold, and (2) the amount of time remaining until expiration. As we'll see, both the strike price and the time remaining to expiration have a significant bearing on the market value of an option.

Strike Price The **strike price** is the fixed, contract price at which an option holder has the right to buy (in the case of a call option) or sell (in the case of a put option) the underlying stock. With conventional (OTC) options, there are no constraints on the strike price, meaning that two parties can agree to whatever strike price they desire. With listed options, strike prices are standardized by the exchanges on which options trade. Generally speaking, options strike prices are set as follows:

- Stocks selling for less than $25 per share carry strike prices that are set in $2.50 increments ($7.50, $10.00, $12.50, $15, and so on).

- In general, the increments jump to $5 for stocks selling between $25 and $200 per share, although a number of securities in the $25 to $50 range are now allowed to use $2.50 increments.

- For stocks that trade at more than $200 a share, the strike price is set in $10 increments.

- Unlike most equity options, options on exchange-traded funds (discussed more fully later in this chapter) usually have strike prices set in $1 increments.

In all cases, the strike price is adjusted for stock splits. Strike prices are not adjusted for cash dividends (except for large "special" dividends), but they are adjusted when firms pay significant stock dividends (e.g., dividends paid in additional shares).

Expiration Date The **expiration date** is also an important provision. It specifies the life of the option, just as the maturity date indicates the life of a bond. The expiration date, in effect, specifies the length of the contract between the holder and the writer of the option. Thus, if you hold a six-month call on Sears with a strike price of, say, $70, that option gives you the right to buy 100 shares of Sears common stock at $70 per share at any time over the next six months. No matter what happens to the market price of the stock, you can use your call option to buy 100 shares of Sears at $70 a share. If the price of the stock moves up, you stand to make money. If it goes down, you'll be out the cost of the option.

Technically, some options can be exercised at any time up until the expiration date, while others can be exercised only on the expiration date. *American options* allow investors to exercise their right to buy or sell the underlying asset at any time up to the expiration date, while *European options* only permit investors to exercise on the expiration date. All exchange-listed options in the United States are American options, so unless otherwise noted, we will focus on those.

Expiration dates are standardized in the listed options market. The exchanges initially created three expiration cycles for all listed options:

- January, April, July, and October

- February, May, August, and November

- March, June, September, and December

Each issue is assigned to one of these cycles. The exchanges still use the same three expiration cycles, but they've been altered so that investors are always able to trade in the two nearest (current and following) months, plus the next two closest months in the option's regular expiration cycle. For reasons that are pretty obvious, this is sometimes referred to as a *two-plus-two* schedule.

For example, if the current month (also called the *front month*) is January, then available options in the *January cycle* would be January, February, April, and July. These represent the two current months (January and February) and the next two months in the cycle (April and July). Likewise, maintaining the assumption that the current month is January, available contracts for the *February cycle* would be January, February, May, and August; available contracts for the *March cycle* would be January, February, March, and June. The expiration dates, based on the front months, continue rolling over in this way during the course of the year. The following table demonstrates the available contracts under the two-plus-two system for the months of February and June:

Front Month	Cycle	Available Contracts
February	January	February, March, April, July
February	February	February, March, May, August
February	March	February, March, June, September
June	January	June, July, October, January
June	February	June, July, August, November
June	March	June, July, September, December

Given the month of expiration, the actual day of expiration is always the same: the third Friday of each expiration month. Thus, for all practical purposes, *listed options always expire on the third Friday of the month of expiration.*

Look Up an Option Chain

Put and Call Transactions Option traders are subject to commission and transaction costs when they buy or sell an option. These costs effectively represent compensation to the broker or dealer for selling the option.

Listed options have their own marketplace and quotation system. Finding the price (or *premium*) of a listed stock option is fairly easy since there are lots of online sources for option quotations. Figure 14.1 illustrates a quotation from **Nasdaq.com** for an *option chain* in which Facebook stock serves as the underlying asset. An **option chain** is a listing of all options (calls and puts) on an underlying asset for a given expiration period. The quotation in Figure 14.1 shows only a small subset of the entire option chain for Facebook, seven call option contracts on the left and seven put option contracts on the right along with their strike prices and premiums for contracts that expire on August 21, 2015. Generating a quotation for all current option contracts on Facebook produces an option chain with several hundred call and put option quotes.

Each row of Figure 14.1 provides important details about a particular option contract. Notice that in the upper left portion of the figure is a column heading that says "Calls," indicating that the first several columns in the figure contain information about various call options on Facebook stock. Moving to the right, notice the column header, "Puts," which indicates that the right side of the figure provides information about put options on Facebook shares. All of the options shown in Figure 14.1 expire on August 21, 2015. The columns headed "Last" provide the most recent market price (or premium) for each option, and the columns headed "Chg" show the change in the price of each option from the previous day's closing price. Other columns show the bid and ask prices for the options, the day's trading volume, and the open interest, which is a measure of the number of outstanding option contracts. Notice that the column headed "Root" shows the ticker symbol for Facebook, which is the underlying asset for all of these options.

Perhaps the most salient information in Figure 14.1 is the market price of each option. For example, on July 6, 2015, an August Facebook call with a strike price of $85 was quoted at $4.90 (which translates into a price of $490 because stock options trade in 100 share lots), and an August put option with the same strike price sold for $2.68.

FIGURE 14.1   Quotations for Facebook Stock Options

The quotes for calls and puts of a specified expiration period are listed down either side of the strike price. In addition to the last price the option traded at for the day and its end-of-day bid and ask price, the change from the previous day's last transaction price is shown. (Source: Data from http://www.nasdaq.com, accessed July 6, 2015.)

Option Chain | Most Actives | Greeks

FB Options: [Composite⇕] [Calls & Puts⇕] [Near the Money⇕] Type: [Monthly⇕] [Go]

Jul 15 | **Aug 15** | Sep 15 | Oct 15 | Nov 15 | Dec 15 | Jan 16 | Jan 17 | Near Term | All

Option Chain for Facebook, Inc. (FB)

Calls	Last	Chg	Bid	Ask	Vol	Open Int	Root	Strike	Puts	Last	Chg	Bid	Ask	Vol	Open Int
Aug 21, 2015	8.40	-0.20	8.35	8.50	233	3142	FB	80	Aug 21, 2015	1.22	0.03	1.21	1.22	1110	6230
Aug 21, 2015	6.60	-0.10	6.50	6.60	109	5118	FB	82.5	Aug 21, 2015	1.85	0.04	1.84	1.85	365	4491
Aug 21, 2015	4.90	-0.20	4.90	4.95	2330	66167	FB	85	Aug 21, 2015	2.68	0.03	2.70	2.71	1212	54821
Aug 21, 2015	3.53	-0.17	3.50	3.55	1493	14194	FB	87.5	Aug 21, 2015	3.85		3.80	3.85	255	2178
Aug 21, 2015	2.44	-0.14	2.42	2.43	2518	18663	FB	90	Aug 21, 2015	5.15	-0.05	5.15	5.25	168	539
Aug 21, 2015	1.56	-0.16	1.57	1.58	439	8698	FB	92.5	Aug 21, 2015	6.85		6.80	6.90	132	326
Aug 21, 2015	0.96	-0.09	0.96	0.97	431	12742	FB	95	Aug 21, 2015	8.38		8.70	8.85	0	99

CONCEPTS IN REVIEW

Answers available at http://www.pearsonhighered.com/smart

14.1 Describe call and put options. Are they issued like other corporate securities?

14.2 What are listed options, and how do they differ from conventional options?

14.3 What are the main investment attractions of call and put options? What are the risks?

14.4 What is a stock option? What is the difference between a stock option and a derivative security? Describe a derivative security and give several examples.

14.5 What is a strike price? How does it differ from the market price of the stock?

14.6 Why do call and put options have expiration dates? Is there a market for options that have passed their expiration dates?

Options Pricing and Trading

LG3 **LG4** **LG5**   The value of an option depends to a large extent on the price of the underlying asset, but several other factors also influence option prices. Being a good options trader requires an understanding of these factors and how they influence option values. Let's look now at the basic principles of options pricing. We'll start with a brief review of how profits are derived from puts and calls. Then we'll take a look at several ways in which investors can use these options.

The Profit Potential from Puts and Calls

Call Option Payoff Diagrams

Although the quoted market price of a call or put is affected by such factors as time to expiration, stock volatility, and market interest rates, by far the most important variable is the price of the underlying common stock. This is the variable that drives the most significant moves in an option's price. When the price of the underlying stock moves up, calls do well. After all, a call option gives an investor the right to buy a stock at a fixed price, and that right is most valuable when the stock price is very high. When the price of the underlying stock drops, puts do well. Again, having the right to sell a stock at a fixed price is most valuable when the market price of the stock is far below the strike price. Clearly investors who are purchasing or selling options need to have some awareness of the potential behavior of the underlying stock.

Figure 14.2 illustrates how the ultimate profits that options provide depend upon the underlying stock price. By "profit" we mean the gain that an investor would receive from exercising the option just before it expires—the difference between the stock price and the strike price (as long as that difference is positive) minus the initial cost of the option. The diagram on the left depicts a call, and the one on the right depicts a put. The call diagram assumes that an investor pays $500 for a call option contract

FIGURE 14.2 **The Valuation Properties of Put and Call Options**

The payoff of a call or put depends on the price of the underlying common stock (or other financial asset). The cost of the option has been recovered when the option passes its breakeven point. After that, the profit potential of a call is unlimited, but the profit potential of a put is limited because the underlying stock price cannot go lower than $0.

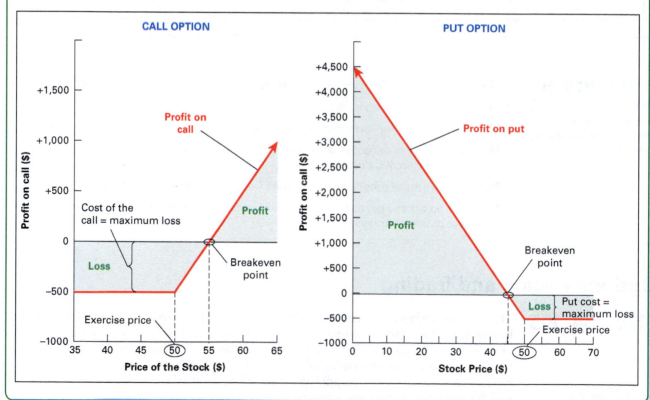

(i.e., 100 calls at $5 per call) and that the call has a strike price of $50. The graph shows how the option profit increases as the stock price rises. Observe that a call provides no cash inflow unless the price of the stock advances past the stated exercise price ($50). In other words, when the underlying stock price is below $50, the call generates a net loss of $500, which is just what the investor spent on the call. If the market price of the stock is below $50, no rational investor would exercise the option and pay $50 to buy the stock—it would be cheaper to simply buy the stock in the open market, and therefore the call expires worthless in that case.

The call option does not begin to move toward profitability until the stock price starts to move above $50. Because it costs $500 to buy the call, the stock has to move up to $55 ($5 above the strike price) for the investor to recover the $500 premium and thereby reach a breakeven point. Note, however, that even if the stock price is between $50 and $55, it's still best to exercise the option because doing so reduces the option holder's net loss. For example, if the stock price is $52, exercising the option generates a cash inflow of $200, which partially offsets the $500 option premium. For each dollar by which the stock price exceeds the breakeven point ($55), the call option's profit goes up by $100. The potential profit from the call position is unlimited because there is no upper limit on the underlying stock's price.

The value of a put is also derived from the price of the underlying stock, except that the put value goes up when the stock price goes down and vice versa. The put diagram in Figure 14.2 assumes you buy a put for $500 and obtain the right to sell the underlying stock at $50 a share. It shows that the profit of the put is −$500 unless the market price of the corresponding stock drops below the exercise price ($50) on the put. The further the stock price is below $50, the more the profit of the put option increases. Again, note that because the put cost $500, the put doesn't reach a break-even point until the stock price reaches $45. At stock prices lower than that, the put is profitable, and it becomes more profitable the further the stock price drops. However, notice an important difference between puts and calls. The put option has a maximum profit of $4,500 because the stock price cannot fall below zero. As noted, a call's profit potential is unlimited because there is no upper limit on the stock price.

Intrinsic Value

As we have seen, the payoff of a put or call depends ultimately on the exercise price stated on the option, as well as on the prevailing market price of the underlying common stock. The relationship between an option's strike price and the underlying stock's market price determines the options intrinsic value. **Intrinsic value** represents the gross amount of money that an investor would receive if he chose to exercise a call option. For example, suppose a call option has a strike price of $50 and the underlying stock price is $60. By exercising this option an investor could receive $10 (or $1,000 for a call contract on 100 shares of stock), and that is the option's intrinsic value. If the stock price were just $45, the investor would not choose to exercise the option (because the stock is cheaper in the open market) and the call's intrinsic value would be zero. More specifically, the intrinsic value of a call is determined according to the following simple formula.

Equation 14.1

> Intrinsic value of a call = (Stock price − Strike price) × 100
>   or 0, whichever is greater

In other words, the intrinsic value of a call is merely the difference between the stock's market price and the option's strike price times 100. When the stock price is below the strike price, the intrinsic value is zero. As implied in Equation 14.1, a call has an intrinsic value whenever the market price of the underlying financial asset exceeds the strike price stipulated on the call. If a call option has a strike price of $50 and the underlying stock sells for $60, then the option's intrinsic value is $1,000.

A put, on the other hand, cannot be valued in the same way because puts and calls allow the holder to do different things. To find the intrinsic value of a put, we must change the order of the equation a bit:

Equation 14.2

$$\text{Intrinsic value of a put} = (\text{Strike price} - \text{Stock price}) \times 100$$
$$\text{or 0, whichever is greater}$$

In this case, a put has intrinsic value as long as the market price of the underlying stock (or financial asset) is less than the strike price stipulated on the put.

In-the-Money/Out-of-the-Money When a call has a strike price that is less than the market price of the underlying common stock, it has a positive intrinsic value and is known as an **in-the-money** option. Look back at Figure 14.1 and notice that the first three call options listed in the figure are highlighted in yellow. Those call options have strike prices of $80, $82.50, and $85, and they are highlighted in yellow because on the day that these option quotes were retrieved, Facebook stock was selling just above $87. This means that the highlighted call options in Figure 14.1 are in the money (i.e., their strike prices are below Facebook's stock price).

When the strike price of the call exceeds the market price of the stock, the call has no intrinsic value, in which case it is known as an **out-of-the-money** option. In Figure 14.1, the calls with strike prices of $87.50, $90, $92.50, and $95 are not highlighted because they were out of the money at the time (i.e., Facebook's stock price was below the strike prices). However, an out-of-the-money call option is not worthless as long as there is still time before it expires because there is a chance that the stock price will rise above the strike price. In other words, when a call is out-of-the-money, its intrinsic value is zero but its market value is greater than zero. In such a case, we say that the option has no intrinsic value but it still has time value. An option's **time value** is the difference between its market price and its intrinsic value. In Figure 14.1, notice that the Facebook call option with a strike price of $87.50 has a quoted price of $3.53. Because the option had more than a month left before it expired, it still had plenty of time value even though its intrinsic value was zero. In the special case when the strike price of the option and the market price of the stock are the same, we say that the call option is **at-the-money**.

As you might expect, the situation is reversed for put options. A put is in-the-money when its strike price is greater than the market price of the stock. Remember, a put option grants the holder the right to sell a stock at the strike price, so that right is most valuable when the strike price is higher than the stock's current market price. In Figure 14.1, the in-the-money put options (highlighted in yellow) have strike prices of $87.50, $90, $92.50, and $95. For all four of those put options, the strike price is above the stock's then-current market price, so the options have a positive intrinsic value. A put option is out-of-the-money when the market price of the stock exceeds the strike price, which is the case in Figure 14.1 for the put options with strike prices of $80, $82.50, and $85. As with calls, an out-of-the-money put still has a positive market value as long as there is some time before the expiration date. For example, the put option with a strike price of $85 in Figure 14.1 has a market price of $2.68. This put's

Ethical Lapse or Extraordinarily Good Timing?

A finance professor conducting research on executive stock option grants discovered that firms awarding these grants seemed to display extraordinarily good timing, setting the exercise prices just before a large run-up in the stock price. Perhaps firms were withholding good news until after they awarded stock option grants, knowing that when they released the news, their stock prices would rise. A few years later, Erik Lie and Randall Heron solved the puzzle of executives' remarkable timing abilities. Some firms apparently backdated their option grants, using hindsight to set the exercise price on the one date in the prior several weeks when their stock price was at its lowest point. Backdating works like this. A firm announces on June 1 that it had granted its executives stock options on April 15, using the market price of the stock that day as the option's exercise price. In fact, the firm did not actually award the options on April 15 but rather chose that date several weeks later. That gave the firm the benefit of hindsight, meaning that the firm knew that the stock's lowest point in the preceding month or two had in fact been April 15. By the time the firm announced the option grant on June 1, the options were already in-the-money because the stock price was much higher than it had been on the retroactively set

grant date. In backdating options, firms failed to disclose the true value of the option grants they awarded, which in turn affected their reported earnings and taxes.

That research and the press coverage it generated prompted investigations of at least 257 firms' options grants. Some firms launched their own internal investigations, but many other companies became the target of SEC investigations. Firms involved in options backdating scandals endured serious consequences. Some executives paid fines or went to prison. Other firms settled lawsuits without admitting wrongdoing, such as Broadcom, which paid $118 million to settle a shareholder lawsuit. Most of the firms investigated saw their stock prices decline by as much as 10%.

The opportunity for senior management to engage in meaningful options backdating was largely eliminated by the Sarbanes-Oxley Act, which requires companies to publicly disclose option grants within two days. Indeed, researchers verified that the unusual market timing associated with stock option grants seemed to vanish soon after the passage of Sarbanes-Oxley.

(Source: Kenneth Carow, Randall Heron, Erik Lie, and Robert Neal, "Option Grant Backdating Investigations and Capital Market Discipline," *Journal of Corporate Finance,* Volume 15, Issue 5, December 2009, pages 562–572.)

---

intrinsic value is zero, but its time value is $2.68. Finally, a put is at-the-money when the strike price equals the stock price.

When firms grant stock options to their employees, they typically grant at-the-money options, meaning that the strike prices of the options are set equal to the price of the underlying stock on the date of the option grant. However, as the accompanying Famous Failures in Finance box explains, many companies got into trouble for using a bit of hindsight (and failing to disclose that) when selecting their option grant dates. This practice came to be known as options backdating.

Put-Call Parity Newcomers to options are often surprised to learn that as different as put and call options are from each other, their prices are linked under certain conditions. As long as a put and call option have the same underlying asset, the same strike price, and the same expiration date, their prices do not, and in fact cannot move independently of each other without creating an arbitrage opportunity. To explain why, consider the following example.

Suppose Nick forms a portfolio containing one share of Dow Chemical common stock and one put option with an exercise price of $50 (which we will denote $X = \$50$). The Dow put option expires in one year. Nick's wife Nora forms a different portfolio. She purchases a Dow call option, also having an exercise price of $50 and a one-year expiration, but Nora also buys a risk-free, zero-coupon bond with a face value of $50 (which matches the option's strike price) and a maturity of one year. Unlike Nora's call

Excel@Investing

TABLE 14.1   ILLUSTRATION OF PUT-CALL PARITY

	Price of Dow Chemical Stock in One Year						
	$35	**$40**	**$45**	**$50**	**$55**	**$60**	**$65**
Nick's portfolio							
Put with X = 50	$15	$10	$ 5	$ 0	$ 0	$ 0	$ 0
Share of stock	$35	$40	$45	$50	$55	$60	$65
Total value	**$50**	**$50**	**$50**	**$50**	**$55**	**$60**	**$65**
Nora's portfolio							
Call with X = $50	$ 0	$ 0	$ 0	$ 0	$ 5	$ 10	$15
Bond with FV = $50	$50	$50	$50	$50	$50	$50	$50
Total value	**$50**	**$50**	**$50**	**$50**	**$55**	**$60**	**$65**

option, the bond is an absolutely safe investment that will pay her $50 in one year with certainty. Let's assume that the put and call options that Nick and Nora have purchased are European options, meaning that they can only be exercised when they expire in one year.

Because Nick and Nora have invested in options on Dow common stock, the value of their portfolios will clearly depend on how Dow's stock performs. Table 14.1 shows what each portfolio will be worth next year, just as the options are about to expire, for a range of possible Dow stock values. Let's look at Nick's portfolio first. Suppose Dow stock does not perform well at all, trading at $35 next year. In that case, Nick will be fortunate to have purchased a put option. If Dow stock is trading at $35, the put option will be in the money by $15, and its market value will be $15 too since it is about to expire. Combined with the share of stock that Nick owns (which is worth $35), the total portfolio value is $50. Notice that Nick's portfolio value is fixed at $50 as long as Dow's stock price is $50 or lower. That should make sense because the put option guarantees that Nick can sell his Dow share for $50. If Dow stock finishes the year above $50 per share, the put option expires out of the money and will be worthless, but the share of Dow that Nick owns gives his portfolio upside potential. To summarize, one year from now, Nick's portfolio will be worth at least $50, and it could be worth more if Dow's stock price ends the year above $50.

Now let's turn to Nora's portfolio, and again let's start by asking what happens to her portfolio when Dow's performance is poor and the stock ends the year at $35. In that case, Nora's call option expires out of the money and has no value. However, Nora at least receives the $50 payment from her risk-free bond, so her total portfolio value is $50. The same will be true at any Dow price of $50 or lower, because when Dow's price is in that range, the call option will be worthless, and Nora will only receive the $50 bond payment. What happens if Dow stock ends the year higher, say at $55? In that scenario, Nora's call option will be worth $5, and her total portfolio will be worth $55. If Dow stock ends the year even higher, then Nora's portfolio will be worth more too because the call value will increase in step with the underlying stock. To summarize Nora's position, her portfolio will be worth at least $50, and it could be worth more if Dow's stock price ends the year above $50.

By now it should be clear that the portfolios that Nick and Nora created have identical future values, no matter what happens to the price of Dow stock. Both investors have guaranteed that their portfolio will be worth at least $50, and both will benefit from an even higher payoff if Dow stock ends the year above $50. In technical terms, we would say that Nick and Nora have *replicating portfolios*, meaning that their portfolios provide identical payoffs (i.e., Nora's portfolio replicates Nick's and vice versa) even though the portfolios contain different securities. This leads to an important concept in option pricing called put-call parity. **Put-call parity** says that the future payoffs of a portfolio containing a put option and a share of the underlying stock are the same as the payoffs of a portfolio containing a call option and a risk-free bond. Again, remember that the put and call options have to have the same underlying asset, the same exercise price, and the same expiration date. But if those conditions hold, as they do for Nick and Nora's portfolios, then put-call parity holds.

Put-call parity is important because it tells us something about the market prices of puts and calls. To be specific, if the future payoff of a put option and a stock equals the future payoff of a call option and a risk-free bond, then the prices of those two portfolios must be the same at any moment in time. If that were not true there would be an arbitrage opportunity. Remember that arbitrage means buying and selling identical assets at different prices to earn an instant, risk-free profit. Hypothetically, if the value of the portfolio containing a put and a share of stock exceeded the value of the portfolio containing a call and a risk-free bond, the traders could sell short the first portfolio and buy the second one to earn a profit. Such transactions would put upward pressure on the prices of the call and the bond, and they would put downward pressure on the prices of the stock and the put, until the values of the two portfolios were equal again. Put-call parity says that because the portfolio containing the put and the stock is essentially the same as the portfolio containing the call and the risk-free bond, the prices of those portfolios must also be the same. We can express this mathematically as follows:

Equation 14.3

> Price of a put option + Price of a stock = Price of a call option + Price of a risk-free bond

Example

> Suppose a certain stock sells for $71.75. You want to know the value of a put option on this stock if the strike price is $70 and the expiration date is three months from now. A call option on the same underlying stock has a strike price of $70, and it expires in three months. That call option currently sells for $6.74. There is also a risk-free, zero-coupon bond available in the market with a maturity in three months and a face value of $70 (notice the bond's face value is the same as the option's strike price). The current risk-free rate is 2% per year, or about 0.5% for a quarter (three months). This means that the bond's market price is just the present value of $70 discounted for three months, or $69.65 ($70/0.005). You can use put-call parity (Equation 14.3) to find the put option's market price:
>
> Price of a put + Price of a stock = Price of a call + Price of a risk-free bond
> Price of a put + $71.75 = $6.74 + 69.65
> Price of a put = $6.74 + $69.65 − $71.75 = $4.64

Now we know one way to find the value of an option. If we know the price of the underlying stock, the risk-free interest rate, and the price of a call option, we can use put-call parity to find the value of a put. Or, if we know the value of the put, we can use it to find the value of a call. But what if we don't know the value of either option? To explore that question, let's turn our attention to the underlying forces that influence option prices.

TABLE 14.2   OPTION PRICE COMPONENTS FOR CALL OPTIONS

Stock Price	Strike Price	Options Expiring in One Month			Options Expiring in Three Months		
		Market Price	Intrinsic Value	Time Value	Market Price	Intrinsic Value	Time Value
$71.75	$65.00	$7.69	$6.75	$0.94	$9.68	$6.75	$2.93
$71.75	$70.00	$4.28	$1.75	$2.53	$6.74	$1.75	$4.99
$71.75	$75.00	$2.04	$0.00	$2.04	$4.50	$0.00	$4.50

Excel@Investing

What Drives Option Prices

Option prices can be reduced to two separate components. The first is the intrinsic value of the option, which is driven by the gap between the current market price of the underlying financial asset and the option's strike price. As we saw in Equations 14.1 and 14.2, the greater the difference between the market price of the underlying asset and the strike price on the option, the greater the intrinsic value of the call or put. We can summarize these relationships by saying that a call value is greater when (1) the strike price is lower or (2) the stock price is higher. Conversely, a put value is greater when (2) the strike price is higher or (3) the stock price is lower.

Time Value and Time to Expiration   The second component of an option price is the time value. It represents the amount by which an option's price exceeds its intrinsic value. Table 14.2 illustrates this concept by listing market prices, intrinsic values, and time values for six different call options. Three of the options expire in one month, and the other three options expire in three months. In addition, there are two call options with a strike price of $65, two with a strike of $70, and two with a $75 strike price. The current market price of the underlying stock is $71.75, so the call options with $65 and $70 strike prices are in the money, but the options with a $75 strike price are out of the money.

Look first at the call option with a strike price of $65 expiring in one month. Table 14.2 lists its market price as $7.69. This option is in-the-money and has an intrinsic value of $6.75 because it allows the option holder to buy a stock for $65 when that stock is actually worth $71.75. The option's market price is $0.94 higher than its intrinsic value, so $0.94 is the option's time value. Why would investors be willing to pay $7.69 for this option when they will only earn $6.75 if they exercise it today?

Because the option does not expire for another month, there is some chance that the underlying stock price will rise, and that possibility gives the option its time value. Moving to the right in Table 14.2, observe that the call with a $65 strike price expiring in three months has an even higher market value, $9.68. The intrinsic value of this option is also $6.75, but its time value is higher because there is more time for the stock price to move in a favorable direction.

Now look at the options with a $75 strike price. These options are out of the money, so their intrinsic values are zero. Yet both have time value. The option expiring in one month is worth $2.04, and the option expiring in three months sells for $4.50. Investors are willing to pay for out-of-the-money options because with time left before they expire, there is still a chance that the underlying stock price will rise, and it will become profitable to exercise the options. Clearly the option expiring in three months is more valuable than the one expiring next month.

There are two important general lessons from Table 14.2. The first is that the market price of an option will almost always be higher than its intrinsic

WATCH YOUR BEHAVIOR

Exercising Too Early Researchers have discovered that customers of discount brokers frequently make the mistake of exercising their options early rather than selling them, and they are particularly prone to this mistake when a stock hits a 52-week high. In contrast, professional options traders almost never make that mistake.

(Source: Allen M. Poteshman and Vitaly Serbin, "Clearly Irrational Financial Market Behavior: Evidence from the Early Exercise of Exchange Traded Stock Options," *Journal of Finance*, February 2003, Volume 58, Issue 37, pp. 37–70.)

value. The main exception to that general rule is that an option's price will equal its intrinsic value just before it expires. As long as an option has some time left before it expires, it will generally be worth more than its intrinsic value. The second important lesson is that an option's price will usually be higher if the option has more time remaining before it expires.

Volatility and Option Prices For most financial assets, higher volatility means higher risk, and higher risk means that investors demand a higher rate of return. Because an asset's value is linked to the present value of its cash flows, if investors discount those cash flows at a higher rate of interest, the asset's value will be lower. Think of a bond, for example. A bond's cash flows are contractually fixed, so if investors perceive that the bond's risk has increased, they will discount those cash flows at a higher rate, which in turn leads to a lower bond price. So in most cases, we can say that if an asset's volatility is higher, its value will be lower, holding everything else constant.

That's not really true with options. The reason is that options have asymmetric payoffs. Consider a call option that is near its expiration date. As the underlying stock price rises above the call's strike price, the option's payoff rises too. So on the upside, the call's payoff moves in step with the stock. But when the stock falls below the call's strike price, the option is out-of-the-money and will not be worth exercising. That is true whether the stock price is $1 below the call's strike price or $10 below it or even $100 below the strike price. On the downside, the call's payoff is fixed at zero no matter how the stock price goes, so there is an asymmetry between a call's upside and its downside.

This asymmetry makes options more valuable if the underlying stock price is more volatile. To see this clearly, consider two stocks, A and B, which are both currently selling for $50 per share. Suppose we want to evaluate the investment potential of call options on these two stocks. Suppose these call options are at-the-money, so their strike prices are $50, and they expire in one year. Suppose A is not a particularly volatile stock, and you think that a year from now, the value of stock A will be in a range between $40 and $60. The following table shows how the payoff on a call option will vary depending on the price of stock A next year.

Price of Stock A	$40	$44	$48	$52	$56	$60
Payoff of Call	$ 0	$ 0	$ 0	$ 2	$ 6	$10

Now stock B is more volatile than stock A, so you believe that in one year its price will be in a range from $32 to $68. The following table below how payoffs on a call option will vary depending on the price of stock B.

Price of Stock B	$32	$36	$40	$44	$48	$52	$56	$60	$64	$68
Payoff of a Call	$ 0	$ 0	$ 0	$ 0	$ 0	$ 2	$ 6	$10	$14	$18

Notice that the payoffs of this option are the same as the call option on stock A when the stock price ends the year below $50, but call options on stock B offer more upside. This means that the market price of a call option on stock B must be higher than the price of a call option on stock A. To say this more generally, *the value of an option (call or put) is greater if the volatility of the underlying stock is greater.*

Interest Rates and Option Prices Previously we said that one way to value options is by using put-call parity, and part of that valuation process involves pricing a risk-free

The Volatility Index

Because the volatility of the underlying asset plays a major role in option valuation, options traders track the volatility of individual stocks and of the market as a whole very closely. In fact, there is an index, called the VIX (which stands for volatility index), which provides an estimate of the volatility of the overall market. From about 1990 to 2007, the average volatility of the U.S. stock market as measured by VIX was close to 20% per year. But in the fall of 2008, after the failure of Lehman Brothers, the VIX index peaked at nearly 90%, more than four times its long-run average! Throughout the Great Recession (December 2007 through June 2009) the VIX index spiked several times to levels above its historical average, but it has been mainly below average in recent years.

bond. In general, options prices do depend on interest rates, just as the prices of other financial assets do. The general relationship is that the value of a call rises when the risk-free rate rises, and the value of a put falls with rising interest rates. Intuitively, a call option grants the holder the right to buy something at some future date. In a sense then, part of what a call option provides is the right to defer payment for a stock. When is the right to defer paying for something most valuable? It's when interest rates are high. With high rates, investors prefer to keep their money invested as long as possible, so having the right to defer payment for something is particularly valuable.

Puts work in just the opposite way. A put option gives the holder the right to sell something, that is, to receive cash in exchange for stock at some future date. Therefore, part of what a put option provides is a deferred receipt. Having to wait to receive money is never a good thing, but it is worse when interest rates are high. Thus, put values fall when the risk-free interest rate rises.

To summarize what we've learned so far, there are five major forces that influence the price of an option. They are (1) the price of the underlying financial asset, (2) the option's strike price, (3) the amount of time remaining to expiration, (4) the underlying asset's volatility, and (5) the risk-free interest rate. For stocks that pay dividends, the dividend yield can also influence the price of an option, with higher dividends leading to lower call values and higher put values.

Option-Pricing Models Some fairly sophisticated option-pricing models have been developed, notably by Myron Scholes and the late Fisher Black, to value options. Options traders use these models to try to identify and trade over- and undervalued options. Not surprisingly, these models are based on the same five variables we identified above. The Black and Scholes option-pricing model prices a European call option using this equation:

Equation 14.4

$$\text{Call price} = SN(d_1) - PV(X)N(d_2)$$

In Equation 14.4, S represents the market price of the underling stock, $PV(X)$ represents the present value of the option's strike price, and $N(d_1)$ and $N(d_2)$ are probabilities ranging from 0 to 1. Loosely speaking, these probabilities are related to the odds that the call option will expire in-the-money. In other words, as these probabilities get closer and closer to 1.0, the option is more and more likely to be exercised, and hence it is more and more valuable. The probabilities $N(d_1)$ and $N(d_2)$ depend on the numerical values of d_1 and d_2, which come from these equations:

Equation 14.4a

$$d_1 = \frac{\ln\left(\frac{S}{X}\right) + \left(r + \frac{\sigma^2}{2}\right)T}{\sigma\sqrt{T}}$$

Equation 14.4b

$$d_2 = d_1 - \sigma\sqrt{T}$$

In these two equations, S and X again represent the stock price and the strike price, respectively, T represents the time remaining before the option expires (expressed in years), σ represents the annual standard deviation of the stock's return (so σ^2 represents the variance of the stock's return), and r represents the annual risk-free interest rate. Once values for d_1 and d_2 are calculated, they must then be converted into probabilities using the standard normal distribution function. The normal distribution is simply the familiar bell curve, and the standard normal distribution is a bell curve with a mean of zero and a standard deviation of 1. The probabilities we need in Equation 14.4 represent the likelihood of drawing a number less than or equal to d_1 (and d_2) from this distribution. Figure 14.3 provides a graphical illustration of the probability that we seek. Suppose we use Equation 14.4a and find that d_1 equals 0.9. To obtain $N(d_1)$ for Equation 14.4, we need to know the area under the curve in Figure 14.3 to the left of the value 0.9.

Fortunately, Excel provides a useful function that makes it easy to calculate these standard normal probabilities. That function is denoted with = normsdist(0.9), and Excel reveals that the appropriate probability is 0.8159.

FIGURE 14.3

The Standard Normal Distribution

The standard normal distribution has a 0 mean and a standard deviation of 1. The shaded area to the left of d_1 represents the probability of drawing a value at random from this distribution that is less than or equal to d_1.

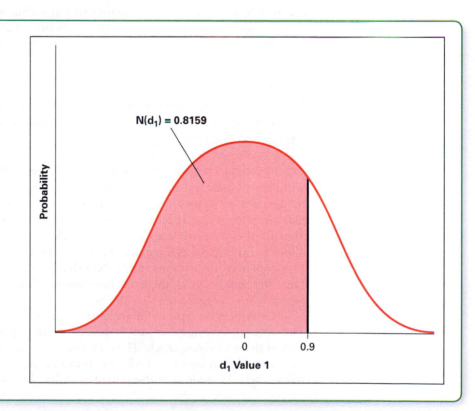

$N(d_1) = 0.8159$

Probability

0   0.9

d_1 Value 1

Now we are ready to price a call option using Black and Scholes.

Example

Suppose we want to price a call option that expires in three months (one-quarter of a year). The option has a strike price of $45, and the market price of the underlying stock is currently $44. The standard deviation of this stock's returns is about 50% per year, and the risk-free rate is 2%.

To price this option, start by solving for the quantities d_1 and d_2:

$$d_1 = \frac{\ln\left(\left(\frac{44}{45}\right) + \left(0.02 + \frac{0.50^2}{2}\right)0.25\right)}{0.50\sqrt{0.25}} = \frac{-0.0225 + (0.145)0.25}{0.25} = 0.0551$$

$$d_2 = 0.0551 - 0.50\sqrt{0.25} = -0.1949$$

Next, use Excel to find the standard normal probabilities attached to these values:

$$N(d_1) = \text{normsdist } (0.0551) = 0.5220$$

$$N(d_2) = \text{normsdist } (-0.1949) = 0.4227$$

Finally, plug the values for $N(d_1)$ and $N(d_2)$ into Equation 14.4 to obtain the call price:

Call price $= \$44(0.5220) - [\$45 \div (1.02)^{0.25}](0.4227) = \$22.97 - \$18.93 = \$4.04$

In this last equation, we calculate the present value of the strike price by discounting $45 at 2% for one quarter of a year. So, according to the Black-Scholes option-pricing model, the call should be priced at $4.04.

Trading Strategies

For the most part, investors can use stock options in three kinds of trading strategies: (1) buying puts and calls for speculation, (2) hedging with puts and calls, and (3) option writing and spreading.

Buying for Speculation Buying for speculation is the simplest and most straightforward use of puts and calls. Basically, it is like buying stock ("buy low, sell high") and, in fact, represents an alternative to investing in stock. For example, if investors feel the market price of a particular stock is going to move up, they can capture that price appreciation by buying a call on the stock. In contrast, if investors feel the stock is about to drop in price, a put could convert that price decline into a profitable situation. Investors may buy options rather than shares due to the leverage that options provide. On a percentage basis, the gains (and losses) that investors can realize on options are typically much higher than on stocks.

Sometimes investors will argue that options offer valuable downside protection. The most an investor can lose is the cost of the option, which is always less than the cost of the underlying stock. Thus, by using options as a tool for speculation, investors can put a cap on losses and still get almost as much profit potential as with the underlying stock. It's true that the potential dollar losses on one option are less than the potential losses on one share of stock, but don't be fooled into thinking that options are less risky than stock. The likelihood of buying an option and earning a return of −100% (i.e., losing the entire investment) is quite high, whereas buying a share of stock and seeing its value drop to nothing is very unusual.

Speculating with Calls To illustrate the essentials of speculating with options, imagine that you own a stock that you feel will move up in price over the next six months. What would happen if you were to buy a call on this stock rather than investing directly in the stock? To find out, let's see what the numbers show. The price of the stock is now $49, and you anticipate that within six months it will rise to about $65. You need to determine the expected return associated with each of your investment alternatives. Because (most) options have relatively short lives, and because we're dealing with an investment horizon of only six months, we can use holding period return to measure the investment's performance. Thus, if your expectations about the stock are correct, it should go up by $16 a share and will provide you with a 33% holding period return: ($65 − $49) ÷ $49 = $16 ÷ $49 = 0.33.

But there are also some listed options available on this stock. Let's see how they would do. For illustrative purposes, we will use two six-month calls that carry a $40 and a $50 strike price, respectively. Table 14.3 compares the behavior of these two calls with the behavior of the underlying common stock. Clearly, from a holding period return perspective, either call option represents a superior investment to buying the stock itself. The dollar amount of profit may be a bit more with the stock, but note that the size of the required investment, $4,900, is a lot more too, so that alternative has the lowest HPR.

Observe that one of the calls is an in-the-money option (the one with the $40 strike price). The other is out-of-the-money. The difference in returns generated by these calls is rather typical. That is, investors are usually able to generate much better rates of return with lower-priced (out-of-the-money) options, but of course there is a greater

Excel@Investing

TABLE 14.3   SPECULATING WITH CALL OPTIONS

	100 Shares of Underlying Common Stock	Six-Month Call Options on the Stock	
		$40 Strike Price	$50 Strike Price
Today			
Market value of stock (at $49/share)	$4,900		
Market price of calls*		$1,100	$ 530
Six Months Later			
Expected value of stock (at $65/share)	$6,500		
Expected price of calls		$2,500	$1,500
Profit	$1,600	$1,400	$ 970
Holding Period Return**	33%	127%	183%

*The price of the calls was computed using the Black and Scholes option-pricing model, assuming a six-month expiration, 2% risk-free rate, and 40% standard deviation.
**Holding period return (HPR) = (Ending price of the stock or option − Beginning price of the stock or option) ÷ Beginning price of the stock or option.

risk that these options will expire worthless. A major drawback of out-of-the-money options is that their price is made up solely of investment premium—a sunk cost that will be lost if the stock does not move in price.

Speculating with Puts To see how you can speculate in puts, consider the following situation. You're looking at a stock that's now priced at $51, but you anticipate a drop in price to about $35 per share within the next six months. If that occurs, you could sell the stock short and make a profit of $16 per share.

Alternatively, you can purchase an out-of-the-money put (with a strike price of $50) for, say, $500. Again, if the price of the underlying stock drops, you will make money with the put. The profit and rate of return on the put are summarized below, along with the comparative returns from short selling the stock. Once again, in terms of holding period return, the stock option is the superior investment vehicle by a wide margin.

Comparative Performance Given Price of Stock Moves from $51 to $35/Share over a 6-Month Period	Buy 1 Put ($50 strike price)	Short Sell 100 Shares of Stock
Purchase price (today)*	−$ 500	
Selling price (six months later)	$1,500	
Short sell (today)		$5,100
Cover (six months later)	——	−$3,500
Profit	$1,000	$1,600
Holding period return	200%	63%**

*The purchase price of the put was computed using the Black and Scholes option-pricing model to value an identical call, then using put-call parity to value the put. Assumed 2% risk-free rate and 40% standard deviation.
**Assumes the short sale was made with a required margin deposit of 50% ($2,550).

Of course, not all option investments perform as well as the ones in our examples. Success with this strategy rests on picking the right underlying common stock. Thus, security analysis and proper stock selection are critical dimensions of this technique. It is a highly risky investment strategy, but it may be well suited for the more speculatively inclined investor.

Hedging: Modifying Risks   A **hedge** is simply a combination of two or more securities into a single investment position for the purpose of reducing risk. Let's say you hold a stock and want to reduce the amount of downside risk in this investment. You can do that by setting up a hedge. In essence, you are using the hedge as a way to modify your exposure to risk. To be more specific, you are trying to change not only the chance of loss but also the amount lost if the worst does occur. A simple hedge might involve nothing more than buying stock and simultaneously buying a put on that stock with a strike price equal to the current stock price. This strategy guarantees that you can sell the stock for at least the strike price of the option, but you might be able to sell the stock for more than the strike price if the stock performs well. Another hedge strategy might consist of selling some stock short and then buying a call. There are many types of hedges, some of which are very simple and others very sophisticated. Investors use them for one basic reason: to earn or protect a profit without exposing the investor to excessive loss.

An options hedge may be appropriate if you have generated a profit from an earlier common stock investment and wish to protect that profit. Or it may be appropriate if you are about to make a common stock investment and wish to protect your money by limiting potential capital loss. If you hold a stock that has gone up in price, the purchase of a put would provide the type of downside protection you need; the purchase of a call, in contrast, would provide protection to a short seller of common stock. Thus, option hedging always involves two transactions: (1) the initial common stock position (long or short) and (2) the simultaneous or subsequent purchase of the option.

Protective Puts: Limiting Capital Loss Let's examine a simple option hedge in which you use a put to limit your exposure to capital loss. Assume that you want to buy 100 shares of stock. Being a bit apprehensive about the stock's outlook, you decide to use an option hedge to protect your capital against loss. Therefore, you simultaneously (1) buy the stock and (2) buy a put on the stock (which fully covers the 100 shares owned) with strike price equal to the stock's current market price. This type of hedge is known as a *protective put*. Suppose you purchase 100 shares of the common stock at $25 a share and pay $150 for a put with a $25 strike price. Now, no matter what happens to the price of the stock over the life of the put, you can always sell the stock for at least $25. Your maximum loss is $150, which occurs if the stock price stays at $25. In that case, there is no gain on the stock and the put expires worthless too, so your loss equals your investment in the put. At the same time, there's no limit on the gains. If the price of the stock goes up (as hoped), the put becomes worthless, and you will earn the capital gains on the stock (less the cost of the put, of course).

Table 14.4 shows the essentials of this option hedge. The $150 paid for the put is sunk cost. That's lost no matter what happens to the price of the stock. In effect, it is the price paid for the insurance this hedge offers. Moreover, this hedge is good only for the life of the put. When this put expires, you will have to replace it with another put or forget about hedging your capital.

Excel@Investing

TABLE 14.4   LIMITING CAPITAL LOSS WITH A PUT HEDGE

	Stock	Put*
Today		
Purchase price of the stock	$25	
Purchase price of the put		$1.50
Sometime Later		
A. Price of stock goes up to:	$50	
Value of put		$ 0
Profit:		
100 shares of stock ($50 – $25) $2,500		
Less: Cost of Put −$ 150		
Profit: $2,350		
B. Price of stock goes down to:	$10	
Value of put		$ 15
Profit:		
100 shares of stock (loss $10 – $25) −$1,500		
Value of put (profit) $1,500		
Less: Cost of put −$ 150		
Loss: $ 150		

*The put is purchased simultaneously and carries a strike price of $25.

TABLE 14.5   PROTECTING PROFITS WITH A PUT HEDGE

		Stock	3-month Put with $75 Strike Price
Purchase price of the stock		$ 35	
Today			
Marketprice of the stock		$ 75	
Market price of the put			$2.50
Three Months Later			
A. Price of stock goes down to:		$ 50	
Value of put			$ 25
Profit:			
100 shares of stock ($50 – $35)	$1,500		
Value of put (profit)	$2,500		
Less: Cost of put	−$ 250		
Profit	**$3,750**		
B. Price of stock goes up to:		$100	
Value of put			$ 0
Profit:			
100 shares of stock ($100 – $35)	$6,500		
Less: Cost of Put	−$ 250		
Profit:	**$6,250**		

Protective Puts: Protecting Profits   The other basic use of an option hedge involves entering into the options position after a profit has been made on the underlying stock. This could be done because of investment uncertainty or for tax purposes (to carry over a profit to the next taxable year). For example, if you bought 100 shares of a stock at $35 and it moved to $75, there would be a profit of $40 per share to protect. You could protect the profit with an option hedge by buying a put. Assume you buy a three-month put with a $75 strike price at a cost of $250. Now, regardless of what happens to the price of the stock over the life of the put, you are guaranteed a minimum profit of $3,750 (the $4,000 profit in the stock made so far, less the $250 cost of the put).

You can see this in Table 14.5. Note that if the price of the stock should fall to $50, you still earn a profit of $3,750. Plus, there is still no limit on how much profit can be made. For example, if the stock goes up to $100, you earn a profit of $6,250.

Unfortunately, the cost of this kind of insurance can become very expensive just when it's needed the most—that is, when market prices are falling. Under such circumstances, it's not uncommon to find put options trading at price premiums of 20% to 30%, or more, above their prevailing intrinsic values. Essentially, that means the price of the stock position you're trying to protect has to fall 20% to 30% before the protection even starts to kick in. Clearly, as long as high option price premiums prevail, the hedging strategies described above are a lot less attractive. They still may prove to be helpful, but only for very wide swings in value—and for those that occur over fairly short periods of time, as defined by the life of the put option.

Although the preceding discussion pertained to put hedges, call hedges can also be set up to limit the loss or protect a profit on a short sale. For example, when selling a stock short, you can purchase a call to protect yourself against a rise in the price of the stock—with the same basic results as outlined above.

Enhancing Returns: Options Writing and Spreading The advent of listed options has led to many intriguing options-trading strategies. Yet, despite the appeal of these techniques, the experts agree on one important point: Such specialized trading strategies should be left to experienced investors who fully understand their subtleties. Our goal at this point is not to master these specialized strategies but to explain in general terms what they are and how they operate. We will look at two types of specialized options strategies here: (1) writing options and (2) spreading options.

Writing Options Generally, investors write options because they believe the price of the underlying stock is going to move in their favor. That is, it is not going to rise as much as the buyer of a call expects, nor will it fall as much as the buyer of a put hopes. Option writing represents an investment transaction to the writers. They receive the full option premium (less normal transaction costs) in exchange for agreeing to live up to the terms of the option.

Naked Options Investors can write options in two ways. One is to write **naked options,** which involves writing options on stock not owned by the writer. An investor simply writes the put or call, collects the option premium, and hopes the price of the underlying stock does not move against him or her. If successful, naked writing can be highly profitable because it requires essentially no capital up front. Remember, though, the amount of return to the writer is always limited to the amount of option premium received. The catch is that there is really no limit to loss exposure. The price of the underlying stock can rise or fall by just about any amount over the life of the option and, thus, can deal a real blow to the writer of a naked put or call.

Covered Options The amount of risk exposure is a lot less for those who write **covered options.** That's because these options are written against stocks the investor (writer) already owns or has a position in. For example, an investor could write a call against stock he owns or write a put against stock he has short sold. The investor can use the long or short position to meet the terms of the option. Such a strategy is a fairly conservative way to generate attractive rates of return. The object is to write a slightly out-of-the-money option, pocket the option premium, and hope the price of the underlying stock will move up or down to (but not exceed) the option's strike price. In effect, you are adding an option premium to the other usual sources of return (dividends and/ or capital gains). But there's more. While the option premium adds to the return, it also reduces risk. It can cushion a loss if the price of the stock moves against the investor.

There is a hitch to all this, of course. The amount of return the covered option investor can realize is limited. Once the price of the underlying common stock exceeds the strike price on the option, the option becomes valuable. When that happens, the investor starts to lose money on the options. From this point on, for every dollar the investor makes on the stock position, he loses an equal amount on the option position. That's a major risk of writing covered call options—if the price of the underlying stock takes off, the call writer misses out on the added profits.

To illustrate the ins and outs of covered call writing, let's assume you own 100 shares of PFP, Inc., an actively traded, high-yielding common stock. The stock is currently trading at $73.50 and pays quarterly dividends of $1 a share. You decide to write a three-month call on PFP, giving the buyer the right to take the stock off your hands at $80 a share. Such options are trading in the market at $2.50, so you receive $250 for writing the call. You fully intend to hold on to the stock, so you'd like to see the price of

TABLE 14.6 COVERED CALL WRITING

	Stock	3-Month Call with $80 Strike Price
Current market price of the stock	$73.50	
Current market price of the call		$2.50
Three Months Later		
A. Price of the stock is *unchanged*:	**$73.50**	
Value of the call		$0
Profit:		
Quarterly dividends received	$ 100	
Proceeds from sale of call	$ 250	
Total Profit:	**$ 350**	
B. Price of the stock goes up to:	**$80**	**Price Where Maximum Profit Occurs**
Value of the call		$0
Profit:		
Quarterly dividends received	$ 100	
Proceeds from sale of call	$ 250	
Capital gains on stock ($80 – $73.5)	$ 650	
Total Profit:	**$1,000**	
C. Price of the stock goes up to:	**$90**	
Value of the call		**$10.00**
Profit:		
Quarterly dividends received	$ 100	
Proceeds from sale of call	$ 250	
Capital gains on stock ($90 – $73.5)	$ 1,650	
Less: Loss on call	–$1,000	
Net Profit:	**$1,000**	
D. Price of the stock drops to:	**$71**	**Breakeven Price**
Value of the call		$0
Profit:		
Quarterly dividends received	$ 100	
Proceeds from sale of call	$ 250	
Capital loss on stock ($71 – $73.50)	–$ 250	
Net Profit:	**$ 100**	

Excel@Investing

PFP stock rise to no more than $80 by the expiration date on the call. If that happens, the call option will expire worthless. As a result, not only will you earn the dividends and capital gains on the stock, but you also get to pocket the $250 you received when you wrote the call. Basically, you've just added $250 to the quarterly return on your stock.

Table 14.6 summarizes the profit and loss characteristics of this covered call position. Note that the maximum profit on this transaction occurs when the market price of the stock equals the strike price on the call. If the price of the stock keeps going up, you miss out on the added profits. Even so, the $1,000 profit you earn at a stock price of $80 or above translates into a (three-month) holding period return of 13.6% ($1,000 ÷ $7,350). That represents an annualized return of nearly 55%! With this kind of return potential, it's not difficult to see why covered call writing is so popular. Moreover, as situation D in the table illustrates, covered call writing adds a little cushion to losses. The price of the stock has to drop more than $2.50 (which is what you received when you wrote/sold the call) before you start losing money.

Besides covered calls and protective puts, there are many ways to combine options with other types of securities to achieve a given investment objective. Probably none is more unusual than the creation of so-called synthetic securities. Here's an example. Say you want to buy a convertible bond on a certain company but that company doesn't have any convertibles outstanding. You can create your own customized convertible by combining a straight (nonconvertible) bond with a listed call option on your targeted company.

Spreading Options Option spreading is nothing more than the combination of two or more options into a single transaction. You could create an option spread, for example, by simultaneously buying and writing options on the same underlying stock. These would not be identical options; they would differ with respect to strike price and/or expiration date. Spreads are a very popular use of listed options, and they account for a substantial amount of the trading activity on the listed options exchanges. These spreads go by a variety of exotic names, such as *bull spreads*, *bear spreads*, *money spreads*, *vertical spreads*, and *butterfly spreads*. Each spread is different and each is constructed to meet a certain type of investment goal.

Consider, for example, a *vertical spread*. It would be set up by buying a call at one strike price and then writing a call (on the same stock and for the same expiration date) at a higher strike price. For instance, you could buy an August call on Facebook at a strike price of, say, $80 and simultaneously sell (write) an August call on Facebook at a strike price of $85. If you refer back to Figure 14.1, you will see that the first option would cost you $8.40, while the option that you sell would bring in $4.90. Therefore, the net cost of this position is $3.50. Strange as it may sound, such a position would generate a hefty return if the price of the underlying stock went up by just a few points. Suppose, for example, that when these options expire, the price of Facebook stock is $88. The call option that you purchased would pay you $8, but you'd have to pay $3 to the buyer of the option you wrote, so your net cash payoff at expiration would be $5. A $5 return on an investment of $3.50 represents a rate of return of almost 43%! Other spreads are used to profit from a falling market. Still others try to make money when the price of the underlying stock moves either up or down.

Whatever the objective, most spreads are created to take advantage of differences in prevailing option prices. The payoff from spreading is usually substantial, but so is the risk. In fact, some spreads that seem to involve almost no risk may end up with devastating results if the market and the difference between option premiums move against the investor.

Option Straddles A variation on this theme involves an **option straddle**. This is the simultaneous purchase (or sale) of both a put and a call on the same underlying common stock. Unlike spreads, straddles normally involve the same strike price and expiration date. Here the object is to earn a profit from either a big or a small swing in the price of the underlying common stock.

How Do Straddles Work?

For example, in a *long straddle* you buy an equal number of puts and calls. You make money in a long straddle when the underlying stock undergoes a big change in price—either up or down. If the price of the stock shoots way up, you make money on the call side of the straddle but are out the cost of the puts. If the price of the stock plummets, you make money on the puts, but the calls are useless. In either case, so long as you make more money on one side than the cost of the options for the other side, you're ahead of the game.

As an example, refer again to Figure 14.1. Imagine that you buy a Facebook call and a put, both having a strike of $87.50 and an August expiration date. The call costs

$3.53, and the put costs $3.85, so the total cost of this position is $7.38. To make money on this transaction, Facebook stock would have to fall more than $7.38 below the $87.50 strike price or rise more than $7.38 above it. If Facebook stock stays within that range, your position loses money.

In a similar fashion, in a *short straddle,* you sell/write an equal number of puts and calls with the same underlying stock, the same strike price, and the same expiration date. You make money in this position when the price of the underlying stock goes nowhere. In effect, you get to keep all or most of the option premiums you collected when you wrote the options.

Except for obvious structural differences, the principles that underlie the creation of straddles are much like those for spreads. The object is to combine options that will enable you to capture the benefits of certain types of stock price behavior. But keep in mind that if the prices of the underlying stock and/or the option premiums do not behave in the anticipated manner, you lose. Spreads and straddles are extremely tricky and should be used only by knowledgeable investors.

CONCEPTS IN REVIEW

Answers available at http://www.pearsonhighered.com/smart

14.7 Briefly explain how you would make money on (a) a call option and (b) a put option. Do you have to exercise the option to capture the profit?

14.8 How do you find the intrinsic value of a call? Of a put? Does an out-of-the-money option have intrinsic value?

14.9 Name five variables that can affect the price of options, and briefly explain how each affects prices. How important are intrinsic value and time value to in-the-money options? To out-of-the-money options?

14.10 Describe three ways in which investors can use stock options.

14.11 What's the most that can be made from writing calls? Why would an investor want to write covered calls? Explain how you can reduce the risk on an underlying common stock by writing covered calls.

Stock-Index and Other Types of Options

LG6 Imagine being able to buy or sell a major stock market index like the S&P 500—and at a reasonable cost. Think of what you could do. If you felt the market was heading up, you could invest in a security that tracks the price of the S&P 500 Index and make money when the market goes up. No longer would you have to go through the process of selecting specific stocks that you hope will capture the market's performance. Rather, you could play the market as a whole. Of course, you can do this by purchasing a mutual fund or an ETF that is indexed to the S&P 500, but you can also accomplish that goal with stock-index options—puts and calls that are written on major stock market indexes. Index options have been around since 1983 and have become immensely popular with both individual and institutional investors. Here we will take a closer look at these popular and often highly profitable investments.

Contract Provisions of Stock-Index Options

Basically, a **stock-index option** is a put or call written on a specific stock market index. The underlying security in this case is the specific market index. Thus, when the market index moves in one direction or another, the value of the index option moves accordingly. Because there are no stocks or other financial assets backing these options, settlement is defined in terms of cash. Specifically, the cash value of an index option is equal to 100 times the published market index that underlies the option. For example, if the S&P 500 is at 2,100, then the value of an S&P 500 Index option will be $100 × 2,100 = $210,000. If the underlying index moves up or down in the market, so will the cash value of the option. In addition, whereas most options on individual stocks are American options and can be exercised at any time, stock index options may be American or European options, so they may be exercisable only on the expiration date.

Today put and call options are available on more than 100 stock indexes. These include options on just about every major U.S. stock market index or average (such as the Dow Jones Industrial Average, the S&P 500, the Russell 2000, and the Nasdaq 100), options on a handful of foreign markets (e.g., China, Mexico, Japan, Hong Kong, and the Europe sector), and options on different segments of the market (pharmaceuticals, oil services, semiconductors, bank, and utility indexes). In 2015 about 10% of traded option contracts were index options, and a large percentage of these contracts were on five of the leading stock indexes:

- S&P 500 Index (SPX)

- Russell 2000 Index (RUT)

- Nasdaq 100 Index (NDX)

- S&P 100 Index (OEX)

- Dow Jones Industrial Average (DJX)

The S&P 500 Index captures the market behavior of large-cap stocks. The Russell 2000 Index measures the performance of the small-cap stocks in the United States. The Nasdaq 100 Index tracks the behavior of the 100 largest nonfinancial stocks listed on Nasdaq and is composed of mostly large, high-tech companies (such as Intel and Cisco). The S&P 100 Index is another large-cap index composed of 100 stocks, drawn from the S&P 500, that have actively traded stock options. Another popular index is the DJIA Index, which measures the blue-chip segment of the market and is one of the most actively traded index options. Options on the S&P 500 are, by far, the most popular instruments. Indeed, there's more trading in SPX options contracts than in all the other index options combined. Among the options exchanges that currently deal in index options, the CBOE dominates the market, accounting for more than 98% of the trades in 2015.

Both puts and calls are available on index options. They are valued and have issue characteristics like any other put or call. That is, a put lets a holder profit from a drop in the market. (When the underlying market index goes down, the value of a put goes up.) A call enables the holder to profit from a market that's going up. Also, as Figure 14.4 shows, index options have a quotation system that is the same as for stock options, except for the fact that the strike price is an index level.

Putting a Value on Stock-Index Options As is true of equity options, the market price of index options is a function of the difference between the strike price on the option (stated in terms of the underlying index) and the latest published stock market index. To illustrate, consider the highly popular S&P 500 Index traded on the CBOE.

Let's say the S&P 500 Index recently closed at 2058 and the August call has a strike price of 2055. A stock-index call will have a positive value so long as the underlying index exceeds the index strike price (just the opposite for puts). The intrinsic value of this call is 2058 − 2053 = 3.

Suppose that the call actually trades at 49.92, which is 46.92 points above the call's intrinsic value. This difference is the option's time value.

Example

If the S&P 500 Index in our example were to go up to, say, 2200 by late August (the expiration date of the call), this option would be quoted at 2200 − 2055 = 145. Because index options (like stock options) are valued in multiples of $100, this contract would be worth $14,500. Thus, if you had purchased this option when it was trading at $49.92, it would have cost you $49.92 × $100 = $4,992 and, in less than a month, would have generated a profit of $14,500 −$4,992 = $9,508. That translates into a holding period return of a whopping 90%.

FIGURE 14.4   Quotations on Index Options

The quotation system used with index options is just like that used with stock options: strikes and expiration dates are shown along with option prices and volumes. The biggest differences are that the option strikes and closing values for the underlying asset are shown as index levels. The closing S&P 500 Index level on the day of this quotation was 2051. (Source: Data from http://www.nasdaq.com, accessed July 9, 2015.)

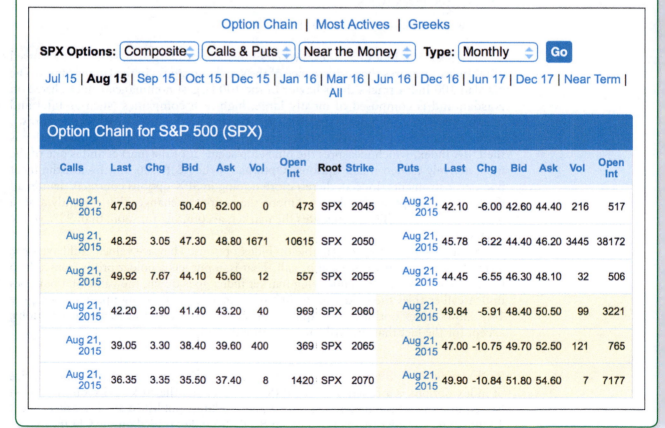

Option Chain | Most Actives | Greeks

SPX Options: [Composite⇕] [Calls & Puts ⇕] [Near the Money ⇕] Type: [Monthly ⇕] **Go**

Jul 15 | **Aug 15** | Sep 15 | Oct 15 | Dec 15 | Jan 16 | Mar 16 | Jun 16 | Dec 16 | Jun 17 | Dec 17 | Near Term | All

Option Chain for S&P 500 (SPX)

Calls	Last	Chg	Bid	Ask	Vol	Open Int	Root	Strike	Puts	Last	Chg	Bid	Ask	Vol	Open Int
Aug 21, 2015	47.50		50.40	52.00	0	473	SPX	2045	Aug 21, 2015	42.10	-6.00	42.60	44.40	216	517
Aug 21, 2015	48.25	3.05	47.30	48.80	1671	10615	SPX	2050	Aug 21, 2015	45.78	-6.22	44.40	46.20	3445	38172
Aug 21, 2015	49.92	7.67	44.10	45.60	12	557	SPX	2055	Aug 21, 2015	44.45	-6.55	46.30	48.10	32	506
Aug 21, 2015	42.20	2.90	41.40	43.20	40	969	SPX	2060	Aug 21, 2015	49.64	-5.91	48.40	50.50	99	3221
Aug 21, 2015	39.05	3.30	38.40	39.60	400	369	SPX	2065	Aug 21, 2015	47.00	-10.75	49.70	52.50	121	765
Aug 21, 2015	36.35	3.35	35.50	37.40	8	1420	SPX	2070	Aug 21, 2015	49.90	-10.84	51.80	54.60	7	7177

Full Value versus Fractional Value Most broad-based index options use the full market value of the underlying index for purposes of options trading and valuation. That's not the case, however, with two of the Dow Jones measures: The option on the Dow Jones Industrial Average is based on 1% of the actual Industrial Average, and the Dow Transportation Average option is based on 10% of the actual average. For example, if the DJIA is at 11,260, the index option would be valued at 1% of that amount, or 112.60. Thus, the cash value of this option is not $100 times the underlying DJIA but $100 times 1% of the DJIA, which equals the Dow Jones Industrial Average itself: $100 \times 112.60 = $11,260.

Fortunately, the option strike prices are also based on the same 1% of the Dow, so there is no effect on option valuation. What matters is the difference between the strike price on the option and 1% of the DJIA. For instance, suppose that the DJIA closes at 11,260, which means that the DJIA option index would close at 112.60. A call option on this index might have a strike price of 110, which would mean that the call is slightly in-the-money with an intrinsic value of 2.60. If the option were not set to expire immediately, its market price would be higher, with the difference between the market price and 2.60 being the option's time value.

Another type of option that is traded at 10% (1 ÷ 10) of the value of the underlying index is the "mini" index option. For example, the Mini-NDX Index (MNX) is set at 10% of the value of the Nasdaq 100. "Minis" also exist for the Nasdaq composite, the S&P 500, the Russell 2000, and the FTSE 250 (an index of mid-cap stocks in the United Kingdom), among others.

Investment Uses

Although index options, like equity options, can be used in spreads, straddles, or even covered calls, they are perhaps used most often for speculating or for hedging. When used as a speculative investment, index options give investors an opportunity to play the market as a whole, with a relatively small amount of capital. Like any other put or call, index options provide attractive leverage opportunities and at the same time limit exposure to loss to the price paid for the option.

Index Options as Hedging Vehicles Index options are equally effective as hedging vehicles. In fact, hedging is a major use of index options and accounts for a good deal of the trading in these securities. To see how these options can be used for hedging, assume that you hold a diversified portfolio of, say, a dozen different stocks and you think the market is heading down. One way to protect your capital would be to sell all of your stocks. However, that could be expensive, especially if you plan to get back into the market after it drops, and it could lead to a good deal of unnecessary taxes. Fortunately, there is a way to "have your cake and eat it, too" and that is to hedge your stock portfolio with a stock index put. In this way, if the market does go down, you'll make money on your puts, which you then can use to buy more stocks at the lower prices. On the other hand, if the market continues to go up, you'll be out only the cost of the puts. That amount could well be recovered from the increased value of your stock holdings. The principles of hedging with stock-index options are exactly the same as those for hedging with equity options. The only difference is that with stock-index options, you're trying to protect a whole portfolio of stocks rather than individual stocks.

Like hedging with individual equity options, the cost of protecting your portfolio with index options can become very expensive (with price premiums of 20% to 30% or more) when markets are falling and the need for this type of portfolio insurance is the greatest. That, of course, will have an impact on the effectiveness of this strategy.

Also, the amount of profit you make or the protection you obtain depends in large part on how closely the behavior of your stock portfolio is matched by the behavior of the stock-index option you employ. There is no guarantee that the two will behave in the same way. You should therefore select an index option that closely reflects the nature of the stocks in your portfolio. If, for example, you hold a number of small-cap stocks, you might select something like the Russell 2000 index option as the hedging vehicle. If you hold mostly blue chips, you might choose the DJIA index option. You probably can't get dollar-for-dollar portfolio protection, but you should try to get as close a match as possible.

A Word of Caution Given their effectiveness for either speculating or hedging, it's little wonder that index options have become popular with investors. But a word of caution is in order. Although trading index options appears simple and seems to provide high rates of return, these investments involve high risk and are subject to considerable price volatility. Amateurs should not use them. True, there's only so much you can lose with these options. The trouble is that it's very easy to lose all of that investment, however small it may be. These securities are not investments you can buy and then forget about until just before they expire. With the wide market swings that are so common today, you must monitor these securities daily.

Other Types of Options

Options on stocks and stock indexes account for most of the market activity in listed options. But you also can obtain put and call options on various other securities. Let's now take a brief look at these other kinds of options, starting with options on ETFs.

Options on Exchange-Traded Funds In addition to various market indexes, put and call options are also available on several hundred exchange-traded funds (ETFs). As you've already learned, ETFs are like mutual funds that have been structured to track the performance of a wide range of market indexes—in other words, ETFs are a type of index fund. They trade like shares of common stock on listed exchanges and cover everything from broad market measures, such as the DJIA, the S&P 500, and the Nasdaq 100, to market sectors like energy, financials, health care, and semiconductors.

There's a good deal of overlap in the markets and market segments covered by index options and ETF options. In addition to their similar market coverage, they perform very much the same in the market, are valued the same, and are used for many of the same reasons (particularly for speculation and hedging). After all, an ETF option is written on an underlying index fund (for example, one that tracks the S&P 500) just like an index option is written on the same underlying market index (the S&P 500). Both do pretty much the same thing—either directly or indirectly track the performance of a market measure—so of course they should behave in the same way. The only real difference is a structural detail. Options on ETFs are operationally like stock options in that each option covers 100 shares of the underlying exchange-traded fund rather than $100 of the underlying market index, as is the case with index options. In the end, though, both trade at 100 times the underlying index (or ETF). Thus, while operationally ETF options may be closer to stock options, they function more like index options. As such, the market views them as viable alternatives to index options. These contracts have definitely caught the fancy of investors, especially those who track the major market indexes.

Interest Rate Options Puts and calls on fixed-income (debt) securities are known as **interest rate options**. At the present time, interest rate options are written only on U.S. Treasury securities with 30-year, 10-year, 5-year, or 13-week maturities. These options are yield-based rather than price-based. This means they track the yield (rather than the price) of the underlying Treasury security. Other types of options (equity and index options) are set up so that they react to movements in the price (or value) of the underlying asset. Interest rate options, in contrast, are set up to react to the yield of the underlying Treasury security (i.e., the exercise price is an interest rate). Thus, when yields rise, the value of a call goes up, and the value of a put goes down. In effect, because bond prices and yields move in opposite directions, the value of an interest rate call option goes up at the very time that the price (or value) of the underlying debt security is going down. The opposite is true for puts.

Currency Options Foreign exchange options, or **currency options** as they're more commonly called, provide a way for investors to speculate on foreign exchange rates or to hedge foreign currency or foreign security holdings. Currency options are available on the currencies of most of the countries with which the United States has strong trading ties. These options are traded on several exchanges and over the counter and include the following currencies:

- British pound
- Swiss franc
- Australian dollar
- Canadian dollar
- Japanese yen
- Euro

Puts and calls on foreign currencies give the holders the right to sell or buy large amounts of the specified currency. However, in contrast to the standardized contracts used with stock and stock-index options, the specific unit of trading in this market varies with the particular underlying currency. Table 14.7 spells out the details. Currency options are traded in full or fractional cents per unit of the underlying currency, relative to the amount of foreign currency involved. Thus, if a put or call on the British pound were quoted at, say, 6.40 (which is read as "6.4 cents"), it would be valued at $640 because 10,000 British pounds underlie this option (that is, $10,000 \times 0.064 = \$640$).

The value of a currency option is linked to the exchange rate between the U.S. dollar and the underlying foreign currency. For example, if the Canadian dollar

TABLE 14.7   FOREIGN CURRENCY OPTION CONTRACTS ON THE PHILADELPHIA EXCHANGE

Underlying Currency*	Size of Contracts	Underlying Currency*	Size of Contracts
British pound	10,000 pounds	Canadian dollar	10,000 dollars
Swiss franc	10,000 francs	Japanese yen	1,000,000 yen
Euro	10,000 euros	Australian dollar	10,000 dollars

*The British pound, Swiss franc, euro, Canadian dollar, and Australian dollar are all quoted in full cents. The Japanese yen is quoted in hundredths of a cent.

becomes stronger relative to the U.S. dollar, causing the exchange rate to go up, the price of a call option on the Canadian dollar will increase, and the price of a put will decline. (*Note:* Some cross-currency options are available in the market, but such options/trading techniques are beyond the scope of this text. Here, we will focus solely on foreign currency options (or futures) linked to U.S. dollars.)

The strike price on a currency option is stated in terms of exchange rates. Thus, a strike price of 150 implies that each unit of the foreign currency (such as one British pound) is worth 150 cents, or $1.50, in U.S. money. If you held a 150 call on this foreign currency, you would make money if the foreign currency strengthened relative to the U.S. dollar so that the exchange rate rose—say, to 155. In contrast, if you held a 150 put, you would profit from a decline in the exchange rate—say, to 145. Success in forecasting movements in foreign exchange rates is obviously essential to a profitable foreign currency options program.

LEAPS They look like regular puts and calls, and they behave pretty much like regular puts and calls, but they're not regular puts and calls. We're talking about **LEAPS**, which are puts and calls with lengthy expiration dates. Basically, LEAPS are long-term options. Whereas standard options have maturities of eight months or less, LEAPS have expiration dates as long as three years. Known formally as *Long-term Equity AnticiPation Securities,* they are listed on all of the major options exchanges. LEAPS are available on hundreds of stocks, stock indexes, and ETFs.

Aside from their time frame, LEAPS work like any other equity or index option. For example, a single (equity) LEAPS contract gives the holder the right to buy or sell 100 shares of stock at a predetermined price on or before the specified expiration date. LEAPS give you more time to be right about your bets on the direction of a stock or stock index, and they give hedgers more time to protect their positions. But there's a price for this extra time. You can expect to pay a lot more for a LEAPS than you would for a regular (short-term) option. That should come as no surprise. LEAPS, being nothing more than long-term options, are loaded with time value. And as we saw earlier in this chapter, other things being equal, *the more time an option has to expiration, the higher the quoted price.*

CONCEPTS IN REVIEW

Answers available at
http://www.pearsonhighered
.com/smart

14.12 Briefly describe the differences and similarities between stock-index options and stock options. Do the same for foreign currency options and stock options.

14.13 Identify and briefly discuss two ways to use stock-index options. Do the same for foreign currency options.

14.14 Why would an investor want to use index options to hedge a portfolio of common stock? Could the same objective be obtained using options on ETFs? If the investor thinks the market is in for a fall, why not just sell the stock?

14.15 What are LEAPS? Why would an investor want to use a LEAPS option rather than a regular listed option?

MyFinanceLab

Here is what you should know after reading this chapter. MyFinanceLab will help you identify what you know and where to go when you need to practice.

What You Should Know	Key Terms	Where to Practice
LG1 **Discuss the basic nature of options in general and puts and calls in particular and understand how these investments work.** An option gives the holder the right to buy or sell a certain amount of some real or financial asset at a set price for a set period of time. Puts and calls are the most widely used types of options. These derivative securities offer considerable leverage potential. A put enables the holder to sell a certain amount of a specified security at a specified price over a specified time period. A call gives the holder the right to buy the security at a specified price over a specified period of time.	call, *p. 551* derivative securities, *p. 551* leverage, *p. 551* option, *p. 551* option premium, *p. 551* option writer (or seller), *p. 551* put, *p. 551*	MyFinanceLab Study Plan 14.1
LG2 **Describe the options market and note key options provisions, including strike prices and expiration dates.** The options market is made up of conventional (OTC) options and listed options. OTC options are used predominantly by institutional investors. Listed options are traded on organized exchanges such as the CBOE. The creation of listed options exchanges led to standardized options features and to widespread use of options by individual investors. Among the option provisions are the strike price (the stipulated price at which the underlying asset can be bought or sold) and the expiration date (the date when the contract expires).	conventional options, *p. 554* expiration date, *p. 555* listed options, *p. 554* option chain, *p. 556* strike price, *p. 555*	MyFinanceLab Study Plan 14.2
LG3 **Explain how put and call options are valued and the forces that drive option prices in the marketplace.** The intrinsic value of a call is the market price of the underlying security less the strike price on the call. The intrinsic value of a put is its strike price less the market price of the security. The market value of an option is its intrinsic value plus its time value. The value of an option is driven by the current market price of the underlying asset, as well as by the option's strike price, its time to expiration, the risk-free interest rate, and the volatility of the underlying asset.	at-the-money out-of-the money, *p. 560* intrinsic value in-the-money, *p. 560* put-call parity time value, *p. 561*	MyFinanceLab Study Plan 14.3 Excel Table 4.2 Video Learning Aid for Problems P14.5, P14.11
LG4 **Describe the profit potential of puts and calls and note some popular put and call investment strategies.** Investors who hold puts make money when the value of the underlying asset goes down over time. Call investors make money when the underlying asset moves up in price. Aggressive investors use puts and calls either for speculation or in highly specialized writing and spreading programs. Conservative investors like the low unit costs and the limited risk that puts and calls offer in absolute dollar terms. Conservative investors often use options to hedge positions in other securities.	hedge, *p. 570*	MyFinanceLab Study Plan 14.4 Excel Tables 4.3, 4.4

What You Should Know	Key Terms	Where to Practice
LG5 Explain the profit potential and loss exposure from writing covered call options and discuss how writing options can be used as a strategy for enhancing investment returns. Covered call writers have limited loss exposure because they write options against securities they already own. The maximum profit occurs when the price of the stock equals the strike price of the call. If the stock price goes above the strike price, then any loss on the option is offset by a gain on the stock position. If the stock price goes down, part of the loss on the stock is offset by the proceeds from the call option. Option writing can be combined with other securities to create investment strategies for specific market conditions.	covered options, *p. 573* naked options, *p. 573* option spreading, *p. 575* option straddle, *p. 573*	MyFinanceLab Study Plan 14.5 Excel Table 14.5 Video Learning Aid for Problem P14.11
LG6 Describe market index options, puts and calls on foreign currencies, and LEAPS and discuss how these securities can be used by investors. Standardized put and call options are available on stock-market indexes, like the S&P 500 (in the form of index options or ETF options), and on a number of foreign currencies (currency options). Also available are LEAPS, which are listed options that carry lengthy expiration dates. Although these securities can be used just like stock options, the index and currency options tend to be used primarily for speculation or to develop hedge positions.	currency options, *p. 581* interest rate options, *p. 581* LEAPS, *p. 582* stock-index option, *p. 576*	MyFinanceLab Study Plan 14.6

Log into MyFinanceLab, take a chapter test, and get a personalized Study Plan that tells you which concepts you understand and which ones you need to review. From there, MyFinanceLab will give you further practice, tutorials, animations, videos, and guided solutions.

Log into **http://www.myfinancelab.com**

Discussion Questions

LG2 **Q14.1** Using the Facebook stock option quotations in Figure 14.1, find the option premium, the time value, and the stock index breakeven point for the following puts and calls.
   a. The August put with a strike price of $82.50
   b. The August call with a strike price of $85

LG3 **Q14.2** In Table 14.2, notice that among the options expiring in one month, the option with the highest time value is the one with a strike price of $70. Likewise, among the options expiring in three months, the option with a $70 strike has more time value than the options with $65 and $75 strike prices. Why do you think this is so?

LG5 **Q14.3** Alcan stock recently closed at $52.51. Assume that you write a covered call on Alcan by writing one September call with a strike price of $55 and buying 100 shares of stock at the market price. The option premium that you obtain from writing the call is $370. Assume the stock will pay no dividends between now and the expiration date of the option.

a. What is the total profit if the stock price remains unchanged?

b. What is the total profit if the stock price goes up to $55?

c. What is the total loss if the stock price goes down to $49?

LG6 **Q14.4** Assume you hold a well-balanced portfolio of common stocks. Under what conditions might you want to use a stock-index (or ETF) option to hedge the portfolio?

a. Briefly explain how such options could be used to hedge a portfolio against a drop in the market.

b. Discuss what happens if the market does, in fact, go down.

c. What happens if the market goes up instead?

LG3 LG4 **Q14.5** Using the resources at your campus or public library (or on the Internet), complete each of the following tasks. (*Note:* Show your work for all calculations.)

a. Find an in-the-money call that has two or three months to expiration. (Select an equity option that is at least $2 or $3 in-the-money.) What's the intrinsic value of this option and what is its time value? Using the current market price of the underlying stock (the one listed with the option), determine what kind of dollar and percentage return the option would generate if the underlying stock goes up 10%. How about if the stock goes down 10%?

b. Repeat part a, but this time use an in-the-money put. (Choose an equity option that's at least $2 or $3 in-the-money and has two or three months to expiration.) Answer the same questions as above.

c. Repeat once more the exercise in part a, but this time use an out-of-the-money call. (Select an equity option, at least $2 or $3 out-of-the-money with two or three months to expiration.) Answer the same questions.

d. Compare the valuation properties and performance characteristics of in-the-money calls and out-of-the-money calls (from parts a and c). Note some of the advantages and disadvantages of each.

Problems

All problems are available on http://www.myfinancelab.com

LG3 **P14.1** Apple stock is selling for $120 per share. Call options with a $117 exercise price are priced at $12. What is the intrinsic value of the option, and what is the time value?

LG3 **P14.2** Twitter is trading at $34.50. Call options with a strike price of $35 are priced at $2.30. What is the intrinsic value of the option, and what is the time value?

LG3 **P14.3** Verizon is trading at $36. Put options with a strike price of $45 are priced at $10.50. What is the intrinsic value of the option, and what is the time value?

LG3 **P14.4** Abercrombie & Fitch is trading at $21.50. Put options with a strike price of $20.50 are priced at $0.85. What is the intrinsic value of the option, and what is the time value?

LG3 **P14.5** A six-month call option contract on 100 shares of Home Depot common stock with a strike price of $60 can be purchased for $600. Assuming that the market price of Home Depot stock rises to $75 per share by the expiration date of the option, what is the call holder's profit? What is the holding period return?

LG4 **P14.6** Suppose that a call option with a strike price of $45 expires in one year and has a current market price of $5.16. The market price of the underlying stock is $46.21, and the risk-free rate is 1%. Use put-call parity to calculate the price of a put option on the same underlying stock with a strike of $45 and an expiration of one year.

LG4   **P14.7**   Look at the Facebook option quotes in Figure 14.1, and focus on the call and put options with a strike price of $80. Can you use put-call parity to infer what the market price of Facebook stock must have been when these option prices were quoted? To keep things simple, assume the options expire in one month, and that the risk-free rate at the time was 0%. (Hint: To use put-call parity, you need to find the market price of a risk-free, zero-coupon bond with a face value equal to the strike price of the options.)

LG4   **P14.8**   Repeat the analysis of problem 14.7, but this time focus on the Facebook call and put options in Figure 14.1 that have a strike price of $87.50. If you use put-call parity to find the price of Facebook stock at the time those call prices were quoted, would you expect to get the same answer that you found in problem 14.6? Do you in fact get the same answer?

LG4 LG6   **P14.9**   You believe that oil prices will be rising more than expected and that rising prices will result in lower earnings for industrial companies that use a lot of petroleum-related products in their operations. You also believe that the effects on this sector will be magnified because consumer demand will fall as oil prices rise. You locate an exchange-traded fund, XLB, that represents a basket of industrial companies. You don't want to short the ETF because you don't have enough margin in your account. XLB is currently trading at $23. You decide to buy a put option (for 100 shares) with a strike price of $24, priced at $1.20. It turns out that you are correct. At expiration, XLB is trading at $20. Calculate your profit.

XLB: Materials—$23.00					
Calls			Puts		
Strike	Expiration	Price	Strike	Expiration	Price
$20	November	$0.25	$20	November	$1.55
$24	November	$0.25	$24	November	$1.20

LG4 LG6   **P14.10**   Refer to Problem 14.9. What happens if you are wrong and the price of XLB increases to $25 on the expiration date?

LG6   **P14.11**   Dorothy Santosuosso does a lot of investing in the stock market and is a frequent user of stock-index options. She is convinced that the market is about to undergo a broad retreat and has decided to buy a put option on the S&P 100 Index. The put option has a strike of 905 and is quoted in the financial press at $14.50. Although the S&P Index of 100 stocks is currently at 900, Dorothy thinks it will drop to 850 by the expiration date on the option. How much profit will she make, and what will be her holding period return if she is right? How much will she lose if the S&P 100 goes up (rather than down) by 25 points and reaches 925 by the date of expiration?

LG3 LG4   **P14.12**   Myles Houck holds 600 shares of Lubbock Gas and Light. He bought the stock several years ago at $48.50, and the shares are now trading at $75. Myles is concerned that the market is beginning to soften. He doesn't want to sell the stock, but he would like to be able to protect the profit he's made. He decides to hedge his position by buying six puts on Lubbock G&L. The three-month puts carry a strike price of $75 and are currently trading at $2.50.
   a. How much profit or loss will Myles make on this deal if the price of Lubbock G&L does indeed drop to $60 a share by the expiration date on the puts?
   b. How would he do if the stock kept going up in price and reached $90 a share by the expiration date?
   c. What do you see as the major advantages of using puts as hedge vehicles?
   d. Would Myles have been better off using in-the-money puts—that is, puts with an $85 strike price that are trading at $10.50? How about using out-of-the-money puts—say, those with a $70 strike price, trading at $1.00? Explain.

LG4 LG6 P14.13 Nick Fitzgerald holds a well-diversified portfolio of high-quality, large-cap stocks. The current value of Fitzgerald's portfolio is $735,000, but he is concerned that the market is heading for a big fall (perhaps as much as 20%) over the next three to six months. He doesn't want to sell all his stocks because he feels they all have good long-term potential and should perform nicely once stock prices have bottomed out. As a result, he's thinking about using index options to hedge his portfolio. Assume that the S&P 500 currently stands at 2,200 and among the many put options available on this index are two that have caught his eye: (1) a six-month put with a strike price of 2,150 that's trading at $76, and (2) a six-month put with a strike price of 2,075 that's quoted at $58.

a. How many S&P 500 puts would Nick have to buy to protect his $735,000 stock portfolio? How much would it cost him to buy the necessary number of puts with a $2,150 strike price? How much would it cost to buy the puts with a $2,075 strike price?

b. Now, considering the performance of both the put options and Nick's portfolio, determine how much *net* profit (or loss) Nick will earn from each of these put hedges if both the market (as measured by the S&P 500) and Nick's portfolio fall by 15% over the next six months. What if the market and Nick's portfolio fall by only 5%? What if they go up by 10%?

c. Do you think Nick should set up the put hedge and, if so, using which put option? Explain.

d. Finally, assume that the DJIA is currently at 17,550 and that a six-month put option on the Dow is available with a strike of 174, and is currently trading at $7.84. How many of these puts would Nick have to buy to protect his portfolio, and what would they cost? Would Nick be better off with the Dow options or the S&P 2,150 puts? Briefly explain.

LG3 LG5 P14.14 Angelo Martino just purchased 500 shares of AT&E at $61.50, and he has decided to write covered calls against these stocks. Accordingly, he sells five AT&E calls at their current market price of $5.75. The calls have three months to expiration and carry a strike price of $65. The stock pays a quarterly dividend of $0.80 a share (the next dividend to be paid in about a month).

a. Determine the total profit and holding period return Angelo will generate if the stock rises to $65 a share by the expiration date on the calls.

b. What happens to Angelo's profit (and return) if the price of the stock rises to more than $65 a share?

c. Does this covered call position offer any protection (or cushion) against a drop in the price of the stock? Explain.

LG6 P14.15 Rick owns stock in a retailer that he believes is highly undervalued. Rick expects that the stock will increase in value nicely over the long term. He is concerned, however, that the entire retail industry may fall out of favor with investors as some larger companies report falling sales. There are no options traded on his stock, but Rick would like to hedge against his fears about retail. He locates a symbol RTH, which is a retail exchange-traded fund. Can Rick hedge against the risk he is concerned with by using RTH? Using options?

LG5 LG6 P14.16 Suppose the DJIA stands at 11,200. You want to set up a long straddle by purchasing 100 calls and an equal number of puts on the index, both of which expire in three months and have a strike of 112. The put price is listed at $1.65 and the call sells for $2.65.

a. What will it cost you to set up the straddle, and how much profit (or loss) do you stand to make if the market falls by 750 points by the expiration dates on the options? What if it goes up by 750 points by expiration? What if it stays at 11,200?

b. Repeat part a, but this time assume that you set up a short straddle by selling/writing 100 July 112 puts and calls.

c. What do you think of the use of option straddles as an investment strategy? What are the risks, and what are the rewards?

LG3 P14.17 A stock trades for $45 per share. A call option on that stock has a strike price of $50 and an expiration date one year in the future. The volatility of the stock's return is 30%, and the risk-free rate is 2%. What is the Black and Scholes value of this option?

LG3 P14.18 Repeat the analysis of problem 14.17 assuming that the volatility of the stock's return is 40%. Intuitively, would you expect this to cause the call price to rise or fall? By how much does the call price change?

Visit **http://www.myfinancelab.com** for web exercises, spreadsheets, and other online resources.

Case Problem 14.1   The Franciscos' Investment Options

LG3 LG4 Hector Francisco is a successful businessman in Atlanta. The box-manufacturing firm he and his wife, Judy, founded several years ago has prospered. Because he is self-employed, Hector is building his own retirement fund. So far, he has accumulated a substantial sum in his investment account, mostly by following an aggressive investment posture. He does this because, as he puts it, "In this business, you never know when the bottom will fall out." Hector has been following the stock of Rembrandt Paper Products (RPP), and after conducting extensive analysis, he feels the stock is about ready to move. Specifically, he believes that within the next six months, RPP could go to about $80 per share, from its current level of $57.50. The stock pays annual dividends of $2.40 per share. Hector figures he would receive two quarterly dividend payments over his six-month investment horizon.

In studying RPP, Hector has learned that the company has six-month call options (with $50 and $60 strike prices) listed on the CBOE. The CBOE calls are quoted at $8 for the options with $50 strike prices and at $5 for the $60 options.

Questions

a. How many alternative investments does Hector have if he wants to invest in RPP for no more than six months? What if he has a two-year investment horizon?

b. Using a six-month holding period and assuming the stock does indeed rise to $80 over this time frame:

1. Find the value of both calls, given that at the end of the holding period neither contains any investment premium.

2. Determine the holding period return for each of the three investment alternatives open to Hector Francisco.

c. Which course of action would you recommend if Hector simply wants to maximize profit? Would your answer change if other factors (e.g., comparative risk exposure) were considered along with return? Explain.

Case Problem 14.2   Luke's Quandary: To Hedge or Not to Hedge

LG3 LG4 A little more than 10 months ago, Luke Weaver, a mortgage banker in Phoenix, bought 300 shares of stock at $40 per share. Since then, the price of the stock has risen to $75 per share. It is now near the end of the year, and the market is starting to weaken. Luke feels there is still plenty of play left in the stock but is afraid the tone of the market will be detrimental to his position.

His wife, Denise, is taking an adult education course on the stock market and has just learned about put and call hedges. She suggests that he use puts to hedge his position. Luke is intrigued by the idea, which he discusses with his broker, who advises him that the needed puts are indeed available on his stock. Specifically, he can buy three-month puts, with $75 strike prices, at a cost of $550 each (quoted at $5.50).

Questions

a. Given the circumstances surrounding Luke's current investment position, what benefits could be derived from using the puts as a hedge device? What would be the major drawback?

b. What will Luke's minimum profit be if he buys three puts at the indicated option price? How much would he make if he did not hedge but instead sold his stock immediately at a price of $75 per share?

c. Assuming Luke uses three puts to hedge his position, indicate the amount of profit he will generate if the stock moves to $100 by the expiration date of the puts. What if the stock drops to $50 per share?

d. Should Luke use the puts as a hedge? Explain. Under what conditions would you urge him not to use the puts as a hedge?

Excel@Investing

 One of the positive attributes of investing in options is the profit potential from the puts or calls. The quoted market price of the option is influenced by the time to expiration, stock volatility, market interest rates, and the behavior of the price of the underlying common stock. The latter variable tends to drive the price movement in options and impacts its potential for profitable returns.

Create a spreadsheet model, similar to that presented below, in order to calculate the profits and/or losses from investing in the option described.

	A	B	C	D	E	F	G	H	I	J
1										
2						Long		100		3-Month Call Option
3						Position		Shares of		on the Stock
4						No		Underlying		Strike Price
5						Option		Common Stock		$$$
6										
7	Today									
8										
9	Market value of stock			$$		$$		$$		
10	Call strike price			$$						
11	Call option premium			$$						
12										
13										
14	Scenario One : 3 months later									
15	Expected market value of stock			$$		$$		$$		
16	Stock value @ strike price			$$						$$
17	Call premium			$$						$$
18	Breakeven point			$$						$$
19										
20	Profit (Loss)					$$		$$		

John has been following the stock market very closely over the past 18 months and has a strong belief that future stock prices will be significantly higher. He has two alternatives that he can follow. The first is to use a long-term strategy—purchase the stock today and sell it sometime in the future at a possibly higher price. The other alternative is to buy a three-month call option. The relevant information needed to analyze these alternatives is presented below:

Current stock price = $49

Desires to buy one round lot = 100 shares

Three-month call option has a strike price of $51 and a call premium of $2

Questions

a. In scenario one, if the stock price three months from now is $58:

1. What is the long-position profit or loss?

2. What is the breakeven point of the call option?

3. Is the option in- or out-of-the-money?

4. What is the option profit or loss?

b. In scenario two, if the stock price three months from now is $42:

1. What is the long-position profit or loss?

2. What is the breakeven point of the call option?

3. Is the option in- or out-of-the-money?

4. What is the option profit or loss?

Chapter-Opening Problem

In the beginning of this chapter you read about Neil Dana, who exercised his option to buy six million shares. In that transaction, Mr. Dana spent $3.6 million to acquire stock valued at $229 million. What was the strike price of the options, and what was the market price of GoPro stock at the time that the options were exercised?

15

Futures Markets and Securities

LEARNING GOALS

After studying this chapter, you should be able to:

LG1 Describe the essential features of a futures contract and explain how the futures market operates.

LG2 Explain the role that hedgers and speculators play in the futures market, including how profits are made and lost.

LG3 Describe the commodities segment of the futures market and the basic characteristics of these investments.

LG4 Discuss the trading strategies investors can use with commodities and explain how investment returns are measured.

LG5 Explain the difference between a physical commodity and a financial future and discuss the growing role of financial futures in the market today.

LG6 Discuss the trading techniques that can be used with financial futures and note how these securities can be used in conjunction with other investments.

I n March 2005 a new commodity, ethanol, began trading on the Chicago Mercantile Exchange (CME). Ethanol (ethyl alcohol) is an alcohol produced by fermenting and distilling starch crops such as sugar cane, corn, wheat, barley, and sugar beet molasses. Ethanol has three major uses: beverages, industrial products, and, increasingly, an alternative fuel source.

With worldwide demand for energy on the rise, ethanol is becoming more attractive as a renewable, environment-friendly fuel that enhances the nation's economy and its energy independence. Ethanol does not provide complete independence from fossil fuels since the ethanol blend with the least amount of fossil fuel is E85, which still requires 15% gasoline and 85% ethanol. Pushed by rising demand and empowered by the U.S. Energy Independence and Security Act of 2007, U.S. ethanol producers have installed 213 plants in 29 states at the start of 2015, with a capacity of more than 15 billion gallons per year—an amount that represents approximately 10% of the U.S. gasoline supply. There are more than 18 million U.S. consumers driving Flexible Fuel Vehicles that can run on ethanol flex fuels, such as E85, which contain anywhere from 51% to 83% ethanol. About 25% of new cars sold in 2015 will be Flexible Fuel Vehicles.

The availability of the CME ethanol futures contracts, which can be traded electronically, will help the ethanol industry continue to grow. Essentially, a future is a contract to buy or sell a certain amount of an item—for example, agricultural products or foreign currencies—at a price for delivery on a specific future date. Before investing in individual commodities or trading financial futures, you should understand how these specialized and often high-risk investments work. This chapter will introduce you to the world of commodities and illustrate how to use futures contracts as a tool for risk management.

(Sources: "Ethanol Futures Scheduled to Launch on March 29th," http://www.prnewswire.com/news-releases/cme-to-launch-its-first-ever-energy-contract-54159072.html, accessed September 17, 2012; Renewable Fuels Association, *Pocket Guide to Ethanol 2015*, http://www.ethanolrfa.org/pocketguide, accessed July 8, 2015.)

The Futures Market

"Psst, hey buddy. Wanna buy some copper? How about some coffee, or lean hogs, or propane? Maybe the Japanese yen or Swiss franc strikes your fancy?" Sound a bit unusual? Perhaps, but these items have one thing in common. They all represent real investments. This is the more exotic side of investing—the market for commodities and financial futures—and it often involves a considerable amount of speculation. The risks are enormous, but with some luck, the payoffs can be phenomenal. Even more important than luck, however, is the need for patience and know-how. Indeed, these are specialized investment products that require specialized investor skills.

The amount of futures trading in the United States has mushroomed over the past few decades. An increasing number of investors have turned to futures trading as a way to earn attractive, highly competitive rates of return. A major reason behind the growth in futures trading has been the number and variety of futures contracts now available for trading. Today futures contracts exist for the traditional primary commodities, such as grains and metals, as well as for processed commodities, crude oil and gasoline, electricity, foreign currencies, money market securities, U.S. and foreign debt securities, Eurodollar securities, and common stocks. You can even buy listed put and call options on just about any actively traded futures contract. All these commodities and financial assets are traded in what is known as the *futures market*.

Why the Economy
Needs Futures Markets

Market Structure

When a bushel of wheat is sold, the transaction takes place in the **cash market**. The bushel changes hands in exchange for the cash price paid to the seller. For all practical purposes, the transaction is completed then and there. Most traditional securities are traded in this type of market. However, a bushel of wheat can also be sold in the **futures market**, the organized market for the trading of futures contracts. In this market, the seller would not deliver the wheat until some mutually agreed-upon date in the future. As a result, the transaction would not be completed for some time. The buyer, in turn, would own a highly liquid futures contract that could be held (and presented for delivery of the bushel of wheat) or traded in the futures market. No matter what the buyer does with the contract, as long as it is outstanding, the seller has a legally binding obligation to make delivery of the stated quantity of wheat on a specified date in the future. The buyer/holder has a similar obligation to take delivery of the underlying commodity.

Futures Contracts A **futures contract** is a commitment to deliver a certain amount of a specified item at a specified date at an agreed-upon price. Each market establishes its own contract specifications. These include not only the quantity and quality of the item but also the delivery procedure and delivery month. The **delivery month** on a futures contract is much like the expiration date on put and call options. It specifies when the commodity or item must be delivered and thus defines the life of the contract. For example, the CME Group's Chicago Board of Trade specifies that each of its full-sized soybean futures contracts will involve 5,000 bushels of USDA No. 2 yellow soybeans; soybean delivery months are January, March, May, July, August, September, and November.

In addition, futures contracts have their own trading hours. Normal trading hours for commodities and financial futures vary widely, unlike listed stocks and bonds, which begin and end trading at the same time. For example, floor trading in futures contracts for oats is Monday through Friday from 9:30 A.M. to 2:00 P.M. (all hours are

How Futures Work

TABLE 15.1 FUTURES CONTRACT DIMENSIONS

	Size of a Single Contract*	Market Value of a Single Contract**
Corn	5,000 bu	$ 21,013
Wheat	5,000 bu	$ 28,863
Live cattle	40,000 lb	$ 59,500
Feeder cattle	50,000 lb	$106,213
Lean hogs	40,000 lb	$ 29,300
Coffee	37,500 lb	$ 46,950
Sugar	112,000 lb	$ 13,328
Gold	100 troy oz	$115,910
Copper	25,000 lb	$ 63,800
Crude oil	1,000 bbls	$ 52,870
Euro	125,000 euro	$137,950
Japanese yen	12.5 million yen	$ 103,113
10-year Treasury notes	$100,000	$126,609
S&P 500 Stock Index	$250 × S&P 500 futures price	$515,625

*Contract sizes are for CME Group futures products.
**Contract values are representative of those that existed on July 9, 2015, for the next expiring futures contract.

central time); silver is from 8:25 A.M. to 1:25 P.M.; live cattle is from 9:05 A.M. to 1:00 P.M.; U.S. Treasury bonds is from 7:20 A.M. to 2:00 P.M.; and the S&P 500 Stock Index is from 8:30 A.M. to 3:15 P.M. In addition to the set of hours for open-outcry or floor trading, there is another set of hours for electronic trading. CME Globex allows traders access to futures products on any exchange nearly 24 hours a day, 5 days a week, from anywhere in the world.

Table 15.1 lists a cross section of 14 commodities and financial futures. The market value of a single contract, as reported in Table 15.1, is found by multiplying the size of the contract by the latest quoted price of the underlying commodity. For example, there are 37,500 pounds of coffee in a single contract, so if coffee's trading at $1.252 a pound, then the market value of one contract is 37,500 × $1.252 = $46,950. As you can see, the typical futures contract covers a large quantity of the underlying product or financial instrument. However, although the value of a single contract is normally quite large, the actual amount of investor capital required to deal in these vehicles is relatively small because all trading in this market is done on a margin basis.

Options versus Futures Contracts In many respects, futures contracts are closely related to call options. For example, both involve the future delivery of an item at an agreed-upon price, and both are derivative securities. But there is a significant difference between a futures contract and an options contract. To begin with, a futures contract obligates a person to buy or sell a specified amount of a given commodity on or before a stated date—unless the contract is canceled or liquidated before it expires. In contrast, an option gives the holder the right to buy or sell a specific amount of a real or financial asset at a specific price over a specified period of time.

In addition, whereas call and put options specify the price at which investors can buy or sell the underlying asset, futures prices are not spelled out in the futures contract. Instead, the price on a futures contract is established through trading on the floor of a commodities exchange. This means that the delivery price is set at whatever price the contract sells for. So, if you bought a corn futures contract three months ago at $4.00 a bushel, then that's the price you'll pay to take delivery of the underlying product, even if the contract trades at, say, $4.50 a bushel at its date of expiration (i.e., delivery date). Equally important, the risk of loss with an option is limited to the price paid for it. A futures contract has no such limit on exposure to loss. Finally, while options have an explicit up-front cost (in the form of an option premium), futures contracts do not. The purchase of a futures contract does involve a margin deposit, but that's nothing more than a refundable security deposit, not a sunk cost (like an option premium).

Major Exchanges Modern futures contracts in this country got their start in the agricultural segment of the economy over 170 years ago when individuals who produced, owned, and/or processed foodstuffs sought a way to protect themselves against adverse price movements. Later, futures contracts came to be traded by individuals who were not necessarily connected with agriculture but who wanted to make money with commodities by speculating on their price swings.

The first organized commodities exchange in this country was the Chicago Board of Trade, which opened its doors in 1848. Over time, additional markets opened. There currently are more than a dozen U.S. exchanges that qualify as designated contract markets (DCM) and deal in listed futures contracts. Designated contract markets are boards of trade (or exchanges) that operate under the regulatory oversight of the U.S. Commodity Futures Trading Commission (CFTC). DCMs may list futures (or options) contracts based on any underlying commodity, index, or instrument. The majority of futures trading occurs on only a few exchanges. The Chicago Mercantile Exchange is the most active exchange, with about as much trading volume as all other futures exchanges combined. The CME is followed in size by the Chicago Board of Trade (CBOT) and the New York Mercantile Exchange (NYMEX), which includes through a previous acquisition the Commodity Exchange, Inc. (COMEX). Together, these four exchanges account for about 95% of the trading conducted on U.S. futures exchanges. Although the exchanges continue to operate separately, in July of 2007 the CME Group was created through a merger of the CME and the CBOT. The CME Group expanded further in August of 2008 by acquiring the NYMEX, which included COMEX.

Most exchanges deal in a number of commodities or financial assets, and many commodities and financial futures are traded on more than one exchange. Annual volume of trading on futures exchanges has surpassed three billion contracts with a total value above the trillion-dollar mark. Most exchanges now conduct trading electronically. The **open-outcry auction** method once used to conduct floor trading, which required traders to shout their orders while using elaborate hand signals (illustrated in Figure 15.1), has all but disappeared. As of July 2015 the CME Group continues open outcry futures trading for the S&P 500 futures contracts. The company also continues floor trading for the options on futures contracts.

In 1992 CME Globex became the first global electronic futures trading platform. Globex offers trading more than 23 hours a day, 5 days a week, and provides an international link among futures exchanges. Since 2000 electronic trading of futures contracts has grown from about 9 percent of trading volume to nearly 100 percent. Globex allowed the CME Eurodollar futures contract to become the most actively traded futures contract in the world. Indeed, the three most actively traded contracts on CME Globex (three-month Eurodollars, the E-Mini S&P 500 Stock Index, and the U.S. 10-year Treasury Note) represent more than 50% of futures trading volume on the U.S. exchanges.

FIGURE 15.1   The Auction Market at Work on the Floor of the Chicago Board of Trade

Traders once employed a system of open-outcry and hand signals to indicate whether they wished to buy or sell and the price at which they wished to do so. Fingers held vertically indicated the number of contracts a trader wanted to buy or sell. Fingers held horizontally indicated the fraction of a cent above or below the last traded full-cent price at which the trader would buy or sell.

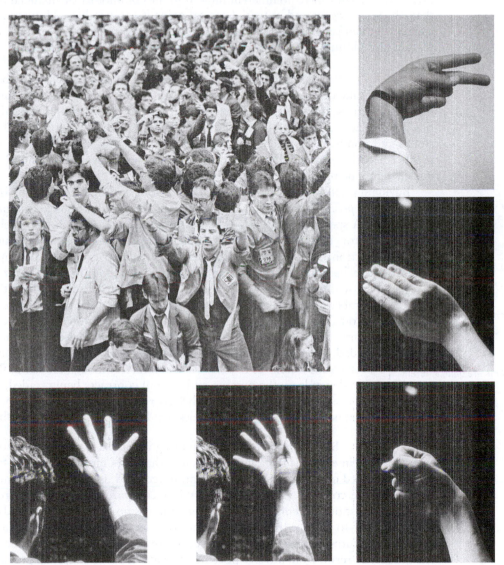

Trading in the Futures Market

Basically, the futures market contains hedgers and speculators. The market could not exist and operate efficiently without either one. The **hedgers** are businesses that either produce a commodity or use it as an input to their production process. For example, a rancher might enter into a futures contract to lock in the price for his herd months before actually selling the herd. That way, the rancher's revenues are predictable and are not affected by swings in the price of cattle. In effect, the hedgers provide the underlying strength of the futures market and represent the very reason for its existence. In the case of financial futures, hedgers are companies whose businesses are affected by swings in financial variables such as interest rates or exchange rates. Accordingly, hedgers also include financial institutions and other large corporations.

Speculators, in contrast, trade futures contracts simply to earn a profit on expected price swings. They have no inherent interest in the commodity or financial future other than the price action and potential capital gains it can produce. However, their presence in the market benefits others because speculators' trades help make the futures market more liquid.

Trading Mechanics Once futures contracts are created, they can readily be traded in the market. Like common stocks, futures contracts are bought and sold through local brokerage offices and on many Internet sites. Except for setting up a special commodities trading account, there is no difference between trading futures and dealing in stocks and bonds. The same types of orders are used, and margin trading is standard practice. Any investor can buy or sell any contract, with any delivery month, as long as it is currently being traded on one of the exchanges.

Buying a contract is referred to as *taking a long position*. Selling one is known as *taking a short position*. It is exactly like going long or short with stocks and has the same connotation. A speculator who is long wants the price to rise, and the short seller wants it to drop. Investors can liquidate both long and short positions simply by executing an offsetting transaction. The short seller, for example, would cover her position by buying an equal amount of the contract. In general, only about 1% of all futures contracts are settled by delivery. The rest are offset prior to the delivery month. The total number of contracts that are open and have not been settled by delivery or by an offsetting transaction is called **open interest**. All trades are subject to normal transaction costs, which include **round-trip commissions** for each contract traded. A round-trip commission includes the commission costs on both ends of the transaction—to buy and sell a contract. Although the size of the commission depends on the number and type of contracts being traded, trades that are executed electronically usually have round-trip commissions under $10 and are much less expensive than trades that have to be routed to a pit broker.

Margin Trading Buying on margin means putting up only a fraction of the total price in cash. Margin, in effect, is the amount of equity that goes into the deal. All futures contracts are traded on a margin basis. The margin required usually ranges from about 2% to 10% of the contract value. This is very low compared to the margin required for stocks and most other securities. Furthermore, there is no borrowing required on the part of the investor to finance the balance of the contract. The **margin deposit**, as margin is called with futures, represents security to cover any loss in the market value of the contract that may result from adverse price movements. It exists simply to guarantee fulfillment of the contract. The margin deposit is not a partial payment for the commodity or financial instrument, nor is it related to the value of the underlying product or item.

The size of the required margin deposit is specified as a dollar amount. It varies according to the type of contract and depends on the price volatility of the underlying commodity or financial asset. In some cases, it also varies according to the exchange on which the commodity is traded. Table 15.2 gives the margin requirements for the same 14 commodities and financial instruments listed in Table 15.1. Compared to the size and value of the futures contracts, margin requirements are very low. The **initial margin** noted in Table 15.2 is the amount of capital the investor must deposit with the broker when initiating the transaction; it represents the amount of money required to make a

Margins and
Margin Calls

TABLE 15.2   MARGIN REQUIREMENTS FOR A SAMPLE OF COMMODITIES AND FINANCIAL FUTURES

Contract	Initial Margin	Maintenance Margin	Exchange
Corn	$ 1,375	$ 1,250	CBOT
Wheat	$ 1,925	$ 1,750	CBOT
Live cattle	$ 1,320	$ 1,200	CME
Feeder cattle	$ 2,475	$ 2,250	CME
Lean hogs	$ 1,320	$ 1,200	CME
Coffee	$ 4,675	$ 4,250	NYMEX
Sugar	$ 770	$ 700	NYMEX
Gold	$ 4,125	$ 3,750	COMEX
Copper	$ 3,410	$ 3,100	COMEX
Crude oil	$ 5,060	$ 4,600	NYMEX
Euro	$ 3,905	$ 3,550	CME
Japanese yen	$ 2,860	$ 2,600	CME
10-year Treasury notes	$ 1,485	$ 1,350	CBOT
S&P 500 Stock Index	$25,300	$23,000	CME

Note: On July 9, 2015, the CME Group specified that speculative and nonmembers initial margin requirements for all products are set at 110% of the maintenance margin requirement for a given product. Hedge and member initial margin requirements for all products are set at 100% of the maintenance margin requirement for a given product. Margins are meant to be typical of the ongoing requirements that customers are expected to live up to. Depending on the volatility of the market, exchange-minimum margin requirements are changed frequently. Thus, the requirements in this table are also subject to change on short notice. The actual margin requirements for a specific type of transaction on a given exchange are typically reported on the exchange's website.

given investment. (The margins quoted in Table 15.2 are for speculative transactions. Typically, the initial margin amount is slightly lower for hedge transactions.)

After the investment is made, the market value of a contract will rise and fall as the quoted price of the underlying commodity or financial instrument goes up or down, and that fluctuation triggers changes in the amount of margin on deposit. To be sure that an adequate margin is always on hand, investors are required to meet a second type of margin requirement, the **maintenance margin.** The maintenance margin, which is slightly less than the initial margin, establishes the minimum amount of margin that an investor must keep in the account at all times. For instance, if the initial margin on a commodity is $1,100 per contract, its maintenance margin might be $1,000. As long as the market value of the contract does not fall by more than $100 (the difference between the contract's initial and maintenance margins), the investor has no problem. But if the value of the contract drops by more than $100, the investor will receive a *margin call.* The investor must then immediately deposit enough cash to bring the position back to the initial margin level.

An investor's margin position is checked daily via a procedure known as **mark-to-the-market.** That is, the gain or loss in a contract's value is determined at the end of each session. At that time the broker debits or credits the account accordingly. In a falling market, an investor may receive a number of margin calls and be required to make additional margin payments. Failure to do so will leave the broker with no choice but to close out the position—that is, to sell the contract.

15.1 What is a futures contract? Briefly explain how it is used as an investment vehicle.

15.2 Discuss the difference between a cash market and a futures market.

15.3 What is the major source of return to commodities speculators? How important is current income from dividends and interest?

15.4 Why are both hedgers and speculators important to the efficient operation of a futures market?

15.5 Explain how margin trading is conducted in the futures market.

    a. What is the difference between an initial margin and a maintenance margin?
    b. Are investors ever required to put up additional margin? If so, when?

Commodities

LG2 LG3 LG4 Physical commodities like grains, metals, wood, and meat make up a major portion of the futures market. They have been actively traded in this country for well over a century. The material that follows focuses on commodities trading. We begin with a review of the basic characteristics and investment merits of these contracts.

Basic Characteristics

Commodities are goods for which there is demand without differentiation of supplier. In other words, a commodity is a fungible good that is qualitatively the same regardless of the supplier. For example, a Troy ounce of gold from a mine in Uzbekistan is the same as a Troy ounce of gold from a mine in Indonesia. As long as the underlying commodity meets the contractual standard, it can be traded with futures. Table 15.3 divides the market for commodity contracts into six categories: agriculture, metals, livestock, food, energy, and other. Such segmentation does not affect trading mechanics and procedures. It merely provides a convenient way of categorizing commodities into groups based on similar underlying characteristics.

TABLE 15.3   MAJOR CLASSES OF COMMODITIES

Agriculture		Metals	
Corn	Soybean oil	Silver	Palladium
Oats	Wheat	Copper	Platinum
Soybeans	Canola	Gold	Iron ore
Soybean meal	Rice		
Livestock		**Food**	
Live cattle	Lean hogs	Cocoa	Sugar
Feeder cattle		Coffee	Cotton
		Milk	Orange juice
Energy		**Other**	
Coal	Natural gas	Weather	Freight
Crude oil	Ethanol	Interest rates	Environment
Heating oil	Electricity	Real estate	Lumber

Table 15.3 shows the diversity of the commodities market and the variety of contracts available. Although the list of available contract types changes yearly, the table indicates that investors have dozens of commodities to choose from. A number of the contracts in Table 15.3 (e.g., soybeans, wheat, and sugar) are available in several forms or grades. Not included in Table 15.3 are dozens of commodities (e.g., butter, cheese, whey, boneless beef, and others) that are not widely traded.

A Commodities Contract Every commodity (whether actively or thinly traded) has certain specifications that spell out in detail the amounts and quality of the product being traded. Figure 15.2 shows the contract specifications of corn futures contracts that trade on the CBOT. You can see that a corn futures contract represents 5,000 bushels of #2 yellow corn, and its price is quoted in cents per bushel. In this case, the contract also allows for deliverable grades of either #1 or #3 yellow corn, but for a premium or discounted price, respectively. The futures contract also specifies the expiration months, trading hours, daily price limits, settlement procedures, and more. In the middle of the page of contract specifications is the exchange rule, which indicates the listing exchange and the trading rules and regulations that apply when trading the contract.

The quotation system used for commodities is based on the size of the contract and the pricing unit. Standard commodities quotations, like the one shown in Figure 15.3, generally report the daily last, open, high, and low prices for each delivery month. With commodities, the last price of the day, or the closing price, is known as the **settlement price**. The daily settlement price is very important since it is used to determine the daily market value of a contract and, therefore, an investor's profit or loss for the day, as well as margin requirements. The prior settle price is the final settlement price at the end of the previous day. The quotation in Figure 15.3 also reports the **volume**—the number of contracts traded—for the day. According to Figure 15.3, the settle price for December 2016 corn futures contract is 439'6. The term after the apostrophe represents a fraction in eighths. Because corn futures are quoted in cents per bushel, the six following the apostrophe means 6/8ths of a cent. According to Figure 15.2 the minimum price fluctuation for corn futures contracts is 1/4th of one cent so 6/8ths is 3/4ths of one cent or 0.75 cents. Each contract represents 5,000 bushels of corn and each bushel is worth $4.3975, so the market value of the contract is $5,000 \times \$4.3975 = \$21,987.50$.

Price Behavior Commodity prices react to a unique set of economic, political, and international pressures—as well as to the weather. The explanation of the reasons that commodity prices change is beyond the scope of this text. But they do move up and down just like any other investment, which is precisely what speculators want. Because we are dealing in such large trading units (5,000 bushels of this or 40,000 pounds of that), even a modest price change can have an enormous impact on the market value of a contract and therefore on investor returns or losses. For example, if the price of corn goes up or down by just $0.20 per bushel, the value of a single contract will change by $1,000. A corn contract can be bought with a $1,375 initial margin deposit, so it is easy to see the effect this kind of price behavior can have on investor return.

Do commodity prices really move all that much? Judge for yourself. The price change columns in Figure 15.3 show some examples of price changes that occurred from the previous day's closing price to the current day's last price. For example, relative to the prior day's settle or closing price, March 2016 corn dropped $75

FIGURE 15.2

Contract Specifications for Corn Futures

The contract specifications for any listed futures contract are typically available online at the listing exchange website. When traders buy or sell futures contracts, they are agreeing to uphold the terms defined by the contract specifications. In this case we see that a corn futures contract calls for the delivery of 5,000 bushels of #2 yellow corn by the end of the second business day following the last trading day of the delivery month, which would be the contract's expiration month.

(Source: Reprinted with permission, CME Group, 2015.)

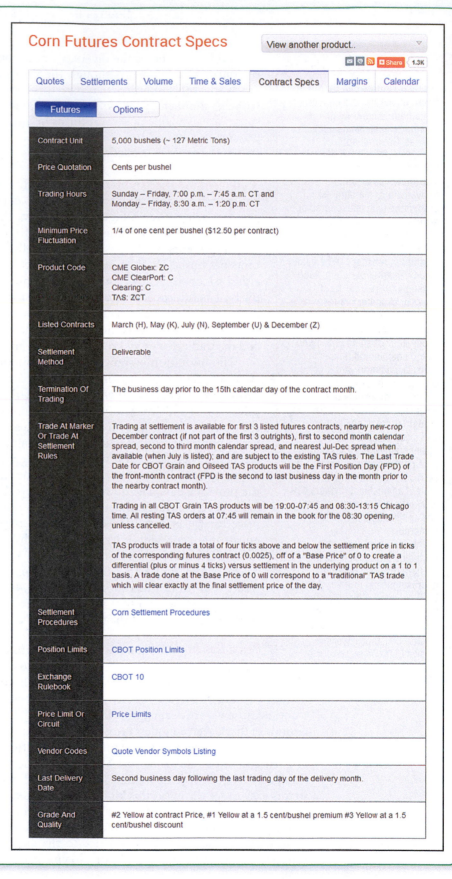

Corn Futures Contract Specs

View another product..

| Quotes | Settlements | Volume | Time & Sales | **Contract Specs** | Margins | Calendar |

| **Futures** | Options |

Contract Unit	5,000 bushels (~ 127 Metric Tons)
Price Quotation	Cents per bushel
Trading Hours	Sunday – Friday, 7:00 p.m. – 7:45 a.m. CT and Monday – Friday, 8:30 a.m. – 1:20 p.m. CT
Minimum Price Fluctuation	1/4 of one cent per bushel ($12.50 per contract)
Product Code	CME Globex: ZC CME ClearPort: C Clearing: C TAS: ZCT
Listed Contracts	March (H), May (K), July (N), September (U) & December (Z)
Settlement Method	Deliverable
Termination Of Trading	The business day prior to the 15th calendar day of the contract month.
Trade At Marker Or Trade At Settlement Rules	Trading at settlement is available for first 3 listed futures contracts, nearby new-crop December contract (if not part of the first 3 outrights), first to second month calendar spread, second to third month calendar spread, and nearest Jul-Dec spread when available (when July is listed); and are subject to the existing TAS rules. The Last Trade Date for CBOT Grain and Oilseed TAS products will be the First Position Day (FPD) of the front-month contract (FPD is the second to last business day in the month prior to the nearby contract month). Trading in all CBOT Grain TAS products will be 19:00-07:45 and 08:30-13:15 Chicago time. All resting TAS orders at 07:45 will remain in the book for the 08:30 opening, unless cancelled. TAS products will trade a total of four ticks above and below the settlement price in ticks of the corresponding futures contract (0.0025), off of a "Base Price" of 0 to create a differential (plus or minus 4 ticks) versus settlement in the underlying product on a 1 to 1 basis. A trade done at the Base Price of 0 will correspond to a "traditional" TAS trade which will clear exactly at the final settlement price of the day.
Settlement Procedures	Corn Settlement Procedures
Position Limits	CBOT Position Limits
Exchange Rulebook	CBOT 10
Price Limit Or Circuit	Price Limits
Vendor Codes	Quote Vendor Symbols Listing
Last Delivery Date	Second business day following the last trading day of the delivery month.
Grade And Quality	#2 Yellow at contract Price, #1 Yellow at a 1.5 cent/bushel premium #3 Yellow at a 1.5 cent/bushel discount

FIGURE 15.3 Quotations on Corn Futures Contracts

Readily available online quotations quickly reveal key information about various commodities in real time (or from some sources, slightly delayed). This quotation for corn futures contracts includes the daily last, open, high, and low prices. It also provides the change in price from the previous day's closing price to the current day's last price and the previous day's settlement price (or prior settle), as well as the current day's volume, and Hi/Lo limit. (Source: Reprinted with permission, CME Group, 2015.)

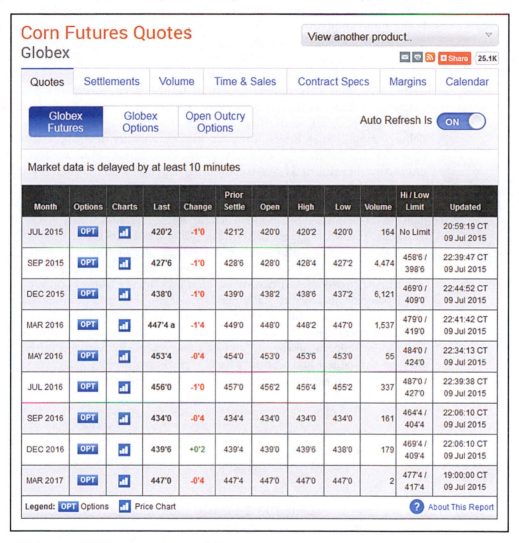

Corn Futures Quotes
Globex

View another product..

Market data is delayed by at least 10 minutes

Month	Options	Charts	Last	Change	Prior Settle	Open	High	Low	Volume	Hi / Low Limit	Updated
JUL 2015	OPT		420'2	-1'0	421'2	420'0	420'2	420'0	164	No Limit	20:59:19 CT 09 Jul 2015
SEP 2015	OPT		427'6	-1'0	428'6	428'0	428'4	427'2	4,474	458'6 / 398'6	22:39:47 CT 09 Jul 2015
DEC 2015	OPT		438'0	-1'0	439'0	438'2	438'6	437'2	6,121	469'0 / 409'0	22:44:52 CT 09 Jul 2015
MAR 2016	OPT		447'4 a	-1'4	449'0	448'0	448'2	447'0	1,537	479'0 / 419'0	22:41:42 CT 09 Jul 2015
MAY 2016	OPT		453'4	-0'4	454'0	453'0	453'6	453'0	55	484'0 / 424'0	22:34:13 CT 09 Jul 2015
JUL 2016	OPT		456'0	-1'0	457'0	456'2	456'4	455'2	337	487'0 / 427'0	22:39:38 CT 09 Jul 2015
SEP 2016	OPT		434'0	-0'4	434'4	434'0	434'0	434'0	161	464'4 / 404'4	22:06:10 CT 09 Jul 2015
DEC 2016	OPT		439'6	+0'2	439'4	439'0	439'6	438'0	179	469'4 / 409'4	22:06:10 CT 09 Jul 2015
MAR 2017	OPT		447'0	-0'4	447'4	447'0	447'0	447'0	2	477'4 / 417'4	19:00:00 CT 09 Jul 2015

Legend: OPT Options   Price Chart   ? About This Report

(i.e., 5,000 bushels × $0.015). The price swing is even larger if you consider the current day's low price relative to the prior day's settle price. In this case March 2016 corn dropped $0.02 per bushel (i.e., $4.49 − $4.47) or $100 per contract (i.e., 5,000 bushels × $0.02). Keep in mind that these intraday price swings are on a single contract. The impact of these small changes can quickly add up to significant profits or losses depending on the number of contracts, especially relative to the small initial investment required.

Clearly, such price behavior is one of the magnets that draw investors to commodities. The exchanges recognize the volatile nature of commodities contracts and try to put lids on price fluctuations by imposing daily price limits and maximum daily price ranges. (Similar limits also are put on some financial futures.) The **daily price limit** restricts the interday change in the price (i.e., the price change from one day to the next day) of the underlying commodity. For example, a corn futures contract has an initial price limit of $0.30 per bushel and an expanded price limit of $0.45 per bushel. The **maximum daily price range** (shown in Figure 15.3 as the difference between the Hi/Lo limits) limits the amount of intraday price movement (i.e., the price can change during the day) and is usually equal to twice the daily price limit. For example, the daily price limit on corn is $0.30 per bushel and its maximum daily range is $0.60 per bushel. In fact, the prior day's settlement price (i.e., the settle price) plus and minus the daily price limit determines the Hi/Lo limits. Because futures prices can become extremely volatile as the contract nears expiration, there are no price limits on the current month contract on or after the second business day preceding the first day of the delivery month. Such limits, however, still leave plenty of room to turn a quick profit. Consider that the daily price limits on one corn futures contract translates into a per-day change in value of $1,500 to unlimited depending on the contract and prior pricing.

Return on Invested Capital Futures contracts have only one source of return: the capital gains that result when prices move in a favorable direction. There is no current income of any kind. The volatile price behavior of futures contracts is one reason why high returns are possible, and the other reason is leverage. Because all futures trading is done on margin, it takes only a small amount of money to control a large investment position—and to participate in the price swings that accompany futures contracts. Of course, the use of leverage also means that an investment can be wiped out in just a matter of days.

We can measure the return on a commodities contract by calculating the **return on invested capital**. This variation of the standard holding period return formula bases the investment's return on the amount of money actually invested in the contract rather than on the value of the contract itself. The return on invested capital for a commodities position can be determined according to the following simple formula.

Equation 15.1

$$\text{Return on invested capital} = \frac{\substack{\text{Selling price of} \\ \text{commodity contract}} - \substack{\text{Purchase price of} \\ \text{commodity contract}}}{\text{Amount of margin deposit}}$$

We can use Equation 15.1 for both long and short transactions. To see how it works, assume you recently bought two March 2017 corn futures contracts at 447'0 ($4.47 per bushel) by depositing the required initial margin of $2,750 ($1,375 for each contract). Your investment, therefore, amounts to only $2,750, but you control 10,000 bushels of corn worth $44,700 (i.e., 10,000 × $4.47) at the time of purchase. Now, assume that March 2017 corn has just closed at 458, making the market value of your position equal to 10,000 × $4.58 = $45,800. At this point, you decide to sell and take your profit. Your return on invested capital is:

$$\text{Return on invested capital} = \frac{\$45,800 - \$44,700}{\$2,750}$$

$$= \frac{\$1,100}{\$2,750} = 0.40 = 40\%$$

FAMOUS FAILURES IN FINANCE

Shady Trading at Enron

Before it was known for its financial problems, Enron, a utility firm operating pipelines and shipping natural gas, had become famous as a business pioneer, blazing new trails in the market for trading risk. In the 1980s the price of natural gas was deregulated, which meant that its price could go down and up, exposing producers and consumers to risks. Enron decided to exploit new opportunities in the commodities business by trading natural gas futures. The natural gas futures that traded on the New York Mercantile Exchange did not take into account regional discrepancies in gas prices. Enron filled this void by agreeing to deliver natural gas to any location in the United States at any time.

In addition to trading natural gas and other energy contracts, in the late 1990s Enron began trading weather derivatives for which no underlying commodities existed. These were just bets on the weather. Its weather-derivatives transactions were worth an estimated $3.5 billion in the United States alone. Thanks to its near-monopoly position in derivatives products, Enron's trading business was initially highly profitable. At one point, the company offered more than 1,800 different contracts for 16 product categories, ranging from oil and natural gas to weather derivatives, broadband services, and emissions rights, and it earned 90% of its revenues from trading derivatives. And unlike traditional commodity and futures exchanges and brokers, Enron's online commodity and derivative business was not subject to federal regulations.

However, Enron eventually lost its unique position as the energy business started to mature. When other firms entered the online derivatives-trading business, they competed by charging lower commissions and exploiting the same regional price discrepancies that had been Enron's bread and butter. Enron's trading operations became less profitable. To find new markets and products, the company expanded into areas such as water, foreign power sources, telecommunications, and broadband services. The farther it moved from its core businesses of supplying gas, the more money Enron lost.

The company sought to hide those losses by entering into more risky and bizarre financial contracts. When financial institutions began to realize that Enron was essentially a shell game, they withdrew their credit. At that point, despite rosy assurances from its founder and CEO Ken Lay, Enron went into a death spiral that ended in bankruptcy on December 2, 2001.

In July 2004 Lay was indicted on 11 counts of securities fraud and related charges. He was found guilty on May 25, 2006, of all but one of the counts. Each count carried a maximum 5- to 10-year sentence and legal experts said Lay could face 20 to 30 years in prison. However, about three and a half months before his scheduled sentencing, Ken Lay died on July 5, 2006, while vacationing in Snowmass, Colorado. On October 17, 2006, as a result of his death, the federal district court judge who presided over the case vacated Lay's conviction.

Critical Thinking Questions Could the Enron debacle have been prevented? If so, what actions should have been taken by auditors, regulators, and lawmakers?

WATCH YOUR BEHAVIOR

It is well known that individual investors are reluctant to sell stocks that have experienced a loss. Perhaps surprisingly, experiments have discovered that professional futures traders exhibit an even stronger tendency to hang onto their losing positions too long.

(Source: Michael S. Haigh and John A. List, "Do Professional Traders Exhibit Myopic Loss Aversion? An Experimental Analysis," *Journal of Finance*, 2005, Vol. 60, No.)

MyFinanceLab

Clearly, this high rate of return was due not only to an increase in the price of the commodity but also to the fact that you were using very low margin, or very high financial leverage. The initial margin in this transaction is only about 6% of the underlying value of the contract.

Trading Commodities

Investing in commodities takes one of three forms. The first, *speculating*, involves using commodities as a way to generate capital gains. In essence, speculators try to capitalize on the wide price swings that are characteristic of so many commodities. As explained in the accompanying Famous Failures in Finance box, this is basically what Enron was doing—until things started turning nasty.

While volatile price movements may appeal to speculators, they frighten many other investors. As a result, some of these more cautious investors turn to *spreading*, the second form of commodities investing. Futures investors use this trading technique as a way to capture some of the benefits of volatile commodities prices but without all the exposure to loss.

Finally, commodities futures can be used for *hedging*. A hedge in the commodities market is more of a technical strategy that is used almost exclusively by producers and processors to protect a position in a product or commodity. For example, a producer or grower would use a commodity hedge to obtain as high a price as possible for its goods. The processor or manufacturer who uses the commodity would use a hedge for the opposite reason: to obtain the goods at as low a price as possible. A successful hedge, in effect, means more predictable income to producers or costs to processors.

Let's now look briefly at the two trading strategies that are most used by individual investors—speculating and spreading—to gain a better understanding of how to use commodities as investments.

Speculating Speculators hope to capitalize on swings in commodity prices by going long or short. To see why a speculator would go long when prices are expected to rise, assume you buy a June 2021 gold futures contract at 1287.4 by depositing the required initial margin of $4,125. One gold contract involves 100 troy ounces of gold, so it has a market value equal to 100 troy ounces × $1,287.4 = $128,740. If gold goes up, you make money. Assume that one month after you purchased the June 2021 contract, its price is 1313.1. You then liquidate the contract and make a profit equal to $1,313.10 − $1,287.40 = $25.70 per ounce. That means a total profit of $2,570 on the long gold contract position with an investment of $4,125—this translates into a return on invested capital of 62.3%. Not bad for a month of speculation.

Of course, instead of rising, the price of gold could have dropped by $25.70 per ounce. On a 100-ounce contract, that amounts to $2,570 loss on the position. As a result, you would have lost a good bit of your original investment: $4,125 − $2,570 leaves $1,555.

But a drop in price would be just what a short seller is after. Here's why. You sell "short" the June 2021 gold contract at 1287.4 and buy it back one month later at 1261.7. Clearly, the difference between the selling price and the purchase price is the same $25.70. But in this case it is profit because the selling price exceeds the purchase price.

Spreading Instead of attempting to speculate on the price behavior of a futures contract, you might follow the more conservative tactic of spreading. Much like spreading with put and call options, the idea is to combine two or more different contracts into a position that offers the potential for a modest amount of profit but restricts your exposure to loss. One very important reason for spreading in the commodities market is that, unlike options, there is no limit to the amount of loss that can occur with a futures contract.

You set up a spread by buying one contract and simultaneously selling another. Although one side of the transaction will lead to a loss, you hope that the profit earned from the other side will more than offset the loss and that the net result will be at least a modest amount of profit. If you're wrong, the spread will limit, but not eliminate, any losses.

Here is a simple example of how a spread might work. Suppose you buy contract A at 533.50 and at the same time short sell contract B for 575.50. Sometime later, you close out your position in contract A by selling it at 542, and you simultaneously cover your short position in B by purchasing a contract at 579. Although you made a profit of 8.50 points (542 − 533.50) on the long position (contract A), you lost 3.50 points (575.50 − 579) on the contract you shorted (B). The net effect, however, is a profit of 5 points. If you were dealing in cents per pound, those 5 points would mean a profit of $250 on a 5,000-pound contract.

All sorts of commodity spreads can be set up for almost any type of investment situation. Most of them, however, are highly sophisticated and require specialized skills.

Diving Oil Prices Send Cal Dive into Bankruptcy

One of the reasons that commodity futures markets exist is the price volatility of the underlying commodity. Futures contracts give firms a way to manage that volatility, but it isn't always possible to insulate a company from commodity price risk. Swings in oil prices, for example, have created many millionaires through the years, but they have also brought about financial ruin. The chart below illustrates the volatility in crude oil prices from 2007 to 2015. In 2007 and 2008 crude oil futures prices were reaching all-time highs of over $100 per barrel, which triggered an explosion in oil futures trading. The average daily trading volume in 2008 was about 15 times the daily world production of oil. But as the global economy turned south and began to slip into recession, demand for oil and other commodities fell off sharply. After peaking during the summer of 2008, the price of oil responded true to form, falling by almost 70% in six months and sending the stock prices of oil-related businesses into freefall. Since then, as the economy has slowly rebounded, so has the oil futures price, again surpassing $100 per barrel. Interestingly, in mid-2014 the price of oil again plummeted, this time blamed mostly on oil futures speculation and a flood of worldwide supply of oil. Even so, the drop in prices sent many oil-related businesses into bankruptcy, among them Cal Dive International, which filed for bankruptcy in March 2015.

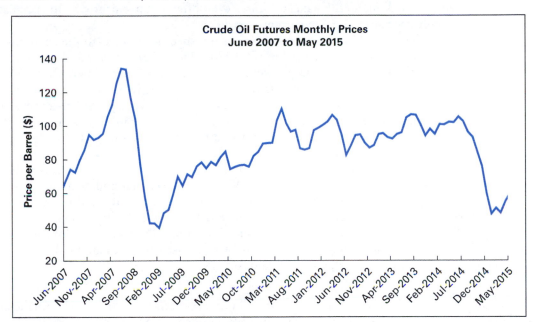

**Crude Oil Futures Monthly Prices
June 2007 to May 2015**

CONCEPTS IN REVIEW

15.6 List and briefly define the five essential parts of a commodities contract. Which parts have a direct bearing on the price behavior of the contract?

15.7 Briefly define each of the following:

a. Settlement price
b. Daily price limit
c. Volume
d. Maximum daily price range
e. Delivery month

15.8 What is the source of return on futures contracts? What measure is used to calculate the return on a commodities contract?

15.9 Note several approaches to investing in commodities and explain the investment objectives of each.

Financial Futures

LG5 LG6 Another dimension of the futures market is **financial futures**, a segment of the market in which futures contracts are traded on financial instruments. Financial futures are an extension of the commodities concept. They were created for much the same reason as commodities futures, they are traded in the same market, their prices behave a lot like commodities, and they have similar investment merits. However, financial futures are unique because of the underlying assets. Let's now look more closely at financial futures and see how investors can use them.

The Financial Futures Market

Although relatively young, financial futures are the dominant type of futures contract. The level of trading in financial futures far surpasses that of traditional commodities. Much of the interest in financial futures is due to hedgers and institutional investors who use these contracts as portfolio management tools. But individual investors can also use financial futures to speculate on the behavior of interest rates and to speculate in the stock market. Financial futures even offer a convenient way to speculate in the highly specialized foreign currency markets.

The financial futures market was established in response to the economic turmoil the United States experienced in the 1970s. The instability of the dollar on the world market was causing serious problems for multinational firms. Interest rates were highly volatile, which caused severe difficulties for corporate treasurers, financial institutions, and money managers. All of these parties needed a way to protect themselves from the wide fluctuations in the value of the dollar and interest rates. Thus, a market for financial futures was born. Hedging provided the economic rationale for the market, but speculators were quick to join in.

Most of the financial futures trading in this country occurs on the Chicago Board of Trade, the Chicago Mercantile Exchange and, to a much lesser extent, the New York Mercantile Exchange. Financial futures also are traded on several foreign exchanges, the most noteworthy of which is the London International Financial Futures Exchange. The basic types of financial futures include foreign currencies, debt securities (more commonly known as interest rate futures), and stock indexes.

Foreign Currencies, Interest Rates, and Stock Indexes The financial futures market started rather inconspicuously in May 1972, with the listing of a handful of foreign currency contracts. Known as **currency futures**, they have become a major hedging vehicle as international trade has mushroomed. Most of the trading in this market is conducted in major market currencies such as the British pound, Swiss franc, Canadian dollar, Japanese yen, and the euro—all of which are issued by countries or regions with strong international trade and economic ties to the United States.

The first futures contract on debt securities, or **interest rate futures**, began trading in October 1975. Today trading is carried out in a variety of interest-rate-based securities, including U.S. Treasury securities, Federal Funds, interest rate swaps, Euromarket deposits (e.g., Eurodollar and Euroyen), and foreign government bonds. Interest rate futures were immediately successful, and their popularity continues to grow.

In February 1982 still another type of trading vehicle was introduced: the stock-index futures contract. **Stock index futures** are contracts pegged to

INVESTOR FACTS

Single Stock Futures Several years ago, single stock futures (SSFs) began trading on an exchange called OneChicago. SSFs allow investors to buy or sell futures contracts written on 100-share lots of a given common stock. SSFs today are available on more than 1,500 well-known companies and ETFs. Because of their lower margin requirements (20% for SSFs versus 50% for regular stock trades), SSFs are highly leveraged investments, with substantial risk but also with very attractive return potential. Depending on their risk profiles, investors can use this futures version of a stock to support both speculative and hedging investment strategies.

(Source: OneChicago, LLC, Press Release 7/1/2015, http://www .Onechicago.Com/?p=10392, accessed July 11, 2015.)

broad-based measures of stock market performance. Today trading is done in most of the (major) U.S. stock indexes, including the Dow Jones Industrial Average, the S&P 500, the Nasdaq 100, and the Russell 2000, among others.

In addition to U.S. indexes, investors can trade stock index futures contracts based on the London, Tokyo, Paris, Sydney, Berlin, Zurich, and Toronto stock exchanges. Stock index futures, which are similar to the stock index options we discussed earlier, allow investors to participate in the general movements of the entire stock market.

Stock index futures, and other futures contracts, are a type of *derivative security*. Like options, they derive their value from the price of the assets that underlie them. In the case of stock index futures, they reflect the general performance of the stock market as a whole or various segments of the market. Thus, when the market for large-cap stocks, as measured by the S&P 500, goes up, the value of an S&P 500 futures contract should go up as well. Accordingly, investors can use stock index futures as a way to buy or sell the market—or reasonable proxies thereof—and thereby participate in broad market moves.

Contract Specifications In principle, financial futures contracts are like commodities contracts. They control large sums of the underlying financial instrument and are issued with a variety of delivery months. The lives of financial futures contracts run from about 12 months or less for most stock index and currency futures to two to three years or more for interest rate instruments. In terms of quotations, Figure 15.4 shows quotes for a foreign currency, an interest rate, and a stock index futures contract. Looking first at the Canadian dollars futures quotation, we see information very similar to that of commodity futures quotations. In particular, currency futures quotations provide the last, prior settle, open, high, and low prices, as well as contract trading volume. The owner of a currency futures contract holds a claim on a certain amount of foreign money, in this case 100,000 Canadian dollars. Underlying currency amounts can vary widely across currency futures contracts, such as 62,500 British pounds or 12.5 million Japanese yen.

Holders of interest rate futures have a claim on a certain amount of the underlying debt security. The contract for interest rate futures shown in Figure 15.4 represents a claim to $100,000 worth of U.S. Treasury bonds. Recall from earlier in the text that bond quotations are expressed as a percentage of the par value, and the same is true for interest rate futures quotations. Figure 15.4 indicates that the September 2015 contract price is 149'21 and in the case of interest rate futures contracts the value following the apostrophe refers to the number 1/32 of a percentage point. So 149'21 is 149.65625% (i.e., 149 + 21/32) and that means that the contract value is $100,000 × 149.65625% = $149,656.25.

Stock index futures are a bit different from most futures contracts because the seller of one of these contracts is not obligated to deliver the underlying stocks at the expiration date. Instead, ultimate delivery is in the form of cash. This is fortunate, as it would indeed be a task to make delivery of the 500 issues in the S&P 500 Index. Basically, the amount of underlying cash is set at a certain multiple of the value of the underlying stock index. Some common examples for U.S. indexes:

Index	Multiple
E-mini Dow ($5)	$5 × index
E-mini S&P 500	$50 × index
E-mini S&P MidCap 400	$100 × index
E-mini NASDAQ 100	$20 × index
S&P 500	$250 × index

FIGURE 15.4

Quotations on Financial Futures Contracts

These quotations for financial futures contracts include the daily last, prior settle, open, high, and low prices, as well as the change in price from the previous day's closing price to the current day's last price and the current day's volume. The top panel shows euro futures contracts that trade on CME, the middle panel shows U.S. Treasury bond futures that trade on CBOT, and the bottom panel shows the E-mini Dow ($5) index futures.

(Source: Reprinted with permission, CME Group, 2015.)

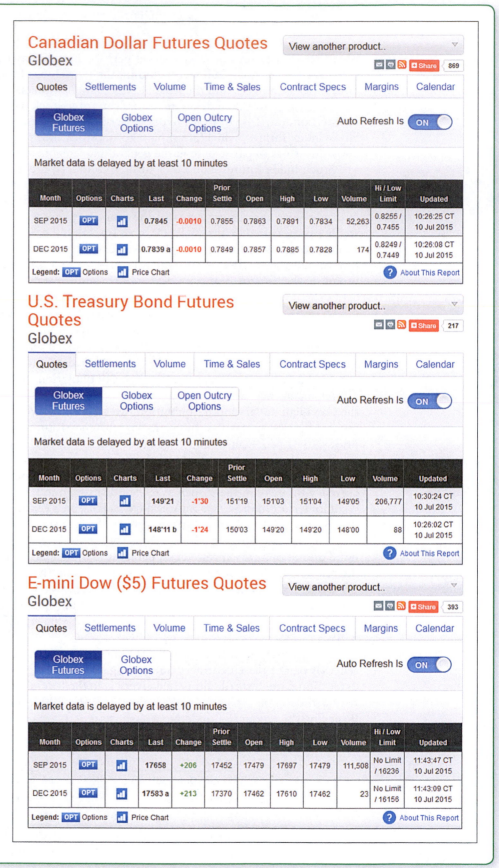

Canadian Dollar Futures Quotes
Globex

Quotes	Settlements	Volume	Time & Sales	Contract Specs	Margins	Calendar

Globex Futures | Globex Options | Open Outcry Options   Auto Refresh Is ON

Market data is delayed by at least 10 minutes

Month	Options	Charts	Last	Change	Prior Settle	Open	High	Low	Volume	Hi / Low Limit	Updated
SEP 2015	OPT	📊	0.7845	-0.0010	0.7855	0.7863	0.7891	0.7834	52,263	0.8255 / 0.7455	10:26:25 CT 10 Jul 2015
DEC 2015	OPT	📊	0.7839 a	-0.0010	0.7849	0.7857	0.7885	0.7828	174	0.8249 / 0.7449	10:26:08 CT 10 Jul 2015

Legend: OPT Options   📊 Price Chart   ? About This Report

U.S. Treasury Bond Futures Quotes
Globex

Quotes	Settlements	Volume	Time & Sales	Contract Specs	Margins	Calendar

Globex Futures | Globex Options | Open Outcry Options   Auto Refresh Is ON

Market data is delayed by at least 10 minutes

Month	Options	Charts	Last	Change	Prior Settle	Open	High	Low	Volume	Updated
SEP 2015	OPT	📊	149'21	-1'30	151'19	151'03	151'04	149'05	206,777	10:30:24 CT 10 Jul 2015
DEC 2015	OPT	📊	148'11 b	-1'24	150'03	149'20	149'20	148'00	88	10:26:02 CT 10 Jul 2015

Legend: OPT Options   📊 Price Chart   ? About This Report

E-mini Dow ($5) Futures Quotes
Globex

Quotes	Settlements	Volume	Time & Sales	Contract Specs	Margins	Calendar

Globex Futures | Globex Options   Auto Refresh Is ON

Market data is delayed by at least 10 minutes

Month	Options	Charts	Last	Change	Prior Settle	Open	High	Low	Volume	Hi / Low Limit	Updated
SEP 2015	OPT	📊	17658	+206	17452	17479	17697	17479	111,508	No Limit / 16236	11:43:47 CT 10 Jul 2015
DEC 2015	OPT	📊	17583 a	+213	17370	17462	17610	17462	23	No Limit / 16156	11:43:09 CT 10 Jul 2015

Legend: OPT Options   📊 Price Chart   ? About This Report

Example

> Consider a December 2015 E-mini NASDAQ 100 stock index futures contract, which stands at 4,407.25. The amount of cash underlying a single futures contract is $20 × 4,407.25 = $88,145. The amount of cash underlying an E-mini NASDAQ 100 futures contract is quite substantial; however, the initial margin amount for a single contract is a much more manageable $3,960.

Prices and Profits Not surprisingly, the price of each type of financial futures contract is quoted somewhat differently.

- *Currency futures.* All currency futures are quoted in U.S. dollars or cents per unit of the underlying foreign currency (e.g., U.S. dollars per Canadian dollar or cents per Japanese yen). For example, the value of a September 2013 Japanese yen contract with a settlement price of 0.012774 is calculated as 12,500,000 yen × $0.012774 = $159,675.

- *Interest-rate futures.* Except for the quotes on Treasury bills and other short-term securities, interest rate futures contracts are priced as a percentage of the par value of the underlying debt instrument (e.g., Treasury notes or bonds). Because these instruments are quoted in increments of 1/32 of 1%, a quote of 148'11 for the settlement price of the December 2015 U.S. Treasury bonds (in Figure 15.4) translates into 148–11/32, which converts to a quote of 148.34375% of par. Multiply this rate times the $100,000 par value of the underlying security, and we see that this contract is worth $148,343.75. The pricing conventions for the variety of other interest rate futures contracts are found in their contract specifications or often included with their quotations.

- *Stock index futures.* Stock index futures are quoted in terms of the actual underlying index. As noted above, they carry a face value of anywhere from $5 to $250 times the index. Thus, according to the settlement price in Figure 15.4, the December 2015 E-mini Dow ($5) contract would be worth $87,915 because the value of this particular contract is equal to $5 times the settlement price of the index or $5 × 17,583.

Example

> Suppose a September 2019 S&P 500 Stock Index contract has a settlement price of 2072.80. The contract's market value can be calculated as follows:
>
> $$\$250 \times 2072.80 = \$518,200$$
>
> The initial margin requirement for this position is $25,300, which is less than 5% of the total contract value.

The value of an interest rate futures contract responds to interest rates exactly as the debt instrument that underlies the contract. That is, when interest rates go up, the value of an interest rate futures contract goes down, and vice versa. The quote system used for interest rate as well as currency and stock index futures is set up to reflect the *market value of the contract* itself. Thus, when the price or quote of a financial futures contract increases (for example, when interest rates fall or a stock index goes up), the investor who is long makes money. In contrast, when the price decreases, the short seller makes money.

Price behavior is the only source of return to speculators. Financial futures contracts have no claim on the dividend and interest income of the underlying issues. Even so, huge profits (or losses) are possible with financial futures because of the equally large size of the contracts. For instance, if the price of Swiss francs goes up by just $0.02 against the U.S. dollar, the investor is ahead $2,500 (i.e., 125,000 Swiss francs × $0.02). Likewise, a 6-point drop in the Nasdaq 100 index means a loss of $20 × 6 or $120 to an E-mini Nasdaq 100 futures investor. When related to the relatively small initial margin deposit required to make transactions in the financial futures markets, such price activity can mean very high rates of return—or very high risk of a total wipeout.

Trading Techniques

Investors can use financial futures, like commodity futures, for hedging, spreading, and speculating. Multinational companies and firms that are active in international trade might hedge with currency or Euromarket futures. Various financial institutions and corporate money managers often use interest rate futures for hedging purposes. In either case, the objective is the same: to lock in the best monetary exchange or interest rate possible. In addition, individual investors and portfolio managers often hedge with stock index futures to protect their security holdings against temporary market declines. Financial futures can also be used for spreading. This tactic is popular with investors who simultaneously buy and sell combinations of two or more contracts to form a desired investment position. Finally, financial futures are widely used for speculation.

Although investors can employ any of the trading strategies noted above, we will focus primarily on the use of financial futures by speculators and hedgers. We will first examine speculating in currency and interest rate futures. Then we'll look at how investors can use futures to hedge investments in stocks, bonds, and foreign securities.

Speculating in Financial Futures   Speculators are especially interested in financial futures because of the size of the contracts. For instance, in mid-2015, euro currency contracts were worth $139,262.50 or 125,000 euros × $1.1141, 10-year Treasury note contracts were going for 125'26 or $100,000 × 125.8125 = $125,812.50 and Dow Jones Real Estate futures contracts were being quoted at $100 × 288.9 or $28,890 each. With contracts of this size, even small movements in the underlying asset can produce big price swings—and therefore big profits.

Currency and interest rate futures can be used for just about any speculative purpose. For example, if you expect the dollar to be devalued relative to the euro, you could buy euro currency futures because the contracts should go up in value, right along with the appreciation of the euro. If you anticipate a rise in interest rates, you might "go short" (sell) interest rate futures, since they should go down in value. Because margin is used and financial futures have the same source of return as commodities (price appreciation), we can measure the profitability of these contracts using return on invested capital (Equation 15.1).

Going Long a Foreign Currency Contract   Suppose you believe that the Swiss franc (CHF) is about to appreciate in value relative to the dollar. You decide to go long (buy) three December 2017 CHF contracts at 0.9728—that is at a quote of just under $1.00 a franc. Each contract would be worth 125,000 CHF × 0.9728 = $121,600, so the total underlying value of the three contracts would be $364,800. Given an initial margin requirement of, say, $5,400 per contract, you would have to deposit only $16,200 to acquire this position.

Now, if Swiss francs do appreciate and move up from 0.9728 to, say, 0.9965, the value of the three contracts will rise to $373,687.50. In a matter of months, you will have made a profit of $8,887.50. Using Equation 15.1 for return on invested capital, we find that such a profit translates into a 54.9% rate of return. Of course, an even smaller fractional change in the other direction would have wiped out this investment. Clearly, these high returns are not without equally high risk.

Going Short an Interest Rate Contract Let's assume that you're anticipating a sharp rise in long-term rates. A rise in rates translates into a drop in the value of interest rate futures. You decide to short sell two June 2016 T-bond contracts at 147'00, which means that the contracts are trading at 147% of par. Thus, the two contracts have a value of $100,000 × 1.47 × 2 = $294,000. You need only $7,560 (the initial margin deposit is $3,780 per contract) to make the investment.

Assume that interest rates do, in fact, move up. As a result, the price on Treasury bond contracts drops to 138'16 (or $138\frac{1}{2}$). You could now buy back the two June 2016 T-bond contracts (to cover the short position) and in the process make a profit of $17,000. You originally sold the two contracts at $294,000 and bought them back sometime later for $100,000 × 1.385 × 2 = $277,000. As with any investment, such a difference between what you pay for a security and what you sell it for is profit. In this case, the return on invested capital amounts to 225%. Again, this return is due in no small part to the enormous risk of loss you assumed.

Trading Stock-Index Futures Most investors use stock index futures for speculation or hedging. (Stock index futures are similar to the index options introduced earlier in the text. Therefore, much of the discussion that follows also applies to index options.) Whether speculating or hedging, the key to success is predicting the future course of the stock market. Because you are "buying the market" with stock index futures, it is important to get a handle on the future direction of the market via technical analysis or some other technique. Once you have a feel for the market's direction, you can formulate a strategy for stock index futures trading or hedging. For example, if you feel that the market is headed up, you would want to go long (buy stock index futures). In contrast, if your analysis suggests a drop in equity values, you could make money by going short (sell stock index futures).

Assume, for instance, that you believe the market is undervalued and a move up is imminent. You can try to identify one or a handful of stocks that should go up with the market (and assume the stock selection risks that go along with this approach), or you can buy an S&P 500 stock index futures contract currently trading at, say, 2101.60. To execute this speculative transaction, you would need to deposit an initial margin of $25,300. Now, if the market does rise so that the S&P 500 Index moves to, say, 2176.6 by the expiration of the futures contract, you earn a profit of (2,176.6 − 2,101.6) × $250 = $18,750. Given the $25,300 investment, your return on invested capital would amount to a hefty 74%. Of course, keep in mind that if the market drops by 75 points (or 3.6%), the investment will be a total loss.

Hedging with Stock Index Futures Stock index futures are also used for hedging. They provide investors with a highly effective way of protecting stock holdings in a declining market. Although this tactic is not perfect, it does enable investors to obtain desired protection against a decline in market value without disturbing their equity holdings.

Here's how a so-called short hedge would work: Assume that you hold a total of 2,000 shares of stock in a dozen companies and that the market value of this portfolio is around $235,000. If you think the market is about to undergo a sharp decline, you can sell all of your shares or buy puts on each of the stocks. You can also protect your stock portfolio by short selling stock index futures.

Suppose, for purposes of our illustration, that you short sell three E-mini Dow ($5) stock index futures contracts at 17672. These contracts would provide a close match to the current value of your portfolio since they would be valued at 3 × $5 × 17,672 = $265,080. Yet these stock index futures contracts would require an initial margin deposit of only $4,290 per contract, or a total deposit of 3 × $4,290 = $12,870. Now, if the DJIA drops, causing the value of your futures contract to drop to 17165, you will make a profit of $7,605 from this short sale. That is, because the futures contract value fell 507 points (17,672 − 17,165), the total profit is 3 × $5 × 507 = $7,605. Ignoring margin costs and taxes, you can add this profit to the portfolio (by purchasing additional shares of stock at their new lower prices). The net result will be a new portfolio position that will approximate the one that existed prior to the decline in the market.

How well the "before" and "after" portfolio positions match will depend on how far the portfolio dropped in value. If the average price dropped about $5 per share in our example, the positions will closely match. But this does not always happen. The price of some stocks will change more than that of others, so the amount of protection provided by this type of short hedge depends on how sensitive the stock portfolio is to movements in the market. Thus, the types of stocks held in the portfolio are an important consideration in structuring a stock index short hedge.

A key to success with this kind of hedging is to make sure that the characteristics of the hedging vehicle (the futures contract) closely match those of the portfolio (or security position) being protected. If the portfolio is made up mostly (or exclusively) of large-cap stocks, use something like the S&P 500 Stock Index futures contract as the hedging vehicle. If the portfolio is mostly blue-chip stocks, use the DJIA contracts. If the portfolio holds mostly tech stocks, consider the Nasdaq 100 Index contract. Again, the point is to pick a hedging vehicle that closely reflects the types of securities you want to protect. If you keep that caveat in mind, hedging with stock index futures can be a low-cost yet effective way of obtaining protection against loss in a declining stock market.

Hedging Other Securities Just as you can use stock index futures to hedge stock portfolios, you can use interest rate futures to hedge bond portfolios. Or, you can use currency futures with foreign securities as a way to protect against foreign exchange risk. Let's consider an interest rate hedge. If you held a substantial portfolio of bonds, the last thing you would want to see is a big jump in interest rates, which could cause a sharp decline in the value of your portfolio. Assume you hold around $300,000 worth of Treasury and agency bonds, with an average maturity of 18 years. If you believe that market rates are headed up, you can hedge your bond portfolio by short selling three U.S. Treasury bond futures contracts. (Each T-bond futures contract is worth about $100,000, so it would take three of them to cover a $300,000 portfolio.) If rates do head up, you will have protected the portfolio against loss. As noted above, the exact amount of protection will depend on how well the T-bond futures contracts parallel the price behavior of your particular bond portfolio.

There is, of course, a downside. If market interest rates go down rather than up, you will miss out on potential profits as long as the short hedge position remains in place. This is so because the profits being made in the portfolio will be offset by losses from the futures contracts. Actually, this will occur with any type of portfolio (stocks, bonds, or anything else) that is tied to an offsetting short hedge. When you create the short hedge, you essentially lock in a position at that point. Although you do not lose anything when the market falls, you also do not make anything when the market goes up. In either case, the profits you make from one position are offset by losses from the other.

 Hedging Foreign Currency Exposure Now let's see how you can use futures contracts to hedge foreign exchange risk. Let's assume that you have just purchased $200,000 of British government one-year notes. (You did this because higher yields were available on the British notes than on comparable U.S. Treasury securities.) Because these notes are denominated in pounds, this investment is subject to loss if currency exchange rates move against you (i.e., if the value of the dollar rises relative to the pound).

If all you wanted was the higher yield offered by the British note, you could eliminate most of the currency exchange risk by setting up a currency hedge. Here's how: Let's say that at the current exchange rate, 1 U.S. dollar will "buy" 0.606 of a British pound. This means that pounds are worth about $1.65 (i.e., $1.00/0.606£ = $1.65). So, if currency contracts on British pounds were trading at around $1.65 a pound, you would have to sell two contracts to protect the $200,000 investment. Each contract covers 62,500 pounds; if they're being quoted at 1.65, then each contract is worth $103,125.

Assume that one year later the value of the dollar has increased relative to the pound, so that 1 U.S. dollar will now "buy" 0.65 pound. Under such conditions, a British pound futures contract would be quoted at around 1.54 (i.e., $1.00/.065£ = $1.54). At this price, each futures contract would have a value of 62,500 × $1.54 = $96,250. Each contract, in effect, would be worth $6,875 less than it was a year ago. But because the contract was sold short when you set up the hedge, you will make a profit of $6,875 per contract—for a total profit of $13,750 on the two contracts. Unfortunately, that's not net profit because this profit will offset the loss you will incur on the British note investment. In very simple terms, when you sent $200,000 overseas to buy the British notes, the money was worth about £121,000. However, when you brought the money back a year later, those 121,000 pounds purchased only about 186,500 U.S. dollars. Thus, you are out some $13,500 on your original investment. Were it not for the currency hedge, you would be out the full $13,500, and the return on this investment would be a lot lower. The hedge covered the loss (plus a little extra), and the net effect was that you were able to enjoy the added yield of the British note without having to worry about potential loss from currency exchange rates.

Financial Futures and the Individual Investor

Like commodities, financial futures can play an important role in your portfolio so long as three factors apply: (1) You thoroughly understand these investments. (2) You clearly recognize the tremendous risk exposure of these investments. (3) You are fully prepared (financially and emotionally) to absorb some losses.

Financial futures are highly volatile securities that have enormous potential for profit and for loss. For instance, the September 2015 S&P 500 futures contract traded at a low of 1963.50 on January 1, 2015, and a high of 2122.00 on June 1, 2015. This range of 158.5 points for a single contract translated into a potential profit—or loss— of $250 × 158.5 = $39,625, and all from an initial margin investment of only $25,300. Investment diversification is obviously essential as a means of reducing the potentially devastating impact of price volatility. Financial futures are exotic investments, but if properly used, they can provide generous returns.

Options on Futures

The evolution that began with listed stock options and financial futures spread, over time, to interest rate options and stock index futures. Eventually, it led to the creation of the ultimate leverage vehicle: options on futures contracts. **Futures options**, as they are called, represent listed puts and calls on actively traded futures contracts. In essence, they give the holders the right to buy (with calls) or sell (with puts) a single standardized futures contract for a specific period of time at a specified strike price.

Such options can be found on both commodities and financial futures. Notice that each of the corn futures contracts quoted in Figure 15.3 include an options icon under each contract delivery month, indicating that a futures option exists for that futures contract. In fact, the CME Group quotations allow you to click on the options icon to access the futures options quotations. Figure 15.5 shows the options quotations for the July 2015 corn futures contract quoted in Figure 15.3. For the most part, these puts and calls cover the same amount of assets as the underlying futures contracts—for example, 112,000 pounds of sugar, 100 troy ounces of gold, 62,500 British pounds, or $100,000 in Treasury bonds. Thus, they also involve the same amount of price volatility as is normally found with commodities and financial futures.

Futures options have the same standardized strike prices, expiration dates, and quotation system as other listed options. Depending on the strike price on the option and the market value of the underlying futures contract, these options can also be in-the-money or out-of-the-money. Futures options are valued like other puts and calls—by the difference between the option's strike price and the market price of the underlying futures contract. They can also be used like any other listed option—for speculating or hedging, in options-writing programs, or for spreading. The biggest difference between a futures option and a futures contract is that the option limits the loss exposure to the price of the option. The most you can lose is the price paid for the put or call option. With the futures contract, there is no real limit to the amount of loss you can incur.

To see how futures options work, assume that you want to trade some gold contracts. You believe that the price of gold will increase over the next four or five months from its present level of $1,160.80 an ounce. You can enter into an August 2016 futures contract to buy gold at $1,163.90 an ounce by depositing the required initial margin of $4,125. Alternatively, you can buy a futures call option with a $1,160 strike price that is currently being quoted at $9.80. Because the underlying futures contract covers 100 ounces of gold, the total cost of this option would be $100 \times \$9.80 = \$980$. The call is an in-the-money option because the market price of gold exceeds the exercise price on the option. The following table summarizes what happens to both investments if the value of the gold futures contract increases to $1,182.54 an ounce by the expiration date and also what happens if the value of the gold futures contract drops to $1,139.75 an ounce.

	Futures Contract		Futures Option	
Price Change	Profit (or Loss)	Return on Invested Capital	Profit (or Loss)	Return on Invested Capital
If futures contract value increases to $1,182.54 an ounce	$1,864	45.2%	$1,274	130%
If futures contract value decreases to $1,139.75 an ounce	($2,415)	−58.5%	($980)	−100%

FIGURE 15.5

Quotations on Corn Futures Options Contracts

This quotation for call and put options on corn futures contracts includes the daily last, open, high, and low prices, as well as the prior settle and strike price. It also provides the change in price from the previous day's closing price to the current day's last price, the current day's volume, and the Hi/Lo limit.

(Source: Reprinted with permission, CME Group, 2015.)

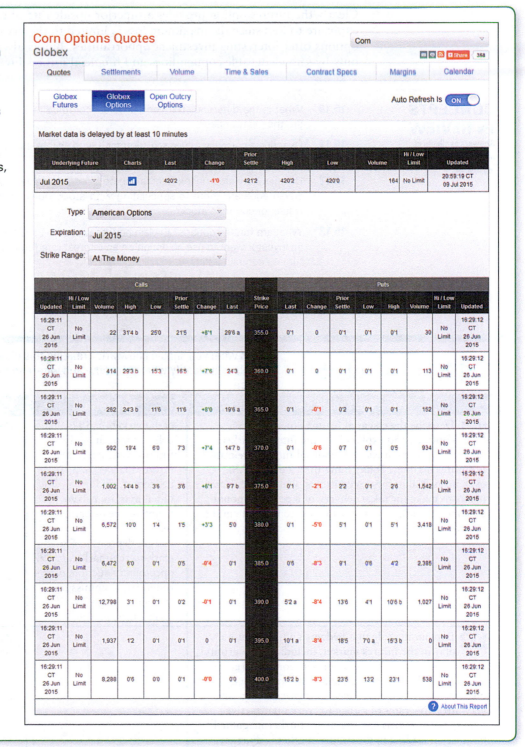

Clearly the futures option provides a superior upside rate of return but also a reduced exposure to loss since the maximum loss is limited to the price of the options. Futures options offer interesting investment opportunities. But as always, they should be used only by knowledgeable commodities and financial futures investors.

CONCEPTS IN REVIEW Answers available at http://www.pearsonhighered .com/smart	**15.10**	What is the difference between physical commodities and financial futures? What are their similarities?
	15.11	Describe a currency future and contrast it with an interest rate future. What is a stock index future, and how can it be used by investors?
	15.12	Discuss how stock index futures can be used for speculation and for hedging. What advantages are there to speculating with stock index futures rather than specific issues of common stock?
	15.13	What are futures options? Explain how they can be used by speculators. Why would an investor want to use an option on an interest rate futures contract rather than the futures contract itself?

MyFinanceLab

Here is what you should know after reading this chapter. MyFinanceLab will help you identify what you know and where to go when you need to practice.

What You Should Know	Key Terms	Where to Practice
LG1 Describe the essential features of a futures contract, and explain how the futures market operates. Commodities and financial futures are traded in futures markets. Today more than a dozen U.S. exchanges deal in futures contracts, which are commitments to make (or take) delivery of a certain amount of some real or financial asset at a specified date in the future.	cash market, *p. 592* delivery month, *p. 592* futures contract, *p. 592* futures market, *p. 592* hedgers, *p. 595* initial margin, *p. 596* maintenance margin, *p. 597* margin deposit, *p. 596* mark-to-the-market, *p. 597* open-outcry auction, *p. 594* round-trip commission, *p. 596* speculators, *p. 596*	MyFinanceLab Study Plan 15.1
LG2 Explain the role that hedgers and speculators play in the futures market, including how profits are made and lost. Futures contracts control large amounts of the underlying commodity or financial instrument. They can produce wide price swings and very attractive rates of return (or very unattractive losses). Such returns (or losses) are further magnified because all trading in the futures market is done on margin. A speculator's profit is derived directly from the wide price fluctuations that occur in the market. Hedgers derive their profit from the protection they gain against adverse price movements.		MyFinanceLab Study Plan 15.2

What You Should Know	Key Terms	Where to Practice
LG3 Describe the commodities segment of the futures market and the basic characteristics of these investments. Commodities such as grains, metals, and meat make up the traditional (commodities) segment of the futures market. A large portion of this market is concentrated in agricultural products. There's also a very active market for various metals and petroleum products. As the prices of commodities go up and down in the market, the respective futures contracts behave in much the same way. Thus, if the price of corn goes up, the value of corn futures contracts rises as well.	daily price limit, *p. 602* maximum daily price range, *p. 602* open interest, *p. 596* settlement price, *p. 599* volume, *p. 599*	MyFinanceLab Study Plan 15.3 Video Learning Aid for Problem P15.1
LG4 Discuss the trading strategies that investors can use with commodities and explain how investment returns are measured. The trading strategies used with commodities contracts are speculating, spreading, and hedging. Regardless of whether investors are in a long or a short position, they have only one source of return from commodities and financial futures: appreciation (or depreciation) in the price of the contract. Rate of return on invested capital is used to assess the actual or potential profitability of a futures transaction.	return on invested capital, *p. 602*	MyFinanceLab Study Plan 15.4 Video Learning Aid for Problem P15.1
LG5 Explain the difference between a physical commodity and a financial future and discuss the growing role of financial futures in the market today. Whereas commodities deal with physical assets, financial futures deal with financial assets, such as stocks, bonds, and currencies. Both are traded in the same place: the futures market. Financial futures are the newcomers, but the volume of trading in financial futures now far exceeds that of commodities.	currency futures, *p. 606* financial futures, *p.606* interest rate futures, *p. 606* stock index futures, *p. 606*	MyFinanceLab Study Plan 15.5 Video Learning Aid for Problem P15.12

What You Should Know	Key Terms	Where to Practice
LG6 Discuss the trading techniques that can be used with financial futures, and note how these securities can be used in conjunction with other investments. There are 3 major types of financial futures: currency futures, interest rate futures, and stock index futures. The first type deals in different kinds of foreign currencies. Interest rate futures involve various types of short- and long-term debt instruments. Stock index futures are pegged to broad movements in the stock market, as measured by such indexes as the S&P 500. These securities can be used for speculating, spreading, or hedging. They hold special appeal as hedges against other security positions. For example, interest rate futures are used to protect bond portfolios against a jump in market interest rates. Currency futures are used to hedge the foreign currency exposure that accompanies investments in foreign securities.	futures options, *p. 614*	MyFinanceLab Study Plan 15.6

Log into MyFinanceLab, take a chapter test, and get a personalized Study Plan that tells you which concepts you understand and which ones you need to review. From there, MyFinanceLab will give you further practice, tutorials, animations, videos, and guided solutions.

Log into **http://www.myfinancelab.com**

Discussion Questions*

LG1 **Q15.1** Three of the biggest U.S. commodities exchanges—the CME, CBOT, and NYMEX—were identified in this chapter. Other U.S. exchanges and several foreign commodities exchanges are also closely followed in the United States. Go to the *Wall Street Journal Online*, wsj .com, and look in the Commodities & Futures section under Markets Data for a list of recent futures quotes. As noted in this chapter, futures quotes include the name of the exchange on which a particular contract is traded.

    a. Using these quotes, how many U.S. commodities exchanges can you identify? List them.

    b. Are quotes from foreign exchanges listed in the *Wall Street Journal*? If so, list them.

    c. For each U.S. and foreign exchange you found in parts **a** and **b**, give an example of one or two contracts traded on that exchange. For example, CBOT—Chicago Board of Trade: oats and Treasury bonds.

LG3 **LG5** **Q15.2** Using settlement or closing prices from Figures 15.3 and 15.4, find the value of the following commodities and financial futures contracts.

    a. March 2013 corn

    b. July 2013 corn

    c. December 2013 corn

    d. December 2012 Treasury bonds

    e. December 2012 DJIA ($10) Index

---

*Current prices and margin requirements of futures contracts in the questions and problems below were established to make computations simpler and do not necessarily reflect current market conditions and requirements.

LG4 LG6 **Q15.3** On the basis of the information provided, indicate how much profit or loss you would make in each of the futures transactions listed below. (*Hint:* You might want to visit **http://www.cmegroup.com** for the size of the contract, pricing unit, and so on.)

a. You buy three yen contracts at a quote of 1.0180 and sell them a few months later at 1.0365 (12,500,000 yen per contract; prices quoted in $ per 100 yen).

b. The price of oats (5,000 bushels/contract; cents/bu) goes up $0.60 a bushel, and you hold three contracts.

c. You short sell two feeder cattle contracts (50,000 lb/contract; cents/lb) at $1.24 a pound and the price drops to $1.03 per pound.

d. You recently purchased a Swiss franc contract (CHF 125,000/contract; $/CHF) at 0.7272, and six weeks later the contract is trading at 0.685.

e. You short sell S&P 500 contracts ($250 × index) when the index is at 1,396.55 and cover when the index moves to 1,371.95.

f. You short three corn contracts (5,000 bushels/contract; cents/bu) at $2.34 a bushel and the price of corn goes to $2.495 a bushel.

Problems

All problems are available on **http://www.myfinancelab.com**

LG3 LG4 **P15.1** Josh Rink considers himself a shrewd commodities investor. Not long ago he bought one July cotton contract at $0.54 a pound and he recently sold it at $0.58 a pound. How much profit did he make? What was his return on invested capital if he had to put up a $1,260 initial margin?

LG3 LG4 **P15.2** You just heard a news story about mad cow disease in a neighboring country, and you believe that feeder cattle prices will rise dramatically in the next few months as buyers of cattle shift to U.S. suppliers. Someone else believes that prices will fall in the next few months because people will be afraid to eat beef. You go to the CME and find out that feeder cattle futures for delivery in April are currently quoted at 88.8. The contract size is 50,000 lbs. What is the market value of one contract?

LG3 LG4 **P15.3** You decide to act on your hunches about feeder cattle, so you purchase four contracts for April delivery at 88.8. You are required to put down 10%. How much equity/capital did you need to make this transaction?

LG3 LG4 **P15.4** As it turns out, you were correct when you purchased four contracts for feeder cattle at 88.8, as the spot price on cattle rose to 101.2 on the delivery date given in your contracts. How much money did you make? What was your return on invested capital?

LG4 **P15.5** Taryn Arsenault is a regular commodities speculator. She is currently considering a short position in July oats, which are now trading at 248. Her analysis suggests that July oats should be trading at about 240 in a couple of months. Assuming that her expectations hold up, what kind of return on invested capital will she make if she shorts three July oats contracts (each contract covers 5,000 bushels of oats) by depositing an initial margin of $540 per contract?

LG5 LG6 **P15.6** You were just notified that you will receive $100,000 in two months from the estate of a deceased relative. You want to invest this money in safe, interest-bearing instruments, so you decide to purchase five-year Treasury notes. You believe, however, that interest rates are headed down, and you will have to pay a lot more in two months than you would today for five-year Treasury notes. You decide to look into futures and find a quote of 111'08 for five-year Treasuries deliverable in two months (contracts trade in $100,000 units). What does the quote mean in terms of price, and how many contracts will you need to buy? How much money will you need to buy the contract, and how much will you need to settle the contract?

LG5 LG6   **P15.7**   George Seby is thinking about doing some speculating in interest rates. He thinks rates will fall and, in response, the price of Treasury bond futures should move from 92'15, their present quote, to a level of about 98. Given a required margin deposit of $1,350 per contract, what would George's return on invested capital be if prices behave as he expects?

LG5 LG6   **P15.8**   Tori Reynolds has been an avid stock market investor for years. She manages her portfolio fairly aggressively and likes to short sell whenever the opportunity presents itself. Recently, she has become fascinated with stock index futures, especially the idea of being able to play the market as a whole. Tori thinks the market is headed down, and she decides to short sell some S&P 500 stock index futures. Assume she shorts three contracts at 1,387.95 and has to make a margin deposit of $19,688 for each contract. How much profit will she make, and what will her return on invested capital be if the market does indeed drop so that the CME contracts are trading at 1,352.00 by the time they expire?

LG6   **P15.9**   A wealthy investor holds $500,000 worth of U.S. Treasury bonds. These bonds are currently being quoted at 105% of par. The investor is concerned, however, that rates are headed up over the next six months, and he would like to do something to protect this bond portfolio. His broker advises him to set up a hedge using T-bond futures contracts. Assume these contracts are now trading at 111'06.
   a. Briefly describe how the investor would set up this hedge. Would he go long or short? How many contracts would he need?
   b. It's now six months later, and rates have indeed gone up. The investor's Treasury bonds are now being quoted at $93\frac{1}{2}$, and the T-bond futures contracts used in the hedge are now trading at 98'00. Show what has happened to the value of the bond portfolio and the profit (or loss) made on the futures hedge.
   c. Was this a successful hedge? Explain.

LG6   **P15.10**   Not long ago, Vanessa Woods sold her company for several million dollars. She took some of that money and put it into the stock market. Today Vanessa's portfolio of blue-chip stocks is worth $3.8 million. Vanessa wants to keep her portfolio intact, but she's concerned about a developing weakness in the market for blue chips. She decides, therefore, to hedge her position with six-month futures contracts on the Dow Jones Industrial Average, which are currently trading at 11,960.
   a. Why would she choose to hedge her portfolio with the DJIA rather than the S&P 500?
   b. Given that Vanessa wants to cover the full $3.8 million in her portfolio, describe how she would go about setting up this hedge.
   c. If each contract required a margin deposit of $4,875, how much money would she need to set up this hedge?
   d. Assume that over the next six months, stock prices do fall and the value of Vanessa's portfolio drops to $3.3 million. If DJIA futures contracts are trading at 10,400, how much will she make (or lose) on the futures hedge? Is it enough to offset the loss in her portfolio? That is, what is her net profit or loss on the hedge?
   e. Will she now get her margin deposit back, or is that a "sunk cost"—gone forever?

LG5 LG6   **P15.11**   A quote for a futures contract for British pounds is 1.6683. The contract size for British pounds is 62,500. What is the dollar equivalent of this contract?

LG5 **P15.12** You have purchased a futures contract for euros. The contract is for 125,000 euros and the quote was 1.1636. On the delivery date, the exchange quote is 1.1050. Assuming you took delivery of the euros, how many dollars would you have after converting back to dollars? What is your profit or loss (before commissions)?

LG4 **P15.13** An American currency speculator feels strongly that the value of the Canadian dollar is going to fall relative to the U.S. dollar over the short run. If he wants to profit from these expectations, what kind of position (long or short) should he take in Canadian dollar futures contracts? How much money would he make from each contract if Canadian dollar futures contracts moved from an initial quote of 0.6775 to an ending quote of 0.6250?

LG6 **P15.14** With regard to futures options, how much profit would an investor make if she bought a call option on gold at 7.20 when gold was trading at $482 an ounce, given that the price of gold went up to $525 an ounce by the expiration date on the call? (*Note:* Assume the call carried a strike price of 480.)

Visit **http://www.myfinancelab.com** for web exercises, spreadsheets, and other online resources.

Case Problem 15.1 T. J.'s Fast-Track Investments: Interest Rate Futures

LG5 LG6 T. J. Patrick is a young, successful industrial designer in Portland, Oregon, who enjoys the excitement of commodities speculation. T. J. has been dabbling in commodities since he was a teenager—he was introduced to this market by his dad, who is a grain buyer for one of the leading food processors. T. J. recognizes the enormous risks involved in commodities speculating but feels that because he's young, he can afford to take a few chances. As a principal in a thriving industrial design firm, T. J. earns more than $150,000 a year. He follows a well-disciplined investment program and annually adds $15,000 to $20,000 to his portfolio.

Recently, T. J. has started playing with financial futures—interest rate futures, to be exact. He admits he is no expert in interest rates, but he likes the price action these investments offer. This all started several months ago, when T. J. met Vinnie Banano, a broker who specializes in financial futures, at a party. T. J. liked what Vinnie had to say (mostly how you couldn't go wrong with interest rate futures) and soon set up a trading account with Vinnie's firm, Banano's of Portland.

The other day, Vinnie called T. J. and suggested he get into five-year Treasury note futures. He reasoned that with the Fed pushing up interest rates so aggressively, the short to intermediate sectors of the term structure would probably respond the most—with the biggest jump in yields. Accordingly, Vinnie recommended that T. J. short sell some five-year T-note contracts. In particular, Vinnie thinks that rates on these T-notes should go up by a full point (moving from about 5.5% to around 6.5%) and that T. J. should short four contracts. This would be a $5,400 investment because each contract requires an initial margin deposit of $1,350.

Questions

a. Assume T-note futures ($100,000/contract; 32's of 1%) are now being quoted at 103'16.

1. Determine the current underlying value of this T-note futures contract.

2. What would this futures contract be quoted at if Vinnie is right and the yield does go up by one percentage point, to 6.5%, on the date of expiration? (*Hint:* It'll be quoted at the same price as its underlying security, which in this case is assumed to be a five-year, 6% semiannual-pay U.S. Treasury note.)

b. How much profit will T. J. make if he shorts four contracts at 103'16 and then covers when five-year T-note contracts are quoted at 98'00? Also, calculate the return on invested capital from this transaction.

c. What happens if rates go down? For example, how much will T. J. make if the yield on T-note futures goes down by just 3/4 of 1%, in which case these contracts would be trading at 105'8?

d. What risks do you see in the recommended short-sale transaction? What is your assessment of T. J.'s new interest in financial futures? How do you think it compares to his established commodities investment program?

Case Problem 15.2   Jim and Polly Pernelli Try Hedging with Stock Index Futures

LG5 LG6   Jim Pernelli and his wife, Polly, live in Augusta, Georgia. Like many young couples, the Pernellis are a two-income family. Jim and Polly are both college graduates and hold high-paying jobs. Jim has been an avid investor in the stock market for a number of years and over time has built up a portfolio that is currently worth nearly $375,000. The Pernellis' portfolio is well diversified, although it is heavily weighted in high-quality, mid-cap growth stocks. The Pernellis reinvest all dividends and regularly add investment capital to their portfolio. Up to now, they have avoided short selling and do only a modest amount of margin trading.

Their portfolio has undergone a substantial amount of capital appreciation in the last 18 months or so, and Jim is eager to protect the profit they have earned. And that's the problem: Jim feels the market has pretty much run its course and is about to enter a period of decline. He has studied the market and economic news very carefully and does not believe the retreat will cover an especially long period of time. He feels fairly certain, however, that most, if not all, of the stocks in his portfolio will be adversely affected by these market conditions—although some will drop more in price than others.

Jim has been following stock index futures for some time and believes he knows the ins and outs of these securities pretty well. After careful deliberation, Jim and Polly decide to use stock index futures—in particular, the S&P MidCap 400 futures contract—as a way to protect (hedge) their portfolio of common stocks.

Questions

a. Explain why the Pernellis would want to use stock index futures to hedge their stock portfolio and how they would go about setting up such a hedge. Be specific.

1. What alternatives do Jim and Polly have to protect the capital value of their portfolio?

2. What are the benefits and risks of using stock index futures to hedge?

b. Assume that S&P MidCap 400 futures contracts are priced at $500 × the index and are currently being quoted at 769.40. How many contracts would the Pernellis have to buy (or sell) to set up the hedge?

1. Say the value of the Pernelli portfolio dropped 12% over the course of the market retreat. To what price must the stock index futures contract move in order to cover that loss?

2. Given that a $16,875 margin deposit is required to buy or sell a single S&P 400 futures contract, what would be the Pernellis' return on invested capital if the price of the futures contract changed by the amount computed in question **b1**?

c. Assume that the value of the Pernelli portfolio declined by $52,000 while the price of an S&P 400 futures contract moved from 769.40 to 691.40. (Assume that Jim and Polly short sold one futures contract to set up the hedge.)

1. Add the profit from the hedge transaction to the new (depreciated) value of the stock portfolio. How does this amount compare to the $375,000 portfolio that existed just before the market started its retreat?

2. Why did the stock index futures hedge fail to give complete protection to the Pernelli portfolio? Is it possible to obtain perfect (dollar-for-dollar) protection from these types of hedges? Explain.

d. The Pernellis might decide to set up the hedge by using futures options instead of futures contracts. Fortunately, such options are available on the S&P MidCap 400 Index. These futures options, like their underlying futures contracts, are also valued/priced at $500 times the underlying S&P 400 Index. Now, suppose a put on the S&P MidCap 400 futures contract (with a strike price of 769) is currently quoted at 5.80, and a comparable call is quoted at 2.35. Use the same portfolio and futures price conditions as set out in question **c** to determine how well the portfolio would be protected if these futures options were used as the hedge vehicle. (*Hint:* Add the net profit from the hedge to the new depreciated value of the stock portfolio.) What are the advantages and disadvantages of using futures options, rather than the stock index futures contract itself, to hedge a stock portfolio?

Excel@Investing

One of the unique features of futures contracts is that they have only one source of return—the capital gains that can accrue when price movements have an upward bias. Remember that there are no current cash flows associated with this financial asset. These instruments are known for their volatility due to swings in prices and the use of leverage upon purchase. With futures trading done on margin, small amounts of capital are needed to control relatively large investment positions.

Assume that you are interested in investing in commodity futures—specifically, oats futures contracts. Refer to the contract terms of oats: "OATS (CBOT) 5000 bu.; cents per bushel." Suppose you had purchased 5 December oats contracts at the settlement price of 186.75. The required amount of investor capital to be deposited with a broker at the time of the initial transaction is 5.35% of a contract's value. Create a spreadsheet to model and answer the following questions concerning the investment in futures contracts.

Questions

a. What is the total amount of your initial margin for the five contracts?

b. What is the total amount of bushels of oats that you control?

c. What is the purchase price of the oats commodity contracts you control according to the December settlement date?

d. Assume that the December oats actually settled at 186.75, and you decide to sell and take your profit. What is the selling price of the oats commodity contracts?

e. Calculate the return on invested capital earned on this transaction. (Remember that the return is based on the amount of funds actually invested in the contract rather than on the value of the contract itself.)

CFA Exam Questions

Derivative Securities

Following is a sample of 12 Level-I CFA exam questions that deal with many of the topics covered in Chapters 14 and 15 of this text, including basic properties of options and futures, pricing characteristics, return behavior, and various option strategies. (When answering the questions, give yourself 1½ minutes for each question; the objective is to correctly answer 8 of the 12 questions in 18 minutes.)

1. Which of the following methods is an investor least likely to use to terminate a futures contract?
   a. Exchanging cash for physical assets
   b. Permitting the contract to expire worthless
   c. Making an offsetting trade using an identical contract

2. Consider a put with a strike price of $20 and a premium of $4. If the stock price is currently $18, what is the breakeven price for the buyer of the put?
   a. $16   b. $22   c. $24

3. Consider a put with a strike price of $20 and a premium of $4. If the stock price is currently $18, what is the maximum loss to the naked writer of the put?
   a. $16   b. $20   c. Unlimited

4. Consider the following statements about a futures clearinghouse:

   Statement 1: "A clearinghouse in futures contracts allows for the offsetting of contracts prior to delivery."

   Statement 2: "A clearinghouse in futures contracts collects initial margin (performance bonds) from both the long and short sides in the contract."

   Are the statements *most likely* correct or incorrect?
   a. Both statements are correct.
   b. Statement 1 is incorrect but Statement 2 is correct.
   c. Statement 1 is correct but Statement 2 is incorrect.

5. Consider the following statements regarding futures contracts that may be settled by delivery:

   Statement 1: "The long initiates the delivery process."

   Statement 2: "For many such contracts, delivery can take place any business day during the delivery month."

   Are the statements *most likely* correct or incorrect?
   a. Both statements are correct.
   b. Statement 1 is incorrect but Statement 2 is correct.
   c. Statement 1 is correct but Statement 2 is incorrect.

6. Unless far out-of-the-money or far in-the-money, for otherwise identical call options, the longer the term to expiration, the lower the price for
   a. American call options but not European call options.
   b. both European call options and American call options.
   c. neither European call options nor American call options.

7. Compare an American call with a strike of 50 that expires in 90 days to an American call on the same underlying asset that has a strike of 60 and expires in 120 days. The underlying asset is selling at 55. Consider the following statements:

   Statement 1: "The 50 strike call is in-the-money and the 60 strike call is out-of-the-money."

   Statement 2: "The time value of the 60 strike call as a proportion of the 60 strike call's premium exceeds the time value of the 50 strike call as a proportion of the 50 strike call's premium."

   Are the statements *most likely* correct or incorrect?
   a. Both statements are correct.
   b. Statement 1 is incorrect but Statement 2 is correct.
   c. Statement 1 is correct but Statement 2 is incorrect.

8. A call with a strike price of $40 is available on a stock currently trading for $35. The call expires in one year and the risk-free rate of return is 10%.

   The lower bound on this call's value
   a. is 0.
   b. is $5 if the call is American-style.
   c. is $1.36 if the call is European-style.

9. An investor writes a call option priced at $3 with an exercise price of $100 on a stock that he owns. The investor paid $85 for the stock. If at expiration of the call option the stock price has risen to $110, the profit for the investor's position would be *closest* to
   a. $3.
   b. $12.
   c. $18.

10. An investor paid $10 for an option that is currently in-the-money $5. If the underlying is priced at $90, which of the following best describes that option?
    a. Call option with an exercise price of $80
    b. Put option with an exercise price of $95
    c. Call option with an exercise price of $95

11. The recent price per share of Dragon Vacations Inc. is $50 per share. Calls with exactly six months left to expiration are available on Dragon with strikes of $45, $50, and $55. The prices of the calls are $8.75, $6.00, and $4.00, respectively. Assume that each call contract is for 100 shares of stock and that at initiation of the strategy the investor purchases 100 shares of Dragon at the current market price. Further assume that the investor will close out the strategy in six months when the options expire, including the sale of any stock not delivered against exercise of a call, whether the stock price goes up or goes down. If the closing price of Dragon stock in six months is exactly $60, the profit to a covered call using the $50 strike call is closest to
    a. $400.
    b. $600.
    c. $1,600.

12. The recent price per share of Win Big, Inc., is €50 per share. Verna Hillsborough buys 100 shares at €50. To protect against a fall in price, Hillsborough buys one put, covering 100 shares of Win Big, with a strike price of €40. The put premium is €1 per share. If Win Big closes at €45 per share at the expiration of the put and Hillsborough sells her shares at €45, Hillsborough's profit from the stay/put is *closest* to:
    a. −€1,100.
    b. −€600.
    c. €900.

Answers: 1. b; 2. a; 3. a; 4. a; 5. b; 6. c; 7. a; 8. a; 9. c; 10. b; 11. b; 12. b.

Glossary

A

abnormal return The difference between an investment's actual return and its expected return. (Chapter 9)

accrued interest Interest earned (but not yet paid) on a bond since the previous coupon payment. (Chapter 11)

active portfolio management Building a portfolio using traditional and modern approaches and managing and controlling it to achieve its objectives; a worthwhile activity that can result in superior returns. (Chapter 13)

actively managed fund A fund that attempts to "beat the market" by selecting stocks or other securities that will earn abnormally high returns. (Chapter 12)

activity ratios Financial ratios that are used to measure how well a firm is managing its assets. (Chapter 7)

agency bonds Debt securities issued by various agencies and organizations of the U.S. government. (Chapter 10)

aggressive-growth fund A highly speculative mutual fund that attempts to achieve the highest capital gains. (Chapter 12)

American depositary receipts (ADRs) U.S. dollar-denominated receipts for the stocks of foreign companies that are held in the vaults of banks in the companies' home countries. Serve as backing for *American depositary shares (ADSs)*. (Chapter 2)

American depositary shares (ADSs) Securities created to permit U.S. investors to hold shares of non-U.S. companies and trade them on U.S. stock exchanges. They are backed by *American depositary receipts (ADRs)*. (Chapter 2)

Amex composite index An index that measures the current price behavior of all shares traded on the NYSE-AMEX, relative to a base of 550 set at December 29, 1995. (Chapter 3)

analytical information Projections and recommendations about potential investments based on available current data. (Chapter 3)

anchoring A phenomenon in which individuals place too much weight on information that they have at hand, even when that information is not particularly relevant. (Chapter 9)

annuity A stream of equal cash flows that occur at equal intervals over time. (Chapter 4)

arbitrage A transaction in which an investor simultaneously buys and sells identical assets at different prices to earn an instant, risk-free profit. (Chapter 9)

arbitration A formal dispute-resolution process in which a client and a broker present their arguments before a panel, which then decides the case. (Chapter 3)

ask price The lowest price offered to sell a security. (Chapter 2)

asset allocation A scheme that involves dividing one's portfolio into various asset classes to preserve capital by protecting against negative developments while taking advantage of positive ones. (Chapter 13)

asset allocation fund A mutual fund that spreads investors' money across stocks, bonds, money market securities, and possibly other asset classes. (Chapter 12)

asset-backed securities (ABSs) Securities similar to mortgage-backed securities that are backed by a pool of bank loans, leases, and other assets. (Chapter 10)

at the money A call or put option is at the money when the strike price of the option and the market price of the underlying stock are equal. (Chapter 14)

automatic investment plan A mutual fund service that allows shareholders to automatically send fixed amounts of money from their paychecks or bank accounts into the fund. (Chapter 12)

automatic reinvestment plan A mutual fund service that enables shareholders to automatically buy additional shares in the fund through the reinvestment of dividends and capital gains income. (Chapter 12)

averages Numbers used to measure the general behavior of stock prices by reflecting the arithmetic average price behavior of a representative group of stocks at a given point in time. (Chapter 3)

B

back-end load A commission charged on the *sale* of shares in a mutual fund. (Chapter 12)

back-office research reports A brokerage firm's analyses of and recommendations on investment prospects; available on request at no cost to existing and potential clients or for purchase at some websites. (Chapter 3)

balance sheet A financial summary of a firm's assets, liabilities, and shareholders' equity at a single point in time. (Chapter 7)

balanced fund A mutual fund whose objective is to generate a balanced return of both current income and long-term capital appreciation. (Chapter 12)

Barron's A weekly business newspaper; a popular source of financial news. (Chapter 3)

basic discount broker Typically, a deep-discount broker through which investors can execute trades electronically online via a commercial service, on the Internet, or by phone. (Also called *online brokers* or *electronic brokers*.) (Chapter 3)

bear markets Markets normally associated with falling prices, investor pessimism, economic slowdown, and government restraint. (Chapter 2)

behavioral finance The body of research into the role that emotions and other subjective factors play in investment decisions. (Chapter 9)

belief perseverance The tendency to ignore or discount evidence contrary to one's existing beliefs. (Chapter 9)

beta A measure of *undiversifiable,* or *market, risk* that indicates how the price of a security responds to market forces. (Chapter 5)

bid price The highest price offered to purchase a security. (Chapter 2)

blue-chip stocks Financially strong, high-quality stocks with long and stable records of earnings and dividends. (Chapter 6)

bond fund A mutual fund that invests in various kinds and grades of bonds, with interest income as the primary objective. (Chapter 12)

bond ladders An investment strategy wherein equal amounts of money are invested in a series of bonds with staggered maturities. (Chapter 11)

bond ratings Letter grades that designate investment quality and are assigned to a bond issue by rating agencies. (Chapter 10)

bond rating agencies Institutions that perform extensive financial analysis on companies issuing bonds to assess the credit risk associated with a particular bond issue. (Chapter 10)

bond swap An investment strategy wherein an investor simultaneously liquidates one bond holding and buys a different issue to take its place. (Chapter 11)

bond yield The return an investor would receive on a bond if it were purchased and held to maturity; reported as an annual rate of return. (Chapter 3)

bond-equivalent yield The annual yield on a bond, calculated as twice the semiannual yield. (Chapter 11)

bonds Long-term debt instruments (IOUs), issued by corporations and governments, that offer a known interest return plus return of the bond's *face value* at maturity. (Chapter 1)

book value The amount of stockholders' equity in a firm; equals the amount of the firm's assets minus the firm's liabilities and preferred stock. (Chapter 6)

broker market The market in which the two sides of a transaction, the buyer and seller, are brought together to execute trades. (Chapter 2)

bull markets Markets normally associated with rising prices, investor optimism, economic recovery, and government stimulus. (Chapter 2)

business cycle An indication of the current state of the economy, reflecting changes in total economic activity over time. (Chapter 7)

business risk The degree of uncertainty associated with an investment's earnings and the investment's ability to pay the returns owed to investors. (Chapter 4)

C

call A negotiable instrument that gives the holder the right to buy securities at a stated price within a certain time period. (Chapter 14)

call feature Feature that specifies whether and under what conditions the issuer can retire a bond prior to maturity. (Chapter 10)

call premium The amount added to a bond's par value and paid to investors when a bond is retired prematurely. (Chapter 10)

call price The price the issuer must pay to retire a bond prematurely; equal to par value plus the call premium. (Chapter 10)

capital asset pricing model (CAPM) Model that formally links the notions of risk and return; it uses beta, the risk-free rate, and the market return to help investors define the required return on an investment. (Chapter 5)

capital gains The amount by which the sale price of an asset *exceeds* its original purchase price. (Chapter 1)

capital gains distributions Payments made to mutual fund shareholders that come from the profits that a fund makes from the sale of its securities. (Chapter 12)

capital loss The amount by which the proceeds from the sale of a capital asset are *less than* its original purchase price. (Chapter 1)

capital market Market in which *long-term* securities (with maturities greater than one year) such as stocks and bonds are bought and sold. (Chapter 2)

cash account A brokerage account in which a customer can make only cash transactions. (Chapter 3)

cash dividend Payment of a dividend in the form of cash. (Chapter 6)

cash market A market where a product or commodity changes hands in exchange for a cash price paid when the transaction is completed. (Chapter 15)

charting The activity of charting price behavior and other market information and then using the patterns these charts form to make investment decisions. (Chapter 9)

churning An illegal and unethical practice engaged in by a broker to increase commissions by causing excessive trading of clients' accounts. (Chapter 3)

classified common stock Common stock issued by a company in different classes, each of which offers different privileges and benefits to its holders. (Chapter 6)

clean price The price of a bond ignoring any accrued interest. The clean price is the present value of the bond's future cash flows, not including any interest accruing on the next coupon date. (Chapter 11)

closed-end fund A mutual fund with a fixed number of shares outstanding. The fund is closed to new contributions from investors, so investors must buy shares in the fund in the open market. (Chapter 12)

collateral trust bonds Senior bonds backed by securities owned by the issuer but held in trust by a third party. (Chapter 10)

collateralized mortgage obligation (CMO) Mortgage-backed bond whose holders are divided into classes based on the length of investment desired; principal is channeled to investors in order of maturity, with short-term classes first. (Chapter 10)

common-size income statement A type of financial report that uses a common denominator (net sales) to convert all entries on a normal income statement from dollars to percentages. (Chapter 8)

common stock Equity investment that represents ownership in a corporation; each share represents a fractional ownership interest in the firm. (Chapter 1)

common-stock (market) ratios Financial ratios that convert key information about a firm to a per-share basis. (Chapter 7)

compound interest Interest paid not only on the initial deposit but also on any interest accumulated from one period to the next. (Chapter 4)

confidence index A ratio of the average yield on high-grade corporate bonds to the average yield on average- or intermediate-grade corporate bonds; a technical indicator based on the theory that market trends usually appear in the bond market before they do in the stock market. (Chapter 9)

constant-dollar plan A formula plan for timing investment transactions, in which the investor establishes a target dollar amount for the speculative portion of the portfolio and establishes trigger points at which funds are transferred to or from the conservative portion as needed to maintain the target dollar amount. (Chapter 13)

constant-ratio plan A formula plan for timing investment transactions, in which a desired fixed ratio of the speculative portion to the conservative portion of the portfolio is established; when the actual ratio differs by a predetermined amount from the desired ratio, transactions are made to rebalance the portfolio to achieve the desired ratio. (Chapter 13)

continuous compounding Interest calculation in which interest is compounded over the smallest possible interval of time. (Chapter 4)

conventional options Put and call options sold over the counter. (Chapter 14)

conversion (exchange) privilege Feature of a mutual fund that allows shareholders to move money from one fund to another, within the same family of funds. (Chapter 12)

conversion equivalent (conversion parity) The price at which the common stock would have to sell in order to make the convertible security worth its present market price. (Chapter 10)

conversion period The time period during which a convertible issue can be converted. (Chapter 10)

conversion price The stated price per share at which common stock will be delivered to the investor in exchange for a convertible issue. (Chapter 10)

conversion privilege The conditions and specific nature of the conversion feature on convertible securities. (Chapter 10)

conversion ratio The number of shares of common stock into which a convertible issue can be converted. (Chapter 10)

conversion value An indication of what a convertible issue would trade for if it were priced to sell on the basis of its stock value. (Chapter 10)

convertible bonds Fixed-income obligations that have a feature permitting the holder to convert the security into a specified number of shares of the issuing company's common stock. (Chapter 10)

convertible security A fixed-income obligation with a feature permitting the investor to convert it into a specified number of shares of common stock. (Chapter 1)

correlation A statistical measure of the relationship, if any, between series of numbers representing data of any kind. (Chapter 5)

correlation coefficient A measure of the degree of correlation between two series. (Chapter 5)

coupon Feature on a bond that defines the amount of annual interest income. (Chapter 10)

coupon rate A bond's coupon expressed as a percentage of its par value. (Chapter 10)

covered options Options written against stock owned (or short-sold) by the writer. (Chapter 14)

crossing markets After-hours trading in stocks that involves filling buy and sell orders by matching identical sell and buy orders at the desired price. (Chapter 2)

currency exchange rate The relationship between two currencies on a specified date. (Chapter 2)

currency exchange risk The risk caused by the varying exchange rates between the currencies of two countries. (Chapter 2)

currency futures Futures contracts on foreign currencies, traded much like commodities. (Chapter 15)

currency options Put and call options written on foreign currencies. (Chapter 14)

current yield Measure of the annual interest income a bond provides relative to its current market price. (Chapter 10)

custodial account The brokerage account of a minor; requires a parent or guardian to be part of all transactions. (Chapter 3)

cyclical stocks Stocks whose earnings and overall market performance are closely linked to the general state of the economy. (Chapter 6)

D

daily price limit Restriction on the day-to-day change in the price of an underlying commodity. (Chapter 15)

date of record The date on which an investor must be a registered shareholder to be entitled to receive a dividend. (Chapter 6)

day trader An investor who buys and sells stocks quickly throughout the day in hopes of making quick profits. (Chapter 3)

dealer market The market in which the buyer and seller are not brought together directly but instead have their orders executed by *dealers* that make markets in the given security. (Chapter 2)

debenture An unsecured (junior) bond. (Chapter 10)

debit balance The amount of money being borrowed in a margin loan. (Chapter 2)

debt Funds lent in exchange for interest income and the promised repayment of the loan at a given future date. (Chapter 1)

defensive stocks Stocks that tend to hold their own, and even do well, when the economy starts to falter. (Chapter 6)

deferred equity Securities issued in one form and later redeemed or converted into shares of common stock. (Chapter 10)

deflation A period of generally declining prices. (Chapter 4)

delivery month The time when a commodity must be delivered; defines the life of a futures contract. (Chapter 15)

derivative securities Securities that are structured to exhibit characteristics similar to those of an underlying security or asset and that derive their value from the underlying security or asset. (Chapter 1)

descriptive information Factual data on the past behavior of the economy, the market, the industry, the company, or a given investment. (Chapter 3)

designated market maker (DMM) NYSE member who specializes in making transactions in one or more stocks and manages the auction process. (Chapter 2)

direct investment Investment in which an investor directly acquires a claim on a security or property. (Chapter 1)

dirty price A bond's dirty price equals its clean price plus accrued interest. (Chapter 11)

discount basis A method of earning interest on a security by purchasing it at a price below its redemption value; the difference is the interest earned. (Chapter 1)

discount bond A bond with a market value lower than par; occurs when market rates are greater than the coupon rate. (Chapter 10)

discount rate The annual rate of return that could be earned currently on a similar investment; used when finding present value; also called *opportunity cost*. (Chapter 4)

diversifiable (unsystematic) risk The portion of an investment's risk that results from uncontrollable or random events that are firm-specific; can be eliminated through diversification. (Chapter 5)

diversification The inclusion of a number of different investment vehicles in a portfolio to increase returns or reduce risk. (Chapter 1)

dividend income Income derived from the dividends and interest earned on the security holdings of a mutual fund. (Chapter 12)

dividend payout ratio The portion of earnings per share (EPS) that a firm pays out as dividends. (Chapter 6)

dividend reinvestment plan (DRIP) Plan in which shareholders have cash dividends automatically reinvested into additional shares of the firm's common stock. (Chapter 6)

dividend valuation model (DVM) A model that values a share of stock on the basis of the future dividend stream it is expected to produce; its three versions are zero-growth, constant-growth, and variable-growth. (Chapter 8)

dividend yield A measure that relates dividends to share price and puts common stock dividends on a relative (percentage) rather than absolute (dollar) basis. (Chapter 6)

dividends Periodic payments made by firms to their shareholders. (Chapter 1)

dividends-and-earnings (D&E) approach Stock valuation approach that uses projected dividends, EPS, and P/E multiples to value a share of stock; also known as the *DCF approach*. (Chapter 8)

dollar-cost averaging A formula plan for timing investment transactions, in which a fixed dollar amount is invested in a security at fixed time intervals. (Chapter 13)

domestic investments Debt, equity, and derivative securities of U.S.-based companies and governments. (Chapter 1)

Dow Jones Corporate Bond Index Mathematical averages of the *closing prices* for 96 bonds—32 industrial, 32 financial, and 32 utility/telecom. (Chapter 3)

Dow Jones Industrial Average (DJIA) A stock market average made up of 30 high-quality stocks selected for total market value and broad public ownership and believed to reflect overall market activity. (Chapter 3)

dual listing Listing of a firm's shares on more than one exchange. (Chapter 2)

duration A measure of bond price volatility that captures both price and reinvestment risks and that is used to indicate how a bond will react in different interest rate environments. (Chapter 11)

E

earnings per share (EPS) The amount of annual earnings available to common stockholders, as stated on a per-share basis. (Chapter 6)

economic analysis A study of general economic conditions that is used in the valuation of common stock. (Chapter 7)

efficient frontier The leftmost boundary of the *feasible (attainable) set* of portfolios that includes all *efficient portfolios*—those providing the best attainable tradeoff between risk (measured by the standard deviation) and return. (Chapter 5)

efficient market A market in which securities reflect all possible information quickly and accurately. (Chapter 9)

efficient markets hypothesis (EMH) Basic theory of the behavior of efficient markets, in which there are a large number of knowledgeable investors who react quickly to new information, causing securities prices to adjust quickly and accurately. (Chapter 9)

efficient portfolio A portfolio that provides the highest return for a given level of risk. (Chapter 5)

electronic communications networks (ECNs) Electronic trading networks that automatically match buy and sell orders that customers place electronically. (Chapter 2)

equipment trust certificates Senior bonds secured by specific pieces of equipment; popular with transportation companies such as airlines. (Chapter 10)

equity Ongoing ownership in a business or property. (Chapter 1)

equity capital Evidence of ownership position in a firm, in the form of shares of common stock. (Chapter 6)

equity kicker Another name for the conversion feature, giving the holder of a convertible security a deferred claim on the issuer's common stock. (Chapter 10)

equity-income fund A mutual fund that emphasizes current income and capital preservation and invests primarily in high-yielding common stocks. (Chapter 12)

ethics Standards of conduct or moral judgment. (Chapter 2)

Eurodollar bonds Foreign bonds denominated in dollars but not registered with the SEC, thus restricting sales of new issues. (Chapter 10)

event risk Risk that comes from an unexpected event that has a significant and usually immediate effect on the underlying value of an investment. (Chapter 4)

ex-dividend date Three business days up to the date of record; determines whether one is an official shareholder and thus eligible to receive a declared dividend. (Chapter 6)

excess margin More equity than is required in a margin account. (Chapter 2)

exchange-traded fund (ETF) An open-end fund that trades as a listed security on a stock exchange. (Chapter 1)

expectations hypothesis Theory that the shape of the yield curve reflects investor expectations of future interest rates. (Chapter 11)

expected inflation premium The average rate of inflation expected in the future. (Chapter 4)

expected return The return an investor thinks an investment will earn in the future. (Chapter 4)

expense ratio A charge, expressed as a percentage of fund assets, that mutual funds charge investors to cover expenses of running the fund. (Chapter 12)

expiration date The date at which an option expires. (Chapter 14)

F

face value The value that a bond issuer must pay to the investor when the bond matures. (Chapter 10)

fair disclosure rule (Regulation FD) Rule requiring senior executives to disclose critical information simultaneously to investment professionals and the public via press releases or SEC filings. (Chapter 3)

familiarity bias The tendency to invest in securities simply because they are familiar to the investor. (Chapter 9)

financial futures A type of futures contract in which the underlying "commodity" is a financial asset, such as debt securities, foreign currencies, or common stocks. (Chapter 15)

financial institutions Organizations that channel the savings of governments, businesses, and individuals into loans or investments. (Chapter 1)

financial leverage The use of debt financing to magnify investment returns. (Chapter 2)

financial markets Forums in which suppliers and demanders of funds trade financial assets. (Chapter 1)

financial portals Supersites on the Web that bring together a wide range of investing features, such as real-time quotes, stock and mutual fund screens, portfolio trackers, news, research, and transaction capabilities, along with other personal finance features. (Chapter 3)

financial risk The degree of uncertainty of payment resulting from a firm's mix of debt and equity; the larger the proportion of debt financing, the greater this risk. (Chapter 4)

fire sale A sale that occurs when a mutual fund experiences withdrawals by investors and must quickly sell illiquid securities to raise cash to meet withdrawal requests. (Chapter 12)

first and refunding bonds Bonds secured in part with both first and second mortgages. (Chapter 10)

fixed-commissions Fixed brokerage commissions that typically apply to the small transactions usually made by individual investors. (Chapter 3)

fixed-income securities Investments that offer fixed periodic cash payments. (Chapter 1)

fixed-weightings approach Asset allocation plan in which a fixed percentage of the portfolio is allocated to each asset category. (Chapter 13)

flexible-weightings approach Asset allocation plan in which weights for each asset category are adjusted periodically based on market analysis. (Chapter 13)

forced conversion The calling in of convertible bonds by the issuing firm. (Chapter 10)

foreign investments Debt, equity, and derivative securities of foreign-based companies. (Chapter 1)

Form 10-K A statement that must be filed annually with the SEC by all firms having securities listed on a securities exchange or traded in the OTC market. (Chapter 3)

formula plans Mechanical methods of portfolio management that try to take advantage of price changes that result from cyclical price movements. (Chapter 13)

fourth market Transactions made directly between large institutional buyers and sellers of securities. (Chapter 2)

free cash flow The cash flow remaining after a firm has paid all of its expenses and makes necessary investments in working capital and fixed assets. (Chapter 8)

free cash flow to equity method A stock valuation approach that estimates the free cash flow that a company will produce over time and discounts that to the present to estimate the firm's total equity value. (Chapter 8)

full-service broker Broker who, in addition to executing clients' transactions, provides them with a full array of brokerage services. (Chapter 3)

fully compounded rate of return The rate of return that includes interest earned on interest. (Chapter 4)

fund families Different kinds of mutual funds offered by a single investment management company. (Chapter 12)

fundamental analysis The in-depth study of the financial condition and operating results of a firm. (Chapter 7)

future value The amount to which a current deposit will grow over a period of time when it is placed in an account paying compound interest. (Chapter 4)

futures Legally binding obligations stipulating that the seller of the contract will make delivery and the buyer of the contract will take delivery of an asset at some specific date, at a price agreed on at the time the contract is sold. (Chapter 1)

futures contracts Contracts that obligate investors to buy or sell some underlying asset at a fixed price on a specific future date. (Chapter 15)

futures market The organized market for the trading of futures contracts. (Chapter 15)

futures options Options that give the holders the right to buy or sell a single standardized futures contract for a specified period of time at a specified strike price. (Chapter 15)

G

general obligation bonds Municipal bonds backed by the full faith, credit, and taxing power of the issuer. (Chapter 10)

growth cycle A reflection of the amount of business vitality that occurs within an industry (or company) over time. (Chapter 7)

growth fund A mutual fund whose primary goal is capital appreciation. (Chapter 12)

growth stocks Stocks that experience high rates of growth in operations and earnings. (Chapter 6)

growth-and-income fund A mutual fund that seeks both long-term growth and current income, with primary emphasis on capital gains. (Chapter 12)

growth-oriented portfolio A portfolio whose primary objective is long-term price appreciation. (Chapter 5)

H

hedge A combination of two or more securities into a single investment position for the purpose of reducing or eliminating risk. (Chapter 14)

hedge fund Lightly regulated investment funds that pool resources from wealthy investors. (Chapter 1)

hedgers Producers and processors who use futures contracts to protect their interest in an underlying commodity or financial instrument. (Chapter 15)

high-yield bonds Bonds with below investment-grade ratings, also known as junk bonds. (Chapter 10)

holding period The period of time over which one wishes to measure the return on an investment vehicle. (Chapter 4)

holding period return (**HPR**) The total return earned from holding an investment for a specified *holding period* (*usually one year or less*). (Chapter 4)

I

immunization Bond portfolio strategy that uses duration to offset price and reinvestment effects; a bond portfolio is immunized when its average duration equals the investment horizon. (Chapter 11)

in-the-money A call option with a strike price less than the market price of the underlying security; a put option whose strike price is greater than the market price of the underlying security. (Chapter 14)

income Usually cash or near-cash that is periodically received as a result of owning an investment. (Chapter 4)

income bonds Unsecured bonds requiring that interest be paid only after a specified amount of income is earned. (Chapter 10)

income statement A financial summary of the operating results of a firm covering a specified period of time, usually a year. (Chapter 7)

income stocks Stocks with long and sustained records of paying higher-than-average dividends. (Chapter 6)

income-oriented portfolio A portfolio that is designed to produce regular dividends and interest payments. (Chapter 5)

index fund A mutual fund that buys and holds a portfolio of stocks (or bonds) equivalent to those in a specific market index. (Chapter 12)

indexes Numbers used to measure the general behavior of stock prices by measuring the current price behavior of a representative group of stocks in relation to a base value set at an earlier point in time. (Chapter 3)

indirect investment Investment made in a collection of securities or properties. (Chapter 1)

individual investors Investors who manage their own funds. (Chapter 1)

industry analysis Study of industry groupings that looks at the competitive position of a particular industry in relation to others and identifies companies that show particular promise within an industry. (Chapter 7)

inflation A period of generally rising prices. (Chapter 4)

initial deposit The amount of investor capital that must be deposited with a broker at the time of a commodity transaction. (Chapter 15)

initial margin The minimum amount of equity that must be provided by a margin investor at the time of purchase. (Chapter 2)

initial public offering (IPO) The first public sale of a company's stock. (Chapter 2)

insider trading The use of nonpublic information about a company to make profitable securities transactions. (Chapter 2)

institutional investors Investment professionals who are paid to manage other people's money. (Chapter 1)

interest The "rent" paid by a borrower for use of the lender's money. (Chapter 4)

interest rate options Put and call options written on fixed-income (debt) securities. (Chapter 14)

interest rate risk The chance that changes in interest rates will adversely affect a security's value. (Chapter 4)

interest-rate futures Futures contracts on debt securities. (Chapter 15)

international fund A mutual fund that does all or most of its investing in foreign securities. (Chapter 12)

intrinsic value The underlying or inherent value of a stock, as determined through fundamental analysis. (Chapter 7) Also, the gross amount of money that an investor would receive if he or she chose to exercise an option. (Chapter 14)

investment Any asset into which funds can be placed with the expectation that it will generate positive income and/or preserve or increase its value. (Chapter 1)

investment advisors Individuals or firms that provide investment advice, typically for a fee. (Chapter 3)

investment banker Financial intermediary that specializes in assisting companies issue new securities and advising companies with regard to major financial transactions. (Chapter 2)

investment club A legal partnership through which a group of investors are bound to a specified organizational structure, operating procedures, and purpose, which is typically to earn favorable long-term returns from moderate-risk investments. (Chapter 3)

investment goals The financial objectives that one wishes to achieve by investing. (Chapter 1)

investment grade bonds Bonds with ratings in the three or four highest ratings categories issued by bond rating agencies. (Chapter 10)

investment letters Newsletters that provide, on a subscription basis, the analyses, conclusions, and recommendations of experts in securities investment. (Chapter 3)

investment plan A written document describing how funds will be invested and specifying the target date for achieving each investment goal and the amount of tolerable risk. (Chapter 1)

investment value The amount that investors believe a security should be trading for, or what they think it's worth. (Chapter 6)

investment value The price at which a convertible would trade if it were nonconvertible and priced at or near the prevailing market yields of comparable nonconvertible issues. (Chapter 10)

J

Jensen's measure (Jensen's alpha) A measure of portfolio performance that uses the portfolio beta and CAPM to calculate its *excess return*, which may be positive, zero, or negative. (Chapter 13)

junior bonds Debt obligations backed only by the promise of the issuer to pay interest and principal on a timely basis. (Chapter 10)

junk bonds High-risk securities that have low ratings but high yields. (Chapter 10)

L

LEAPS Long-term options. (Chapter 14)

leverage The ability to obtain a given equity position at a reduced capital investment, thereby magnifying returns. (Chapter 14)

leverage measures Financial ratios that measure the amount of debt being used to support operations and the ability of the firm to service its debt. (Chapter 7)

limit order An order to buy at or below a specified price or to sell at or above a specified price. (Chapter 3)

liquidity The ability of an investment to be converted into cash quickly and with little or no loss in value. (Chapter 1)

liquidity measures Financial ratios concerned with a firm's ability to meet its day-to-day operating expenses and satisfy its short-term obligations as they come due. (Chapter 7)

liquidity preference theory Theory that investors tend to prefer the greater liquidity of short-term securities and therefore require a premium to invest in long-term securities. (Chapter 11)

liquidity risk The risk of not being able to liquidate an investment quickly and at a reasonable price. (Chapter 4)

listed options Put and call options listed and traded on organized securities exchanges, such as the CBOE. (Chapter 14)

load fund A mutual fund that charges a commission when shares are bought; also known as a *front-end load fund*. (Chapter 12)

long purchase A transaction in which investors buy securities in the hope that they will increase in value and can be sold at a later date for profit. (Chapter 2)

long-term investments Investments with maturities of longer than a year or with no maturity at all. (Chapter 1)

loss aversion A situation in which the desire to avoid losses is so great that investors who are otherwise risk-averse will exhibit risk-seeking behavior in an attempt to avoid a loss. (Chapter 9)

low-load fund A mutual fund that charges a small commission when shares are bought. (Chapter 12)

LYON (liquid yield option note) A zero-coupon bond that carries both a conversion feature and a put option. (Chapter 10)

M

maintenance deposit The minimum amount of margin that must be kept in a margin account at all times. (Chapter 15)

maintenance margin The absolute minimum amount of margin (equity) that an investor must maintain in the margin account at all times. (Chapter 2)

management fee A fee levied annually for professional mutual fund services provided; paid regardless of the performance of the portfolio. (Chapter 12)

margin account A brokerage account for which margin trading is authorized. (Chapter 3)

margin call Notification of the need to bring the equity of an account whose margin is below the maintenance level up above the maintenance margin level or to have enough margined holdings sold to reach this standard. (Chapter 2)

margin deposit Amount deposited with a broker to cover any loss in the market value of a futures contract that may result from adverse price movements. (Chapter 15)

margin loan Vehicle through which borrowed funds are made available, at a stated interest rate, in a margin transaction. (Chapter 2)

margin requirement The minimum amount of equity that must be a margin investor's own funds; set by the Federal Reserve Board (the "Fed"). (Chapter 2)

margin trading The use of borrowed funds to purchase securities; magnifies returns by reducing the amount of equity that the investor must put up. (Chapter 2)

mark-to-the-market A daily check of an investor's margin position, determined at the end of each session, at which time the broker debits or credits the account as needed. (Chapter 15)

market anomalies Irregularities or deviations from the behavior one would expect in an efficient market. (Chapter 9)

market makers *Securities dealers* that "make markets" by offering to buy or sell certain quantities of securities at stated prices. (Chapter 2)

market order An order to buy or sell stock at the best price available when the order is placed. (Chapter 3)

market return The average return for all (or a large sample of) stocks, such as those in the *Standard & Poor's 500-Stock Composite Index*. (Chapter 5)

market risk Risk of decline in investment returns because of market factors independent of the given investment. (Chapter 4)

market segmentation theory Theory that the market for debt is segmented on the basis of maturity, that supply and demand within each segment determine the prevailing interest rate, and that the slope of the yield curve depends on the relationship between the prevailing rates in each segment. (Chapter 11)

market technicians Analysts who believe it is chiefly (or solely) supply and demand that drive stock prices. (Chapter 9)

market value The prevailing market price of a security. (Chapter 6)

maturity date The date on which a bond matures and the principal must be repaid. (Chapter 10)

maximum daily price range The amount a commodity price can change during the day; usually equal to twice the daily price limit. (Chapter 15)

mediation An informal, voluntary dispute-resolution process in which a client and a broker agree to a mediator, who facilitates negotiations between them to resolve the case. (Chapter 3)

Mergent Publisher of a variety of financial material, including *Mergent's Manuals*. (Chapter 3)

mid-cap stocks Medium-sized stocks, generally with market values of less than $4 or $5 billion but more than $1 billion. (Chapter 6)

mixed stream A stream of returns that, unlike an annuity, exhibits no special pattern. (Chapter 4)

modern portfolio theory (MPT) An approach to portfolio management that uses several basic statistical measures to develop a portfolio plan. (Chapter 5)

money market Market where *short-term* debt securities (with maturities less than one year) are bought and sold. (Chapter 2)

money market mutual funds (money funds) Mutual funds that invest solely in short-term investment vehicles. (Chapter 1)

mortgage bonds Senior bonds secured by real estate. (Chapter 10)

mortgage-backed bond A debt issue secured by a pool of home mortgages; issued primarily by federal agencies. (Chapter 10)

moving average (MA) A mathematical procedure that computes and records the average values of a series of prices, or other data, over time; results in a stream of average values that will act to smooth out a series of data. (Chapter 9)

municipal bond guarantees Guarantees from a party other than the issuer that principal and interest payments will be made in a prompt and timely manner. (Chapter 10)

municipal bonds Debt securities issued by states, counties, cities, and other political subdivisions; most of these bonds are tax-exempt (free of federal income tax on interest income). (Chapter 10)

mutual fund A company that raises money from sale of its shares and invests in and professionally manages a diversified portfolio of securities. (Chapter 1)

N

naked options Options written on securities not owned by the writer. (Chapter 14)

narrow framing Analyzing an investment problem in isolation or in a particularly narrow context rather than looking at all aspects of the problem. (Chapter 9)

Nasdaq market A major segment of the *secondary market* that employs an all-electronic trading platform to execute trades. (Chapter 2)

Nasdaq Stock Market indexes Indexes that measure the current price behavior of securities traded in the Nasdaq stock market, relative to a base of 100 set at specified dates. (Chapter 3)

negatively correlated Describes two series that move in opposite directions. (Chapter 5)

negotiated commissions Brokerage commissions agreed to by the client and the broker as a result of their negotiations; typically available to large institutional transactions and to individual investors who maintain large accounts. (Chapter 3)

net asset value (NAV) The underlying value of a share of stock in a particular mutual fund. (Chapter 12)

net losses The amount by which capital losses exceed capital gains; up to $3,000 of net losses can be applied against ordinary income in any year. (Chapter 1)

no-load fund A mutual fund that does not charge a commission when shares are bought. (Chapter 12)

nominal rate of return The actual return earned on an investment expressed in current dollars. (Chapter 4)

note A debt security originally issued with a maturity of from 2 to 10 years. (Chapter 10)

NYSE composite index An index that measures the current price behavior of stocks listed on the NYSE, relative to a base of 5,000 set at December 31, 2002. (Chapter 3)

O

odd lot Less than 100 shares of stock. (Chapter 3)

open interest The number of contracts currently outstanding on a commodity or financial future. (Chapter 15)

open-end fund A mutual fund that issues new shares to investors each time that they send money to the fund. There is no limit to the number of new shares that can be issued and, hence, no limit to the amount of money that people can invest in the fund. (Chapter 12)

open-outcry auction In futures trading, an auction in which trading is done through a series of shouts, body motions, and hand signals. (Chapter 15)

option Securities that give the holder the right to buy or sell a certain amount of an underlying financial asset at a specified price for a specified period of time. (Chapter 14)

option chain A list of all options traded on a particular security. An option chain provides the current market prices and trading volumes for all options linked to a particular stock. (Chapter 14)

option premium The quoted price the investor pays to buy a listed put or call option. (Chapter 14)

option spreading Combining two or more options with different strike prices and/or expiration dates into a single transaction. (Chapter 14)

option straddle The simultaneous purchase (or sale) of a put and a call on the same underlying common stock (or financial asset). (Chapter 14)

option writer (or seller) The individual or institution that writes/creates put and call options. (Chapter 14)

ordinary annuity An annuity for which the cash flows occur at the end of each period. (Chapter 4)

out-of-the-money A call option with no real value because the strike price exceeds the market price of the stock; a put option whose market price exceeds the strike price. (Chapter 14)

overconfidence The tendency to overestimate one's ability to perform a particular task. (Chapter 9)

over-the-counter (OTC) market A segment of the *secondary market* that involves trading in smaller, *unlisted securities*. (Chapter 2)

P

paper return A return that has been achieved but not yet realized by an investor during a given period. (Chapter 4)

par value The stated, or face, value of a stock. (Chapter 6). Also, the value that a bond issuer must pay to the investor when the bond matures. (Chapter 10)

payback period The length of time it takes for the buyer of a convertible to recover the conversion premium from the extra current income earned on the convertible. (Chapter 10)

payment date The actual date on which the company will mail dividend checks to shareholders (also known as the *payable date*). (Chapter 6)

PEG ratio A financial ratio that relates a stock's price/earnings multiple to the company's rate of growth in earnings. (Chapter 7)

perfectly negatively correlated Describes two negatively correlated series that have a correlation coefficient of −1. (Chapter 5)

perfectly positively correlated Describes two positively correlated series that have a correlation coefficient of 1. (Chapter 5)

PIK bond A payment in kind junk bond that gives the issuer the right to make annual interest payments in new bonds rather than in cash. (Chapter 10)

pooled diversification A process whereby investors buy into a portfolio of securities for the collective benefit of the individual investors. (Chapter 12)

portfolio Collection of securities or other investments, typically constructed to meet one or more investment goals. (Chapter 1)

portfolio beta, b_p The beta of a portfolio; calculated as the weighted average of the betas of the individual assets it includes. (Chapter 5)

portfolio revision The process of selling certain issues in a portfolio and purchasing new ones to replace them. (Chapter 13)

positively correlated Describes two series that move in the same direction. (Chapter 5)

preferred stock Ownership interest in a corporation; has a stated dividend rate, payment of which is given preference over common stock dividends of the same firm. (Chapter 1)

premium bond A bond with a market value in excess of par; occurs when interest rates drop below the coupon rate. (Chapter 10)

premium discount broker Broker who charges low commissions to make transactions for customers but provides limited free research information and investment advice. (Chapter 3)

present value The *value today* of a sum to be received at some future date; the inverse of future value. (Chapter 4)

price/earnings (P/E) approach Stock valuation approach that tries to find the P/E ratio that's most appropriate for the stock; this ratio, along with estimated EPS, is then used to determine a reasonable stock price. (Chapter 8)

primary market The market in which *new issues* of securities are sold by the issuers to investors. (Chapter 2)

prime rate The lowest interest rate charged to the best business borrowers. (Chapter 2)

principal On a bond, the amount of capital that must be repaid at maturity. (Chapter 10)

private placement The sale of new securities directly, without SEC registration, to private investors. (Chapter 2)

profitability Financial ratios that measure a firm's returns by relating profits to sales, assets, or equity. (Chapter 7)

promised yield Yield-to-maturity. (Chapter 11)

property Investments in real property or tangible personal property. (Chapter 1)

prospectus A portion of a security registration statement that describes the key aspects of the issue and issuer. (Chapter 2)

public offering The sale of a firm's securities to public investors. (Chapter 2)

publicly traded issues Shares of stock that are readily available to the general public and are bought and sold in the open market. (Chapter 6)

purchasing power risk The chance that unanticipated changes in price levels (inflation or deflation) will adversely affect investment returns. (Chapter 4)

put A negotiable instrument that enables the holder to sell the underlying security at a specified price over a set period of time. (Chapter 14)

put-call parity A relationship linking the market values of puts and calls of European options written on the same underlying stock and having the same exercise price and expiration date. (Chapter 14)

pyramiding The technique of using paper profits in margin accounts to partly or fully finance the acquisition of additional securities. (Chapter 2)

Q

quotations Price information about various types of securities, including current price data and statistics on recent price behavior. (Chapter 3)

R

random walk hypothesis The theory that stock price movements are unpredictable, so there's no way to know where prices are headed. (Chapter 9)

rate of growth The compound annual *rate of change* in the value of a stream of income. (Chapter 4)

ratio analysis The study of the relationships between financial statement accounts. (Chapter 7)

real estate Entities such as residential homes, raw land, and income property. (Chapter 1)

real estate investment trust (REIT) A type of closed-end investment company that sells shares to investors and invests the proceeds in various types of real estate and real estate mortgages; they come in three types: equity REITs, mortgage REITs, and hybrid REITs. (Chapter 12)

real rate of return The nominal return minus the inflation rate; a measure of the increase in purchasing power that an investment provides. (Chapter 4)

realized return Current income actually received by an investor during a given period. (Chapter 4)

realized yield Expected return. (Chapter 11)

red herring A preliminary prospectus made available to prospective investors while waiting for the registration statement's SEC approval. (Chapter 2)

redemption fee A charge that investors pay if they sell shares in the fund only a short time after buying them. (Chapter 12)

refunding provisions Provisions that prohibit the premature retirement of an issue from the proceeds of a lower-coupon refunding bond. (Chapter 10)

reinvestment rate The rate of return earned on interest or other income received from an investment over its investment horizon. (Chapter 4)

relative P/E multiple A measure of how a stock's P/E behaves relative to the average market multiple. (Chapter 8)

relevant risk Risk that is undiversifiable. (Chapter 5)

representativeness Cognitive biases that occur because people have difficulty thinking about randomness in outcomes. (Chapter 9)

required rate of return The rate of return that compensates investors for the risk of a particular investment. The minimum acceptable return on an investment given its risk. (Chapter 8)

required return The rate of return an investor must earn on an investment to be fully compensated for its risk. (Chapter 4)

residual owners Owners/stockholders of a firm, who are entitled to dividend income and a prorated share of the firm's earnings only after all other obligations have been met. (Chapter 6)

restricted account A margin account whose equity is less than the initial margin requirement; the investor may not make further margin purchases and must bring the margin back to the initial level when securities are sold. (Chapter 2)

return on invested capital Return to investors based on the amount of money actually invested in a security, rather than the value of the contract itself. (Chapter 15)

returns The rewards from investing, received as current income and/or increased value. (Chapter 1)

revenue bonds Municipal bonds that require payment of principal and interest only if sufficient revenue is generated by the issuer. (Chapter 10)

rights offering An offer of new shares of stock to existing stockholders on a pro rata basis. (Chapter 2)

risk Reflects the uncertainty surrounding the return that an investment will generate. (Chapter 1)

risk premium A return premium that reflects the issue and issuer characteristics associated with a given investment vehicle. (Chapter 4)

risk-averse Describes an investor who requires greater return in exchange for greater risk. (Chapter 4)

risk-free rate The rate of return that can be earned on a risk-free investment; the sum of the real rate of return and the expected inflation premium. (Chapter 4)

risk-indifferent Describes an investor who does not require a change in return as compensation for greater risk. (Chapter 4)

risk-return tradeoff The relationship between risk and return, in which investments with more risk should provide higher returns, and vice versa. (Chapter 4)

risk-seeking Describes an investor who will accept a lower return in exchange for greater risk. (Chapter 4)

round lot A 100-share unit of stock. (Chapter 3)

round-trip commission The combined commission that investors pay when they buy and sell a security. (Chapter 15)

S

satisfactory investment An investment whose present value of benefits (discounted at the appropriate rate) equals or exceeds the present value of its costs. (Chapter 4)

secondary distributions The public sales of large blocks of previously issued securities held by large investors. (Chapter 2)

secondary market The market in which securities are traded *after they have been issued*; an *aftermarket*. (Chapter 2)

sector fund A mutual fund that restricts its investments to a particular segment of the market. (Chapter 12)

Securities and Exchange Commission (SEC) Federal agency that regulates securities offerings and markets. (Chapter 2)

Securities Investor Protection Corporation (SIPC) A nonprofit membership corporation, authorized by the federal government, that insures each brokerage customer's account for up to $500,000, with claims for cash limited to $100,000 per customer. (Chapter 3)

securities Investments issued by firms, governments, or other organizations that represent a financial claim on the issuer's resources. (Chapter 1)

securities markets Forums that allow suppliers and demanders of *securities* to make financial transactions. (Chapter 2)

securitization The process of transforming lending vehicles such as mortgages into marketable securities. (Chapter 10)

security analysis The process of gathering and organizing information and then using it to determine the intrinsic value of a share of common stock. (Chapter 7)

security market line (SML) The graphical depiction of the capital asset pricing model; reflects the investor's required return for each level of undiversifiable risk, measured by beta. (Chapter 5)

security selection The procedures used to select the specific securities to be held within an asset class. (Chapter 13)

self-attribution bias The tendency to overestimate the role that one's intelligence or skill plays in bringing about a favorable investment result and to underestimate the role of chance in that result. (Chapter 9)

selling group A group of dealers and brokerage firms that join the investment banker(s); each member is responsible for selling a certain portion of a new security issue. (Chapter 2)

semi-strong form (EMH) Form of the EMH holding that abnormally large profits cannot be consistently earned using publicly available information. (Chapter 9)

senior bonds Secured debt obligations, backed by a legal claim on specific property of the issuer. (Chapter 10)

serial bond A bond that has a series of different maturity dates. (Chapter 10)

settlement price The closing price (last price of the day) for commodities and financial futures. (Chapter 15)

Sharpe's measure A measure of portfolio performance that measures the *risk premium per unit of total risk*, which is measured by the portfolio standard deviation of return. (Chapter 13)

short interest The number of stocks sold short in the market at any given time; a technical indicator believed to indicate future market demand. (Chapter 9)

short-selling The sale of borrowed securities, their eventual repurchase by the short-seller, and their return to the lender. (Chapter 2)

short-term investments Investments that typically mature within one year. (Chapter 1)

simple interest Interest paid only on the initial deposit for the amount of time it is held. (Chapter 4)

sinking fund A provision that stipulates the amount of principal that will be retired annually over the life of a bond. (Chapter 10)

small-cap stocks Stocks that generally have market values of less than $1 billion but can offer above-average returns. (Chapter 6)

socially responsible fund A mutual fund that actively and directly incorporates ethics and morality into the investment decision. (Chapter 12)

speculators Investors who trade a particular asset purely to take advantage of a price change that they believe will occur. (Chapter 15)

speculative stocks Stocks that offer the potential for substantial price appreciation, usually because of some special situation, such as new management or the introduction of a promising new product. (Chapter 6)

split ratings Different ratings given to a bond issue by two or more rating agencies. (Chapter 10)

Standard & Poor's Corporation (S&P) Publisher of a large number of financial reports and services, including *corporation records* and *stock reports*. (Chapter 3)

Standard & Poor's indexes Indexes that measure the current price of a group of stocks relative to a base index value (set according to the specific index). (Chapter 3)

standard deviation, s A statistic used to measure the dispersion (variation) of returns around an asset's average or expected return. (Chapter 4)

statement of cash flows A financial summary of a firm's cash flow and other events that caused changes in the company's cash position. (Chapter 7)

stock dividend Payment of a dividend in the form of additional shares of stock. (Chapter 6)

stock spin-off Conversion of one of a firm's subsidiaries to a stand-alone company by distribution of stock in that new company to existing shareholders. (Chapter 6)

stock split A maneuver in which a company increases the number of shares outstanding by exchanging a specified number of new shares of stock for each outstanding share. (Chapter 6)

stock valuation The process by which the underlying value of a stock is established on the basis of its forecasted risk and return performance. (Chapter 8)

stockbrokers Professionals who assist investors in deciding which stocks and other investments to buy and in executing trades. (Chapter 3)

stock-index futures Futures contracts written on broad based measures of stock market performance (e.g., the S&P 500 Stock Index), allowing investors to participate in the general movements of the stock market. (Chapter 15)

stock-index option A put or call option written on a specific stock market index, such as the S&P 500. (Chapter 14)

stockholders' (annual) report A report published yearly by a publicly held corporation; contains a wide range of information, including financial statements for the most recent period of operation. (Chapter 3)

stop-loss (stop) order An order to sell a stock when its market price reaches or drops below a specified level; can also be used to buy stock when its market price reaches or rises above a specified level. (Chapter 3)

street name Security certificates issued in the brokerage firm's name but held in trust for its client, who actually owns them. (Chapter 3)

strike price The stated price at which you can buy a security with a call or sell a security with a put. (Chapter 14)

strong form (EMH) Form of the EMH that holds that there is no information, public or private, that allows investors to consistently earn abnormal profits. (Chapter 9)

subordinated debentures Unsecured bonds whose claim is secondary to other debentures. (Chapter 10)

systematic withdrawal plan A mutual fund service that enables shareholders to automatically receive a predetermined amount of money every month or quarter. (Chapter 12)

T

tactical asset allocation Asset allocation plan that uses stock-index futures and bond futures to change a portfolio's asset allocation based on forecast market behavior. (Chapter 13)

tangibles Investment assets, other than real estate, that can be seen or touched. (Chapter 1)

target date fund A mutual fund that follows an asset allocation plan tied to a specific target date, usually decreasing the asset allocation to equities and increasing the allocation to bonds as the target date approaches. (Chapter 12)

target price The price an analyst expects the stock to reach within a certain period of time, usually a year. (Chapter 8)

tax planning The development of strategies that will defer and minimize an individual's level of taxes over the long run. (Chapter 1)

tax risk The chance that Congress will make unfavorable changes in tax laws, driving down the after-tax returns and market values of certain investments. (Chapter 4)

tax swap Replacement of a bond that has a capital loss for a similar security; used to offset a gain generated in another part of an investor's portfolio. (Chapter 11)

tax-advantaged investments Investment vehicles and strategies designed to produce higher after-tax returns by reducing the amount of taxes that investors must pay. (Chapter 1)

taxable equivalent yield The return a fully taxable bond would have to provide to match the after-tax return of a lower-yielding, tax-free municipal bond. (Chapter 10)

tech stocks Stocks that represent the technology sector of the market. (Chapter 6)

technical analysis The study of the various forces at work in the marketplace and their effect on stock prices. (Chapter 9)

term bond A bond that has a single, fairly lengthy maturity date. (Chapter 10)

term structure of interest rates The relationship between the interest rate or rate of return (yield) on a bond and its time to maturity. (Chapter 11)

theory of contrary opinion A technical indicator that uses the amount and type of odd-lot trading as an indicator of the current state of the market and pending changes. (Chapter 9)

third market Over-the-counter transactions typically handled by market makers and made in securities listed on the NYSE, the NYSE AMEX, or one of the other exchanges. (Chapter 2)

time value The amount by which the option price exceeds the option's fundamental value. (Chapter 14)

time value of money The fact that as long as an opportunity exists to earn interest, the value of money is affected by the point in time when the money is received. (Chapter 4)

total return The sum of the current income and the capital gain (or loss) earned on an investment over a specified period of time. (Chapter 4)

total risk The sum of an investment's undiversifiable risk and diversifiable risk. (Chapter 5)

traditional portfolio management An approach to portfolio management that emphasizes "balancing" the portfolio by assembling a wide variety of stocks and/or bonds of companies from a broad range of industries. (Chapter 5)

Treasury bonds U.S. Treasury securities that are issued with 30-year maturities. (Chapter 10)

Treasury inflation-protected securities (TIPS) A type of Treasury security that provides protection against inflation by adjusting investor returns for the annual rate of inflation. (Chapter 10)

Treasury notes U.S. Treasury debt securities that are issued with maturities of 2 to 10 years. (Chapter 10)

treasury stock Shares of stock that have been sold and subsequently repurchased by the issuing firm. (Chapter 6)

Treasury strips Zero-coupon bonds created from U.S. Treasury securities. (Chapter 10)

Treynor's measure A measure of portfolio performance that measures the *risk premium per unit of undiversifiable risk*, which is measured by the portfolio beta. (Chapter 13)

true rate of interest The actual rate of interest earned. (Chapter 4)

12(b)-1 fee A fee levied annually by many mutual funds to cover management and other operating costs. (Chapter 12)

U

uncorrelated Describes two series that lack any relationship or interaction and therefore have a correlation coefficient close to zero. (Chapter 5)

underwriting The role of the *investment banker* in bearing the risk of reselling the securities purchased from an issuing corporation at an agreed-on price. (Chapter 2)

underwriting syndicate A group of investment banks formed by the originating investment banker to share the financial risk associated with *underwriting* new securities. (Chapter 2)

undiversifiable (systematic) risk The risk that remains even in a well-diversified portfolio. Risk that tends to affect all (or nearly all) securities. (Chapter 5)

unrealized capital gains (paper profits) A capital gain made only "on paper"—that is, not realized until the fund's holdings are sold. (Chapter 12)

V

value fund A mutual fund that invests in stocks that are deemed to be undervalued in the market; value stocks often exhibit low P/E multiples, high dividend yields, and promising futures. (Chapter 12)

Value Line composite index Stock index that reflects the percentage changes in share price of about 1,700 stocks, relative to a base of 100 set at June 30, 1961. (Chapter 3)

Value Line Investment Survey One of the most popular subscription services used by individual investors; subscribers receive three basic reports weekly. (Chapter 3)

variable-ratio plan A formula plan for timing investment transactions, in which the ratio of the speculative portion to the total portfolio value varies depending on the movement in value of the speculative securities; when the ratio rises or falls by a predetermined amount, the amount committed to the speculative portion of the portfolio is reduced or increased, respectively. (Chapter 13)

volume The number of securities traded in a particular time interval. (Chapter 15)

W

Wall Street Journal A daily business newspaper; the most popular source of financial news. (Chapter 3)

weak form (EMH) Form of the EMH holding that past data on stock prices are of no use in predicting future prices. (Chapter 9)

whipsawing The situation where a stock temporarily drops in price and then bounces back upward. (Chapter 13)

wrap account A brokerage account in which customers with large portfolios pay a flat annual fee that covers the cost of a money manager's services and the commissions on all trades. (Also called a *managed account*.) (Chapter 3)

Y

Yankee bonds U.S. dollar-denominated debt securities issued by foreign governments or corporations and traded in U.S. securities markets. (Chapter 2)

yield (internal rate of return) The compound annual rate of return earned by a long-term investment; the discount rate that produces a present value of the investment's benefits that just equals its cost. (Chapter 4)

yield curve A graph that represents the relationship between a bond's term to maturity and its yield at a given point in time. (Chapter 11)

yield pickup swap Replacement of a low-coupon bond for a comparable higher-coupon bond in order to realize an increase in current yield and yield-to-maturity. (Chapter 11)

yield spreads Differences in interest rates that exist among various sectors of the market. (Chapter 11)

yield-to-call (YTC) The yield on a bond if it remains outstanding only until a specified call date. (Chapter 11)

yield-to-maturity (YTM) The fully compounded rate of return earned by an investor over the life of a bond, including interest income and price appreciation. (Chapter 11)

Z

zero-coupon bonds Bonds with no coupons that are sold at a deep discount from par value. (Chapter 10)

Index

Abercrombie & Fitch Co., 225, 226
Abnormal returns, 338–339
Account executives. *See* Stockbrokers
Accounts receivable turnover ratio, 274
Accrual concept, 269
Accrued interest, bond valuation and, 438–439
Acme Brick Company, 511
Active income, 16
Active portfolio management, 521–522
Actively managed funds, 10, 471
Activity ratios, 273–275
Advanced Micro Devices (AMD), 254, 256
Advance/decline (A/D) line, 360
Advantest, 236
AdviceAmerica, 111
Affordable Care Act, 140
AFLAC, 215
Aftermarket. *See* Secondary market
Agency bonds, 396–397
Agency ratings of bonds, 391–393
Aggressive stock management, 244
Aggressive-growth funds, 484
Airline disasters, 358
Alcoa, 237
Alcoholics Anonymous, 103
Almanac of Business & Industrial Financial Ratios, 85, 88
Altria Group, 236
Amazon.com, 191, 236
American Arbitration Association (AAA), 109
American Banker, 84
American Century, 473–474
American Depositary Receipts (ADRs), 51, 92, 98, 240
American Depositary Shares (ADSs), 51, 181
American Eagle Outfitters, Inc., 142–143, 238
American Electric Power, 236
American Express, 511
American Football League, 347
American Funds Growth Fund of America, 190–191
American International Group (AIG), 21, 94
American Municipal Bond Assurance Corporation (AMBAC), 398
American options, 552, 555
American Recovery and Reinvestment Act of 2009, 259
American Stock Exchange (ASE), 37, 45
    advance/decline line and, 360
    short interest on, 359

Analytical information, 80
Anchoring, 355
    on credit spread, 427
Annual compounding
    bond valuation and, 435–437
    yield to maturity and, 440–442
Annual reports, 85–88
Annual Statement Studies, 85
Annual total returns, 123
AnnualReports.com, 85
Annuities
    future value of, 162
    ordinary, 162
    present value of, 165
AP (Associated Press), 83
Apple Inc., 3, 47, 94, 221, 236, 237, 273, 284, 476
Appreciation of currencies, 52
Arbitrage, 342–344
Arbitration, 109
Archipelago Exchange, 48
Arms index, 361
Art as asset, 2
Ask price, 46
Assessment of risk, 144–146
Asset allocation, 512–516
    alternatives for, 514–515
    applying, 515
    approaches to, 513–514
    defined, 513
Asset allocation funds, 488–489, 515
Asset management accounts, 24, 25, 26
Asset-backed securities (ABS), 405
Assets
    on balance sheet, 267
    financial, 550
Assured Guaranty Corp, 398
AT&T, 85–87, 94, 234
Australian Securities Exchange, 50
Automated Data Processing, 378, 392
Automatic investment plans, 489–490
Automatic reinvestment plans, 490
Avanir Pharmaceuticals, 92
Average market multiple, 301–302
Average maturity of a bond, 449
Averages, market, 94–95

Baby blues, 238
Backdating, 561
Back-end loads, 11, 480
Back-office research reports, 89
Balance sheet in fundamental analysis, 267–268
Balanced funds, 485

Balloon payments, 390
Bancorp West, Inc., 522–524
Bank of America, 83, 100, 106, 187, 232
Bank runs, 22
Bankers' acceptances, 25, 26
Banking Act of 1933, 22
Banks, economic letters of, 83
Barchart, 78
Barclays, 42
Barrick Gold Corporation, 51
Barron's, 83, 89, 99, 260, 262
    bond indexes quoted by, 99
    bond market data published by, 517
    confidence index of, 357–358
    mutual fund statistics published by, 494
    short interest reported by, 359
BASF, 240
Basic discount brokers, 101–102
BATS Option Exchange (BATS), 554
Bear markets, 48–49, 217
    price-to-earnings (P/E) ratio and, 280
Bear spreads, 575
Beardstown Ladies investment club, 123
Behavioral finance, 335, 347–356
    airline disasters and, 358
    implications for security analysis, 355–356
    investor behavior and, 348–350, 353
    mutual funds and, 348
Belief perseverance, 354
Ben Bridge Jeweler, 511
Benchmarks, 471
Berkshire Hathaway, Inc., 236, 511
Beta, 183–187
    application of, 186
    capital asset pricing model and, 187–189
    definition of, 183
    derivation of, 183–185
    high, 187
    interpretation of, 185–186
    multiple estimates of, 186
    for portfolios, 193–196
Better Investing Community, 112
Bid price, 46
Bid-ask spread, 226
"Big Board," 37, 45
BigCharts, 78
Binding arbitration, 109
Black, Fisher, 566
Black-Scholes option-pricing model, 566–568
Bloomberg, 48, 88, 90
Bloomberg Financial Services, 83

Bloomberg Television, 1
Blue Chip Advisor, 89
Blue sky laws, 54
Blue-chip stocks, 234, 235
Bogle, John, 348, 468
Bona Film Group, 237
Bond equivalent yield, 441–442
Bond funds, 485–486
Bond indexes, 99
Bond investment strategies, 455–457
  bond swaps and, 456–457
  forecasted interest rate approach
    to, 456
  passive, 455–456
Bond ladders, 456
Bond market, 394–407
  global view of, 406–407
  historical performance of, 380–384
  segments of, 394–402
  specialty issues in, 402–406
Bond market indicators, 98–99
Bond portfolios
  duration for, 451
  immunization of, 453–455
  structuring of, 453
Bond prices, 434–439
  accrued interest and, 438–439
  annual compounding and, 435–437
  basic bond valuation model and, 435
  behavior of, 387–388
  call, 389–390
  clean and dirty, 439
  forecasting, 456
  market yields and, 435
  quoting, 389
  semiannual compounding and,
    437–438
  volatility of, duration and, 451–452
Bond rating agencies, 391–393
Bond ratings, 391–393
Bond sites, 90
Bond swaps, 456–457
Bond valuation, 425–457
  current yield and, 439–440
  duration and, 447–455
  expected return and, 445–447
  investment strategies and, 455–457
  market interest rates and, 426–434
  pricing of bonds and, 434–439
  yield to call and, 444–445
  yield to maturity and, 440–443
Bond yields, 99
  to call, 444–445
  to maturity, 440–443
Bonds, 4, 378–414
  agency, 396–397
  business cycle and, 20
  call features of, 389–390
  closing prices for, 99
  collateral trust, 390
  convertible (*See* Convertible bonds)
  corporate, 402
  coupon and, 386
  deferred call, 389

definition of, 9
discount, 387
dollar-denominated, 406
equipment trust certificates and, 390
Eurodollar, 406
face value of, 9
first and refunding, 390
foreign-pay, 406–407
general obligation, 397
historical returns of, 381–383
income, 391
interest on, 386
investment-grade, 392
junior, 391
junk (high-yield), 392, 396, 405–406
liquidity of, 22
market for (*See* Bond market)
maturity date of, 386–387
measures of return for, 519
mortgage, 390
mortgage-backed, 403–404
municipal, 397–401
noncallable, 389
PIK, 405
premium, 387
principal of, 386
purchasing power risk and, 139
reasons for investing in, 379–385
refunding provisions of, 390
revenue, 397
risks and, 384–385
senior, 390
serial, 387
sinking funds and, 390
stock returns versus, 383–384
term, 387
treasury, 395–396
valuation of (*See* Bond valuation)
weighted-average life of, 449
Yankee, 51, 406
yield spread of, 381, 396
zero-coupon, 402–403, 442, 443
BondsOnline, 91
Book value
  of common stock, 227
  per share, 282
  ratio of price to, 282, 323–324
Borsheim's Fine Jewelry, 511
Boston Scientific, 281
Box Inc., 222, 223
BP, 240
Breaking the buck, 487
Brin, Sergey, 96
Broadcom, 561
Broker market, 44–46
Brokerage commissions, 108
Brokerage firms, types of, 101–102
Brokerage reports, 89
Brokerage services, 100–101
Brokers, 44, 45
Brunswick, 237
Buffett, Warren, 349, 385, 511
Bull markets, 48–49
Bull spreads, 575

Bureau of the Public Debt, 91
Business 2.0, 84
Business as net demander of funds, 5
Business cycle, 259
  investing and, 20–21
Business equipment stocks, 260
Business periodicals, 83–84
Business risk, 139
Business Week, 83, 84, 88–89, 260, 262,
  427
Business/financial risk, 385
Butterfly spreads, 575
Buttonwood Agreement, 37
Buy-and-hold investors, 344
Buy-and-hold strategy, 243
Buybacks, 224

Cal Dive International, 605
Calculating returns, 123
Calendar effect, 344
Call features of bonds, 389–390
Call options (calls), 13. *See also* Put and
    call options
  speculating with, 568–570
Call premium, 389–390
Call price of a bond, 389–390
Call risk, 385
Callaway Golf, 238
Capital, equity. *See* Common stock
Capital asset pricing model (CAPM),
    182–189, 187–189, 307–308
  anchoring and, 355
  beta and, 183–187
  definition of, 187
  estimating return using, 187–189
  risk components and, 182–183
  security market line and, 188–189
Capital gains, 8–9
  as component of return, 122–123
  of portfolio, measuring, 523–524
  realized, 8–9
  on stocks, estimating, 518
  taxation of, 16
  unrealized, 8–9, 499
Capital gains distributions, 499
Capital losses
  as component of return, 122–123
  limiting with puts, 571
  taxes and, 18
Capital markets, 38
  broker, 44–46
  dealer, 44–45, 46–47
  fourth, 48
  primary, 38–43
  secondary, 43
  third, 48
Capra, Frank, 22
Careers in finance, 27–30
  average salaries for, 29
Cash accounts, 103
Cash dividends, 230–232
Cash flow, 269–271
  free (*see* Free cash flow to equity
    method)

price-to-cash-flow (P/CF) procedure, 322–323
Cash interest payments, 122
Cash market, 592
Cash settling options, 553
Caterpillar Inc., 237, 402
Celgene Corporation, 172–178
Certificates of deposit (CDs), 24, 25, 26
Certified Financial Analyst (CFA) designation, 27
Certified Financial Planner (CFP) designation, 27, 110
Certified Investment Management Analyst (CIMA) designation, 110
Certified Public Accountant (CPA) designation, 110
CFA Institute, 27
Challenger disaster, 341
Charles Schwab, 101, 106
Chart formations, 363–364
Chartered Financial Analyst (CFA) designation, 27, 110
Chartered Financial Analyst (CFA) exam questions
   on derivative securities, 624–625
   on investing in common stocks, 376–377
   on investing in fixed-income securities, 466–467
   on investment environment and conceptual tools, 213–214
   on portfolio management, 547–548
Chartered Financial Consultant (ChFC) designation, 110
Chartered Investment Counselor (CIC) designation, 110
Chartered Life Underwriter (CLU) designation, 110
Charting, 78, 363–366
Checking accounts, liquidity of, 22
Checkpoint Systems, 237
Chemical Week, 84
Chevron, 234
Chicago Board of Trade (CBT), 592, 594, 606
Chicago Board Options Exchange (CBOE), 46, 550, 553–554, 577
Chicago Mercantile Exchange (CME), 46, 591, 606
   weather futures and, 599
Chicago Stock Exchange, 45
Chicago Tribune, 83
Chief financial officers (CFOs), 28
Chilango, 122
Churning, 102
CIO Magazine, 84
Cisco Systems, 47, 236, 577
Citibank, 51
Citigroup, 47
Classified common stock, 224
Clean price, 439
Clear Channel Communications, 393
Closed-end funds (CEFs), 476, 495–498
   features of, 497–498

open-end funds compared with, 495–497
   returns on, 502
Closing prices for bonds, 99
CME Globex, 593, 594
CME Group, 594
CNBC, 1
CNET, 85
CNNMoney, 83, 91
Coca-Cola Company, 47, 51, 343, 511
Collateral trust bonds, 390
Collateralized mortgage obligations (CMOs), 404–405
Commercial banking, careers in, 27–28
   average salaries for, 29
Commercial paper, 24, 26
Commission brokers, 45
Commissions
   brokerage, 108
   round-trip, 596
Commodities, 598–605
   basic characteristics of, 598–603
   trading, 603–605
Commodities contracts, 599
Commodities futures, 13
Commodity Exchange, Inc. (COMEX), 594
Commodity Futures Trading Commission (CFTC), 594
Common stock, 4, 8–9, 215–245, 221.
   See also Stocks
   advantages and disadvantages of owning, 219–221
   alternative investment strategies for, 242–245
   appeal of, 216
   blue-chip, 234, 235
   book value of, 227
   classified, 224
   as corporate security, 221–224
   cyclical, 237
   defensive, 237
   definition of, 8
   direct ownership of, 3–4
   dividends on (*See* Dividends)
   economic analysis for, 255–256, 258–263
   foreign, 238–242
   fundamental analysis for (*See* Fundamental analysis)
   growth, 236
   income, 234–236
   industry analysis for, 263–266
   intrinsic value of, 255
   investment value of, 227–228
   issuing new shares of, 222–224
   large-cap, 237, 238
   market value of, 227
   market-cap stocks, 237–238
   mid-cap, 237, 238
   outstanding shares of, 305
   par value of, 226
   price behavior of, 216
   quotes for, 225–226

real estate bubble and, 218–219
   returns on, 216–218
   security analysis for, 255–257
   small-cap, 237, 238
   speculative, 236–237
   spin-offs of, 222
   splits of, 222, 224
   tech, 236, 355
   transaction costs and, 226
   treasury, 224
   types of, 234–245
Common-size income statement, 298–300
Common-stock ratios, 279–282
Company analysis, 256
Company analysis phase of fundamental analysis, 266–267
Company information, 82
   sources of, 84–92
Comparative data sources, 85, 88
Competition, evaluating firms relative to, 285–286
Compound interest, 157–159
Compounding
   annual, bond valuation and, 435–437
   semiannual, bond valuation and, 437–438
Computer programs, 341
   time value of money computations and, 160
Computerworld, 84
Conagra Foods, 236
Confidence index, 357–358
Constant-dollar plan, 529–530, 531
Constant-growth model, 311–314, 319
Constant-ratio plan, 530–532
Consumer Finance, Survey of, 353
Consumer prices, 261
Continuous compounding, 158–159
Conventional options, 553–554
Conversion, forced, 409
Conversion equivalent, 412
Conversion parity, 412
Conversion period, 409
Conversion premium, 412–413
Conversion price, 409–410
Conversion privilege, 409–410
   mutual funds and, 490–491
Conversion ratio, 409
Conversion value, 411–414
Convertible bond funds, 486
Convertible bonds, 408–414
   busted, 411
   as investment outlets, 408–410
   measuring value of, 411–414
   sources of value of, 411
Convertible notes, 408–409
Convertible securities, 9
Corporate bonds, 402
Corporate finance, careers in, 28
   average salaries for, 29
Corporate securities, common stock as, 221–224
Correlation, 174–176
   culture and, 180

Correlation (continued)
  during periods of economic uncertainty and high stock market volatility, 178
Correlation coefficient, 174–175
Cosan Ltd., 51
Cost of goods sold, 275
Costs. See also Commissions; Fees
  of international diversification, 181
  of investment advisers, 111
  opportunity, 162
  transaction (See Transaction costs)
Coupons, bond, 386
Covered options, 573–575
Creation units of exchange-traded funds, 477
Credit risk, 385
Credit spread, 381, 396
  anchoring on, 427
Crossing markets, 53
Culture, correlation and, 180
Currency contracts, long position with, 610–611
Currency exchange rates, 52, 242
  arbitrage and, 342–343
Currency exchange risk, 52–53
Currency futures, 606, 609
Currency options, 581–582
Current event information, 82–84
Current income, common stocks for, 243
Current ratio, 272
Current yield of bonds, 386, 439–440, 518
Custodial brokerage accounts, 103
Custodians, mutual funds and, 475
Cyclical stocks, 237

Daily Finance, 91
Daily price limit, 602
Daimler, 51
Dallas National Corporation, 518, 519, 522–524
Dana, Neil, 549
Date of record for dividends, 230
Dator Companies, Inc., 522–524
Day orders, 105
Day traders, 106
Dealer market, 44–45, 46–47
Debentures, 391
  subordinated, 391, 405
Debit balance, 60
Debt, definition of, 4
Debt-equity ratio, 276
Decline stage of industry growth cycle, 264–265
Deductions, personal taxes and, 16
Default risk, 23, 385
Defensive stocks, 237
Deferred call bonds, 389
Deferred equities, 408. See also Convertible bonds
Deferred refunding issue, 390
Deflation, 125
Delivery month, 592
Dell, 47

Demanders of funds, 5–6
Department of Commerce, publications of, 84
Depreciation
  of assets, 270
  of currencies, 52
Derivative securities, 8, 12–13, 404, 550, 551, 607. See also Put and call options
  definition of, 4
Descriptive information, 80, 81
Designated market makers (DMMs), 46
Destination Maternity, 237
Diageo, 240
Diamond Foods, 271
Dick Davis Digest, 89
Dick's Sporting Goods, 238
Diebold, 260
The Dines Letter, 89
Direct investment, 3–4
  definition of, 3
  in foreign securities, 51, 240
DirectAdvice, 111
Dirty price, 439
Discount basis, 23
Discount bonds, 387
Discount rate, 162
Discounts, closed-end funds trading at, 496
Distributors, mutual funds and, 474
Diversifiable risk, 182–183
Diversification, 174, 176–181, 191
  correlation between assets and, 178–180
  definition of, 4, 49
  exchange-traded funds and, 11
  foreign investments and, 5
  interindustry, 190–191
  international, 180–181
  investment policy statement and, 15
  mutual funds for, 8, 10, 181
  pooled, 8, 470
  of risk, 193–196
"Dividend aristocrats," 215
Dividend income, 499
Dividend payout ratio, 231
Dividend reinvestment plans (DRIPs), 232–233
Dividend valuation model (DVM), 309–317
  constant-growth and, 311–314
  expected growth rate and, 315–317
  variable growth and, 314–317
  zero growth and, 309–311
Dividend yield, 231, 281–282, 518
Dividends, 8, 228–233
  cash, 230–232
  contribution to returns, 523
  dates related to, 230
  decision to pay, 229–230
  forecasted, 300–304
  steady stream of, 311
  stock, 232
  tax rate and, 16
Dividends per share, 281–282

Dodd-Frank Wall Street Reform and Consumer Protection Act of 2010, 22, 54, 55
Dollar-cost averaging, 529
Dollar-denominated bonds, 406
Domestic investments, 5
Dow Chemical, 51, 561–562
Dow Jones & Company, 82, 83, 94–95
Dow Jones Composite Average, 95
Dow Jones Corporate Bond Index, 99, 517
Dow Jones Industrial Average (DJIA), 94–95, 97, 216, 517
  PIIGS nation crisis and, 97
  stock-index futures and, 607
  stock-index options and, 577, 579, 580
Dow Jones MarketWatch, 92
Dow Jones Transportation Average, 95
Dow Jones Utilities Average, 95
Dow Theory Letters, 89
Drexel Burnham Lambert, 396
Dreyfus, 474
Dreyfus fund family, 491
Dreyfus GNMA fund, 470
DTE Energy, 236
Dual listings, 46
Duke Energy, 236
Dun & Bradstreet, 85
Duration (of bonds), 447–455
  concept of, 448–449
  effective, 452–453
  Macaulay, 449
  measurement of, 449–451
  modified, 452
  for a portfolio, 451
  price volatility and, 451–452
  for a single bond, 450–451
  uses of measures of, 453–455

Earnings. See Price-to-earnings (P/E) approach to stock valuation; Price-to-earnings (P/E) ratio
Earnings before interest, taxes, depreciation, and amortization (EBITDA), 277, 322–323
Earnings per share (EPS), 229
  estimating, 302–304
  price-to-earnings approach to stock valuation and, 321–322
EBay, 47, 236
EchoStar Communications, 281
Economic activity, evaluating performance of individual investments and, 517
Economic activity level, interest rates and, 429
Economic analysis, 255–256, 258–263
  business cycle and, 259
  defined, 258
  developing an economic outlook and, 260–263
  key economic factors and, 259–260, 261
Economic information, 82
  sources of, 82–84

Economic Report of the President, 84
Economic uncertainty, correlation
        between assets and, 178
The Economist, 83
EDGAR (Electronic Data Gathering and
        Analysis Retrieval), 85, 267
Efficient frontier, 191–193
Efficient market hypothesis (EMH),
        257, 338–342
    semi-strong form of, 340–341
    strong form of, 341–342
    weak form of, 339–340
Efficient markets, 335–366
    arbitrage and, 342–344
Efficient portfolios, 171, 191–192
Elan Corporation, 240
Electronic Arts, 236
Electronic brokers, 101–102
Electronic communications networks
        (ECNs), 48
Electronic spreadsheets, time value calcu-
        lations using, 127
Employment, 261
Energy Future Holdings Corporation,
        385
Enron, 603
Equipment trust certificates, 390, 402
Equities, deferred, 408. *See also*
        Convertible bonds
Equity. *See also* Book value
    definition of, 4
    ratio of debt to, 276
    return on, 278–279
    seasoned equity issues and, 38
    stockholders, on balance sheet,
        267–268
Equity capital. *See* Common stock
Equity kickers, 408, 550
Equity options. *See* Stock options
Equity real estate investment trusts
        (REITs), 482
Equity securities. *See* Common stock
Equity-income funds, 485
Ericsson Telephone, 240
ETF sponsors, 477
Ethics, 55
Etsy, IPO of, 323
Eurodollar bonds, 406
Euroland.com, 92
Euronext, 50, 52
Euronext.liffe, 37
European Central Bank, 131
European Monetary Union (EMU),
        50, 52
European options, 552, 555
Europe/Australia/Far East (EAFE/MSCI)
        Index, 98
Event risk, 141
Excelsior Industries, 522–524
Excess margin, 61
Exchange privileges, mutual funds
        and, 490–491
Exchange-traded funds (ETFs), 8, 11–12,
        335, 468, 477–479

diversification and, 11
    options on, 580
    overreaction to news and, 53
Ex-dividend date, 230
Exercise price, 550
    of stock options, 554–555
Expectations hypothesis, 432
Expected inflation premium, 130
Expected returns, 124, 340
    of bonds, 445–447
    determining, 320–321
Expedia, 222
Expense ratios, 10–11
    defined, 10
    of mutual funds, 472
Expiration date of stock options,
        555–556
Extendicare, 237
ExxonMobil Corporation, 47, 123–124,
        137, 215, 221, 237, 378, 476, 511

Face value of a bond, 386
Facebook, 5, 556–557, 575–576
    IPO of, 74, 75, 224, 226
    moving averages and, 354–355
Fair disclosure rules, 84–85
Fama, Eugene, 335
Familiarity bias, 355
Fast Company, 84
February cycle, 556
Federal budget deficit, interest rates
        and, 429
Federal Deposit Insurance Corporation
        (FDIC), 22
Federal Farm Credit Systems, 396
Federal Financing Bank, 397
Federal Home Loan Bank, 396
Federal Home Loan Mortgage Corpora-
        tion (Freddie Mac), 396–397, 404
Federal National Mortgage Association
        (Fannie Mae), 396–397, 404
Federal Reserve (Fed), 94, 131
    bond market data published by, 517
    interest rates and, 429
    margin trading and, 58
    Survey of Consumer Finance by, 353
Federal Reserve Bulletin, 84
FedEx Corporation, 183–185
Fees
    of hedge funds, 12
    of index funds, 493
    of investment advisers, 111
    of mutual funds, 181, 472, 480–481
Fidelity, 92, 232, 473
    planning tools provided by, 76
Fidelity Contrafund, 470
Fifth Third Bank of Cincinnati, 271
Fill-or-kill orders, 105
Financial assets, 550
Financial calculators, time value of money
        computations and, 159–160
Financial consultants. *See* Stockbrokers
Financial Engines, 111
Financial fraud, stock prices and, 21

Financial futures, 13, 606–616
    individual investors and, 613
    market for, 606–610
    options on, 614–616
    trading techniques for, 610–613
Financial Industry Regulatory Authority
        (FINRA), 107, 109, 480
    over-the-counter market regulation
        by, 43
    planning tools provided by, 76, 77
Financial institutions
    definition of, 5
    safety of, 22
Financial journals, 82–83
Financial leverage, 56
Financial markets. *See also* Securities
        markets
    definition of, 5
    functions of, 5
    U.S., development of, 37
Financial news, 1
Financial planning, careers in, 27, 28
    average salaries for, 29
Financial portals, 90, 91, 92
Financial press, lack of bond quotes
        in, 389
Financial ratios, 270–282
    activity, 273–275
    breaking down return on assets and
        return on equity and, 278–279
    common-stock, 279–282
    leverage, 275–277
    liquidity, 272–273
    profitability, 277–279
    uses of, 272
Financial risk, 139
Financial statements
    common-size income statement,
        298–300
    in fundamental analysis, 267–270
Financial Times, 1, 83, 92
Financing of margin trading, 58–59
Fine art as asset, 2
Fire sales, 11, 475
First and refunding bonds, 390
First Index Investment Trust, 468
First-day return, 39, 41
Firstrade, 106
Fiscal quarters, 269
Fitbit, 551–552
Fitch, 90
    bond ratings of, 391
Fixed commissions, 108
Fixed-income securities, 8, 9–10.
        See also Bonds
Fixed-weightings approach, 513–514
Flexible weightings approach, 514
"Flight to quality," 383
FlightSafety International, 511
Flip This House (TV show), 121
Florida Southcoast Banks, 522–524
Forbes, 83, 84, 511
    market interest rate reporting by, 427
    mutual fund statistics published by, 494

Forced conversion, 409
Ford Motor Company, 187
Forecasted interest rate approach to bond investment, 456
Forecasting
  of bond prices, 456
  of future behavior, 304–306
Foreign investments, 5
Foreign stocks, 238–242
  American Depositary Receipts and, 240
  comparative returns on, 239–240
  currency exchange rates and, 242
  direct investment in, 240
  global returns and, 240–242
Foreign-pay bonds, 406–407
Form 10-K, 85
Formula plans, 529–533
Fortune, 83, 84, 260
  market interest rate reporting by, 427
  mutual fund statistics published by, 494
401(k) plans, 4, 19, 534
Fourth market, 48
Fox Business Network, 1
Frank Russell Company, 98
Frankfurt Stock Exchange, 242
Franklin Templeton, 4
Fraud, 271
  detection of, 283
  at Enron, 603
  financial, stock prices and, 21
  Insider Trading and Fraud Act of 1988 and, 54
Freddie Mac, 21
Free cash flow to equity method, 317–320
Front month, 555
Front-end loads, 11, 480
Fruit of the Loom, 511
FTSE 250, stock-index options and, 579
FTSE Global Index, 56
Fujitsu, 51
Full-service brokers, 101–102
Fully compounded rate of return, 136
Fund families, 491
Fundamental analysis, 256, 266–286
  concept of, 266–267
  definition of, 266
  financial ratios in, 270–282
  financial statements in, 267–270
  interpreting data for, 283–286
Funds of funds, 474
Future options, 614–616
Future value, 160–163
  of an annuity, 162
  present value and, 162–163
Futures contracts, 13, 46, 592–594
  currency, 606, 609
  financial (*See* Financial futures)
  interest-rate, 606, 609
  measures of return for, 520
  options compared with, 593–594
  single stock, 606

specifications of, 607–609
stock-index, 606–607, 609, 611–612
tendency to hold too long, 603
Futures exchanges, 46
Futures market, 592–597
  major exchanges in, 594–595
  structure of, 592–595
  trading in, 595–597

Gabelli & Co., 170
Gains, capital. *See* Capital gains
Garmin Ltd., 238
GEICO, 511
Genentech, 281
General Electric (GE), 47, 378, 379
General Mills, 236, 312, 313
General Motors, 187, 393
General obligation bonds, 397
General Steel Holdings, 51
General-purpose money funds, 486
Genuine Parts, 237
Get-rich-quick scams, 92–93
Gilead Sciences, 191
Glenn, David, 21
Global Power Equipment Group, 237
Globalization. *See* International securities markets
GMAC, 405
Goldman, Sachs & Co., 42
Good-'til-canceled (GTC) orders, 105, 533
Google Finance, 90
Google Inc., 47, 96, 191, 236
  classified common stock and, 224
  IPO of, 255
GoPro Inc., 549
Government
  as net demander of funds, 5
  publications of, 84
  taxes levied by, 16
Government bond funds, 486
Government National Mortgage Association (Ginnie Mae), 403–404
Government securities money funds, 487
"Great Depression," 22, 38
"Great Recession," 38
  oil prices and, 123
Greenberg, Hank, 21
Gross domestic product (GDP), 259, 261
Gross proceeds of IPOs, 41
Gross spread, 42
Growth cycle of an industry, 264–265
Growth funds, 484
Growth rates, 137
Growth stocks, 236, 317, 346
Growth-and-income funds, 485
Growth-oriented portfolios, 171
Grupo Televisa, 240
Guidelines for investment selection, 15

Hanson, Lars Peter, 335
Hasbro, 238
Hedge funds, 4, 8, 12, 482–483
  fees on, 12

Hedgers in futures market, 595–596
Hedging
  commodities and, 603, 604
  of foreign exchange risk, 613
  options for, 570–573
  with stock-index futures, 611–612
  with stock-index options, 579–580
Heineken, 52–53
Helmerich & Payne, 297
Helzberg Diamonds, 511
Herman Miller, 260
Heron, Randall, 561
1/N heuristic, 514
Hidden loads, 480
High-grade corporate bond funds, 486
High-risk investments, 4–5
High-water mark fees, 12
High-yield bonds, 392, 396, 405–406
High-yield corporate bond funds, 486
Historical data, 283–285
Historical returns, 126
  risk and, 142–144
Holders of record, 230
Holding period, 131
Holding period return (HPR), 131–133
  for evaluating portfolio performance, 517–520
  global returns and, 241–242
  mutual fund returns and, 500–501
  of portfolio, measuring, 524–525
Home Depot, 47, 234
Hong Kong Exchanges and Clearing Ltd., 50
Hoover's Online, 85
Housing market
  loss aversion and, 350
  owners' reluctance to sell at a loss and, 218
Housing starts, 261
The Hulbert Financial Digest, 89
Hutchison Wampoa, Ltd., 240
Hybrid securities, 408. *See also* Convertible bonds

I bonds, 24, 26
Ihle, Heiko, 170
Illiquid types of investments, 3
Income, 2
  active, 16
  as component of return, 122
  dividend, 499
  measuring, 523
  ordinary, 16–17
  passive, 16
  personal, 261
  portfolio, 16
  types of, 16–19
Income bonds, 391
Income statement
  common-size, 298–300
  in fundamental analysis, 268–269
Income stocks, 234–236
Income-oriented portfolios, 171
Independent brokers, 45

Index funds, 10, 27, 335, 348, 487–488
  fees for, 493
Indexes. See also specific indexes
  of investment performance, 517
  of leading indicators, 261
  market, 94, 96–98
  price-weighted, 94
IndexFunds.com, 91
Indirect investment, 3–4
  definition of, 3
  in foreign securities, 51
Individual investors, 6
Individual retirement accounts (IRAs),
    19, 491–492
Individuals as net suppliers of funds, 5
Industrial production, 259, 261
Industry analysis, 263–266
  key issues in, 263–265
  for stock, 256
Industry data, 283–285
Industry growth cycle, 264–265
Industry information, 82
  sources of, 84–92
Industry outlook, developing, 265–266
Industry Week, 84
Inflation, 125
  interest rates and, 428
  returns and, 129
Inflation risk, 23
Inflation-indexed securities, 395
Inflation-protected securities, 396
ING, 28
Initial development stage of industry
    growth cycle, 264
Initial margin, 59, 596
Initial public offerings (IPOs), 38–42
  of Etsy, 323
  of Facebook, 74, 75
  first-day return for, 39, 41
  of Google, 255
  gross proceeds of, 41
  money left on the table and, 41
  of Shake Shack Inc., 38–42
  small-cap stocks and, 238
  underpricing of, 41
Insider trading, 103, 342
Insider Trading and Fraud Act of 1988,
    54
Instinet, 48
Institutional investors, 6
Institutional news, 83
Insurance, careers in, 28
Intel Corporation, 44, 236, 254, 577
InterAmerican Bank, 406
Intercontinental Exchange, Inc., 37
Interest
  accrued, bond valuation and, 438–439
  on bonds, 386
  compound, 157–159
  continuous compounding of, 158–159
  definition of, 157
  on interest, 135–136
  on short-term investments, 23
  simple, 157

stated rate of, 158
  true rate of, 158
Interest payments, cash, 122
Interest rate currency contracts, short
    position with, 611
Interest rate futures, 606, 609
Interest rate options, 581
Interest rate risk, 139–140, 384
Interest rates
  foreign, domestic interest rates and, 429
  inflation and, 428
  market (See Market interest rates)
  prime, 58
  stated, 23
  term structure of, 429
Interindustry diversification, 190–191
Intermediate-term bond funds, 486
Internal rate of return (IRR), 133–136,
    320–321
  mutual fund returns and, 501
  reinvestment and, 136
  for single cash flow, 133–134
  for stream of income, 134–135
International Business Machines Corpora-
    tion (IBM), 47, 51, 172–178, 511
International Dairy Queen, 511
International diversification, 180–181
International funds, 489
International Securities Exchange (ISE), 554
International securities markets, 49–53
  growing importance of, 50
  investment performance and, 50–51
  risk of investing in, 51–53
  ways to invest in foreign securities
    and, 51
International sites, 92
Internet as investment tool, pros and
    cons of, 79
In-the-money options, 560–561
Intrinsic value of puts and calls, 559–564
Intrinsic value of stock, 255
Inventory turnover, 274–275
Investing Online Resource Center, 75
Investinginbonds.com, 91
Investment advisers, 110–111
  cost of, 111
  mutual funds and, 474
  online, 111
  regulation of, 110
  use of, 111
Investment Advisers Act of 1940, 54, 110
Investment bankers, 41–43
Investment banking, careers in, 28–29
  average salaries for, 29
Investment clubs, 110, 111–112, 123
Investment companies. See Mutual funds
Investment Company Act of 1940, 54
Investment discussion forums, 92
Investment executives. See Stockbrokers
Investment goals, 14–15
Investment horizon, price-to-earnings
    over, 302
Investment information, 80–93
  alternative, 82

analytical, 80
  descriptive, 80, 81
  online, 89–92
  sources of, 82–93
  types of, 82
Investment letters, 89
Investment management, careers in, 29–30
  average salaries for, 29
Investment philosophy, 15
Investment planning, 14–21
  business cycle and, 20–21
  stages of life and, 19
  taxes and, 16–19
Investment policy statement (IPS), 14–15
Investment process, structure of, 5–7
Investment research, 75–79
  online education sites for, 75–76
  pros and cons of Internet as tool for,
    79
  tools for, 76–79
Investment selection guidelines, 15
Investment value
  of common stock, 227–228
  of convertible bonds, 414
Investment-grade bonds, 392
Investments
  attributes of, 2–5
  definition of, 2
  direct, 3–4
  domestic, 5
  foreign, 5
  high-risk, 4–5
  indirect, 3–4
  long-term, 5
  low-risk, 4–5
  monitoring, 15
  satisfactory, 127–128
  short-term (See Short-term
    investments)
  tax-advantaged, 8, 13
  types of, 2–5, 7–13
Investopedia, 75
Investor relations (IR) firms, 83
Investor services provided by mutual
    funds, 489–492
InvestorGuide.com, 75
Investors
  buy-and-hold, 344
  characteristics and objectives of, 512
  heavy traders, 344
  individual, 6
  institutional, 6
  protections for, 108–109
  utility functions of, 192–193
Investor's Business Daily, 83
IQ, stock ownership and, 3
Iridium Communications, 237
Irrational Exuberance (Shiller), 335
Island, 48
Issue characteristics, risk premium
    and, 130
Issuer characteristics, risk premium
    and, 130
It's A Wonderful Life (Capra film), 22

J. P. Morgan, 42
Jama Motors, 533
January cycle, 555–556
January effect, 344
JC Penney, 393
Jefferies & Company, Inc., 42
Jensen, Michael C., 527
Jensen's measure (Jensen's alpha),
    527–528
Johns Manville, 511
Johnson & Johnson, 215, 234, 378
Joint brokerage accounts, 103
JP Morgan Chase & Company, 51, 92
Junior bonds, 391
Junk bonds, 392, 396, 405–406

Kahneman, Daniel, 348
Kase Capital, 63
Keogh accounts, 19, 492
Key Business Ratios, 85
Key economic factors, 259–260, 261
Kiplinger Washington Letter, 84
Kiplinger's Personal Finance Magazine,
    76, 83–84
Kraft Foods, 47, 94

L-3 Communications, 236
Land's End, 222
Large-cap stocks, 237, 238
Latin-Focus.com, 92
Lay, Ken, 603
Leading indicators, market as, 262–263
Legal discretion, 270
Lehman Brothers, 21, 218, 393, 396,
    487, 566
Lennar, 237
Leverage, put and call options and, 551,
    552
Leverage ratios, 275–277
LG Electronics, 51
Liabilities on balance sheet, 267
Lie, Erik, 561
Life cycle, investing over, 19–20
Limit orders, 74, 104–105, 533
LinkedIn, 236
Lintner, John, 187
Liquidity
    secondary market and, 43
    securities and, 2
    short-term investments and,
        7–8, 22–26
    warehousing, 533–534
Liquidity preference theory, 433
Liquidity ratios, 272–273
Liquidity risk, 140, 385
Listed options, 554
Listed securities, 43
Load funds, 11, 480–481
Logitech, 238
London Stock Exchange, 50
Long position, 596
    with foreign currency contracts,
        610–611
Long purchase, 55–56

Long straddles, 575–576
Long-term Equity AnticiPation Securities
    (LEAPS), 582
Long-term growth, common stocks for,
    243–244
Long-term investments, 5
Long-term securities, 38
Los Angeles Times, 83
Loss aversion, 349–350
Losses
    capital (*See* Capital losses)
    net, 19
Lowe's Companies, 234
Low-load funds, 480, 495
Low-risk investments, 4–5
Lumber Liquidators, 63
LYONs (liquid yield option notes), 410

Macaulay, Frederick, 448
Macaulay duration, 449
Madoff, Bernie, 21
Maintenance margin, 59, 597
Maloney Act of 1938, 54
Managed accounts, 104
Management companies, 473–474
Management fees of mutual funds,
    472, 480–481
Manchester United, 51
MannKind, 238
March cycle, 556
Margin accounts, 58, 103–104
Margin calls, 59, 597
Margin deposit, 596
Margin loans, 58
Margin requirements, 56
    short selling and, 63–64
Margin trading, 56–62
    advantages and disadvantages of, 58
    basic margin formula and, 60
    essentials of, 56–58
    financing of transaction and, 58–59
    magnified profits and losses
        and, 56–58
    making margin transactions and,
        58–60
    return on invested capital and, 60–61
    risk and, 62
    uses of, 61–62
Marginal tax rate, 399
Market activity, evaluating performance
    of individual investments and, 517
Market anomalies, 344–347
    calendar effect, 344
    explanations for, 346–347
    post earnings announcement drift,
        344–346
    small-firm effect, 344
    value effect, 346
Market averages, 94–95
Market capitalization, 225–226
Market indexes, 94, 96–98
Market interest rates, 426–434
    movement of, causes of, 427–429
    multiple, 426–427

term structure of, 429
    yield curves and, 429–434
Market makers, 44, 100
    designated, 46
Market orders, 104, 105
Market ratios, 279
Market returns, beta and, 183
Market risk, 141, 182
Market segmentation theory, 433
Market technicians, 360
Market timing, 456
Market value
    of common stock, 227
    S&P indexes and, 96
Market volume, 358
Market Watch, 83, 85
Market-cap stocks, 237–238. *See also*
    Mid-cap stocks
Markets
    bear, 48–49, 217
    bond (*See* Bond market)
    breadth of, 358–359
    broker, 44–46
    bull, 48–49
    capital (*See* Capital markets)
    cash, 592
    crossing, 53
    dealer, 44–45, 46–47
    efficient (*See* Efficient market hypothesis
        (EMH); Efficient markets)
    financial (*See* Financial markets;
        Securities markets)
    fourth, 48
    futures (*See* Futures market)
    housing, 218–219, 350
    as leading indicator, 262–263
    money, 38
    over-the-counter, 43, 44, 47–48, 85
    primary, 38–43
    secondary (*See* Secondary market)
    securities (*See* International securities
        markets; Securities markets)
    stock (*See* Stock market)
    third, 48
MarketXT, 48
Markowitz, Harry, 191
Mark-to-the-market, 597
Marvell Technology, 236
Maryland-Pacific, 522–524
Mature growth stage of industry growth
    cycle, 264
Maturity, average, of a bond, 449
Maturity date of a bond, 386–387
MAXfunds, 91
Maximum daily price range, 602
McDonald's Corporation, 80, 81, 234
McGee, Timothy, 103
Measuring returns, 128–137
Mediation, 109
Medicare surtax, 228
Merck & Co., 234
Mergent, 88–89, 265
    bond market data published by, 517
Merrill Lynch, 45, 100

Michigan, University of, 353
Microsoft, 47, 378
Mid-cap stocks, 237, 238. *See also* Market-cap stocks
Milken, Michael, 396
"Mini" index options, 579
Mini-NDX Index (MNX), 579
Mitsubishi, 51
Mixed stream of returns, 163–165
Modern portfolio theory (MPT), 191–196
  reconciliation with traditional approach, 196–197
Modified duration, 452
Momentum anomaly, 346
Money, 1, 76, 84
  mutual fund statistics published by, 494
Money, time value of. *See* Time value of money
Money left on the table, 41
Money managers, mutual funds and, 474
Money market deposit accounts (MMDAs), 24, 25, 26
Money market funds, 487
Money market mutual funds (MMMFs, money funds), 10–11, 26, 486–487
Money markets, 38
Money spreads, 575
Money supply, 261
  changes in, interest rates and, 429
Monitoring investments, 15
Montreal Exchange, 50
Moody's, 90, 283
  bond ratings of, 391–393
  market interest rate reporting by, 427
Moody's Financial Information Services Division, 89
Moody's Investors Service, 85
Morgan Stanley, 42
Morningstar, 79, 91, 265
Morningstar Mutual Funds, 494
Moronson, 522–524
Mortgage bonds, 390
Mortgage real estate investment trusts (REITs), 482
Mortgage-backed bond funds, 486
Mortgage-backed bonds, 403–404
Mortgage-backed securities, 393
Morton Thiokol, 341
Motley Fool, 75, 91, 92
Moving averages (MAs), 364–366
MSN Money, 79, 91
Multinational corporations, 51
Municipal bond funds, 486
Municipal bond guarantees, 398
Municipal Bond Investors Assurance Corporation (MBIA), 398
Municipal bonds, 397–401
Murdoch, Rupert, 83
Mutual fund cash ratio (MFCR), 361–362
Mutual fund companies, 4
Mutual Fund Investor's Center, 91

Mutual fund managers, 257
Mutual Fund Observer, 91
Mutual fund sites, 92
Mutual funds, 3–4, 8, 10–11, 468–502
  abuses of, 474
  active versus passive management of, 10, 471, 472
  aggressive-growth, 484
  asset allocation, 488–489, 515
  attractions and drawbacks of owning, 471–472
  balanced, 485
  behavioral finance and, 348
  benefits of, 181
  bond, 485–486
  closed-end (*See* Closed-end funds (CEFs))
  definition of, 469
  equity-income, 485
  exchange-traded, 468, 477–479
  expense ratio of, 472
  funds of funds and, 474
  growth, 484
  growth-and-income, 485
  index, 487–488
  international, 489
  investment company types and, 481–483
  investor services provided by, 489–492
  investor uses of, 492–493
  load and no-load, 11, 480–481
  location and, 191
  management fees of, 472, 480–481
  managing, 257
  measures of return and, 499–502, 519–520
  money market, 10–11, 26, 486–487
  no-load, 11, 495
  open-end, 475
  organization and running of, 473–475
  other fees and costs associated with, 480–481
  performance of, 472–473, 498–502
  pooled diversification and, 8, 10, 470
  risk and, 502
  sales load of, 472
  sector, 488
  selection process for, 493–495
  socially responsible, 488
  sources of return and, 498–499
  taxes and, 494
  types of, 484–489
  value, 484–485

Naked options, 573
Narrow framing, 354
Nasdaq 100 index, 98
  stock-index futures and, 607
  stock-index options and, 577, 579
Nasdaq biotech index, 98
Nasdaq Capital Market, 47
Nasdaq Composite Index, 98, 236, 517
  stock-index options and, 579
Nasdaq computer index, 98

Nasdaq Global Market, 47
Nasdaq Global Select Market, 47
Nasdaq market, 47
Nasdaq National Market, short interest on, 359
Nasdaq OMX, 44
Nasdaq OMX BX, 46
Nasdaq OMX market, 47
  margin transactions in, 59
Nasdaq OMX PHLX (PHLX), 45, 46
Nasdaq PHLX (PHLX), 554
Nasdaq.com, 76, 556
National Association of Securities Dealers, 460
National Association of Securities Dealers Automated Quotations (Nasdaq), 47, 50, 97–98, 236
  advance/decline line and, 360
  stock market indexes of, 97–98
  trading hours of, 53
National Football League, 347
National securities exchanges, 43
National Stock Exchange, 45
Natural gas futures, 603
Negotiated commissions, 108
Nestle, 51, 240
Net asset value (NAV), 475–476
Net cash flow from operating activities, 270
Net losses, 19
Net profit margin, 277, 305
Net sales, 298
Net working capital, 273
Net worth. *See* Book value
New highs-new lows (NH-NL) indicator, 361
New York Mercantile Exchange (NYMEX), 46, 594, 603, 606
New York Stock Exchange (NYSE), 37, 45–46, 47, 50, 97–98, 236. *see also specific NYSE indexes*
  advance/decline line and, 360
  listing policies of, 46
  short interest on, 359
  trading activity on, 45–46
  trading hours of, 53
New York Times, 83
News, overreaction to, 53
News Corporation, 83, 222
Newspapers, 83
Newsweek, 83
Nike, 131, 234
"No arbitrage" condition, 343
Nobel Prize, 335
Nokia, 240
No-load funds, 480, 495
Nominal rate of return, 129
Nominal rates, 131
Noncallable bonds, 389
Nordic American Tankers (NAT), 231
Norex, 50
Norsk Hydro, 240
North American Grocery Business Group, 94

Northern Trust, 83
Northwest Mining and Manufacturing, 522–524
Notes, 387
    convertible, 408–409
NOW accounts, 24, 25, 26
NVIDIA, 236
NYSE Amex Exchange. *See* American Stock Exchange (ASE)
NYSE Arca Options (NYSE Arca), 45, 46
NYSE composite index, 98
NYSE Euronext N.V., 37, 45
NYSE Exchange, 98
NYSE Group, Inc., 37, 42, 50
NYSE Liffe, 37
NYSE Liffe U.S., 37

Obama, Barack, 259
Odd lots, 104
Odd-lot dealers, 226
Odd-lot differentials, 104, 226
Odd-lot trading, 359–360
Oil and Gas Journal, 84
Oil futures, 605
Old Mutual Growth fund, 460
On-balance volume (OBV), 362
1/N heuristic, 514
OneChicago, 606
Oneok, 236
Online brokers, 101–102
Online calculators and worksheets, 76, 77
Online discussion forums, 92
Online education sites for investment research, 75–76
Online investment advice, 111
Online investment information sources, 89–92
    avoiding scams from, 92–93
Online transactions, 106–107
    day trading and, 106
    technical and service problems with, 107
    tips for, 107
Open interest, 596
Open-end funds, 475
    closed-end funds compared with, 495–497
Open-outcry auction, 594–595
Opportunity cost, 162
Option chains, 556
Option premiums, 551
Option prices
    pricing models for, 566–568
    time value and, 564–565
Option sellers, 551
Option spreading, 575
Option straddles, 575–576
Option writers, 551
Options, 12–13, 46, 549–582
    backdating of, 561
    basic features of, 550–553
    call (*See* Put and call options)
    cash settling, 553
    exercising too early, 564

on futures, 614–616
    futures contracts compared with, 593–594
    measures of return for, 520
    put (*See* Put and call options)
    types of, 550
Options exchanges, 46
Ordinary annuities, 162
Ordinary income, 16–17
Osaka Securities Exchange, 50
OTC Bulletin Board (OTCBB), 47
OTC Markets Group, 47–48
OTC Pink, 48
OTC QB, 48
OTC QX, 48
Out-of-the-money options, 560–561
Overbought condition, 363
Overconfidence, 348–349
Overreaction, 350–353
Oversold condition, 363
Over-the-counter (OTC) markets, 43, 44, 47–48, 48–49, 85

Pacific Stock Exchange, 45
Page, Larry, 96
The Pampered Chef, 511
Paper profits, 499
Paper return, 131
Par value
    of a bond, 386
    of common stock, 226
Paragon Shipping, 51
Parity, put-call, 561–564
Participation certificates, 403
Passbook savings accounts, 24, 25, 26
Passive bond investment strategies, 455–456
Passive income, 16
Passive portfolio management, 521
Passively managed funds, 10, 471, 472
Pass-through securities, 403
Payable date, 230
Payback period for convertible bonds, 413–414
Payment date for dividends, 230
Payment in kind bonds, 405
Payout ratio, 281–282, 305
PEG ratio, 280–281
Pension funds, 4
Pepsico Inc., 231, 343
Percentage returns, 123
Perfectly negatively correlated series, 175–176
Perfectly positively correlated series, 175–176
Personal income, 261
Personal property, tangible, 3
Personal taxes, 16–19
    deductions and, 16
    investments and, 19
    sources of taxation and, 16
    tax-advantaged retirement savings plans and, 19
    types of income and, 16–19

Personalfund.com, 91
Pfizer, 47, 234, 378
PFP, Inc., 573–574
Philadelphia Consolidated Holding Corporation, 103
Philadelphia Exchange, 581
Philadelphia Stock Exchange, 45
PIIGS nation crisis, 97
PIK bonds, 405
Pitney Bowes, 260
Pooled diversification, 470
    mutual funds and, 8, 10
Portfolio beta, 193–196
Portfolio income, 16
Portfolio management, 190–197, 511–534
    assessing performance and, 521–528
    asset allocation scheme for, 512–516
    comparing performance to investment goals and, 520–521
    comparing return with overall market performance and, 525–528
    evaluating performance of individual investments for, 516–521
    formula plans for, 529–533
    gender and marriage and, 512
    investor characteristics and objectives and, 512
    measuring return and, 522–525
    modern portfolio theory and, 191–196
    portfolio objectives and policies and, 512–513
    reconciliation of approaches to, 196–197
    revising the portfolio and, 528
    sales timing and, 534
    timing of transactions and, 529–534
    traditional approach to, 190–191
    warehousing liquidity and, 533–534
Portfolio planning, 171–181
    correlation and, 174–176
    diversification and, 174, 176–181
    objectives and, 171
    return and standard deviation and, 171–174, 176–177
Portfolios
    betas for, 193–196
    bond (*See* Bond portfolios)
    definition of, 2, 171
    efficient, 171, 191–192
    growth-oriented, 171
    income-oriented, 171
    replicating, 563
    risk and, 182–189 (*See also* Capital asset pricing model (CAPM))
    tracking of, 78–79
Post earnings announcement drift, 344–346
Poston, Daniel, 271
Power Financial Corporation, 311
Preferred stock, definition of, 10
Premium bonds, 387
Premium discount brokers, 101–102

Premiums
  call, 389–390
  closed-end funds trading at, 496
  option, 551
Prepayment risk, 385
Present value, 162–165
  of an annuity, 165
  of a stream of returns, 163–165
Price effect, 453
Price information, 82
  sources of, 89
Prices, 125. *See also* Inflation
  ask, 46
  bid, 46
  of bonds (*See* Bond prices)
  of commodities, 599, 602
  consumer, 125, 261
  deflation and, 125
  exercise (strike), 550, 554–555
  of financial futures, 609–610
  options (*See* Option prices)
  producer, 261
  settlement, 599
Price-to-book-value (P/BV) ratio, 282,
    323–324
Price-to-cash-flow (P/CF) procedure,
    322–323
Price-to-earnings (P/E) approach to stock
    valuation, 321–322
Price-to-earnings (P/E) ratio, 280–281,
    300–302, 305
  misleading, 302
Price-to-sales (P/S) ratio, 323–324
Price-weighted index, 94
Primary market, 38–43
Prime rate, 58
Private placement, 38
Problem investments, isolating, 521
Procter & Gamble, 47, 234, 235, 511
Producer prices, 261
Profit takeout, 457
Profitability, definition of, 277
Profitability ratios, 277–279
Profits
  forecasted, 298–300
  paper, 499
  protecting with puts, 572–573
  from puts and calls, 558–559
Profit-sharing plans, 19
Promised yield, of bonds, 440–443
Property
  definition of, 3
  personal, tangible, 3
  real, 3
Property real estate investment trusts
    (REITs), 482
Prospectus, 39, 40, 89
Protective puts, 571–573
The Prudent Speculator, 89
Public offerings, 38
Public Utilities Fortnightly, 84
Publicly traded issues, 221
Pump-and-dump scams, 92–93
Purchasing power risk, 139, 384–385

Put and call options, 550–557
  advantages and disadvantages of, 553
  American, 552, 555
  backdating of, 561
  components driving prices of, 564–568
  conventional, 553–554
  covered, 573–575
  currency, 581–582
  definitions of, 551
  European, 552, 555
  on exchange-traded funds, 580
  in- and out-of-the-money, 560–561
  interest rate, 581
  intrinsic value of, 559–564
  investment uses of, 579–580
  LEAPS, 582
  listed, 554
  markets for, 553–554
  naked, 573
  operation of, 552–553
  profit potential from, 558–559
  put-call parity and, 561–564
  return chasing and, 569
  seller versus buyer, 551–552
  spreading, 575
  stock, 550–551, 554–557
  stock-index, 577–578
  straddles, 575–576
  time value and prices of, 564–565
  trading strategies for, 568–576
  volume of trades involving, 554
  writing, 573
Puts (put options), 13. *See also* Put and
    call options
  protective, 572–573
  speculating with, 570
Pyramiding, 61

*Quarterly Financial Report for U.S.
    Manufacturing, Mining, and
    Wholesale Trade Corporations*,
    84, 85
Quick ratio, 272–273
Quiet period, 39
Quotations, 89
Quotes
  of bond prices, 389
  stock, 78–79, 225–226

Raging Bull, 92
Random walk hypothesis, 338
Rapid expansion stage of industry
    growth cycle, 264
Rate of growth, 137
Ratio analysis, 270. *See also* Financial
    ratios
Rau, Ramalinga, 21
Rawland Petroleum, 522–524
Real estate
  definition of, 13
  liquidity of, 22
Real estate bubble, 218–219
Real Estate Investment Trust Act of
    1960, 482

Real estate investment trusts (REITs),
    482
  in Nasdaq composite index, 98
Real property, 3
Real rate of return, 129
Real returns, 428
Realized capital gains, 8–9
Realized return, 131
  of bonds, 445–447
Recession, 38
  decline in prices due to, 125
  oil prices and, 123
  signs of, 427
Red Herring, 84
Red herrings, 39
Redemption fee, 475
Redemptive fee load, 11
Refunding provisions of bonds, 390
Regional exchanges, 45
Regional stock exchanges, 46
Regulation Fair Disclosure (SEC), 310
Regulation Fair Disclosure of 2002, 54
Regulation FD, 84–85
Regulation of securities markets, 53–55
Reinvestment effect, 453
Reinvestment rate, 136
Relative P/E multiples, 302
Relative strength index (RSI), 362–363
Relevant risk, 194
Replicating portfolios, 563
Representativeness, 350–354
Repurchase of shares, 224
Required rate of return, 307–308
Required return, 130
The Reserve Fund, 487
Residual owners, 216
Restricted accounts, 59
Retail sales, 261
Retirement savings, 160
  401(k) plans and, 534
  mutual funds and, 491
  tax-advantaged plans for, 19
Return chasing, 352
  put and call options and, 569
Return on assets (ROA), 277–279
  breaking down, 278–279
Return on equity (ROE), 278–279
  breaking down, 278–279
Returns, 122–136
  abnormal, 338–339
  annual total, 123
  on bonds, historical, 381–383
  on bonds, measures of, 447
  calculating, 123
  in closed-end funds, 502
  combining risk and, 146
  comparison with overall market
    measures, 525–528
  components of, 122–123
  data for analyzing, 517
  definition of, 2, 122
  dividend contribution to, 523
  expected (*See* Expected returns)
  on foreign stocks, 239–240, 240–242

Returns *(continued)*
  fully compounded rate of, 136
  growth rate of, 137
  historical, 126
  holding period, 131–133
  importance of, 123–124
  inflation and, 129
  internal rate of (*see* Internal rate of return (IRR))
  on invested capital, 602–603
  level of, 124–125
  market, beta and, 183
  measuring, 128–137
  on mutual funds, 498–502
  nominal rate of, 129
  paper, 131
  percentage, 123
  portfolio, 171–174, 176–177, 522–525
  real, 428
  real rate of, 129
  realized, 131, 445–447
  required, 130–131
  required rate of, 307–308
  risk and, 1, 130–131 (*See also* Risk-return tradeoff)
  risk-return tradeoff and, 138
  stocks versus bonds, 383–384
  stream of, present value of, 163–165
  time value of money and, 126–128
Reuters.com, 89
Revenue bonds, 397
Rights, 550, 551
Rights offerings, 38, 222
Risk, 138–146. *See also* Capital asset pricing model (CAPM)
  acceptable level of, 144–146
  assessment of, 144–146
  bonds and, 384–385
  business, 139
  business/financial (credit, default), 23, 385
  call (prepayment), 385
  combining return and, 146
  currency exchange, 52–53
  of default, 23, 385
  definition of, 4
  diversifiable (unsystematic), 182–183
  diversification of, 193–196
  event, 141
  financial, 139
  historical returns and, 142–144
  inflation, 23
  interest rate, 139–140, 384
  of international investment, 51–53
  liquidity, 140, 385
  margin trading and, 62
  market, 141
  mutual funds and, 502
  purchasing power, 139, 384–385
  relevant, 194
  of a single asset, 141–144
  standard deviation as measure of, 141–142
  tax, 140

  total, 182
  undiversifiable (market, systematic), 182–186
Risk premium, 130, 138
  capital asset pricing model and, 187
Risk-averse investors, 130, 145, 146
Risk-free rate, 130, 196
Risk-indifference curves, 192
Risk-indifferent investors, 145
Risk-return tradeoff, 1, 138
  in portfolio management, 520–521
  for portfolios, 196
  for various investments, 144–145
Risk-seeking investors, 145
Road shows, 39
Roth IRAs, 19, 491
Round lots, 104
Round-trip commissions, 596
Royal Dutch Shell, 51, 240
Rudy Nutrition, 93
Ruettiger, Daniel, 92–93
Russell 1000 Index, 98
Russell 2000 Index, 98, 471
  stock-index futures and, 607
  stock-index options and, 577, 579, 580
Russell 3000 Index, 98

Sales
  forecasted, 298–300
  of investments, timing, 534
  net, 298
  ratio of price to, 323–324
  retail, 261
Sales load funds, 11
Sales load of mutual funds, 472
SanDisk, 236
Sarbanes-Oxley Act of 2002, 21, 54, 55, 561
Satisfactory investment, determining, 127–128
Satyam Computer Services, 21
Scams, avoiding, 92–93
Scana, 236
Scholes, Myron, 566
Screening tools, 76, 78
Sears, 222, 393
Seasoned equity issues, 38
Seasoned equity offerings (SEOs), 38
SEC/EDGAR (Electronic Data Gathering and Analysis Retrieval), 85, 267
Secondary distributions, 47
Secondary market, 43
  broker, 43
  dealer, 44–45, 47
  liquidity and, 43
  over-the-counter, 43, 44
Sector funds, 488
Securities
  asset-backed, 405
  convertible, 9
  definition of, 2
  derivative, 4, 12–13, 404
  equity, 221 (*See also* Common stock)

  fixed-income, 8, 9–10 (*See also* Bonds)
  hybrid, 408 (*See also* Convertible bonds)
  inflation-indexed, 395
  inflation-protected, 396
  liquidity and, 2
  listed, 43
  long-term, 38
  mortgage-backed, 393
  options, 12–13
  pass-through, 403
  short-term, 38
  Treasury Inflation-Protected Securities (TIPS), 139
  unlisted, 43
Securities Act of 1933, 54
Securities Acts Amendments of 1975, 54, 108
Securities analysts
  mutual funds and, 474
  reports of, 89
Securities and Exchange Commission (SEC), 38, 487, 561
  EDGAR (Electronic Data Gathering and Analysis Retrieval), 85, 267
  exchanges registered with, 43
  fraud and, 271
  insider trading and, 342
  mutual funds and, 481
  Office of Internet Enforcement of, 93
  Regulation Fair Disclosure of, 310
Securities dealers, 44
Securities Exchange Act of 1934, 54
Securities Investor Protection Act of 1970, 108
Securities Investor Protection Corporation (SIPC), 108–109
Securities markets, 5–6, 37–55
  bull and bear, 48–49
  capital, 38
  globalization of, 49–53 (*See also* International securities markets)
  money, 38
  regulation of, 53–55
  trading hours of, 53
  types of, 38–44
Securities transactions, types of, 55–65
Security analysis, 255–257
  need for, 256–257
  top-down approach to, 255–256
Security market line (SML), 188–189
Security selection, 513
See's Candies, 511
Self-attribution bias, 348–349
Self-directed retirement plans (SEPs), 491
Selling groups, 41
Semiannual compounding
  bond valuation and, 437–438
  yield to maturity and, 441–442
Semi-strong form of the EMH, 340–341
Senior bonds, 390
SEP-IRAs, 19
Serial bonds, 387
Serial obligations, 397

Settlement price, 599
Shake Shack Inc., 89
  IPO of, 38–42
Shanghai Stock Exchange, 50
Share repurchases, 224
Sharpe, William F., 187, 525
Sharpe's measure, 525–526
Shiller, Robert, 335
Shoe Carnival, 238
Short interest, 359
Short position, 596
  with interest rate currency
    contracts, 611
Short straddles, 576
Shorting-against-the-box, 62
Short-selling, 62–65
  advantages and disadvantages of, 64
  basics of, 62
  definition of, 62
  lenders of securities for, 62–63
  margin requirements and, 63–64
  uses of, 65
Short-term investments, 5, 7–8, 22–26
  advantages and disadvantages of, 23
  common types of, 23, 24–25
  interest on, 23
  liquidity and, 7–8, 22–26
  risk characteristics of, 23
  role of, 22–23
  suitability as investments, 23, 25–26
Short-term securities, 38
Short-term trading
  in common stock, 244–245
  mutual funds for, 493
Siemens AG, 242
Silicon Investor, 92
Silicon Valley, CA, 355
Simple average, 365
Simple interest, 157
Single stock futures (SSFs), 606
Sinking funds, 390
Sirius XM Radio, 237, 379
Site-By-Site! International Investment
  Portal & Research Center, 92
60 Minutes, 63
Size effect, 344
Small Business Administration, 396
Small-cap stocks, 237, 238
Small-firm effect, 344
Smart Money, 1, 76, 83–84
Socially responsible funds, 488
Sony, 240
South Pacific Stock Exchange, 50
Southern Company, 236
S&P 100 Index, 96
  stock-index options and, 577
S&P 400 MidCap Index, 96
S&P 500 Index (S&P 500), 10, 83,
  96–97, 121, 183–185, 215,
  216–217, 471, 487, 517
  dividends and, 282
  exchange-traded funds and, 11
  stock-index futures and, 607
  stock-index options and, 576–577, 579

S&P 600 SmallCap Index, 96
S&P Industry Surveys, 265
S&P Total Market Index, 97
S&P/Case-Shiller Index, 121
Special subscription services, 84
Speculation
  commodities and, 603
  common stock and, 244–245
  in financial futures, 610–611
  mutual funds for, 493
  options for, 568–570
Speculative stocks, 236–237
Speculators in futures market, 596
Spiders (SPDRS, Standard & Poor's
  Depositary Receipts), 468
"Spin," 83
Spitzer, Eliot, 474
Spread, gross, 42
Spreading, commodities and, 603–604
Spreadsheets, time value of money
  computations and, 160
Sprint Corporation, 393
Stability stage of industry growth cycle,
  264–265
Standard and Poor's Case-Shiller Home
  Price Index, 218–219
Standard deviation
  as measure of risk, 141–142
  portfolio returns and, 171–174,
    176–177
Standard & Poor's Corporation (S&P),
  85, 88, 90, 215, 267, 283. See
  also specific S&P indexes
  bond market data published by, 517
  bond ratings of, 391–392, 393
  Fannie Mae and, 397
  Freddie Mac and, 397
  indexes published by, 10, 96–97
  market interest rate reporting by, 427
  ratings by, 378
  research on mutual funds by, 257
Standard & Poor's Depositary Receipts
  (SPDRs), 468
Staples, 47
Star Furniture, 511
Starbucks Corporation, 47, 224, 236, 281
Stated rate of interest, 158
Statement of cash flows, 269–271
Steelcase, 260
Stifel, 42
Stock charts, 78
Stock dividends, 230, 232
Stock exchanges, regional, 46
Stock market
  bear, 217
  falling, 217
  volatility of, correlation between assets
    and, 178
Stock options, 4, 550–551, 554–557
  expiration date of, 555–556
  put and call transactions involving,
    556–557
  strike price of, 554–555
  triple witching day and, 612

Stock prices
  economic variables affecting, 261–262
  forecasted, 300–304
  target, 304
Stock quotes, 78–79, 225–226
Stock returns, 216–218
Stock spin-offs, 222
Stock splits, 222, 224
Stock valuation, 297–324
  definition of, 298
  developing an estimate of future
    behavior and, 304–306
  dividend valuation model for, 309–317
  expected return determination and,
    320–321
  forecasted dividends and prices in,
    300–304
  forecasted sales and profits in,
    298–300
  free cash flow to equity method of,
    317–320
  increase in, 2
  of non-dividend-paying stocks,
    317–322
  price-to-book-value ratio for, 323–324
  price-to-cash-flow procedures for,
    322–323
  price-to-earnings approach for,
    321–322
  price-to-sales ratio for, 323–324
  valuation process and, 307–308
Stockbrokers, 100–104
  brokerage services and, 100–101
  churning by, 102
  opening an account with, 102–104
  selecting, 102
  types of, 101–102
Stockholders' equity on balance sheet,
  267–268
Stockholders' reports, 85–88
Stock-index futures, 606–607, 609,
  611–612
  triple witching day and, 612
Stock-index options, 576–577
  as hedging vehicles, 579–580
  triple witching day and, 612
Stocks. See also Common stock
  beta of (See Beta)
  bond returns versus, 383–384
  business cycle and, 20–21
  capital gains on, estimating, 518
  financial fraud and, 21
  growth, 324
  increased value of, 2
  international, performance of, 50–51
  IQ and, 3
  liquidity of, 22
  measures of return for, 518–519
  non-dividend-paying, finding value of,
    317–322
  ownership of, 3–4
  preferred, 10
  selling at a loss, 19
  value, 324

Stop-limit orders, 105–106
Stop-loss orders, 533
Stream of returns, present value of, 163–165
Street name, 101
Street-name accounts, 63
Strike price, 550
    of stock options, 554–555
Strong form of the EMH, 341–342
Student Loan Marketing Association, 396
Subordinated debentures, 391, 405
Subscription services, 88–89
Substitution swaps, 457
Summary of current financial situation, 14
Summary of Income and Capital Changes, 498–499
Suntech Power, 240
Super Bowl anomaly, 347
Suppliers of funds, 5–6
Survey of Current Business, 84
Survivorship bias, 471
Sweeteners, 550
Swiss Exchange, 50
Systematic risk, 182
Systematic withdrawal plans, 490

T. Rowe Price, 4, 111, 473
Tactical asset allocation, 514
Taiwan Stock Exchange Corporation, 50
Tangible personal property, 3
Tangibles, definition of, 13
Target Corporation, 142–143
Target prices, 304
Tax planning, 19
Tax Relief, Unemployment Insurance Reauthorization, and Job Creation Act of 2010, 259
Tax risk, 140
Tax swaps, 457
Taxable equivalent yields, 400–401
Tax-advantaged investments, 13
Tax-advantaged retirement savings plans, 19
Taxes
    Affordable Care Act and, 140
    Medicare surtax, 228
    municipal bonds and, 398–401
    mutual funds and, 494
    personal (*See* Personal taxes)
    timing investment sales and, 534
Tax-exempt money funds, 487
TD Ameritrade, 106
Tech stocks, 236, 355
Technical analysis, 356–366
    charting and, 363–366
    measuring the market and, 357–360
    trading rules and measures and, 360–363
Term bonds, 387
Term structure of interest rates, 429
    yield curves and, 431–434
Term to maturity, 387
Teva Pharmaceuticals, 240

Texas Instruments, 47
Theory of contrary opinion, 360
Third market, 48
Thrift and savings plans, 19
Ticker symbols, confusion over, 107
Tilson, Whitney, 63
Time Inc., 39, 83, 222
Time value of money, 126–128, 157–165
    annuities and, 162, 165
    computational aids for, 159–160
    defined, 157
    future value and, 160–161
    interest and, 157–159
    option prices and, 564–565
    present value of a stream of returns and, 163–165
Time Warner Inc., 39, 222
Times interest earned, 276–277
Timing of setting option exercise prices, 561
Timken, 237
Tokio Marine, 103
Tokyo Stock Exchange, 50
Toronto Stock Exchange, 50
Total asset turnover, 275
Total risk, 182
Toys R Us, 393
Trade magazines, 84
Tradebook, 48
Traders, mutual funds and, 474
Trading hours
    for futures contracts, 592–593
    of securities markets, 53
Trading index, 361
Trading orders, odd-lot, 360
Traditional portfolio management, 190–191
    reconciliation with modern approach, 196–197
Trailing earnings, 321
Tranches, 404
Transaction costs, 108
    for common stock purchases and sales, 226
    odd-lot trading and, 360
Transfer agents, mutual funds and, 475
Treasury Inflation-Protected Securities (TIPS), 139, 396
Treasury stock, 224
Treasury strips, 403
Treynor, Jack L., 526
Treynor's measure, 526–527
TRIN, 361
TripAdvisor, 222
Triple witching day, 612
True rate of interest, 158
Twain, Mark, 121
12(b)-1 fees, 480
21st Century Fox, 222
Twins, risk-aversion among, 146
Twitter, 341
Two and twenty rule, 12
Two Sigma Investments, LLC, 341

Two-plus-two cycle, 555
Tyco International, 51

U. S. Treasury bills, 131
U. S. Treasury Inflation-Protected Securities (TIPS), 139, 396
U. S. Treasury stock, 224
U. S. Treasury strips, 403
UBS, 254, 256
UK-Invest.com, 92
Underdiversification, 191
Underpricing of IPOs, 41
Underreaction, 353–354
    post earnings announcement drift and, 345
Underwriting by investment bankers, 41
Underwriting syndicates, 41
Undiversifiable risk, 182–186
United Parcel Service Inc. (UPS), 183–185, **234**
United Rentals Inc. (URI), 170
UnitedHealth Group, 94
Unlisted securities, 43
Unrealized capital gains, 8–9, 499
Unsystematic risk, 182–183
UPI (United Press International), 83
UPS, 47
U.S. News & World Report, 83
U.S. Total Stock Market Index, 95
U.S. Treasury bills, 24, 26, 425
U.S. Treasury bonds, 395–396
    record low yield on, 99
U.S. Treasury notes, 395–396
U.S. Treasury securities, 24, 26
USA Today, 83

Valuation, 307–308. *See also* Bond valuation; Dividend valuation model (DVM); Stock valuation
Value, mutual funds as storehouse of, 493
Value effect, 346
Value funds, 484–485
Value Line, 88, 265, 267
Value Line composite index, 98
Value Line Investment Survey, 88, 89, 98
Value Line Mutual Fund Survey, 494
Value stocks, 324
Vanguard, 348, 473
Vanguard Group, 111, 468
Vanguard S&P 500 Index fund, 471
Variable growth model
    dividend valuation model (DVM) and, 314–317
    free cash flow to equity method and, 319–320
Variable-growth model, 314–317
Variable-ratio plan, 532–533
Vertical spreads, 575
Viacom, 47
Vimpel-Communications, 240
VIX index, 566
Volume of commodities traded, 599
Vornox, 522–524
Voya Corporate Leader Trust, 487

Walgreen's, 234
Wall Street Journal, 1, 82–83, 84, 90, 99, 260, 321, 389
  for assessing performance of securities, 516
  bond market data published by, 99, 517
  market interest rate reporting by, 427
  mutual fund statistics published by, 494
  short interest reported by, 359
  stock market indexes published by, 98
Wall Street*E, 106
Walmart, 47, 237, 336–338, 511
Walt Disney, 186
Warehousing liquidity, 534
Warrants, 550, 551
Washington Post, 83
WD-40, 237
Weak form of the EMH, 339–340
Wealth accumulation, mutual funds for, 492–493
Weather futures, 599
Wells Fargo & Company, 83, 511
Wendy's International, 238
Whipsawing, 533
Whirlpool Corporation, 9
William Blair, 42

Williams-Sonoma, 238
Window dressing, 191
Wire services, 83
Wolverine Mutual Fund, 529, 530
Woodman, Nick, 549
World Bank, 406
World Federation of Stock Exchanges, 221
World Index, 98
Worth, 83–84
Wrap accounts, 104
Writing options, 573
WSJ Online, 82–83
WSJ.com, 76
  for assessing performance of securities, 516

Yahoo!, 47
Yahoo! Finance, 78, 79, 80, 85, 90, 91, 92, 183, 321
  bond market data published by, 517
Yahoo.com, for assessing performance of securities, 516
Yankee bonds, 51, 181, 406
Yield. *See also* Internal rate of return (IRR)
  bond equivalent, 441–442
  bond prices and, 435
  current, of bonds, 386, 439–440

promised, of bonds, 440–443
  on zero-coupon bonds, 442, 443
Yield curves, 429–434
  expectations hypothesis and, 432
  investment decisions and, 434
  liquidity preference theory and, 433
  market segmentation theory and, 433
  plotting, 430–431
  term structure of interest rates and, 431–434
  types of, 429–430
Yield pickup swaps, 457
Yield properties, 442–443
Yield spreads, 381, 396, 426
Yield to call (YTC) of bonds, 444–445
Yield to maturity (YTM), 518
  of bonds, 440–443
Yodlee, 91
York Water Company, 228

Zacks Investment Research, 234, 235, 310
  Research Digest Reports of, 89
  screening tools provided by, 76, 78
Zero-coupon bonds, 402–403
  yield on, 442, 443
Zero-growth model, 309–311, 318–319
Zuckerberg, Mark, 224

Key Equations

Equation 2.1 $\text{Margin} = \dfrac{\text{Value of securities} - \text{Debit balance}}{\text{Value of securities}}$

Equation 2.1a $\phantom{\text{Margin}} = \dfrac{V - D}{V}$

Equation 2.2 $\begin{array}{l}\text{Return on} \\ \text{invested capital} \\ \text{from a margin} \\ \text{transaction}\end{array} = \dfrac{\begin{array}{l}\text{Total} \\ \text{current} \\ \text{income} \\ \text{received}\end{array} - \begin{array}{l}\text{Total} \\ \text{interest} \\ \text{paid on} \\ \text{margin loan}\end{array} + \begin{array}{l}\text{Market} \\ \text{value of} \\ \text{securities} \\ \text{at sale}\end{array} - \begin{array}{l}\text{Market} \\ \text{value of} \\ \text{securities} \\ \text{at purchase}\end{array}}{\text{Amount of equity at purchase}}$

Equation 4.1 $\begin{array}{l}\text{Required return} \\ \text{on investment } j\end{array} = \begin{array}{l}\text{Real rate} \\ \text{of return}\end{array} + \begin{array}{l}\text{Expected inflation} \\ \text{premium}\end{array} + \begin{array}{l}\text{Risk premium} \\ \text{for investment } j\end{array}$

Equation 4.2 $\text{Risk-free rate} = \begin{array}{l}\text{Real rate} \\ \text{of return}\end{array} + \begin{array}{l}\text{Expected inflation} \\ \text{premium}\end{array}$

Equation 4.3 $\begin{array}{l}\text{Required return} \\ \text{on investment } j\end{array} = \begin{array}{l}\text{Risk-free} \\ \text{rate}\end{array} + \begin{array}{l}\text{Risk premium} \\ \text{for investment } j\end{array}$

Equation 4.4 $\text{Holding period return} = \dfrac{\begin{array}{l}\text{Income} \\ \text{during period}\end{array} + \begin{array}{l}\text{Capital gain (or loss)} \\ \text{during period}\end{array}}{\text{Beginning investment value}}$

Equation 4.5 $\begin{array}{l}\text{Capital gain (or loss)} \\ \text{during period}\end{array} = \begin{array}{l}\text{Ending} \\ \text{investment value}\end{array} - \begin{array}{l}\text{Beginning} \\ \text{investment value}\end{array}$

Equation 4.6 $\text{Standard deviation} = \sqrt{\dfrac{\sum\limits_{t=1}^{n}\left(\begin{array}{l}\text{Return for} \\ \text{outcome } t\end{array} - \begin{array}{l}\text{Average or} \\ \text{expected return}\end{array}\right)^2}{\begin{array}{l}\text{Total number} \\ \text{of outcomes}\end{array} - 1}}$

Equation 5.1 $\begin{array}{l}\text{Portfolio} \\ \text{Return}\end{array} = \left(\begin{array}{l}\text{Proportion of} \\ \text{portfolio's total} \\ \text{dollar value} \\ \text{invested in} \\ \text{asset 1}\end{array} \times \begin{array}{l}\text{Return} \\ \text{on asset} \\ 1\end{array}\right) + \left(\begin{array}{l}\text{Proportion of} \\ \text{portfolio's total} \\ \text{dollar value} \\ \text{invested in} \\ \text{asset 2}\end{array} \times \begin{array}{l}\text{Return} \\ \text{on asset} \\ 2\end{array}\right) + \cdots +$

$\left(\begin{array}{l}\text{Proportion of} \\ \text{portfolio's total} \\ \text{dollar value} \\ \text{invested in} \\ \text{asset } n\end{array} \times \begin{array}{l}\text{Return} \\ \text{on asset} \\ n\end{array}\right) = \sum\limits_{j=1}^{n}\left(\begin{array}{l}\text{Proportion of} \\ \text{portfolio's total} \\ \text{dollar value} \\ \text{invested in} \\ \text{asset } j\end{array} \times \begin{array}{l}\text{Return} \\ \text{on asset} \\ j\end{array}\right)$

Equation 5.2 $\text{Total risk} = \text{Diversifiable risk} + \text{Undiversifiable risk}$

Equation 5.3 $\begin{array}{l}\text{Expected return} \\ \text{on investment } j\end{array} = \begin{array}{l}\text{Risk-free} \\ \text{rate}\end{array} + \left[\begin{array}{l}\text{Beta for} \\ \text{investment } j\end{array} \times \left(\begin{array}{l}\text{Expected market} \\ \text{return}\end{array} - \begin{array}{l}\text{Risk-free} \\ \text{rate}\end{array}\right)\right]$

Key Equations

Equation 5.4

$$\begin{pmatrix} \text{Proportion of} \\ \text{portfolio's total} \\ \text{dollar value} \\ \text{in asset 1} \end{pmatrix} \times \begin{pmatrix} \text{Beta} \\ \text{for} \\ \text{asset 1} \end{pmatrix} + \begin{pmatrix} \text{Proportion of} \\ \text{portfolio's total} \\ \text{dollar value} \\ \text{in asset 2} \end{pmatrix} \times \begin{pmatrix} \text{Beta} \\ \text{for} \\ \text{asset 2} \end{pmatrix} + \cdots +$$

$$\text{Portfolio beta} = \begin{pmatrix} \text{Proportion of} \\ \text{portfolio's total} \\ \text{dollar value} \\ \text{in asset } n \end{pmatrix} \times \begin{pmatrix} \text{Beta} \\ \text{for} \\ \text{asset } n \end{pmatrix} = \sum_{j=1}^{n} \begin{pmatrix} \text{Proportion of} \\ \text{portfolio's total} \\ \text{dollar value} \\ \text{in asset } j \end{pmatrix} \times \begin{pmatrix} \text{Beta} \\ \text{for} \\ \text{asset } j \end{pmatrix}$$

Equation 6.1

$$\text{EPS} = \frac{\text{Net profit after taxes} - \text{Preferred dividends}}{\text{Number of shares of common stock outstanding}}$$

Equation 6.2

$$\text{Dividend yield} = \frac{\text{Annual dividends received per share}}{\text{Current market price of the stock}}$$

Equation 6.3

$$\text{Dividend payout ratio} = \frac{\text{Dividends per share}}{\text{Earnings per share}}$$

Equation 6.4

$$\begin{matrix} \text{Total returns} \\ (\text{in U.S. dollars}) \end{matrix} = \begin{matrix} \text{Current income} \\ (\text{dividends}) \end{matrix} + \begin{matrix} \text{Capital gains} \\ (\text{or losses}) \end{matrix} \pm \begin{matrix} \text{Changes in currency} \\ \text{exchange rates} \end{matrix}$$

Equation 6.5

$$\begin{matrix} \text{Total return} \\ (\text{in U.S. dollars}) \end{matrix} = \begin{matrix} \text{Returns from current} \\ \text{income and capital gains} \\ (\text{in local currency}) \end{matrix} \pm \begin{matrix} \text{Returns from} \\ \text{changes in currency} \\ \text{exchange rates} \end{matrix}$$

Equation 6.6

$$\begin{matrix} \text{Total return} \\ (\text{in U.S. dollars}) \end{matrix} = \left[\frac{\begin{matrix}\text{Ending value of} \\ \text{stock in foreign} \\ \text{currency}\end{matrix} + \begin{matrix}\text{Amount of dividends} \\ \text{received in} \\ \text{foreign currency}\end{matrix}}{\begin{matrix}\text{Beginning value of stock} \\ \text{in foreign currency}\end{matrix}} \times \frac{\begin{matrix}\text{Exchange rate} \\ \text{at end of} \\ \text{holding period}\end{matrix}}{\begin{matrix}\text{Exchange rate} \\ \text{at beginning of} \\ \text{holding period}\end{matrix}} \right] - 1$$

Equation 7.1

$$\text{Current ratio} = \frac{\text{Current assets}}{\text{Current liabilities}}$$

Equation 7.2

$$\text{Quick ratio} = \frac{\text{Current assets} - \text{inventory}}{\text{Current liabilities}}$$

Equation 7.3

$$\text{Net working capital} = \text{Current assets} - \text{Current liabilities}$$

Equation 7.4

$$\text{Accounts receivable turnover} = \frac{\text{Sales revenue}}{\text{Accounts receivable}}$$

Equation 7.5

$$\text{Inventory turnover} = \frac{\text{Sales revenue}}{\text{Inventory}}$$

Equation 7.6	$\text{Total asset turnover} = \dfrac{\text{Sales revenue}}{\text{Total assets}}$
Equation 7.7	$\text{Debt-equity ratio} = \dfrac{\text{Long-term debt}}{\text{Stockholders' equity}}$
Equation 7.8	$\text{Equity multiplier} = \dfrac{\text{Total assets}}{\text{Stockholders' equity}}$
Equation 7.9	$\text{Times interest earned} = \dfrac{\text{Earnings before interest and taxes}}{\text{Interest expense}}$
Equation 7.10	$\text{Net profit margin} = \dfrac{\text{Net profit after taxes}}{\text{Sales revenue}}$
Equation 7.11	$\text{ROA} = \dfrac{\text{Net profit after taxes}}{\text{Total assets}}$
Equation 7.12	$\text{ROE} = \dfrac{\text{Net profit after taxes}}{\text{Stockholders' equity}}$
Equation 7.13	$\text{ROA} = \text{Net profit margin} \times \text{Total asset turnover}$
Equation 7.14	$\text{ROE} = \text{ROA} \times \text{Equity multiplier}$
Equation 7.15	$\text{ROE} = \text{ROA} \times \text{Equity multiplier}$ $= (\text{Net profit margin} \times \text{Total asset turnover}) \times \text{Equity multiplier}$
Equation 7.16	$\text{P/E} = \dfrac{\text{Price of common stock}}{\text{EPS}}$
Equation 7.17	$\text{PEG ratio} = \dfrac{\text{Stock's P/E ratio}}{\text{3- to 5-year growth rate in earnings}}$
Equation 7.18	$\text{Dividends per share} = \dfrac{\text{Annual dividends paid to common stock}}{\text{Number of common shares outstanding}}$
Equation 7.19	$\text{Dividend payout ratio} = \dfrac{\text{Dividends per share}}{\text{Earnings per share}}$
Equation 7.20	$\text{Book value per share} = \dfrac{\text{Stockholders' equity}}{\text{Number of common shares outstanding}}$
Equation 7.21	$\text{Price-to-book-value} = \dfrac{\text{Market price of common stock}}{\text{Book value per share}}$
Equation 8.1	$\begin{matrix} \text{Future after-tax} \\ \text{earnings in year } t \end{matrix} = \begin{matrix} \text{Estimated sales} \\ \text{in year } t \end{matrix} \times \begin{matrix} \text{Net profit margin} \\ \text{expected in year } t \end{matrix}$

Key Equations

Equation 8.2
$$\text{Estimated EPS in year } t = \frac{\text{Future after-tax earnings in year } t}{\text{Number of shares of common stock outstanding in year } t}$$

Equation 8.3
$$\text{EPS} = \frac{\text{After-tax earnings}}{\text{Book value of equity}} \times \frac{\text{Book value of equity}}{\text{Shares outstanding}} = \text{ROE} \times \text{Book value per share}$$

Equation 8.4
$$\frac{\text{Estimated dividends}}{\text{per share in year } t} = \frac{\text{Estimated EPS}}{\text{for year } t} \times \frac{\text{Estimated}}{\text{payout ratio}}$$

Equation 8.5
$$\frac{\text{Estimated share price}}{\text{at end of year } t} = \frac{\text{Estimated EPS}}{\text{in year } t} \times \frac{\text{Estimated P/E}}{\text{ratio}}$$

Equation 8.6
$$\frac{\text{Required}}{\text{rate of return}} = \frac{\text{Risk-free}}{\text{rate}} + \left[\frac{\text{Stock's}}{\text{beta}} \times \left(\frac{\text{Market}}{\text{return}} - \frac{\text{Risk-free}}{\text{rate}} \right) \right]$$

Equation 8.7
$$\frac{\text{Value of a}}{\text{share of stock}} = \frac{\text{Annual dividends}}{\text{Required rate of return}}$$

Equation 8.8
$$\frac{\text{Value of a}}{\text{share of stock}} = \frac{\text{Next year's dividends}}{\dfrac{\text{Required rate}}{\text{of return}} - \dfrac{\text{Dividend growth}}{\text{rate}}}$$

Equation 8.9
$$\frac{\text{Value of a share}}{\text{of stock}} = \frac{\text{Present value of future dividends during the initial variable-growth period}}{} + \frac{\text{Present value of the price of the stock at the end of the variable-growth period}}{}$$

Equation 8.10 $g = \text{ROE} \times \text{The firm's retention rate, } rr$

Equation 8.10a $rr = 1 - \text{Dividend payout ratio}$

Equation 8.11
$$\text{Value of a share of stock} = \frac{\text{present value of future free cash flows going to equity}}{\text{shares outstanding}}$$

$$\text{Free cash flow} = \text{after-tax earnings} + \text{depreciation}$$
$$- \text{ investments in working capital} - \text{ investments in fixed assets}$$

Equation 8.12 $\text{Stock price} = \text{EPS} \times \text{P/E ratio}$

Equation 8.13
$$\text{P/CF ratio} = \frac{\text{Market price of common stock}}{\text{Cash flow per share}}$$

Equation 8.14
$$\text{P/S ratio} = \frac{\text{Market price of common stock}}{\text{Sales per share}}$$

Equation 9.1 $\text{Abnormal return (or alpha)} = \text{Actual return} - \text{Expected return}$

Equation 9.3
$$\frac{\text{Confidence}}{\text{index}} = \frac{\text{Average yield on 10 high-grade corporate bonds}}{\text{Average yield on 10 intermediate-grade bonds}}$$

Equation 9.4
$$\text{TRIN} = \frac{\text{Number of up stocks}}{\text{Number of down stocks}} \div \frac{\text{Volume in up stocks}}{\text{Volume in down stocks}}$$

Equation 9.5
$$\text{MFCR} = \text{Mutual fund cash position} \div \text{Total assets under management}$$

Equation 9.6
$$\text{RSI} = 100 - \left[100 \div \left(1 + \frac{\text{Average price change on up days}}{\text{Average price change on down days}} \right) \right]$$

Equation 10.1
$$\text{Taxable equivalent yield} = \frac{\text{Yield on municipal bond}}{1 - \text{Marginal federal tax rate}}$$

Equation 10.2
$$\text{Taxable equivalent yield for both federal and state taxes} = \frac{\text{Municipal bond yield}}{1 - [\text{Federal tax rate} + \text{State tax rate} (1 - \text{Federal tax rate})]}$$

Equation 10.3
$$\text{Total return (in U.S. dollars)} = \left[\frac{\substack{\text{Ending value of} \\ \text{bond in foreign} \\ \text{currency}} + \substack{\text{Amount of interest} \\ \text{received in} \\ \text{foreign currency}}}{\substack{\text{Beginning value of bond} \\ \text{in foreign currency}}} \times \frac{\substack{\text{Exchange rate} \\ \text{at end of} \\ \text{holding period}}}{\substack{\text{Exchange rate} \\ \text{at beginning of} \\ \text{holding period}}} \right] - 1.00$$

Equation 10.4
$$\text{Conversion value} = \text{Conversion ratio} \times \text{Current market price of the stock}$$

Equation 10.5
$$\text{Conversion equivalent} = \frac{\text{Current market price of the convertible bond}}{\text{Conversion ratio}}$$

Equation 10.6
$$\text{Conversion premium (in \$)} = \substack{\text{Current market price} \\ \text{of the convertible bond}} - \substack{\text{Conversion} \\ \text{value}}$$

Equation 10.7
$$\text{Conversion premium (in \%)} = \frac{\text{Conversion premium (in \$)}}{\text{Conversion value}}$$

Equation 10.8
$$\text{Payback period} = \frac{\text{Conversion premium (in \$)}}{\substack{\text{Annual interest} \\ \text{income from the} \\ \text{convertible bond}} - \substack{\text{Annual dividend} \\ \text{income from the} \\ \text{underlying common stock}}}$$

Equation 11.2
$$BP_i = \substack{\text{Present value of} \\ \text{coupon payments}} + \substack{\text{Present value of} \\ \text{bond's par value}}$$

Equation 11.2a
$$BP_i = \sum_{t=1}^{N} \frac{C}{(1 + r_i)^t} + \frac{PV_N}{(1 + r_i)^N}$$

Equation 11.4
$$\substack{\text{Bond price (with semi-} \\ \text{annual compounding)}} = \substack{\text{Present value of the annuity of} \\ \text{semiannual coupon payments}} + \substack{\text{Present value of the} \\ \text{bond's par value}}$$

Equation 11.4a
$$BP_i = \frac{C/2}{\left(1 + \dfrac{r_i}{2}\right)^1} + \frac{C/2}{\left(1 + \dfrac{r_i}{2}\right)^2} + \cdots + \frac{C/2}{\left(1 + \dfrac{r_i}{2}\right)^{2N}} + \frac{\$1,000}{\left(1 + \dfrac{r_i}{2}\right)^{2N}}$$

Equation 11.5
$$\text{Current yield} = \frac{\text{Annual interest income}}{\text{Current market price of the bond}}$$

Key Equations

Equation 11.7   Bond price = Present value of the bond's annual coupon payments over the holding period + Present value of the bond's future price at the end of the holding period

Equation 11.8 $\text{Duration} = \sum_{t=1}^{N}\left[\dfrac{PV(C_t)}{BP} \times t\right]$

Equation 11.9 $\text{Modified duration} = \dfrac{(\text{Macaulay})\ \text{Duration in years}}{1 + \text{Yield to maturity}}$

Equation 11.10 $\dfrac{\text{Percent change}}{\text{in bond price}} = -1 \times \text{Modified duration} \times \text{Change in interest rates}$

Equation 11.11 $ED = \dfrac{BP(r_i\downarrow) - BP(r_i\uparrow)}{2 \times BP \times \Delta r_i}$

Equation 12.1 $\text{Premium (or discount)} = (\text{Share price} - \text{NAV}) \div \text{NAV}$

Equation 12.2 $\text{Holding period return} = \dfrac{\left(\begin{array}{c}\text{Number of}\\ \text{shares at end}\\ \text{of period}\end{array} \times \begin{array}{c}\text{Ending}\\ \text{price}\end{array}\right) - \left(\begin{array}{c}\text{Number of}\\ \text{shares at beginning}\\ \text{of period}\end{array} \times \begin{array}{c}\text{Initial}\\ \text{price}\end{array}\right)}{\left(\begin{array}{c}\text{Number of shares}\\ \text{at beginning of}\\ \text{period}\end{array} \times \begin{array}{c}\text{Initial}\\ \text{price}\end{array}\right)}$

Equation 13.1 $\text{Holding period return} = \dfrac{\begin{array}{c}\text{Current income}\\ \text{during period}\end{array} + \begin{array}{c}\text{Capital gain (or loss)}\\ \text{during period}\end{array}}{\text{Beginning investment value}}$

Equation 13.1a $HPR = \dfrac{C + CG}{V_0}$

Equation 13.2 $\dfrac{\text{Capital gain (or loss)}}{\text{during period}} = \begin{array}{c}\text{Ending}\\ \text{investment value}\end{array} - \begin{array}{c}\text{Beginning}\\ \text{investment value}\end{array}$

Equation 13.2a $CG = V_n - V_0$

Equation 13.3 $\begin{array}{c}\text{Holding}\\ \text{period}\\ \text{return for}\\ \text{a portfolio}\end{array} = \dfrac{\begin{array}{c}\text{Dividends and}\\ \text{interest}\\ \text{received}\end{array} + \begin{array}{c}\text{Realized}\\ \text{gain}\end{array} + \begin{array}{c}\text{Unrealized}\\ \text{gain}\end{array}}{\begin{array}{c}\text{Initial}\\ \text{equity}\\ \text{investment}\end{array} + \left(\begin{array}{c}\text{New}\\ \text{funds}\end{array} \times \dfrac{\begin{array}{c}\text{Number of}\\ \text{months in}\\ \text{portfolio}\end{array}}{12}\right) - \left(\begin{array}{c}\text{Withdrawn}\\ \text{funds}\end{array} \times \dfrac{\begin{array}{c}\text{Number of months}\\ \text{Withdrawn}\\ \text{form portfolio}\end{array}}{12}\right)}$

Equation 13.3a $HPR_p = \dfrac{C + RG + UG}{E_0 + \left(NF \times \dfrac{ip}{12}\right) - \left(WF \times \dfrac{wp}{12}\right)}$

Equation 13.4 $\qquad$ Sharpe's measure $= \dfrac{\text{Total portfolio return } - \text{ Risk-free rate}}{\text{Standard deviation of portfolio return}}$

Equation 13.4a $\qquad\qquad\qquad SM = \dfrac{r_p - r_f}{s_p}$

Equation 13.5 $\qquad$ Treynor's measure $= \dfrac{\text{Total portfolio return } - \text{ Risk-free rate}}{\text{Portfolio beta}}$

Equation 13.5a $\qquad\qquad\qquad TM = \dfrac{r_p - r_f}{b_p}$

Equation 14.1 $\qquad$ Intrinsic value of a call $=$ (Stock price $-$ Strike price) $\times$ 100
or 0, whichever is greater

Equation 14.2 $\qquad$ Intrinsic value of a put $=$ (Strike price $-$ Stock price) $\times$ 100
or 0, whichever is greater

Equation 14.3 $\qquad$ Price of a put option $+$ Price of a stock $=$ Price of a call option $+$ Price of a
risk-free bond

Equation 14.4 $\qquad$ Call price $= SN(d_1) - PV(X)N(d_2)$

Equation 14.4a $\qquad d_1 = \dfrac{\ln\left(\dfrac{S}{X}\right) + \left(r + \dfrac{\sigma^2}{2}\right)T}{\sigma\sqrt{T}}$

Equation 14.4b $\qquad d_2 = d_1 - \sigma\sqrt{T}$

Equation 15.1 $\qquad$ Return on invested capital $= \dfrac{\begin{array}{c}\text{Selling price of}\\\text{commodity contract}\end{array} - \begin{array}{c}\text{Purchase price of}\\\text{commodity contract}\end{array}}{\text{Amount of margin deposit}}$